D1578460

THE
WISDEN
BOOK OF
TEST
CRICKET
VOLUME I 1877-1977

THE
WISDEN
BOOK OF
TEST
CRICKET
VOLUME I   1877-1977

Compiled and edited by
BILL FRINDALL

Macdonald
Queen Anne Press

A Queen Anne Press Book

First published in Great Britain in 1979 by
Macdonald and Jane's Publishers Ltd
Reprinted 1980 (twice), Revised 1985
Third (revised) edition published in 1990 by
Queen Anne Press, a division of
Macdonald & Co (Publishers) Ltd
Orbit House
1 New Fetter Lane
London EC4A 1AR

A member of Maxwell Macmillan Pergamon Publishing Corporation

British Library Cataloguing in Publication Data
The Wisden book of test cricket.——3rd ed.——
  (Wisden cricket library)
  1. Cricket——Records   2. Test matches
  (Cricket)——History
  I. Frindall, Bill   II. Series
  796.35'865   GV925

  ISBN 0-356-18150-2

Printed and bound in Great Britain by
Mackays of Chatham PLC, Chatham, Kent

CONTENTS

FOREWORD
by
SIR DONALD BRADMAN, A.C.

One of the great joys for cricket followers is the volume of literature about the game which has been handed down to us over the years. This is not to say all of it is good. There have been some dreadful publications, obviously ghosted, and clearly produced with the box office in mind. But thankfully they are more than counterbalanced by thoughtful, intelligent and beautifully written books which are a must for the library shelves.

Not the least valuable and interesting is the statistical information which leads to so much discussion as to the merits of performers, past and present.

Bill Frindall is a leading contender for the Oscar as a statistician and the world of cricket is very much in his debt for producing *The Wisden Book of Test Cricket*.

Unfortunately the validity of statistics as a measuring stick is becoming more and more clouded by changes in rules and/or playing conditions—for instance covered versus uncovered pitches, the size of the wicket, the 'lbw' law, etc. The latest bugbear is the 'no-ball' law. Whereas for a century the bowler who delivered a 'no-ball' was in danger of being hit for six, the modern bowler is decidedly unlucky if the striker hears the call before the ball hits his bat.

Conversely the bowler's figures are debited with each violation of the 'front foot' monstrosity. I remain of the opinion that 90% of the public and the players would like to see a return to a sensible back foot control and thus rid the game of the frustrations and irritations which are etched on the bowlers' faces, especially in the limited-overs games.

The highly-experienced West Indians have had such difficulty coping with the rule that 15 to 20 no-balls in a fifty-over innings are not uncommon—a percentage factor of great significance.

As I write these lines the first day–night match ever at Melbourne has just been played before an audience of over 82,000. This spectacular was followed by the results of a gallup poll showing that 57% of the people favour a multi-nation one-day series to a two-nation Test series. How long I wonder before we have day–night Test matches?

There can be no doubt that Test cricket should remain the pinnacle of achievement and the true fulfilment of cricket skill because to win you have to dismiss your opponents. No such requirement exists in the limited-overs game. It seems a travesty of justice that a team can win a match by scoring 9 for 201 against its rival's 0 for 200, simply because time has run out. But I have great sympathy for the paying customer who will not support watching 240 runs per day when next week he can see the same players in the same time amass over 500 runs—especially when he is interested in entertainment, not technique.

One thing the limited-overs game has done is to highlight good fielding. The current West Indian team is the best all round fielding side in my memory. Another facet of great interest is the running between wickets. It is thrilling and exciting to see almost impossible singles being risked and achieved.

Of great moment to me, and I think of importance to the future conduct of the game, are two other matters. One is the 'no-ball' and/or 'wide' call. In recent years we have seen far too many short-pitched deliveries in first-class cricket without any action by umpires, probably because they were unwilling to exercise a moral judgement regarding intimidation. The rule applicable in one-day games has curbed bouncers in a sensible, realistic and practical way. I would like to see it adopted for first-class games, with the rider that the call for an offending delivery should be 'no-ball' instead of 'wide'.

This matter is important for the game of cricket which I'm sure was never intended to be indulged in by players garbed as though they were taking part in grid-iron football. Apart from the uncomfortable helmets and voluminous padding we now find more and more players using the protective arm guard. To be fair, I think the arm guard is less of a necessity and more of a reflection on batting technique. Throughout my career I was never once hit on the forearm nor did I ever remotely feel in danger of being hit. Too many moderns are slaves to the forward prod, left elbow forward (come what may) with a resultant lack of versatility and stroke play; and may I add evasive capability. Indeed the whole gamut of protective devices must militate against mobility and speed.

The second matter is the 'wide' ball itself. This is much more severe (especially on the leg side) in one-day games and in my view could, with advantage, be adopted in first-class cricket.

There has been much speculation as to whether the current West Indian team is the best of all time. Comparisons have been made with the Australian teams of 1921 and 1948. The question provokes animated and interesting discussion but can never produce an authoritative answer.

Of course they are a great side. As I've said earlier, the best fielding team I've seen. Added to that, they have probably the best combination of fast bowlers in one side. But that particular strength immediately predicates a lack of balance when conditions don't favour speed—a fact so nakedly exposed when the West Indians were handsomely beaten in a Sydney Test, mainly through the bowling of Australia's spinners. The West Indian attack lacked adequate spin under these conditions and the batsmen (including even the great Richards) could not handle the unfamiliar spin of Holland and Bennett. Yet nobody with a knowledge of his subject and in his right mind would rate Holland and Bennett in the same class as Grimmett and O'Reilly.

Comparing great sides of different eras must be inconclusive. I always thought my 1948 side the best I saw, though conceding it would have been hard pressed to beat Armstrong's 1921 combination. Yet Armstrong, when asked whether his team was better than Joe Darling's 1902 side replied 'the 1902 side could play 22 of our chaps and give them a beating'. Armstrong played in both so he should know.

Where do we go from here?

I'm sorry for modern players who are caught up in the proliferation of Test and one-day cricket because they have to endure incessant travel, publicity and pressure. The reward is vastly increased remuneration. The corollary is, I fear, less satisfaction in personal achievement, and more subservience to commercialism. But that is the age in which we live.

Only history will be able to determine whether the scales have been tilted in the right direction. Meanwhile it is essential to chronicle events as they happen, and to that end we owe thanks to the Bill Frindalls of this world because their evidence will be valuable in the world court of jurisdiction in the 21st century.

Don Bradman

Kensington Park,
Adelaide,
South Australia.
February 1985.

PREFACE AND ACKNOWLEDGEMENTS

The phrase 'Test match' was coined during the very first cricket tour to Australia, when, in 1861–62, games between H.H. Stephenson's team and each of the Australian colonies were described as 'Test matches'. Those early contests were played against odds, i.e. with the opposition batting and fielding more than 11 men. It was not until the fourth expedition to Australia, by James Lillywhite's professionals in 1876–77, that an English team played on level terms overseas. The first such encounter, against a combined eleven from Melbourne and Sydney, has become accepted as the first official Test match.

This first volume includes the full scores of the 803 official Test matches played from when Alfred Shaw bowled the very first ball to Charles Bannerman at Melbourne in March 1877, until Australia won the commemorative Centenary Test by the identical margin of 45 runs on the same ground almost exactly a hundred years later.

With regard to the earliest matches, I have accepted the list first published in 1894 by Mr Clarence Moody (*Australian Cricket and Cricketers*) and which the following year was adopted by Mr John Pentelow in the first book of Test cricket (*England v. Australia – the Story of the Test Matches*). Although purists may object to the inclusion of matches in which England was represented by privately arranged teams in Australia and South Africa, prior to the first official MCC tours to those countries in 1903–04 and 1905–06 respectively, the status of those matches has now become sanctified by time. Similarly, the coincidental England rubbers in New Zealand and the West Indies in the early months of 1930 have long been accepted and should not now have their status challenged. On the other hand, England's matches against the Rest of the World in 1970, which were substituted for the cancelled rubber against South Africa and played with the full panoply of Test matches, have to be excluded because they were unofficial. Moreover, the International Cricket Conference, which claims control of the title 'Test match', ruled that they should not be included in Test match records. Spare a thought for Alan Jones of Glamorgan. Although he won a full England cap for appearing at Lord's in the opening match of that rubber, his name does not appear elsewhere in this volume because he was never selected for an official Test match.

With three exceptions the matches are arranged chronologically by rubber; to ensure that each player's Test career is shown in unbroken chronological order, the nine matches constituting the 1912 Triangular Tournament, England's eight matches in Pakistan and India in 1961–62, and the six Tests in which Australia alernately played West Indies and England in 1979–80, are set strictly in the order in which they took place. Each match has a reference number to show its position in the general order and its place in that particular series; e.g. 638/200 is the 638th match listed and was the 200th in the series between England and Australia. To identify a match in either the statistical notes preceding each score or in the Index of Test Cricketers, only the prefix of each reference number is given.

Ideally each score should be an exact reproduction of the match details recorded in the original scorebook. Where that document no longer survives, research has turned to contemporary match reports and I am particularly indebted to the staff of The British Library, custodians of that most comprehensive collection of newspapers and microfilm at Colindale. With the aid of Geoffrey Saulez, virtually every surviving Test match scorebook throughout the world has been checked. Apart from removing many errors of transcription, all substitute catchers have been identified, changes of batting order for the second innings determined, and all but one set of umpires traced. Because it has not always been possible to establish which opening batsman faced first in the second innings of the early matches, I though it better for consistency not to show such changes for any match.

In addition to features introduced in the first two editions, such as noting days when no play was possible, listing those players making their first appearance at this level, denoting left-handers by annotating symbols in the career records section, and showing the number of Test appearances to date for each umpire officiating in a particular match, this edition includes the close of play and 'not out' batsmen's scores for every single day of Test cricket.

I have not indicated the winners of match awards because I regard them as commercial gimmicks which detract from a team game. Nor have I listed twelfth men; frequently there are several for each side during a match and, in recent years, the officially named reserve has merely fetched and carried an assortment of drinks and protective equipment while someone else has acted as emergency fielder.

In his 77th year, Sir Donald Bradman honoured the second edition by contributing a Foreword which reveals the concise mind that controlled the most successful and feared batting technique of all time. It is indeed a delight to have this work graced by 'The Don', the most esteemed name in the history of international cricket.

Many friends and colleagues have been unstinting with their help and kindness in assisting with the preparation of all three editions. Besides recording my gratitude to Celia Kent, whose calm expertise and good humour have guided the last two editions of this chronicle through all the potential hazards of book production, I am extremely grateful to the cricketers who made it possible and to all of the following, some alas no longer with us:

John Arlott	Syd Levey
G.W. Ashok	Rex Lister
Philip Bailey	Trevor Lockett
Robert Brooke	Bapoo Mama
Debbie Brown	Christopher Martin-Jenkins
Sue Bullen	Francis Payne
Tony Cozier	S.S. Perera
Harold de Andrado	Ken Piesse
Paula Dixon	Mike Ringham
Anandji Dossa	Ray Robinson
Graham Dowling	David Roylance
Michael Fordham	Dickie Rutnagur
David Frith	Geoffrey Saulez
Ghulam Mustafa Khan	Bob Spence
Stephen Green	Sa'adi Thawfeeq
Chris Harte	Gordon Tratalos
Denys Heesom	Ray Webster
Victor Isaacs	Roy Wilkinson
Hayward Kidson	Graeme Wright
Rajesh Kumar	Peter Wynne-Thomas

Auckland Public Library
The British Library
Lancashire Country Cricket Club
Marylebone Cricket Club
New South Wales Cricket Association
Nottinghamshire County Cricket Club
Queensland Cricket Association
Royal Geographical Society
South Australia Cricket Association
Victoria State Library
Western Australia Cricket Association

BILL FRINDALL

Test Match Scores 1876-77 to 1976-77

* denotes the Captain and   † shows the Wicket-Keeper

NUMBER OF BALLS TO AN OVER IN TEST MATCHES

In England	Balls
1880 to 1888	4
1890 to 1899	5
1902 to 1938	6
1939	8
1946 to date	6

In Australia	
1876–77 to 1887–88	4
1891–92 to 1920–21	6
1924–25	8
1928–29 to 1932–33	6
1936–37 to 1978–79	8
1979–80 to date	6

In South Africa	
1888–89	4
1891–92 to 1898–99	5
1902–03 to 1935–36	6
1938–39 to 1957–58	8
1961–62 to 1969–70	6

In West Indies	Balls
1929–30 to date	6

In New Zealand	
1929–30 to 1967–68	6
1968–69 to 1978–79	8
1979–80 to date	6

In India	
1933–34 to date	6

In Pakistan	
1954–55 to 1972–73	6
1974–75 to 1977–78	8
1978–79 to date	6

In Sri Lanka	
1981–82 to date	6

AUSTRALIA v ENGLAND 1876–77 (1st Test)

Played at Melbourne Cricket Ground on 15, 16, 17, 19 March.
Toss: Australia.   Result: AUSTRALIA won by 45 runs.
Debuts: All.

The first match played on level terms between English and Australian teams was only subsequently recognised as the first Test match. In fact it was between a Grand Combined Melbourne and Sydney XI and James Lillywhite's professional touring team. The Australians lacked three of their best bowlers in Allan, Evans and Spofforth, while the leading English batsmen were absent amateurs, and the tourists' only wicket-keeper, Pooley, had been 'confiscated' by the authorities in New Zealand – whence the team had returned somewhat sea-sick the previous day.

Note that the match continued into the fourth day, that Horan was dismissed by Hill (not Ulyett, as most scores show), that Jupp kept wicket for England in place of Selby from lunch on the first day, and that overs were of four balls.

AUSTRALIA

C. Bannerman	retired hurt	165	b Ulyett	4
N. Thompson	b Hill	1	c Emmett b Shaw	7
T.P. Horan	c Hill b Shaw	12	c Selby b Hill	20
D.W. Gregory*	run out	1	(9) b Shaw	3
B.B. Cooper	b Southerton	15	b Shaw	3
W.E. Midwinter	c Ulyett b Southerton	5	c Southerton b Ulyett	17
E.J. Gregory	c Greenwood b Lillywhite	0	c Emmett b Ulyett	11
J.M. Blackham†	b Southerton	17	lbw b Shaw	6
T.W. Garrett	not out	18	(4) c Emmett b Shaw	0
T. Kendall	c Southerton b Shaw	3	not out	17
J.H. Hodges	b Shaw	0	b Lillywhite	8
Extras	(B 4, LB 2, W 2)	8	(B 5, LB 3)	8
Total		**245**		**104**

ENGLAND

H. Jupp	lbw b Garrett	63	(3) lbw b Midwinter	4
J. Selby†	c Cooper b Hodges	7	(5) c Horan b Hodges	38
H.R.J. Charlwood	c Blackham b Midwinter	36	(4) b Kendall	13
G. Ulyett	lbw b Thompson	10	(6) b Kendall	24
A. Greenwood	c E.J. Gregory b Midwinter	1	(2) c Midwinter b Kendall	5
T. Armitage	c Blackham b Midwinter	9	(8) c Blackham b Kendall	3
A. Shaw	b Midwinter	10	st Blackham b Kendall	2
T. Emmett	b Midwinter	8	(9) b Kendall	9
A. Hill	not out	35	(1) c Thompson b Kendall	0
James Lillywhite*	c and b Kendall	10	b Hodges	4
J. Southerton	c Cooper b Garrett	6	not out	1
Extras	(LB 1)	1	(B 4, LB 1)	5
Total		**196**		**108**

ENGLAND	O	M	R	W	O	M	R	W
Shaw	55·3	34	51	3	34	16	38	5
Hill	23	10	42	1	14	6	18	1
Ulyett	25	12	36	0	19	7	39	3
Southerton	37	17	61	3				
Armitage	3	0	15	0				
Lillywhite	14	5	19	1	1	0	1	1
Emmett	12	7	13	0				
AUSTRALIA								
Hodges	9	0	27	1	7	5	7	2
Garrett	18·1	10	22	2	2	0	9	0
Kendall	38	16	54	1	33·1	12	55	7
Midwinter	54	23	78	5	19	7	23	1
Thompson	17	10	14	1				
D.W. Gregory					5	1	9	0

FALL OF WICKETS

	A	E	A	E
Wkt	1st	1st	2nd	2nd
1st	2	23	7	0
2nd	40	79	27	7
3rd	41	98	31	20
4th	118	109	31	22
5th	142	121	35	62
6th	143	135	58	68
7th	197	145	71	92
8th	243	145	75	93
9th	245	168	75	100
10th	–	196	104	108

Umpires: C.A. Reid (1) and R.B. Terry (1).

Close: 1st day – A(1) 166-6 (Bannerman 126, Blackham 3); 2nd – E(1) 109-4 (Jupp 54); 3rd – A(2) 83-9 (Kendall 5, Hodges 3).

In his seventh first-class match (tenth innings), Charles Bannerman, born in Kent 25 years earlier, faced the first ball in Test cricket from the round-arm, 'length' bowler, Alfred Shaw, scored the first run (second ball) and the first hundred by an Australian. against any English team. He reached the only first-class century of his career in 160 minutes (playing hours the first day were 1.05 to 5.00 pm with lunch 2.00 to 2.40 pm) and, when a rising ball from Ulyett split the second finger of his right hand, he retired hurt with 165 of Australia's total of 240 for 7 after batting chancelessly for $4\frac{3}{4}$ hours and hitting 15 fours. His score remains the highest by an Australian on debut against England; it was the Test record until W.L. Murdoch scored 211 in 1884 (*Test No. 16*) and the record score in Australia until S.E. Gregory made 201 for Australia in 1894-95 (*Test No. 42*). He scored 67·3 per cent of his side's total (69·6 per cent of the runs scored from the bat) – this remains the highest individual proportion of any Test innings.

One hundred years later this result and its margin were exactly emulated on the same ground in the Centenary Test (*Test No. 803*).

THE FIRST TEST CRICKETERS

AUSTRALIA

	Born	Died
BANNERMAN, Charles	Woolwich, England 23 July 1851	Surry Hills, Sydney 20 August 1930
BLACKHAM, John McCarthy	North Fitzroy, Melbourne 11 May 1854	Melbourne 28 December, 1932
COOPER, Bransby Beauchamp	Dacca, India 15 March 1844	Geelong, Victoria 7 August 1914
GARRETT, Thomas William	Wollongong, N.S.W. 26 July 1858	Warrawee, Sydney 6 August 1943
GREGORY, David William	Fairy Meadow, N.S.W. 15 April 1845	Turramurra, Sydney 4 August 1919
GREGORY, Edward James	Waverley, Sydney 29 May 1839	S.C.G., Sydney 22 April 1899
HODGES, John Henry	Collingwood, Melbourne 31 May 1856	Collingwood, Melbourne 17 January 1933
HORAN, Thomas Patrick	Midleton, Ireland 8 March 1854	Malvern, Melbourne 16 April 1916
KENDALL, Thomas	Bedford, England 24 August 1851	Hobart 17 August 1924
MIDWINTER, William Evans	St Briavels, Glos, England 19 June 1851	Kew, Melbourne 3 December 1890
THOMPSON, Nathaniel	Birmingham, England 21 April 1838	Burwood, Sydney 2 September 1896

ENGLAND

	Born	Died
ARMITAGE, Thomas	Walkley, Sheffield, Yorkshire 25 April 1848	Pullman, Chicago, U.S.A. 21 September 1922
CHARLWOOD, Henry Rupert James	Horsham, Sussex 19 December 1846	Scarborough, Yorkshire 6 June 1888
EMMETT, Thomas	Halifax, Yorkshire 3 September 1841	Leicester 30 June 1904
GREENWOOD, Andrew	Cowmes Lepton, Yorkshire 20 August 1847	Huddersfield, Yorkshire 12 February 1889
HILL, Allen	Kirkheaton, Yorkshire 14 November 1843	Leyland, Lancashire 29 August 1910
JUPP, Henry	Dorking, Surrey 19 November 1841	Bermondsey, London 8 April 1889
LILLYWHITE, James, jr	Westhampnett, Sussex 23 February 1842	Westerton, Sussex 25 October 1929
SELBY, John	Nottingham 1 July 1849	Nottingham 11 March 1894
SHAW, Alfred	Burton Joyce, Nottinghamshire 29 August 1842	Gedling, Nottinghamshire 16 January 1907
SOUTHERTON, James	Petworth, Sussex 16 November 1827	Mitcham, Surrey 16 June 1880
ULYETT, George	Pitsmoor, Sheffield, Yorkshire 21 October 1851	Pitsmoor, Yorkshire 18 June 1898

AUSTRALIA v ENGLAND 1876–77 (2nd Test)

Played at Melbourne Cricket Ground on 31 March, 2, 3, 4 April.
Toss: Australia.   Result: ENGLAND won by four wickets.
Debuts: Australia – T.J.D. Kelly, W.L. Murdoch, F.R. Spofforth.

This return match was played for the benefit of the English professionals, and attracted a total attendance of about 15,000. Jupp took over as England's wicket-keeper after lunch on the first day. In Australia's second innings Kelly made eight successive scoring strokes for four, and Bannerman scored 30 in thirteen minutes. Yorkshiremen contributed 329 of the 356 runs scored from the bat by England.

AUSTRALIA

N. Thompson	lbw b Hill	18	b Lillywhite	41
C. Bannerman	b Hill	10	(3) c Jupp b Ulyett	30
J.M. Blackham†	c Lillywhite b Hill	5	(10) lbw b Southerton	26
T.W. Garrett	b Hill	12	(7) c Jupp b Lillywhite	18
T.J.D. Kelly	b Ulyett	19	(4) b Southerton	35
W.E. Midwinter	c Emmett b Lillywhite	31	c Greenwood b Lillywhite	12
F.R. Spofforth	b Ulyett	0	(8) b Hill	17
W.L. Murdoch	run out	3	(5) c Shaw b Southerton	8
T. Kendall	b Lillywhite	7	b Southerton	12
D.W. Gregory*	not out	1	(2) c Ulyett b Lillywhite	43
J.H. Hodges	run out	2	not out	0
Extras	(B 8, LB 5, W 1)	14	(B 10, LB 7)	17
Total		**122**		**259**

ENGLAND

H. Jupp	b Kendall	0	b Kendall	1
A. Shaw	st Blackham b Spofforth	1	(8) not out	0
A. Greenwood	b Hodges	49	c Murdoch b Hodges	22
H.R.J. Charlwood	c Kelly b Kendall	14	b Kendall	0
J. Selby†	b Kendall	7	(2) b Spofforth	2
G. Ulyett	b Spofforth	52	(5) c Spofforth b Hodges	63
T. Emmett	c Kendall b Spofforth	48	(6) b Midwinter	8
T. Hill	run out	49	(7) not out	17
T. Armitage	c Thompson b Midwinter	21		
James Lillywhite*	not out	2		
J. Southerton	c Thompson b Kendall	0		
Extras	(B 5, LB 12, NB 1)	18	(B 8, LB 1)	9
Total		**261**	(6 wickets)	**122**

ENGLAND	O	M	R	W	O	M	R	W	FALL OF WICKETS				
										A	E	A	E
Shaw	42	27	30	0	32	19	27	0		1st	1st	2nd	2nd
Lillywhite	29	17	36	2	41	15	70	4	*Wkt*	*1st*	*1st*	*2nd*	*2nd*
Hill	27	12	27	4	21	9	43	1	1st	29	0	88	2
Ulyett	14·1	6	15	2	19	9	33	1	2nd	29	4	112	8
Emmett					13	6	23	0	3rd	50	55	135	9
Southerton					28·3	13	46	4	4th	60	72	164	54
									5th	96	88	169	76
AUSTRALIA									6th	104	162	196	112
Kendall	52·2	21	82	4	17	7	24	2	7th	108	196	203	–
Spofforth	29	6	67	3	15	3	44	1	8th	114	255	221	–
Midwinter	21	8	30	1	13·1	6	25	1	9th	119	259	259	–
Hodges	12	2	37	1	6	2	13	2	10th	122	261	259	–
Garrett	5	2	10	0	1	0	7	0					
Thompson	11	6	17	0									

Umpires: S. Cosstick (1) and R.B. Terry (2).

Close: 1st day – E(1) 7-2 (Greenwood 4, Charlwood 2); 2nd – E(1) 261 all out; 3rd – A(2) 207-7 (Spofforth 3, Kendall 4).

AUSTRALIA v ENGLAND 1878–79 (Only Test)

Played at Melbourne Cricket Ground on 2, 3, 4 January.
Toss: England.   Result: AUSTRALIA won by ten wickets.
Debuts: Australia – F.E. Allan, A.C. Bannerman, H.F. Boyle; England – C.A. Absolom, The Fourth
  Lord Harris, L. Hone, A.N. Hornby, A.P. Lucas, F.A. MacKinnon (The MacKinnon of
  MacKinnon, 35th Chief of the Clan MacKinnon), V.P.F.A. Royle, S.S. Schultz, A.J. Webbe.

Originally billed as 'Gentlemen of England (with Ulyett and Emmett) v The Australian XI', this match has
become accepted as the third Test match between the two countries. Ignoring the possible effects of an early
morning thunderstorm, Lord Harris chose to bat. Ulyett played on to the second ball of the match and England's
first seven wickets fell for 26 runs – the worst start to a Test innings until *Test No. 25*. Spofforth achieved the
first Test match hat-trick when he dismissed Royle, MacKinnon and Emmett in the first innings and became
the first bowler to take 13 wickets at this level.

ENGLAND

G. Ulyett	b Spofforth	0	b Spofforth	14
A.P. Lucas	b Allan	6	c Boyle b Allan	13
A.J. Webbe	b Allan	4	lbw b Allan	0
A.N. Hornby	b Spofforth	2	b Spofforth	4
Lord Harris*	b Garrett	33	c Horan b Spofforth	36
V.P.F.A. Royle	b Spofforth	3	c Spofforth b Boyle	18
F.A. MacKinnon	b Spofforth	0	b Spofforth	5
T. Emmett	c Horan b Spofforth	0	(9) not out	24
C.A. Absolom	c A.C. Bannerman b Boyle	52	(8) c and b Spofforth	6
L. Hone†	c Blackham b Spofforth	7	b Spofforth	6
S.S. Schultz	not out	0	c and b Spofforth	20
Extras	(B 4, LB 2)	6	(B 10, LB 4)	14
Total		**113**		**160**

AUSTRALIA

C. Bannerman	b Emmett	15	not out	15
W.L. Murdoch	c Webbe b Ulyett	4	not out	4
T.P. Horan	c Hone b Emmett	10		
A.C. Bannerman	b Schultz	73		
F.R. Spofforth	c Royle b Emmett	39		
T.W. Garrett	c Hone b Emmett	26		
F.E. Allan	b Hornby	5		
H.F. Boyle	c Royle b Emmett	28		
J.M. Blackham†	b Emmett	6		
T.J.D. Kelly	c Webbe b Emmett	10		
D.W. Gregory*	not out	12		
Extras	(B19, LB 2, W 7)	28		
Total		**256**	(0 wickets)	**19**

AUSTRALIA	O	M	R	W	O	M	R	W	FALL OF WICKETS				
Spofforth	25	9	48	6	35	16	62	7		E	A	E	A
Allan	17	4	30	2	28	11	50	2	*Wkt*	*1st*	*1st*	*2nd*	*2nd*
Garrett	5	0	18	1	10	6	18	0	1st	0	16	26	–
Boyle	7	1	11	1	10	4	16	1	2nd	7	30	28	–
									3rd	10	37	28	–
ENGLAND									4th	14	101	34	–
Emmett	59	31	68	7					5th	26	131	78	–
Ulyett	62	24	93	1	1	0	9	0	6th	26	158	103	–
Lucas	18	6	31	0					7th	26	215	103	–
Schultz	6·3	3	16	1	2	0	10	0	8th	89	224	118	–
Hornby	7	7	0	1					9th	113	234	128	–
Harris	3	0	14	0					10th	113	256	160	–
Royle	4	1	6	0									

Umpires: P. Coady (1) and G. Coulthard (1).

Close: 1st day – A(1) 95-3 (A.C. Bannerman 23, Spofforth 36); 2nd – E(2) 103-6 (MacKinnon 5).

ENGLAND v AUSTRALIA 1880 (Only Test)

Played at Kennington Oval, London, on 6, 7, 8 September.
Toss: England.   Result: ENGLAND won by five wickets.
Debuts: England – W. Barnes, E.M. Grace, G.F. Grace, W.G. Grace, Hon. A. Lyttelton, F. Morley,
   F. Penn, A.G. Steel; Australia – G. Alexander, G.J. Bonnor, T.U. Groube, P.S. McDonnell,
   W.H. Moule, G.E. Palmer, J. Slight.

Charles William Alcock, secretary of Surrey CCC, was the main instigator of the first Test match to be played
in England. It was held on dates originally set aside for the Australians' match against Sussex. The visitors were
without Spofforth (damaged finger). William Gilbert Grace, who scored England's first Test century on his debut,
and his two brothers, Edward Mills and George Frederick, provided the first instance of three brothers playing
in the same Test. 'W.G.' and Lucas shared the first hundred partnership in Test cricket – 120 for the second
wicket. Murdoch became the first Test captain to score a hundred (his first in first-class cricket), and did so in
his first match in that role.

ENGLAND

E.M. Grace	c Alexander b Bannerman	36	(6) b Boyle		0
W.G. Grace	b Palmer	152	(7) not out		9
A.P. Lucas	b Bannerman	55	c Blackham b Palmer		2
W. Barnes	b Alexander	28	(5) c Moule b Boyle		5
Lord Harris*	c Bonnor b Alexander	52			
F. Penn	b Bannerman	23	(4) not out		27
A.G. Steel	c Boyle b Moule	42			
Hon. A. Lyttelton†	not out	11	(1) b Palmer		13
G.F. Grace	c Bannerman b Moule	0	(2) b Palmer		0
A. Shaw	b Moule	0			
F. Morley	run out	2			
Extras	(B 8, LB 11)	19	(NB 1)		1
Total		**420**	(5 wickets)		**57**

AUSTRALIA

A.C. Bannerman	b Morley	32	c Lucas b Shaw		8
W.L. Murdoch*	c Barnes b Steel	0	(3) not out		153
T.U. Groube	b Steel	11	(4) c Shaw b Morley		0
P.S. McDonnell	c Barnes b Morley	27	(5) lbw b W.G. Grace		43
J. Slight	c G.F. Grace b Morley	11	(6) c Harris b W.G. Grace		0
J.M. Blackham†	c and b Morley	0	(7) c E.M. Grace b Morley		19
G.J. Bonnor	c G.F. Grace b Shaw	2	(8) b Steel		16
H.F. Boyle	not out	36	(2) run out		3
G.E. Palmer	b Morley	6	c and b Steel		4
G. Alexander	c W.G. Grace b Steel	6	c Shaw b Morley		33
W.H. Moule	c Morley b W.G. Grace	6	b Barnes		34
Extras	(B 9, LB 3)	12	(B 7, LB 7)		14
Total		**149**			**327**

AUSTRALIA	O	M	R	W	O	M	R	W		FALL OF WICKETS			
Boyle	44	17	71	0	17	7	21	2		E	A	A	E
Palmer	70	27	116	1	16·3	5	35	3	*Wkt*	*1st*	*1st*	*2nd*	*2nd*
Alexander	32	10	69	2					1st	91	28	8	2
Bannerman	50	12	111	3					2nd	211	39	13	10
McDonnell	2	0	11	0					3rd	269	59	14	22
Moule	12·3	4	23	3					4th	281	84	97	31
									5th	322	84	101	31
ENGLAND									6th	404	89	143	–
Morley	32	9	56	5	61	30	90	3	7th	410	97	181	–
Steel	29	9	58	3	31	6	73	2	8th	410	113	187	–
Shaw	13	5	21	1	33	18	42	1	9th	413	126	239	–
W.G. Grace	1·1	0	2	1	28	10	66	2	10th	420	149	327	–
Barnes					8·3	3	17	1					
Lucas					12	7	23	0					
Penn					3	1	2	0					

Umpires: H.H. Stephenson (1) and R. Thoms (1).

Close: 1st day – E(1) 410-8 (Lyttelton 4); 2nd – A(2) 170-6 (Murdoch 79, Bonnor 13).

AUSTRALIA v ENGLAND 1881–82 (1st Test)

Played at Melbourne Cricket Ground on 31 December, 2, 3, 4 January.
Toss: England.   Result: MATCH DRAWN.
Debuts: Australia – W.H. Cooper, E. Evans, G. Giffen, H.H. Massie; England – R.G. Barlow, W. Bates, E. Peate, R. Pilling, A. Shrewsbury, W.H. Scotton. *W.E. Midwinter made his debut for England having played for Australia in the first two Test matches and became the only man to represent both sides in this series.*

Horan and Giffen recorded Australia's first century-partnership: 107 for the fifth wicket. Ulyett scored 80 not out in two hours before lunch on the first day. His second-wicket partnership of 137 with Selby was a Test record for any wicket. James Lillywhite, England's captain in the first two matches of Test cricket, became the first former Test cricketer to umpire at that level. This was the first Test in which 1,000 runs were scored.

ENGLAND

R.G. Barlow	c Bannerman b Palmer	0	st Blackham b Palmer		33
G. Ulyett	c McDonnell b Cooper	87	st Blackham b Cooper		23
J. Selby	run out	55	c Boyle b Cooper		70
W. Bates	c Giffen b Boyle	58	c Bannerman b Cooper		47
A. Shrewsbury	c Blackham b Evans	11	b Cooper		16
W.E. Midwinter	b Evans	36	c Massie b Cooper		4
T. Emmett	b Evans	5	b Cooper		6
W.H. Scotton	run out	21	not out		50
A. Shaw*	c Boyle b Cooper	5	c Cooper b Boyle		40
R. Pilling†	c Giffen b Cooper	5	b Palmer		3
E. Peate	not out	4	run out		2
Extras	(LB 6, NB 1)	7	(B 7, LB 2, NB 5)		14
Total		**294**			**308**

AUSTRALIA

H.H. Massie	st Pilling b Midwinter	2			
A.C. Bannerman	b Ulyett	38	b Ulyett		8
W.L. Murdoch*	b Ulyett	39	(4) not out		22
P.S. McDonnell	b Midwinter	19	(5) not out		33
T.P. Horan	run out	124	(3) c Emmett b Bates		26
G. Giffen	b Emmett	30			
J.M. Blackham†	b Emmett	2	(1) b Bates		25
G.E. Palmer	c Pilling b Bates	34			
E. Evans	b Bates	3			
H.F. Boyle	not out	4			
W.H. Cooper	st Pilling b Peate	7			
Extras	(B 4, LB 11, W 3)	18	(B 9, LB 3, W 1)		13
Total		**320**	(3 wickets)		**127**

AUSTRALIA	O	M	R	W	O	M	R	W		FALL OF WICKETS			
Palmer	36	9	73	1	77	19	77	2		E	A	E	A
Boyle	18	9	18	1	15	6	19	1	Wkt	1st	1st	2nd	2nd
Bannerman	10	3	23	0					1st	5	9	37	35
Evans	71	35	81	3	75·2	45	63	0	2nd	142	82	96	70
Cooper	32·2	8	80	3	66	19	120	6	3rd	151	97	179	72
Giffen	3	0	12	0					4th	187	113	183	–
McDonnell					4	1	15	0	5th	227	220	188	–
									6th	232	226	197	–
ENGLAND									7th	277	305	217	–
Peate	59	24	64	1	11	5	22	0	8th	284	309	300	–
Midwinter	39	21	50	2					9th	289	309	305	–
Bates	41	20	43	2	13	3	43	2	10th	294	320	308	–
Emmett	35	12	61	2	16	11	19	0					
Ulyett	20	5	41	2	15	3	30	1					
Barlow	23	13	22	0									
Shaw	20	11	21	0									

Umpires: James Lillywhite, jr (1) and J.S. Swift (1).

Close: 1st day – E(1) 294 all out; 2nd – A(1) 277-6 (Horan 106, Palmer 23); 3rd – E(2) 238-7 (Scotton 13, Shaw 14).

AUSTRALIA v ENGLAND 1881–82 (2nd Test)

Played at Sydney Cricket Ground on 17, 18, 20, 21 February.
Toss: England.   Result: AUSTRALIA won by five wickets.
Debuts: Australia – G. Coulthard, S.P. Jones.

England undertook a seven-match tour of New Zealand immediately before this, the first Test to be played in Sydney. Ulyett and Barlow scored 122 for England's first wicket in the second innings – the first hundred opening partnership in Test cricket. Blackham kept wicket for part of England's second innings. Palmer and Evans bowled unchanged throughout England's first innings which lasted over three hours. Coulthard was the first Test umpire (*Test No. 3*) who subsequently played Test cricket.

ENGLAND

G. Ulyett	c Murdoch b Evans	25	lbw b Palmer		67
R.G. Barlow	b Palmer	31	c Boyle b Garrett		62
J. Selby	c and b Evans	6	c Blackham b Palmer		2
W. Bates	st Murdoch b Palmer	4	b Palmer		5
A. Shrewsbury	b Palmer	7	c McDonnell b Garrett		22
W.E. Midwinter	c Blackham b Palmer	4	b Palmer		8
W.H. Scotton	b Palmer	30	lbw b Garrett		12
T. Emmett	b Evans	10	c McDonnell b Garrett		9
A. Shaw*	c Massie b Palmer	11	b Evans		30
R. Pilling†	b Palmer	3	b Jones		9
E. Peate	not out	1	not out		1
Extras	(LB 1)	1	(B 3, LB 2)		5
Total		**133**			**232**

AUSTRALIA

H.H. Massie	c Shrewsbury b Bates	49	b Ulyett		22
J.M. Blackham	c Shaw b Midwinter	40	c and b Bates		4
E. Evans	run out	11			
W.L. Murdoch*†	c Emmett b Bates	10	(3) c Barlow b Midwinter		49
T.P. Horan	run out	4	(4) b Ulyett		21
P.S. McDonnell	b Bates	14	(5) b Shaw		25
S.P. Jones	c Emmett b Ulyett	37	(6) not out		13
T.W. Garrett	c Shrewsbury b Peate	4	(7) not out		31
G.E. Palmer	b Bates	16			
H.F. Boyle	c Shrewsbury b Ulyett	0			
G. Coulthard	not out	6			
Extras	(B 1, LB 2, W 2, NB 1)	6	(B 3, LB 1)		4
Total		**197**	(5 wickets)		**169**

AUSTRALIA	O	M	R	W	O	M	R	W	FALL OF WICKETS				
Palmer	58	36	68	7	66	29	97	4		E	A	E	A
Evans	57	32	64	3	40·1	19	49	1	*Wkt*	*1st*	*1st*	*2nd*	*2nd*
Garrett					36	12	62	4	1st	39	78	122	10
Jones					11	4	19	1	2nd	47	102	124	28
									3rd	64	103	130	67
ENGLAND									4th	73	111	156	113
Peate	52	28	53	1	20	12	22	0	5th	77	132	165	127
Midwinter	34	16	43	1	18	8	23	1	6th	90	133	175	–
Emmett	6	2	24	0	6	3	17	0	7th	115	140	183	–
Ulyett	22·2	16	11	2	15	4	48	2	8th	123	167	204	–
Bates	72	43	52	4	24	11	37	1	9th	132	168	230	–
Barlow	8	4	8	0	4	1	6	0	10th	133	197	232	–
Shaw					21	15	12	1					

Umpires: James Lillywhite, jr (2) and J.S. Swift (2).

Close: 1st day – A(1) 86-1 (Blackham 30, Evans 5); 2nd – E(1) 8-0 (Ulyett 5, Barlow 1); 3rd – A(2) 35-2 (Murdoch 2, Horan 6).

AUSTRALIA v ENGLAND 1881–82 (3rd Test)

Played at Sydney Cricket Ground on 3, 4, 6, 7 March.
Toss: England.   Result: AUSTRALIA won by six wickets.
Debuts: Nil.

The partnership of 199 between Bannerman and McDonnell, who scored his first hundred in first-class cricket, was the highest for any wicket in Test matches until W.L. Murdoch and H.J.H. Scott added 207 in 1884 (*Test No. 16*). It remains the fourth-wicket record by either side in Australia v England Tests in Australia.

ENGLAND

G. Ulyett	b Palmer	0	b Garrett	23
R.G. Barlow	c Blackham b Garrett	4	c and b Garrett	8
J. Selby	c Massie b Palmer	13	b Palmer	1
W. Bates	c and b Palmer	1	c Bannerman b Garrett	2
A. Shrewsbury	c and b Boyle	82	c Boyle b Garrett	47
W.E. Midwinter	b Palmer	12	b Palmer	10
W.H. Scotton	c Jones b Garrett	18	b Palmer	1
T. Emmett	b Garrett	4	b Garrett	2
A. Shaw*	b Boyle	3	b Garrett	6
R. Pilling†	b Palmer	12	b Palmer	23
E. Peate	not out	11	not out	8
Extras	(B 22, LB 6)	28	(B 2, NB 1)	3
Total		**188**		**134**

AUSTRALIA

A.C. Bannerman	b Midwinter	70	c Pilling b Peate	14
H.H. Massie	b Bates	0	c Midwinter b Peate	9
W.L. Murdoch*	c Ulyett b Bates	6	c Midwinter b Bates	4
T.P. Horan	c and b Bates	1	not out	16
P.S. McDonnell	c Midwinter b Peate	147	c Emmett b Peate	4
G. Giffen	c Pilling b Peate	2		
J.M. Blackham†	b Peate	4		
T.W. Garrett	b Peate	0		
G.E. Palmer	b Midwinter	6		
S.P. Jones	not out	7	(6) not out	10
H.F. Boyle	c Pilling b Peate	3		
Extras	(B 6, LB 8)	14	(B 2, LB 5, W 1, NB 1)	9
Total		**260**	(4 wickets)	**66**

AUSTRALIA	O	M	R	W	O	M	R	W
Palmer	45·2	23	46	5	40	19	44	4
Garrett	60	25	85	3	36·1	10	78	6
Boyle	27	18	18	2	4	1	9	0
Jones	8	5	11	0				
ENGLAND								
Peate	45	24	43	5	25	18	14	3
Bates	38	17	67	3	24·3	13	43	1
Ulyett	3	1	10	0				
Midwinter	62	25	75	2				
Shaw	8	4	14	0				
Emmett	16	6	37	0				

FALL OF WICKETS

Wkt	E 1st	A 1st	E 2nd	A 2nd
1st	2	0	28	14
2nd	8	10	29	21
3rd	17	16	32	39
4th	35	215	42	49
5th	56	228	60	–
6th	148	235	70	–
7th	154	244	73	–
8th	159	245	79	–
9th	164	252	113	–
10th	188	260	134	–

Umpires: James Lillywhite, jr (3) and J.S. Swift (3).

Close: 1st day – A(1) 24-3 (Bannerman 15, McDonnell 0); 2nd – A(1) 146-3 (Bannerman 59, McDonnell 72); 3rd – E(2) 121-9 (Shrewsbury 39, Peate 4).

AUSTRALIA v ENGLAND 1881–82 (4th Test)

Played at Melbourne Cricket Ground on 10, 11, 13, 14 (*no play*) March.
Toss: England.   Result: MATCH DRAWN.
Debuts: Nil.

This was the last drawn Test in Australia until 1946-47. Ulyett's 149 was the first Test hundred for England in Australia and it was the highest score for England on the first day of a Test in Australia until R.W. Barber scored 185 in 1965-66 (*Test No. 599*).

ENGLAND

G. Ulyett	c Blackham b Garrett	149	c Palmer b Boyle	64
R.G. Barlow	c Blackham b Garrett	16	run out	56
J. Selby	b Spofforth	7	not out	48
W. Bates	st Blackham b Garrett	23	not out	52
A. Shrewsbury	lbw b Palmer	1		
W.E. Midwinter	c Palmer b Boyle	21		
W.H. Scotton	st Blackham b Giffen	26		
T. Emmett	b Giffen	27		
A. Shaw*	c Murdoch b Garrett	3		
R. Pilling†	not out	6		
E. Peate	c and b Garrett	13		
Extras	(B 10, LB 7)	17	(B 12, LB 2)	14
Total		**309**	(2 wickets)	**234**

AUSTRALIA

W.L. Murdoch*	b Midwinter	85
A.C. Bannerman	c and b Midwinter	37
T.P. Horan	c and b Midwinter	20
P.S. McDonnell	c Barlow b Ulyett	52
H.H. Massie	c Emmett b Shaw	19
G. Giffen	c Scotton b Peate	14
J.M. Blackham†	c Pilling b Midwinter	6
T.W. Garrett	c Ulyett b Bates	10
G.E. Palmer	c Ulyett b Bates	32
H.F. Boyle	c Shrewsbury b Bates	6
F.R. Spofforth	not out	3
Extras	(B 2, LB 7, W 6, NB 1)	16
Total		**300**

AUSTRALIA	O	M	R	W	O	M	R	W		FALL OF WICKETS		
Garrett	54·2	23	80	5	27	6	62	0		E	A	E
Spofforth	51	14	92	1	15	3	36	0	*Wkt*	*1st*	*1st*	*2nd*
Boyle	18	4	33	1	25	9	38	1	1st	32	110	98
Palmer	23	5	70	1	20	5	47	0	2nd	49	149	152
Giffen	13	6	17	2	8·3	1	25	0	3rd	98	153	–
Bannerman					2	0	12	0	4th	109	189	–
									5th	177	228	–
ENGLAND									6th	239	237	–
Bates	28·1	14	49	3					7th	281	247	–
Peate	20	6	38	1					8th	284	280	–
Emmett	19	14	22	0					9th	288	297	–
Ulyett	24	8	40	1					10th	309	300	–
Barlow	15	6	25	0								
Shaw	16	6	29	1								
Midwinter	41	9	81	4								

Umpires: G. Coulthard (2) and James Lillywhite, jr (4).

Close: 1st day – E(1) 283-7 (Emmett 27, Shaw 1); 2nd – A(1) 228-5 (McDonnell 41, Blackham 0); 3rd – E(2) 234-2 (Selby 48, Bates 52).

ENGLAND v AUSTRALIA 1882 (Only Test)

Played at Kennington Oval, London, on 28, 29 August.
Toss: Australia.   Result: AUSTRALIA won by 7 runs.
Debuts: England – J.M. Read, C.T. Studd.

The Ashes came into being as a result of this first Australian victory over a full-strength England side in England. The *Sporting Times* carried a mock obituary notice stating that the body of English cricket would be cremated and the ashes taken to Australia. Spofforth, the first bowler to take 14 wickets in a Test, conceded only one scoring stroke while taking four wickets for two runs off his last 11 overs in the first innings – a spell which included the first Test match instance of three wickets in four balls. 'The Demon' had taken the first hat-trick in *Test No. 3*. Jones was run out by Grace when, after completing a run, he left his crease to pat the pitch down. The paying attendance for the two days totalled 39,194. During the tense final stages one spectator died of heart failure and another bit through his umbrella handle.

AUSTRALIA

Batsman	Dismissal 1		Dismissal 2	
A.C. Bannerman	c Grace b Peate	9	c Studd b Barnes	13
H.H. Massie	b Ulyett	1	b Steel	55
W.L. Murdoch*	b Peate	13	(4) run out	29
G.J. Bonnor	b Barlow	1	(3) b Ulyett	2
T.P. Horan	b Barlow	3	c Grace b Peate	2
G. Giffen	b Peate	2	c Grace b Peate	0
J.M. Blackham†	c Grace b Barlow	17	c Lyttelton b Peate	7
T.W. Garrett	c Read b Peate	10	(10) not out	2
H.F. Boyle	b Barlow	2	(11) b Steel	0
S.P. Jones	c Barnes b Barlow	0	(8) run out	6
F.R. Spofforth	not out	4	(9) b Peate	0
Extras	(B 1)	1	(B 6)	6
Total		**63**		**122**

ENGLAND

Batsman	Dismissal 1		Dismissal 2	
R.G. Barlow	c Bannerman b Spofforth	11	(3) b Spofforth	0
W.G. Grace	b Spofforth	4	(1) c Bannerman b Boyle	32
G. Ulyett	st Blackham b Spofforth	26	(4) c Blackham b Spofforth	11
A.P. Lucas	c Blackham b Boyle	9	(5) b Spofforth	5
Hon. A. Lyttelton†	c Blackham b Spofforth	2	(6) b Spofforth	12
C.T. Studd	b Spofforth	0	(10) not out	0
J.M. Read	not out	19	(8) b Spofforth	0
W. Barnes	b Boyle	5	(9) c Murdoch b Boyle	2
A.G. Steel	b Garrett	14	(7) c and b Spofforth	0
A.N. Hornby*	b Spofforth	2	(2) b Spofforth	9
E. Peate	c Boyle b Spofforth	0	b Boyle	2
Extras	(B 6, LB 2, NB 1)	9	(B 3, NB 1)	4
Total		**101**		**77**

ENGLAND	O	M	R	W	O	M	R	W
Peate	38	24	31	4	21	9	40	4
Ulyett	9	5	11	1	6	2	10	1
Barlow	31	22	19	5	13	5	27	0
Steel	2	1	1	0	7	0	15	2
Barnes					12	5	15	1
Studd					4	1	9	0
AUSTRALIA								
Spofforth	36·3	18	46	7	28	15	44	7
Garrett	16	7	22	1	7	2	10	0
Boyle	19	7	24	2	20	11	19	3

FALL OF WICKETS

Wkt	A 1st	E 1st	A 2nd	E 2nd
1st	6	13	66	15
2nd	21	18	70	15
3rd	22	57	70	51
4th	26	59	79	53
5th	30	60	79	66
6th	30	63	99	70
7th	48	70	114	70
8th	53	96	117	75
9th	59	101	122	75
10th	63	101	122	77

Umpires: L. Greenwood (1) and R. Thoms (2).

Close: 1st day – E(1) 101 all out.

AUSTRALIA v ENGLAND 1882–83 (1st Test)

Played at Melbourne Cricket Ground on 30 December, 1, 2 January.
Toss: Australia.   Result: AUSTRALIA won by nine wickets.
Debuts: England – Hon. I.F.W. Bligh, C.F.H. Leslie, W.W. Read, G.B. Studd, E.F.S. Tylecote,
G.F. Vernon. *The Hon. Ivo Bligh later became the eighth Earl of Darnley.*

Originally billed as 'Mr Murdoch's Eleven v The Hon. Ivo F.W. Bligh's Team', this was the first of three matches under that title against the Australian team which toured England in 1882. It attracted a total attendance of around 54,000. Leslie's analysis remained his best in first-class cricket.

AUSTRALIA

A.C. Bannerman	st Tylecote b Leslie	30	not out	25
H.H. Massie	c and b C.T. Studd	4	c and b Barnes	0
W.L. Murdoch*	b Leslie	48	not out	33
T.P. Horan	c Barlow b Leslie	0		
P.S. McDonnell	b Bates	43		
G. Giffen	st Tylecote b Steel	36		
G.J. Bonnor	c Barlow b Barnes	85		
J.M. Blackham†	c Tylecote b C.T. Studd	25		
F.R. Spofforth	c Steel b Barnes	9		
T.W. Garrett	c C.T. Studd b Steel	0		
G.E. Palmer	not out	0		
Extras	(B 4, LB 2, W 2, NB 3)	11		
Total		**291**	(1 wicket)	**58**

ENGLAND

R.G. Barlow	st Blackham b Palmer	10	b Spofforth	28
Hon. I.F.W. Bligh*	b Palmer	0	(5) b Spofforth	3
C.F.H. Leslie	c Garrett b Palmer	4	(7) b Giffen	4
C.T. Studd	b Spofforth	0	(3) b Palmer	21
A.G. Steel	b Palmer	27	(4) lbw b Giffen	29
W.W. Read	b Palmer	19	b Giffen	29
W.Bates	c Bannerman b Garrett	28	(8) c Massie b Palmer	11
E.F.S. Tylecote†	b Palmer	33	(2) b Spofforth	38
G.B. Studd	run out	7	c Palmer b Giffen	0
W. Barnes	b Palmer	26	not out	2
G.F. Vernon	not out	11	lbw b Palmer	3
Extras	(B 8, LB 1, NB 3)	12	(LB 1)	1
Total		**177**		**169**

ENGLAND	O	M	R	W	O	M	R	W
C.T. Studd	46	30	35	2	14	11	7	0
Barnes	30	11	51	2	13	8	6	1
Steel	33	16	68	2	9	4	17	0
Read	8	2	27	0				
Barlow	20	6	37	0	4	2	6	0
Bates	21	7	31	1	13.1	7	22	0
Leslie	11	1	31	3				
AUSTRALIA								
Spofforth	28	11	56	1	41	15	65	3
Palmer	52·2	25	65	7	36·1	11	61	3
Garrett	27	6	44	1	2	1	4	0
Giffen					20	7	38	4

FALL OF WICKETS

	A	E	E	A
Wkt	1st	1st	2nd	2nd
1st	5	2	64	0
2nd	81	7	75	–
3rd	81	8	105	–
4th	96	36	108	–
5th	162	45	132	–
6th	190	96	150	–
7th	251	96	164	–
8th	289	117	164	–
9th	289	156	164	–
10th	291	177	169	–

Umpires: E.H. Elliott (1) and J.S. Swift (4).

Close: 1st day – A(1) 258-7 (Bonnor 60, Spofforth 1); 2nd – E(2) 11-0 (Barlow 8, Tylecote 3).

AUSTRALIA v ENGLAND 1882–83 (2nd Test)

Played at Melbourne Cricket Ground on 19, 20, 22 January.
Toss: England.　　Result: ENGLAND won by an innings and 27 runs.
Debuts: Nil.

Bates achieved the first Test hat-trick by an England bowler when he dismissed McDonnell, Giffen and Bonnor in the first innings. He went on to become the first player to score a fifty and take ten or more wickets in the same Test match. This was the first victory by an innings margin in Test cricket.

ENGLAND

R.G. Barlow	b Palmer	14
C.T. Studd	b Palmer	14
C.F.H. Leslie	run out	54
A.G. Steel	c McDonnell b Giffen	39
W.W. Read	c and b Palmer	75
W. Barnes	b Giffen	32
E.F.S. Tylecote†	b Giffen	0
Hon. I.F.W. Bligh*	b Giffen	0
W. Bates	c Horan b Palmer	55
G.B. Studd	b Palmer	1
F. Morley	not out	0
Extras	(B 3, LB 3, NB 4)	10
Total		**294**

AUSTRALIA

H.H. Massie	b Barlow	43	(7)	c C.T. Studd b Barlow	10
A.C. Bannerman	b Bates	14		c Bligh b Bates	14
W.L. Murdoch*	not out	19	(1)	b Bates	17
T.P. Horan	c and b Barnes	3	(5)	c Morley b Bates	15
P.S. McDonnell	b Bates	3	(6)	b Bates	13
G. Giffen	c and b Bates	0	(8)	c Bligh b Bates	19
G.J. Bonnor	c Read b Bates	0	(4)	c Morley b Barlow	34
J.M. Blackham†	b Barnes	5	(3)	b Barlow	6
T.W. Garrett	b Bates	10		c Barnes b Bates	6
G.E. Palmer	b Bates	7		c G.B. Studd b Bates	4
F.R. Spofforth	b Bates	0		not out	14
Extras	(B 6, LB 3, NB 1)	10		(B 1)	1
Total		**114**			**153**

AUSTRALIA	O	M	R	W	O	M	R	W
Spofforth	34	11	57	0				
Palmer	66·3	25	103	5				
Giffen	49	13	89	4				
Garrett	34	16	35	0				
ENGLAND								
C.T. Studd	4	1	22	0				
Morley	23	16	13	0	2	0	7	0
Barnes	23	7	32	2	3	1	4	0
Barlow	22	18	9	1	31	6	67	3
Bates	26·2	14	28	7	33	14	74	7

FALL OF WICKETS

	E	A	A
Wkt	1st	1st	2nd
1st	28	56	21
2nd	35	72	28
3rd	106	75	66
4th	131	78	72
5th	193	78	93
6th	199	78	104
7th	199	85	113
8th	287	104	132
9th	293	114	139
10th	294	114	153

Umpires: E.H. Elliott (2) and J.S. Swift (5).

Close: 1st day – E(1) 248-7 (Read 51, Bates 35); 2nd – A(2) 28-1 (Bannerman 5, Blackham 6).

AUSTRALIA v ENGLAND 1882–83 (3rd Test)

Played at Sydney Cricket Ground on 26, 27, 29, 30 January.
Toss: England.   Result: ENGLAND won by 69 runs.
Debuts: Nil.

With the rubber level, two pitches were prepared for this final Test, each captain having the choice of pitch on which to bat. Approximately 50,000 attended, with nearly 23,000 watching the first day's play. Tylecote's half-century was the first in Test cricket by a wicket-keeper. After this match, the last of the rubber originally scheduled, some Melbourne ladies burned a bail, sealed the ashes in an urn and presented it to the victorious captain of the English team. The urn, together with its embroidered velvet bag, is housed in the Memorial Gallery at Lord's.

ENGLAND

R.G. Barlow	c Murdoch b Spofforth	28	(3) c Palmer b Horan	24
C.T. Studd	c Blackham b Garrett	21	b Spofforth	25
C.F.H. Leslie	b Spofforth	0	(1) b Spofforth	8
A.G. Steel	b Garrett	17	lbw b Spofforth	6
W.W. Read	c Massie b Bannerman	66	b Horan	21
W. Barnes	c Blackham b Spofforth	2	lbw b Spofforth	3
E.F.S. Tylecote†	run out	66	c Bonnor b Spofforth	0
W. Bates	c McDonnell b Spofforth	17	c Murdoch b Horan	4
G.B. Studd	b Palmer	3	(10) c Garrett b Spofforth	8
Hon. I.F.W. Bligh*	b Palmer	13	(9) not out	17
F. Morley	not out	2	b Spofforth	0
Extras	(B 8, LB 3, NB 1)	12	(B 5, LB 2)	7
Total		**247**		**123**

AUSTRALIA

A.C. Bannerman	c Bates b Morley	94	c Bligh b Barlow	5
G. Giffen	st Tylecote b Bates	41	b Barlow	7
W.L. Murdoch*	lbw b Steel	19	c G.B. Studd b Morley	0
P.S. McDonnell	b Steel	0	(5) c Bligh b Morley	0
T.P. Horan	c Steel b Morley	19	(4) run out	8
H.H. Massie	c Bligh b Steel	1	c C.T. Studd b Barlow	11
G.J. Bonnor	c G.B. Studd b Morley	0	b Barlow	8
J.M. Blackham†	b Barlow	27	b Barlow	26
T.W. Garrett	c Barlow b Morley	0	(11) b Barlow	0
G.E. Palmer	c G.B. Studd b Barnes	7	not out	2
F.R. Spofforth	not out	0	(9) c Steel b Barlow	7
Extras	(B 6, LB 2, W 1, NB 1)	10	(B 6, LB 2, W 1)	9
Total		**218**		**83**

AUSTRALIA	O	M	R	W	O	M	R	W		FALL OF WICKETS			
										E	A	E	A
Giffen	12	3	37	0					Wkt	1st	1st	2nd	2nd
Palmer	38	21	38	2	9	3	19	0	1st	41	76	13	11
Spofforth	51	19	73	4	41·1	23	44	7	2nd	44	140	45	12
Garrett	27	8	54	2	13	3	31	0	3rd	67	140	55	18
Bannerman	11	2	17	1					4th	69	176	87	18
McDonnell	4	0	16	0					5th	75	177	92	30
Horan					17	10	22	3	6th	191	178	94	33
									7th	223	196	97	56
ENGLAND									8th	224	196	98	72
Morley	34	16	47	4	35	19	34	2	9th	244	218	115	80
Barlow	47·1	31	52	1	34·2	20	40	7	10th	247	218	123	83
Bates	45	20	55	1									
Barnes	13	6	22	1									
C.T. Studd	14	11	5	0									
Steel	26	14	27	3									

Umpires: E.H. Elliott (3) and J.S. Swift (6).

Close: 1st day – A(1) 8-0 (Bannerman 1, Giffen 6); 2nd – A(1) 133-1 (Bannerman 40, Murdoch 17); 3rd – E(2) 123 all out.

AUSTRALIA v ENGLAND 1882–83 (4th Test)

Played at Sydney Cricket Ground on 17, 19, 20, 21 February.
Toss: England.   Result: AUSTRALIA won by four wickets.
Debuts: Nil.

Having completed the three-match rubber against W.L. Murdoch's 1882 touring team, England played a fourth fixture against a combined side. For this match the captains decided to experiment by using a separate pitch for each of the four innings. After two appearances for Australia followed by four for England, Midwinter embarked upon the final phase of his unique Test career. Bonnor gave eight chances during his innings of 87. Murdoch batted for 70 minutes before scoring his first run in the second innings. Blackham was the first wicket-keeper to score two fifties in a Test; his feat remained unequalled until 1933-34 (Dilawar Hussain in *Test No. 231*).

ENGLAND

R.G. Barlow	c Murdoch b Midwinter	2	c Bonnor b Midwinter		20
C.T. Studd	run out	48	c Murdoch b Midwinter		31
C.F.H. Leslie	c Bonnor b Boyle	17	b Horan		19
A.G. Steel	not out	135	b Spofforth		21
W.W. Read	c Bonnor b Boyle	11	b Spofforth		7
E.F.S. Tylecote†	b Boyle	5	b Palmer		0
W. Barnes	b Spofforth	2	(9) c and b Boyle		20
W.Bates	c Bonnor b Midwinter	9	(7) not out		48
Hon. I.F.W. Bligh*	b Palmer	19	(8) c Murdoch b Horan		10
G.B. Studd	run out	3	c Murdoch b Boyle		9
F. Morley	b Palmer	0	c Blackham b Palmer		2
Extras	(B 4, LB 7, NB 1)	12	(B 8, LB 1, NB 1)		10
Total		**263**			**197**

AUSTRALIA

A.C. Bannerman	c Barlow b Morley	10	c Bligh b C.T. Studd		63
G.J. Bonnor	c Barlow b Steel	87	(3) c G.B. Studd b Steel		3
W.L. Murdoch*	b Barlow	0	(2) c Barlow b Bates		17
T.P. Horan	c G.B. Studd b Morley	4	c and b Bates		0
G. Giffen	c G.B. Studd b Leslie	27	st Tylecote b Steel		32
W.E. Midwinter	b Barlow	10	(8) not out		8
J.M. Blackham†	b Bates	57	(6) not out		58
G.E. Palmer	c Bligh b Steel	0			
E. Evans	not out	22	(7) c Leslie b Steel		0
F.R. Spofforth	c Bates b Steel	1			
H.F. Boyle	c G.B. Studd b Barlow	29			
Extras	(B 10, LB 3, W 2)	15	(B 10, LB 4, W 4)		18
Total		**262**	(6 wickets)		**199**

AUSTRALIA	O	M	R	W	O	M	R	W		FALL OF WICKETS			
										E	A	E	A
Palmer	24	9	52	2	43·3	19	59	2	*Wkt*	*1st*	*1st*	*2nd*	*2nd*
Midwinter	47	24	50	2	23	13	21	2	1st	13	31	54	44
Spofforth	21	8	56	1	28	6	57	2	2nd	37	34	55	51
Boyle	40	19	52	3	23	6	35	2	3rd	110	39	77	51
Horan	12	4	26	0	9	2	15	2	4th	150	113	99	107
Evans	11	3	15	0					5th	156	128	100	162
									6th	159	160	112	164
ENGLAND									7th	199	164	137	–
Barlow	48	21	88	3	37·1	20	44	0	8th	236	220	178	–
Morley	44	25	45	2	12	9	4	0	9th	263	221	192	–
Barnes	10	2	33	0	16	5	22	0	10th	263	262	197	–
Bates	15	6	24	1	39	19	52	2					
Leslie	5	2	11	1	8	7	2	0					
Steel	19	6	34	3	43	9	49	3					
C.T. Studd	6	2	12	0	8	4	8	1					

Umpires: E.H. Elliott (4) and J.S. Swift (7).

Close: 1st day – E(1) 263-9 (Steel 135, Morley 0); 2nd – A(1) 248-9 (Evans 20, Boyle 20); 3rd – E(2) 197 all out.

ENGLAND v AUSTRALIA 1884 (1st Test)

Played at Old Trafford, Manchester, on 10 (*no play*), 11, 12 July.
Toss: England.   Result: MATCH DRAWN.
Debuts: England – T.C. O'Brien; Australia – H.J.H. Scott. *O'Brien later became Sir Timothy Carew O'Brien, Third Baronet.*

Old Trafford immediately established its unenviable reputation as the rain-centre of Britain when the first day of Test match cricket there was washed out. This was the first rubber of more than one match to be played in England.

ENGLAND

W.G. Grace	c Palmer b Boyle	8		b Palmer	31
A.N. Hornby*	st Blackham b Boyle	0	(9)	st Blackham b Palmer	4
G. Ulyett	b Spofforth	5		c Bannerman b Boyle	1
A. Shrewsbury	b Boyle	43		b Palmer	25
A.G. Steel	c Midwinter b Spofforth	15		c Blackham b Bonnor	18
A.P. Lucas	not out	15	(2)	b Giffen	24
W. Barnes	c and b Boyle	0	(6)	b Palmer	8
T.C. O'Brien	b Spofforth	0		c Bannerman b Spofforth	20
R.G. Barlow	c Bonnor b Boyle	6	(7)	not out	14
R. Pilling†	c Scott b Boyle	0		b Spofforth	3
E. Peate	b Spofforth	2		not out	8
Extras	(LB 1)	1		(B 18, LB 5, NB 1)	24
Total		**95**		(9 wickets)	**180**

AUSTRALIA

P.S. McDonnell	c Pilling b Steel	36
A.C. Bannerman	lbw b Ulyett	6
W.L. Murdoch*	c Grace b Peate	28
G. Giffen	c and b Barnes	16
W.E. Midwinter	c Grace b Ulyett	37
G.J. Bonnor	hit wkt b Peate	6
J.M. Blackham†	lbw b Steel	8
H.J.H. Scott	b Grace	12
G.E. Palmer	not out	14
F.R. Spofforth	c Shrewsbury b Peate	13
H.F. Boyle	b Ulyett	4
Extras	(LB 2)	2
Total		**182**

AUSTRALIA	O	M	R	W	O	M	R	W
Spofforth	32	10	42	4	41	17	52	2
Boyle	25	9	42	6	20	8	27	1
Palmer	6	2	10	0	36	17	47	4
Giffen					29	15	25	1
Bonnor					4	1	5	1
ENGLAND								
Peate	49	25	62	3				
Ulyett	30	17	41	3				
Barlow	8	3	18	0				
Steel	13	5	32	2				
Barnes	19	10	25	1				
Grace	11	10	2	1				

FALL OF WICKETS

Wkt	E 1st	A 1st	E 2nd
1st	6	10	41
2nd	13	56	44
3rd	13	86	70
4th	45	90	106
5th	83	97	108
6th	83	118	114
7th	84	141	139
8th	93	157	145
9th	93	172	154
10th	95	182	–

Umpires: C.K. Pullin (1) and J. Rowbotham (1).

Close: 1st day – no play; 2nd – A(1) 141-7 (Midwinter 29, Palmer 0).

ENGLAND v AUSTRALIA 1884 (2nd Test)

Played at Lord's, London, on 21, 22, 23 July.
Toss: Australia.   Result: ENGLAND won by an innings and 5 runs.
Debuts: England – S. Christopherson.

The first Test to be played at Thomas Lord's third ground. Murdoch became the first substitute fielder to take a catch in Test cricket and did so while fielding for the opposition, Grace having injured a finger. Blackham, batting without gloves, retired at 94 when his left hand was damaged by a ball from Ulyett.

AUSTRALIA

P.S. McDonnell	b Peate	0	b Steel		20
A.C. Bannerman	b Peate	12	c and b Ulyett		27
W.L. Murdoch*	lbw b Peate	10	c Shrewsbury b Ulyett		17
G. Giffen	b Peate	63	c Peate b Ulyett		5
W.E. Midwinter	b Peate	3	(7) b Ulyett		6
G.J. Bonnor	c Grace b Christopherson	25	(5) c and b Ulyett		4
J.M. Blackham†	run out	0	(8) retired hurt		0
H.J.H. Scott	c sub (W.L. Murdoch) b Steel	75	(6) not out		31
G.E. Palmer	c Grace b Peate	7	b Ulyett		13
F.R. Spofforth	c Barlow b Grace	0	c Shrewsbury b Barlow		11
H.F. Boyle	not out	26	b Ulyett		10
Extras	(B 5, LB 3)	8	(B 1)		1
Total		**229**			**145**

ENGLAND

W.G. Grace	c Bonnor b Palmer	14
A.P. Lucas	c Bonnor b Palmer	28
A. Shrewsbury	st Blackham b Giffen	27
G. Ulyett	b Palmer	32
A.G. Steel	b Palmer	148
Lord Harris*	b Spofforth	4
R.G. Barlow	c Palmer b Bonnor	38
W.W. Read	b Palmer	12
Hon. A. Lyttelton†	b Palmer	31
E. Peate	not out	8
S. Christopherson	c Bonnor b Spofforth	17
Extras	(B 15, LB 5)	20
Total		**379**

ENGLAND	O	M	R	W	O	M	R	W		FALL OF WICKETS		
Peate	40	14	85	6	16	4	34	0		A	E	A
Barlow	20	6	44	0	21	8	31	1	*Wkt*	*1st*	*1st*	*2nd*
Ulyett	11	3	21	0	39·1	23	36	7	1st	0	37	33
Christopherson	26	10	52	1	8	3	17	0	2nd	25	56	60
Grace	7	4	13	1					3rd	32	90	65
Steel	1·2	0	6	1	10	2	26	1	4th	46	120	73
									5th	88	135	84
AUSTRALIA									6th	93	233	90
Spofforth	55·1	19	112	2					7th	132	272	118
Palmer	75	26	111	6					8th	155	348	133
Giffen	22	4	68	1					9th	160	351	145
Boyle	11	3	16	0					10th	229	379	–
Bonnor	8	1	23	1								
Midwinter	13	2	29	0								

Umpires: F.H. Farrands (1) and C.K. Pullin (2).

Close: 1st day – E(1) 90-3 (Ulyett 18); 2nd – A(2) 73-4 (Giffen 4).

ENGLAND v AUSTRALIA 1884 (3rd Test)

Played at Kennington Oval, London, on 11, 12, 13 August.
Toss: Australia.   Result: MATCH DRAWN.
Debuts: Nil.

Murdoch scored the first double-century in Test cricket. His stand with Scott of 207 was a Test record for any wicket. Read reached his hundred in 113 minutes with 36 scoring strokes; it remains the highest Test innings by a No. 10 batsman and his partnership of 151 with Scotton, who batted 340 minutes, is still England's highest for the ninth wicket against Australia and against all countries in England. For the first time in Test cricket all 11 players bowled during Australia's innings. Grace kept wicket while Lyttelton took four wickets for eight runs with lobs and 'made a good leg-side catch to the first ball' (*The Times*). Read had kept wicket during Lyttelton's first spell the previous evening. Declarations were not permitted until 1889.

AUSTRALIA

A.C. Bannerman	c Read b Peate	4
P.S. McDonnell	c Ulyett b Peate	103
W.L. Murdoch*	c Peate b Barnes	211
H.J.H. Scott	c Lyttelton b Barnes	102
G. Giffen	c Steel b Ulyett	32
G.J. Bonnor	c Read b Grace	8
W.E. Midwinter	c Grace b Lyttelton	30
J.M. Blackham†	lbw b Lyttelton	31
G.E. Palmer	not out	8
F.R. Spofforth	b Lyttelton	4
H.F. Boyle	c Harris b Lyttelton	1
Extras	(B 7, LB 10)	17
Total		**551**

ENGLAND

W.G. Grace	run out	19		
W.H. Scotton	c Scott b Giffen	90		
W.Barnes	c Midwinter b Spofforth	19		
A. Shrewsbury	c Blackham b Midwinter	10	(3) c Scott b Giffen	37
A.G. Steel	lbw b Palmer	31		
G. Ulyett	c Bannerman b Palmer	10		
R.G. Barlow	c Murdoch b Palmer	0	(1) not out	21
Lord Harris*	lbw b Palmer	14	(4) not out	6
Hon. A. Lyttelton†	b Spofforth	8	(2) b Boyle	17
W.W. Read	b Boyle	117		
E. Peate	not out	4		
Extras	(B 8, LB 7, W 6, NB 3)	24	(B 3, LB 1)	4
Total		**346**	(2 wickets)	**85**

ENGLAND	O	M	R	W	O	M	R	W
Peate	63	25	99	2				
Ulyett	56	24	96	1				
Steel	34	7	71	0				
Barnes	52	25	81	2				
Barlow	50	22	72	0				
Grace	24	14	23	1				
Read	7	0	36	0				
Scotton	5	1	20	0				
Harris	5	1	15	0				
Lyttelton	12	5	19	4				
Shrewsbury	3	2	2	0				
AUSTRALIA								
Bonnor	13	4	33	0				
Palmer	54	19	90	4	2	1	2	0
Spofforth	58	31	81	2	6	2	14	0
Boyle	13	7	24	1	8	1	32	1
Midwinter	31	16	41	1	3	0	15	0
Giffen	26	13	36	1	7	1	18	1
Scott	3	0	17	0				

FALL OF WICKETS

Wkt	A 1st	E 1st	E 2nd
1st	15	32	22
2nd	158	60	73
3rd	365	75	–
4th	432	120	–
5th	454	136	–
6th	494	136	–
7th	532	160	–
8th	545	181	–
9th	549	332	–
10th	551	346	–

Umpires: F.H. Farrands (2) and C.K. Pullin (3).

Close: 1st day – A(1) 363-2 (Murdoch 145, Scott 101); 2nd – E(1) 71-2 (Scotton 21, Shrewsbury 6).

AUSTRALIA v ENGLAND 1884–85 (1st Test)

Played at Adelaide Oval on 12, 13, 15, 16 December.
Toss: Australia.   Result: ENGLAND won by eight wickets.
Debuts: England – W. Attewell, J. Briggs, W. Flowers, J. Hunter, R. Peel.

McDonnell became the first batsman to score two hundreds in successive Test innings. Originally billed as 'Murdoch's Australian Team v Alfred Shaw's Team' this was the first Test to be played at Adelaide. England's revised batting order for the second innings enabled Nottinghamshire to provide the first four batsmen to go to the wicket. Bannerman split a finger fielding a powerful hit by Ulyett. Three officially appointed umpires shared their duties equally.

AUSTRALIA

A.C. Bannerman	lbw b Peel	2	absent hurt	–
P.S. McDonnell	b Attewell	124	run out	83
W.L. Murdoch*	c Hunter b Peel	5	b Peel	7
H.J.H. Scott	b Peel	19	(5) lbw b Peel	1
J.M. Blackham†	c Attewell b Bates	66	(1) b Peel	11
G. Giffen	b Bates	4	(4) c Shrewsbury b Peel	47
G.J. Bonnor	c Read b Bates	4	c Peel b Barnes	19
G.E. Palmer	c Shrewsbury b Bates	6	b Barnes	0
H.F. Boyle	c Hunter b Bates	1	(10) not out	0
G. Alexander	run out	3	(9) st Hunter b Peel	10
W.H. Cooper	not out	0	(6) c Shrewsbury b Barnes	6
Extras	(B 7, W 2)	9	(B 7)	7
Total		**243**		**191**

ENGLAND

W.H. Scotton	st Blackham b Giffen	82	c Scott b Boyle	2
A. Shrewsbury*	b Boyle	0	(3) not out	26
G.Ulyett	c Alexander b Boyle	68		
W. Barnes	b Palmer	134	(4) not out	28
W. Bates	c Giffen b Palmer	18		
W. Flowers	lbw b Palmer	15	(2) c Scott b Palmer	7
J.M. Read	c and b Giffen	14		
J. Briggs	c Blackham b Palmer	1		
W. Attewell	not out	12		
R. Peel	b Palmer	4		
J. Hunter†	run out	1		
Extras	(B 18, LB 1, NB 1)	20	(B 4)	4
Total		**369**	(2 wickets)	**67**

ENGLAND	O	M	R	W	O	M	R	W		FALL OF WICKETS			
Peel	41	15	68	3	40·1	15	51	5		A	E	A	E
Attewell	50	23	48	1	18	10	26	0	*Wkt*	*1st*	*1st*	*2nd*	*2nd*
Ulyett	10	3	23	0	2	1	3	0	1st	33	11	28	8
Flowers	10	1	27	0	16	4	27	0	2nd	47	107	56	14
Barnes	14	2	37	0	31	10	51	3	3rd	95	282	125	–
Bates	24·1	10	31	5	9	3	26	0	4th	190	306	139	–
									5th	224	325	160	–
AUSTRALIA									6th	227	344	171	–
Boyle	63	25	95	2	9	3	21	1	7th	233	349	182	–
Giffen	56·2	26	80	2	6	0	19	0	8th	239	349	191	–
Cooper	18	4	26	0					9th	242	361	191	–
Bonnor	16	10	23	0					10th	243	369	–	–
Palmer	73	37	81	5	16	5	23	1					
McDonnell	3	0	11	0									
Scott	4	1	9	0									
Alexander	10	3	24	0									

Umpires: T.N. Cole (1), I. Fisher (1) and J. Travers (1).

Close: 1st day – A(1) 243 all out; 2nd – E(1) 233-2 (Scotton 71, Barnes 86); 3rd – A(2) 152-4 (Giffen 43, Cooper 3).

AUSTRALIA v ENGLAND 1884–85 (2nd Test)

Played at Melbourne Cricket Ground on 1, 2, 3, 5 January.
Toss: England.   Result: ENGLAND won by ten wickets.
Debuts: Australia – W. Bruce, A.H. Jarvis, A.P. Marr, S. Morris, H. Musgrove, R.J. Pope, W.R. Robertson, J.W. Trumble, J. Worrall.

Australia's team showed eleven changes as a result of the 1884 touring team (who had contested the 1st Test) demanding fifty per cent of the gate money for this match. Thus was ended the unique run of J.M. Blackham who played in each of the first 17 Test matches. For the first time players from the same county (Shrewsbury, Scotton and Barnes of Nottinghamshire) occupied the first three places in England's first innings batting order.

ENGLAND

A. Shrewsbury*	c Worrall b Morris	72	not out	0
W.H. Scotton	b Bruce	13	not out	7
W. Barnes	b Morris	58		
W. Bates	b Bruce	35		
W. Flowers	c Worrall b Bruce	5		
J.M. Read	b Jones	3		
J. Briggs	c Horan b Jones	121		
G. Ulyett	b Jones	0		
W. Attewell	c Jones b Worrall	30		
R. Peel	b Jones	5		
J. Hunter†	not out	39		
Extras	(B 7, LB 12, NB 1)	20		
Total		**401**	(0 wickets)	7

AUSTRALIA

S.P. Jones	lbw b Peel	19	b Ulyett	9
S. Morris	lbw b Attewell	4	(10) not out	10
T.P. Horan*	c Shrewsbury b Peel	63	c Hunter b Barnes	16
J.W. Trumble	c and b Barnes	59	c and b Barnes	11
A.H. Jarvis†	c Briggs b Flowers	82	lbw b Peel	10
R.J. Pope	c Flowers b Attewell	0	b Peel	3
A.P. Marr	b Barnes	0	c and b Barnes	5
H. Musgrove	c Read b Barnes	4	c Bates b Peel	9
J. Worrall	b Flowers	34	c and b Barnes	6
W. Bruce	not out	3	(2) c Hunter b Barnes	45
W.R. Robertson	c Barnes b Peel	0	b Barnes	2
Extras	(B 3, LB 4, W 2, NB 2)	11		
Total		**279**		**126**

AUSTRALIA	O	M	R	W	O	M	R	W
Bruce	55	22	88	3	0·1	0	4	0
Worrall	56	28	97	1				
Marr	11	6	11	0	1	0	3	0
Trumble	23	9	41	0				
Robertson	11	3	24	0				
Morris	34	14	73	2				
Jones	25·2	9	47	4				
Horan	1	1	0	0				
ENGLAND								
Peel	102·1	56	78	3	44	26	45	3
Attewell	61	35	54	2	5	2	7	0
Flowers	29	12	46	2	11	6	11	0
Barnes	50	27	50	3	38·3	26	31	6
Ulyett	15	7	23	0	8	3	19	1
Bates	17	11	17	0				
Briggs					8	3	13	0

FALL OF WICKETS

	E	A	A	E
Wkt	1st	1st	2nd	2nd
1st	28	4	29	–
2nd	144	46	66	–
3rd	161	124	80	–
4th	191	190	83	–
5th	194	193	86	–
6th	204	193	95	–
7th	204	203	99	–
8th	254	276	108	–
9th	303	278	116	–
10th	401	279	126	–

Umpires: E.H. Elliott (5) and James Lillywhite, jr (5).

Close: 1st day – E(1) 303-9 (Briggs 65); 2nd – A(1) 151-3 (Trumble 41, Jarvis 15); 3rd – A(2) 66-2 (Bruce 41).

AUSTRALIA v ENGLAND 1884–85 (3rd Test)

Played at Sydney Cricket Ground on 20, 21, 23, 24 February.
Toss: Australia.   Result: AUSTRALIA won by 6 runs.
Debuts: Nil.

This match resulted in the smallest margin of victory in a Test until Australia beat England by three runs in 1902 (*Test No. 73*). Spofforth took England's first three first innings wickets in four balls. He won the match when he produced a sharply lifting ball for Flowers to edge a difficult catch to point. According to Australian newspaper reports, Barnes, the most successful wicket-taker on the tour, refused to bowl on a pitch that was ideally suited to him because of a quarrel with his captain. A storm interrupted play for two hours on the first afternoon.

AUSTRALIA

A.C. Bannerman	c Peel b Flowers	13	c Shrewsbury b Ulyett	16
S.P. Jones	st Hunter b Flowers	28	(4) b Attewell	22
T.P. Horan	c Hunter b Attewell	7	b Bates	36
H.J.H. Scott	c Ulyett b Attewell	5	(5) c Barnes b Attewell	4
G.J. Bonnor	c Barnes b Flowers	18	(2) b Ulyett	29
J.W. Trumble	c Read b Attewell	13	c Ulyett b Bates	32
H.H. Massie*	c Scotton b Flowers	2	b Bates	21
A.H. Jarvis†	b Attewell	0	c and b Peel	2
F.R. Spofforth	st Hunter b Flowers	3	(11) c Attewell b Bates	0
T.W. Garrett	not out	51	not out	0
E. Evans	c Hunter b Ulyett	33	(9) b Bates	1
Extras	(B 3, LB 5)	8	(B 1, LB 1)	2
Total		**181**		**165**

ENGLAND

W.H. Scotton	c Jarvis b Horan	22	b Spofforth	2
A. Shrewsbury*	c and b Spofforth	18	b Spofforth	24
G.Ulyett	b Spofforth	2	run out	4
W. Barnes	st Jarvis b Spofforth	0	c Jarvis b Trumble	5
W. Bates	c Evans b Horan	12	c Jarvis b Spofforth	31
J. Briggs	c Scott b Horan	3	b Spofforth	1
W. Flowers	c Jarvis b Spofforth	24	c Evans b Spofforth	56
J.M. Read	c Evans b Horan	4	b Spofforth	56
W. Attewell	b Horan	14	run out	0
R. Peel	not out	8	c Jarvis b Trumble	3
J. Hunter†	b Horan	13	not out	5
Extras	(B 8, LB 3, NB 2)	13	(B 7, LB 9, W 1, NB 3)	20
Total		**133**		**207**

ENGLAND	O	M	R	W	O	M	R	W
Attewell	71	47	53	4	58	36	54	2
Ulyett	12·2	8	17	1	39	25	42	2
Flowers	46	24	46	5	20	14	19	0
Bates	6	2	6	0	20	10	24	5
Peel	32	13	51	0	20	10	24	1
AUSTRALIA								
Spofforth	48	23	54	4	48·1	22	90	6
Garrett	6	2	17	0	16	8	31	0
Horan	37·1	22	40	6	9	4	23	0
Evans	4	1	9	0	4	1	8	0
Trumble					26	13	26	2
Jones					3	0	9	0

FALL OF WICKETS

	A	E	A	E
Wkt	*1st*	*1st*	*2nd*	*2nd*
1st	45	31	36	14
2nd	46	33	56	18
3rd	56	33	91	29
4th	73	46	95	59
5th	77	56	119	61
6th	83	70	151	92
7th	83	82	161	194
8th	94	111	165	194
9th	101	111	165	199
10th	181	133	165	207

Umpires: J. Bryant (1) and E. Payne (1).

Close: 1st day – A(1) 97-8 (Spofforth 3, Garrett 2); 2nd – E(1) 133 all out; 3rd – E(2) 29-2 (Shrewsbury 12, Barnes 5).

AUSTRALIA v ENGLAND 1884–85 (4th Test)

Played at Sydney Cricket Ground on 14, 16, 17 March.
Toss: England.   Result: AUSTRALIA won by eight wickets.
Debuts: Nil.

Bonnor, 6 ft 6 in tall, scored his hundred in 100 minutes and it remained the fastest in Tests until J.T. Brown reached his in 95 minutes in 1894-95 (*Test No. 46*). His only Test century and highest first-class innings included four fives (hits out of the ground scored five runs) and 14 fours. England were caught on a drying pitch on the third day. Another version of Australia's second innings gives a total of 40 with the inclusion of two byes. However, as Jones won the match with a two and only 38 runs were required for victory, the score shown below is believed to be correct.

ENGLAND

G. Ulyett	b Giffen	10	c Garrett b Palmer		2
A. Shrewsbury*	b Giffen	40	c Bonnor b Spofforth		16
W.H. Scotton	c Blackham b Giffen	4	c Jones b Spofforth		0
W. Barnes	b Giffen	50	c Bannerman b Spofforth		20
W. Bates	c and b Jones	64	c Blackham b Palmer		1
J.M. Read	b Giffen	47	c Bannerman b Spofforth		6
W. Flowers	b Giffen	14	c Jones b Palmer		7
J. Briggs	c Palmer b Spofforth	3	run out		5
W. Attewell	b Giffen	1	not out		1
R. Peel	not out	17	c and b Spofforth		0
J. Hunter†	b Spofforth	13	b Palmer		4
Extras	(B 5, NB 1)	6	(B 14, NB 1)		15
Total		**269**			**77**

AUSTRALIA

G.E. Palmer	b Ulyett	0			
T.W. Garrett	b Barnes	32			
J.W. Trumble	b Peel	5			
P.S. McDonnell	c Attewell b Ulyett	20	(1) c Ulyett b Peel		3
A.C. Bannerman	c Shrewsbury b Flowers	51	(2) b Barnes		8
G. Giffen	c Attewell b Barnes	1			
T.P. Horan	c Barnes b Ulyett	9	(3) not out		12
G.J. Bonnor	c Bates b Barnes	128			
S.P. Jones	run out	40	(4) not out		15
J.M. Blackham*†	not out	11			
F.R. Spofforth	c Read b Barnes	1			
Extras	(B 5, LB 1, W 2, NB 3)	11			
Total		**309**	(2 wickets)		**38**

AUSTRALIA	O	M	R	W	O	M	R	W		FALL OF WICKETS			
										E	A	E	A
Giffen	52	14	117	7					*Wkt*	*1st*	*1st*	*2nd*	*2nd*
Palmer	16	5	35	0	19·1	7	32	4	1st	19	0	5	7
Spofforth	29	10	61	2	20	8	30	5	2nd	52	16	16	16
Garrett	2	1	5	0					3rd	76	40	19	–
Trumble	12	5	16	0					4th	159	98	20	–
Horan	5	2	12	0					5th	186	108	27	–
Jones	10	5	17	1					6th	219	119	42	–
									7th	222	134	63	–
ENGLAND									8th	229	288	69	–
Ulyett	54	25	91	3					9th	252	308	69	–
Peel	31	12	53	1	9	4	16	1	10th	269	309	77	–
Attewell	18	13	22	0	3	1	4	0					
Bates	17	5	44	0									
Barnes	35·3	17	61	4	9	3	15	1					
Flowers	14	5	27	1	3·3	2	3	0					

Umpires: E.H. Elliott (6) and P.G. McShane (1).

Close: 1st day – A(1) 12-1 (Garrett 9, Trumble 2); 2nd – A(1) 308-8 (Jones 40, Blackham 11).

AUSTRALIA v ENGLAND 1884–85 (5th Test)

Played at Melbourne Cricket Ground on 21, 23, 24, 25 March.
Toss: Australia.   Result: ENGLAND won by an innings and 98 runs.
Debuts: Australia – P.G. McShane, F.H. Walters.

Shrewsbury became the first England captain to score a Test match hundred. Garrett deputised for umpire Hodges when the latter refused to stand after tea on the third day because of England's complaints about his decisions. Allen stood for Phillips on the third and fourth days. McShane played in this Test after umpiring in the previous one. Bates retired ill with 54 not out when England were 214 and resumed at 324. England fielded an unchanged team throughout Test cricket's first five-match rubber. Jarvis was the second Australian substitute fielder after W.L. Murdoch (*Test No. 15*) to hold a catch for England.

AUSTRALIA

A.C. Bannerman	c Peel b Ulyett	5		c sub (G.F. Vernon) b Ulyett	2
W. Bruce	c Briggs b Peel	15	(6)	c Bates b Attewell	35
G. Giffen	b Ulyett	13		c Peel b Ulyett	12
T.P. Horan*	lbw b Ulyett	0	(5)	b Attewell	20
S.P. Jones	lbw b Peel	0	(4)	b Peel	17
F.H. Walters	b Ulyett	7	(8)	c Attewell b Flowers	5
A.H. Jarvis†	c Hunter b Peel	15	(9)	c Peel b Flowers	1
J.W. Trumble	not out	34	(7)	lbw b Attewell	10
P.G. McShane	c Hunter b Barnes	9	(11)	not out	12
T.W. Garrett	c Briggs b Barnes	6	(2)	b Ulyett	5
F.R. Spofforth	b Attewell	50	(10)	c sub (A.H. Jarvis) b Flowers	1
Extras	(B 5, LB 1, NB 3)	9		(B 5)	5
Total		**163**			**125**

ENGLAND

W.H. Scotton	b Bruce	27
W. Barnes	c Horan b Bruce	74
J.M. Read	b Giffen	13
G. Ulyett	b Spofforth	1
A. Shrewsbury*	not out	105
W. Bates	c Walters b Bruce	61
W. Flowers	b Spofforth	16
J. Briggs	c Walters b Trumble	43
W. Attewell	c Bannerman b Trumble	0
R. Peel	b Trumble	0
J. Hunter†	b Giffen	18
Extras	(B 10, LB 14, NB 4)	28
Total		**386**

ENGLAND	O	M	R	W	O	M	R	W	FALL OF WICKETS			
Peel	41	26	28	3	30	16	37	1		A	E	A
Ulyett	23	7	52	4	15	7	25	3	*Wkt*	*1st*	*1st*	*2nd*
Barnes	28	12	47	2					1st	21	60	4
Flowers	9	6	9	0	21	7	34	3	2nd	21	96	17
Attewell	5	1	18	1	36·1	22	24	3	3rd	21	97	26
									4th	34	141	60
AUSTRALIA									5th	34	256	60
Giffen	74·3	31	132	2					6th	45	324	91
Bruce	51	13	99	3					7th	67	324	100
Spofforth	49	21	71	2					8th	87	335	106
Trumble	28	14	29	3					9th	99	337	108
Garrett	8	6	12	0					10th	163	386	125
McShane	3	2	3	0								
Jones	5	2	7	0								
Horan	3	0	5	0								

Umpires: J.H. Hodges (1) and J. Phillips (1) (T.W. Garrett and J.C. Allen deputised).

Close: 1st day – E(1) 44-0 (Scotton 21, Barnes 19); 2nd – E(1) 270-5 (Shrewsbury 54, Briggs 11); 3rd – A(2) 105-7 (Bruce 25, Jarvis 1).

ENGLAND v AUSTRALIA 1886 (1st Test)

Played at Old Trafford, Manchester, on 5, 6, 7 July.
Toss: Australia.   Result: ENGLAND won by four wickets.
Debuts: England – G.A. Lohmann.

A.N. Hornby (injured leg) and W. Barnes (strained side) were replaced by Barlow and Briggs, the former playing a major part in England's narrowest victory in a home Test until 1890 (*Test No. 34*).

AUSTRALIA

S.P. Jones	lbw b Grace	87	c Ulyett b Steel	12
H.J.H. Scott*	c Barlow b Ulyett	21	b Barlow	47
G. Giffen	b Steel	3	c Shrewsbury b Barlow	1
A.H. Jarvis†	c Scotton b Ulyett	45	c Lohmann b Barlow	2
G.J. Bonnor	c Lohmann b Barlow	4	c Barlow b Peate	2
J.W. Trumble	c Scotton b Steel	24	c Ulyett b Barlow	4
W. Bruce	run out	2	(8) c Grace b Barlow	0
T.W. Garrett	c Pilling b Lohmann	5	(9) c Grace b Ulyett	22
J.M. Blackham	not out	7	(7) lbw b Barlow	2
G.E. Palmer	c Lohmann b Ulyett	4	c Pilling b Barlow	8
F.R. Spofforth	c Barlow b Ulyett	2	not out	20
Extras	(W1)	1	(B 3)	3
Total		**205**		**123**

ENGLAND

W.H. Scotton	c Trumble b Garrett	21	b Palmer	20
W.G. Grace	c Bonnor b Spofforth	8	c Palmer b Giffen	4
A. Shrewsbury	b Spofforth	31	c and b Giffen	4
W.W. Read	c Scott b Garrett	51	c Jones b Spofforth	9
A.G. Steel*	c Jarvis b Palmer	12	(6) not out	19
R.G. Barlow	not out	38	(5) c Palmer b Spofforth	30
G. Ulyett	b Spofforth	17	c Scott b Garrett	8
J. Briggs	c Garrett b Spofforth	1	not out	2
G.A. Lohmann	b Giffen	32		
E. Peate	st Jarvis b Palmer	6		
R. Pilling†	c Bruce b Palmer	2		
Extras	(B 2, LB 2)	4	(B 10, LB 1)	11
Total		**223**	(6 wickets)	**107**

ENGLAND	O	M	R	W	O	M	R	W		FALL OF WICKETS			
Peate	19	7	30	0	46	25	45	1		A	E	A	E
Lohmann	23	9	41	1	5	3	14	0	*Wkt*	*1st*	*1st*	*2nd*	*2nd*
Steel	27	5	47	2	8	3	9	1	1st	58	9	37	7
Ulyett	36·1	20	46	4	6·3	3	7	1	2nd	71	51	42	15
Barlow	23	15	19	1	52	34	44	7	3rd	134	80	44	24
Grace	9	3	21	1	1	0	1	0	4th	141	109	55	62
									5th	181	131	68	90
AUSTRALIA									6th	187	156	70	105
Spofforth	53	22	82	4	29·2	13	40	2	7th	188	160	70	–
Giffen	32	15	44	1	24	9	31	2	8th	192	206	73	–
Garrett	45	23	43	2	17	9	14	1	9th	201	219	103	–
Bruce	10	7	9	0					10th	205	223	123	–
Palmer	17·2	4	41	3	7	3	11	1					

Umpires: C.K. Pullin (4) and J. West (1).

Close: 1st day – E(1) 36-1 (Scotton 10, Shrewsbury 17); 2nd – A(2) 55-4 (Scott 36).

ENGLAND v AUSTRALIA 1886 (2nd Test)

Played at Lord's, London, on 19, 20, 21 July.
Toss: England.   Result: ENGLAND won by an innings and 106 runs.
Debuts: Nil.

Shrewsbury's 164 was an England Test record for just one match. Showing a magnificent defensive technique on a rain-affected pitch, he scored 91 of England's 202 for 4 on the interrupted first day. Last out, he batted for 410 minutes and hit 16 fours. His partnership of 161 with Barnes, his Nottinghamshire colleague, was England's first of three figures for the fifth wicket.

ENGLAND

W.G. Grace	c Jarvis b Palmer	18
W.H. Scotton	b Garrett	19
A. Shrewsbury	c Bonnor b Trumble	164
W.W. Read	c Spofforth b Giffen	22
A.G. Steel*	lbw b Spofforth	5
W. Barnes	c Palmer b Garrett	58
R.G. Barlow	c Palmer b Spofforth	12
G. Ulyett	b Spofforth	19
E.F.S. Tylecote†	b Spofforth	0
J. Briggs	c Jones b Trumble	0
G.A. Lohmann	not out	7
Extras	(B 24, LB 4, NB 1)	29
Total		**353**

AUSTRALIA

S.P. Jones	c Grace b Briggs	25	(4) b Briggs		17
H.J.H. Scott*	lbw b Briggs	30	(5) b Briggs		2
G. Giffen	b Steel	3	(6) b Barlow		1
A.H. Jarvis†	b Briggs	3	(7) not out		13
G.J. Bonnor	c Grace b Steel	0	(8) b Briggs		3
J.W. Trumble	c Tylecote b Briggs	0	(3) c Tylecote b Barnes		20
G.E. Palmer	c Shrewsbury b Barnes	20	(1) c Lohmann b Barlow		48
J.M. Blackham	b Briggs	23	(9) b Briggs		5
T.W. Garrett	not out	7	(2) b Briggs		4
F.R. Spofforth	b Barnes	5	(11) c and b Briggs		0
E. Evans	c Ulyett b Barnes	0	(10) run out		0
Extras	(B 4, LB 1)	5	(B 13)		13
Total		**121**			**126**

AUSTRALIA	O	M	R	W	O	M	R	W
Garrett	72	40	77	2				
Evans	36	20	37	0				
Palmer	38	15	45	1				
Spofforth	56	26	73	4				
Trumble	14	4	27	2				
Giffen	40	18	63	1				
Jones	3	1	2	0				
ENGLAND								
Barnes	14·3	7	25	3	10	5	18	1
Lohmann	7	3	21	0	14	9	11	0
Briggs	34	22	29	5	38·1	17	45	6
Steel	21	8	34	2	16	9	14	0
Barlow	6	3	7	0	25	20	12	2
Ulyett					8	3	13	0

	FALL OF WICKETS		
	E	A	A
Wkt	1st	1st	2nd
1st	27	45	6
2nd	77	52	56
3rd	112	59	91
4th	119	60	95
5th	280	62	98
6th	303	67	105
7th	333	99	120
8th	333	109	126
9th	340	121	126
10th	353	121	126

Umpires: F.H. Farrands (3) and C.K. Pullin (5).

Close: 1st day – E(1) 202-4 (Shrewsbury 91, Barnes 28); 2nd – A(2) 12-1 (Palmer 2, Trumble 6).

ENGLAND v AUSTRALIA 1886 (3rd Test)

Played at Kennington Oval, London, on 12, 13, 14 August.
Toss: England.   Result: ENGLAND won by an innings and 217 runs.
Debuts: Australia – J. McIlwraith.

The opening partnership of 170 between Grace and Scotton was the highest first-wicket stand by either country until 1899 (*Test No. 64*). Grace, who recaptured the England record score which he had lost to A. Shrewsbury in the previous Test, batted for 270 minutes, hit 24 fours, and made his 170 out of 216. Scotton scored 34 in 225 minutes; at one stage of his innings he spent 67 minutes with his score on 24.

ENGLAND

W.G. Grace	c Blackham b Spofforth	170
W.H. Scotton	b Garrett	34
A. Shrewsbury	c Jones b Trumble	44
W.W. Read	c Jones b Spofforth	94
W. Barnes	c Evans b Trumble	3
A.G. Steel*	st Blackham b Trumble	9
R.G. Barlow	c Trumble b Garrett	3
G. Ulyett	c McIlwraith b Garrett	0
J. Briggs	c Trumble b Spofforth	53
E.F.S. Tylecote†	not out	10
G.A. Lohmann	b Spofforth	7
Extras	(B 3, LB 2, NB 2)	7
Total		**434**

AUSTRALIA

S.P. Jones	c Grace b Lohmann	2	(3) c Read b Lohmann	2
G.E. Palmer	c Barlow b Briggs	15	(6) st Tylecote b Steel	35
G. Giffen	c Shrewsbury b Briggs	5	(4) c and b Lohmann	47
H.J.H. Scott*	c Tylecote b Lohmann	6	(5) c Grace b Lohmann	4
J.W. Trumble	c Read b Lohmann	13	(7) c Read b Briggs	18
J. McIlwraith	b Lohmann	2	(1) c Tylecote b Briggs	7
J.M. Blackham†	c and b Briggs	0	(8) c Grace b Briggs	5
T.W. Garrett	c Grace b Lohmann	2	(10) c Shrewsbury b Lohmann	4
W. Bruce	c Ulyett b Lohmann	9	b Lohmann	11
E. Evans	not out	9	(2) run out	3
F.R. Spofforth	b Lohmann	1	not out	5
Extras	(B 4)	4	(B 7, LB 1)	8
Total		**68**		**149**

AUSTRALIA	O	M	R	W	O	M	R	W
Giffen	62	32	96	0				
Garrett	99	55	88	3				
Palmer	47	21	80	0				
Bruce	6	2	9	0				
Spofforth	30·1	12	65	4				
Evans	13	10	6	0				
Trumble	47	14	83	3				
ENGLAND								
Lohmann	30·2	17	36	7	37	14	68	5
Briggs	30	17	28	3	32	19	30	3
Barlow					14	8	13	0
Barnes					7	4	10	0
Steel					7	1	20	1

FALL OF WICKETS

	E	A	A
Wkt	*1st*	*1st*	*2nd*
1st	170	2	11
2nd	216	11	14
3rd	287	22	26
4th	293	34	30
5th	305	35	84
6th	314	35	120
7th	320	44	129
8th	410	49	131
9th	418	67	137
10th	434	68	149

Umpires: R.P. Carpenter (1) and F.H. Farrands (4).

Close: 1st day – E(1) 279-2 (Shrewsbury 42, Read 30); 2nd – A(2) 8-0 (McIlwraith 3, Evans 1).

AUSTRALIA v ENGLAND 1886–87 (1st Test)

Played at Sydney Cricket Ground on 28, 29, 31 January.
Toss: Australia.   Result: ENGLAND won by 13 runs.
Debuts: Australia – J.J. Ferris, H. Moses, C.T.B. Turner; England – W. Gunn, M. Sherwin.

Leading 'The Combined Australian Eleven' for the first time, McDonnell became the first captain to invite the opposition to bat on winning the toss in a Test match. Turner and Ferris bowled unchanged throughout their first innings at Test level to dismiss 'Shaw's Team' for what remains England's lowest total in any Test match. In the second innings, A.C. Bannerman batted for an hour without adding to his score. His elder brother, Charles Bannerman – the man who had faced the first ball, scored the first run, reached the first hundred and had been the first batsman to retire hurt in Test cricket – made his first appearance as an umpire at this level.

ENGLAND

W. Bates	c Midwinter b Ferris	8	b Ferris	24
A. Shrewsbury*	c McShane b Ferris	2	b Ferris	29
W. Barnes	c Spofforth b Turner	0	c Moses b Garrett	32
R.G. Barlow	b Turner	2	c Jones b Ferris	4
J.M. Read	c Spofforth b Ferris	5	b Ferris	0
W. Gunn	b Turner	0	b Turner	4
W.H. Scotton	c Jones b Turner	1	(9) c Spofforth b Garrett	6
J. Briggs	c Midwinter b Turner	5	b Spofforth	33
G.A. Lohmann	c Garrett b Ferris	17	(7) lbw b Ferris	3
W. Flowers	b Turner	2	c McDonnell b Turner	14
M. Sherwin†	not out	0	not out	21
Extras	(B2, LB 1)	3	(B 9, LB 5)	14
Total		**45**		**184**

AUSTRALIA

J.M. Blackham†	c Sherwin b Lohmann	4	b Barnes	5
P.S. McDonnell*	b Barnes	14	lbw b Barnes	0
H. Moses	b Barlow	31	c Shrewsbury b Barnes	24
S.P. Jones	c Shrewsbury b Bates	31	c Read b Barnes	18
C.T.B. Turner	b Barlow	3	c and b Barnes	7
A.C. Bannerman	not out	15	b Lohmann	4
P.G. McShane	lbw b Briggs	5	b Briggs	0
W.E. Midwinter	c Shrewsbury b Barlow	0	lbw b Barnes	10
T.W. Garrett	b Lohmann	12	c Gunn b Lohmann	10
F.R. Spofforth	b Lohmann	2	b Lohmann	5
J.J. Ferris	c Barlow b Barnes	1	not out	0
Extras	(B 1)	1	(B 12, LB 2)	14
Total		**119**		**97**

AUSTRALIA	O	M	R	W	O	M	R	W	FALL OF WICKETS				
Turner	18	11	15	6	44·2	22	53	2		E	A	E	A
Ferris	17·3	7	27	4	61	30	76	5	*Wkt*	*1st*	*1st*	*2nd*	*2nd*
Spofforth					12	3	17	1	1st	11	8	31	4
Midwinter					4	1	10	0	2nd	11	18	80	5
Garrett					12	7	8	2	3rd	13	64	92	29
McShane					3	0	6	0	4th	13	67	92	38
									5th	13	86	98	58
ENGLAND									6th	17	95	99	61
Barnes	22·1	16	19	2	46	29	28	6	7th	21	96	103	80
Lohmann	21	12	30	3	24	11	20	3	8th	29	116	128	83
Briggs	14	5	25	1	7	5	7	1	9th	41	118	153	95
Barlow	35	23	25	3	13	6	20	0	10th	45	119	184	97
Bates	21	9	19	1	17	11	8	0					

Umpires: C. Bannerman (1) and H. Rawlinson (1).

Close: 1st day – A(1) 76-4 (Moses 21, Bannerman 2); 2nd – E(2) 103-7 (Briggs 0).

AUSTRALIA v ENGLAND 1886–87 (2nd Test)

Played at Sydney Cricket Ground on 25, 26, 28 February, 1 March.
Toss: England.   Result: ENGLAND won by 71 runs.
Debuts: Australia – R.C. Allen, F.J. Burton, J.T. Cottam, W.F. Giffen, J.J. Lyons; England – R. Wood.

Rain prevented the match from starting until 2.55 pm. Lohmann became the first bowler to take eight wickets in an innings of a Test match; his analysis is still the record for England in Australia. W. Gunn both played and deputised as umpire in this match (on the final morning when Swift was absent). Turner emulated W.L. Murdoch (*Test No. 15*) and A.H. Jarvis (*21*) by holding a catch while substituting for the opposition.

ENGLAND

A. Shrewsbury*	b Turner	9	b Turner	6
W. Bates	c Ferris b Turner	8	b Turner	30
J.M. Read	b Turner	11	(4) st Burton b Ferris	2
W. Gunn	b Turner	9	(5) c Cottam b Ferris	10
G.A. Lohmann	b Ferris	2	(6) b Ferris	6
W.H. Scotton	b Turner	0	(7) b Ferris	2
J. Briggs	b Ferris	17	(8) b Garrett	16
R.G. Barlow	c Allen b Ferris	34	(3) not out	42
W. Flowers	c Allen b Ferris	37	b Turner	18
R. Wood	lbw b Ferris	6	hit wkt b Midwinter	0
M. Sherwin†	not out	4	b Turner	5
Extras	(B 9, LB 3, NB 2)	14	(B 12, LB 5)	17
Total		**151**		**154**

AUSTRALIA

W.F. Giffen	b Lohmann	2	(6) b Briggs	0
J.J. Lyons	b Lohmann	11	(4) c Gunn b Bates	0
H. Moses	b Flowers	28	(2) st Sherwin b Bates	33
R.C. Allen	b Lohmann	14	(3) c sub (C.T.B. Turner) b Bates	30
P.S. McDonnell*	c Gunn b Lohmann	10	(1) c Gunn b Lohmann	35
W.E. Midwinter	b Lohmann	1	(7) c Sherwin b Lohmann	4
J.T. Cottam	hit wkt b Lohmann	1	(5) st Sherwin b Briggs	3
C.T.B. Turner	c and b Flowers	9	c Briggs b Bates	9
T.W. Garrett	b Lohmann	1	c Sherwin b Briggs	20
J.J. Ferris	b Lohmann	1	run out	2
F.J. Burton†	not out	0	not out	2
Extras	(B 5, LB 1)	6	(B 9, LB 3)	12
Total		**84**		**150**

AUSTRALIA	O	M	R	W	O	M	R	W
Ferris	45	16	71	5	60	33	69	4
Turner	53	29	41	5	64·1	33	52	4
Garrett	6	2	12	0	10	6	7	1
Midwinter	3	1	2	0	6	3	9	1
Lyons	2	0	11	0				
ENGLAND								
Lohmann	25	12	35	8	40	16	52	2
Briggs	20	6	34	0	22	9	31	3
Flowers	8	3	9	2	13	5	17	0
Bates					26	13	26	4
Barlow					9	2	12	0

FALL OF WICKETS

	E	A	E	A
Wkt	1st	1st	2nd	2nd
1st	14	12	21	51
2nd	19	15	42	86
3rd	35	40	47	86
4th	38	56	59	95
5th	43	59	73	95
6th	50	65	77	106
7th	73	82	98	121
8th	130	83	136	129
9th	145	83	137	135
10th	151	84	154	150

Umpires: C. Bannerman (2) and J.S. Swift (8) (W. Gunn deputised).

Close: 1st day – E(1) 128-7 (Barlow 24, Flowers 37); 2nd – E(2) 73-5 (Barlow 10, Scotton 0); 3rd – A(2) 101-5 (Allen 19, Midwinter 4).

AUSTRALIA v ENGLAND 1887–88 (Only Test)

Played at Sydney Cricket Ground on 10, 11 (*no play*), 13 (*no play*), 14, 15 February.
Toss: Australia.   Result: ENGLAND won by 126 runs.
Debuts: England – W. Newham, A.E. Stoddart.

Two English touring teams (led by G.F. Vernon and A. Shrewsbury) in Australia during the 1887-88 season combined to play this match. Australia's total of 42, on a rain-affected pitch, remains their lowest in any Test in Australia and was their lowest in all Tests until they were dismissed for 36 by England in 1902 (*Test No. 70*). Turner's match analysis of 12 for 87 remains the record for any Test at Sydney.

ENGLAND

A.E. Stoddart	c McShane b Turner	16	c Blackham b Turner		17
A. Shrewsbury	c Turner b Ferris	44	b Ferris		1
G. Ulyett	c Burton b Turner	5	b Ferris		5
W.W. Read*	b Turner	10	b Turner		8
J.M. Read	c and b Turner	0	c Bannerman b Turner		39
R. Peel	hit wkt b Ferris	3	st Blackham b Turner		9
W. Newham	c Worrall b Ferris	9	(8) lbw b Turner		17
G.A. Lohmann	c Jones b Ferris	12	(7) c Blackham b Turner		0
J. Briggs	b Turner	0	c Worrall b McShane		14
W. Attewell	not out	7	not out		10
R. Pilling†	run out	3	b Turner		5
Extras	(B 4)	4	(B 7, LB 5)		12
Total		**113**			**137**

AUSTRALIA

A.C. Bannerman	c Ulyett b Lohmann	2	c Attewell b Lohmann		2
S.P. Jones	c Shrewsbury b Peel	0	(4) c Shrewsbury b Lohmann		15
H. Moses	c W.W. Read b Lohmann	3	c Briggs b Lohmann		11
F.J. Burton	c Stoddart b Lohmann	1	(5) c Pilling b Peel		1
J. Worrall	st Pilling b Peel	6	(10) b Lohmann		1
P.G. McShane	c Shrewsbury b Peel	0	(8) b Peel		0
P.S. McDonnell*	b Lohmann	3	(2) b Peel		6
J.M. Blackham†	c Shrewsbury b Peel	2	(9) not out		25
T.W. Garrett	c Pilling b Lohmann	10	(7) c Shrewsbury b Peel		1
C.T.B. Turner	not out	8	(6) lbw b Attewell		12
J.J. Ferris	c W.W. Read b Peel	0	c Shrewsbury b Peel		5
Extras	(B 6, W 1)	7	(B 2, LB 1)		3
Total		**42**			**82**

AUSTRALIA	O	M	R	W	O	M	R	W		FALL OF WICKETS			
Turner	50	27	44	5	38	23	43	7		E	A	E	A
Ferris	47	25	60	4	16	4	43	2	*Wkt*	*1st*	*1st*	*2nd*	*2nd*
Garrett	3	1	5	0					1st	27	2	9	8
McShane					21	7	39	1	2nd	36	2	15	8
									3rd	54	10	27	20
ENGLAND									4th	54	16	54	21
Lohmann	19	13	17	5	32	18	35	4	5th	57	18	82	44
Peel	18·3	9	18	5	33	14	40	5	6th	88	21	82	47
Attewell					4·2	2	4	1	7th	102	23	84	53
									8th	103	26	111	60
									9th	103	37	131	61
									10th	113	42	137	82

Umpires: C. Bannerman (3) and J. Phillips (2).

Close: 1st day – A(1) 35-8 (Garrett 9, Turner 3); 2nd – no play; 3rd – no play; 4th – A(2) 47-5 (Jones 13, Garrett 1).

ENGLAND v AUSTRALIA 1888 (1st Test)

Played at Lord's, London, 16, 17 July.
Toss: Australia.   Result: AUSTRALIA won by 61 runs.
Debuts: England – R. Abel; Australia – J.D. Edwards, G.H.S. Trott, S.M.J. Woods.

Heavy overnight rain prevented the match from starting until 3 pm. The second day saw 27 wickets fall for 157 runs in just over three hours of actual playing time on a mud pitch – the highest number of wickets to fall in any day of Test cricket. The match ended at 4.25 pm and produced the lowest aggregate of runs (291) for any completed Test match until 1931-32 (*Test No. 216*).

AUSTRALIA

A.C. Bannerman	c Grace b Lohmann	0	b Peel	0
P.S. McDonnell*	c O'Brien b Peel	22	b Lohmann	1
G.H.S. Trott	c Lohmann b Peel	0	b Lohmann	3
G.J. Bonnor	b Lohmann	6	c Lohmann b Peel	8
J.M. Blackham†	b Briggs	22	run out	1
S.M.J. Woods	c Gunn b Briggs	18	c Grace b Peel	3
C.T.B. Turner	c Lohmann b Peel	3	c Grace b Briggs	12
J.D. Edwards	not out	21	c Sherwin b Lohmann	0
A.H. Jarvis	c Lohmann b Peel	3	(11) c Barnes b Peel	4
J. Worrall	c Abel b Briggs	2	b Lohmann	4
J.J. Ferris	c Sherwin b Steel	14	(9) not out	20
Extras	(B 5)	5	(B 3, LB 1)	4
Total		**116**		**60**

ENGLAND

W.G. Grace	c Woods b Ferris	10	c Bannerman b Ferris	24
R. Abel	b Ferris	3	c Bonnor b Ferris	8
W. Barnes	c Jarvis b Turner	3	(9) st Blackham b Ferris	1
G.A. Lohmann	lbw b Turner	2	(10) st Blackham b Ferris	0
W.W. Read	st Blackham b Turner	4	(4) b Turner	3
T.C. O'Brien	b Turner	0	(5) b Turner	4
R. Peel	run out	8	(3) b Turner	4
A.G. Steel*	st Blackham b Turner	3	(6) not out	10
W. Gunn	c Blackham b Ferris	2	(7) b Ferris	8
J. Briggs	b Woods	17	(8) b Turner	0
M. Sherwin†	not out	0	c Ferris b Turner	0
Extras	(LB 1)	1		
Total		**53**		**62**

ENGLAND	O	M	R	W	O	M	R	W
Lohmann	20	9	28	2	14	4	33	4
Peel	21	7	36	4	10·2	3	14	4
Briggs	21	8	26	3	4	1	9	1
Barnes	6	0	17	0				
Steel	3·2	2	4	1	1	1	0	0
AUSTRALIA								
Turner	25	9	27	5	24	8	36	5
Ferris	21	13	19	3	23	11	26	5
Woods	4	2	6	1				

FALL OF WICKETS

	A	E	A	E
Wkt	*1st*	*1st*	*2nd*	*2nd*
1st	0	5	1	29
2nd	3	14	1	34
3rd	28	18	13	38
4th	32	22	15	39
5th	65	22	18	44
6th	76	22	18	55
7th	76	26	18	56
8th	79	35	42	57
9th	82	49	49	57
10th	116	53	60	62

Umpires: F.H. Farrands (5) and C.K. Pullin (6).

Close: 1st day – E(1) 18-3 (Grace 10).

ENGLAND v AUSTRALIA 1888 (2nd Test)

Played at Kennington Oval, London, on 13, 14 August.
Toss: Australia.   Result: ENGLAND won by an innings and 137 runs.
Debuts: England – J. Shuter, F.H. Sugg, H. Wood.

The England team, chosen by the home club's committee, included five Surrey players: Shuter, Read, Abel, Lohmann and Wood. Lohmann's highest Test innings took 55 minutes and included 10 fours. Bannerman batted for 75 minutes in the second innings. The total paying attendance was 30,957.

AUSTRALIA

A.C. Bannerman	c Lohmann b Barnes	13	b Barnes	5
P.S. McDonnell*	c Lohmann b Peel	0	b Peel	32
G.H.S. Trott	b Briggs	13	st Wood b Peel	4
G.J. Bonnor	b Briggs	0	c Wood b Barnes	5
J.D. Edwards	b Lohmann	26	c Read b Barnes	0
A.H. Jarvis	b Briggs	5	(9) b Peel	8
S.M.J. Woods	run out	0	c Abel b Barnes	7
C.T.B. Turner	b Briggs	0	b Peel	18
J.M. Blackham†	b Briggs	0	(10) c Lohmann b Barnes	4
J. Worrall	c Grace b Barnes	8	(11) not out	0
J.J. Ferris	not out	13	(6) run out	16
Extras	(B 1, LB 1)	2	(LB 1)	1
Total		**80**		**100**

ENGLAND

W.G. Grace*	c Edwards b Turner	1
J. Shuter	b Turner	28
G. Ulyett	c Blackham b Turner	0
W.W. Read	b Turner	18
R. Abel	run out	70
W. Barnes	c Worrall b Turner	62
F.H. Sugg	b Turner	31
R. Peel	b Woods	25
J. Briggs	b Woods	0
G.A. Lohmann	not out	62
H. Wood†	c Bannerman b Ferris	8
Extras	(B 6, LB 4, W 2)	12
Total		**317**

ENGLAND	O	M	R	W	O	M	R	W		FALL OF WICKETS		
Lohmann	29·3	21	21	1	6	4	11	0		A	E	A
Peel	8	4	14	1	28·2	13	49	4	*Wkt*	*1st*	*1st*	*2nd*
Briggs	37	24	25	5	6	3	7	0	1st	0	2	34
Barnes	16	9	18	2	29	16	32	5	2nd	22	6	38
									3rd	22	46	43
AUSTRALIA									4th	40	53	45
Turner	60	24	112	6					5th	49	165	62
Ferris	35·2	15	73	1					6th	49	191	62
Trott	7	2	25	0					7th	50	241	72
Woods	32	10	80	2					8th	50	242	89
Worrall	4	1	15	0					9th	63	259	98
									10th	80	317	100

Umpires: R.P. Carpenter (2) and F.H. Farrands (6).

Close: 1st day – E(1) 185-5 (Abel 65, Sugg 5).

ENGLAND v AUSTRALIA 1888 (3rd Test)

Played at Old Trafford, Manchester, on 30, 31 August.
Toss: England.   Result: ENGLAND won by an innings and 21 runs.
Debuts: Nil.

Heavy rain before the match produced a soft, wet pitch and gave the side batting first an enormous advantage. A hot, drying sun on the second day made the pitch a vicious 'sticky'; 18 wickets fell before lunch – the record for all Test cricket. Australia were unable to avoid following-on, the compulsory margin in 1888 being 80 runs. The match ended at 1.52 pm (before lunch on the second day), after Australia had been bowled out in 69 minutes – their briefest innings in all Tests. The shortest completed Test match in England required only 6 hours 34 minutes of playing time.

ENGLAND

W.G. Grace*	c Bonnor b Turner	38
R. Abel	b Turner	0
G. Ulyett	b Turner	0
W.W. Read	b Turner	19
W. Barnes	b Ferris	24
F.H. Sugg	b Woods	24
W. Gunn	lbw b Turner	15
R. Peel	lbw b Ferris	11
J. Briggs	not out	22
G.A. Lohmann	run out	0
R. Pilling†	c Bonnor b Woods	17
Extras	(B 2)	2
Total		**172**

AUSTRALIA

P.S. McDonnell*	c Grace b Peel	15		b Lohmann	0
A.C. Bannerman	b Peel	1		c Grace b Peel	0
G.H.S. Trott	st Pilling b Peel	17		run out	0
G.J. Bonnor	run out	5		c Grace b Peel	0
J.D. Edwards	b Peel	0	(9)	c Grace b Peel	1
C.T.B. Turner	b Peel	0	(8)	b Briggs	26
S.M.J. Woods	c Read b Briggs	4		b Lohmann	0
J.M. Blackham†	c Read b Lohmann	15	(5)	b Lohmann	5
J.J. Lyons	c Lohmann b Peel	22	(6)	b Briggs	32
J. Worrall	b Peel	0	(11)	not out	0
J.J. Ferris	not out	0	(10)	c Abel b Peel	3
Extras	(B 2)	2		(B 2, LB 1)	3
Total		**81**			**70**

AUSTRALIA	O	M	R	W	O	M	R	W
Ferris	40	20	49	2				
Turner	55	21	86	5				
Woods	18.1	6	35	2				
ENGLAND								
Peel	26·2	17	31	7	16	4	37	4
Lohmann	17	9	31	1	8	3	20	3
Briggs	9	4	17	1	7·1	2	10	2

Umpires: F.H. Farrands (7) and C.K. Pullin (7).

Close: 1st day – A(1) 32-2 (Trott 14).

FALL OF WICKETS

Wkt	E 1st	A 1st	A 2nd
1st	0	16	0
2nd	6	32	0
3rd	58	35	1
4th	59	39	7
5th	96	39	7
6th	115	43	7
7th	127	45	55
8th	135	81	56
9th	136	81	70
10th	172	81	70

SOUTH AFRICA v ENGLAND 1888–89 (1st Test)

Played at St George's Park, Port Elizabeth, on 12, 13 March.
Toss: South Africa.   Result: ENGLAND won by eight wickets.
Debuts: South Africa – All; England – M.P. Bowden, Hon. C.J. Coventry, A.J. Fothergill, B.A.F. Grieve, F. Hearne, C.A. Smith. *Coventry and Grieve were making their debuts in first-class cricket; both ended their first-class careers with the 2nd Test of this series. C.A. Smith (later Sir Aubrey Smith) of Hollywood fame is the only player to captain England on his only appearance in Test cricket.*

South Africa's introduction to Test cricket ended in a comprehensive defeat by Major Robert Gardner Warton's touring team. This match, the seventeenth of the tour but the first to be played on equal 11-a-side terms, was also the first in South Africa to be considered (subsequently) first-class. Played on matting, it finished just before 3.30 on the second afternoon. Milton kept wicket for South Africa in the second innings and was in turn caught by Bowden who deputised for Wood after lunch on the second day. Webster stood for umpire Deare on the second day.

SOUTH AFRICA

A. Rose-Innes	b Briggs	0	b Smith	13
A.B. Tancred	b Smith	29	c and b Briggs	29
P.Hutchinson	b Briggs	0	(5) b Smith	11
C.H. Vintcent	c Abel b Briggs	3	c and b Ulyett	4
A.E. Ochse	c Abel b Briggs	4	(3) lbw b Fothergill	8
W.H. Milton	c Abel b Fothergill	1	(7) c Bowden b Briggs	19
O.R. Dunell*	not out	26	(6) c and b Ulyett	11
R.B. Stewart	lbw b Smith	4	c Ulyett b Fothergill	9
F.W. Smith†	b Smith	7	b Fothergill	12
C.E. Finlason	b Smith	0	b Fothergill	6
G.A. Kempis	c Hearne b Smith	0	not out	0
Extras	(B 8, W 2)	10	(B 7)	7
Total		**84**		**129**

ENGLAND

R. Abel	c Milton b Rose-Innes	46	not out	23
G. Ulyett	b Kempis	4	b Vintcent	22
J.M. Read	c Dunell b Kempis	1	b Kempis	3
F. Hearne	c Stewart b Rose-Innes	27		
H. Wood†	c Hutchinson b Rose-Innes	3		
M.P. Bowden	run out	0		
J. Briggs	c Smith b Rose-Innes	0		
C.A. Smith*	c Stewart b Kempis	3		
B.A.F. Grieve	not out	14	(4) not out	12
Hon. C.J. Coventry	c Smith b Rose-Innes	12		
A.J. Fothergill	c Tancred b Milton	32		
Extras	(B 5, W 1)	6	(B 7)	7
Total		**148**	(2 wickets)	**67**

ENGLAND	O	M	R	W	O	M	R	W		FALL OF WICKETS			
Briggs	37	21	39	4	27	14	34	2		SA	E	SA	E
Fothergill	24	15	15	1	18·1	11	19	4	*Wkt*	*1st*	*1st*	*2nd*	*2nd*
Smith	13·2	6	19	5	25	10	42	2	1st	0	10	21	32
Ulyett	1	0	1	0	20	9	27	2	2nd	0	14	42	35
									3rd	10	65	51	–
SOUTH AFRICA									4th	16	75	67	–
Kempis	31	14	53	3	11	3	23	1	5th	17	75	67	–
Finlason	3	0	7	0					6th	58	77	88	–
Vintcent	12	4	34	0	8·1	2	21	1	7th	66	85	110	–
Rose-Innes	18	5	43	5	2	0	16	0	8th	78	87	116	–
Milton	2·2	1	5	1					9th	82	103	126	–
									10th	84	148	129	–

Umpires: C.R. Deare (1) and R.G. Warton (1) (H.H. Webster deputised).

Close: 1st day – E(1) 148 all out.

SOUTH AFRICA v ENGLAND 1888–89 (2nd Test)

Played at Newlands, Cape Town, on 25, 26 March.
Toss: England.   Result: ENGLAND won by an innings and 202 runs.
Debuts: South Africa – W.H. Ashley, W.H.M. Richards, N.H. Theunissen; England – J.E.P. McMaster (*his only first-class match*).

Fever prevented C.A. Smith from playing. Bowden, aged 23 years 144 days, became England's youngest captain three years before dying in Umtali Hospital – a glorified mud hut where his body had to be protected from marauding lions prior to being interred in a coffin made from whisky cases. Abel scored the first hundred in first-class cricket in South Africa and Tancred became the first batsman to carry his bat through a completed Test innings. Briggs set new Test records by taking 8 for 11 (all bowled) in the second innings (the first completed Test innings without a catch being taken, it contained a record number of batsmen bowled), and 15 for 28 in the match – the most wickets in one day of Test cricket. Ashley took 7 for 95 in his only Test.

ENGLAND

R. Abel	b Ashley	120
G. Ulyett	b Ashley	22
J. Briggs	b Vintcent	6
J.M. Read	c Hutchinson b Ashley	12
F. Hearne	b Vintcent	20
H. Wood†	c Rose-Innes b Vintcent	59
M.P. Bowden*	c Hutchinson b Ashley	25
B.A.F. Grieve	c Tancred b Ashley	14
J.E.P. McMaster	c Rose-Innes b Ashley	0
Hon. C.J. Coventry	not out	1
A.J. Fothergill	b Ashley	1
Extras	(B 12)	12
Total		**292**

SOUTH AFRICA

A.B. Tancred	not out	26	b Briggs	3
A. Rose-Innes	lbw b Fothergill	1	run out	0
A.E. Ochse	run out	1	b Briggs	3
P. Hutchinson	b Briggs	3	b Briggs	0
O.R. Dunell	b Briggs	0	b Fothergill	5
W.H. Milton*	b Briggs	7	b Briggs	4
W.H.M. Richards	c Abel b Fothergill	0	b Briggs	4
C.H. Vintcent	b Briggs	4	b Briggs	9
F.W. Smith†	b Briggs	0	b Briggs	11
N.H. Theunissen	lbw b Briggs	0	not out	2
W.H. Ashley	b Briggs	1	b Briggs	0
Extras	(B 2, NB 2)	4	(B 2)	2
Total		**47**		**43**

SOUTH AFRICA	O	M	R	W	O	M	R	W
Theunissen	20	5	51	0				
Rose-Innes	12	3	30	0				
Ashley	43·1	18	95	7				
Vintcent	42	9	88	3				
Milton	6	2	16	0				
ENGLAND								
Fothergill	24	12	26	2	14	4	30	1
Ulyett	4	4	0	0				
Briggs	19·1	11	17	7	14·2	5	11	8

FALL OF WICKETS

	E	SA	SA
Wkt	1st	1st	2nd
1st	54	2	1
2nd	62	3	4
3rd	79	11	6
4th	110	19	12
5th	215	31	16
6th	257	32	20
7th	287	41	20
8th	287	41	37
9th	288	41	43
10th	292	47	43

Umpires: J. Hickson (1) and R.G. Warton (2).

Close: 1st day – SA(1) 2-1 (Tancred 1).

ENGLAND v AUSTRALIA 1890 (1st Test)

Played at Lord's, London, on 21, 22, 23 July.
Toss: Australia.   Result: ENGLAND won by seven wickets.
Debuts: England–G. MacGregor;   Australia–J.E. Barrett, E.J.K. Burn, P.C. Charlton, S.E. Gregory, H. Trumble.

Barrett, playing his first Test match, became the first to carry his bat through a completed innings in a Test between Australia and England. Lyons took only 36 minutes to reach his fifty and set the record for Australia's fastest half-century against England (equalled by J. Ryder in 1928-29 in *Test No. 177*). For the first time no byes were conceded in a Test match.

AUSTRALIA

J.J. Lyons	b Barnes	55	(4)	c Attewell b Peel	33
C.T.B. Turner	b Attewell	24		lbw b Peel	2
W.L. Murdoch*	c and b Attewell	9	(5)	b Lohmann	19
J.E. Barrett	c Grace b Ulyett	9	(1)	not out	67
G.H.S. Trott	run out	12	(3)	b Peel	0
S.E. Gregory	b Attewell	0		c Lohmann b Barnes	9
P.C. Charlton	st MacGregor b Peel	6		lbw b Grace	2
J.M. Blackham†	b Peel	5		c Barnes b Grace	10
J.J. Ferris	b Attewell	8		lbw b Lohmann	8
E.J.K. Burn	st MacGregor b Peel	0	(11)	c MacGregor b Attewell	19
H. Trumble	not out	1	(10)	c Barnes b Lohmann	5
Extras	(LB 3)	3		(LB 2)	2
Total		**132**			**176**

ENGLAND

W.G. Grace*	c and b Turner	0		not out	75
A. Shrewsbury	st Blackham b Ferris	4		lbw b Ferris	13
W. Gunn	run out	14		c and b Ferris	34
W.W. Read	c and b Ferris	1		b Trumble	13
J.M. Read	b Lyons	34		not out	2
G. Ulyett	b Lyons	74			
R. Peel	c and b Trumble	16			
W. Barnes	b Lyons	9			
G.A. Lohmann	c and b Lyons	19			
G. MacGregor†	b Lyons	0			
W. Attewell	not out	0			
Extras	(LB 2)	2			
Total		**173**		(3 wickets)	**137**

ENGLAND	O	M	R	W	O	M	R	W		FALL OF WICKETS			
Lohmann	21	10	43	0	29	19	28	3		A	E	A	E
Peel	24	11	28	3	43	23	59	3	*Wkt*	*1st*	*1st*	*2nd*	*2nd*
Attewell	32	15	42	4	42·2	22	54	1	1st	66	0	6	27
Barnes	6	2	16	1	6	3	10	1	2nd	82	14	8	101
Ulyett	3	3	0	1	6	2	11	0	3rd	93	20	48	135
Grace					14	10	12	2	4th	109	20	84	–
									5th	111	92	106	–
AUSTRALIA									6th	113	109	109	–
Turner	35	17	53	1	22	12	31	0	7th	120	147	119	–
Ferris	40	17	55	2	25	11	42	2	8th	131	162	136	–
Trott	3	0	16	0					9th	131	166	142	–
Lyons	20·1	7	30	5	20	6	43	0	10th	132	173	176	–
Trumble	12	7	17	1	8	1	21	1					

Umpires: A. Hill (1) and C.K. Pullin (8).

Close: 1st day – E(1) 108-5 (Ulyett 45, Peel 8); 2nd – A(2) 168-9 (Barrett 63, Burn 15).

ENGLAND v AUSTRALIA 1890 (2nd Test)

Played at Kennington Oval, London, on 11, 12 August.
Toss: Australia.   Result: ENGLAND won by two wickets.
Debuts: England – J. Cranston, F. Martin, J.W. Sharpe.

Yorkshire refused to release Peel and Ulyett for this match; Stoddart opted to play for Middlesex against them at Bradford. Martin, a left-arm, medium-fast bowler from Kent, became the first to take 12 wickets on debut. His record remained until 1972 when R.A.L. Massie took 16 for 137 in his first Test (*No. 699*). Rain before the start produced a pitch on which 22 wickets fell for 197 runs on the first day. England won the match from an overthrow when Barrett missed an easy run-out.

AUSTRALIA

J.J. Lyons	c W.W. Read b Martin	13	(4) b Martin	21
C.T.B. Turner	c Sharpe b Lohmann	12	(7) b Martin	0
W.L. Murdoch*	b Martin	2	(5) b Lohmann	6
J.E. Barrett	c Lohmann b Martin	0	(1) b Martin	4
G.H.S. Trott	c MacGregor b Martin	39	(6) c Cranston b Martin	25
E.J.K. Burn	c MacGregor b Lohmann	7	(2) b Martin	15
J.M. Blackham†	b Martin	1	(8) b Lohmann	1
J.J. Ferris	c Lohmann b Sharpe	6	(3) lbw b Lohmann	1
P.C. Charlton	b Martin	10	b Sharpe	11
S.E. Gregory	b Lohmann	2	(11) not out	4
H. Trumble	not out	0	(10) b Martin	6
Extras		–	(B 7, LB 1)	8
Total		**92**		**102**

ENGLAND

A. Shrewsbury	c Trott b Turner	4	lbw b Ferris	9
W.G. Grace*	c Trumble b Ferris	0	c Trumble b Ferris	16
W. Gunn	b Ferris	32	st Blackham b Ferris	1
W.W. Read	b Turner	1	b Turner	6
J. Cranston	run out	16	(6) c Trumble b Turner	15
J.M. Read	c Murdoch b Charlton	19	(5) c Barrett b Turner	35
W. Barnes	c Murdoch b Charlton	5	(8) lbw b Ferris	5
G.A. Lohmann	c Gregory b Ferris	3	(7) c Blackham b Ferris	2
G. MacGregor†	c Turner b Ferris	1	not out	2
J.W. Sharpe	not out	5	not out	2
F. Martin	c Turner b Charlton	1		
Extras	(B 9, LB 3, NB 1)	13	(LB 1, NB 1)	2
Total		**100**	(8 wickets)	**95**

ENGLAND	O	M	R	W	O	M	R	W		FALL OF WICKETS			
Martin	27	9	50	6	30·2	12	52	6		A	E	A	E
Lohmann	32·2	19	34	3	21	8	32	3	*Wkt*	*1st*	*1st*	*2nd*	*2nd*
Sharpe	6	3	8	1	9	5	10	1	1st	16	0	4	24
									2nd	27	10	5	25
AUSTRALIA									3rd	27	16	36	28
Turner	22	12	37	2	25	9	38	3	4th	32	55	43	32
Ferris	25	14	25	4	23	8	49	5	5th	39	79	49	83
Trumble	2	0	7	0					6th	46	90	53	83
Charlton	6	0	18	3	3	1	6	0	7th	70	91	54	86
									8th	85	93	90	93
Umpires: C.K. Pullin (9) and J. Street (1).									9th	92	94	92	–
									10th	92	100	102	–

Close: 1st day – A(2) 5-2 (Burn 0).

The Third Test at Old Trafford, scheduled for 25, 26, 27 August, was abandoned without a ball being bowled. The teams are shown on page 816.

AUSTRALIA v ENGLAND 1891–92 (1st Test)

Played at Melbourne Cricket Ground on 1, 2, 4, 5, 6 January.
Toss: Australia.   Result: AUSTRALIA won by 54 runs.
Debuts: Australia – S.T. Callaway, H. Donnan, R.W. McLeod; England – G. Bean.

Dr W.G. Grace captained Lord Sheffield's Team on his Test debut in Australia. This match saw the introduction of 6-ball overs in Test cricket in Australia; the 8-ball over did not gain favour until 1924-25. Bannerman's tally of 86 runs took him 435 minutes.

AUSTRALIA

A.C. Bannerman	c Read b Sharpe	45	c Grace b Sharpe	41
J.J. Lyons	c Grace b Peel	19	c Abel b Briggs	51
G. Giffen	lbw b Peel	2	b Attewell	1
W. Bruce	b Sharpe	57	c Lohmann b Sharpe	40
H. Donnan	b Sharpe	9	(9) c and b Lohmann	2
H. Moses	c Lohmann b Sharpe	23	run out	15
G.H.S. Trott	c MacGregor b Sharpe	6	lbw b Attewell	23
R.W. McLeod	b Sharpe	14	b Peel	31
S.T. Callaway	b Attewell	21	(10) not out	13
C.T.B. Turner	b Peel	29	(5) c Peel b Lohmann	19
J.M. Blackham*†	not out	4	c MacGregor b Peel	0
Extras	(B 5, LB 6)	11		–
Total		**240**		**236**

ENGLAND

W.G. Grace*	b McLeod	50	c Bannerman b Turner	25
R. Abel	b McLeod	32	(5) c Blackham b Turner	28
A.E. Stoddart	c Giffen b McLeod	0	(2) b Callaway	35
G. Bean	c Bruce b Giffen	50	(3) c McLeod b Trott	3
J.M. Read	c and b Giffen	38	(4) b Trott	11
R.Peel	b McLeod	19	b Turner	6
G.A. Lohmann	lbw b Giffen	3	c Bannerman b Turner	0
J.Briggs	c Bruce b Turner	41	c Trott b McLeod	4
W.Attewell	c Bannerman b Turner	8	(10) c Donnan b Turner	24
J.W. Sharpe	c Blackham b McLeod	2	(11) not out	5
G. MacGregor†	not out	9	(9) c sub (S.E. Gregory) b Trott	16
Extras	(B 7, LB 2, NB 3)	12	(B 1)	1
Total		**264**		**158**

ENGLAND	O	M	R	W	O	M	R	W	FALL OF WICKETS				
Sharpe	51	20	84	6	54	25	81	2		A	E	A	E
Peel	43	23	54	3	16·5	7	25	2	*Wkt*	*1st*	*1st*	*2nd*	*2nd*
Attewell	21·1	11	28	1	61	32	51	2	1st	32	84	66	60
Lohmann	28	14	40	0	39	15	53	2	2nd	36	85	67	60
Briggs	3	1	13	0	21	9	26	1	3rd	123	85	120	71
Stoddart	5	2	10	0					4th	136	171	152	75
									5th	136	179	152	93
AUSTRALIA									6th	148	187	182	93
Trott	10	2	25	0	19	2	52	3	7th	164	232	197	98
Giffen	20	3	75	3	3	0	8	0	8th	191	249	210	125
Turner	16	3	40	2	33·2	14	51	5	9th	232	256	236	139
McLeod	28·4	12	55	5	23	8	39	1	10th	240	264	236	158
Callaway	14	2	39	0	4	1	7	1					
Bruce	3	0	18	0									

Umpires: T. Flynn (1) and J. Phillips (3).

Close: 1st day – A(1) 191-7 (Moses 23, Callaway 11); 2nd – E(1) 248-7 (Briggs 41, Attewell 7); 3rd – A(2) 152-5 (Moses 0, Trott 0); 4th – E(2) 104-7 (Abel 16, MacGregor 3).

AUSTRALIA v ENGLAND 1891–92 (2nd Test)

Played at Sydney Cricket Ground on 29, 30 January, 1, 2, 3 February.
Toss: Australia.   Result: AUSTRALIA won by 72 runs.
Debuts: Nil.

Abel became the first England player to carry his bat through a completed Test innings. Briggs ended Australia's second innings with a hat-trick, dismissing W.F. Giffen, Callaway and Blackham. Bannerman scored only 67 runs in the complete third day's play and batted 448 minutes for his 91 in what remains the slowest completed innings of that score in all first-class cricket. Australia achieved a most notable victory after being 162 runs behind on first innings. Moreover, in the later stages, they lacked the services of Moses, who had aggravated the leg injury he had sustained in the previous Test, and McLeod, who returned to Melbourne on learning of his brother's death.

AUSTRALIA

A.C. Bannerman	c Abel b Lohmann	12	c Grace b Briggs	91
J.J. Lyons	c Grace b Lohmann	41	(3) c Grace b Lohmann	134
G. Giffen	c Abel b Lohmann	6	(4) lbw b Attewell	49
H. Moses	c Grace b Lohmann	29	absent hurt	–
C.T.B. Turner	c MacGregor b Lohmann	15	(7) not out	14
W. Bruce	c Bean b Attewell	15	(5) c Briggs b Sharpe	72
G.H.S. Trott	b Lohmann	2	(2) c Sharpe b Lohmann	1
R.W. McLeod	c Attewell b Lohmann	13	(6) c Read b Peel	18
W.F. Giffen	c and b Lohmann	1	(8) b Briggs	3
S.T. Callaway	run out	1	c Grace b Briggs	0
J.M. Blackham*†	not out	3	(9) lbw b Briggs	0
Extras	(B 6, W 1)	7	(B 6, LB 2, W 1)	9
Total		**145**		**391**

ENGLAND

R. Abel	not out	132	c W.F. Giffen b G.Giffen	1
W.G. Grace*	b Turner	26	c Blackham b Turner	5
G. Bean	b G. Giffen	19	c Lyons b Turner	4
A.E. Stoddart	c Blackham b McLeod	27	b Turner	69
J.M. Read	c Turner b G. Giffen	3	c and b G. Giffen	22
R. Peel	c G. Giffen b Turner	20	st Blackham b G. Giffen	6
G.A. Lohmann	b G. Giffen	10	c Bruce b G. Giffen	15
G. MacGregor†	lbw b McLeod	3	c and b G. Giffen	12
J. Briggs	lbw b Trott	28	c Trott b Turner	12
W. Attewell	b Trott	0	c and b G. Giffen	0
J.W. Sharpe	c Bannerman b G. Giffen	26	not out	4
Extras	(B 10, LB 2, W 1)	13	(B 5, LB 2)	7
Total		**307**		**157**

ENGLAND	O	M	R	W	O	M	R	W		FALL OF WICKETS			
Lohmann	43·2	18	58	8	51	14	84	2		A	E	A	E
Attewell	31	20	25	1	46	24	43	1	*Wkt*	*1st*	*1st*	*2nd*	*2nd*
Briggs	10	2	24	0	32·4	8	69	4	1st	31	50	1	2
Sharpe	10	1	31	0	35	7	91	1	2nd	57	79	175	6
Peel					35	13	49	1	3rd	62	123	254	11
Grace					16	2	34	0	4th	90	127	347	64
Stoddart					4	1	12	0	5th	117	152	364	83
									6th	123	167	376	117
AUSTRALIA									7th	126	178	391	133
Turner	37	11	90	2	23·2	7	46	4	8th	132	235	391	140
McLeod	18	6	55	2					9th	141	235	391	140
G. Giffen	28·2	5	88	4	28	10	72	6	10th	145	307	–	157
Trott	14	3	42	2	5	0	11	0					
Callaway	17	10	19	0	10	6	21	0					

Umpires: T. Flynn (2) and J. Tooher (1).

Close: 1st day – E(1) 38-0 (Abel 15, Grace 23); 2nd – A(2) 1-1 (Bannerman 0); 3rd – A(2) 263-3 (Bannerman 67, Bruce 5); 4th – E(2) 11-3 (Stoddart 1).

AUSTRALIA v ENGLAND 1891–92 (3rd Test)

Played at Adelaide Oval on 24, 25, 26, 28 March.
Toss: England.   Result: ENGLAND won by an innings and 230 runs.
Debuts: England – H. Philipson.

England gained the biggest margin of victory in any Test so far. Torrential rain on the second day caused play to be abandoned after England had amassed 490 for 9 and ruined the pitch for batting.

ENGLAND

W.G. Grace*	b McLeod	58
R. Abel	st Blackham b Trott	24
A.E. Stoddart	lbw b G. Giffen	134
J.M. Read	c Gregory b Turner	57
G. Bean	c McLeod b Lyons	16
R. Peel	c G. Giffen b Turner	83
G.A. Lohmann	lbw b G. Giffen	0
J. Briggs	b Turner	39
H. Philipson†	c Blackham b McLeod	1
G. MacGregor	run out	31
W. Attewell	not out	43
Extras	(B 5. LB 7, W 1)	13
Total		**499**

AUSTRALIA

A.C. Bannerman	c Bean b Lohmann	12	b Briggs	1
J.J. Lyons	c Peel b Briggs	23	c Stoddart b Briggs	19
G. Giffen	run out	5	c Bean b Attewell	27
W. Bruce	lbw b Lohmann	5	lbw b Attewell	37
C.T.B. Turner	c Lohmann b Briggs	10	c Grace b Briggs	5
S.E. Gregory	c Abel b Briggs	3	c Peel b Briggs	7
R.W. McLeod	b Briggs	20	c Grace b Lohmann	30
G.H.S. Trott	b Briggs	0	st Philipson b Briggs	16
W.F. Giffen	b Lohmann	3	c Peel b Briggs	2
H. Donnan	c Bean b Briggs	7	not out	11
J.M. Blackham*†	not out	7	b Attewell	9
Extras	(B 5)	5	(B 3, LB 2)	5
Total		**100**		**169**

AUSTRALIA	O	M	R	W	O	M	R	W
G. Giffen	51·1	17	154	2				
McLeod	41	11	78	2				
Trott	12	0	80	1				
Turner	46	17	111	3				
Donnan	9	2	22	0				
Lyons	5	0	22	1				
Bruce	4	3	19	0				
ENGLAND								
Briggs	21·5	4	49	6	28	7	87	6
Lohmann	21	8	46	3	6	2	8	1
Attewell					34	10	69	3

FALL OF WICKETS

	E	A	A
Wkt	1st	1st	2nd
1st	47	30	1
2nd	121	38	42
3rd	218	48	51
4th	272	48	85
5th	327	51	91
6th	333	66	99
7th	412	66	120
8th	425	73	124
9th	425	90	157
10th	499	100	169

Umpires: G. Downes (1) and W.O. Whitridge (1).

Close: 1st day – E(1) 313-4 (Stoddart 129, Peel 29); 2nd – E(1) 490-9 (MacGregor 29, Attewell 36); 3rd – A(2) 124-8 (McLeod 8).

SOUTH AFRICA v ENGLAND 1891–92 (Only Test)

Played at Newlands, Cape Town, on 19, 21, 22 March.
Toss: South Africa.   Result: ENGLAND won by an innings and 189 runs.
Debuts: South Africa–G. Cripps, J.F. du Toit, C.G. Fichardt, E.A. Halliwell, C.H. Mills, D.C. Parkin, T.W. Routledge, C.S. Wimble; England – V.A. Barton, W. Chatterton, A. Hearne, G.G. Hearne, J.T. Hearne, A.D. Pougher. *F. Hearne was making his debut for South Africa after playing twice for England. J.J. Ferris and W.L. Murdoch were making their debuts for England after appearing for Australia.*

For the first time England contested two Test series simultaneously; two days after W.W. Read's Team played this Test Lord Sheffield's side began their third match against Australia. The Hearnes provided the second instance of three brothers playing in the same match: Alec and George Gibbons for England, and Frank for South Africa. John Thomas was their cousin. Harry Wood scored the first century by a wicket-keeper in Test matches; it was his only hundred in first-class cricket. Murdoch, the former Australian captain, kept wicket for England in the second innings.

SOUTH AFRICA

T.W. Routledge	b Ferris	5	c Pougher b Ferris		1
F. Hearne	b Pougher	24	b Ferris		23
C.G. Fichardt	c and b Pougher	0	run out		10
C.H. Mills	b Ferris	4	b Ferris		21
E.A. Halliwell†	c J.T. Hearne b Ferris	8	b Ferris		0
C.S. Wimble	c Wood b Pougher	0	(10) st Murdoch b Martin		0
G. Cripps	b J.T. Hearne	18	b Ferris		3
W.H. Milton*	c Martin b Ferris	21	c A. Hearne b Ferris		16
C.H. Vintcent	lbw b Ferris	6	(6) b Ferris		0
D.C. Parkin	b Ferris	6	(9) c and b Martin		0
J.F. du Toit	not out	0	not out		2
Extras	(B 5)	5	(B 7)		7
Total		**97**			**83**

ENGLAND

W. Chatterton	c Du Toit b Mills	48
A. Hearne	lbw b Parkin	9
W.L. Murdoch	c and b Parkin	12
G.G. Hearne	c Mills b Parkin	0
V.A. Barton	c Vintcent b Mills	23
W.W. Read*	b Du Toit	40
A.D. Pougher	b Hearne	17
H. Wood†	not out	134
J.J. Ferris	run out	16
J.T. Hearne	c Fichardt b Milton	40
F. Martin	c Mills b Hearne	13
Extras	(B 13, NB 4)	17
Total		**369**

ENGLAND	O	M	R	W	O	M	R	W
Ferris	29·2	11	54	6	25	16	37	7
Pougher	21	8	26	3				
J.T. Hearne	8	2	12	1				
Martin					24·3	9	39	2

SOUTH AFRICA	O	M	R	W
Vintcent	24	8	50	0
Parkin	26	4	82	3
Mills	28	7	83	2
Hearne	12·2	0	40	2
Du Toit	17	5	47	1
Milton	9	2	27	1
Cripps	3	0	23	0

FALL OF WICKETS

	SA	E	SA
Wkt	1st	1st	2nd
1st	7	19	1
2nd	14	33	30
3rd	29	33	40
4th	33	86	45
5th	39	110	45
6th	47	144	59
7th	78	215	70
8th	89	280	79
9th	93	351	81
10th	97	369	83

Umpires: J. Leaney (1) and C.N. Thomas (1).

Close: 1st day – E(1) 110-5 (Read 15); 2nd – SA(2) 48-5 (Mills 8, Cripps 0).

ENGLAND v AUSTRALIA 1893 (1st Test)

Played at Lord's, London, on 17, 18, 19 July.
Toss: England.   Result: MATCH DRAWN.
Debuts: England–F.S. Jackson, W.H. Lockwood, A.W. Mold, E. Wainwright; Australia–
H. Graham. *Jackson was to become Colonel the Right Honourable Sir Francis Stanley Jackson, PC, GCSI, GCIE.*

On the first day Shrewsbury became the first batsman to score 1,000 runs in Test matches, the first to reach that aggregate in England v Australia Tests, and the first to score three hundreds for England. Graham emulated C. Bannerman (*Test No. 1*) by scoring his maiden first-class hundred in his first Test innings. Deputising for the injured W.G. Grace, Stoddart was the first captain to declare a Test innings closed. Rain prevented play after lunch on the third day. James Phillips was the first umpire to officiate in Tests in more than one country. Renowned and respected in his native Australia as a fearless no-baller of 'chuckers', he later stood in Tests in South Africa – a unique treble.

ENGLAND

A. Shrewsbury	c Blackham b Turner	106	b Giffen		81
A.E. Stoddart*	b Turner	24	b Turner		13
W. Gunn	c Lyons b Turner	2	c Graham b Giffen		77
F.S. Jackson	c Blackham b Turner	91	c Bruce b Giffen		5
J.M. Read	b Bruce	6	c McLeod b Bruce		1
R. Peel	c Bruce b Trumble	12	(9) not out		0
W. Flowers	b McLeod	35	(6) b Turner		4
E. Wainwright	c Giffen b Turner	1	b Giffen		26
W.H. Lockwood	b Bruce	22	(7) b Giffen		0
G. MacGregor†	not out	5			
A.W. Mold	b Turner	0			
Extras	(B 19, LB 9, NB 2)	30	(B 16, LB 9, W 1, NB 1)		27
Total		**334**	(8 wickets declared)		**234**

AUSTRALIA

J.J. Lyons	b Lockwood	7
A.C. Bannerman	c Shrewsbury b Lockwood	17
G. Giffen	b Lockwood	0
G.H.S. Trott	c MacGregor b Lockwood	33
R.W. McLeod	b Lockwood	5
S.E. Gregory	c MacGregor b Lockwood	57
H. Graham	c MacGregor b Mold	107
W. Bruce	c Peel b Mold	23
C.T.B. Turner	b Flowers	0
H. Trumble	not out	2
J.M. Blackham*†	lbw b Mold	2
Extras	(B 15, LB 1)	16
Total		**269**

AUSTRALIA	O	M	R	W	O	M	R	W		FALL OF WICKETS		
Turner	36	16	67	6	32	15	64	2		E	A	E
Bruce	22	4	58	2	20	10	34	1	*Wkt*	*1st*	*1st*	*2nd*
Trumble	19	7	42	1	11	2	33	0	1st	29	7	27
Trott	9	2	38	0	2	0	5	0	2nd	31	7	179
McLeod	21	6	51	1	25	11	28	0	3rd	168	50	195
Giffen	18	3	48	0	26·4	6	43	5	4th	189	60	198
									5th	213	75	198
ENGLAND									6th	293	217	198
Peel	22	12	36	0					7th	298	264	234
Lockwood	45	11	101	6					8th	313	265	234
Mold	20·1	7	44	3					9th	333	265	–
Jackson	5	1	10	0					10th	334	269	–
Wainwright	11	3	41	0								
Flowers	11	3	21	1								

Umpires: W. Hearn (1) and J. Phillips (4).

Close: 1st day – A(1) 33-2 (Bannerman 9, Trott 4); 2nd – E(2) 113-1 (Shrewsbury 45, Gunn 43).

ENGLAND v AUSTRALIA 1893 (2nd Test)

Played at Kennington Oval, London, on 14, 15, 16 August.
Toss: England.   Result: ENGLAND won by an innings and 43 runs.
Debuts: England – Albert Ward (*England's second 'A. Ward'*, Alan, *made his debut in Test No. 656*).

Jackson's hundred, which took 135 minutes, was the first in a Test in England to be completed with a hit over the boundary (then worth only four runs). His score was 98 when the ninth wicket fell. Bannerman became the first Australian to score 1,000 runs in Tests. This match, played in almost tropical heat, was awarded as a benefit to J.M. Read and produced takings of £1,200.

ENGLAND

W.G. Grace*	c Giffen b Trumble	68
A.E. Stoddart	b Turner	83
A. Shrewsbury	c Graham b Giffen	66
W. Gunn	b Giffen	16
A. Ward	c and b Giffen	55
W.W. Read	b Giffen	52
F.S. Jackson	run out	103
J. Briggs	b Giffen	0
W.H. Lockwood	c and b Giffen	10
G. MacGregor†	lbw b Giffen	5
A.W. Mold	not out	0
Extras	(B 19, LB 4, W 2)	25
Total		**483**

AUSTRALIA

A.C. Bannerman	c MacGregor b Lockwood	10	c Read b Lockwood	55
J.J. Lyons	b Briggs	19	(7) c Grace b Lockwood	31
G.H.S. Trott	b Lockwood	0	(4) c Read b Lockwood	92
S.E. Gregory	lbw b Briggs	9	(5) c Shrewsbury b Briggs	6
H. Graham	c MacGregor b Lockwood	0	(6) b Briggs	42
G. Giffen	c MacGregor b Lockwood	4	(3) b Lockwood	53
W. Bruce	not out	10	(2) c Jackson b Mold	22
H. Trumble	b Briggs	5	b Briggs	8
R.W. McLeod	c Lockwood b Briggs	2	c Jackson b Briggs	5
C.T.B. Turner	b Briggs	7	b Briggs	0
J.M. Blackham*†	run out	17	not out	2
Extras	(B 5, LB 3)	8	(B 18, LB 15)	33
Total		**91**		**349**

AUSTRALIA	O	M	R	W	O	M	R	W
Turner	47	18	94	1				
Trumble	47	16	101	1				
McLeod	23	6	57	0				
Giffen	54	17	128	7				
Trott	6	1	33	0				
Bruce	3	0	19	0				
Lyons	7	1	26	0				
ENGLAND								
Lockwood	19	9	37	4	29	7	96	4
Mold	4	0	12	0	23	8	73	1
Briggs	14·3	5	34	5	35	6	114	5
Jackson					11	3	33	0

FALL OF WICKETS

	E	A	A
Wkt	*1st*	*1st*	*2nd*
1st	151	30	54
2nd	151	31	126
3rd	200	32	165
4th	303	32	189
5th	311	40	295
6th	442	48	311
7th	442	57	340
8th	456	59	342
9th	478	69	342
10th	483	91	349

Umpires: H. Draper (1) and C.K. Pullin (10).

Close: 1st day – E(1) 378-5 (Read 21, Jackson 49); 2nd – A(2) 158-2 (Giffen 49, Trott 21).

ENGLAND v AUSTRALIA 1893 (3rd Test)

Played at Old Trafford, Manchester, on 24, 25, 26 August.
Toss: Australia.   Result: MATCH DRAWN.
Debuts: England – W. Brockwell, T. Richardson.

Gunn's hundred took 250 minutes and was the first in a Test at Old Trafford. During his match-saving second innings, Turner was struck on the hand and dislocated a finger. Dr Grace pulled the joint back into place and he was able to continue his last-wicket partnership of 36 with Blackham which occupied valuable time for Australia. England, one up in the three-match rubber, made no attempt to score 198 runs in 135 minutes.

AUSTRALIA

A.C. Bannerman	c MacGregor b Briggs	19	b Richardson	60
J.J. Lyons	c MacGregor b Briggs	27	b Mold	33
G. Giffen	b Richardson	17	c Brockwell b Richardson	17
G.H.S. Trott	c Grace b Richardson	9	b Mold	12
W. Bruce	c Read b Richardson	68	(6) c Shrewsbury b Richardson	36
H. Graham	lbw b Mold	18	(7) st MacGregor b Briggs	3
S.E. Gregory	b Briggs	0	(8) lbw b Richardson	3
H. Trumble	b Richardson	35	(9) run out	8
R.W. McLeod	b Briggs	2	(5) c Read b Richardson	6
C.T.B. Turner	b Richardson	0	c Mold b Briggs	27
J.M. Blackham*†	not out	0	not out	23
Extras	(B 5, LB 4)	9	(B 4, LB 4)	8
Total		**204**		**236**

ENGLAND

A.E. Stoddart	run out	0	c Gregory b Trumble	42
W.G. Grace*	b Bruce	40	c Trott b McLeod	45
A. Shrewsbury	c Bruce b Giffen	12	not out	19
W. Gunn	not out	102	b Trumble	11
A. Ward	c Blackham b Turner	13	b Trumble	0
W.W. Read	b Giffen	12	not out	0
W. Brockwell	c Gregory b Giffen	11		
J. Briggs	b Giffen	2		
G. MacGregor†	st Blackham b Turner	12		
T. Richardson	b Bruce	16		
A.W. Mold	b Trumble	0		
Extras	(B 17, LB 6)	23	(B 1)	1
Total		**243**	(4 wickets)	**118**

ENGLAND	O	M	R	W	O	M	R	W
Mold	28	11	48	1	23	6	57	2
Richardson	23·4	5	49	5	44	15	107	5
Briggs	42	18	81	4	28·3	11	64	2
Brockwell	3	0	17	0				
AUSTRALIA								
Giffen	67	30	113	4	6	3	10	0
Turner	53	22	72	2	7	1	18	0
Bruce	17	5	26	2	9	4	19	0
Trumble	3·2	1	9	1	25	4	49	3
McLeod					16	7	21	1

FALL OF WICKETS

	A	E	A	E
Wkt	1st	1st	2nd	2nd
1st	32	4	56	78
2nd	59	43	79	100
3rd	69	73	92	117
4th	73	93	99	117
5th	129	112	153	–
6th	130	136	170	–
7th	194	165	173	–
8th	198	196	182	–
9th	201	238	200	–
10th	204	243	236	–

Umpires: C. Clements (1) and J. Phillips (5).

Close: 1st day – E(1) 54-2 (Grace 29, Gunn 5); 2nd – A(2) 93-3 (Bannerman 26, McLeod 1).

AUSTRALIA v ENGLAND 1894–95 (1st Test)

Played at Sydney Cricket Ground on 14, 15, 17, 18, 19, 20 December.
Toss: Australia.   Result: ENGLAND won by 10 runs.
Debuts: Australia – J. Darling, F.A. Iredale, E. Jones, C.E. McLeod, J.C. Reedman; England – J.T. Brown, F.G.J. Ford, L.H.Gay, A.C. MacLaren.

The first Test to involve six playing days resulted in the first instance of a team winning a Test after following-on (repeated by England in 1981 – *Test No. 905*). Gregory, who batted for 244 minutes and hit 28 fours, scored the first double century in a Test in Australia; his partnership of 154 in 73 minutes with Blackham remains the ninth-wicket record for this series and Australia's record for that wicket in all Tests. Giffen is the only player to score 200 runs and take eight wickets in a Test between these two countries. Peel and Briggs took full advantage of a 'sticky' pitch on the sixth day. McLeod deputised for Blackham (damaged thumb) for part of the second innings. The match aggregate of 1,514 runs was then a record for all first-class cricket.

AUSTRALIA

J.J. Lyons	b Richardson	1	b Richardson	25
G.H.S. Trott	b Richardson	12	c Gay b Peel	8
G Giffen	c Ford b Brockwell	161	lbw b Briggs	41
J. Darling	b Richardson	0	c Brockwell b Peel	53
F.A. Iredale	c Stoddart b Ford	81	(6) c and b Briggs	5
S.E. Gregory	c Peel b Stoddart	201	(5) c Gay b Peel	16
J.C. Reedman	c Ford b Peel	17	st Gay b Peel	4
C.E. McLeod	b Richardson	15	not out	2
C.T.B. Turner	c Gay b Peel	1	c Briggs b Peel	2
J.M. Blackham*†	b Richardson	74	(11) c and b Peel	2
E. Jones	not out	11	(10) c MacLaren b Briggs	1
Extras	(B 8, LB 3, W 1)	12	(B 2, LB 1, NB 4)	7
Total		**586**		**166**

ENGLAND

A.C. MacLaren	c Reedman b Turner	4	b Giffen	20
A. Ward	c Iredale b Turner	75	b Giffen	117
A.E. Stoddart*	c Jones b Giffen	12	c Giffen b Turner	36
J.T. Brown	run out	22	c Jones b Giffen	53
W. Brockwell	c Blackham b Jones	49	b Jones	37
R. Peel	c Gregory b Giffen	4	b Giffen	17
F.G.J. Ford	st Blackham b Giffen	30	c and b McLeod	48
J. Briggs	b Giffen	57	b McLeod	42
W.H. Lockwood	c Giffen b Trott	18	b Trott	29
L.H. Gay†	c Gregory b Reedman	33	b Trott	4
T. Richardson	not out	0	not out	12
Extras	(B 17, LB 3, W 1)	21	(B 14, LB 8)	22
Total		**325**		**437**

ENGLAND	O	M	R	W	O	M	R	W
Richardson	55·3	13	181	5	11	3	27	1
Peel	53	14	140	2	30	9	67	6
Briggs	25	4	96	0	11	2	25	3
Brockwell	22	7	78	1				
Lockwood	3	2	1	0	16	3	40	0
Ford	11	2	47	1				
Stoddart	3	0	31	1				
AUSTRALIA								
Turner	44	16	89	2	35	14	78	1
Jones	18	6	44	1	19	0	57	1
Giffen	43	17	75	4	75	25	164	4
McLeod	14	2	25	0	30	6	67	2
Trott	15	4	59	1	12·4	3	22	2
Reedman	3·3	1	12	1	6	1	12	0
Lyons	2	2	0	0	2	0	12	0
Iredale					2	1	3	0

FALL OF WICKETS

	A	E	E	A
Wkt	1st	1st	2nd	2nd
1st	10	14	44	26
2nd	21	43	115	45
3rd	21	78	217	130
4th	192	149	245	135
5th	331	155	290	147
6th	379	211	296	158
7th	400	211	385	159
8th	409	252	398	161
9th	563	325	420	162
10th	586	325	437	166

Umpires: C. Bannerman (4) and J. Phillips (6).

Close: 1st day – A(1) 346-5 (Gregory 85, Reedman 4); 2nd – E(1) 130-3 (Ward 67, Brockwell 18); 3rd – E(1) 325 all out; 4th – E(2) 268-4 (Brockwell 20, Peel 9); 5th – A(2) 113-2 (Giffen 30, Darling 44).

AUSTRALIA v ENGLAND 1894–95 (2nd Test)

Played at Melbourne Cricket Ground on 29, 31 December, 1, 2, 3 January.
Toss: Australia.   Result: ENGLAND won by 94 runs.
Debuts: Australia – A. Coningham.

Stoddart's 173 in 320 minutes was the highest score for England in Tests, beating W.G. Grace's 170 in 1886 (*Test No. 24*). It remained the England record until K.S. Ranjitsinhji scored 175 in 1897-98 (*Test No. 53*) and the highest by an England captain in Australia until 1974-75 when M.H. Denness scored 188 (*Test No. 755*). Coningham took MacLaren's wicket with his first ball in his only Test to claim the first instances of a wicket falling to the first ball of a Test match and to a bowler's first delivery at this level. In England's second innings all eleven batsmen reached double figures for the first time in a Test match innings.

ENGLAND

A.C. MacLaren	c Trott b Coningham	0	b Turner	15
A. Ward	c Darling b Trumble	30	b Turner	41
A.E. Stoddart*	b Turner	10	b Giffen	173
J.T. Brown	c Trumble b Turner	0	c Jarvis b Bruce	37
W. Brockwell	c Iredale b Coningham	0	b Turner	21
R. Peel	c Trumble b Turner	6	st Jarvis b Giffen	53
F.G.J. Ford	c Giffen b Trumble	9	c Trott b Giffen	24
W.H. Lockwood	not out	3	(9) not out	33
J. Briggs	c Bruce b Turner	5	(8) lbw b Giffen	31
H. Philipson†	c Darling b Turner	1	b Giffen	30
T. Richardson	c Iredale b Trumble	0	c Gregory b Giffen	11
Extras	(LB 9, NB 2)	11	(B 1, LB 2, NB 3)	6
Total		**75**		**475**

AUSTRALIA

J.J. Lyons	b Richardson	2	(7) b Peel	14
W. Bruce	c Ford b Peel	4	c Stoddart b Peel	54
G. Giffen*	c Philipson b Briggs	32	c Brown b Brockwell	43
S.E. Gregory	c Ward b Richardson	2	b Richardson	12
J. Darling	b Lockwood	32	b Brockwell	5
F.A. Iredale	b Richardson	10	b Peel	68
G.H.S. Trott	run out	16	(1) c and b Brockwell	95
A. Coningham	c Philipson b Richardson	10	(9) b Peel	3
H. Trumble	b Richardson	1	(10) run out	2
A.H. Jarvis†	c Brown b Briggs	11	(8) b Richardson	4
C.T.B. Turner	not out	1	not out	26
Extras	(W 2)	2	(B 5, LB 1, NB 1)	7
Total		**123**		**333**

AUSTRALIA	O	M	R	W	O	M	R	W	FALL OF WICKETS				
										E	A	E	A
Coningham	11	5	17	2	20	4	59	0	*Wkt*	*1st*	*1st*	*2nd*	*2nd*
Turner	20	9	32	5	55	21	99	3	1st	0	4	24	98
Trumble	9·1	4	15	3	26	6	72	0	2nd	19	12	101	191
Giffen					78·2	21	155	6	3rd	23	14	191	206
Lyons					2	1	3	0	4th	26	53	222	214
Trott					17	0	60	0	5th	44	80	320	216
Bruce					4	0	21	1	6th	58	96	362	241
ENGLAND									7th	60	108	385	254
Richardson	23	6	57	5	40	10	100	2	8th	70	110	402	263
Peel	14	4	21	1	40·1	9	77	4	9th	71	116	455	268
Lockwood	5	0	17	1	25	5	60	0	10th	75	123	475	333
Briggs	13·5	2	26	2	12	0	49	0					
Ford					6	2	7	0					
Brockwell					14	3	33	3					

Umpires: T. Flynn (3) and J. Phillips (7).

Close: 1st day – A(1) 123 all out; 2nd – E(2) 287-4 (Stoddart 151, Peel 18); 3rd – A(2) 86-0 (Trott 43, Bruce 43); 4th – A(2) 328-9 (Iredale 63, Turner 26).

AUSTRALIA v ENGLAND 1894–95 (3rd Test)

Played at Adelaide Oval on 11, 12, 14, 15 January.
Toss: Australia.   Result: AUSTRALIA won by 382 runs.
Debuts: Australia – J. Harry, A.E. Trott.

This match, played in temperatures that reached 155°F in the open, was notable for the all-round performance of Albert Trott who scored 110 runs without being dismissed and bowled unchanged virtually throughout the second innings to take 8 for 43. Only two other bowlers have taken eight wickets in an innings of their maiden Test: A.L. Valentine for West Indies in 1950 (*Test No. 323*) and R.A.L. Massie (twice) for Australia in 1972 (*Test No. 699*).

AUSTRALIA

W. Bruce	b Richardson	11	c Brockwell b Briggs		80
G.H.S. Trott	run out	48	b Peel		0
G. Giffen*	c Lockwood b Brockwell	58	c Ford b Peel		24
F.A. Iredale	b Richardson	7	c and b Peel		140
J. Darling	c Philipson b Briggs	10	c Philipson b Lockwood		3
S.E. Gregory	c Brown b Richardson	6	b Richardson		20
J. Harry	b Richardson	2	b Richardson		6
J. Worrall	run out	0	c Peel b Briggs		11
A.H. Jarvis†	c and b Lockwood	13	c Brown b Peel		29
A.E. Trott	not out	38	not out		72
S.T. Callaway	b Richardson	41	b Richardson		11
Extras	(B 2, W 1, NB 1)	4	(B 7, LB 7, NB 1)		15
Total		**238**			**411**

ENGLAND

J. Briggs	b Callaway	12	(9) b A.E. Trott		0
A.C. MacLaren	b Callaway	25	c Iredale b A.E. Trott		35
W. Brockwell	c Harry b Callaway	12	(6) c and b A.E. Trott		24
A. Ward	c Bruce b Giffen	5	(1) b A.E. Trott		13
A.E. Stoddart*	b Giffen	1	(3) not out		34
J.T. Brown	not out	39	(5) b A.E. Trott		2
R. Peel	b Callaway	0	(7) c and b A.E. Trott		0
F.G.J. Ford	c Worrall b Giffen	21	c G.H.S. Trott b A.E. Trott		14
W.H. Lockwood	c Worrall b Giffen	0	(10) c Iredale b A.E. Trott		1
H. Philipson†	c Gregory b Giffen	7	(4) b Giffen		1
T. Richardson	c Worrall b Callaway	0	c A.E. Trott b Giffen		12
Extras	(B 2)	2	(B 5, LB 2)		7
Total		**124**			**143**

ENGLAND	O	M	R	W	O	M	R	W	FALL OF WICKETS				
Richardson	21	4	75	5	31·2	8	89	3		A	E	A	E
Peel	16	1	43	0	34	6	96	4	*Wkt*	*1st*	*1st*	*2nd*	*2nd*
Brockwell	20	13	30	1	10	1	50	0	1st	31	14	0	52
Ford	8	2	19	0	6	0	33	0	2nd	69	30	44	52
Briggs	8	2	34	1	19	3	57	2	3rd	84	49	142	53
Lockwood	8	2	33	1	15	2	71	1	4th	103	50	145	64
									5th	120	56	197	102
AUSTRALIA									6th	124	64	215	102
A.E. Trott	3	1	9	0	27	10	43	8	7th	137	111	238	128
Giffen	28	11	76	5	22·1	12	74	2	8th	157	111	283	128
Callaway	26·3	13	37	5	7	1	19	0	9th	157	124	347	130
									10th	238	124	411	143

Umpires: J. Phillips (8) and G. Searcy (1).

Close: 1st day – E(1) 5-0 (Briggs 4, MacLaren 1); 2nd – A(2) 145-4 (Iredale 31); 3rd – E(2) 56-3 (Stoddart 1, Brown 2).

AUSTRALIA v ENGLAND 1894–95 (4th Test)

Played at Sydney Cricket Ground on 1, 2 (*no play*), 4 February.
Toss: England.   Result: AUSTRALIA won by an innings and 147 runs.
Debuts: Nil.

Stoddart, who had made Test cricket's first declaration (*Test No. 39*), became the first England captain to invite the opposition to bat. Graham completed a rare double, scoring hundreds in his first Test innings in both England and Australia. Briggs, in his 25th Test, was the first to take 100 wickets when he dismissed Jarvis. Lancashire players occupied the first three places in England's first innings order. Playing in his 17th and final Test, 'Terror' Turner became the first Australian to take 100 wickets when he had Peel stumped the first time. England, 11 for 1 overnight, lost 17 wickets in under three hours in dreadful batting conditions on the third day. Lockwood, whose hand had been badly gashed by an exploding soda water bottle before the match, was unable to bat.

AUSTRALIA

G.H.S. Trott	c Brown b Peel	1
W. Bruce	c Brockwell b Peel	15
G Giffen*	b Peel	8
H. Moses	b Richardson	1
H. Graham	st Philipson b Briggs	105
S.E. Gregory	st Philipson b Briggs	5
F.A. Iredale	c and b Briggs	0
J. Darling	b Richardson	31
A.E. Trott	not out	85
A.H. Jarvis†	c Philipson b Briggs	5
C.T.B. Turner	c Richardson b Lockwood	22
Extras	(B 3, LB 1, W 1, NB 1)	6
Total		**284**

ENGLAND

A.C. MacLaren	st Jarvis b G.H.S. Trott	1	(4) c Bruce b Giffen		0
A. Ward	c and b Turner	7	c Darling b Giffen		6
J. Briggs	b G.H.S. Trott	11	(8) c Bruce b Giffen		6
A.E. Stoddart*	st Jarvis b G.H.S. Trott	7	(3) c Iredale b Turner		0
J.T. Brown	not out	20	(1) b Giffen		0
W. Brockwell	c Darling b Turner	1	(5) c Bruce b Turner		17
F.G.J. Ford	c G.H.S. Trott b Giffen	0	c Darling b Giffen		11
R. Peel	st Jarvis b Turner	0	(6) st Jarvis b Turner		0
H. Philipson†	c Graham b Giffen	4	c and b Turner		9
T. Richardson	c and b Giffen	2	not out		10
W.H. Lockwood	absent hurt	–	absent hurt		–
Extras	(B 7, LB 3, NB 2)	12	(B 5, LB 7, NB 1)		13
Total		**65**			**72**

ENGLAND	O	M	R	W	O	M	R	W
Peel	24	5	74	3				
Richardson	22	5	78	2				
Briggs	22	4	65	4				
Brockwell	5	1	25	0				
Ford	2	0	14	0				
Lockwood	8·2	3	22	1				
AUSTRALIA								
G.H.S. Trott	14	5	21	3				
Turner	19	10	18	3	14·1	6	33	4
Giffen	5·5	1	14	3	15	7	26	5

FALL OF WICKETS

Wkt	A 1st	E 1st	E 2nd
1st	2	2	0
2nd	20	20	5
3rd	26	24	5
4th	26	31	12
5th	51	40	14
6th	51	43	29
7th	119	56	47
8th	231	63	52
9th	239	65	72
10th	284	–	–

Umpires: C. Bannerman (5) and J. Phillips (9).

Close: 1st day – E(1) 11-1 (Ward 5, Briggs 4); 2nd – no play.

AUSTRALIA v ENGLAND 1894–95 (5th Test)

Played at Melbourne Cricket Ground on 1, 2, 4, 5, 6 March.
Toss: Australia.   Result: ENGLAND won by six wickets.
Debuts: Australia – T.R. McKibbin.

With the rubber level, 'the match of the century' attracted vast crowds and even the interest of Queen Victoria. John Thomas Brown (140) scored his first fifty in only 28 minutes – still the fastest half-century in Test cricket. His hundred took 95 minutes and was the fastest Test century until J. Darling eclipsed it by four minutes in 1897-98 (*Test No. 57*). Brown's third-wicket partnership of 210 with Ward set a new Test record for any wicket. Giffen achieved what is still the best all-round performance in a Test rubber by scoring 475 runs and taking 34 wickets.

AUSTRALIA

G.H.S. Trott	b Briggs	42	b Peel	42
W. Bruce	c MacLaren b Peel	22	c and b Peel	11
G. Giffen*	b Peel	57	b Richardson	51
F.A. Iredale	b Richardson	8	b Richardson	18
S.E. Gregory	c Philipson b Richardson	70	b Richardson	30
J. Darling	c Ford b Peel	74	b Peel	50
J.J. Lyons	c Philipson b Lockwood	55	b Briggs	15
H. Graham	b Richardson	6	lbw b Richardson	10
A.E. Trott	c Lockwood b Peel	10	b Richardson	0
A.H. Jarvis†	not out	34	not out	14
T.R. McKibbin	c Peel b Briggs	23	c Philipson b Richardson	13
Extras	(B 3, LB 10)	13	(B 5, LB 6, NB 2)	13
Total		**414**		**267**

ENGLAND

A. Ward	b McKibbin	32	b G.H.S. Trott	93
W. Brockwell	st Jarvis b G.H.S. Trott	5	c and b Giffen	5
A.E. Stoddart*	st Jarvis b G.H.S. Trott	68	lbw b G.H.S. Trott	11
J.T. Brown	b A.E. Trott	30	c Giffen b McKibbin	140
A.C. MacLaren	hit wkt b G.H.S. Trott	120	not out	20
R. Peel	c Gregory b Giffen	73	not out	15
W.H. Lockwood	c G.H.S. Trott b Giffen	5		
F.G.J. Ford	c A.E. Trott b Giffen	11		
J. Briggs	c G.H.S. Trott b Giffen	0		
H. Philipson†	not out	10		
T. Richardson	lbw b G.H.S. Trott	11		
Extras	(B 8, LB 8, W 4)	20	(B 6, LB 5, W 2, NB 1)	14
Total		**385**	(4 wickets)	**298**

ENGLAND	O	M	R	W	O	M	R	W
Richardson	42	7	138	3	45·2	7	104	6
Peel	48	13	114	4	46	16	89	3
Lockwood	27	7	72	1	16	7	24	0
Briggs	23·4	5	46	2	16	3	37	1
Brockwell	6	1	22	0				
Ford	2	0	9	0				
AUSTRALIA								
Giffen	45	13	130	4	31	4	106	1
G.H.S. Trott	24	5	71	4	20	1	63	2
A.E. Trott	30	4	84	1	19	2	56	0
McKibbin	29	6	73	1	14	2	47	1
Bruce	5	1	7	0	3	1	10	0
Lyons					1	0	2	0

FALL OF WICKETS

Wkt	A 1st	E 1st	A 2nd	E 2nd
1st	40	6	32	5
2nd	101	110	75	28
3rd	126	112	125	238
4th	142	166	148	278
5th	284	328	179	–
6th	286	342	200	–
7th	304	364	219	–
8th	335	364	219	–
9th	367	366	248	–
10th	414	385	267	–

Umpires: T. Flynn (4) and J. Phillips (10).

Close: 1st day – A(1) 282-4 (Gregory 70, Darling 72); 2nd – E(1) 206-4 (MacLaren 40, Peel 18); 3rd – A(2) 69-1 (Trott 37, Giffen 14); 4th – E(2) 28-1 (Ward 6, Stoddart 11).

SOUTH AFRICA v ENGLAND 1895–96 (1st Test)

Played at St George's Park, Port Elizabeth, on 13, 14 February.
Toss: South Africa.   Result: ENGLAND won by 288 runs.
Debuts: South Africa – F.J. Cook, R.A. Gleeson, C.F.W. Hime, J. Middleton, R.M. Poore, J.H. Sinclair, J.T. Willoughby; England – H.R. Bromley-Davenport, H.R. Butt, C.B. Fry, The Seventh Lord Hawke, T.W. Hayward, A.J.L. Hill, A.M. Miller, C.W. Wright. *S.M.J. Woods was making his debut for England after playing for Australia.*

South Africa were dismissed in only 94 balls for 30 – the lowest total in Test cricket until 1954-55 when New Zealand were dismissed for 26 (*Test No. 402*). Lohmann's analysis of 8 for 7 set a new Test record and he ended the match – on the second day – with a hat-trick. His match figures of 15 for 45 remain the best in any Test at Port Elizabeth. A record number of batsmen (23) were bowled in the match. The most diligent research has failed to identify either umpire who officiated in this match.

ENGLAND

Sir T.C. O'Brien*	c Gleeson b Willoughby	17	(3) b Sinclair	16
G.A. Lohmann	c Routledge b Willoughby	0	(6) b Willoughby	0
T.W. Hayward	c Sinclair b Middleton	30	(4) c Halliwell b Willoughby	6
C.B. Fry	b Middleton	43	(5) c Halliwell b Middleton	15
A.J.L. Hill	run out	25	(7) b Middleton	37
S.M.J. Woods	b Hime	7	(8) c Poore b Sinclair	53
H.R. Bromley-Davenport	c Fichardt b Middleton	26	(9) c Poore b Middleton	7
Lord Hawke	b Middleton	0	(10) c Gleeson b Poore	30
C.W. Wright	b Sinclair	19	(1) b Sinclair	33
A.M. Miller	not out	4	(11) not out	20
H.R. Butt†	c Halliwell b Middleton	1	(2) b Middleton	0
Extras	(B 13)	13	(B 9)	9
Total		**185**		**226**

SOUTH AFRICA

T.W. Routledge	b Bromley-Davenport	22	b Lohmann	2
F. Hearne	c O'Brien b Bromley-Davenport	23	b Lohmann	5
R.M. Poore	b Lohmann	11	c O'Brien b Lohmann	10
J.H. Sinclair	b Lohmann	4	b Lohmann	0
C.F.W. Hime	b Lohmann	0	(6) b Hayward	8
E.A. Halliwell*†	b Lohmann	13	(7) c Hayward b Lohmann	3
C.G. Fichardt	b Lohmann	4	(5) lbw b Bromley-Davenport	1
R.A. Gleeson	c Lohmann b Hayward	3	not out	1
F.J. Cook	b Lohmann	7	b Lohmann	0
J. Middleton	not out	4	b Lohmann	0
J.T. Willoughby	b Lohmann	0	c Hayward b Lohmann	0
Extras	(B 2)	2		–
Total		**93**		**30**

SOUTH AFRICA	O	M	R	W	O	M	R	W		FALL OF WICKETS			
Sinclair	16	5	34	1	20	2	68	3		E	SA	E	SA
Willoughby	22	6	54	2	19	4	68	2	*Wkt*	*1st*	*1st*	*2nd*	*2nd*
Middleton	25·4	6	64	5	36	12	66	4	1st	0	29	0	4
Hime	7	3	20	1	4	1	11	0	2nd	25	58	39	11
Poore					1·4	0	4	1	3rd	68	58	52	11
									4th	120	62	68	18
ENGLAND									5th	125	62	68	18
Lohmann	15·4	6	38	7	9·4	5	7	8	6th	131	77	72	28
Bromley-Davenport	12	2	46	2	7	1	23	1	7th	140	80	161	29
Hayward	3	1	7	1	2	2	0	1	8th	145	80	169	30
									9th	184	92	184	30
									10th	185	93	226	30

Umpires: Not known.

Close: 1st day – E(2) 0-1 (Wright 0).

SOUTH AFRICA v ENGLAND 1895–96 (2nd Test)

Played at Old Wanderers, Johannesburg, on 2, 3, 4 March.
Toss: England.   Result: ENGLAND won by an innings and 197 runs.
Debuts: South Africa – W.H.B. Frank, C.L. Johnson, C.B. Llewellyn, G.A. Rowe, G.H. Shepstone;
England – C. Heseltine.

Lord Hawke's team arrived at the Wanderers to find the club buildings filled with injured survivors from a dynamite explosion nearby. Lohmann improved on his record analysis of the previous match by becoming the first bowler to take nine wickets in a Test innings. Only J.C. Laker with 10 for 53 against Australian in 1956 (*Test No. 428*) has returned better figures at Test level. Lohmann took his hundredth Test wicket during the second innings of this his 16th Test. Wright kept wicket after Butt had injured his hand during South Africa's first innings. Umpire Miller had played in the previous Test.

ENGLAND

Sir T.C. O'Brien	b Rowe	0
G.A. Lohmann	c Hearne b Sinclair	2
T.W. Hayward	c Routledge b Rowe	122
C.B. Fry	c and b Rowe	64
A.J.L. Hill	b Sinclair	65
S.M.J. Woods	c Rowe b Sinclair	32
Lord Hawke*	lbw b Sinclair	4
C.W. Wright	b Frank	71
H.R. Bromley-Davenport	c Johnson b Rowe	84
C. Heseltine	lbw b Rowe	0
H.R. Butt†	not out	8
Extras	(B 22, LB 4, W 1, NB 3)	30
Total		**482**

SOUTH AFRICA

T.W. Routledge	b Woods	14	c sub (H.F. Mosenthal) b Heseltine	0
J.H. Sinclair	c and b Lohmann	40	c sub (H.F. Mosenthal) b Woods	29
R.M. Poore	b Lohmann	20	b Heseltine	10
F. Hearne	c Butt b Lohmann	0	c Heseltine b Lohmann	16
E.A. Halliwell*†	c O'Brien b Lohmann	13	c Hawke b Heseltine	41
C.L. Johnson	b Lohmann	3	run out	7
G.H. Shepstone	b Lohmann	21	c Fry b Lohmann	9
F.W. Smith	b Lohmann	4	not out	11
W.H.B. Frank	c and b Lohmann	5	c Hill b Lohmann	2
C.B. Llewellyn	c Heseltine b Lohmann	24	c Lohmann b Heseltine	4
G.A. Rowe	not out	0	b Heseltine	0
Extras	(W 2, NB 5)	7	(LB 3, NB 2)	5
Total		**151**		**134**

SOUTH AFRICA	O	M	R	W	O	M	R	W	FALL OF WICKETS			
Rowe	49	9	115	5						E	SA	SA
Sinclair	35	6	118	4					*Wkt*	*1st*	*1st*	*2nd*
Frank	11·3	3	52	1					1st	0	19	0
Llewellyn	14	3	71	0					2nd	8	70	23
Johnson	28	12	57	0					3rd	127	70	48
Shepstone	20	8	39	0					4th	249	77	63
									5th	291	85	83
ENGLAND									6th	304	101	116
Heseltine	9	0	29	0	16·2	3	38	5	7th	307	105	118
Woods	20	2	74	1	6	1	27	1	8th	461	111	124
Lohmann	14·2	6	28	9	17	4	43	3	9th	461	142	134
Bromley-Davenport	3	0	13	0					10th	482	151	134
Hayward					4	1	21	0				

Umpires: A.M. Miller (1) and (probably) G. Allsop (1).

Close: 1st day – E(1) 355-7 (Wright 30, Bromley-Davenport 19); 2nd – SA(2) 63-3 (Sinclair 29, Halliwell 4).

SOUTH AFRICA v ENGLAND 1895–96 (3rd Test)

Played at Newlands, Cape Town, on 21, 23 March.
Toss: England.   Result. ENGLAND won by an innings and 33 runs.
Debuts: South Africa – G.K. Glover. A.R. Richards. A.W. Seccull: England – E.J. Tyler.

Lohmann took his total of wickets for the three-match rubber to 35 at 5.8 runs apiece. Hill scored his first hundred in first-class cricket. Stumps were drawn at 5.30 pm with South Africa's score at 111 for 9, but play continued when the crowd demanded a finish.

SOUTH AFRICA

T.W. Routledge	b Lohmann	24	(5) b Woods		4
F. Hearne	c and b Lohmann	0	c Hayward b Tyler		30
R.M. Poore	c Woods b Lohmann	17	b Woods		8
J.H. Sinclair	c Woods b Tyler	2	(6) c Hawke b Bromley-Davenport		28
A.R. Richards*	c Woods b Lohmann	6	(1) b Woods		0
E.A. Halliwell†	c Heseltine b Tyler	23	(7) b Hill		11
A.W. Seccull	c and b Lohmann	6	(8) not out		17
G.K. Glover	not out	18	(4) c Woods b Lohmann		3
J. Middleton	c Hayward b Tyler	2	c Hawke b Hill		6
J.T. Willoughby	b Lohmann	5	st Butt b Hill		3
G.A. Rowe	b Lohmann	5	b Hill		3
Extras	(B 5, W 1, NB 1)	7	(B 2, NB 2)		4
Total		**115**			**117**

ENGLAND

C.W. Wright	c Seccull b Willoughby	2
A.J.L. Hill	c Poore b Middleton	124
T.W. Hayward	b Seccull	31
H.R. Bromley-Davenport	b Seccull	7
S.M.J. Woods	b Rowe	30
Sir T.C. O'Brien	c sub (J.H. Anderson) b Glover	2
G.A. Lohmann	b Willoughby	8
C. Heseltine	c Hearne b Rowe	18
Lord Hawke*	not out	12
E.J. Tyler	b Middleton	0
H.R. Butt†	c Sinclair b Middleton	13
Extras	(B 12, LB 4, NB 2)	18
Total		**265**

ENGLAND	O	M	R	W	O	M	R	W	FALL OF WICKETS			
										SA	E	SA
Lohmann	24	9	42	7	23	8	45	1	*Wkt*	*1st*	*1st*	*2nd*
Tyler	18	3	49	3	11	3	16	1	1st	6	2	1
Heseltine	6	0	17	0					2nd	43	79	13
Woods					13	5	28	3	3rd	48	95	28
Bromley-Davenport					9	3	16	1	4th	48	159	35
Hill					8	4	8	4	5th	74	168	75
									6th	80	190	80
SOUTH AFRICA									7th	90	226	97
Willoughby	14	2	37	2					8th	98	244	105
Rowe	32	9	72	2					9th	104	244	111
Seccull	12	2	37	2					10th	115	265	117
Sinclair	7	1	23	0								
Middleton	23·4	6	50	3								
Glover	13	4	28	1								

Umpires: A.M. Miller (2) and (probably) G. Beves (1).

Close: 1st day – E(1) 126-3 (Hill 56, Woods 18).

ENGLAND v AUSTRALIA 1896 (1st Test)

Played at Lord's, London, on 22, 23, 24 June.
Toss: Australia.   Result: ENGLAND won by six wickets.
Debuts: England – A.F.A. Lilley; Australia – C.J. Eady, C. Hill, J.J. Kelly.

Grace completed his 1,000 runs in Test cricket in front of 30,000 spectators on the first day. The fourth-wicket partnership of 221 in 161 minutes between Trott and Gregory was a new record for any wicket in Test matches, the former scoring a hundred on his debut as captain. George Lohmann ended his final Test with career figures of 112 wickets, average 10.75, in 18 matches. Besides recording the lowest average by any bowler taking 25 or more wickets, he remains the most frequent wicket-taker, at 34 balls per dismissal, that Test cricket has produced. Less than five years later he died of consumption at the age of 36.

AUSTRALIA

H. Donnan	run out	1	(11) b Hearne		8
J. Darling	b Richardson	22	b Richardson		0
G. Giffen	c Lilley b Lohmann	0	b Richardson		32
G.H.S. Trott*	b Richardson	0	c Hayward b Richardson		143
S.E. Gregory	b Richardson	14	c Lohmann b Hearne		103
H. Graham	b Richardson	0	b Richardson		10
C. Hill	b Lohmann	1	b Hearne		5
C.J. Eady	not out	10	(1) c Lilley b Richardson		2
H. Trumble	b Richardson	0	(8) c Lilley b Hearne		4
J.J. Kelly†	c Lilley b Lohmann	0	(9) not out		24
E. Jones	b Richardson	4	(10) c Jackson b Hearne		4
Extras	(B 1)	1	(B 7, LB 4, W 1)		12
Total		**53**			**347**

ENGLAND

W.G. Grace*	c Trumble b Giffen	66	c Hill b Trumble		7
A.E. Stoddart	b Eady	17	(5) not out		30
R. Abel	b Eady	94	(2) c sub (F.A. Iredale) b Jones		4
J.T. Brown	b Jones	9	c Kelly b Eady		36
W. Gunn	c Kelly b Trumble	25	(6) not out		13
F.S. Jackson	c Darling b Giffen	44			
T.W. Hayward	not out	12	(3) b Jones		13
A.F.A. Lilley†	b Eady	0			
G.A. Lohmann	c sub (F.A. Iredale) b Giffen	1			
J.T. Hearne	c Giffen b Trott	11			
T. Richardson	c Hill b Trot	6			
Extras	(B 5, LB 2)	7	(B 3, LB 4, W 1)		8
Total		**292**	(4 wickets)		**111**

ENGLAND	O	M	R	W	O	M	R	W
Richardson	11·3	3	39	6	47	15	134	5
Lohmann	11	6	13	3	22	6	39	0
Hayward					11	3	44	0
Hearne					36	14	76	5
Jackson					11	5	28	0
Grace					6	1	14	0
AUSTRALIA								
Jones	26	6	64	1	23	10	42	2
Giffen	26	5	95	3	1	0	9	0
Eady	29	12	58	3	3	0	11	1
Trott	7·4	2	13	2	0·1	0	4	0
Trumble	19	3	55	1	20	10	37	1

FALL OF WICKETS

	A	E	A	E
Wkt	1st	1st	2nd	2nd
1st	3	38	0	16
2nd	3	143	3	20
3rd	4	152	62	42
4th	26	197	283	82
5th	26	256	289	–
6th	31	266	300	–
7th	41	266	304	–
8th	45	267	308	–
9th	46	286	318	–
10th	53	292	347	–

Umpires: J. Phillips (11) and W.A.J. West (1).

Close: 1st day – E(1) 286-8 (Hayward 12, Hearne 11); 2nd – E(2) 16-1 (Grace 7, Hayward 4).

ENGLAND v AUSTRALIA 1896 (2nd Test)

Played at Old Trafford, Manchester, on 16, 17, 18 July.
Toss: Australia.   Result: AUSTRALIA won by three wickets.
Debuts: England – K.S. Ranjitsinhji (*Kumar Shri Ranjitsinhji, later His Highness The Jam Saheb of Nawanagar*).

'Ranji', the first Indian to play Test cricket, became the second batsman after W.G. Grace (*Test No. 4*) to score a hundred on debut for England. He was the first player to score a hundred before lunch in a Test match; on the third morning he took his overnight score of 41 to 154, adding 113 runs in 130 minutes and setting a record that remains unbeaten for the most runs in a pre-lunch session in Tests between these two countries. Brown kept wicket when Lilley's leg-spin was required to break a stand. George Giffen became the first to complete the Test career double of 1,000 runs and 100 wickets – in his 30th and penultimate match. All his appearances were against England.

AUSTRALIA

F.A. Iredale	b Briggs	108	b Richardson	11
J. Darling	c Lilley b Richardson	27	c Lilley b Richardson	16
G. Giffen	c and b Richardson	80	c Ranjitsinhji b Richardson	6
G.H.S. Trott*	c Brown b Lilley	53	c Lilley b Richardson	2
S.E. Gregory	c Stoddart b Briggs	25	c Ranjitsinhji b Briggs	33
H. Donnan	b Richardson	12	c Jackson b Richardson	15
C. Hill	c Jackson b Richardson	9	c Lilley b Richardson	14
H. Trumble	b Richardson	24	not out	17
J.J. Kelly†	c Lilley b Richardson	27	not out	8
T.R. McKibbin	not out	28		
E. Jones	b Richardson	4		
Extras	(B 6, LB 8, W 1)	15	(LB 3)	3
Total		**412**	(7 wickets)	**125**

ENGLAND

A.E. Stoddart	st Kelly b Trott	15	b McKibbin	41
W.G. Grace*	st Kelly b Trott	2	c Trott b Jones	11
K.S. Ranjitsinhji	c Trott b McKibbin	62	not out	154
R. Abel	c Trumble b McKibbin	26	c McKibbin b Giffen	13
F.S. Jackson	run out	18	c McKibbin b Giffen	1
J.T. Brown	c Kelly b Trumble	22	c Iredale b Jones	19
A.C. MacLaren	c Trumble b McKibbin	0	c Jones b Trumble	15
A.F.A. Lilley†	not out	65	c Trott b Giffen	19
J. Briggs	b Trumble	0	st Kelly b McKibbin	16
J.T. Hearne	c Trumble b Giffen	18	c Kelly b McKibbin	9
T. Richardson	run out	2	c Jones b Trumble	1
Extras	(B 1)	1	(B 2, LB 3, W 1)	6
Total		**231**		**305**

ENGLAND	O	M	R	W	O	M	R	W
Richardson	68	23	168	7	42·3	16	76	6
Briggs	40	18	99	2	18	8	24	1
Jackson	16	6	34	0				
Hearne	28	11	53	0	24	13	22	0
Grace	7	3	11	0				
Stoddart	6	2	9	0				
Lilley	5	1	23	1				
AUSTRALIA								
Jones	5	2	11	0	17	0	78	2
Trott	10	0	46	2	7	1	17	0
Giffen	19	3	48	1	16	1	65	3
Trumble	37	14	80	2	29·1	12	78	2
McKibbin	19	8	45	3	21	4	61	3

FALL OF WICKETS

	A	E	E	A
Wkt	1st	1st	2nd	2nd
1st	41	2	33	20
2nd	172	23	76	26
3rd	242	104	97	28
4th	294	111	109	45
5th	294	140	132	79
6th	314	140	179	95
7th	325	154	232	100
8th	352	166	268	–
9th	403	219	304	–
10th	412	231	305	–

Umpires: A. Chester (1) and J. Phillips (12).

Close: 1st day – A(1) 366-8 (Kelly 14, McKibbin 7); 2nd – E(2) 109-4 (Ranjitsinhji 41).

ENGLAND v AUSTRALIA 1896 (3rd Test)

Played at Kennington Oval, London, on 10, 11, 12 August.
Toss: England.   Result: ENGLAND won by 66 runs.
Debuts: England – E.G. Wynyard.

Five players threatened strike action before the start because of a dispute over match fees. Although Abel, Hayward and Richardson relented, Gunn and Lohmann refused to play. Rain prevented play until 4.55 pm on the first day, hastened the fall of 24 wickets on the second, and led to Australia being dismissed for their lowest total in England until 1902 (36 in *Test No. 70*). Peel ended his Test career with the splendid analysis of 6 for 23; the fourth of those wickets was his hundredth in Test matches.

ENGLAND

W.G. Grace*	c Trott b Giffen	24	b Trumble	9
F.S. Jackson	c McKibbin b Trumble	45	b Trumble	2
K.S. Ranjitsinhji	b Giffen	8	st Kelly b McKibbin	11
R. Abel	c and b Trumble	26	c Giffen b Trumble	21
A.C. MacLaren	b Trumble	20	b Jones	6
T.W. Hayward	b Trumble	0	c Trott b Trumble	13
E.G. Wynyard	c Darling b McKibbin	10	c Kelly b McKibbin	3
R. Peel	b Trumble	0	b Trumble	0
A.F.A. Lilley†	c Iredale b Trumble	2	c McKibbin b Trumble	6
J.T. Hearne	b McKibbin	8	b McKibbin	1
T. Richardson	not out	1	not out	10
Extras	(LB 1)	1	(LB 2)	2
Total		**145**		**84**

AUSTRALIA

J. Darling	c MacLaren b Hearne	47	b Hearne	0
F.A. Iredale	run out	30	c Jackson b Hearne	3
G. Giffen	b Hearne	0	(4) b Hearne	1
G.H.S. Trott*	b Peel	5	(3) c sub (W. Brockwell) b Peel	3
S.E. Gregory	b Hearne	1	c Richardson b Peel	6
C. Hill	run out	1	b Peel	0
H. Donnan	b Hearne	10	c Hayward b Peel	0
J.J. Kelly†	not out	10	lbw b Peel	3
H. Trumble	b Hearne	3	not out	7
E. Jones	c MacLaren b Peel	3	b Peel	3
T.R. McKibbin	b Hearne	0	c Abel b Hearne	16
Extras	(B 8, LB 1)	9	(B 2)	2
Total		**119**		**44**

AUSTRALIA	O	M	R	W	O	M	R	W
Giffen	32	12	64	2	1	0	4	0
Trumble	40	10	59	6	25	9	30	6
McKibbin	9·3	0	21	2	20	8	35	3
Jones					3	0	13	1
ENGLAND								
Peel	20	9	30	2	12	5	23	6
Hearne	26·1	10	41	6	13	8	19	4
Richardson	5	0	22	0	1	1	0	0
Hayward	2	0	17	0				

FALL OF WICKETS

	E	A	E	A
Wkt	1st	1st	2nd	2nd
1st	54	75	11	0
2nd	78	77	12	3
3rd	78	82	24	7
4th	114	83	50	7
5th	114	84	56	11
6th	131	85	67	11
7th	132	112	67	14
8th	135	116	67	19
9th	138	119	68	25
10th	145	119	84	44

Umpires: W. Hearn (2) and J. Phillips (13).

Close: 1st day – E(1) 69-1 (Jackson 39, Ranjitsinhji 5); 2nd – E(2) 60-5 (Hayward 9, Wynyard 0).

AUSTRALIA v ENGLAND 1897–98 (1st Test)

Played at Sydney Cricket Ground on 13, 14, 15, 16, 17 December.
Toss: England.   Result: ENGLAND won by nine wickets.
Debuts: England – N.F. Druce, G.H. Hirst, J.R. Mason, W. Storer.

MacLaren, deputising for A.E. Stoddart whose mother had died, scored a hundred in his first Test as captain. Ranjitsinhji, who had not fully recovered from a bout of quinsy, emulated H. Graham by scoring a hundred in his first Test in Australia having also done so in England. His 175 set a new England record which stood until R.E. Foster scored 287 in 1903-04 (*Test No. 78*). Darling had the distinction of being the first left-hander to score a hundred in a Test match. McLeod was run out by Storer when he left his crease after being bowled by a no-ball. His deafness prevented him from hearing the umpire's call. Kelly became the first wicket-keeper to prevent any byes in a total of over 500 and still holds Australia's record (no byes in highest total).

ENGLAND

J.R. Mason	b Jones	6	b McKibbin		32
A.C. MacLaren*	c Kelly b McLeod	109	not out		50
T.W. Hayward	c Trott b Trumble	72			
W. Storer†	c and b Trott	43			
N.F. Druce	c Gregory b McLeod	20			
G.H. Hirst	b Jones	62			
K.S. Ranjitsinhji	c Gregory b McKibbin	175	(3) not out		8
E. Wainwright	b Jones	10			
J.T. Hearne	c and b McLeod	17			
J. Briggs	run out	1			
T. Richardson	not out	24			
Extras	(LB 11, W 1)	12	(B 5, NB 1)		6
Total		**551**	(1 wicket)		**96**

AUSTRALIA

J. Darling	c Druce b Richardson	7	c Druce b Briggs		101
J.J. Lyons	b Richardson	3	(7) c Hayward b Hearne		25
F.A. Iredale	c Druce b Hearne	25	(2) b Briggs		18
C. Hill	b Hearne	19	b Hearne		96
S.E. Gregory	c Mason b Hearne	46	run out		31
G.H.S. Trott*	b Briggs	10	(8) b Richardson		27
J.J. Kelly†	b Richardson	1	(9) not out		46
H. Trumble	c Storer b Mason	70	(6) c Druce b Hearne		2
C.E. McLeod	not out	50	(3) run out		26
T.R. McKibbin	b Hearne	0	(11) b Hearne		6
E. Jones	c Richardson b Hearne	0	(10) lbw b Richardson		3
Extras	(B 1, LB 1, NB 4)	6	(B 12, LB 1, W 4, NB 10)		27
Total		**237**			**408**

AUSTRALIA	O	M	R	W	O	M	R	W
McKibbin	34	5	113	1	5	1	22	1
Jones	50	8	130	3	9	1	28	0
McLeod	28	12	80	3				
Trumble	40	7	138	1	14	4	40	0
Trott	23	2	78	1				
ENGLAND								
Richardson	27	8	71	3	41	9	121	2
Hirst	28	7	57	0	13	3	49	0
Hearne	20·1	7	42	5	38	8	99	4
Briggs	20	7	42	1	22	3	86	2
Hayward	3	1	11	0	5	1	16	0
Mason	2	1	8	1	2	0	10	0

FALL OF WICKETS

Wkt	E 1st	A 1st	A 2nd	E 2nd
1st	26	8	37	80
2nd	162	24	135	–
3rd	224	56	191	–
4th	256	57	269	–
5th	258	86	271	–
6th	382	87	318	–
7th	422	138	321	–
8th	471	228	382	–
9th	477	237	390	–
10th	551	237	408	–

Umpires: C. Bannerman (6) and J. Phillips (14).

Close: 1st day – E(1) 337-5 (Hirst 37, Ranjitsinhji 39); 2nd – A(1) 86-5 (Gregory 18); 3rd – A(2) 126-1 (Darling 80, McLeod 20); 4th – E(2) 30-0 (Mason 13, MacLaren 16).

AUSTRALIA v ENGLAND 1897–98 (2nd Test)

Played at Melbourne Cricket Ground on 1, 3, 4, 5 January.
Toss: Australia.   Result: AUSTRALIA won by an innings and 55 runs.
Debuts: Australia – M.A. Noble.

McLeod avenged his unfortunate dismissal of the previous match by making the most of his surprising promotion in the order. After an extremely slow start he completed Australia's first hundred at Melbourne since 1881-82 (*Test No. 5*) in 225 minutes. Jones was the first bowler to be no-balled for throwing in a Test match – umpire Phillips called him once.

AUSTRALIA

J. Darling	c Hirst b Briggs	36
C.E. McLeod	b Storer	112
C. Hill	c Storer b Hayward	58
S.E. Gregory	b Briggs	71
F.A. Iredale	c Ranjitsinhji b Hirst	89
G.H.S. Trott*	c Wainwright b Briggs	79
M.A. Noble	b Richardson	17
H. Trumble	c Hirst b Mason	14
J.J. Kelly†	c Richardson b Hearne	19
E. Jones	run out	7
T.R. McKibbin	not out	2
Extras	(B 14, W 1, NB 1)	16
Total		**520**

ENGLAND

A.C. MacLaren*	c Trumble b McKibbin	35		c Trott b Trumble	38
J.R. Mason	b McKibbin	3		b Trumble	3
E. Wainwright	c Jones b Noble	21	(8)	b Noble	11
K.S. Ranjitsinhji	b Trumble	71	(3)	b Noble	27
T.W. Hayward	c Jones b Trott	23	(4)	c Trumble b Noble	33
W. Storer†	c Kelly b Trumble	51	(5)	c Trumble b Noble	1
G.H. Hirst	b Jones	0	(6)	lbw b Trumble	3
N.F. Druce	lbw b Trumble	44	(7)	c McLeod b Noble	15
J.T. Hearne	b Jones	1	(10)	c Jones b Noble	0
J. Briggs	not out	46	(9)	c Trott b Trumble	12
T. Richardson	b Trumble	3		not out	2
Extras	(B 10, LB 3, NB 4)	17		(B 3, LB 1, W 1)	5
Total		**315**			**150**

ENGLAND	O	M	R	W	O	M	R	W
Richardson	48	12	114	1				
Hirst	25	1	89	1				
Briggs	40	10	96	3				
Hearne	36	6	94	1				
Mason	11	1	33	1				
Hayward	9	4	23	1				
Storer	16	4	55	1				
AUSTRALIA								
McKibbin	28	7	66	2	4	0	13	0
Trumble	26·5	5	54	4	30·4	12	53	4
Jones	22	5	54	2				
Trott	17	3	49	1	7	0	17	0
Noble	12	3	31	1	17	1	49	6
McLeod	14	2	44	0	7	2	13	0

FALL OF WICKETS

	A	E	E
Wkt	1st	1st	2nd
1st	43	10	10
2nd	167	60	65
3rd	244	74	71
4th	310	133	75
5th	434	203	80
6th	453	208	115
7th	478	223	123
8th	509	224	141
9th	515	311	148
10th	520	315	150

Umpires: C. Bannerman (7) and J. Phillips (15).

Close: 1st day – A(1) 283-3 (Gregory 54, Iredale 12); 2nd – E(1) 22-1 (MacLaren 9, Wainwright 3); 3rd – E(1) 311-8 (Druce 44, Briggs 45).

AUSTRALIA v ENGLAND 1897–98 (3rd Test)

Played at Adelaide Oval on 14, 15, 17, 18, 19 January.
Toss: Australia.   Result: AUSTRALIA won by an innings and 13 runs.
Debuts: Australia – W.P. Howell.

Darling became the first batsman to score two hundreds in the same rubber (MacLaren equalled this feat later in the match), and the first to reach his century with a six which in those days involved hitting the ball right out of the ground as opposed to over the boundary. This was the first six ever hit in Test cricket without the aid of overthrows. His tea score of 117 is still the highest for his country at that interval on the first day of a Test against England in Australia.

AUSTRALIA

C.E. McLeod	b Briggs	31
J. Darling	c Storer b Richardson	178
C. Hill	c Storer b Richardson	81
S.E. Gregory	c Storer b Hirst	52
F.A. Iredale	b Richardson	84
G.H.S. Trott*	b Hearne	3
M.A. Noble	b Richardson	39
H. Trumble	not out	37
J.J. Kelly†	b Stoddart	22
E. Jones	run out	8
W.P. Howell	b Hearne	16
Extras	(B 16, LB 5, NB 1)	22
Total		**573**

ENGLAND

A.C. MacLaren	b Howell	14		c Kelly b Noble	124
J.R. Mason	b Jones	11		c Jones b Noble	0
K.S. Ranjitsinhji	c Noble b Trumble	6		c Trumble b McLeod	77
W. Storer†	b Howell	4	(5)	c Hill b McLeod	6
T.W. Hayward	b Jones	70	(4)	c and b McLeod	1
N.F Druce	c Darling b Noble	24		b Noble	27
G.H. Hirst	c Trumble b Noble	85		lbw b McLeod	6
A.E. Stoddart*	c Jones b Howell	15		c Jones b McLeod	24
J. Briggs	c Kelly b Noble	14		not out	0
J.T. Hearne	b Howell	0		c and b Noble	4
T. Richardson	not out	25		c Jones b Noble	0
Extras	(B 2, LB 6, W 2)	10		(B 2, LB 6, W 3, NB 2)	13
Total		**278**			**282**

ENGLAND	O	M	R	W	O	M	R	W		FALL OF WICKETS		
Richardson	56	11	164	4						A	E	E
Briggs	63	26	128	1					*Wkt*	*1st*	*1st*	*2nd*
Hearne	44·1	15	94	2					1st	97	24	10
Hirst	22	6	62	1					2nd	245	30	152
Hayward	8	1	36	0					3rd	310	34	154
Mason	11	2	41	0					4th	374	42	160
Storer	3	0	16	0					5th	389	106	212
Stoddart	4	1	10	1					6th	474	172	235
									7th	493	206	262
AUSTRALIA									8th	537	223	278
Howell	54	23	70	4	40	18	60	0	9th	552	224	282
Jones	27	3	67	2	1	0	5	0	10th	573	278	282
Trumble	17	3	39	1	16	5	37	0				
Noble	24·5	5	78	3	33	7	84	5				
Trott	4	0	14	0	6	0	18	0				
McLeod					48	24	65	5				

Umpires: C. Bannerman (8) and J. Phillips (16).

Close: 1st day – A(1) 310-2 (Darling 178, Gregory 16); 2nd – A(1) 552-9 (Trumble 32); 3rd – E(1) 197-6 (Hirst 50, Stoddart 11); 4th – E(2) 161-4 (MacLaren 70, Druce 0).

AUSTRALIA v ENGLAND 1897–98 (4th Test)

Played at Melbourne Cricket Ground on 29, 31 January, 1, 2 February.
Toss: Australia.   Result: AUSTRALIA won by eight wickets.
Debuts: Nil.

Hill's 188 remains the highest score by a batsman under 21 in Tests between England and Australia; he was 20 years 317 days old. His 182 not out was the highest score on the first day of a Test in Australia and his partnership of 165 with Trumble is still the best for Australia's seventh wicket against England.

AUSTRALIA

C.E. McLeod	b Hearne	1	not out		64
J. Darling	c Hearne b Richardson	12	c Druce b Hayward		29
C. Hill	c Stoddart b Hearne	188	lbw b Hayward		0
S.E. Gregory	b Richardson	0	not out		21
F.A. Iredale	c Storer b Hearne	0			
M.A. Noble	c and b Hearne	4			
G.H.S. Trott*	c Storer b Hearne	7			
H. Trumble	c Mason b Storer	46			
J.J. Kelly†	c Storer b Briggs	32			
E. Jones	c Hayward b Hearne	20			
W.P. Howell	not out	9			
Extras	(B 3, W 1)	4	(NB 1)		1
Total		**323**	(2 wickets)		**115**

ENGLAND

A.C. MacLaren	b Howell	8	(3) c Iredale b Trumble		45
E. Wainwright	c Howell b Trott	6	c McLeod b Jones		2
K.S. Ranjitsinhji	c Iredale b Trumble	24	(4) b Noble		55
T.W. Hayward	c Gregory b Noble	22	(5) c and b Trumble		25
N.F. Druce	lbw b Jones	24	(7) c Howell b Trott		16
W. Storer†	c and b Trumble	2	(9) c Darling b McLeod		26
J.R. Mason	b Jones	30	(8) b Howell		26
A.E. Stoddart*	c Darling b Jones	17	(6) b Jones		25
J. Briggs	not out	21	(1) c Darling b Howell		23
J.T. Hearne	c Trott b Jones	0	not out		4
T. Richardson	b Trott	20	c Trumble b McLeod		2
Extras		–	(B 1, LB 11, W 1, NB 1)		14
Total		**174**			**263**

ENGLAND	O	M	R	W	O	M	R	W
Richardson	26	2	102	2				
Hearne	35·4	13	98	6	7	3	19	0
Hayward	10	4	24	0	10	4	24	2
Briggs	17	4	38	1	6	1	31	0
Stoddart	6	1	22	0				
Storer	4	0	24	1				
Wainwright	3	1	11	0	9	2	21	0
Mason					4	1	10	0
Ranjitsinhji					3·4	1	9	0
AUSTRALIA								
Howell	16	7	34	1	30	12	58	2
Trott	11·1	1	33	2	12	2	39	1
Noble	7	1	21	1	16	6	31	1
Trumble	15	4	30	2	23	6	40	2
Jones	12	2	56	4	25	7	70	2
McLeod					8·2	4	11	2

FALL OF WICKETS

	A	E	E	A
Wkt	1st	1st	2nd	2nd
1st	1	14	7	50
2nd	25	16	63	50
3rd	25	60	94	–
4th	26	60	147	–
5th	32	67	157	–
6th	58	103	192	–
7th	223	121	211	–
8th	283	148	259	–
9th	303	148	259	–
10th	323	174	263	–

Umpires: C. Bannerman (9) and J. Phillips (17).

Close: 1st day – A(1) 275-7 (Hill 182, Kelly 22); 2nd – E(2) 7-1 (Briggs 4); 3rd – E(2) 254-7 (Mason 25, Storer 24).

AUSTRALIA v ENGLAND 1897–98 (5th Test)

Played at Sydney Cricket Ground on 26, 28 February, 1, 2 March.
Toss: England.   Result: AUSTRALIA won by six wickets.
Debuts: Nil.

Tom Richardson ended his Test career by returning his best analysis. His 88 wickets in only 14 matches included 11 instances of five or more in an innings. Darling's hundred took only 91 minutes and remains the fastest for Australia against England. Only G.L. Jessop (75 minutes in *Test No. 74*) has scored a faster hundred in Tests between England and Australia. Darling was the first batsman to score three hundreds in the same Test rubber and the first to aggregate 500 runs in one. His innings lasted only 175 minutes and included 30 fours. His century contained 20 fours, a record number for this series equalled only by A.R. Morris in 1948 (*Test No. 302*).

ENGLAND

A.C. MacLaren*	b Trott	65	c Darling b Jones		0
E. Wainwright	c Hill b Trumble	49	b Noble		6
K.S. Ranjitsinhji	c Gregory b Trott	2	lbw b Jones		12
T.W. Hayward	b Jones	47	c Worrall b Trumble		43
W. Storer†	b Jones	44	c Gregory b Trumble		31
N.F. Druce	lbw b Noble	64	c Howell b Trumble		18
G.H. Hirst	b Jones	44	c Trott b Jones		7
J.R. Mason	c Howell b Jones	7	b Trumble		11
J. Briggs	b Jones	0	b Howell		29
J.T. Hearne	not out	2	not out		3
T. Richardson	b Jones	1	b Howell		6
Extras	(B 2, LB 5, W 2, NB 1)	10	(LB 12)		12
Total		**335**			**178**

AUSTRALIA

C.E. McLeod	b Richardson	64	b Hearne		4
J. Darling	c Mason b Briggs	14	c Wainwright b Richardson		160
C. Hill	b Richardson	8	b Richardson		2
J. Worrall	c Ranjitsinhji b Richardson	26	c Hirst b Hayward		62
S.E. Gregory	c Storer b Richardson	21	not out		22
M.A. Noble	c Storer b Richardson	31	not out		15
G.H.S. Trott*	c Ranjitsinhji b Hearne	18			
H. Trumble	b Richardson	12			
J.J. Kelly†	not out	27			
W.P. Howell	c MacLaren b Richardson	10			
E. Jones	c Storer b Richardson	1			
Extras	(B 5, W 1, NB 1)	7	(B 6, W 1, NB 4)		11
Total		**239**	(4 wickets)		**276**

AUSTRALIA	O	M	R	W	O	M	R	W		FALL OF WICKETS			
Noble	26	6	57	1	15	4	34	1		E	A	E	A
Howell	17	6	40	0	6·1	0	22	2	*Wkt*	*1st*	*1st*	*2nd*	*2nd*
Trumble	26	4	67	1	24	7	37	4	1st	111	36	0	23
Jones	26·2	3	82	6	26	3	61	3	2nd	117	45	16	40
Trott	23	6	56	2	7	1	12	0	3rd	119	99	30	233
McLeod	11	4	23	0					4th	197	132	99	252
									5th	230	137	104	–
ENGLAND									6th	308	188	121	–
Richardson	36·1	7	94	8	21·4	1	110	2	7th	318	188	137	–
Briggs	17	4	39	1	5	1	25	0	8th	324	221	148	–
Hearne	21	9	40	1	15	5	52	1	9th	334	232	172	–
Storer	5	1	13	0					10th	335	239	178	–
Mason	13	7	20	0	11	1	27	0					
Hayward	4	0	12	0	3	0	18	1					
Hirst	4	1	14	0	7	0	33	0					

Umpires: C. Bannerman (10) and J. Phillips (18).

Close: 1st day – E(1) 301-5 (Druce 43, Hirst 43); 2nd – A(1) 184-5 (Noble 31, Trott 14); 3rd – E(2) 172-9 (Hearne 3).

SOUTH AFRICA v ENGLAND 1898–99 (1st Test)

Played at Old Wanderers, Johannesburg, on 14, 15, 16 February.
Toss: England.   Result: ENGLAND won by 32 runs.
Debuts: South Africa – M. Bisset, R.R. Dower, H.H. Francis, R. Graham, W.R.T. Solomon, V.M. Tancred; England – J.H. Board, W.R. Cuttell, S. Haigh, F.W. Milligan, F. Mitchell, J.T. Tyldesley, P.F. Warner, C.E.M. Wilson. *A.E. Trott was making his debut for England after appearing in three Test for Australia.*

South Africa gained their first lead on first innings, Sinclair contributing their first half-century in Tests. Warner was the first to score a hundred in his first Test, that match being against South Africa, and the first to carry his bat through a completed innings on debut for England (J.E. Barrett did so for Australia in *Test No. 33*).

ENGLAND

F. Mitchell	b Graham	28	lbw b Llewellyn		1
P.F. Warner	c and b Llewellyn	21	not out		132
J.T. Tyldesley	run out	17	c Shepstone b Middleton		17
C.E.M. Wilson	b Middleton	8	b Middleton		18
W.R. Cuttell	c Llewellyn b Graham	19	c Dower b Middleton		21
A.E. Trott	run out	0	c Solomon b Rowe		6
F.W. Milligan	c Graham b Middleton	11	(8) st Bisset b Llewellyn		8
Lord Hawke*	c Bisset b Llewellyn	0	(9) b Llewellyn		5
J.H. Board†	c Dower b Rowe	29	(10) c and b Middleton		17
H.R. Bromley-Davenport	c Graham b Rowe	4	(11) b Middleton		0
S. Haigh	not out	2	(7) c Shepstone b Rowe		1
Extras	(B 4, LB 1, W 1)	6	(B 9, NB 2)		11
Total		**145**			**237**

SOUTH AFRICA

J.H. Sinclair	run out	86	c Cuttell b Haigh		4
V.M. Tancred	b Haigh	18	c Board b Haigh		7
H.H. Francis	lbw b Trott	7	b Cuttell		29
R.R. Dower	b Trott	0	c Cuttell b Trott		9
M. Bisset*†	b Haigh	35	not out		21
W.R.T. Solomon	c Tyldesley b Haigh	2	(8) b Cuttell		2
G.H. Shepstone	b Cuttell	8	lbw b Cuttell		0
C.B. Llewellyn	st Board b Trott	38	(6) b Trott		0
R. Graham	c Board b Cuttell	4	(10) c Tyldesley b Trott		0
J. Middleton	c Mitchell b Trott	22	(9) c Bromley-Davenport b Trott		14
G.A. Rowe	not out	13	b Trott		0
Extras	(B 5, LB 11, NB 2)	18	(B 4, LB 5, NB 4)		13
Total		**251**			**99**

SOUTH AFRICA	O	M	R	W	O	M	R	W
Middleton	23	9	48	2	26	8	51	5
Rowe	18·2	6	34	2	28	12	40	2
Graham	16	7	22	2	11	2	38	0
Llewellyn	20	6	35	2	36	11	89	3
Shepstone					3	1	8	0
ENGLAND								
Trott	30·1	13	61	4	33·1	14	49	5
Haigh	30	5	101	3	12	5	20	2
Cuttell	17	5	42	2	32	24	17	3
Milligan	7	0	29	0				

FALL OF WICKETS

	E	SA	E	SA
Wkt	*1st*	*1st*	*2nd*	*2nd*
1st	51	46	1	13
2nd	53	55	41	21
3rd	77	59	104	58
4th	77	114	139	62
5th	81	118	149	65
6th	96	143	153	66
7th	96	169	171	78
8th	138	183	189	97
9th	138	224	233	99
10th	145	251	237	99

Umpires: A. Soames (1) and A.A. White (1).

Close: 1st day – SA(1) 86-3 (Sinclair 38, Bisset 21); 2nd – E(2) 171-7 (Warner 97).

SOUTH AFRICA v ENGLAND 1898–99 (2nd Test)

Played at Newlands, Cape Town, on 1, 3, 4 April.
Toss: England.   Result: ENGLAND won by 210 runs.
Debuts: South Africa – F. Kuys, A.W. Powell, C.F.H. Prince, W.A. Shalders;
England – A.G. Archer.

Sinclair, having scored South Africa's first Test fifty in the previous match, hit his country's first Test hundred – his first in first-class cricket. He also became the first player to score a century and take six wickets in the first innings of the same Test and the only one to do so for South Africa. This was South Africa's eighth consecutive defeat – a record equalled by England in the 1920-21 and 1921 series against Australia. South Africa's second innings, which lasted only 114 balls, is the fourth-lowest in Test cricket.

ENGLAND

F. Mitchell	c Rowe b Middleton	18	lbw b Rowe		41
P.F. Warner	c Halliwell b Sinclair	31	b Rowe		23
J.T. Tyldesley	b Sinclair	13	c Shalders b Kuys		112
C.E.M. Wilson	not out	10	b Powell		6
W.R. Cuttell	b Sinclair	7	b Kuys		18
A.E. Trott	c Powell b Sinclair	1	b Rowe		16
S. Haigh	c Halliwell b Middleton	0	c Francis b Sinclair		25
F.W. Milligan	b Sinclair	1	b Sinclair		38
J.H. Board†	b Sinclair	0	b Graham		6
A.G. Archer	c Powell b Middleton	7	not out		24
Lord Hawke*	b Middleton	1	c and b Sinclair		3
Extras	(LB 3)	3	(B 6, LB 10, W 1, NB 1)		18
Total		**92**			**330**

SOUTH AFRICA

W.A. Shalders	b Haigh	9	lbw b Haigh		8
H.H. Francis	b Trott	1	(5) c Haigh b Trott		2
M Bisset*	b Haigh	15	b Trott		1
J.H. Sinclair	c Tyldesley b Trott	106	c Milligan b Haigh		4
A.W. Powell	c Haigh b Trott	5	(2) b Haigh		11
E.A. Halliwell†	st Board b Haigh	0	(7) b Haigh		1
F. Kuys	b Cuttell	26	(6) b Trott		0
C.F.H. Prince	run out	5	b Haigh		1
R. Graham	b Trott	0	b Trott		2
J. Middleton	run out	3	not out		0
G.A. Rowe	not out	1	c Mitchell b Haigh		0
Extras	(B 4, W 1, NB 1)	6	(B 5)		5
Total		**177**			**35**

SOUTH AFRICA	O	M	R	W	O	M	R	W	FALL OF WICKETS				
Graham	5	0	26	0	16	4	41	1		E	SA	E	SA
Rowe	12	4	19	0	41	8	93	3	*Wkt*	*1st*	*1st*	*2nd*	*2nd*
Middleton	19	9	18	4	28	7	74	0	1st	36	1	63	18
Sinclair	12	4	26	6	31·2	8	63	3	2nd	61	27	68	21
Powell					4	1	10	1	3rd	62	34	96	21
Kuys					12	4	31	2	4th	70	60	146	27
									5th	72	61	178	27
ENGLAND									6th	74	110	234	28
Trott	20·2	5	69	4	11	5	19	4	7th	81	115	281	28
Haigh	27	4	88	3	11·4	6	11	6	8th	81	127	288	31
Cuttell	8	3	14	1					9th	90	173	322	35
Milligan	2	2	0	0					10th	92	177	330	35

Umpires: F. Hearne (1) and A.A. White (2).

Close: 1st day – SA(1) 126-7 (Sinclair 59, Graham 0); 2nd – E(2) 221-5 (Tyldesley 87, Haigh 17).

ENGLAND v AUSTRALIA 1899 (1st Test)

Played at Trent Bridge, Nottingham, on 1, 2, 3 June.
Toss: Australia.   Result: MATCH DRAWN.
Debuts: England – W. Rhodes; Australia – F. Laver, V.T. Trumper.

The first five-match rubber in England began with the first Test ever staged at Nottingham. Dr W.G. Grace, playing his last Test, was 50 years and 320 days old when the match ended – the oldest Test captain; only Wilfred Rhodes played for England at a greater age, and by coincidence, he was making his debut in Grace's last match.

AUSTRALIA

J. Darling*	b Hearne	47	b Rhodes	14
F.A. Iredale	c Hayward b Hearne	6	(4) run out	20
M.A. Noble	b Rhodes	41	(2) lbw b Rhodes	45
S.E. Gregory	b Hirst	48		
C. Hill	run out	52	(3) c Grace b Jackson	80
V.T. Trumper	b Hearne	0	(5) b Jackson	11
J.J. Kelly†	c Hirst b Hearne	26	(9) not out	11
F. Laver	b Rhodes	3	(7) b Jackson	3
W.P. Howell	c Hayward b Rhodes	0	(10) not out	4
H. Trumble	not out	16	(8) c Ranjitsinhji b Rhodes	38
E. Jones	c Fry b Rhodes	4	(6) c Ranjitsinhji b Hearne	3
Extras	(B 8, LB 1)	9	(LB 1)	1
Total		**252**	(8 wickets declared)	**230**

ENGLAND

W.G. Grace*	c Kelly b Noble	28	b Howell	1
C.B. Fry	b Jones	50	c Jones b Trumble	9
F.S. Jackson	c Darling b Noble	8	b Howell	0
W. Gunn	b Jones	14	b Jones	3
K.S. Ranjitsinhji	b Jones	42	not out	93
T.W. Hayward	run out	0	b Trumble	28
J.T. Tyldesley	c Laver b Howell	22	c Kelly b Trumble	10
W. Storer†	b Jones	4	lbw b Jones	3
G.H. Hirst	b Howell	6		
W. Rhodes	c Kelly b Jones	6		
J.T. Hearne	not out	4		
Extras	(LB 3, NB 6)	9	(B 5, W 1, NB 2)	8
Total		**193**	(7 wickets)	**155**

ENGLAND	O	M	R	W	O	M	R	W		FALL OF WICKETS			
										A	E	A	E
Rhodes	35·2	13	58	4	20	3	60	3	Wkt	1st	1st	2nd	2nd
Hearne	59	28	71	4	29	10	70	1	1st	14	75	18	1
Grace	20	8	31	0	2	0	6	0	2nd	85	91	111	1
Hirst	24	9	42	1	11	4	20	0	3rd	109	93	151	10
Jackson	11	3	27	0	26	8	57	3	4th	166	116	170	19
Hayward	3	0	14	0	6	2	16	0	5th	167	117	173	82
									6th	229	172	177	140
AUSTRALIA									7th	229	176	180	155
Jones	33	6	88	5	22	9	31	2	8th	229	178	226	–
Howell	28·4	12	43	2	37	18	54	2	9th	248	185	–	–
Trumble	13	7	17	0	29	16	39	3	10th	252	193	–	–
Noble	16	4	36	2	11	5	23	0					

Umpires: R.G. Barlow (1) and V.A. Titchmarsh (1).

Close: 1st day – A(1) 238-8 (Laver 0, Trumble 9); 2nd – A(2) 93-1 (Noble 38, Hill 41).

ENGLAND v AUSTRALIA 1899 (2nd Test)

Played at Lord's, London, on 15, 16, 17 June.
Toss: England.   Result: AUSTRALIA won by ten wickets.
Debuts: England – G.L. Jessop, W. Mead, C.L. Townsend.

Trumper, aged 21, scored a chanceless 135 not out in his second Test match after Jones had returned the best figures of his 19-match career.

ENGLAND

A.C. MacLaren*	b Jones	4	(6)	not out	88
C.B. Fry	c Trumble b Jones	13		b Jones	4
K.S. Ranjitsinhji	c and b Jones	8		c Noble b Howell	0
C.L. Townsend	st Kelly b Howell	5		b Jones	8
F.S. Jackson	b Jones	73		c and b Trumble	37
T.W. Hayward	b Noble	1	(1)	c Trumble b Laver	77
J.T. Tyldesley	c Darling b Jones	14		c Gregory b Laver	4
G.L. Jessop	c Trumper b Trumble	51		c Trumble b Laver	4
A.F.A. Lilley†	not out	19		b Jones	12
W. Mead	b Jones	7	(11)	lbw b Noble	0
W. Rhodes	b Jones	2	(10)	c and b Noble	2
Extras	(B 2, LB 6, W 1)	9		(B 2, LB 2)	4
Total		**206**			**240**

AUSTRALIA

J. Worrall	c Hayward b Rhodes	18		not out	11
J. Darling*	c Ranjitsinhji b Rhodes	9		not out	17
C. Hill	c Fry b Townsend	135			
S.E. Gregory	c Lilley b Jessop	15			
M.A. Noble	c Lilley b Rhodes	54			
V.T. Trumper	not out	135			
J.J. Kelly†	c Lilley b Mead	9			
H. Trumble	c Lilley b Jessop	24			
F. Laver	b Townsend	0			
E. Jones	c Mead b Townsend	17			
W.P. Howell	b Jessop	0			
Extras	(LB 4, NB 1)	5			
Total		**421**	(0 wickets)		**28**

AUSTRALIA	O	M	R	W	O	M	R	W
Jones	36·1	11	88	7	36	15	76	3
Howell	14	4	43	1	31	12	67	1
Noble	15	7	39	1	19·4	8	37	2
Trumble	15	9	27	1	15	6	20	1
Laver					16	4	36	3
ENGLAND								
Jessop	37·1	10	105	3	6	0	19	0
Mead	53	24	91	1				
Rhodes	39	10	108	3	5	1	9	0
Jackson	18	6	31	0				
Townsend	15	1	50	3				
Ranjitsinhji	2	0	6	0				
Hayward	6	0	25	0				

FALL OF WICKETS

Wkt	E 1st	A 1st	E 2nd	A 2nd
1st	4	27	5	–
2nd	14	28	6	–
3rd	20	59	23	–
4th	44	189	94	–
5th	45	271	160	–
6th	66	306	166	–
7th	161	386	170	–
8th	184	387	212	–
9th	194	421	240	–
10th	206	421	240	–

Umpires: T. Mycroft (1) and W.A.J. West (2).

Close: 1st day – A(1) 156-3 (Hill 72, Noble 42); 2nd – E(2) 94-4 (Hayward 42).

ENGLAND v AUSTRALIA 1899 (3rd Test)

Played at Headingley, Leeds, 29, 30 June, 1 (*no play*) July.
Toss: Australia.   Result: MATCH DRAWN.
Debuts: England – W.G. Quaife, H.I. Young.

Briggs suffered a violent epileptic fit on the first night of this first Test in Yorkshire, was detained in Cheadle Asylum and played no further cricket until the next season. Hearne did the hat-trick in the second innings when he dismissed Hill, Gregory and Noble for 'ducks'. England required a further 158 runs for victory when rain caused the final day's play to be abandoned.

AUSTRALIA

J. Worrall	run out	76	c sub (J.T. Tyldesley) b Young	16	
J.J. Kelly†	c Fry b Briggs	0	(7) c Lilley b Hayward	33	
M.A. Noble	run out	0	(5) c Ranjitsinhji b Hearne	0	
S.E. Gregory	c Lilley b Hearne	0	(4) c MacLaren b Hearne	0	
C. Hill	c Lilley b Young	34	(3) b Hearne	0	
J. Darling*	c Young b Briggs	9	(2) c Fry b Young	16	
V.T. Trumper	b Young	12	(6) c Ranjitsinhji b Jackson	32	
H. Trumble	not out	20	run out	56	
F. Laver	st Lilley b Briggs	7	c Lilley b Hearne	45	
E. Jones	b Young	5	c Brown b Hayward	2	
W.P. Howell	c Ranjitsinhji b Young	7	not out	2	
Extras	(B 2)	2	(B 17, LB 3, W 1, NB 1)	22	
Total		**172**		**224**	

ENGLAND

J.T. Brown	c Trumble b Noble	27	not out	14
A.C. MacLaren*	c and b Trumble	9		
K.S. Ranjitsinhji	c Worrall b Noble	11		
W.G. Quaife	b Jones	20	(2) not out	1
F.S. Jackson	b Trumble	9		
C.B. Fry	b Noble	38		
T.W. Hayward	not out	40		
A.F.A. Lilley†	c Hill b Trumble	55		
J.T. Hearne	b Trumble	3		
H.I. Young	c Kelly b Trumble	0		
J. Briggs	absent ill	–		
Extras	(B 3, LB 5)	8	(LB 4)	4
Total		**220**	(0 wickets)	**19**

ENGLAND	O	M	R	W	O	M	R	W		FALL OF WICKETS			
Hearne	23	5	69	1	31·3	12	50	4		A	E	A	E
Briggs	30	11	53	3					*Wkt*	*1st*	*1st*	*2nd*	*2nd*
Young	19·1	11	30	4	26	5	72	2	1st	8	27	34	–
Jackson	5	1	18	0	11	6	13	1	2nd	17	38	34	–
Brown					7	0	22	0	3rd	24	53	34	–
Hayward					10	1	45	2	4th	95	69	34	–
									5th	114	119	39	–
AUSTRALIA									6th	131	119	97	–
Trumble	39·3	16	60	5					7th	132	212	140	–
Noble	42	17	82	3	3	1	8	0	8th	151	220	213	–
Howell	13	3	29	0					9th	164	220	215	–
Jones	21	9	34	1	4	2	7	0	10th	172	–	224	–
Laver	3	1	7	0									

Umpires: W. Hearn (3) and M. Sherwin (1).

Close: 1st day – E(1) 119-4 (Quaife 20, Fry 38); 2nd – E(2) 19-0 (Brown 14, Quaife 1).

ENGLAND v AUSTRALIA 1899 (4th Test)

Played at Old Trafford, Manchester, on 17, 18, 19 July.
Toss: England.   Result: MATCH DRAWN.
Debuts: England – W.M. Bradley.

This match provoked a change in the follow-on law, which was then applied automatically in cases of first innings arrears of 120 runs and which often inadvertently penalised the ascendant team. Bradley dismissed Laver with his first ball in Test cricket – the first such instance for England. Noble became the only batsman to score two separate fifties on the same day of a Test. On the second day he scored 60 not out in 190 minutes (11.25 am to 3.30 pm), before going in first when Australia were compelled to follow-on. At the close he had scored a further 59 in 150 minutes. He was not dismissed until 2.45 pm on the final day, his two innings occupying 510 minutes and saving the match.

ENGLAND

W.G. Quaife	c Darling b Noble	8	c Iredale b Jones		15
C.B. Fry	b Jones	9	c Iredale b Trumble		4
K.S. Ranjitsinhji	c Worrall b Jones	21	not out		49
A.C. MacLaren*	b Noble	8	c Iredale b Trumble		6
F.S. Jackson	c Trumble b Jones	44	not out		14
T.W. Hayward	c Jones b Howell	130			
W. Brockwell	c Worrall b Noble	20			
A.F.A. Lilley†	lbw b Laver	58			
H.I. Young	b Howell	43			
J.T. Hearne	c Iredale b Trumble	1			
W.M. Bradley	not out	23			
Extras	(B 3, LB 3, W 1)	7	(B4, NB 2)		6
Total		**372**	(3 wickets)		**94**

AUSTRALIA

F. Laver	c Lilley b Bradley	0	(9) not out		14
J.J. Kelly†	b Young	9	(8) c Lilley b Ranjitsinhji		26
W.P. Howell	b Bradley	0			
J. Worrall	b Bradley	14	(1) c Brockwell b Young		53
M.A. Noble	not out	60	(2) c and b Hearne		89
S.E. Gregory	lbw b Young	5	(5) c Ranjitsinhji b Hearne		1
V.T. Trumper	b Young	14	(4) b Hearne		63
J. Darling*	b Young	4	(6) c sub (W. Rhodes) b Young		39
H. Trumble	c MacLaren b Bradley	44	(3) c Ranjitsinhji b Bradley		7
F.A. Iredale	c Lilley b Bradley	31	(7) not out		36
E. Jones	b Jackson	0			
Extras	(B 14, W 1)	15	(B 14, LB 2, W 1, NB 1)		18
Total		**196**	(7 wickets declared)		**346**

AUSTRALIA	O	M	R	W	O	M	R	W
Jones	42	9	136	3	8	0	33	1
Noble	38	19	85	3				
Trumble	29	10	72	1	13	3	33	2
Howell	19·1	7	45	2	6	2	22	0
Laver	13	2	27	1				
ENGLAND								
Young	29	10	79	4	37	12	81	2
Bradley	33	13	67	5	46	16	82	1
Brockwell	6	2	18	0	15	3	36	0
Hearne	10	6	7	0	47	26	54	3
Jackson	3·3	1	9	1	18	8	36	0
Ranjitsinhji	1	0	1	0	12	5	23	1
Hayward					3	1	10	0
Quaife					3	1	6	0

FALL OF WICKETS

Wkt	E 1st	A 1st	A 2nd	E 2nd
1st	14	1	93	12
2nd	18	6	117	39
3rd	47	14	205	54
4th	47	26	213	–
5th	107	35	255	–
6th	154	53	278	–
7th	267	57	319	–
8th	324	139	–	–
9th	337	195	–	–
10th	372	196	–	–

Umpires: A.B. Hide (1) and James Lillywhite, jr (6).

Close: 1st day – A(1) 1-1 (Kelly 0, Howell 0); 2nd – A(2) 142-2 (Noble 59, Trumper 18).

ENGLAND v AUSTRALIA 1899 (5th Test)

Played at Kennington Oval, London, on 14, 15, 16 August.
Toss: England.   Result: MATCH DRAWN.
Debuts: England – A.O. Jones.

Hayward and Jackson, opening a Test innings together for the first time, shared a partnership of 185, then England's highest for any wicket in England and the best opening stand by either country in these matches. Hayward's hundred was his second in successive innings. England scored 435 for 4 on the first day and went on to record the highest total in a Test in England until 1930 (*Test No. 195*).

ENGLAND

F.S. Jackson	b Jones	118
T.W. Hayward	c Iredale b McLeod	137
K.S. Ranjitsinhji	c Howell b Jones	54
C.B. Fry	c Worrall b Jones	60
A.C. MacLaren*	c Trumper b Trumble	49
C.L. Townsend	b Jones	38
W.M. Bradley	run out	0
W.H. Lockwood	b Trumble	24
A.O. Jones	b Noble	31
A.F.A. Lilley†	c Iredale b Noble	37
W. Rhodes	not out	8
Extras	(B 9, LB 6, W 4, NB 1)	20
Total		**576**

AUSTRALIA

J. Worrall	c Hayward b Lockwood	55		c Lilley b Hayward	75
H. Trumble	c and b Jones	24	(7)	not out	3
V.T. Trumper	c Lilley b Jones	6	(4)	c and b Rhodes	7
M.A. Noble	b Lockwood	9	(3)	not out	69
J. Darling*	c Fry b Lockwood	71	(6)	run out	6
S.E. Gregory	c Jones b Lockwood	117	(5)	b Rhodes	2
F.A. Iredale	b Lockwood	9			
J.J. Kelly†	lbw b Jones	4			
C.E. McLeod	not out	31	(2)	b Rhodes	77
E. Jones	b Lockwood	0			
W.P. Howell	b Lockwood	4			
Extras	(B 5, LB 10, W 1, NB 6)	22		(B 7, W 4, NB 4)	15
Total		**352**		**(5 wickets)**	**254**

AUSTRALIA	O	M	R	W	O	M	R	W
Jones	53	12	164	4				
Noble	35·4	12	96	2				
Trumble	39	11	107	2				
McLeod	48	15	131	1				
Howell	15	3	43	0				
Worrall	3	0	15	0				
ENGLAND								
Bradley	29	12	52	0	17	8	32	0
Rhodes	25	2	79	0	22	8	27	3
Lockwood	40·3	17	71	7	15	7	33	0
Jones	30	12	73	3	12	2	43	0
Townsend	5	0	16	0	8	4	9	0
Jackson	14	7	39	0	13	2	54	0
Hayward					11	3	38	1
Fry					2	1	3	0

FALL OF WICKETS

Wkt	E 1st	A 1st	A 2nd
1st	185	38	116
2nd	316	44	208
3rd	318	85	224
4th	428	120	228
5th	436	220	243
6th	436	242	–
7th	479	257	–
8th	511	340	–
9th	551	340	–
10th	576	352	–

Umpires: W. Richards (1) and A.A. White (3).

Close: 1st day – E(1) 435-4 (Fry 60, Townsend 3); 2nd – A(1) 220-5 (Gregory 37).

AUSTRALIA v ENGLAND 1901–02 (1st Test)

Played at Sydney Cricket Ground on 13, 14, 16 December.
Toss: England.   Result: ENGLAND won by an innings and 124 runs.
Debuts: England – S.F. Barnes, C. Blythe, L.C. Braund, J.R. Gunn.

MacLaren became the first batsman to score four centuries in Test cricket. Not until 1958-59 did another England captain score a Test hundred in Australia (P.B.H. May in *Test No. 465*). Sydney Francis Barnes, a virtually unknown bowler selected by MacLaren, immediately demonstrated his artistry.

ENGLAND

A.C. MacLaren*	lbw b McLeod	116
T.W. Hayward	c Hill b Trumble	69
J.T. Tyldesley	c McLeod b Laver	1
W.G. Quaife	b Howell	21
G.L. Jessop	b McLeod	24
A.O. Jones	c Kelly b Noble	9
A.F.A. Lilley†	c Laver b McLeod	84
L.C. Braund	c Jones b McLeod	58
J.R. Gunn	c and b Jones	21
S.F. Barnes	not out	26
C. Blythe	c Trumble b Laver	20
Extras	(B 6, LB 7, W 1, NB 1)	15
Total		**464**

AUSTRALIA

S.E. Gregory	c Braund b Blythe	48	(5)	c MacLaren b Braund	43
V.T. Trumper	c and b Barnes	2		c Lilley b Blythe	34
C. Hill	b Barnes	46		b Braund	0
M.A. Noble	st Lilley b Braund	2		c Lilley b Blythe	14
W.P. Howell	c Braund b Blythe	9	(10)	not out	31
C.E. McLeod	b Barnes	0		b Blythe	0
J.J. Kelly†	b Blythe	0		c Barnes b Blythe	12
J. Darling*	c Quaife b Barnes	39	(1)	c Jessop b Braund	3
F. Laver	c Quaife b Braund	6		st Lilley b Braund	0
H. Trumble	not out	5	(8)	c Lilley b Barnes	26
E. Jones	c Jessop b Barnes	5		c Jones b Braund	2
Extras	(B 1, LB 3, NB 2)	6		(B 5, LB 2)	7
Total		**168**			**172**

AUSTRALIA	O	M	R	W	O	M	R	W
Jones	36	8	98	1				
Noble	33	17	91	1				
McLeod	44	17	84	4				
Howell	21	8	52	1				
Trumble	34	12	85	1				
Laver	17	6	39	2				
Trumper	1	1	0	0				
ENGLAND								
Barnes	35·1	9	65	5	16	2	74	1
Braund	15	4	40	2	28·4	8	61	5
Gunn	5	0	27	0				
Blythe	16	8	26	3	13	5	30	4
Jessop	1	0	4	0				

FALL OF WICKETS

Wkt	E 1st	A 1st	A 2nd
1st	154	3	12
2nd	163	89	12
3rd	193	97	52
4th	220	112	59
5th	236	112	59
6th	272	112	89
7th	396	112	129
8th	405	142	136
9th	425	163	147
10th	464	168	172

Umpires: R. Callaway (1) and R.W. Crockett (1).

Close: 1st day – E(1) 272-6 (Lilley 22); 2nd – A(1) 103-3 (Hill 42, Howell 4).

AUSTRALIA v ENGLAND 1901–02 (2nd Test)

Played at Melbourne Cricket Ground on 1, 2, 3, 4 January.
Toss: England. Result: AUSTRALIA won by 229 runs.
Debuts: Australia – W.W. Armstrong, R.A. Duff.

Barnes dismissed Trumper with the second ball of the match. On a rain-affected pitch 25 wickets fell on the first day – a record in Australia – England being dismissed in just 68 minutes. Hill was the first to be out for 99 in a Test. Duff, top-scorer in both innings, became the third Australian to score a hundred on his Test debut. He remains the only Australian to score a century against England batting at No. 10. He and Armstrong had been held back until the pitch eased and they responded with the first hundred partnership for the tenth wicket in Tests. Trumble completed Australia's victory by taking a hat-trick to dismiss Jones, Gunn and Barnes.

AUSTRALIA

V.T. Trumper	c Tyldesley b Barnes	0	(8) c Lilley b Barnes	16
J. Darling*	c Lilley b Blythe	19	c Tyldesley b Barnes	23
C. Hill	b Barnes	15	(7) c Jones b Barnes	99
H. Trumble	c Braund b Blythe	16	(1) c Braund b Barnes	16
M.A. Noble	c Lilley b Blythe	0	(9) lbw b Blythe	16
S.E. Gregory	st Lilley b Blythe	0	c Jones b Barnes	17
R.A. Duff	c Braund b Barnes	32	(10) b Braund	104
J.J. Kelly†	c Quaife b Barnes	5	(4) run out	3
W.W. Armstrong	not out	4	(11) not out	45
W.P. Howell	b Barnes	1	(3) c Hayward b Barnes	0
E. Jones	c MacLaren b Barnes	14	(5) c MacLaren b Barnes	5
Extras	(B 6)	6	(B 7, LB 1, NB 1)	9
Total		**112**		**353**

ENGLAND

A.C. MacLaren*	c Jones b Trumble	13	c Trumble b Noble	1
T.W. Hayward	c Darling b Trumble	0	st Kelly b Trumble	12
J.T. Tyldesley	c Gregory b Trumble	2	c Trumble b Noble	66
W.G. Quaife	b Noble	0	b Noble	25
G.L. Jessop	st Kelly b Noble	27	c Gregory b Noble	32
J.R. Gunn	st Kelly b Noble	0	(9) c Jones b Trumble	2
A.F.A. Lilley†	c Trumper b Noble	6	(6) c Darling b Noble	0
A.O. Jones	c Kelly b Noble	0	c Darling b Trumble	6
L.C. Braund	not out	2	(7) c Darling b Noble	25
S.F. Barnes	c and b Noble	1	c and b Trumble	0
C. Blythe	c Trumper b Noble	4	not out	0
Extras	(B 6)	6	(B 1, LB 1, NB 4)	6
Total		**61**		**175**

ENGLAND	O	M	R	W	O	M	R	W	FALL OF WICKETS				
Barnes	16·1	5	42	6	64	17	121	7		A	E	A	E
Blythe	16	2	64	4	31	7	85	1	*Wkt*	*1st*	*1st*	*2nd*	*2nd*
Braund					53·2	17	114	1	1st	0	5	32	2
Jessop					1	0	9	0	2nd	32	16	42	29
Gunn					6	1	13	0	3rd	34	16	42	80
Jones					1	0	2	0	4th	34	24	42	123
									5th	38	36	48	123
AUSTRALIA									6th	81	51	98	156
Trumble	8	1	38	3	22·5	10	49	4	7th	85	51	128	173
Noble	7·4	2	17	7	26	5	60	6	8th	90	56	167	175
Jones					12	2	33	0	9th	94	57	233	175
Howell					15	6	23	0	10th	112	61	353	175
Armstrong					2	1	3	0					
Trumper					2	1	1	0					

Umpires: R. Callaway (2) and R.W. Crockett (2).

Close: 1st day – A(2) 48-5 (Gregory 0); 2nd – A(2) 300-9 (Duff 71, Armstrong 25); 3rd – E(2) 147-5 (Tyldesley 60, Braund 13).

AUSTRALIA v ENGLAND 1901–02 (3rd Test)

Played at Adelaide Oval on 17, 18, 20, 21, 22, 23 January.
Toss: England.   Result: AUSTRALIA won by four wickets.
Debuts: Nil.

Barnes was unable to take any further part in the rubber after injuring his knee while bowling. Hill became the first batsman to be dismissed for three successive nineties in Test matches: 99, 98 and 97. Australia provided the first instance of a team scoring over 300 in the fourth innings to win a Test. A dust storm caused play to be abandoned at 3.00 pm on the fourth day.

ENGLAND

A.C. MacLaren*	run out	67	b Trumble	44
T.W. Hayward	run out	90	b Trumble	47
J.T. Tyldesley	c and b Trumble	0	run out	25
G.L. Jessop	c Trumper b Trumble	1	(5) b Trumble	16
A.F.A. Lilley†	lbw b Trumble	10	(7) b McLeod	21
W.G. Quaife	c Kelly b Howell	68	(4) lbw b Trumble	44
L.C. Braund	not out	103	(6) b Howell	17
A.O. Jones	run out	5	c and b Trumble	11
J.R. Gunn	b Noble	24	lbw b Trumble	5
S.F. Barnes	c Hill b Noble	5	absent hurt	–
C. Blythe	c Hill b Noble	2	(10) not out	10
Extras	(B 9, W 1, NB 3)	13	(B 7)	7
Total		**388**		**247**

AUSTRALIA

J. Darling*	c MacLaren b Blythe	1	(5) c Hayward b Jessop	69
V.T. Trumper	run out	65	b Gunn	25
C. Hill	c Tyldesley b Braund	98	b Jessop	97
R.A. Duff	lbw b Braund	43	(1) hit wkt b Gunn	4
S.E. Gregory	c Blythe b Braund	55	(4) c Braund b Gunn	23
W.W. Armstrong	c and b Gunn	9	(8) not out	9
H. Trumble	b Gunn	13	(6) not out	62
W.P. Howell	c Braund b Gunn	3		
M.A. Noble	b Gunn	14	(7) run out	13
J.J. Kelly†	not out	5		
C.E. McLeod	b Gunn	7		
Extras	(B 2, LB 6)	8	(B 9, LB 3, NB 1)	13
Total		**321**	(6 wickets)	**315**

AUSTRALIA	O	M	R	W	O	M	R	W		FALL OF WICKETS			
Trumble	65	23	124	3	44	18	74	6		E	A	E	A
Noble	26	10	58	3	21	7	72	0	*Wkt*	*1st*	*1st*	*2nd*	*2nd*
Howell	36	10	82	1	27	9	54	1	1st	149	1	80	5
Armstrong	18	5	45	0	5	0	9	0	2nd	160	138	113	50
Trumper	6	3	17	0					3rd	164	197	126	98
McLeod	19	5	49	0	14	3	31	1	4th	171	229	144	194
									5th	186	260	165	255
ENGLAND									6th	294	288	204	287
Braund	46	9	143	3	25	5	79	0	7th	302	289	218	–
Blythe	11	3	54	1	41	16	66	0	8th	371	302	224	–
Barnes	7	0	21	0					9th	384	309	247	–
Gunn	42	14	76	5	38	14	88	3	10th	388	321	–	–
Jessop	7	0	19	0	24.4	9	41	2					
Hayward					7	0	28	0					

Umpires: P. Argall (1) and R.W. Crockett (3).

Close: 1st day – E(1) 266-5 (Quaife 51, Braund 35); 2nd – A(1) 172-2 (Hill 83, Duff 22); 3rd – E(2) 98-1 (Hayward 44, Tyldesley 4); 4th – E(2) 204-5 (Quaife 27, Lilley 21); 5th – A(2) 201-4 (Darling 40, Trumble 4).

AUSTRALIA v ENGLAND 1901–02 (4th Test)

Played at Sydney Cricket Ground on 14, 15, 17, 18 February.
Toss: England.   Result: AUSTRALIA won by seven wickets.
Debuts: Australia – A.J.Y. Hopkins, J.V. Saunders; England – C.P. McGahey.

Howell scored 35 in 14 minutes, being out to his 15th ball; he hit 23 off his first eight balls. Saunders took nine wickets in his first Test but was not selected for the next match. Kelly was the first wicket-keeper to make eight dismissals in a Test. Although equalled, his record remained intact until 1956 when G.R.A. Langley claimed nine wickets at Lord's (*Test No. 426*).

ENGLAND

A.C. MacLaren*	c Duff b Saunders	92	c Kelly b Noble	5
T.W. Hayward	b Saunders	41	b Noble	12
J.T. Tyldesley	c Kelly b Noble	79	c Trumble b Saunders	10
W.G. Quaife	c Kelly b Saunders	4	lbw b Noble	15
G.L. Jessop	c Noble b Saunders	0	b Saunders	15
L.C. Braund	lbw b Trumble	17	b Saunders	0
C.P. McGahey	b Trumble	18	c Kelly b Saunders	13
A.F.A. Lilley†	c Kelly b Noble	40	c Trumble b Noble	0
A.O. Jones	c Kelly b Trumble	15	c Kelly b Noble	6
J.R. Gunn	not out	0	not out	13
C. Blythe	b Noble	4	c Kelly b Saunders	8
Extras	(B 5, NB 2)	7	(LB 2)	2
Total		**317**		**99**

AUSTRALIA

H. Trumble*	c MacLaren b Jessop	6		
V.T. Trumper	c Braund b Jessop	7	lbw b Blythe	25
C. Hill	c Jones b Jessop	21	c Lilley b Gunn	30
S.E. Gregory	c Braund b Jessop	5	(5) not out	12
M.A. Noble	lbw b Braund	56		
R.A. Duff	c Lilley b Blythe	39	(1) not out	51
W.W. Armstrong	b Braund	55		
A.J.Y. Hopkins	c Lilley b Braund	43		
J.J. Kelly†	not out	24		
W.P. Howell	c MacLaren b Gunn	35	(4) c sub (H.G. Garnett) b Gunn	0
J.V. Saunders	b Braund	0		
Extras	(B 7, NB 1)	8	(LB 1, NB 2)	3
Total		**299**	(3 wickets)	**121**

AUSTRALIA	O	M	R	W	O	M	R	W
Noble	33·2	12	78	3	24	7	54	5
Saunders	43	11	119	4	24·1	8	43	5
Howell	22	10	40	0				
Trumble	38	18	65	3				
Armstrong	2	1	8	0				
ENGLAND								
Braund	60	25	118	4	15	2	55	0
Gunn	16	5	48	1	8·3	1	17	2
Jessop	26	5	68	4	7	0	23	0
Blythe	37	17	57	1	6	0	23	1

FALL OF WICKETS

Wkt	E 1st	A 1st	E 2nd	A 2nd
1st	73	7	5	50
2nd	179	18	24	105
3rd	188	30	36	105
4th	188	48	57	–
5th	225	119	57	–
6th	245	160	57	–
7th	267	205	60	–
8th	312	252	78	–
9th	312	288	88	–
10th	317	299	99	–

Umpires: C. Bannerman (11) and R. Callaway (3).

Close: 1st day – E(1) 266-6 (McGahey 18, Lilley 10); 2nd – A(1) 148-5 (Noble 51, Armstrong 11); 3rd – E(2) 77-7 (McGahey 12, Jones 6).

AUSTRALIA v ENGLAND 1901–02 (5th Test)

Played at Melbourne Cricket Ground on 28 February, 1, 3, 4 March.
Toss: Australia.   Result: AUSTRALIA won by 32 runs.
Debuts: Australia – J.P.F. Travers.

Hill became the first player to score 500 runs in a rubber without making a century; C.C. Hunte (550 for West Indies v Australia in 1964-65) is the only other batsman to do so.

AUSTRALIA

V.T. Trumper	b Blythe	27	c McGahey b Braund		18
R.A. Duff	b Braund	10	c and b Braund		28
C. Hill	c Jones b Gunn	28	c Lilley b Hayward		87
S.E. Gregory	c Jones b Gunn	25	b Gunn		41
M.A. Noble	lbw b Hayward	7	c MacLaren b Gunn		16
H. Trumble*	c Quaife b Hayward	3	(7) b Blythe		22
W.W. Armstrong	not out	17	(6) lbw b Braund		20
A.J.Y. Hopkins	c Lilley b Hayward	4	(9) c MacLaren b Blythe		0
J.J. Kelly†	c Gunn b Hayward	0	(8) not out		11
C.J. Eady	b Gunn	5	c Gunn b Braund		3
J.P.F. Travers	c Braund b Gunn	9	c and b Braund		1
Extras	(B 7, W 1, NB 1)	9	(B 3, LB 1, NB 4)		8
Total		**144**			**255**

ENGLAND

A.C. MacLaren*	c and b Trumble	25	run out		49
G.L. Jessop	c Hopkins b Trumble	35	(4) c Trumper b Trumble		16
W.G. Quaife	c Trumble b Noble	3	lbw b Noble		4
J.T. Tyldesley	c Kelly b Eady	13	(5) c Eady b Trumble		36
T.W. Hayward	c Trumper b Travers	19	(2) c Travers b Trumble		15
L.C. Braund	c Hopkins b Trumble	32	c Hill b Noble		2
A.F.A. Lilley†	c Eady b Trumble	41	c Duff b Noble		9
C.P. McGahey	b Trumble	0	c Hill b Noble		7
A.O. Jones	c Kelly b Eady	10	c and b Noble		28
J.R. Gunn	lbw b Eady	8	c Hill b Noble		4
C. Blythe	not out	0	not out		5
Extras	(B 1, LB 2)	3	(LB 2, NB 1)		3
Total		**189**			**178**

ENGLAND	O	M	R	W	O	M	R	W
Jessop	1	0	13	0				
Braund	10	2	33	1	26·1	4	95	5
Blythe	9	2	29	1	13	3	36	2
Hayward	16	9	22	4	22	4	63	1
Gunn	17	6	38	4	28	11	53	2
AUSTRALIA								
Noble	26	4	80	1	33	4	98	6
Trumble	25	4	62	5	30·3	7	64	3
Travers	8	2	14	1				
Eady	8·3	2	30	3	2	0	13	0

FALL OF WICKETS

Wkt	A 1st	E 1st	A 2nd	E 2nd
1st	16	50	30	40
2nd	54	62	52	64
3rd	81	64	131	87
4th	98	91	149	87
5th	104	96	208	93
6th	108	164	224	104
7th	112	168	249	120
8th	112	173	249	157
9th	124	186	255	161
10th	144	189	255	178

Umpires: C. Bannerman (12) and R.W. Crockett (4).

Close: 1st day – E(1) 133-5 (Braund 26, Lilley 10); 2nd – A(2) 226-6 (Trumble 10, Kelly 2); 3rd – E(2) 87-3 (Jessop 16).

ENGLAND v AUSTRALIA 1902 (1st Test)

Played at Edgbaston, Birmingham, on 29, 30, 31 May.
Toss: England.   Result: MATCH DRAWN.
Debuts: Nil.

MacLaren's team in this, Birmingham's first Test match, is usually considered to be the strongest batting side ever to represent England – all eleven scored centuries in first-class cricket. The unbroken partnership of 81 between Lockwood and Rhodes is still a tenth-wicket record against Australia in England. Australia were dismissed in 80 minutes for their lowest score in Tests. Rain delayed the start on the third day until 5.15 pm and restricted play to 75 minutes. Three days after this Test, Yorkshire gained a five-wicket win against the Australians at Leeds after Hirst and Jackson had bowled them out for 23.

ENGLAND

A.C. MacLaren*	run out	9	
C.B. Fry	c Kelly b Jones	0	
K.S. Ranjitsinhji	b Armstrong	13	
Hon. F.S. Jackson	b Jones	53	
J.T. Tyldesley	lbw b Howell	138	
A.F.A. Lilley†	c Jones b Noble	2	
G.H. Hirst	c Armstrong b Trumper	48	
G.L. Jessop	c Hopkins b Trumper	6	
L.C. Braund	b Jones	14	
W.H. Lockwood	not out	52	
W. Rhodes	not out	38	
Extras	(LB 3)	3	
Total	**(9 wickets declared)**	**376**	

AUSTRALIA

V.T. Trumper	b Hirst	18	c Braund b Rhodes		14
R.A. Duff	c Jessop b Rhodes	2	c Fry b Braund		15
C. Hill	c Braund b Hirst	1	not out		10
S.E. Gregory	lbw b Hirst	0	not out		1
J. Darling*	c Jessop b Rhodes	3			
M.A. Noble	st Lilley b Rhodes	3			
W.W. Armstrong	c Lilley b Rhodes	0			
A.J.Y. Hopkins	c Lilley b Rhodes	5			
J.J. Kelly†	not out	1			
E. Jones	c Jackson b Rhodes	0			
W.P. Howell	c Fry b Rhodes	0			
Extras	(B 3)	3	(LB 4, W 1, NB 1)		6
Total		**36**	**(2 wickets)**		**46**

AUSTRALIA	O	M	R	W	O	M	R	W
Jones	28	9	76	3				
Noble	44	15	112	1				
Trumper	13	5	35	2				
Armstrong	25	6	64	1				
Howell	26	8	58	1				
Hopkins	6	2	28	0				
ENGLAND								
Hirst	11	4	15	3	9	6	10	0
Rhodes	11	3	17	7	10	5	9	1
Braund	1	0	1	0	5	0	14	1
Jackson					4	2	7	0

FALL OF WICKETS

Wkt	E 1st	A 1st	A 2nd
1st	5	9	16
2nd	13	10	41
3rd	35	14	–
4th	112	17	–
5th	121	25	–
6th	212	25	–
7th	230	31	–
8th	264	35	–
9th	295	35	–
10th	–	36	–

Umpires: W. Hearn (4) and J. Phillips (19).

Close: 1st day – E(1) 351-9 (Lockwood 41, Rhodes 24); 2nd – A(1) 8-0 (Trumper 8, Duff 0).

ENGLAND v AUSTRALIA 1902 (2nd Test)

Played at Lord's, London, on 12, 13 (*no play*), 14 (*no play*) June.
Toss: England.   Result: MATCH DRAWN.
Debuts: Nil.

Rain delayed the start until 2.45 pm, restricted play to 105 minutes on the first day, completely washed out the second, and caused the match to be abandoned before the scheduled start of the third and final day. MacLaren overtook S.E. Gregory's record aggregate of 1,366 runs for this series after Hopkins (off-cutters and inswing) had taken two wickets without cost in his first two overs.

ENGLAND

A.C. MacLaren*	not out	47
C.B. Fry	c Hill b Hopkins	0
K.S. Ranjitsinhji	b Hopkins	0
Hon. F.S. Jackson	not out	55
J.T. Tyldesley	)	
A.F.A. Lilley†	)	
G.H. Hirst	)	
G.L. Jessop	) did not bat	
L.C. Braund	)	
W.H. Lockwood	)	
W. Rhodes	)	
Extras		–
Total	(2 wickets)	**102**

AUSTRALIA

V.T. Trumper
R.A. Duff
A.J.Y. Hopkins
C. Hill
S.E. Gregory
J. Darling*
M.A. Noble
W.W. Armstrong
J.J. Kelly†
E. Jones
J.V. Saunders

AUSTRALIA	O	M	R	W
Jones	11	4	31	0
Hopkins	9	3	18	2
Saunders	3	0	15	0
Trumper	8	1	33	0
Armstrong	5	0	5	0
Noble	2	2	0	0

Umpires: C.E. Richardson (1) and V.A. Titchmarsh (2).

FALL OF WICKETS	
	E
Wkt	1st
1st	0
2nd	0
3rd	–
4th	–
5th	–
6th	–
7th	–
8th	–
9th	–
10th	–

Close: 1st day – E(1) 102-2 (MacLaren 47, Jackson 55); 2nd – no play.

ENGLAND v AUSTRALIA 1902 (3rd Test)

Played at Bramall Lane, Sheffield, on 3, 4, 5 July.
Toss: Australia.   Result: AUSTRALIA won by 143 runs.
Debuts: Nil.

Hill had the distinction of scoring the only hundred in Sheffield's only Test. Now solely the home of Sheffield United Football Club, Bramall Lane staged its last first-class cricket match in 1973. Trumper made 50 in 40 minutes, taking only 50 minutes to score 62.

AUSTRALIA

V.T. Trumper	b Braund	1	c Lilley b Jackson		62
R.A. Duff	c Lilley b Barnes	25	c Hirst b Rhodes		1
C. Hill	c Rhodes b Barnes	18	c MacLaren b Jackson		119
J. Darling*	c Braund b Barnes	0	c Braund b Barnes		0
S.E. Gregory	c Abel b Barnes	11	run out		29
M.A. Noble	c Braund b Rhodes	47	b Jackson		8
A.J.Y. Hopkins	c Braund b Barnes	27	not out		40
W.W. Armstrong	c and b Braund	25	b Rhodes		26
J.J. Kelly†	b Barnes	0	c Hirst b Rhodes		0
H. Trumble	c and b Jackson	32	b Rhodes		0
J.V. Saunders	not out	0	b Rhodes		1
Extras	(B 3, LB 5)	8	(LB 3)		3
Total		**194**			**289**

ENGLAND

A.C. MacLaren*	b Noble	31	(4) c Trumper b Noble		63
R. Abel	b Noble	38	c Hill b Noble		8
J.T. Tyldesley	c Armstrong b Noble	22	b Trumble		14
Hon. F.S. Jackson	c Gregory b Saunders	3	(6) b Noble		14
C.B. Fry	st Kelly b Saunders	1	lbw b Trumble		4
A.F.A. Lilley†	b Noble	8	(7) b Noble		9
L.C. Braund	st Kelly b Saunders	0	(8) c Armstrong b Noble		9
G.H. Hirst	c Trumble b Saunders	8	(9) b Noble		0
G.L. Jessop	c Saunders b Noble	12	(1) lbw b Trumble		55
W. Rhodes	not out	7	not out		7
S.F. Barnes	c Darling b Saunders	7	b Trumble		5
Extras	(B 4, LB 3, NB 1)	8	(B 4, LB 1, W 1, NB 1)		7
Total		**145**			**195**

ENGLAND	O	M	R	W	O	M	R	W
Hirst	15	1	59	0	10	1	40	0
Braund	13	4	34	2	12	0	58	0
Barnes	20	9	49	6	12	4	50	1
Jackson	5·1	1	11	1	17	2	60	3
Rhodes	13	3	33	1	17·1	3	63	5
Jessop					4	0	15	0
AUSTRALIA								
Trumble	18	10	21	0	21·5	3	49	4
Saunders	15·3	4	50	5	12	0	68	0
Trumper	4	1	8	0	6	0	19	0
Noble	19	6	51	5	21	4	52	6
Armstrong	5	2	7	0				

FALL OF WICKETS

	A	E	A	E
Wkt	1st	1st	2nd	2nd
1st	3	61	20	14
2nd	39	86	80	75
3rd	39	101	80	84
4th	52	101	187	98
5th	73	102	214	162
6th	127	106	225	165
7th	137	110	277	174
8th	137	130	287	174
9th	194	131	287	186
10th	194	145	289	195

Umpires: J. Phillips (20) and W. Richards (2).

Close: 1st day – E(1) 102-5 (Lilley 0, Braund 0); 2nd – E(2) 73-1 (Jessop 53, Tyldesley 11).

ENGLAND v AUSTRALIA 1902 (4th Test)

Played at Old Trafford, Manchester, on 24, 25, 26 July.
Toss: Australia.   Result: AUSTRALIA won by 3 runs.
Debuts: England – L.C.H. Palairet, F.W. Tate.

Trumper reached his century in 108 minutes before lunch on the first day – a feat since equalled on only three occasions: C.G. Macartney in 1926 (*Test No. 165*), D.G. Bradman in 1930 (*196*), and Majid Khan in 1976-77 (*784*). At lunch Trumper was 103 not out and Australia's score was 173 for 1. He was out to the fifth ball after the resumption having batted for 115 minutes. His partnership of 135 in 78 minutes with Duff was a record for Australia's first wicket and is still the fastest century opening stand in this series (57 minutes). Darling's first innings included the first two hits for six out of the ground made in Tests in England. Fred Tate, who dropped Darling in the second innings and was bowled with only four runs needed, was not again selected. This result, emulated by England at Melbourne in 1982-83 (*Test No. 941*), remains the closest by a runs margin in Tests.

AUSTRALIA

V.T. Trumper	c Lilley b Rhodes	104		c Braund b Lockwood	4
R.A. Duff	c Lilley b Lockwood	54		b Lockwood	3
C. Hill	c Rhodes b Lockwood	65		b Lockwood	0
M.A. Noble	c and b Rhodes	2	(6)	c Lilley b Lockwood	4
S.E. Gregory	c Lilley b Rhodes	3		lbw b Tate	24
J. Darling*	c MacLaren b Rhodes	51	(4)	c Palairet b Rhodes	37
A.J.Y. Hopkins	c Palairet b Lockwood	0		c Tate b Lockwood	2
W.W. Armstrong	b Lockwood	5		b Rhodes	3
J.J. Kelly†	not out	4		not out	2
H. Trumble	c Tate b Lockwood	0		lbw b Tate	4
J.V. Saunders	b Lockwood	3		c Tyldesley b Rhodes	0
Extras	(B 5, LB 2, W 1)	8		(B 1, LB 1, NB 1)	3
Total		**299**			**86**

ENGLAND

L.C.H. Palairet	c Noble b Saunders	6		b Saunders	17
R. Abel	c Armstrong b Saunders	6	(5)	b Trumble	21
J.T. Tyldesley	c Hopkins b Saunders	22		c Armstrong b Saunders	16
A.C. MacLaren*	b Trumble	1	(2)	c Duff b Trumble	35
K.S. Ranjitsinhji	lbw b Trumble	2	(4)	lbw b Trumble	4
Hon. F.S. Jackson	c Duff b Trumble	128		c Gregory b Saunders	7
L.C. Braund	b Noble	65		st Kelly b Trumble	3
A.F.A. Lilley†	b Noble	7		c Hill b Trumble	4
W.H. Lockwood	run out	7		b Trumble	0
W. Rhodes	c and b Trumble	5		not out	4
F.W. Tate	not out	5		b Saunders	4
Extras	(B 6, LB 2)	8		(B 5)	5
Total		**262**			**120**

ENGLAND	O	M	R	W	O	M	R	W
Rhodes	25	3	104	4	14·4	5	26	3
Jackson	11	0	58	0				
Tate	11	1	44	0	5	3	7	2
Braund	9	0	37	0	11	3	22	0
Lockwood	20·1	5	48	6	17	5	28	5
AUSTRALIA								
Trumble	43	16	75	4	25	9	53	6
Saunders	34	5	104	3	19·4	4	52	4
Noble	24	8	47	2	5	3	10	0
Trumper	6	4	6	0				
Armstrong	5	2	19	0				
Hopkins	2	0	3	0				

FALL OF WICKETS

	A	E	A	E
Wkt	*1st*	*1st*	*2nd*	*2nd*
1st	135	12	7	44
2nd	175	13	9	68
3rd	179	14	10	72
4th	183	30	64	92
5th	256	44	74	97
6th	256	185	76	107
7th	288	203	77	109
8th	292	214	79	109
9th	292	235	85	116
10th	299	262	86	120

Umpires: J. Moss (1) and T. Mycroft (2).

Close: 1st day – E(1) 70-5 (Jackson 16, Braund 13); 2nd – A(2) 85-8 (Kelly 1, Trumble 4).

ENGLAND v AUSTRALIA 1902 (5th Test).

Played at Kennington Oval, London, on 11, 12, 13 August.
Toss: Australia.   Result: ENGLAND won by one wicket.
Debuts: Nil.

Going in with England 48 for 5 and needing another 215 to win, Jessop hit fifty in 43 minutes and went on to record the fastest century in Test cricket in 75 minutes. There has been only one faster Test hundred since – J.M. Gregory reaching his in just 70 minutes in 1921-22 (*Test No. 146*). Trumble, who bowled unchanged throughout both innings, became the first Australian to score a fifty and take ten wickets in the same Test. This was the first of six one-wicket victories in Test cricket and the only one in England. At the end of the rubber, the fourth in succession won by Australia, Hill (1,562) and MacLaren (1,543) were the leading scorers in this series. Hirst and Rhodes calmly acquired the 15 runs needed for victory (not all in singles) during one of cricket's most historic last-wicket partnerships.

AUSTRALIA

V.T. Trumper	b Hirst	42	run out	2
R.A. Duff	c Lilley b Hirst	23	b Lockwood	6
C. Hill	b Hirst	11	c MacLaren b Hirst	34
J. Darling*	c Lilley b Hirst	3	c MacLaren b Lockwood	15
M.A. Noble	c and b Jackson	52	b Braund	13
S.E. Gregory	b Hirst	23	b Braund	9
W.W. Armstrong	b Jackson	17	b Lockwood	21
A.J.Y. Hopkins	c MacLaren b Lockwood	40	c Lilley b Lockwood	3
H. Trumble	not out	64	(10) not out	7
J.J. Kelly†	c Rhodes b Braund	39	(11) lbw b Lockwood	0
J.V. Saunders	lbw b Braund	0	(9) c Tyldesley b Rhodes	2
Extras	(B 5, LB 3, NB 2)	10	(B 7, LB 2)	9
Total		**324**		**121**

ENGLAND

A.C. MacLaren*	c Armstrong b Trumble	10	b Saunders	2
L.C.H. Palairet	b Trumble	20	b Saunders	6
J.T. Tyldesley	b Trumble	33	b Saunders	0
T.W. Hayward	b Trumble	0	c Kelly b Saunders	7
Hon. F.S. Jackson	c Armstrong b Saunders	2	c and b Trumble	49
L.C. Braund	c Hill b Trumble	22	c Kelly b Trumble	2
G.L. Jessop	b Trumble	13	c Noble b Armstrong	104
G.H. Hirst	c and b Trumble	43	not out	58
W.H. Lockwood	c Noble b Saunders	25	lbw b Trumble	2
A.F.A. Lilley†	c Trumper b Trumble	0	c Darling b Trumble	16
W. Rhodes	not out	0	not out	6
Extras	(B 13, LB 2)	15	(B 5, LB 6)	11
Total		**183**	(9 wickets)	**263**

ENGLAND	O	M	R	W	O	M	R	W		FALL OF WICKETS			
Lockwood	24	2	85	1	20	6	45	5		A	E	A	E
Rhodes	28	9	46	0	22	7	38	1	*Wkt*	*1st*	*1st*	*2nd*	*2nd*
Hirst	29	5	77	5	5	1	7	1	1st	47	31	6	5
Braund	16·5	5	29	2	9	1	15	2	2nd	63	36	9	5
Jackson	20	4	66	2	4	3	7	0	3rd	69	62	31	10
Jessop	6	2	11	0					4th	82	67	71	31
									5th	126	67	75	48
AUSTRALIA									6th	174	83	91	157
Trumble	31	13	65	8	33·5	4	108	4	7th	175	137	99	187
Saunders	23	7	79	2	24	3	105	4	8th	256	179	114	214
Noble	7	3	24	0	5	0	11	0	9th	324	183	115	248
Armstrong					4	0	28	1	10th	324	183	121	–

Umpires: C.E. Richardson (2) and A.A. White (4).

Close: 1st day – A(1) 324 all out; 2nd – A(2) 114-8 (Armstrong 21).

SOUTH AFRICA v AUSTRALIA 1902–03 (1st Test)

Played at Old Wanderers, Johannesburg, on 11, 13, 14 October.
Toss: South Africa.   Result: MATCH DRAWN.
Debuts: South Africa – C.M.H. Hathorn, A.W. Nourse, C.J.E. Smith, H.M. Taberer, L.J. Tancred,
P.G. Thornton. *Arthur William Nourse was known as 'Dave' and he is usually incorrectly shown as
'A.D. Nourse, sr' to differentiate him from his son, Arthur Dudley.*

The 1902 Australians sailed home via the Cape and this match was played almost immediately after their
arrival – on matting at an altitude of nearly 6,000 feet. Taberer emulated C.A. Smith of England (*Test No. 31*)
by captaining his country in his only Test. With a lead of 158 he was able to enforce the follow-on in this initial
match of the series. South Africa had to wait another 26 Tests and 48 years before they were in a similar position.
Hill became the first Australian to score a century before lunch when he took his total from 22 to 138 on the
third day.

SOUTH AFRICA

W.A. Shalders	c and b Jones	19	c Kelly b Jones	0
L.J. Tancred	c Duff b Trumper	97	b Armstrong	24
C.B. Llewellyn	b Trumper	90	(6) not out	4
J.H. Sinclair	c and b Hopkins	44	b Armstrong	19
C.M.H. Hathorn	c Gregory b Jones	45	(3) c Armstrong b Noble	31
C.J.E. Smith	b Hopkins	13	(5) not out	16
H.M. Taberer*	b Hopkins	2		
A.W. Nourse	c Hopkins b Noble	72		
E.A. Halliwell†	c Darling b Jones	57		
P.G. Thornton	not out	1		
G.A. Rowe	c Jones b Noble	4		
Extras	(B 5, LB 4, NB 1)	10	(B 4, LB 3)	7
Total		**454**	(4 wickets)	**101**

AUSTRALIA

V.T. Trumper	c Rowe b Llewellyn	63	b Taberer	37
W.W. Armstrong	b Sinclair	11	(4) c Halliwell b Thornton	59
C. Hill	c Nourse b Sinclair	76	c and b Sinclair	142
R.A. Duff	not out	82	(2) c Halliwell b Rowe	15
M.A. Noble	b Sinclair	1	(6) not out	53
J. Darling*	st Halliwell b Sinclair	0	(5) b Llewellyn	14
S.E. Gregory	lbw b Llewellyn	0	b Llewellyn	4
A.J.Y. Hopkins	c Tancred b Llewellyn	1	lbw b Llewellyn	30
H. Trumble	c Thornton b Llewellyn	13	not out	0
J.J. Kelly†	c Halliwell b Llewellyn	25		
E. Jones	c Sinclair b Llewellyn	0		
Extras	(B 22, LB 2)	24	(B 13, LB 5)	18
Total		**296**	(7 wickets declared)	**372**

AUSTRALIA	O	M	R	W	O	M	R	W		FALL OF WICKETS			
Jones	21	5	78	3	7	3	22	1		SA	A	A	SA
Armstrong	13	3	88	0	7	2	24	2	*Wkt*	*1st*	*1st*	*2nd*	*2nd*
Trumble	23	1	103	0	11	3	24	0	1st	31	60	42	5
Trumper	12	0	62	2					2nd	204	106	67	44
Hopkins	12	1	59	3	2	0	17	0	3rd	223	195	231	74
Noble	14	2	54	2	5	1	7	1	4th	296	196	277	90
SOUTH AFRICA									5th	304	196	281	–
Rowe	5	1	28	0	11	1	55	1	6th	306	199	297	–
Taberer	4	1	23	0	6	1	25	1	7th	325	217	354	–
Llewellyn	22	3	92	6	26	3	124	3	8th	449	242	–	–
Sinclair	20	1	129	4	23	2	115	1	9th	449	296	–	–
Nourse					8	2	15	0	10th	454	296	–	–
Thornton					4	0	20	1					

Umpires: F. Hearne (2) and A. Soames (2).

Close: 1st day – SA(1) 428-7 (Nourse 64, Halliwell 44); 2nd – A(2) 76-2 (Hill 22, Armstrong 0).

SOUTH AFRICA v AUSTRALIA 1902–03 (2nd Test)

Played at Old Wanderers, Johannesburg, on 18, 20, 21 October.
Toss: Australia.   Result: AUSTRALIA won by 159 runs.
Debuts: South Africa – J.H. Anderson, J.J. Kotze.

Armstrong became the second Australian after J.E. Barrett (*Test No. 33*) to carry his bat through a completed innings and the only one to do so against South Africa. Anderson emulated H.M. Taberer (*Test No. 75*) by captaining South Africa in his only Test.

AUSTRALIA

V.T. Trumper	b Kotze	18	(3) c Shalders b Sinclair		13
R.A. Duff	b Middleton	43	(4) b Sinclair		44
C. Hill	st Halliwell b Kotze	6	(8) c Kotze b Llewellyn		12
W.W. Armstrong	run out	49	(1) not out		159
M.A. Noble	c Kotze b Llewellyn	5	lbw b Llewellyn		24
J. Darling*	c Anderson b Llewellyn	6	b Llewellyn		4
S.E. Gregory	b Kotze	1	(2) c Llewellyn b Kotze		13
A.J.Y. Hopkins	c Nourse b Llewellyn	20	(9) c Llewellyn b Nourse		8
J.J. Kelly†	c Halliwell b Llewellyn	16	(10) c Hathorn b Llewellyn		9
W.P. Howell	c Nourse b Llewellyn	0	(11) b Llewellyn		9
J.V. Saunders	not out	0	(7) b Sinclair		1
Extras	(B 10, W 1)	11	(B 8, LB 5)		13
Total		**175**			**309**

SOUTH AFRICA

L.J. Tancred	lbw b Noble	19	c Kelly b Howell		29
W.A. Shalders	b Howell	42	(3) b Saunders		3
C.M.H. Hathorn	c Armstrong b Noble	12	(2) b Saunders		1
J.H. Sinclair	b Howell	101	b Howell		18
C.J.E. Smith	c Kelly b Trumper	12	(6) b Howell		4
C.B. Llewellyn	c and b Trumper	10	(5) b Saunders		0
A.W. Nourse	c and b Trumper	5	(8) not out		18
E.A. Halliwell†	c Kelly b Noble	4	(9) b Saunders		0
J.H. Anderson*	c Howell b Saunders	32	(7) c Darling b Saunders		11
J.J. Kotze	b Saunders	0	(11) st Kelly b Saunders		0
J. Middleton	not out	0	(10) b Saunders		0
Extras	(B 3)	3	(LB 1)		1
Total		**240**			**85**

SOUTH AFRICA	O	M	R	W	O	M	R	W
Kotze	20	2	64	3	17	2	71	1
Middleton	13	3	27	1	4	0	15	0
Llewellyn	18·1	3	43	5	31·4	9	73	5
Sinclair	4	0	30	0	26	0	118	3
Nourse					3	0	19	1
AUSTRALIA								
Trumper	12	1	60	3	3	0	27	0
Saunders	9	1	32	2	11	2	34	7
Howell	13	1	52	2	8	3	23	3
Noble	15	2	75	3				
Armstrong	2	0	16	0				
Hopkins	2	1	2	0				

FALL OF WICKETS

Wkt	A 1st	SA 1st	A 2nd	SA 2nd
1st	29	58	40	4
2nd	35	66	87	20
3rd	125	91	143	46
4th	125	136	180	51
5th	138	154	188	51
6th	138	170	201	66
7th	140	179	238	66
8th	172	231	263	77
9th	172	240	290	77
10th	175	240	309	85

Umpires: F. Hearne (3) and F.E. Smith (1).

Close: 1st day – SA(1) 136-3 (Sinclair 49, Smith 12); 2nd – A(2) 201-5 (Armstrong 94, Saunders 1).

SOUTH AFRICA v AUSTRALIA 1902–03 (3rd Test)

Played at Newlands, Cape Town, on 8, 10, 11 November.
Toss: Australia.   Result: AUSTRALIA won by ten wickets.
Debuts: South Africa – P.S. Twentyman-Jones.

Sinclair scored his century in only 80 minutes – still the fastest for South Africa and the fourth-fastest in all Tests; it included six sixes – the South African record. His fifty took 35 minutes – also a national record. He scored South Africa's first three hundreds; not until South Africa's 14th match (*Test No. 90*) did another batsman score a century. Howell took three wickets in four balls in the first innings (Tancred, Sinclair and Twentyman-Jones being dismissed in the same over – WWOWOO), and three in five balls in the second. Llewellyn, slow left-arm, was the first to take 25 wickets in a rubber for South Africa.

AUSTRALIA

R.A. Duff	c Tancred b Kotze	34	not out		20
V.T. Trumper	b Llewellyn	70	not out		38
C. Hill	not out	91			
W.W. Armstrong	b Llewellyn	3			
M.A. Noble	c Smith b Sinclair	9			
A.J.Y. Hopkins	b Llewellyn	16			
S.E. Gregory	c Smith b Llewellyn	11			
J. Darling*	b Llewellyn	1			
J.J. Kelly†	b Kotze	1			
W.P. Howell	b Llewellyn	2			
J.V. Saunders	run out	4			
Extras	(B 6, LB 4)	10	(NB 1)		1
Total		**252**	(0 wickets)		**59**

SOUTH AFRICA

L.J. Tancred	b Howell	0	c and b Howell		2
W.A. Shalders	c Darling b Saunders	11	c Darling b Hopkins		40
C.J.E. Smith	b Saunders	16	c and b Trumper		45
J.H. Sinclair	b Howell	0	st Kelly b Saunders		104
P.S. Twentyman-Jones	b Howell	0	b Hopkins		0
C.B. Llewellyn	b Howell	1	st Kelly b Howell		8
C.M.H. Hathorn	run out	19	st Kelly b Saunders		18
A.W. Nourse	b Saunders	15	b Howell		5
E.A. Halliwell*†	run out	13	b Howell		1
J.J. Kotze	b Saunders	2	b Howell		0
J. Middleton	not out	1	not out		0
Extras	(B 4, LB 3)	7	(LB 1, NB 1)		2
Total		**85**			**225**

SOUTH AFRICA	O	M	R	W	O	M	R	W
Llewellyn	30·5	4	97	6	4	1	19	0
Kotze	17	1	49	2	2·5	1	16	0
Sinclair	12	0	55	1	2	0	22	0
Middleton	8	1	28	0	1	0	1	0
Nourse	3	0	13	0				
AUSTRALIA								
Howell	17	6	18	4	26	6	81	5
Saunders	12·2	2	37	4	17·1	3	73	2
Noble	4	0	23	0	6	3	6	0
Trumper					6	1	26	1
Hopkins					8	0	37	2

FALL OF WICKETS

Wkt	A 1st	SA 1st	SA 2nd	A 2nd
1st	100	12	2	–
2nd	121	12	81	–
3rd	129	12	115	–
4th	142	12	115	–
5th	179	14	134	–
6th	223	36	216	–
7th	226	60	221	–
8th	227	79	225	–
9th	230	83	225	–
10th	252	85	225	–

Umpires: W.H. Creese (1) and F. Hearne (4).

Close: 1st day – SA(1) 11-0 (Tancred 0, Shalders 11); 2nd – SA(2) 216-6 Hathorn 13).

AUSTRALIA v ENGLAND 1903–04 (1st Test)

Played at Sydney Cricket Ground on 11, 12, 14, 15, 16, 17 December.
Toss: Australia.   Result: ENGLAND won by five wickets.
Debuts: England – E.G. Arnold, B.J.T. Bosanquet, R.E. Foster, A.E. Relf.

Arnold took Trumper's wicket with his first ball in Tests. Noble scored his only Test hundred on his debut as captain. This was the first touring team to be selected and managed by the MCC. Foster's 287 in 419 minutes was the highest score in Test cricket until A. Sandham scored 325 in 1929-30 (*Test No. 193*) and remains the highest by any player in his first Test, and the highest for England in Australia. He was the first batsman to share in three century partnerships in the same Test innings and his tenth-wicket stand of 130 in 66 minutes with Rhodes remains the record for either country in this series. Foster's 214 runs in a day is England's best against Australia and the record for either country in Australia. Trumper reached his century in 94 minutes.

AUSTRALIA

R.A. Duff	c Lilley b Arnold	3	(3) c Relf b Rhodes	84
V.T. Trumper	c Foster b Arnold	1	(5) not out	185
C. Hill	c Lilley b Hirst	5	(4) run out	51
M.A. Noble*	c Foster b Arnold	133	(6) st Lilley b Bosanquet	22
W.W. Armstrong	b Bosanquet	48	(7) c Bosanquet b Rhodes	27
A.J.Y. Hopkins	b Hirst	39	(8) c Arnold b Rhodes	20
W.P. Howell	c Relf b Arnold	5	(10) c Lilley b Arnold	4
S.E. Gregory	b Bosanquet	23	(1) c Lilley b Rhodes	43
F. Laver	lbw b Rhodes	4	c Relf b Rhodes	6
J.J. Kelly†	c Braund b Rhodes	10	(2) b Arnold	13
J.V. Saunders	not out	11	run out	2
Extras	(NB 3)	3	(B 10, LB 15, W 2, NB 1)	28
Total		**285**		**485**

ENGLAND

T.W. Hayward	b Howell	15	st Kelly b Saunders	91
P.F. Warner*	c Kelly b Laver	0	b Howell	8
J.T. Tyldesley	b Noble	53	c Noble b Saunders	9
E.G. Arnold	c Laver b Armstrong	27		
R.E. Foster	c Noble b Saunders	287	(4) st Kelly b Armstrong	19
L.C. Braund	b Howell	102	(5) c Noble b Howell	0
G.H. Hirst	b Howell	0	(6) not out	60
B.J.T. Bosanquet	c Howell b Noble	2	(7) not out	1
A.F.A. Lilley†	c Hill b Noble	4		
A.E. Relf	c Armstrong b Saunders	31		
W. Rhodes	not out	40		
Extras	(B 6, LB 7, W 1, NB 2)	16	(B 3, LB 1, W 2)	6
Total		**577**	(5 wickets)	**194**

ENGLAND	O	M	R	W	O	M	R	W
Hirst	24	8	47	2	29	1	79	0
Arnold	32	7	76	4	28	2	93	2
Braund	26	9	39	0	12	2	56	0
Bosanquet	13	0	52	2	23	1	100	1
Rhodes	17·2	3	41	2	40·2	10	94	5
Relf	6	1	27	0	13	5	35	0
AUSTRALIA								
Saunders	36·2	8	125	2	18·5	3	51	2
Laver	37	12	119	1	16	4	37	0
Howell	31	7	111	3	31	18	35	2
Noble	34	8	99	3	12	2	37	0
Armstrong	23	3	47	1	18	6	28	1
Hopkins	11	1	40	0				
Trumper	7	2	12	0				
Gregory	2	0	8	0				

FALL OF WICKETS

	A	E	A	E
Wkt	1st	1st	2nd	2nd
1st	2	0	36	21
2nd	9	49	108	39
3rd	12	73	191	81
4th	118	117	254	82
5th	200	309	334	181
6th	207	311	393	–
7th	259	318	441	–
8th	263	332	468	–
9th	271	447	473	–
10th	285	577	485	–

Umpires: R.W. Crockett (5) and A.C. Jones (1).

Close: 1st day – A(1) 259-7 (Noble 132); 2nd – E(1) 243-4 (Foster 73, Braund 67); 3rd – A(2) 16-0 (Gregory 6, Kelly 5); 4th – A(2) 367-5 (Trumper 119, Armstrong 14); 5th – E(2) 122-4 (Hayward 60, Hirst 21).

AUSTRALIA v ENGLAND 1903–04 (2nd Test)

Played at Melbourne Cricket Ground on 1, 2, 4, 5 January.
Toss: England.   Result: ENGLAND won by 185 runs.
Debuts: England – A. Fielder, A.E. Knight.

A severe chill prevented Foster from playing after the first day and he retired when the score was 221 for 2. Rain seriously curtailed the second day's play and prevented a start on the fourth until just before 3.30 pm. Rhodes set an England record against Australia by taking 15 wickets in the match – despite having eight catches dropped! His record stood until 1934 when H. Verity slightly improved the figures with 15 for 104 (*Test No. 234*). Rhodes' match analysis of 15 for 124 remains the best in any Melbourne Test.

ENGLAND

P.F. Warner*	c Duff b Trumble	68		c Trumper b Saunders	3
T.W. Hayward	c Gregory b Hopkins	58		c Trumper b Trumble	0
J.T. Tyldesley	c Trumble b Howell	97		c Trumble b Howell	62
R.E. Foster	retired ill	49		absent ill	–
L.C. Braund	c Howell b Trumble	20	(4)	b Saunders	3
A.E. Knight	b Howell	2	(7)	lbw b Trumble	0
G.H. Hirst	c Noble b Howell	7	(5)	c Gregory b Howell	4
W. Rhodes	lbw b Trumble	2	(6)	lbw b Trumble	9
A.F.A. Lilley†	c Howell b Trumble	4	(8)	st Kelly b Trumble	0
A.E. Relf	not out	3	(9)	not out	10
A. Fielder	b Howell	1	(10)	c Hill b Trumble	4
Extras	(LB 3, W 1)	4		(B 7, LB 1)	8
Total		**315**			**103**

AUSTRALIA

V.T. Trumper	c Tyldesley b Rhodes	74		c Relf b Rhodes	35
R.A. Duff	st Lilley b Rhodes	10		c Braund b Rhodes	8
C. Hill	c Rhodes b Hirst	5		c Relf b Rhodes	20
M.A. Noble*	c sub (H. Strudwick) b Rhodes	0		not out	31
S.E. Gregory	c Hirst b Rhodes	1		c Rhodes b Hirst	0
A.J.Y. Hopkins	c sub (H. Strudwick) b Relf	18		c and b Rhodes	7
H. Trumble	c sub (H. Strudwick) b Rhodes	2		c Braund b Rhodes	0
W.W. Armstrong	c Braund b Rhodes	1		c Hayward b Rhodes	0
J.J. Kelly†	run out	8		c Lilley b Rhodes	7
W.P. Howell	c Fielder b Rhodes	0		c Hirst b Rhodes	3
J.V. Saunders	not out	2		c Fielder b Hirst	0
Extras	(LB 1)	1			–
Total		**122**			**111**

AUSTRALIA	O	M	R	W	O	M	R	W
Trumble	50	10	107	4	10·5	2	34	5
Noble	6	3	4	0				
Saunders	16	3	60	0	8	0	33	2
Howell	34·5	14	43	4	8	3	25	2
Armstrong	25	6	43	0				
Hopkins	20	2	50	1	2	1	3	0
Trumper	1	0	4	0				
ENGLAND								
Rhodes	15·2	3	56	7	15	0	68	8
Hirst	8	1	33	1	14·4	4	38	2
Relf	2	0	12	1	1	0	5	0
Braund	5	0	20	0				

FALL OF WICKETS

	E	A	E	A
Wkt	1st	1st	2nd	2nd
1st	122	14	5	14
2nd	132	23	7	59
3rd	277	23	27	73
4th	279	33	40	77
5th	297	67	74	86
6th	306	73	74	90
7th	306	97	74	90
8th	314	105	90	102
9th	315	116	103	105
10th	–	122	–	111

Umpires: P. Argall (2) and R.W. Crockett (6).

Close: 1st day – E(1) 221-2 (Tyldesley 46, Foster 49); 2nd – E(1) 306-6 (Tyldesley 97); 3rd – E(2) 74-5 (Tyldesley 48).

AUSTRALIA v ENGLAND 1903–04 (3rd Test)

Played at Adelaide Oval on 15, 16, 18, 19, 20 January.
Toss: Australia.   Result: AUSTRALIA won by 216 runs.
Debuts: Nil.

On the first day Hill became the first batsman to score 2,000 runs in Tests when he reached 31. Trumper was the first to score four Test hundreds against England. It was the fourth successive Test innings in which he had made top score. Gregory equalled Trumper's record in the second innings with his own fourth hundred which took 115 minutes.

AUSTRALIA

V.T. Trumper	b Hirst	113		lbw b Rhodes	59
R.A. Duff	b Hirst	79		c Braund b Hirst	14
C. Hill	c Lilley b Arnold	88		b Fielder	16
M.A. Noble*	st Lilley b Arnold	59		c Bosanquet b Braund	65
S.E. Gregory	c Tyldesley b Arnold	8		c Rhodes b Braund	112
A.J.Y. Hopkins	b Bosanquet	0	(7)	run out	7
W.W. Armstrong	lbw b Rhodes	10	(6)	c Hirst b Bosanquet	39
H. Trumble	b Bosanquet	4		c and b Bosanquet	9
C.E. McLeod	run out	8		b Bosanquet	2
J.J. Kelly†	lbw b Bosanquet	1		st Lilley b Bosanquet	13
W.P. Howell	not out	3		not out	1
Extras	(B 7, LB 5, W 3)	15		(B 8, LB 2, W 3, NB 1)	14
Total		**388**			**351**

ENGLAND

P.F. Warner*	c McLeod b Trumble	48		c and b Trumble	79
T.W. Hayward	b Howell	20		lbw b Hopkins	67
J.T. Tyldesley	c Kelly b Hopkins	0	(4)	c Noble b Hopkins	10
R.E. Foster	c Howell b Noble	21	(5)	b McLeod	16
L.C. Braund	c Duff b Hopkins	13	(6)	b Howell	25
G.H. Hirst	c Trumper b Trumble	58	(7)	b Trumble	44
B.J.T. Bosanquet	c Duff b Hopkins	10	(9)	c Trumper b Hopkins	10
W. Rhodes	c Armstrong b McLeod	9	(10)	run out	8
E.G. Arnold	not out	23	(3)	b Hopkins	1
A.F.A. Lilley†	run out	28	(8)	c and b Howell	0
A. Fielder	b Trumble	6		not out	14
Extras	(B 4, LB 1, W 4)	9		(LB 2, W 2)	4
Total		**245**			**278**

ENGLAND	O	M	R	W	O	M	R	W
Fielder	7	0	33	0	25	11	51	1
Arnold	27	4	93	3	19	3	74	0
Rhodes	14	3	45	1	21	4	46	1
Bosanquet	30·1	4	95	3	15·5	0	73	4
Braund	13	1	49	0	21	6	57	2
Hirst	15	1	58	2	13	1	36	1
AUSTRALIA								
McLeod	24	6	56	1	25	4	46	1
Trumble	28	9	49	3	33	8	73	2
Howell	13	4	28	1	20	5	52	2
Hopkins	24	5	68	3	28·1	9	81	4
Armstrong	10	3	25	0	7	2	15	0
Noble	3	0	10	1				
Trumper					4	0	7	0

FALL OF WICKETS

	A	E	A	E
Wkt	1st	1st	2nd	2nd
1st	129	47	48	148
2nd	272	48	81	150
3rd	296	88	101	160
4th	308	99	263	160
5th	310	116	289	195
6th	343	146	320	231
7th	360	173	324	231
8th	384	199	326	256
9th	384	234	350	256
10th	388	245	351	278

Umpires: P. Argall (3) and R.W. Crockett (7).

Close: 1st day – A(1) 355-6 (Noble 38, Trumble 4); 2nd – E(1) 199-8 (Arnold 11); 3rd – A(2) 263-4 (Noble 52); 4th – E(2) 150-2 (Warner 79).

AUSTRALIA v ENGLAND 1903–04 (4th Test)

Played at Sydney Cricket Ground on 26, 27, 29 (*no play*) February, 1, 2, 3 March.
Toss: England.   Result: ENGLAND won by 157 runs.
Debuts: Australia – A. Cotter, P.A. McAlister.

Frequent interruptions by rain – there was no play at all on the third day and the fourth day's start was delayed until 4 pm – extended this comparatively low-scoring game into the sixth morning. Knight batted 260 minutes for the highest innings of the match. A spell of 5 for 12 by the inventor of the googly, Bosanquet, enabled England to regain the Ashes.

ENGLAND

P.F. Warner*	b Noble	0	(9) not out		31
T.W. Hayward	c McAlister b Trumble	18	lbw b Trumble		52
J.T. Tyldesley	c Gregory b Noble	16	(4) b Cotter		5
R.E. Foster	c McAlister b Noble	19	(1) c Noble b Hopkins		27
A.E. Knight	not out	70	c McAlister b Cotter		9
L.C. Braund	c Trumble b Noble	39	c McLeod b Hopkins		19
G.H. Hirst	b Noble	25	c Kelly b McLeod		18
B.J.T. Bosanquet	b Hopkins	12	c Hill b McLeod		7
E.G. Arnold	lbw b Noble	0	(3) c Kelly b Noble		0
A.F.A. Lilley†	c Hopkins b Trumble	24	b McLeod		6
W. Rhodes	st Kelly b Noble	10	c McAlister b Cotter		29
Extras	(B 6, LB 7, W 2, NB 1)	16	(B 1, LB 6)		7
Total		**249**			**210**

AUSTRALIA

V.T. Trumper	b Braund	7	(4) lbw b Arnold		12
R.A. Duff	b Arnold	47	b Arnold		19
C. Hill	c Braund b Arnold	33	st Lilley b Bosanquet		26
P.A. McAlister	c Arnold b Rhodes	2	(1) b Hirst		1
A.J.Y. Hopkins	b Braund	9	(7) st Lilley b Bosanquet		0
C.E. McLeod	b Rhodes	18	(8) c Lilley b Bosanquet		6
J.J. Kelly†	c Foster b Arnold	5	(10) c Foster b Bosanquet		10
M.A. Noble*	not out	6	(5) not out		53
S.E. Gregory	c Foster b Rhodes	2	(6) lbw b Bosanquet		0
H. Trumble	c Lilley b Rhodes	0	(9) st Lilley b Bosanquet		0
A. Cotter	c Tyldesley b Arnold	0	b Hirst		34
Extras	(B 1, W 1)	2	(B 10)		10
Total		**131**			**171**

AUSTRALIA	O	M	R	W	O	M	R	W				
Cotter	14	1	44	0	17·3	3	41	3				
Noble	41·1	10	100	7	19	8	40	1				
Trumble	43	20	58	2	28	10	49	1				
Hopkins	8	3	22	1	14	5	31	2				
McLeod	8	5	9	0	20	5	42	3				

FALL OF WICKETS

		E	A	E	A
Wkt	*1st*	*1st*	*2nd*	*2nd*	
1st	4	28	49	7	
2nd	34	61	50	35	
3rd	42	72	57	59	
4th	66	97	73	76	
5th	155	101	106	76	
6th	185	116	120	76	
7th	207	124	138	86	
8th	208	126	141	90	
9th	237	130	155	114	
10th	249	131	210	171	

ENGLAND	O	M	R	W	O	M	R	W
Hirst	13	1	36	0	12·5	2	32	2
Braund	11	2	27	2	16	3	24	0
Rhodes	11	3	33	4	11	7	12	0
Arnold	15·3	5	28	4	12	3	42	2
Bosanquet	2	1	5	0	15	1	51	6

Umpires: P. Argall (4) and R.W. Crockett (8).

Close: 1st day – E(1) 207-7 (Knight 64); 2nd – A(1) 114-5 (McLeod 12, Kelly 4); 3rd – no play; 4th – E(2) 50-1 (Hayward 23, Arnold 0); 5th – E(2) 155-9 (Warner 6).

AUSTRALIA v ENGLAND 1903–04 (5th Test)

Played at Melbourne Cricket Ground on 5, 7, 8 March.
Toss: Australia.   Result: AUSTRALIA won by 218 runs.
Debuts: Australia – D.R.A. Gehrs.

Rain during the first night of the match delayed the next day's start until 4 pm and greatly affected the pitch – the 19-year-old fast bowler, Cotter, being particularly dangerous. Hugh Trumble took his second Test hat-trick in his final first-class match, dismissing Bosanquet, Warner and Lilley. Tonsillitis prevented Hayward from batting a second time. Noble became the second player after G. Giffen to complete the Test double for Australia.

AUSTRALIA

R.A. Duff	b Braund	9	(7) c Warner b Rhodes	31
V.T. Trumper	c and b Braund	88	(5) b Hirst	0
C. Hill	c Braund b Rhodes	16	(6) c Warner b Hirst	16
M.A. Noble*	c Foster b Arnold	29	(8) st Lilley b Rhodes	19
P.A. McAlister	st Lilley b Braund	36	(1) c Foster b Arnold	9
D.R.A. Gehrs	c and b Braund	3	(10) c and b Hirst	5
A.J.Y. Hopkins	c Knight b Braund	32	(9) not out	25
C.E. McLeod	c Rhodes b Braund	8	(2) c Bosanquet b Braund	0
H. Trumble	c Foster b Braund	6	(11) c Arnold b Hirst	0
J.J. Kelly†	not out	6	(3) c and b Arnold	24
A. Cotter	b Braund	6	(4) b Hirst	0
Extras	(B 4, LB 4)	8	(B 1, LB 3)	4
Total		**247**		**133**

ENGLAND

T.W. Hayward	b Noble	0	absent ill	–
W. Rhodes	c Gehrs b Cotter	3	(8) not out	16
E.G. Arnold	c Kelly b Noble	0	(10) c Duff b Trumble	19
P.F. Warner*	c McAlister b Cotter	1	(5) c and b Trumble	11
J.T. Tyldesley	c Gehrs b Noble	10	(3) c Hopkins b Cotter	15
R.E. Foster	b Cotter	18	(2) c Trumper b Trumble	30
G.H. Hirst	c Trumper b Cotter	0	(6) c McAlister b Trumble	1
L.C. Braund	c Hopkins b Noble	5	(1) c McAlister b Cotter	0
A.E. Knight	b Cotter	0	(4) c Kelly b Trumble	0
B.J.T. Bosanquet	c Noble b Cotter	16	(7) c Gehrs b Trumble	4
A.F.A. Lilley†	not out	6	(9) lbw b Trumble	0
Extras	(B 1, NB 1)	2	(B 1, LB 4)	5
Total		**61**		**101**

ENGLAND	O	M	R	W	O	M	R	W
Hirst	19	6	44	0	16·5	4	48	5
Braund	28·5	6	81	8	4	1	6	1
Rhodes	12	1	41	1	15	2	52	2
Arnold	18	4	46	1	8	3	23	2
Bosanquet	4	0	27	0				
AUSTRALIA								
Noble	15	8	19	4	6	2	19	0
Cotter	15·2	2	40	6	5	0	25	2
McLeod	1	1	0	0	5	0	24	0
Trumble					6·5	0	28	7

FALL OF WICKETS

	A	E	A	E
Wkt	1st	1st	2nd	2nd
1st	13	0	9	0
2nd	67	0	9	24
3rd	142	4	13	38
4th	144	5	13	47
5th	159	23	43	54
6th	218	26	49	61
7th	221	36	92	61
8th	231	36	115	61
9th	235	48	133	101
10th	247	61	133	–

Umpires: P. Argall (5) and R.W. Crockett (9).

Close: 1st day – E(1) 4-2 (Rhodes 3, Warner 1); 2nd – A(2) 13-3 (Kelly 4).

ENGLAND v AUSTRALIA 1905 (1st Test)

Played at Trent Bridge, Nottingham, on 29, 30, 31 May.
Toss: England.   Result: ENGLAND won by 213 runs.
Debuts: Nil.

MacLaren's hundred was the first in Tests at Nottingham and the fifth of his Test career – a record. Trumper retired hurt because of back strain at 23 for 1. Hill and Noble thus added 106 for the second wicket. Jackson dismissed Noble, Hill and Darling in one over: WO1WOW. For the second time in three Tests Bosanquet gained England a notable victory, his analysis of 8 for 107 being the best of his brief Test career. The two captains for this rubber were born on the same day: 21 November 1870.

ENGLAND

Batsman	Dismissal 1		Dismissal 2	
T.W. Hayward	b Cotter	5	c Darling b Armstrong	47
A.O. Jones	b Laver	4	(4) b Duff	30
J.T. Tyldesley	c Duff b Laver	56	c and b Duff	61
A.C. MacLaren	c Kelly b Laver	2	(2) c Duff b Laver	140
Hon. F.S. Jackson*	b Cotter	0	not out	82
B.J.T. Bosanquet	b Laver	27	b Cotter	6
J.R. Gunn	b Cotter	8		
G.L. Jessop	b Laver	0		
A.F.A. Lilley†	c and b Laver	37		
W. Rhodes	c Noble b Laver	29	(7) not out	39
E.G. Arnold	not out	2		
Extras	(B 21, LB 5)	26	(B 11, LB 9, W 1)	21
Total		**196**	(5 wickets declared)	**426**

AUSTRALIA

Batsman	Dismissal 1		Dismissal 2	
R.A. Duff	c Hayward b Gunn	1	c and b Bosanquet	25
V.T. Trumper	retired hurt	13	absent hurt	–
C. Hill	b Jackson	54	(5) c and b Bosanquet	8
M.A. Noble	c Lilley b Jackson	50	(3) st Lilley b Bosanquet	7
W.W. Armstrong	st Lilley b Rhodes	27	(4) c Jackson b Bosanquet	6
J. Darling*	c Bosanquet b Jackson	0	(2) b Bosanquet	40
A. Cotter	c and b Jessop	45	b Rhodes	18
S.E. Gregory	c Jones b Jackson	2	(6) c Arnold b Bosanquet	51
C.E. McLeod	b Arnold	4	lbw b Bosanquet	13
F. Laver	c Jones b Jackson	5	(8) st Lilley b Bosanquet	5
J.J. Kelly†	not out	1	(10) not out	6
Extras	(B 16, LB 2, W 1)	19	(B 4, LB 3, L 2)	9
Total		**221**		**188**

AUSTRALIA	O	M	R	W	O	M	R	W
Cotter	23	2	64	3	17	1	59	1
Laver	31·3	14	64	7	34	7	121	1
McLeod	8	2	19	0	28	9	84	0
Armstrong	6	3	4	0	52	24	67	1
Noble	3	0	19	0	7	1	31	0
Duff					15	2	43	2
ENGLAND								
Arnold	11	2	39	1	4	2	7	0
Gunn	6	2	27	1				
Jessop	7	2	18	1	1	0	1	0
Bosanquet	7	0	29	0	32·4	2	107	8
Rhodes	18	6	37	1	30	8	58	1
Jackson	14·5	2	52	5	5	3	6	0

FALL OF WICKETS

	E	A	E	A
Wkt	1st	1st	2nd	2nd
1st	6	1	145	62
2nd	24	129	222	75
3rd	40	130	276	82
4th	49	130	301	93
5th	98	200	313	100
6th	119	204	–	139
7th	119	209	–	144
8th	139	216	–	175
9th	187	221	–	188
10th	196	–	–	–

Umpires: J. Carlin (1) and J. Phillips (21).

Close: 1st day – A(1) 158-4 (Armstrong 20, Cotter 6); 2nd – E(2) 318-5 (Jackson 19, Rhodes 2).

ENGLAND v AUSTRALIA 1905 (2nd Test)

Played at Lord's, London, on 15, 16, 17 (*no play*) June.
Toss: England.   Result: MATCH DRAWN.
Debuts: Nil.

Rain, which had accounted for the last two days of the 1902 Lord's Test, took its tally at Headquarters to three days out of the last five in Test matches. Ten days of rain preceded this match and thunderstorms occurred each night during it.

ENGLAND

A.C. MacLaren	b Hopkins	56	b Armstrong	79
T.W. Hayward	lbw b Duff	16	c Laver b McLeod	8
J.T. Tyldesley	c Laver b Armstrong	43	b Noble	12
C.B. Fry	c Kelly b Hopkins	73	not out	36
Hon. F.S. Jackson*	c Armstrong b Laver	29	b Armstrong	0
A.O. Jones	b Laver	1	c Trumper b Armstrong	5
B.J.T. Bosanquet	c and b Armstrong	6	not out	4
W. Rhodes	b Hopkins	15		
A.F.A. Lilley†	lbw b McLeod	0		
S.Haigh	b Laver	14		
E.G. Arnold	not out	7		
Extras	(B 20, LB 2)	22	(B 2, LB 4, NB 1)	7
Total		**282**	(5 wickets)	**151**

AUSTRALIA

V.T. Trumper	b Jackson	31
R.A. Duff	c Lilley b Rhodes	27
C. Hill	c Bosanquet b Jackson	7
M.A. Noble	c Fry b Jackson	7
W.W. Armstrong	lbw b Jackson	33
J. Darling*	c Haigh b Arnold	41
S.E. Gregory	c Jones b Rhodes	5
A.J.Y. Hopkins	b Haigh	16
C.E. McLeod	b Haigh	0
F. Laver	not out	4
J.J. Kelly†	lbw b Rhodes	2
Extras	(B 3, LB 5)	8
Total		**181**

AUSTRALIA	O	M	R	W	O	M	R	W
McLeod	20	7	40	1	15	5	33	1
Laver	34	8	64	3	10	4	39	0
Armstrong	30	11	41	2	10	2	30	3
Noble	34	13	61	0	13	2	31	1
Duff	7	4	14	1				
Hopkins	15	4	40	3	2	0	11	0
ENGLAND								
Haigh	12	3	40	2				
Rhodes	16·1	1	70	3				
Jackson	15	0	50	4				
Arnold	7	3	13	1				

FALL OF WICKETS

Wkt	E 1st	A 1st	E 2nd
1st	59	57	18
2nd	97	73	63
3rd	149	73	136
4th	208	95	136
5th	210	131	146
6th	227	138	–
7th	257	171	–
8th	258	175	–
9th	258	175	–
10th	282	181	–

Umpires: J. Phillips (22) and W. Richards (3).

Close: 1st day – E(1) 258-8 (Lilley 0); 2nd – E(2) 151-5 (Fry 36, Bosanquet 4).

ENGLAND v AUSTRALIA 1905 (3rd Test)

Played at Headingley, Leeds, on 3, 4, 5 July.
Toss: England.   Result: MATCH DRAWN.
Debuts: England – D. Denton, A. Warren.

Jackson batted 268 minutes for his highest score in Tests. The fourth of his five centuries for England, it was also the first in any Test at Headingley. Warren took five wickets in the first innings of his only Test match and went on to dismiss Trumper cheaply a second time. Tyldesley's second hundred against Australia required considerable improvisation against the leg-theory of Armstrong and off-theory of McLeod.

ENGLAND

T.W. Hayward	b McLeod	26	c Hopkins b Armstrong	60
C.B. Fry	c Noble b McLeod	32	c Kelly b Armstrong	30
J.T. Tyldesley	b Laver	0	st Kelly b Armstrong	100
D. Denton	c Duff b McLeod	0	c Hill b Armstrong	12
Hon. F.S. Jackson*	not out	144	c Duff b Armstrong	17
G.H. Hirst	c Trumper b Laver	35	not out	40
B.J.T. Bosanquet	b Duff	20	not out	22
A.F.A. Lilley†	b Noble	11		
S. Haigh	c Noble b Armstrong	11		
A. Warren	run out	7		
C. Blythe	b Armstrong	0		
Extras	(B 10, LB 1, W 2, NB 2)	15	(B 1, LB 6, W 6, NB 1)	14
Total		**301**	(5 wickets declared)	**295**

AUSTRALIA

V.T. Trumper	b Warren	8	c Hirst b Warren	0
R.A. Duff	c Lilley b Blythe	48	b Hirst	17
C Hill	c and b Hirst	7	c Warren b Haigh	33
M.A. Noble	c Hayward b Warren	2	st Lilley b Bosanquet	62
W.W. Armstrong	c Hayward b Warren	66	lbw b Blythe	32
J. Darling*	c Bosanquet b Warren	5	b Blythe	2
A.J.Y. Hopkins	c Lilley b Jackson	36	b Blythe	17
S.E. Gregory	run out	4	not out	32
C.E. McLeod	b Haigh	8	not out	10
J.J. Kelly†	not out	1		
F. Laver	b Warren	3		
Extras	(B 4, LB 1, W 2)	7	(B 11, W 6, NB 2)	19
Total		**195**	(7 wickets)	**224**

AUSTRALIA	O	M	R	W	O	M	R	W
Armstrong	26·3	6	44	2	51	14	122	5
Noble	23	6	59	1	20	3	68	0
Laver	29	10	61	2	10	4	29	0
McLeod	37	13	88	3	23	6	62	0
Hopkins	9	4	21	0				
Duff	4	1	13	1				
ENGLAND								
Hirst	7	1	37	1	10	2	26	1
Warren	19·2	5	57	5	20	4	56	1
Blythe	8	0	36	1	24	11	41	3
Jackson	4	0	10	1	8	2	10	0
Haigh	11	5	19	1	14	4	36	1
Bosanquet	4	0	29	0	15	1	36	1

FALL OF WICKETS

	E	A	E	A
Wkt	*1st*	*1st*	*2nd*	*2nd*
1st	51	26	80	0
2nd	54	33	126	36
3rd	57	36	170	64
4th	64	96	202	117
5th	133	105	258	121
6th	201	161	–	152
7th	232	166	–	199
8th	282	191	–	–
9th	301	191	–	–
10th	301	195	–	–

Umpires: J. Phillips (23) and V.A. Titchmarsh (3).

Close: 1st day – E(1) 301 all out; 2nd – E(2) 169-2 (Tyldesley 62, Denton 11).

ENGLAND v AUSTRALIA 1905 (4th Test)

Played at Old Trafford, Manchester, 24, 25, 26 July.
Toss: England.   Result: ENGLAND won by an innings and 80 runs.
Debuts: England – W. Brearley, R.H. Spooner.

Jackson hit his second hundred in successive Tests and became the first to score five Test hundreds in England. Apart from G. Boycott, he is the only batsman to score five hundreds against Australia in England. Under his captaincy England retained the Ashes before lunch on the last day.

ENGLAND

A.C. MacLaren	c Hill b McLeod	14
T.W. Hayward	c Gehrs b McLeod	82
J.T. Tyldesley	b Laver	24
C.B. Fry	b Armstrong	17
Hon. F.S. Jackson*	c Cotter b McLeod	113
R.H. Spooner	c and b McLeod	52
G.H. Hirst	c Laver b McLeod	25
E.G. Arnold	run out	25
W. Rhodes	not out	27
A.F.A. Lilley†	lbw b Noble	28
W. Brearley	c Darling b Noble	0
Extras	(B 17, LB 20, W 1, NB 1)	39
Total		**446**

AUSTRALIA

M.A. Noble	b Brearley	7	(4) c Rhodes b Brearley		10
V.T. Trumper	c Rhodes b Brearley	11	lbw b Rhodes		30
C. Hill	c Fry b Arnold	0	c sub (A.O. Jones) b Arnold		27
W.W. Armstrong	b Rhodes	29	(5) b Brearley		9
R.A. Duff	c MacLaren b Brearley	11	(1) c Spooner b Brearley		60
J. Darling*	c Tyldesley b Jackson	73	c Rhodes b Brearley		0
D.R.A. Gehrs	b Arnold	0	(8) c and b Rhodes		11
C.E. McLeod	b Brearley	6	(9) c Arnold b Rhodes		6
A. Cotter	c Fry b Jackson	11	(10) run out		0
F. Laver	b Rhodes	24	(11) not out		6
J.J. Kelly†	not out	16	(7) c Rhodes b Arnold		5
Extras	(B 9)	9	(B 4, NB 1)		5
Total		**197**			**169**

AUSTRALIA	O	M	R	W	O	M	R	W
Cotter	26	4	83	0				
McLeod	47	8	125	5				
Armstrong	48	14	93	1				
Laver	21	5	73	1				
Noble	15·5	3	33	2				
ENGLAND								
Hirst	2	0	12	0	7	2	19	0
Brearley	17	3	72	4	14	3	54	4
Arnold	14	2	53	2	15	5	35	2
Rhodes	5·5	1	25	2	11·3	3	36	3
Jackson	7	0	26	2	5	0	20	0

FALL OF WICKETS

	E	A	A
Wkt	1st	1st	2nd
1st	24	20	55
2nd	77	21	121
3rd	136	27	122
4th	176	41	133
5th	301	88	133
6th	347	93	146
7th	382	146	146
8th	387	146	158
9th	446	166	158
10th	446	197	169

Umpires: J. Carlin (2) and J.E. West (1).

Close: 1st day – E(1) 352-6 (Jackson 103, Arnold 0); 2nd – A(2) 113-1 (Duff 58, Hill 26).

ENGLAND v AUSTRALIA 1905 (5th Test)

Played at Kennington Oval, London, on 14, 15, 16 August.
Toss: England.   Result: MATCH DRAWN.
Debuts: Nil.

In his final Test, Jackson became the first captain to win every toss in a five-match rubber. Duff was the first of four batsmen (W.H. Ponsford, M. Leyland and R. Subba Row being the others) to score centuries on both their first and their last appearances in Tests between England and Australia. A.O. Jones was the first substitute to keep wicket in a Test and the first such to make a dismissal (Armstrong). Spooner kept wicket in the second innings and caught Trumper. When he dismissed Spooner, Noble became the second player after G. Giffen to complete the double of 1,000 runs and 100 wickets against England.

ENGLAND

A.C. MacLaren	c Laver b Cotter	6	(3) c Kelly b Armstrong		6
T.W. Hayward	hit wkt b Hopkins	59	lbw b Armstrong		2
J.T. Tyldesley	b Cotter	16	(4) not out		112
C.B. Fry	b Cotter	144	(5) c Armstrong b Noble		16
Hon. F.S. Jackson*	c Armstrong b Laver	76	(6) b Cotter		31
R.H. Spooner	b Cotter	0	(7) c sub (D.R.A. Gehrs) b Noble		79
G.H. Hirst	c Noble b Laver	5			
E.G. Arnold	c Trumper b Cotter	40	(1) b Cotter		0
W. Rhodes	b Cotter	36			
A.F.A. Lilley†	b Cotter	17			
W. Brearley	not out	11			
Extras	(B 11, LB 1, W 1, NB 7)	20	(B 4, LB 5, W 1, NB 5)		15
Total		**430**	(6 wickets declared)		**261**

AUSTRALIA

V.T. Trumper	b Brearley	4	c Spooner b Brearley		28
R.A. Duff	c and b Hirst	146	b Arnold		34
C. Hill	c Rhodes b Brearley	18	b Arnold		34
M.A. Noble	c MacLaren b Jackson	25	b Hirst		3
W.W. Armstrong	c sub (A.O. Jones) b Hirst	18	not out		32
J. Darling*	b Hirst	57	not out		12
A.J.Y. Hopkins	b Brearley	1	(2) run out		10
C.E. McLeod	b Brearley	0			
J.J. Kelly†	run out	42			
A. Cotter	c Fry b Brearley	6			
F. Laver	not out	15			
Extras	(B 17, LB 9, W 1, NB 4)	31	(B 4, LB 1)		5
Total		**363**	(4 wickets)		**124**

AUSTRALIA	O	M	R	W	O	M	R	W
Cotter	40	4	148	7	21	2	73	2
Noble	18	6	51	0	14·3	3	56	2
Armstrong	27	7	76	0	30	13	61	2
McLeod	13	2	47	0	11	2	27	0
Laver	17	3	41	2	3	0	18	0
Hopkins	11	2	32	1	1	0	11	0
Duff	4	1	15	0				
ENGLAND								
Hirst	23	6	86	3	9	2	32	1
Brearley	31·1	8	110	5	11	2	41	1
Arnold	9	0	50	0	9	2	17	1
Rhodes	21	2	59	0	8	0	29	0
Jackson	9	1	27	1				

FALL OF WICKETS

	E	A	E	A
Wkt	1st	1st	2nd	2nd
1st	12	5	0	27
2nd	32	44	8	49
3rd	132	159	13	58
4th	283	214	48	92
5th	291	237	103	–
6th	306	247	261	–
7th	322	265	–	–
8th	394	293	–	–
9th	418	304	–	–
10th	430	363	–	–

Umpires: J. Phillips (24) and W.A.J. West (3).

Close: 1st day – E(1) 381-7 (Arnold 25, Rhodes 32); 2nd – E(2) 0-1 (Hayward 0).

SOUTH AFRICA v ENGLAND 1905–06 (1st Test)

Played at Old Wanderers, Johannesburg, on 2, 3, 4 January.
Toss: England.   Result: SOUTH AFRICA won by one wicket.
Debuts: South Africa – G.A. Faulkner, R.O. Schwarz, P.W. Sherwell, S.J. Snooke, A.E.E. Vogler,
  G.C. White; England – J.N. Crawford, F.L. Fane, E.G. Hayes, W.S. Lees.

South Africa's first Test victory came in their twelfth match. They defeated the first official MCC team by a
margin which has occurred only six times in Tests. Nourse, who shared the decisive last-wicket stand with
Sherwell, made the highest score for South Africa on debut against England. That unbroken partnership of 48
is the highest for the tenth wicket to win a Test. South Africa's team contained eight members of the Transvaal
side that had defeated the MCC by 60 runs in their previous match.

ENGLAND

P.F. Warner*	c Snooke b Schwarz	6	b Vogler	51
F.L. Fane	c Schwarz b Faulkner	1	b Snooke	3
D. Denton	c Faulkner b Schwarz	0	b Faulkner	34
E.G. Wynyard	st Sherwell b Schwarz	29	b Vogler	0
E.G. Hayes	c and b Vogler	20	c Schwarz b Snooke	3
J.N. Crawford	c Nourse b Sinclair	44	b Nourse	43
A.E. Relf	b White	8	c Sherwell b Faulkner	17
S. Haigh	b Faulkner	23	lbw b Nourse	0
J.H. Board†	not out	9	lbw b Faulkner	7
W.S. Lees	st Sherwell b White	11	not out	1
C. Blythe	b Sinclair	17	b Faulkner	0
Extras	(B 6, LB 9, NB 1)	16	(B 23, LB 8)	31
Total		**184**		**190**

SOUTH AFRICA

L.J. Tancred	c Board b Lees	3	c Warner b Blythe	10
W.A. Shalders	c Haigh b Blythe	4	run out	38
C.M.H. Hathorn	b Lees	5	c Crawford b Lees	4
G.C. White	c Blythe b Lees	8	b Relf	81
S.J. Snooke	c Board b Blythe	19	lbw b Lees	9
J.H. Sinclair	c and b Lees	0	c Fane b Lees	5
G.A. Faulkner	b Blythe	4	run out	6
A.W. Nourse	not out	18	not out	93
A.E.E. Vogler	b Crawford	14	b Hayes	2
R.O. Schwarz	c Relf b Crawford	5	c and b Relf	2
P.W. Sherwell*†	lbw b Lees	1	not out	22
Extras	(B 9, LB 1)	10	(B 6, LB 2, NB 7)	15
Total		**91**	(9 wickets)	**287**

SOUTH AFRICA	O	M	R	W	O	M	R	W	FALL OF WICKETS				
										E	SA	E	SA
Schwarz	21	5	72	3	8	1	24	0	*Wkt*	*1st*	*1st*	*2nd*	*2nd*
Faulkner	22	7	35	2	12·5	5	26	4	1st	6	5	3	11
Sinclair	11	1	36	2	5	1	25	0	2nd	6	11	55	22
Vogler	3	0	10	1	11	3	24	2	3rd	15	13	56	68
White	5	1	13	2	4	0	15	0	4th	53	35	73	81
Nourse	1	0	2	0	6	4	7	2	5th	76	39	113	89
Snooke					12	4	38	2	6th	97	43	166	105
ENGLAND									7th	145	44	174	226
Lees	23·1	10	34	5	33	10	74	3	8th	147	62	185	230
Blythe	16	5	33	3	28	12	50	1	9th	159	82	190	239
Crawford	7	1	14	2	17	4	49	0	10th	184	91	190	–
Haigh					1	0	9	0					
Relf					21·5	7	47	2					
Wynyard					3	0	15	0					
Hayes					9	1	28	1					

Umpires: J. Phillips (25) and F.E. Smith (2).

Close: 1st day – SA(1) 71-8 (Nourse 2, Schwarz 3); 2nd – SA(2) 68-2 (Shalders 38, White 16).

SOUTH AFRICA v ENGLAND 1905–06 (2nd Test)

Played at Old Wanderers, Johannesburg, on 6, 7, 8 March.
Toss: England.   Result: SOUTH AFRICA won by nine wickets.
Debuts: England – L.J. Moon.

South Africa's second Test victory is still their largest by a wickets margin against England.

ENGLAND

P.F. Warner*	c White b Snooke	2	b Snooke		0
J.N. Crawford	c Faulkner b Schwarz	23	c Sherwell b Snooke		6
D. Denton	c and b Sinclair	1	c Sherwell b Snooke		4
F.L. Fane	c and b Faulkner	8	b Sinclair		65
L.J. Moon	lbw b Sinclair	30	c Sherwell b Sinclair		0
E.G. Wynyard	b Vogler	0	c and b Vogler		30
A.E. Relf	c White b Faulkner	24	c White b Schwarz		37
S. Haigh	c Hathorn b Faulkner	3	(10) not out		0
J.H. Board†	b Sinclair	0	b Schwarz		2
W.S. Lees	not out	25	(8) b Schwarz		4
C. Blythe	b Schwarz	12	b Schwarz		0
Extras	(B 10, LB 5, NB 5)	20	(B 12)		12
Total		**148**			**160**

SOUTH AFRICA

L.J. Tancred	b Crawford	28	not out	18
W.A. Shalders	b Crawford	37	c Board b Lees	0
G.C. White	b Relf	21	not out	9
A.W. Nourse	c Denton b Haigh	21		
C.M.H. Hathorn	run out	17		
G.A. Faulkner	c Denton b Lees	17		
J.H. Sinclair	st Board b Blythe	66		
S.J. Snooke	b Haigh	24		
R.O. Schwarz	b Haigh	2		
P.W. Sherwell*†	not out	20		
A.E.E. Vogler	b Haigh	6		
Extras	(B 9, LB 8, NB 1)	18	(B 2, LB 4, NB 1)	7
Total		**277**	(1 wicket)	**34**

SOUTH AFRICA	O	M	R	W	O	M	R	W
Snooke	7	2	15	1	15	3	40	3
Sinclair	25	11	35	3	22	6	36	2
Faulkner	17	6	38	3	7	0	19	0
Schwarz	5·2	0	16	2	14·5	3	30	4
Vogler	9	3	18	1	6	2	7	1
Nourse	3	1	6	0	6	1	16	0
ENGLAND								
Lees	26	13	47	1	4	0	16	1
Blythe	25	6	66	1	4·5	3	7	0
Haigh	19·2	4	64	4				
Relf	18	4	36	1				
Crawford	11	1	44	2	2	1	4	0
Wynyard	1	0	2	0				

FALL OF WICKETS

	E	SA	E	SA
Wkt	*1st*	*1st*	*2nd*	*2nd*
1st	2	70	0	0
2nd	13	71	10	–
3rd	28	100	19	–
4th	62	131	25	–
5th	66	133	97	–
6th	102	175	138	–
7th	109	232	151	–
8th	109	242	157	–
9th	111	252	160	–
10th	148	277	160	–

Umpires: J. Phillips (26) and F.E. Smith (3).

Close: 1st day – SA(1) 4-0 (Tancred 0, Shalders 4); 2nd – SA(1) 277 all out.

SOUTH AFRICA v ENGLAND 1905–06 (3rd Test)

Played at Old Wanderers, Johannesburg, on 10, 12, 13, 14 March.
Toss: South Africa.   Result: SOUTH AFRICA won by 243 runs.
Debuts: England – J.C. Hartley.

The third of South Africa's victories, gained in successive matches, remains their largest by a runs margin against England. 'Tip' Snooke was the first South African bowler to take eight wickets in a Test innings – no other did so until 1956-57 – and twelve in a Test match. All eleven batsmen reached double figures in South Africa's first innings. Hathorn and White broke Sinclair's monopoly on centuries for South Africa.

SOUTH AFRICA

L.J. Tancred	c Hartley b Blythe	13	c Fane b Lees		73
W.A. Shalders	c Denton b Lees	13	c Hartley b Blythe		11
G.C. White	c Relf b Lees	46	c Crawford b Lees		147
A.W. Nourse	c Moon b Relf	61	c Denton b Haigh		55
C.M.H. Hathorn	c Haigh b Hartley	102			
J.H. Sinclair	b Blythe	28	(5) c Denton b Lees		48
G.A. Faulkner	c and b Lees	19	not out		0
S.J. Snooke	b Lees	29			
P.W. Sherwell*†	b Lees	11			
R.O. Schwarz	c Haigh b Lees	10			
A.E.E. Vogler	not out	28	(6) not out		4
Extras	(B 10, LB 9, NB 6)	25	(B 9, LB 2)		11
Total		**385**	(5 wickets declared)		**349**

ENGLAND

P.F. Warner*	b Schwarz	19	b Schwarz		2
J.N. Crawford	b Schwarz	4	(7) c White b Sinclair		34
D. Denton	b Schwarz	4	(6) c Sherwell b Snooke		61
F.L. Fane	c Vogler b Snooke	143	(5) c Sherwell b Snooke		7
L.J. Moon†	b Schwarz	36	(8) b Snooke		15
E.G. Hayes	c Snooke b Sinclair	35	(9) not out		11
A.E. Relf	c Schwarz b Snooke	33	(3) c Schwarz b Snooke		18
J.C. Hartley	b Shalders	0	(2) c Vogler b Snooke		9
S. Haigh	c Sherwell b Snooke	0	(4) c Sherwell b Snooke		16
W.S. Lees	c Sherwell b Snooke	6	c Vogler b Snooke		3
C. Blythe	not out	3	c Shalders b Snooke		7
Extras	(B 3, LB 3, W 2, NB 4)	12	(B 8, LB 3, NB 2)		13
Total		**295**			**196**

ENGLAND	O	M	R	W	O	M	R	W
Lees	31·3	7	78	6	26	6	85	3
Blythe	26	8	72	2	31	6	96	1
Haigh	15	2	50	0	24	5	72	1
Relf	14	1	47	1	9	0	37	0
Crawford	13	1	51	0	4	0	17	0
Hartley	19	1	62	1	7	1	31	0
SOUTH AFRICA								
Snooke	21·2	1	57	4	31·4	8	70	8
Schwarz	20	2	67	4	15	4	31	1
Vogler	19	8	33	0	7	5	9	0
Faulkner	15	3	46	0	8	0	21	0
Nourse	4	2	11	0				
Sinclair	12	0	61	1	17	3	52	1
White	2	0	2	0				
Shalders	8	3	6	1				

FALL OF WICKETS

Wkt	SA 1st	E 1st	SA 2nd	E 2nd
1st	27	7	24	3
2nd	29	16	134	14
3rd	126	51	254	34
4th	157	135	341	48
5th	209	223	345	75
6th	253	280	–	139
7th	325	284	–	171
8th	339	285	–	171
9th	349	288	–	182
10th	385	295	–	196

Umpires: J. Phillips (27) and F.E. Smith (4).

Close: 1st day – SA(1) 338-7 (Snooke 28, Sherwell 4); 2nd – E(1) 295 all out; 3rd – E(2) 14-2 (Relf 2, Haigh 0).

SOUTH AFRICA v ENGLAND 1905–06 (4th Test)

Played at Newlands, Cape Town, on 24, 26, 27 March.
Toss: South Africa.   Result: ENGLAND won by four wickets.
Debuts: Nil.

England gained their lone success of the rubber. Blythe, given the new ball throughout this matting-based series, returned his best match analysis in a Test in South Africa. In the second innings White scored 73 of the 97 runs added while he was at the wicket.

SOUTH AFRICA

L.J. Tancred	lbw b Blythe	11	c Haigh b Blythe	10
W.A. Shalders	lbw b Blythe	16	c Blythe b Crawford	0
G.C. White	c Board b Lees	41	b Lees	73
A.W. Nourse	c Hayes b Blythe	2	c Crawford b Blythe	3
C.M.H. Hathorn	b Blythe	3	b Lees	10
J.H. Sinclair	c Board b Blythe	0	b Lees	1
G.A. Faulkner	b Blythe	34	b Blythe	4
S.J. Snooke	b Crawford	44	b Blythe	5
R.O. Schwarz	c Moon b Relf	33	c Haigh b Lees	8
A.E.E. Vogler	b Haigh	9	(11) not out	12
P.W. Sherwell*†	not out	0	(10) b Blythe	9
Extras	(B 20, LB 3, W 2)	25	(LB 3)	3
Total		**218**		**138**

ENGLAND

J.H. Board†	b Snooke	0	(8) not out	14
A.E. Relf	lbw b Faulkner	28	(6) b Vogler	18
C. Blythe	b Faulkner	27		
F.L. Fane	b Sinclair	9	not out	66
D. Denton	c Vogler b Snooke	34	(3) b Snooke	20
P.F. Warner*	c Snooke b Faulkner	1	(1) b Sinclair	4
J.N. Crawford	not out	36	(2) b Sinclair	4
L.J. Moon	b Sinclair	33	(5) lbw b Faulkner	28
E.G. Hayes	lbw b Sinclair	0	(7) b Sinclair	0
S. Haigh	c Nourse b Sinclair	0		
W.S. Lees	c Hathorn b Faulkner	5		
Extras	(B 14, LB 6, W 1, NB 4)	25	(B 3, LB 2, NB 1)	6
Total		**198**	(6 wickets)	**160**

ENGLAND	O	M	R	W	O	M	R	W		FALL OF WICKETS			
Lees	27	12	42	1	14	5	27	4		SA	E	SA	E
Blythe	32	13	68	6	28·5	10	50	5	*Wkt*	*1st*	*1st*	*2nd*	*2nd*
Crawford	13·3	3	28	1	15	5	46	1	1st	28	0	0	5
Haigh	19	8	38	1	2	0	12	0	2nd	34	59	28	20
Relf	6	2	17	1					3rd	40	70	40	34
									4th	44	98	94	100
SOUTH AFRICA									5th	44	101	97	131
Snooke	18	5	41	2	19	6	41	1	6th	116	137	102	134
Schwarz	12	2	34	0	2	0	6	0	7th	136	193	106	–
Sinclair	27	10	41	4	26·1	5	67	3	8th	199	193	115	–
Faulkner	25·5	11	49	4	5	0	21	1	9th	218	193	121	–
Vogler	5	3	7	0	6	1	13	1	10th	218	198	138	–
Nourse	2	1	1	0	1	0	6	0					

Umpires: F. Hearne (5) and J. Phillips (28).

Close: 1st day – E(1) 7-1 (Relf 0, Blythe 6); 2nd – SA(2) 97-5 (Sinclair 1).

SOUTH AFRICA v ENGLAND 1905–06 (5th Test)

Played at Newlands, Cape Town, on 30, 31 March, 2 April.
Toss: England.   Result: SOUTH AFRICA won by an innings and 16 runs.
Debuts: Nil.

South Africa's selectors had named the side for all five matches at the start of the series. On only one other occasion (England in Australia in 1884-85) has a team remained unchanged throughout a five-match rubber. Vogler's 62 not out remained the highest score by a number eleven batsman until 1972-73 when R.O. Collinge scored 68 not out (*Test No. 713*). His partnership of 94 in 75 minutes with Sherwell was South Africa's record for the tenth wicket until 1929 (*Test No. 183*). The Springboks gained their only innings victory against England in 102 Tests between 1888-89 and 1965.

ENGLAND

J.N. Crawford	b Sinclair	74		b Snooke	13
P.F. Warner*	b Schwarz	0	(7)	c Snooke b Schwarz	4
D. Denton	b Snooke	4		b Vogler	10
F.L. Fane	b Vogler	30		b Nourse	10
L.J. Moon	lbw b Vogler	7	(2)	lbw b Sinclair	33
A.E. Relf	c Faulkner b Sinclair	25	(5)	b Nourse	21
J.H. Board†	c Nourse b Snooke	20	(6)	b Nourse	4
J.C. Hartley	run out	6	(9)	c Vogler b Schwarz	0
W.S. Lees	not out	9	(8)	b Nourse	2
S. Haigh	c Tancred b Sinclair	1		c Nourse b Schwarz	2
C. Blythe	b Sinclair	1		not out	11
Extras	(B 6, NB 4)	10		(B 14, LB 2, W 2, NB 2)	20
Total		**187**			**130**

SOUTH AFRICA

L.J. Tancred	c Moon b Crawford	26
W.A. Shalders	c and b Crawford	21
G.C. White	c Crawford b Lees	11
A.W. Nourse	c Relf b Crawford	36
C.M.H. Hathorn	c Board b Blythe	1
J.H. Sinclair	b Blythe	12
G.A. Faulkner	c Moon b Relf	45
S.J. Snooke	lbw b Relf	60
R.O. Schwarz	c Crawford b Relf	15
P.W. Sherwell*†	c Blythe b Lees	30
A.E.E. Vogler	not out	62
Extras	(B 12, LB 1, NB 1)	14
Total		**333**

SOUTH AFRICA	O	M	R	W	O	M	R	W
Snooke	12	4	41	2	9	3	26	1
Schwarz	7	2	14	1	8·2	2	16	3
Sinclair	21·2	8	45	4	11	4	20	1
Vogler	19	6	63	2	8	3	17	1
Faulkner	4	1	11	0	3	1	6	0
Nourse	2	1	3	0	10	3	25	4
ENGLAND								
Lees	24·4	6	64	2				
Blythe	35	11	106	2				
Crawford	18	3	69	3				
Haigh	6	1	18	0				
Hartley	6	0	22	0				
Relf	21	6	40	3				

FALL OF WICKETS

Wkt	E 1st	SA 1st	E 2nd
1st	0	45	33
2nd	5	52	62
3rd	91	65	64
4th	108	66	90
5th	137	87	94
6th	160	140	103
7th	176	182	105
8th	176	226	106
9th	181	239	109
10th	187	333	130

Umpires: F. Hearne (6) and J. Phillips (29).

Close: 1st day – SA(1) 87-4 (Nourse 12, Sinclair 12); 2nd – E(2) 103-5 (Relf 21, Warner 1).

ENGLAND v SOUTH AFRICA 1907 (1st Test)

Played at Lord's, London, on 1, 2, 3 (*no play*) July.
Toss: England.   Result: MATCH DRAWN.
Debuts: Nil.

On their first Test appearance abroad, South Africa lost their last six first-innings wickets in the course of 24 balls. Jessop and Braund scored 145 for the sixth wicket in 75 minutes. Sherwell, the number eleven of 1905-06, averted defeat and needed only 90 minutes to reach the first Test century by a wicket-keeper in England. H. Wood, in *Test No. 38*, was the only earlier wicket-keeper to score a hundred. Sherwell's century, like that of Wood, was his first in first-class cricket.

ENGLAND

C.B Fry	b Vogler	33		
T.W. Hayward	st Sherwell b Vogler	21		
J.T. Tyldesley	b Vogler	52		
R.E. Foster*	st Sherwell b Vogler	8		
L.C. Braund	c Kotze b Faulkner	104		
G.H. Hirst	b Vogler	7		
G.L. Jessop	c Faulkner b Vogler	93		
J.N. Crawford	c Sherwell b Schwarz	22		
E.G. Arnold	b Schwarz	4		
A.F.A. Lilley†	c Nourse b Vogler	48		
C. Blythe	not out	4		
Extras	(B 24, LB 6, W 2)	32		
Total		**428**		

SOUTH AFRICA

W.A. Shalders	c Lilley b Arnold	2	b Hirst	0
P.W. Sherwell*†	run out	6	b Blythe	115
C.M.H. Hathorn	c Foster b Hirst	6	c Fry b Blythe	30
A.W. Nourse	b Blythe	62	not out	11
G.A. Faulkner	c Jessop b Braund	44	not out	12
S.J. Snooke	lbw b Blythe	5		
G.C. White	b Arnold	0		
J.H. Sinclair	b Arnold	0		
R.O. Schwarz	not out	0		
A.E.E. Vogler	c Lilley b Arnold	3		
J.J. Kotze	b Arnold	0		
Extras	(B 9, LB 2, W 1)	12	(B 15, LB 2)	17
Total		**140**	(3 wickets)	**185**

SOUTH AFRICA	O	M	R	W	O	M	R	W		FALL OF WICKETS		
Kotze	12	2	43	0						E	SA	SA
Schwarz	34	7	90	2					*Wkt*	*1st*	*1st*	*2nd*
Vogler	47·2	12	128	7					1st	54	8	1
White	15	2	52	0					2nd	55	8	140
Nourse	1	0	2	0					3rd	79	18	153
Faulkner	12	1	59	1					4th	140	116	–
Sinclair	6	1	22	0					5th	158	134	–
ENGLAND									6th	303	135	–
Hirst	18	7	35	1	16	8	26	1	7th	335	135	–
Arnold	22	7	37	5	13	2	41	0	8th	347	137	–
Jessop	2	0	8	0					9th	401	140	–
Crawford	8	1	20	0	4	0	19	0	10th	428	140	–
Blythe	8	3	18	2	21	5	56	2				
Braund	7	4	10	1	4	0	26	0				

Umpires: A. Millward (1) and A.A. White (5).

Close: 1st day – E(1) 428 all out; 2nd – SA(2) 185-3 (Nourse 11, Faulkner 12).

ENGLAND v SOUTH AFRICA 1907 (2nd Test)

Played at Headingley, Leeds, on 29, 30, 31 July.
Toss: England.   Result: ENGLAND won by 53 runs.
Debuts: England – N.A. Knox.

Blythe is the only bowler to take 15 South African wickets in a Test in England. His match analysis of 15 for 99 remains the record for a Test at Leeds. Fry played a most courageous and masterly innings on a rain-affected pitch and in murky light to reach the only half-century of the match.

ENGLAND

T.W. Hayward	st Sherwell b Faulkner	24	st Sherwell b Vogler		15
C.B. Fry	b Vogler	2	lbw b White		54
J.T. Tyldesley	b Faulkner	12	c Snooke b Schwarz		30
R.E. Foster*	b Sinclair	0	lbw b Faulkner		22
L.C. Braund	lbw b Faulkner	1	c Schwarz b White		0
G.H. Hirst	c Hathorn b Sinclair	17	b White		2
G.L. Jessop	c Sherwell b Faulkner	0	c Hathorn b Faulkner		10
E.G. Arnold	b Faulkner	0	c Schwarz b Faulkner		12
A.F.A. Lilley†	c Schwarz b Faulkner	3	lbw b White		0
C. Blythe	not out	5	not out		4
N.A. Knox	c Faulkner b Sinclair	8	run out		5
Extras	(B 1, LB 2, NB 1)	4	(B 7, LB 1)		8
Total		76			162

SOUTH AFRICA

L.J. Tancred	st Lilley b Blythe	0		run out	0
P.W. Sherwell*†	lbw b Blythe	26		c Foster b Blythe	1
C.M.H. Hathorn	c Lilley b Hirst	0		b Arnold	7
A.W. Nourse	c Arnold b Blythe	18		lbw b Blythe	2
G.C. White	c Hirst b Blythe	3		c Arnold b Blythe	7
J.H. Sinclair	st Lilley b Blythe	2	(7)	c Braund b Blythe	15
G.A. Faulkner	c Braund b Blythe	6	(6)	c Foster b Blythe	11
S.J. Snooke	c Lilley b Knox	13		c Hirst b Blythe	14
W.A. Shalders	c Fry b Blythe	21		lbw b Hirst	5
A.E.E. Vogler	c Hayward b Blythe	11		c Tyldesley b Blythe	9
R.O. Schwarz	not out	5		not out	0
Extras	(B 3, LB 1, NB 1)	5		(B 3, NB 1)	4
Total		110			75

SOUTH AFRICA	O	M	R	W	O	M	R	W
Vogler	8	3	14	1	4	0	18	1
Schwarz	7	0	18	0	5·4	0	18	1
Faulkner	11	4	17	6	20	3	58	3
Sinclair	10·3	2	23	3	4	0	13	0
White					16	3	47	4
ENGLAND								
Hirst	9	3	22	1	9	2	21	1
Blythe	15·5	1	59	8	22·4	9	40	7
Arnold	4	1	11	0	13	7	10	1
Knox	3	0	13	1				

FALL OF WICKETS

	E	SA	E	SA
Wkt	1st	1st	2nd	2nd
1st	9	6	37	0
2nd	41	9	100	3
3rd	42	34	106	10
4th	42	47	107	16
5th	53	49	115	18
6th	53	56	126	38
7th	57	59	151	56
8th	63	73	152	66
9th	63	102	154	75
10th	76	110	162	75

Umpires: J. Carlin (3) and J. Moss (2).

Close: 1st day – E(2) 25-0 (Hayward 13, Fry 12); 2nd – E(2) 110-4 (Foster 5, Hirst 1).

ENGLAND v SOUTH AFRICA 1907 (3rd Test)

Played at Kennington Oval, London, on 19, 20, 21 August.
Toss: England.   Result: MATCH DRAWN.
Debuts: South Africa – S.D. Snooke.

Hayward was out to the first ball of the match and remains the only England batsman to suffer this fate in a home Test. Attempting to score 256 in just over 150 minutes, South Africa reached 100 in an hour before the dismissal of S.J. Snooke and fading light compelled more defensive measures. This rubber was dominated by spin bowling with Blythe (slow left-arm) taking 26 wickets for England, while the leg-spin and googly quartet of Faulkner (12), Schwarz (9), Vogler (15) and White (4) accounted for all but nine of the wickets that fell to South African bowlers.

ENGLAND

T.W. Hayward	lbw b Vogler	0	c Sherwell b Nourse	3
C.B. Fry	c and b Faulkner	129	b Vogler	3
J.T. Tyldesley	b Faulkner	8	c White b Nourse	11
R.E. Foster*	lbw b Vogler	51	c and b S.J. Snooke	35
L.C. Braund	b Schwarz	18	c Schwarz b Vogler	34
G.H. Hirst	c S.J. Snooke b Schwarz	4	(7) hit wkt b Schwarz	16
G.L. Jessop	c S.D. Snooke b Sinclair	2	(6) st Sherwell b Schwarz	11
J.N. Crawford	c S.D. Snooke b Schwarz	2	c Nourse b Vogler	2
A.F.A. Lilley†	b Nourse	42	not out	9
C. Blythe	b Nourse	10	b Schwarz	0
N.A. Knox	not out	8	b Vogler	3
Extras	(B 6, LB 12, W 1, NB 2)	21	(B 3, LB 6, NB 2)	11
Total		**295**		**138**

SOUTH AFRICA

P.W. Sherwell*†	b Blythe	6		
G.A. Faulkner	c and b Hirst	2	b Hirst	42
S.J. Snooke	c Jessop b Hirst	63	c Foster b Blythe	36
A.W. Nourse	c Lilley b Knox	34	(7) not out	0
J.H. Sinclair	c Crawford b Knox	22	(1) b Hirst	28
W.A. Shalders	c Jessop b Blythe	31	not out	24
A.E.E. Vogler	b Blythe	5	(5) b Blythe	19
R.O. Schwarz	c Blythe b Hirst	2		
G.C. White	st Lilley b Blythe	4	(4) b Hirst	1
C.M.H. Hathorn	not out	3		
S.D. Snooke	c Foster b Blythe	0		
Extras	(B 3, LB 1, NB 2)	6	(B 5, LB 3, NB 1)	9
Total		**178**	(5 wickets)	**159**

SOUTH AFRICA	O	M	R	W	O	M	R	W
Vogler	31	7	86	2	14·3	2	49	4
Faulkner	27	2	78	2	3	1	6	0
Schwarz	27	8	45	3	14	7	21	3
White	9	2	28	0				
Sinclair	14	4	27	1				
Nourse	4	1	10	2	18	6	43	2
S.J. Snooke					5	3	8	1
ENGLAND								
Blythe	20·3	5	61	5	12·3	3	36	2
Hirst	22	7	39	3	13	1	42	3
Crawford	11	2	33	0	6	3	14	0
Knox	10	2	39	2	8	0	53	0
Braund					1	0	5	0

FALL OF WICKETS

	E	SA	E	SA
Wkt	1st	1st	2nd	2nd
1st	0	8	6	61
2nd	19	8	6	72
3rd	105	69	20	76
4th	154	105	89	110
5th	170	149	100	159
6th	177	160	108	–
7th	181	163	118	–
8th	271	174	131	–
9th	274	175	131	–
10th	295	178	138	–

Umpires: W. Richards (4) and W.A.J. West (4).

Close: 1st day – E(1) 226-7 (Fry 108, Lilley 16); 2nd – SA(1) 149-5 (Shalders 18).

AUSTRALIA v ENGLAND 1907–08 (1st Test)

Played at Sydney Cricket Ground on 13, 14, 16, 17, 18 (*no play*), 19 December.
Toss: England.   Result: AUSTRALIA won by two wickets.
Debuts: Australia – H. Carter, G.R. Hazlitt, C.G. Macartney, V.S. Ransford; England – G. Gunn,
  J. Hardstaff, sr, K.L. Hutchings, R.A. Young.

Fane became the first Essex player to lead England when the appointed captain, A.O. Jones, was hospitalised
in Brisbane. G. Gunn, in Australia for health reasons and not a member of the MCC touring team, was a last
minute selection and made top score in both innings, becoming the fifth batsman to score a century for England
on debut. His inclusion relegated J.B. Hobbs to the role of twelfth man. Australia owed their dramatic victory
to a sterling innings by Carter, their new wicket-keeper, and to a partnership of 56 in 39 minutes between Hazlitt
and Cotter.

ENGLAND

F.L. Fane*	c Trumper b Cotter	2		c Noble b Saunders	33
R.A. Young†	c Carter b Cotter	13	(7)	b Noble	3
G. Gunn	c Hazlitt b Cotter	119		c Noble b Cotter	74
K.L. Hutchings	c and b Armstrong	42		c Armstrong b Saunders	17
L.C. Braund	b Cotter	30	(6)	not out	32
J. Hardstaff, sr	b Armstrong	12	(5)	b Noble	63
W. Rhodes	run out	1	(2)	c McAlister b Macartney	29
J.N. Crawford	b Armstrong	31		c Hazlitt b Cotter	5
S.F. Barnes	b Cotter	1		b Saunders	11
C. Blythe	b Cotter	5		c Noble b Saunders	15
A. Fielder	not out	1		lbw b Armstrong	6
Extras	(B 7, LB 6, W 1, NB 2)	16		(B 2, W 3, NB 7)	12
Total		**273**			**300**

AUSTRALIA

V.T. Trumper	b Fielder	43		b Barnes	3
P.A. McAlister	c Hutchings b Barnes	3	(7)	b Crawford	41
C. Hill	c Gunn b Fielder	87		b Fielder	1
M.A. Noble*	c Braund b Fielder	37		b Barnes	27
W.W. Armstrong	c Braund b Fielder	7		b Crawford	44
V.S. Ransford	c Braund b Rhodes	24		c and b Blythe	13
C.G. Macartney	c Young b Fielder	35	(2)	c Crawford b Fielder	9
H. Carter†	b Braund	25		c Young b Fielder	61
G.R. Hazlitt	not out	18	(10)	not out	34
A. Cotter	b Braund	2	(9)	not out	33
J.V. Saunders	c Braund b Fielder	9			
Extras	(B 4, LB 2, W 2, NB 2)	10		(B 6, NB 3)	9
Total		**300**		**(8 wickets)**	**275**

AUSTRALIA	O	M	R	W	O	M	R	W		FALL OF WICKETS			
Cotter	21·5	0	101	6	26	1	101	2			E	A	E	A
Saunders	11	0	42	0	23	6	68	4	*Wkt*	*1st*	*1st*	*2nd*	*2nd*
Hazlitt	9	2	32	0	4	2	24	0	1st	11	4	56	7
Armstrong	26	10	63	3	27	14	33	1	2nd	18	72	82	12
Macartney	3	0	5	0	14	2	39	1	3rd	91	164	105	27
Noble	6	1	14	0	15	5	23	2	4th	208	171	218	75
ENGLAND									5th	221	184	223	95
Fielder	30·2	4	82	6	27·3	4	88	3	6th	223	222	227	124
Barnes	22	3	74	1	30	7	63	2	7th	246	253	241	185
Blythe	12	1	33	0	19	5	55	1	8th	253	279	262	219
Braund	17	2	74	2	7	2	14	0	9th	271	281	293	–
Crawford	5	1	14	0	8	2	33	2	10th	273	300	300	–
Rhodes	5	2	13	1	7	3	13	0					

Umpires: R.W. Crockett (10) and W. Hannah (1).

Close: 1st day – A(1) 50-1 (Trumper 31, Hill 16); 2nd – E(2) 19-0 (Fane 8, Rhodes 10); 3rd – E(2) 293-9 (Braund
31); 4th – A(2) 63-3 (Noble 27, Armstrong 17); 5th – no play.

AUSTRALIA v ENGLAND 1907–08 (2nd Test)

Played at Melbourne Cricket Ground on 1, 2, 3, 4, 6, 7 January.
Toss: Australia.   Result: ENGLAND won by one wicket.
Debuts: England – J.B. Hobbs, J. Humphries.

Had cover-point (Hazlitt) thrown accurately as the winning run was being scampered, this match would have provided Test cricket with its first tie. John Berry Hobbs batted for 195 minutes in the first of his 102 Test innings. Hutchings, playing in his second Test, reached his only hundred for England in 128 minutes, his second fifty taking just 43 minutes.

AUSTRALIA

V.T. Trumper	c Humphries b Crawford	49		lbw b Crawford	63
C.G. Macartney	b Crawford	37	(6)	c Humphries b Barnes	54
C. Hill	b Fielder	16		b Fielder	3
M.A. Noble*	c Braund b Rhodes	61	(2)	b Crawford	64
W.W. Armstrong	c Hutchings b Crawford	31		b Barnes	77
P.A. McAlister	run out	10	(4)	run out	15
V.S. Ransford	run out	27		c Hutchings b Barnes	18
A. Cotter	b Crawford	17	(9)	lbw b Crawford	27
H. Carter†	not out	15	(8)	c Fane b Barnes	53
G.R. Hazlitt	b Crawford	1		b Barnes	3
J.V. Saunders	b Fielder	0		not out	0
Extras	(LB 1, W 1)	2		(B 12, LB 8)	20
Total		**266**			**397**

ENGLAND

F.L. Fane*	b Armstrong	13		b Armstrong	50
J.B. Hobbs	b Cotter	83		b Noble	28
G. Gunn	lbw b Cotter	15		lbw b Noble	0
K.L. Hutchings	b Cotter	126		c Cotter b Macartney	39
L.C. Braund	b Cotter	49		b Armstrong	30
J. Hardstaff, sr	b Saunders	12		c Ransford b Cotter	19
W. Rhodes	b Saunders	32		run out	15
J.N. Crawford	c Ransford b Saunders	16		c Armstrong b Saunders	10
S.F. Barnes	c Hill b Armstrong	14		not out	38
J. Humphries†	b Cotter	6		lbw b Armstrong	16
A. Fielder	not out	6		not out	18
Extras	(B 3, LB 3, W 1, NB 3)	10		(B 9, LB 7, W 1, NB 2)	19
Total		**382**	(9 wickets)		**282**

ENGLAND	O	M	R	W	O	M	R	W
Fielder	27·5	4	77	2	27	6	74	1
Barnes	17	7	30	0	27·4	4	72	5
Rhodes	11	0	37	1	16	6	38	0
Braund	16	5	41	0	18	2	68	0
Crawford	29	1	79	5	33	6	125	3
AUSTRALIA								
Cotter	33	4	142	5	28	3	82	1
Saunders	34	7	100	3	30	9	58	1
Noble	9	3	26	0	22	7	41	2
Armstrong	34·2	15	36	2	30·4	10	53	3
Hazlitt	13	1	34	0	2	1	8	0
Macartney	12	2	34	0	9	3	21	1

FALL OF WICKETS

	A	E	A	E
Wkt	1st	1st	2nd	2nd
1st	84	27	126	54
2nd	93	61	131	54
3rd	111	160	135	121
4th	168	268	162	131
5th	197	287	268	162
6th	214	325	303	196
7th	240	353	312	198
8th	261	360	361	209
9th	265	369	392	243
10th	266	382	397	–

Umpires: P. Argall (6) and R.W. Crockett (11).

Close: 1st day – A(1) 255-7 (Ransford 27, Carter 10); 2nd – E(1) 246-3 (Hutchings 117, Braund 15); 3rd – A(2) 96-0 (Trumper 46, Noble 50); 4th – A(2) 360-7 (Carter 22, Cotter 27); 5th – E(2) 159-4 (Braund 17, Hardstaff 17).

AUSTRALIA v ENGLAND 1907–08 (3rd Test)

Played at Adelaide Oval on 10, 11, 13, 14, 15, 16 January.
Toss: Australia.   Result: AUSTRALIA won by 245 runs.
Debuts: Australia – R.J. Hartigan, J.D.A. O'Connor.

Hartigan became the fourth Australian to score a century on debut. His partnership of 243 with Hill set a new Test record for any wicket and remains Australia's highest eighth-wicket stand in all Test matches. Hill, suffering from influenza and unable to field, batted in extreme heat for 319 minutes. His score of 160 is the highest by anyone batting number nine in a Test match. Having scored England's first run in the second innings, Hobbs was struck by Saunders' first ball and retired after a ten-minute delay. He resumed the following day at 146.

AUSTRALIA

V.T. Trumper	b Fielder	4		b Barnes	0
M.A. Noble*	c Hutchings b Barnes	15		c Gunn b Fielder	65
C.G. Macartney	lbw b Braund	75		b Barnes	9
P.A. McAlister	c Hutchings b Crawford	28		c Hutchings b Crawford	17
W.W. Armstrong	c Humphries b Fielder	17		c Hutchings b Braund	34
V.S. Ransford	b Barnes	44	(7)	c Rhodes b Braund	25
C. Hill	c Humphries b Barnes	5	(9)	c Gunn b Crawford	160
R.J. Hartigan	b Fielder	48		c sub (R.A. Young) b Barnes	116
H. Carter†	lbw b Hutchings	24	(10)	not out	31
J.D.A. O'Connor	not out	10	(6)	b Crawford	20
J.V. Saunders	b Fielder	1		run out	0
Extras	(B 3, LB 5, W 3, NB 3)	14		(B 20, LB 7, W 2)	29
Total		**285**			**506**

ENGLAND

J.B. Hobbs	c Carter b Saunders	26		not out	23
F.L. Fane*	run out	48		b Saunders	0
G. Gunn	b O'Connor	65		c Trumper b O'Connor	11
K.L. Hutchings	c and b Macartney	23		b O'Connor	0
L.C. Braund	b Macartney	0		c Hartigan b O'Connor	47
J. Hardstaff, sr	b O'Connor	61		c Macartney b Saunders	72
W. Rhodes	c Carter b O'Connor	38		c Armstrong b O'Connor	9
J.N. Crawford	b Armstrong	62		c and b Saunders	7
S.F. Barnes	c and b Armstrong	12		c McAlister b Saunders	8
J. Humphries†	run out	7		b O'Connor	1
A. Fielder	not out	0		c Ransford b Saunders	1
Extras	(B 12, LB 2, W 2, NB 5)	21		(B 3, NB 1)	4
Total		**363**			**183**

ENGLAND	O	M	R	W	O	M	R	W		FALL OF WICKETS			
Barnes	27	8	60	3	42	9	83	3		A	E	A	E
Fielder	27·5	5	80	4	23	3	81	1	*Wkt*	*1st*	*1st*	*2nd*	*2nd*
Rhodes	15	5	35	0	27	9	81	0	1st	11	58	7	8
Crawford	14	0	65	1	45·5	4	113	3	2nd	35	98	35	9
Braund	9	1	26	1	23	3	85	2	3rd	114	138	71	15
Hutchings	2	1	5	1	7	0	34	0	4th	140	138	127	128
									5th	160	194	135	138
AUSTRALIA									6th	191	277	179	146
Saunders	36	6	83	1	21·4	4	65	5	7th	215	282	180	162
Macartney	18	3	49	2	4	1	17	0	8th	273	320	423	177
O'Connor	40	8	110	3	21	6	40	5	9th	275	363	501	182
Noble	18	4	38	0	7	1	14	0	10th	285	363	506	183
Armstrong	18	4	55	2	10	1	43	0					
Hartigan	2	0	7	0									

Umpires: R.W. Crockett (12) and T. Laing (1).

Close: 1st day – A(1) 279-9 (O'Connor 5, Saunders 1); 2nd – E(1) 259-5 (Hardstaff 51, Rhodes 34); 3rd – A(2) 133-4 (Noble 63, O'Connor 4); 4th – A(2) 397-7 (Hill 106, Hartigan 105); 5th – E(2) 139-5 (Braund 41, Crawford 1).

AUSTRALIA v ENGLAND 1907–08 (4th Test)

Played at Melbourne Cricket Ground on 7, 8, 10, 11 February.
Toss: Australia.   Result: AUSTRALIA won by 308 runs.
Debuts: Nil.

After dismissing Australia for 214 on a perfect pitch, England had to bat on one ruined by heavy rain. Hobbs struck ten boundaries in a brilliant 70-minute display in difficult conditions. Armstrong's innings, his first hundred against England, lasted 289 minutes. It left England with an impossible target of 495 and no hope of retaining the Ashes.

AUSTRALIA

M.A. Noble*	b Crawford	48	b Crawford		10
V.T. Trumper	c Crawford b Fielder	0	b Crawford		0
C. Hill	b Barnes	7	run out		25
P.A. McAlister	c Jones b Fielder	37	c Humphries b Fielder		4
S.E. Gregory	c Fielder b Crawford	10	lbw b Fielder		29
W.W. Armstrong	b Crawford	32	not out		133
V.S. Ransford	c Braund b Fielder	51	c Humphries b Rhodes		54
C.G. Macartney	c Hardstaff b Fielder	12	c Gunn b Crawford		29
H. Carter†	c and b Crawford	2	c Braund b Fielder		66
J.D.A. O'Connor	c Fielder b Crawford	2	c Humphries b Barnes		18
J.V. Saunders	not out	1	c Jones b Fielder		2
Extras	(B 1, LB 10, NB 1)	12	(B 7, LB 2, NB 6)		15
Total		**214**			**385**

ENGLAND

J.B. Hobbs	b Noble	57	c and b Saunders		0
G. Gunn	c and b Saunders	13	b Saunders		43
J. Hardstaff, sr	c Carter b O'Connor	8	c Carter b Saunders		39
K.L. Hutchings	b Saunders	8	b Noble		3
L.C. Braund	run out	4	b Macartney		10
W. Rhodes	c McAlister b Saunders	0	c Carter b O'Connor		2
J.N. Crawford	b Saunders	1	c Carter b O'Connor		0
A.O. Jones*	b Noble	3	c Saunders b O'Connor		31
S.F. Barnes	c O'Connor b Noble	3	not out		22
J. Humphries†	not out	3	c Carter b Saunders		11
A. Fielder	st Carter b Saunders	1	b Armstrong		20
Extras	(B 1, LB 2, NB 1)	4	(LB 4, NB 1)		5
Total		**105**			**186**

ENGLAND	O	M	R	W	O	M	R	W
Fielder	22	3	54	4	31	2	91	4
Barnes	23	11	37	1	35	13	69	1
Braund	12	3	42	0	7	0	48	0
Crawford	23·5	3	48	5	25	5	72	3
Rhodes	5	0	21	0	24	5	66	1
Hutchings					2	0	24	0
AUSTRALIA								
O'Connor	6	1	40	1	21	3	58	3
Armstrong	1	0	4	0	3·1	0	18	1
Macartney	6	1	18	0	6	1	15	1
Saunders	15·2	8	28	5	26	2	76	4
Noble	6	0	11	3	12	6	14	1

FALL OF WICKETS

	A	E	A	E
Wkt	1st	1st	2nd	2nd
1st	1	58	4	0
2nd	14	69	21	61
3rd	89	88	28	64
4th	103	90	65	79
5th	105	90	77	85
6th	196	92	162	85
7th	196	96	217	128
8th	198	100	329	132
9th	212	103	374	146
10th	214	105	385	186

Umpires: P. Argall (7) and R.W. Crockett (13).

Close: 1st day – E(1) 9-0 (Hobbs 9, Gunn 0); 2nd – A(2) 49-3 (Hill 18, Gregory 13); 3rd – A(2) 358-8 (Armstrong 114, O'Connor 12).

AUSTRALIA v ENGLAND 1907–08 (5th Test)

Played at Sydney Cricket Ground on 21, 22, 24, 25, 26, 27 February.
Toss: England.   Result: AUSTRALIA won by 49 runs.
Debuts: Nil.

England were again unable to restrict Australia's second innings to moderate proportions; for the fourth successive Test that innings provided the highest total of the match. Trumper batted for 241 minutes. His fifth hundred against England enabled him to become the second batsman after C. Hill to score 2,000 runs in Tests.

AUSTRALIA

M.A. Noble*	b Barnes	35		lbw b Rhodes	34
C.G. Macartney	c Crawford b Barnes	1	(5)	c Jones b Crawford	12
J.D.A. O'Connor	c Young b Crawford	9	(2)	b Barnes	6
S.E. Gregory	c and b Barnes	44		b Crawford	56
C. Hill	c Hutchings b Barnes	12	(6)	c Young b Crawford	44
W.W. Armstrong	c and b Crawford	3	(7)	c Gunn b Crawford	32
V.T. Trumper	c Braund b Barnes	10	(3)	c Gunn b Rhodes	166
V.S. Ransford	c Gunn b Barnes	11		not out	21
R.J. Hartigan	c and b Crawford	1		b Crawford	5
H. Carter†	not out	1		c Hobbs b Rhodes	22
J.V. Saunders	c Young b Barnes	0		c Young b Rhodes	0
Extras	(B 9, LB 1)	10		(B 21, LB 3)	24
Total		**137**			**422**

ENGLAND

J.B. Hobbs	b Saunders	72		c Gregory b Saunders	13
F.L. Fane	b Noble	0		b Noble	46
G. Gunn	not out	122		b Macartney	0
K.L. Hutchings	run out	13		b Macartney	2
J. Hardstaff, sr	c O'Connor b Saunders	17		b Saunders	8
J.N. Crawford	c Hill b Saunders	6	(10)	not out	24
L.C. Braund	st Carter b Macartney	31	(6)	c Noble b Saunders	0
W. Rhodes	c Noble b Armstrong	10	(7)	b Noble	69
R.A. Young†	st Carter b Macartney	0	(8)	c O'Connor b Saunders	11
A.O. Jones*	b Macartney	0	(9)	b Armstrong	34
S.F. Barnes	run out	1		b Saunders	11
Extras	(B 6, LB 3)	9		(B 5, LB 6)	11
Total		**281**			**229**

ENGLAND	O	M	R	W	O	M	R	W	FALL OF WICKETS				
Barnes	22·4	6	60	7	27	6	78	1		A	E	A	E
Rhodes	10	5	15	0	37·4	7	102	4	*Wkt*	*1st*	*1st*	*2nd*	*2nd*
Crawford	18	4	52	3	36	10	141	5	1st	10	1	25	21
Braund					20	3	64	0	2nd	46	135	52	26
Hobbs					7	3	13	0	3rd	46	168	166	30
									4th	64	189	192	51
AUSTRALIA									5th	73	197	300	57
Noble	28	9	62	1	24	6	56	2	6th	94	245	342	87
Saunders	35	5	114	3	35·1	5	82	5	7th	124	264	373	123
O'Connor	6	0	23	0	13	3	29	0	8th	129	271	387	176
Macartney	15·1	3	44	3	15	4	24	2	9th	137	271	422	198
Armstrong	12	2	29	1	18	7	27	1	10th	137	281	422	229

Umpires: W. Hannah (2) and A.C. Jones (2).

Close: 1st day – E(1) 116-1 (Hobbs 65, Gunn 50); 2nd – E(1) 187-3 (Gunn 77, Hardstaff 17); 3rd – A(2) 18-0 (Noble 11, O'Connor 4); 4th – A(2) 357-6 (Armstrong 19, Ransford 4); 5th – E(2) 117-6 (Rhodes 32, Young 9).

ENGLAND v AUSTRALIA 1909 (1st Test)

Played at Edgbaston, Birmingham, on 27, 28, 29 May.
Toss: Australia.   Result: ENGLAND won by ten wickets.
Debuts: England – G.J. Thompson; Australia – W. Bardsley, W.J. Whitty.

England's selectors called upon 25 players during the rubber and invited 15 to Birmingham. W. Brearley, H.A. Gilbert, T.W. Hayward and A.E. Relf were eventually omitted. The left-arm combination of Hirst and Blythe accounted for all 20 Australian wickets. Hobbs and Fry, both dismissed first ball by Macartney, shared a decisive partnership in the final innings. Jones caught Noble left-handed at short-leg off a full-blooded hit – a supreme piece of anticipation.

AUSTRALIA

A. Cotter	c Hirst b Blythe	2	(9) c Tyldesley b Hirst		15
W. Bardsley	c MacLaren b Hirst	2	(6) c Thompson b Blythe		6
W.W. Armstrong	b Hirst	24	(7) c Jessop b Blythe		0
V.T. Trumper	c Hirst b Blythe	10	(5) c Rhodes b Hirst		1
M.A. Noble*	c Jessop b Blythe	15	(1) c Jones b Hirst		11
S.E. Gregory	c Rhodes b Blythe	0	(3) c Thompson b Blythe		43
V.S. Ransford	b Hirst	1	(4) b Blythe		43
C.G. Macartney	c MacLaren b Blythe	10	(2) lbw b Blythe		1
H. Carter†	lbw b Hirst	0	(8) c Hobbs b Hirst		1
J.D.A. O'Connor	lbw b Blythe	8	c Lilley b Hirst		13
W.J. Whitty	not out	0	not out		9
Extras	(LB 1, NB 1)	2	(B 7, LB 1)		8
Total		**74**			**151**

ENGLAND

A.C. MacLaren*	b Macartney	5			
J.B. Hobbs	lbw b Macartney	0	(1) not out		62
J.T. Tyldesley	b O'Connor	24			
C.B. Fry	b Macartney	0	(2) not out		35
A.O. Jones	c Carter b Armstrong	28			
G.H. Hirst	lbw b Armstrong	15			
G.L. Jessop	b Armstrong	22			
W. Rhodes	not out	15			
A.F.A. Lilley†	c Ransford b Armstrong	0			
G.J. Thompson	run out	6			
C. Blythe	c Macartney b Armstrong	1			
Extras	(B 4, LB 1)	5	(B 5, LB 3)		8
Total		**121**	(0 wickets)		**105**

ENGLAND	O	M	R	W	O	M	R	W
Hirst	23	8	28	4	23·5	4	58	5
Blythe	23	6	44	6	24	3	58	5
Thompson					4	0	19	0
Rhodes					1	0	8	0
AUSTRALIA								
Whitty	17	5	43	0	5	1	18	0
Macartney	17	6	21	3	11	2	35	0
Noble	1	0	2	0				
O'Connor	5	2	23	1	3·2	1	17	0
Armstrong	15·3	7	27	5	13	5	27	0

FALL OF WICKETS

Wkt	A 1st	E 1st	A 2nd	E 2nd
1st	5	0	4	–
2nd	7	13	16	–
3rd	30	13	97	–
4th	46	61	99	–
5th	47	61	103	–
6th	52	90	103	–
7th	58	103	106	–
8th	59	107	123	–
9th	71	116	125	–
10th	74	121	151	–

Umpires: J. Carlin (4) and F. Parris (1).

Close: 1st day – A(1) 22-2 (Armstrong 10, Trumper 7); 2nd – A(2) 67-2 (Gregory 26, Ransford 28).

ENGLAND v AUSTRALIA 1909 (2nd Test)

Played at Lord's, London, on 14, 15, 16 June.
Toss: Australia.   Result: AUSTRALIA won by nine wickets.
Debuts: England – J.H. King.

King, Leicestershire's 38-year-old left-handed all-rounder, was top scorer in the first innings of his only Test. His fellow left-hander, Ransford, batted 245 minutes, hit 21 fours, and was dropped three times (twice off King), in compiling his only three-figure score in Tests. Armstrong's leg-spin reaped its best analysis at Test level.

ENGLAND

T.W. Hayward	st Carter b Laver	16		run out	6
J.B. Hobbs	c Carter b Laver	19		c and b Armstrong	9
J.T. Tyldesley	lbw b Laver	46		st Carter b Armstrong	3
G. Gunn	lbw b Cotter	1		b Armstrong	0
J.H. King	c Macartney b Cotter	60		b Armstrong	4
A.C. MacLaren*	c Armstrong b Noble	7	(8)	b Noble	24
G.H. Hirst	b Cotter	31		b Armstrong	1
A.O. Jones	b Cotter	8	(6)	lbw b Laver	26
A.E. Relf	c Armstrong b Noble	17	(10)	b Armstrong	3
A.F.A. Lilley†	c Bardsley b Noble	47	(9)	not out	25
S. Haigh	not out	1		run out	5
Extras	(B 8, LB 3, W 3, NB 2)	16		(B 2, LB 3, NB 10)	15
Total		**269**			**121**

AUSTRALIA

P.A. McAlister	lbw b King	22		not out	19
F. Laver	b Hirst	14			
W. Bardsley	b Relf	46	(2)	c Lilley b Relf	0
W.W. Armstrong	c Lilley b Relf	12			
V.S. Ransford	not out	143			
V.T. Trumper	c MacLaren b Relf	28			
M.A. Noble*	c Lilley b Relf	32			
S.E. Gregory	c Lilley b Relf	14	(3)	not out	18
A. Cotter	run out	0			
C.G. Macartney	b Hirst	5			
H. Carter†	b Hirst	7			
Extras	(B 16, LB 8, W 1, NB 2)	27		(B 4)	4
Total		**350**		(1 wicket)	**41**

AUSTRALIA	O	M	R	W	O	M	R	W		FALL OF WICKETS			
Laver	32	9	75	3	13	4	24	1		E	A	E	A
Macartney	8	3	10	0					Wkt	1st	1st	2nd	2nd
Cotter	23	1	80	4	18	3	35	0	1st	23	18	16	4
Noble	24·2	9	42	3	5	1	12	1	2nd	41	84	22	–
Armstrong	20	6	46	0	24·5	11	35	6	3rd	44	90	22	–
									4th	123	119	23	–
ENGLAND									5th	149	198	34	–
Hirst	26·5	2	83	3	8	1	28	0	6th	175	269	41	–
King	27	5	99	1					7th	199	317	82	–
Relf	45	14	85	5	7·4	4	9	1	8th	205	317	90	–
Haigh	19	5	41	0					9th	258	342	101	–
Jones	2	0	15	0					10th	269	350	121	–

Umpires: C.E. Dench (1) and J. Moss (3).

Close: 1st day – A(1) 17-0 (McAlister 4, Laver 13); 2nd – E(2) 16-1 (Hayward 5).

ENGLAND v AUSTRALIA 1909 (3rd Test)

Played at Headingley, Leeds, on 1, 2, 3 July.
Toss: Australia.   Result: AUSTRALIA won by 126 runs.
Debuts: England – J. Sharp.

Gregory completed 2,000 runs in Tests. Jessop strained his back on the first day and was unable to bat. Macartney (slow left-arm) achieved his best innings and match analyses in Test matches. England's 87 remains their lowest total in a Headingley Test.

AUSTRALIA

P.A. McAlister	lbw b Hirst	3	c Sharp b Barnes		5
S.E. Gregory	b Barnes	46	b Hirst		0
V.S. Ransford	run out	45	lbw b Barnes		24
M.A. Noble*	b Hirst	3	(5) c Rhodes b Barnes		31
W. Bardsley	hit wkt b Rhodes	30	(7) c Lilley b Barnes		2
W.W. Armstrong	c Lilley b Brearley	21	(4) b Rhodes		45
V.T. Trumper	not out	27	(6) b Barnes		2
C.G. Macartney	c Fry b Rhodes	4	b Brearley		18
A. Cotter	b Rhodes	2	c MacLaren b Rhodes		19
H. Carter†	lbw b Rhodes	1	c Lilley b Barnes		30
F. Laver	c Lilley b Brearley	0	not out		13
Extras	(LB 4, W 1, NB 1)	6	(B 15, LB 2, NB 1)		18
Total		**188**			**207**

ENGLAND

C.B. Fry	lbw b Cotter	1	b Cotter		7
J.B. Hobbs	b Macartney	12	b Cotter		30
J.T. Tyldesley	c Armstrong b Macartney	55	c and b Macartney		7
J. Sharp	st Carter b Macartney	61	b Cotter		11
A.C. MacLaren*	b Macartney	17	c Cotter b Macartney		1
W. Rhodes	c Carter b Laver	12	c Armstrong b Macartney		16
G.H. Hirst	b Macartney	4	(8) b Cotter		0
A.F.A. Lilley†	not out	4	(7) lbw b Cotter		2
S.F. Barnes	b Macartney	1	b Macartney		1
W. Brearley	b Macartney	6	not out		4
G.L. Jessop	absent hurt	–	absent hurt		–
Extras	(B 1, LB 4, NB 4)	9	(B 1, LB 1, W 1, NB 5)		8
Total		**182**			**87**

ENGLAND	O	M	R	W	O	M	R	W	FALL OF WICKETS				
Hirst	26	6	65	2	17	3	39	1		A	E	A	E
Barnes	25	12	37	1	35	16	63	6	Wkt	1st	1st	2nd	2nd
Brearley	14·1	1	42	2	24·1	6	36	1	1st	6	8	0	17
Rhodes	8	2	38	4	19	3	44	2	2nd	86	31	14	26
Sharp					1	0	7	0	3rd	100	137	52	60
									4th	104	146	118	61
AUSTRALIA									5th	140	157	122	61
Cotter	17	1	45	1	16	2	38	5	6th	154	169	126	82
Macartney	25·3	6	58	7	16·5	5	27	4	7th	167	171	127	82
Armstrong	16	5	33	0	3	1	8	0	8th	169	174	150	82
Laver	13	4	15	1	2	0	6	0	9th	171	182	183	87
Noble	13	5	22	0					10th	188	–	207	–

Umpires: W. Richards (5) and W.A.J. West (5).

Close: 1st day – E(1) 88-2 (Tyldesley 38, Sharp 30); 2nd – A(2) 175-8 (Macartney 7, Carter 22).

ENGLAND v AUSTRALIA 1909 (4th Test)

Played at Old Trafford, Manchester, on 26, 27, 28 July.
Toss: Australia.   Result: MATCH DRAWN.
Debuts: Nil.

Frank Laver, right-arm medium pace, recorded the best innings analysis by any visiting bowler in a Test in England.

AUSTRALIA

S.E. Gregory	b Blythe	21	b Hirst		5
W. Bardsley	b Barnes	9	c MacLaren b Blythe		35
V.S. Ransford	lbw b Barnes	4	(7) not out		54
M.A. Noble*	b Blythe	17	b Blythe		13
V.T. Trumper	c Hutchings b Barnes	2	(6) c Tyldesley b Rhodes		48
W.W. Armstrong	not out	32	(5) lbw b Rhodes		30
A.J.Y. Hopkins	b Blythe	3	(8) c Barnes b Rhodes		9
C.G. Macartney	b Barnes	5	(3) b Rhodes		51
A. Cotter	c Tyldesley b Blythe	17	c MacLaren b Rhodes		4
H. Carter†	lbw b Barnes	13	lbw b Barnes		12
F. Laver	b Blythe	11			
Extras	(B 6, LB 7)	13	(B 9, LB 8, NB 1)		18
Total		**147**	(9 wickets declared)		**279**

ENGLAND

P.F. Warner	b Macartney	9	b Hopkins		25
R.H. Spooner	c and b Cotter	25	b Laver		58
J.T. Tyldesley	c Armstrong b Laver	15	b Hopkins		11
J. Sharp	c Armstrong b Laver	3	not out		8
W. Rhodes	c Carter b Laver	5	not out		0
K.L. Hutchings	b Laver	9			
A.C. MacLaren*	lbw b Laver	16			
A.F.A. Lilley†	not out	26			
G.H. Hirst	c Hopkins b Laver	1			
S.F. Barnes	b Laver	0			
C. Blythe	b Laver	1			
Extras	(B 2, LB 3, NB 4)	9	(B 2, LB 4)		6
Total		**119**	(3 wickets)		**108**

ENGLAND	O	M	R	W	O	M	R	W
Hirst	7	0	15	0	12	3	32	1
Barnes	27	9	56	5	22·3	5	66	1
Blythe	20·3	5	63	5	24	5	77	2
Sharp					1	0	3	0
Rhodes					25	0	83	5
AUSTRALIA								
Noble	8	2	11	0				
Macartney	18	6	31	1	7	2	16	0
Laver	18·2	7	31	8	21	12	25	1
Cotter	8	1	37	1	5	0	14	0
Armstrong					10	6	16	0
Hopkins					12	4	31	2

FALL OF WICKETS

	A	E	A	E
Wkt	1st	1st	2nd	2nd
1st	13	24	16	78
2nd	21	39	77	90
3rd	45	44	106	102
4th	48	50	126	–
5th	58	63	148	–
6th	66	72	237	–
7th	86	99	256	–
8th	110	103	262	–
9th	128	103	279	–
10th	147	119	–	–

Umpires: W. Richards (6) and W.A.J. West (6).

Close: 1st day – E(1) 119 all out; 2nd – A(2) 77-2 (Macartney 33).

ENGLAND v AUSTRALIA 1909 (5th Test)

Played at Kennington Oval, London, on 9, 10, 11 August.
Toss: Australia.   Result: MATCH DRAWN.
Debuts: England – D.W. Carr, F.E. Woolley.

Noble emulated F.S. Jackson's feat of 1905 by winning all five tosses in the rubber. Carr, aged 37 and a googly bowler in his first season of county cricket, took 3 for 19 in the first seven overs of his only Test but was then grossly overbowled. Bardsley became the first batsman to score a hundred in each innings of a Test match. He batted for 225 minutes in each innings but was to wait 17 years for his next century against England. His second innings opening partnership of 180 with Gregory was the Australian record until 1964 (*Test No. 564*).

AUSTRALIA

S.E. Gregory	b Carr	1	run out		74
W. Bardsley	b Sharp	136	lbw b Barnes		130
M.A. Noble*	lbw b Carr	2	c MacLaren b Barnes		55
W.W. Armstrong	lbw b Carr	15	c Woolley b Carr		10
V.S. Ransford	b Barnes	3	not out		36
V.T. Trumper	c Rhodes b Barnes	73	st Lilley b Carr		20
C.G. Macartney	c Rhodes b Sharp	50	not out		4
A.J.Y. Hopkins	c Rhodes b Sharp	21			
A. Cotter	b Carr	7			
H. Carter†	lbw b Carr	4			
F. Laver	not out	8			
Extras	(B 1, LB 3, NB 1)	5	(B 4, LB 3, W 1, NB 2)		10
Total		**325**	(5 wickets declared)		**339**

ENGLAND

R.H. Spooner	b Cotter	13	c and b Macartney		3
A.C. MacLaren*	lbw b Cotter	15			
W. Rhodes	c Carter b Cotter	66	(2) st Carter b Armstrong		54
C.B. Fry	run out	62	not out		35
J. Sharp	c Gregory b Hopkins	105	not out		0
F.E. Woolley	b Cotter	8			
E.G. Hayes	lbw b Armstrong	4	(3) c sub (R.J. Hartigan) b Armstrong	9
K.L. Hutchings	c Macartney b Cotter	59			
A.F.A. Lilley†	not out	2			
S.F. Barnes	c Carter b Hopkins	0			
D.W. Carr	b Cotter	0			
Extras	(B 8, LB 4, NB 6)	18	(LB 2, NB 1)		3
Total		**352**	(3 wickets)		**104**

ENGLAND	O	M	R	W	O	M	R	W		FALL OF WICKETS			
Carr	34	2	146	5	35	1	136	2		A	E	A	E
Barnes	19	3	57	2	27	7	61	2	*Wkt*	*1st*	*1st*	*2nd*	*2nd*
Sharp	16·3	3	67	3	12	0	34	0	1st	9	15	180	14
Woolley	4	1	6	0	6	0	31	0	2nd	27	36	267	27
Hayes	4	0	10	0	2	0	14	0	3rd	55	140	268	88
Rhodes	12	3	34	0	14	1	35	0	4th	58	187	294	–
Hutchings					4	0	18	0	5th	176	201	335	–
									6th	259	206	–	–
AUSTRALIA									7th	289	348	–	–
Cotter	27·4	1	95	6	8	1	21	0	8th	300	348	–	–
Armstrong	31	7	93	1	7	4	8	2	9th	304	351	–	–
Laver	8	1	13	0					10th	325	352	–	–
Macartney	16	2	49	0	8	2	11	1					
Hopkins	15	2	51	2	8	0	40	0					
Noble	8	1	29	0									
Gregory	1	0	4	0	2	0	21	0					

Umpires: J. Moss (4) and W. Richards (7).

Close: 1st day – E(1) 40-2 (Rhodes 7, Fry 3); 2nd – A(2) 76-0 (Gregory 35, Bardsley 33).

SOUTH AFRICA v ENGLAND 1909–10 (1st Test)

Played at Old Wanderers, Johannesburg, on 1, 3, 4, 5 January.
Toss: South Africa.   Result: SOUTH AFRICA won by 19 runs.
Debuts: South Africa – T. Campbell, J.M.M. Commaille, L.A. Stricker, J.W. Zulch;
England – M.C. Bird, C.P. Buckenham, H.D.G. Leveson Gower, G.H.T. Simpson-Hayward, H. Strudwick.

Simpson-Hayward, the last of the great lob bowlers and playing in his only Test series, dismissed Zulch with his fifth ball and returned his best Test analysis at his first attempt. England again fell to the leg-spin and googly wiles of Vogler (12 for 181) and Faulkner (8 for 160). The latter emulated G. Giffen (*Test No. 42*) by scoring over 200 runs and taking eight wickets in the same Test.

SOUTH AFRICA

J.W. Zulch	b Simpson-Hayward	19		lbw b Buckenham	27
L.A. Stricker	b Buckenham	12		b Simpson-Hayward	17
G.A. Faulkner	lbw b Simpson-Hayward	78	(6)	b Bird	123
A.W. Nourse	c Leveson Gower b Rhodes	53		c Strudwick b Buckenham	34
S.J. Snooke*	c Strudwick b Buckenham	12	(7)	c Rhodes b Buckenham	47
G.C. White	c Woolley b Buckenham	0	(3)	c Woolley b Buckenham	39
J.H. Sinclair	b Simpson-Hayward	3	(8)	b Simpson-Hayward	0
J.M.M. Commaille	st Strudwick b Simpson-Hayward	8	(9)	b Bird	19
R.O. Schwarz	b Simpson-Hayward	0	(11)	not out	6
A.E.E. Vogler	c Denton b Simpson-Hayward	10		c Rhodes b Bird	14
T. Campbell†	not out	8	(5)	b Thompson	8
Extras	(B 1, LB 2, NB 2)	5		(B 2, W 1, NB 8)	11
Total		**208**			**345**

ENGLAND

J.B. Hobbs	c Campbell b Vogler	89		b Vogler	35
W. Rhodes	b Vogler	66		c Nourse b Vogler	2
D. Denton	c Vogler b Faulkner	28		c and b Vogler	26
F.L. Fane	c Vogler b Faulkner	23		lbw b Vogler	0
F.E. Woolley	c Schwarz b Vogler	14		b Vogler	25
G.J. Thompson	lbw b Vogler	16		b Faulkner	63
M.C. Bird	c Vogler b Faulkner	4		c Snooke b Faulkner	5
C.P. Buckenham	b Faulkner	0		b Vogler	1
H.D.G. Leveson Gower*	c Campbell b Faulkner	17		b Faulkner	31
G.H.T. Simpson-Hayward	not out	29		c White b Vogler	14
H. Strudwick†	b Vogler	7		not out	1
Extras	(B 9, LB 8)	17		(B 14, LB 2, W 1, NB 4)	21
Total		**310**			**224**

ENGLAND	O	M	R	W	O	M	R	W
Buckenham	19	1	77	3	39	5	110	4
Hobbs	6	1	20	0	6	2	16	0
Simpson-Hayward	16	3	43	6	24	3	59	2
Thompson	11	3	25	0	28	6	100	1
Rhodes	9	1	34	1	9	3	25	0
Woolley	1	0	4	0	4	1	13	0
Bird	1	1	0	0	4	1	11	3
SOUTH AFRICA								
Vogler	30·1	4	87	5	22	2	94	7
Snooke	6	1	28	0	3	0	10	0
Nourse	9	3	13	0	5	0	20	0
Faulkner	33	4	120	5	17·2	7	40	3
White	3	0	15	0	4	0	33	0
Sinclair	4	0	10	0				
Schwarz	2	0	8	0	1	0	4	0
Stricker	3	0	12	0	1	0	2	0

FALL OF WICKETS

Wkt	SA 1st	E 1st	SA 2nd	E 2nd
1st	25	159	30	36
2nd	33	190	88	47
3rd	133	206	95	47
4th	155	237	129	91
5th	155	241	143	94
6th	164	245	242	102
7th	187	247	247	108
8th	187	265	321	178
9th	195	275	332	210
10th	208	310	345	224

Umpires: A.J. Atfield (1) and F.W. Grey (1).

Close: 1st day – E(1) 147-0 (Hobbs 77, Rhodes 65); 2nd – SA(2) 124-3 (Nourse 27, Campbell 8); 3rd – E(2) 144-7 (Thompson 25, Leveson Gower 12).

SOUTH AFRICA v ENGLAND 1909–10 (2nd Test)

Played at Lord's, Durban, on 21, 22, 24, 25, 26 January.
Toss: South Africa.   Result: SOUTH AFRICA won by 95 runs.
Debuts: Nil.

The first Test to be staged in Natal produced the first instance of a tie on first innings at this level. Only Hobbs batted consistently against Faulkner and Vogler as they shared another 15 wickets. N.C. Tufnell, who made his only Test appearance in the final match of this rubber, was the first substitute to make a stumping in a Test match; he kept wicket after Strudwick had been hit in the face.

SOUTH AFRICA

L.A. Stricker	b Buckenham	31	c Strudwick b Thompson	5
J.W. Zulch	b Thompson	13	c Rhodes b Buckenham	3
G.C. White	c Hobbs b Thompson	7	(5) b Simpson-Hayward	118
A.W. Nourse	c Strudwick b Buckenham	0	c Rhodes b Bird	69
G.A. Faulkner	c Woolley b Thompson	47	(3) c Fane b Backenham	9
T. Campbell†	b Simpson-Hayward	48	(9) b Simpson-Hayward	1
S.J. Snooke*	b Woolley	19	st sub (N.C. Tufnell) b Thompson	53
J.H. Sinclair	b Simpson-Hayward	12	b Woolley	22
J.M.M. Commaille	c Thompson b Simpson-Hayward	3	(6) b Buckenham	30
R.O. Schwarz	b Simpson-Hayward	0	(11) not out	9
A.E.E. Vogler	not out	7	(10) c Woolley b Simpson-Hayward	11
Extras	(B 7, LB 5)	12	(B 12, LB 1, NB 4)	17
Total		**199**		**347**

ENGLAND

J.B. Hobbs	b Sinclair	53	c Vogler b Faulkner	70
W. Rhodes	c Schwarz b Vogler	44	c White b Sinclair	17
D. Denton	run out	0	c Vogler b Faulkner	6
F.L. Fane	c and b Vogler	6	c Schwarz b Vogler	6
F.E. Woolley	c Zulch b Vogler	22	c Vogler b Faulkner	4
G.J. Thompson	c and b Vogler	38	not out	46
M.C. Bird	c Stricker b Nourse	1	c Nourse b Faulkner	42
C.P. Buckenham	b Faulkner	16	c Faulkner b Vogler	3
H.D.G. Leveson Gower*	not out	6	b Nourse	23
G.H.T. Simpson-Hayward	c Campbell b Vogler	0	lbw b Faulkner	16
H. Strudwick†	hit wkt b Faulkner	1	c Vogler b Faulkner	7
Extras	(B 4, LB 6, NB 2)	12	(B 9, LB 1, NB 2)	12
Total		**199**		**252**

ENGLAND	O	M	R	W	O	M	R	W		FALL OF WICKETS			
										SA	E	SA	E
Buckenham	27	4	51	2	31	4	94	3	Wkt	1st	1st	2nd	2nd
Hobbs	5	2	5	0	2	0	5	0	1st	20	94	6	48
Simpson-Hayward	23·5	3	42	4	23	4	66	3	2nd	36	95	16	59
Thompson	28	13	52	3	38·2	13	78	2	3rd	37	108	23	84
Woolley	15	5	23	1	10	3	34	1	4th	76	117	166	106
Rhodes	5	1	11	0	19	6	43	0	5th	116	138	245	111
Bird	3	2	3	0	7	3	10	1	6th	150	148	269	174
									7th	187	188	302	180
SOUTH AFRICA									8th	190	198	305	220
Snooke	6	1	11	0	1	0	9	0	9th	192	198	317	244
Vogler	30	6	83	5	29	6	93	2	10th	199	199	347	252
Faulkner	17·1	4	51	2	33·4	8	87	6					
Sinclair	16	4	32	1	5	0	18	1					
White	4	1	9	0	6	3	10	0					
Stricker	1	0	1	0									
Nourse	1	1	0	1	6	2	11	1					
Schwarz					2	0	12	0					

Umpires: F.W. Grey (2) and F.E. Smith (5).

Close: 1st day – SA(1) 89-4 (Faulkner 32, Campbell 3); 2nd – E(1) 148-6 (Thompson 1); 3rd – SA(2) 171-4 (White 74, Commaille 1); 4th – E(2) 15-0 (Hobbs 12, Rhodes 3).

SOUTH AFRICA v ENGLAND 1909–10 (3rd Test)

Played at Old Wanderers, Johannesburg, on 26, 28 February, 1, 2, 3 March.
Toss: South Africa.   Result: ENGLAND won by three wickets.
Debuts: South Africa – C.E. Floquet, S.J. Pegler.

Denton, who batted for 100 minutes, achieved his only Test century. It was his third hundred in successive innings; in the previous match, against Transvaal, he had become the first batsman to make a hundred in each innings of a first-class match in South Africa. For the first time Hobbs did not open the batting in either innings (also in *Test No. 131*). Commaille retired on the third day and resumed his brief second innings on the fourth.

SOUTH AFRICA

Batsman	Dismissal 1	Score	Dismissal 2	Score
L.A. Stricker	c Woolley b Buckenham	1	b Thompson	12
J.W. Zulch	c Woolley b Thompson	3	run out	34
G.C. White	c Buckenham b Simpson-Hayward	72	(7) c Woolley b Simpson-Hayward	2
A.W. Nourse	b Thompson	12	(6) c Thompson b Simpson-Hayward	5
G.A. Faulkner	c Rhodes b Buckenham	76	c Thompson b Simpson-Hayward	44
J.M.M. Commaille	c Strudwick b Buckenham	39	(3) b Simpson-Hayward	2
S.J. Snooke*	c Rhodes b Buckenham	13	(8) b Thompson	52
A.E.E. Vogler	c Woolley b Rhodes	65	(9) b Thompson	22
C.E. Floquet	b Buckenham	1	(11) not out	11
S.J. Pegler	not out	11	run out	28
T. Campbell†	c Strudwick b Woolley	0	(4) b Simpson-Hayward	19
Extras	(B 9, LB 1, W 1, NB 1)	12	(B 1, LB 3, NB 2)	6
Total		**305**		**237**

ENGLAND

Batsman	Dismissal 1	Score	Dismissal 2	Score
W. Rhodes	c Faulkner b Vogler	14	(4) c Snooke b Faulkner	1
F.L. Fane	c Campbell b Pegler	39	(6) b Faulkner	17
D. Denton	b Vogler	104	c White b Vogler	24
G.J. Thompson	c Vogler b Faulkner	21	(1) lbw b Vogler	10
M.C. Bird	b Faulkner	20	(8) run out	45
H.D.G. Leveson Gower*	lbw b Vogler	6	(9) not out	12
J.B. Hobbs	b Faulkner	11	(5) not out	93
F.E. Woolley	not out	58	(7) c Nourse b Vogler	0
G.H.T. Simpson-Hayward	c Zulch b Vogler	5		
C.P. Buckenham	c Pegler b Faulkner	1		
H. Strudwick†	c Snooke b Pegler	18	(2) b Vogler	5
Extras	(B 17, LB 7, NB 1)	25	(B 10, LB 3, NB 1)	14
Total		**322**	(7 wickets)	**221**

ENGLAND	O	M	R	W	O	M	R	W
Buckenham	31	2	115	5	23	4	73	0
Thompson	17	6	74	2	23	9	54	3
Simpson-Hayward	14	1	46	1	22	2	69	5
Woolley	21	4	54	1	18	6	29	0
Rhodes	1	0	4	1	4	1	6	0
Bird					1	1	0	0
SOUTH AFRICA								
Vogler	28	4	98	4	25	2	109	4
Faulkner	30	4	89	4	23·4	5	75	2
Pegler	9·4	0	40	2	4	1	15	0
White	4	0	28	0				
Floquet	8	2	24	0				
Nourse	3	1	18	0				
Snooke					6	3	8	0

	FALL OF WICKETS			
	SA	E	SA	E
Wkt	1st	1st	2nd	2nd
1st	4	32	24	16
2nd	4	96	57	37
3rd	30	187	61	42
4th	144	193	104	42
5th	198	201	119	92
6th	212	233	120	93
7th	239	234	123	188
8th	245	251	178	–
9th	304	253	214	–
10th	305	322	237	–

Umpires: A.J. Atfield (2) and F.W. Grey (3).

Close: 1st day – SA(1) 144-4 (White 47); 2nd – E(1) 201-5 (Bird 2); 3rd – SA(2) 35-1 (Zulch 20, Campbell 2); 4th – E(2) 7-0 (Thompson 6, Strudwick 0).

SOUTH AFRICA v ENGLAND 1909–10 (4th Test)

Played at Newlands, Cape Town, on 7, 8, 9 March.
Toss: England.   Result: SOUTH AFRICA won by four wickets.
Debuts: Nil.

South Africa won their second successive home rubber against England. They were to wait until 1930-31 for their next success.

ENGLAND

J.B. Hobbs	c Faulkner b Vogler	1	c Campbell b Snooke	0
W. Rhodes	c Faulkner b Snooke	0	b Snooke	5
D. Denton	c Commaille b Snooke	0	c Faulkner b Vogler	10
F.L. Fane*	c Campbell b Sinclair	14	(5) c Snooke b Faulkner	37
F.E. Woolley	c Zulch b Sinclair	69	(4) b Vogler	64
G.J. Thompson	run out	16	c Snooke b Faulkner	6
M.C. Bird	c Campbell b White	57	c Schwarz b Vogler	11
G.H.T. Simpson-Hayward	b Faulkner	13	(9) c Faulkner b Vogler	9
C.P. Buckenham	b Vogler	5	(10) c Faulkner b Vogler	17
H. Strudwick†	c and b White	7	(8) c Nourse b Faulkner	3
C. Blythe	not out	1	not out	4
Extras	(B 13, LB 5, NB 2)	20	(B 4, LB 8)	12
Total		**203**		**178**

SOUTH AFRICA

J.W. Zulch	b Simpson-Hayward	30	c Strudwick b Thompson	13
J.M.M. Commaille	c and b Buckenham	42	b Buckenham	3
G.C. White	b Bird	15	c Woolley b Thompson	31
A.W. Nourse	b Thompson	27	c Rhodes b Blythe	24
G.A. Faulkner	c Fane b Buckenham	10	not out	49
S.J. Snooke*	b Woolley	9	lbw b Blythe	7
J.H. Sinclair	b Thompson	10	b Thompson	19
L.A. Stricker	lbw b Thompson	0		
R.O. Schwarz	c Rhodes b Thompson	27	(8) not out	9
A.E.E. Vogler	b Buckenham	23		
T.Campbell†	not out	3		
Extras	(B 10, NB 1,)	11	(B 15, LB 3, NB 2)	20
Total		**207**	(6 wickets)	**175**

SOUTH AFRICA	O	M	R	W	O	M	R	W
Snooke	8	1	35	2	8	0	23	2
Vogler	11	3	28	2	21·3	3	72	5
Faulkner	15	1	61	1	14	6	40	3
Sinclair	15	3	41	2	4	1	16	0
Nourse	3	0	13	0				
White	1	0	5	2	4	1	15	0
ENGLAND								
Buckenham	20	3	61	3	7	2	12	1
Blythe	15	7	26	0	20	7	38	2
Simpson-Hayward	9	1	33	1	5	0	12	0
Thompson	16	3	50	4	20·3	2	62	3
Bird	1	0	3	1	1	0	5	0
Woolley	6	2	23	1	3	0	24	0
Rhodes					3	2	2	0

FALL OF WICKETS

Wkt	E 1st	SA 1st	E 2nd	SA 2nd
1st	1	47	0	18
2nd	1	93	15	18
3rd	2	101	17	76
4th	43	113	117	76
5th	112	131	125	91
6th	118	143	140	162
7th	146	143	142	–
8th	161	160	146	–
9th	198	195	167	–
10th	203	207	178	–

Umpires: A.J. Atfield (3) and S.L. Harris (1).

Close: 1st day – SA(1) 93-2 (Commaille 39); 2nd – E(2) 159-8 (Simpson-Hayward 2, Buckenham 9).

SOUTH AFRICA v ENGLAND 1909–10 (5th Test)

Played at Newlands, Cape Town, on 11, 12, 14 March.
Toss: England.   Result: ENGLAND won by nine wickets.
Debuts: South Africa – N.O. Norton, S.V. Samuelson; England – N.C. Tufnell.

Hobbs scored the first of his 15 Test hundreds and was out 'hit wicket' for the only time in his 102 innings for England. Zulch became the second South African to carry his bat through a completed innings against England; both instances took place at Newlands (also *Test No. 32*).

ENGLAND

J.B. Hobbs	hit wkt b Norton	187		
W. Rhodes	b Nourse	77	not out	0
D. Denton	c Samuelson b Nourse	26	not out	16
F.L. Fane*	b Norton	6		
F.E. Woolley	b Norton	0		
G.J. Thompson	c Sinclair b Faulkner	51		
M.C. Bird	b Norton	0	(1) c Bisset b Vogler	0
G.H.T. Simpson-Hayward	c Snooke b Faulkner	19		
N.C. Tufnell†	c and b Vogler	14		
H. Strudwick	c Zulch b Faulkner	2		
C. Blythe	not out	2		
Extras	(B 30, LB 3)	33		
Total		**417**	(1 wicket)	**16**

SOUTH AFRICA

J.W. Zulch	not out	43	b Woolley	14
J.M.M. Commaille	b Blythe	4	lbw b Thompson	5
S.J. Snooke*	b Blythe	0	b Woolley	47
A.W. Nourse	lbw b Thompson	8	c Simpson-Hayward b Woolley	0
G.A. Faulkner	c Rhodes b Blythe	10	c Woolley b Thompson	99
J.H. Sinclair	c Denton b Thompson	1	st Tufnell b Blythe	37
M. Bisset†	c Rhodes b Blythe	4	not out	27
A.E.E. Vogler	b Blythe	0	b Thompson	2
R.O. Schwarz	c Denton b Blythe	13	c Bird b Hobbs	44
N.O. Norton	b Blythe	2	c Fane b Blythe	7
S.V. Samuelson	b Simpson-Hayward	15	b Blythe	7
Extras	(LB 2, NB 1)	3	(B 25, LB 5, NB 8)	38
Total		**103**		**327**

SOUTH AFRICA	O	M	R	W	O	M	R	W
Snooke	5	0	17	0	2	2	0	0
Vogler	26	2	103	1	2·1	1	16	1
Faulkner	25·2	6	72	3				
Samuelson	18	2	64	0				
Norton	15	4	47	4				
Sinclair	8	1	36	0				
Nourse	8	1	35	2				
Schwarz	3	0	10	0				
ENGLAND								
Hobbs	4	0	11	0	8	3	19	1
Blythe	18	5	46	7	30	13	58	3
Thompson	12	6	28	2	30	5	96	3
Simpson-Hayward	4·5	0	15	1	8	1	35	0
Woolley					13	3	47	3
Bird					3	0	12	0
Rhodes					7	0	22	0

FALL OF WICKETS

	E	SA	SA	E
Wkt	1st	1st	2nd	2nd
1st	221	4	25	0
2nd	265	4	29	–
3rd	286	23	31	–
4th	286	30	151	–
5th	327	41	199	–
6th	327	48	226	–
7th	381	48	229	–
8th	408	83	296	–
9th	411	86	307	–
10th	417	103	327	–

Umpires: A.J. Atfield (4) and S.L. Harris (2).

Close: 1st day – E(1) 406-7 (Thompson 48, Tufnell 12); 2nd – SA(2) 102-3 (Snooke 31, Faulkner 39).

AUSTRALIA v SOUTH AFRICA 1910–11 (1st Test)

Played at Sydney Cricket Ground on 9, 10, 12 (*no play*), 13, 14 December.
Toss: Australia.   Result: AUSTRALIA won by an innings and 114 runs.
Debuts: Australia – C. Kelleway; South Africa – C.O.C. Pearse.

Australia scored 494 for 6 on the first day of this first match between these countries in Australia. This is still the highest total for the first day of any Test match and there has been only one instance of more runs being scored by one side in a day's play – England scoring 502 for 2 v South Africa on the second day at Lord's in 1924 (*Test No. 154*). Bardsley, who scored two hundreds in his previous match (*Test No. 105*), became the first to make three centuries in successive innings.

AUSTRALIA

V.T. Trumper	run out	27
W. Bardsley	b Pearse	132
C. Hill*	b Pearse	191
D.R.A. Gehrs	b Pearse	67
W.W. Armstrong	b Schwarz	48
V.S. Ransford	b Schwarz	11
C.G. Macartney	b Schwarz	1
C. Kelleway	not out	14
H. Carter†	st Sherwell b Schwarz	5
A. Cotter	st Sherwell b Schwarz	0
W.J. Whitty	c Snooke b Sinclair	15
Extras	(B 12, LB 4, NB 1)	17
Total		**528**

SOUTH AFRICA

L.A. Stricker	b Cotter	2	(7) lbw b Whitty		4
J.W. Zulch	b Cotter	4	(4) run out		1
C.O.C. Pearse	c Trumper b Cotter	16	(10) run out		31
A.W. Nourse	c Kelleway b Cotter	5	(6) not out		64
G.A. Faulkner	c Kelleway b Whitty	62		c Bardsley b Whitty	43
C.B. Llewellyn	b Cotter	0	(8) c Macartney b Whitty		19
S.J. Snooke	b Whitty	3	(3) b Cotter		4
J.H. Sinclair	b Cotter	1	(2) b Cotter		6
R.O. Schwarz	c Trumper b Whitty	61		c Carter b Whitty	0
P.W. Sherwell*†	not out	8	(1) c Whitty b Kelleway		60
A.E.E. Vogler	b Whitty	0		b Kelleway	0
Extras	(LB 7, NB 5)	12	(LB 1, NB 7)		8
Total		**174**			**240**

SOUTH AFRICA	O	M	R	W	O	M	R	W
Llewellyn	14	0	54	0				
Sinclair	19·4	0	80	1				
Schwarz	25	6	102	5				
Nourse	12	0	61	0				
Vogler	15	0	87	0				
Faulkner	12	0	71	0				
Pearse	12	0	56	3				
AUSTRALIA								
Cotter	20	2	69	6	17	2	73	2
Whitty	24	11	33	4	21	4	75	4
Armstrong	8	3	16	0	9	1	35	0
Kelleway	9	1	33	0	15·1	4	37	2
Macartney	7	4	11	0	5	1	12	0

FALL OF WICKETS

Wkt	A 1st	SA 1st	SA 2nd
1st	52	5	24
2nd	276	10	28
3rd	420	29	44
4th	427	38	98
5th	445	38	124
6th	453	44	144
7th	499	49	183
8th	511	149	185
9th	511	174	237
10th	528	174	240

Umpires: R.W. Crockett (14) and W. Curran (1).

Close: 1st day – A(1) 494-6 (Armstrong 43, Kelleway 6); 2nd – SA(1) 140-7 (Faulkner 45, Schwarz 52); 3rd – no play; 4th – SA(1) 146-7 (Faulkner 45, Schwarz 58).

Test No. 112/5

AUSTRALIA v SOUTH AFRICA 1910–11 (2nd Test)

Played at Melbourne Cricket Ground on 31 December, 2, 3, 4 January.
Toss: Australia.   Result: AUSTRALIA won by 89 runs.
Debuts: Nil.

Faulkner, who batted for 315 minutes and hit 26 fours, scored South Africa's first double century. It remained the national Test record until 1935-36 (*Test No. 248*). The left-arm fast-medium swing of Whitty, aided by a strong cross-wind, achieved a career-best analysis as South Africa collapsed for their lowest total so far against Australia.

AUSTRALIA

V.T. Trumper	b Pegler	34	b Faulkner	159
W. Bardsley	c Snooke b Sinclair	85	st Sherwell b Schwarz	14
C. Hill*	b Llewellyn	39	b Schwarz	0
D.R.A. Gehrs	b Llewellyn	4	st Sherwell b Schwarz	22
C.G. Macartney	run out	7	c Snooke b Llewellyn	5
V.S. Ransford	run out	58	c Sinclair b Schwarz	23
W.W. Armstrong	c Sherwell b Faulkner	75	(8) b Llewellyn	29
C. Kelleway	c Faulkner b Stricker	18	(7) b Pegler	48
H. Carter†	not out	15	c Sherwell b Llewellyn	0
A. Cotter	c Stricker b Schwarz	3	c sub (J.M.M. Commaille) b Llewellyn	15
W.J. Whitty	c Nourse b Faulkner	6	not out	5
Extras	(LB 3, NB 1)	4	(LB 6, NB 1)	7
Total		**348**		**327**

SOUTH AFRICA

P.W. Sherwell*†	c Carter b Cotter	24	b Whitty	16
J.W. Zulch	b Cotter	42	(8) not out	6
G.A. Faulkner	c Armstrong b Whitty	204	c Kelleway b Whitty	8
A.W. Nourse	b Kelleway	33	lbw b Cotter	2
L.A. Stricker	b Armstrong	26	(2) lbw b Cotter	0
C.B. Llewellyn	b Armstrong	5	b Cotter	17
S.J. Snooke	b Whitty	77	c Armstrong b Whitty	9
J.H. Sinclair	not out	58	(5) lbw b Whitty	3
R.O. Schwarz	b Whitty	0	c Kelleway b Cotter	7
C.O.C. Pearse	b Armstrong	6	c Kelleway b Whitty	0
S.J. Pegler	lbw b Armstrong	8	lbw b Whitty	0
Extras	(B 2, LB 10, W 2, NB 9)	23	(B 6, LB 3, NB 3)	12
Total		**506**		**80**

SOUTH AFRICA	O	M	R	W	O	M	R	W		FALL OF WICKETS			
Nourse	8	3	24	0	5	1	18	0		A	SA	A	SA
Snooke	5	1	19	0	8	1	24	0	*Wkt*	*1st*	*1st*	*2nd*	*2nd*
Pegler	10	0	43	1	6·3	1	24	1	1st	59	34	35	1
Schwarz	13	0	66	1	22	2	76	4	2nd	160	141	35	28
Llewellyn	10	0	69	2	16	0	81	4	3rd	164	251	89	31
Sinclair	13	1	53	1	8	0	32	0	4th	164	298	94	34
Stricker	10	0	36	1	2	1	10	0	5th	183	312	176	46
Faulkner	10·4	0	34	2	12	1	55	1	6th	262	402	237	66
									7th	309	469	279	69
AUSTRALIA									8th	337	469	279	77
Cotter	43	5	158	2	15	3	47	4	9th	340	482	305	80
Whitty	29	6	81	3	16	7	17	6	10th	348	506	327	80
Kelleway	17	3	67	1									
Armstrong	48	9	134	4	1	0	4	0					
Macartney	16	5	43	0									

Umpires: R.W. Crockett (15) and W. Hannah (3).

Close: 1st day – SA(1) 17-0 (Sherwell 10, Zulch 5); 2nd – SA(1) 352-5 (Faulkner 188, Snooke 18); 3rd – A(2) 208-5 (Trumper 133, Kelleway 6).

AUSTRALIA v SOUTH AFRICA 1910–11 (3rd Test)

Played at Adelaide Oval on 7, 9, 10, 11, 12, 13 January.
Toss: South Africa.   Result: SOUTH AFRICA won by 38 runs.
Debuts: Nil.

South Africa gained their first win against Australia in a match which produced the highest aggregate to date in Test cricket: 1,646 runs for 40 wickets. It remains the record for any Test between Australia and South Africa. Trumper's 214 not out was a new Test record for Australia. Hill became the first batsman to score 3,000 runs in Test cricket when he had made 41 in the second innings.

SOUTH AFRICA

P.W. Sherwell*†	lbw b Armstrong	11		lbw b Whitty	1
J.W. Zulch	c Macartney b Whitty	105		c Carter b Whitty	14
G.A. Faulkner	c Hill b Armstrong	56		c Armstrong b Whitty	115
A.W. Nourse	b Cotter	10		c Armstrong b Kelleway	39
C.M.H. Hathorn	b Whitty	9	(10)	b Whitty	2
C.B. Llewellyn	run out	43		b Whitty	80
S.J. Snooke	c Kelleway b Cotter	103	(8)	run out	25
J.H. Sinclair	c Armstrong b Kelleway	20	(9)	c Hill b Whitty	29
L.A. Stricker	c Kelleway b Armstrong	48	(5)	b Macartney	6
R.O. Schwarz	b Armstrong	15	(11)	not out	11
S.J. Pegler	not out	24	(7)	c Cotter b Kelleway	26
Extras	(B 6, LB 10, W 4, NB 18)	38		(B 4, LB 2, W 1, NB 5)	12
Total		**482**			**360**

AUSTRALIA

C.G. Macartney	b Llewellyn	2	(9)	lbw b Schwarz	0
C. Kelleway	c Sherwell b Llewellyn	47	(4)	c Sherwell b Sinclair	65
V.S. Ransford	b Llewellyn	50	(5)	c Llewellyn b Schwarz	0
W. Bardsley	lbw b Nourse	54	(2)	c and b Faulkner	58
V.T. Trumper	not out	214	(1)	b Llewellyn	28
D.R.A. Gehrs	c Schwarz b Faulkner	20	(8)	c Sherwell b Schwarz	22
C. Hill*	c Snooke b Schwarz	16	(3)	c Schwarz b Sinclair	55
W.W. Armstrong	b Sinclair	30	(7)	b Schwarz	48
H. Carter†	lbw b Schwarz	17	(6)	c Llewellyn b Faulkner	11
A. Cotter	c Snooke b Llewellyn	8		not out	36
W.J. Whitty	c Sherwell b Sinclair	1		c Schwarz b Pegler	11
Extras	(B 4, LB 2)	6		(LB 5)	5
Total		**465**			**339**

AUSTRALIA	O	M	R	W	O	M	R	W	FALL OF WICKETS				
Cotter	38	4	100	2	23	3	64	0		SA	A	SA	A
Whitty	34	7	114	2	39·2	5	104	6	*Wkt*	*1st*	*1st*	*2nd*	*2nd*
Armstrong	42·4	9	103	4	33	9	90	0	1st	31	7	10	63
Kelleway	24	6	72	1	23	4	64	2	2nd	166	94	29	122
Macartney	27	9	51	0	12	3	26	1	3rd	189	111	106	170
Gehrs	1	0	4	0					4th	191	229	119	171
									5th	205	276	228	187
SOUTH AFRICA									6th	303	319	273	263
Llewellyn	31	4	107	4	12	0	48	1	7th	338	384	317	285
Schwarz	19	2	68	2	15	3	48	4	8th	400	430	319	285
Sinclair	25·5	3	86	2	21	2	72	2	9th	429	458	327	292
Pegler	20	2	92	0	10·4	0	58	1	10th	482	465	360	339
Faulkner	11	0	59	1	15	3	56	2					
Nourse	12	2	43	1	5	0	31	0					
Stricker	1	0	4	0									
Snooke					5	0	21	0					

Umpires: R.W. Crockett (16) and G.A. Watson (1).

Close: 1st day – SA(1) 279-5 (Llewellyn 36, Snooke 36); 2nd – A(1) 72-1 (Kelleway 39, Ransford 31); 3rd – A(1) 458-8 (Trumper 208, Cotter 8); 4th – SA(2) 232-5 (Llewellyn 44, Pegler 2); 5th – A(2) 187-4 (Kelleway 33, Carter 11).

AUSTRALIA v SOUTH AFRICA 1910–11 (4th Test)

Played at Melbourne Cricket Ground on 17, 18, 20, 21 February.
Toss: South Africa.   Result: AUSTRALIA won by 530 runs.
Debuts: Australia – H.V. Hordern.

Australia gained the first Test win by a margin exceeding 500 runs. Their second innings total of 578 remains their highest in a home Test against South Africa and was then the highest ever reached in the second innings of a Test. Llewellyn injured his left hand fielding a drive off his own bowling. W.L. Murdoch, Australia's captain in 16 Tests, died a few hours after collapsing at the match during the second day.

AUSTRALIA

V.T. Trumper	b Faulkner	7	(6) c Sherwell b Vogler	87
W. Bardsley	c Schwarz b Pegler	82	(3) run out	15
C. Hill*	b Llewellyn	11	(5) st Sherwell b Pegler	100
W.W. Armstrong	run out	48	(4) c Sherwell b Vogler	132
D.R.A. Gehrs	st Sherwell b Vogler	9	(2) c Snooke b Faulkner	58
C. Kelleway	run out	59	(1) run out	18
V.S. Ransford	lbw b Schwarz	75	b Faulkner	95
A. Cotter	b Pegler	10	c sub (C.O.C. Pearse) b Vogler	0
H.V. Hordern	c Vogler b Pegler	7	c sub (C.O.C. Pearse) b Schwarz	24
H. Carter†	run out	5	c Snooke b Faulkner	2
W.J. Whitty	not out	0	not out	39
Extras	(B 7, LB 7, W 1)	15	(B 4, LB 3, NB 1)	8
Total		**328**		**578**

SOUTH AFRICA

J.W. Zulch	run out	2	c Trumper b Cotter	15
L.A. Stricker	b Hordern	4	c Carter b Cotter	0
G.A. Faulkner	c Gehrs b Hordern	20	b Whitty	80
A.W. Nourse	not out	92	c and b Hordern	28
S.J. Snooke	b Whitty	1	b Hordern	7
J.H. Sinclair	b Hordern	0	lbw b Hordern	19
R.O. Schwarz	b Whitty	18	c Carter b Whitty	1
P.W. Sherwell*†	c sub (T.J. Matthews) b Whitty	41	c Kelleway b Hordern	0
C.B. Llewellyn	b Whitty	7	absent hurt	
S.J. Pegler	c Hill b Cotter	15	(9) c Gehrs b Hordern	8
A.E.E. Vogler	b Cotter	0	(10) not out	2
Extras	(B 4, LB 1)	5	(B 7, LB 1, W 2, NB 1)	11
Total		**205**		**171**

SOUTH AFRICA	O	M	R	W	O	M	R	W
Llewellyn	15	1	65	1				
Faulkner	18	2	82	1	28·2	5	101	3
Schwarz	15	2	34	1	38	4	168	1
Vogler	8	2	30	1	15	3	59	3
Sinclair	14	2	40	0	13	1	71	0
Pegler	17·4	3	40	3	17	1	88	1
Stricker	5	1	18	0	3	0	14	0
Nourse	2	0	4	0	7	0	31	0
Zulch					3	0	26	0
Snooke					2	0	12	0
AUSTRALIA								
Cotter	6·5	0	16	2	6	1	22	2
Whitty	22	5	78	4	9	2	32	2
Hordern	15	1	39	3	14·2	2	66	5
Armstrong	8	2	25	0	3	0	15	0
Kelleway	11	1	42	0	8	0	25	0

FALL OF WICKETS

	A	SA	A	SA
Wkt	1st	1st	2nd	2nd
1st	9	7	48	2
2nd	24	23	88	25
3rd	126	36	106	88
4th	146	37	260	108
5th	182	38	403	151
6th	289	65	418	158
7th	310	156	420	161
8th	317	171	491	165
9th	328	205	496	171
10th	328	205	578	–

Umpires: R.W. Crockett (17) and D. Elder (1).

Close: 1st day – A(1) 317-8 (Hordern 1); 2nd – A(2) 48-1 (Gehrs 30); 3rd – A(2) 476-7 (Ransford 38, Hordern 23).

AUSTRALIA v SOUTH AFRICA 1910–11 (5th Test)

Played at Sydney Cricket Ground on 3, 4, 6, 7 March.
Toss: South Africa.   Result: AUSTRALIA won by seven wickets.
Debuts: Nil.

In the second innings Macartney took only 35 minutes to reach his fifty. This remains the fastest for Australia, although it was equalled by J.M. Gregory in 1921-22 (*Test No. 146*). Faulkner's series aggregate of 732 (average 73.20) is the South African record against all countries. Whitty's total of 37 wickets (average 17.08) remains the Australian record for a home series against South Africa. Sherwell's nine stumpings in this series is still the world record.

AUSTRALIA

C. Kelleway	c Snooke b Llewellyn	2	(5) not out	24
C.G. Macartney	lbw b Schwarz	137	c Nourse b Schwarz	56
H.V. Hordern	lbw b Sinclair	50		
W. Bardsley	c and b Sinclair	94	(1) b Nourse	39
W.J. Whitty	c Nourse b Llewellyn	13		
V.T. Trumper	b Schwarz	31	(3) not out	74
C. Hill*	st Sherwell b Schwarz	13		
W.W. Armstrong	c Pearse b Schwarz	0		
V.S. Ransford	st Sherwell b Schwarz	6	(4) b Nourse	0
A. Cotter	st Sherwell b Schwarz	8		
H. Carter†	not out	1		
Extras	(B 7, LB 2)	9	(B 1, LB 3, W 1)	5
Total		**364**	(3 wickets)	**198**

SOUTH AFRICA

C.O.C. Pearse	b Whitty	0	(11) lbw b Hordern	2
J.W. Zulch	st Carter b Hordern	15	b Ransford	150
G.A. Faulkner	b Armstrong	52	(4) b Cotter	92
A.W. Nourse	b Armstrong	3	(5) c Cotter b Whitty	28
L.A. Stricker	c Macartney b Hordern	19	(6) b Cotter	42
J.H. Sinclair	c Ransford b Hordern	1	(8) c and b Whitty	12
S.J. Snooke	b Hordern	18	c Carter b Whitty	12
C.B. Llewellyn	c Carter b Kelleway	24	(9) b Whitty	3
R.O. Schwarz	run out	13	(10) not out	6
P.W. Sherwell*†	c Bardsley b Whitty	5	(1) b Armstrong	14
S.J. Pegler	not out	0	(3) c Cotter b Hordern	26
Extras	(B 1, LB 9)	10	(B 3, LB 4, W 2, NB 5)	14
Total		**160**		**401**

SOUTH AFRICA	O	M	R	W	O	M	R	W
Llewellyn	25	0	92	2	8	1	43	0
Faulkner	12	2	38	0	5	0	18	0
Sinclair	27	6	83	2	6	1	22	0
Pegler	6	1	31	0	4	0	22	0
Schwarz	11·4	0	47	6	9	0	42	1
Nourse	5	1	26	0	8·1	0	32	2
Pearse	9	0	36	0	3	0	14	0
Zulch	1	0	2	0				
AUSTRALIA								
Cotter	8	2	24	0	18	1	60	2
Whitty	11·1	3	32	2	27	5	66	4
Hordern	21	3	73	4	30·1	1	117	2
Kelleway	4	1	4	1	7	1	46	0
Armstrong	6	1	17	2	26	4	68	1
Macartney					10	0	21	0
Ransford					4	2	9	1

FALL OF WICKETS

Wkt	A 1st	SA 1st	SA 2nd	A 2nd
1st	2	4	19	74
2nd	126	47	64	134
3rd	271	70	207	134
4th	296	81	278	–
5th	317	87	357	–
6th	346	115	368	–
7th	346	128	385	–
8th	351	144	392	–
9th	361	160	398	–
10th	364	160	401	–

Umpires: R.W. Crockett (18) and D. Elder (2).

Close: 1st day – A(1) 281-3 (Bardsley 83, Whitty 2); 2nd – SA(2) 33-1 (Zulch 7, Pegler 10); 3rd – SA(2) 368-6 (Snooke 2).

AUSTRALIA v ENGLAND 1911–12 (1st Test)

Played at Sydney Cricket Ground on 15, 16, 18, 19, 20, 21 December.
Toss: Australia.   Result: AUSTRALIA won by 146 runs.
Debuts: Australia – R.B. Minnett; England – J.W.H.T. Douglas, F.R. Foster, J.W. Hearne,
    S.P. Kinneir, C.P. Mead.

Douglas took over the captaincy of the touring team when P.F. Warner fell ill after the first match. Trumper's century was his eighth in Tests and his sixth against England – both being records at the time. He became the second batsman after C. Hill to score 3,000 runs in Tests when his score reached 106. The googly bowler, Dr H.V. Hordern, took 12 wickets in his first Test against England (he had played twice against South Africa in the previous season).

AUSTRALIA

W. Bardsley	c Strudwick b Douglas	30	b Foster		12
C. Kelleway	c and b Woolley	20	b Douglas		70
C. Hill*	run out	46	b Foster		65
W.W. Armstrong	st Strudwick b Hearne	60	b Foster		28
V.T. Trumper	c Hobbs b Woolley	113	c and b Douglas		14
V.S. Ransford	c Hearne b Barnes	26	c Rhodes b Barnes		34
R.B. Minnett	c Foster b Barnes	90	(8) b Douglas		17
H.V. Hordern	not out	17	(7) b Foster		18
A. Cotter	c and b Barnes	6	lbw b Douglas		2
H. Carter†	b Foster	13	c Gunn b Foster		15
W.J. Whitty	b Foster	0	not out		9
Extras	(B 9, LB 15, NB 2)	26	(B 16, LB 7, NB 1)		24
Total		**447**			**308**

ENGLAND

J.B. Hobbs	c Hill b Whitty	63	c Carter b Cotter		22
S.P. Kinneir	b Kelleway	22	c Trumper b Hordern		30
G. Gunn	b Cotter	4	c Whitty b Hordern		62
W. Rhodes	c Hill b Hordern	41	(5) c Trumper b Hordern		0
C.P. Mead	c and b Hordern	0	(4) run out		25
J.W. Hearne	c Trumper b Kelleway	76	(7) b Hordern		43
F.R. Foster	b Hordern	56	(6) c Ransford b Hordern		21
F.E. Woolley	b Hordern	39	c Armstrong b Cotter		7
J.W.H.T. Douglas*	c Trumper b Hordern	0	b Hordern		32
S.F. Barnes	b Kelleway	9	b Hordern		14
H. Strudwick†	not out	0	not out		12
Extras	(B 3, LB 3, W 1, NB 1)	8	(B 14, LB 8, NB 1)		23
Total		**318**			**291**

ENGLAND	O	M	R	W	O	M	R	W
Foster	29	6	105	2	31·3	5	92	5
Douglas	24	5	62	1	21	3	50	4
Barnes	35	5	107	3	30	8	72	1
Hearne	10	1	44	1	13	2	51	0
Woolley	21	2	77	2	6	1	15	0
Rhodes	8	0	26	0	3	1	4	0
AUSTRALIA								
Cotter	19	0	88	1	27	3	71	2
Whitty	28	13	60	1	20	8	41	0
Kelleway	16·5	3	46	3	19	6	27	0
Hordern	27	4	85	5	42·2	11	90	7
Armstrong	9	3	28	0	15	3	39	0
Minnett	2	1	3	0				

FALL OF WICKETS

	A	E	A	E
Wkt	1st	1st	2nd	2nd
1st	44	45	29	29
2nd	77	53	150	69
3rd	121	115	169	141
4th	198	129	191	141
5th	278	142	218	148
6th	387	231	246	167
7th	420	293	268	177
8th	426	293	274	263
9th	447	310	283	276
10th	447	318	308	291

Umpires: R.W. Crockett (19) and W. Curran (2).

Close: 1st day – A(1) 317-5 (Trumper 95, Minnett 22); 2nd – E(1) 142-4 (Hobbs 63, Hearne 9); 3rd – A(2) 119-1 (Kelleway 47, Hill 49); 4th – E(2) 65-1 (Kinneir 27, Gunn 16); 5th – E(2) 263-8 (Douglas 32).

AUSTRALIA v ENGLAND 1911–12 (2nd Test)

Played at Melbourne Cricket Ground on 30 December, 1, 2, 3 January.
Toss: Australia.   Result: ENGLAND won by eight wickets.
Debuts: England – J.W. Hitch, E.J. Smith.

Barnes, then 38 and unwell before play began, gave the match a sensational start by dismissing Bardsley (with his first ball), Kelleway, Hill, and Armstrong for just one run in five overs and taking 5 for 6 in his opening spell of 11 overs. Hearne's hundred was scored in his second Test and at the age of 20 years 324 days. Only D.C.S. Compton, who was 20 years 19 days old when he scored 102 at Nottingham in 1938 (*Test No. 263*), has scored a century for England against Australia at an earlier age. Hobbs batted for 227 minutes, steering England to victory with the first of his 12 hundreds against Australia.

AUSTRALIA

C. Kelleway	lbw b Barnes	2		c Gunn b Foster	13
W. Bardsley	b Barnes	0		run out	16
C. Hill*	b Barnes	4		c Gunn b Barnes	0
W.W. Armstrong	c Smith b Barnes	4		b Foster	90
V.T. Trumper	b Foster	13		b Barnes	2
V.S. Ransford	c Smith b Hitch	43		c Smith b Foster	32
R.B. Minnett	c Hobbs b Barnes	2	(8)	b Foster	34
H.V. Hordern	not out	49	(7)	c Mead b Foster	31
A. Cotter	run out	14		c Hobbs b Foster	41
H. Carter†	c Smith b Douglas	29		b Barnes	16
W.J. Whitty	b Woolley	14		not out	0
Extras	(B 5, LB 4, NB 1)	10		(B 14, LB 7, W 1, NB 2)	24
Total		**184**			**299**

ENGLAND

W. Rhodes	c Trumper b Cotter	61		c Carter b Cotter	28
J.B. Hobbs	c Carter b Cotter	6		not out	126
J.W. Hearne	c Carter b Cotter	114	(4)	not out	12
G. Gunn	lbw b Armstrong	10	(3)	c Carter b Whitty	43
C.P. Mead	c Armstrong b Whitty	11			
F.R. Foster	c Hill b Cotter	9			
J.W.H.T. Douglas*	b Hordern	9			
F.E. Woolley	c Ransford b Hordern	23			
E.J. Smith†	b Hordern	5			
S.F. Barnes	lbw b Hordern	1			
J.W. Hitch	not out	0			
Extras	(B 2, LB 10, NB 4)	16		(B 5, LB 5)	10
Total		**265**		(2 wickets)	**219**

ENGLAND	O	M	R	W	O	M	R	W
Foster	16	2	52	1	38	9	91	6
Barnes	23	9	44	5	32·1	7	96	3
Hitch	7	0	57	1	5	0	21	0
Douglas	15	4	33	1	10	0	38	0
Hearne	1	0	8	0	1	0	5	0
Woolley	0·1	0	0	1	3	0	21	0
Rhodes					3	1	3	0
AUSTRALIA								
Cotter	22	2	73	4	14	5	45	1
Whitty	19	2	47	1	18	3	37	1
Hordern	23·1	1	66	4	17	0	66	0
Kelleway	15	7	27	0	7	0	15	0
Armstrong	15	6	20	1	8	1	22	0
Minnett	5	0	16	0	2	0	13	0
Ransford					1·1	0	11	0

FALL OF WICKETS

	A	E	A	E
Wkt	1st	1st	2nd	2nd
1st	0	10	28	57
2nd	5	137	34	169
3rd	8	174	34	–
4th	11	213	38	–
5th	33	224	135	–
6th	38	227	168	–
7th	80	258	232	–
8th	97	260	235	–
9th	140	262	298	–
10th	184	265	299	–

Umpires: R.W. Crockett (20) and D. Elder (3).

Close: 1st day – E(1) 38-1 (Rhodes 16, Hearne 12); 2nd – E(1) 265 all out; 3rd – A(2) 269-8 (Cotter 18, Carter 12).

AUSTRALIA v ENGLAND 1911–12 (3rd Test)

Played at Adelaide Oval on 12, 13, 15, 16, 17 January.
Toss: Australia.   Result: ENGLAND won by seven wickets.
Debuts: Australia – T.J. Matthews.

Hobbs scored his second hundred in successive Test innings. It was the highest of his 12 centuries against Australia and it remains England's highest score at Adelaide. Ransford retired at 17 for 2 when 6 not out and resumed at 113 for 8. Hill made his fifth score of between 96 and 99 against England. Trumper batted last after a fierce drive by Woolley had damaged a vein in his leg. Joseph Vine, the Sussex all-rounder who made his debut for England in the next Test, substituted for Trumper and caught Smith.

AUSTRALIA

W. Bardsley	c Smith b Barnes	5		b Foster	63
C. Kelleway	b Foster	1		b Douglas	37
H.V. Hordern	c Rhodes b Foster	25	(7)	c and b Barnes	5
V.S. Ransford	not out	8	(8)	b Hitch	38
W.W. Armstrong	b Foster	33		b Douglas	25
V.T. Trumper	b Hitch	26	(11)	not out	1
C. Hill*	st Smith b Foster	0	(4)	c Hitch b Barnes	98
R.B. Minnett	b Foster	0	(6)	c Hobbs b Barnes	38
T.J. Matthews	c Mead b Barnes	5		b Barnes	53
A. Cotter	b Barnes	11		b Barnes	15
H. Carter†	c Gunn b Douglas	8	(3)	c Smith b Woolley	72
Extras	(B 3, LB 6, NB 2)	11		(B 26, LB 3, NB 2)	31
Total		**133**			**476**

ENGLAND

J.B. Hobbs	c Hordern b Minnett	187		lbw b Hordern	3
W. Rhodes	lbw b Cotter	59		not out	57
G. Gunn	c Hill b Cotter	29		c Cotter b Kelleway	45
J.W. Hearne	c Hill b Kelleway	12		c Kelleway b Matthews	2
C.P. Mead	c and b Hordern	46		not out	2
F.R. Foster	b Armstrong	71			
J.W.H.T. Douglas*	b Minnett	35			
F.E. Woolley	b Cotter	20			
E.J. Smith†	c sub (J. Vine) b Cotter	22			
S.F. Barnes	not out	2			
J.W. Hitch	c sub (C.G. Macartney) b Hordern	0			
Extras	(B 7, LB 8, NB 3)	18		(B 1, LB 1, NB 1)	3
Total		**501**		(3 wickets)	**112**

ENGLAND	O	M	R	W	O	M	R	W
Foster	26	9	36	5	49	15	103	1
Barnes	23	4	71	3	46·4	7	105	5
Douglas	7	2	7	1	29	10	71	2
Hearne	2	0	6	0	10	0	61	0
Hitch	2	1	2	1	11	0	69	1
Woolley					7	1	30	1
Rhodes					1	0	6	0
AUSTRALIA								
Cotter	43	11	125	4	5	0	21	0
Hordern	47·1	5	143	2	11	3	32	1
Kelleway	23	3	46	1	7	3	8	1
Matthews	33	8	72	0	9·2	3	24	1
Minnett	17	3	54	2	4	1	12	0
Armstrong	14	0	43	1	6	1	12	0

FALL OF WICKETS

Wkt	A 1st	E 1st	A 2nd	E 2nd
1st	6	147	86	5
2nd	6	206	122	102
3rd	65	260	279	105
4th	84	323	303	–
5th	88	350	342	–
6th	88	435	360	–
7th	97	455	363	–
8th	113	492	447	–
9th	123	501	475	–
10th	133	501	476	–

Umpires: R.W. Crockett (21) and G.A. Watson (2).

Close: 1st day – E(1) 49-0 (Hobbs 29, Rhodes 20); 2nd – E(1) 327-4 (Mead 31, Foster 0); 3rd – A(2) 96-1 (Bardsley 46, Carter 4); 4th – A(2) 360-5 (Minnett 38, Hordern 3).

AUSTRALIA v ENGLAND 1911–12 (4th Test)

Played at Melbourne Cricket Ground on 9, 10, 12, 13 February.
Toss: England.   Result: ENGLAND won by an innings and 225 runs.
Debuts: England – J. Vine.

England's total of 589 and the first-wicket partnership of 323 between Hobbs and Rhodes set new Test records. That partnership took 268 minutes and remained the highest opening stand by either country in Tests between England and Australia until 1989 (*Test No. 1125*), and is still England's highest stand for any wicket in Australia. There has been only one higher opening partnership for England, L. Hutton and C. Washbrook scoring 359 against South Africa in 1948-49 (*Test No. 310*). Douglas achieved his best analysis in Tests, his last wicket regaining the Ashes for England.

AUSTRALIA

C. Kelleway	c Hearne b Woolley	29		c Smith b Barnes	5
H.V. Hordern	b Barnes	19	(11)	c Foster b Douglas	5
W. Bardsley	b Foster	0		b Foster	3
V.T. Trumper	b Foster	17		b Barnes	28
C. Hill*	c Hearne b Barnes	22		b Douglas	11
W.W. Armstrong	b Barnes	7		b Douglas	11
R.B. Minnett	c Rhodes b Foster	56		b Douglas	7
V.S. Ransford	c Rhodes b Foster	4		not out	29
T.J. Matthews	c Gunn b Barnes	3	(10)	b Foster	10
A. Cotter	b Barnes	15	(9)	c Mead b Foster	8
H. Carter†	not out	6	(2)	c Hearne b Douglas	38
Extras	(B 1, LB 5, NB 7)	13		(B 9, LB 2, NB 7)	18
Total		**191**			**173**

ENGLAND

J.B. Hobbs	c Carter b Hordern	178
W. Rhodes	c Carter b Minnett	179
G. Gunn	c Hill b Armstrong	75
J.W. Hearne	c Armstrong b Minnett	0
F.R. Foster	c Hordern b Armstrong	50
J.W.H.T. Douglas*	c Bardsley b Armstrong	0
F.E. Woolley	c Kelleway b Minnett	56
C.P. Mead	b Hordern	21
J. Vine	not out	4
E.J. Smith†	c Matthews b Kelleway	7
S.F. Barnes	c Hill b Hordern	0
Extras	(B 2, LB 4, W 4, NB 9)	19
Total		**589**

ENGLAND	O	M	R	W	O	M	R	W		FALL OF WICKETS		
Foster	22	2	77	4	19	3	38	3		A	E	A
Barnes	29·1	4	74	5	20	6	47	2	*Wkt*	*1st*	*1st*	*2nd*
Woolley	11	3	22	1	2	0	7	0	1st	53	323	12
Rhodes	2	1	1	0					2nd	53	425	20
Hearne	1	0	4	0	3	0	17	0	3rd	69	425	76
Douglas					17·5	6	46	5	4th	74	486	86
									5th	83	486	101
AUSTRALIA									6th	124	513	112
Cotter	37	5	125	0					7th	152	565	117
Kelleway	26	2	80	1					8th	165	579	127
Armstrong	36	12	93	3					9th	170	589	156
Matthews	22	1	68	0					10th	191	589	173
Hordern	47·5	5	137	3								
Minnett	20	5	59	3								
Ransford	2	1	8	0								

Umpires: R.W. Crockett (22) and W. Young (1).

Close: 1st day – E(1) 54-0 (Hobbs 30, Rhodes 23); 2nd – E(1) 370-1 (Rhodes 157, Gunn 22); 3rd – A(2) 8-0 (Kelleway 2, Carter 5).

AUSTRALIA v ENGLAND 1911–12 (5th Test)

Played at Sydney Cricket Ground on 23, 24, 26 (*no play*), 27, 28, 29 (*no play*) February, 1 March.
Toss: England.   Result: ENGLAND won by 70 runs.
Debuts: Australia – J.W. McLaren.

Woolley's hundred was the first by an England left-hander against Australia. His partnership of 143 with Vine remains the England seventh-wicket record against Australia. This match marked the end of the Test careers of the two heaviest-scoring batsmen – Hill (3,412 runs), and Trumper (3,163). The latter celebrated his fortieth consecutive appearance against England with a fifty. Barnes took 34 wickets in the rubber to set an England record that stood until M.W. Tate (38) beat it in 1924-25. Foster, with 226 runs and 32 wickets, achieved a notable all-round performance.

ENGLAND

J.B. Hobbs	c Ransford b Hordern	32	c Hazlitt b Hordern		45
W. Rhodes	b Macartney	8	lbw b Armstrong		30
G. Gunn	st Carter b Hordern	52	b Hordern		61
J.W. Hearne	c Macartney b Armstrong	4	b Hordern		18
F.R. Foster	st Carter b Hazlitt	15	b McLaren		4
J.W.H.T. Douglas*	c Ransford b Hordern	18	b Armstrong		8
F.E. Woolley	not out	133	c Armstrong b Hazlitt		11
J. Vine	b Hordern	36	not out		6
E.J. Smith†	b Hordern	0	b Hordern		13
S.F. Barnes	c Hordern b Hazlitt	5	b Hordern		4
J.W. Hitch	c Hill b Hazlitt	4	c Ransford b Armstrong		4
Extras	(B 10, LB 4, W 1, NB 2)	17	(B 8, NB 2)		10
Total		**324**			**214**

AUSTRALIA

V.T. Trumper	c Woolley b Barnes	5	c Woolley b Barnes		50
S.E. Gregory	c Gunn b Douglas	32	c Smith b Barnes		40
C. Hill*	c Smith b Hitch	20	b Foster		8
W.W. Armstrong	lbw b Barnes	33	b Barnes		33
R.B. Minnett	c Douglas b Hitch	0	c Woolley b Barnes		61
V.S. Ransford	c Hitch b Foster	29	b Woolley		9
H. Carter†	c sub (C.P. Mead) b Barnes	11	(8) c Woolley b Foster		23
C.G. Macartney	c and b Woolley	26	(7) c Woolley b Foster		27
H.V. Hordern	b Woolley	0	run out		4
G.R. Hazlitt	run out	1	c Rhodes b Foster		4
J.W. McLaren	not out	0	not out		0
Extras	(B 14, LB 2, W 2, NB 1)	19	(B 22, LB 8, W 1, NB 2)		33
Total		**176**			**292**

AUSTRALIA	O	M	R	W	O	M	R	W
McLaren	16	2	47	0	8	1	23	1
Macartney	12	3	26	1	7	0	28	0
Hordern	37	8	95	5	25	5	66	5
Hazlitt	31	6	75	3	12	2	52	1
Armstrong	25	8	42	1	17·3	7	35	3
Minnett	8	1	22	0	1	1	0	0
ENGLAND								
Foster	16	0	55	1	30·1	7	43	4
Barnes	19	2	56	3	39	12	106	4
Hitch	9	0	31	2	6	1	23	0
Douglas	7	0	14	1	9	0	34	0
Woolley	2	1	1	2	16	5	36	1
Rhodes					2	0	17	0

FALL OF WICKETS

Wkt	E 1st	A 1st	E 2nd	A 2nd
1st	15	17	76	88
2nd	69	59	76	101
3rd	83	81	105	117
4th	114	82	110	209
5th	125	133	146	220
6th	162	133	178	231
7th	305	171	186	278
8th	305	175	201	287
9th	312	176	209	287
10th	324	176	214	292

Umpires: R.W. Crockett (23) and A.C. Jones (3).

Close: 1st day – E(1) 204-6 (Woolley 62, Vine 8); 2nd – A(1) 133-5 (Ransford 29, Carter 0); 3rd – no play; 4th – E(2) 209-9 (Vine 5); 5th – A(2) 193-3 (Armstrong 23, Minnett 49); 6th – no play.

AUSTRALIA v SOUTH AFRICA 1912 (1st Test)
Triangular Tournament – 1st Match

Played at Old Trafford, Manchester, on 27, 28 May.
Toss: Australia.   Result: AUSTRALIA won by an innings and 88 runs.
Debuts: Australia – W. Carkeek, S.H. Emery, C.B. Jennings; South Africa – R. Beaumont,
   G.P.D. Hartigan, H.W. Taylor, T.A. Ward. *F. Mitchell was playing in his first Test match for South
   Africa having made his debut for England in Test No. 58.*

Matthews created a unique Test record by taking a hat-trick in each innings – both instances being on the second
day. Ward bagged a 'king pair', being the third victim of both hat-tricks. This was the first of nine Test matches
between England, Australia and South Africa which constituted the Triangular Tournament of 1912, the
brainchild of Sir Abe Bailey. The first day produced 464 runs.

AUSTRALIA

C.B. Jennings	c Schwarz b Pegler	32
C. Kelleway	c Ward b Pegler	114
C.G. Macartney	b Pegler	21
W. Bardsley	c and b White	121
S.E. Gregory*	st Ward b Pegler	37
R.B. Minnett	c and b Schwarz	12
T.J. Matthews	not out	49
S.H. Emery	b Schwarz	1
G.R. Hazlitt	lbw b Schwarz	0
W. Carkeek†	b Pegler	4
W.J. Whitty	st Ward b Pegler	33
Extras	(B 14, LB 9, W 1)	24
Total		**448**

SOUTH AFRICA

G.P.D. Hartigan	c Carkeek b Emery	25		b Kelleway	4
H.W. Taylor	c Carkeek b Whitty	0	(5)	b Matthews	21
A.W. Nourse	b Whitty	17		c Bardsley b Whitty	18
S.J. Snooke	b Whitty	7		b Whitty	9
G.A. Faulkner	not out	122	(2)	b Kelleway	0
G.C. White	lbw b Whitty	22		c Carkeek b Kelleway	9
F. Mitchell*	b Whitty	11		b Kelleway	0
R.O. Schwarz	b Hazlitt	19		c and b Matthews	0
R. Beaumont	b Matthews	31	(10)	b Kelleway	17
S.J. Pegler	lbw b Matthews	0	(11)	not out	8
T.A. Ward†	lbw b Matthews	0	(9)	c and b Matthews	0
Extras	(B 2, LB 5, W 1, NB 3)	11		(B 5, LB 1, NB 3)	9
Total		**265**			**95**

SOUTH AFRICA	O	M	R	W	O	M	R	W
Faulkner	16	2	55	0				
Nourse	14	1	62	0				
Pegler	45·3	9	105	6				
Schwarz	32	0	142	3				
Hartigan	9	0	31	0				
White	6	1	29	1				
AUSTRALIA								
Hazlitt	16	4	46	1				
Whitty	34	12	55	5	6	3	15	2
Emery	37	10	94	1				
Kelleway	11	3	27	0	14·2	4	33	5
Matthews	12	3	16	3	8	1	38	3
Minnett	6	2	16	0				

FALL OF WICKETS

Wkt	A 1st	SA 1st	SA 2nd
1st	62	4	1
2nd	92	30	22
3rd	294	42	22
4th	314	54	43
5th	328	143	70
6th	375	167	70
7th	376	200	70
8th	376	265	70
9th	385	265	78
10th	448	265	95

Umpires: G. Webb (1) and A.A. White (6).

Close: 1st day – SA(1) 16-1 (Hartigan 8, Nourse 8).

ENGLAND v SOUTH AFRICA 1912 (1st Test)
Triangular Tournament – 2nd Match

Played at Lord's, London, on 10, 11, 12 June.
Toss: South Africa.   Result: ENGLAND won by an innings and 62 runs.
Debuts: South Africa – C.P. Carter.

Following their two-day defeat by Australia, South Africa were bowled out by England in 90 minutes for the lowest total of the Tournament. For the first time in a Test match, extras top-scored in an innings. Pegler, whose leg-spin bowling accounted for 189 wickets on South Africa's tour, including 29 in this Tournament, returned the best analysis of his Test career.

SOUTH AFRICA

G.P.D. Hartigan	c Foster b Barnes	0	b Foster	1
H.W. Taylor	lbw b Barnes	1	b Barnes	5
A.W. Nourse	b Foster	13	run out	17
C.B. Llewellyn	b Foster	9	c Smith b Foster	75
G.A. Faulkner	b Foster	7	b Barnes	15
S.J. Snooke	b Barnes	2	b Foster	16
F. Mitchell*	c and b Barnes	1	b Barnes	1
R.O. Schwarz	c Foster b Barnes	4	b Barnes	28
S.J. Pegler	b Foster	4	b Barnes	10
C.P. Carter	b Foster	0	not out	27
T. Campbell†	not out	0	c Jessop b Barnes	3
Extras	(B 12, LB 3, NB 2)	17	(B 17, LB 1, NB 1)	19
Total		**58**		**217**

ENGLAND

J.B. Hobbs	b Nourse	4
W. Rhodes	b Nourse	36
R.H. Spooner	c Llewellyn b Nourse	119
C.B. Fry*	b Pegler	29
P.F. Warner	st Campbell b Pegler	39
F.E. Woolley	b Pegler	73
G.L. Jessop	b Pegler	3
F.R. Foster	lbw b Pegler	11
E.J. Smith†	b Pegler	2
S.F. Barnes	not out	0
W. Brearley	b Pegler	0
Extras	(B 11, LB 9, W 1)	21
Total		**337**

ENGLAND	O	M	R	W	O	M	R	W
Foster	13·1	7	16	5	27	10	54	3
Barnes	13	3	25	5	34	9	85	6
Brearley					6	2	4	0
Woolley					4	0	19	0
Hobbs					11	2	36	0
SOUTH AFRICA								
Nourse	16	5	46	3				
Pegler	31	8	65	7				
Faulkner	29	6	72	0				
Carter	4	0	15	0				
Llewellyn	9	0	60	0				
Schwarz	20	3	44	0				
Hartigan	10	2	14	0				

FALL OF WICKETS

Wkt	SA 1st	E 1st	SA 2nd
1st	2	4	5
2nd	3	128	17
3rd	28	183	36
4th	35	207	104
5th	36	320	132
6th	42	323	135
7th	45	324	147
8th	54	330	176
9th	55	337	197
10th	58	337	217

Umpires: W. Richards (8) and W.A.J. West (7).

Close: 1st day – E(1) 122-1 (Rhodes 36, Spooner 67); 2nd – SA(2) 114-4 (Llewellyn 60, Snooke 5).

ENGLAND v AUSTRALIA 1912 (1st Test)
Triangular Tournament – 3rd Match

Played at Lord's, London, on 24, 25, 26 June.
Toss: England.   Result: MATCH DRAWN.
Debuts: England – H. Dean; Australia – D.B.M. Smith

The weather at Lord's consolidated its unenviable Test record by restricting play in this match to $3\frac{1}{2}$ hours on the first day and to 20 minutes on the second. Over 35,000 paid for admission to this key match of the Tournament at Headquarters. The Prince of Wales was present on the third day. Hobbs batted for 165 minutes, his innings twice interrupted by heavy showers and played in its latter stages on a most treacherous surface.

ENGLAND

J.B. Hobbs	b Emery	107
W. Rhodes	c Carkeek b Kelleway	59
R.H. Spooner	c Bardsley b Kelleway	1
C.B. Fry*	run out	42
P.F. Warner	b Emery	4
F.E. Woolley	c Kelleway b Hazlitt	20
F.R. Foster	c Macartney b Whitty	20
J.W. Hearne	not out	21
E.J. Smith†	not out	14
S.F. Barnes	) did not bat	
H. Dean	)	
Extras	(B 16, LB 4, NB 2)	22
Total	(7 wickets declared)	**310**

AUSTRALIA

C.B. Jennings	c Smith b Foster	21
C. Kelleway	b Rhodes	61
C.G. Macartney	c Smith b Foster	99
W. Bardsley	lbw b Rhodes	21
S.E. Gregory*	c Foster b Dean	10
D.B.M. Smith	not out	24
T.J. Matthews	b Dean	0
G.R. Hazlitt	b Rhodes	19
S.H. Emery	) did not bat	
W.J. Whitty	)	
W. Carkeek†	)	
Extras	(B 17, LB 5, W 1, NB 4)	27
Total	(7 wickets)	**282**

AUSTRALIA	O	M	R	W
Whitty	12	2	69	1
Hazlitt	25	6	68	1
Matthews	13	4	26	0
Kelleway	21	5	66	2
Emery	12	1	46	2
Macartney	7	1	13	0
ENGLAND				
Foster	36	18	42	2
Barnes	31	10	74	0
Dean	29	10	49	2
Hearne	12	1	31	0
Rhodes	19·2	5	59	3

FALL OF WICKETS

	E	A
Wkt	1st	1st
1st	112	27
2nd	123	173
3rd	197	226
4th	211	233
5th	246	243
6th	255	243
7th	285	282
8th	–	–
9th	–	–
10th	–	–

Umpires: J. Moss (5) and A.E. Street (1).

Close: 1st day – E(1) 211-4 (Fry 24); 2nd – E(1) 241-4 (Fry 41, Woolley 8).

Test No. 124/23

ENGLAND v SOUTH AFRICA 1912 (2nd Test)
Triangular Tournament – 4th Match

Played at Headingley, Leeds, on 8, 9, 10 July.
Toss: England.   Result: ENGLAND won by 174 runs.
Debuts: Nil.

Although they managed to make their opponents bat twice, South Africa were completely outplayed for the third successive time. Hobbs scored 55 out of 78 in just over an hour. Barnes took his tally of South African wickets in this Tournament to 21 in two matches.

ENGLAND

J.B. Hobbs	c Ward b Nourse	27	c Nourse b Faulkner	55
W. Rhodes	c and b Pegler	7	b Pegler	10
R.H. Spooner	c Stricker b Nourse	21	b Faulkner	82
C.B. Fry*	lbw b Pegler	10	c Nourse b Pegler	7
J.W. Hearne	b Pegler	45	b Nourse	35
F.E. Woolley	b Nourse	57	c Nourse b Pegler	4
G.L. Jessop	b Faulkner	16	b Nourse	1
F.R. Foster	c Pegler b Nourse	30	b Nourse	0
E.J. Smith†	run out	13	c Ward b Faulkner	11
S.F. Barnes	b Faulkner	0	not out	15
H. Dean	not out	2	b Faulkner	8
Extras	(B 12, LB 2)	14	(B 5, LB 5)	10
Total		**242**		**238**

SOUTH AFRICA

L.J. Tancred*	c Spooner b Barnes	15	st Smith b Barnes	39
H.W. Taylor	c Hobbs b Dean	31	c Smith b Foster	2
A.W. Nourse	b Barnes	5	(6) c Foster b Dean	15
C.B. Llewellyn	c Smith b Barnes	0	b Barnes	4
G.A. Faulkner	c and b Barnes	5	b Barnes	0
L.A. Stricker	b Dean	10	(7) run out	0
G.C. White	c Barnes b Woolley	6	(3) c and b Foster	17
S.J. Snooke	b Barnes	23	b Dean	8
S.J. Pegler	not out	35	b Hearne	32
C.P. Carter	c Dean b Barnes	5	b Barnes	31
T.A. Ward†	b Dean	0	not out	0
Extras	(B 4, LB 3, NB 5)	12	(B 5, LB 3, NB 3)	11
Total		**147**		**159**

SOUTH AFRICA	O	M	R	W	O	M	R	W
Nourse	26·1	8	52	4	30	11	52	3
Pegler	35	6	112	3	31	0	110	3
Faulkner	13	2	50	2	24·2	2	50	4
Carter	4	0	14	0	5	1	16	0
ENGLAND								
Foster	16	7	29	0	23	4	51	2
Barnes	22	7	52	6	21·2	5	63	4
Dean	12·3	1	41	3	8	3	15	2
Woolley	6	2	13	1				
Rhodes					4	1	14	0
Hearne					2	0	5	1

FALL OF WICKETS

Wkt	E 1st	SA 1st	E 2nd	SA 2nd
1st	20	18	46	18
2nd	44	25	78	38
3rd	67	25	95	44
4th	68	43	165	49
5th	179	69	180	67
6th	181	76	181	69
7th	198	80	181	85
8th	226	130	207	110
9th	227	146	224	159
10th	242	147	238	159

Umpires: W. Richards (9) and A.A. White (7).

Close: 1st day – SA(1) 141-8 (Pegler 33, Carter 2); 2nd – SA(2) 105-7 (Tancred 38, Pegler 12).

136

AUSTRALIA v SOUTH AFRICA 1912 (2nd Test)
Triangular Tournament – 5th Match

Played at Lord's, London, on 15, 16, 17 July.
Toss: South Africa.   Result: AUSTRALIA won by ten wickets.
Debuts: Australia – E.R. Mayne.

South Africa suffered their fourth heavy defeat in spite of nine chances being missed in their first innings. Bardsley made the highest score of the Tournament and moved towards its best aggregate – 392 runs, average 65.33. On the second day, when King George V visited the ground, Bardsley scored a century before lunch, taking his total from 32 to 150.

SOUTH AFRICA

Batsman	Dismissal 1st	Score	Dismissal 2nd	Score
G.A. Faulkner	b Whitty	5	(6) c and b Matthews	6
L.J. Tancred	lbw b Matthews	31	c Bardsley b Hazlitt	19
G.C. White	c Carkeek b Minnett	0	b Matthews	18
C.B. Llewellyn	c Jennings b Minnett	8	b Macartney	59
A.W. Nourse	b Hazlitt	11	lbw b Kelleway	10
H.W. Taylor	c Kelleway b Hazlitt	93	(7) not out	10
L.A. Stricker	lbw b Kelleway	48	(1) b Hazlitt	13
F. Mitchell*	b Whitty	12	b Matthews	3
R.O. Schwarz	b Whitty	0	c Macartney b Matthews	1
S.J. Pegler	c Bardsley b Whitty	25	c Kelleway b Macartney	14
T.A. Ward†	not out	1	b Macartney	7
Extras	(B 12, LB 14, W 1, NB 2)	29	(B 9, LB 4)	13
Total		**263**		**173**

AUSTRALIA

Batsman	Dismissal 1st	Score	Dismissal 2nd	Score
C.B. Jennings	b Nourse	0	not out	22
C. Kelleway	lbw b Faulkner	102		
C.G. Macartney	b Nourse	9		
W. Bardsley	lbw b Llewellyn	164		
S.E. Gregory*	b Llewellyn	5		
E.R. Mayne	st Ward b Pegler	23	(2) not out	25
R.B. Minnett	b Pegler	39		
T.J. Matthews	c Faulkner b Pegler	9		
G.R. Hazlitt	b Nourse	0		
W. Carkeek†	not out	6		
W.J. Whitty	lbw b Pegler	3		
Extras	(B 24, LB 3, W 2, NB 1)	30	(B 1)	1
Total		**390**	(0 wickets)	**48**

AUSTRALIA	O	M	R	W	O	M	R	W
Minnett	15	6	49	2				
Whitty	31	9	68	4	9	0	41	0
Hazlitt	19	9	47	2	13	1	39	2
Matthews	13	5	32	1	13	2	29	4
Kelleway	11	3	38	1	8	1	22	1
Macartney					14·1	5	29	3
SOUTH AFRICA								
Nourse	36	12	60	3	6·1	2	22	0
Pegler	29·5	7	79	4	4	1	15	0
Schwarz	11	1	44	0				
Faulkner	28	3	86	1	2	0	10	0
Llewellyn	19	2	71	2				
Taylor	2	0	12	0				
Stricker	3	1	8	0				

FALL OF WICKETS

Wkt	SA 1st	A 1st	SA 2nd	A 2nd
1st	24	0	28	–
2nd	25	14	54	–
3rd	35	256	62	–
4th	56	277	102	–
5th	74	316	134	–
6th	171	353	136	–
7th	203	375	142	–
8th	213	379	146	–
9th	250	381	163	–
10th	263	390	173	–

Umpires: J. Moss (6) and A.E. Street (2).

Close: 1st day – A(1) 86-2 (Kelleway 33, Bardsley 32); 2nd – SA(2) 146-8 (Taylor 5).

ENGLAND v AUSTRALIA 1912 (2nd Test)
Triangular Tournament – 6th Match

Played at Old Trafford, Manchester, on 29, 30, 31 (*no play*) July.
Toss: England.   Result: MATCH DRAWN.
Debuts: Nil.

Rain restricted play to 3¾ hours on the first day and to 75 minutes on the second, before completely washing out the third.

ENGLAND

J.B. Hobbs	b Whitty	19
W. Rhodes	b Whitty	92
R.H. Spooner	b Whitty	1
C.B. Fry*	c sub (J.W. McLaren) b Matthews	19
J.W. Hearne	b Hazlitt	9
F.E. Woolley	c Kelleway b Whitty	13
F.R. Foster	c and b Matthews	13
E.J. Smith†	c Emery b Hazlitt	4
S. Haigh	c Kelleway b Hazlitt	9
S.F. Barnes	not out	1
J.W. Hitch	b Hazlitt	4
Extras	(B 9, LB 9, NB 1)	19
Total		**203**

AUSTRALIA

C.B. Jennings	not out	9
C. Kelleway	not out	3
W. Bardsley	)	
S.E. Gregory*	)	
C.G. Macartney	)	
E.R. Mayne	)	
T.J. Matthews	) did not bat	
S.H. Emery	)	
W.J. Whitty	)	
G.R. Hazlitt	)	
W. Carkeek†	)	
Extras	(B 2)	2
Total	(0 wickets)	**14**

AUSTRALIA	O	M	R	W
Hazlitt	40·5	12	77	4
Whitty	27	15	43	4
Kelleway	6	1	19	0
Matthews	12	4	23	2
Emery	7	1	22	0
ENGLAND				
Foster	1	0	3	0
Haigh	6	4	3	0
Woolley	6	3	6	0

FALL OF WICKETS

	E	A
Wkt	*1st*	*1st*
1st	37	–
2nd	39	–
3rd	83	–
4th	140	–
5th	155	–
6th	181	–
7th	185	–
8th	189	–
9th	199	–
10th	203	–

Umpires: G. Webb (2) and W.A.J. West (8).

Close: 1st day – E(1) 185-6 (Rhodes 92, Smith 0); 2nd – SA(1) 14-0 (Jennings 9, Kelleway 3).

AUSTRALIA v SOUTH AFRICA 1912 (3rd Test)
Triangular Tournament – 7th Match

Played at Trent Bridge, Nottingham, on 5, 6, 7 (*no play*) August.
Toss: South Africa.   Result: MATCH DRAWN.
Debuts: Nil.

Rain prevented South Africa from capitalising on their only first innings lead of the Tournament. The Bank Holiday paying attendance totalled a mere 2,365.

SOUTH AFRICA

L.J. Tancred*	c Kelleway b Matthews	30
H.W. Taylor	b Whitty	2
A.W. Nourse	b Whitty	64
G.A. Faulkner	c Kelleway b Emery	15
C.B. Llewellyn	b Emery	12
L.A. Stricker	lbw b Macartney	37
S.J. Snooke	b Kelleway	20
G.C. White	not out	59
R. Beaumont	b Hazlitt	2
S.J. Pegler	b Hazlitt	26
T.A. Ward†	c Emery b Matthews	24
Extra	(B 30, LB 7, NB 1)	38
Total		**329**

AUSTRALIA

C.B. Jennings	run out	9
C. Kelleway	c Faulkner b Pegler	37
C.G. Macartney	c Faulkner b Llewellyn	34
W. Bardsley	run out	56
S.E. Gregory*	b Pegler	18
R.B. Minnett	c Nourse b Faulkner	31
T.J. Matthews	b Pegler	21
S.H. Emery	b Faulkner	5
G.R. Hazlitt	not out	2
W.J. Whitty	b Pegler	0
W. Carkeek†	st Ward b Faulkner	1
Extras	(B 2, LB 3)	5
Total		**219**

AUSTRALIA	O	M	R	W
Whitty	30	10	64	2
Minnett	8	3	12	0
Hazlitt	28	10	48	2
Matthews	20·5	7	27	2
Emery	21	1	87	2
Kelleway	8	2	18	1
Macartney	13	2	35	1
SOUTH AFRICA				
Pegler	36	6	80	4
Faulkner	20·1	2	43	3
Taylor	12	5	19	0
Llewellyn	22	3	60	1
Nourse	4	1	12	0

FALL OF WICKETS

	SA	A
Wkt	*1st*	*1st*
1st	2	19
2nd	79	61
3rd	116	101
4th	140	127
5th	154	171
6th	196	199
7th	225	212
8th	232	216
9th	282	216
10th	329	219

Umpires: G. Webb (3) and W.A.J. West (9).

Close: 1st day – SA(1) 266-8 (White 30, Pegler 16); 2nd – A(1) 219 all out.

ENGLAND v SOUTH AFRICA 1912 (3rd Test)
Triangular Tournament – 8th Match

Played at Kennington Oval, London, on 12, 13 August.
Toss: South Africa.   Result: ENGLAND won by ten wickets.
Debuts: Nil.

The combination of a wet pitch and poor light produced a pre-lunch finish on the second day to rival *Test No. 30* as the shortest completed match in England. Barnes, moving the ball both ways from an immaculate length, bowled unchanged through both innings to bring his total of wickets in his first three matches against South Africa to 34 at 8.29 runs apiece. His second innings pre-lunch analysis of 8 for 29 is the best in any Test at The Oval. Spooner kept wicket for most of the first session while Smith, his mouth damaged by a simultaneous collision with a ball from Barnes and Taylor's bat, had six stitches inserted in his lip.

SOUTH AFRICA

H.W. Taylor	c Foster b Woolley	23		lbw b Barnes	6
L.J. Tancred*	b Barnes	0		st Smith b Woolley	0
A.W. Nourse	lbw b Woolley	8		c and b Foster	42
G.A. Faulkner	c Hayes b Barnes	9	(5)	b Barnes	10
L.A. Stricker	b Barnes	5	(4)	c Spooner b Barnes	0
C.B. Llewellyn	c Rhodes b Woolley	0		c Hitch b Barnes	0
G.C. White	b Barnes	4		c Smith b Barnes	1
S.J. Snooke	c Foster b Woolley	23		c Hearne b Barnes	7
R. Beaumont	c Hearne b Barnes	3		b Barnes	6
S.J. Pegler	c Hitch b Woolley	3		b Barnes	0
T.A. Ward†	not out	6		not out	0
Extras	(B 8, LB 3)	11		(B 18, LB 3)	21
Total		**95**			**93**

ENGLAND

J.B. Hobbs	c and b Faulkner	68		not out	9
W. Rhodes	b Faulkner	0			
R.H. Spooner	c Nourse b Llewellyn	26			
C.B. Fry*	c Snooke b Faulkner	9			
E.G. Hayes	b Faulkner	4			
F.E. Woolley	b Pegler	13			
J.W. Hearne	lbw b Faulkner	20	(2)	not out	5
F.R. Foster	st Ward b Faulkner	8			
E.J. Smith†	b Faulkner	9			
S.F. Barnes	c Taylor b Pegler	8			
J.W. Hitch	not out	0			
Extras	(B 10, LB 1)	11			
Total		**176**		(0 wickets)	**14**

ENGLAND	O	M	R	W	O	M	R	W			
Foster	6	2	15	0	7	2	19	1			
Barnes	21	10	28	5	16·4	4	29	8			
Woolley	15·3	1	41	5	9	2	24	1			
SOUTH AFRICA											
Pegler	19	3	53	2							
Faulkner	27·1	4	84	7	2	0	4	0			
Llewellyn	10	1	28	1							
Nourse					2·3	0	10	0			

FALL OF WICKETS				
	SA	E	SA	E
Wkt	1st	1st	2nd	2nd
1st	2	4	0	–
2nd	31	65	10	–
3rd	38	85	10	–
4th	47	89	54	–
5th	50	111	54	–
6th	53	127	58	–
7th	76	135	70	–
8th	86	163	89	–
9th	86	176	93	–
10th	95	176	93	–

Umpires: W. Richards (10) and A.A. White (8).

Close: 1st day – E(1) 176 all out.

ENGLAND v AUSTRALIA 1912 (3rd Test)
Triangular Tournament – 9th Match

Played at Kennington Oval, London, on 19, 20, 21, 22 August.
Toss: England.   Result: ENGLAND won by 244 runs.
Debuts: Nil.

Shortly before this final match came the pronouncement that whichever side won would be the Tournament champions. To ensure a result the match would be played out – the first 'timeless' Test to be staged in England. Fry, driving magnificently, played a brilliant innings of 79 when the ball was turning viciously. Woolley became the third player after W. Bates and H. Trumble to score a fifty and take ten wickets in an England-Australia Test.

TOURNAMENT RESULTS		*Played*	*Won*	*Lost*	*Drawn*
ENGLAND		6	4	0	2
Australia		6	2	1	3
South Africa		6	0	5	1

ENGLAND

J.B. Hobbs	c Carkeek b Macartney	66	c Matthews b Whitty	32
W. Rhodes	b Minnett	49	b Whitty	4
R.H. Spooner	c Hazlitt b Macartney	1	c Jennings b Whitty	0
C.B. Fry*	c Kelleway b Whitty	5	c Jennings b Hazlitt	79
F.E. Woolley	lbw b Minnett	62	b Hazlitt	4
J.W. Hearne	c Jennings b Whitty	1	c Matthews b Hazlitt	14
J.W.H.T. Douglas	lbw b Whitty	18	lbw b Hazlitt	24
F.R. Foster	b Minnett	19	not out	3
E.J. Smith†	b Whitty	4	b Hazlitt	0
S.F. Barnes	c Jennings b Minnett	7	c Whitty b Hazlitt	0
H. Dean	not out	0	b Hazlitt	0
Extras	(B 2, LB 10, NB 1)	13	(B 14, NB 1)	15
Total		**245**		**175**

AUSTRALIA

S.E. Gregory*	c Rhodes b Barnes	1	(5) c Douglas b Dean	1
C. Kelleway	lbw b Woolley	43	c Douglas b Dean	0
C.G. Macartney	b Barnes	4	b Dean	30
W. Bardsley	b Barnes	30	run out	0
C.B. Jennings	c and b Woolley	0	(1) c Fry b Woolley	14
R.B. Minnett	c Rhodes b Woolley	0	lbw b Woolley	4
D.B.M. Smith	c Smith b Woolley	6	c Douglas b Dean	0
T.J. Matthews	c Fry b Barnes	2	c and b Woolley	1
W.J. Whitty	c Foster b Barnes	0	b Woolley	3
G.R. Hazlitt	not out	2	c Dean b Woolley	5
W. Carkeek†	c Barnes b Woolley	5	not out	0
Extras	(B 12, LB 6)	18	(B 1, LB 5, W 1)	7
Total		**111**		**65**

AUSTRALIA	O	M	R	W	O	M	R	W
Whitty	38	12	69	4	33	13	71	3
Matthews	14	5	43	0	10	3	21	0
Hazlitt	26	10	48	0	21·4	8	25	7
Macartney	19	6	22	2	22	5	43	0
Minnett	10·1	3	34	4				
Kelleway	7	2	16	0				
ENGLAND								
Barnes	27	15	30	5	4	1	18	0
Dean	16	7	29	0	9	2	19	4
Foster	2	0	5	0				
Woolley	9·4	3	29	5	7·4	1	20	5
Rhodes					2	1	1	0

FALL OF WICKETS

Wkt	E 1st	A 1st	E 2nd	A 2nd
1st	107	9	7	0
2nd	109	19	7	46
3rd	127	90	51	46
4th	131	90	56	47
5th	144	92	91	51
6th	180	96	170	51
7th	216	104	171	51
8th	233	104	171	54
9th	239	104	175	65
10th	245	111	175	65

Umpires: J. Moss (7) and A.E. Street (3).

Close: 1st day – E(1) 233-8 (Smith 0); 2nd – A(1) 51-2 (Kelleway 26, Bardsley 10); 3rd – E(2) 64-4 (Fry 17, Hearne 2).

SOUTH AFRICA v ENGLAND 1913–14 (1st Test)

Played at Lord's, Durban, 13, 15, 16, 17 December.
Toss: South Africa.   Result: ENGLAND won by an innings and 157 runs.
Debuts: South Africa – H.V. Baumgartner, J.M. Blanckenberg, A.H.C. Cooper, J.L. Cox, P.A.M. Hands, P.T. Lewis, G.L. Tapscott; England – M.W. Booth, Hon. L.H. Tennyson (*later The Third Baron Tennyson*).

This match provided the first instance of both captains scoring hundreds, Taylor doing so on his first appearance in that role. Barnes became the first bowler to take 150 Test wickets when he made the last of his ten dismissals in this, his 24th match for England.

SOUTH AFRICA

H.W. Taylor*	c Strudwick b Douglas	109	lbw b Barnes	8
G.P.D. Hartigan	c Strudwick b Barnes	0	(3) c Hobbs b Woolley	13
P.A.M. Hands	c Barnes b Booth	3	(2) lbw b Relf	14
A.W. Nourse	b Douglas	19	hit wkt b Barnes	46
P.T. Lewis	c Woolley b Barnes	0	c Woolley b Barnes	0
A.H.C. Cooper	b Barnes	6	c Strudwick b Barnes	0
G.L. Tapscott	b Barnes	4	c Relf b Woolley	1
T.A. Ward†	c Woolley b Booth	9	c Rhodes b Barnes	12
H.V. Baumgartner	lbw b Woolley	16	b Relf	3
J.M. Blanckenberg	not out	6	not out	0
J.L. Cox	b Barnes	1	c and b Relf	0
Extras	(B 6, LB 1, NB 2)	9	(B 6, LB 6, W 2)	14
Total		**182**		**111**

ENGLAND

J.B. Hobbs	b Baumgartner	82
W. Rhodes	c Tapscott b Cox	18
A.E. Relf	c Baumgartner b Cox	1
Hon. L.H. Tennyson	lbw b Nourse	52
C.P. Mead	c and b Blanckenberg	41
J.W.H.T. Douglas*	b Baumgartner	119
F.E. Woolley	c Cooper b Hartigan	31
M.C. Bird	c Ward b Nourse	61
M.W. Booth	run out	14
S.F. Barnes	run out	0
H. Strudwick†	not out	2
Extras	(B 25, LB 2, W 2)	29
Total		**450**

ENGLAND	O	M	R	W	O	M	R	W
Barnes	19·4	1	57	5	25	11	48	5
Booth	10	0	38	2				
Woolley	7	0	24	1	9	3	16	2
Relf	5	2	9	0	16·2	3	31	3
Douglas	8	2	19	2	2	1	2	0
Rhodes	7	0	26	0				
SOUTH AFRICA								
Cox	43	9	123	2				
Nourse	29	7	74	2				
Hartigan	18	5	72	1				
Baumgartner	27·4	3	99	2				
Blanckenberg	21	5	46	1				
Taylor	6	3	7	0				

FALL OF WICKETS

	SA	E	SA
Wkt	1st	1st	2nd
1st	5	24	21
2nd	22	40	31
3rd	62	136	57
4th	65	173	71
5th	73	236	77
6th	77	301	78
7th	113	416	104
8th	144	448	111
9th	181	448	111
10th	182	450	111

Umpires: A.J. Atfield (5) and F.W. Grey (4).

Close: 1st day – E(1) 94-2 (Hobbs 59, Tennyson 6); 2nd – E(1) 419-7 (Douglas 108, Booth 0); 3rd – SA(2) 18-0 (Taylor 6, Hands 6).

SOUTH AFRICA v ENGLAND 1913–14 (2nd Test)

Played at Old Wanderers, Johannesburg, on 26, 27, 29, 30 December.
Toss: South Africa.   Result: ENGLAND won by an innings and 12 runs.
Debuts: South Africa – C.J. Newberry.

By taking 17 wickets, Barnes established a Test record which stood until 1956 when J.C. Laker took 19 for 90 against Australia at Manchester (*Test No. 428*). The only previous instance of nine wickets in an innings, by G.A. Lohmann in 1895-96, also took place at Johannesburg (*Test No. 48*). When he dismissed Hartigan, Rhodes, playing in his 44th Test, became the first to complete the double of 1,000 runs and 100 wickets for England.

SOUTH AFRICA

J.W. Zulch	c Woolley b Barnes	14		c Relf b Barnes	34
H.W. Taylor*	b Barnes	29		c Rhodes b Barnes	40
P.A.M. Hands	c Rhodes b Barnes	0	(6)	c Rhodes b Barnes	40
R. Beaumont	c Strudwick b Barnes	0	(3)	c Strudwick b Relf	5
A.W. Nourse	b Barnes	17	(4)	c Strudwick b Barnes	56
L.J. Tancred	st Strudwick b Barnes	13	(7)	b Barnes	20
G.P.D. Hartigan	c Smith b Rhodes	51	(5)	lbw b Barnes	2
T.A. Ward†	b Woolley	19		b Barnes	0
C.J. Newberry	st Strudwick b Barnes	1		st Strudwick b Barnes	5
J.M. Blanckenberg	not out	0		not out	12
J.L. Cox	c Strudwick b Barnes	0		b Barnes	0
Extras	(B 10, LB 4, NB 2)	16		(B 9, LB 6, NB 2)	17
Total		**160**			**231**

ENGLAND

W. Rhodes	c and b Blanckenberg	152
A.E. Relf	b Blanckenberg	63
J.B. Hobbs	lbw b Newberry	23
C.P. Mead	c Beaumont b Blanckenberg	102
Hon. L.H. Tennyson	lbw b Cox	13
J.W.H.T. Douglas*	c Taylor b Blanckenberg	3
F.E. Woolley	b Newberry	0
M.C. Bird	c Ward b Newberry	1
E.J. Smith	lbw b Cox	9
H. Strudwick†	c Cox b Blanckenberg	14
S.F. Barnes	not out	0
Extras	(B 18, LB 4, W 1)	23
Total		**403**

ENGLAND	O	M	R	W	O	M	R	W		FALL OF WICKETS		
Douglas	2	0	11	0	6	0	27	0		SA	E	SA
Barnes	26·5	9	56	8	38·4	7	103	9	*Wkt*	*1st*	*1st*	*2nd*
Relf	14	1	34	0	9	3	19	1	1st	22	141	70
Woolley	3	1	5	1	21	5	45	0	2nd	22	181	77
Rhodes	13	5	23	1	9	2	20	0	3rd	24	333	93
Bird	4	1	15	0					4th	56	354	106
									5th	63	373	177
SOUTH AFRICA									6th	78	374	194
Cox	30	8	74	2					7th	155	376	201
Nourse	21	2	62	0					8th	159	376	212
Blanckenberg	38	13	83	5					9th	160	395	223
Newberry	26	2	93	3					10th	160	403	231
Hartigan	5	0	24	0								
Hands	6	0	17	0								
Taylor	8	0	27	0								
Beaumont	1	1	0	0								

Umpires: A.J. Atfield (6) and F.W. Grey (5).

Close: 1st day – SA(1) 160 all out; 2nd – E(1) 317-2 (Rhodes 143, Mead 73); 3rd – SA(2) 177-4 (Nourse 52, Hands 40).

SOUTH AFRICA v ENGLAND 1913–14 (3rd Test)

Played at Old Wanderers, Johannesburg, on 1, 2, 3, 5 January.
Toss: England.   Result: ENGLAND won by 91 runs.
Debuts: South Africa – C.D. Dixon, L.R. Tuckett.

England avenged the loss of their two previous rubbers in the Union with three straight wins. Taylor and Zulch led a spirited attempt to score 396 runs for victory before Barnes devastated the middle order.

ENGLAND

J.B. Hobbs	c Ward b Dixon	92		c Nourse b Dixon	41
W. Rhodes	lbw b Taylor	35		c Ward b Taylor	0
J.W. Hearne	c and b Dixon	27	(4)	lbw b Newberry	0
C.P. Mead	b Blanckenberg	0	(3)	c Tuckett b Newberry	86
Hon. L.H. Tennyson	b Nourse	21	(6)	c Beaumont b Nourse	6
J.W.H.T. Douglas*	c Ward b Blanckenberg	30	(5)	b Newberry	77
F.E. Woolley	lbw b Taylor	7		st Ward b Newberry	37
A.E. Relf	lbw b Nourse	0		b Blanckenberg	25
M.C. Bird	st Ward b Taylor	1		not out	20
S.F. Barnes	b Blanckenberg	5		b Blanckenberg	0
H. Strudwick†	not out	9		c Tuckett b Blanckenberg	0
Extras	(B 4, LB 7)	11		(B 10, LB 5, W1)	16
Total		**238**			**308**

SOUTH AFRICA

H.W. Taylor*	c Woolley b Relf	14		c Tennyson b Relf	70
J.W. Zulch	c and b Hearne	38		c and b Relf	82
T.A. Ward†	b Hearne	15	(6)	c Strudwick b Douglas	40
R. Beaumont	c Rhodes b Hearne	6	(5)	b Barnes	0
A.W. Nourse	b Hearne	1	(4)	c Strudwick b Barnes	6
P.A.M. Hands	hit wkt b Hearne	26	(3)	c Tennyson b Barnes	7
G.P.D. Hartigan	b Barnes	18		c Douglas b Barnes	0
C.J. Newberry	c Hearne b Rhodes	15		b Barnes	13
C.D. Dixon	c Rhodes b Barnes	0	(10)	b Hearne	0
L.R. Tuckett	b Barnes	0	(11)	not out	0
J.M. Blanckenberg	not out	4	(9)	b Douglas	59
Extras	(B 4, LB 9, NB 1)	14		(B 17, LB 8, NB 2)	27
Total		**151**			**304**

SOUTH AFRICA	O	M	R	W	O	M	R	W
Nourse	9	1	22	2	13	4	36	1
Dixon	19	2	62	2	21	4	56	1
Blanckenberg	22·1	4	54	3	21·3	7	66	3
Tuckett	10	1	45	0	10	3	24	0
Newberry	10	1	29	0	22	2	72	4
Taylor	10	5	15	3	6	1	38	1
ENGLAND								
Barnes	16	3	26	3	38	8	102	5
Hearne	16	4	49	5	14	2	58	1
Relf	14	7	24	1	29	12	40	2
Douglas	7	2	16	0	13·4	2	34	2
Woolley	5	1	13	0	7	0	24	0
Rhodes	3·5	1	9	1	6	1	17	0
Bird					2	1	2	0

FALL OF WICKETS

Wkt	E 1st	SA 1st	E 2nd	SA 2nd
1st	100	24	4	153
2nd	158	67	83	162
3rd	159	81	84	167
4th	163	82	177	170
5th	201	91	198	173
6th	208	112	250	173
7th	209	143	262	217
8th	210	143	304	295
9th	219	147	304	300
10th	238	151	308	304

Umpires: A.J. Atfield (7) and F.W. Grey (6).

Close: 1st day – SA(1) 12-0 (Taylor 6, Zulch 5); 2nd – E(2) 117-3 (Mead 54, Douglas 14); 3rd – E(2) 308 all out.

SOUTH AFRICA v ENGLAND 1913–14 (4th Test)

Played at Lord's, Durban, on 14, 16, 17, 18 February.
Toss: South Africa.   Result: MATCH DRAWN.
Debuts: South Africa – H.W. Chapman, F.L. le Roux, D. Taylor.

Barnes, in the last of his 27 Tests, took his total of wickets to 189, including 49, average 10.93, in only four Tests of this rubber (still the world record). In seven Tests against South Africa Barnes took 83 wickets, average 9.85, with six instances of ten or more wickets in a match, and 12 of five or more in an innings. His match analysis of 14 for 144 remains the record for a Test at Durban.

SOUTH AFRICA

H.W. Taylor*	c Strudwick b Barnes	16	lbw b Barnes	93
T.A. Ward†	b Barnes	5	b Barnes	1
D. Taylor	c Rhodes b Barnes	36	c Strudwick b Barnes	36
A.W. Nourse	b Barnes	9	c Tennyson b Rhodes	45
F.L. le Roux	b Barnes	1	c and b Barnes	0
P.A.M. Hands	st Strudwick b Rhodes	51	c Rhodes b Barnes	8
C.J. Newberry	b Rhodes	0	c Bird b Barnes	16
H.W. Chapman	b Barnes	17	(9) not out	16
J.M. Blanckenberg	c Douglas b Rhodes	4	(10) c Tennyson b Barnes	13
C.P. Carter	not out	19	(8) b Douglas	45
J.L. Cox	c Strudwick b Barnes	4	not out	12
Extras	(B 6, LB 2)	8	(B12, LB 5, NB 3)	20
Total		**170**	(9 wickets declared)	**305**

ENGLAND

J.B. Hobbs	c Nourse b Blanckenberg	64	b Blanckenberg	97
W. Rhodes	lbw b Carter	22	lbw b Carter	35
J.W. Hearne	c Newberry b Carter	2	not out	8
C.P. Mead	c Newberry b Blanckenberg	31	c Blanckenberg b Newberry	1
Hon. L.H. Tennyson	c and b Newberry	1	(6) b Blanckenberg	0
J.W.H.T. Douglas*	c and b Carter	0	(5) lbw b Blanckenberg	7
F.E. Woolley	c Hands b Newberry	9	not out	0
M.C. Bird	b Carter	8		
A.E. Relf	b Carter	11		
S.F. Barnes	not out	4		
H. Strudwick†	b Carter	0		
Extras	(B 7, LB 3, NB 1)	11	(B 2, LB 4)	6
Total		**163**	(5 wickets)	**154**

ENGLAND	O	M	R	W	O	M	R	W		FALL OF WICKETS			
Barnes	29·5	7	56	7	32	10	88	7		SA	E	SA	E
Woolley	10	3	27	0	13	2	26	0	Wkt	1st	1st	2nd	2nd
Relf	8	3	15	0					1st	20	92	15	133
Rhodes	14	5	33	3	26	6	53	1	2nd	25	92	84	141
Douglas	7	0	31	0	14	1	51	1	3rd	35	104	181	142
Hearne					11	0	46	0	4th	45	109	183	152
Bird					6	1	21	0	5th	84	116	195	154
									6th	84	127	203	–
SOUTH AFRICA									7th	135	146	244	–
Le Roux	6	1	19	0	3	2	5	0	8th	145	146	269	–
Cox	10	1	30	0	13	6	18	0	9th	164	163	283	–
Carter	28	8	50	6	29	12	27	1	10th	170	163	–	–
Blanckenberg	20	4	35	2	15	4	43	3					
Newberry	11	4	18	2	10	4	22	1					
Nourse					6	0	13	0					
Chapman					4	0	20	0					

Umpires: A.J. Atfield (8) and F.W. Grey (7).

Close: 1st day – SA(1) 162-8 (Chapman 17, Carter 15); 2nd – SA(2) 32-1 (H.W. Taylor 17, D. Taylor 10); 3rd – SA(2) 249-7 (Carter 32, Chapman 0).

SOUTH AFRICA v ENGLAND 1913-14 (5th Test)

Played at St George's Park, Port Elizabeth, on 27, 28 February, 2, 3 March.
Toss: South Africa.   Result: ENGLAND won by ten wickets.
Debuts: South Africa – R.H.M. Hands, E.B. Lundie.

Even without S.F. Barnes, who declined to play after a difference of opinion concerning administrative matters, England gained a comfortable fourth win. This remains their best return in any rubber against South Africa. The first Test at Port Elizabeth since 1895-96 proved to be the last anywhere for 6 years 289 days – the longest interval in Test cricket. South Africa provided the first instance of a side playing two pairs of brothers in the same Test.

SOUTH AFRICA

H.W. Taylor*	c Strudwick b Woolley	42		c Rhodes b Bird	87
J.W. Zulch	c Strudwick b Booth	11		c Rhodes b Booth	60
D. Taylor	b Relf	12		b Bird	1
A.W. Nourse	b Hearne	26		c Relf b Bird	0
P.A.M. Hands	c Bird b Douglas	83		c Woolley b Booth	49
R.H.M. Hands	st Strudwick b Woolley	0		st Strudwick b Douglas	7
C.J. Newberry	b Woolley	11	(8)	c Hearne b Relf	1
T.A. Ward†	c Bird b Douglas	3	(7)	c Woolley b Booth	1
C.P. Carter	c Bird b Douglas	0		b Booth	5
J.M. Blanckenberg	b Douglas	0		not out	6
E.B. Lundie	not out	0		c Strudwick b Relf	1
Extras	(B 2, LB 2, NB 1)	5		(B 6, LB 3, NB 1)	10
Total		**193**			**228**

ENGLAND

J.B. Hobbs	c Nourse b Lundie	33		not out	11
W. Rhodes	b Carter	27		not out	0
H. Strudwick†	b Carter	3			
J.W. Hearne	c H.W. Taylor b Blanckenberg	32			
C.P. Mead	c and b Blanckenberg	117			
F.E. Woolley	lbw b Newberry	54			
J.W.H.T. Douglas*	c Blanckenberg b Lundie	30			
Hon. L.H. Tennyson	lbw b Lundie	23			
M.C. Bird	run out	4			
M.W. Booth	b Lundie	32			
A.E. Relf	not out	23			
Extras	(B20, LB 6, NB 7)	33			
Total		**411**		(0 wickets)	**11**

ENGLAND	O	M	R	W	O	M	R	W
Relf	11	5	26	1	23·1	11	29	2
Booth	18	3	43	1	24	5	49	4
Woolley	22	4	71	3	5	2	23	0
Hearne	9	2	34	1	12	4	30	0
Douglas	5·4	2	14	4	9	1	34	1
Bird					11	1	38	3
Tennyson					1	0	1	0
Rhodes					10	4	14	0
SOUTH AFRICA								
Lundie	46·3	9	101	4	1·1	0	6	0
Nourse	9	1	31	0				
Carter	41	9	111	2				
Blanckenberg	34	7	101	2				
Newberry	14	2	34	1				
H.W. Taylor					1	0	5	0

FALL OF WICKETS

Wkt	SA 1st	E 1st	SA 2nd	E 2nd
1st	19	48	129	–
2nd	36	52	133	–
3rd	95	90	133	–
4th	116	134	173	–
5th	116	238	204	–
6th	167	317	213	–
7th	176	329	215	–
8th	176	353	215	–
9th	180	361	223	–
10th	193	411	228	–

Umpires: F.W. Grey (8) and D. Smith (1).

Close: 1st day – E(1) 48-1 (Rhodes 7, Strudwick 0); 2nd – E(1) 357-8 (Tennyson 23, Booth 1); 3rd – SA(2) 204-5 (P.A.M. Hands 44).

AUSTRALIA v ENGLAND 1920-21 (1st Test)

Played at Sydney Cricket Ground on 17, 18, 20, 21, 22 December.
Toss: Australia.   Result: AUSTRALIA won by 377 runs.
Debuts: Australia – H.L. Collins, J.M. Gregory, A.A. Mailey, W.A.S. Oldfield, C.E. Pellew, J. Ryder, J.M. Taylor; England – E.H. Hendren, C.H. Parkin, C.A.G. Russell, A. Waddington.
Note that Ryder has no second initial. Russell has usually appeared as 'A.C. Russell'.

Collins was the fifth Australian to score a hundred against England in his first Test match. At the age of 31, he was the oldest to do so. Australia's total of 581 was a record for the second innings of any Test match. Armstrong scored a hundred in his first match as captain and led Australia to the first of eight successive victories. During his second innings Rhodes became the first to score 2,000 runs and take 100 wickets in Test cricket.

AUSTRALIA

C.G. Macartney	b Waddington	19	(3) b Douglas		69
H.L. Collins	run out	70	c Waddington b Douglas		104
W. Bardsley	c Strudwick b Hearne	22	(1) b Hearne		57
C. Kelleway	run out	33	(6) c Russell b Woolley		78
W.W. Armstrong*	st Strudwick b Woolley	12	(7) b Parkin		158
J.M. Gregory	c Strudwick b Woolley	8	(9) run out		0
J.M. Taylor	lbw b Hearne	34	(4) c Woolley b Parkin		51
C.E. Pellew	c Hendren b Hearne	36	(5) lbw b Woolley		16
J. Ryder	run out	5	(8) run out		6
W.A.S. Oldfield†	c Hobbs b Parkin	7	c Strudwick b Parkin		16
A.A. Mailey	not out	10	not out		0
Extras	(B 4, LB 6, NB 1)	11	(B 17, LB 7, NB 2)		26
Total		**267**			**581**

ENGLAND

C.A.G. Russell	b Kelleway	0	c Oldfield b Gregory		5
J.B. Hobbs	b Gregory	49	lbw b Armstrong		59
J.W. Hearne	c Gregory b Mailey	14	b Gregory		57
E.H. Hendren	c Gregory b Ryder	28	b Kelleway		56
F.E. Woolley	c Mailey b Ryder	52	st Oldfield b Mailey		16
J.W.H.T. Douglas*	st Oldfield b Mailey	21	c Armstrong b Mailey		7
W. Rhodes	c Gregory b Mailey	3	c Ryder b Mailey		45
J.W. Hitch	c Kelleway b Gregory	3	c Taylor b Gregory		19
A. Waddington	run out	7	b Kelleway		3
C.H. Parkin	not out	4	b Kelleway		4
H. Strudwick†	lbw b Gregory	2	not out		1
Extras	(B 3, LB 4)	7	(B 6, LB 3)		9
Total		**190**			**281**

ENGLAND	O	M	R	W	O	M	R	W	FALL OF WICKETS				
Hitch	10	0	37	0	8	0	40	0		A	E	A	E
Waddington	18	3	35	1	23	4	53	0	*Wkt*	*1st*	*1st*	*2nd*	*2nd*
Parkin	26·5	5	58	1	35·3	5	102	3	1st	40	0	123	5
Hearne	34	8	77	3	42	7	124	1	2nd	80	50	234	105
Douglas	3	0	14	0	26	3	79	2	3rd	140	70	241	149
Woolley	23	7	35	2	36	10	90	2	4th	162	144	282	170
Rhodes					22	2	67	0	5th	173	145	332	178
									6th	176	158	519	231
AUSTRALIA									7th	244	165	536	264
Kelleway	6	2	10	1	15·5	3	45	3	8th	249	180	540	271
Gregory	23·1	3	56	3	33	6	70	3	9th	250	188	578	279
Mailey	23	4	95	3	24	2	105	3	10th	267	190	581	281
Ryder	6	1	20	2	17	6	24	0					
Armstrong	1	0	2	0	10	0	21	1					
Macartney					3	0	7	0					

Umpires: R.W. Crockett (24) and A.C. Jones (4).

Close: 1st day – A(1) 250-8 (Ryder 5, Oldfield 0); 2nd – A(2) 46-0 (Bardsley 23, Collins 17); 3rd – A(2) 332-5 (Kelleway 23); 4th – E(2) 47-1 (Hobbs 18, Hearne 23).

AUSTRALIA v ENGLAND 1920–21 (2nd Test)

Played at Melbourne Cricket Ground on 31 December, l, 3, 4 January.
Toss: Australia.   Result: AUSTRALIA won by an innings and 91 runs.
Debuts: Australia – R.L. Park; England – H. Howell, J.W.H. Makepeace (*usually given as* 'H. Makepeace').

Pellew and Gregory each scored their maiden Test centuries in their second match. Gregory became the third player to score a hundred and take eight wickets in the same Test. Hobbs scored his third century in successive innings at Melbourne, his last 69 runs coming in 96 minutes during the third day on a sticky wicket. Hearne was taken ill after the first day and took no further part in the tour.

AUSTRALIA

H.L. Collins	c Hearne b Howell	64
W. Bardsley	c Strudwick b Woolley	51
R.L. Park	b Howell	0
J.M. Taylor	c Woolley b Parkin	68
W.W. Armstrong*	lbw b Douglas	39
C. Kelleway	c Strudwick b Howell	9
C.E. Pellew	b Parkin	116
J. Ryder	c Woolley b Douglas	13
J.M. Gregory	c Russell b Woolley	100
W.A.S. Oldfield†	c and b Rhodes	24
A.A. Mailey	not out	8
Extras	(B 1, LB 3, W 1, NB 2)	7
Total		**499**

ENGLAND

J.B. Hobbs	c Ryder b Gregory	122	b Kelleway	20
W. Rhodes	b Gregory	7	c Collins b Armstrong	28
J.W.H. Makepeace	lbw b Armstrong	4	c Gregory b Armstrong	4
E.H. Hendren	c Taylor b Gregory	67	c and b Collins	1
C.A.G. Russell	c Collins b Gregory	0	c Armstrong b Collins	5
F.E. Woolley	b Gregory	5	b Ryder	50
J.W.H.T. Douglas*	lbw b Gregory	15	b Gregory	9
C.H. Parkin	c Mailey b Gregory	4	c Taylor b Armstrong	9
H. Strudwick†	not out	21	c Oldfield b Armstrong	24
H. Howell	st Oldfield b Armstrong	5	not out	0
J.W. Hearne	absent ill	–	absent ill	–
Extras	(NB 1)	1	(B 3, LB 3, NB 1)	7
Total		**251**		**157**

ENGLAND	O	M	R	W	O	M	R	W
Howell	37	5	142	3				
Douglas	24	1	83	2				
Parkin	27	0	116	2				
Hearne	14	0	38	0				
Woolley	27	8	87	2				
Rhodes	8·3	1	26	1				
AUSTRALIA								
Gregory	20	1	69	7	12	0	32	1
Kelleway	19	1	54	0	12	1	25	1
Armstrong	24·3	8	50	2	15·2	5	26	4
Ryder	14	2	31	0	10	2	17	1
Park	1	0	9	0				
Collins	9	0	37	0	17	5	47	2
Pellew					1	0	3	0

FALL OF WICKETS

	A	E	E
Wkt	1st	1st	2nd
1st	116	20	36
2nd	116	32	53
3rd	118	174	54
4th	194	185	58
5th	220	201	70
6th	251	208	104
7th	282	213	141
8th	455	232	151
9th	469	251	157
10th	499	–	–

Umpires: R.W. Crockett (25) and D. Elder (4).

Close: 1st day – A(1) 282-6 (Pellew 33, Ryder 13); 2nd – E(1) 93-2 (Hobbs 53, Hendren 29); 3rd – E(2) 76-5 (Woolley 15, Douglas 0).

AUSTRALIA v ENGLAND 1920–21 (3rd Test)

Played at Adelaide Oval on 14, 15, 17, 18, 19, 20 January.
Toss: Australia.   Result: AUSTRALIA won by 119 runs.
Debuts: Australia – E.A. McDonald; England – P.G.H. Fender.

This match produced six centuries – a record which stood until 1938 when seven were scored at Nottingham (*Test No. 263*). Australia's total of 582 beat by one run the record set in the 1st Test of this rubber and remains the second innings record for Tests between England and Australia – as does the match aggregate of 1,753 runs. Armstrong's century was the 100th in this series.

AUSTRALIA

H.L. Collins	c Rhodes b Parkin	162	c Hendren b Parkin		24
W. Bardsley	st Strudwick b Douglas	14	b Howell		16
C. Kelleway	c Fender b Parkin	4	b Howell		147
J.M. Taylor	run out	5	(6) c Strudwick b Fender		38
W.W. Armstrong*	c Strudwick b Douglas	11	b Howell		121
C.E. Pellew	run out	35	(7) c Strudwick b Parkin		104
J.M. Gregory	c Strudwick b Fender	10	(8) not out		78
J. Ryder	c Douglas b Parkin	44	(4) c Woolley b Howell		3
W.A.S. Oldfield†	lbw b Parkin	50	b Rhodes		10
E.A. McDonald	b Parkin	2	b Rhodes		4
A.A. Mailey	not out	3	b Rhodes		13
Extras	(B 6, LB 8)	14	(B 5, LB 10, W 4, NB 5)		24
Total		**354**			**582**

ENGLAND

J.B. Hobbs	c and b Mailey	18	b Gregory		123
W. Rhodes	run out	16	lbw b McDonald		4
J.W.H. Makepeace	c Gregory b Armstrong	60	c and b McDonald		30
E.H. Hendren	b Gregory	36	b Mailey		51
F.E. Woolley	c Kelleway b Gregory	79	b Gregory		0
C.A.G. Russell	not out	135	b Mailey		59
J.W.H.T. Douglas*	lbw b Mailey	60	c Armstrong b Gregory		32
P.G.H. Fender	b McDonald	2	c Ryder b Mailey		42
C.H. Parkin	st Oldfield b Mailey	12	(10) st Oldfield b Mailey		17
H. Strudwick†	c Pellew b Mailey	9	(9) c Armstrong b Mailey		1
H. Howell	c Gregory b Mailey	2	not out		4
Extras	(B 8, LB 5, NB 5)	18	(LB 3, NB 4)		7
Total		**447**			**370**

ENGLAND	O	M	R	W	O	M	R	W
Howell	26	1	89	0	34	6	115	4
Douglas	24	6	69	2	19	2	61	0
Parkin	20	2	60	5	40	8	109	2
Woolley	21	6	47	0	38	4	91	0
Fender	12	0	52	1	22	0	105	1
Rhodes	5	1	23	0	25·5	8	61	3
Hobbs					7	2	16	0
AUSTRALIA								
McDonald	24	1	78	1	24	0	95	2
Gregory	36	5	108	2	20	2	50	3
Kelleway	11	4	25	0	8	2	16	0
Mailey	32·1	3	160	5	29·2	3	142	5
Armstrong	23	10	29	1	16	1	41	0
Ryder	6	0	29	0	9	2	19	0

FALL OF WICKETS

Wkt	A 1st	E 1st	A 2nd	E 2nd
1st	32	25	34	20
2nd	45	49	63	125
3rd	55	111	71	183
4th	96	161	265	185
5th	176	250	328	243
6th	209	374	454	292
7th	285	391	477	308
8th	347	416	511	321
9th	349	437	570	341
10th	354	447	582	370

Umpires: R.W. Crockett (26) and D. Elder (5).

Close: 1st day – A(1) 313-7 (Ryder 36, Oldfield 22); 2nd – E(1) 233-4 (Woolley 73, Russell 21); 3rd – A(2) 71-3 (Kelleway 19); 4th – A(2) 364-5 (Kelleway 115, Pellew 26); 5th – E(2) 66-1 (Hobbs 50, Makepeace 11).

AUSTRALIA v ENGLAND 1920–21 (4th Test)

Played at Melbourne Cricket Ground on 11, 12, 14, 15, 16 February.
Toss: England.   Result: AUSTRALIA won by eight wickets.
Debuts: England – A. Dolphin.

Mailey's analysis of 9 for 121 remains Australia's record in all Test matches and, until *Test No. 849*, was the best achieved in any Test at Melbourne. No other Australian bowler has taken nine wickets in a Test innings. At 39 years 173 days, Makepeace was the oldest player to score a maiden Test hundred. Armstrong overcame an attack of malaria to score his second century in successive innings. It was his fourth and last against England.

ENGLAND

J.B. Hobbs	c Carter b McDonald	27	lbw b Mailey	13
W. Rhodes	c Carter b Gregory	11	c Gregory b Mailey	73
J.W.H. Makepeace	c Collins b Mailey	117	lbw b Mailey	54
E.H. Hendren	c Carter b Mailey	30	b Kelleway	32
F.E. Woolley	lbw b Kelleway	29	st Carter b Mailey	0
J.W.H.T. Douglas*	c and b Mailey	50	st Carter b Mailey	60
A. Waddington	b Mailey	0	(8) st Carter b Mailey	6
P.G.H. Fender	c Gregory b Kelleway	3	(7) c Collins b Mailey	59
A. Dolphin†	b Kelleway	1	c Gregory b Mailey	0
C.H. Parkin	run out	10	c Bardsley b Mailey	4
H. Howell	not out	0	not out	0
Extras	(B 1, LB 5)	6	(B 5, LB 5, W 1, NB 3)	14
Total		**284**		**315**

AUSTRALIA

H.L. Collins	c Rhodes b Woolley	59	c Rhodes b Parkin	32
W. Bardsley	b Fender	56	run out	38
J. Ryder	lbw b Woolley	7	not out	52
J.M. Taylor	hit wkt b Fender	2		
J.M. Gregory	c Dolphin b Parkin	77	(4) not out	76
C.E. Pellew	b Fender	12		
W.W. Armstrong*	not out	123		
C. Kelleway	b Fender	27		
H. Carter†	b Fender	0		
A.A. Mailey	run out	13		
E.A. McDonald	b Woolley	0		
Extras	(B 1, LB 6, W 1, NB 5)	13	(B 5, LB 5, W 2, NB 1)	13
Total		**389**	(2 wickets)	**211**

AUSTRALIA	O	M	R	W	O	M	R	W
McDonald	19	2	46	1	23	2	77	0
Gregory	18	1	61	1	14	4	31	0
Mailey	29·2	1	115	4	47	8	121	9
Ryder	10	5	10	0	10	3	25	0
Armstrong	5	1	9	0				
Kelleway	18	2	37	3	23	8	47	1
ENGLAND								
Howell	17	2	86	0	10	1	36	0
Douglas	4	0	17	0	5	1	13	0
Waddington	5	0	31	0				
Parkin	22	5	64	1	12	2	46	1
Fender	32	3	122	5	13·2	2	39	0
Woolley	32·1	14	56	3	14	4	39	0
Rhodes					10	2	25	0

FALL OF WICKETS

Wkt	E 1st	A 1st	E 2nd	A 2nd
1st	18	117	32	71
2nd	61	123	145	81
3rd	104	128	152	–
4th	164	133	152	–
5th	270	153	201	–
6th	270	298	305	–
7th	273	335	307	–
8th	274	335	307	–
9th	275	376	315	–
10th	284	389	315	–

Umpires: R.W. Crockett (27) and D. Elder (6).

Close: 1st day – E(1) 270-6 (Douglas 50); 2nd – A(1) 267-5 (Gregory 67, Armstrong 54); 3rd – E(2) 123-1 (Rhodes 66, Makepeace 40); 4th – A(2) 92-2 (Ryder 12, Gregory 6).

AUSTRALIA v ENGLAND 1920–21 (5th Test)

Played at Sydney Cricket Ground on 25, 26, 28 February, 1 March.
Toss: England.   Result: AUSTRALIA won by nine wickets.
Debuts: England – E.R. Wilson.

This victory gave Australia an unprecedented and unequalled five wins in one rubber between these two countries. Mailey's total of 36 wickets remains Australia's record in any five-match rubber against England. Gregory is the only non-wicket-keeper to make 15 catches in a Test rubber. Macartney, the 'Governor-General', compiled his chanceless and highest innings in Tests in only 244 minutes.

ENGLAND

J.B. Hobbs	lbw b Gregory	40	(5)	c Taylor b Mailey	34
W. Rhodes	c Carter b Kelleway	26		run out	25
J.W.H. Makepeace	c Gregory b Mailey	3		c Gregory b Kelleway	7
E.H. Hendren	c Carter b Gregory	5	(6)	st Carter b Mailey	13
F.E. Woolley	b McDonald	53	(1)	c and b Kelleway	1
C.A.G. Russell	c Gregory b Mailey	19	(8)	c Gregory b Armstrong	35
J.W.H.T. Douglas*	not out	32		c and b Mailey	68
P.G.H. Fender	c Gregory b Kelleway	2	(9)	c Kelleway b McDonald	40
E.R. Wilson	c Carter b Kelleway	5	(4)	st Carter b Mailey	5
C.H. Parkin	c Taylor b Kelleway	9		c Gregory b Mailey	36
H. Strudwick†	b Gregory	2		not out	5
Extras	(B 3, LB 2, W 1, NB 2)	8		(B 3, LB 5, NB 3)	11
Total		**204**			**280**

AUSTRALIA

H.L. Collins	c Fender b Parkin	5	c Strudwick b Wilson	37
W. Bardsley	c Fender b Douglas	7	not out	50
C.G. Macartney	c Hobbs b Fender	170	not out	2
J.M. Taylor	c Hendren b Douglas	32		
J.M. Gregory	c Strudwick b Fender	93		
W.W. Armstrong*	c Woolley b Fender	0		
J. Ryder	b Fender	2		
C. Kelleway	c Strudwick b Wilson	32		
H. Carter†	c Woolley b Fender	17		
A.A. Mailey	b Wilson	5		
E.A. McDonald	not out	3		
Extras	(B 18, LB 6, NB 2)	26	(B 3, NB 1)	4
Total		**392**	(1 wicket)	**93**

AUSTRALIA	O	M	R	W	O	M	R	W
Gregory	16·1	4	42	3	16	3	37	0
McDonald	11	2	38	1	25	3	58	1
Kelleway	20	6	27	4	14	3	29	2
Mailey	23	1	89	2	36·2	5	119	5
Ryder					2	2	0	0
Armstrong					8	2	26	1
ENGLAND								
Douglas	16	0	84	2				
Parkin	19	1	83	1	9	1	32	0
Woolley	15	1	58	0	11	3	27	0
Wilson	14·3	4	28	2	6	1	8	1
Fender	20	1	90	5	1	0	2	0
Rhodes	7	0	23	0	7·2	1	20	0

FALL OF WICKETS

Wkt	E 1st	A 1st	E 2nd	A 2nd
1st	54	16	1	91
2nd	70	22	14	–
3rd	74	89	29	–
4th	76	287	75	–
5th	125	287	82	–
6th	161	313	91	–
7th	164	356	160	–
8th	172	384	224	–
9th	201	384	251	–
10th	204	392	280	–

Umpires: R.W. Crockett (28) and D. Elder (7).

Close: 1st day – A(1) 70-2 (Macartney 31, Taylor 22); 2nd – E(2) 24-2 (Rhodes 10, Wilson 2); 3rd – A(2) 25-0 (Collins 7, Bardsley 17).

ENGLAND v AUSTRALIA 1921 (1st Test)

Played at Trent Bridge, Nottingham, on 28, 30 May.
Toss: England.   Result: AUSTRALIA won by ten wickets.
Debuts: England – P. Holmes, V.W.C. Jupp, D.J. Knight, T.L. Richmond, G.E. Tyldesley;
Australia – T.J.E. Andrews, H.S.T.L. Hendry. *Tyldesley has usually appeared as 'E. Tyldesley'.*

The hundredth match in this series ended on the second afternoon. Gregory dismissed Knight, Tyldesley and
Hendren with his last four balls of an over. Holmes top-scored in the first innings of his only Test against
Australia. Tyldesley's second innings ended when he deflected a short ball into the wicket with his face.

ENGLAND

D.J. Knight	c Carter b Gregory	8	run out		38
P. Holmes	b McDonald	30	c Taylor b McDonald		8
G.E. Tyldesley	b Gregory	0	b Gregory		7
E.H. Hendren	b Gregory	0	b McDonald		7
J.W.H.T. Douglas*	c Gregory b Armstrong	11	c Hendry b McDonald		13
F.E. Woolley	c Hendry b McDonald	20	c Carter b Hendry		34
V.W.C. Jupp	c Armstrong b McDonald	8	c Pellew b Gregory		15
W. Rhodes	c Carter b Gregory	19	c Carter b McDonald		10
H. Strudwick†	c Collins b Gregory	0	b Hendry		0
H. Howell	not out	0	not out		4
T.L. Richmond	c and b Gregory	4	b McDonald		2
Extras	(B 6, LB 6)	12	(B 4, LB 3, NB 2)		9
Total		**112**			**147**

AUSTRALIA

W. Bardsley	lbw b Woolley	66	not out		8
H.L. Collins	lbw b Richmond	17			
C.G. Macartney	lbw b Douglas	20	(2) not out		22
J.M. Taylor	c Jupp b Douglas	4			
W.W. Armstrong*	b Jupp	11			
J.M. Gregory	lbw b Richmond	14			
C.E. Pellew	c and b Rhodes	25			
H. Carter†	b Woolley	33			
T.J.E. Andrews	c and b Rhodes	6			
H.S.T.L. Hendry	not out	12			
E.A. McDonald	c Knight b Woolley	10			
Extras	(B 8, LB 5, NB 1)	14			
Total		**232**	(0 wickets)		**30**

AUSTRALIA	O	M	R	W	O	M	R	W
Gregory	19	5	58	6	22	8	45	2
McDonald	15	5	42	3	22·4	10	32	5
Armstrong	3	3	0	1	27	10	33	0
Macartney					5	2	10	0
Hendry					9	1	18	2
ENGLAND								
Howell	9	3	22	0				
Douglas	13	2	34	2				
Richmond	16	3	69	2	3	0	17	0
Woolley	22	8	46	3				
Jupp	5	0	14	1	3·1	0	13	0
Rhodes	13	3	33	2				

FALL OF WICKETS

Wkt	E 1st	A 1st	E 2nd	A 2nd
1st	18	49	23	–
2nd	18	86	41	–
3rd	18	98	60	–
4th	43	126	63	–
5th	77	138	76	–
6th	78	152	110	–
7th	101	183	138	–
8th	107	202	138	–
9th	108	212	140	–
10th	112	232	147	–

Umpires: H.R. Butt (1) and J. Moss (8).

Close: 1st day – A(1) 167-6 (Pellew 21, Carter 3).

ENGLAND v AUSTRALIA 1921 (2nd Test)

Played at Lord's, London, on 11, 13, 14 June.
Toss: England.   Result: AUSTRALIA won by eight wickets.
Debuts: England – A.E. Dipper, F.J. Durston, A.J. Evans, N.E. Haig.

England, still bereft of J.B. Hobbs (torn thigh muscle), made six changes but could not avoid their seventh consecutive defeat. Woolley was the first to score two nineties in a match for England.

ENGLAND

D.J. Knight	c Gregory b Armstrong	7	c Carter b Gregory	1
A.E. Dipper	b McDonald	11	b McDonald	40
F.E. Woolley	st Carter b Mailey	95	c Hendry b Mailey	93
E.H. Hendren	b McDonald	0	c Gregory b Mailey	10
J.W.H.T. Douglas*	b McDonald	34	b Gregory	14
A.J. Evans	b McDonald	4	lbw b McDonald	14
Hon. L.H. Tennyson	st Carter b Mailey	5	not out	74
N.E. Haig	c Carter b Gregory	3	b McDonald	0
C.H. Parkin	b Mailey	0	c Pellew b McDonald	11
H. Strudwick†	c McDonald b Mailey	8	b Gregory	12
F.J. Durston	not out	6	b Gregory	2
Extras	(B 1, LB 11, W 1, NB 1)	14	(B 4, LB 3, NB 5)	12
Total		**187**		**283**

AUSTRALIA

W. Bardsley	c Woolley b Douglas	88	not out	63
T.J.E. Andrews	c Strudwick b Durston	9	lbw b Parkin	49
C.G. Macartney	c Strudwick b Durston	31	b Durston	8
C.E. Pellew	b Haig	43	not out	5
J.M. Taylor	lbw b Douglas	36		
W.W. Armstrong*	b Durston	0		
J.M. Gregory	c and b Parkin	52		
H.S.T.L. Hendry	b Haig	5		
H. Carter†	b Durston	46		
A.A. Mailey	c and b Parkin	5		
E.A. McDonald	not out	17		
Extras	(B 2, LB 5, NB 3)	10	(B 3, LB 2, NB 1)	6
Total		**342**	(2 wickets)	**131**

AUSTRALIA	O	M	R	W	O	M	R	W		FALL OF WICKETS			
Gregory	16	1	51	1	26·2	4	76	4		E	A	E	A
McDonald	20	2	58	4	23	3	89	4	*Wkt*	*1st*	*1st*	*2nd*	*2nd*
Armstrong	18	12	9	1	12	6	19	0	1st	20	19	3	103
Mailey	14·2	1	55	4	25	4	72	2	2nd	24	73	97	114
Hendry					4	0	15	0	3rd	25	145	124	–
									4th	108	191	165	–
ENGLAND									5th	120	192	165	–
Durston	24·1	2	102	4	9·3	0	34	1	6th	145	230	198	–
Douglas	9	1	53	2	6	0	23	0	7th	156	263	202	–
Parkin	20	5	72	2	9	0	31	1	8th	157	277	235	–
Haig	20	4	61	2	3	0	27	0	9th	170	289	263	–
Woolley	11	2	44	0	3	0	10	0	10th	187	342	283	–

Umpires: J. Moss (9) and W. Phillips (1).

Close: 1st day – A(1) 191-3 (Bardsley 88, Taylor 15); 2nd – E(2) 243-8 (Tennyson 44, Strudwick 6).

ENGLAND v AUSTRALIA 1921 (3rd Test)

Played at Headingley, Leeds, on 2, 4, 5 July.
Toss: Australia.   Result: AUSTRALIA won by 219 runs.
Debuts: England – G. Brown, A. Ducat, H.T.W. Hardinge, J.C. White.

Although England introduced a new captain and made seven team changes, they could not avoid equalling South Africa's record of eight successive defeats (1888-89 to 1898-99). Australia's record run of eight wins stood until 1984. Macartney's hundred, following his 345 against Nottinghamshire, was his fourth in consecutive innings, the first for Australia at Leeds, and, surprisingly, was their only century of the rubber. Hobbs, having missed the first two Tests because of injury, was taken ill with appendicitis on the first afternoon and played no more cricket that season. Tennyson split his left hand fielding against Macartney and scored 63 and 36 batting virtually with one hand.

AUSTRALIA

W. Bardsley	c Woolley b Douglas	6	b Jupp		25
T.J.E. Andrews	c Woolley b Douglas	19	b Jupp		92
C.G. Macartney	lbw b Parkin	115	c and b Woolley		30
C.E. Pellew	c Hearne b Woolley	52	(5) c Ducat b White		16
J.M. Taylor	c Douglas b Jupp	50	(6) c Tennyson b White		4
J.M. Gregory	b Parkin	1	(8) c Jupp b White		3
W.W. Armstrong*	c Brown b Douglas	77	not out		28
H.S.T.L. Hendry	b Parkin	0	(9) not out		11
H. Carter†	b Jupp	34	(4) lbw b Parkin		47
E.A. McDonald	not out	21			
A.A. Mailey	c and b Parkin	6			
Extras	(B 16, LB 7, NB 3)	26	(B 10, LB 4, NB 3)		17
Total		**407**	(7 wickets declared)		**273**

ENGLAND

F.E. Woolley	b Gregory	0	(4) b Mailey		37
H.T.W. Hardinge	lbw b Armstrong	25	c Gregory b McDonald		5
J.W. Hearne	b McDonald	7	c Taylor b McDonald		27
A. Ducat	c Gregory b McDonald	3	(6) st Carter b Mailey		2
J.W.H.T. Douglas	b Armstrong	75	b Gregory		8
V.W.C. Jupp	c Carter b Gregory	14	(7) c Carter b Armstrong		28
G. Brown†	c Armstrong b Mailey	57	(1) lbw b Gregory		46
J.C. White	b McDonald	1	(9) not out		6
Hon. L.H. Tennyson*	c Gregory b McDonald	63	(8) b Armstrong		36
C.H. Parkin	not out	5	b Mailey		4
J.B. Hobbs	absent ill	–	absent ill		–
Extras	(LB 3, NB 6)	9	(B 3)		3
Total		**259**			**202**

ENGLAND	O	M	R	W	O	M	R	W		FALL OF WICKETS			
Douglas	20	3	80	3	11	0	38	0		A	E	A	E
White	25	4	70	0	11	3	37	3	*Wkt*	*1st*	*1st*	*2nd*	*2nd*
Parkin	20·1	0	106	4	20	0	91	1	1st	22	0	71	15
Hearne	5	0	21	0					2nd	45	13	139	57
Jupp	18	2	70	2	13	2	45	2	3rd	146	30	193	98
Woolley	5	0	34	1	18	4	45	1	4th	255	47	223	124
									5th	256	67	227	126
AUSTRALIA									6th	271	164	227	128
Gregory	21	6	47	2	14	1	55	2	7th	271	165	230	190
McDonald	26·1	6	105	4	15	2	67	2	8th	333	253	–	197
Armstrong	19	4	44	2	3	0	6	2	9th	388	259	–	202
Mailey	17	4	38	1	20·2	3	71	3	10th	407	–	–	–
Hendry	10	4	16	0									

Umpires: H.R. Butt (2) and A. Millward (2).

Close: 1st day – E(1) 22-2 (Hardinge 11, Ducat 3); 2nd – A(2) 143-2 (Andrews 78, Carter 3).

ENGLAND v AUSTRALIA 1921 (4th Test)

Played at Old Trafford, Manchester, on 23 (*no play*), 25, 26 July.
Toss: England.   Result: MATCH DRAWN.
Debuts: England – C. Hallows, C.W.L. Parker.

When Tennyson attempted to close England's innings at 5.50 pm on the second day, the first having been washed out, Armstrong pointed out that, under two-day rules, no declaration was permissible unless 100 minutes batting was available to the fielding side on that day. The players left the field, 25 minutes were lost, and, when the England innings eventually resumed, Armstrong bowled his second consecutive over – one either side of the hiatus. Russell scored 81 of his runs on the leg side. Tyldesley and Fender added 102 in 39 minutes.

ENGLAND

C.A.G. Russell	b Gregory	101			
G. Brown†	c Gregory b Armstrong	31			
F.E. Woolley	c Pellew b Armstrong	41			
C.P. Mead	c Andrews b Hendry	47			
G.E. Tyldesley	not out	78			
P.G.H. Fender	not out	44			
C. Hallows			(1) not out	16	
C.H. Parkin			(2) c Collins b Andrews	23	
C.W.L. Parker			(3) not out	3	
Hon. L.H. Tennyson*	did not bat				
J.W.H.T. Douglas					
Extras	(B 12, LB 5, NB 3)	20	(LB 2)	2	
Total	(4 wickets declared)	**362**	(1 wicket)	**44**	

AUSTRALIA

W. Bardsley	b Parkin	3
H.L. Collins	lbw b Parkin	40
C.G. Macartney	b Parker	13
T.J.E. Andrews	c Tennyson b Fender	6
J.M. Taylor	b Fender	4
C.E. Pellew	c Tyldesley b Parker	17
W.W. Armstrong*	b Douglas	17
J.M. Gregory	b Parkin	29
H. Carter†	b Parkin	0
H.S.T.L. Hendry	c Russell b Parkin	4
E.A. McDonald	not out	8
Extras	(B 22, LB 5, NB 7)	34
Total		**175**

AUSTRALIA	O	M	R	W	O	M	R	W
Gregory	23	5	79	1				
McDonald	31	1	112	0				
Macartney	8	2	20	0				
Hendry	25	5	74	1	4	1	12	0
Armstrong	33	13	57	2				
Andrews					5	0	23	1
Pellew					3	0	6	0
Taylor					1	0	1	0
ENGLAND								
Parkin	29·4	12	38	5				
Woolley	39	22	38	0				
Parker	28	16	32	2				
Fender	15	6	30	2				
Douglas	5	2	3	1				

FALL OF WICKETS

	E	A	E
Wkt	1st	1st	2nd
1st	65	9	36
2nd	145	33	–
3rd	217	44	–
4th	260	48	–
5th	–	78	–
6th	–	125	–
7th	–	161	–
8th	–	161	–
9th	–	166	–
10th	–	175	–

Umpires: J. Moss (10) and A.E. Street (4).

Close: 1st day – no play; 2nd – E(1) 362-4 (Tyldesley 78, Fender 44).

ENGLAND v AUSTRALIA 1921 (5th Test)

Played at Kennington Oval, London, on 13, 15, 16 August.
Toss: England.   Result: MATCH DRAWN.
Debuts: England – A. Sandham.

England's selectors employed the record number of 30 players during this five-match rubber. Mead's 182 not out was a new record for England against Australia at home and stood until 1938. He scored a century before lunch on the second day, moving from 19 to 128 in 147 minutes. Although 471 runs were scored on the third day, the match quickly declined from being a serious contest to a farce. Armstrong left his team to organise itself, fielded in the deep and picked up a stray newspaper 'to see who we're playing'. Hitch reached his fifty in 35 minutes – the second-fastest in this series of Tests.

ENGLAND

C.A.G. Russell	c Oldfield b McDonald	13	not out		102
G. Brown†	b Mailey	32	c Mailey b Taylor		84
G.E. Tyldesley	c Macartney b Gregory	39			
F.E. Woolley	run out	23			
C.P. Mead	not out	182			
A. Sandham	b McDonald	21			
Hon. L.H. Tennyson*	b McDonald	51			
P.G.H. Fender	c Armstrong b McDonald	0	(3) c Armstrong b Mailey		6
J.W. Hitch	b McDonald	18	(4) not out		51
J.W.H.T. Douglas	not out	21			
C.H. Parkin	did not bat				
Extras	(LB 3)	3	(B 1)		1
Total	(8 wickets declared)	**403**	(2 wickets)		**244**

AUSTRALIA

H.L. Collins	hit wkt b Hitch	14
W. Bardsley	b Hitch	22
C.G. Macartney	b Douglas	61
T.J.E. Andrews	lbw b Parkin	94
J.M. Taylor	c Woolley b Douglas	75
C.E. Pellew	c Woolley b Parkin	1
W.W. Armstrong*	c Brown b Douglas	19
J.M. Gregory	st Brown b Parkin	27
W.A.S. Oldfield†	not out	28
E.A. McDonald	st Brown b Woolley	36
A.A. Mailey	b Woolley	0
Extras	(B 6, LB 3, W 2, NB 1)	12
Total		**389**

AUSTRALIA	O	M	R	W	O	M	R	W	FALL OF WICKETS			
Gregory	38	5	128	1	3	0	13	0		E	A	E
McDonald	47	9	143	5	6	0	20	0	*Wkt*	*1st*	*1st*	*2nd*
Mailey	30	4	85	1	18	2	77	1	1st	27	33	158
Armstrong	12	2	44	0					2nd	54	54	173
Pellew					9	3	25	0	3rd	84	162	–
Andrews					8	0	44	0	4th	121	233	–
Taylor					7	1	25	1	5th	191	239	–
Collins					7	0	39	0	6th	312	288	–
									7th	312	311	–
ENGLAND									8th	339	338	–
Hitch	19	3	65	2					9th	–	389	–
Douglas	30	2	117	3					10th	–	389	–
Fender	19	3	82	0								
Parkin	23	4	82	3								
Woolley	11	2	31	2								

Umpires: J. Moss (11) and W. Phillips (2).

Close: 1st day – E(1) 129-4 (Mead 19, Sandham 1); 2nd – A(1) 162-3 (Andrews 59).

SOUTH AFRICA v AUSTRALIA 1921–22 (1st Test)

Played at Lord's, Durban, on 5, 7, 8, 9 November.
Toss: Australia.   Result: MATCH DRAWN.
Debuts: South Africa – C.N. Frank, W.V.S. Ling, W.F.E. Marx, E.P. Nupen.

The 1921 Australians played three Tests in South Africa on their way home. Armstrong handed over the captaincy to Collins.

AUSTRALIA

H.L. Collins*	b Carter	31	c Chapman b Nupen	47
J.M. Gregory	b Blanckenberg	51	(4) b Blanckenberg	6
C.G. Macartney	c Nourse b Nupen	59	c Ward b Marx	116
W. Bardsley	b Blanckenberg	5	(2) lbw b Carter	23
T.J.E. Andrews	b Blanckenberg	3	(6) not out	35
J. Ryder	not out	78	(5) b Blanckenberg	58
J.M. Taylor	b Carter	18	b Carter	11
H.S.T.L. Hendry	c Nourse b Chapman	23	b Carter	13
H. Carter†	c Nourse b Blanckenberg	9	not out	1
E.A. McDonald	b Carter	2		
A.A. Mailey	b Blanckenberg	2		
Extras	(B 16, LB 2)	18	(B 12, LB 1, NB 1)	14
Total		**299**	(7 wickets declared)	**324**

SOUTH AFRICA

H.W. Taylor*	c Hendry b Gregory	1	(4) c and b McDonald	29
J.W. Zulch	c Gregory b Macartney	80	(5) c Taylor b McDonald	17
C.N. Frank	c Gregory b McDonald	1	(1) c Gregory b Mailey	38
A.W. Nourse	c Hendry b Gregory	32	(6) not out	31
W.V.S. Ling	b Gregory	33	(7) c Gregory b McDonald	28
W.F.E. Marx	c Macartney b Gregory	0	(3) c Carter b Mailey	28
H.W. Chapman	c Gregory b Hendry	4	(8) b Gregory	2
E.P. Nupen	c and b Hendry	6	(9) not out	0
T.A. Ward†	not out	22	(2) b Gregory	0
J.M. Blanckenberg	c Ryder b Gregory	28		
C.P. Carter	c Mailey b Gregory	14		
Extras	(B 4, LB 3, NB 4)	11	(LB 8, NB 3)	11
Total		**232**	(7 wickets)	**184**

SOUTH AFRICA	O	M	R	W	O	M	R	W
Marx	3	0	6	0	6	0	20	1
Nourse	11	1	36	0	8	1	32	0
Nupen	15	2	42	1	16	3	59	1
Chapman	11	0	51	1	6	1	33	0
Blanckenberg	24·4	6	78	5	30	3	100	2
Carter	20	1	68	3	21	3	66	3
AUSTRALIA								
Gregory	25·1	4	77	6	19	7	28	2
McDonald	20	5	55	1	34	17	64	3
Mailey	17	2	55	0	31	10	54	2
Macartney	11	6	13	1				
Hendry	7	0	21	2	4	0	20	0
Ryder					8	3	7	0

FALL OF WICKETS

Wkt	A 1st	SA 1st	A 2nd	SA 2nd
1st	85	2	44	1
2nd	95	9	118	43
3rd	116	62	144	82
4th	128	136	250	112
5th	175	136	270	131
6th	214	154	283	179
7th	276	154	314	182
8th	291	163	–	–
9th	296	214	–	–
10th	299	232	–	–

Umpires: F.W. Grey (9) and A.G. Laver (1).

Close: 1st day – SA(1) 8-1 (Zulch 7, Frank 0); 2nd – A(2) 13-0 (Collins 8, Bardsley 5); 3rd – A(2) 324-7 (Andrews 35, Carter 1).

SOUTH AFRICA v AUSTRALIA 1921–22 (2nd Test)

Played at Old Wanderers, Johannesburg, on 12, 14, 15, 16 November.
Toss: Australia.   Result: MATCH DRAWN.
Debuts: South Africa – N.V. Lindsay.

Collins scored Australia's only double-century in a Test in South Africa. The left-handed Gregory scored 50 in 35 minutes and took only 70 minutes to reach his hundred; it is still the fastest century in Test cricket. Zulch was victim of a freak dismissal in the first innings when a piece of his bat broke off and flew into his stumps. Frank took 518 minutes to score 152; his partnership of 206 with Nourse remains South Africa's highest for the fourth wicket against Australia. Nourse was the first left-hander to score a century for South Africa.

AUSTRALIA

H.L. Collins*	c Lindsay b Carter	203	not out	5
W. Bardsley	b Marx	8	not out	2
J. Ryder	b Blanckenberg	56		
J.M. Gregory	st Ward b Carter	119		
T.J.E. Andrews	st Ward b Carter	3		
J.M. Taylor	c Nupen b Marx	11		
E.R. Mayne	b Carter	1		
H.S.T.L. Hendry	b Carter	15		
W.A.S. Oldfield†	b Marx	2		
E.A. McDonald	not out	9		
A.A. Mailey	st Ward b Carter	4		
Extras	(B 3, LB 15, NB 1)	19		
Total		**450**	(0 wickets)	**7**

SOUTH AFRICA

J.W. Zulch	hit wkt b McDonald	4		b Gregory	2
C.N. Frank	run out	1		c Collins b Mailey	152
N.V. Lindsay	hit wkt b Gregory	6		b Gregory	29
H.W. Taylor*	c Mailey b Gregory	47		c Hendry b Gregory	80
A.W. Nourse	c sub (C.E. Pellew) b McDonald	64		c Gregory b Ryder	111
W.V.S. Ling	c Hendry b Gregory	0		st Oldfield b Ryder	19
W.F.E. Marx	c Collins b Mailey	36	(8)	c Bardsley b Mailey	34
T.A. Ward†	c Taylor b Collins	7	(9)	not out	9
J.M. Blanckenberg	b Gregory	45	(7)	c Andrews b Mailey	4
E.P. Nupen	b Mailey	22		not out	13
C.P. Carter	not out	0			
Extras	(B 4, LB 4, NB 3)	11		(B10, LB 5, NB 4)	19
Total		**243**		(8 wickets declared)	**472**

SOUTH AFRICA	O	M	R	W	O	M	R	W		FALL OF WICKETS				
Marx	21	0	85	3	1	0	4	0			A	SA	SA	A
Nupen	16	0	86	0	0·4	0	3	0	Wkt	1st	1st	2nd	2nd	
Carter	29·5	4	91	6					1st	15	6	6	–	
Blanckenberg	21	2	105	1					2nd	128	6	44	–	
Nourse	7	1	44	0					3rd	337	16	149	–	
Ling	3	0	20	0					4th	347	95	355	–	
									5th	382	109	387	–	
AUSTRALIA									6th	383	135	393	–	
Gregory	19·3	1	71	4	28	7	68	3	7th	407	164	446	–	
McDonald	19	7	43	2	44	14	121	0	8th	422	189	450	–	
Mailey	22	4	72	2	43	8	113	3	9th	446	243	–	–	
Hendry	12	2	37	0	23	6	58	0	10th	450	243	–	–	
Collins	6	2	9	1	15	12	7	0						
Taylor					11	4	19	0						
Mayne					1	0	1	0						
Ryder					30	9	66	2						

Umpires: S.L. Harris (3) and A.G. Laver (2).

Close: 1st day – A(1) 450 all out; 2nd – SA(2) 39-1 (Frank 13, Lindsay 24); 3rd – SA(2) 311-3 (Frank 106, Nourse 79).

SOUTH AFRICA v AUSTRALIA 1921–22 (3rd Test)

Played at Newlands, Cape Town, on 26, 28, 29 November.
Toss: South Africa.   Result: AUSTRALIA won by ten wickets.
Debuts: South Africa – N. Reid.

The strongest team to visit the Union so far, Australia easily dominated the final Test, South Africa avoiding an innings defeat by a single run.

SOUTH AFRICA

C.N. Frank	b Ryder	21		b Macartney	23
J.W. Zulch	c Ryder b Macartney	50	(3)	c and b Macartney	40
P.A.M. Hands	c Gregory b Ryder	0	(6)	c Andrews b Macartney	19
H.W. Taylor*	c Andrews b McDonald	26		run out	17
A.W. Nourse	c Mayne b Mailey	11		st Carter b Mailey	31
W.V.S. Ling	b McDonald	0	(7)	b Macartney	35
W.F.E. Marx	st Carter b Mailey	11	(8)	run out	16
J.M. Blanckenberg	st Carter b Mailey	25	(9)	c Carter b Mailey	20
T.A. Ward†	b McDonald	2	(2)	b McDonald	4
C.P. Carter	not out	19		not out	1
N. Reid	c Mayne b Mailey	11		b Macartney	6
Extras	(LB 2, NB 2)	4		(B 1, LB 2, NB 1)	4
Total		**180**			**216**

AUSTRALIA

H.L. Collins*	b Blanckenberg	54			
W. Bardsley	lbw b Blanckenberg	30			
C.G. Macartney	c Nourse b Blanckenberg	44			
J. Ryder	c Taylor b Carter	142			
J.M. Gregory	c Hands b Blanckenberg	29			
E.R. Mayne	lbw b Reid	15			
T.J.E. Andrews	c Hands b Carter	10			
C.E. Pellew	c Nourse b Reid	6			
H. Carter†	not out	31	(2)	not out	0
E.A. McDonald	c Ward b Carter	4			
A.A. Mailey	c Taylor b Nourse	14	(1)	not out	1
Extras	(B 9, LB 5, NB 3)	17			
Total		**396**		(0 wickets)	**1**

AUSTRALIA	O	M	R	W	O	M	R	W		FALL OF WICKETS			
Gregory	15	9	11	0	9	1	29	0		SA	A	SA	A
McDonald	19	3	53	3	13	2	35	1	*Wkt*	*1st*	*1st*	*2nd*	*2nd*
Macartney	24	10	47	1	24·3	10	44	5	1st	50	71	10	–
Ryder	16	7	25	2	7	0	15	0	2nd	54	108	58	–
Mailey	14	1	40	4	26	0	89	2	3rd	82	153	84	–
Collins					1	1	0	0	4th	106	201	92	–
									5th	107	242	122	–
SOUTH AFRICA									6th	110	281	162	–
Marx	7	1	29	0					7th	143	320	182	–
Nourse	30	5	89	1					8th	146	358	203	–
Blanckenberg	31	5	82	4					9th	151	361	209	–
Carter	26	5	104	3					10th	180	396	216	–
Reid	21	3	63	2									
Taylor	5	2	12	0									
Hands					0·1	0	1	0					

Umpires: H.V. Adams (1) and A.G. Laver (3).

Close: 1st day – A(1) 15-0 (Collins 7, Bardsley 6); 2nd – SA(2) 3-0 (Frank 0, Ward 3).

SOUTH AFRICA v ENGLAND 1922–23 (1st Test)

Played at Old Wanderers, Johannesburg, on 23, 26, 27, 28 December.
Toss: South Africa.   Result: SOUTH AFRICA won by 168 runs.
Debuts: South Africa – W.H. Brann, I.D. Buys, R.H. Catterall, C.M. Francois, G.A.L. Hearne;
    England – A.W. Carr, A.E.R. Gilligan, A.S. Kennedy, F.T. Mann, G.T.S. Stevens.

This was England's only defeat during a 22-match tour and South Africa's first win for 16 Tests (then the longest run without a victory). Blanckenberg, bowling at medium-pace on an accurate length, achieved his best analysis in Test cricket. South Africa scored their highest total to date against England. Taylor's innings of 176 remains the highest for his country in a home Test against England.

SOUTH AFRICA

R.H. Catterall	c and b Kennedy	39		c Woolley b Gilligan	17
G.A.L. Hearne	b Jupp	28		c Kennedy b Gilligan	27
H.W. Taylor*	c Brown b Fender	21		c Gilligan b Kennedy	176
A.W. Nourse	c Brown b Kennedy	14		c Fender b Jupp	20
W.V.S. Ling	b Kennedy	0		b Kennedy	38
W.H. Brann	lbw b Kennedy	1		c Fender b Gilligan	50
C.M. Francois	c Fender b Jupp	19	(8)	c Mann b Jupp	9
J.M. Blanckenberg	lbw b Jupp	1	(9)	b Kennedy	30
E.P. Nupen	c Kennedy b Jupp	0	(10)	st Brown b Kennedy	23
T.A. Ward†	not out	13	(7)	b Jupp	10
I.D. Buys	run out	0		not out	4
Extras	(B 5, LB 2, NB 5)	12		(B 14, LB 1, W 1)	16
Total		**148**			**420**

ENGLAND

A. Sandham	b Blanckenberg	26		lbw b Blanckenberg	25
F.T. Mann*	c Francois b Nupen	4	(6)	not out	28
F.E. Woolley	lbw b Francois	26	(4)	c Nupen b Francois	15
A.W. Carr	b Francois	27	(3)	c Taylor b Nupen	27
C.P. Mead	b Blanckenberg	1	(2)	b Nupen	49
P.G.H. Fender	c Brann b Blanckenberg	0	(7)	run out	9
V.W.C. Jupp	c and b Blanckenberg	1	(9)	st Ward b Blanckenberg	33
G.T.S. Stevens	b Francois	11	(10)	c Nourse b Nupen	2
G. Brown†	b Blanckenberg	22	(8)	b Blanckenberg	1
A.S. Kennedy	not out	41	(5)	c Blanckenberg b Nupen	0
A.E.R. Gilligan	b Blanckenberg	18		b Nupen	7
Extras	(B 3, LB 1, W 1)	5		(B 14, LB 6, NB 2)	22
Total		**182**			**218**

ENGLAND	O	M	R	W	O	M	R	W
Gilligan	7	1	23	0	20	3	69	3
Kennedy	20·4	5	37	4	41·3	9	132	4
Jupp	21	6	59	4	31	7	87	3
Fender	7	1	17	1	12	0	64	0
Woolley					16	4	33	0
Stevens					4	0	19	0
SOUTH AFRICA								
Buys	7	1	20	0	17	3	32	0
Nupen	17	3	58	1	30	11	53	5
Blanckenberg	22·5	5	76	6	24	3	59	3
Francois	10	1	23	3	29	9	52	1

FALL OF WICKETS

Wkt	SA 1st	E 1st	SA 2nd	E 2nd
1st	55	15	33	56
2nd	92	45	52	99
3rd	97	79	91	114
4th	97	84	202	114
5th	111	84	300	124
6th	120	85	326	147
7th	121	93	352	161
8th	121	100	380	207
9th	145	152	393	210
10th	148	182	420	218

Umpires: F.W. Grey (10) and A.G. Laver (4).

Close: 1st day – E(1) 132-8 (Brown 13, Kennedy 19); 2nd – SA(2) 270-4 (Taylor 121, Brann 35); 3rd – E(2) 123-4 (Woolley 15, Mann 0).

SOUTH AFRICA v ENGLAND 1922–23 (2nd Test)

Played at Newlands, Cape Town, on 1, 2, 3, 4 January.
Toss: South Africa.   Result: ENGLAND won by one wicket.
Debuts: South Africa – A.E. Hall; England – G.G. Macaulay.

Macaulay took the wicket of Hearne with his first ball in Test cricket and also made the final hit in one of only six Test matches to be won by the margin of one wicket. Hall, the other debutant in this match and Lancashire-born, took 11 wickets bowling left-arm fast-medium, and came within the narrowest possible margin of winning the game for South Africa. Hearne kept wicket for part of the match after Ward injured a finger.

SOUTH AFRICA

R.H. Catterall	c Brown b Fender	10	b Macaulay	76
G.A.L. Hearne	c Fender b Macaulay	0	b Kennedy	0
H.W. Taylor*	b Fender	9	c Jupp b Macaulay	68
A.W. Nourse	lbw b Fender	16	b Fender	19
W.V.S. Ling	c Mann b Fender	13	c Fender b Macaulay	2
W.H. Brann	b Kennedy	0	lbw b Macaulay	4
J.M. Blanckenberg	c Carr b Jupp	9	(8) b Kennedy	5
C.M. Francois	run out	28	(7) c and b Macaulay	19
T.A. Ward†	b Jupp	4	not out	15
E.P. Nupen	c and b Macaulay	2	b Kennedy	6
A.E. Hall	not out	0	b Kennedy	5
Extras	(B 14, LB 6, NB 2)	22	(B 15, LB 6, NB 2)	23
Total		**113**		**242**

ENGLAND

C.A.G. Russell	c Catterall b Hall	39	lbw b Blanckenberg	8
A. Sandham	c Francois b Blanckenberg	19	lbw b Hall	17
F.E. Woolley	c Francois b Hall	0	b Hall	5
C.P. Mead	c Francois b Blanckenberg	21	lbw b Hall	31
A.W. Carr	c Ward b Hall	42	c Brann b Hall	6
F.T. Mann*	lbw b Blanckenberg	4	(7) c Blanckenberg b Hall	45
P.G.H. Fender	c Hearne b Hall	3	(6) c Nourse b Hall	2
V.W.C. Jupp	c Hearne b Nupen	12	st Ward b Hall	38
A.S. Kennedy	c Hearne b Blanckenberg	2	not out	11
G. Brown†	not out	10	run out	0
G.G. Macaulay	b Blanckenberg	19	not out	1
Extras	(B 5, LB 4, W 1, NB 2)	12	(B 4, LB 5)	9
Total		**183**	(9 wickets)	**173**

ENGLAND	O	M	R	W	O	M	R	W		FALL OF WICKETS			
Kennedy	18	10	24	1	35·2	13	58	4		SA	E	SA	E
Macaulay	13	5	19	2	37	11	64	5	*Wkt*	*1st*	*1st*	*2nd*	*2nd*
Fender	14	4	29	4	20	3	52	1	1st	0	59	2	20
Woolley	2	1	1	0	11	3	22	0	2nd	22	59	157	29
Jupp	9	3	18	2	11	3	23	0	3rd	31	60	158	49
									4th	60	128	162	56
SOUTH AFRICA									5th	67	134	170	59
Nupen	15	2	48	1	24	8	41	0	6th	67	137	200	86
Hall	25	8	49	4	37·3	12	63	7	7th	96	147	212	154
Blanckenberg	24·1	5	61	5	24	7	56	1	8th	108	149	212	167
Francois	4	1	13	0	3	0	4	0	9th	111	155	224	168

Umpires: A.G. Laver (5) and G.J. Thompson (1).

Close: 1st day – E(1) 128-4 (Mead 17); 2nd – SA(2) 134-1 (Catterall 74, Taylor 48); 3rd – E(2) 86-6 (Mann 12).

SOUTH AFRICA v ENGLAND 1922–23 (3rd Test)

Played at Kingsmead, Durban, on 18, 19, 20 (*no play*), 22 January.
Toss: England.   Result: MATCH DRAWN.
Debuts: England – G.B. Street.

This was the first Test to be played on the Kingsmead Ground in Durban. Mead scored the first Test hundred on the new ground but his innings of 181 took 454 minutes. Ling was summoned home to Kimberley when his mother became seriously ill; it proved to be his last Test.

ENGLAND

C.A.G. Russell	c Ward b Nupen	34		
A. Sandham	c Nourse b Snooke	0		
F.E. Woolley	c Nourse b Hall	0		
C.P. Mead	c Nourse b Blanckenberg	181		
A.W. Carr	c Snooke b Nupen	7	(3) not out	2
P.G.H. Fender	c Ling b Hall	60		
F.T. Mann*	c Snooke b Hall	84		
V.W.C. Jupp	st Ward b Blanckenberg	16		
A.S. Kennedy	c Catterall b Blanckenberg	8		
G.B. Street†	c Nourse b Hall	4	(1) not out	7
G.G. Macaulay	not out	3	(2) c Blanckenberg b Hall	2
Extras	(B 16, LB 6, NB 9)	31		
Total		**428**	(1 wicket)	**11**

SOUTH AFRICA

R.H. Catterall	c Woolley b Kennedy	52
H.W. Taylor*	c Woolley b Macaulay	91
S.J. Snooke	lbw b Kennedy	8
A.W. Nourse	c Woolley b Kennedy	52
W.H. Brann	c Kennedy b Fender	16
C.M. Francois	c Jupp b Kennedy	72
T.A. Ward†	b Jupp	26
J.M. Blanckenberg	b Kennedy	8
E.P. Nupen	st Street b Jupp	6
A.E. Hall	not out	1
W.V.S. Ling	absent	–
Extras	(B 15, LB 8, NB 13)	36
Total		**368**

SOUTH AFRICA	O	M	R	W	O	M	R	W				
Snooke	9	1	20	1	2	0	9	0				
Hall	53·5	23	105	4	2	1	2	1				
Blanckenberg	48	12	122	3								
Francois	30	13	55	0								
Nupen	41	9	86	2								
Nourse	4	0	9	0								

FALL OF WICKETS

	E	SA	E
Wkt	1st	1st	2nd
1st	1	110	8
2nd	2	120	–
3rd	63	220	–
4th	71	228	–
5th	225	263	–
6th	381	338	–
7th	397	360	–
8th	418	362	–
9th	421	368	–
10th	428	–	–

ENGLAND	O	M	R	W
Kennedy	39	14	88	5
Macaulay	29	8	55	1
Fender	29	7	72	1
Jupp	22·4	6	70	2
Woolley	15	3	47	0

Umpires: G.J. Thompson (2) and W. Wainwright (1).

Close: 1st day – E(1) 256-5 (Mead 128, Mann 11); 2nd – SA(1) 70-0 (Catterall 33, Taylor 25); 3rd – no play.

SOUTH AFRICA v ENGLAND 1922–23 (4th Test)

Played at Old Wanderers, Johannesburg, on 9, 10, 12, 13 February.
Toss: England.   Result: MATCH DRAWN.
Debuts: South Africa – D.J. Meintjes, L.E. Tapscott.

Before a capacity Saturday crowd of nearly 20,000, the largest then on record for any cricket match in the Union, South Africa gained their only first innings lead of the rubber. Woolley survived his first ball (from Hall) by the narrowest margin, when it grazed his off bail without removing it, and reached his only Test century in South Africa. During his innings of 63, Nourse became the first South African to score 2,000 runs in Test cricket.

ENGLAND

C.A.G. Russell	b Hall	8	c Hall b Nupen		96
A. Sandham	c Ward b Meintjes	6	lbw b Hall		58
F.E. Woolley	c Nourse b Hall	15	not out		115
A.W. Carr	lbw b Blanckenberg	63	c Ward b Meintjes		6
C.P. Mead	b Nupen	38	c and b Meintjes		0
P.G.H. Fender	c Hall b Blanckenberg	44	b Meintjes		9
F.T. Mann*	c Catterall b Hall	34	c Meintjes b Blanckenberg		59
V.W.C. Jupp	c Nourse b Hall	7	not out		10
A.S. Kennedy	c Nourse b Hall	16			
G. Brown†	b Hall	0			
G.G. Macaulay	not out	1			
Extras	(B 4, LB 7, NB 1)	12	(B 12, LB 8, NB 3)		23
Total		**244**	(6 wickets declared)		**376**

SOUTH AFRICA

D.J. Meintjes	c Russell b Kennedy	3			
T.A. Ward†	b Jupp	64	(3) c Macaulay b Kennedy		8
R.H. Catterall	b Fender	31	(1) c Brown b Macaulay		8
H.W. Taylor*	c Russell b Fender	11	(2) c Russell b Kennedy		101
A.W. Nourse	c Woolley b Jupp	51	(4) c Fender b Kennedy		63
S.J. Snooke	lbw b Jupp	2	(5) not out		39
C.M. Francois	c Brown b Kennedy	41	(6) not out		3
L.E. Tapscott	not out	50			
J.M. Blanckenberg	c Russell b Kennedy	7			
E.P. Nupen	c Mann b Macaulay	12			
A.E. Hall	c Kennedy b Macaulay	0			
Extras	(B 11, LB 6, NB 6)	23	(B 16, LB 3, NB 6)		25
Total		**295**	(4 wickets)		**247**

SOUTH AFRICA	O	M	R	W	O	M	R	W
Meintjes	8	1	31	1	11	3	38	3
Snooke	3	0	10	0	6	3	11	0
Hall	36·4	11	82	6	44	8	114	1
Blanckenberg	30	10	46	2	29	6	78	1
Nupen	16	4	50	1	28	4	88	1
Francois	10	6	13	0	9	3	17	0
Nourse					5	3	7	0
Taylor					2	2	0	0
ENGLAND								
Kennedy	24	5	68	3	27·5	7	70	3
Macaulay	27	5	80	2	17	6	27	1
Woolley	6	3	10	0	6	2	26	0
Fender	20	4	78	2	17	2	60	0
Jupp	15	5	36	3	12	3	39	0

FALL OF WICKETS

Wkt	E 1st	SA 1st	E 2nd	SA 2nd
1st	9	16	153	19
2nd	19	78	189	32
3rd	35	116	203	166
4th	108	139	209	238
5th	177	157	221	–
6th	192	212	345	–
7th	207	220	–	–
8th	237	230	–	–
9th	243	293	–	–
10th	244	295	–	–

Umpires: S.L. Harris (4) and A.G. Laver (6).

Close: 1st day – SA(1) 8-0 (Meintjes 2, Ward 2); 2nd – E(2) 6-0 (Russell 3, Sandham 2); 3rd – E(2) 294-5 (Woolley 80, Mann 23).

SOUTH AFRICA v ENGLAND 1922–23 (5th Test)

Played at Kingsmead, Durban, on 16, 17, 19, 20, 21, 22 February.
Toss: England. Result: ENGLAND won by 109 runs.
Debuts: South Africa – D.P. Conyngham.

Russell, in what proved to be his final Test match, emulated W. Bardsley of Australia (*Test No. 105*) by scoring a hundred in each innings of a Test. Russell's last three scores in Test cricket were 96, 140 and 111. His stand of 92 with Gilligan remains England's best for the tenth wicket against South Africa. A comfortable victory in this timeless Test gave England their first successful rubber for nine years. Taylor's aggregate of 582 (average 64.66) remains the South African record for a home rubber against England.

ENGLAND

C.A.G. Russell	c Catterall b Blanckenberg	140	(6) c Francois b Blanckenberg		111
A. Sandham	c Ward b Snooke	1	(4) b Francois		40
F.E. Woolley	c and b Meintjes	2	c Nourse b Snooke		8
C.P. Mead	lbw b Francois	66	(5) c Conyngham b Meintjes		5
A.W. Carr	lbw b Conyngham	14	(7) b Blanckenberg		5
P.G.H. Fender	b Hall	1	(8) b Blanckenberg		0
F.T. Mann*	b Nourse	8	(9) lbw b Conyngham		15
A.S. Kennedy	c Nourse b Snooke	14	(2) c Taylor b Hall		1
G.G. Macaulay	lbw b Snooke	0	(10) b Hall		1
G. Brown†	not out	15	(1) lbw b Snooke		1
A.E.R. Gilligan	c Taylor b Hall	4	not out		39
Extras	(B 12, LB 3, NB 1)	16	(B 13, LB 1, NB 1)		15
Total		**281**			**241**

SOUTH AFRICA

R.H. Catterall	b Macaulay	17	c Macaulay b Gilligan		22
H.W. Taylor*	c Russell b Gilligan	3	(4) c Fender b Kennedy		102
T.A. Ward†	c Macaulay b Gilligan	1	b Macaulay		10
A.W. Nourse	c Mann b Fender	44	(5) c Brown b Kennedy		25
S.J. Snooke	c Woolley b Kennedy	4	(7) lbw b Kennedy		1
C.M. Francois	c Fender b Gilligan	43	b Gilligan		18
L.E. Tapscott	c Brown b Macaulay	2	(8) b Macaulay		6
D.J. Meintjes	run out	19	(2) lbw b Kennedy		21
J.M. Blanckenberg	c Mead b Kennedy	21	b Gilligan		9
D.P. Conyngham	not out	3	not out		3
A.E. Hall	c Fender b Macaulay	0	c Woolley b Kennedy		0
Extras	(B 14, LB 2, NB 6)	22	(B 11, LB 3, NB 3)		17
Total		**179**			**234**

SOUTH AFRICA	O	M	R	W	O	M	R	W
Meintjes	13	1	33	1	9	2	13	1
Snooke	12	3	17	3	23	6	41	2
Conyngham	31	10	63	1	30	12	40	1
Blanckenberg	24	5	65	1	25·4	7	50	3
Hall	24·5	9	31	2	27	10	55	2
Francois	11	1	33	1	8	2	15	1
Nourse	11	4	23	1	6	2	10	0
Tapscott					2	1	2	0
ENGLAND								
Gilligan	23	7	35	3	36	10	78	3
Kennedy	25	9	46	2	49·1	19	76	5
Macaulay	20	5	42	3	18	6	39	2
Fender	11	3	25	1	11	3	21	0
Woolley	6	3	9	0	3	2	3	0

FALL OF WICKETS				
	E	SA	E	SA
Wkt	1st	1st	2nd	2nd
1st	14	7	2	42
2nd	17	13	10	48
3rd	156	41	14	64
4th	191	58	26	122
5th	194	97	102	149
6th	224	107	111	150
7th	253	135	111	175
8th	253	169	148	204
9th	268	178	149	232
10th	281	179	241	234

Umpires: A.G. Laver (7) and J. Reid (1).

Close: 1st day – E(1) 261-8 (Russell 136, Brown 3); 2nd – E(2) 0-0 (Brown 0, Kennedy 0); 3rd – E(2) 201-9 (Russell 90, Gilligan 20); 4th – SA(2) 111-3 (Taylor 28, Nourse 17); 5th – SA(2) 203-7 (Taylor 76, Blanckenberg 9).

ENGLAND v SOUTH AFRICA 1924 (1st Test)

Played at Edgbaston, Birmingham, on 14, 16, 17 June.
Toss: South Africa.   Result: ENGLAND won by an innings and 18 runs.
Debuts: England – A.P.F. Chapman, R. Kilner, H. Sutcliffe, M.W. Tate, G.E.C. Wood; South
  Africa – H.G. Deane, G.M. Parker, M.J. Susskind.

Parker, an expatriate fast bowler from Cape Town then playing for Eccleshill in the Bradford League, was called up to strengthen the bowling and responded with six wickets. Hobbs and Sutcliffe achieved the first of their 15 three-figure opening partnerships for England at their first attempt. South Africa equalled their own record for the lowest Test score set in 1895-96 (*Test No. 47*). It stood until England dismissed New Zealand for 26 in 1954-55 (*Test No. 402*). The innings was over in 75 balls and took 48 minutes. Tate dismissed Susskind with his first ball in Test cricket.

ENGLAND

J.B. Hobbs	lbw b Blanckenberg	76
H. Sutcliffe	b Parker	64
F.E. Woolley	c Ward b Parker	64
E.H. Hendren	c Nourse b Parker	74
A.P.F. Chapman	b Parker	8
P.G.H. Fender	c Taylor b Blanckenberg	36
R. Kilner	c and b Pegler	59
M.W. Tate	c Taylor b Parker	19
A.E.R. Gilligan*	b Pegler	13
G.E.C. Wood†	b Parker	1
C.H. Parkin	not out	8
Extras	(B 4, LB 11, NB 1)	16
Total		**438**

SOUTH AFRICA

H.W. Taylor*	b Tate	7		c and b Tate	34
R.H. Catterall	b Gilligan	0	(5)	c Hobbs b Tate	120
M.J. Susskind	c Kilner b Tate	3		b Gilligan	51
A.W. Nourse	lbw b Gilligan	1		c Wood b Gilligan	34
J.M.M. Commaille	not out	1	(2)	c Hendren b Tate	29
J.M. Blanckenberg	b Tate	4		c Chapman b Gilligan	56
H.G. Deane	b Gilligan	2		run out	5
E.P. Nupen	b Gilligan	0		lbw b Tate	5
S.J. Pegler	b Tate	0	(10)	c Hobbs b Gilligan	6
T.A. Ward†	b Gilligan	1	(9)	b Gilligan	19
G.M. Parker	lbw b Gilligan	0		not out	2
Extras	(B 1, LB 7, NB 3)	11		(B 4, LB 18, W 1, NB 6)	29
Total		**30**			**390**

SOUTH AFRICA	O	M	R	W	O	M	R	W	FALL OF WICKETS			
										E	SA	SA
Parker	37	2	152	6					*Wkt*	*1st*	*1st*	*2nd*
Pegler	36	8	106	2					1st	136	1	54
Blanckenberg	32	5	95	2					2nd	164	4	101
Nupen	18	2	66	0					3rd	247	6	152
Nourse	1	0	3	0					4th	255	14	161
ENGLAND									5th	315	20	275
Gilligan	6·3	4	7	6	28	6	83	5	6th	356	23	284
Tate	6	1	12	4	50·4	19	103	4	7th	386	23	295
Parkin					16	5	38	0	8th	407	24	350
Kilner					22	10	40	0	9th	410	30	372
Fender					17	5	56	0	10th	438	30	390
Woolley					10	2	41	0				

Umpires: H.R. Butt (3) and W. Reeves (1).

Close: 1st day – E(1) 398-7 (Kilner 40, Gilligan 4); 2nd – SA(2) 274-4 (Catterall 52, Blanckenberg 56).

ENGLAND v SOUTH AFRICA 1924 (2nd Test)

Played at Lord's, London, on 28, 30 June, 1 July.
Toss: South Africa.   Result: ENGLAND won by an innings and 18 runs.
Debuts: England – R.K. Tyldesley.

Catterall made his second successive top-score of 120 and his country suffered their second successive defeat by the identical margin of an innings and 18 runs. England gained their victory for the loss of only two wickets; no other country has equalled this record. On the second day England became the only Test team to score 500 runs in a day (503-2). The stand of 268 between Hobbs and Sutcliffe remains England's first-wicket record at Lord's and was the highest against South Africa until 1948-49 (*Test No. 310*). Although he reached three figures on 15 occasions for England, this was the only time that Hobbs scored 200. He took his score from 12 to 114 before lunch on the second day. Parker ended his third and final first-class match as the only South African Test cricketer not to play first-class cricket in his own country.

SOUTH AFRICA

H.W. Taylor*	c Wood b Gilligan	4	(5) b Gilligan		8
J.M.M. Commaille	b Gilligan	0	lbw b Tyldesley		37
M.J. Susskind	c Tate b Hearne	64	lbw b Tyldesley		53
A.W. Nourse	c Woolley b Tate	4	lbw b Gilligan		11
R.H. Catterall	b Gilligan	120	(6) c Gilligan b Tyldesley		45
J.M. Blanckenberg	b Tate	12	(7) c Hobbs b Fender		15
H.G. Deane	b Tylesley	33	(1) c Sutcliffe b Hearne		24
G.A. Faulkner	b Fender	25	run out		12
T.A. Ward†	b Tyldesley	1	(10) not out		3
S.J. Pegler	c Fender b Tyldesley	0	(9) b Tate		8
G.M. Parker	not out	1	b Tate		0
Extras	(B 3, LB 2, NB 4)	9	(B 13, LB 8, NB 3)		24
Total		**273**			**240**

ENGLAND

J.B. Hobbs	c Taylor b Parker	211
H. Sutcliffe	b Parker	122
F.E. Woolley	not out	134
E.H. Hendren	not out	50
J.W. Hearne	)	
A.P.F. Chapman	)	
P.G.H. Fender	)	
A.E.R. Gilligan*	) did not bat	
G.E.C. Wood†	)	
M.W. Tate	)	
R.K. Tyldesley	)	
Extras	(B 11, LB 1, NB 2)	14
Total	(2 wickets declared)	**531**

ENGLAND	O	M	R	W	O	M	R	W
Gilligan	31	7	70	3	24	6	54	2
Tate	34	12	62	2	26·4	8	43	2
Tyldesley	24	10	52	3	36	18	50	3
Hearne	18	3	35	1	19	4	35	1
Fender	9	1	45	1	14	5	25	1
Woolley					4	1	9	0

SOUTH AFRICA	O	M	R	W
Parker	24	0	121	2
Blanckenberg	28	3	113	0
Pegler	31	4	120	0
Nourse	15	1	57	0
Faulkner	17	0	87	0
Catterall	3	0	19	0

FALL OF WICKETS

	SA	E	SA
Wkt	1st	1st	2nd
1st	4	268	50
2nd	5	410	78
3rd	17	–	103
4th	129	–	117
5th	182	–	171
6th	212	–	204
7th	265	–	224
8th	271	–	231
9th	272	–	240
10th	273	–	240

Umpires: F. Chester (1) and H.I. Young (1).

Close: 1st day – E(1) 28-0 (Hobbs 12, Sutcliffe 12); 2nd – SA(2) 19-0 (Deane 13, Commaille 5).

ENGLAND v SOUTH AFRICA 1924 (3rd Test)

Played at Headingley, Leeds, on 12, 14, 15 July.
Toss: England.   Result: ENGLAND won by nine wickets.
Debuts: Nil.

In glorious weather England won the rubber decisively. Countering some persistent leg-theory tactics with adroit footwork, Hendren reached the first of his seven Test hundreds. Tate's first innings analysis remained his best for England.

ENGLAND

J.B. Hobbs	c Pegler b Nourse	31	b Blanckenberg	7
H. Sutcliffe	c Nupen b Blanckenberg	83	not out	29
J.W. Hearne	lbw b Pegler	20	not out	23
F.E. Woolley	b Pegler	0		
E.H. Hendren	c Deane b Nupen	132		
G.E. Tyldesley	run out	15		
M.W. Tate	c Taylor b Carter	29		
A.E.R. Gilligan*	c Catterall b Pegler	28		
R.K. Tyldesley	c Carter b Pegler	29		
G.E.C. Wood†	run out	6		
G.G. Macaulay	not out	0		
Extras	(B 13, LB 8, W 1, NB 1)	23	(LB 1)	1
Total		**396**	(1 wicket)	**60**

SOUTH AFRICA

J.M.M. Commaille	run out	4	st Wood b R.K. Tyldesley	31
H.G. Deane	c and b Tate	2	(7) not out	47
T.A. Ward†	b Tate	17	(2) lbw b Hearne	25
M.J. Susskind	b Gilligan	4	lbw b R.K. Tyldesley	23
A.W. Nourse	run out	3	(3) c Wood b R.K. Tyldesley	30
H.W. Taylor*	not out	59	(5) run out	56
R.H. Catterall	c Wood b Tate	29	(6) b Tate	56
E.P. Nupen	c Wood b Tate	0	(9) b Macaulay	11
S.J. Pegler	lbw b Tate	0	(10) run out	14
J.M. Blanckenberg	b Tate	0	(8) b Tate	6
C.P. Carter	c Hendren b Macaulay	11	b Tate	0
Extras	(LB 1, NB 2)	3	(B 14, LB 7, NB 3)	24
Total		**132**		**323**

SOUTH AFRICA	O	M	R	W	O	M	R	W	FALL OF WICKETS				
Nupen	30	8	85	1	1	0	6	0		E	SA	SA	E
Pegler	35	6	116	4	11·2	3	30	0	*Wkt*	*1st*	*1st*	*2nd*	*2nd*
Nourse	24	7	67	1					1st	72	6	35	17
Blanckenberg	12	0	58	1	10	2	23	1	2nd	130	10	81	–
Carter	15	2	47	1					3rd	130	16	82	–
ENGLAND									4th	201	30	135	–
									5th	248	34	234	–
Gilligan	10	3	27	1	18	7	37	0	6th	305	88	238	–
Tate	17	4	42	6	30	6	64	3	7th	350	88	244	–
Macaulay	11·3	2	23	1	27	8	60	1	8th	365	90	276	–
R.K. Tyldesley	13	4	37	0	24	8	63	3	9th	386	90	318	–
Hearne					19	3	54	1	10th	396	132	323	–
Woolley					9	2	21	0					

Umpires: W. Reeves (2) and A.E. Street (5).

Close: 1st day – SA(1) 15-2 (Ward 5, Susskind 4); 2nd – SA(2) 232-4 (Taylor 54, Catterall 54).

ENGLAND v SOUTH AFRICA 1924 (4th Test)

Played at Old Trafford, Manchester, on 26, 28 (*no play*), 29 (*no play*) July.
Toss: South Africa.   Result: MATCH DRAWN.
Debuts: England – G. Duckworth, G. Geary, J.C.W. MacBryan.

Torrential rain ended this match at 4.00 pm on the first day. About 8,000 spectators, 3,000 of them members, witnessed 165 minutes of play. That period encompassed the entire Test career of John Crawford William MacBryan, the stylish Somerset batsman. He is the only Test cricketer who never batted, bowled or dismissed anyone in the field.

SOUTH AFRICA

J.M.M. Commaille	lbw b Tate	8
T.A. Ward†	b Tate	50
M.J. Susskind	lbw b Tyldesley	5
A.W. Nourse	b Tate	18
H.W. Taylor*	not out	18
R.H. Catterall	not out	6
H.G. Deane	)	
P.A.M. Hands	)	
J.M. Blanckenberg	) did not bat	
S.J. Pegler	)	
C.P. Carter	)	
Extras	(B 8, LB 3)	11
Total	(4 wickets)	**116**

ENGLAND

H. Sutcliffe
A. Sandham
J.C.W. MacBryan
F.E. Woolley
E.H. Hendren
J.W.H.T. Douglas*
R. Kilner
M.W. Tate
G. Geary
R.K. Tyldesley
G. Duckworth†

ENGLAND	O	M	R	W
Tate	24	8	34	3
Douglas	8	2	20	0
Geary	11	5	21	0
Tyldesley	11·5	4	11	1
Kilner	12	6	19	0

	FALL OF WICKETS	
		SA
Wkt		1st
1st		8
2nd		40
3rd		71
4th		98
5th		–
6th		–
7th		–
8th		–
9th		–
10th		–

Umpires: H.R. Butt (4) and A.E. Street (6).

Close: 1st day – SA(1) 116-4 (Taylor 18, Catterall 6); 2nd – no play.

ENGLAND v SOUTH AFRICA 1924 (5th Test)

Played at Kennington Oval, London, on 16, 18, 19 August.
Toss: South Africa.   Result: MATCH DRAWN.
Debuts: Nil.

Catterall narrowly missed a third hundred when he was caught at backward point after scoring 95 out of 151 in just over two hours. Kilner was substituting for Tyldesley who had injured his left wrist attempting a fast slip catch. Hendren's hundred was his second in successive innings. Rain prevented play after tea on Monday and a thunderstorm flooded the ground after 50 minutes of play on the last day.

SOUTH AFRICA

J.M.M. Commaille	b Tate	3
G.A.L. Hearne	run out	4
M.J. Susskind	c Woolley b Hearne	65
A.W. Nourse	c Sutcliffe b Woolley	37
H.W. Taylor*	c and b Tyldesley	11
R.H. Catterall	c sub (R. Kilner) b Tate	95
H.G. Deane	c Strudwick b Hearne	30
J.M. Blanckenberg	not out	46
T.A. Ward†	lbw b Tate	5
S.J. Pegler	b Tyldesley	25
C.P. Carter	c Sandham b Hearne	4
Extras	(B 4, LB 9, W 1, NB 3)	17
Total		**342**

ENGLAND

J.B. Hobbs	c Ward b Pegler	30
H. Sutcliffe	c Ward b Nourse	5
J.W. Hearne	c Susskind b Pegler	35
F.E. Woolley	b Carter	51
A. Sandham	c Ward b Nourse	46
E.H. Hendren	c Nourse b Carter	142
M.W. Tate	b Carter	50
A.E.R. Gilligan*	c Nourse b Pegler	36
R.K. Tyldesley	not out	1
H. Strudwick†	not out	2
H. Howell	did not bat	
Extras	(B 8, LB 13, NB 2)	23
Total	(8 wickets)	**421**

ENGLAND	O	M	R	W
Gilligan	16	5	44	0
Tate	29	10	64	3
Howell	20	5	69	0
Tyldesley	22	6	36	2
Hearne	23	3	90	3
Woolley	14	4	22	1
SOUTH AFRICA				
Nourse	24	3	63	2
Blanckenberg	36	2	122	0
Carter	23	2	85	3
Pegler	48	14	128	3

FALL OF WICKETS

Wkt	SA 1st	E 1st
1st	7	5
2nd	7	72
3rd	86	79
4th	108	137
5th	181	238
6th	259	328
7th	259	402
8th	268	418
9th	337	–
10th	342	–

Umpires: H.R. Butt (5) and F. Chester (2).

Close: 1st day – SA(1) 342 all out; 2nd – E(1) 332-6 (Hendren 92, Gilligan 4).

AUSTRALIA v ENGLAND 1924–25 (1st Test)

Played at Sydney Cricket Ground on 19, 20, 22, 23, 24, 26, 27 December.
Toss: Australia.   Result: AUSTRALIA won by 193 runs.
Debuts: Australia – W.H. Ponsford, A.J. Richardson, V.Y. Richardson; England – A.P. Freeman.

This rubber, in which the 8-ball over was introduced to Test cricket, saw the start of the famous association between Hobbs (aged 42) and Sutcliffe (30) against Australia. They began with opening partnerships of 157 and 110. Ponsford, protected by Collins from Tate's early hostility, was the third Australian to score a hundred on debut. The stand of 127 between Taylor (suffering from a boil behind his knee), and Mailey remains the best for Australia's last wicket against England. Hearne injured his hand and was unable to complete his over in the first innings.

AUSTRALIA

H.L. Collins*	c Hendren b Tate	114	(4) c Chapman b Tate	60
W. Bardsley	c Woolley b Freeman	21	b Tate	22
W.H. Ponsford	b Gilligan	110	(5) c Woolley b Freeman	27
A.J. Richardson	b Hearne	22	(1) c and b Freeman	98
J.M. Taylor	c Strudwick b Tate	43	(8) b Tate	108
V.Y. Richardson	b Freeman	42	c Hendren b Tate	18
C. Kelleway	c Woolley b Tate	17	(3) b Gilligan	23
H.S.T.L. Hendry	c Strudwick b Tate	3	(7) c Strudwick b Tate	22
J.M. Gregory	c Strudwick b Tate	0	c Woolley b Freeman	2
W.A.S. Oldfield†	not out	39	c Strudwick b Gilligan	18
A.A. Mailey	b Tate	21	not out	46
Extras	(B 10, LB 8)	18	(B 2, LB 5, W 1)	8
Total		450		452

ENGLAND

J.B. Hobbs	c Kelleway b Gregory	115	c Hendry b Mailey	57
H. Sutcliffe	c V.Y. Richardson b Mailey	59	c Gregory b Mailey	115
J.W. Hearne	c sub (T.J.E. Andrews) b Mailey	7	b Gregory	0
F.E. Woolley	b Gregory	0	(6) c Mailey b Gregory	123
E.H. Hendren	not out	74	c Gregory b Hendry	9
A. Sandham	b Mailey	7	(7) c Oldfield b Mailey	2
A.P.F. Chapman	run out	13	(4) c Oldfield b Hendry	44
M.W. Tate	c sub (T.J.E. Andrews) b Mailey	7	c Ponsford b Kelleway	0
A.E.R. Gilligan*	b Gregory	1	b Kelleway	1
A.P. Freeman	b Gregory	0	not out	50
H. Strudwick†	lbw b Gregory	6	c Oldfield b Hendry	2
Extras	(B 1, LB 5, NB 3)	9	(B 4, LB 3, NB 1)	8
Total		298		411

ENGLAND	O	M	R	W	O	M	R	W
Tate	55·1	11	130	6	33·7	8	98	5
Gilligan	23	0	92	1	27	6	114	2
Freeman	49	11	124	2	37	4	134	3
Hearne	12·1	3	28	1	25	2	88	0
Woolley	9	0	35	0				
Hobbs	2	0	13	0				
Chapman	2	0	10	0	3	1	10	0
AUSTRALIA								
Gregory	28·7	2	111	5	28	2	115	2
Kelleway	14	3	44	0	21	5	60	2
Mailey	31	2	129	4	32	0	179	3
Hendry	5	1	5	0	10·7	2	36	3
A.J. Richardson	1	1	0	0	5	0	13	0

FALL OF WICKETS

Wkt	A 1st	E 1st	A 2nd	E 2nd
1st	46	157	40	110
2nd	236	171	115	127
3rd	275	172	168	195
4th	286	202	210	212
5th	364	235	241	263
6th	374	254	260	269
7th	387	272	281	270
8th	387	274	286	276
9th	388	274	325	404
10th	450	298	452	411

Umpires: A.C. Jones (5) and A.P. Williams (1).

Close: 1st day – A(1) 282-3 (A.J. Richardson 21, Taylor 1); 2nd – E(1) 72-0 (Hobbs 42, Sutcliffe 28); 3rd – A(2) 61-1 (A.J Richardson 30, Kelleway 9); 4th – A(2) 258-5 (Collins 58, Hendry 6); 5th – E(2) 42-0 (Hobbs 13, Sutcliffe 27); 6th – E(2) 362-8 (Woolley 94, Freeman 33).

AUSTRALIA v ENGLAND 1924–25 (2nd Test)

Played at Melbourne Cricket Ground on 1, 2, 3, 5, 6, 7, 8 January.
Toss: Australia.   Result: AUSTRALIA won by 81 runs.
Debuts: Australia – A.E.V. Hartkopf.

Ponsford was the first to score centuries in each of his first two Tests. V.Y. Richardson scored 21 (44442300) off an over from Douglas – still the most runs by one batsman in an over for this series. Australia's total was the highest in Tests until 1928-29 (*Test No. 177*). Hobbs, the first to score 2,000 runs against Australia, and Sutcliffe batted throughout the third day – the first such instance in Tests. Their 289-minute partnership was the longest for the first wicket in this series until 1989. Sutcliffe was the first batsman to score a hundred in each innings of a Test against Australia and became the first Englishman to score three successive hundreds in Test cricket; his first four innings against Australia were 59, 115, 176 and 127, and his first three partnerships with Hobbs against Australia produced stands of 157, 110 and 283.

AUSTRALIA

Batsman	Dismissal 1	Score 1	Dismissal 2	Score 2
H.L. Collins*	c Strudwick b Tate	9	b Hearne	30
W. Bardsley	c Strudwick b Gilligan	19	lbw b Tate	2
A.J. Richardson	run out	14	b Tate	9
W.H. Ponsford	b Tate	128	b Tate	4
J.M. Taylor	run out	72	b Tate	90
V.Y. Richardson	run out	138	c Strudwick b Hearne	8
C. Kelleway	c Strudwick b Gilligan	32	c and b Hearne	17
A.E.V. Hartkopf	c Chapman b Gilligan	80	lbw b Tate	0
J.M. Gregory	c Gilligan b Tate	44	not out	36
W.A.S. Oldfield†	not out	39	lbw b Hearne	39
A.A. Mailey	lbw b Douglas	1	b Tate	3
Extras	(B 18, LB 5, NB 1)	24	(B 11, LB 1)	12
Total		**600**		**250**

ENGLAND

Batsman	Dismissal 1	Score 1	Dismissal 2	Score 2
J.B. Hobbs	b Mailey	154	lbw b Mailey	22
H. Sutcliffe	b Kelleway	176	c Gregory b Mailey	127
F.E. Woolley	b Gregory	0	(5) lbw b A.J. Richardson	50
J.W. Hearne	b Mailey	9	lbw b Gregory	23
E.H. Hendren	c Oldfield b Kelleway	32	(6) b Gregory	18
A.P.F. Chapman	c Oldfield b Gregory	28	(9) not out	4
J.W.H.T. Douglas	c Collins b A.J. Richardson	8	(8) b Mailey	14
R.K. Tyldesley	c Collins b Gregory	5	(7) c Ponsford b Mailey	0
M.W. Tate	b A.J. Richardson	34	(11) b Gregory	0
A.E.R. Gilligan*	not out	17	c and b Mailey	0
H. Strudwick†	b Hartkopf	4	(3) lbw b Gregory	22
Extras	(B 4, LB 4, NB 4)	12	(B 6, LB 2, NB 2)	10
Total		**479**		**290**

ENGLAND	O	M	R	W	O	M	R	W					
Tate	45	10	142	3	33·3	8	99	6					
Douglas	19·5	0	95	1	4	0	9	0					
Tyldesley	35	3	130	0	2	0	6	0					
Gilligan	26	1	114	3	11	2	40	0					
Hearne	13	1	69	0	29	5	84	4					
Woolley	11	3	26	0									

FALL OF WICKETS

Wkt	A 1st	E 1st	A 2nd	E 2nd
1st	22	283	3	36
2nd	47	284	13	75
3rd	47	305	27	121
4th	208	373	106	211
5th	301	404	126	254
6th	424	412	166	255
7th	439	418	168	280
8th	499	453	168	289
9th	599	458	239	289
10th	600	479	250	290

AUSTRALIA	O	M	R	W	O	M	R	W
Gregory	34	4	124	3	27·3	6	87	4
Kelleway	30	10	62	2	18	4	42	0
Mailey	34	5	141	2	24	2	92	5
Hartkopf	26	1	120	1	4	1	14	0
A.J. Richardson	14	6	20	2	22	7	35	1
Collins					11	3	10	0

Umpires: R.W. Crockett (29) and C. Garing (1).

Close: 1st day – A(1) 300-4 (Ponsford 128, V.Y. Richardson 39); 2nd – A(1) 600 all out; 3rd – E(1) 283-0 (Hobbs 154, Sutcliffe 123); 4th – A(2) 63-3 (Collins 17, Taylor 25); 5th – E(2) 54-1 (Sutcliffe 12, Strudwick 15); 6th – E(2) 259-6 (Sutcliffe 114, Douglas 0).

AUSTRALIA v ENGLAND 1924–25 (3rd Test)

Played at Adelaide Oval on 16, 17, 19, 20, 21, 22, 23 January.
Toss: Australia.   Result: AUSTRALIA won by 11 runs.
Debuts: England – W.W. Whysall.

Ryder, who batted for 395 minutes, equalled S.E. Gregory's (then) record score against England in Australia set in *Test No. 42*. Australia recovered from 119 for 6 when England lost the services of Tate (blistered foot), Gilligan (strained thigh – unable to complete his eighth over), and Freeman (bruised wrist). This was the third successive match to require a seventh day.

AUSTRALIA

H.L. Collins*	b Tate	3		b Freeman	26
A.J. Richardson	b Kilner	69		c Kilner b Woolley	14
J.M. Gregory	b Freeman	6	(9)	c Hendren b Woolley	2
J.M. Taylor	lbw b Tate	0		b Freeman	34
W.H. Ponsford	c Strudwick b Gilligan	31		c Hendren b Kilner	43
V.Y. Richardson	c Whysall b Kilner	4	(7)	c Tate b Woolley	0
J. Ryder	not out	201	(3)	c and b Woolley	88
T.J.E. Andrews	b Kilner	72	(6)	c Whysall b Kilner	1
C. Kelleway	c Strudwick b Woolley	16	(8)	not out	22
W.A.S. Oldfield†	lbw b Kilner	47		b Kilner	4
A.A. Mailey	st Strudwick b Hendren	27		c Sutcliffe b Kilner	5
Extras	(LB 9, NB 4)	13		(B 4, LB 4, NB 3)	11
Total		**489**			**250**

ENGLAND

W.W. Whysall	b Gregory	9	(5)	c and b Gregory	75
M.W. Tate	c Andrews b Mailey	27	(8)	b Mailey	21
H. Strudwick†	c Gregory b Kelleway	1	(11)	not out	2
A.P.F. Chapman	b Gregory	26	(6)	c Ryder b Kelleway	58
J.B. Hobbs	c Gregory b Mailey	119	(1)	c Collins b A. J. Richardson	27
H. Sutcliffe	c Oldfield b Ryder	33	(2)	c Ponsford b Mailey	59
F.E. Woolley	c Andrews b Mailey	16	(3)	b Kelleway	21
E.H. Hendren	c Taylor b Gregory	92	(4)	lbw b Kelleway	4
R. Kilner	lbw b A.J. Richardson	6	(7)	c V.Y. Richardson b A.J. Richardson	24
A.E.R. Gilligan*	c Collins b A.J. Richardson	9	(9)	c V.Y. Richardson b Gregory	31
A.P. Freeman	not out	6	(10)	c Oldfield b Mailey	24
Extras	(B 8, LB 10, NB 3)	21		(B 5, LB 5, W 1, NB 6)	17
Total		**365**			**363**

ENGLAND	O	M	R	W	O	M	R	W
Tate	18	1	43	2	10	4	17	0
Gilligan	7·7	1	17	1				
Freeman	18	0	107	1	17	1	94	2
Woolley	43	5	135	1	19	1	77	4
Kilner	56	7	127	4	22·1	7	51	4
Hobbs	3	0	11	0				
Hendren	5·1	0	27	1				
Whysall	2	0	9	0				
AUSTRALIA								
Gregory	26·2	0	111	3	23	6	71	2
Kelleway	15	6	24	1	22	4	57	3
Mailey	44	5	133	3	30·2	4	126	3
A.J. Richardson	21	7	42	2	25	5	62	2
Ryder	6	2	15	1	2	0	11	0
Collins	5	1	19	0	9	4	19	0

FALL OF WICKETS

	A	E	A	E
Wkt	1st	1st	2nd	2nd
1st	10	15	36	63
2nd	19	18	63	92
3rd	22	67	126	96
4th	114	69	215	155
5th	118	159	216	244
6th	119	180	217	254
7th	253	297	217	279
8th	308	316	220	312
9th	416	326	242	357
10th	489	365	250	363

Umpires: R.W. Crockett (30) and D. Elder (8).

Close: 1st day – A(1) 275-7 (Ryder 72, Kelleway 8); 2nd – E(1) 36-2 (Tate 14, Chapman 7); 3rd – E(1) 270-6 (Hobbs 99, Hendren 47); 4th – A(2) 211-3 (Ryder 86, Ponsford 40); 5th – E(2) 133-3 (Sutcliffe 56, Whysall 22); 6th – E(2) 348-8 (Gilligan 29, Freeman 17).

AUSTRALIA v ENGLAND 1924–25 (4th Test)

Played at Melbourne Cricket Ground on 13, 14, 16, 17, 18 February.
Toss: England.   Result: ENGLAND won by an innings and 29 runs.
Debuts: Nil.

Sutcliffe was the first to score four hundreds in one rubber of Test matches. This was his third century in consecutive Test innings at Melbourne and it took his aggregate after only nine Test matches (12 innings) to 1,015 runs. Oldfield was the first wicket-keeper to make either five dismissals or four stumpings in a Test innings. England's long-awaited victory ended Australia's run of 16 Tests without defeat against both England and South Africa since August 1912 (*Test No. 129*).

ENGLAND

J.B. Hobbs	st Oldfield b Ryder	66
H. Sutcliffe	lbw b Mailey	143
J.W. Hearne	c Bardsley b Richardson	44
F.E. Woolley	st Oldfield b Mailey	40
E.H. Hendren	b Ryder	65
A.P.F. Chapman	st Oldfield b Mailey	12
W.W. Whysall	st Oldfield b Kelleway	76
R. Kilner	lbw b Kelleway	74
A.E.R. Gilligan*	c Oldfield b Kelleway	0
M.W. Tate	c Taylor b Mailey	8
H. Strudwick†	not out	7
Extras	(B 6, LB 2, W 3, NB 2)	13
Total		**548**

AUSTRALIA

H.L. Collins*	c Kilner b Tate	22	c Whysall b Kilner		1
A.J. Richardson	b Hearne	19	(9) lbw b Hearne		3
J. Ryder	b Tate	0	(5) lbw b Woolley		38
W. Bardsley	run out	24	(2) b Tate		0
W.H. Ponsford	c Strudwick b Hearne	21	(8) b Tate		19
J.M. Taylor	c Hendren b Woolley	86	(4) c Woolley b Gilligan		68
T.J.E. Andrews	c Hearne b Kilner	35	(7) c Strudwick b Tate		3
C. Kelleway	lbw b Kilner	1	(6) c Strudwick b Tate		42
J.M. Gregory	c Woolley b Hearne	38	(3) c Sutcliffe b Kilner		45
W.A.S. Oldfield†	c Chapman b Kilner	3	b Tate		8
A.A. Mailey	not out	4	not out		8
Extras	(B 13, LB 2, NB 1)	16	(B 15)		15
Total		**269**			**250**

AUSTRALIA	O	M	R	W	O	M	R	W
Gregory	22	1	102	0				
Kelleway	29	5	70	3				
Mailey	43·6	2	186	4				
Ryder	25	3	83	2				
Richardson	26	8	76	1				
Collins	6	1	18	0				
ENGLAND								
Tate	16	2	70	2	25·5	6	75	5
Gilligan	6	1	24	0	7	0	26	1
Hearne	19·3	1	77	3	20	0	76	1
Kilner	13	1	29	3	16	3	41	2
Woolley	9	1	53	1	6	0	17	1

FALL OF WICKETS

Wkt	E 1st	A 1st	A 2nd
1st	126	38	5
2nd	232	38	5
3rd	284	64	64
4th	307	74	133
5th	346	109	190
6th	394	170	195
7th	527	172	225
8th	527	244	234
9th	529	257	238
10th	548	269	250

Umpires: R.W. Crockett (31) and D. Elder (9).

Close: 1st day – E(1) 282-2 (Sutcliffe 141, Woolley 26); 2nd – E(1) 548 all out; 3rd – A(1) 168-5 (Taylor 42, Andrews 33); 4th – A(2) 175-4 (Taylor 59, Kelleway 23).

AUSTRALIA v ENGLAND 1924–25 (5th Test)

Played at Sydney Cricket Ground on 27, 28 February, 2, 3, 4 March.
Toss: Australia.　Result: AUSTRALIA won by 307 runs.
Debuts: Australia – C.V. Grimmett, A.F. Kippax.

Grimmett, a 33-year-old Dunedin-born leg-break and googly bowler, took 11 for 82 in his first Test match. Sutcliffe's aggregate of 734 runs, average 81.55, was the record for any rubber until W.R. Hammond surpassed it in 1928-29. Tate's total of 38 wickets remains the most by an England bowler in a rubber in Australia.

AUSTRALIA

H.L. Collins*	c Strudwick b Gilligan	1	(7) lbw b Tate		28
J. Ryder	b Kilner	29	b Gilligan		7
J.M. Gregory	run out	29	(1) lbw b Hearne		22
T.J.E. Andrews	c Whysall b Kilner	26	(3) c Woolley b Hearne		80
J.M. Taylor	c Whysall b Tate	15	(4) st Strudwick b Tate		25
W.H. Ponsford	c Woolley b Kilner	80	(5) run out		5
A.F. Kippax	b Kilner	42	(6) c Whysall b Woolley		8
C. Kelleway	lbw b Tate	9	c Whysall b Tate		73
W.A.S. Oldfield†	c Strudwick b Tate	29	not out		65
A.A. Mailey	b Tate	14	b Tate		0
C.V. Grimmett	not out	12	b Tate		0
Extras	(B 2, LB 5, NB 2)	9	(B 6, LB 4, W 1, NB 1)		12
Total		**295**			**325**

ENGLAND

J.B. Hobbs	c Oldfield b Gregory	0	st Oldfield b Grimmett		13
H. Sutcliffe	c Mailey b Kelleway	22	b Gregory		0
A. Sandham	run out	4	lbw b Grimmett		15
F.E. Woolley	b Grimmett	47	c Andrews b Kelleway		28
E. H. Hendren	c Ponsford b Gregory	10	c Oldfield b Grimmett		10
J. W. Hearne	lbw b Grimmett	16	lbw b Grimmett		24
W.W. Whysall	lbw b Grimmett	8	st Oldfield b Grimmett		18
R. Kilner	st Oldfield b Grimmett	24	c Ponsford b Collins		1
M.W. Tate	b Ryder	25	c Mailey b Kelleway		33
A.E.R. Gilligan*	st Oldfield b Grimmett	5	not out		0
H. Strudwick†	not out	1	c Mailey b Grimmett		0
Extras	(LB 4, NB 1)	5	(B 1, LB 3)		4
Total		**167**			**146**

ENGLAND	O	M	R	W	O	M	R	W
Tate	39·5	6	92	4	39·3	6	115	5
Gilligan	13	1	46	1	15	2	46	1
Kilner	38	4	97	4	34	13	54	0
Hearne	7	0	33	0	22	0	84	2
Woolley	5	0	18	0	8	1	14	1
AUSTRALIA								
Gregory	9	1	42	2	10	0	53	1
Kelleway	15	1	38	1	7	1	16	2
Mailey	5	0	13	0				
Ryder	7	0	24	1				
Grimmett	11·7	2	45	5	19·4	3	37	6
Collins					8	2	36	1

FALL OF WICKETS

Wkt	A 1st	E 1st	A 2nd	E 2nd
1st	3	0	7	3
2nd	55	15	43	31
3rd	64	28	110	32
4th	99	58	130	60
5th	103	96	152	84
6th	208	109	156	99
7th	239	122	209	100
8th	239	157	325	146
9th	264	163	325	146
10th	295	167	325	146

Umpires: R.W. Crockett (32) and D. Elder (10).

Close: 1st day – A(1) 239-7 (Kelleway 9); 2nd – E(1) 167 all out; 3rd – A(2) 203-6 (Collins 27, Kelleway 22); 4th – E(2) 88-5 (Hearne 18, Whysall 4).

ENGLAND v AUSTRALIA 1926 (1st Test)

Played at Trent Bridge, Nottingham, on 12, 14 (*no play*), 15 (*no play*) June.
Toss: England.   Result: MATCH DRAWN.
Debuts: England – C.F. Root; Australia – W.M. Woodfull.

Following a delayed start there was only 50 minutes of play on the first day before heavy rain ended the match.

ENGLAND

J.B. Hobbs	not out	19
H. Sutcliffe	not out	13
F.E. Woolley	)	
J.W. Hearne	)	
E.H. Hendren	)	
A.P.F. Chapman	)	
R. Kilner	) did not bat	
A.W. Carr*	)	
M.W. Tate	)	
C.F. Root	)	
H. Strudwick†	)	
Extras		–
Total	(0 wickets)	**32**

AUSTRALIA

H.L. Collins*
W. Bardsley
C.G. Macartney
J.M. Taylor
T.J.E. Andrews
W.M. Woodfull
J. Ryder
J.M. Gregory
A.J. Richardson
W.A.S. Oldfield
A.A. Mailey

AUSTRALIA	O	M	R	W
Gregory	8	1	18	0
Macartney	8·2	2	14	0
Richardson	1	1	0	0

Umpires: R.D. Burrows (1) and F. Chester (3).

Close: 1st day – E(1) 32-0 (Hobbs 19, Sutcliffe 13); 2nd – no play.

ENGLAND v AUSTRALIA 1926 (2nd Test)

Played at Lord's, London, on 26, 28, 29 June.
Toss: Australia.   Result: MATCH DRAWN.
Debuts: England – H. Larwood.

Bardsley carried his bat through Australia's first innings and, at the age of 43 years 201 days, remains the oldest to score a hundred for Australia against England. His score of 193 not out, made in 398 minutes, is the highest by a player of over 40 in this series. Hobbs was the first to score 4,000 runs in Tests when he reached 83. Hendren scored the only hundred by a Middlesex batsman against Australia at Lord's. At 37 he was the youngest of the four century-makers in this match.

AUSTRALIA

H.L. Collins*	b Root	1	c Sutcliffe b Larwood	24
W. Bardsley	not out	193		
C.G. Macartney	c Sutcliffe b Larwood	39	not out	133
W.M. Woodfull	c Strudwick b Root	13	(6) c Root b Woolley	0
T.J.E. Andrews	c and b Kilner	10	(4) b Root	9
J.M. Gregory	b Larwood	7	(2) c Sutcliffe b Root	0
J.M. Taylor	c Carr b Tate	9		
A.J. Richardson	b Kilner	35		
J. Ryder	c Strudwick b Tate	28	(7) not out	0
W.A.S. Oldfield†	c Sutcliffe b Kilner	19	(5) c Sutcliffe b Tate	11
A.A. Mailey	lbw b Kilner	1		
Extras	(B 12, LB 16)	28	(B 5, LB 12)	17
Total		**383**	(5 wickets)	**194**

ENGLAND

J.B. Hobbs	c Richardson b Macartney	119
H. Sutcliffe	b Richardson	82
F.E. Woolley	lbw b Ryder	87
E.H. Hendren	not out	127
A.P.F. Chapman	not out	50
A.W. Carr*	)	
R. Kilner	)	
M.W. Tate	) did not bat	
H. Larwood	)	
C.F. Root	)	
H. Strudwick†	)	
Extras	(B 4, LB 4, W 1, NB 1)	10
Total	(3 wickets declared)	**475**

ENGLAND	O	M	R	W	O	M	R	W
Tate	50	12	111	2	25	11	38	1
Root	36	11	70	2	19	9	40	2
Kilner	34·5	11	70	4	22	2	49	0
Larwood	32	2	99	2	15	3	37	1
Woolley	2	0	5	0	7	1	13	1
AUSTRALIA								
Gregory	30	3	125	0				
Macartney	33	8	90	1				
Mailey	30	6	96	0				
Richardson	48	18	73	1				
Ryder	25	3	70	1				
Collins	2	0	11	0				

FALL OF WICKETS

	A	E	A
Wkt	*1st*	*1st*	*2nd*
1st	11	182	2
2nd	84	219	125
3rd	127	359	163
4th	158	–	187
5th	187	–	194
6th	208	–	–
7th	282	–	–
8th	338	–	–
9th	379	–	–
10th	383	–	–

Umpires: L.C. Braund (1) and A.E. Street (7).

Close: 1st day – A(1) 338-8 (Bardsley 173); 2nd – E(1) 297-2 (Woolley 50, Hendren 42).

ENGLAND v AUSTRALIA 1926 (3rd Test)

Played at Headingley, Leeds, on 10, 12, 13 July.
Toss: England.   Result: MATCH DRAWN.
Debuts: Nil.

Bardsley, captain in the absence of H.L. Collins (neuritis), lost the toss and was out to the first ball of the match. Macartney, who had been dropped fourth ball, reached his hundred out of 131 in 103 minutes and scored 112 not out in 116 minutes before lunch on the first day. He was the second of four batsmen to achieve this feat in Test matches and his was the highest pre-lunch score. His partnership of 235 with Woodfull was then the highest in this series for any wicket by either side in England. Macaulay and Geary shared a match-saving ninth-wicket partnership of 108. In the second innings, Hobbs broke C. Hill's record aggregate of 2,660 in Tests between England and Australia.

AUSTRALIA

W. Bardsley*	c Sutcliffe b Tate	0
W.M. Woodfull	b Tate	141
C.G. Macartney	c Hendren b Macaulay	151
T.J.E. Andrews	lbw b Kilner	4
A.J. Richardson	run out	100
J.M. Taylor	c Strudwick b Geary	4
J.M. Gregory	c Geary b Kilner	26
J. Ryder	b Tate	42
W.A.S. Oldfield†	lbw b Tate	14
C.V. Grimmett	c Sutcliffe b Geary	1
A.A. Mailey	not out	1
Extras	(B 2, LB 4, NB 4)	10
Total		**494**

ENGLAND

J.B. Hobbs	c Andrews b Mailey	49	b Grimmett	88
H. Sutcliffe	c and b Grimmett	26	b Richardson	94
F.E. Woolley	run out	27	c Macartney b Grimmett	20
E.H. Hendren	c Andrews b Mailey	0	not out	4
A.W. Carr*	lbw b Macartney	13		
A.P.F. Chapman	b Macartney	15	(5) not out	42
R. Kilner	c Ryder b Grimmett	36		
M.W. Tate	st Oldfield b Grimmett	5		
G. Geary	not out	35		
G.G. Macaulay	c and b Grimmett	76		
H. Strudwick†	c Gregory b Grimmett	1		
Extras	(B 4, LB 6, NB 1)	11	(B 5, LB 1)	6
Total		**294**	**(3 wickets)**	**254**

ENGLAND	O	M	R	W	O	M	R	W
Tate	51	13	99	4				
Macaulay	32	8	123	1				
Kilner	37	6	106	2				
Geary	41	5	130	2				
Woolley	4	0	26	0				
AUSTRALIA								
Gregory	17	5	37	0	6	2	12	0
Macartney	31	13	51	2	4	1	13	0
Grimmett	39	11	88	5	29	10	59	2
Richardson	20	5	44	0	16	7	22	1
Mailey	21	4	63	2	18	2	80	0
Ryder					9	2	26	0
Andrews					4	0	36	0

FALL OF WICKETS

Wkt	A 1st	E 1st	E 2nd
1st	0	59	156
2nd	235	104	208
3rd	249	108	210
4th	378	110	–
5th	385	131	–
6th	423	140	–
7th	452	175	–
8th	485	182	–
9th	492	290	–
10th	494	294	–

Umpires: H.R. Butt (6) and W. Reeves (3).

Close: 1st day – A(1) 366-3 (Woodfull 134, Richardson 70); 2nd – E(1) 203-8 (Geary 6, Macaulay 18).

ENGLAND v AUSTRALIA 1926 (4th Test)

Played at Old Trafford, Manchester, on 24, 26, 27 July.
Toss: Australia.   Result: MATCH DRAWN.
Debuts: Nil.

Manchester's weather permitted ten balls to be bowled on the first afternoon. Macartney scored his third hundred in successive Test innings and became the first to score three hundreds in a Test rubber in England. Woodfull's century was his second in consecutive innings. Hobbs took over the captaincy on the second and third days after Carr developed tonsillitis, the first professional to lead England since A. Shrewsbury in 1886-87 (*Test No. 26*).

AUSTRALIA

W.M. Woodfull	c Hendren b Root	117
W. Bardsley*	c Tyldesley b Stevens	15
C.G. Macartney	b Root	109
T.J.E. Andrews	c sub (A.P.F. Chapman) b Stevens	8
W.H. Ponsford	c and b Kilner	23
A.J. Richardson	c Woolley b Stevens	0
J. Ryder	c Strudwick b Root	3
J.M. Gregory	c Kilner b Root	34
W.A.S. Oldfield†	not out	12
C.V. Grimmett	c Stevens b Tate	6
A.A. Mailey	b Tate	1
Extras	(B 2, LB 1, W 1, NB 3)	7
Total		**335**

ENGLAND

J.B. Hobbs	c Ryder b Grimmett	74
H. Sutcliffe	c Oldfield b Mailey	20
G.E. Tyldesley	c Oldfield b Macartney	81
F.E. Woolley	c Ryder b Mailey	58
E.H. Hendren	not out	32
G.T.S. Stevens	c Bardsley b Mailey	24
R. Kilner	not out	9
A.W. Carr*	)	
M.W. Tate	) did not bat	
C.F. Root	)	
H. Strudwick†	)	
Extras	(B 4, LB 3)	7
Total	(5 wickets)	**305**

ENGLAND	O	M	R	W
Tate	36·2	7	88	2
Root	52	27	84	4
Kilner	28	12	51	1
Stevens	32	3	86	3
Woolley	2	0	19	0

AUSTRALIA	O	M	R	W
Gregory	11	4	17	0
Grimmett	38	9	85	1
Mailey	27	4	87	3
Ryder	15	3	46	0
Richardson	17	3	43	0
Macartney	8	5	7	1
Andrews	9	5	13	0

FALL OF WICKETS

	A	E
Wkt	*1st*	*1st*
1st	29	58
2nd	221	135
3rd	252	225
4th	256	243
5th	257	272
6th	266	–
7th	300	–
8th	317	–
9th	329	–
10th	335	–

Umpires: H. Chidgey (1) and H.I. Young (2).

Close: 1st day – A(1) 6-0 (Woodfull 5, Bardsley 0); 2nd – A(1) 322-8 (Oldfield 2, Grimmett 4).

ENGLAND v AUSTRALIA 1926 (5th Test)

Played at Kennington Oval, London, on 14, 16, 17, 18 August.
Toss: England.   Result: ENGLAND won by 289 runs.
Debuts: Nil.

England appointed Chapman as captain, recalled Rhodes at the age of 48 and regained the Ashes with one of their finest victories. The highlight of this timeless Test was the opening partnership of 172 between Hobbs and Sutcliffe on a rain-affected pitch; it was Hobbs's only Test hundred against Australia on his home ground. This match ended a remarkable unbroken run of 52 Test appearances by Woolley; he had played in all England's matches since the 5th Test of 1909.

ENGLAND

J.B. Hobbs	b Mailey	37	b Gregory	100
H. Sutcliffe	b Mailey	76	b Mailey	161
F.E. Woolley	b Mailey	18	lbw b Richardson	27
E.H. Hendren	b Gregory	8	c Oldfield b Grimmett	15
A.P.F. Chapman*	st Oldfield b Mailey	49	b Richardson	19
G.T.S. Stevens	c Andrews b Mailey	17	c Mailey b Grimmett	22
W. Rhodes	c Oldfield b Mailey	28	lbw b Grimmett	14
G. Geary	run out	9	c Oldfield b Gregory	1
M.W. Tate	b Grimmett	23	not out	33
H. Larwood	c Andrews b Grimmett	0	b Mailey	5
H. Strudwick†	not out	4	c Andrews b Mailey	2
Extras	(B 6, LB 5)	11	(B 19, LB 18)	37
Total		**280**		**436**

AUSTRALIA

W.M. Woodfull	b Rhodes	35	c Geary b Larwood	0
W. Bardsley	c Strudwick b Larwood	2	(4) c Woolley b Rhodes	21
C.G. Macartney	b Stevens	25	c Geary b Larwood	16
W.H. Ponsford	run out	2	(2) c Larwood b Rhodes	12
T.J.E. Andrews	b Larwood	3	(6) c Tate b Larwood	15
H.L. Collins*	c Stevens b Larwood	61	(5) c Woolley b Rhodes	4
A.J. Richardson	c Geary b Rhodes	16	(8) b Rhodes	4
J.M. Gregory	c Stevens b Tate	73	(7) c Sutcliffe b Tate	9
W.A.S. Oldfield†	not out	33	b Stevens	23
C.V. Grimmett	b Tate	35	not out	8
A.A. Mailey	c Strudwick b Tate	0	b Geary	6
Extras	(B 5, LB 12)	17	(LB 7)	7
Total		**302**		**125**

AUSTRALIA	O	M	R	W	O	M	R	W
Gregory	15	4	31	1	18	1	58	2
Grimmett	33	12	74	2	55	17	108	3
Mailey	33·5	3	138	6	42·5	6	128	3
Macartney	7	4	16	0	26	16	24	0
Richardson	7	2	10	0	41	21	81	2
ENGLAND								
Tate	37·1	17	40	3	9	4	12	1
Larwood	34	11	82	3	14	3	34	3
Geary	27	8	43	0	6·3	2	15	1
Stevens	29	3	85	1	3	1	13	1
Rhodes	25	15	35	2	20	9	44	4

FALL OF WICKETS

Wkt	E 1st	A 1st	E 2nd	A 2nd
1st	53	9	172	1
2nd	91	44	220	31
3rd	108	51	277	31
4th	189	59	316	35
5th	213	90	373	63
6th	214	122	375	83
7th	231	229	382	83
8th	266	231	425	87
9th	266	298	430	114
10th	280	302	436	125

Umpires: F. Chester (4) and H.I. Young (3).

Close: 1st day – A(1) 60-4 (Woodfull 22, Collins 1); 2nd – E(2) 49-0 (Hobbs 28, Sutcliffe 20); 3rd – E(2) 375-6 (Rhodes 0).

SOUTH AFRICA v ENGLAND 1927–28 (1st Test)

Played at Old Wanderers, Johannesburg, on 24, 26, 27 December.
Toss: South Africa.   Result: ENGLAND won by ten wickets.
Debuts: South Africa – H.B. Cameron, S.K. Coen, J.P. Duminy, D.P.B. Morkel, H.L.E. Promnitz, C.L. Vincent; England – W.E. Astill, W.R. Hammond, G.B. Legge, I.A.R. Peebles, R.T. Stanyforth, R.E.S. Wyatt.

Four players dominated this match: Hammond took three wickets for no runs in 23 balls and finished with five wickets and a fifty in his maiden Test; Sutcliffe, whose 102 included 47 singles, and Tyldesley scored 230 in a second-wicket partnership; while Geary claimed 12 wickets, achieving the best innings and match analyses of his Test career. During Catterall's innings of 86 out of 137 in 130 minutes, 'aeroplanes flew over the ground, scattering the fieldsmen' (*The Cricketer*).

SOUTH AFRICA

H.W. Taylor	c and b Stevens	31	(3) b Hammond		3
J.P. Duminy	b Geary	0	b Hammond		4
J.M.M. Commaille	lbw b Stevens	23	(1) c Stanyforth b Geary		4
R.H. Catterall	c and b Geary	86	b Hammond		1
H.G. Deane*	b Geary	7	b Geary		5
D.P.B. Morkel	lbw b Geary	2	(7) lbw b Geary		29
S.K. Coen	b Geary	7	(10) not out		41
H.B. Cameron†	lbw b Stevens	20	(6) lbw b Geary		5
E.P. Nupen	b Geary	6	(8) b Geary		1
C.L. Vincent	not out	2	(9) lbw b Hammond		53
H.L.E. Promnitz	b Geary	4	b Hammond		5
Extras	(LB 6, NB 2)	8	(B 5, LB 13, NB 1)		19
Total		**196**			**170**

ENGLAND

P. Holmes	lbw b Morkel	0	not out	15
H. Sutcliffe	c Vincent b Promnitz	102	not out	41
G.E. Tyldesley	lbw b Duminy	122		
W.R. Hammond	c Promnitz b Vincent	51		
R.E.S. Wyatt	lbw b Promnitz	0		
G.T.S. Stevens	c Nupen b Promnitz	0		
G.B. Legge	c and b Nupen	0		
W.E. Astill	c Cameron b Promnitz	7		
R.T. Stanyforth*†	c Cameron b Promnitz	1		
G. Geary	lbw b Vincent	3		
I.A.R. Peebles	not out	2		
Extras	(B 11, LB 10, W 1, NB 3)	25	(B 1)	1
Total		**313**	(0 wickets)	**57**

ENGLAND	O	M	R	W	O	M	R	W
Geary	27·3	7	70	7	27	9	60	5
Hammond	8	2	21	0	21·2	9	36	5
Stevens	19	3	58	3	8	3	13	0
Peebles	12	5	22	0	7	1	25	0
Wyatt	4	1	6	0				
Astill	8	4	11	0	6	0	17	0
SOUTH AFRICA								
Morkel	14	3	38	1				
Nupen	49	12	111	1	11	1	29	0
Vincent	31·3	5	57	2				
Promnitz	37	14	58	5	6	1	14	0
Coen	2	0	7	0				
Duminy	4	0	17	1	4	0	13	0

FALL OF WICKETS

	SA	E	SA	E
Wkt	1st	1st	2nd	2nd
1st	1	0	10	–
2nd	53	230	10	–
3rd	58	252	11	–
4th	89	252	20	–
5th	93	254	20	–
6th	120	263	26	–
7th	170	280	38	–
8th	185	292	78	–
9th	190	308	158	–
10th	196	313	170	–

Umpires: A.G. Laver (8) and G.B. Treadwell (1).

Close: 1st day – E(1) 9-1 (Sutcliffe 9); 2nd – SA(2) 8-0 (Commaille 4, Duminy 4).

SOUTH AFRICA v ENGLAND 1927–28 (2nd Test)

Played at Newlands, Cape Town, on 31 December, 2, 3, 4 January.
Toss: South Africa.   Result: ENGLAND won by 87 runs.
Debuts: South Africa – G.F. Bissett, A.W. Palm.

An appeal against the dark colour of the ball by the batsmen in the opening over was turned down as it had been chosen by the captains. Bissett, whose current playing experience was limited to second division league matches in Cape Town, took the first five wickets to fall. Geary injured his elbow and took no further part in the rubber. South Africa, needing 312 to win in 275 minutes, were dismissed with half-an-hour to spare.

ENGLAND

P. Holmes	b Bissett	9	c Vincent b Nupen		88
H. Sutcliffe	c Nupen b Bissett	29	b Bissett		99
G.E. Tyldesley	b Bissett	0	lbw b Promnitz		87
W.R. Hammond	lbw b Morkel	43	c Palm b Promnitz		14
G.T.S. Stevens	c Cameron b Bissett	0	c Morkel b Bissett		2
R.E.S. Wyatt	lbw b Bissett	2	c Promnitz b Bissett		91
W.E. Astill	lbw b Vincent	25	c Cameron b Vincent		9
R.T. Stanyforth*†	b Vincent	4	b Vincent		1
G. Geary	lbw b Vincent	0	b Vincent		1
I.A.R. Peebles	not out	3	c Vincent b Promnitz		6
A.P. Freeman	st Cameron b Vincent	7	not out		0
Extras	(B 5, LB 1, NB 5)	11	(B 19, LB 5, NB 6)		30
Total		**133**			**428**

SOUTH AFRICA

H.W. Taylor	hit wkt b Freeman	68	run out		71
J.M.M. Commaille	lbw b Freeman	13	c Astill b Hammond		47
H.B. Cameron†	c Geary b Stevens	19	b Hammond		19
R.H. Catterall	b Hammond	9	lbw b Astill		10
D.P.B. Morkel	b Freeman	36	c Holmes b Astill		23
A.W. Palm	c Stevens b Freeman	2	(7) c Hammond b Freeman		13
H.G. Deane*	c Stanyforth b Hammond	41	(6) c Hammond b Freeman		4
C.L. Vincent	b Astill	13	c Hammond b Freeman		11
E.P. Nupen	not out	39	b Astill		1
G.F. Bissett	b Hammond	3	not out		11
H.L.E. Promnitz	run out	3	b Peebles		2
Extras	(B 2, LB 2)	4	(B 6, LB 4, NB 2)		12
Total		**250**			**224**

SOUTH AFRICA	O	M	R	W	O	M	R	W
Bissett	17	5	37	5	31·5	5	99	3
Morkel	9	3	20	1	21	4	60	0
Vincent	15·1	4	22	4	40	10	93	3
Nupen	3	0	10	0	36	8	90	1
Promnitz	15	5	33	0	30	10	56	3
ENGLAND								
Geary	23	2	50	0				
Hammond	17	4	53	3	30	13	50	2
Freeman	29	12	58	4	22	7	66	3
Peebles	14	3	27	0	12·1	4	26	1
Stevens	10	1	26	1	5	0	17	0
Astill	8	0	32	1	29	11	48	3
Wyatt					3	0	5	0

FALL OF WICKETS

Wkt	E 1st	SA 1st	E 2nd	SA 2nd
1st	14	32	140	115
2nd	14	72	233	126
3rd	50	99	278	147
4th	59	128	282	161
5th	66	140	326	166
6th	97	153	348	190
7th	106	197	350	197
8th	106	211	360	206
9th	123	221	415	210
10th	133	250	428	224

Umpires: H.V. Adams (2) and G.B. Treadwell (2).

Close: 1st day – SA(1) 128-4 (Morkel 17); 2nd – E(2) 220-1 (Sutcliffe 92, Tyldesley 24); 3rd – E(2) 412-8 (Wyatt 76, Peebles 6).

SOUTH AFRICA v ENGLAND 1927–28 (3rd Test)

Played at Kingsmead, Durban, on 21, 23, 24, 25 January.
Toss: South Africa.   Result: MATCH DRAWN
Debuts: South Africa – J.F.W. Nicolson, A.L. Ochse, I.J. Siedle; England – S.J. Staples.

After an opening spell of 11-10-1-1, Wyatt was not recalled until the total had reached 241; he then took two wickets in his first over. Facing a deficit of 184, South Africa made their highest total against England so far. Nicolson defended for 230 minutes in making 78 out of 257, before Deane and Nupen added 123 in what remains the highest seventh-wicket partnership by either side in this series.

SOUTH AFRICA

H.W. Taylor	b Wyatt	7	c Astill b Peebles		60
I.J. Siedle	lbw b Staples	11	st Stanyforth b Freeman		10
H.B. Cameron†	b Peebles	21	c Stanyforth b Freeman		9
J.F.W. Nicolson	c Astill b Staples	39	c Hammond b Astill		78
R.H. Catterall	b Staples	14	b Staples		76
D.P.B. Morkel	b Peebles	14	b Freeman		42
H.G. Deane*	st Stanyforth b Wyatt	77	lbw b Astill		73
C.L. Vincent	c Stevens b Peebles	2	(9) not out		8
E.P. Nupen	lbw b Wyatt	51	(8) b Staples		69
A.L. Ochse	b Freeman	4	not out		4
G.F. Bissett	not out	1			
Extras	(B 1, LB 1, NB 3)	5	(B 22, LB 12, NB 1)		35
Total		**246**	(8 wickets declared)		**464**

ENGLAND

P. Holmes	c Catterall b Nupen	70	c Catterall b Vincent		56
H. Sutcliffe	b Vincent	25	c Morkel b Nupen		8
G.E. Tyldesley	c Siedle b Vincent	78	not out		62
W.R. Hammond	b Vincent	90	not out		1
R.E.S. Wyatt	lbw b Vincent	0			
G.T.S. Stevens	b Vincent	69			
W.E. Astill	c Ochse b Vincent	40			
R.T. Stanyforth*†	c Vincent b Nupen	0			
S.J. Staples	b Nupen	11			
I.A.R. Peebles	not out	18			
A.P. Freeman	b Nupen	3			
Extras	(B 15, LB 9, NB 2)	26	(B 5)		5
Total		**430**	(2 wickets)		**132**

ENGLAND	O	M	R	W	O	M	R	W		FALL OF WICKETS			
										SA	E	SA	E
Hammond	16	3	54	0	16	2	37	0	Wkt	1st	1st	2nd	2nd
Wyatt	13	10	4	3	15	6	31	0	1st	13	67	30	25
Freeman	16·3	3	44	1	33	3	122	3	2nd	22	131	50	127
Staples	36	17	50	3	47	9	111	2	3rd	55	258	118	–
Peebles	16	3	69	3	11	2	29	1	4th	93	260	225	–
Stevens	4	0	12	0	11	0	58	0	5th	98	303	284	–
Astill	3	1	8	0	24	6	41	2	6th	135	365	307	–
									7th	146	365	430	–
SOUTH AFRICA									8th	241	379	454	–
Bissett	30	4	89	0	11	2	41	0	9th	242	421	–	–
Ochse	11	1	45	0					10th	246	430	–	–
Vincent	45	10	131	6	13	0	31	1					
Nupen	44·3	9	94	4	10·2	2	29	1					
Morkel	3	0	17	0	8	0	26	0					
Nicolson	2	0	5	0									
Catterall	2	0	15	0									
Taylor	2	0	8	0									

Umpires A.G. Laver (9) and C. Saunders (1).

Close: 1st day – E(1) 42-0 (Holmes 23, Sutcliffe 17); 2nd – E(1) 381-8 (Stevens 42, Peebles 0); 3rd – SA(2) 279-4 (Nicolson 66, Morkel 39).

SOUTH AFRICA v ENGLAND 1927–28 (4th Test)

Played at Old Wanderers, Johannesburg, on 28, 30, 31 January, 1 February.
Toss: South Africa.   Result: SOUTH AFRICA won by four wickets.
Debuts: Nil.

Deane sent England in to prevent the possibility of them playing for a draw in the fourth innings. Hall's recall was immediately effective. Taylor scored 101 out of 175 in 145 minutes to record South Africa's first century of the rubber. Freeman kept wicket on the third day after Stanyforth sustained a severe blow under the right eye, but the wicket-keeper returned on the final day.

ENGLAND

P. Holmes	b Bissett	1	b Vincent	63
H. Sutcliffe	lbw b Hall	37	c Vincent b Bissett	3
G.E. Tyldesley	lbw b Bissett	42	c Morkel b Nupen	8
W.R. Hammond	c Cameron b Hall	28	lbw b Vincent	25
R.E.S. Wyatt	c Cameron b Hall	58	lbw b Bissett	39
G.T.S. Stevens	c Vincent b Hall	14	c Deane b Bissett	20
W.E. Astill	c Hall b Bissett	3	c Duminy b Bissett	17
I.A.R. Peebles	c Deane b Hall	26	lbw b Hall	7
S.J. Staples	b Bissett	39	b Hall	6
R.T. Stanyforth*†	b Hall	1	not out	6
A.P. Freeman	not out	9	lbw b Hall	4
Extras	(LB 5, NB 2)	7	(B 16, LB 1)	17
Total		**265**		**215**

SOUTH AFRICA

H.W. Taylor	b Hammond	101	c Stanyforth b Hammond	6
J.P. Duminy	c Stevens b Hammond	7	(4) b Freeman	5
D.P.B. Morkel	b Hammond	0	lbw b Staples	45
J.F.W. Nicolson	b Staples	13	(2) c Hammond b Staples	28
R.H. Catterall	c Stanyforth b Astill	39	lbw b Staples	23
H.B. Cameron†	c and b Astill	64	c Wyatt b Astill	18
H.G. Deane*	c and b Wyatt	39	not out	8
E.P. Nupen	c Stanyforth b Staples	0	not out	4
C.L. Vincent	not out	26		
G.F. Bissett	c Stevens b Freeman	23		
A.E. Hall	c Stanyforth b Staples	5		
Extras	(B 8, LB 3)	11	(B 16, LB 3)	19
Total		**328**	(6 wickets)	**156**

SOUTH AFRICA	O	M	R	W	O	M	R	W		FALL OF WICKETS			
Bissett	23	5	43	4	17	1	70	4		E	SA	E	SA
Hall	42·4	9	100	6	26	6	67	3	*Wkt*	*1st*	*1st*	*2nd*	*2nd*
Nupen	38	8	52	0	19	4	39	1	1st	6	33	21	14
Vincent	20	2	54	0	10	5	22	2	2nd	83	33	83	85
Duminy	2	0	9	0					3rd	83	62	83	98
ENGLAND									4th	136	152	141	124
Hammond	22	4	62	3	9	3	20	1	5th	167	170	172	126
Wyatt	11	0	44	1	2	0	6	0	6th	174	259	185	151
Staples	32·3	7	81	3	21	1	67	3	7th	198	268	192	–
Peebles	12	0	48	0					8th	253	268	198	–
Freeman	3	0	18	1	13	2	34	1	9th	254	313	209	–
Astill	11	0	55	2	3·2	1	10	1	10th	265	328	215	–
Stevens	1	0	9	0	1	1	0	0					

Umpires: J. Page (1) and G.A. Verheyen (1).

Close: 1st day – E(1) 233-7 (Peebles 19, Staples 24); 2nd – SA(1) 328 all out; 3rd – SA(2) 55-1 (Nicolson 20, Morkel 15).

SOUTH AFRICA v ENGLAND 1927–28 (5th Test)

Played at Kingsmead, Durban on 4 (*no play*), 6, 7, 8 February.
Toss: South Africa.   Result: SOUTH AFRICA won by eight wickets.
Debuts: England – E.W. Dawson, H. Elliott.

Deane became the third captain to win all five tosses in a rubber; on two occasions out of three South Africa won after he had put England in to bat. South Africa squared the rubber in spite of the first day's play being lost to rain. Stanyforth stood down because of his damaged eye, Stevens making his only appearance as captain. Tyldesley completed his second hundred of the rubber before 'Buster' Nupen, a tall fast-medium bowler, extremely effective on matting pitches where he could cut the ball sharply either way, produced a spell of 5 for 7. Bissett dismissed Holmes for a 'pair' and returned the best analysis by a South African fast bowler until G.B. Lawrence took 8 for 53 in 1961–62 (*Test No. 521*). Wyatt (4) retired at 49 after two painful blows from Bissett's bowling. He resumed his second innings at 89.

ENGLAND

P. Holmes	c Cameron b Bissett	0	lbw b Bissett		0
H. Sutcliffe	c Cameron b Vincent	51	lbw b Nupen		23
G.E. Tyldesley	c Morkel b Vincent	100	c Deane b Bissett		21
W.R. Hammond	c Catterall b Nupen	66	c Vincent b Bissett		3
R.E.S. Wyatt	c Catterall b Bissett	22	not out		20
G.T.S. Stevens*	c Taylor b Vincent	13	c Deane b Bissett		18
E.W. Dawson	lbw b Nupen	14	c Vincent b Bissett		9
W.E. Astill	lbw b Nupen	1	c Coen b Bissett		0
S.J. Staples	b Nupen	2	b Bissett		7
H. Elliott†	c Catterall b Nupen	1	b Vincent		3
A.P. Freeman	not out	0	c Hall b Vincent		1
Extras	(B 4, LB 4, NB 4)	12	(B 10, LB 1, NB 2)		13
Total		**282**			**118**

SOUTH AFRICA

H.W. Taylor	lbw b Staples	36	c Wyatt b Staples		29
S.K. Coen	b Astill	28	not out		25
D.P.B. Morkel	c Hammond b Staples	2			
J.F.W. Nicolson	b Astill	21			
R.H. Catterall	c Holmes b Astill	119	(4) not out		2
H.B. Cameron†	c Holmes b Freeman	53			
H.G. Deane*	b Staples	23			
E.P. Nupen	not out	19	(3) c Freeman b Hammond		10
C.L. Vincent	not out	19			
G.F. Bissett	) did not bat				
A.E. Hall	)				
Extras	(B 1, LB 9, NB 2)	12	(B 3)		3
Total	(7 wickets declared)	**332**	(2 wickets)		**69**

SOUTH AFRICA	O	M	R	W	O	M	R	W	FALL OF WICKETS				
Bissett	16	1	61	2	19	5	29	7		E	SA	E	SA
Hall	18	0	48	0	10	3	18	0	*Wkt*	*1st*	*1st*	*2nd*	*2nd*
Nupen	33·5	9	83	5	9	2	14	1	1st	2	57	0	51
Vincent	31	4	63	3	17	3	44	2	2nd	132	60	40	66
Morkel	2	0	3	0					3rd	177	87	43	–
Nicolson	2	0	12	0					4th	240	95	70	–
									5th	262	230	89	–
ENGLAND									6th	264	278	90	–
Hammond	12	2	41	0	10	2	25	1	7th	265	296	90	–
Staples	44	13	96	3	11	3	30	1	8th	269	–	103	–
Wyatt	3	0	16	0					9th	282	–	114	–
Freeman	16	2	57	1					10th	282	–	118	–
Astill	36	10	99	3	2	0	9	0					
Stevens	2	0	11	0									
Tyldesley					0·3	0	2	0					

Umpires: A.G. Laver (10) and G.B. Treadwell (3).

Close: 1st day – no play; 2nd – SA(1) 6-0 (Taylor 3, Coen 2); 3rd – E(2) 30-1 (Sutcliffe 10, Tyldesley 14).

ENGLAND v WEST INDIES 1928 (1st Test)

Played at Lord's, London, 23, 25, 26 June.
Toss: England.   Result: ENGLAND won by an innings and 58 runs.
Debuts: England – D.R. Jardine, H. Smith; West Indies – All.

West Indies conceded 382 runs during their first day of Test cricket, in spite of possessing the fastest opening attack since Gregory and McDonald. Tyldesley, making his first appearance in a Test at Lord's, drove powerfully and reached his third and final hundred for England in 160 minutes. Although without Larwood (strain), England completed an innings victory before lunch on the last day.

ENGLAND

H. Sutcliffe	c Constantine b Francis	48
C. Hallows	c Griffith b Constantine	26
G.E. Tyldesley	c Constantine b Francis	122
W.R. Hammond	b Constantine	45
D.R. Jardine	lbw b Griffith	22
A.P.F. Chapman*	c Constantine b Small	50
V.W.C. Jupp	b Small	14
M.W. Tate	c Browne b Griffith	22
H. Smith†	b Constantine	7
H. Larwood	not out	17
A.P. Freeman	b Constantine	1
Extras	(B 6, LB 19, NB 2)	27
Total		**401**

WEST INDIES

G. Challenor	c Smith b Larwood	29	b Tate	0
F.R. Martin	lbw b Tate	44	b Hammond	12
M.P. Fernandes	b Tate	0	c Hammond b Freeman	8
R.K. Nunes*†	b Jupp	37	lbw b Jupp	10
W.H. St Hill	c Jardine b Jupp	4	lbw b Freeman	9
C.A. Roach	run out	0	c Chapman b Tate	16
L.N. Constantine	c Larwood b Freeman	13	b Freeman	0
J.A. Small	lbw b Jupp	0	c Hammond b Jupp	52
C.R. Browne	b Jupp	10	b Freeman	44
G.N. Francis	not out	19	c Jardine b Jupp	0
H.C. Griffith	c Sutcliffe b Freeman	2	not out	0
Extras	(B 13, LB 6)	19	(B 10, LB 5)	15
Total		**177**		**166**

WEST INDIES	O	M	R	W	O	M	R	W
Francis	25	4	72	2				
Constantine	26·4	9	82	4				
Griffith	29	9	78	2				
Browne	22	5	53	0				
Small	15	1	67	2				
Martin	8	2	22	0				
ENGLAND								
Larwood	15	4	27	1				
Tate	27	8	54	2	22	10	28	2
Freeman	18·3	5	40	2	21·1	10	37	4
Jupp	23	9	37	4	15	4	66	3
Hammond					15	6	20	1

FALL OF WICKETS

	E	WI	WI
Wkt	1st	1st	2nd
1st	51	86	0
2nd	97	86	22
3rd	174	88	35
4th	231	95	43
5th	327	96	44
6th	339	112	44
7th	360	123	100
8th	380	151	147
9th	389	156	147
10th	401	177	166

Umpires: L.C. Braund (2) and F. Chester (5).

Close: 1st day – E(1) 382-8 (Smith 7, Larwood 2); 2nd – WI(2) 53-6 (Roach 3, Small 8).

ENGLAND v WEST INDIES 1928 (2nd Test)

Played at Old Trafford, Manchester, on 21, 23, 24 July.
Toss: West Indies.   Result: ENGLAND won by an innings and 30 runs.
Debuts: West Indies – E.L.G. Hoad, O.C. Scott.

West Indies lost 19 wickets for 221 runs after being 100 for 1. 'Tich' Freeman (leg-breaks and googlies), was the first to take five wickets in an innings and ten wickets in a match against West Indies. Hobbs and Sutcliffe completed their tenth three-figure opening partnership for England on their first joint appearance in this series. White took over the captaincy after Chapman had pulled a muscle in his left thigh while taking a run.

WEST INDIES

G. Challenor	run out	24	c Elliott b Hammond		0
C.A. Roach	lbw b Freeman	50	c Jardine b Tate		0
F.R. Martin	run out	21	c Hammond b Freeman		32
W.H. St Hill	c Jupp b Tate	3	c Hammond b White		38
E.L.G. Hoad	lbw b Jupp	13	lbw b Freeman		4
R.K. Nunes*†	b Freeman	17	(7) c sub (M.L. Taylor) b Freeman		11
L.N. Constantine	lbw b Jupp	4	(8) c Sutcliffe b Freeman		18
C.R. Browne	c White b Freeman	23	(9) c Elliott b White		7
O.C. Scott	c Chapman b Freeman	32	(10) not out		3
G.N. Francis	b Freeman	1	(6) c Tate b Freeman		0
H.C. Griffith	not out	1	c Hammond b White		0
Extras	(B 10, LB 7)	17	(B 1, LB1)		2
Total		**206**			**115**

ENGLAND

J.B. Hobbs	c St Hill b Browne	53
H. Sutcliffe	c Nunes b Griffith	54
G.E. Tyldesley	b Browne	3
W.R. Hammond	c Roach b Constantine	63
D.R. Jardine	run out	83
A.P.F. Chapman*	retired hurt	3
M.W. Tate	b Griffith	28
V.W.C. Jupp	c Constantine b Griffith	12
J.C. White	not out	21
H. Elliott†	lbw b Scott	6
A.P. Freeman	lbw b Scott	0
Extras	(B 15, LB 3, W 1, NB 6)	25
Total		**351**

ENGLAND	O	M	R	W	O	M	R	W		FALL OF WICKETS		
Tate	35	13	68	1	9	4	10	1		WI	E	WI
Hammond	6	2	16	0	6	0	23	1	*Wkt*	*1st*	*1st*	*2nd*
Freeman	33·4	18	54	5	18	5	39	5	1st	48	119	0
Jupp	18	5	39	2					2nd	100	124	2
White	13	6	12	0	14·3	4	41	3	3rd	105	131	57
									4th	113	251	67
WEST INDIES									5th	129	285	71
Francis	23	4	68	0					6th	133	311	79
Constantine	25	7	89	1					7th	158	326	93
Browne	25	2	72	2					8th	185	351	108
Griffith	25	7	69	3					9th	203	351	115
Scott	9·2	0	28	2					10th	206	–	115

Umpires: A. Morton (1) and W.R. Parry (1).

Close: 1st day – E(1) 84-0 (Hobbs 32, Sutcliffe 39); 2nd – WI(2) 71-4 (St Hill 33, Francis 0).

ENGLAND v WEST INDIES 1928 (3rd Test)

Played at Kennington Oval, London, 11, 13, 14 August.
Toss: West Indies.   Result: ENGLAND won by an innings and 71 runs.
Debuts: England – M. Leyland; West Indies – E.L. Bartlett, C.V. Wight.

England completed their third successive innings victory of the rubber after West Indies had recorded their largest total to date. Hobbs scored the last of only five Test hundreds in England.

WEST INDIES

G. Challenor	c Hammond b Leyland	46	c Hammond b Freeman	2
C.A. Roach	b Larwood	53	b Larwood	12
F.R. Martin	c Chapman b Freeman	25	b Tate	41
R.K. Nunes*†	b Tate	0	c Hendren b Larwood	12
E.L. Bartlett	b Larwood	13	c Larwood b Freeman	8
O.C. Scott	c Duckworth b Tate	35	c Duckworth b Larwood	4
L.N. Constantine	c Chapman b Hammond	37	c Larwood b Tate	17
C.V. Wight	c Chapman b Tate	23	not out	12
J.A. Small	lbw b Freeman	0	c Freeman b Tate	2
H.C. Griffith	not out	0	c Hammond b Freeman	5
G.N. Francis	c Chapman b Tate	4	c Hammond b Freeman	4
Extras	(B 2)	2	(B 6, LB 4)	10
Total		**238**		**129**

ENGLAND

J.B. Hobbs	c Small b Francis	159
H. Sutcliffe	b Francis	63
G.E. Tyldesley	c Constantine b Griffith	73
W.R. Hammond	c Small b Griffith	3
M. Leyland	b Griffith	0
E.H. Hendren	c Roach b Griffith	14
A.P.F. Chapman*	c Constantine b Griffith	5
M.W. Tate	c Griffith b Francis	54
H. Larwood	c and b Francis	32
G. Duckworth†	not out	7
A.P. Freeman	c Francis b Griffith	19
Extras	(B 1, LB 2, NB 6)	9
Total		**438**

ENGLAND	O	M	R	W	O	M	R	W		FALL OF WICKETS		
										WI	E	WI
Larwood	21	6	46	2	14	3	41	3	*Wkt*	*1st*	*1st*	*2nd*
Tate	21	4	59	4	13	4	27	3	1st	91	155	12
Freeman	27	8	85	2	21·4	4	47	4	2nd	112	284	26
Hammond	8	0	40	1	4	2	4	0	3rd	113	305	46
Leyland	3	0	6	1					4th	132	305	59
									5th	160	310	70
WEST INDIES									6th	177	322	102
Francis	27	4	112	4					7th	231	333	102
Constantine	20	3	91	0					8th	234	394	110
Griffith	25·5	4	103	6					9th	234	413	123
Scott	14	1	75	0					10th	238	438	129
Small	15	2	39	0								
Martin	2	1	9	0								

Umpires: J. Hardstaff, sr (1) and T.W. Oates (1).

Close: 1st day – E(1) 155-1 (Hobbs 89, Tyldesley 0); 2nd – WI(2) 61-4 (Martin 21, Scott 1).

AUSTRALIA v ENGLAND 1928–29 (1st Test)

Played at Exhibition Ground, Brisbane, on 30 November, 1, 3, 4, 5 December.
Toss: England.   Result: ENGLAND won by 675 runs.
Debuts: Australia – D.G. Bradman, H. Ironmonger.

Brisbane's introduction to Test cricket brought the first declaration in a Test in Australia and the record margin of victory by runs alone. Woodfull carried his bat through Australia's completed second innings in which two men (Kelleway with food poisoning, Gregory through cartilage problems) were absent. Gregory was unable to play cricket again. Oldfield set a Test record by not allowing a bye during England's match aggregate of 863 runs. Larwood, whose partnership of 124 with Hendren remains England's highest for the eighth wicket against Australia, returned the best analysis of his Test career in perfect batting conditions, in addition to scoring 107 runs.

ENGLAND

J.B. Hobbs	run out	49	lbw b Grimmett		11
H. Sutcliffe	c Ponsford b Gregory	38	c sub (R.K. Oxenham)		
			b Ironmonger		32
C.P. Mead	lbw b Grimmett	8	lbw b Grimmett		73
W.R. Hammond	c Woodfull b Gregory	44	c sub (F.C. Thompson)		
			b Ironmonger		28
D.R. Jardine	c Woodfull b Ironmonger	35	not out		65
E.H. Hendren	c Ponsford b Ironmonger	169	c Ponsford b Grimmett		45
A.P.F. Chapman*	c Kelleway b Gregory	50	c Oldfield b Grimmett		27
M.W. Tate	c Ryder b Grimmett	26	c Bradman b Grimmett		20
H. Larwood	lbw b Hendry	70	c Ponsford b Grimmett		37
J.C. White	lbw b Grimmett	14			
G. Duckworth†	not out	5			
Extras	(LB 10, NB 3)	13	(LB 3, NB 1)		4
Total		**521**	(8 wickets declared)		**342**

AUSTRALIA

W.M. Woodfull	c Chapman b Larwood	0	not out		30
W.H. Ponsford	b Larwood	2	c Duckworth b Larwood		6
A.F. Kippax	c and b Tate	16	c and b Larwood		15
H.S.T.L. Hendry	lbw b Larwood	30	c Larwood b White		6
C. Kelleway	b Larwood	8	absent ill		–
J. Ryder*	c Jardine b Larwood	33	(5) c Larwood b Tate		1
D.G. Bradman	lbw b Tate	18	(6) c Chapman b White		1
W.A.S. Oldfield†	lbw b Tate	2	(7) c Larwood b Tate		5
C.V. Grimmett	not out	7	(8) c Chapman b White		1
H. Ironmonger	b Larwood	4	(9) c Chapman b White		0
J.M. Gregory	absent hurt	–	absent hurt		–
Extras	(B 1, LB 1)	2	(NB 1)		1
Total		**122**			**66**

AUSTRALIA	O	M	R	W	O	M	R	W
Gregory	41	3	142	3				
Kelleway	34	9	77	0				
Grimmett	40	2	167	3	44·1	9	131	6
Ironmonger	44·3	18	79	2	50	20	85	2
Ryder	6	2	23	0	14	3	43	0
Hendry	10	1	20	1	27	6	79	0
ENGLAND								
Larwood	14·4	4	32	6	7	0	30	2
Tate	21	6	50	3	11	3	26	2
Hammond	15	5	38	0	1	0	2	0
White					6·3	2	7	4

FALL OF WICKETS

	E	A	E	A
Wkt	1st	1st	2nd	2nd
1st	85	0	25	6
2nd	95	7	69	33
3rd	108	24	117	46
4th	161	40	165	47
5th	217	71	228	49
6th	291	101	263	62
7th	319	105	285	66
8th	443	116	342	66
9th	495	122	–	–
10th	521	–	–	–

Umpires: D. Elder (11) and G.A. Hele (1).

Close: 1st day – E(1) 272-5 (Hendren 52, Chapman 29); 2nd – A(1) 44-4 (Hendry 14, Ryder 4); 3rd – E(2) 103-2 (Mead 40, Hammond 19); 4th – A(2) 17-1 (Woodfull 4, Kippax 0).

AUSTRALIA v ENGLAND 1928–29 (2nd Test)

Played at Sydney Cricket Ground on 14, 15, 17, 18, 19, 20 December.
Toss: Australia.   Result: ENGLAND won by eight wickets.
Debuts: Australia – D.D. Blackie, O.E. Nothling.

England's total of 636 established a new Test record. All England's batsmen reached double figures for the second time in this series (also *Test No. 43*). Hammond's 251 came in his second match against Australia, in 461 minutes, and included 30 fours. Ryder reached his fifty in 36 minutes to equal J.J. Lyons's record for the fastest Australian fifty against England set in *Test No. 33*. Following his unsuccessful debut at Brisbane, the selectors dropped Bradman for this match – he fielded for Ponsford whose left hand had been fractured by a ball from Larwood when the score was 74. A record Sydney crowd of 58,446 acclaimed Hobbs on the second day – the eve of his 46th birthday.

AUSTRALIA

W.M. Woodfull	lbw b Geary	68		run out	111
V.Y. Richardson	b Larwood	27		c Hendren b Tate	0
A.F. Kippax	b Geary	9	(4)	lbw b Tate	10
W.H. Ponsford	retired hurt	5		absent hurt	–
H.S.T.L. Hendry	b Geary	37	(3)	lbw b Tate	112
J. Ryder*	lbw b Geary	25	(5)	c Chapman b Larwood	79
O.E. Nothling	b Larwood	8	(6)	run out	44
W.A.S. Oldfield†	not out	41	(7)	lbw b Tate	0
C.V. Grimmett	run out	9	(8)	c Chapman b Geary	18
D.D. Blackie	b Geary	8	(9)	not out	11
H. Ironmonger	c Duckworth b Larwood	1	(10)	b Geary	0
Extras	(B 4, LB 9, W 2)	15		(B 5, LB 6, W 1)	12
Total		**253**			**397**

ENGLAND

J.B. Hobbs	c Oldfield b Grimmett	40			
H. Sutcliffe	c Hendry b Ironmonger	11			
W.R. Hammond	b Ironmonger	251			
D.R. Jardine	run out	28			
E.H. Hendren	c Richardson b Blackie	74			
A.P.F. Chapman*	c Ryder b Blackie	20			
H. Larwood	c Ryder b Grimmett	43			
G. Geary	lbw b Blackie	66	(1)	b Hendry	8
M.W. Tate	lbw b Blackie	25	(2)	c sub (D.G. Bradman) b Hendry	4
G. Duckworth†	not out	39	(3)	not out	2
J.C. White	st Oldfield b Hendry	29	(4)	not out	2
Extras	(B 2, LB 3, W 4, NB 1)	10			
Total		**636**		(2 wickets)	**16**

ENGLAND	O	M	R	W	O	M	R	W
Larwood	26·2	4	77	3	35	5	105	1
Tate	21	9	29	0	46	14	99	4
White	38	10	79	0	30	5	83	0
Geary	18	5	35	5	31·4	11	55	2
Hammond	5	0	18	0	9	0	43	0
AUSTRALIA								
Nothling	42	15	60	0	4	0	12	0
Grimmett	64	14	191	2				
Ironmonger	68	21	142	2				
Blackie	59	10	148	4				
Hendry	23·1	4	52	1	3	2	4	2
Ryder	11	3	22	0				
Kippax	5	3	11	0				

FALL OF WICKETS

	A	E	A	E
Wkt	*1st*	*1st*	*2nd*	*2nd*
1st	51	37	0	8
2nd	65	65	215	13
3rd	152	148	234	–
4th	153	293	246	–
5th	171	341	347	–
6th	192	432	348	–
7th	222	496	370	–
8th	251	523	397	–
9th	253	592	397	–
10th	–	636	–	–

Umpires: D. Elder (12) and G.A. Hele (2).

Close: 1st day – A(1) 251-8 (Oldfield 40); 2nd – E(1) 113-2 (Hammond 33, Jardine 23); 3rd – E(1) 420-5 (Hammond 201, Larwood 37); 4th – A(2) 39-1 (Woodfull 17, Hendry 21); 5th – A(2) 339-4 (Ryder 77, Nothling 20).

AUSTRALIA v ENGLAND 1928–29 (3rd Test)

Played at Melbourne Cricket Ground on 29, 31 December, 1, 2, 3, 4, 5 January.
Toss: Australia.   Result: ENGLAND won by three wickets.
Debuts: Australia – E.L. a'Beckett, R.K. Oxenham.

Hammond, whose innings of 200 lasted 398 minutes and included 17 fours, was the first to score double-centuries in consecutive Test innings. Bradman, playing in his second match, scored the first of his 29 Test hundreds at the age of 20 years 129 days. Sutcliffe's fourth hundred in five successive Test innings at Melbourne was chanceless and began on one of the most spiteful rain-affected pitches experienced in these matches.

AUSTRALIA

W.M. Woodfull	c Jardine b Tate	7	c Duckworth b Tate	107
V.Y. Richardson	c Duckworth b Larwood	3	b Larwood	5
H.S.T.L. Hendry	c Jardine b Larwood	23	st Duckworth b White	12
A.F. Kippax	c Jardine b Larwood	100	b Tate	41
J. Ryder*	c Hendren b Tate	112	b Geary	5
D.G. Bradman	b Hammond	79	c Duckworth b Geary	112
W.A.S. Oldfield†	b Geary	3	b White	7
E.L. a'Beckett	c Duckworth b White	41	b White	6
R.K. Oxenham	b Geary	15	b White	39
C.V. Grimmett	c Duckworth b Geary	5	not out	4
D.D. Blackie	not out	2	b White	0
Extras	(B 4, LB 3)	7	(B 6, LB 7)	13
Total		**397**		**351**

ENGLAND

J.B. Hobbs	c Oldfield b A'Beckett	20	lbw b Blackie	49
H. Sutcliffe	b Blackie	58	lbw b Grimmett	135
W.R. Hammond	c A'Beckett b Blackie	200	(4) run out	32
A.P.F. Chapman*	b Blackie	24	(6) c Woodfull b Ryder	5
E.H. Hendren	c A'Beckett b Hendry	19	b Oxenham	45
D.R. Jardine	c and b Blackie	62	(3) b Grimmett	33
H. Larwood	c and b Blackie	0		
G. Geary	lbw b Grimmett	1	not out	4
M.W. Tate	c Kippax b Grimmett	21	(7) run out	0
G. Duckworth†	b Blackie	3	(9) not out	0
J.C. White	not out	8		
Extras	(B 1)	1	(B 15, LB 14)	29
Total		**417**	(7 wickets)	**332**

ENGLAND	O	M	R	W	O	M	R	W	FALL OF WICKETS				
Larwood	37	3	127	3	16	3	37	1		A	E	A	E
Tate	46	17	87	2	47	15	70	2	*Wkt*	*1st*	*1st*	*2nd*	*2nd*
Geary	31·5	4	83	3	30	4	94	2	1st	5	28	7	105
Hammond	8	4	19	1	16	6	30	0	2nd	15	161	60	199
White	57	30	64	1	56·5	20	107	5	3rd	57	201	138	257
Jardine	1	0	10	0					4th	218	238	143	318
									5th	282	364	201	326
AUSTRALIA									6th	287	364	226	328
A'Beckett	37	7	92	1	22	5	39	0	7th	373	381	252	328
Hendry	20	8	35	1	23	5	33	0	8th	383	385	345	–
Grimmett	55	14	114	2	42	12	96	2	9th	394	391	351	–
Oxenham	35	11	67	0	28	10	44	1	10th	397	417	351	–
Blackie	44	13	94	6	39	11	75	1					
Ryder	4	0	14	0	5·5	1	16	1					

Umpires: D. Elder (13) and G.A. Hele (3).

Close: 1st day – A(1) 276-4 (Ryder 111, Bradman 26); 2nd – E(1) 47-1 (Sutcliffe 15, Hammond 12); 3rd – E(1) 312-4 (Hammond 169, Jardine 21); 4th – A(2) 118-2 (Woodfull 64, Kippax 34); 5th – A(2) 347-8 (Oxenham 39, Grimmett 0); 6th – E(2) 171-1 (Sutcliffe 83, Jardine 18).

AUSTRALIA v ENGLAND 1928–29 (4th Test)

Played at Adelaide Oval on 1, 2, 4, 5, 6, 7, 8 February.
Toss: England.   Result: ENGLAND won by 12 runs.
Debuts: Australia – A.A. Jackson.

At 19 years 152 days of age, Jackson, playing his first Test match, became the youngest player to score a century in Tests between England and Australia. Hammond was the fourth batsman to score a hundred in each innings of a Test and the second after H. Sutcliffe (1924-25) to score four centuries in a rubber. His aggregate of 779 runs in five innings remains the record for England v Australia and included four centuries, two of them double-hundreds. His partnership of 262 with Jardine is still England's highest for the third wicket against Australia.

ENGLAND

J.B. Hobbs	c Ryder b Hendry	74	c Oldfield b Hendry	1
H. Sutcliffe	st Oldfield b Grimmett	64	c Oldfield b A'Beckett	17
W.R. Hammond	not out	119	c and b Ryder	177
D.R. Jardine	lbw b Grimmett	1	c Woodfull b Oxenham	98
E.H. Hendren	b Blackie	13	c Bradman b Blackie	11
A.P.F. Chapman*	c A'Beckett b Ryder	39	c Woodfull b Blackie	0
G. Duckworth†	c Ryder b Grimmett	5	(11) lbw b Oxenham	1
H. Larwood	b Hendry	3	(7) lbw b Oxenham	5
G. Geary	run out	3	(8) c and b Grimmett	6
M.W. Tate	b Grimmett	2	(9) lbw b Oxenham	47
J.C. White	c Ryder b Grimmett	0	(10) not out	4
Extras	(B 3, LB 7, W 1)	11	(B 6, LB 10)	16
Total		**334**		**383**

AUSTRALIA

W.M. Woodfull	c Duckworth b Tate	1	c Geary b White	30
A.A. Jackson	lbw b White	164	c Duckworth b Geary	36
H.S.T.L. Hendry	c Duckworth b Larwood	2	c Tate b White	5
A.F. Kippax	b White	3	c Hendren b White	51
J. Ryder*	lbw b White	63	c and b White	87
D.G. Bradman	c Larwood b Tate	40	run out	58
E.L. a'Beckett	hit wkt b White	36	c Hammond b White	21
R.K. Oxenham	c Chapman b White	15	c Chapman b White	12
W.A.S. Oldfield†	b Tate	32	not out	15
C.V. Grimmett	b Tate	4	c Tate b White	9
D.D. Blackie	not out	3	c Larwood b White	0
Extras	(LB 5, W 1)	6	(B 9, LB 3)	12
Total		**369**		**336**

AUSTRALIA	O	M	R	W	O	M	R	W	FALL OF WICKETS				
A'Beckett	31	8	44	0	27	9	41	1		E	A	E	A
Hendry	31	14	49	2	28	11	56	1	*Wkt*	*1st*	*1st*	*2nd*	*2nd*
Grimmett	52·1	12	102	5	52	15	117	1	1st	143	1	1	65
Oxenham	35	14	51	0	47·4	21	67	4	2nd	143	6	21	71
Blackie	29	6	57	1	39	11	70	2	3rd	149	19	283	74
Ryder	5	1	20	1	5	1	13	1	4th	179	145	296	211
Kippax					2	0	3	0	5th	246	227	297	224
									6th	263	287	302	258
ENGLAND									7th	270	323	327	308
Larwood	37	6	92	1	20	4	60	0	8th	308	336	337	320
Tate	42	10	77	4	37	9	75	0	9th	312	365	381	336
White	60	16	130	5	64·5	21	126	8	10th	334	369	383	336
Geary	12	3	32	0	16	2	42	1					
Hammond	9	1	32	0	14	3	21	0					

Umpires: D. Elder (14) and G.A. Hele (4).

Close: 1st day – E(1) 246-5 (Hammond 47, Duckworth 0); 2nd – A(1) 131-3 (Jackson 70, Ryder 54); 3rd – A(1) 365-9 (Oldfield 31); 4th – E(2) 206-2 (Hammond 105, Jardine 73); 5th – A(2) 24-0 (Woodfull 7, Jackson 16); 6th – A(2) 260-6 (Bradman 16, Oxenham 2).

AUSTRALIA v ENGLAND 1928–29 (5th Test)

Played at Melbourne Cricket Ground on 8, 9, 11, 12, 13, 14, 15, 16 March.
Toss: England.   Result: AUSTRALIA won by five wickets.
Debuts: Australia – A.G. Fairfax, P.M. Hornibrook, T.W. Wall.

This was the first Test to be played on eight days and remains the longest match played in Australia. At the age of 46 years 82 days, Hobbs became the oldest batsman to score a century in Test cricket. The last of his 15 Test hundreds was his twelfth against Australia and this remains the record for England. Five of his centuries were scored in his aggregate of 1,178 runs at Melbourne. He became the first to score 5,000 runs in Tests when he had made 18 in the second innings. Leyland, in his first innings against Australia, completed the first of his seven hundreds in this series. Hammond finished with the record aggregate of 905 runs, average 113.12, in the rubber. Only Bradman (974 in 1930) surpassed it.

ENGLAND

J.B. Hobbs	lbw b Ryder	142		c Fairfax b Grimmett	65
D.R. Jardine	c Oldfield b Wall	19		c Oldfield b Wall	0
W.R. Hammond	c Fairfax b Wall	38	(4)	c Ryder b Fairfax	16
G.E. Tyldesley	c Hornibrook b Ryder	31	(5)	c Oldfield b Wall	21
G. Duckworth†	c Fairfax b Hornibrook	12	(11)	lbw b Oxenham	9
E.H. Hendren	c Hornibrook b Fairfax	95		b Grimmett	1
M. Leyland	c Fairfax b Oxenham	137		not out	53
H. Larwood	b Wall	4	(3)	b Wall	11
G. Geary	b Hornibrook	4	(9)	b Wall	3
M.W. Tate	c sub (E.L. a'Beckett) b Hornibrook	15	(8)	c Fairfax b Hornibrook	54
J.C. White*	not out	9	(10)	c Oxenham b Wall	4
Extras	(B 4, LB 6, W 1, NB 2)	13		(B 19, LB 1)	20
Total		**519**			**257**

AUSTRALIA

W.M. Woodfull	c Geary b Larwood	102	(3)	b Hammond	35
A.A. Jackson	run out	30	(4)	b Geary	46
A.F. Kippax	c Duckworth b White	38	(5)	run out	28
J. Ryder*	c Tate b Hammond	30	(6)	not out	57
D.G. Bradman	c Tate b Geary	123	(7)	not out	37
A.G. Fairfax	lbw b Geary	65			
R.K. Oxenham	c Duckworth b Geary	7			
W.A.S. Oldfield†	c and b Gary	6	(1)	b Hammond	48
C.V. Grimmett	not out	38			
T.W. Wall	c Duckworth b Geary	9			
P.M. Hornibrook	lbw b White	26	(2)	b Hammond	18
Extras	(B 6, LB 9, W 2)	17		(B 12, LB 6)	18
Total		**491**		(5 wickets)	**287**

AUSTRALIA	O	M	R	W	O	M	R	W		FALL OF WICKETS			
Wall	49	8	123	3	26	5	66	5		E	A	E	A
Hornibrook	48	8	142	3	19	5	51	1	*Wkt*	*1st*	*1st*	*2nd*	*2nd*
Oxenham	45·1	15	86	1	10.3	1	34	1	1st	64	54	1	51
Grimmett	25	11	40	0	24	7	66	2	2nd	146	143	19	80
Fairfax	27	4	84	1	7	0	20	1	3rd	235	203	75	129
Ryder	18	5	29	2					4th	240	203	119	158
Kippax	3	1	2	0					5th	261	386	123	204
									6th	401	399	131	–
ENGLAND									7th	409	409	212	–
Larwood	34	7	83	1	32·1	5	81	0	8th	428	420	217	–
Tate	62	26	108	0	38	13	76	0	9th	470	432	231	–
Geary	81	36	105	5	20	5	31	1	10th	519	491	257	–
White	75·3	22	136	2	18	8	28	0					
Hammond	16	3	31	1	26	8	53	3					
Leyland	3	0	11	0									

Umpires: G.A. Hele (5) and A.C. Jones (6).

Close: 1st day – E(1) 240-4 (Duckworth 3); 2nd – E(1) 485-9 (Leyland 110, White 3); 3rd – A(1) 152-2 (Woodfull 78, Ryder 4); 4th – A(1) 367-4 (Bradman 109, Fairfax 50); 5th – E(2) 18-1 (Hobbs 3, Larwood 11); 6th – A(2) 7-0 (Oldfield 6, Hornibrook 1); 7th – A(2) 173-4 (Kippax 12, Ryder 8).

ENGLAND v SOUTH AFRICA 1929 (1st Test)

Played at Edgbaston, Birmingham, on 15, 17, 18 June.
Toss: England.   Result: MATCH DRAWN.
Debuts: England – K.S. Duleepsinhji, E.T. Killick; South Africa – J.A.J. Christy, B. Mitchell, H.G. Owen-Smith, N.A. Quinn.

Mitchell shared in opening partnerships of 119 and 171 in his first Test but took 575 minutes to score his 149 runs in the match. South Africa were set 304 to win in less than three hours.

ENGLAND

H. Sutcliffe	c Cameron b Ochse	26	b Morkel	114
E.T. Killick	c Morkel b Ochse	31	b Quinn	23
W.R. Hammond	b Quinn	18	not out	138
K.S. Duleepsinhji	c Vincent b Morkel	12	(5) lbw b Ochse	1
E.H. Hendren	b Morkel	70	(6) not out	8
M. Leyland	c Taylor b Ochse	3		
P.G.H. Fender	c Cameron b Quinn	6	(4) c Vincent b Ochse	12
M.W. Tate	c Mitchell b Morkel	40		
H. Larwood	lbw b Ochse	6		
J.C. White*	run out	5		
G. Duckworth†	not out	11		
Extras	(B 9, LB 3, W 4, NB 1)	17	(LB 10, W 2)	12
Total		**245**	(4 wickets declared)	**308**

SOUTH AFRICA

R.H. Catterall	lbw b Fender	67	c White b Fender	98
B. Mitchell	b Tate	88	not out	61
J.A.J. Christy	b Larwood	1		
H.W. Taylor	b Larwood	2		
D.P.B. Morkel	b Tate	5		
H.G. Deane*	c and b Fender	29		
H.B. Cameron†	b Larwood	5		
H.G. Owen-Smith	b Tate	25		
C.L. Vincent	not out	14		
N.A. Quinn	b Larwood	1		
A.L. Ochse	b Larwood	2		
Extras	(B 6, LB 2, W 1, NB 2)	11	(B 9, NB 3)	12
Total		**250**	(1 wicket)	**171**

SOUTH AFRICA	O	M	R	W	O	M	R	W
Morkel	20	4	40	3	22	6	54	1
Quinn	27	8	62	2	20	2	55	1
Ochse	25·1	2	79	4	28	2	88	2
Vincent	7	0	37	0	19	3	55	0
Mitchell	2	0	10	0				
Owen-Smith					6	0	29	0
Christy					5	1	15	0
ENGLAND								
Larwood	42·4	17	57	5	11	6	12	0
Tate	44	14	65	3	16	4	43	0
Fender	32	10	64	2	15·4	3	55	1
Hammond	22	12	25	0	3	0	19	0
White	32	19	28	0	13	5	23	0
Duleepsinhji					1	0	7	0

FALL OF WICKETS

Wkt	E 1st	SA 1st	E 2nd	SA 2nd
1st	59	119	34	171
2nd	66	120	255	–
3rd	92	122	278	–
4th	96	130	280	–
5th	111	174	–	–
6th	128	182	–	–
7th	215	224	–	–
8th	215	239	–	–
9th	222	248	–	–
10th	245	250	–	–

Umpires: J. Hardstaff, sr (2) and T.W. Oates (2).

Close: 1st day – SA(1) 59-0 (Catterall 33, Mitchell 25); 2nd – E(2) 34-0 (Sutcliffe 10, Killick 23).

ENGLAND v SOUTH AFRICA 1929 (2nd Test)

Played at Lord's, London, on 29 June, 1, 2 July.
Toss: England.   Result: MATCH DRAWN.
Debuts: England – J. O'Connor, R.W.V. Robins; South Africa – A.J. Bell, E.L. Dalton, Q. McMillan.

Sutcliffe scored his second hundred in successive innings after being dropped at slip when 14. Leyland and Tate, who hit his only Test hundred in less than two hours, added 129 in 70 minutes. 'Sandy' Bell, swerving the ball at fast-medium pace, took the last six wickets and returned his best analysis in his first Test innings. Cameron was carried from the field at 86 for 5, poleaxed by a lifting ball from Larwood which struck him a very severe blow on the head and put him out of cricket for over three weeks. Bad light ended this match at 5.45 pm on the third day when an England victory appeared highly probable.

ENGLAND

Batsman	Dismissal	R		R
H. Sutcliffe	c Mitchell b Bell	100	c Catterall b Morkel	10
E.T. Killick	b Morkel	3	c Morkel b Christy	24
W.R. Hammond	c Christy b Morkel	8	(5) b Morkel	5
J. O'Connor	b Morkel	0	(6) c Cameron b Ochse	11
E.H. Hendren	b Morkel	43	(4) b Morkel	11
M. Leyland	b Bell	73	(3) c Cameron b Ochse	102
M.W. Tate	c Cameron b Bell	15	not out	100
R.W.V. Robins	c Mitchell b Bell	4	c Mitchell b Ochse	0
H. Larwood	b Bell	35	b Ochse	9
J.C. White*	b Bell	8	not out	18
G. Duckworth†	not out	8		
Extras	(LB 4, W 1)	5	(B 11, LB 6, W 2, NB 3)	22
Total		**302**	(8 wickets declared)	**312**

SOUTH AFRICA

Batsman	Dismissal	R		R
R.H. Catterall	b Larwood	0	b Tate	3
B. Mitchell	st Duckworth b Hammond	29	c Hendren b Robins	22
J.A.J. Christy	run out	70	c Hendren b Robins	41
D.P.B. Morkel	lbw b Tate	88	not out	17
H.G. Deane*	b Tate	1	(6) st Duckworth b Robins	2
H.B. Cameron†	c Leyland b Robins	32	(7) retired hurt	0
H.G. Owen-Smith	not out	52	(8) not out	1
E.L. Dalton	b Tate	6	(5) c Killick b Larwood	1
Q. McMillan	c Killick b White	17		
A.L. Ochse	c Duckworth b White	1		
A.J. Bell	b Robins	13		
Extras	(B 9, LB 4)	13	(B 2, LB 1)	3
Total		**322**	(5 wickets)	**90**

SOUTH AFRICA	O	M	R	W	O	M	R	W
Ochse	24	5	51	0	20	0	99	4
Morkel	31	6	93	4	24	6	63	3
Bell	30·4	7	99	6	18·2	2	60	0
Christy	6	2	20	0	3	0	15	1
McMillan	7	0	31	0	13	0	34	0
Owen-Smith	1	0	3	0				
Mitchell					4	0	19	0
ENGLAND								
Larwood	20	4	65	1	12	3	17	1
Tate	39	9	108	3	11	3	27	1
Hammond	8	3	19	1				
White	35	12	61	2	9	3	11	0
Robins	24	5	47	2	19	4	32	3
Leyland	5	2	9	0				

FALL OF WICKETS

Wkt	E 1st	SA 1st	E 2nd	SA 2nd
1st	8	0	28	9
2nd	18	82	46	60
3rd	18	125	83	77
4th	111	126	93	82
5th	199	189	117	85
6th	243	237	246	–
7th	249	253	250	–
8th	252	272	260	–
9th	287	279	–	–
10th	302	322	–	–

Umpires: W. Bestwick (1) and F. Chester (6).

Close: 1st day – SA(1) 57-1 (Mitchell 15, Christy 42); 2nd – E(2) 49-2 (Leyland 12, Hendren 0).

ENGLAND v SOUTH AFRICA 1929 (3rd Test)

Played at Headingley, Leeds, on 13, 15, 16 July.
Toss: South Africa.   Result: ENGLAND won by five wickets.
Debuts: England – E.H. Bowley; South Africa – E.A. van der Merwe.

Freeman celebrated his recall by taking seven wickets in the post-lunch session. A strained tendon prevented Larwood from fielding in the second innings when Owen-Smith, playing in his only rubber, scored his maiden first-class hundred at the age of 20 years 148 days. On the third day he took his score from 27 to 129 to become the only South African to score a century before lunch in Test cricket. His partnership of 103 in 65 minutes with Bell is South Africa's record for the tenth wicket in all Tests. Woolley and Tate hit 76 in 45 minutes to take England to victory.

SOUTH AFRICA

R.H. Catterall	b Freeman	74	b Tate	10
I.J. Siedle	b Larwood	0	c White b Freeman	14
B. Mitchell	b Tate	22	lbw b White	24
D.P.B. Morkel	st Duckworth b Freeman	17	lbw b Freeman	14
J.P. Duminy	b Freeman	2	b Woolley	12
H.G. Deane*	c Duckworth b Tate	20	b White	4
H.G. Owen-Smith	c Hammond b Freeman	6	c Sutcliffe b Woolley	129
C.L. Vincent	b Freeman	60	b Woolley	0
N.A. Quinn	c Leyland b Freeman	5	st Duckworth b White	28
E.A. van der Merwe†	c Hammond b Freeman	19	c Duckworth b Freeman	1
A.J. Bell	not out	2	not out	26
Extras	(LB 9)	9	(B 6, LB 6, NB 1)	13
Total		236		275

ENGLAND

H. Sutcliffe	c Mitchell b Quinn	37	c Owen-Smith b Morkel	4
E.H. Bowley	c Bell b Quinn	31	c Mitchell b Vincent	46
W.R. Hammond	c Van der Merwe b Quinn	65	c and b Morkel	0
G. Duckworth†	b Bell	21		
F.E. Woolley	b Vincent	83	(4) not out	95
E.H. Hendren	c Van der Merwe b Quinn	0	(5) c Owen-Smith b Vincent	5
M. Leyland	c Duminy b Quinn	45	(6) b Vincent	0
M.W. Tate	c Owen-Smith b Vincent	3	(7) not out	24
J.C. White*	not out	20		
H. Larwood	c Deane b Mitchell	0		
A.P. Freeman	b Quinn	15		
Extras	(B 2, LB 4, NB 2)	8	(B 8, LB 4)	12
Total		328	(5 wickets)	186

ENGLAND	O	M	R	W	O	M	R	W					
Larwood	17	4	35	1					FALL OF WICKETS				
Tate	26	8	40	2	26	5	50	1		SA	E	SA	E
Freeman	32·3	6	115	7	35	7	92	1	Wkt	1st	1st	2nd	2nd
Hammond	8	2	13	0	7	0	19	0	1st	1	42	15	13
White	17	6	24	0	23	7	40	3	2nd	75	94	25	13
Bowley					4	1	7	0	3rd	120	149	66	98
Woolley					13·1	3	35	3	4th	124	170	66	110
Leyland					3	0	19	0	5th	125	170	73	110
									6th	143	276	116	–
SOUTH AFRICA									7th	151	285	116	–
Morkel	19	5	41	0	14	1	43	2	8th	170	295	167	–
Bell	14	0	58	1	2	0	12	0	9th	219	300	172	–
Quinn	29·5	5	92	6	17	2	46	0	10th	236	328	275	–
Vincent	30	5	76	2	19	0	67	3					
Owen-Smith	2	0	8	0									
Mitchell	13	1	45	1	0·4	0	6	0					

Umpires: L.C. Braund (3) and W.R. Parry (2).

Close: 1st day – E(1) 106-2 (Hammond 30, Duckworth 5); 2nd – SA(2) 116-7 (Owen-Smith 27).

ENGLAND v SOUTH AFRICA 1929 (4th Test)

Played at Old Trafford, Manchester, on 27, 29, 30 July.
Toss: England.   Result: ENGLAND won by an innings and 32 runs.
Debuts: England – F. Barratt.

England, with Hammond, Tate and Larwood absent injured, clinched the rubber with a convincing innings victory. Wyatt, appearing in his first home Test, added 245 in 165 minutes with Woolley before Freeman decided the match with the best innings and match analyses of his Test career.

ENGLAND

H. Sutcliffe	b Morkel	9
E.H. Bowley	b Bell	13
R.E.S. Wyatt	c Cameron b Vincent	113
F.E. Woolley	c and b Vincent	154
E.H. Hendren	b Quinn	12
M. Leyland	c Cameron b Mitchell	55
A.W. Carr*	c Bell b Quinn	10
G. Geary	not out	31
F. Barratt	not out	2
A.P. Freeman	) did not bat	
G. Duckworth†	)	
Extras	(B 16, LB 10, NB 2)	28
Total	(7 wickets declared)	**427**

SOUTH AFRICA

I.J. Siedle	lbw b Freeman	6		b Barratt	1
R.H. Catterall	c Sutcliffe b Barratt	3		b Geary	1
B. Mitchell	c Geary b Freeman	1		b Geary	2
H.W. Taylor	b Freeman	28		c Leyland b Freeman	70
H.G. Deane*	st Duckworth b Freeman	0	(9)	c Duckworth b Wyatt	29
H.B. Cameron†	c Bowley b Freeman	13	(7)	c Woolley b Freeman	83
D.P.B. Morkel	lbw b Geary	63	(6)	st Duckworth b Woolley	36
H.G. Owen-Smith	c Barratt b Freeman	6		st Duckworth b Freeman	7
C.L. Vincent	c Geary b Freeman	6	(10)	c Duckworth b Freeman	4
N.A. Quinn	not out	1	(5)	b Freeman	11
A.J. Bell	c Duckworth b Geary	0		not out	0
Extras	(LB 2, NB 1)	3		(B 13, LB 3, NB 5)	21
Total		**130**			**265**

SOUTH AFRICA	O	M	R	W	O	M	R	W
Morkel	18	5	61	1				
Quinn	31	3	95	2				
Bell	32	3	113	1				
Vincent	34	4	93	2				
Owen-Smith	5	0	16	0				
Mitchell	8	3	21	1				
ENGLAND								
Barratt	10	4	8	1	20	7	30	1
Geary	22·3	13	18	2	37	18	50	2
Freeman	32	12	71	7	39·4	13	100	5
Woolley	9	3	22	0	18	5	51	1
Wyatt	2	1	8	0	4	0	13	1

FALL OF WICKETS			
	E	SA	SA
Wkt	1st	1st	2nd
1st	30	4	1
2nd	36	7	3
3rd	281	34	13
4th	304	34	66
5th	342	39	113
6th	365	65	145
7th	424	84	180
8th	–	98	245
9th	–	130	256
10th	–	130	265

Umpires: J. Hardstaff, sr (3) and W.R. Parry (3).

Close: 1st day – E(1) 427-7 dec; 2nd – SA(2) 15-3 (Taylor 10, Quinn 0).

ENGLAND v SOUTH AFRICA 1929 (5th Test)

Played at Kennington Oval, London, on 17, 19, 20 August.
Toss: South Africa.   Result: MATCH DRAWN.
Debuts: England – L.E.G. Ames, E.W. Clark.

After losing Catterall to Clark's fourth ball in Test cricket, South Africa amassed their highest score against England so far. Taylor scored his only Test century overseas and shared a partnership of 214 with Deane which is still South Africa's record for the fourth wicket in all Tests. Sutcliffe became the first batsman to score hundreds in each innings of a Test match on two occasions (also *Test No. 159*).

ENGLAND

J.B. Hobbs	c Quinn b McMillan	10	c Mitchell b Vincent	52
H. Sutcliffe	c Owen-Smith b Vincent	104	not out	109
W.R. Hammond	st Cameron b Vincent	17	not out	101
F.E. Woolley	hit wkt b Vincent	46		
R.E.S. Wyatt	c Deane b Vincent	6		
M. Leyland	b Vincent	16		
A.W. Carr*	c Morkel b McMillan	15		
L.E.G. Ames†	c Mitchell b McMillan	0		
G. Geary	not out	12		
A.P. Freeman	c Cameron b Quinn	15		
E.W. Clark	b Quinn	7		
Extras	(B 9, NB 1)	10	(B 1, LB 1)	2
Total		**258**	(1 wicket)	**264**

SOUTH AFRICA

R.H. Catterall	c Carr b Clark	0
I.J. Siedle	b Geary	14
B. Mitchell	b Geary	2
H.W. Taylor	c Ames b Clark	121
H.G. Deane*	c Woolley b Wyatt	93
H.B. Cameron†	c Freeman b Geary	62
D.P.B. Morkel	c Ames b Clark	81
H.G. Owen-Smith	b Woolley	26
Q. McMillan	not out	50
C.L. Vincent	not out	24
N.A. Quinn	did not bat	
Extras	(B 4, LB 12, W 2, NB 1)	19
Total	(8 wickets declared)	**492**

SOUTH AFRICA	O	M	R	W	O	M	R	W
Morkel	9	2	20	0	16	6	43	0
Quinn	15·3	4	30	2	24	3	61	0
Vincent	45	10	105	5	15	3	42	1
McMillan	28	7	78	3	10	1	39	0
Owen-Smith	4	0	15	0	8	0	42	0
Mitchell					4	0	17	0
Catterall					3	0	18	0
ENGLAND								
Clark	36	8	79	3				
Geary	49	15	121	3				
Freeman	49	9	169	0				
Woolley	13	4	25	1				
Leyland	9	4	25	0				
Wyatt	16	4	54	1				

FALL OF WICKETS

Wkt	E 1st	SA 1st	E 2nd
1st	38	0	77
2nd	69	9	–
3rd	140	20	–
4th	166	234	–
5th	194	246	–
6th	217	326	–
7th	221	397	–
8th	222	439	–
9th	239	–	–
10th	258	–	–

Umpires: W. Bestwick (2) and T.W. Oates (3).

Close: 1st day – E(1) 166-4 (Sutcliffe 84, Leyland 0); 2nd – SA(1) 283-5 (Cameron 31, Morkel 9).

NEW ZEALAND v ENGLAND 1929–30 (1st Test)

Played at Lancaster Park, Christchurch, on 10, 11 (*no play*), 13 January.
Toss: New Zealand.   Result: ENGLAND won by eight wickets.
Debuts: New Zealand – All; England – M.J.C. Allom, W.L. Cornford, A.H.H. Gilligan, M.S. Nichols, M.J.L. Turnbull, T.S. Worthington.

As in 1891-92, England contested two Test rubbers simultaneously, another MCC team starting a four-match programme in the West Indies just a day after New Zealand began its first Test. Extremely tall and making the ball swerve sharply in a strong wind, Maurice Allom took four wickets in five balls (WOWWW) in his eighth over on his first day of Test cricket. C.M. Old emulated this feat in 1978 (*Test No. 825*). Allom's hat-trick victims were Lowry, James and Badcock. Henderson took his country's first Test wicket (Dawson) with his first ball. England's win was completed in two days with 55 minutes to spare.

NEW ZEALAND

C.S. Dempster	b Allom	11	c Duleepsinhji b Allom		25
H. Foley	c Duleepsinhji b Nichols	2	c Nichols b Allom		2
A.W. Roberts	c Duleepsinhji b Nichols	3	(6) c and b Worthington		5
M.L. Page	c and b Nichols	1	st Cornford b Barratt		21
R.C. Blunt	not out	45	(3) c Legge b Woolley		7
T.C. Lowry*	lbw b Allom	0	(5) b Nichols		40
K.C. James†	c Cornford b Allom	0	lbw b Worthington		0
F.T. Badcock	b Allom	0	(9) b Nichols		0
G.R. Dickinson	b Nichols	11	(8) c Barratt b Woolley		8
W.E. Merritt	b Allom	19	b Allom		2
M. Henderson	b Worthington	6	not out		2
Extras	(B 7, LB 4, NB 3)	14	(B 9, LB 6, NB 4)		19
Total		**112**			**131**

ENGLAND

E.W. Dawson	c Lowry b Henderson	7	lbw b Blunt		10
A.H.H. Gilligan*	c Henderson b Badcock	10	b Blunt		4
K.S. Duleepsinhji	c Dickinson b Henderson	49	not out		33
F.E. Woolley	c Merritt b Dickinson	31	not out		17
G.B. Legge	b Blunt	36			
M.S. Nichols	c Dickinson b Page	21			
T.S. Worthington	b Blunt	0			
M.J.L. Turnbull	c Merritt b Badcock	7			
F. Barratt	st James b Merritt	4			
W.L. Cornford†	c Lowry b Blunt	6			
M.J.C. Allom	not out	4			
Extras	(B 3, LB 1, NB 2)	6	(W 1, NB 1)		2
Total		**181**	(2 wickets)		**66**

ENGLAND	O	M	R	W	O	M	R	W		FALL OF WICKETS			
Nichols	17	5	28	4	14·3	6	23	2		NZ	E	NZ	E
Allom	19	4	38	5	15	6	17	3	*Wkt*	*1st*	*1st*	*2nd*	*2nd*
Barratt	4	1	8	0	9	2	16	1	1st	5	20	8	14
Worthington	7·1	1	24	1	13	4	19	2	2nd	11	20	28	17
Woolley					9	2	37	2	3rd	15	81	65	–
									4th	21	113	79	–
NEW ZEALAND									5th	21	148	86	–
Badcock	18	7	29	2					6th	21	148	86	–
Dickinson	11	1	40	1	2	0	4	0	7th	21	163	111	–
Merritt	13	1	48	1	2	0	7	0	8th	64	168	111	–
Henderson	8	1	38	2	7	2	26	0	9th	103	172	125	–
Blunt	11·1	4	17	3	7	1	17	2	10th	112	181	131	–
Page	2	1	3	1									
Dempster					0·5	0	10	0					

Umpires: W. Butler (1) and K.H. Cave (1).

Close: 1st day – E(1) 147-4 (Legge 35, Nichols 10); 2nd – no play.

NEW ZEALAND v ENGLAND 1929–30 (2nd Test)

Played at Basin Reserve, Wellington, on 24, 25, 27 January.
Toss: New Zealand.   Result: MATCH DRAWN.
Debuts: New Zealand – E.G. McLeod, J.E. Mills, G.L. Weir.

Mills was the first New Zealander to score a hundred in his first Test. His opening partnership of 276 with Dempster, who registered his country's first century, is still New Zealand's highest for any wicket against England. The first day produced 339 runs. Woolley returned the best analysis of his 64-Test career. Only 110 minutes remained when Lowry declared with a lead of 284.

NEW ZEALAND

C.S. Dempster	st Cornford b Woolley	136	not out	80
J.E. Mills	b Woolley	117	b Nichols	7
T.C. Lowry*	c Duleepsinhji b Woolley	6		
M.L. Page	c Cornford b Allom	67	c Bowley b Woolley	32
R.C. Blunt	c Duleepsinhji b Woolley	36	b Worthington	12
E.G. McLeod	b Woolley	16	not out	2
G.L. Weir	lbw b Woolley	3	(3) c Duleepsinhji b Woolley	21
K.C. James†	c Cornford b Worthington	7		
G.R. Dickinson	c Worthington b Woolley	5		
W.E. Merritt	lbw b Worthington	0		
F.T. Badcock	not out	4		
Extras	(B 17, LB 18, NB 8)	43	(B 1, LB 2, NB 7)	10
Total		**440**	(4 wickets declared)	**164**

ENGLAND

E.H. Bowley	b Blunt	9	c Weir b Dickinson	2
E.W. Dawson	b Badcock	44	c Lowry b Badcock	7
K.S. Duleepsinhji	c Blunt b Badcock	40	not out	56
F.E. Woolley	c Lowry b Dickinson	6	b Merritt	23
G.B. Legge	c James b Dickinson	39	c Lowry b Weir	9
M.S. Nichols	not out	78	not out	3
T.S. Worthington	st James b Merritt	32		
A.H.H. Gilligan*	b Merritt	32		
F. Barratt	b Badcock	5		
W.L. Cornford†	c Page b Badcock	10		
M.J.C. Allom	c Lowry b Dickinson	2		
Extras	(B 11, LB 4, NB 8)	23	(B 4, LB 2, NB 1)	7
Total		**320**	(4 wickets)	**107**

ENGLAND	O	M	R	W	O	M	R	W
Nichols	20	5	66	0	9	1	22	1
Allom	28	4	73	1	6	1	21	0
Barratt	33	4	87	0				
Worthington	22	3	63	2	10	0	44	1
Bowley	5	0	32	0	5	0	19	0
Woolley	28·3	5	76	7	23	9	48	2
NEW ZEALAND								
Dickinson	19·5	3	66	3	8	0	24	1
Badcock	36	6	80	4	17	8	22	1
Blunt	14	3	44	1	3	0	12	0
Page	2	0	8	0				
Merritt	34	3	94	2	9	1	41	1
McLeod	2	0	5	0				
Weir					2	1	1	1

FALL OF WICKETS

Wkt	NZ 1st	E 1st	NZ 2nd	E 2nd
1st	276	20	23	8
2nd	288	81	91	12
3rd	295	91	135	58
4th	385	135	155	98
5th	407	149	–	–
6th	410	219	–	–
7th	425	288	–	–
8th	431	293	–	–
9th	431	303	–	–
10th	440	320	–	–

Umpires: K.H. Cave (2) and L.T. Cobcroft (1).

Close: 1st day – NZ(1) 339-3 (Page 33, Blunt 15); 2nd – E(1) 255-6 (Nichols 48, Gilligan 20).

NEW ZEALAND v ENGLAND 1929–30 (3rd Test)

Played at Eden Park, Auckland, on 14 (*no play*), 15 (*no play*), 17 February.
Toss: New Zealand.   Result: MATCH DRAWN.
Debuts: New Zealand – C.F.W. Allcott, H.M. McGirr.

Rain prevented play on the first two days and the MCC's itinerary was changed to accommodate an extra Test match at Auckland the following weekend. So that the crowd could watch England's batsmen, Lowry generously opted to field when he won the toss. They were treated to a dazzling exhibition of strokeplay from Duleepsinhji and a chanceless innings by Bowley. England declared at tea after 3½ hours' play had produced the first hundreds to be scored against New Zealand in official Tests. Dempster drove Legge for six off the final ball of the match.

ENGLAND

E.H. Bowley	st James b Merritt	109
E.W. Dawson	b Merritt	23
K.S. Duleepsinhji	c and b Allcott	117
F.E. Woolley	run out	59
G.B. Legge	not out	19
M.S. Nichols	not out	1
A.H.H. Gilligan*	)	
M.J.C. Allom	)	
F. Barratt	) did not bat	
T.S. Worthington	)	
W.L. Cornford†	)	
Extras	(LB 2)	2
Total	(4 wickets declared)	**330**

NEW ZEALAND

C.S. Dempster	not out	62
J.E. Mills	lbw b Barratt	3
G.L. Weir	not out	27
T.C. Lowry*	)	
R.C. Blunt	)	
M.L. Page	)	
K.C. James†	) did not bat	
C.F.W. Allcott	)	
H.M. McGirr	)	
F.T. Badcock	)	
W.E. Merritt	)	
Extras	(LB 3, NB 1)	4
Total	(1 wicket)	**96**

NEW ZEALAND	O	M	R	W
McGirr	12	2	46	0
Badcock	11	2	22	0
Merritt	28	1	119	2
Blunt	6	2	16	0
Page	5	1	16	0
Weir	4	0	20	0
Allcott	22	2	89	1
ENGLAND				
Nichols	5	0	18	0
Allom	6	4	3	0
Barratt	12	3	26	1
Worthington	6	1	11	0
Legge	5	0	34	0

FALL OF WICKETS

	E	NZ
Wkt	1st	1st
1st	82	27
2nd	193	–
3rd	286	–
4th	320	–
5th	–	–
6th	–	–
7th	–	–
8th	–	–
9th	–	–
10th	–	–

Umpires: K.H. Cave (3) and L.T. Cobcroft (2).

Close: play on final day only.

NEW ZEALAND v ENGLAND 1929–30 (4th Test)

Played at Eden Park, Auckland, on 21, 22, 24 February.
Toss: England.   Result: MATCH DRAWN.
Debuts: New Zealand – A.M. Matheson.

This extra match was dominated by the bat and in particular by a brilliant 280-minute display from Legge. His only three-figure innings for England included 23 fours. Both sides batted for 445 minutes in their first innings.

ENGLAND

E.H. Bowley	run out	42		
E.W. Dawson	c Allcott b Blunt	55	b Matheson	6
K.S. Duleepsinhji	b Allcott	63		
F.E. Woolley	b Allcott	10		
G.B. Legge	c Matheson b Weir	196	(4) b Blunt	0
M.S. Nichols	b McGirr	75	(3) not out	7
T.S. Worthington	b Merritt	0		
A.H.H. Gilligan*	b Merritt	25		
F. Barratt	c Mills b Blunt	17		
W.L. Cornford†	c Matheson b Page	18	(1) b Matheson	2
M.J.C. Allom	not out	8		
Extras	(B 19, LB 11, NB 1)	31	(B 6, LB 1)	7
Total		**540**	(3 wickets)	**22**

NEW ZEALAND

C.S. Dempster	c Cornford b Allom	27
J.E. Mills	c Duleepsinhji b Allom	12
G.L. Weir	b Barratt	63
M.L. Page	c Cornford b Woolley	25
R.C. Blunt	b Nichols	0
C.F.W. Allcott	run out	33
T.C. Lowry*	lbw b Allom	80
H.M. McGirr	st Cornford b Woolley	51
K.C. James†	lbw b Worthington	14
W.E. Merritt	not out	18
A.M. Matheson	b Allom	7
Extras	(B 31, LB 16, NB 10)	57
Total		**387**

NEW ZEALAND	O	M	R	W	O	M	R	W		FALL OF WICKETS		
										E	NZ	E
McGirr	15	2	65	1	3	1	4	0	*Wkt*	*1st*	*1st*	*2nd*
Matheson	30	6	89	0	5	2	7	2	1st	60	20	12
Merritt	34	2	127	2					2nd	150	71	21
Allcott	47	17	102	2					3rd	170	127	22
Weir	10	1	29	1					4th	190	131	–
Blunt	21	8	61	2	3·3	2	4	1	5th	374	186	–
Page	14·4	4	36	1					6th	375	193	–
Lowry					1	1	0	0	7th	432	293	–
									8th	475	349	–
ENGLAND									9th	526	373	–
Nichols	19	4	45	1					10th	540	387	–
Barratt	37	12	60	1								
Allom	26·1	5	42	4								
Woolley	41	10	100	2								
Bowley	28	6	58	0								
Worthington	15	5	25	1								

Umpires: K.H. Cave (4) and L.T. Cobcroft (3).

Close: 1st day – E(1) 375-6 (Legge 104); 2nd – NZ(1) 174-4 (Weir 59, Allcott 21).

WEST INDIES v ENGLAND 1929–30 (1st Test)

Played at Kensington Oval, Bridgetown, Barbados, on 11, 13, 14, 15, 16 January.
Toss: West Indies.   Result: MATCH DRAWN.
Debuts: West Indies – F.I. de Caires, G.A. Headley, E.A.C. Hunte, E.L. St Hill, J.E.D. Sealy,
   L.A. Walcott; England – Hon. F.S.G. Calthorpe, W. Voce.

This rubber was concurrent with England's inaugural one in New Zealand and was the first to be staged in the Caribbean. Sealy, aged 17 years 122 days, was then the youngest Test cricketer and remains the youngest to represent West Indies. Gunn, whose last appearance was before Sealy's birth in 1911-12 (*Test No. 120*), was recalled at the age of 50 after a record interval of 17 years 316 days. Roach was the first West Indian to score a Test century (it was his first in first-class cricket), and Headley, aged 20 years 230 days, is still the youngest to do so. Stevens' match analysis of 10 for 195 remains the best by a touring bowler in any Bridgetown Test. England were set 287 in 165 minutes.

WEST INDIES

C.A. Roach	c Hendren b Astill	122		c Rhodes b Haig	77
E.L.G. Hoad*	c Rhodes b Voce	24		c Astill b Calthorpe	0
G.A. Headley	b O'Connor	21		c O'Connor b Rhodes	176
F.I. de Caires	c Sandham b Voce	80		c and b Stevens	70
J.E.D. Sealy	c Haig b Stevens	58	(6)	b Rhodes	15
L.N. Constantine	lbw b Stevens	13	(5)	c sub (L.F. Townsend) b Stevens	6
C.R. Browne	b Stevens	0	(8)	c Hendren b Rhodes	0
L.A. Walcott	run out	24	(7)	not out	16
E.L. St Hill	c Calthorpe b Stevens	0		c Ames b Stevens	12
H.C. Griffith	lbw b Stevens	8		c O'Connor b Stevens	0
E.A.C. Hunte†	not out	10		lbw b Stevens	1
Extras	(B 6, LB 3)	9		(B 4, LB 6, W 1)	11
Total		**369**			**384**

ENGLAND

G. Gunn	lbw b St Hill	35		b Walcott	29
A. Sandham	lbw b Constantine	152		b Griffith	51
G.T.S. Stevens	run out	9		c Constantine b Griffith	5
E.H. Hendren	c Constantine b St Hill	80		not out	36
J. O'Connor	c Constantine b Griffith	37			
L.E.G. Ames†	b Constantine	16	(5)	not out	44
N.E. Haig	c Hunte b Browne	47			
W.E. Astill	c Constantine b Griffith	1			
Hon. F.S.G. Calthorpe*	b Constantine	40			
W. Rhodes	not out	14			
W. Voce	c Hoad b Browne	10			
Extras	(B 20, LB 3, NB 3)	26		(W 2)	2
Total		**467**		**(3 wickets)**	**167**

ENGLAND	O	M	R	W	O	M	R	W		FALL OF WICKETS			
										WI	E	WI	E
Voce	27	1	120	2	3	0	15	0	*Wkt*	*1st*	*1st*	*2nd*	*2nd*
Haig	10	4	27	0	20	4	40	1	1st	90	78	6	77
Rhodes	27·1	9	44	0	51	10	110	3	2nd	157	96	162	85
Stevens	27	5	105	5	26·4	1	90	5	3rd	179	264	304	98
O'Connor	10	0	31	1					4th	303	307	320	–
Astill	9	1	19	1	30	10	72	0	5th	320	333	352	–
Calthorpe	4	0	14	0	20	7	38	1	6th	320	349	360	–
Gunn					2	0	8	0	7th	327	353	362	–
									8th	327	431	381	–
WEST INDIES									9th	343	448	381	–
Constantine	39	9	121	3	12	3	47	0	10th	369	467	384	–
Griffith	36	11	102	2	15	4	37	2					
St Hill	35	7	110	2	11	3	24	0					
Browne	37	8	83	2	13	6	19	0					
Headley	3	0	10	0	2	0	6	0					
Walcott	3	0	15	0	5	1	17	1					
Roach					5	1	6	0					
De Caires					2	0	9	0					

Umpires: W. Badley (1) and J. Hardstaff, sr (4).

Close: 1st day – WI(1) 338-8 (Walcott 7, Griffith 5); 2nd – E(1) 233-2 (Sandham 111, Hendren 64); 3rd – WI (2) 46-1 (Roach 29, Headley 16); 4th – WI(2) 326-4 (Headley 157, Sealy 5).

WEST INDIES v ENGLAND 1929–30 (2nd Test)

Played at Queen's Park Oval, Port-of-Spain, Trinidad, on 1, 3, 4, 5, 6 February.
Toss: England.   Result: ENGLAND won by 167 runs.
Debuts: West Indies – E.E. Achong, N. Betancourt, M.G. Grell.

Hendren scored the first double-century in Tests between England and West Indies. Previous versions of this score have included 'R.L.' and not 'E.A.C.' Hunte in the West Indies side. This error was caused by a copy typist mishearing 'Errol' as 'R.L.' and resulted in E.A.C. Hunte being given two separate career records! Betancourt captained West Indies in his only match. Voce (7 for 70) returned his best analysis in Tests.

ENGLAND

G. Gunn	run out	1		c Achong b Constantine	23
A. Sandham	b Griffith	0		b Griffith	5
G.T.S. Stevens	c Small b Constantine	8	(6)	c De Caires b Griffith	29
E.H. Hendren	b Achong	77		not out	205
J.O'Connor	c Headley b Achong	30	(3)	c Headley b Constantine	21
L.E.G. Ames†	c Achong b Constantine	42	(5)	c sub (J.E.D. Sealy) b Small	105
N.E. Haig	c Grell b Griffith	5		c and b Constantine	5
W.E. Astill	c sub (J.E.D. Sealy) b Griffith	19		c Griffith b Constantine	14
Hon.F.S.G. Calthorpe*	c Constantine b Griffith	12		c sub (J.E.D. Sealy) b Griffith	0
W. Rhodes	lbw b Griffith	2		not out	6
W. Voce	not out	2			
Extras	(B 7, LB 2, NB 1)	10		(B 9, LB 2, W 1)	12
Total		**208**		(8 wickets declared)	**425**

WEST INDIES

C.A. Roach	b Voce	0	(4)	c Sandham b Voce	0
E.A.C. Hunte†	c Hendren b Astill	58		b Stevens	30
W.H. St Hill	lbw b Astill	33	(1)	c Ames b Voce	30
G.A. Headley	hit wkt b Voce	8	(3)	c Ames b Haig	39
F.I. de Caires	c and b Voce	0	(6)	c Astill b Voce	45
M.G. Grell	c Ames b Haig	21	(7)	b Voce	13
J.A. Small	c Voce b Astill	20	(8)	c Calthorpe b Haig	5
L.N. Constantine	c Hendren b Voce	52	(5)	c Gunn b Voce	16
N. Betancourt*	lbw b Rhodes	39		c sub (L.F. Townsend) b Voce	13
H.C. Griffith	not out	3		st Ames b Voce	3
E.E. Achong	c sub (L.F. Townsend) b Astill	1		not out	4
Extras	(B 4, LB 14, NB 1)	19		(B 8, LB 4, NB 2)	14
Total		**254**			**212**

WEST INDIES	O	M	R	W	O	M	R	W
Griffith	22	4	63	5	38	8	99	3
Constantine	16·1	3	42	2	40	4	165	4
Small	12	6	22	0	19	2	56	1
Achong	20	3	64	2	4	0	12	0
Grell	2	0	7	0	3	1	10	0
Headley					11	2	30	0
St Hill					2	0	9	0
Roach					8	1	32	0
ENGLAND								
Voce	28	5	79	4	37·2	15	70	7
Haig	8	1	33	1	21	8	33	2
Stevens	7	1	25	0	8	2	21	1
Astill	24·2	6	58	4	20	3	34	0
Rhodes	20	5	40	1	22	12	31	0
O'Connor					4	1	9	0

FALL OF WICKETS

Wkt	E 1st	WI 1st	E 2nd	WI 2nd
1st	1	0	9	57
2nd	3	89	49	79
3rd	12	104	52	85
4th	61	104	289	109
5th	142	110	375	135
6th	147	141	380	165
7th	180	160	408	183
8th	200	231	409	193
9th	206	253	–	207
10th	208	254	–	212

Umpires: K.L. Grant (1) and J. Hardstaff, sr (5).

Close: 1st day – WI(1) 27-1 (Hunte 19, St Hill 8); 2nd – E(2) 20-1 (Gunn 7, O'Connor 8); 3rd – E(2) 339-4 (Hendren 155, Stevens 18); 4th – WI(2) 47-0 (St Hill 18, Hunte 27).

WEST INDIES v ENGLAND 1929–30 (3rd Test)

Played at Bourda, Georgetown, British Guiana, on 21, 22, 24, 25, 26 February.
Toss: West Indies.   Result: WEST INDIES won by 289 runs.
Debuts: West Indies – C.E.L. Jones (*usually given as 'C.M. Jones'*) England – L.F. Townsend.

West Indies gained their first Test match victory after Roach had scored their first double-century and Headley had become the first West Indian to score a hundred in each innings of a Test. He was also the first batsman to score three Test hundreds before his 21st birthday; he added a fourth in the next Test. Browne reached his fifty in only 34 minutes – then the fastest half-century for West Indies.

WEST INDIES

C.A. Roach	c Haig b Townsend	209		st Ames b Astill	22
E.A.C. Hunte†	c Townsend b Wyatt	53		hit wkt b Townsend	14
G.A. Headley	run out	114		c Townsend b Haig	112
M.P. Fernandes*	c Ames b Rhodes	22		c Calthorpe b Rhodes	19
J.E.D. Sealy	c and b Rhodes	0	(7)	c Hendren b Rhodes	10
C.V. Wight	b Townsend	10	(8)	b Haig	22
L.N. Constantine	st Ames b Wyatt	13	(6)	b Astill	0
C.R. Browne	b Voce	22	(9)	not out	70
C.E.L. Jones	c Ames b Voce	6	(11)	b Townsend	2
G.N. Francis	not out	5		lbw b Astill	2
E.L. St Hill	st Ames b Haig	3	(5)	b Astill	3
Extras	(B 3, LB 11)	14		(B 9, LB 5)	14
Total		**471**			**290**

ENGLAND

G. Gunn	hit wkt b Francis	11		c Hunte b Francis	45
A. Sandham	c Hunte b Browne	9		c and b Constantine	0
R.E.S. Wyatt	c Francis b Constantine	0		c Jones b Constantine	28
E.H. Hendren	b Constantine	56		lbw b St Hill	123
L.E.G. Ames†	c Hunte b Francis	31		c Francis b Constantine	3
L.F. Townsend	c Hunte b Francis	3		b Constantine	21
N.E. Haig	b Constantine	4		b Browne	0
W.E. Astill	run out	0		hit wkt b Constantine	5
Hon. F.S.G. Calthorpe*	c Headley b Constantine	15		c Jones b Roach	49
W. Rhodes	b Francis	0		not out	10
W. Voce	not out	1		lbw b Francis	2
Extras	(B 11, LB 2, NB 2)	15		(B 30, LB 5, W 3, NB 3)	41
Total		**145**			**327**

ENGLAND	O	M	R	W	O	M	R	W
Voce	26	4	81	2	16	4	44	0
Haig	23	7	61	1	10	1	44	2
Townsend	16	6	48	2	7·3	2	25	2
Rhodes	40	8	96	2	51	23	93	2
Astill	28	3	92	0	43	17	70	4
Calthorpe	6	0	23	0				
Wyatt	9	0	56	2				
WEST INDIES								
Francis	21	5	40	4	26·5	11	69	2
Constantine	16·3	6	35	4	40	17	87	5
Browne	10	2	29	1	33	15	32	1
St Hill	14	4	26	0	33	15	61	1
Roach					9	2	18	1
Headley					2	0	8	0
Jones					10	7	5	0
Wight					5	1	6	0

FALL OF WICKETS

Wkt	WI 1st	E 1st	WI 2nd	E 2nd
1st	144	19	23	0
2nd	336	20	76	82
3rd	400	33	135	82
4th	406	103	138	106
5th	417	107	138	162
6th	427	117	155	168
7th	446	120	209	181
8th	459	126	248	269
9th	464	141	281	320
10th	471	145	290	327

Umpires: J. Hardstaff, sr (6) and R.D.R. Hill (1).

Close: 1st day – WI(1) 336-2 (Headley 60); 2nd – E(1) 120-7 (Haig 1, Calthorpe 0); 3rd – WI(2) 150-5 (Headley 70, Sealy 9); 4th – E(2) 102-3 (Hendren 17, Ames 3).

WEST INDIES v ENGLAND 1929–30 (4th Test)

Played at Sabina Park, Kingston, Jamaica, on 3, 4, 5, 7, 8, 9, 10, 11 (*no play*), 12 (*no play*) April.
Toss: England.   Result: MATCH DRAWN.
Debuts: West Indies – I. Barrow, O.C. Da Costa, G. Gladstone, C.C. Passailaigue.

This timeless Test was abandoned as a draw when rain prevented play on the last two days before England's voyage home. It set records, all subsequently beaten, for the longest match, highest total, highest individual score and highest individual match aggregate. West Indies appointed their fourth captain of the rubber. Sandham (39) batted more than two days for the highest score of his first-class career. Ames recorded the (still) highest Test score by an England wicket-keeper. With a modest lead of 563 Calthorpe decided not to enforce the follow-on. Scott, who set records for the longest and most expensive bowl, still holds the record for conceding most runs in a Test match (374). Headley was the youngest to score a double-century in Tests until Javed Miandad did so at the age of 19 years 141 days (*Test No. 784*). He remains the only batsman to score four Test hundreds before attaining the age of 21. Rhodes ended the world's longest Test career (31 years 315 days) and, at the age of 52 years 165 days, remains the world's oldest Test cricketer.

ENGLAND

G. Gunn	st Barrow b Martin	85	run out		47
A. Sandham	b Griffith	325	(7) lbw b Griffith		50
R.E.S. Wyatt	c Barrow b Da Costa	58	(2) c Passailaigue b Da Costa		10
E.H. Hendren	c Passailaigue b Scott	61	b Roach		55
L.E.G. Ames†	b Griffith	149	c Nunes b Scott		27
J. O'Connor	c Da Costa b Scott	51	(3) c Headley b Scott		3
Hon. F.S.G. Calthorpe*	c Griffith b Scott	5	(8) st Barrow b Scott		8
N.E. Haig	c Da Costa b Gladstone	28	(6) c Passailaigue b Scott		34
W.E. Astill	b Scott	39	b Griffith		10
W. Rhodes	not out	8	not out		11
W. Voce	c Da Costa b Scott	20	not out		6
Extras	(B 6, LB 12, W 1, NB 1)	20	(B 5, LB 6)		11
Total		**849**	(9 wickets declared)		**272**

WEST INDIES

R.K. Nunes*	c Ames b Voce	66	b Astill		92
C.A. Roach	lbw b Haig	15	c Gunn b Rhodes		22
G.A. Headley	c Haig b Voce	10	st Ames b Wyatt		223
F.R. Martin	lbw b Haig	33	(5) c Sandham b Wyatt		24
F.I. de Caires	run out	21	(4) b Haig		16
C.C. Passailaigue	b Haig	44	not out		2
I. Barrow†	b Astill	0			
O.C. Da Costa	c Haig b Astill	39			
O.C. Scott	c and b Astill	8			
H.C. Griffith	c Hendren b Rhodes	7			
G. Gladstone	not out	12			
Extras	(B 19, LB 5, W 2, NB 5)	31	(B 17, LB 11, NB 1)		29
Total		**286**	(5 wickets)		**408**

WEST INDIES	O	M	R	W	O	M	R	W
Griffith	58	6	155	2	21·1	5	52	2
Da Costa	21	0	81	1	6	2	14	1
Gladstone	42	5	139	1	8	0	50	0
Scott	80·2	13	266	5	25	0	108	4
Martin	45	6	128	1	9	1	12	0
Headley	5	0	23	0				
Roach	5	0	22	0	10	1	25	1
Passailaigue	2	0	15	0				
ENGLAND								
Voce	22	3	81	2	29	3	94	0
Haig	30	10	73	3	26	15	49	1
Rhodes	20·5	12	17	1	24	13	22	1
Astill	33	12	73	3	46	13	108	1
Wyatt	4	0	11	0	24·3	7	58	2
O'Connor	2	2	0	0	11	3	32	0
Calthorpe					4	1	16	0

FALL OF WICKETS				
	E	WI	E	WI
Wkt	1st	1st	2nd	2nd
1st	173	53	22	44
2nd	321	80	35	271
3rd	418	141	116	320
4th	667	156	121	397
5th	720	181	176	408
6th	748	181	180	–
7th	755	254	198	–
8th	813	265	233	–
9th	821	270	256	–
10th	849	286	–	–

Umpires: J. Hardstaff, sr (7) and E. Knibbs (1).
Close: 1st day – E(1) 289-1 (Sandham 151, Wyatt 47); 2nd – E(1) 700-4 (Sandham 309, O'Connor 22); 3rd – WI(1) 141-3 (Martin 28); 4th – E(2) 121-4 (Ames 3); 5th – E(2) 256-9 (Rhodes 1); 6th – WI(2) 234-1 (Nunes 78, Headley 117); 7th – WI(2) 408-5 (Passailaigue 2); 8th – no play.

ENGLAND v AUSTRALIA 1930 (1st Test)

Played at Trent Bridge, Nottingham, on 13, 14, 16, 17 June.
Toss: England.   Result: ENGLAND won by 93 runs.
Debuts: Australia – S.J. McCabe.

England gained their ninth victory in successive matches under Chapman's captaincy. Sutcliffe retired hurt at 134 in the second innings after a blow on the right thumb. Bradman scored Australia's first century at Trent Bridge in his first Test in England. Sydney Copley, a 24-year-old member of the Nottinghamshire groundstaff who was fielding at mid-on as substitute for Larwood (upset stomach), 'made a lot of ground, took the ball at full-length and, although rolling over, retained possession' (*Wisden*). His historic catch ended a potentially match-winning stand between McCabe and Bradman. A week later Copley made the only first-class appearance of his career.

ENGLAND

J.B. Hobbs	c Richardson b McCabe	78	st Oldfield b Grimmett		74
H. Sutcliffe	c Hornibrook b Fairfax	29	retired hurt		58
W.R. Hammond	lbw b Grimmett	8	lbw b Grimmett		4
F.E. Woolley	st Oldfield b Grimmett	0	b Wall		5
E.H. Hendren	b Grimmett	5	c Richardson b Wall		72
A.P.F. Chapman*	c Ponsford b Hornibrook	52	b Wall		29
H. Larwood	b Grimmett	18	(9) b Grimmett		7
R.W.V. Robins	not out	50	b McCabe		4
M.W. Tate	b Grimmett	13	(7) c Kippax b Grimmett		24
R.K. Tyldesley	c Fairfax b Wall	1	b Grimmett		5
G. Duckworth†	lbw b Fairfax	4	not out		14
Extras	(B 4, LB 7, NB 1)	12	(B 5, LB 1)		6
Total		**270**			**302**

AUSTRALIA

W.M. Woodfull*	c Chapman b Tate	2	c Chapman b Larwood		4
W.H. Ponsford	b Tate	3	b Tate		39
A.G. Fairfax	c Hobbs b Robins	14	(7) c Robins b Tate		14
D.G. Bradman	b Tate	8	(3) b Robins		131
A.F. Kippax	not out	64	(4) c Hammond b Robins		23
S.J. McCabe	c Hammond b Robins	4	(5) c sub (S.H. Copley) b Tate		49
V.Y. Richardson	b Tyldesley	37	(6) lbw b Tyldesley		29
W.A.S. Oldfield†	c Duckworth b Robins	4	c Hammond b Tyldesley		11
C.V. Grimmett	st Duckworth b Robins	0	c Hammond b Tyldesley		0
P.M. Hornibrook	lbw b Larwood	0	c Duckworth b Robins		5
T.W. Wall	b Tyldesley	0	not out		8
Extras	(B 4, LB 4)	8	(B 17, LB 5)		22
Total		**144**			**335**

AUSTRALIA	O	M	R	W	O	M	R	W	FALL OF WICKETS				
										E	A	E	A
Wall	17	4	47	1	26	4	67	3	*Wkt*	*1st*	*1st*	*2nd*	*2nd*
Fairfax	21·4	5	51	2	15	4	58	0	1st	53	4	125	12
Grimmett	32	6	107	5	30	4	94	5	2nd	63	6	137	93
Hornibrook	12	3	30	1	11	4	35	0	3rd	63	16	147	152
McCabe	7	3	23	1	14	3	42	1	4th	71	57	211	229
ENGLAND									5th	153	61	250	267
Larwood	15	8	12	1	5	1	9	1	6th	188	105	260	296
Tate	19	8	20	3	50	20	69	3	7th	218	134	283	316
Tyldesley	21	8	53	2	35	10	77	3	8th	241	140	283	322
Robins	17	4	51	4	17·2	1	81	3	9th	242	141	302	324
Hammond					29	5	74	0	10th	270	144	–	335
Woolley					3	1	3	0					

Umpires: J. Hardstaff, sr (8) and W.R. Parry (4).

Close: 1st day – E(1) 241-8 (Robins 28); 2nd – A(1) 140-8 (Kippax 60, Hornibrook 0); 3rd – A(2) 60-1 (Ponsford 21, Bradman 3).

ENGLAND v AUSTRALIA 1930 (2nd Test)

Played at Lord's, London, on 27, 28, 30 June, 1 July.
Toss: England.   Result: AUSTRALIA won by seven wickets.
Debuts: England – G.O.B. Allen.

Ponsford lost his wicket immediately after the teams had been presented to King George V. Australia's 729 remains the highest total in any cricket match at Lord's and their highest against England. Duleepsinhji emulated his uncle, K.S. Ranjitsinhji, by scoring a hundred in his first Test against Australia. Bradman batted for 339 minutes and hit 25 fours in what remains the highest innings in any Test at Lord's. He reached 50 in 46 minutes, 100 in 106, and 200 in 234 before Chapman held a sensational right-handed catch at wide mid-off. Woodfull was the first Australian captain to score a Test century in England since 1896 (G.H.S. Trott in *Test No. 50*). Chapman, whose only Test hundred included three sixes off Grimmett into the Mound Stand, was dismissed soon after swallowing a bluebottle. This was the first match in this series in which both captains made centuries.

ENGLAND

J.B. Hobbs	c Oldfield b Fairfax	1	b Grimmett	19
F.E. Woolley	c Wall b Fairfax	41	hit wkt b Grimmett	28
W.R. Hammond	b Grimmett	38	c Fairfax b Grimmett	32
K.S. Duleepsinhji	c Bradman b Grimmett	173	c Oldfield b Hornibrook	48
E.H. Hendren	c McCabe b Fairfax	48	c Richardson b Grimmett	9
A.P.F. Chapman*	c Oldfield b Wall	11	c Oldfield b Fairfax	121
G.O.B. Allen	b Fairfax	3	lbw b Grimmett	57
M.W. Tate	c McCabe b Wall	54	c Ponsford b Grimmett	10
R.W.V. Robins	c Oldfield b Hornibrook	5	not out	11
J.C. White	not out	23	run out	10
G. Duckworth†	c Oldfield b Wall	18	lbw b Fairfax	0
Extras	(B 2, LB 7, NB 1)	10	(B 16, LB 13, W 1)	30
Total		**425**		**375**

AUSTRALIA

W.M. Woodfull*	st Duckworth b Robins	155	not out	26
W.H. Ponsford	c Hammond b White	81	b Robins	14
D.G. Bradman	c Chapman b White	254	c Chapman b Tate	1
A.F. Kippax	b White	83	c Duckworth b Robins	3
S.J. McCabe	c Woolley b Hammond	44	not out	25
V.Y. Richardson	c Hobbs b Tate	30		
W.A.S. Oldfield†	not out	43		
A.G. Fairfax	not out	20		
C.V. Grimmett	)			
P.M. Hornibrook	) did not bat			
T.W. Wall	)			
Extras	(B 6, LB 8, W 5)	19	(B 1, LB 2)	3
Total	(6 wickets declared)	**729**	(3 wickets)	**72**

AUSTRALIA	O	M	R	W	O	M	R	W		FALL OF WICKETS			
										E	A	E	A
Wall	29·4	2	118	3	25	2	80	0	*Wkt*	*1st*	*1st*	*2nd*	*2nd*
Fairfax	31	6	101	4	12·4	2	37	2	1st	13	162	45	16
Grimmett	33	4	105	2	53	13	167	6	2nd	53	393	58	17
Hornibrook	26	6	62	1	22	6	49	1	3rd	105	585	129	22
McCabe	9	1	29	0	3	1	11	0	4th	209	588	141	–
Bradman					1	0	1	0	5th	236	643	147	–
ENGLAND									6th	239	672	272	–
Allen	34	7	115	0					7th	337	–	329	–
Tate	64	16	148	1	13	6	21	1	8th	363	–	354	–
White	51	7	158	3	2	0	8	0	9th	387	–	372	–
Robins	42	1	172	1	9	1	34	2	10th	425	–	375	–
Hammond	35	8	82	1	4·2	1	6	0					
Woolley	6	0	35	0									

Umpires: F. Chester (7) and T.W. Oates (4).

Close: 1st day – E(1) 405-9 (White 14, Duckworth 7); 2nd – A(1) 404-2 (Bradman 155, Kippax 7); 3rd – E(2) 98-2 (Hammond 20, Duleepsinhji 27).

ENGLAND v AUSTRALIA 1930 (3rd Test)

Played at Headingley, Leeds, on 11, 12, 14, 15 July.
Toss: Australia.   Result: MATCH DRAWN.
Debuts: Nil.

Bradman scored 309 runs on the first day (still a record for all Test cricket); he made 105 before lunch, 115 between lunch and tea, and 89 in the final session. His 334 was the highest Test innings to date. At 21 years 318 days he was then the youngest to score a triple-century in Test cricket. With his score 138, he reached 1,000 runs in only seven Test matches (13 innings). His double-century took 214 minutes and remains the fastest in Test cricket. His 50 took 49 minutes and his century came 50 minutes later; in all he batted for 383 minutes and hit 46 fours. Hammond completed 1,000 runs against Australia in his 14th innings (8 Tests).

AUSTRALIA

W.M. Woodfull*	b Hammond	50
A.A. Jackson	c Larwood b Tate	1
D.G. Bradman	c Duckworth b Tate	334
A.F. Kippax	c Chapman b Tate	77
S.J. McCabe	b Larwood	30
V.Y. Richardson	c Larwood b Tate	1
E.L. a'Beckett	c Chapman b Geary	29
W.A.S. Oldfield†	c Hobbs b Tate	2
C.V. Grimmett	c Duckworth b Tyldesley	24
T.W. Wall	b Tyldesley	3
P.M. Hornibrook	not out	1
Extras	(B 5, LB 8, W 1)	14
Total		**566**

ENGLAND

J.B. Hobbs	c A'Beckett b Grimmett	29	run out	13
H. Sutcliffe	c Hornibrook b Grimmett	32	not out	28
W.R. Hammond	c Oldfield b McCabe	113	c Oldfield b Grimmett	35
K.S. Duleepsinhji	b Hornibrook	35	c Grimmett b Hornibrook	10
M. Leyland	c Kippax b Wall	44	not out	1
G. Geary	run out	0		
G. Duckworth†	c Oldfield b A'Beckett	33		
A.P.F. Chapman*	b Grimmett	45		
M.W. Tate	c Jackson b Grimmett	22		
H. Larwood	not out	10		
R.K. Tyldesley	c Hornibrook b Grimmett	6		
Extras	(B 9, LB 10, NB 3)	22	(LB 8)	8
Total		**391**	(3 wickets)	**95**

ENGLAND	O	M	R	W	O	M	R	W
Larwood	33	3	139	1				
Tate	39	9	124	5				
Geary	35	10	95	1				
Tyldesley	33	5	104	2				
Hammond	17	3	46	1				
Leyland	11	0	44	0				
AUSTRALIA								
Wall	40	12	70	1	10	3	20	0
A'Beckett	28	8	47	1	11	4	19	0
Grimmett	56·2	16	135	5	17	3	33	1
Hornibrook	41	7	94	1	11·5	5	14	1
McCabe	10	4	23	1	2	1	1	0

FALL OF WICKETS

	A	E	E
Wkt	1st	1st	2nd
1st	2	53	24
2nd	194	64	72
3rd	423	123	94
4th	486	206	–
5th	491	206	–
6th	508	289	–
7th	519	319	–
8th	544	370	–
9th	565	375	–
10th	566	391	–

Umpires: W. Bestwick (3) and T.W. Oates (5).

Close: 1st day – A(1) 458-3 (Bradman 309, McCabe 12); 2nd – E(1) 212-5 (Hammond 61, Duckworth 0); 3rd – E(1) 242-5 (Hammond 73, Duckworth 15).

ENGLAND v AUSTRALIA 1930 (4th Test)

Played at Old Trafford, Manchester, on 25, 26, 28, 29 (*no play*) July.
Toss: Australia.   Result: MATCH DRAWN.
Debuts: England -- T.W.J. Goddard.

Hobbs and Sutcliffe shared their eleventh and last first-wicket hundred partnership against Australia. Only 45 minutes' play was possible on the third day and none at all on the fourth.

AUSTRALIA

W.M. Woodfull*	c Duckworth b Tate	54
W.H. Ponsford	b Hammond	83
D.G. Bradman	c Duleepsinhji b Peebles	14
A.F. Kippax	c Chapman b Nichols	51
S.J. McCabe	lbw b Peebles	4
V.Y. Richardson	b Hammond	1
A.G. Fairfax	lbw b Goddard	49
W.A.S. Oldfield†	b Nichols	2
C.V. Grimmett	c Sutcliffe b Peebles	50
P.M. Hornibrook	c Duleepsinhji b Goddard	3
T.W. Wall	not out	1
Extras	(B 23, LB 3, NB 7)	33
Total		**345**

ENGLAND

J.B. Hobbs	c Oldfield b Wall	31
H. Sutcliffe	c Bradman b Wall	74
W.R. Hammond	b Wall	3
K.S. Duleepsinhji	c Hornibrook b McCabe	54
M. Leyland	b McCabe	35
A.P.F. Chapman*	c Grimmett b Hornibrook	1
M.W. Tate	c Ponsford b McCabe	15
M.S. Nichols	not out	7
I.A.R. Peebles	c Richardson b McCabe	6
G. Duckworth†	not out	0
T.W.J. Goddard	did not bat	
Extras	(B 13, LB 12)	25
Total	(8 wickets)	**251**

ENGLAND	O	M	R	W
Nichols	21	5	33	2
Tate	30	11	39	1
Goddard	32·1	14	49	2
Peebles	55	9	150	3
Leyland	8	2	17	0
Hammond	21	6	24	2
AUSTRALIA				
Wall	33	9	70	3
Fairfax	13	5	15	0
Grimmett	19	2	59	0
Hornibrook	26	9	41	1
McCabe	17	3	41	4

FALL OF WICKETS

	A	E
Wkt	1st	1st
1st	106	108
2nd	138	115
3rd	184	119
4th	189	192
5th	190	199
6th	239	222
7th	243	237
8th	330	247
9th	338	–
10th	345	–

Umpires: F. Chester (8) and J. Hardstaff, sr (9).

Close: 1st day – A(1) 275-7 (Fairfax 21, Grimmett 21); 2nd – E(1) 221-5 (Leyland 35, Tate 5); 3rd – E(1) 251-8 (Nichols 7, Duckworth 0).

ENGLAND v AUSTRALIA 1930 (5th Test)

Played at Kennington Oval, London, on 16, 18, 19, 20, 21 (*no play*), 22 August.
Toss: England.   Result: AUSTRALIA won by an innings and 39 runs.
Debuts: Nil.

Australia regained the Ashes on their captain's 33rd birthday. This timeless Test was the longest staged in England until 1972 (*Test No. 702*). Wyatt captained England in his first Test against Australia. Sutcliffe batted through the first day for 138, having made only 21 before lunch. Bradman batted 438 minutes and hit 16 fours in his third score of over 200 in the rubber. His aggregate of 974 runs, average 139·14, remains the world record for any Test rubber. Hobbs ended his Test career with the then record totals of 5,410 runs and 15 hundreds. His record against Australia still survives: 3,636 runs, average 54.26, with 12 centuries. For the first time in 50 years of Test cricket at The Oval a day's play was lost to rain.

ENGLAND

J.B. Hobbs	c Kippax b Wall	47	b Fairfax		9
H. Sutcliffe	c Oldfield b Fairfax	161	c Fairfax b Hornibrook		54
W.W. Whysall	lbw b Wall	13	c Hornibrook b Grimmett		10
K.S. Duleepsinhji	c Fairfax b Grimmett	50	c Kippax b Hornibrook		46
W.R. Hammond	b McCabe	13	c Fairfax b Hornibrook		60
M. Leyland	b Grimmett	3	b Hornibrook		20
R.E.S. Wyatt*	c Oldfield b Fairfax	64	b Hornibrook		7
M.W. Tate	st Oldfield b Grimmett	10	run out		0
H. Larwood	lbw b Grimmett	19	c McCabe b Hornibrook		9
G. Duckworth†	b Fairfax	3	b Hornibrook		15
I.A.R. Peebles	not out	3	not out		0
Extras	LB 17, NB 2)	19	(B 16, LB 3, NB 2)		21
Total		**405**			**251**

AUSTRALIA

W.M. Woodfull*	c Duckworth b Peebles	54
W.H. Ponsford	b Peebles	110
D.G. Bradman	c Duckworth b Larwood	232
A.F. Kippax	c Wyatt b Peebles	28
A.A. Jackson	c Sutcliffe b Wyatt	73
S.J. McCabe	c Duckworth b Hammond	54
A.G. Fairfax	not out	53
W.A.S. Oldfield†	c Larwood b Peebles	34
C.V. Grimmett	lbw b Peebles	6
T.W. Wall	lbw b Peebles	0
P.M. Hornibrook	c Duckworth b Tate	7
Extras	(B 22, LB 18, NB 4)	44
Total		**695**

AUSTRALIA	O	M	R	W	O	M	R	W
Wall	37	6	96	2	12	2	25	0
Fairfax	31	9	52	3	10	3	21	1
Grimmett	66·2	18	135	4	43	12	90	1
McCabe	22	4	49	1	3	1	2	0
Hornibrook	15	1	54	0	31·2	9	92	7
ENGLAND								
Larwood	48	6	132	1				
Tate	65·1	12	153	1				
Peebles	71	8	204	6				
Wyatt	14	1	58	1				
Hammond	42	12	70	1				
Leyland	16	7	34	0				

FALL OF WICKETS

	E	A	E
Wkt	1st	1st	2nd
1st	68	159	17
2nd	97	190	37
3rd	162	263	118
4th	190	506	135
5th	197	570	189
6th	367	594	207
7th	379	670	208
8th	379	684	220
9th	391	684	248
10th	405	695	251

Umpires: J. Hardstaff, sr (10) and W.R. Parry (5).

Close: 1st day – E(1) 316-5 (Sutcliffe 138, Wyatt 39); 2nd – A(1) 215-2 (Bradman 27, Kippax 11); 3rd – A(1) 403-3 (Bradman 130, Jackson 43); 4th – E(2) 24-1 (Sutcliffe 8, Whysall 6); 5th – no play.

AUSTRALIA v WEST INDIES 1930–31 (1st Test)

Played at Adelaide Oval on 12, 13, 15, 16 December.
Toss: West Indies.   Result: AUSTRALIA won by ten wickets.
Debuts: Australia – A. Hurwood; West Indies – L.S. Birkett, G.C. Grant.

Playing in West Indies' first match against Australia, Grant was the first to score a not out fifty in each innings of any Test Match. Scott ended Australia's first innings with a spell of 4 for 0. Bradman captured his first Test wicket and recorded what remained his best analysis for Australia.

WEST INDIES

C.A. Roach	st Oldfield b Hurwood	56	b Hurwood		9
L.S. Birkett	c and b Grimmett	27	st Oldfield b Grimmett		64
G.A. Headley	c Wall b Grimmett	0	st Oldfield b Grimmett		11
F.R. Martin	b Grimmett	39	run out		3
L.N. Constantine	c Wall b Grimmett	1	b Grimmett		14
G.C. Grant*	not out	53	not out		71
E.L. Bartlett	lbw b Grimmett	84	c Grimmett b Hurwood		11
I. Barrow†	c Bradman b Grimmett	12	lbw b Bradman		27
G.N. Francis	lbw b Hurwood	5	b Hurwood		3
O.C. Scott	c Fairfax b Grimmett	3	c Kippax b Hurwood		8
H.C. Griffith	b Hurwood	1	st Oldfield b Grimmett		10
Extras	(B 6, LB 8, NB 1)	15	(B 16, LB 2)		18
Total		**296**			**249**

AUSTRALIA

W.H. Ponsford	c Birkett b Francis	24	not out	92
A.A. Jackson	c Barrow b Francis	31	not out	70
D.G. Bradman	c Grant b Griffith	4		
A.F. Kippax	c Barrow b Griffith	146		
S.J. McCabe	c and b Constantine	90		
W.M. Woodfull*	run out	6		
A.G. Fairfax	not out	41		
W.A.S. Oldfield†	c Francis b Scott	15		
C.V. Grimmett	c Barrow b Scott	0		
A. Hurwood	c Martin b Scott	0		
T.W. Wall	lbw b Scott	0		
Extras	(B 2, LB 10, NB 7)	19	(B 8, W 1, NB 1)	10
Total		**376**	(0 wickets)	**172**

AUSTRALIA	O	M	R	W	O	M	R	W
Wall	16	0	64	0	10	1	20	0
Fairfax	11	1	36	0	3	2	6	0
Grimmett	48	19	87	7	38	7	96	4
Hurwood	36·1	14	55	3	34	11	86	4
McCabe	12	3	32	0	8	2	15	0
Bradman	4	0	7	0	5	1	8	1
WEST INDIES								
Francis	18	7	43	2	10	1	30	0
Constantine	22	0	89	1	9·3	3	27	0
Griffith	28	4	69	2	10	1	20	0
Martin	29	3	73	0	11	0	28	0
Scott	20·5	2	83	4	13	0	55	0
Birkett					2	0	2	0

FALL OF WICKETS

Wkt	WI 1st	A 1st	WI 2nd	A 2nd
1st	58	56	15	–
2nd	58	59	47	–
3rd	118	64	52	–
4th	123	246	74	–
5th	131	269	115	–
6th	245	341	138	–
7th	269	374	203	–
8th	290	374	208	–
9th	295	374	220	–
10th	296	376	249	–

Umpires: G.A. Hele (6) and A.G. Jenkins (1).

Close: 1st day – WI(1) 286-7 (Grant 49, Francis 3); 2nd – A(1) 297-5 (Kippax 118, Fairfax 7); 3rd – WI(2) 203-7 (Grant 50).

AUSTRALIA v WEST INDIES 1930–31 (2nd Test)

Played at Sydney Cricket Ground on 1, 2 (*no play*), 3, 5 January.
Toss: Australia.   Result: AUSTRALIA won by an innings and 172 runs.
Debuts: Nil.

Rain completely altered the character of a perfect batting pitch after Australia had scored 323 for 4 on the first day. When play resumed, 20 wickets fell on the third day for 220 runs. Bartlett crushed a finger against his boot in catching Kippax at mid-on and was unable to bat.

AUSTRALIA

W.H. Ponsford	b Scott	183
A.A. Jackson	c Francis b Griffith	8
D.G. Bradman	c Barrow b Francis	25
A.F. Kippax	c Bartlett b Griffith	10
S.J. McCabe	lbw b Scott	31
W.M. Woodfull*	c Barrow b Constantine	58
A.G. Fairfax	c Constantine b Francis	15
W.A.S. Oldfield†	run out	0
C.V. Grimmett	b Scott	12
A. Hurwood	c Martin b Scott	5
H. Ironmonger	not out	3
Extras	(B 6, LB 5, W 5, NB 3)	19
Total		**369**

WEST INDIES

C.A. Roach	run out	7	c Kippax b McCabe	25
L.S. Birkett	c Hurwood b Fairfax	3	c McCabe b Hurwood	8
G.A. Headley	b Fairfax	14	c Jackson b Hurwood	2
F.R. Martin	lbw b Grimmett	10	c McCabe b Hurwood	0
G.C. Grant*	c Hurwood b Ironmonger	6	not out	15
L.N. Constantine	c Bradman b Grimmett	12	b Hurwood	8
I. Barrow†	c Jackson b Fairfax	17	c McCabe b Ironmonger	10
G.N. Francis	b Grimmett	8	c Oldfield b Ironmonger	0
O.C. Scott	not out	15	c Woodfull b Ironmonger	17
H.C. Griffith	c Kippax b Grimmett	8	lbw b Grimmett	0
E.L. Bartlett	absent hurt	–	absent hurt	–
Extras	(B 6, NB 1)	7	(B 1, LB 2, W 1, NB 1)	5
Total		**107**		**90**

WEST INDIES	O	M	R	W	O	M	R	W
Griffith	28	4	57	2				
Constantine	18	2	56	1				
Francis	27	3	70	2				
Scott	15·4	0	66	4				
Martin	18	1	60	0				
Birkett	10	1	41	0				
AUSTRALIA								
Fairfax	13	4	19	3	5	1	21	0
Hurwood	5	1	7	0	11	2	22	4
Grimmett	19·1	3	54	4	3·3	1	9	1
Ironmonger	13	3	20	1	4	1	13	3
McCabe					7	0	20	1

FALL OF WICKETS

	A	WI	WI
Wkt	1st	1st	2nd
1st	12	3	26
2nd	52	26	32
3rd	69	36	32
4th	140	36	42
5th	323	57	53
6th	341	63	67
7th	344	80	67
8th	361	88	90
9th	364	107	90
10th	369	–	–

Umpires: G. Borwick (1) and W.G. French (1).

Close: 1st day – A(1) 323-4 (Ponsford 174, Woodfull 58); 2nd – no play; 3rd – WI(2) 67-5 (Grant 10, Barrow 10).

AUSTRALIA v WEST INDIES 1930–31 (3rd Test)

Played at Exhibition Ground, Brisbane, on 16, 17, 19, 20 January.
Toss: Australia.   Result: AUSTRALIA won by an innings and 217 runs.
Debuts: Nil.

Missed in the slips when four, Bradman batted for five hours and hit 24 fours in making the highest score to date by an Australian in a home Test. Headley scored West Indies' first hundred against Australia.

AUSTRALIA

W.H. Ponsford	c Birkett b Francis	109
A.A. Jackson	lbw b Francis	0
D.G. Bradman	c Grant b Constantine	223
A.F. Kippax	b Birkett	84
S.J. McCabe	c Constantine b Griffith	8
W.M. Woodfull*	c Barrow b Griffith	17
A.G. Fairfax	c Sealy b Scott	9
R.K. Oxenham	lbw b Griffith	48
W.A.S. Oldfield†	not out	38
C.V. Grimmett	c Constantine b Francis	4
H. Ironmonger	c Roach b Griffith	2
Extras	(B 2, LB 7, NB 7)	16
Total		**558**

WEST INDIES

C.A. Roach	lbw b Oxenham	4	b McCabe	1
F.R. Martin	lbw b Grimmett	21	lbw b Oxenham	11
G.A. Headley	not out	102	c Oldfield b Ironmonger	28
J.E.D. Sealy	c McCabe b Ironmonger	3	(9) not out	16
G.C. Grant*	c McCabe b Grimmett	8	(6) run out	10
L.N. Constantine	c Fairfax b Ironmonger	9	(4) lbw b Oxenham	7
L.S. Birkett	lbw b Oxenham	8	(5) b Grimmett	13
I. Barrow†	st Oldfield b Grimmett	19	(7) st Oldfield b Grimmett	17
O. C. Scott	b Oxenham	0	(8) lbw b Grimmett	15
G.N. Francis	b Oxenham	8	c Oldfield b Grimmett	7
H.C. Griffith	lbw b Grimmett	8	c Bradman b Grimmett	12
Extras	(B 1, LB 2)	3	(B 5, LB 4, NB 2)	11
Total		**193**		**148**

WEST INDIES	O	M	R	W	O	M	R	W
Francis	26	4	76	3				
Constantine	26	2	74	1				
Griffith	33	4	133	4				
Scott	24	1	125	1				
Martin	27	3	85	0				
Sealy	3	0	32	0				
Birkett	7	0	16	1				
Grant	1	0	1	0				
AUSTRALIA								
Fairfax	7	2	13	0	6	2	6	0
Oxenham	30	15	39	4	18	5	37	2
Ironmonger	26	15	43	2	15	8	29	1
Grimmett	41·3	9	95	4	14·3	4	49	5
McCabe					7	1	16	1

FALL OF WICKETS

	A	WI	WI
Wkt	1st	1st	2nd
1st	1	5	13
2nd	230	36	29
3rd	423	41	47
4th	431	60	58
5th	441	94	72
6th	462	116	82
7th	468	159	94
8th	543	162	112
9th	551	182	128
10th	558	193	148

Umpires: J.P. Orr (1) and A.E. Wyeth (1).

Close: 1st day – A(1) 428-3 (Bradman 223, McCabe 1); 2nd – WI(1) 51-3 (Headley 19, Grant 2); 3rd – WI(2) 115-8 (Sealy 2, Francis 2).

AUSTRALIA v WEST INDIES 1930–31 (4th Test)

Played at Melbourne Cricket Ground on 13, 14 February.
Toss: West Indies.   Result: AUSTRALIA won by an innings and 122 runs.
Debuts: Nil.

West Indies never recovered from their first innings collapse against the left-arm medium-paced spin of 'Dainty' Ironmonger, and suffered their fourth defeat of the rubber, this time in two days. Ironmonger's match figures (11 for 79) were the best for Australia against West Indies until 1988-89. His first innings analysis of 7 for 23 remained the best of his Test career.

WEST INDIES

C.A. Roach	c Kippax b Grimmett	20		lbw b Fairfax	7
F.R. Martin	lbw b Ironmonger	17	(6)	c Oldfield b Fairfax	10
G.A. Headley	c Jackson b Ironmonger	33		c Fairfax b Ironmonger	11
L.S. Birkett	c McCabe b Ironmonger	0		c Jackson b Ironmonger	13
E.L. Bartlett	st Oldfield b Ironmonger	9	(7)	b Fairfax	6
G.C. Grant*	c Oldfield b Ironmonger	0	(5)	c McCabe b Ironmonger	3
L.N. Constantine	c Jackson b Grimmett	7	(2)	c Kippax b Fairfax	10
I. Barrow†	c Fairfax b Ironmonger	0		c Oxenham b Ironmonger	13
O.C. Scott	run out	11		not out	20
G.N. Francis	not out	0	(11)	c Jackson b Grimmett	0
H.C. Griffith	c Fairfax b Ironmonger	0	(10)	b Grimmett	4
Extras	(NB 2)	2		(B 3, LB 6, NB 1)	10
Total		**99**			**107**

AUSTRALIA

W.M. Woodfull*	run out	83
W.H. Ponsford	st Barrow b Constantine	24
D.G. Bradman	c Roach b Martin	152
A.A. Jackson	c Birkett b Constantine	15
S.J. McCabe	run out	2
A.G. Fairfax	c Birkett b Martin	16
A.F. Kippax	b Martin	24
R.K. Oxenham	c Constantine b Griffith	0
W.A.S. Oldfield†	not out	1
H. Ironmonger	) did not bat	
C.V. Grimmett	)	
Extras	(B 7, LB 3, NB 1)	11
Total	(8 wickets declared)	**328**

AUSTRALIA	O	M	R	W	O	M	R	W
Fairfax	5	0	14	0	14	2	31	4
Oxenham	6	1	14	0				
Ironmonger	20	7	23	7	17	4	56	4
Grimmett	19	7	46	2	4·4	0	10	2
WEST INDIES								
Francis	13	0	51	0				
Griffith	8	1	33	1				
Scott	11	0	47	0				
Constantine	25	4	83	2				
Martin	30·2	3	91	3				
Birkett	2	0	12	0				

FALL OF WICKETS

	WI	A	WI
Wkt	1st	1st	2nd
1st	32	50	8
2nd	51	206	32
3rd	53	265	36
4th	81	275	49
5th	81	286	60
6th	88	325	60
7th	88	326	67
8th	88	328	92
9th	99	–	97
10th	99	–	107

Umpires: A.N. Barlow (1) and J. Richards (1).

Close: 1st day – A(1) 197-1 (Woodfull 75, Bradman 92).

AUSTRALIA v WEST INDIES 1930–31 (5th Test)

Played at Sydney Cricket Ground on 27, 28 February, 2, 3 (*no play*), 4 March.
Toss: West Indies.   Result: WEST INDIES won by 30 runs.
Debuts: Australia—K.E. Rigg.

After losing their first four Tests against Australia, West Indies gained a surprise victory when Grant timed his declarations to allow his bowlers maximum assistance from a 'sticky' pitch. In the final innings he gambled by asking Australia to score only 247 runs in unlimited time. Earlier Martin had defended skilfully in difficult conditions to complete his only Test hundred.

WEST INDIES

F.R. Martin	not out	123	c McCabe b Grimmett		20
C.A. Roach	lbw b Grimmett	31	c Oldfield b Ironmonger		34
G.A. Headley	lbw b McCabe	105	b Oxenham		30
G.C. Grant*	c McCabe b Ironmonger	62	not out		27
J.E.D. Sealy	c Kippax b Grimmett	4	run out		7
L.N. Constantine	c McCabe b Ironmonger	0	c Bradman b Ironmonger		4
E.L. Bartlett	b Grimmett	0	not out		0
I. Barrow†	not out	7			
O.C. Scott	)				
G.N. Francis	) did not bat				
H.C. Griffith	)				
Extras	(B 6, LB 5, W 1, NB 6)	18	(B 1, LB 1)		2
Total	(6 wickets declared)	**350**	(5 wickets declared)		**124**

AUSTRALIA

W.M. Woodfull*	c Constantine b Martin	22	c Constantine b Griffith		18
W.H. Ponsford	c Bartlett b Francis	7	c Constantine b Martin		28
D.G. Bradman	c Francis b Martin	43	b Griffith		0
A.F. Kippax	c Sealy b Constantine	3	(5) c Roach b Constantine		10
K.E. Rigg	c Barrow b Francis	14	(6) c Barrow b Constantine		16
S.J. McCabe	c Headley b Francis	21	(7) c Grant b Martin		44
A.G. Fairfax	st Barrow b Scott	54	(8) not out		60
R.K. Oxenham	c Barrow b Francis	0	(9) lbw b Scott		14
W.A.S. Oldfield†	run out	36	(4) lbw b Griffith		0
C.V. Grimmett	not out	15	c Constantine b Griffith		12
H. Ironmonger	b Griffith	1	run out		4
Extras	(B 1, LB 7)	8	(B 3, LB 7, W 2, NB 2)		14
Total		**224**			**220**

AUSTRALIA	O	M	R	W	O	M	R	W	FALL OF WICKETS				
										WI	A	WI	A
Fairfax	21	2	60	0						1st	1st	2nd	2nd
Oxenham	24	10	51	0	10	4	14	1	*Wkt*	*1st*	*1st*	*2nd*	*2nd*
Ironmonger	42	16	95	2	16	7	44	2	1st	70	7	46	49
Grimmett	33	7	100	3	18	4	47	1	2nd	222	66	66	49
McCabe	15	5	26	1	7	2	17	0	3rd	332	69	103	53
									4th	337	89	113	53
WEST INDIES									5th	338	89	124	65
Francis	19	6	48	4	16	2	32	0	6th	341	130	–	76
Griffith	13·2	3	31	1	13·3	3	50	4	7th	–	134	–	155
Martin	27	3	67	2	18	4	44	2	8th	–	196	–	180
Constantine	10	2	28	1	17	2	50	2	9th	–	215	–	214
Scott	10	1	42	1	11	0	30	1	10th	–	224	–	220

Umpires: H. Armstrong (1) and W.G. French (2).

Close: 1st day – WI(1) 298-2 (Martin 100, Grant 48); 2nd – A(1) 89-5 (McCabe 0, Fairfax 0); 3rd – WI(2) 124-5 (Grant 27, Bartlett 0); 4th – no play.

SOUTH AFRICA v ENGLAND 1930–31 (1st Test)

Played at Old Wanderers, Johannesburg, on 24, 26, 27 December.
Toss: England.   Result: SOUTH AFRICA won by 28 runs.
Debuts: South Africa – X.C. Balaskas, S.H. Curnow, E.S. Newson, K.G. Viljoen.

Nupen, born of Norwegian parents and blind in one eye since the age of four, led South Africa to an unexpected victory in his only match as captain. Ironically for England, although he was renowned as probably the greatest bowler of all time on matting pitches, he was selected for this Test only because H.G. Deane, the current captain, was unavailable. Nupen's 11 wickets proved decisive.

SOUTH AFRICA

I.J. Siedle	b Voce	13		lbw b Voce	35
S.H. Curnow	lbw b Tate	13		run out	8
B. Mitchell	c Hammond b Voce	6		c Duckworth b Hammond	72
R.H. Catterall	b Voce	5		c Hendren b Hammond	54
K.G. Viljoen	c Duckworth b Peebles	7	(6)	b Hammond	44
X.C. Balaskas	lbw b Peebles	7	(5)	lbw b Tate	3
H.B. Cameron†	b Peebles	0		c Duckworth b Voce	51
Q. McMillan	not out	45		b Voce	14
E.P. Nupen*	b Peebles	0		b Hammond	1
C.L. Vincent	c Hammond b Voce	2		b Voce	1
E.S. Newson	b Tate	10		not out	0
Extras	(B 12, LB 5, NB 1)	18		(B 16, LB 7)	23
Total		**126**			**306**

ENGLAND

R.E.S. Wyatt	lbw b Nupen	8		c McMillan b Catterall	5
M. Leyland	c Cameron b Nupen	29		c and b Catterall	15
W.R. Hammond	lbw b Nupen	49		st Cameron b Vincent	63
E.H. Hendren	c Cameron b McMillan	8		c Mitchell b Nupen	3
M.J.L. Turnbull	st Cameron b Vincent	28		b Nupen	61
A.P.F. Chapman*	c Newson b Vincent	28		c Mitchell b Nupen	11
J.C. White	c Curnow b Nupen	14		lbw b Nupen	2
M.W. Tate	c Mitchell b Vincent	8		c Mitchell b Nupen	28
I.A.R. Peebles	b Nupen	0	(11)	not out	13
W. Voce	run out	8	(9)	c Nupen b Vincent	0
G. Duckworth†	not out	0	(10)	lbw b Nupen	4
Extras	(B 9, LB 3, W 1)	13		(LB 6)	6
Total		**193**			**211**

ENGLAND	O	M	R	W	O	M	R	W
Tate	12·2	4	20	2	18	2	47	1
Voce	26	11	45	4	27·2	8	59	4
Peebles	14	2	43	4	7	0	41	0
Hammond					25	5	63	4
White					16	3	53	0
Wyatt					2	0	20	0
SOUTH AFRICA								
Newson	8	2	11	0	14	2	30	0
Viljoen	4	1	10	0				
McMillan	9	0	47	1	4	0	25	0
Nupen	26·1	1	63	5	25·3	3	87	6
Vincent	21	8	49	3	17	1	44	2
Catterall					5	0	12	2
Balaskas					2	0	7	0

FALL OF WICKETS

Wkt	SA 1st	E 1st	SA 2nd	E 2nd
1st	19	33	34	13
2nd	28	42	50	22
3rd	37	51	172	30
4th	42	103	174	131
5th	51	149	182	152
6th	53	176	263	154
7th	78	179	291	164
8th	78	185	305	169
9th	81	193	306	195
10th	126	193	306	211

Umpires: W.B. Ryan (1) and G.B. Treadwell (4).

Close: 1st day – E(1) 167-5 (Hammond 45, White 8); 2nd – SA(2) 303-7 (Viljoen 43, Nupen 0).

SOUTH AFRICA v ENGLAND 1930–31 (2nd Test)

Played at Newlands, Cape Town, on 1, 2, 3, 5 January.
Toss: South Africa.   Result: MATCH DRAWN.
Debuts: Nil.

This was the first Test in South Africa to be played on a turf pitch; all 40 previous matches in the Union were played on matting, as were the following two games in this rubber. Nupen's success in the previous match did not prevent Deane being persuaded out of retirement to return as captain. Gaining first use of an excellent batting surface, South Africa amassed their highest total so far and were able to control the match. Tate became the second player after W. Rhodes to complete the double for England. The partnership of 260 between Mitchell and Siedle remains the highest by South Africa for the first wicket in all Tests. Hammond kept wicket on the second day after Duckworth had torn a ligament in his hand.

SOUTH AFRICA

B. Mitchell	b Tate	123
I.J. Siedle	c Chapman b White	141
E.P. Nupen	b Tate	12
H.W. Taylor	c White b Leyland	117
R.H. Catterall	b Tate	56
H.B. Cameron†	c Peebles b White	26
X.C. Balaskas	c Turnbull b Leyland	0
H.G. Deane*	b Leyland	7
Q. McMillan	not out	7
C.L. Vincent	not out	3
A.J. Bell	did not bat	
Extras	(B 8, LB 12, NB 1)	21
Total	(8 wickets declared)	**513**

ENGLAND

R.E.S. Wyatt	b McMillan	40		b Bell	29
W.R. Hammond	c and b McMillan	57		c Deane b Vincent	65
M. Leyland	b Bell	52		c Mitchell b McMillan	28
E.H. Hendren	b Balaskas	93		b Vincent	86
M.J.L. Turnbull	b Bell	7		b McMillan	14
A.P.F. Chapman*	b Bell	0	(8)	b Catterall	4
J.C. White	lbw b Balaskas	23	(6)	lbw b Catterall	8
M.W. Tate	c Taylor b McMillan	15	(9)	lbw b Nupen	3
W. Voce	c and b Vincent	30	(10)	not out	1
I.A.R. Peebles	not out	7	(7)	b Catterall	0
G. Duckworth†	lbw b Vincent	0		absent hurt	–
Extras	(B9, LB 16, NB 1)	26		(B 9, LB 4, NB 1)	14
Total		**350**			**252**

ENGLAND	O	M	R	W	O	M	R	W		FALL OF WICKETS		
Tate	43	13	79	3							SA	E	E
Hammond	10	2	27	0					*Wkt*	*1st*	*1st*	*2nd*
Voce	33	11	95	0					1st	260	75	58
Peebles	28	2	95	0					2nd	280	120	105
White	46	15	101	2					3rd	299	202	152
Leyland	30	6	91	3					4th	447	214	184
Wyatt	2	0	4	0					5th	473	214	225
									6th	479	288	225
SOUTH AFRICA									7th	502	293	235
Bell	27	9	53	3	29	8	58	1	8th	506	312	250
Catterall	5	3	2	0	12	2	15	3	9th	–	350	252
Nupen	22	7	43	0	17	2	26	1	10th	–	350	–
Balaskas	16	0	75	2	9	1	29	0				
Vincent	17·4	4	40	2	17	6	26	2				
McMillan	33	6	111	3	32	7	64	2				
Mitchell					8	0	20	0				

Umpires: J.C. Collings (1) and W.B. Ryan (2).

Close: 1st day – SA(1) 280-1 (Mitchell 119, Nupen 12); 2nd – E(1) 98-1 (Hammond 43, Leyland 12); 3rd – E(2) 28-0 (Wyatt 16, Hammond 7).

SOUTH AFRICA v ENGLAND 1930–31 (3rd Test)

Played at Kingsmead, Durban, on 16, 17 (*no play*), 19, 20 January.
Toss: South Africa.   Result: MATCH DRAWN.
Debuts: Nil.

Returning to the mat England dominated the rain-ruined Kingsmead Test. Hammond's eighth Test century was his first in South Africa. Taylor fought bravely for two hours to prevent England from squaring the rubber.

SOUTH AFRICA

I.J. Siedle	b White	38	lbw b Tate		0
B. Mitchell	c Duckworth b Tate	5	(3) c Chapman b White		13
S.H. Curnow	c Duckworth b Voce	2	(2) c Hammond b Voce		9
H.W. Taylor	c Duckworth b Voce	3	not out		64
R.H. Catterall	b White	11	b Hammond		19
H.B. Cameron†	c Voce b Tate	41	b Hammond		8
H.G. Deane*	b Voce	15	c Duckworth b Allom		8
Q. McMillan	c Wyatt b White	20	c Chapman b White		1
C.L. Vincent	c Duckworth b Voce	18	c sub (H.W. Lee) b White		5
N.A. Quinn	b Voce	3			
A.J. Bell	not out	0	(10) not out		0
Extras	(B 5, LB 8, NB 8)	21	(B 8, LB 8, NB 2)		18
Total		**177**	(8 wickets)		**145**

ENGLAND

R.E.S. Wyatt	c Siedle b Vincent	54
W.R. Hammond	not out	136
M. Leyland	not out	31
E.H. Hendren	)	
M.J.L. Turnbull	)	
A.P.F. Chapman*	)	
J.C. White	) did not bat	
M.J.C. Allom	)	
M.W. Tate	)	
W. Voce	)	
G. Duckworth†	)	
Extras	(LB 2)	2
Total	(1 wicket declared)	**223**

ENGLAND	O	M	R	W	O	M	R	W
Tate	27	13	33	2	9	3	12	1
Allom	25	4	44	0	11	0	27	1
Voce	29·2	3	58	5	12	3	14	1
White	16	6	21	3	18	4	33	3
Hammond					11	6	9	2
Leyland					9	1	32	0
SOUTH AFRICA								
Bell	22	3	45	0				
Catterall	10	0	37	0				
Quinn	19	4	42	0				
Vincent	25	7	66	1				
McMillan	6	0	31	0				

FALL OF WICKETS

Wkt	SA 1st	E 1st	SA 2nd
1st	14	160	0
2nd	23	–	27
3rd	33	–	47
4th	51	–	106
5th	86	–	116
6th	118	–	136
7th	141	–	137
8th	161	–	145
9th	172	–	–
10th	177	–	–

Umpires: J.C. Collings (2) and A.C. King (1).

Close: 1st day – SA(1) 59-4 (Siedle 29, Cameron 4); 2nd – no play; 3rd – E(1) 130-0 (Wyatt 45, Hammond 83).

SOUTH AFRICA v ENGLAND 1930–31 (4th Test)

Played at Old Wanderers, Johannesburg, on 13, 14, 16, 17 February.
Toss: England.   Result: MATCH DRAWN.
Debuts: England – W. Farrimond, H.W. Lee.

Cameron became South Africa's third captain in four Tests after Deane had resigned. Peebles ended the first innings with a spell of leg-spin which produced figures of 5 for 18 in 9.5 overs, including three wickets with his last five balls. Nupen also achieved his best analysis in Test cricket in this, the last Test in South Africa to be played on matting. Chasing 317 in four hours, the home side needed 37 with three wickets left when time ran out.

ENGLAND

R.E.S. Wyatt	lbw b Nupen	37	lbw b Vincent		7
H.W. Lee	lbw b Nupen	18	c Mitchell b Catterall		1
W.R. Hammond	c McMillan b Hall	75	c Mitchell b Catterall		15
E.H. Hendren	c Cameron b Hall	64	c Vincent b Nupen		45
M. Leyland	lbw b Hall	91	c Mitchell b Nupen		46
M.J.L. Turnbull	st Cameron b McMillan	25	(9) not out		0
W. Farrimond†	c Mitchell b McMillan	28			
I.A.R. Peebles	c Nupen b Vincent	3	(10) c and b Nupen		2
A.P.F. Chapman*	b Nupen	5	(7) c Taylor b Nupen		3
M.W. Tate	c Mitchell b Hall	26	(6) c McMillan b Nupen		38
W. Voce	not out	41	(8) c Siedle b Nupen		5
Extras	(B 21, LB 8)	29	(B 1, LB 6)		7
Total		**442**	(9 wickets declared)		**169**

SOUTH AFRICA

S.H. Curnow	lbw b Hammond	7	lbw b Tate		12
I.J. Siedle	lbw b Peebles	62	c Hammond b Tate		8
B. Mitchell	lbw b Tate	68	c Hammond b Voce		74
H.W. Taylor	hit wkt b Peebles	72	b Voce		13
R.H. Catterall	c Hammond b Tate	11	lbw b Peebles		21
K.G. Viljoen	b Voce	30	(7) c Hammond b Voce		31
H.B. Cameron*†	b Peebles	2	(6) not out		69
Q. McMillan	c Hendren b Peebles	12	c Hendren b Voce		24
E.P. Nupen	not out	11	not out		11
C.L. Vincent	lbw b Peebles	0			
A.E. Hall	b Peebles	0			
Extras	(B 6, LB 14)	20	(B 6, LB 9, NB 2)		17
Total		**295**	(7 wickets)		**280**

SOUTH AFRICA	O	M	R	W	O	M	R	W
Hall	37	5	105	4	9	2	47	0
Catterall	7	1	16	0	10	1	28	2
Nupen	51	7	148	3	16·1	1	46	6
McMillan	16·4	1	62	2	2	0	12	0
Vincent	26	8	69	1	14	4	29	1
Viljoen	4	0	13	0				
ENGLAND								
Tate	27	9	46	2	22	6	52	2
Hammond	28	6	50	1	11	2	27	0
Voce	42	11	106	1	32	7	87	4
Peebles	38·5	10	63	6	27	6	86	1
Wyatt	2	0	10	0				
Leyland					4	0	11	0

FALL OF WICKETS

	E	SA	E	SA
Wkt	*1st*	*1st*	*2nd*	*2nd*
1st	41	16	3	14
2nd	64	112	23	63
3rd	183	167	23	102
4th	231	185	120	135
5th	329	243	125	153
6th	337	249	135	209
7th	341	280	167	261
8th	352	295	167	–
9th	385	295	169	–
10th	442	295	–	–

Umpires: J.C. Collings (3) and A.C. King (2).

Close: 1st day – E(1) 338-6 (Farrimond 4, Peebles 0); 2nd – SA(1) 166-2 (Mitchell 68, Taylor 20); 3rd – E(2) 110-3 (Hendren 39, Leyland 41).

SOUTH AFRICA v ENGLAND 1930–31 (5th Test)

Played at Kingsmead, Durban, on 21, 23, 24, 25 February.
Toss: England.   Result: MATCH DRAWN.
Debuts: South Africa – J.A.K. Cochran.

The start of this match was delayed by 20 minutes because the correct size of bails was unavailable and the umpires had to make two sets. Needing a win to share the rubber and having won the toss on a rain-affected turf pitch, Chapman protested strongly about this waste of valuable bowling time. Rain ended play after 70 minutes on the first day and bad light curtailed the third. South Africa thus won their first rubber against England since 1909-10.

SOUTH AFRICA

I.J. Siedle	c and b White	57	c Chapman b White		30
B. Mitchell	b Hammond	73	c Hammond b Voce		21
J.A.J. Christy	b Peebles	16	st Farrimond b Peebles		37
H.W. Taylor	c and b Peebles	16	lbw b Peebles		14
K.G. Viljoen	c Hammond b Tate	16	c Chapman b Voce		18
H.B. Cameron*†	b Voce	4	(7) not out		41
E.L. Dalton	c Farrimond b Hammond	31	(6) st Farrimond b Peebles		11
Q. McMillan	not out	29	c Chapman b Wyatt		28
C.L. Vincent	c Chapman b Peebles	6	not out		5
A.J. Bell	b Voce	0			
J.A.K. Cochran	b Peebles	4			
Extras		–	(B 8, LB 3, NB 3)		14
Total		**252**	(7 wickets declared)		**219**

ENGLAND

R.E.S. Wyatt	c Cameron b Bell	24	c Mitchell b Christy		1
W.R. Hammond	c Mitchell b Vincent	29	c Vincent b Bell		28
M. Leyland	lbw b Bell	8			
E.H. Hendren	c McMillan b Vincent	30			
M.J.L. Turnbull	b McMillan	6	(4) c and b Siedle		7
W. Farrimond†	c Taylor b Vincent	35	(3) c Cameron b Taylor		9
A.P.F. Chapman*	c McMillan b Vincent	24			
M.W. Tate	b Vincent	50	(5) not out		24
W. Voce	c Bell b McMillan	0			
J.C. White	c and b Vincent	10			
I.A.R. Peebles	not out	2			
Extras	(B 5, LB 4, NB 3)	12	(B 2, LB 1)		3
Total		**230**	(4 wickets)		**72**

ENGLAND	O	M	R	W	O	M	R	W
Tate	22	6	35	1	9	2	17	0
Hammond	19	6	36	2	5	0	28	0
Voce	27	10	51	2	22	1	46	2
Peebles	27·4	3	67	4	25	4	71	3
White	35	9	63	1	17	6	37	1
Wyatt					4	2	6	1
SOUTH AFRICA								
Bell	30	4	63	2	3	0	14	1
Cochran	23	5	47	0				
Vincent	31·2	9	51	6				
McMillan	17	3	57	2				
Christy					4	1	17	1
Taylor					3	0	13	1
Siedle					3·1	1	7	1
Mitchell					1	0	18	0

FALL OF WICKETS

Wkt	SA 1st	E 1st	SA 2nd	E 2nd
1st	127	56	43	7
2nd	131	56	64	31
3rd	157	87	91	40
4th	163	101	110	72
5th	168	101	126	–
6th	203	126	143	–
7th	221	188	208	–
8th	242	188	–	–
9th	243	223	–	–
10th	252	230	–	–

Umpires: J.C. Collings (4) and A.C. King (3).

Close: 1st day – SA(1) 32-0 (Siedle 23, Mitchell 9); 2nd – SA(1) 252 all out; 3rd – SA(2) 3-0 (Siedle 0, Mitchell 2).

ENGLAND v NEW ZEALAND 1931 (1st Test)

Played at Lord's, London, on 27, 29, 30 June.
Toss: New Zealand.   Result: MATCH DRAWN.
Debuts: England – J. Arnold, A.H. Bakewell; New Zealand – I.B. Cromb, J.L. Kerr.

Although New Zealand's first official Test overseas was the only one originally scheduled, their form resulted in two additional matches being arranged. Both sides collapsed on the first day; New Zealand lost eight wickets for 92 after being 132 for 2 at lunch, and only a superb innings of 80 in even time by Woolley enabled England to reach 190 for 7 at stumps. The course of the game was changed by a partnership of 246 between Ames and Allen which is still the world eighth-wicket record in Test cricket and the oldest such record to survive. The tourists' second total was their highest in any Test until 1949 (*Test No. 315*). It allowed a token declaration which left England to score 240 in 140 minutes.

NEW ZEALAND

J.E. Mills	b Peebles	34	(2) b Allen	0
C.S. Dempster	lbw b Peebles	53	(1) b Hammond	120
G.L. Weir	lbw b Peebles	37	b Allen	40
J.L. Kerr	st Ames b Robins	2	(6) lbw b Peebles	0
R.C. Blunt	c Hammond b Robins	7	b Robins	96
M.L. Page	b Allen	23	(4) c and b Peebles	104
T.C. Lowry*	c Hammond b Robins	1	(9) b Peebles	34
I.B. Cromb	c Ames b Peebles	20	(7) c Voce b Robins	14
C.F.W. Allcott	c Hammond b Peebles	13	(10) not out	20
W.E. Merritt	c Jardine b Hammond	17	(8) b Peebles	5
K.C. James†	not out	1		
Extras	(B 2, LB 12, W 1, NB 1)	16	(B 23, LB 10, W 1, NB 2)	36
Total		**224**	(9 wickets declared)	**469**

ENGLAND

A.H. Bakewell	lbw b Cromb	9	c Blunt b Cromb	27
J. Arnold	c Page b Cromb	0	c and b Blunt	34
W.R. Hammond	b Cromb	7	run out	46
K.S. Duleepsinhji	c Kerr b Merritt	25	c James b Allcott	11
D.R. Jardine*	c Blunt b Merritt	38	(7) not out	0
F.E. Woolley	lbw b Merritt	80	(5) b Cromb	9
L.E.G. Ames†	c James b Weir	137	(6) not out	17
I.A.R. Peebles	st James b Merritt	0		
G.O.B. Allen	c Lowry b Weir	122		
R.W.V. Robins	c Lowry b Weir	12		
W. Voce	not out	1		
Extras	(B 15, LB 8)	23	(LB 2)	2
Total		**454**	(5 wickets)	**146**

ENGLAND	O	M	R	W	O	M	R	W		FALL OF WICKETS			
Voce	10	1	40	0	32	11	60	0		NZ	E	NZ	E
Allen	15	2	45	1	25	8	47	2	*Wkt*	*1st*	*1st*	*2nd*	*2nd*
Hammond	10·3	5	8	1	21	2	50	1	1st	58	5	1	62
Peebles	26	3	77	5	42·4	6	150	4	2nd	130	14	100	62
Robins	13	3	38	3	37	5	126	2	3rd	136	62	218	94
NEW ZEALAND									4th	140	62	360	105
Cromb	37	7	113	3	25	5	44	2	5th	153	129	360	144
Weir	8	1	38	3	5	1	18	0	6th	161	188	389	–
Blunt	46	9	124	0	14	5	54	1	7th	190	190	404	–
Allcott	17	3	34	0	10	2	26	1	8th	191	436	406	–
Merritt	23	2	104	4	1	0	2	0	9th	209	447	469	–
Page	3	0	18	0					10th	224	454	–	–

Umpires: F. Chester (9) and J. Hardstaff, sr (11).

Close: 1st day – E(1) 190-7 (Ames 15); 2nd – NZ(2) 161-2 (Dempster 86, Page 31).

ENGLAND v NEW ZEALAND 1931 (2nd Test)

Played at Kennington Oval, London, on 29, 30, 31 July.
Toss: England.   Result: ENGLAND won by an innings and 26 runs.
Debuts: England – F.R. Brown, H. Verity; New Zealand – H.G. Vivian.

Showers had interrupted an impressive display of batting by Sutcliffe (his 14th Test hundred), Duleepsinhji (his third and last), and Hammond (his ninth – in just 100 minutes). The pitch had livened considerably when New Zealand began their reply and it deteriorated further on the last day before the match ended at 3.15 pm. Tate reached 150 Test wickets when he dismissed Merritt.

ENGLAND

H. Sutcliffe	st James b Vivian	117
A.H. Bakewell	run out	40
K.S. Duleepsinhji	c Weir b Allcott	109
W.R. Hammond	not out	100
L.E.G. Ames†	c James b Vivian	41
D.R. Jardine*	not out	7
F.R. Brown	)	
G.O.B. Allen	)	
M.W. Tate	) did not bat	
I.A.R. Peebles	)	
H. Verity	)	
Extras	(B 1, LB 1)	2
Total	(4 wickets declared)	**416**

NEW ZEALAND

J.E. Mills	b Allen	27	b Brown		30
G.L. Weir	b Allen	13	b Peebles		6
R.C. Blunt	c Ames b Allen	2	(4) b Peebles		43
M.L. Page	c Peebles b Tate	12	(3) b Tate		3
H.G. Vivian	c Ames b Allen	3	c Brown b Peebles		51
T.C. Lowry*	c Jardine b Brown	62	c Duleepsinhji b Peebles		0
J.L. Kerr	c Ames b Allen	34	b Tate		28
K.C. James†	lbw b Brown	4	c Peebles b Verity		10
I.B. Cromb	c Hammond b Verity	8	not out		3
W.E. Merritt	c Hammond b Verity	8	lbw b Tate		4
C.F.W. Allcott	not out	5	c Allen b Verity		1
Extras	(B 2, LB 9, NB 4)	15	(B 6, LB 10, NB 2)		18
Total		**193**			**197**

NEW ZEALAND	O	M	R	W	O	M	R	W
Cromb	30	5	97	0				
Allcott	44	7	108	1				
Vivian	34·3	8	96	2				
Weir	10	1	36	0				
Merritt	12	0	75	0				
Blunt	1	0	2	0				
ENGLAND								
Tate	18	9	15	1	21	6	22	3
Brown	29	12	52	2	16	6	38	1
Verity	22·1	8	52	2	12·3	4	33	2
Peebles	12	3	35	0	22	4	63	4
Allen	13	7	14	5	13	4	23	0
Hammond	1	0	10	0				

FALL OF WICKETS

Wkt	E 1st	NZ 1st	NZ 2nd
1st	84	42	19
2nd	262	44	38
3rd	271	45	51
4th	401	53	139
5th	–	92	143
6th	–	157	162
7th	–	167	189
8th	–	168	189
9th	–	188	196
10th	–	193	197

Umpires: F. Chester (10) and J. Hardstaff, sr (12).

Close: 1st day – E(1) 312-3 (Hammond 35, Ames 9); 2nd – NZ(2) 22-1 (Mills 10, Page 0).

ENGLAND v NEW ZEALAND 1931 (3rd Test)

Played at Old Trafford, Manchester, on 15 (*no play*), 17 (*no play*), 18 August.
Toss: New Zealand.   Result: MATCH DRAWN.
Debuts: England – E. Paynter.

Manchester's rainfall eventually relented in time for a start at 3.15 on the third afternoon. In the remaining 195 minutes Paynter made his Test debut on his home ground and Sutcliffe completed his second hundred in successive innings for England.

ENGLAND

H. Sutcliffe	not out	109
E. Paynter	c James b Cromb	3
K.S. Duleepsinhji	c Allcott b Vivian	63
W.R. Hammond	c Cromb b Vivian	16
D.R. Jardine*	not out	28
L.E.G. Ames†	)	
G.O.B. Allen	)	
F.R. Brown	) did not bat	
H. Larwood	)	
I.A.R. Peebles	)	
H. Verity	)	
Extras	(B 4, NB 1)	5
Total	(3 wickets)	**224**

NEW ZEALAND

T.C. Lowry*
C.S. Dempster
J.E. Mills
M.L. Page
G.L. Weir
K.C. James†
A.M. Matheson
I.B. Cromb
C.F.W. Allcott
H.G. Vivian
R.C. Blunt

NEW ZEALAND	O	M	R	W
Matheson	12	1	40	0
Cromb	16	6	33	1
Allcott	27	6	75	0
Vivian	14	1	54	2
Blunt	1	0	12	0
Lowry	1	0	5	0

FALL OF WICKETS

	E
Wkt	1st
1st	8
2nd	134
3rd	166
4th	–
5th	–
6th	–
7th	–
8th	–
9th	–
10th	–

Umpires: F. Chester (11) and J. Hardstaff, sr (13).

Close: play on final day only.

AUSTRALIA v SOUTH AFRICA 1931–32 (1st Test)

Play at Woolloongabba, Brisbane, on 27, 28, 30 (*no play*) November, 1 (*no play*), 2, 3 December.
Toss: Australia.   Result: AUSTRALIA won by an innings and 163 runs.
Debuts: Australia – H.C. Nitschke.

Bradman, missed when 11 and 15, marked the introduction of Test cricket to the 'Gabba' by exceeding his own record score by an Australian in a home Test. It remains the highest innings in a Test at Brisbane. South Africa, 126 for 3 at Saturday's close, had to wait until 4 pm on Wednesday before resuming their innings on a rain-soaked pitch. Mitchell established a world Test record by not adding to his score for a period of 90 minutes.

AUSTRALIA

W.M. Woodfull*	lbw b Vincent	76
W.H. Ponsford	c Mitchell b Bell	19
D.G. Bradman	lbw b Vincent	226
A.F. Kippax	c Cameron b Vincent	1
S.J. McCabe	c Vincent b Morkel	27
H.C. Nitschke	c Cameron b Bell	6
R.K. Oxenham	b Bell	1
W.A.S. Oldfield†	not out	56
C.V. Grimmett	b Bell	14
T.W. Wall	lbw b Quinn	14
H. Ironmonger	b Quinn	2
Extras	(B 5, LB 1, W 1, NB 1)	8
Total		**450**

SOUTH AFRICA

J.A.J. Christy	b Wall	24	c McCabe b Ironmonger	15
S.H. Curnow	b Ironmonger	11	b Grimmett	8
B. Mitchell	run out	58	b Wall	0
H.B. Cameron*†	st Oldfield b Grimmett	4	b Ironmonger	21
H.W. Taylor	b Wall	41	c Oxenham b Ironmonger	47
E.L. Dalton	c and b Ironmonger	11	b Wall	6
Q. McMillan	c Oxenham b Ironmonger	0	(8) c Nitschke b Wall	0
D.P.B. Morkel	c McCabe b Ironmonger	3	(7) b Wall	5
C.L. Vincent	c Nitschke b Grimmett	10	c sub (K.E. Rigg) b Wall	1
N.A. Quinn	c sub (K.E. Rigg) b Ironmonger	1	c McCabe b Ironmonger	0
A.J. Bell	not out	1	not out	0
Extras	(B 2, LB 4)	6	(B 6, LB 5, NB 3)	14
Total		**170**		**117**

SOUTH AFRICA	O	M	R	W	O	M	R	W
Bell	42	5	120	4				
Morkel	13	1	57	1				
Quinn	38·3	6	113	2				
Vincent	34	0	100	3				
McMillan	10	0	52	0				
AUSTRALIA								
Wall	28	14	39	2	15·1	7	14	5
McCabe	11	4	16	0				
Grimmett	41·1	21	49	2	15	3	45	1
Ironmonger	47	29	42	5	30	16	44	4
Oxenham	11	5	18	0				

FALL OF WICKETS

	A	SA	SA
Wkt	*1st*	*1st*	*2nd*
1st	32	25	16
2nd	195	44	29
3rd	211	49	34
4th	292	129	78
5th	316	140	97
6th	320	140	111
7th	380	152	111
8th	407	157	117
9th	446	169	117
10th	450	170	117

Umpires: G. Borwick (2) and G.A. Hele (7).

Close: 1st day – A(1) 341-6 (Bradman 200, Oldfield 3); 2nd – SA(1) 126-3 (Mitchell 45, Taylor 38); 3rd – no play; 4th – no play; 5th – SA(1) 152-6 (Mitchell 53, Morkel 3).

AUSTRALIA v SOUTH AFRICA 1931–32 (2nd Test)

Played at Sydney Cricket Ground on 18, 19, 21 December.
Toss: South Africa.   Result: AUSTRALIA won by an innings and 155 runs.
Debuts: Australia – P.K. Lee; South Africa – L.S. Brown.

Australia gained their second victory by an innings in this rubber; it was completed soon after tea on the third day and this time without assistance from the elements. Grimmett mesmerised the Springbok batsmen and, before lunch on the first day, they scored off only four of the 66 balls he bowled. Rigg, a tall right-hander from Victoria, scored his only hundred for Australia in his second Test while Bradman, although nursing a slight leg strain, flayed the bowling for his fourth hundred against the tourists in successive first-class innings.

SOUTH AFRICA

Batsman	Dismissal 1	R	Dismissal 2	R
J.A.J. Christy	c Nitschke b Grimmett	14	c Woodfull b Ironmonger	41
B. Mitchell	b McCabe	1	c Oldfield b Wall	24
D.P.B. Morkel	st Oldfield b Grimmett	20	lbw b Grimmett	17
H.B. Cameron*†	b Wall	11	b Wall	0
H.W. Taylor	c Lee b Grimmett	7	c Grimmett b Ironmonger	6
K.G. Viljoen	b Ironmonger	37	b Grimmett	0
E.L. Dalton	b Grimmett	21	c Bradman b Ironmonger	14
C.L. Vincent	not out	31	c Ponsford b Grimmett	35
L.S. Brown	b McCabe	2	c Wall b Lee	8
N.A. Quinn	lbw b McCabe	5	st Oldfield b Grimmett	1
A.J. Bell	b McCabe	0	not out	1
Extras	(LB 3, W 1)	4	(B 5, LB 8, NB 1)	14
Total		**153**		**161**

AUSTRALIA

W.M. Woodfull*	c Mitchell b Vincent	58
W.H. Ponsford	b Quinn	5
K.E. Rigg	b Bell	127
D.G. Bradman	c Viljoen b Morkel	112
S.J. McCabe	c Christy b Vincent	79
H.C. Nitschke	b Bell	47
P.K. Lee	c Cameron b Brown	0
W.A.S. Oldfield†	c Cameron b Bell	8
C.V. Grimmett	not out	9
T.W. Wall	c Morkel b Bell	6
H. Ironmonger	c Cameron b Bell	0
Extras	(B 5, LB 12, W 1)	18
Total		**469**

AUSTRALIA	O	M	R	W	O	M	R	W
Wall	18	4	46	1	18	5	31	2
McCabe	12	5	13	4	3	0	25	0
Grimmett	24	12	28	4	20·3	7	44	4
Ironmonger	12	1	38	1	19	10	22	3
Lee	7	1	24	0	13	4	25	1

SOUTH AFRICA	O	M	R	W
Bell	46·5	6	140	5
Quinn	42	10	95	1
Brown	29	3	100	1
Vincent	24	5	75	2
Morkel	12	2	33	1
Mitchell	1	0	8	0

FALL OF WICKETS

Wkt	SA 1st	A 1st	SA 2nd
1st	6	6	70
2nd	31	143	89
3rd	36	254	89
4th	54	347	100
5th	62	432	100
6th	91	433	100
7th	136	444	122
8th	143	457	144
9th	153	469	160
10th	153	469	161

Umpires: G. Borwick (3) and G.A. Hele (8).

Close: 1st day – A(1) 78-1 (Woodfull 36, Rigg 35); 2nd – A(1) 444-7 (Oldfield 4).

AUSTRALIA v SOUTH AFRICA 1931–32 (3rd Test)

Played at Melbourne Cricket Ground on 31 December, 1, 2, 4, 5, 6 January.
Toss: Australia.   Result: AUSTRALIA won by 169 runs.
Debuts: Nil.

For the only time in the rubber, South Africa achieved a first innings lead and dismissed Bradman cheaply, two events which were not totally unrelated. Viljoen recorded his maiden Test hundred, the only century by a South African in this rubber, and the entire side reached double figures for the fourth time in Tests. The match was transformed by a partnership of 274 between Woodfull and Bradman, then Australia's highest for the second wicket against all countries, before Grimmett and Ironmonger completed a decisive third victory.

AUSTRALIA

W.M. Woodfull*	c Cameron b Bell	7	c Mitchell b McMillan	161
W.H. Ponsford	b Bell	7	c Mitchell b Bell	34
D.G. Bradman	c Cameron b Quinn	2	lbw b Vincent	167
A.F. Kippax	c Bell b Quinn	52	c Curnow b McMillan	67
S.J. McCabe	c Morkel b Bell	22	c Mitchell b McMillan	71
K.E. Rigg	c Mitchell b Bell	68	c Mitchell b Vincent	1
E.L. a'Beckett	c Mitchell b Quinn	6	b Vincent	4
W.A.S. Oldfield†	c Vincent b Quinn	0	lbw b McMillan	0
C.V. Grimmett	c Morkel b Bell	9	not out	16
T.W. Wall	not out	6	b Vincent	12
H. Ironmonger	run out	12	b Quinn	0
Extras	(B 1, LB 4, W 1, NB 1)	7	(B 17, LB 3, NB 1)	21
Total		**198**		**554**

SOUTH AFRICA

S.H. Curnow	b Grimmett	47	b Grimmett	9
B. Mitchell	c McCabe b Wall	17	c and b Grimmett	46
J.A.J. Christy	c McCabe b Ironmonger	16	c Oldfield b Ironmonger	63
H.W. Taylor	lbw b Grimmett	11	b Grimmett	38
D.P.B. Morkel	lbw b Ironmonger	33	b Ironmonger	4
H.B. Cameron*†	st Oldfield b Ironmonger	39	lbw b Ironmonger	13
K.G. Viljoen	c Wall b McCabe	111	b Ironmonger	2
C.L. Vincent	c Oldfield b Wall	16	c Ponsford b Grimmett	34
Q. McMillan	c Oldfield b Wall	29	c Wall b Grimmett	1
N.A. Quinn	b McCabe	11	not out	0
A.J. Bell	not out	10	b Grimmett	0
Extras	(B 3, LB 13, NB 2)	18	(B 8, LB 6, NB 1)	15
Total		**358**		**225**

SOUTH AFRICA	O	M	R	W	O	M	R	W		FALL OF WICKETS			
Bell	26·1	9	69	5	36	6	101	1		A	SA	A	SA
Quinn	31	13	42	4	36·4	6	113	1	*Wkt*	*1st*	*1st*	*2nd*	*2nd*
Morkel	3	0	12	0	4	0	15	0	1st	11	39	54	18
Vincent	12	1	32	0	55	16	154	4	2nd	16	79	328	120
McMillan	2	0	22	0	33	3	150	4	3rd	25	89	408	133
Christy	3	0	14	0					4th	74	108	519	138
									5th	135	163	521	178
AUSTRALIA									6th	143	183	521	186
Wall	37	5	98	3	13	3	35	0	7th	143	225	524	188
A'Beckett	18	5	29	0	3	1	6	0	8th	173	329	530	208
Grimmett	63	23	100	2	46	14	92	6	9th	179	336	550	225
Ironmonger	49	26	72	3	42	18	54	4	10th	198	358	554	225
McCabe	21·3	4	41	2	10	1	21	0					
Bradman					1	0	2	0					

Umpires: G. Borwick (4) and G.A. Hele (9).

Close: 1st day – SA(1) 46-1 (Curnow 22, Christy 3); 2nd – SA(1) 268-7 (Viljoen 65, McMillan 10); 3rd – A(2) 206-1 (Woodfull 73, Bradman 97); 4th – A(2) 554-9 (Grimmett 16, Ironmonger 0); 5th – SA(2) 198-7 (Vincent 10, McMillan 1).

AUSTRALIA v SOUTH AFRICA 1931–32 (4th Test)

Played at Adelaide Oval on 29, 30 January, 1, 2 February.
Toss: South Africa.   Result: AUSTRALIA won by ten wickets.
Debuts: Australia – W.A. Hunt, W.J. O'Reilly, H.M. Thurlow.

Bradman ran out his last partner when attempting the vital single off the last ball of an over. His innings remains the highest in any Test at Adelaide and was the highest for Australia in a home Test until R.M. Cowper scored 307 at Melbourne in 1965-66 (*Test No. 601*). Grimmett's match analysis of 14 for 199 is still the Test record for Adelaide. Bell bowled with great courage, sending down 40 overs only with the aid of pain-killing injections in a severely-bruised left foot. Bill 'Tiger' O'Reilly captured the first of his 144 wickets for Australia.

SOUTH AFRICA

S.H. Curnow	c Ponsford b Grimmett	20	b McCabe	3
B. Mitchell	c and b McCabe	75	c O'Reilly b Grimmett	95
J.A.J. Christy	b O'Reilly	7	b Grimmett	51
H.W. Taylor	c Rigg b Grimmett	78	b O'Reilly	84
H.B. Cameron*†	lbw b Grimmett	52	b O'Reilly	4
D.P.B. Morkel	c and b Grimmett	0	(8) b Grimmett	15
K.G. Viljoen	c and b Grimmett	0	b Grimmett	1
C.L. Vincent	not out	48	(6) b Grimmett	5
Q. McMillan	b Grimmett	19	c Hunt b Grimmett	3
N.A. Quinn	c Ponsford b Grimmett	1	b Grimmett	1
A.J. Bell	lbw b O'Reilly	2	not out	0
Extras	(LB 2, NB 4)	6	(B 4, LB 3, NB 5)	12
Total		**308**		**274**

AUSTRALIA

W.M. Woodfull*	c Morkel b Bell	82	not out	37
W.H. Ponsford	b Quinn	5	not out	27
D.G. Bradman	not out	299		
A.F. Kippax	run out	0		
S.J. McCabe	c Vincent b Bell	2		
K.E. Rigg	c Taylor b Bell	35		
W.A.S. Oldfield†	lbw b Vincent	23		
C.V. Grimmett	b Bell	21		
W.A. Hunt	c Vincent b Quinn	0		
W.J. O'Reilly	b Bell	23		
H.M. Thurlow	run out	0		
Extras	(B 18, LB 3, W 1, NB 1)	23	(B 4, LB 5)	9
Total		**513**	(0 wickets)	**73**

AUSTRALIA	O	M	R	W	O	M	R	W		FALL OF WICKETS			
Thurlow	27	6	53	0	12	1	33	0		SA	A	SA	A
McCabe	17	6	34	1	14	1	51	1	*Wkt*	*1st*	*1st*	*2nd*	*2nd*
O'Reilly	39·4	10	74	2	42	13	81	2	1st	27	9	22	–
Grimmett	47	11	116	7	49·2	17	83	7	2nd	45	185	103	–
Hunt	10	1	25	0	6	1	14	0	3rd	165	191	224	–
									4th	202	194	232	–
SOUTH AFRICA									5th	204	308	240	–
Bell	40	2	142	5					6th	204	357	246	–
Quinn	37	5	114	2	3	0	5	0	7th	243	418	262	–
Vincent	34	5	110	1	7	0	31	0	8th	286	421	268	–
McMillan	9	0	53	0	7·2	0	23	0	9th	300	499	274	–
Morkel	18	1	71	0	2	0	5	0	10th	308	513	274	–

Umpires: G. Borwick (5) and G.A. Hele (10).

Close: 1st day – SA(1) 265-7 (Vincent 18, McMillan 10); 2nd – A(1) 302-4 (Bradman 170, Rigg 32); 3rd – SA(2) 124-2 (Mitchell 54, Taylor 11).

AUSTRALIA v SOUTH AFRICA 1931–32 (5th Test)

Played at Melbourne Cricket Ground on 12, 13 (*no play*), 15 February.
Toss: South Africa.   Result: AUSTRALIA won by an innings and 72 runs.
Debuts: Australia – J.H.W. Fingleton, L.J. Nash.

A vicious Melbourne 'sticky' produced the lowest aggregate (81) by any side losing all 20 wickets in a Test match. The match aggregate of 234 is still the lowest in all Test cricket. It is also the shortest completed Test match; the innings, in chronological order, lasted 89, 159 and 105 minutes respectively – a total playing time of 5 hours 53 minutes. Ironmonger had the incredible match figures of 11 for 24 and Grimmett, who took 33 wickets in the first four Tests, was not invited to bowl. Bradman severely twisted his ankle when his studs caught in the coir matting of the dressing room as he was going out to field.

SOUTH AFRICA

B. Mitchell	c Rigg b McCabe	2	(4) c Oldfield b Ironmonger		4
S.H. Curnow	c Oldfield b Nash	3	c Fingleton b Ironmonger		16
J.A.J. Christy	c Grimmett b Nash	4	(1) c and b Nash		0
H.W. Taylor	c Kippax b Nash	0	(7) c Bradman b Ironmonger		2
K.G. Viljoen	c sub (L.S. Darling) b Ironmonger	1	(8) c Oldfield b O'Reilly		0
H.B. Cameron*†	c McCabe b Nash	11	(5) c McCabe b O'Reilly		0
D.P.B. Morkel	c Nash b Ironmonger	1	(6) c Rigg b Ironmonger		0
C.L. Vincent	c Nash b Ironmonger	1	(9) not out		8
Q. McMillan	st Oldfield b Ironmonger	0	(10) c Oldfield b Ironmonger		0
N.A. Quinn	not out	5	(11) c Fingleton b Ironmonger		5
A.J. Bell	st Oldfield b Ironmonger	0	(3) c McCabe b O'Reilly		6
Extras	(B 2, LB 3, NB 3)	8	(B 3, LB 1)		4
Total		**36**			**45**

AUSTRALIA

W.M. Woodfull*	b Bell	0
J.H.W. Fingleton	c Vincent b Bell	40
K.E. Rigg	c Vincent b Quinn	22
A.F. Kippax	c Curnow b McMillan	42
S.J. McCabe	c Cameron b Bell	0
L.J. Nash	b Quinn	13
W.A.S. Oldfield†	c Curnow b McMillan	11
C.V. Grimmett	c Cameron b Quinn	9
W.J. O'Reilly	c Curnow b McMillan	13
H. Ironmonger	not out	0
D.G. Bradman	absent hurt	–
Extras	(LB 3)	3
Total		**153**

AUSTRALIA	O	M	R	W	O	M	R	W		FALL OF WICKETS		
Nash	12	6	18	4	7	4	4	1		SA	A	SA
McCabe	4	1	4	1					*Wkt*	*1st*	*1st*	*2nd*
Ironmonger	7·2	5	6	5	15·3	7	18	6	1st	7	0	0
O'Reilly					9	5	19	3	2nd	16	51	12
									3rd	16	75	25
SOUTH AFRICA									4th	17	75	30
Bell	16	0	52	3					5th	19	112	30
Quinn	19·3	4	29	3					6th	25	125	30
Vincent	11	2	40	0					7th	31	131	32
McMillan	8	0	29	3					8th	31	148	32
									9th	33	153	33
									10th	36	–	45

Umpires: G. Borwick (6) and G.A. Hele (11).

Close: 1st day – SA(2) 5-1 (Curnow 1, Bell 4); 2nd – no play.

NEW ZEALAND v SOUTH AFRICA 1931–32 (1st Test)

Played at Lancaster Park, Christchurch, on 27, 29 February, 1 March.
Toss: New Zealand.   Result: SOUTH AFRICA won by an innings and 12 runs.
Debuts: New Zealand – D.C. Cleverley, J. Newman.

This first match between South Africa and New Zealand was the last of H.W. Taylor's Test career. Of the pre-First-World-War players only F.E. Woolley (who played his last Test in 1934) remained in Test cricket longer. The partnership of 196 between Christy and Mitchell remains the highest for the first wicket by either side in this series.

NEW ZEALAND

C.S. Dempster	b McMillan	8		b Quinn	12
J.L. Kerr	b Bell	0		c Vincent b Bell	3
R.C. Blunt	run out	23		c Mitchell b Vincent	17
G.L. Weir	c Mitchell b Vincent	46		not out	74
A.W. Roberts	st Cameron b Mitchell	54		c and b McMillan	17
M.L. Page*	c Taylor b McMillan	22		st Cameron b McMillan	0
F.T. Badcock	c Dalton b Bell	64		st Cameron b McMillan	5
K.C. James†	c Cameron b McMillan	3	(9)	lbw b Quinn	0
I.B. Cromb	c Morkel b McMillan	25	(8)	c Vincent b McMillan	0
D.C. Cleverley	not out	10		b Quinn	7
J. Newman	c Balaskas b Mitchell	19		lbw b McMillan	4
Extras	(B 4, LB 13, NB 2)	19		(B 1, LB 5, NB 1)	7
Total		**293**			**146**

SOUTH AFRICA

J.A.J. Christy	run out	103
B. Mitchell	c James b Cromb	113
H.W. Taylor	b Badcock	9
H.B. Cameron*†	c James b Badcock	47
X.C. Balaskas	run out	5
E.L. Dalton	c Page b Newman	82
D.P.B. Morkel	b Newman	51
C.L. Vincent	c Page b Blunt	3
Q. McMillan	c Badcock b Blunt	6
N.A. Quinn	run out	3
A.J. Bell	not out	2
Extras	(B 14, LB 10, NB 3)	27
Total		**451**

SOUTH AFRICA	O	M	R	W	O	M	R	W	FALL OF WICKETS			
Bell	32	8	64	2	9	3	11	1		NZ	SA	NZ
Quinn	29	7	46	0	15	6	17	3	*Wkt*	*1st*	*1st*	*2nd*
McMillan	19	2	61	4	20·5	4	66	5	1st	1	196	16
Vincent	23	7	57	1	14	3	33	1	2nd	26	227	16
Balaskas	4	0	15	0					3rd	38	249	41
Mitchell	7·4	0	31	2	1	0	6	0	4th	128	262	70
Morkel					2	0	6	0	5th	149	299	70
NEW ZEALAND									6th	189	376	76
Cleverley	22	2	79	0					7th	198	395	94
Badcock	38	8	88	2					8th	251	423	103
Newman	28·5	4	76	2					9th	265	432	117
Blunt	16	0	60	2					10th	293	451	146
Cromb	26	4	94	1								
Page	6	0	27	0								

Umpires: W. Butler (2) and J.T. Forrester (1).

Close: 1st day – NZ(1) 293 all out; 2nd – NZ(2) 16-0 (Dempster 12, Kerr 3).

NEW ZEALAND v SOUTH AFRICA 1931–32 (2nd Test)

Played at Basin Reserve, Wellington, on 4, 5, 7 March.
Toss: New Zealand.   Result: SOUTH AFRICA won by eight wickets.
Debuts: Nil.

Vivian, who hit his country's first hundred against South Africa and who was top-scorer in both innings, shared
in a partnership of 100 with Badcock which remains the highest for the sixth wicket by either side in this series.
A left-hander, he was 19 years 121 days old when he scored his only Test century; he remains the youngest to
make a hundred for New Zealand. Needing to score 148 runs in 135 minutes, South Africa reached their objective
with 40 minutes to spare.

NEW ZEALAND

C.S. Dempster	c Vincent b McMillan	64	c Cameron b Quinn	20
G.L. Weir	b McMillan	8	b Quinn	1
R.C. Blunt	lbw b Quinn	25	b Brown	17
H.G. Vivian	c Dalton b McMillan	100	c Vincent b Balaskas	73
A.W. Roberts	lbw b Quinn	1	b Quinn	26
M.L. Page*	c Mitchell b Brown	7	(7) c and b Balaskas	23
F.T. Badcock	c and b McMillan	53	(6) run out	0
G.R. Dickinson	st Cameron b McMillan	2	b McMillan	5
C.F.W. Allcott	c Dalton b Mitchell	26	b Quinn	15
I.B. Cromb	not out	51	c Christy b McMillan	2
K.C. James†	b Mitchell	11	not out	0
Extras	(B 12, LB 4)	16	(B 4, LB 6, NB 1)	11
Total		**364**		**193**

SOUTH AFRICA

J.A.J. Christy	c Dempster b Badcock	62	c Roberts b Badcock	53
B. Mitchell	b Cromb	0	c James b Dickinson	53
H.B. Cameron*†	c Blunt b Vivian	44	not out	22
K.G. Viljoen	b Page	81	not out	16
E.L. Dalton	c James b Dickinson	42		
X.C. Balaskas	not out	122		
Q. McMillan	c Dickinson b Allcott	1		
C.L. Vincent	c and b Vivian	33		
L.S. Brown	c Page b Vivian	7		
N.A. Quinn	b Vivian	8		
A.J. Bell	lbw b Dickinson	2		
Extras	(B 2, LB 2, W 1, NB 3)	8	(LB 6)	6
Total		**410**	**(2 wickets)**	**150**

SOUTH AFRICA	O	M	R	W	O	M	R	W
Bell	16	1	47	0	10	0	30	0
Quinn	28	6	51	2	24	9	37	4
Brown	14	1	59	1	10	3	30	1
McMillan	29	2	125	5	21	2	71	2
Vincent	6	1	32	0				
Christy	2	0	11	0				
Mitchell	4·5	0	23	2				
Balaskas					7	2	14	2
NEW ZEALAND								
Dickinson	26·2	7	78	2	8	2	33	1
Cromb	23	9	48	1	3	0	13	0
Badcock	24	6	70	1	11	2	31	1
Allcott	27	4	80	1	7	0	27	0
Blunt	10	0	38	0	2·2	0	11	0
Vivian	20·	7	58	4	7	0	15	0
Page	11	3	30	1	3	0	14	0

FALL OF WICKETS

	NZ	SA	NZ	SA
Wkt	1st	1st	2nd	2nd
1st	42	2	14	104
2nd	79	78	23	115
3rd	135	133	66	–
4th	139	220	122	–
5th	158	256	122	–
6th	258	257	157	–
7th	269	362	171	–
8th	270	386	186	–
9th	339	394	192	–
10th	364	410	193	–

Umpires: K.H. Cave (5) and W.P. Page (1).

Close: 1st day – SA(1) 78-2 (Christy 32); 2nd – SA(1) 410-9 (Balaskas 122, Bell 2).

ENGLAND v INDIA 1932 (Only Test)

Played at Lord's, London, on 25, 27, 28 June.
Toss: England.   Result: ENGLAND won by 158 runs.
Debuts: England – W.E. Bowes; India – All.

In the absence of their captain, the Maharajah of Porbandar, and vice-captain, K.S. Ganshyamsinhji of Limbdi, India were led by C.K. Nayudu in their first official Test match. Nayudu badly damaged his hand attempting a catch in the first innings, and India were further weakened by leg injuries to Nazir Ali and Palia. Amar Singh scored India's first fifty and added 74 in 40 minutes with Lall Singh, the first Malayan Test cricketer.

ENGLAND

P. Holmes	b Nissar	6	b Jahangir		11
H. Sutcliffe	b Nissar	3	c Nayudu b Amar Singh		19
F.E. Woolley	run out	9	c Colah b Jahangir		21
W.R. Hammond	b Amar Singh	35	b Jahangir		12
D.R. Jardine*	c Navle b Nayudu	79	not out		85
E. Paynter	lbw b Nayudu	14	b Jahangir		54
L.E.G. Ames†	b Nissar	65	b Amar Singh		6
R.W.V. Robins	c Lall Singh b Nissar	21	c Jahangir b Nissar		30
F.R. Brown	c Amar Singh b Nissar	1	c Colah b Naoomal		29
W. Voce	not out	4	not out		0
W.E. Bowes	c Nissar b Amar Singh	7			
Extras	(B 3, LB 9, NB 3)	15	(B 2, LB 6)		8
Total		**259**	(8 wickets declared)		**275**

INDIA

J.G. Navle†	b Bowes	12	lbw b Robins		13
Naoomal Jeoomal	lbw b Robins	33	b Brown		25
S. Wazir Ali	lbw b Brown	31	c Hammond b Voce		39
C.K. Nayudu*	c Robins b Voce	40	b Bowes		10
S.H.M. Colah	c Robins b Bowes	22	b Brown		4
S. Nazir Ali	b Bowes	13	c Jardine b Bowes		6
P.E. Palia	b Voce	1	(11) not out		1
Lall Singh	c Jardine b Bowes	15	(7) b Hammond		29
M. Jahangir Khan	b Robins	1	(8) b Voce		0
L. Amar Singh	c Robins b Voce	5	(9) c and b Hammond		51
Mahomed Nissar	not out	1	(10) b Hammond		0
Extras	(B 5, LB 7, W 1, NB 2)	15	(B 5, LB 2, NB 2)		9
Total		**189**			**187**

INDIA	O	M	R	W	O	M	R	W		FALL OF WICKETS			
Nissar	26	3	93	5	18	5	42	1		E	I	E	I
Amar Singh	31·1	10	75	2	41	13	84	2	Wkt	1st	1st	2nd	2nd
Jahangir	17	7	26	0	30	12	60	4	1st	8	39	30	41
Nayudu	24	8	40	2	9	0	21	0	2nd	11	63	34	41
Palia	4	3	2	0	3	0	11	0	3rd	19	110	54	52
Naoomal	3	0	8	0	8	0	40	1	4th	101	139	67	65
Wazir Ali					1	0	9	0	5th	149	160	156	83
									6th	166	165	169	108
ENGLAND									7th	229	181	222	108
Bowes	30	13	49	4	14	5	30	2	8th	231	182	271	182
Voce	17	6	23	3	12	3	28	2	9th	252	188	–	182
Brown	25	7	48	1	14	1	54	2	10th	259	189	–	187
Robins	17	4	39	2	14	5	57	1					
Hammond	4	0	15	0	5·3	3	9	3					

Umpires: F. Chester (12) and J. Hardstaff, sr (14).

Close: 1st day – I(1) 30-0 (Navle 11, Naoomal 11); 2nd – E(2) 141-4 (Jardine 25, Paynter 50).

AUSTRALIA v ENGLAND 1932–33 (1st Test)

Played at Sydney Cricket Ground on 2, 3, 5, 6, 7 December.
Toss: Australia.   Result: ENGLAND won by ten wickets.
Debuts: Australia – L.E. Nagel; England – Nawab Iftikhar Ali of Pataudi.

Illness prevented Bradman from playing in the opening match of what has become known as 'The Bodyline Series'. McCabe's innings was the greatest (in both senses) against such bowling. He batted for 242 minutes, hit 25 fours and scored his last 51 runs out of a tenth-wicket stand of 55 in 33 minutes. Pataudi, the third Indian Prince to play cricket for England, emulated 'Ranji' and 'Duleep' by scoring a hundred in his first Test against Australia. The last of Sutcliffe's 16 Test centuries was his highest and his eighth against Australia. With it he overtook the world record 15 of J.B. Hobbs. Hammond scored the 100th century in Test matches involving England in Australia.

AUSTRALIA

W.M. Woodfull*	c Ames b Voce	7	b Larwood		0
W.H. Ponsford	b Larwood	32	b Voce		2
J.H.W. Fingleton	c Allen b Larwood	26	c Voce b Larwood		40
A.F. Kippax	lbw b Larwood	8	(6) b Larwood		19
S.J. McCabe	not out	187	(4) lbw b Hammond		32
V.Y. Richardson	c Hammond b Voce	49	(5) c Voce b Hammond		0
W.A.S. Oldfield†	c Ames b Larwood	4	c Leyland b Larwood		1
C.V. Grimmett	c Ames b Voce	19	c Allen b Larwood		5
L.E. Nagel	b Larwood	0	not out		21
W.J. O'Reilly	b Voce	4	(11) b Voce		7
T.W. Wall	c Allen b Hammond	4	(10) c Ames b Allen		20
Extras	(B 12, LB 4, NB 4)	20	(B 12, LB 2, W 1, NB 2)		17
Total		**360**			**164**

ENGLAND

H. Sutcliffe	lbw b Wall	194	not out	1
R.E.S. Wyatt	lbw b Grimmett	38	not out	0
W.R. Hammond	c Grimmett b Nagel	112		
Nawab of Pataudi, sr	b Nagel	102		
M.Leyland	c Oldfield b Wall	0		
D.R. Jardine*	c Oldfield b McCabe	27		
H. Verity	lbw b Wall	2		
G.O.B. Allen	c and b O'Reilly	19		
L.E.G. Ames†	c McCabe b O'Reilly	0		
H.Larwood	lbw b O'Reilly	0		
W. Voce	not out	0		
Extras	(B 7, LB 17, NB 6)	30		
Total		**524**	(0 wickets)	**1**

ENGLAND	O	M	R	W	O	M	R	W	FALL OF WICKETS			
Larwood	31	5	96	5	18	4	28	5		A	E	A	E
Voce	29	4	110	4	17·3	5	54	2	Wkt	1st	1st	2nd	2nd
Allen	15	1	65	0	9	5	13	1	1st	22	112	2	–
Hammond	14·2	0	34	1	15	6	37	2	2nd	65	300	10	–
Verity	13	4	35	0	4	1	15	0	3rd	82	423	61	–
									4th	87	423	61	–
AUSTRALIA									5th	216	470	100	–
Wall	38	4	104	3					6th	231	479	104	–
Nagel	43·4	9	110	2					7th	299	519	105	–
O'Reilly	67	32	117	3					8th	300	522	113	–
Grimmett	64	22	118	1					9th	305	522	151	–
McCabe	15	2	42	1	0·1	0	1	0	10th	360	524	164	–
Kippax	2	1	3	0									

Umpires: G. Borwick (7) and G.A. Hele (12).

Close: 1st day – A(1) 290-6 (McCabe 127, Grimmett 17); 2nd – E(1) 252-1 (Sutcliffe 116, Hammond 87); 3rd – E(1) 479-6 (Pataudi 80); 4th – A(2) 164-9 (Nagel 21, O'Reilly 7).

AUSTRALIA v ENGLAND 1932–33 (2nd Test)

Played at Melbourne Cricket Ground on 30, 31 December, 2, 3 January.
Toss: Australia.   Result: AUSTRALIA won by 111 runs.
Debuts: Australia – L.P.J. O'Brien.

Bradman, who played on trying to hook his first ball in the first innings, batted for 185 minutes and hit seven fours. Australia's total of 191 remains their lowest against England to contain a century. For the first time England failed to include a specialist slow bowler in their side; on each of three subsequent occasions when this has occurred they have also been defeated. The medium-paced high-bouncing leg-breaks and googlies of O'Reilly reaped the first of three Test match hauls of ten or more wickets.

AUSTRALIA

J.H.W. Fingleton	b Allen	83	c Ames b Allen		1
W.M. Woodfull*	b Allen	10	c Allen b Larwood		26
L.P.J. O'Brien	run out	10	b Larwood		11
D.G. Bradman	b Bowes	0	not out		103
S.J. McCabe	c Jardine b Voce	32	b Allen		0
V.Y. Richardson	c Hammond b Voce	34	lbw b Hammond		32
W.A.S. Oldfield†	not out	27	b Voce		6
C.V. Grimmett	c Sutcliffe b Voce	2	b Voce		0
T.W. Wall	run out	1	lbw b Hammond		3
W.J. O'Reilly	b Larwood	15	c Ames b Hammond		0
H. Ironmonger	b Larwood	4	run out		0
Extras	(B 5, LB 1, W 2, NB 2)	10	(B 3, LB 1, W 4, NB 1)		9
Total		**228**			**191**

ENGLAND

H. Sutcliffe	c Richardson b Wall	52	b O'Reilly		33
R.E.S. Wyatt	lbw b O'Reilly	13	(7) lbw b O'Reilly		25
W.R. Hammond	b Wall	8	(4) c O'Brien b O'Reilly		23
Nawab of Pataudi, sr	b O'Reilly	15	(3) c Fingleton b Ironmonger		5
M. Leyland	b O'Reilly	22	(2) b Wall		19
D.R. Jardine*	c Oldfield b Wall	1	(5) c McCabe b Ironmonger		0
L.E.G. Ames†	b Wall	4	(6) c Fingleton b O'Reilly		2
G.O.B. Allen	c Richardson b O'Reilly	30	st Oldfield b Ironmonger		23
H. Larwood	b O'Reilly	9	c Wall b Ironmonger		4
W. Voce	c McCabe b Grimmett	6	c O'Brien b O'Reilly		0
W.E. Bowes	not out	4	not out		0
Extras	(B 1, LB 2, NB 2)	5	(LB 4, NB 1)		5
Total		**169**			**139**

ENGLAND	O	M	R	W	O	M	R	W
Larwood	20·3	2	52	2	15	2	50	2
Voce	20	3	54	3	15	2	47	2
Allen	17	3	41	2	12	1	44	2
Hammond	10	3	21	0	10·5	2	21	3
Bowes	19	2	50	1	4	0	20	0
AUSTRALIA								
Wall	21	4	52	4	8	2	23	1
O'Reilly	34·3	17	63	5	24	5	66	5
Grimmett	16	4	21	1	4	0	19	0
Ironmonger	14	4	28	0	19·1	8	26	4

FALL OF WICKETS

	A	E	A	E
Wkt	1st	1st	2nd	2nd
1st	29	30	1	53
2nd	67	43	27	53
3rd	67	83	78	70
4th	131	98	81	70
5th	156	104	135	77
6th	188	110	150	85
7th	194	122	156	135
8th	200	138	184	137
9th	222	161	186	138
10th	228	169	191	139

Umpires: G. Borwick (8) and G.A. Hele (13).

Close: 1st day – A(1) 194-7 (Oldfield 13); 2nd – E(1) 161-9 (Allen 26); 3rd – E(2) 43-0 (Sutcliffe 33, Leyland 10).

AUSTRALIA v ENGLAND 1932–33 (3rd Test)

Played at Adelaide Oval on 13, 14, 16, 17, 18, 19 January.
Toss: England,   Result: ENGLAND won by 338 runs.
Debuts: Nil.

This match brought the 'bodyline' or fast leg-theory controversy to its crest. Although Woodfull was struck over the heart and Oldfield, attempting to hook, sustained a fractured skull when the score was 222 for 7, both were accidental injuries involving short balls pitched outside the off stump. When the governing bodies of the two countries exchanged terse cables it seemed that the tour might be abandoned. Woodfull carried his bat through a completed innings against England for the second time. Richardson kept wicket in England's second innings. The match was attended by a record aggregate of 172,926, including 50,962 on the second day.

ENGLAND

H. Sutcliffe	c Wall b O'Reilly	9	c sub (L.P.J. O'Brien) b Wall	7
D.R. Jardine*	b Wall	3	lbw b Ironmonger	56
W.R. Hammond	c Oldfield b Wall	2	(5) b Bradman	85
L.E.G. Ames†	b Ironmonger	3	(7) b O'Reilly	69
M. Leyland	b O'Reilly	83	(6) c Wall b Ironmonger	42
R.E.S. Wyatt	c Richardson b Grimmett	78	(3) c Wall b O'Reilly	49
E. Paynter	c Fingleton b Wall	77	(10) not out	1
G.O.B. Allen	lbw b Grimmett	15	(4) lbw b Grimmett	15
H. Verity	c Richardson b Wall	45	(8) lbw b O'Reilly	40
W. Voce	b Wall	8	(11) b O'Reilly	8
H. Larwood	not out	3	(9) c Bradman b Ironmonger	8
Extras	(B 1, LB 7, NB 7)	15	(B 17, LB 11, NB 4)	32
Total		**341**		**412**

AUSTRALIA

J.H.W. Fingleton	c Ames b Allen	0	b Larwood	0
W.M. Woodfull*	b Allen	22	not out	73
D.G. Bradman	c Allen b Larwood	8	(4) c and b Verity	66
S.J. McCabe	c Jardine b Larwood	8	(5) c Leyland b Allen	7
W.H. Ponsford	b Voce	85	(3) c Jardine b Larwood	3
V.Y. Richardson	b Allen	28	c Allen b Larwood	21
W.A.S. Oldfield†	retired hurt	41	absent hurt	–
C.V. Grimmett	c Voce b Allen	10	(7) b Allen	6
T.W. Wall	b Hammond	6	(8) b Allen	0
W.J. O'Reilly	b Larwood	0	(9) b Larwood	5
H. Ironmonger	not out	0	(10) b Allen	0
Extras	(B 2, LB 11, NB 1)	14	(B 4, LB 2, W 1, NB 5)	12
Total		**222**		**193**

AUSTRALIA	O	M	R	W	O	M	R	W		FALL OF WICKETS			
Wall	34·1	10	72	5	29	6	75	1		E	A	E	A
O'Reilly	50	19	82	2	50·3	21	79	4	*Wkt*	*1st*	*1st*	*2nd*	*2nd*
Ironmonger	20	6	50	1	57	21	87	3	1st	4	1	7	3
Grimmett	28	6	94	2	35	9	74	1	2nd	16	18	91	12
McCabe	14	3	28	0	16	0	42	0	3rd	16	34	123	100
Bradman					4	0	23	1	4th	30	51	154	116
									5th	186	131	245	171
ENGLAND									6th	196	194	296	183
Larwood	25	6	55	3	19	3	71	4	7th	228	212	394	183
Allen	23	4	71	4	17·2	5	50	4	8th	324	222	395	192
Hammond	17·4	4	30	1	9	3	27	0	9th	336	222	403	193
Voce	14	5	21	1	4	1	7	0	10th	341	–	412	–
Verity	16	7	31	0	20	12	26	1					

Umpires: G. Borwick (9) and G.A. Hele (14).

Close: 1st day – E(1) 236-7 (Paynter 25, Verity 5); 2nd – A(1) 109-4 (Ponsford 45, Richardson 21); 3rd – E(2) 85-1 (Jardine 24, Wyatt 47); 4th – E(2) 296-6 (Ames 18); 5th – A(2) 120-4 (Woodfull 36, Richardson 0).

AUSTRALIA v ENGLAND 1932–33 (4th Test)

Played at Woolloongabba, Brisbane, on 10, 11, 13, 14, 15, 16 February.
Toss: Australia.   Result: ENGLAND won by six wickets.
Debuts: Australia – E.H. Bromley, L.S. Darling, H.S.B. Love; England – T.B. Mitchell.

Suffering from acute tonsillitis, Paynter left a nursing home sick-bed to play an historic four-hour innings of 83. Later he struck the six which won the match and regained the Ashes on the day when Archie Jackson had died in Brisbane at the age of 23.

AUSTRALIA

V.Y. Richardson	st Ames b Hammond	83	c Jardine b Verity	32
W.M. Woodfull*	b Mitchell	67	c Hammond b Mitchell	19
D.G. Bradman	b Larwood	76	c Mitchell b Larwood	24
S.J. McCabe	c Jardine b Allen	20	(5) b Verity	22
W.H. Ponsford	b Larwood	19	(4) c Larwood b Allen	0
L.S. Darling	c Ames b Allen	17	run out	39
E.H. Bromley	c Verity b Larwood	26	c Hammond b Allen	7
H.S.B. Love†	lbw b Mitchell	5	lbw b Larwood	3
T.W. Wall	not out	6	c Jardine b Allen	2
W.J. O'Reilly	c Hammond b Larwood	6	b Larwood	4
H. Ironmonger	st Ames b Hammond	8	not out	0
Extras	(B 5, LB 1, NB 1)	7	(B 13, LB 9, NB 1)	23
Total		**340**		**175**

ENGLAND

D.R. Jardine*	c Love b O'Reilly	46	lbw b Ironmonger	24
H. Sutcliffe	lbw b O'Reilly	86	c Darling b Wall	2
W.R. Hammond	b McCabe	20	(4) c Bromley b Ironmonger	14
R.E.S. Wyatt	c Love b Ironmonger	12		
M. Leyland	c Bradman b O'Reilly	12	(3) c McCabe b O'Reilly	86
L.E.G. Ames†	c Darling b Ironmonger	17	(5) not out	14
G.O.B. Allen	c Love b Wall	13		
E. Paynter	c Richardson b Ironmonger	83	(6) not out	14
H. Larwood	b McCabe	23		
H. Verity	not out	23		
T.B. Mitchell	lbw b O'Reilly	0		
Extras	(B 6, LB 12, NB 3)	21	(B 2, LB 4, NB 2)	8
Total		**356**	(4 wickets)	**162**

ENGLAND	O	M	R	W	O	M	R	W
Larwood	31	7	101	4	17·3	3	49	3
Allen	24	4	83	2	17	3	44	3
Hammond	23	5	61	2	10	4	18	0
Mitchell	16	5	49	2	5	0	11	1
Verity	27	12	39	0	19	6	30	2
AUSTRALIA								
Wall	33	6	66	1	7	1	17	1
O'Reilly	67·4	27	120	4	30	11	65	1
Ironmonger	43	19	69	3	35	13	47	2
McCabe	23	7	40	2	7·4	2	25	0
Bromley	10	4	19	0				
Bradman	7	1	17	0				
Darling	2	0	4	0				

FALL OF WICKETS

	A	E	A	E
Wkt	1st	1st	2nd	2nd
1st	133	114	46	5
2nd	200	157	79	78
3rd	233	165	81	118
4th	264	188	91	138
5th	267	198	136	–
6th	292	216	163	–
7th	315	225	169	–
8th	317	264	169	–
9th	329	356	171	–
10th	340	356	175	–

Umpires: G. Borwick (10) and G.A. Hele (15).

Close: 1st day – A(1) 251-3 (Bradman 71, Ponsford 8); 2nd – E(1) 99-0 (Jardine 41, Sutcliffe 51); 3rd – E(1) 271-8 (Paynter 24, Verity 1); 4th – A(2) 108-4 (McCabe 14, Darling 8); 5th – E(2) 107-2 (Leyland 66, Hammond 8).

AUSTRALIA v ENGLAND 1932–33 (5th Test)

Played at Sydney Cricket Ground on 23, 24, 25, 27, 28 February.
Toss: Australia.   Result: ENGLAND won by eight wickets.
Debuts: Australia – H.H. Alexander.

Larwood's innings of 98 in 135 minutes (after bowling 32.2 overs) was the highest by a 'night-watchman' in Tests until 1962, when Nasim-ul-Ghani scored 101 (*Test No. 531*). Although forced to reduce his pace because of a splintered bone in the ball of his left foot, Larwood, in his final Test, extended his analysis for the rubber to 33 wickets at 19.51 runs apiece. Hammond, who earlier had scored his third hundred in successive Test innings at Sydney, ended this infamous rubber by winning the match with a straight drive for six.

AUSTRALIA

V.Y. Richardson	c Jardine b Larwood	0	c Allen b Larwood	0
W.M. Woodfull*	b Larwood	14	b Allen	67
D.G. Bradman	b Larwood	48	b Verity	71
L.P.J. O'Brien	c Larwood b Voce	61	c Verity b Voce	5
S.J. McCabe	c Hammond b Verity	73	c Jardine b Voce	4
L.S. Darling	b Verity	85	c Wyatt b Verity	7
W.A.S. Oldfield†	run out	52	c Wyatt b Verity	5
P.K. Lee	c Jardine b Verity	42	b Allen	15
W.J. O'Reilly	b Allen	19	b Verity	1
H.H. Alexander	not out	17	lbw b Verity	0
H. Ironmonger	b Larwood	1	not out	0
Extras	(B 13, LB 9, W 1)	23	(B 4, NB 3)	7
Total		**435**		**182**

ENGLAND

D.R. Jardine*	c Oldfield b O'Reilly	18	c Richardson b Ironmonger	24
H. Sutcliffe	c Richardson b O'Reilly	56		
W.R. Hammond	lbw b Lee	101	(4) not out	75
H. Larwood	c Ironmonger b Lee	98		
M. Leyland	run out	42	(3) b Ironmonger	0
R.E.S. Wyatt	c Ironmonger b O'Reilly	51	(2) not out	61
L.E.G. Ames†	run out	4		
E. Paynter	b Lee	9		
G.O.B. Allen	c Bradman b Lee	48		
H. Verity	c Oldfield b Alexander	4		
W. Voce	not out	7		
Extras	(B 7, LB 7, NB 2)	16	(B 6, LB 1, NB 1)	8
Total		**454**	(2 wickets)	**168**

ENGLAND	O	M	R	W	O	M	R	W
Larwood	32·2	10	98	4	11	0	44	1
Voce	24	4	80	1	10	0	34	2
Allen	25	1	128	1	11·4	2	54	2
Hammond	8	0	32	0	3	0	10	0
Verity	17	3	62	3	19	9	33	5
Wyatt	2	0	12	0				
AUSTRALIA								
Alexander	35	1	129	1	11	2	25	0
McCabe	12	1	27	0	5	2	10	0
O'Reilly	45	7	100	3	15	5	32	0
Ironmonger	31	13	64	0	26	12	34	2
Lee	40·2	11	111	4	12·2	3	52	0
Darling	7	5	3	0	2	0	7	0
Bradman	1	0	4	0				

FALL OF WICKETS

	A	E	A	E
Wkt	1st	1st	2nd	2nd
1st	0	31	0	43
2nd	59	153	115	43
3rd	64	245	135	–
4th	163	310	139	–
5th	244	330	148	–
6th	328	349	161	–
7th	385	374	177	–
8th	414	418	178	–
9th	430	434	178	–
10th	435	454	182	

Umpires: G. Borwick (11) and G.A. Hele (16).

Close: 1st day – A(1) 296-5 (Darling 66, Oldfield 13); 2nd – E(1) 159-2 (Hammond 72, Larwood 5); 3rd – E(1) 418-8 (Allen 25); 4th – E(2) 11-0 (Jardine 6, Wyatt 5).

NEW ZEALAND v ENGLAND 1932–33 (1st Test)

Played at Lancaster Park, Christchurch, on 24, 25, 27 March.
Toss: England.   Result: MATCH DRAWN.
Debuts: New Zealand – D.L. Freeman, H.D. Smith, P.E. Whitelaw.

Sutcliffe was the fourth batsman to be dismissed by the first ball of a Test match. Smith took the wicket of Paynter with his first ball in his only match for New Zealand. Hammond, who reached his century in 160 minutes, and Ames added 242 runs in 144 minutes for what is still the record fifth-wicket partnership by either side in this series. When bad light stopped play 20 minutes early, England were 418 for 5 (Hammond 223 not out), and their final total was their highest against New Zealand until 1962-63 (*Test No. 540*). A violent dust storm, followed by poor light and then rain, ended the match at 3.30 on the last afternoon.

ENGLAND

H. Sutcliffe	c James b Badcock	0
E. Paynter	b Smith	0
W.R. Hammond	b Badcock	227
R.E.S. Wyatt	run out	20
D.R. Jardine*	c James b Badcock	45
L.E.G. Ames†	b Vivian	103
F.R. Brown	c Kerr b Page	74
W. Voce	c Dempster b Page	66
M.W. Tate	not out	10
G.O.B. Allen	} did not bat	
H. Verity	}	
Extras	(B 8, LB 7)	15
Total	(8 wickets declared)	**560**

NEW ZEALAND

C.S. Dempster	c Wyatt b Allen	8	not out	14
P.E. Whitelaw	c Brown b Verity	30	not out	17
G.L. Weir	c Hammond b Voce	66		
J.L. Kerr	c Hammond b Brown	59		
M.L. Page*	c Voce b Allen	22		
K.C. James†	lbw b Tate	2		
H.D. Smith	b Tate	4		
J. Newman	b Voce	5		
D.L. Freeman	b Voce	1		
F.T. Badcock	not out	10		
H.G. Vivian	absent hurt	–		
Extras	(B 3, LB 10, NB 3)	16	(LB 1, NB 3)	4
Total		**223**	(0 wickets)	**35**

NEW ZEALAND	O	M	R	W	O	M	R	W
Badcock	54	11	142	3				
Smith	20	0	113	1				
Newman	25	5	91	0				
Freeman	20	2	78	0				
Vivian	19	1	72	1				
Weir	7	0	28	0				
Page	2·3	0	21	2				
ENGLAND								
Tate	37	16	42	2	3	1	5	0
Voce	17·1	3	27	3	4	0	13	0
Allen	20	5	46	2	4·1	1	5	0
Brown	19	10	34	1				
Verity	23	7	58	1	3	1	6	0
Hammond					2	0	2	0

FALL OF WICKETS

Wkt	E 1st	NZ 1st	NZ 2nd
1st	0	25	–
2nd	4	59	–
3rd	46	153	–
4th	133	186	–
5th	375	194	–
6th	424	205	–
7th	532	211	–
8th	560	212	–
9th	–	223	–
10th	–	–	–

Umpires: T.W. Burgess (1) and R.C. Torrance (1).

Close: 1st day – E(1) 418-5 (Hammond 223, Brown 12); 2nd – NZ(1) 153-3 (Kerr 42).

NEW ZEALAND v ENGLAND 1932–33 (2nd Test)

Played at Eden Park, Auckland, on 31 March, 1, 3 April.
Toss: New Zealand.   Result: MATCH DRAWN.
Debuts: New Zealand – J.A. Dunning.

Hammond's innings set a new record for the highest score in Test matches and was made out of 492 in only 318 minutes. He hit ten sixes (the Test record), three of them off successive balls from Newman, and 34 fours. His 300 took 288 minutes and remains the fastest Test triple century. His third hundred took only 47 minutes. Rain caused the match to be abandoned after New Zealand had doubled their overnight total on the final morning. Hammond's average of 563.00 is the highest for any Test rubber.

NEW ZEALAND

P.E. Whitelaw	b Bowes	12	not out	5
J.E. Mills	b Bowes	0	not out	11
G.L. Weir	b Bowes	0		
C.S. Dempster	not out	83		
J.L. Kerr	lbw b Voce	10		
M.L. Page*	st Duckworth b Mitchell	20		
F.T. Badcock	b Bowes	1		
K.C. James†	b Bowes	0		
J.A. Dunning	b Bowes	12		
J. Newman	b Voce	5		
D.L. Freeman	run out	1		
Extras	(B 9, LB 4, NB 1)	14		
Total		**158**	(0 wickets)	**16**

ENGLAND

H. Sutcliffe	c Weir b Freeman	24
R.E.S. Wyatt*	b Dunning	60
W.R. Hammond	not out	336
E. Paynter	b Dunning	36
L.E.G. Ames	b Badcock	26
G.O.B. Allen	b Badcock	12
F.R. Brown	c Page b Weir	13
W. Voce	b Weir	16
G. Duckworth†	not out	6
W.E. Bowes)	did not bat	
T.B. Mitchell)		
Extras	(B 7, LB 6, W 1, NB 5)	19
Total	(7 wickets declared)	**548**

ENGLAND	O	M	R	W	O	M	R	W		FALL OF WICKETS		
										NZ	E	NZ
Allen	5	2	11	0	3	1	4	0	*Wkt*	*1st*	*1st*	*2nd*
Bowes	19	5	34	6	2	0	4	0	1st	0	56	–
Mitchell	18	1	49	1					2nd	0	139	–
Voce	9·5	3	20	2	1·3	0	2	0	3rd	31	288	–
Brown	2	0	19	0					4th	62	347	–
Hammond	3	0	11	0	2	0	6	0	5th	98	407	–
NEW ZEALAND									6th	101	456	–
Badcock	59	16	126	2					7th	103	500	–
Dunning	43	5	156	2					8th	123	–	–
Freeman	20	1	91	1					9th	149	–	–
Newman	17	2	87	0					10th	158	–	–
Page	6	2	30	0								
Weir	11	2	39	2								

Umpires: K.H. Cave (6) and J.T. Forrester (2).

Close: 1st day – E(1) 127-1 (Wyatt 56, Hammond 41); 2nd – NZ(2) 8-0 (Whitelaw 4, Mills 4).

ENGLAND v WEST INDIES 1933 (1st Test)

Played at Lord's, London, on 24, 26, 27 June.
Toss: England.   Result: ENGLAND won by an innings and 27 runs.
Debuts: England – C.F. Walters; West Indies – E.A. Martindale, C.A. Merry.

Nelson Cricket Club refused to release Constantine for this match. Francis, currently professional to Radcliffe in the Bolton League was brought in to strengthen the bowling. Rain allowed only 45 minutes' play in two instalments on the first day when King George V visited the ground. Roach completed a 'pair' off the first ball when West Indies followed on.

ENGLAND

C.F. Walters	c Barrow b Martindale	51
H. Sutcliffe	c Grant b Martindale	21
W.R. Hammond	c Headley b Griffith	29
M. Leyland	c Barrow b Griffith	1
D.R. Jardine*	c Da Costa b Achong	21
M.J.L. Turnbull	c Barrow b Achong	28
L.E.G. Ames†	not out	83
G.O.B. Allen	run out	16
R.W.V. Robins	b Martindale	8
H. Verity	c Achong b Griffith	21
G.G. Macaulay	lbw b Martindale	9
Extras	(B 3, LB 5)	8
Total		**296**

WEST INDIES

C.A. Roach	b Allen	0	c Sutcliffe b Macaulay	0
I. Barrow†	c and b Verity	7	lbw b Robins	12
G.A. Headley	lbw b Allen	13	b Allen	50
E.L.G. Hoad	lbw b Robins	6	c and b Verity	36
G.C. Grant*	hit wkt b Robins	26	lbw b Macaulay	28
O.C. Da Costa	b Robins	6	lbw b Verity	1
C.A. Merry	lbw b Macaulay	9	b Macaulay	1
E.E. Achong	b Robins	15	c Hammond b Verity	10
G.N. Francis	b Robins	4	(10) not out	11
E.A. Martindale	b Robins	4	(9) b Macaulay	4
H.C. Griffith	not out	1	b Verity	18
Extras	(B 3, LB 1, NB 2)	6	(B 1)	1
Total		**97**		**172**

WEST INDIES	O	M	R	W	O	M	R	W
Martindale	24	3	85	4				
Francis	18	3	52	0				
Griffith	20	7	48	3				
Achong	35	9	88	2				
Da Costa	4	0	15	0				
ENGLAND								
Macaulay	18	7	25	1	20	6	57	4
Allen	13	6	13	2	11	2	33	1
Verity	16	8	21	1	18·1	4	45	4
Robins	11·5	1	32	6	12	2	36	1

FALL OF WICKETS

Wkt	E 1st	WI 1st	WI 2nd
1st	49	1	0
2nd	103	17	56
3rd	105	27	64
4th	106	31	116
5th	154	40	119
6th	155	51	120
7th	194	87	133
8th	217	92	138
9th	265	96	146
10th	296	97	172

Umpires: F. Chester (13) and A. Dolphin (1).

Close: 1st day – E(1) 43-0 (Walters 21, Sutcliffe 19); 2nd – WI(1) 55-6 (Grant 11, Achong 2).

ENGLAND v WEST INDIES 1933 (2nd Test)

Played at Old Trafford, Manchester, on 22, 24, 25 July.
Toss: West Indies.   Result: MATCH DRAWN.
Debuts: England – James Langridge (*elder brother of John George Langridge, also of Sussex*); West
Indies – V.A. Valentine, C.A. Wiles.

Barrow and Headley added 200 in 205 minutes and made the first hundreds for West Indies in England.
Martindale and Constantine gave England's batsmen an exhibition of the 'bodyline' bowling in which their
bowlers had indulged in Australia earlier that year. Hammond retired with a cut chin but Jardine gave the perfect
rejoinder by scoring his only Test century. Macaulay injured his foot while fielding in what proved to be his last
Test. Langridge, in his first, completed the double of 1,000 runs and 100 wickets in first-class matches for the
season during his best analysis for England.

WEST INDIES

C.A. Roach	b Clark	13	lbw b Langridge		64
I. Barrow†	b Wyatt	105	c Langridge b Clark		0
G.A. Headley	not out	169	c and b Langridge		24
E.L.G. Hoad	b Clark	1	c Hammond b Langridge		14
G.C. Grant*	c Ames b Robins	16	c Hammond b Langridge		14
L.N. Constantine	c Robins b Clark	31	(7) b Langridge		64
C.A. Wiles	c Hammond b Verity	0	(6) st Ames b Langridge		2
O.C. Da Costa	b Clark	20	c Sutcliffe b Clark ·		0
E.E. Achong	b Verity	6	c Ames b Langridge		10
V.A. Valentine	b Robins	6	not out		19
E.A. Martindale	b Robins	2	c Verity b Robins		1
Extras	(LB 6)	6	(B 8, LB 4, NB 1)		13
Total		**375**			**225**

ENGLAND

C.F. Walters	lbw b Martindale	46
H. Sutcliffe	run out	20
W.R. Hammond	c Martindale b Constantine	34
R.E.S. Wyatt	c Constantine b Martindale	18
D.R. Jardine*	c Constantine b Martindale	127
L.E.G. Ames†	c Headley b Martindale	47
J. Langridge	c Grant b Achong	9
R.W.V. Robins	st Barrow b Achong	55
H. Verity	not out	0
E.W. Clark	b Martindale	0
G.G. Macaulay	absent hurt	–
Extras	(B 7, LB 6, W 1, NB 4)	18
Total		**374**

ENGLAND	O	M	R	W	O	M	R	W		FALL OF WICKETS		
Clark	40	8	99	4	15	1	64	2		WI	E	WI
Macaulay	14	2	48	0					*Wkt*	*1st*	*1st*	*2nd*
Robins	28·4	2	111	3	11·1	0	41	1	1st	26	63	5
Verity	32	14	47	2	13	2	40	0	2nd	226	83	86
Hammond	5	0	27	0					3rd	227	118	95
Langridge	9	1	23	0	17	4	56	7	4th	266	134	112
Wyatt	7	1	14	1	4	1	11	0	5th	302	217	118
									6th	306	234	131
WEST INDIES									7th	341	374	132
Martindale	23·4	4	73	5					8th	354	374	191
Constantine	25	5	55	1					9th	363	374	214
Valentine	28	8	49	0					10th	375	–	225
Achong	37	9	90	2								
Headley	15	1	65	0								
Grant	2	0	12	0								
Da Costa	10	6	12	0								

Umpires: J. Hardstaff, sr (15) and E.J. Smith (1).

Close: 1st day – WI(1) 333-6 (Headley 145, Da Costa 16); 2nd – E(1) 263-6 (Jardine 68, Robins 6).

ENGLAND v WEST INDIES 1933 (3rd Test)

Played at Kennington Oval, London, on 12, 14, 15 August.
Toss: England.   Result: ENGLAND won by an innings and 17 runs.
Debuts: England – C.J. Barnett, C.S. Marriott; West Indies – B.J. Sealey

England, without a Surrey player in a Test at The Oval for the first time, completed their second innings victory of the rubber after ten minutes of play on the third day. 'Father' Marriott, playing in his only Test, took 11 for 96 with his leg-breaks and googlies. Only F. Martin, with 12 for 102 in 1890 (*Test No. 34*), has achieved better figures on debut for England. In the second innings Grant retired after being struck on the arm, and Roach took only 33 minutes to score 50 – then the fastest for West Indies.

ENGLAND

C.F. Walters	c Merry b Martindale	2
A.H. Bakewell	c Headley b Sealey	107
W.R. Hammond	c Barrow b Valentine	11
R.E.S. Wyatt*	c Achong b Martindale	15
M.J.L. Turnbull	b Martindale	4
J. Langridge	c Barrow b Da Costa	22
L.E.G. Ames†	c Headley b Martindale	37
C.J. Barnett	run out	52
M.S. Nichols	b Achong	49
E.W. Clark	not out	8
C.S. Marriott	b Martindale	0
Extras	(LB 5)	5
Total		**312**

WEST INDIES

C.A. Roach	c Bakewell b Clark	8		lbw b Marriott	56
I. Barrow†	c Ames b Clark	3		c Ames b Clark	16
G.A. Headley	st Ames b Marriott	9	(5)	c Ames b Clark	12
O.C. Da Costa	c Bakewell b Clark	8	(3)	b Marriott	35
B.J. Sealey	c Ames b Nichols	29	(4)	b Marriott	12
C.A. Merry	b Marriott	13	(7)	c Barnett b Nichols	11
G.C. Grant*	b Marriott	4	(6)	c Ames b Nichols	14
E.E. Achong	run out	4		c Ames b Marriott	22
V.A. Valentine	c Langridge b Marriott	10		c Barnett b Marriott	0
E.A. Martindale	not out	1		not out	9
H.C. Griffith	st Ames b Marriott	0		c and b Marriott	0
Extras	(B 1, LB 10)	11		(LB 7, NB 1)	8
Total		**100**			**195**

WEST INDIES	O	M	R	W	O	M	R	W	FALL OF WICKETS			
										E	WI	WI
Martindale	24·5	2	93	5					*Wkt*	*1st*	*1st*	*2nd*
Griffith	20	4	44	0					1st	2	7	77
Valentine	20	6	55	1					2nd	27	26	79
Da Costa	12	2	30	1					3rd	64	38	113
Achong	23	3	59	1					4th	68	44	138
Headley	4	0	16	0					5th	147	68	138
Sealey	5	1	10	1					6th	194	74	151
									7th	208	88	160
ENGLAND									8th	303	95	183
Clark	8	3	16	3	21	10	54	2	9th	305	100	195
Nichols	10	1	36	1	14	3	51	2	10th	312	100	195
Marriott	11·5	2	37	5	29·2	6	59	6				
Langridge					7	1	23	0				

Umpires: F. Chester (14) and J. Hardstaff, sr (16).

Close: 1st day – E(1) 312 all out; 2nd – WI(2) 190-8 (Achong 22, Martindale 4).

INDIA v ENGLAND 1933–34 (1st Test)

Played at Gymkhana Ground, Bombay, on 15, 16, 17, 18 December.
Toss: India.   Result: ENGLAND won by nine wickets.
Debuts: India – L. Amarnath, L.P. Jai, R.J.D. Jamshedji, V.M. Merchant, L. Ramji;
  England – A. Mitchell, B.H. Valentine.

India's first official home Test was played on the first of three Test match grounds in Bombay. It was the first Test match to include Sunday play and the only one to be staged on the Gymkhana Ground. Valentine and Amarnath scored the first hundreds of this series, both achieving the feat on debut. The fast bowling of Nichols brought the reward of eight wickets in return for 47.1 overs of unstinting effort in great heat; he also contributed three catches, including a superb one low at fine-leg to dismiss Amarnath.

INDIA

S. Wazir Ali	lbw b Nichols	36	c Nichols b Clark		5
J.G. Navle†	c Nichols b Verity	13	c Elliott b Clark		4
L. Amarnath	lbw b Langridge	38	c Nichols b Clark		118
C.K. Nayudu*	lbw b Clark	28	c Valentine b Nichols		67
L.P. Jai	c Mitchell b Langridge	19	c Jardine b Nichols		0
V.M. Merchant	lbw b Nichols	23	c Elliott b Langridge		30
S.H.M. Colah	c Elliott b Nichols	31	(8) c Elliott b Nichols		12
L. Amar Singh	st Elliott b Langridge	0	(7) lbw b Verity		1
Mahomed Nissar	c Mitchell b Verity	13	lbw b Nichols		1
L. Ramji	b Verity	1	(11) lbw b Nichols		0
R.J.D. Jamshedji	not out	4	(10) not out		1
Extras	(B 2, LB 5, NB 6)	13	(B 4, LB 6, W 1, NB 8)		19
Total		**219**			**258**

ENGLAND

A. Mitchell	b Nissar	5	lbw b Amar Singh		9
C.F. Walters	c Merchant b Amar Singh	78	not out		14
C.J. Barnett	c and b Jamshedji	33	not out		17
J. Langridge	lbw b Nissar	31			
D.R. Jardine*	b Nissar	60			
B.H. Valentine	c Merchant b Jamshedji	136			
L.F. Townsend	c and b Jamshedji	15			
M.S. Nichols	run out	2			
H. Verity	c Ramji b Nissar	24			
H. Elliott†	not out	37			
E.W. Clark	b Nissar	1			
Extras	(B 7, LB 9)	16			
Total		**438**	(1 wicket)		**40**

ENGLAND	O	M	R	W	O	M	R	W	FALL OF WICKETS				
Nichols	23·2	8	53	3	23·5	7	55	5		I	E	I	E
Clark	13	3	41	1	19	5	69	3	Wkt	1st	1st	2nd	2nd
Barnett	2	1	1	0					1st	44	12	9	15
Verity	27	11	44	3	20	9	50	1	2nd	71	67	21	–
Langridge	17	4	42	3	16	7	32	1	3rd	117	143	207	–
Townsend	9	2	25	0	12	5	33	0	4th	135	164	208	–
									5th	148	309	208	–
INDIA									6th	175	362	214	–
Nissar	33·5	3	90	5	4	1	25	0	7th	186	371	248	–
Ramji	23	5	64	0					8th	209	373	249	–
Amar Singh	36	5	119	1	3·2	1	15	1	9th	212	431	258	–
Jamshedji	35	4	137	3					10th	219	438	258	–
Nayudu	7	2	10	0									
Amarnath	2	1	2	0									

Umpires: J.W. Hitch (1) and F.A. Tarrant (1).

Close: 1st day – I(1) 212-9 (Colah 28, Jamshedji 0); 2nd – E(1) 294-4 (Jardine 53, Valentine 79); 3rd – I(2) 159-2 (Amarnath 102, Nayudu 44).

INDIA v ENGLAND 1933–34 (2nd Test)

Played at Eden Gardens, Calcutta, on 5, 6, 7, 8 January.
Toss: England.   Result: MATCH DRAWN.
Debuts: India – Dilawar Hussain, M.J. Gopalan, Mushtaq Ali, C.S. Nayudu;
  England – W.H.V. Levett.

Dilawar Hussain retired hurt at 11, struck on the back of the head by a ball from Nichols, after scoring 7 in the first innings but recovered to become the first to score two fifties in a Test for India. Following on, India were 30 for 4 and still 126 runs in arrears at the start of the last day. Hussain and the brothers Nayudu ensured that England's eventual target was an impossible 82 runs in half an hour, 'C.S.' making only four scoring strokes in 135 minutes.

ENGLAND

C.F. Walters	c Gopalan b Amar Singh	29	not out		2
A. Mitchell	c Gopalan b C.K. Nayudu	47			
C.J. Barnett	lbw b Amar Singh	8	(2) c Gopalan b Nissar		0
J. Langridge	c Nissar b Gopalan	70			
D.R. Jardine*	c C.S. Nayudu b Mushtaq Ali	61			
B.H. Valentine	lbw b C.K. Nayudu	40	(3) st Hussain b Naoomal		3
W.H.V. Levett†	b C.K. Nayudu	5	(4) not out		2
M.S. Nichols	lbw b Nissar	13			
L.F. Townsend	c Hussain b Amar Singh	40			
H. Verity	not out	55			
E.W. Clark	c Merchant b Amar Singh	10			
Extras	(B 13, LB 10, NB 2)	25			
Total		**403**	(2 wickets)		**7**

INDIA

Naoomal Jeoomal	c Jardine b Nichols	2	c Levett b Townsend		43
Dilawar Hussain†	c Jardine b Clark	59	(7) b Clark		57
S. Wazir Ali	c Nichols b Verity	39	c Nichols b Verity		0
C.K. Nayudu*	b Clark	5	lbw b Verity		38
L. Amarnath	c Jardine b Clark	0	c Levett b Clark		9
V.M. Merchant	b Verity	54	c Jardine b Verity		17
Mushtaq Ali	lbw b Nichols	9	(2) c Barnett b Nichols		18
C.S. Nayudu	c Verity b Nichols	36	lbw b Verity		15
L. Amar Singh	c Nichols b Verity	10	c Jardine b Townsend		18
M.J. Gopalan	not out	11	c Levett b Clark		7
Mahomed Nissar	c Walters b Verity	2	not out		0
Extras	(B 5, LB 5, NB 10)	20	(B 10, LB 4, NB 1)		15
Total		**247**			**237**

INDIA	O	M	R	W	O	M	R	W		FALL OF WICKETS			
Nissar	34	6	112	1	2	1	2	1		E	I	I	E
Amar Singh	54·5	13	106	4	2	1	1	0	*Wkt*	*1st*	*1st*	*2nd*	*2nd*
Gopalan	19	7	39	1					1st	45	12	57	0
Mushtaq Ali	19	5	45	1					2nd	55	23	58	5
Amarnath	2	0	10	0					3rd	135	27	76	–
C.S. Nayudu	8	1	26	0					4th	185	90	88	–
C.K. Nayudu	23	7	40	3					5th	256	131	129	–
Naoomal					1	0	4	1	6th	281	158	149	–
									7th	281	211	201	–
ENGLAND									8th	301	223	214	–
Clark	26	8	39	3	19·3	4	50	3	9th	371	236	230	–
Nichols	28	6	78	3	20	6	48	1	10th	403	247	237	–
Verity	28·4	13	64	4	31	12	76	4					
Langridge	17	7	27	0	10	4	19	0					
Townsend	8	4	19	0	8	3	22	2					
Barnett					2	0	7	0					

Umpires: J.W. Hitch (2) and F.A. Tarrant (2).

Close: 1st day – E(1) 257-5 (Jardine 42, Levett 0); 2nd – I(1) 90-4 (Merchant 26); 3rd – I(2) 30-0 (Naoomal 14, Mushtaq Ali 10).

INDIA v ENGLAND 1933–34 (3rd Test)

Played at Chepauk, Madras, on 10, 11, 12, 13 February.
Toss: England.   Result: ENGLAND won by 202 runs.
Debuts: India – The Yuvraj of Patiala (*later Lt-Gen. Yadavendra Singh, Maharaja of Patiala*).

Naoomal Jeoomal played no further part in the match after retiring with a gashed head when he edged a ball from Clark. Amar Singh, who cut and swung the ball at fast-medium pace off a short run, conceded less than two runs an over in returning the best figures of his Test career. The left-arm spin of Verity and Langridge accounted for all but one of the 18 Indian wickets to fall. In his final match for England Jardine contributed exactly 100 runs. India provided the second instance after South Africa in *Test No. 134* of a side playing two pairs of brothers in the same Test (C.K. and C.S. Nayudu, and Nazir and Wazir Ali).

ENGLAND

A.H. Bakewell	c C.S. Nayudu b Amarnath	85		c Patiala b Amar Singh	4
C.F. Walters	lbw b Amar Singh	59		c sub (M.J. Gopalan) b Amarnath	102
A. Mitchell	lbw b Amarnath	25	(8)	c and b Amarnath	28
J. Langridge	lbw b Amar Singh	1	(6)	c Hussain b Nazir Ali	46
D.R. Jardine*	c Wazir Ali b Amar Singh	65	(7)	not out	35
C.J. Barnett	c Patiala b Amar Singh	4	(3)	c Mushtaq Ali b Nazir Ali	26
M.S. Nichols	b Amar Singh	1	(5)	c Hussain b Nazir Ali	8
L.F. Townsend	b Amar Singh	10	(4)	c C.K. Nayudu b Nazir Ali	8
H. Verity	lbw b Mushtaq Ali	42			
H. Elliott†	c Mushtaq Ali b Amar Singh	14			
E.W. Clark	not out	4			
Extras	(B 22, LB 2, NB 1)	25		(B 1, LB 3)	4
Total		**335**		(7 wickets declared)	**261**

INDIA

Dilawar Hussain†	c Barnett b Verity	13		b Langridge	36
Naoomal Jeoomal	retired hurt	5		absent hurt	–
S. Wazir Ali	b Nichols	2		c Mitchell b Verity	21
C.K. Nayudu*	b Verity	20	(5)	st Elliott b Langridge	2
L. Amarnath	c Elliott b Langridge	12	(8)	not out	26
V.M. Merchant	b Verity	26		c and b Verity	28
Yuvraj of Patiala	b Verity	24		c Elliott b Langridge	60
S. Nazir Ali	c Mitchell b Verity	3	(9)	c Nichols b Langridge	8
C.S. Nayudu	c Nichols b Verity	11	(10)	st Elliott b Verity	0
Mushtaq Ali	not out	7	(2)	c Mitchell b Verity	8
L. Amar Singh	c Barnett b Verity	16	(4)	c Barnett b Langridge	48
Extras	(B 1, LB 3, NB 2)	6		(B 10, LB 1, NB 1)	12
Total		**145**			**249**

INDIA	O	M	R	W	O	M	R	W			
Amar Singh	44·4	13	86	7	23	6	55	1			
C.K. Nayudu	11	1	32	0	9	0	38	0			
Amarnath	31	14	69	2	11·5	3	32	2			
Mushtaq Ali	25	3	64	1	4	0	16	0			
C.S. Nayudu	13	1	43	0	2	0	17	0			
Naoomal	6	0	16	0							
Wazir Ali	1	1	0	0	3	0	16	0			
Nazir Ali					23	1	83	4			

FALL OF WICKETS

Wkt	E 1st	I 1st	E 2nd	I 2nd
1st	111	15	10	16
2nd	167	39	76	45
3rd	170	42	90	119
4th	174	66	102	120
5th	178	99	184	125
6th	182	107	209	209
7th	208	122	261	237
8th	305	127	–	248
9th	317	145	–	249
10th	335	–	–	–

ENGLAND	O	M	R	W	O	M	R	W
Clark	15	4	37	0	8	2	27	0
Nichols	12	3	30	1	6	1	23	0
Verity	23·5	10	49	7	27·2	6	104	4
Langridge	6	1	9	1	24	5	63	5
Townsend	3	0	14	0	3	0	19	0
Barnett					1	0	1	0

Umpires: J.B. Higgins (1) and J.W. Hitch (3).

Close: 1st day – E(1) 281-7 (Jardine 44, Verity 31); 2nd – I(1) 145-9 (Mushtaq Ali 7); 3rd – I(2) 65-2 (Dilawar Hussain 16, Amar Singh 18).

ENGLAND v AUSTRALIA 1934 (1st Test)

Played at Trent Bridge, Nottingham, on 8, 9, 11, 12 June.
Toss: Australia.   Result: AUSTRALIA won by 238 runs.
Debuts: England – K. Farnes; Australia – W.A. Brown, A.G. Chipperfield.

England were without the three major exponents of 'bodyline'; Jardine, Larwood and Voce. This was Australia's only victory against England between 1928 and 1938 gained without Bradman contributing a century, and it was completed with only ten minutes to spare. Walters captained England in his first Test against Australia because Wyatt (fractured thumb), was unavailable. Chipperfield was the first batsman to miss a hundred on Test debut by just one run; not out 99 at lunch, he was dismissed by the third ball afterwards.

AUSTRALIA

W.M. Woodfull*	c Verity b Farnes	26	b Farnes		2
W.H. Ponsford	c Ames b Farnes	53	b Hammond		5
W.A. Brown	lbw b Geary	22	c Ames b Verity		73
D.G. Bradman	c Hammond b Geary	29	c Ames b Farnes		25
S.J. McCabe	c Leyland b Farnes	65	c Hammond b Farnes		88
L.S. Darling	b Verity	4	c Hammond b Farnes		14
A.G. Chipperfield	c Ames b Farnes	99	c Hammond b Farnes		4
W.A.S. Oldfield†	c Hammond b Mitchell	20	not out		10
C.V. Grimmett	b Geary	39	(10) not out		3
W.J. O'Reilly	b Farnes	7	(9) c Verity b Geary		18
T.W. Wall	not out	0			
Extras	(B 4, LB 5, NB 1)	10	(B 22, LB 9)		31
Total		**374**	(8 wickets declared)		**273**

ENGLAND

C.F. Walters*	lbw b Grimmett	17	b O'Reilly		46
H. Sutcliffe	c Chipperfield b Grimmett	62	c Chipperfield b O'Reilly		24
W.R. Hammond	c McCabe b O'Reilly	25	st Oldfield b Grimmett		16
Nawab of Pataudi, sr	c McCabe b Wall	12	c Ponsford b Grimmett		10
M. Leyland	c and b Grimmett	6	(6) c Oldfield b O'Reilly		18
E.H. Hendren	b O'Reilly	79	(5) c Chipperfield b O'Reilly		3
L.E.G. Ames†	c Wall b O'Reilly	7	b O'Reilly		12
G. Geary	st Oldfield b Grimmett	53	c Chipperfield b Grimmett		0
H. Verity	b O'Reilly	0	not out		0
K. Farnes	b Grimmett	1	c Oldfield b O'Reilly		0
T.B. Mitchell	not out	1	lbw b O'Reilly		4
Extras	(B 5)	5	(B 4, LB 3, NB 1)		8
Total		**268**			**141**

ENGLAND	O	M	R	W	O	M	R	W
Farnes	40·2	10	102	5	25	3	77	5
Geary	43	8	101	3	23	5	46	1
Hammond	13	4	29	0	12	5	25	1
Verity	34	9	65	1	17	8	48	1
Mitchell	21	4	62	1	13	2	46	0
Leyland	1	0	5	0				
AUSTRALIA								
Wall	33	7	82	1	13	2	27	0
McCabe	7	2	7	0	2	0	7	0
Grimmett	58·3	24	81	5	47	28	39	3
O'Reilly	37	16	75	4	41·4	24	54	7
Chipperfield	3	0	18	0	4	1	6	0

FALL OF WICKETS

	A	E	A	E
Wkt	1st	1st	2nd	2nd
1st	77	45	2	51
2nd	88	102	32	83
3rd	125	106	69	91
4th	146	114	181	103
5th	153	145	219	110
6th	234	165	231	134
7th	281	266	244	135
8th	355	266	267	137
9th	374	266	–	137
10th	374	268	–	141

Umpires: F. Chester (15) and A. Dolphin (2).

Close: 1st day – A(1) 207-5 (McCabe 50, Chipperfield 17); 2nd – E(1)128-4 (Pataudi 6, Hendren 0); 3rd – A(2) 159-3 (Brown 37, McCabe 74).

ENGLAND v AUSTRALIA 1934 (2nd Test)

Played at Lord's, London, on 22, 23, 25 June.
Toss: England.   Result: ENGLAND won by an innings and 38 runs.
Debuts: Nil.

Verity took 14 wickets for 80 runs on the third day – six of them in the last hour – to give England their first win against Australia at Lord's since 1896. His performance still stands as the record for most Test wickets in a day in Tests between England and Australia and led to the BBC allowing commentator Howard Marshall a scorer/assistant (Arthur Wrigley) at the next Test. His match analysis of 15 for 104 was then the best for England against Australia and has been surpassed only by J.C. Laker's 19 for 90 (*Test No. 428*). Ames was the only wicket-keeper to score a hundred in this series until 1974-75 (A.P.E. Knott in *Test No. 754*). Oldfield became the first to make 100 dismissals and to complete the wicket-keepers' double in Test cricket when he stumped Verity on the second day.

ENGLAND

C.F. Walters	c Bromley b O'Reilly	82
H. Sutcliffe	lbw b Chipperfield	20
W.R. Hammond	c and b Chipperfield	2
E.H. Hendren	c McCabe b Wall	13
R.E.S. Wyatt*	c Oldfield b Chipperfield	33
M. Leyland	b Wall	109
L.E.G. Ames†	c Oldfield b McCabe	120
G. Geary	c Chipperfield b Wall	9
H. Verity	st Oldfield b Grimmett	29
K. Farnes	b Wall	1
W.E. Bowes	not out	10
Extras	(LB 12)	12
Total		**440**

AUSTRALIA

W.M. Woodfull*	b Bowes	22		c Hammond b Verity	43
W.A. Brown	c Ames b Bowes	105		c Walters b Bowes	2
D.G. Bradman	c and b Verity	36	(4)	c Ames b Verity	13
S.J. McCabe	c Hammond b Verity	34	(3)	c Hendren b Verity	19
L.S. Darling	c Sutcliffe b Verity	0		b Hammond	10
A.G. Chipperfield	not out	37		c Geary b Verity	14
E.H. Bromley	c Geary b Verity	4		c and b Verity	1
W.A.S. Oldfield†	c Sutcliffe b Verity	23		lbw b Verity	0
C.V. Grimmett	b Bowes	9		c Hammond b Verity	0
W.J. O'Reilly	b Verity	4		not out	8
T.W. Wall	lbw b Verity	0		c Hendren b Verity	1
Extras	(B 1, LB 9)	10		(B 6, NB 1)	7
Total		**284**			**118**

AUSTRALIA	O	M	R	W	O	M	R	W
Wall	49	7	108	4				
McCabe	18	3	38	1				
Grimmett	53·3	13	102	1				
O'Reilly	38	15	70	1				
Chipperfield	34	10	91	3				
Darling	6	2	19	0				
ENGLAND								
Farnes	12	3	43	0	4	2	6	0
Bowes	31	5	98	3	14	4	24	1
Geary	22	4	56	0				
Verity	36	15	61	7	22·3	8	43	8
Hammond	4	1	6	0	13	0	38	1
Leyland	4	1	10	0				

FALL OF WICKETS

	E	A	A
Wkt	*1st*	*1st*	*2nd*
1st	70	68	10
2nd	78	141	43
3rd	99	203	57
4th	130	204	94
5th	182	205	94
6th	311	218	95
7th	359	258	95
8th	409	273	95
9th	410	284	112
10th	440	284	118

Umpires: F. Chester (16) and J. Hardstaff, sr (17).

Close: 1st day – E(1) 293-5 (Leyland 95, Ames 44); 2nd – A(1) 192-2 (Brown 103, McCabe 24).

ENGLAND v AUSTRALIA 1934 (3rd Test)

Played at Old Trafford, Manchester, on 6, 7, 9, 10 July.
Toss: England.   Result: MATCH DRAWN.
Debuts: England – J.L. Hopwood.

O'Reilly took the wickets of Walters, Wyatt and Hammond in four balls (WW4W). At 45 years 151 days, Hendren became the second oldest batsman after J.B. Hobbs (*Test No. 180*) to score a century in this series. Leyland's hundred was his second in successive innings. Bradman and Chipperfield delayed their first innings because of throat infections. Allen's first over lasted 13 balls; he was called for three wides and four no-balls. Possibly he was overcome by the phenomenal Manchester weather. 'From first to last the sun blazed down, the heat being at times almost unbearable.' (*Wisden*).

ENGLAND

C.F. Walters	c Darling b O'Reilly	52	not out	50
H. Sutcliffe	c Chipperfield b O'Reilly	63	not out	69
R.E.S. Wyatt*	b O'Reilly	0		
W.R. Hammond	b O'Reilly	4		
E.H. Hendren	c and b O'Reilly	132		
M. Leyland	c sub (B.A. Barnett) b O'Reilly	153		
L.E.G. Ames†	c Ponsford b Grimmett	72		
J.L. Hopwood	b O'Reilly	2		
G.O.B. Allen	b McCabe	61		
H. Verity	not out	60		
E.W. Clark	not out	2		
Extras	(B 6, LB 18, W 2)	26	(B 2, LB 1, W 1)	4
Total	(9 wickets declared)	**627**	(0 wickets declared)	**123**

AUSTRALIA

W.A. Brown	c Walters b Clark	72	c Hammond b Allen	0
W.H. Ponsford	c Hendren b Hammond	12	not out	30
S.J. McCabe	c Verity b Hammond	137	not out	33
W.M. Woodfull*	run out	73		
L.S. Darling	b Verity	37		
D.G. Bradman	c Ames b Hammond	30		
W.A.S. Oldfield†	c Wyatt b Verity	13		
A.G. Chipperfield	c Walters b Verity	26		
C.V. Grimmett	b Verity	0		
W.J. O'Reilly	not out	30		
T.W. Wall	run out	18		
Extras	(B 20, LB 13, W 4, NB 6)	43	(B 1, LB 2)	3
Total		**491**	(1 wicket)	**66**

AUSTRALIA	O	M	R	W	O	M	R	W
Wall	36	3	131	0	9	0	31	0
McCabe	32	3	98	1	13	4	35	0
Grimmett	57	20	122	1	17	5	28	0
O'Reilly	59	9	189	7	13	4	25	0
Chipperfield	7	0	29	0				
Darling	10	0	32	0				
ENGLAND								
Clark	40	9	100	1	4	1	16	0
Allen	31	3	113	0	6	0	23	1
Hammond	28·3	6	111	3	2	1	2	0
Verity	53	24	78	4	5	4	2	0
Hopwood	38	20	46	0	9	5	16	0
Hendren					1	0	4	0

FALL OF WICKETS

Wkt	E 1st	A 1st	E 2nd	A 2nd
1st	68	34	–	1
2nd	68	230	–	–
3rd	72	242	–	–
4th	149	320	–	–
5th	340	378	–	–
6th	482	409	–	–
7th	492	411	–	–
8th	510	419	–	–
9th	605	454	–	–
10th	–	491	–	–

Umpires: J. Hardstaff, sr (18) and F.I. Walden (1).

Close: 1st day – E(1) 355-5 (Leyland 93, Ames 4); 2nd – A(1) 136-1 (Brown 56, McCabe 55); 3rd – A(1) 423-8 (Chipperfield 7, O'Reilly 1).

ENGLAND v AUSTRALIA 1934 (4th Test)

Played at Headingley, Leeds, on 20, 21, 23, 24 July.
Toss: England.   Result: MATCH DRAWN.
Debuts: England – W.W. Keeton.

Heavy rain at 1 pm on the last day saved England from probable defeat after Bradman had scored his second triple century in successive Tests at Leeds. He batted for 430 minutes, hit two sixes and 43 fours, and added 388 runs with Ponsford (then the highest partnership for any wicket by either side in this series, and still the record for the fourth wicket). Australia's total was the highest in Tests at Headingley until 1989.

ENGLAND

C.F. Walters	c and b Chipperfield	44	b O'Reilly	45
W.W. Keeton	c Oldfield b O'Reilly	25	b Grimmett	12
W.R. Hammond	b Wall	37	run out	20
E.H. Hendren	b Chipperfield	29	lbw b O'Reilly	42
R.E.S. Wyatt*	st Oldfield b Grimmett	19	b Grimmett	44
M. Leyland	lbw b O'Reilly	16	not out	49
L.E.G. Ames†	c Oldfield b Grimmett	9	c Brown b Grimmett	8
J.L. Hopwood	lbw b O'Reilly	8	not out	2
H. Verity	not out	2		
T.B. Mitchell	st Oldfield b Grimmett	9		
W.E. Bowes	c Ponsford b Grimmett	0		
Extras	(LB 2)	2	(B 1, LB 6)	7
Total		**200**	(6 wickets)	**229**

AUSTRALIA

W.A. Brown	b Bowes	15
W.H. Ponsford	hit wkt b Verity	181
W.A.S. Oldfield†	c Ames b Bowes	0
W.M. Woodfull*	b Bowes	0
D.G. Bradman	b Bowes	304
S.J. McCabe	b Bowes	27
L.S. Darling	b Bowes	12
A.G. Chipperfield	c Wyatt b Verity	1
C.V. Grimmett	run out	15
W.J. O'Reilly	not out	11
T.W. Wall	lbw b Verity	1
Extras	(B 8, LB 9)	17
Total		**584**

AUSTRALIA	O	M	R	W	O	M	R	W
Wall	18	1	57	1	14	5	36	0
McCabe	4	2	3	0	5	4	5	0
Grimmett	30·4	11	57	4	56·5	24	72	3
O'Reilly	35	16	46	3	51	25	88	2
Chipperfield	18	6	35	2	9	2	21	0
ENGLAND								
Bowes	50	13	142	6				
Hammond	29	5	82	0				
Mitchell	23	1	117	0				
Verity	46·5	15	113	3				
Hopwood	30	7	93	0				
Leyland	5	0	20	0				

FALL OF WICKETS

Wkt	E 1st	A 1st	E 2nd
1st	43	37	28
2nd	85	39	70
3rd	135	39	87
4th	135	427	152
5th	168	517	190
6th	170	550	213
7th	189	551	–
8th	189	557	–
9th	200	574	–
10th	200	584	–

Umpires: A. Dolphin (3) and J. Hardstaff, sr (19).

Close: 1st day – A(1) 39-3 (Ponsford 22); 2nd – A(1) 494-4 (Bradman 271, McCabe 18); 3rd – E(2) 188-4 (Hendren 42, Leyland 22).

ENGLAND v AUSTRALIA 1934 (5th Test)

Played at Kennington Oval, London, on 18, 20, 21, 22 August.
Toss: Australia.   Result: AUSTRALIA won by 562 runs.
Debuts: Australia – H.I. Ebeling.

For the second time in four years Australia regained the Ashes on their captain's birthday; they were to keep them for 19 years. Their victory in this timeless Test remains their biggest by a runs margin. The second-wicket partnership of 451 in 316 minutes between Ponsford (460 minutes, a five and 27 fours) and Bradman (316 minutes, a six and 32 fours) remains the world record for any wicket in Test cricket, although it was equalled in 1982-83 (*Test No. 946*). Ponsford, who was at the wicket while the first 574 runs were scored in his final Test, also scored a hundred on his debut. Ames retired with a strained back at 227. Woolley, recalled at the age of 47 to make the last Test appearance by a pre-1914 Test player, deputised for Ames when Australia batted again and conceded what is still the record number of byes in a Test innings.

AUSTRALIA

W.A. Brown	b Clark	10	c Allen b Clark	1
W.H. Ponsford	hit wkt b Allen	266	c Hammond b Clark	22
D.G. Bradman	c Ames b Bowes	244	b Bowes	77
S.J. McCabe	b Allen	10	c Walters b Clark	70
W.M. Woodfull*	b Bowes	49	b Bowes	13
A.F. Kippax	lbw b Bowes	28	c Walters b Clark	8
A.G. Chipperfield	b Bowes	3	c Woolley b Clark	16
W.A.S. Oldfield†	not out	42	c Hammond b Bowes	0
C.V. Grimmett	c Ames b Allen	7	c Hammond b Bowes	14
H.I. Ebeling	b Allen	2	c Allen b Bowes	41
W.J. O'Reilly	b Clark	7	not out	15
Extras	(B 4, LB 14, W 2, NB 13)	33	(B 37, LB 8, W 1, NB 4)	50
Total		**701**		**327**

ENGLAND

C.F. Walters	c Kippax b O'Reilly	64	b McCabe	1
H. Sutcliffe	c Oldfield b Grimmett	38	c McCabe b Grimmett	28
F.E. Woolley	c McCabe b O'Reilly	4	c Ponsford b McCabe	0
W.R. Hammond	c Oldfield b Ebeling	15	c and b O'Reilly	43
R.E.S. Wyatt*	b Grimmett	17	(6) c Ponsford b Grimmett	22
M. Leyland	b Grimmett	110	(5) c Brown b Grimmett	17
L.E.G. Ames†	retired hurt	33	absent hurt	–
G.O.B. Allen	b Ebeling	19	(7) st Oldfield b Grimmett	26
H. Verity	b Ebeling	11	(8) c McCabe b Grimmett	1
E.W. Clark	not out	2	not out	2
W.E. Bowes	absent ill	–	(9) c Bradman b O'Reilly	2
Extras	(B 4, LB 3, NB 1)	8	(LB 1, NB 2)	3
Total		**321**		**145**

ENGLAND	O	M	R	W	O	M	R	W		FALL OF WICKETS			
Bowes	38	2	164	4	11·3	3	55	5		A	E	A	E
Allen	34	5	170	4	16	2	63	0	*Wkt*	*1st*	*1st*	*2nd*	*2nd*
Clark	37·2	4	110	2	20	1	98	5	1st	21	104	13	1
Hammond	12	0	53	0	7	1	18	0	2nd	472	108	42	3
Verity	43	7	123	0	14	3	43	0	3rd	488	111	192	67
Wyatt	4	0	28	0					4th	574	136	213	89
Leyland	3	0	20	0					5th	626	142	224	109
									6th	631	263	236	122
AUSTRALIA									7th	638	311	236	138
Ebeling	21	4	74	3	10	5	15	0	8th	676	321	256	141
McCabe	6	1	21	0	5	3	5	2	9th	682	–	272	145
Grimmett	49·3	13	103	3	26·3	10	64	5	10th	701	–	327	–
O'Reilly	37	10	93	2	22	9	58	2					
Chipperfield	4	0	22	0									

Umpires: F. Chester (17) and F.I. Walden (2).

Close: 1st day – A(1) 475-2 (Ponsford 205, McCabe 1); 2nd – E(1) 90-0 (Walters 59, Sutcliffe 31); 3rd – A(2) 186-2 (Bradman 76, McCabe 60).

WEST INDIES v ENGLAND 1934–35 (1st Test)

Played at Kensington Oval, Bridgetown, Barbados, on 8, 9, 10 January.
Toss: England.   Result: ENGLAND won by four wickets.
Debuts: West Indies – G.M. Carew, C.M. Christiani, R.S. Grant, L.G. Hylton;
  England – W.E. Hollies, E.R.T. Holmes, J. Iddon, G.A.E. Paine, C.I.J. Smith.

A remarkable match on a 'sticky' pitch, it produced only 309 runs and just one innings was completed, when West Indies were dismissed for what remains their lowest total in any home Test. Rain prevented play before tea on the second day and until 3.30 on the last afternoon. England were set 73 to win after tea on a pitch drying from a burning sun and a strong breeze. Hammond, displaying his best form, steered England home, finally driving Martindale for an enormous winning six. This was the first Test to be won against a second innings declaration.

WEST INDIES

C.A. Roach	c Paine b Farnes	9	(6) not out		10
G.M. Carew	c Holmes b Farnes	0			
G.A. Headley	run out	44	(7) c Paine b Farnes		0
C.E.L. Jones	c Leyland b Farnes	3			
J.E.D. Sealy	c Paine b Farnes	0			
G.C. Grant*	c Hendren b Hollies	4	(8) not out		0
R.S. Grant	c Hammond b Hollies	5	(2) c Paine b Smith		0
L.G. Hylton	st Ames b Paine	15	(1) lbw b Smith		19
C.M. Christiani†	not out	9	(5) b Smith		11
E.E. Achong	st Ames b Paine	0	(4) b Smith		0
E.A. Martindale	c Leyland b Paine	9	(3) lbw b Smith		0
Extras	(LB 2, NB 2)	4	(B 4, LB 4, NB 3)		11
Total		**102**	(6 wickets declared)		**51**

ENGLAND

R.E.S. Wyatt*	c R.S. Grant b Martindale	8	(8) not out		6
M. Leyland	c and b Martindale	3	(5) c R.S. Grant b Martindale		2
W.R. Hammond	c R.S. Grant b Hylton	43	(6) not out		29
E.H. Hendren	c R.S. Grant b Martindale	3	(4) b Martindale		20
L.E.G. Ames†	lbw b R.S. Grant	8			
C.I.J. Smith	c Jones b Hylton	0	(2) c Christiani b Martindale		0
J. Iddon	not out	14			
E.R.T. Holmes	c Achong b Hylton	0	(3) c G.C. Grant b Martindale		6
K. Farnes	)		(1) c G.C. Grant b Hylton		5
G.A.E. Paine	) did not bat		(7) c R.S. Grant b Martindale		2
W.E. Hollies	)				
Extras	(B 1, NB 1)	2	(B 2, NB 3)		5
Total	(7 wickets declared)	**81**	(6 wickets)		**75**

ENGLAND	O	M	R	W	O	M	R	W
Farnes	15	4	40	4	9	2	23	1
Smith	7	3	8	0	8	4	16	5
Hollies	16	4	36	2				
Paine	9	3	14	3	1	1	0	0
Hammond					1	0	1	0
WEST INDIES								
Martindale	9	0	39	3	8·3	1	22	5
Hylton	7·3	3	8	3	8	0	48	1
Achong	6	1	14	0				
R.S. Grant	7	0	18	1				

FALL OF WICKETS				
	WI	E	WI	E
Wkt	1st	1st	2nd	2nd
1st	1	12	4	3
2nd	11	14	4	7
3rd	20	28	4	25
4th	20	52	40	29
5th	31	54	47	43
6th	49	81	51	48
7th	81	81	–	–
8th	86	–	–	–
9th	88	–	–	–
10th	102	–	–	–

Umpires: C.W. Reece (1) and E.L. Ward (1).

Close: 1st day – E(1) 81-5 (Hammond 43, Iddon 14); 2nd – WI(2) 33-3 (Hylton 17, Christiani 6).

WEST INDIES v ENGLAND 1934–35 (2nd Test)

Played at Queen's Park Oval, Port-of-Spain, Trinidad, on 24, 25, 26, 28 January.
Toss: England.   Result: WEST INDIES won by 217 runs.
Debuts: England – D.C.H. Townsend.

England, who put West Indies in to bat for the second successive time and virtually reversed their batting order in the second innings, lost their last wicket to the fifth ball of the last possible over. Constantine was cautioned by the umpire in the second innings for excessive use of the short-pitched ball. West Indies batsmen created a bizarre record by suffering three dismissals in the nineties.

WEST INDIES

C.M. Christiani†	c Holmes b Smith	11	c Farrimond b Smith	8
C.E.L. Jones	c Farrimond b Paine	19	c Wyatt b Paine	19
G.A. Headley	c Holmes b Paine	25	lbw b Smith	93
J.E.D. Sealy	b Wyatt	92	c Hammond b Leyland	35
G.C. Grant*	b Smith	8	c Hammond b Paine	23
O.C. Da Costa	b Holmes	25	(7) not out	19
L.N. Constantine	c Hendren b Smith	90	(6) c Ames b Paine	31
R.S. Grant	b Wyatt	0	not out	38
L.G. Hylton	c Hendren b Smith	8		
E.E. Achong	lbw b Wyatt	9		
E.A. Martindale	not out	0		
Extras	(B 2, LB 5, NB 8)	15	(B 3, LB 8, W 1, NB 2)	14
Total		**302**	(6 wickets declared)	**280**

ENGLAND

R.E.S. Wyatt*	c R.S. Grant b Hylton	15	(7) c Headley b Constantine	2
D.C.H. Townsend	lbw b Constantine	5	c Da Costa b Achong	36
W.R. Hammond	c R.S. Grant b Hylton	1	(5) b Constantine	9
L.E.G. Ames	c R.S. Grant b Martindale	2	(8) c Achong b Hylton	6
M. Leyland	lbw b Constantine	0	(9) lbw b Constantine	18
E.H. Hendren	c G.C. Grant b R.S. Grant	41	run out	11
J. Iddon	c Headley b R.S. Grant	73	(10) c Christiani b Hylton	0
E.R.T. Holmes	not out	85	(11) not out	0
C.I.J. Smith	b R.S. Grant	8	(4) run out	3
W. Farrimond†	c Constantine b Sealy	16	(1) c Headley b Hylton	2
G.A.E. Paine	lbw b Sealy	4	(3) hit wkt b R.S. Grant	14
Extras	(B 3, LB 4, NB 1)	8	(B 4, LB 2)	6
Total		**258**		**107**

ENGLAND	O	M	R	W	O	M	R	W
Smith	26	3	100	4	30	9	73	2
Wyatt	17	7	33	3	8	2	26	0
Hammond	14	5	28	0	10	0	17	0
Paine	26	6	85	2	42	10	109	3
Leyland	9	1	31	0	13	3	41	1
Holmes	3	1	10	1				
WEST INDIES								
Martindale	17	5	26	1	5	1	5	0
Hylton	23	6	55	2	14	4	25	3
Constantine	19	5	41	2	14·5	9	11	3
Achong	16	4	27	0	12	5	24	1
R.S. Grant	28	7	68	3	12	4	18	1
Da Costa	8	2	23	0	1	1	0	0
Sealy	6	2	7	2	5	0	16	0
Headley	4	2	3	0				
Jones					2	0	2	0

FALL OF WICKETS

Wkt	WI 1st	E 1st	WI 2nd	E 2nd
1st	32	15	19	14
2nd	38	19	34	53
3rd	102	23	99	54
4th	115	23	163	62
5th	174	23	216	71
6th	233	95	225	75
7th	233	168	–	79
8th	253	178	–	103
9th	281	240	–	103
10th	302	258	–	107

Umpires: V. Guillen (1) and A.J. Richardson (1).

Close: 1st day – WI(1) 284-9 (Constantine 72, Martindale 0); 2nd – E(1) 200-8 (Holmes 41, Farrimond 11); 3rd – WI(2) 150-3 (Headley 50, G.C. Grant 21).

WEST INDIES v ENGLAND 1934–35 (3rd Test)

Played at Bourda, Georgetown, British Guiana, on 14, 15, 16, 18 February.
Toss: England.   Result: MATCH DRAWN.
Debuts: West Indies – J.M. Neblett, K.L. Wishart.

Rain delayed the start of the match until after lunch. Smith, promoted in the order after the openers had struggled 90 minutes for 38 runs, struck three sixes and scored 25 in only ten minutes. The leg-breaks and googlies of Hollies achieved their best analysis at Test level. West Indies were set 203 runs to win in less than two hours.

ENGLAND

D.C.H. Townsend	lbw b R.S. Grant	16	lbw b Constantine		1
R.E.S. Wyatt*	c G.C. Grant b Martindale	21	b R.S. Grant		71
C.I.J. Smith	c Headley b Hylton	25	(5) b Constantine		4
G.A.E. Paine	st Christiani b Constantine	49	(3) c G. C. Grant b Neblett		18
W.R. Hammond	run out	47	(4) b Constantine		1
E.H. Hendren	c Martindale b Hylton	38	not out		38
M. Leyland	c Christiani b Hylton	13	b R.S. Grant		0
L.E.G. Ames†	c Christiani b Hylton	0	not out		5
J. Iddon	lbw b Martindale	0			
E.R.T. Holmes	b Martindale	2			
W.E. Hollies	not out	1			
Extras	(B 5, LB 5, NB 4)	14	(B 18, LB 3, W 1)		22
Total		**226**	(6 wickets declared)		**160**

WEST INDIES

C.E.L. Jones	lbw b Hollies	6	(3) b Paine		8
K.L. Wishart	run out	52	lbw b Wyatt		0
G.C. Grant*	c Paine b Hollies	16	(7) not out		5
G.A. Headley	lbw b Paine	53			
J.E.D. Sealy	c Ames b Hollies	19	(4) run out		33
L.N. Constantine	lbw b Hollies	7	(5) st Ames b Paine		7
J.M. Neblett	not out	11	(6) c Hammond b Holmes		5
R.S. Grant	lbw b Hollies	2			
C.M. Christiani†	lbw b Hollies	0	(1) not out		32
L.G. Hylton	b Paine	6			
E.A. Martindale	b Hollies	0			
Extras	(B 4, LB 7, NB 1)	12	(B 9, LB 1, W 4)		14
Total		**184**	(5 wickets)		**104**

WEST INDIES	O	M	R	W	O	M	R	W
Martindale	20	7	47	3	8	3	16	0
Hylton	13·2	4	27	4	8	3	18	0
Constantine	22	4	45	1	26	11	32	3
Neblett	20	9	31	0	16	2	44	1
R.S. Grant	26	7	46	1	22	6	28	2
Jones	5	4	4	0				
Sealy	6	2	12	0				
Headley	1	1	0	0				
ENGLAND								
Smith	22	8	37	0	4	2	13	0
Wyatt	10	5	10	0	4	2	7	1
Hollies	26	7	50	7	5	2	17	0
Paine	33	7	63	2	7	0	28	2
Leyland	2	0	12	0				
Townsend					1	0	9	0
Holmes					3	1	16	1

FALL OF WICKETS

Wkt	E 1st	WI 1st	E 2nd	WI 2nd
1st	38	18	3	4
2nd	63	43	39	27
3rd	72	122	54	70
4th	152	153	60	80
5th	172	157	140	85
6th	209	170	144	–
7th	209	173	–	–
8th	212	173	–	–
9th	215	183	–	–
10th	226	184	–	–

Umpires: J.G. Blackman (1) and A.J. Richardson (2).

Close: 1st day – E(1) 64-2 (Wyatt 17, Paine 0); 2nd – WI(1) 26-1 (Wishart 14, G.C. Grant 6); 3rd – E(2) 5-1 (Wyatt 4, Paine 0).

WEST INDIES v ENGLAND 1934–35 (4th Test)

Played at Sabina Park, Kingston, Jamaica, on 14, 15, 16, 18 March.
Toss: West Indies.   Result: WEST INDIES won by an innings and 161 runs.
Debuts: West Indies – R.L. Fuller, G.H. Mudie.

Headley's innings remained the highest West Indies score against England until L.G. Rowe made 302 in 1973-74 (*Test No. 733*). Wyatt's jaw was fractured by a short-pitched ball from Martindale. His opposite number, G.C. Grant, was forced to retire with an ankle injury in the second innings and handed over the captaincy to Constantine. West Indies dismissed England for what remains their lowest total in a Test in the Caribbean and so won their first rubber.

WEST INDIES

I. Barrow	b Farnes	3
C.M. Christiani†	b Paine	27
G.A. Headley	not out	270
J.E.D. Sealy	b Paine	91
L.N. Constantine	lbw b Paine	34
G.H. Mudie	c Townsend b Paine	5
R.L. Fuller	lbw b Hollies	1
R.S. Grant	c Wyatt b Paine	77
L.G. Hylton	not out	5
G.C. Grant*	) did not bat	
E.A. Martindale	)	
Extras	(B 8, LB 13, NB 1)	22
Total	(7 wickets declared)	**535**

ENGLAND

R.E.S. Wyatt*	retired hurt	1	absent hurt	–
D.C.H. Townsend	c Christiani b Martindale	8	b Martindale	11
W.R. Hammond	c Hylton b Constantine	11	b Martindale	34
G.A.E. Paine	lbw b Martindale	0	(7) not out	10
E.R.T. Holmes	b Martindale	0	(6) lbw b Sealy	3
L.E.G. Ames†	c Constantine b Mudie	126	(5) c R.S. Grant b Constantine	17
E.H. Hendren	c Barrow b R.S. Grant	40	(4) c Constantine b Mudie	11
J. Iddon	lbw b Mudie	54	(1) lbw b Constantine	0
C.I.J. Smith	b Constantine	10	(8) b Martindale	4
K. Farnes	b Constantine	5	(9) c Christiani b Martindale	0
W.E. Hollies	not out	1	(10) c Martindale b Constantine	6
Extras	(B 4, LB 6, NB 5)	15	(B 4, LB 1, W 2)	7
Total		**271**		**103**

ENGLAND	O	M	R	W	O	M	R	W
Smith	22	2	83	0				
Farnes	24	4	72	1				
Wyatt	5	1	12	0				
Hollies	46	11	114	1				
Holmes	8	0	40	0				
Paine	56	12	168	5				
Iddon	7	1	24	0				
WEST INDIES								
Martindale	17	1	56	3	16	5	28	4
Hylton	19	1	59	0	4	1	11	0
Constantine	23·2	4	55	3	9	3	13	3
Fuller	6	2	10	0	2	0	2	0
R.S. Grant	16	1	48	1	9	2	19	0
Mudie	17	7	23	2	12	5	17	1
G.C. Grant	1	0	5	0				
Sealy					2	0	6	1

FALL OF WICKETS

Wkt	WI 1st	E 1st	E 2nd
1st	5	23	14
2nd	92	26	18
3rd	294	26	45
4th	352	26	68
5th	376	95	83
6th	381	252	83
7th	528	265	89
8th	–	267	93
9th	–	271	103
10th	–	–	–

Umpires: S.C. Burke (1) and E. Knibbs (2).

Close: 1st day – WI(1) 235-2 (Headley 132, Sealy 60); 2nd – E(1) 27-4 (Ames 0, Hendren 1); 3rd – E(2) 14-0 (Iddon 0, Townsend 11).

ENGLAND v SOUTH AFRICA 1935 (1st Test)

Played at Trent Bridge, Nottingham, on 15, 17, 18 (*no play*) June.
Toss: England.   Result: MATCH DRAWN.
Debuts: England – N.S. Mitchell-Innes; South Africa – R.J. Crisp, A.B.C. Langton, A.D. (Dudley) Nourse, E.A.B. Rowan, D.S. Tomlinson, H.F. Wade.

This was South Africa's first Test against England at Trent Bridge. Mitchell-Innes played in his only Test match whilst in his second year at Brasenose College, Oxford. Batting almost five hours and hitting 17 fours, Wyatt compiled his highest innings for England. Nichols demolished the second half of South Africa's innings after tea on the second day with a spell of 7.5-4-13-5. Rain prevented play on the final day and rescued the visitors from a precarious situation.

ENGLAND

H. Sutcliffe	lbw b Langton	61
R.E.S. Wyatt*	c Wade b Crisp	149
W.R. Hammond	lbw b Vincent	28
N.S. Mitchell-Innes	lbw b Mitchell	5
M. Leyland	c Mitchell b Crisp	69
L.E.G. Ames†	c Viljoen b Vincent	17
J. Iddon	c Rowan b Vincent	29
M.S. Nichols	not out	13
R.W.V. Robins	)	
H. Verity	) did not bat	
W.E. Bowes	)	
Extras	(B 3, LB 10)	13
Total	(7 wickets declared)	**384**

SOUTH AFRICA

I.J. Siedle	b Verity	59	c Verity b Nichols	2
B. Mitchell	b Nichols	25	not out	8
E.A.B. Rowan	c Ames b Robins	20	not out	6
A.D. Nourse	c Hammond b Verity	4		
H.F. Wade*	c Nichols b Verity	18		
H.B. Cameron†	b Nichols	52		
K.G. Viljoen	b Nichols	13		
C.L. Vincent	lbw b Nichols	0		
D.S. Tomlinson	b Nichols	9		
A.B.C. Langton	not out	0		
R.J. Crisp	c Robins b Nichols	4		
Extras	(B 4, LB 10, NB 2)	16	(NB 1)	1
Total		**220**	(1 wicket)	**17**

SOUTH AFRICA	O	M	R	W	O	M	R	W
Crisp	18	4	49	2				
Langton	39	3	117	1				
Vincent	43	9	101	3				
Tomlinson	10	0	38	0				
Mitchell	22	1	66	1				
ENGLAND								
Bowes	22	9	31	0	4	3	2	0
Nichols	23·5	9	35	6	5	1	14	1
Verity	41	18	52	3				
Robins	19	4	65	1				
Iddon	4	2	3	0				
Leyland	7	2	18	0				

FALL OF WICKETS

Wkt	E 1st	SA 1st	SA 2nd
1st	118	42	3
2nd	170	98	–
3rd	179	103	–
4th	318	120	–
5th	325	174	–
6th	355	198	–
7th	384	198	–
8th	–	215	–
9th	–	216	–
10th	–	220	–

Umpires: A. Dolphin (4) and J. Hardstaff, sr (20).

Close: 1st day – E(1) 384-7 (Nichols 13); 2nd – SA(2) 17-1 (Mitchell 8, Rowan 6).

ENGLAND v SOUTH AFRICA 1935 (2nd Test)

Played at Lord's, London, on 29 June, 1, 2 July.
Toss: South Africa.   Result: SOUTH AFRICA won by 157 runs.
Debuts: Nil.

South Africa gained their first win in England in Sutcliffe's final Test. Both Sutcliffe and Ames batted with a runner in the second innings when England were set 309 runs to win in $4\frac{3}{4}$ hours. With the exception of Langton's dismissal of Sutcliffe, all the 'lbw' decisions in the match were given under the new experimental law which decreed that a batsman could be out 'lbw' to a ball pitching outside the off stump, provided that it hit the striker in line with the two wickets and would have hit his stumps. Cameron took only 105 minutes to score 90. Mitchell's 164 not out is the highest score for South Africa at Lord's.

SOUTH AFRICA

B. Mitchell	lbw b Nichols	30	not out		164
I.J. Siedle	b Mitchell	6	c Farrimond b Mitchell		13
E.A.B. Rowan	c Farrimond b Verity	40	lbw b Nichols		44
A.D. Nourse	b Verity	3	b Verity		2
H.F. Wade*	c Hammond b Langridge	23	(7) b Verity		0
H.B. Cameron†	b Nichols	90	(5) c Ames b Mitchell		3
E.L. Dalton	c and b Langridge	19	(6) c Wyatt b Verity		0
X.C. Balaskas	b Verity	4			
A.B.C. Langton	c Holmes b Hammond	4	(8) c and b Hammond		44
R.J. Crisp	not out	4			
A.J. Bell	b Hammond	0			
Extras	(B 1, LB 1, W 1, NB 2)	5	(B 3, LB 5)		8
Total		**228**	(7 wickets declared)		**278**

ENGLAND

R.E.S. Wyatt*	c Nourse b Dalton	53	b Balaskas		16
H. Sutcliffe	lbw b Bell	3	lbw b Langton		38
M. Leyland	b Balaskas	18	b Crisp		4
W.R. Hammond	b Dalton	27	c Cameron b Langton		27
L.E.G. Ames	b Balaskas	5	lbw b Langton		8
E.R.T. Holmes	c Bell b Balaskas	10	b Langton		8
J. Langridge	c Mitchell b Balaskas	27	lbw b Balaskas		17
W. Farrimond†	b Balaskas	13	b Crisp		13
M.S. Nichols	c Cameron b Langton	10	not out		7
H. Verity	lbw b Langton	17	c Langton b Balaskas		8
T.B. Mitchell	not out	5	st Cameron b Balaskas		1
Extras	(B 4, LB 5, W 1)	10	(LB 4)		4
Total		**198**			**151**

ENGLAND	O	M	R	W	O	M	R	W					
Nichols	21	5	47	2	18	4	64	1					
Wyatt	4	2	9	0	4	2	2	0					
Hammond	5·3	3	8	2	14·4	4	26	1					
Mitchell	20	3	71	1	33	5	93	2					
Verity	28	10	61	3	38	16	56	3					
Langridge	13	3	27	2	10	4	19	0					
Holmes					4	2	10	0					

FALL OF WICKETS

Wkt	SA 1st	E 1st	SA 2nd	E 2nd
1st	27	5	32	24
2nd	59	46	136	45
3rd	62	100	169	89
4th	98	109	169	90
5th	158	116	169	102
6th	187	121	177	111
7th	196	158	278	129
8th	224	161	–	141
9th	228	177	–	149
10th	228	198	–	151

SOUTH AFRICA	O	M	R	W	O	M	R	W
Crisp	8	1	32	0	15	4	30	2
Bell	6	0	16	1	12	3	21	0
Langton	21·3	3	58	2	11	3	31	4
Balaskas	32	8	49	5	27	8	54	4
Dalton	13	1	33	2				
Mitchell					2	0	11	0

Umpires: E.J. Smith (2) and F.I. Walden (3).

Close: 1st day – E(1) 75-2 (Wyatt 37, Hammond 12); 2nd – SA(2) 208-6 (Mitchell 129, Langton 11).

ENGLAND v SOUTH AFRICA 1935 (3rd Test)

Played at Headingley, Leeds, on 13, 15, 16 July.
Toss: England.   Result: MATCH DRAWN.
Debuts: England – W. Barber, J. Hardstaff, jr, J.M. Sims, D. Smith.

South Africa were set 340 runs to win in just over 4½ hours. Barber took Cameron's wicket with his second ball in Test cricket after the latter's stumps had been hit by a ball from Hammond which did not dislodge a bail.

ENGLAND

R.E.S. Wyatt*	c Cameron b Crisp	0	(5)	c Vincent b Bell	44
D. Smith	c Cameron b Vincent	36		b Vincent	57
W. Barber	c Bell b Langton	24		c Dalton b Vincent	14
W.R. Hammond	lbw b Vincent	63		not out	87
A. Mitchell	c Mitchell b Langton	58	(1)	c Viljoen b Vincent	72
J. Hardstaff, jr	c and b Vincent	10		b Bell	0
L.E.G. Ames†	b Vincent	0		b Bell	13
M.S. Nichols	lbw b Langton	4		b Vincent	2
J.M. Sims	b Langton	12			
H. Verity	c Cameron b Crisp	1			
W.E. Bowes	not out	0			
Extras	(B 2, LB 6)	8		(B 1, LB 4)	5
Total		**216**		(7 wickets declared)	**294**

SOUTH AFRICA

I.J. Siedle	run out	33		c Hammond b Bowes	21
B. Mitchell	lbw b Hammond	8		b Hammond	58
E.A.B. Rowan	c Hammond b Bowes	62		b Bowes	5
K.G. Viljoen	c Smith b Wyatt	19		b Sims	9
H. F. Wade*	c Mitchell b Verity	3		not out	32
H.B. Cameron†	lbw b Nichols	9		st Ames b Barber	49
E.L. Dalton	b Bowes	4			
C.L. Vincent	c Barber b Verity	0			
A.B.C. Langton	b Nichols	0			
R.J. Crisp	c Hammond b Nichols	18			
A.J. Bell	not out	3			
Extras	(B 8, LB 3, NB 1)	12		(B 14, LB 4, W 1, NB 1)	20
Total		**171**		(5 wickets)	**194**

SOUTH AFRICA	O	M	R	W	O	M	R	W
Crisp	13·5	3	26	2	11	1	52	0
Bell	16	3	48	0	14	4	38	3
Langton	26	5	59	4	31	8	95	0
Vincent	32	12	45	4	23·3	3	104	4
Mitchell	6	0	30	0				
ENGLAND								
Bowes	29	5	62	2	19	9	31	2
Nichols	21·4	4	58	3	22	5	65	0
Hammond	12	6	13	1	7	4	10	1
Sims	9	4	20	0	27	13	48	1
Verity	12	9	5	2	13	11	4	0
Wyatt	4	3	1	1	6	2	12	0
Mitchell					1	0	4	0
Barber					0·2	0	0	1

FALL OF WICKETS

	E	SA	E	SA
Wkt	1st	1st	2nd	2nd
1st	0	21	128	53
2nd	52	65	139	61
3rd	78	120	148	91
4th	147	123	277	111
5th	177	141	277	194
6th	177	149	291	–
7th	188	150	294	–
8th	215	150	–	–
9th	216	150	–	–
10th	216	171	–	–

Umpires: F. Chester (18) and J.W. Hitch (4).

Close: 1st day – SA(1) 26-1 (Siedle 14, Rowan 3); 2nd – E(2) 177-3 (Hammond 15, Wyatt 14).

ENGLAND v SOUTH AFRICA 1935 (4th Test)

Played at Old Trafford, Manchester, on 27, 29, 30 July.
Toss: England.   Result: MATCH DRAWN.
Debuts: Nil.

Tate, recalled to the England team after an interval of more than two years, made his final Test appearance.
Both Robins, who batted only 130 minutes, and Viljoen achieved their highest scores in Test cricket. Because
of fluid on the elbow Bell was unable to bowl more than one over in the second innings. Although England's
lunchtime declaration set a target of 271 runs at 72 per hour, Mitchell managed only 48 runs in 225 minutes.

ENGLAND

D. Smith	c Mitchell b Bell	35	lbw b Crisp	0
A.H. Bakewell	b Crisp	63	b Langton	54
W. Barber	c Langton b Bell	1	b Vincent	44
W.R. Hammond	b Crisp	29	not out	63
R.E.S. Wyatt*	lbw b Crisp	3	(8) not out	15
M. Leyland	c Mitchell b Crisp	53	(5) c Mitchell b Vincent	37
R.W.V. Robins	b Bell	108	(6) c Wade b Vincent	14
H. Verity	lbw b Langton	16		
M.W. Tate	c Viljoen b Vincent	34	(7) b Vincent	0
G. Duckworth†	c Nourse b Crisp	2		
W.E. Bowes	not out	0		
Extras	(B 2, LB 9, W 1, NB 1)	13	(B 1, LB 1, W 1, NB 1)	4
Total		**357**	(6 wickets declared)	**231**

SOUTH AFRICA

B. Mitchell	c Duckworth b Hammond	10	not out	48
E.A.B. Rowan	b Bowes	13	hit wkt b Robins	49
K.G. Viljoen	c Verity b Bowes	124	lbw b Robins	10
A.D. Nourse	lbw b Verity	29	not out	53
H.F. Wade*	lbw b Bowes	16		
H.B. Cameron†	c Bowes b Tate	53		
E.L. Dalton	lbw b Robins	47		
C.L. Vincent	not out	14		
A.B.C. Langton	c Bakewell b Bowes	0		
R.J. Crisp	c Verity b Bowes	3		
A.J. Bell	lbw b Tate	1		
Extras	(B 3, LB 5)	8	(B 6, LB 1, W 2)	9
Total		**318**	(2 wickets)	**169**

SOUTH AFRICA	O	M	R	W	O	M	R	W		FALL OF WICKETS			
										E	SA	E	SA
Crisp	26·1	1	99	5	11	0	43	1	*Wkt*	*1st*	*1st*	*2nd*	*2nd*
Bell	26	3	90	3	1	0	3	0	1st	71	21	1	67
Vincent	28	4	85	1	26	6	78	4	2nd	77	41	90	103
Langton	11	0	59	1	25	2	80	1	3rd	123	91	110	–
Mitchell	1	0	11	0					4th	132	124	172	–
Dalton					4	0	23	0	5th	141	223	200	–
									6th	246	288	200	–
ENGLAND									7th	302	311	–	–
Bowes	36	7	100	5	15	1	34	0	8th	338	311	–	–
Tate	22·3	5	67	2	9	2	20	0	9th	357	315	–	–
Hammond	17	2	49	1	5	0	15	0	10th	357	318	–	–
Verity	20	4	48	1	20	10	24	0					
Robins	10	0	34	1	19	8	31	2					
Wyatt	4	1	12	0									
Leyland					12	4	28	0					
Bakewell					3	0	8	0					

Umpires: F. Chester (19) and F.I. Walden (4).

Close: 1st day – SA(1) 3-0 (Mitchell 2, Rowan 1); 2nd – E(2) 43-1 (Bakewell 21, Barber 21).

ENGLAND v SOUTH AFRICA 1935 (5th Test)

Played at Kennington Oval, London, on 17, 19, 20 August.
Toss: England.   Result: MATCH DRAWN.
Debuts: England – J.C. Clay, H.D. Read.

After waiting for 28 years, South Africa won their first rubber in England by drawing the match after being invited to bat on a perfect pitch. The partnership of 137 in 70 minutes between Dalton and Langton remains the ninth-wicket record for this series. Leyland and Ames contributed 151 in 100 minutes towards the highest total by either country in the series to date. Cameron contracted enteric fever on the voyage home and died ten weeks after this match at the age of 30.

SOUTH AFRICA

I.J. Siedle	c Ames b Robins	35	b Bowes	36
B. Mitchell	c Ames b Read	128	b Read	9
E.A.B. Rowan	lbw b Robins	0	b Bowes	7
A.D. Nourse	c Wyatt b Bowes	32	b Read	34
K.G. Viljoen	c Clay b Read	60	st Ames b Robins	45
H.B. Cameron†	c Mitchell b Read	8	st Ames b Robins	42
H.F. Wade*	c Hammond b Bowes	0	not out	40
E.L. Dalton	c Robins b Read	117	not out	57
C.L. Vincent	b Robins	5		
A.B.C. Langton	not out	73		
R.J. Crisp	c Ames b Bowes	0		
Extras	(B 6, LB 10, NB 2)	18	(B 6, LB 9, NB 2)	17
Total		**476**	(6 wickets)	**287**

ENGLAND

A.H. Bakewell	c Cameron b Langton	20	
A. Mitchell	b Crisp	40	
R.E.S. Wyatt*	c Cameron b Vincent	37	
W.R. Hammond	st Cameron b Vincent	65	
M. Leyland	st Cameron b Mitchell	161	
L.E.G. Ames†	not out	148	
M.S. Nichols	c Siedle b Langton	30	
R.W.V. Robins	not out	10	
J.C. Clay	)		
W.E. Bowes	) did not bat		
H.D. Read	)		
Extras	(B 5, LB 16, NB 2)	23	
Total	(6 wickets declared)	**534**	

ENGLAND	O	M	R	W	O	M	R	W
Read	35	13	136	4	10	1	64	2
Nichols	23	3	79	0	5	1	20	0
Bowes	40·4	7	112	3	13	2	40	2
Hammond	9	2	25	0				
Clay	14	1	30	0	18	6	45	0
Robins	22	3	73	3	17	1	61	2
Wyatt	2	0	3	0	3	0	25	0
Leyland					7	2	15	0
SOUTH AFRICA								
Crisp	28	0	113	1				
Langton	38	5	124	2				
Dalton	16	1	50	0				
Vincent	42	5	188	2				
Mitchell	8	0	36	1				

FALL OF WICKETS

	SA	E	SA
Wkt	1st	1st	2nd
1st	116	34	16
2nd	116	98	23
3rd	164	98	67
4th	234	249	112
5th	248	428	178
6th	254	506	193
7th	312	–	–
8th	333	–	–
9th	470	–	–
10th	476	–	–

Umpires: F. Chester (20) and J. Hardstaff, sr (21).

Close: 1st day – SA(1) 297-6 (Viljoen 60, Dalton 21); 2nd – E(1) 313-4 (Leyland 119, Ames 25).

SOUTH AFRICA v AUSTRALIA 1935–36 (1st Test)

Played at Kingsmead, Durban, on 14, 16, 17, 18 December.
Toss: South Africa.   Result: AUSTRALIA won by nine wickets.
Debuts: South Africa – F. Nicholson, J.B. Robertson; Australia – L. O'B. Fleetwood-Smith, E.L. McCormick.

Even without Bradman (unavailable), the Australians remained unbeaten on this tour of 16 first-class matches; 13 were won – ten by an innings. Chipperfield's only Test hundred was scored in his first match against South Africa. The Springboks lost 18 wickets to Australia's varied trio of spinners.

SOUTH AFRICA

B. Mitchell	b Fleetwood-Smith	19	run out	19
I.J. Siedle	lbw b O'Reilly	31	b Grimmett	59
E.A.B. Rowan	c and b Grimmett	66	b Grimmett	49
K.G. Viljoen	b Fleetwood-Smith	4	b Fleetwood-Smith	1
A.D. Nourse	b McCormick	30	c Fingleton b O'Reilly	91
H.F. Wade*	b O'Reilly	31	lbw b O'Reilly	11
E.L. Dalton	st Oldfield b Fleetwood-Smith	4	c Darling b Grimmett	5
A.B.C. Langton	b Grimmett	0	not out	12
F. Nicholson†	not out	16	b O'Reilly	0
R.J. Crisp	b Fleetwood-Smith	35	b O'Reilly	16
J.B. Robertson	b O'Reilly	9	c Richardson b O'Reilly	9
Extras	(B 1, LB 2)	3	(B 8, LB 1, NB 1)	10
Total		**248**		**282**

AUSTRALIA

W.A. Brown	c Langton b Robertson	66	c Crisp b Dalton	55
J.H.W. Fingleton	c Nicholson b Crisp	2	not out	36
S.J. McCabe	c Rowan b Langton	149	not out	7
L.S. Darling	c Viljoen b Crisp	60		
V.Y. Richardson*	b Langton	2		
A.G. Chipperfield	b Crisp	109		
W.A.S. Oldfield†	lbw b Langton	0		
W.J. O'Reilly	c Rowan b Robertson	11		
C.V. Grimmett	c Nicholson b Robertson	15		
E.L. McCormick	not out	2		
L.O'B. Fleetwood-Smith	b Langton	1		
Extras	(B 5, LB 2, W 1, NB 4)	12	(B 3, LB 1)	4
Total		**429**	(1 wicket)	**102**

AUSTRALIA	O	M	R	W	O	M	R	W
McCormick	15	4	50	1	6	0	26	0
McCabe	10	1	28	0	2	0	5	0
Grimmett	28	10	48	2	52	20	83	3
O'Reilly	33·2	17	55	3	17	5	49	5
Fleetwood-Smith	28	6	64	4	37	7	101	1
Chipperfield					1	0	8	0
SOUTH AFRICA								
Crisp	36	7	87	3	6	1	10	0
Langton	48·2	10	113	4	9	0	29	0
Robertson	55	11	143	3	13	4	24	0
Dalton	6	0	25	0	1·3	0	12	1
Mitchell	17	2	49	0	7	0	23	0

FALL OF WICKETS

Wkt	SA 1st	A 1st	SA 2nd	A 2nd
1st	45	12	65	93
2nd	59	173	86	–
3rd	71	269	89	–
4th	108	277	207	–
5th	168	299	233	–
6th	185	299	242	–
7th	186	329	242	–
8th	187	412	242	–
9th	234	428	263	–
10th	248	429	282	–

Umpires: J.C. Collings (5) and W.J. Routledge (1).

Close: 1st day – A(1) 0-0 (Brown 0, Fingleton 0); 2nd – A(1) 280-4 (Darling 51, Chipperfield 2); 3rd – SA(2) 167-3 (Rowan 33, Nourse 48).

Test No. 248/21

SOUTH AFRICA v AUSTRALIA 1935–36 (2nd Test)

Played at Old Wanderers, Johannesburg, on 24, 26, 27, 28 December.
Toss: South Africa.   Result: MATCH DRAWN.
Debuts: South Africa – E.G. Bock, A.W. Briscoe.

A heavy storm ended the match at 2.45 on the last afternoon when Australia were 125 runs away from victory with eight wickets in hand. Nourse's 231 (289 minutes, 36 fours), was South Africa's highest Test score until 1951 when E.A.B. Rowan made 236 (*Test No. 337*) and it is still the record innings in a Test at Johannesburg. Mitchell's slow miscellany brought him four wickets (including three in four balls) for five runs in nine balls. McCabe scored his first 50 in 40 minutes.

SOUTH AFRICA

B. Mitchell	c Oldfield b McCormick	8	(4) c Oldfield b McCabe	45
I.J. Siedle	c Chipperfield b McCormick	22	b Grimmett	34
E.A.B. Rowan	lbw b Grimmett	38	lbw b Grimmett	13
A.D. Nourse	b McCormick	0	(5) c McCormick b McCabe	231
A.W. Briscoe	b O'Reilly	15	(6) b McCormick	16
H.F. Wade*	b O'Reilly	0	(1) lbw b Grimmett	30
A.B.C. Langton	c Fingleton b O'Reilly	7	(8) b McCormick	16
F. Nicholson†	st Oldfield b Grimmett	27	(7) lbw Fleetwood-Smith	29
R.J. Crisp	b Grimmett	8	b O'Reilly	35
J.B. Robertson	b O'Reilly	17	b McCormick	3
E.G. Bock	not out	9	not out	2
Extras	(LB 6)	6	(B 13, LB 19, NB 5)	37
Total		**157**		**491**

AUSTRALIA

J.H.W. Fingleton	c and b Langton	62	b Mitchell	40
W.A. Brown	c Crisp b Robertson	51	c Nicholson b Crisp	6
S.J. McCabe	c Robertson b Langton	34	not out	189
L.S. Darling	run out	42	not out	37
V.Y. Richardson*	b Langton	2		
A.G. Chipperfield	c Rowan b Langton	0		
W.A.S. Oldfield†	c Briscoe b Mitchell	40		
C.V. Grimmett	b Mitchell	7		
W.J. O'Reilly	b Mitchell	0		
E.L. McCormick	b Mitchell	4		
L.O'B. Fleetwood-Smith	not out	5		
Extras	(LB 3)	3	(LB 2)	2
Total		**250**	(2 wickets)	**274**

AUSTRALIA	O	M	R	W	O	M	R	W		FALL OF WICKETS			
McCormick	16	5	36	3	26	3	129	3		SA	A	SA	A
O'Reilly	20·2	9	54	4	35·3	15	91	1	*Wkt*	*1st*	*1st*	*2nd*	*2nd*
Grimmett	15	5	29	3	58	28	111	3	1st	11	105	50	17
McCabe	6	2	11	0	9	1	30	2	2nd	46	127	89	194
Fleetwood-Smith	6	2	21	0	21	5	93	1	3rd	50	168	90	–
									4th	68	170	219	–
SOUTH AFRICA									5th	70	174	291	–
Crisp	15	1	49	0	17	3	62	1	6th	78	209	397	–
Langton	32	6	85	4	22	6	54	0	7th	112	241	440	–
Mitchell	7·3	0	26	4	15	1	73	1	8th	126	241	454	–
Bock	14	2	49	0	9	0	42	0	9th	139	242	466	–
Robertson	13	0	38	1	13	3	41	0	10th	157	250	491	–

Umpires: R.G.A. Ashman (1) and J.C. Collings (6).

Close: 1st day – A(1) 168-3 (Darling 19); 2nd – SA(2) 254-4 (Nourse 98, Briscoe 10); 3rd – A(2) 85-1 (Fingleton 20, McCabe 59).

SOUTH AFRICA v AUSTRALIA 1935–36 (3rd Test)

Played at Newlands, Cape Town, on 1 (*no play*), 2, 3, 4 January.
Toss: Australia.   Result: AUSTRALIA won by an innings and 78 runs.
Debuts: Nil.

The decisive opening stand of 233 by Brown and Fingleton is the best by either country in this series. After torrential rain and a delay until 3 pm, Australia again found conditions ideal for their spin bowlers. Grimmett established a new record in this his 35th Test, when he took his seventh wicket and passed S.F. Barnes' record of 189 wickets in 27 matches.

AUSTRALIA

W.A. Brown	c and b Robertson	121
J.H.W. Fingleton	c Wade b Balaskas	112
S.J. McCabe	c and b Balaskas	0
L.S. Darling	lbw b Balaskas	12
V.Y. Richardson*	lbw b Crisp	14
A.G. Chipperfield	b Langton	30
W.A.S. Oldfield†	b Robertson	8
C.V. Grimmett	not out	30
W.J. O'Reilly	b Balaskas	17
E.L. McCormick	not out	0
L.O'B. Fleetwood-Smith	did not bat	
Extras	(B 14, LB 4)	18
Total	(8 wickets declared)	**362**

SOUTH AFRICA

I. J. Siedle	lbw b Grimmett	1		b Grimmett	59
H.F. Wade*	c and b McCabe	0		lbw b Fleetwood-Smith	31
E.A.B. Rowan	b Grimmett	12		c Richardson b O'Reilly	19
B. Mitchell	c Fingleton b O'Reilly	14	(5)	b Grimmett	0
K.G. Viljoen	st Oldfield b Fleetwood-Smith	14	(6)	c O'Reilly b Grimmett	23
A.D. Nourse	not out	44	(4)	c and b Grimmett	25
F. Nicholson†	b Fleetwood-Smith	0		c and b O'Reilly	4
A.B.C. Langton	b Grimmett	3		b O'Reilly	4
R.J. Crisp	b Grimmett	0		c Richardson b O'Reilly	0
X.C. Balaskas	b Grimmett	0	(11)	b Grimmett	2
J.B. Robertson	run out	1	(10)	not out	12
Extras	(LB 13)	13		(B 1, LB 2)	3
Total		**102**			**182**

SOUTH AFRICA	O	M	R	W	O	M	R	W
Crisp	14	2	30	1				
Langton	30	2	94	1				
Robertson	29	8	75	2				
Balaskas	38	1	126	4				
Mitchell	4	0	19	0				
AUSTRALIA								
McCormick	2	1	3	0	2	0	8	0
McCabe	2	1	9	1				
O'Reilly	11	4	24	1	25	15	35	4
Grimmett	17	4	32	5	36·4	17	56	5
Fleetwood-Smith	6·2	0	21	2	24	4	80	1

FALL OF WICKETS

	A	SA	SA
Wkt	1st	1st	2nd
1st	233	0	87
2nd	235	12	97
3rd	251	21	137
4th	259	29	137
5th	299	86	139
6th	313	88	146
7th	313	95	156
8th	361	95	156
9th	–	95	174
10th	–	102	182

Umpires: R.G.A. Ashman (2) and J.C. Collings (7).

Close: 1st day – no play; 2nd – A(1) 362-8 (Grimmett 30, McCormick 0); 3rd – SA(2) 11-0 (Siedle 6, Wade 5).

SOUTH AFRICA v AUSTRALIA 1935–36 (4th Test)

Played at Old Wanderers, Johannesburg, on 15, 17 February.
Toss: South Africa.   Result: AUSTRALIA won by an innings and 184 runs.
Debuts: South Africa – E.Q. Davies, R.L. Harvey.

Australia gained their third and most decisive win of this rubber a few minutes after the scheduled close on the second day, the captains agreeing to play on to obtain a finish. O'Reilly recorded the remarkable first innings analysis of 5 for 20 in 21 overs. He failed to take another wicket as Grimmett achieved his best figures for Australia in his penultimate match and became the first to reach 200 Test wickets.

SOUTH AFRICA

I.J. Siedle	lbw b Grimmett	44		b McCormick	0
H.F. Wade*	b McCormick	39		b McCormick	2
A.D. Nourse	c Oldfield b McCormick	3	(5)	b McCormick	3
K.G. Viljoen	b O'Reilly	33	(3)	st Oldfield b Grimmett	7
R.L. Harvey	b O'Reilly	5	(6)	c Darling b Grimmett	17
B. Mitchell	st Oldfield b Grimmett	16	(4)	not out	48
A.B.C. Langton	lbw b O'Reilly	7	(8)	lbw b Grimmett	9
F. Nicholson†	b Grimmett	0	(7)	b Grimmett	0
E.P. Nupen	b O'Reilly	1		b Grimmett	6
X.C. Balaskas	lbw b O'Reilly	0		c O'Brien b Grimmett	0
E.Q. Davies	not out	0		c Oldfield b Grimmett	3
Extras	(LB 5, W 4)	9		(LB 3)	3
Total		**157**			**98**

AUSTRALIA

J.H.W. Fingleton	c Langton b Davies	108
W.A. Brown	lbw b Langton	34
S.J. McCabe	b Davies	40
L.P.J. O'Brien	b Balaskas	59
W.A.S. Oldfield†	c Balaskas b Nupen	44
L.S. Darling	c Wade b Balaskas	16
A.G. Chipperfield	lbw b Balaskas	39
V.Y. Richardson*	b Davies	21
C.V. Grimmett	lbw b Balaskas	4
W.J. O'Reilly	not out	56
E.L. McCormick	c Mitchell b Davies	13
Extras	(B 1, LB 4)	5
Total		**439**

AUSTRALIA	O	M	R	W	O	M	R	W
McCormick	11	0	37	2	12	2	28	3
McCabe	5	2	21	0	2	1	1	0
Grimmett	26·4	6	70	3	19·5	9	40	7
O'Reilly	21	11	20	5	10	3	26	0
SOUTH AFRICA								
Davies	24·4	4	75	4				
Langton	30	5	88	1				
Balaskas	44	4	165	4				
Nupen	14	1	53	1				
Mitchell	14	1	53	0				

FALL OF WICKETS

	SA	A	SA
Wkt	1st	1st	2nd
1st	81	99	0
2nd	91	179	5
3rd	96	184	21
4th	128	260	24
5th	137	282	49
6th	153	333	50
7th	154	352	76
8th	155	368	82
9th	157	370	82
10th	157	439	98

Umpires: R.G.A. Ashman (3) and J.C. Collings (8).

Close: 1st day – A(1) 185-3 (O'Brien 1, Oldfield 0).

SOUTH AFRICA v AUSTRALIA 1935–36 (5th Test)

Played at Kingsmead, Durban, on 28, 29 February, 2, 3 March.
Toss: South Africa.   Result: AUSTRALIA won by an innings and 6 runs.
Debuts: Nil.

For the third match in succession, Fingleton scored a century (three in consecutive innings), Grimmett took ten or more wickets and Australia won by an innings. Richardson established a Test record, since equalled, by holding five catches in the second innings. In the last of his 37 Tests Grimmett returned the best analysis (13 for 173) for this series in South Africa. His tally of 44 wickets, average 14.59, remains the highest for Australia in any rubber and the record for this series. His final total of 216 wickets at 24.21 runs apiece was the Test record until 1953 when A.V. Bedser broke it in *Test No. 375*. Wade also ended his Test career after captaining South Africa in each of his ten matches.

SOUTH AFRICA

I.J. Siedle	c Fingleton b Grimmett	36	c Brown b Grimmett	46
H.F. Wade*	c Richardson b Grimmett	26	b O'Reilly	25
B. Mitchell	c and b Grimmett	10	not out	72
A.D. Nourse	lbw b Grimmett	50	b O'Reilly	41
K.G. Viljoen	c Chipperfield b McCormick	56	lbw b Grimmett	25
R.L. Harvey	c Oldfield b McCormick	28	c Richardson b Grimmett	1
A.B.C. Langton	st Oldfield b Grimmett	1	b Grimmett	3
X.C. Balaskas	st Oldfield b Grimmett	2	c Richardson b Grimmett	0
R.J. Crisp	b Grimmett	0	(11) c Richardson b O'Reilly	0
E.A. van der Merwe†	not out	7	(9) c Richardson b Grimmett	0
E.Q. Davies	b McCormick	0	(10) c Richardson b O'Reilly	2
Extras	(B 1, LB 5)	6	(B 5, LB 7)	12
Total		**222**		**227**

AUSTRALIA

J.H.W. Fingleton	b Crisp	118
W.A. Brown	c Langton b Mitchell	84
S.J. McCabe	c and b Mitchell	1
L.P.J. O'Brien	c Van der Merwe b Balaskas	48
L.S. Darling	lbw b Mitchell	62
A.G. Chipperfield	c Balaskas b Mitchell	18
V.Y. Richardson*	b Crisp	45
W.A.S. Oldfield†	c Crisp b Langton	29
C.V. Grimmett	c Siedle b Mitchell	14
W.J. O'Reilly	c Siedle b Langton	13
E.L. McCormick	not out	0
Extras	(B 19, LB 3, NB 1)	23
Total		**455**

AUSTRALIA	O	M	R	W	O	M	R	W		FALL OF WICKETS		
McCormick	20·1	8	37	3	15	1	64	0		SA	A	SA
McCabe	7	0	20	0	2	0	11	0	*Wkt*	*1st*	*1st*	*2nd*
Grimmett	45	18	100	7	48	23	73	6	1st	44	162	63
O'Reilly	37	15	59	0	40·1	18	47	4	2nd	57	164	73
Chipperfield					8	1	20	0	3rd	124	240	146
									4th	125	316	196
SOUTH AFRICA									5th	178	333	206
Davies	18	0	54	0					6th	183	361	212
Crisp	19	2	65	2					7th	199	423	220
Langton	33	9	69	2					8th	199	433	220
Balaskas	51	4	157	1					9th	220	451	227
Mitchell	25·5	2	87	5					10th	222	455	227

Umpires: J.C. Collings (9) and W.J. Routledge (2).

Close: 1st day – SA(1) 199-8 (Viljoen 42, Van der Merwe 0); 2nd – A(1) 239-2 (Fingleton 117, O'Brien 23); 3rd – SA(2) 110-2 (Mitchell 16, Nourse 20).

ENGLAND v INDIA 1936 (1st Test)

Played at Lord's, London, on 27, 29, 30 June.
Toss: England.   Result: ENGLAND won by nine wickets.
Debuts: England – H. Gimblett; India – D.D. Hindlekar, The Maharajkumar of Vizianagram (*who, before the 2nd Test, received a knighthood and became Sir Gajapatairaj Vijaya Ananda, The Maharajkumar of Vizianagram*).

For the first time in a Test in England, artificial means were used to dry the pitch. Allen, making the first of eleven appearances as captain, achieved his best match analysis in Test cricket (10 for 78). Amar Singh took England's first four wickets for 13 runs in an opening spell of nine overs and his analysis of 6 for 35 remains the best for India in England. In the second innings Hindlekar withstood England's attack for 90 minutes after chipping a bone in his finger. Gimblett hooked bravely and, batting with fine aggression, contributed the highest innings of the match on his debut. Hitting 11 fours, including four off successive balls from Nissar, he completed England's task in 100 minutes with 50 minutes to spare.

INDIA

V.M. Merchant	b Allen	35	c Duckworth b Allen	0
D.D. Hindlekar†	b Robins	26	lbw b Robins	17
Mushtaq Ali	c Langridge b Allen	0	lbw b Allen	8
C.K. Nayudu	lbw b Allen	1	c Robins b Allen	3
S. Wazir Ali	b Allen	11	c Verity b Allen	4
L. Amar Singh	c Langridge b Robins	12	lbw b Verity	7
P.E. Palia	c Mitchell b Verity	11	c Leyland b Verity	16
M. Jahangir Khan	b Allen	13	c Duckworth b Verity	13
Maharaj Vizianagram*	not out	19	c Mitchell b Verity	6
C.S. Nayudu	c Wyatt b Robins	6	c Hardstaff b Allen	9
Mahomed Nissar	st Duckworth b Verity	9	not out	2
Extras	(B 4)	4	(B 4, LB 3, NB 1)	8
Total		**147**		**93**

ENGLAND

A. Mitchell	b Amar Singh	14	c Merchant b Nissar	0
H. Gimblett	c Mushtaq Ali b Amar Singh	11	not out	67
M.J.L. Turnbull	b Amar Singh	0	not out	37
M. Leyland	lbw b Amar Singh	60		
R.E.S. Wyatt	c Jahangir b Amar Singh	0		
J. Hardstaff, jr	b Nissar	2		
J. Langridge	c Jahangir b C.K. Nayudu	19		
G.O.B. Allen*	c Jahangir b Amar Singh	13		
G. Duckworth†	c Vizianagram b Nissar	2		
R.W.V. Robins	c C.K. Nayudu b Nissar	0		
H. Verity	not out	2		
Extras	(B 4, LB 4, NB 3)	11	(B 4)	4
Total		**134**	(1 wicket)	**108**

ENGLAND	O	M	R	W	O	M	R	W
Allen	17	7	35	5	18	1	43	5
Wyatt	3	2	7	0	7	4	8	0
Verity	18·1	5	42	2	16	8	17	4
Langridge	4	1	9	0				
Robins	13	4	50	3	5	1	17	1
INDIA								
Nissar	17	5	36	3	6	3	26	1
Amar Singh	25·1	11	35	6	16·3	6	36	0
Jahangir	9	0	27	0	10	3	20	0
C.K. Nayudu	7	2	17	1	7	2	22	0
C.S. Nayudu	3	0	8	0				

FALL OF WICKETS				
	I	E	I	E
Wkt	1st	1st	2nd	2nd
1st	62	16	0	0
2nd	62	16	18	–
3rd	64	30	22	–
4th	66	34	28	–
5th	85	41	39	–
6th	97	96	45	–
7th	107	129	64	–
8th	119	132	80	–
9th	137	132	90	–
10th	147	134	93	–

Umpires: A. Dolphin (5) and F.I. Walden (5).

Close: 1st day – E(1) 132-7 (Allen 13, Duckworth 2); 2nd – I(2) 80-7 (Palia 15, Vizianagram 6).

ENGLAND v INDIA 1936 (2nd Test)

Played at Old Trafford, Manchester, on 25, 27, 28 July.
Toss: India.   Result: MATCH DRAWN.
Debuts: England – A.E. Fagg, L.B. Fishlock, A.R. Gover: India – K.R. Meherhomji,
C. Ramaswami.

England scored 571 for 8 in only 375 minutes and India's opening partnership of 203 (then their record against England) took just 150 minutes; on the second day 588 runs were scored for the loss of six wickets (England 398 for 6, India 190 for 0) – this is still the most runs scored in a day of Test cricket. The first wicket of the match fell to a freak run out when Merchant drove a ball via the bat of Mushtaq Ali, the non-striker, to mid-on (Fagg), who threw down the bowler's wicket. Hammond reached his first hundred against India out of 138 runs in 100 minutes.

INDIA

V.M. Merchant	c Hammond b Verity	33	lbw b Hammond	114
Mushtaq Ali	run out	13	c and b Robins	112
L. Amar Singh	c Duckworth b Worthington	27	(6) not out	48
C.K. Nayudu	lbw b Allen	16	st Duckworth b Verity	34
S. Wazir Ali	c Worthington b Verity	42	b Robins	4
C. Ramaswami	b Verity	40	(3) b Robins	60
M. Jahangir Khan	c Duckworth b Allen	2		
C.S. Nayudu	b Verity	10		
Maharaj Vizianagram*	b Robins	6	(7) not out	0
K.R. Meherhomji†	not out	0		
Mahomed Nissar	c Hardstaff b Robins	13		
Extras	(B 1)	1	(B 9, LB 7, NB 2)	18
Total		**203**	(5 wickets)	**390**

ENGLAND

H. Gimblett	b Nissar	9
A.E. Fagg	lbw b Mushtaq Ali	39
W.R. Hammond	b C.K. Nayudu	167
T.S. Worthington	c C.K. Nayudu b C.S. Nayudu	87
L.B. Fishlock	b C.K. Nayudu	6
J. Hardstaff, jr	c and b Amar Singh	94
G.O.B. Allen*	c Meherhomji b Amar Singh	1
R.W.V. Robins	c Merchant b Nissar	76
H. Verity	not out	66
G. Duckworth†	not out	10
A.R. Gover	did not bat	
Extras	(B 5, LB 9, W 1, NB 1)	16
Total	(8 wickets declared)	**571**

ENGLAND	O	M	R	W	O	M	R	W	FALL OF WICKETS			
Allen	14	3	39	2	19	2	96	0		I	E	I
Gover	15	2	39	0	20	2	61	0	Wkt	1st	1st	2nd
Hammond	9	1	34	0	12	2	19	1	1st	18	12	203
Robins	9·1	1	34	2	29	2	103	3	2nd	67	146	279
Verity	17	5	41	4	22	8	66	1	3rd	73	273	313
Worthington	4	0	15	1	13	4	27	0	4th	100	289	317
									5th	161	375	390
INDIA									6th	164	376	–
Nissar	28	5	125	2					7th	181	409	–
Amar Singh	41	8	121	2					8th	188	547	–
C.S. Nayudu	17	1	87	1					9th	190	–	–
C.K. Nayudu	22	1	84	2					10th	203	–	–
Jahangir	18	5	57	0								
Mushtaq Ali	13	1	64	1								
Merchant	3	0	17	0								

Umpires: F. Chester (21) and F.I. Walden (6).

Close: 1st day – E(1) 173-2 (Hammond 118, Worthington 5); 2nd – I(2) 190-0 (Merchant 79, Mushtaq Ali 105).

ENGLAND v INDIA 1936 (3rd Test)

Played at Kennington Oval, London, on 15, 17, 18 August.
Toss: England.   Result: ENGLAND won by nine wickets.
Debuts: India – M. Baqa Jilani.

Hammond's 15th hundred for England, and second in successive innings, was the first double century against India. He batted for 290 minutes, hit 30 fours and shared with Worthington in a partnership of 266 which is still the fourth-wicket record for this series. Nayudu refused to retire after sustaining a crippling blow from a ball from Allen, defended stoically for over $2\frac{1}{2}$ hours, and averted an innings defeat. Allen's analysis of 7 for 80 remained his best in Tests. England needed only 40 minutes to score 64 runs and win the rubber.

ENGLAND

C.J. Barnett	lbw b Nayudu	43	not out	32
A.E. Fagg	c Hussain b Amar Singh	8	c Amar Singh b Nissar	22
W.R. Hammond	b Nissar	217	not out	5
M. Leyland	b Nissar	26		
T.S. Worthington	b Nissar	128		
L.B. Fishlock	not out	19		
G.O.B. Allen*	c Hussain b Nissar	13		
H. Verity	c Hussain b Nissar	4		
J.M. Sims	lbw b Amar Singh	1		
W. Voce	not out	1		
G. Duckworth†	did not bat			
Extras	(LB 10, NB 1)	11	(B 4, NB 1)	5
Total	(8 wickets declared)	**471**	(1 wicket)	**64**

INDIA

V.M. Merchant	b Allen	52		c Worthington b Allen	48
Mushtaq Ali	st Duckworth b Verity	52		c Hammond b Allen	17
Dilawar Hussain†	st Duckworth b Verity	35		lbw b Sims	54
C.K. Nayudu	c Allen b Voce	5	(6)	b Allen	81
C. Ramaswami	b Sims	29	(8)	not out	41
S. Wazir Ali	lbw b Sims	2	(7)	c Duckworth b Allen	1
L. Amar Singh	b Verity	5	(4)	c Sims b Verity	44
M. Jahangir Khan	c Fagg b Sims	9	(10)	c Voce b Allen	1
Maharaj Vizianagram*	b Sims	1		b Allen	1
M. Baqa Jilani	not out	4	(5)	c Fagg b Allen	12
Mahomed Nissar	c Worthington b Sims	14		c Voce b Sims	0
Extras	(B 8, LB 6)	14		(B 3, LB 7, NB 2)	12
Total		**222**			**312**

INDIA	O	M	R	W	O	M	R	W
Nissar	26	2	120	5	7	0	36	1
Amar Singh	39	8	102	2	6	0	23	0
Baqa Jilani	15	4	55	0				
Nayudu	24	1	82	1				
Jahangir	17	1	65	0				
Mushtaq Ali	2	0	13	0				
Merchant	6	0	23	0				
ENGLAND								
Voce	20	5	46	1	20	5	40	0
Allen	12	3	37	1	20	3	80	7
Hammond	8	2	17	0	7	0	24	0
Verity	25	12	30	3	16	6	32	1
Sims	18·5	1	73	5	25	1	95	2
Leyland	2	0	5	0	3	0	19	0
Worthington					2	0	10	0

FALL OF WICKETS

Wkt	E 1st	I 1st	I 2nd	E 2nd
1st	19	81	64	48
2nd	93	125	71	–
3rd	156	130	122	–
4th	422	185	159	–
5th	437	187	212	–
6th	455	192	222	–
7th	463	195	295	–
8th	468	203	307	–
9th	–	206	309	–
10th	–	222	312	–

Umpires: F. Chester (22) and F.I. Walden (7).

Close: 1st day – E(1) 471-8 (Fishlock 19, Voce 1); 2nd – I(2) 156-3 (Dilawar Hussain 30, Baqa Jilani 12).

AUSTRALIA v ENGLAND 1936–37 (1st Test)

Played at Woolloongabba, Brisbane, on 4, 5, 7, 8, 9 December.
Toss: England.   Result: ENGLAND won by 322 runs.
Debuts: Australia – C.L. Badcock, R.H. Robinson, M.W. Sievers, F.A. Ward.

Worthington was out when he attempted to hook the first ball of Bradman's first match as captain. Leyland scored England's only century at 'The Gabba' until 1974-75. Fingleton became the first to score four hundreds in successive Test innings. His run was ended by the very first ball of his next innings. When he stumped Hardstaff, Oldfield beat A.F.A. Lilley's record of 84 dismissals in this series. With McCormick unable to bat because of acute lumbago, Australia were dismissed on a rain-affected pitch for their lowest total at home this century.

ENGLAND

T.S. Worthington	c Oldfield b McCormick	0	st Oldfield b McCabe	8
C.J. Barnett	c Oldfield b O'Reilly	69	c Badcock b Ward	26
A.E. Fagg	c Oldfield b McCormick	4	st Oldfield b Ward	27
W.R. Hammond	c Robinson b McCormick	0	hit wkt b Ward	25
M. Leyland	b Ward	126	c Bradman b Ward	33
L.E.G. Ames†	c Chipperfield b Ward	24	b Sievers	9
J. Hardstaff, jr	c McCabe b O'Reilly	43	(8) st Oldfield b Ward	20
R.W.V. Robins	c sub (W.A. Brown) b O'Reilly	38	(9) c Chipperfield b Ward	0
G.O.B. Allen*	c McCabe b O'Reilly	35	(7) c Fingleton b Sievers	68
H. Verity	c Sievers b O'Reilly	7	lbw b Sievers	19
W. Voce	not out	4	not out	2
Extras	(B 1, LB 3, NB 4)	8	(B 14, LB 4, NB 1)	19
Total		**358**		**256**

AUSTRALIA

J.H.W. Fingleton	b Verity	100	b Voce	0
C.L. Badcock	b Allen	8	c Fagg b Allen	0
D.G. Bradman*	c Worthington b Voce	38	(5) c Fagg b Allen	0
S.J. McCabe	c Barnett b Voce	51	(6) c Leyland b Allen	7
R.H. Robinson	c Hammond b Voce	2	(7) c Hammond b Voce	3
A.G. Chipperfield	c Ames b Voce	7	(8) not out	26
M.W. Sievers	b Allen	8	(3) c Voce b Allen	5
W.A.S. Oldfield†	c Ames b Voce	6	(4) b Voce	10
W.J. O'Reilly	c Leyland b Voce	3	b Allen	0
F.A. Ward	c Hardstaff b Allen	0	b Voce	1
E.L. McCormick	not out	1	absent ill	–
Extras	(B 4, LB 1, NB 5)	10	(NB 6)	6
Total		**234**		**58**

AUSTRALIA	O	M	R	W	O	M	R	W					
McCormick	8	1	26	3					**FALL OF WICKETS**				
Sievers	16	5	42	0	19·6	9	29	3		E	A	E	A
O'Reilly	40·6	13	102	5	35	15	59	0	*Wkt*	*1st*	*1st*	*2nd*	*2nd*
Ward	36	3	138	2	46	16	102	6	1st	0	13	17	0
Chipperfield	11	3	32	0	10	2	33	0	2nd	20	89	50	3
McCabe	2	0	10	0	6	1	14	1	3rd	20	166	82	7
ENGLAND									4th	119	176	105	7
									5th	162	202	122	16
Allen	16	2	71	3	6	0	36	5	6th	252	220	144	20
Voce	20·6	5	41	6	6·3	0	16	4	7th	311	229	205	35
Hammond	4	0	12	0					8th	311	231	205	41
Verity	28	11	52	1					9th	343	231	247	58
Robins	17	0	48	0					10th	358	234	256	–

Umpires: G. Borwick (12) and J.D. Scott (1).

Close: 1st day – E(1) 263-6 (Hardstaff 27, Robins 6); 2nd – A(1) 151-2 (Fingleton 61, McCabe 37); 3rd – E(2) 75-2 (Fagg 24, Hammond 12); 4th – A(2) 3-1 (Badcock 0, Sievers 2).

AUSTRALIA v ENGLAND 1936–37 (2nd Test)

Played at Sydney Cricket Ground on 18, 19, 21, 22 December.
Toss: England.   Result: ENGLAND won by an innings and 22 runs.
Debuts: Nil.

The third of Hammond's four double-centuries against Australia took 458 minutes and included 27 fours. His scores in four Tests at Sydney to date were 251, 112, 101, 75 not out and 231 not out. A thunderstorm on the third morning transformed the pitch. Bradman was dismissed first ball for his second duck in successive innings, the second of three wickets in four balls during Voce's opening spell (O'Brien and McCabe were the other victims). Badcock was taken ill before Australia's first innings but left his sick-bed to bat in the second.

ENGLAND

A.E. Fagg	c Sievers b McCormick	11
C.J. Barnett	b Ward	57
W.R. Hammond	not out	231
M. Leyland	lbw b McCabe	42
L.E.G. Ames†	c sub (R.H. Robinson) b Ward	29
G.O.B. Allen*	lbw b O'Reilly	9
J. Hardstaff, jr	b McCormick	26
H. Verity	not out	0
J.M. Sims	)	
R.W.V. Robins	) did not bat	
W. Voce	)	
Extras	(B 8, LB 8, W 1, NB 4)	21
Total	(6 wickets declared)	**426**

AUSTRALIA

J.H.W. Fingleton	c Verity b Voce	12		b Sims	73
L.P.J. O'Brien	c Sims b Voce	0		c Allen b Hammond	17
D.G. Bradman*	c Allen b Voce	0		b Verity	82
S.J. McCabe	c Sims b Voce	0		lbw b Voce	93
A.G. Chipperfield	c Sims b Allen	13		b Voce	21
M.W. Sievers	c Voce b Verity	4	(7)	run out	24
W.A.S. Oldfield†	b Verity	1	(8)	c Ames b Voce	1
W.J. O'Reilly	not out	37	(9)	b Hammond	3
E.L. McCormick	b Allen	10	(10)	lbw b Hammond	0
F.A. Ward	b Allen	0	(11)	not out	1
C.L. Badcock	absent ill	–	(6)	lbw b Allen	2
Extras	(B 1, LB 1, NB 1)	3		(LB 3, NB 4)	7
Total		**80**			**324**

AUSTRALIA	O	M	R	W	O	M	R	W
McCormick	20	1	79	2				
Sievers	16·2	4	30	0				
Ward	42	8	132	2				
O'Reilly	41	17	86	1				
Chipperfield	13	2	47	0				
McCabe	9	1	31	1				
ENGLAND								
Voce	8	1	10	4	19	4	66	3
Allen	5·7	1	19	3	19	4	61	1
Verity	3	0	17	2	19	7	55	1
Hammond	4	0	6	0	15.7	3	29	3
Sims	2	0	20	0	17	0	80	1
Robins	1	0	5	0	7	0	26	0

FALL OF WICKETS

	E	A	A
Wkt	1st	1st	2nd
1st	27	1	38
2nd	118	1	162
3rd	247	1	186
4th	351	16	220
5th	368	28	226
6th	424	30	318
7th	–	31	319
8th	–	80	323
9th	–	80	323
10th	–	–	324

Umpires: G. Borwick (13) and J.D. Scott (2).

Close: 1st day – E(1) 279-3 (Hammond 147, Ames 8); 2nd – E(1) 426-6 (Hammond 231, Verity 0); 3rd – A(2) 145-1 (Fingleton 67, Bradman 57).

AUSTRALIA v ENGLAND 1936–37 (3rd Test)

Played at Melbourne Cricket Ground on 1, 2, 4, 5, 6, 7 January.
Toss: Australia.   Result: AUSTRALIA won by 365 runs.
Debuts: Nil.

For the first time in Test cricket each side declared its first innings closed. Bradman countered a 'gluepot' pitch by opening with his tailenders and went to the wicket at 2.50 pm the following day when Australia were 97 for 5. He batted for 458 minutes, hit 22 fours and 110 singles, made the (then) highest score for Australia against England at home, and shared in what remains the world record sixth-wicket partnership in all Tests of 346 with Fingleton. His innings, made while he was suffering from a severe chill, remains the highest second innings score in this series and the record for any number seven batsman in Tests. The attendance of 350,534 was the record for any cricket match until 1981-82 (*Test No. 915*).

AUSTRALIA

J.H.W. Fingleton	c Sims b Robins	38	(6) c Ames b Sims		136
W.A. Brown	c Ames b Voce	1	(5) c Barnett b Voce		20
D.G. Bradman*	c Robins b Verity	13	(7) c Allen b Verity		270
K.E. Rigg	c Verity b Allen	16	lbw b Sims		47
S.J. McCabe	c Worthington b Voce	63	(8) lbw b Allen		22
L.S. Darling	c Allen b Verity	20	(9) b Allen		0
M.W. Sievers	st Ames b Robins	1	(10) not out		25
W.A.S. Oldfield†	not out	27	(11) lbw b Verity		7
W.J. O'Reilly	c Sims b Hammond	4	(1) c and b Voce		0
F.A. Ward	st Ames b Hammond	7	(3) c Hardstaff b Verity		18
L.O'B. Fleetwood-Smith	did not bat		(2) c Verity b Voce		0
Extras	(B 2, LB 6, NB 2)	10	(B 6, LB 2, W 1, NB 10)		19
Total	(9 wickets declared)	**200**			**564**

ENGLAND

T.S. Worthington	c Bradman b McCabe	0	c Sievers b Ward		16
C.J. Barnett	c Darling b Sievers	11	lbw b O'Reilly		23
W.R. Hammond	c Darling b Sievers	32	b Sievers		51
M. Leyland	c Darling b O'Reilly	17	not out		111
J.M. Sims	c Brown b Sievers	3	(10) lbw b Fleetwood-Smith		0
L.E.G. Ames†	b Sievers	3	(5) b Fleetwood-Smith		19
R.W.V. Robins	c O'Reilly b Sievers	0	(8) b O'Reilly		61
J. Hardstaff, jr	b O'Reilly	3	(6) c Ward b Fleetwood-Smith		17
G.O.B. Allen*	not out	0	(7) c Sievers b Fleetwood-Smith		11
H. Verity	c Brown b O'Reilly	0	(9) c McCabe b O'Reilly		11
W. Voce	not out	0	c Bradman b Fleetwood-Smith		0
Extras	(B 5, LB 1, NB 1)	7	(LB 3)		3
Total	(9 wickets declared)	**76**			**323**

ENGLAND	O	M	R	W	O	M	R	W	FALL OF WICKETS				
Voce	18	3	49	2	29	2	120	3		A	E	A	E
Allen	12	2	35	1	23	2	84	2	*Wkt*	*1st*	*1st*	*2nd*	*2nd*
Sims	9	1	35	0	23	1	109	2	1st	7	0	0	29
Verity	14	4	24	2	37·7	9	79	3	2nd	33	14	3	65
Robins	7	0	31	2	11	2	46	0	3rd	69	56	38	117
Hammond	5·3	0	16	2	22	3	89	0	4th	79	68	74	155
Worthington					4	0	18	0	5th	122	71	97	179
AUSTRALIA									6th	130	71	443	195
McCabe	2	1	7	1	8	0	32	0	7th	183	76	511	306
Sievers	11·2	5	21	5	12	2	39	1	8th	190	76	511	322
O'Reilly	12	5	28	3	21	6	65	3	9th	200	76	549	323
Fleetwood-Smith	3	1	13	0	25·6	2	124	5	10th	–	–	564	323
Ward					12	1	60	1					

Umpires: G. Borwick (14) and J.D. Scott (3).

Close: 1st day – A(1) 181-6 (McCabe 63, Oldfield 21); 2nd – A (2) 3-1 (Fleetwood-Smith 0, Ward 1); 3rd – A(2) 194-5 (Fingleton 39, Bradman 56); 4th – A(2) 500-6 (Bradman 248, McCabe 14); 5th – E(2) 236-6 (Leyland 69, Robins 27).

AUSTRALIA v ENGLAND 1936–37 (4th Test)

Played at Adelaide Oval on 29, 30 January, 1, 2, 3, 4 February.
Toss: Australia.   Result: AUSTRALIA won by 148 runs.
Debuts: Australia – R.G. Gregory.

For the third time against England, Bradman scored a double-century in two successive Test matches; it was his 17th Test hundred, beating the record set by H. Sutcliffe which was equalled during this rubber by Hammond. Fleetwood-Smith returned the best innings and match analyses of his ten-match Test career.

AUSTRALIA

J.H.W. Fingleton	run out	10		lbw b Hammond	12
W.A. Brown	c Allen b Farnes	42		c Ames b Voce	32
K.E. Rigg	c Ames b Farnes	20	(5)	c Hammond b Farnes	7
D.G. Bradman*	b Allen	26	(3)	c and b Hammond	212
S.J. McCabe	c Allen b Robins	88	(4)	c Wyatt b Robins	55
R.G. Gregory	lbw b Hammond	23		run out	50
A.G. Chipperfield	not out	57		c Ames b Hammond	31
W.A.S. Oldfield†	run out	5		c Ames b Hammond	1
W.J. O'Reilly	c Leyland b Allen	7		c Hammond b Farnes	1
E.L. McCormick	c Ames b Hammond	4		b Hammond	1
L.O'B. Fleetwood-Smith	b Farnes	1		not out	4
Extras	(LB 2, NB 3)	5		(B 10, LB 15, W 1, NB 1)	27
Total		**288**			**433**

ENGLAND

H. Verity	c Bradman b O'Reilly	19		b Fleetwood-Smith	17
C.J. Barnett	lbw b Fleetwood-Smith	129		c Chipperfield b Fleetwood-Smith	21
W.R. Hammond	c McCormick b O'Reilly	20	(4)	b Fleetwood-Smith	39
M.Leyland	c Chipperfield b Fleetwood-Smith	45	(5)	c Chipperfield b Fleetwood-Smith	32
R.E.S. Wyatt	c Fingleton b O'Reilly	3	(6)	c Oldfield b McCabe	50
L.E.G. Ames†	b McCormick	52	(7)	lbw b Fleetwood-Smith	0
J. Hardstaff, jr	c and b McCormick	20	(3)	b O'Reilly	43
G.O.B. Allen*	lbw b Fleetwood-Smith	11		c Gregory b McCormick	9
R.W.V. Robins	c Oldfield b O'Reilly	10		b McCormick	4
W. Voce	c Rigg b Fleetwood-Smith	8		b Fleetwood-Smith	1
K. Farnes	not out	0		not out	7
Extras	(B 6, LB 2, W 1, NB 4)	13		(B 12, LB 2, NB 6)	20
Total		**330**			**243**

ENGLAND	O	M	R	W	O	M	R	W
Voce	12	0	49	0	20	2	86	1
Allen	16	0	60	2	14	1	61	0
Farnes	20·6	1	71	3	24	2	89	2
Hammond	6	0	30	2	15·2	1	57	5
Verity	16	4	47	0	37	17	54	0
Robins	7	1	26	1	6	0	38	1
Barnett					5	1	15	0
Leyland					2	0	6	0
AUSTRALIA								
McCormick	21	2	81	2	13	1	43	2
McCabe	9	2	18	0	5	0	15	1
Fleetwood-Smith	41·4	10	129	4	30	1	110	6
O'Reilly	30	12	51	4	26	8	55	1
Chipperfield	9	1	24	0				
Gregory	3	0	14	0				

FALL OF WICKETS

	A	E	A	E
Wkt	1st	1st	2nd	2nd
1st	26	53	21	45
2nd	72	108	88	50
3rd	73	190	197	120
4th	136	195	237	149
5th	206	259	372	190
6th	226	299	422	190
7th	249	304	426	225
8th	271	318	427	231
9th	283	322	429	235
10th	288	330	433	243

Umpires: G. Borwick (15) and J.D. Scott (4).

Close: 1st day – A(1) 267-7 (Chipperfield 45, O'Reilly 3); 2nd – E(1) 174-2 (Barnett 92, Leyland 35); 3rd – A(2) 63-1 (Brown 23, Bradman 26); 4th – A(2) 341-4 (Bradman 174, Gregory 36); 5th – E(2) 148-3 (Hammond 39, Leyland 17).

AUSTRALIA v ENGLAND 1936–37 (5th Test)

Played at Melbourne Cricket Ground on 26, 27 February, 1, 2, 3 March.
Toss: Australia.   Result: AUSTRALIA won by an innings and 200 runs.
Debuts: Nil.

This was the first time that any country had won a Test rubber after losing the first two matches. The five matches attracted 943,513 spectators – the biggest attendance for any Test rubber. Bradman's hundred was his 12th against England, equalling the series record held by J.B. Hobbs. 'The Don's' aggregate of 810, average 90.00, is the highest by a captain in any Test rubber.

AUSTRALIA

J.H.W. Fingleton	c Voce b Farnes	17
K.E. Rigg	c Ames b Farnes	28
D.G. Bradman*	b Farnes	169
S.J. McCabe	c Farnes b Verity	112
C.L. Badcock	c Worthington b Voce	118
R.G. Gregory	c Verity b Farnes	80
W.A.S. Oldfield†	c Ames b Voce	21
L.J. Nash	c Ames b Farnes	17
W.J. O'Reilly	b Voce	1
E.L. McCormick	not out	17
L. O'B. Fleetwood-Smith	b Farnes	13
Extras	(B 1, LB 5, W 1, NB 4)	11
Total		**604**

ENGLAND

C.J. Barnett	c Oldfield b Nash	18	lbw b O'Reilly		41
T.S. Worthington	hit wkt b Fleetwood-Smith	44	c Bradman b McCormick		6
J. Hardstaff, jr	c McCormick b O'Reilly	83	b Nash		1
W.R. Hammond	c Nash b O'Reilly	14	c Bradman b O'Reilly		56
M. Leyland	b O'Reilly	7	c McCormick b Fleetwood-Smith		28
R.E.S. Wyatt	c Bradman b O'Reilly	38	run out		9
L.E.G. Ames†	b Nash	19	c McCabe b McCormick		11
G.O.B. Allen*	c Oldfield b Nash	0	c Nash b O'Reilly		7
H. Verity	c Rigg b Nash	0	not out		2
W. Voce	st Oldfield b O'Reilly	3	c Badcock b Fleetwood-Smith		1
K. Farnes	not out	0	c Nash b Fleetwood-Smith		0
Extras	(LB 12, NB 1)	13	(LB 3)		3
Total		**239**			**165**

ENGLAND	O	M	R	W	O	M	R	W
Allen	17	0	99	0				
Farnes	28·5	5	96	6				
Voce	29	3	123	3				
Hammond	16	1	62	0				
Verity	41	5	127	1				
Worthington	6	0	60	0				
Leyland	3	0	26	0				
AUSTRALIA								
McCormick	13	1	54	0	9	0	33	2
Nash	17·5	1	70	4	7	1	34	1
O'Reilly	23	7	51	5	19	6	58	3
Fleetwood-Smith	18	3	51	1	13·2	3	36	3
McCabe					1	0	1	0

FALL OF WICKETS

	A	E	E
Wkt	1st	1st	2nd
1st	42	33	9
2nd	54	96	10
3rd	303	130	70
4th	346	140	121
5th	507	202	142
6th	544	236	142
7th	563	236	153
8th	571	236	162
9th	576	239	165
10th	604	239	165

Umpires: G. Borwick (16) and J.D. Scott (5).

Close: 1st day – A(1) 342-3 (Bradman 165, Badcock 12); 2nd – A(1) 593-9 (McCormick 9, Fleetwood-Smith 11); 3rd – E(1) 184-4 (Hardstaff 73, Wyatt 20); 4th – E (2) 165-8 (Verity 2, Voce 1).

ENGLAND v NEW ZEALAND 1937 (1st Test)

Played at Lord's, London, on 26, 28, 29 June.
Toss: England.   Result: MATCH DRAWN.
Debuts: England – L. Hutton (*later Sir Leonard Hutton*), J.H. Parks; New Zealand – J. Cowie (*not 'J.A'*), M.P. Donnelly, W.A. Hadlee, D.A.R. Moloney, E.W.T. Tindill, W.M. Wallace.

The partnership of 245 in 210 minutes between Hammond and Hardstaff is still the highest third-wicket stand by either country in this series. When his score reached 23 Hammond passed J.B. Hobbs' record Test aggregate of 5,410. Fluid on the knee prevented him from batting in the second innings. Moloney and Roberts averted the follow on with a partnership of 104 which is still New Zealand's highest for the eighth wicket against England.

ENGLAND

J.H. Parks	b Cowie	22	b Cowie	7
L. Hutton	b Cowie	0	c Vivian b Cowie	1
J. Hardstaff, jr	c Moloney b Roberts	114	c Tindill b Roberts	64
W.R. Hammond	c Roberts b Vivian	140		
E. Paynter	c Dunning b Roberts	74		
C.J. Barnett	b Cowie	5	(4) not out	83
L.E.G. Ames†	b Vivian	5	(5) c sub (J.R. Lamason) b Roberts	20
R.W.V. Robins*	c Tindill b Roberts	18	(6) not out	38
W. Voce	c Tindill b Cowie	27		
H. Verity	c Cowie b Roberts	3		
A.R. Gover	not out	2		
Extras	(B 4, LB 9, W 1)	14	(B 5, LB 8)	13
Total		**424**	(4 wickets declared)	**226**

NEW ZEALAND

J.L. Kerr	c Ames b Robins	31	(7) not out	38
H.G. Vivian	lbw b Gover	5	c Verity b Voce	11
W.A. Hadlee	c Verity b Voce	34	(2) b Voce	3
M.L. Page*	c Paynter b Robins	9	c and b Robins	13
W.M. Wallace	lbw b Parks	52	lbw b Parks	56
M.P. Donnelly	lbw b Parks	0	(9) c Ames b Voce	21
D.A.R. Moloney	c and b Verity	64	(3) run out	0
E.W.T. Tindill†	c Hammond b Robins	8	lbw b Verity	3
A.W. Roberts	not out	66	(6) c sub (G.E. Hart) b Gover	17
J.A. Dunning	b Gover	0		
J. Cowie	lbw b Voce	2		
Extras	(B 4, LB 18, NB 2)	24	(B 4, LB 8, W 1)	13
Total		**295**	(8 wickets)	**175**

NEW ZEALAND	O	M	R	W	O	M	R	W
Cowie	41	10	118	4	15	2	49	2
Roberts	43·3	11	101	4	14	3	73	2
Dunning	20	3	64	0	9	0	60	0
Vivian	46	10	106	2	4	0	31	0
Moloney	2	1	9	0				
Page	3	0	12	0				
ENGLAND								
Gover	22	8	49	2	18	7	27	1
Voce	24·2	2	74	2	18·5	8	41	3
Hammond	6	2	12	0				
Robins	21	5	58	3	16	3	51	1
Verity	25	13	48	1	14	7	33	1
Parks	11	3	26	2	10	6	10	1
Hutton	2	1	4	0				

FALL OF WICKETS

Wkt	E 1st	NZ 1st	E 2nd	NZ 2nd
1st	13	9	8	15
2nd	31	36	19	15
3rd	276	66	123	15
4th	284	131	163	85
5th	302	131	–	87
6th	307	147	–	143
7th	339	176	–	146
8th	402	280	–	175
9th	415	281	–	–
10th	424	295	–	–

Umpires: F. Chester (23) and F.I. Walden (8).

Close: 1st day – E(1) 370-7 (Paynter 42, Voce 12); 2nd – NZ (1) 282-9 (Roberts 58, Cowie 1).

ENGLAND v NEW ZEALAND 1937 (2nd Test)

Played at Old Trafford, Manchester, on 24, 26, 27 July.
Toss: England.   Result: ENGLAND won by 130 runs.
Debuts: England – A.W. Wellard; New Zealand – N. Gallichan.

Hutton, who had struggled for more than half an hour for a match aggregate of one run at Lord's, batted 210 minutes for the first of his 19 Test hundreds. Set 265 runs in 245 minutes, New Zealand were all out soon after tea with off-spinner Goddard achieving the best figures of his brief international career.

ENGLAND

C.J. Barnett	c Kerr b Cowie	62	lbw b Dunning		12
L. Hutton	c Dunning b Vivian	100	c Vivian b Cowie		14
J. Hardstaff, jr	st Tindill b Vivian	58	c Tindill b Cowie		11
W.R. Hammond	b Gallichan	33	c Moloney b Cowie		0
E. Paynter	lbw b Cowie	33	c Cowie b Vivian		7
L.E.G. Ames†	not out	16	lbw b Dunning		39
A.W. Wellard	b Cowie	5	(8) c Wallace b Vivian		0
R.W.V. Robins*	b Cowie	14	(7) c Moloney b Cowie		12
F.R. Brown	b Gallichan	1	b Cowie		57
C.I.J. Smith	c Kerr b Gallichan	21	c and b Cowie		27
T.W.J. Goddard	not out	4	not out		1
Extras	(B 4, LB 7)	11	(LB 7)		7
Total	(9 wickets declared)	**358**			**187**

NEW ZEALAND

H.G. Vivian	b Wellard	58	c Ames b Smith		50
D.A.R. Moloney	lbw b Smith	11	run out		20
W.M. Wallace	st Ames b Brown	23	b Goddard		5
J.L. Kerr	b Wellard	4	b Smith		3
M.P. Donnelly	lbw b Wellard	4	not out		37
W.A. Hadlee	hit wkt b Wellard	93	b Goddard		3
M.L. Page*	c Smith b Hammond	33	b Goddard		2
E.W.T. Tindill†	b Brown	6	lbw b Brown		0
N. Gallichan	c Brown b Smith	30	c Wellard b Goddard		2
J.A. Dunning	not out	4	b Goddard		3
J. Cowie	st Ames b Brown	0	c Wellard b Goddard		0
Extras	(B 4, LB 11)	15	(B 7, LB 1, NB 1)		9
Total		**281**			**134**

NEW ZEALAND	O	M	R	W	O	M	R	W
Cowie	32	6	73	4	23·5	6	67	6
Dunning	28	5	84	0	12	2	35	2
Gallichan	36	7	99	3	8	4	14	0
Vivian	28	7	75	2	17	5	64	2
Page	5	0	16	0				
ENGLAND								
Smith	22	7	29	2	14	2	34	2
Wellard	30	4	81	4	14	2	30	0
Hammond	15	5	27	1	6	1	18	0
Goddard	18	5	48	0	14·4	5	29	6
Brown	22·4	4	81	3	5	0	14	1

FALL OF WICKETS

Wkt	E 1st	NZ 1st	E 2nd	NZ 2nd
1st	100	19	17	50
2nd	228	65	29	68
3rd	231	91	29	73
4th	296	105	46	94
5th	302	119	46	102
6th	307	218	68	104
7th	327	242	75	109
8th	328	268	147	116
9th	352	280	186	134
10th	–	281	187	134

Umpires: W. Reeves (4) and E.J. Smith (3).

Close: 1st day – E(1) 358-9 (Ames 16, Goddard 4); 2nd – E(2) 37-3 (Hardstaff 6, Paynter 3).

ENGLAND v NEW ZEALAND 1937 (3rd Test)

Played at Kennington Oval, London, on 14, 16, 17 August.
Toss: New Zealand.   Result: MATCH DRAWN.
Debuts: England – D.C.S. Compton, A.D.G. Matthews, C. Washbrook.

Only half an hour's play was possible on the first day. Robins ended New Zealand's first innings with a spell of three wickets for one run in seven balls. Compton, who scored 65 in 120 minutes in the first of 131 innings for England, was run out backing up when the bowler, Vivian, deflected Hardstaff's drive into the stumps. Vivian took over the captaincy after Page pulled a muscle.

NEW ZEALAND

H.G. Vivian	c Ames b Gover	13	lbw b Hammond	57
W.A. Hadlee	b Matthews	18	c Compton b Matthews	0
W.M. Wallace	run out	8	lbw b Gover	7
G.L. Weir	c Matthews b Gover	3	c Hutton b Goddard	8
M.P. Donnelly	c Hutton b Robins	58	(6) c Ames b Hammond	0
D.A.R. Moloney	b Hammond	23	(5) b Compton	38
M.L. Page*	c Washbrook b Robins	53	absent hurt	–
A.W. Roberts	c Barnett b Gover	50	(7) lbw b Goddard	9
E.W.T. Tindill†	b Robins	4	(8) not out	37
J.A. Dunning	c Gover b Robins	0	(9) b Compton	19
J. Cowie	not out	4	(10) c Robins b Hutton	2
Extras	(B 2, LB 11, NB 2)	15	(B 4, LB 5, NB 1)	10
Total		**249**		**187**

ENGLAND

C.J. Barnett	c Hadlee b Cowie	13	c Roberts b Dunning	21
L. Hutton	c and b Vivian	12		
C. Washbrook	lbw b Vivian	9	(2) not out	8
D.C.S. Compton	run out	65		
J. Hardstaff, jr	b Cowie	103		
W.R. Hammond	c Wallace b Cowie	31		
L.E.G. Ames†	not out	6		
R.W.V. Robins*	c and b Roberts	9		
A.D.G. Matthews	not out	2		
T.W.J. Goddard	) did not bat			
A.R. Gover	)			
Extras	(B 2, LB 1, W 1)	4	(LB 2)	2
Total	(7 wickets declared)	**254**	(1 wicket)	**31**

ENGLAND	O	M	R	W	O	M	R	W
Gover	28	3	85	3	12	1	42	1
Matthews	22	6	52	1	8	2	13	1
Goddard	10	2	25	0	18	8	41	2
Hammond	7	1	25	1	11	3	19	2
Robins	14·1	2	40	4	11	2	24	0
Hutton	2	0	7	0	2·4	1	4	1
Compton					6	0	34	2
NEW ZEALAND								
Cowie	24	5	73	3	4	1	15	0
Roberts	15	4	26	1	4	1	9	0
Dunning	25	5	89	0	1·2	0	5	1
Vivian	29	5	62	2				

FALL OF WICKETS

	NZ	E	NZ	E
Wkt	1st	1st	2nd	2nd
1st	22	15	4	31
2nd	36	31	19	–
3rd	42	36	46	–
4th	47	161	87	–
5th	97	222	94	–
6th	145	240	107	–
7th	222	249	150	–
8th	244	–	182	–
9th	244	–	187	–
10th	249	–	–	–

Umpires: A. Dolphin (6) and E.J. Smith (4).

Close: 1st day – NZ(1) 20-0 (Vivian 13, Hadlee 7); 2nd – E(1) 86-3 (Compton 28, Hardstaff 23).

ENGLAND v AUSTRALIA 1938 (1st Test)

Played at Trent Bridge, Nottingham, on 10, 11, 13, 14 June.
Toss: England.   Result: MATCH DRAWN.
Debuts: England – W.J. Edrich, R.A. Sinfield, D.V.P. Wright; Australia – B.A. Barnett, A.L. Hassett.

Barnett, 98 at lunch, completed his hundred off the first ball after the interval; it is the nearest that any batsman has come to scoring a century before lunch for England on the first day. This was the only occasion on which four batsmen have scored hundreds in the same innings in this series, or seven centuries have been compiled in the same match; Hutton and Compton did so in their first Test against Australia. At 20 years 19 days, Compton remains England's youngest century-maker. His stand of 206 in 138 minutes with Paynter, whose score was the highest against Australia in England, is still England's record for the sixth wicket against Australia. Wright bowled Fingleton with his fourth ball in Test cricket. McCabe batted for 235 minutes, hit a six and 34 fours, gave no chance, made his second 100 in 84 minutes (the last 50 of it in 24), and scored 72 of the last 77 runs. Bradman set a new series record when he reached his 13th hundred. Hammond's first appearance as England's captain came in his 66th Test.

ENGLAND

C.J. Barnett	b McCormick	126
L. Hutton	lbw b Fleetwood-Smith	100
W.J. Edrich	b O'Reilly	5
W.R. Hammond*	b O'Reilly	26
E. Paynter	not out	216
D.C.S. Compton	c Badcock b Fleetwood-Smith	102
L.E.G. Ames†	b Fleetwood-Smith	46
H. Verity	b Fleetwood-Smith	3
R.A. Sinfield	lbw b O'Reilly	6
D.V.P. Wright	not out	1
K. Farnes	did not bat	
Extras	(B 1, LB 22, NB 4)	27
Total	(8 wickets declared)	**658**

AUSTRALIA

J.H.W. Fingleton	b Wright	9	c Hammond b Edrich	40
W.A. Brown	c Ames b Farnes	48	c Paynter b Verity	133
D.G. Bradman*	c Ames b Sinfield	51	not out	144
S.J. McCabe	c Compton b Verity	232	c Hammond b Verity	39
F.A. Ward	b Farnes	2	(8) not out	7
A.L. Hassett	c Hammond b Wright	1	(5) c Compton b Verity	2
C.L. Badcock	b Wright	9	(6) b Wright	5
B.A. Barnett†	c Wright b Farnes	22	(7) lbw b Sinfield	31
W.J. O'Reilly	c Paynter b Farnes	9		
E.L. McCormick	b Wright	2		
L.O'B. Fleetwood-Smith	not out	5		
Extras	(B 10, LB 10, W 1)	21	(B 5, LB 16, NB 5)	26
Total		**411**	(6 wickets declared)	**427**

AUSTRALIA	O	M	R	W	O	M	R	W
McCormick	32	4	108	1				
O'Reilly	56	11	164	3				
McCabe	21	5	64	0				
Fleetwood-Smith	49	9	153	4				
Ward	30	2	142	0				
ENGLAND								
Farnes	37	11	106	4	24	2	78	0
Hammond	19	7	44	0	12	6	15	0
Sinfield	28	8	51	1	35	8	72	1
Wright	39	6	153	4	37	8	85	1
Verity	7·3	0	36	1	62	27	102	3
Edrich					13	2	39	1
Barnett					1	0	10	0

FALL OF WICKETS

	E	A	A
Wkt	1st	1st	2nd
1st	219	34	89
2nd	240	111	259
3rd	244	134	331
4th	281	144	337
5th	487	151	369
6th	577	194	417
7th	597	263	–
8th	626	319	–
9th	–	334	–
10th	–	411	–

Umpires: F. Chester (24) and E. Robinson (1).

Close: 1st day – E(1) 422-4 (Paynter 75, Compton 69); 2nd – A(1) 138-3 (McCabe 19, Ward 0); 3rd – A(2) 102-1 (Brown 51, Bradman 3).

ENGLAND v AUSTRALIA 1938 (2nd Test)

Played at Lord's, London, on 24, 25, 27, 28 June.
Toss: England.   Result: MATCH DRAWN.
Debuts: Nil.

Hammond batted 367 minutes, hit 32 fours, and gave no chance in making the highest score against Australia at Lord's and the highest by an England captain in this series. His partnership of 222 in 182 minutes with Paynter is still England's highest for the fourth wicket against Australia. Chipperfield injured a finger during his ninth over. Brown batted 369 minutes in scoring Australia's 100th century against England. The total of 422 remains the highest throughout which anyone has carried his bat in a Test. A dropped slip catch deprived Farnes of a hat-trick. Bradman scored the 200th hundred of this series and passed the record aggregate of 3,636 by J.B. Hobbs for these Tests. Paynter kept wicket and caught Barnett after Ames had fractured a finger.

ENGLAND

C.J. Barnett	c Brown b McCormick	18	c McCabe b McCormick		12
L. Hutton	,c Brown b McCormick	4	c McCormick b O'Reilly		5
W.J. Edrich	b McCormick	0	(4) c McCabe b McCormick		10
W.R. Hammond*	b McCormick	240	(6) c sub (M.G. Waite) b McCabe		2
E. Paynter	lbw b O'Reilly	99	run out		43
D.C.S. Compton	lbw b O'Reilly	6	(7) not out		76
L.E.G. Ames†	c McCormick b Fleetwood-Smith	83	(8) c McCabe b O'Reilly		6
H. Verity	b O'Reilly	5	(3) b McCormick		11
A.W. Wellard	c McCormick b O'Reilly	4	b McCabe		38
D.V.P. Wright	b Fleetwood-Smith	6	not out		10
K. Farnes	not out	5			
Extras	(B 1, LB 12, W 1, NB 10)	24	(B 12, LB 12, W 1, NB 4)		29
Total		**494**	(8 wickets declared)		**242**

AUSTRALIA

J.H.W. Fingleton	c Hammond b Wright	31	c Hammond b Wellard	4
W.A. Brown	not out	206	b Verity	10
D.G. Bradman*	b Verity	18	not out	102
S.J. McCabe	c Verity b Farnes	38	c Hutton b Verity	21
A.L. Hassett	lbw b Wellard	56	b Wright	42
C.L. Badcock	b Wellard	0	c Wright b Edrich	0
B.A. Barnett†	c Compton b Verity	8	c Paynter b Edrich	14
A.G. Chipperfield	lbw b Verity	1		
W.J. O'Reilly	b Farnes	42		
E.L. McCormick	c Barnett b Farnes	0		
L.O'B. Fleetwood-Smith	c Barnett b Verity	7		
Extras	(B 1, LB 8, NB 6)	15	(B 5, LB 3, W 2, NB 1)	11
Total		**422**	(6 wickets)	**204**

AUSTRALIA	O	M	R	W	O	M	R	W					
McCormick	27	1	101	4	24	5	72	3					
McCabe	31	4	86	0	12	1	58	2					
Fleetwood-Smith	33.5	2	139	2	7	1	30	0					
O'Reilly	37	6	93	4	29	10	53	2					
Chipperfield	8.4	0	51	0									

FALL OF WICKETS				
	E	A	E	A
Wkt	1st	1st	2nd	2nd
1st	12	69	25	8
2nd	20	101	28	71
3rd	31	152	43	111
4th	253	276	64	175
5th	271	276	76	180
6th	457	307	128	204
7th	472	308	142	–
8th	476	393	216	–
9th	483	393	–	–
10th	494	422	–	–

ENGLAND	O	M	R	W	O	M	R	W
Farnes	43	6	135	3	13	3	51	0
Wellard	23	2	96	2	9	1	30	1
Wright	16	2	68	1	8	0	56	1
Verity	35.4	9	103	4	13	5	29	2
Edrich	4	2	5	0	5.2	0	27	2

Umpires: E.J. Smith (5) and F.I. Walden (9).

Close: 1st day – E(1) 409-5 (Hammond 210, Ames 50); 2nd – A(1) 299-5 (Brown 140, Barnett 6); 3rd – E(2) 39-2 (Verity 5, Edrich 6).

The 3rd Test at Old Trafford, Manchester, scheduled for 8, 9, 11, 12 July, was abandoned without a ball being bowled (see page 816).

ENGLAND v AUSTRALIA 1938 (4th Test)

Played at Headingley, Leeds, on 22, 23, 25 July.
Toss: England.   Result: AUSTRALIA won by five wickets.
Debuts: England – W.F.F. Price; Australia – M.G. Waite.

Bradman scored his third hundred in successive Test innings at Leeds and extended to six his record sequence of matches in which he had made centuries. On a damp pitch and in deepening gloom he manipulated the strike and the bowling to reach his 15th century against England. O'Reilly took ten wickets for the third time in this series as Australia retained the Ashes.

ENGLAND

W.J. Edrich	b O'Reilly	12	st Barnett b Fleetwood-Smith		28
C.J. Barnett	c Barnett b McCormick	30	c Barnett b McCormick		29
J. Hardstaff, jr	run out	4	b O'Reilly		11
W.R. Hammond*	b O'Reilly	76	c Brown b O'Reilly		0
E. Paynter	st Barnett b Fleetwood-Smith	28	not out		21
D.C.S. Compton	b O'Reilly	14	c Barnett b O'Reilly		15
W.F.F. Price†	c McCabe b O'Reilly	0	lbw b Fleetwood-Smith		6
H. Verity	not out	25	b Fleetwood-Smith		0
D.V.P. Wright	c Fingleton b Fleetwood-Smith	22	c Waite b Fleetwood-Smith		0
K. Farnes	c Fingleton b Fleetwood-Smith	2	b O'Reilly		7
W.E. Bowes	b O'Reilly	3	lbw b O'Reilly		0
Extras	(LB 4, NB 3)	7	(LB 4, W 1, NB 1)		6
Total		**223**			**123**

AUSTRALIA

J.H.W. Fingleton	b Verity	30		lbw b Verity	9
W.A. Brown	b Wright	22		lbw b Farnes	9
B.A. Barnett†	c Price b Farnes	57	(7)	not out	15
D.G. Bradman*	b Bowes	103	(3)	c Verity b Wright	16
S.J. McCabe	b Farnes	1	(4)	c Barnett b Wright	15
C.L. Badcock	b Bowes	4		not out	5
A.L. Hassett	c Hammond b Wright	13	(5)	c Edrich b Wright	33
M.G. Waite	c Price b Farnes	3			
W.J. O'Reilly	c Hammond b Farnes	2			
E.L. McCormick	b Bowes	0			
L.O'B. Fleetwood-Smith	not out	2			
Extras	(B 2, LB 3)	5		(B 4, NB 1)	5
Total		**242**		(5 wickets)	**107**

AUSTRALIA	O	M	R	W	O	M	R	W
McCormick	20	6	46	1	11	4	18	1
Waite	18	7	31	0	2	0	9	0
O'Reilly	34·1	17	66	5	21·5	8	56	5
Fleetwood-Smith	25	7	73	3	16	4	34	4
McCabe	1	1	0	0				
ENGLAND								
Farnes	26	3	77	4	11·3	4	17	1
Bowes	35·4	6	79	3	11	0	35	0
Wright	15	4	38	2	5	0	26	3
Verity	19	6	30	1	5	2	24	1
Edrich	3	0	13	0				

FALL OF WICKETS

	E	A	E	A
Wkt	1st	1st	2nd	2nd
1st	29	28	60	17
2nd	34	87	73	32
3rd	88	128	73	50
4th	142	136	73	61
5th	171	145	96	91
6th	171	195	116	–
7th	172	232	116	–
8th	213	240	116	–
9th	215	240	123	–
10th	223	242	123	–

Umpires: F. Chester (25) and E.J. Smith (6).

Close: 1st day – A(1) 32-1 (Fingleton 9, Barnett 1); 2nd – E(2) 49-0 (Edrich 25, Barnett 20).

ENGLAND v AUSTRALIA 1938 (5th Test)

Played at Kennington Oval, London, on 20, 22, 23, 24 August.
Toss: England.   Result: ENGLAND won by an innings and 579 runs.
Debuts: England – A. Wood; Australia – S.G. Barnes.

England's total and margin of victory remain records for all Test cricket – as does the 298 runs conceded by Fleetwood-Smith. Hutton's score, length of innings (13 hours 17 minutes), and partnership of 382 with Leyland remain England records against Australia, the partnership being their best for any wicket. He batted while a record 770 runs were scored, made England's 100th century against Australia and hit 35 fours. Leyland was the first to score hundreds in his first and last innings against Australia. Bradman sustained a flake fracture of the right ankle when his boot caught in a foothole while he was bowling, and a strained leg muscle prevented Fingleton from batting. Brown, last out in the first innings, was on the field for the first 18 hours 40 minutes of play.

ENGLAND

L. Hutton	c Hassett b O'Reilly	364
W.J. Edrich	lbw b O'Reilly	12
M. Leyland	run out	187
W.R. Hammond*	lbw b Fleetwood-Smith	59
E. Paynter	lbw b O'Reilly	0
D.C.S. Compton	b Waite	1
J. Hardstaff, jr	not out	169
A. Wood†	c and b Barnes	53
H. Verity	not out	8
K. Farnes	} did not bat	
W.E. Bowes		
Extras	(B 22, LB 19, W 1, NB 8)	50
Total	(7 wickets declared)	**903**

AUSTRALIA

W.A. Brown	c Hammond b Leyland	69	c Edrich b Farnes	15
C.L. Badcock	c Hardstaff b Bowes	0	b Bowes	9
S.J. McCabe	c Edrich b Farnes	14	c Wood b Farnes	2
A.L. Hassett	c Compton b Edrich	42	lbw b Bowes	10
S.G. Barnes	b Bowes	41	lbw b Verity	33
B.A. Barnett†	c Wood b Bowes	2	b Farnes	46
M.G. Waite	b Bowes	8	c Edrich b Verity	0
W.J. O'Reilly	c Wood b Bowes	0	not out	7
L.O'B. Fleetwood-Smith	not out	16	c Leyland b Farnes	0
D.G. Bradman*	absent hurt	–	absent hurt	–
J.H.W. Fingleton	absent hurt	–	absent hurt	–
Extras	(B 4, LB 2, NB 3)	9	(B 1)	1
Total		**201**		**123**

AUSTRALIA	O	M	R	W	O	M	R	W
Waite	72	16	150	1				
McCabe	38	8	85	0				
O'Reilly	85	26	178	3				
Fleetwood-Smith	87	11	298	1				
Barnes	38	3	84	1				
Hassett	13	2	52	0				
Bradman	2·2	1	6	0				
ENGLAND								
Farnes	13	2	54	1	12·1	1	63	4
Bowes	19	3	49	5	10	3	25	2
Edrich	10	2	55	1				
Verity	5	1	15	0	7	3	15	2
Leyland	3·1	0	11	1	5	0	19	0
Hammond	2	0	8	0				

FALL OF WICKETS

Wkt	E 1st	A 1st	A 2nd
1st	29	0	15
2nd	411	19	18
3rd	546	70	35
4th	547	145	41
5th	555	147	115
6th	770	160	115
7th	876	160	117
8th	–	201	123
9th	–	–	–
10th	–	–	–

Umpires: F. Chester (26) and F.I. Walden (10).

Close: 1st day – E(1) 347-1 (Hutton 160, Leyland 156); 2nd – E(1) 634-5 (Hutton 300, Hardstaff 40); 3rd – A(1) 117-3 (Brown 29, Barnes 25).

SOUTH AFRICA v ENGLAND 1938–39 (1st Test)

Played at Old Wanderers, Johannesburg, on 24, 26, 27, 28 December.
Toss: England.   Result: MATCH DRAWN.
Debuts: South Africa – G.E. Bond, N. Gordon, A. Melville, P.G.V. van der Bijl, W.W. Wade;
England – P.A. Gibb, L.L. Wilkinson, N.W.D. Yardley.

Goddard achieved the second hat-trick in this series when he dismissed Nourse, Gordon and Wade. South Africa's innings showed a unique distribution – five fifties and five ducks. Paynter was the fifth batsman to score a hundred in each innings for England while Gibb, on his Test debut, almost joined him. Hammond, during his first innings, became the first to score 6,000 runs in Tests.

ENGLAND

W.J. Edrich	c Mitchell b Davies	4	c Mitchell b Gordon	10
P.A. Gibb	c Melville b Mitchell	93	b Dalton	106
E. Paynter	b Mitchell	117	c Langton b Gordon	100
W.R. Hammond*	lbw b Gordon	24	lbw b Dalton	58
L.E.G. Ames†	c Wade b Gordon	42	not out	3
N.W.D. Yardley	c and b Mitchell	7		
B.H. Valentine	c Wade b Gordon	97		
H. Verity	b Dalton	26		
L.L. Wilkinson	lbw b Gordon	2		
K. Farnes	b Gordon	0		
T.W.J. Goddard	not out	0		
Extras	(B 3, LB 6, NB 1)	10	(B 7, LB 2, W 2, NB 3)	14
Total		**422**	(4 wickets declared)	**291**

SOUTH AFRICA

B. Mitchell	b Farnes	73	not out	48
P.G.V. van der Bijl	lbw b Verity	4	b Hammond	38
A. Melville*	c and b Verity	0		
A.D. Nourse	c and b Goddard	73	(3) not out	17
N. Gordon	st Ames b Goddard	0		
W.W. Wade†	b Goddard	0		
K.G. Viljoen	b Wilkinson	50		
E.L. Dalton	c Edrich b Verity	102		
G.E. Bond	lbw b Wilkinson	0		
A.B.C. Langton	not out	64		
E.Q. Davies	b Verity	0		
Extras	(B 5, LB 18, NB 1)	24	(LB 5)	5
Total		**390**	(1 wicket)	**108**

SOUTH AFRICA	O	M	R	W	O	M	R	W		FALL OF WICKETS			
										E	SA	E	SA
Davies	19	0	102	1	14	2	67	0	*Wkt*	*1st*	*1st*	*2nd*	*2nd*
Langton	27	5	74	0	16	3	64	0	1st	4	42	38	67
Gordon	33·4	3	103	5	14	0	59	2	2nd	188	44	206	–
Mitchell	22	2	75	3	11	1	58	0	3rd	234	160	281	–
Dalton	10	1	42	1	6·5	0	29	2	4th	278	160	291	–
Bond	2	0	16	0					5th	292	160	–	–
ENGLAND									6th	294	173	–	–
Farnes	23	1	87	1	7	3	17	0	7th	378	281	–	–
Edrich	9	0	44	0	3	0	7	0	8th	389	281	–	–
Verity	44·1	16	61	4	16	8	17	0	9th	415	378	–	–
Hammond	10	3	27	0	6	3	13	1	10th	422	390	–	–
Wilkinson	22	0	93	2	8	3	18	0					
Goddard	27	5	54	3	11	3	31	0					

Umpires: R.G.A. Ashman (4) and G.L. Sickler (1).

Close: 1st day – E(1) 326-6 (Valentine 12, Verity 19); 2nd – SA(1) 166-5 (Mitchell 72, Viljoen 0); 3rd – E(2) 103-1 (Gibb 53, Paynter 32).

SOUTH AFRICA v ENGLAND 1938–39 (2nd Test)

Played at Newlands, Cape Town, on 31 December, 2, 3, 4 January.
Toss: England.   Result: MATCH DRAWN.
Debuts: Nil.

Rain prevented play before 3.30 on the first afternoon. England made their highest total so far against South Africa and the partnership of 197 in 145 minutes between Hammond and Ames is still England's best for the fourth wicket in this series. Gordon again swung the ball late and kept a steady length to earn his second five-wicket haul in as many Tests.

ENGLAND

L. Hutton	b Gordon	17
P.A. Gibb	c Wade b Gordon	58
E. Paynter	lbw b Langton	1
W.R. Hammond*	b Davies	181
L.E.G. Ames†	b Gordon	115
W.J. Edrich	b Gordon	0
B.H. Valentine	lbw b Gordon	112
H. Verity	b Langton	29
D.V.P. Wright	c Nourse b Langton	33
K. Farnes	not out	1
T.W.J. Goddard	did not bat	
Extras	(LB 9, NB 3)	12
Total	(9 wickets declared)	**559**

SOUTH AFRICA

B. Mitchell	b Wright	42	c Ames b Farnes	1
P.G.V. van der Bijl	c Valentine b Verity	37	hit wkt b Goddard	87
E.A.B. Rowan	b Wright	6	not out	89
A.D. Nourse	lbw b Verity	120	not out	19
A.W. Briscoe	lbw b Goddard	2		
W.W. Wade†	c Edrich b Verity	10		
A.B.C. Langton	lbw b Goddard	0		
X.C. Balaskas	c Paynter b Verity	29		
A. Melville*	b Verity	23		
N. Gordon	st Ames b Goddard	0		
E.Q. Davies	not out	0		
Extras	(B 2, LB 7, NB 8)	17	(B 1, LB 3, NB 1)	5
Total		**286**	(2 wickets)	**201**

SOUTH AFRICA	O	M	R	W	O	M	R	W
Davies	16	1	77	1				
Langton	30·7	3	117	3				
Gordon	40	3	157	5				
Balaskas	24	0	115	0				
Mitchell	20	0	81	0				
ENGLAND								
Farnes	13	3	37	0	8	1	23	1
Edrich	5	1	15	0	3	1	5	0
Goddard	38	15	64	3	11	1	68	1
Wright	26	3	83	2	12	0	62	0
Verity	36·6	13	70	5	10	5	13	0
Hammond					9	0	25	0

FALL OF WICKETS

Wkt	E 1st	SA 1st	SA 2nd
1st	29	66	2
2nd	30	79	149
3rd	139	151	–
4th	336	160	–
5th	338	176	–
6th	410	177	–
7th	504	214	–
8th	537	283	–
9th	559	286	–
10th	–	286	–

Umpires: R.G.A. Ashman (5) and G.L. Sickler (2).

Close: 1st day – E(1) 131-2 (Gibb 56, Hammond 54); 2nd – E(1) 553-8 (Wright 27, Farnes 1); 3rd – SA(1) 213-6 (Nourse 74, Balaskas 28).

SOUTH AFRICA v ENGLAND 1938–39 (3rd Test)

Played at Kingsmead, Durban, on 20, 21, 23 January.
Toss: England.   Result: ENGLAND won by an innings and 13 runs.
Debuts: Nil.

Paynter's 243 is the highest score for either country in this series of Tests. His partnership of 242 with Hammond was scored in less than two hours, the second hundred coming in 52 minutes. Paynter was the first to score double-centuries against both Australia and South Africa.

ENGLAND

L. Hutton	lbw b Gordon	31
P.A. Gibb	c Wade b Davies	38
E. Paynter	c Melville b Langton	243
W.R. Hammond*	c Mitchell b Gordon	120
L.E.G. Ames†	not out	27
W.J. Edrich	)	
B.H. Valentine	)	
H. Verity	) did not bat	
D.V.P. Wright	)	
K. Farnes	)	
L.L. Wilkinson	)	
Extras	(B 5, LB 4, NB 1)	10
Total	(4 wickets declared)	**469**

SOUTH AFRICA

B. Mitchell	c Ames b Edrich	30		c Ames b Farnes	109
P.G.V. van der Bijl	run out	28		b Verity	13
E.A.B. Rowan	lbw b Wright	4		c Ames b Hammond	67
A.D. Nourse	c Hammond b Farnes	0		c Ames b Edrich	27
K.G. Viljoen	c Hammond b Wright	2		c Hammond b Farnes	61
E.L. Dalton	b Wilkinson	12	(7)	c Hammond b Verity	8
W.W. Wade†	c Hammond b Farnes	14	(8)	lbw b Farnes	28
A. Melville*	not out	5	(6)	b Wilkinson	10
A.B.C. Langton	c Hutton b Farnes	0		b Wilkinson	12
N. Gordon	b Farnes	1		c Edrich b Verity	0
E.Q. Davies	lbw b Wilkinson	2		not out	2
Extras	(B 1, LB 3, W 1)	5		(B 7, LB 9)	16
Total		**103**			**353**

SOUTH AFRICA	O	M	R	W	O	M	R	W		FALL OF WICKETS		
Davies	15	0	106	1						E	SA	SA
Langton	23·5	0	107	1					*Wkt*	*1st*	*1st*	*2nd*
Gordon	29	0	127	2					1st	38	60	46
Mitchell	8	0	45	0					2nd	153	61	165
Dalton	13	0	74	0					3rd	395	65	223
									4th	469	65	247
ENGLAND									5th	–	79	282
Farnes	13	1	29	4	28·2	8	80	3	6th	–	87	306
Hammond	2	1	2	0	3	0	11	1	7th	–	98	308
Wright	12	1	37	2	15	2	56	0	8th	–	98	345
Verity	8	4	9	0	35	10	71	3	9th	–	100	346
Edrich	4	0	9	1	7	2	16	1	10th	–	103	353
Wilkinson	6·5	2	12	2	26	4	103	2				

Umpires: R.G.A. Ashman (6) and G.L. Sickler (3).

Close: 1st day – E(1) 373-2 (Paynter 197, Hammond 99); 2nd – SA(2) 73-1 (Mitchell 53, Rowan 7).

SOUTH AFRICA v ENGLAND 1938–39 (4th Test)

Played at Old Wanderers, Johannesburg, on 18, 20, 21 (*no play*), 22 February.
Toss: England.   Result: MATCH DRAWN.
Debuts: South Africa – R.E. Grieveson.

Hammond won the toss for the eighth successive time. Langton returned his best analysis in Tests. Ames became England's most successful wicket-keeper when he passed A.F.A. Lilley's total of 92 Test match dismissals. Rain prevented play until 2 pm on the second day and washed out the next completely.

ENGLAND

L. Hutton	b Mitchell	92	c Grieveson b Gordon		32
P.A. Gibb	c Mitchell b Langton	9	c Grieveson b Gordon		45
E. Paynter	c Newson b Langton	40	c Grieveson b Newson		15
W.R. Hammond*	c Newson b Gordon	1	not out		61
L.E.G. Ames†	b Langton	34	b Gordon		17
B.H. Valentine	c Grieveson b Gordon	11	not out		25
W.J. Edrich	lbw b Langton	6			
H. Verity	c Rowan b Mitchell	8			
K. Farnes	c Grieveson b Newson	4			
T.W.J. Goddard	c Van der Bijl b Langton	8			
L.L. Wilkinson	not out	1			
Extras	(W 1)	1	(B 2, LB 6)		8
Total		**215**	(4 wickets)		**203**

SOUTH AFRICA

P.G.V. van der Bijl	lbw b Goddard	31
A. Melville*	c Verity b Wilkinson	67
E.A.B. Rowan	b Farnes	85
B. Mitchell	c Ames b Farnes	63
A.D. Nourse	hit wkt b Verity	38
A.B.C. Langton	c Hutton b Verity	6
E.L. Dalton	not out	20
E.S. Newson	b Hammond	16
K.G. Viljoen	lbw b Verity	5
R.E. Grieveson†	) did not bat	
N.Gordon	)	
Extras	(B 5, LB 12, NB 1)	18
Total	(8 wickets declared)	**349**

SOUTH AFRICA	O	M	R	W	O	M	R	W
Newson	13	0	53	1	11	2	22	1
Langton	19·2	1	58	5	12	1	49	0
Gordon	15	1	47	2	22	4	58	3
Mitchell	12	3	37	2	12	1	42	0
Dalton	5	0	19	0	3	0	24	0

ENGLAND	O	M	R	W
Farnes	26	7	64	2
Edrich	4	0	11	0
Verity	37·5	10	127	3
Goddard	18	2	65	1
Wilkinson	9	0	45	1
Hammond	7	1	19	1

FALL OF WICKETS

Wkt	E 1st	SA 1st	E 2nd
1st	18	108	64
2nd	96	108	91
3rd	99	224	103
4th	159	280	145
5th	187	294	–
6th	187	311	–
7th	197	340	–
8th	201	349	–
9th	205	–	–
10th	215	–	–

Umpires: R.G.A. Ashman (7) and G.L. Sickler (4).

Close: 1st day – SA(1) 11-0 (Van der Bijl 2, Melville 9); 2nd – SA(1) 249-3 (Rowan 53, Nourse 20); 3rd – no play.

SOUTH AFRICA v ENGLAND 1938–39 (5th Test)

Played at Kingsmead, Durban, on 3, 4, 6, 7, 8, 9, 10, 11 (*no play*), 13, 14 March.
Toss: South Africa.   Result: MATCH DRAWN.
Debuts: England – R.T.D. Perks.

The most famous timeless Test, it began when the Editor was $3\frac{1}{2}$ hours old and ended, still undecided, some eleven days later when the tourists had to begin their two-day rail journey back to their ship at Cape Town. It is the longest first-class match ever played (ten days) and produced the highest aggregate (1,981 runs). England's 654 for 5 remains the highest fourth innings total in all first-class cricket. The partnership of 280 between Gibb and Edrich, who ended a nightmarish baptism in Test cricket, remains the second-wicket record for this series. England, set 696 to win, were only 42 runs short of victory when rain during the tea interval caused the match to be abandoned as a draw after 43 hours 16 minutes of actual playing time.

SOUTH AFRICA

A. Melville*	hit wkt b Wright	78	(6) b Farnes		103
P.G.V. van der Bijl	b Perks	125	c Paynter b Wright		97
E.A.B. Rowan	lbw b Perks	33	c Edrich b Verity		0
B. Mitchell	b Wright	11	(1) hit wkt b Verity		89
A.D. Nourse	b Perks	103	(4) c Hutton b Farnes		25
K.G. Viljoen	c Ames b Perks	0	(5) b Perks		74
E.L. Dalton	c Ames b Farnes	57	c and b Wright		21
R.E. Grieveson†	b Perks	75	b Farnes		39
A.B.C. Langton	c Paynter b Verity	27	c Hammond b Farnes		6
E.S. Newson	c and b Verity	1	b Wright		3
N. Gordon	not out	0	not out		7
Extras	(B 2, LB 12, NB 6)	20	(B 5, LB 8, NB 4)		17
Total		**530**			**481**

ENGLAND

L. Hutton	run out	38	b Mitchell		55
P.A. Gibb	c Grieveson b Newson	4	b Dalton		120
E. Paynter	lbw b Langton	62	(5) c Grieveson b Gordon		75
W.R. Hammond*	st Grieveson b Dalton	24	st Grieveson b Dalton		140
L.E.G. Ames†	c Dalton b Langton	84	(6) not out		17
W.J. Edrich	c Rowan b Langton	1	(3) c Gordon b Langton		219
B.H. Valentine	st Grieveson b Dalton	26	not out		4
H. Verity	b Dalton	3			
D.V.P. Wright	c Langton b Dalton	26			
K. Farnes	b Newson	20			
R.T.D. Perks	not out	2			
Extras	(B 7, LB 17, W 1, NB 1)	26	(B 8, LB 12, W 1, NB 3)		24
Total		**316**	(5 wickets)		**654**

ENGLAND	O	M	R	W	O	M	R	W		FALL OF WICKETS			
										SA	E	SA	E
Farnes	46	9	108	1	22·1	2	74	4	*Wkt*	*1st*	*1st*	*2nd*	*2nd*
Perks	41	5	100	5	32	6	99	1	1st	131	9	191	78
Wright	37	6	142	2	32	7	146	3	2nd	219	64	191	358
Verity	55·6	14	97	2	40	9	87	2	3rd	236	125	191	447
Hammond	14	4	34	0	9	1	30	0	4th	274	169	242	611
Edrich	9	2	29	0	6	1	18	0	5th	278	171	346	650
Hutton					1	0	10	0	6th	368	229	382	–
SOUTH AFRICA									7th	475	245	434	–
Newson	25·6	5	58	2	43	4	91	0	8th	522	276	450	–
Langton	35	12	71	3	56	12	132	1	9th	523	305	462	–
Gordon	37	7	82	0	55·2	10	174	1	10th	530	316	481	–
Mitchell	7	0	20	0	37	4	133	1					
Dalton	13	1	59	4	27	3	100	2					

Umpires: R.G.A. Ashman (8) and G.L. Sickler (5).

Close: 1st day – SA(1) 229-2 (Van der Bijl 105, Mitchell 4); 2nd – SA(1) 423-6 (Nourse 77, Grieveson 26); 3rd – E(1) 35-1 (Hutton 24, Paynter 6); 4th – E(1) 268-7 (Ames 82, Wright 5); 5th – SA(2) 193-3 (Nourse 1, Viljoen 1); 6th – E(2) 0-0 (Hutton 0, Gibb 0); 7th – E(2) 253-1 (Gibb 78, Edrich 107); 8th – no play; 9th – E(2) 496-3 (Hammond 58, Paynter 24).

ENGLAND v WEST INDIES 1939 (1st Test)

Played at Lord's, London, on 24, 26, 27 June.
Toss: West Indies.   Result: ENGLAND won by eight wickets.
Debuts: England – W.H. Copson; West Indies – J.H. Cameron, C.B. Clarke, J.B. Stollmeyer, K.H. Weekes.

Headley scored a hundred in each innings for the second time (also *Test No. 192*), and became the first to do so in a Test at Lord's. Hutton and Compton added 248 for the fourth wicket in only 140 minutes. Needing 99 in 110 minutes, England won with 35 minutes to spare. Copson took nine wickets in the first of three Test appearances. As a result of a two-year experiment – aborted because of the War – eight-ball overs were employed in England for just one season. Cameron bowled Gimblett with his second ball in Test cricket.

WEST INDIES

R.S. Grant*	c Compton b Copson	22	b Bowes		23
J.B. Stollmeyer	b Bowes	59	c Verity b Copson		0
G.A. Headley	c Wood b Copson	106	c Hutton b Wright		107
J.E.D. Sealy	c Wood b Wright	13	c Wood b Copson		29
K.H. Weekes	c Gimblett b Copson	20	c Wood b Verity		16
L.N. Constantine	lbw b Copson	14	c Hammond b Verity		17
J.H. Cameron	c Hutton b Bowes	1	c and b Wright		0
I. Barrow†	lbw b Copson	2	not out		6
E.A. Martindale	lbw b Wright	22	c Bowes b Wright		3
L.G. Hylton	not out	2	c Hardstaff b Copson		13
C.B. Clarke	b Bowes	1	c and b Copson		0
Extras	(B 3, LB 9, NB 3)	15	(B 6, LB 4, W 1)		11
Total		**277**			**225**

ENGLAND

L. Hutton	c Grant b Hylton	196	b Hylton	16
H. Gimblett	b Cameron	22	b Martindale	20
E. Paynter	c Barrow b Cameron	34	not out	32
W.R. Hammond*	c Grant b Cameron	14	not out	30
D.C.S. Compton	c Stollmeyer b Clarke	120		
J. Hardstaff, jr	not out	3		
A. Wood†	not out	0		
D.V.P. Wright	)			
H. Verity	) did not bat			
W.H. Copson	)			
W.E. Bowes	)			
Extras	(B 8, LB 6, W 1)	15	(LB 2)	2
Total	(5 wickets declared)	**404**	(2 wickets)	**100**

ENGLAND	O	M	R	W	O	M	R	W
Bowes	28·4	5	86	3	19	7	44	1
Copson	24	2	85	5	16·4	2	67	4
Wright	13	1	57	2	17	0	75	3
Verity	16	3	34	0	14	4	20	2
Compton					3	0	8	0
WEST INDIES								
Martindale	20	2	86	0	7·7	0	51	1
Hylton	24	4	98	1	7	1	36	1
Constantine	13	0	67	0	3	0	11	0
Cameron	26	6	66	3				
Clarke	6	0	28	1				
Sealy	3	0	21	0				
Grant	3	0	23	0				

FALL OF WICKETS

Wkt	WI 1st	E 1st	WI 2nd	E 2nd
1st	29	49	0	35
2nd	147	119	42	39
3rd	180	147	105	–
4th	226	395	154	–
5th	245	402	190	–
6th	250	–	199	–
7th	250	–	200	–
8th	261	–	204	–
9th	276	–	225	–
10th	277	–	225	–

Umpires: E.J. Smith (7) and F.I. Walden (11).

Close: 1st day – E(1) 11-0 (Hutton 4, Gimblett 5); 2nd – E(1) 404-5 (Hardstaff 3, Wood 0).

ENGLAND v WEST INDIES 1939 (2nd Test)

Played at Old Trafford, Manchester, on 22, 24, 25 July.
Toss: West Indies.   Result: MATCH DRAWN.
Debuts: West Indies – G.E. Gomez, E.A.V. Williams.

Manchester continued its tradition of providing abundant rain during Test matches by allowing only 35 minutes of play on the first day and delaying the start of the second. Hardstaff scored 76 out of 111 in 100 minutes and, as the pitch worsened, Grant struck three sixes off Goddard, four fours, and short leg (Compton) a tremendous blow on the thigh. Bowes celebrated his 31st birthday by producing the best analysis of his England career. When he caught Headley via Wood's gloves at slip, Hammond became the first to hold 100 catches in Tests as a fielder.

ENGLAND

L. Hutton	c Martindale b Grant	13	c Sealy b Martindale		17
A.E. Fagg	b Hylton	7	b Constantine		32
E. Paynter	c Sealy b Clarke	9	c Gomez b Martindale		0
W.R. Hammond*	st Sealy b Clarke	22	b Constantine		32
D.C.S. Compton	hit wkt b Clarke	4	not out		34
J. Hardstaff, jr	c Williams b Grant	76	c Grant b Constantine		1
A. Wood†	c and b Constantine	26	b Constantine		1
D.V.P. Wright	not out	1	not out		0
W.E. Bowes	)				
W.H. Copson	) did not bat				
T.W.J. Goddard	)				
Extras	(B 3, LB 2, NB 1)	6	(B 8, LB 2, NB 1)		11
Total	(7 wickets declared)	**164**	(6 wickets declared)		**128**

WEST INDIES

R.S. Grant*	c Fagg b Goddard	47	c Hardstaff b Bowes		0
J.B. Stollmeyer	c and b Goddard	5	lbw b Wright		10
G.A. Headley	c Wood b Bowes	51	c Hammond b Copson		5
G.E. Gomez	c Wood b Bowes	0	b Goddard		11
J.E.D. Sealy†	c Hammond b Bowes	16	not out		13
J.H. Cameron	c Hutton b Bowes	5			
E.A.V. Williams	b Copson	1			
L.N. Constantine	b Bowes	0			
E.A. Martindale	c Hammond b Copson	0			
L.G. Hylton	lbw b Bowes	2			
C.B. Clarke	not out	0			
Extras	(LB 6)	6	(LB 3, NB 1)		4
Total		**133**	(4 wickets)		**43**

WEST INDIES	O	M	R	W	O	M	R	W	FALL OF WICKETS				
Martindale	8	2	10	0	12	2	34	2		E	WI	E	WI
Hylton	11	3	15	1	6	1	18	0	*Wkt*	*1st*	*1st*	*2nd*	*2nd*
Clarke	13	1	59	3					1st	21	35	26	0
Grant	13·2	4	16	2					2nd	34	56	30	11
Cameron	3	0	22	0					3rd	34	56	74	27
Constantine	7	2	36	1	11	1	42	4	4th	53	96	89	43
Williams					9	1	23	0	5th	62	108	113	–
ENGLAND									6th	150	113	126	–
Bowes	17·4	4	33	6	5	0	13	1	7th	164	124	–	–
Copson	9	2	31	2	3	1	2	1	8th	–	125	–	–
Goddard	4	0	43	2	4·6	1	15	1	9th	–	132	–	–
Wright	5	1	20	0	3	0	9	1	10th	–	133	–	–

Umpires: F. Chester (27) and E.J. Smith (8).

Close: 1st day – E(1) 11-0 (Hutton 6, Fagg 2); 2nd – WI(1) 85-3 (Headley 16, Sealy 13).

ENGLAND v WEST INDIES 1939 (3rd Test)

Played at Kennington Oval, London, on 19, 21, 22 August.
Toss: England.   Result: MATCH DRAWN.
Debuts: England – N. Oldfield; West Indies – T.F. Johnson, V.H. Stollmeyer.

Keeton played on to Johnson's first ball in Test cricket. The tall left-arm fast bowler from Trinidad had also taken a wicket with his first ball of the tour. Nichols was brilliantly run out by Constantine's direct throw from cover – off his own bowling. Weekes took only 110 minutes to reach his only Test century before Constantine flayed the bowling for a six and 11 fours. Hutton and Hammond added 264 in three hours – then the world Test record for the third wicket and still the highest for this series. Hutton's last eight Tests had brought him 1,109 runs. World War 2 demanded an interval of 6 years 219 days in Test cricket's history – 70 days fewer than its predecessor.

ENGLAND

L. Hutton	c and b Johnson	73	not out		165
W.W. Keeton	b Johnson	0	b Constantine		20
N. Oldfield	c Sealy b Constantine	80	c Sealy b Johnson		19
W.R. Hammond*	c Grant b Constantine	43	b Clarke		138
D.C.S. Compton	c Gomez b Martindale	21	not out		10
J. Hardstaff, jr	b Constantine	94			
M.S. Nichols	run out	24			
A. Wood†	b Constantine	0			
D.V.P. Wright	lbw b Constantine	6			
T.W.J. Goddard	b Clarke	0			
R.T.D. Perks	not out	1			
Extras	(B 4, LB 5, NB 1)	10	(B 4, LB 5 W 4, NB 1)		14
Total		**352**	(3 wickets declared)		**366**

WEST INDIES

R.S. Grant*	c Goddard b Perks	6
J.B. Stollmeyer	c Perks b Hutton	59
G.A. Headley	run out	65
V.H. Stollmeyer	st Wood b Goddard	96
G.E. Gomez	b Perks	11
K.H. Weekes	c Hammond b Nichols	137
J.E.D. Sealy†	c Wright b Nichols	24
L.N. Constantine	c Wood b Perks	79
E.A. Martindale	b Perks	3
C.B. Clarke	b Perks	2
T.F. Johnson	not out	9
Extras	(LB 6, NB 1)	7
Total		**498**

WEST INDIES	O	M	R	W	O	M	R	W	FALL OF WICKETS			
										E	WI	E
Martindale	13	0	87	1	10	2	46	0	*Wkt*	*1st*	*1st*	*2nd*
Johnson	16	1	53	2	14	2	76	1	1st	2	15	39
Constantine	17·3	2	75	5	20	3	97	1	2nd	133	128	77
Clarke	21	0	96	1	17	1	78	1	3rd	168	134	341
Grant	6	0	31	0	11	1	38	0	4th	215	164	–
Headley					4	0	17	0	5th	244	327	–
									6th	333	389	–
ENGLAND									7th	333	434	–
Nichols	34	4	161	2					8th	345	451	–
Perks	30·5	6	156	5					9th	346	475	–
Wright	13	2	53	0					10th	352	498	–
Goddard	12	1	56	1								
Hutton	7	0	45	1								
Compton	5	1	20	0								

Umpires: F. Chester (28) and W. Reeves (5).

Close: 1st day – WI(1) 27-1 (J.B. Stollmeyer 14, Headley 7); 2nd – WI(1) 395-6 (Sealy 17, Constantine 1).

NEW ZEALAND v AUSTRALIA 1945–46 (Only Test)

Played at Basin Reserve, Wellington, on 29, 30 March.
Toss: New Zealand.   Result: AUSTRALIA won by an innings and 103 runs.
Debuts: New Zealand – W.M. Anderson, C. Burke, L.A. Butterfield, D.A.N. McRae, C.G. Rowe,
   V.J. Scott; Australia – I.W. Johnson, R.R. Lindwall, C.L. McCool, K.D. Meuleman, K.R. Miller,
   D. Tallon, E.R.H. Toshack.

This match was not granted Test status by the ICC until March 1948. New Zealand chose to take first innings on a rain-affected pitch, were dismissed for their lowest aggregate, and did not meet Australia again in an official Test until 1973-74. New Zealand's last eight wickets fell for five runs. In the last of his 27 Test matches, O'Reilly took five wickets in an innings for the eleventh time and his tally of wickets to 144. McCool took a wicket with his second ball in Test cricket. The match, which ended at 3.35 on the second afternoon after $8\frac{1}{2}$ hours of play, produced the third-lowest aggregate (295) of any completed Test.

NEW ZEALAND

W.A. Hadlee*	c Miller b Toshack	6	b Miller		3
W.M. Anderson	b Lindwall	4	b Lindwall		1
V.J. Scott	c Barnes b O'Reilly	14	c Tallon b Miller		4
W.M. Wallace	c Barnes b Toshack	10	run out		14
E.W.T. Tindill†	b Toshack	1	lbw b Toshack		13
C.G. Rowe	b O'Reilly	0	b O'Reilly		0
L.A. Butterfield	lbw b O'Reilly	0	lbw b O'Reilly		0
D.A.N. McRae	c Hassett b O'Reilly	0	(9) c Meuleman b McCool		8
C. Burke	lbw b Toshack	1	(8) b Toshack		3
J. Cowie	st Tallon b O'Reilly	2	c Toshack b O'Reilly		0
D.C. Cleverley	not out	1	not out		1
Extras	(B 3)	3	(B 5, NB 2)		7
Total		**42**			**54**

AUSTRALIA

W.A. Brown*	c Rowe b Burke	67
K.D. Meuleman	b Cowie	0
S.G. Barnes	b Cowie	54
K.R. Miller	c Hadlee b Burke	30
A.L. Hassett	c Tindill b Cowie	19
C.L. McCool	c Hadlee b Cowie	7
I.W. Johnson	not out	7
D. Tallon†	c Scott b Cowie	5
R.R. Lindwall	c Anderson b Cowie	0
W.J. O'Reilly	} did not bat	
E.R.H. Toshack	}	
Extras	(B 5, LB 3, NB 2)	10
Total	(8 wickets declared)	**199**

AUSTRALIA	O	M	R	W	O	M	R	W		FALL OF WICKETS		
Lindwall	8	1	13	1	9	3	16	1		NZ	A	NZ
Toshack	19	13	12	4	10	5	6	2	*Wkt*	*1st*	*1st*	*2nd*
O'Reilly	12	5	14	5	7	1	19	3	1st	7	9	3
Miller					6	2	6	2	2nd	15	118	5
McCool					0·2	0	0	1	3rd	37	142	12
									4th	37	174	36
NEW ZEALAND									5th	37	186	37
McRae	14	3	44	0					6th	37	186	37
Cowie	21	8	40	6					7th	37	196	39
Cleverley	15	1	51	0					8th	39	199	41
Butterfield	13	6	24	0					9th	40	–	42
Burke	11	2	30	2					10th	42	–	54

Umpires: H.W. Gourlay (1) and M.F. Pengelly (1).

Close: 1st day – A(1) 149-3 (Miller 14, Hassett 6).

ENGLAND v INDIA 1946 (1st Test)

Played at Lord's, London, on 22, 24, 25 June.
Toss: India.   Result: ENGLAND won by ten wickets.
Debuts: England – A.V. Bedser, J.T. Ikin, T.F. Smailes; India – Gul Mahomed, V.S. Hazare,
A.H. Kardar *(Abdul Hafeez Kardar, who played for India as 'Abdul Hafeez' but later took the name
of 'Kardar' and appeared for Pakistan as 'A.H. Kardar'. For consistency he is listed throughout this
book under the latter name)*, M.H. Mankad *(real names Mulwantrai Himmatlal Mankad but was
known as 'Vinoo'; his son, Ashok, has taken 'Vinoo' as his second name)*, R.S. Modi, S.G. Shinde.
Nawab Iftikhar Ali of Pataudi made his debut for India after appearing in three Tests for England.

The return of Test cricket to England after an interval of seven years brought capacity crowds on the first two
days. Hardstaff batted for 315 minutes for the last and highest of his three-figure innings for England; it remains
the only double-century against India at Lord's. Alec Bedser, younger of the Surrey twins, took 11 for 145 in
his first Test, the harbinger of many fine exhibitions of fast-medium bowling. England completed their first
post-war victory at 1.30 pm on the third day – just in time for a relaxed lunch.

INDIA

V.M. Merchant	c Gibb b Bedser	12	lbw b Ikin	27
M.H. Mankad	b Wright	14	c Hammond b Smailes	63
L. Amarnath	lbw b Bedser	0	(8) b Smailes	50
V.S. Hazare	b Bedser	31	c Hammond b Bedser	34
R.S. Modi	not out	57	(3) lbw b Smailes	21
Nawab of Pataudi, sr*	c Ikin b Bedser	9	b Wright	22
Gul Mahomed	b Wright	1	lbw b Wright	9
A.H. Kardar	b Bowes	43	(5) b Bedser	0
D.D. Hindlekar†	lbw b Bedser	3	c Ikin b Bedser	17
C.S. Nayudu	st Gibb b Bedser	4	b Bedser	13
S.G. Shinde	b Bedser	10	not out	4
Extras	(B 10, LB 6)	16	(B 10, LB 2, NB 3)	15
Total		**200**		**275**

ENGLAND

L. Hutton	c Nayudu b Amarnath	7	not out	22
C. Washbrook	c Mankad b Amarnath	27	not out	24
D.C.S. Compton	b Amarnath	0		
W.R. Hammond*	b Amarnath	33		
J. Hardstaff, jr	not out	205		
P.A. Gibb†	c Hazare b Mankad	60		
J.T. Ikin	c Hindlekar b Shinde	16		
T.F. Smailes	c Mankad b Amarnath	25		
A.V. Bedser	b Hazare	30		
D.V.P. Wright	b Mankad	3		
W.E. Bowes	lbw b Hazare	2		
Extras	(B 11, LB 8, NB 1)	20	(LB 1, W 1)	2
Total		**428**	(0 wickets)	**48**

ENGLAND	O	M	R	W	O	M	R	W	FALL OF WICKETS			
Bowes	25	7	64	1	4	1	9	0		I	E	I	E
Bedser	29·1	11	49	7	32·1	3	96	4	*Wkt*	*1st*	*1st*	*2nd*	*2nd*
Smailes	5	1	18	0	15	2	44	3	1st	15	16	67	–
Wright	17	4	53	2	20	3	68	2	2nd	15	16	117	–
Ikin					10	1	43	1	3rd	44	61	126	–
									4th	74	70	129	–
INDIA									5th	86	252	174	–
Hazare	34·4	4	100	2	4	2	7	0	6th	87	284	185	–
Amarnath	57	18	118	5	4	0	15	0	7th	144	344	190	–
Gul Mahomed	2	0	2	0					8th	147	416	249	–
Mankad	48	11	107	2	4·5	1	11	0	9th	157	421	263	–
Shinde	23	2	66	1					10th	200	428	275	–
Nayudu	5	1	15	0	4	0	13	0					

Umpires: H.G. Baldwin (1) and J.A. Smart (1).

Close: 1st day – E(1) 135-4 (Hardstaff 42, Gibb 23); 2nd – I(2) 162-4 (Hazare 26, Pataudi 16).

ENGLAND v INDIA 1946 (2nd Test)

Played at Old Trafford, Manchester, on 20, 22, 23 July.
Toss: India.   Result: MATCH DRAWN.
Debuts: England – R. Pollard; India – C.T. Sarwate, S.W. Sohoni.

Rain prevented play until after lunch on the opening day. Prompted by a spell of 5-2-7-4 from Pollard, India lost all ten wickets for 46 runs after being 124 for 0. Although limping because of a damaged knee, Amarnath bowled unchanged through England's second innings. India, set 278 in three hours, were saved only by two dropped catches as their last pair played out the final 13 minutes. Bedser, who took the 100th wicket of his first first-class season during this match, took 11 wickets for the second match running. His career figures after two Tests were 22 wickets at 10.81 apiece.

ENGLAND

L. Hutton	c Mushtaq Ali b Mankad	67	c Hindlekar b Amarnath		2
C. Washbrook	c Hindlekar b Mankad	52	lbw b Mankad		26
D.C.S. Compton	lbw b Amarnath	51	not out		71
W.R. Hammond*	b Amarnath	69	c Kardar b Mankad		8
J. Hardstaff, jr	c Merchant b Amarnath	5	b Amarnath		0
P.A. Gibb†	b Mankad	24	c Modi b Amarnath		0
J.T. Ikin	c Mankad b Amarnath	2	not out		29
W. Voce	b Mankad	0			
R. Pollard	not out	10			
A.V. Bedser	lbw b Amarnath	8			
D.V.P. Wright	lbw b Mankad	0			
Extras	(B 2, LB 4)	6	(B 6, LB 10, W 1)		17
Total		**294**	(5 wickets declared)		**153**

INDIA

V.M. Merchant	c Bedser b Pollard	78	c Ikin b Pollard		0
Mushtaq Ali	b Pollard	46	b Pollard		1
A.H. Kardar	c and b Pollard	1	(7) c and b Bedser		35
M.H. Mankad	b Pollard	0	(8) c Pollard b Bedser		5
V.S. Hazare	b Voce	3	b Bedser		44
R.S. Modi	c Ikin b Bedser	2	(4) b Bedser		30
Nawab of Pataudi, sr*	b Pollard	11	(3) b Bedser		4
L. Amarnath	b Bedser	8	(6) b Bedser		3
S.W. Sohoni	c and b Bedser	3	not out		11
C.T. Sarwate	c Ikin b Bedser	0	c Gibb b Bedser		2
D.D. Hindlekar†	not out	1	not out		4
Extras	(B 10, LB 5, NB 2)	17	(B 5, LB 8)		13
Total		**170**	(9 wickets)		**152**

INDIA	O	M	R	W	O	M	R	W
Sohoni	11	1	31	0				
Amarnath	51	17	96	5	30	9	71	3
Hazare	14	2	48	0	10	3	20	0
Mankad	46	15	101	5	21	6	45	2
Sarwate	7	0	12	0				
ENGLAND								
Voce	20	3	44	1	6	5	2	0
Bedser	26	9	41	4	25	4	52	7
Pollard	27	16	24	5	25	10	63	2
Wright	2	0	12	0	2	0	17	0
Compton	4	0	18	0	3	1	5	0
Ikin	2	0	11	0				
Hammond	1	0	3	0				

FALL OF WICKETS

	E	I	E	I
Wkt	1st	1st	2nd	2nd
1st	81	124	7	0
2nd	156	130	48	3
3rd	186	130	68	5
4th	193	141	68	79
5th	250	141	84	84
6th	265	146	–	87
7th	270	156	–	113
8th	274	168	–	132
9th	287	169	–	138
10th	294	170	–	–

Umpires: G. Beet (1) and F. Chester (29).

Close: 1st day – E(1) 236-4 (Hammond 45, Gibb 13); 2nd – I(1) 160-7 (Pataudi 9, Sohoni 0).

ENGLAND v INDIA 1946 (3rd Test)

Played at Kennington Oval, London, on 17, 19, 20 (*no play*) August.
Toss: India.   Result: MATCH DRAWN.
Debuts: England – T.G. Evans, T.P.B. Smith.

Playing conditions prevented a start until 5 pm on the first day and rain completely washed out the third day. Compton, an Arsenal and England (war-time and Victory internationals) soccer player, ran out Merchant by kicking the ball into the stumps. Merchant's innings was then the highest for India in England. Hammond became the first to score 7,000 runs in Test cricket.

INDIA

V.M. Merchant	run out	128
Mushtaq Ali	run out	59
Nawab of Pataudi, sr*	b Edrich	9
L. Amarnath	b Edrich	8
V.S. Hazare	c Compton b Gover	11
R.S. Modi	b Smith	27
A.H. Kardar	b Edrich	1
M.H. Mankad	b Bedser	42
S.W. Sohoni	not out	29
C.S. Nayudu	c Washbrook b Bedser	4
D.D. Hindlekar†	lbw b Edrich	3
Extras	(b 1, LB 5, NB 4)	10
Total		**331**

ENGLAND

L. Hutton	lbw b Mankad	25
C. Washbrook	c Mushtaq Ali b Mankad	17
L.B. Fishlock	c Merchant b Nayudu	8
D.C.S. Compton	not out	24
W.R. Hammond*	not out	9
W.J. Edrich	)	
J. Langridge	)	
T.P.B. Smith	)	
T.G. Evans†	) did not bat	
A.V. Bedser	)	
A.R. Gover	)	
Extras	(B 11, LB 1)	12
Total	(3 wickets)	**95**

ENGLAND	O	M	R	W
Gover	21	3	56	1
Bedser	32	6	60	2
Smith	21	4	58	1
Edrich	19·2	4	68	4
Langridge	29	9	64	0
Compton	5	0	15	0
INDIA				
Amarnath	15	6	30	0
Sohoni	4	3	2	0
Hazare	2	1	4	0
Mankad	20	7	28	2
Nayudu	9	2	19	1

FALL OF WICKETS

Wkt	I 1st	E 1st
1st	94	48
2nd	124	55
3rd	142	67
4th	162	–
5th	225	–
6th	226	–
7th	272	–
8th	313	–
9th	325	–
10th	331	–

Umpires: F. Chester (30) and J.A. Smart (2).

Close: 1st day – I(1) 79-0 (Merchant 30, Mushtaq Ali 48); 2nd – E(1) 95-3 (Compton 24, Hammond 9).

AUSTRALIA v ENGLAND 1946–47 (1st Test)

Played at Woolloongabba, Brisbane, on 29, 30 November 2, 3, 4 December.
Toss: Australia.   Result: AUSTRALIA won by an innings and 332 runs.
Debuts: Australia – A.R. Morris, G.E. Tribe.

Bradman, given not out in response to an appeal for a catch to Ikin at second slip off Voce when 28, added 276 for the third wicket with Hassett in what is still the record partnership for that wicket by either country in this series. Australia's total was then their highest in any home Test. Twice England had to bat after violent storms; only 99 minutes of play was possible on the third day and three hours were lost on the fourth. The second storm flooded the ground and, accompanied by an 80 mph gale which helped the covers and stumps to float away, bombarded the corrugated roofs of the pavilion and stands with giant hailstones. In its wake 15 England wickets fell in $3\frac{1}{2}$ hours to give a record Australian margin of victory at 4.40 on the last afternoon.

AUSTRALIA

S.G. Barnes	c Bedser b Wright	31
A.R. Morris	c Hammond b Bedser	2
D.G. Bradman*	b Edrich	187
A.L. Hassett	c Yardley b Bedser	128
K.R. Miller	lbw b Wright	79
C.L. McCool	lbw b Wright	95
I.W. Johnson	lbw b Wright	47
D. Tallon†	lbw b Edrich	14
R.R. Lindwall	c Voce b Wright	31
G.E. Tribe	c Gibb b Edrich	1
E.R.H. Toshack	not out	1
Extras	(B 5, LB 11, W 2, NB 11)	29
Total		**645**

ENGLAND

L. Hutton	b Miller	7	c Barnes b Miller	0
C. Washbrook	c Barnes b Miller	6	c Barnes b Miller	13
W.J. Edrich	c McCool b Miller	16	lbw b Toshack	7
D.C.S. Compton	lbw b Miller	17	c Barnes b Toshack	15
W.R. Hammond*	lbw b Toshack	32	b Toshack	23
J.T. Ikin	c Tallon b Miller	0	b Tribe	32
N.W.D. Yardley	c Tallon b Toshack	29	c Hassett b Toshack	0
P.A. Gibb†	b Miller	13	lbw b Toshack	11
W. Voce	not out	1	c Hassett b Tribe	18
A.V. Bedser	lbw b Miller	0	c and b Toshack	18
D.V.P. Wright	c Tallon b Toshack	4	not out	10
Extras	(B 8, LB 3, W 2, NB 3)	16	(B 15, LB 7, W 1, NB 2)	25
Total		**141**		**172**

ENGLAND	O	M	R	W	O	M	R	W
Voce	28	9	92	0				
Bedser	41	5	159	2				
Wright	43·6	4	167	5				
Edrich	25	2	107	3				
Yardley	13	1	47	0				
Ikin	2	0	24	0				
Compton	6	0	20	0				
AUSTRALIA								
Lindwall	12	4	23	0				
Miller	22	4	60	7	11	3	17	2
Toshack	16·5	11	17	3	20·7	2	82	6
Tribe	9	2	19	0	12	2	48	2
McCool	1	0	5	0				
Barnes	1	0	1	0				

FALL OF WICKETS

Wkt	A 1st	E 1st	E 2nd
1st	9	10	0
2nd	46	25	13
3rd	322	49	33
4th	428	56	62
5th	465	56	65
6th	596	121	65
7th	599	134	112
8th	629	136	114
9th	643	136	143
10th	645	141	172

Umpires: G. Borwick (17) and J.D. Scott (6).

Close: 1st day – A(1) 292-2 (Bradman 162, Hassett 81); 2nd – A(1) 595-5 (McCool 92, Johnson 47); 3rd – E(1) 21-1 (Washbrook 5, Edrich 8); 4th – E(1) 117-5 (Hammond 30, Yardley 25).

AUSTRALIA v ENGLAND 1946–47 (2nd Test)

Played at Sydney Cricket Ground on 13, 14, 16, 17, 18, 19 December.
Toss: England.   Result: AUSTRALIA won by an innings and 33 runs.
Debuts: Australia – F.W. Freer.

Barnes and Bradman established a fifth-wicket partnership of 405 in 393 minutes which remains the record for all Test cricket. Barnes took 570 minutes to reach his 200 – then the slowest double-century in first-class cricket. His innings lasted 642 minutes and was the longest for Australia until R.B. Simpson scored 311 in 762 minutes in 1964 (*Test No. 564*). Evans, playing in his first Test against Australia, conceded no byes in Australia's total of 659; it is still the highest Test total which does not include a bye and was then their highest total in any home Test. England were defeated by an innings in successive matches for the first time since 1897-98 (*Tests 54* and *55*). Freer (fourth ball) and Johnson (third) each took a wicket in their first over in Test cricket. Two tropical storms curtailed the second day's play.

ENGLAND

L. Hutton	c Tallon b Johnson	39	hit wkt b Miller		37
C. Washbrook	b Freer	1	c McCool b Johnson		41
W.J. Edrich	lbw b McCool	71	b McCool		119
D.C.S. Compton	c Tallon b McCool	5	c Bradman b Freer		54
W.R. Hammond*	c Tallon b McCool	1	c Toshack b McCool		37
J.T. Ikin	c Hassett b Johnson	60	b Freer		17
N.W.D. Yardley	c Tallon b Johnson	25	b McCool		35
T.P.B. Smith	lbw b Johnson	4	c Hassett b Johnson		2
T.G. Evans†	b Johnson	5	st Tallon b McCool		9
A.V. Bedser	b Johnson	14	not out		3
D.V.P. Wright	not out	15	c Tallon b McCool		0
Extras	(B 4, LB 11)	15	(B 8, LB 6, W 1, NB 2)		17
Total		**255**			**371**

AUSTRALIA

S.G. Barnes	c Ikin b Bedser	234
A.R. Morris	b Edrich	5
I.W. Johnson	c Washbrook b Edrich	7
A.L. Hassett	c Compton b Edrich	34
K.R. Miller	c Evans b Smith	40
D.G. Bradman*	lbw b Yardley	234
C.L. McCool	c Hammond b Smith	12
D. Tallon†	c and b Wright	30
F.W. Freer	not out	28
G.E. Tribe	not out	25
E.R.H. Toshack	did not bat	
Extras	(LB 7, W 1, NB 2)	10
Total	(8 wickets declared)	**659**

AUSTRALIA	O	M	R	W	O	M	R	W
Miller	9	2	24	0	11	3	37	1
Freer	7	1	25	1	13	2	49	2
Toshack	7	2	6	0	6	1	16	0
Tribe	20	3	70	0	12	0	40	0
Johnson	30·1	12	42	6	29	7	92	2
McCool	23	2	73	3	32·4	4	109	5
Barnes					3	0	11	0
ENGLAND								
Bedser	46	7	153	1				
Edrich	26	3	79	3				
Wright	46	8	169	1				
Smith	37	1	172	2				
Ikin	3	0	15	0				
Compton	6	0	38	0				
Yardley	9	0	23	1				

FALL OF WICKETS

	E	A	E
Wkt	*1st*	*1st*	*2nd*
1st	10	24	49
2nd	88	37	118
3rd	97	96	220
4th	99	159	280
5th	148	564	309
6th	187	564	327
7th	197	595	346
8th	205	617	366
9th	234	–	369
10th	255	–	371

Umpires: G. Borwick (18) and J.D. Scott (7).

Close: 1st day – E(1) 219-8 (Ikin 52, Bedser 1); 2nd – A(1) 27-1 (Barnes 21, Johnson 0); 3rd – A(1) 252-4 (Barnes 109, Bradman 52); 4th – A(1) 571-6 (McCool 3, Tallon 4); 5th – E(2) 247-3 (Edrich 86, Hammond 15).

AUSTRALIA v ENGLAND 1946–47 (3rd Test)

Played at Melbourne Cricket Ground on 1, 2, 3, 4, 6, 7 January.
Toss: Australia.   Result: MATCH DRAWN.
Debuts: Australia – B. Dooland.

The first drawn Test in Australia since 1881-82. Hammond overtook W.G. Grace's record 39 catches against Australia when he dismissed Hassett. England were without Voce (strained groin muscle) and Edrich (bruised shin) for most of the first innings. Australia were rescued by McCool's only Test hundred. In the second innings Bradman completed 1,000 runs in Tests at Melbourne before Tallon (104 minutes) and Lindwall (113 minutes – second 50 in 37 minutes) added 154 runs in just 88 minutes. Yardley became the first England player to score 50 in each innings and take five wickets in the same Test.

AUSTRALIA

S.G. Barnes	lbw b Bedser	45	c Evans b Yardley		32
A.R. Morris	lbw b Bedser	21	b Bedser		155
D.G. Bradman*	b Yardley	79	c and b Yardley		49
A.L. Hassett	c Hammond b Wright	12	b Wright		9
K.R. Miller	c Evans b Wright	33	c Hammond b Yardley		34
I.W. Johnson	lbw b Yardley	0	(7) run out		0
C.L. McCool	not out	104	(6) c Evans b Bedser		43
D. Tallon†	c Evans b Edrich	35	c and b Wright		92
R.R. Lindwall	b Bedser	9	c Washbrook b Bedser		100
B. Dooland	c Hammond b Edrich	19	c Compton b Wright		1
E.R.H. Toshack	c Hutton b Edrich	6	not out		2
Extras	(NB 2)	2	(B 14, LB 2, NB 3)		19
Total		**365**			**536**

ENGLAND

L. Hutton	c McCool b Lindwall	2	c Bradman b Toshack		40
C. Washbrook	c Tallon b Dooland	62	b Dooland		112
W.J. Edrich	lbw b Lindwall	89	lbw b McCool		13
D.C.S. Compton	lbw b Toshack	11	run out		14
W.R. Hammond*	c and b Dooland	9	b Lindwall		26
J.T. Ikin	c Miller b Dooland	48	c Hassett b Miller		5
N.W.D. Yardley	b McCool	61	not out		53
T.G. Evans†	b McCool	17	(9) not out		0
W. Voce	lbw b Dooland	0			
A.V. Bedser	not out	27	(8) lbw b Miller		25
D.V.P. Wright	b Johnson	10			
Extras	(B 1, LB 12, NB 2)	15	(B 15, LB 6, W 1)		22
Total		**351**	(7 wickets)		**310**

ENGLAND	O	M	R	W	O	M	R	W		FALL OF WICKETS			
Voce	10	2	40	0	6	1	29	0		A	E	A	E
Bedser	31	4	99	3	34·3	4	176	3	*Wkt*	*1st*	*1st*	*2nd*	*2nd*
Wright	26	2	124	2	32	3	131	3	1st	32	8	68	138
Yardley	20	4	50	2	20	0	67	3	2nd	108	155	159	163
Edrich	10·3	2	50	3	18	1	86	0	3rd	143	167	177	186
Hutton					3	0	28	0	4th	188	176	242	197
									5th	188	179	333	221
AUSTRALIA									6th	192	292	335	249
Lindwall	20	1	64	2	16	2	59	1	7th	255	298	341	294
Miller	10	0	34	0	11	0	41	2	8th	272	298	495	–
Toshack	26	5	88	1	16	5	39	1	9th	355	324	511	–
McCool	19	3	53	2	24	9	41	1	10th	365	351	536	–
Dooland	27	5	69	4	21	1	84	1					
Johnson	6·5	1	28	1	12	4	24	0					

Umpires: G. Borwick (19) and J.D. Scott (8).

Close: 1st day – A(1) 253-6 (McCool 28, Tallon 35); 2nd – E(1) 147-1 (Washbrook 54, Edrich 83); 3rd – A(2) 33-0 (Barnes 19, Morris 14); 4th – A(2) 293-4 (Morris 132, McCool 25); 5th – E(2) 91-0 (Hutton 25, Washbrook 60).

AUSTRALIA v ENGLAND 1946–47 (4th Test)

Played at Adelaide Oval on 31 January, 1, 3, 4, 5, 6 February.
Toss: England.   Result: MATCH DRAWN.
Debuts: Australia – M.R. Harvey.

Compton and Morris both scored hundreds in each innings – the only occasion that a batsman on each side has done this in the same Test match. Evans established a world record for all first-class cricket (still unbeaten) by taking 97 minutes to score his first run in the second innings. In the first innings Lindwall bowled the last three batsmen in four balls. Morris became the third batsman after H. Sutcliffe (1924-25) and C.G. Macartney (1926) to score three hundreds in successive innings in this series. Hutton and Washbrook extended their run of successive century opening partnerships to three. Hammond made the last of his 33 appearances against Australia: 2,852 runs, 9 hundreds, 36 wickets and a record (until surpassed by I.T. Botham) 43 catches.

ENGLAND

L. Hutton	lbw b McCool	94	b Johnson		76
C. Washbrook	c Tallon b Dooland	65	c Tallon b Lindwall		39
W.J. Edrich	c and b Dooland	17	c Bradman b Toshack		46
W.R. Hammond*	b Toshack	18	c Lindwall b Toshack		22
D.C.S. Compton	c and b Lindwall	147	not out		103
J. Hardstaff, jr	b Miller	67	b Toshack		9
J.T. Ikin	c Toshack b Dooland	21	lbw b Toshack		1
N.W.D. Yardley	not out	18	c Tallon b Lindwall		18
A.V. Bedser	b Lindwall	2	c Tallon b Miller		3
T.G. Evans†	b Lindwall	0	not out		10
D.V.P. Wright	b Lindwall	0			
Extras	(B 4, LB 5, W 2)	11	(B 5, LB 3, W 2, NB 3)		13
Total		**460**	(8 wickets declared)		**340**

AUSTRALIA

M.R. Harvey	b Bedser	12	b Yardley		31
A.R. Morris	c Evans b Bedser	122	not out		124
D.G. Bradman*	b Bedser	0	not out		56
A.L. Hassett	c Hammond b Wright	78			
K.R. Miller	not out	141			
I.W. Johnson	lbw b Wright	52			
C.L. McCool	c Bedser b Yardley	2			
D. Tallon†	b Wright	3			
R.R. Lindwall	c Evans b Yardley	20			
B. Dooland	c Bedser b Yardley	29			
E.R.H. Toshack	run out	0			
Extras	(B 16, LB 6, W 2, NB 4)	28	(LB 2, NB 2)		4
Total		**487**	(1 wicket)		**215**

AUSTRALIA	O	M	R	W	O	M	R	W		FALL OF WICKETS			
Lindwall	23	5	52	4	17·1	4	60	2		E	A	E	A
Miller	16	0	45	1	11	0	34	1	*Wkt*	*1st*	*1st*	*2nd*	*2nd*
Toshack	30	13	59	1	36	6	76	4	1st	137	18	100	116
McCool	29	1	91	1	19	3	41	0	2nd	173	18	137	–
Johnson	22	3	69	0	25	8	51	1	3rd	196	207	178	–
Dooland	33	1	133	3	17	2	65	0	4th	202	222	188	–
									5th	320	372	207	–
ENGLAND									6th	381	389	215	–
Bedser	30	6	97	3	15	1	68	0	7th	455	396	250	–
Edrich	20	3	88	0	7	2	25	0	8th	460	423	255	–
Wright	32·4	1	152	3	9	0	49	0	9th	460	486	–	–
Yardley	31	7	101	3	13	0	69	1	10th	460	487	–	–
Ikin	2	0	9	0									
Compton	3	0	12	0									

Umpires: G. Borwick (20) and J.D. Scott (9).

Close: 1st day – E(1) 239-4 (Compton 15, Hardstaff 22); 2nd – A(1) 24-2 (Morris 11, Hassett 0); 3rd – A(1) 293-4 (Miller 33, Johnson 35); 4th – E(2) 96-0 (Hutton 58, Washbrook 38); 5th – E(2) 274-8 (Compton 52, Evans 0).

AUSTRALIA v ENGLAND 1946–47 (5th Test)

Played at Sydney Cricket Ground on 28 February, 1 (*no play*), 3, 4, 5 March.
Toss: England.   Result: AUSTRALIA won by five wickets.
Debuts: Australia – R.A. Hamence.

Australia won in the last over of the penultimate day. Hutton, 122 not out on Friday evening when England were 237 for 6, had been hospitalised with tonsillitis and a temperature of 103 degrees by the time play resumed on Monday. Wright's first innings analysis was the best of his 34-match career for England. Yardley took over the captaincy in the absence of Hammond (fibrositis).

ENGLAND

L. Hutton	retired ill	122	absent ill	–
C. Washbrook	b Lindwall	0	b McCool	24
W.J. Edrich	c Tallon b Lindwall	60	st Tallon b McCool	24
L.B. Fishlock	b McCool	14	(1) lbw b Lindwall	0
D.C.S. Compton	hit wkt b Lindwall	17	(4) c Miller b Toshack	76
N.W.D. Yardley*	c Miller b Lindwall	2	b McCool	11
J.T. Ikin	b Lindwall	0	(5) st Tallon b McCool	0
T.G. Evans†	b Lindwall	29	(7) b Miller	20
T.P.B. Smith	b Lindwall	2	(8) c Tallon b Lindwall	24
A.V. Bedser	not out	10	(9) st Tallon b McCool	4
D.V.P. Wright	c Tallon b Miller	7	(10) not out	1
Extras	(B 7, LB 8, W 1, NB 1)	17	(B 1, LB 1)	2
Total		**280**		**186**

AUSTRALIA

S.G. Barnes	c Evans b Bedser	71	c Evans b Bedser	30
A.R. Morris	lbw b Bedser	57	run out	17
D.G. Bradman*	b Wright	12	c Compton b Bedser	63
A.L. Hassett	c Ikin b Wright	24	c Ikin b Wright	47
K.R. Miller	c Ikin b Wright	23	not out	34
R.A. Hamence	not out	30	c Edrich b Wright	1
C.L. McCool	c Yardley b Wright	3	not out	13
D. Tallon†	c Compton b Wright	0		
R.R. Lindwall	c Smith b Wright	0		
G.E. Tribe	c Fishlock b Wright	9		
E.R.H. Toshack	run out	5		
Extras	(B 7, LB 6, NB 6)	19	(B 4, LB 1, NB 4)	9
Total		**253**	(5 wickets)	**214**

AUSTRALIA	O	M	R	W	O	M	R	W
Lindwall	22	3	63	7	12	1	46	2
Miller	15·3	2	31	1	6	1	11	1
Tribe	28	2	95	0	14	0	58	0
Toshack	16	4	40	0	4	1	14	1
McCool	13	0	34	1	21·4	5	44	5
Barnes					3	0	11	0
ENGLAND								
Bedser	27	7	49	2	22	4	75	2
Edrich	7	0	34	0	2	0	14	0
Smith	8	0	38	0	2	0	8	0
Wright	29	4	105	7	22	1	93	2
Yardley	5	2	8	0	3	1	7	0
Compton					1·2	0	8	0

FALL OF WICKETS

	E	A	E	A
Wkt	*1st*	*1st*	*2nd*	*2nd*
1st	1	126	0	45
2nd	151	146	42	51
3rd	188	146	65	149
4th	215	187	65	173
5th	225	218	85	180
6th	225	230	120	–
7th	244	230	157	–
8th	269	233	184	–
9th	280	245	186	–
10th	–	253	–	–

Umpires: G. Borwick (21) and J.D. Scott (10).

Close: 1st day – E(1) 237-6 (Hutton 122, Evans 0); 2nd – no play; 3rd – A(1) 189-4 (Hassett 12, Hamence 0); 4th – E(2) 144-6 (Compton 51, Smith 14).

NEW ZEALAND v ENGLAND 1946–47 (Only Test)

Played at Lancaster Park, Christchurch, on 21, 22, 24 (*no play*), 25 (*no play*) March.
Toss: England.   Result: MATCH DRAWN.
Debuts: New Zealand – T.B. Burtt, R.H. Scott, F.B. Smith, C.A. Snedden, B. Sutcliffe, D.D. Taylor.

For the first time in Test cricket an extra day was added to this match after the third day had been washed out, but rain prevented play on that one too. Hammond was top scorer in his last innings for England. Applauded to the wicket and given three cheers by the fielding side, he took his (then) world record aggregate from 85 Tests to 7,249 runs. Cowie, right-arm fast-medium, took six of the first seven England wickets to fall after Hadlee had reached his only Test hundred in 130 minutes.

NEW ZEALAND

W.A. Hadlee*	c Bedser b Yardley	116
B. Sutcliffe	c Evans b Bedser	58
V.J. Scott	c Hammond b Pollard	18
W.M. Wallace	c Evans b Bedser	9
D.D. Taylor	lbw b Bedser	12
F.B. Smith	b Bedser	18
E.W.T. Tindill†	b Pollard	1
R.H. Scott	b Edrich	18
J. Cowie	b Pollard	45
T.B. Burtt	not out	24
C.A. Snedden	did not bat	
Extras	(B 10, LB 11, NB 5)	26
Total	(9 wickets declared)	**345**

ENGLAND

C. Washbrook	c Smith b Cowie	2
N.W.D. Yardley	b Cowie	22
W.J. Edrich	c Taylor b R.H. Scott	42
D.C.S. Compton	b Cowie	38
W.R. Hammond*	c Sutcliffe b Cowie	79
J.T. Ikin	c Tindill b Cowie	45
T.G. Evans†	not out	21
T.P.B. Smith	c sub (C. Burke) b Cowie	1
A.V. Bedser	not out	8
D.V.P. Wright	) did not bat	
R. Pollard	)	
Extras	(B 5, LB 1, NB 1)	7
Total	(7 wickets declared)	**265**

ENGLAND	O	M	R	W
Bedser	39	5	95	4
Pollard	29·4	8	73	3
Edrich	11	2	35	1
Wright	13	1	61	0
Smith	6	0	43	0
Yardley	4	0	12	1
NEW ZEALAND				
Cowie	30	4	83	6
R.H. Scott	23	3	74	1
Burtt	14	1	55	0
Snedden	16	5	46	0

FALL OF WICKETS

	NZ	E
Wkt	*1st*	*1st*
1st	133	2
2nd	195	46
3rd	212	79
4th	212	125
5th	234	222
6th	238	241
7th	258	249
8th	281	–
9th	345	–
10th	–	–

Umpires: O.R. Montgomery (1) and M.F. Pengelly (2).

Close: 1st day – NZ(1) 306-8 (Cowie 24, Burtt 9); 2nd – E(1) 265-7 (Evans 21, Bedser 8); 3rd – no play.

ENGLAND v SOUTH AFRICA 1947 (1st Test)

Played at Trent Bridge, Nottingham, on 7, 9, 10, 11 June.
Toss: South Africa.   Result: MATCH DRAWN.
Debuts: England – C. Cook, H.E. Dollery, J.W. Martin; South Africa – O.C. Dawson, T.A. Harris, J.D. Lindsay, N.B.F. Mann, A.M.B. Rowan, V.I. Smith, L. Tuckett.

Melville was the first South African to score a hundred in each innings of a Test match. Mann opened his Test career with eight consecutive maiden overs. After Hollies and Martin had added 51 for the last wicket in England's second innings, South Africa were left 138 minutes in which to score 227 to win. The third-wicket partnership of 319 between Melville and Nourse was then South Africa's highest in all Test cricket for any wicket; it remains their highest against England. Compton and Yardley set the present fifth-wicket record for this series by adding 237 together. England's total was the highest after following on until 1957-58 (*Test No. 449*).

SOUTH AFRICA

B. Mitchell	b Bedser	14	c Evans b Bedser		4
A. Melville*	b Martin	189	not out		104
K.G. Viljoen	lbw b Edrich	10	not out		51
A.D. Nourse	b Hollies	149			
O.C. Dawson	st Evans b Hollies	48			
T.A. Harris	c Hutton b Hollies	60			
A.M.B. Rowan	not out	34			
L. Tuckett	lbw b Hollies	0			
N.B.F. Mann	b Bedser	8			
J.D. Lindsay†	b Bedser	0			
V.I. Smith	c Yardley b Hollies	1			
Extras	(B 7, LB 12, W 1)	20	(B 1, W 5, NB 1)		7
Total		**533**	(1 wicket)		**166**

ENGLAND

L. Hutton	lbw b Rowan	17	b Tuckett		9
C. Washbrook	lbw b Tuckett	25	c Lindsay b Rowan		59
W.J. Edrich	b Smith	57	b Smith		50
D.C.S. Compton	c Mitchell b Tuckett	65	c Mitchell b Mann		163
H.E. Dollery	b Dawson	9	c and b Dawson		17
N.W.D. Yardley*	lbw b Tuckett	22	c Tuckett b Dawson		99
T.G. Evans†	st Lindsay b Smith	2	c and b Smith		74
A.V. Bedser	c Melville b Smith	7	c Harris b Smith		2
C. Cook	b Tuckett	0	c Dawson b Smith		4
J.W. Martin	c Lindsay b Tuckett	0	(11) b Rowan		26
W.E. Hollies	not out	0	(10) not out		18
Extras	(B 1, LB 2, W 1)	4	(B 15, LB 13, W 2)		30
Total		**208**			**551**

ENGLAND	O	M	R	W	O	M	R	W	FALL OF WICKETS				
Martin	36	4	111	1	9	2	18	0		SA	E	E	SA
Bedser	57·1	14	106	3	14	3	31	1	*Wkt*	*1st*	*1st*	*2nd*	*2nd*
Edrich	20	8	56	1	4	0	8	0	1st	23	40	20	21
Hollies	55·2	16	123	5	9	1	33	0	2nd	44	48	116	–
Cook	21	4	87	0	9	0	40	0	3rd	363	154	133	–
Yardley	5	0	24	0					4th	384	165	170	–
Compton	2	1	6	0	4	0	14	0	5th	450	198	407	–
Hutton					2	0	15	0	6th	505	198	434	–
									7th	505	207	472	–
SOUTH AFRICA									8th	528	208	499	–
Tuckett	37	9	68	5	47	12	127	1	9th	530	208	500	–
Dawson	13	2	35	1	25	7	57	2	10th	533	208	551	–
Rowan	16	6	45	1	43·2	8	100	2					
Mann	20	13	10	0	60	22	94	1					
Smith	27·1	10	46	3	51	15	143	4					

Umpires: C.A.R. Coleman (1) and J.A. Smart (3).

Close: 1st day – SA(1) 376-3 (Melville 183, Dawson 3); 2nd – E(1) 154-2 (Edrich 44, Compton 65); 3rd – E(2) 278-4 (Compton 83, Yardley 45).

ENGLAND v SOUTH AFRICA 1947 (2nd Test)

Played at Lord's, London, on 21, 23, 24, 25 June.
Toss: England.   Result: ENGLAND won by ten wickets.
Debuts: England – G.H. Pope.

Edrich and Compton, in the prime of their halcyon summer in which they aggregated 7,355 runs and 30 centuries in first-class matches, shared a partnership of 370 which was then the record for the third wicket in all Test cricket. Melville scored his fourth hundred in consecutive Test innings, spread over nine years, equalling the record set by J.H.W. Fingleton in 1936-37 (*Test No. 255*). Wright achieved his best match figures for England.

ENGLAND

L. Hutton	b Rowan	18	not out	13
C. Washbrook	c Tuckett b Dawson	65	not out	13
W.J. Edrich	b Mann	189		
D.C.S. Compton	c Rowan b Tuckett	208		
C.J. Barnett	b Tuckett	33		
N.W.D. Yardley*	c Rowan b Tuckett	5		
T.G. Evans†	b Tuckett	16		
G.H. Pope	not out	8		
A.V. Bedser	b Tuckett	0		
D.V.P. Wright	} did not bat			
W.E. Hollies				
Extras	(B 2, LB 10)	12		
Total	(8 wickets declared)	**554**	(0 wickets)	**26**

SOUTH AFRICA

B. Mitchell	st Evans b Compton	46	c Edrich b Wright	80
A. Melville*	c Bedser b Hollies	117	b Edrich	8
K.G. Viljoen	b Wright	1	b Edrich	6
A.D. Nourse	lbw b Wright	61	b Edrich	58
O.C. Dawson	c Barnett b Hollies	36	c Edrich b Compton	33
T.A. Harris	st Evans b Compton	30	c Yardley b Compton	3
A.M.B. Rowan	b Wright	8	not out	38
L. Tuckett	b Wright	5	lbw b Wright	9
N.B.F. Mann	b Wright	4	b Wright	5
J.D. Lindsay†	not out	7	c Yardley b Wright	5
V.I. Smith	c Edrich b Pope	11	c Edrich b Wright	0
Extras	(LB 1)	1	(B 3, LB 4)	7
Total		**327**		**252**

SOUTH AFRICA	O	M	R	W	O	M	R	W			FALL OF WICKETS		
Tuckett	47	8	115	5	3	0	4	0		E	SA	SA	E
Dawson	33	11	81	1	6	2	6	0	*Wkt*	*1st*	*1st*	*2nd*	*2nd*
Mann	53	16	99	1	3·1	1	16	0	1st	75	95	16	–
Rowan	65	11	174	1					2nd	96	104	28	–
Smith	17	2	73	0					3rd	466	222	120	–
									4th	515	230	192	–
ENGLAND									5th	526	290	192	–
Edrich	9	1	22	0	13	5	31	3	6th	541	300	201	–
Bedser	26	1	76	0	14	6	20	0	7th	554	302	224	–
Pope	19·2	5	49	1	17	7	36	0	8th	554	308	236	–
Wright	39	10	95	5	32·2	6	80	5	9th	–	309	252	–
Hollies	28	10	52	2	20	7	32	0	10th	–	327	252	–
Compton	21	11	32	2	32	10	46	2					

Umpires: H.G. Baldwin (2) and D. Davies (1).

Close: 1st day – E(1) 312-2 (Edrich 109, Compton 110); 2nd – SA(1) 167-2 (Melville 96, Nourse 24); 3rd – SA(2) 120-2 (Mitchell 47, Nourse 58).

ENGLAND v SOUTH AFRICA 1947 (3rd Test)

Played at Old Trafford, Manchester, on 5, 7, 8, 9 July.
Toss: South Africa.   Result: ENGLAND won by seven wickets.
Debuts: England – K. Cranston, C. Gladwin; South Africa – D.V. Dyer, J.B. Plimsoll.

Edrich, who pull-drove three sixes when Plimsoll took the second new ball, and Compton, who scored his third successive hundred, added 228 runs in 196 minutes. Edrich became the third player after G. Giffen (*Test No. 42*) and G.A. Faulkner (*106*) to score 200 runs and take eight wickets in a Test. Nourse considered his fifth hundred for South Africa, on a difficult drying pitch, to be the finest of his career.

SOUTH AFRICA

A. Melville*	c Hutton b Gladwin	17	b Edrich		59
D.V. Dyer	b Edrich	62	b Gladwin		1
B. Mitchell	run out	80	c Hutton b Compton		6
A.D. Nourse	c Yardley b Cranston	23	b Edrich		115
K.G. Viljoen	c Compton b Edrich	93	c Hutton b Wright		32
O.C. Dawson	b Cranston	1	b Edrich		9
A.M.B. Rowan	lbw b Hollies	13	c Evans b Wright		0
L. Tuckett	b Edrich	13	lbw b Edrich		17
N.B.F. Mann	c Hollies b Gladwin	8	c Barnett b Wright		9
J.D. Lindsay†	not out	9	b Hollies		0
J.B. Plimsoll	c Evans b Edrich	8	not out		8
Extras	(B 3, LB 9)	12	(B 5, LB 5, NB 1)		11
Total		**339**			**267**

ENGLAND

L. Hutton	c Lindsay b Plimsoll	12	c Dawson b Mann		24
C. Washbrook	c Nourse b Tuckett	29	c Lindsay b Dawson		40
W.J. Edrich	b Tuckett	191	not out		22
D.C.S. Compton	c Tuckett b Dawson	115	hit wkt b Mann		6
C.J. Barnett	c sub (T.A. Harris) b Mann	5	not out		19
N.W.D. Yardley*	c Melville b Plimsoll	41			
K. Cranston	c Dawson b Rowan	23			
T.G. Evans†	b Tuckett	27			
C. Gladwin	b Tuckett	16			
D.V.P. Wright	not out	4			
W.E. Hollies	c Nourse b Plimsoll	5			
Extras	(B 2, LB 7, NB 1)	10	(B 9, LB 8, NB 2)		19
Total		**478**	(3 wickets)		**130**

ENGLAND	O	M	R	W	O	M	R	W
Edrich	35·1	9	95	4	22·4	4	77	4
Gladwin	50	24	58	2	16	6	28	1
Cranston	34	12	64	2				
Barnett	8	3	11	0	5	1	12	0
Wright	9	1	30	0	10	2	32	3
Hollies	23	8	42	1	14	4	49	1
Compton	7	1	27	0	17	2	58	1
SOUTH AFRICA								
Tuckett	50	5	148	4	5	0	26	0
Plimsoll	35·3	9	128	3	4	0	15	0
Rowan	17	1	63	1	4	0	13	0
Mann	35	12	85	1	14	8	19	2
Dawson	14	2	44	1	9·5	2	38	1

FALL OF WICKETS				
	SA	E	SA	E
Wkt	1st	1st	2nd	2nd
1st	32	40	12	63
2nd	125	48	42	80
3rd	163	276	96	103
4th	214	289	217	–
5th	215	363	225	–
6th	260	415	228	–
7th	287	439	232	–
8th	298	466	244	–
9th	327	471	244	–
10th	339	478	267	–

Umpires: F. Chester (31) and C.A.R. Coleman (2).

Close: 1st day – SA(1) 278-6 (Viljoen 66, Tuckett 6); 2nd – E(1) 311-4 (Edrich 141, Yardley 1); 3rd – SA(2) 14-1 (Melville 12, Mitchell 0).

Test No. 288/68

ENGLAND v SOUTH AFRICA 1947 (4th Test)

Played at Headingley, Leeds, on 26, 28, 29 July.
Toss: South Africa.   Result: ENGLAND won by ten wickets.
Debuts: England – H.J. Butler, J.A. Young; South Africa – G.M. Fullerton.

England won this match and the rubber with a day in hand when Hutton hit Mann for a six. Earlier he had scored a hundred in his first Test at Leeds. Cranston ended South Africa's second innings by taking four wickets in six balls (WOWOWW).

SOUTH AFRICA

A. Melville*	b Edrich	0	c Compton b Young	30
D.V. Dyer	c Evans b Wright	9	c Yardley b Edrich	2
B. Mitchell	b Butler	53	b Young	5
A.D. Nourse	b Butler	51	lbw b Butler	57
K.G. Viljoen	b Wright	5	lbw b Butler	29
O.C. Dawson	c Young b Butler	5	b Butler	17
G.M. Fullerton†	c Cranston b Edrich	13	lbw b Cranston	13
A.M.B. Rowan	c Yardley b Edrich	0	not out	21
N.B.F. Mann	c Edrich b Cranston	29	c Evans b Cranston	0
L. Tuckett	c Evans b Butler	3	b Cranston	0
V.I. Smith	not out	0	b Cranston	0
Extras	(LB 5, NB 2)	7	(B 4, LB 6)	10
Total		**175**		**184**

ENGLAND

L. Hutton	run out	100	not out	32
C. Washbrook	b Mann	75	not out	15
W.J. Edrich	c Melville b Mann	43		
D.C.S. Compton	c Mitchell b Mann	30		
C.J. Barnett	c Tuckett b Rowan	6		
N.W.D. Yardley*	c Nourse b Smith	36		
K. Cranston	c Melville b Mann	3		
T.G. Evans†	not out	6		
J.A. Young	not out	0		
D.V.P. Wright	) did not bat			
H.J. Butler	)			
Extras	(B 8, LB 8, NB 2)	18		
Total	(7 wickets declared)	**317**	(0 wickets)	**47**

ENGLAND	O	M	R	W	O	M	R	W
Butler	28	15	34	4	24	9	32	3
Edrich	17	4	46	3	14	2	35	1
Young	17	5	31	0	19	7	54	2
Wright	20	9	24	2	14	7	31	0
Cranston	11·1	3	24	1	7	3	12	4
Compton	4	0	9	0	2	0	10	0
SOUTH AFRICA								
Tuckett	18	4	48	0	6	1	12	0
Dawson	4	0	12	0	4	1	13	0
Mann	50	20	68	4	3·4	0	17	0
Smith	36	9	82	1				
Rowan	46	12	89	1				
Mitchell					2	1	5	0

FALL OF WICKETS

Wkt	SA 1st	E 1st	SA 2nd	E 2nd
1st	1	141	6	–
2nd	23	218	16	–
3rd	113	241	59	–
4th	121	253	130	–
5th	125	289	139	–
6th	130	306	156	–
7th	131	316	184	–
8th	158	–	184	–
9th	175	–	184	–
10th	175	–	184	–

Umpires: F. Chester (32) and J.J. Hills (1).

Close: 1st day – E(1) 53-0 (Hutton 32, Washbrook 21); 2nd – E(1) 317-7 (Evans 6, Young 0).

ENGLAND v SOUTH AFRICA 1947 (5th Test)

Played at Kennington Oval, London, on 16, 18, 19, 20 August.
Toss: England.   Result: MATCH DRAWN.
Debuts: England – R. Howorth, J.D.B. Robertson.

Mitchell emulated Melville's feat of the 1st Test by scoring a century in both innings. He was on the field for the entire match bar 8 minutes (12 balls). Howorth dismissed Dyer with his first ball in Test cricket, the last England bowler to achieve this. Copson took the last three wickets without cost. Compton batted 105 minutes and hit 15 fours in scoring his 14th hundred of the first-class season; he was to set a world record by making four more. Nourse's aggregate of 621 runs in this rubber remains his country's record against England. South Africa finished just 28 runs short of victory.

ENGLAND

L. Hutton	b Mann	83	c Tuckett b Mann		36
C. Washbrook	lbw b Mann	32	c Fullerton b Rowan		43
J.D.B. Robertson	c Melville b Smith	4	b Rowan		30
D.C.S. Compton	c Tuckett b Rowan	53	c Nourse b Dawson		113
N.W.D. Yardley*	b Mann	59	c sub (D.W. Begbie) b Mann		11
K. Cranston	st Fullerton b Rowan	45	c Mitchell b Rowan		0
R. Howorth	c Fullerton b Rowan	23	not out		45
T.G. Evans†	run out	45	not out		39
C. Gladwin	not out	51			
D.V.P. Wright	b Mann	14			
W.H. Copson	b Dawson	6			
Extras	(B 4, LB 7, NB 1)	12	(B 6, W 2)		8
Total		**427**	(6 wickets declared)		**325**

SOUTH AFRICA

B. Mitchell	c Evans b Copson	120	not out		189
D.V. Dyer	c Gladwin b Howorth	18	lbw b Wright		4
K.G. Viljoen	c Evans b Wright	10	st Evans b Howorth		33
A.D. Nourse	c Yardley b Howorth	10	b Howorth		97
A. Melville*	lbw b Cranston	39	c Evans b Cranston		6
O.C. Dawson	lbw b Wright	55	c Howorth b Cranston		0
G.M. Fullerton†	c Howorth b Cranston	6	c Evans b Howorth		14
A.M.B. Rowan	b Howorth	0			
N.B.F. Mann	b Copson	36	(8) c Hutton b Wright		10
L. Tuckett	not out	0	(9) not out		40
V.I. Smith	lbw b Copson	0			
Extras	(B 3, LB 2, W 1, NB 2)	8	(B 12, LB 14, W 4)		30
Total		**302**	(7 wickets)		**423**

SOUTH AFRICA	O	M	R	W	O	M	R	W		FALL OF WICKETS			
Tuckett	32	6	82	0	7	0	34	0		E	SA	E	SA
Dawson	35	5	80	1	15	1	59	1	*Wkt*	*1st*	*1st*	*2nd*	*2nd*
Mann	64	28	93	4	27	7	102	2	1st	63	47	73	8
Rowan	38	9	92	3	25	1	95	3	2nd	80	62	89	48
Smith	21	0	68	1	3	0	27	0	3rd	178	78	158	232
									4th	178	164	179	247
ENGLAND									5th	271	243	180	249
Copson	27	13	46	3	30	11	66	0	6th	290	253	267	266
Gladwin	16	2	39	0	16	5	33	0	7th	322	254	–	314
Wright	29	7	89	2	30	8	103	2	8th	358	293	–	–
Howorth	39	16	64	3	37	12	85	3	9th	408	302	–	–
Compton	11	4	31	0	4	0	30	0	10th	427	302	–	–
Cranston	9	2	25	2	21	3	61	2					
Hutton					2	0	14	0					
Yardley					1	0	1	0					

Umpires: H.G. Baldwin (3) and J.A. Smart (4).

Close: 1st day – E(1) 311-6 (Howorth 17, Evans 10); 2nd – SA(1) 204-4 (Mitchell 92, Dawson 28); 3rd – SA(2) 8-1 (Mitchell 1).

AUSTRALIA v INDIA 1947–48 (1st Test)

Played at Woolloongabba, Brisbane, on 28, 29 November, 1, 2, 3 (*no play*), 4 December.
Toss: Australia.   Result: AUSTRALIA won by an innings and 226 runs.
Debuts: Australia – W.A. Johnston; India – H.R. Adhikari, J.K. Irani, G. Kishenchand,
K.M. Rangnekar.

Brisbane provided its customary sticky pitch for India's first official encounter with Australia. Before the rain, Bradman, who batted for 285 minutes and hit 20 fours, scored a hundred in his first Test against India. Only an hour's play was possible on the second and fourth days. In taking 5 for 2 in 19 balls, Toshack (left-arm slow-medium) returned the most economical five wicket analysis in Test cricket. His match figures of 11 for 31 were the best in any Test at Brisbane until 1985-86. India's total of 58 remains their lowest against Australia.

AUSTRALIA

W.A. Brown	c Irani b Amarnath	11
A.R. Morris	hit wkt b Sarwate	47
D.G. Bradman*	hit wkt b Amarnath	185
A.L. Hassett	c Gul Mahomed b Mankad	48
K.R. Miller	c Mankad b Amarnath	58
C.L. McCool	c Sohoni b Amarnath	10
R.R. Lindwall	st Irani b Mankad	7
D. Tallon†	not out	3
I.W. Johnson	c Rangnekar b Mankad	6
E.R.H. Toshack	not out	0
W.A. Johnston	did not bat	
Extras	(B 5, LB 1, W 1)	7
Total	(8 wickets declared)	**382**

INDIA

M.H. Mankad	c Tallon b Lindwall	0	b Lindwall	7
C.T. Sarwate	c Johnston b Miller	12	b Johnston	26
Gul Mahomed	b Lindwall	0	b Toshack	13
H.R. Adhikari	c McCool b Johnston	8	lbw b Toshack	13
G. Kishenchand	c Tallon b Johnston	1	c Bradman b Toshack	0
V.S. Hazare	c Brown b Toshack	10	c Morris b Toshack	18
L. Amarnath*	c Bradman b Toshack	22	b Toshack	5
K.M. Rangnekar	c Miller b Toshack	1	c Hassett b Toshack	0
S.W. Sohoni	c Miller b Toshack	2	c Brown b Miller	4
C.S. Nayudu	not out	0	c Hassett b Lindwall	6
J.K. Irani†	c Hassett b Toshack	0	not out	2
Extras	(B 1, LB 1)	2	(B 3, NB 1)	4
Total		**58**		**98**

INDIA	O	M	R	W	O	M	R	W
Sohoni	23	4	81	0				
Amarnath	39	10	84	4				
Mankad	34	3	113	3				
Sarwate	5	1	16	1				
Hazare	11	1	63	0				
Nayudu	3	0	18	0				
AUSTRALIA								
Lindwall	5	2	11	2	10·7	2	19	2
Johnston	8	4	17	2	9	6	11	1
Miller	6	1	26	1	10	2	30	1
Toshack	2·3	1	2	5	17	6	29	6
Johnson					3	1	5	0

FALL OF WICKETS

	A	I	I
Wkt	1st	1st	2nd
1st	38	0	14
2nd	97	0	27
3rd	198	19	41
4th	318	23	41
5th	344	23	72
6th	373	53	80
7th	373	56	80
8th	380	58	89
9th	–	58	94
10th	–	58	98

Umpires: A.N. Barlow (2) and G. Borwick (22).

Close: 1st day – A(1) 273-3 (Bradman 160, Miller 6); 2nd – A(1) 309-3 (Bradman 179, Miller 19); 3rd – I(2) 41-4 (Sarwate 8, Hazare 0); 4th – I(2) 70-4 (Sarwate 16, Hazare 18); 5th – no play.

AUSTRALIA v INDIA 1947–48 (2nd Test)

Played at Sydney Cricket Ground on 12, 13, 15 (*no play*), 16 (*no play*), 17, 18 (*no play*) December.
Toss: India.   Result: MATCH DRAWN.
Debuts: India – Amir Elahi, D.G. Phadkar.

This was the first Test in Australia to be completely ruined by rain; only ten hours of play were possible during the six days. Mankad created Test history by running out non-striker Brown for backing-up. He had rehearsed this successfully when the Indians played an Australian XI, but on that occasion he had warned the batsman first. India were 142 runs ahead with three wickets in hand when rain washed out the final day.

INDIA

M.H. Mankad	b Lindwall	5	b Lindwall	5
C.T. Sarwate	b Johnston	0	(3) c Johnson b Johnston	3
Gul Mahomed	c Brown b Miller	29	(4) c Bradman b Johnson	5
V.S. Hazare	b Miller	16	(5) not out	13
L. Amarnath*	b Johnson	25	(7) c Morris b Johnson	14
G. Kishenchand	b Johnson	44	(8) c McCool b Johnston	0
H.R. Adhikari	lbw b Johnston	0	(9) not out	0
D.G. Phadkar	c Miller b McCool	51	(6) c Tallon b Miller	2
C.S. Nayudu	c and b McCool	6		
Amir Elahi	c Miller b McCool	4	(2) c Miller b Johnston	13
J.K. Irani†	not out	1		
Extras	(B 5, LB 2)	7	(B 3, LB 3)	6
Total		**188**	(7 wickets)	**61**

AUSTRALIA

W.A. Brown	run out	18
A.R. Morris	lbw b Amarnath	10
D.G. Bradman*	b Hazare	13
A.L. Hassett	c Adhikari b Hazare	6
K.R. Miller	lbw b Phadkar	17
R.A. Hamence	c Adhikari b Mankad	25
I.W. Johnson	lbw b Phadkar	1
C.L. McCool	b Phadkar	9
R.R. Lindwall	b Hazare	0
D. Tallon†	c Irani b Hazare	6
W.A. Johnston	not out	0
Extras	(B 1, LB 1)	2
Total		**107**

AUSTRALIA	O	M	R	W	O	M	R	W			FALL OF WICKETS	
Lindwall	12	3	30	1	5	1	13	1		I	A	I
Johnston	17	4	33	2	13	5	15	3	Wkt	1st	1st	2nd
Miller	9	3	25	2	6	2	5	1	1st	2	25	17
McCool	18	2	71	3					2nd	16	30	19
Johnson	14	3	22	2	13	7	22	2	3rd	52	43	26
INDIA									4th	57	48	29
Phadkar	10	2	14	3					5th	94	86	34
Amarnath	14	4	31	1					6th	95	92	53
Mankad	9	0	31	1					7th	165	92	55
Hazare	13·2	3	29	4					8th	174	97	–
									9th	182	105	–
									10th	188	107	–

Umpires: A.N. Barlow (3) and G. Borwick (23).

Close: 1st day – I(1) 38-2 (Gul Mahomed 24, Hazare 5); 2nd – A(1) 28-1 (Morris 10, Bradman 0); 3rd – no play; 4th – no play; 5th – I(2) 61-7 (Hazare 13, Adhikari 0).

AUSTRALIA v INDIA 1947–48 (3rd Test)

Played at Melbourne Cricket Ground on 1, 2, 3, 5 January.
Toss: Australia.   Result: AUSTRALIA won by 233 runs.
Debuts: India – K. Rai Singh, P. Sen.

Bradman added to his considerable collection of records by becoming the first to score a hundred in each innings of a Test against India. After Mankad had scored India's first hundred against Australia, overnight rain changed the character of the pitch and prompted Amarnath's declaration. Bradman countered with a change of batting order, a move that was fully vindicated when he added 223 in an unbroken stand with Morris that remains the fifth-wicket record for this series.

AUSTRALIA

S.G. Barnes	b Mankad	12	(4) c Sen b Amarnath	15
A.R. Morris	b Amarnath	45	(5) not out	100
D.G. Bradman*	lbw b Phadkar	132	(6) not out	127
A.L. Hassett	lbw b Mankad	80		
K.R. Miller	lbw b Mankad	29		
R.A. Hamence	st Sen b Amarnath	25		
R.R. Lindwall	b Amarnath	26		
D. Tallon†	c Mankad b Amarnath	2		
B. Dooland	not out	21	(2) lbw b Phadkar	6
I.W. Johnson	lbw b Mankad	16	(1) c Hazare b Amarnath	0
W.A. Johnston	run out	5	(3) lbw b Amarnath	3
Extras	(B 1)	1	(B 3, NB 1)	4
Total		**394**	(4 wickets declared)	**255**

INDIA

M.H. Mankad	c Tallon b Johnston	116	b Johnston	13
C.T. Sarwate	c Tallon b Johnston	36	b Johnston	1
Gul Mahomed	c and b Dooland	12	c Morris b Johnson	28
V.S. Hazare	c Tallon b Barnes	17	c Barnes b Miller	10
L. Amarnath*	lbw b Barnes	0	b Lindwall	8
D.G. Phadkar	not out	55	c Barnes b Johnston	13
H.R. Adhikari	st Tallon b Johnson	26	c Lindwall b Johnson	1
K. Rai Singh	c Barnes b Johnson	2	c Tallon b Johnston	24
K.M. Rangnekar	c and b Johnson	6	c Hamence b Johnson	18
P. Sen†	b Johnson	4	c Hassett b Johnson	2
C.S. Nayudu	not out	4	not out	0
Extras	(B 9, LB 3, NB 1)	13	(B 6, LB 1)	7
Total	(9 wickets declared)	**291**		**125**

INDIA	O	M	R	W	O	M	R	W					
Phadkar	15	1	80	1	10	1	28	1					
Amarnath	21	3	78	4	20	3	52	3					
Hazare	16·1	0	62	0	11	1	55	0					
Mankad	37	4	135	4	18	4	74	0					
Sarwate	3	0	16	0	5	0	41	0					
Nayudu	2	0	22	0									
Gul Mahomed					1	0	1	0					

FALL OF WICKETS

Wkt	A 1st	I 1st	A 2nd	I 2nd
1st	29	124	1	10
2nd	99	145	11	27
3rd	268	188	13	44
4th	289	188	32	60
5th	302	198	–	60
6th	339	260	–	69
7th	341	264	–	100
8th	352	280	–	107
9th	387	284	–	125
10th	394	–	–	125

AUSTRALIA	O	M	R	W	O	M	R	W
Lindwall	12	0	47	0	3	0	10	1
Miller	13	2	46	0	7	0	29	1
Johnston	12	0	33	2	10	1	44	4
Johnson	14	1	59	4	5·7	0	35	4
Dooland	12	0	68	1				
Barnes	6	1	25	2				

Umpires: A.N. Barlow (4) and H. Elphinston (1).

Close: 1st day – A(1) 355-8 (Dooland 2, Johnson 2); 2nd – I(1) 262-6 (Phadkar 43, Rai Singh 2); 3rd – A(2) 255-4 (Morris 100, Bradman 127).

AUSTRALIA v INDIA 1947–48 (4th Test)

Played at Adelaide Oval on 23, 24, 26, 27, 28 January,
Toss: Australia.   Result: AUSTRALIA won by an innings and 16 runs.
Debuts: Australia – R.N. Harvey; India – C.R. Rangachari.

Australia's total of 674 remains the record for any Test in Australia. Hazare became the first batsman to score a hundred in each innings of a Test for India, and the only one to do so on successive days: 108 on the third day and 102 on the fourth. His sixth-wicket partnership of 188 with Phadkar and seventh-wicket one of 132 with Adhikari were then India's highest against Australia. Barnes and Bradman shared Australia's best second-wicket stand (236) for this series. This was Bradman's 27th hundred and the last of his 12 double-centuries in Tests. Hassett (198 not out) and Lindwall (7 for 38) both recorded career-best performances for Australia.

AUSTRALIA

S.G. Barnes	lbw b Mankad	112
A.R. Morris	b Phadkar	7
D.G. Bradman*	b Hazare	201
A.L. Hassett	not out	198
K.R. Miller	b Rangachari	67
R.N. Harvey	lbw b Rangachari	13
C.L. McCool	b Phadkar	27
I.W. Johnson	b Rangachari	22
R.R. Lindwall	b Rangachari	2
D. Tallon†	lbw b Mankad	1
E.R.H. Toshack	lbw b Hazare	8
Extras	(B 8, LB 6, NB 2)	16
Total		**674**

INDIA

M.H. Mankad	b McCool	49		c Tallon b Lindwall	0
C.T. Sarwate	b Miller	1		b Toshack	11
P. Sen†	b Miller	0	(10)	not out	0
L. Amarnath*	c Bradman b Johnson	46	(3)	b Lindwall	0
V.S. Hazare	lbw b Johnson	116	(4)	b Lindwall	145
Gul Mahomed	st Tallon b Johnson	4	(5)	b Barnes	34
D.G. Phadkar	lbw b Toshack	123	(6)	lbw b Lindwall	14
G. Kishenchand	b Lindwall	10	(7)	b Lindwall	0
H.R. Adhikari	run out	2	(8)	lbw b Miller	51
K.M. Rangnekar	st Tallon b Johnson	8	(9)	b Lindwall	0
C.R. Rangachari	not out	0		c McCool b Lindwall	0
Extras	(B 11, LB 8, NB 3)	22		(B 18, LB 3, NB 1)	22
Total		**381**			**277**

INDIA	O	M	R	W	O	M	R	W
Phadkar	15	0	74	2				
Amarnath	9	0	42	0				
Rangachari	41	5	141	4				
Mankad	43	8	170	2				
Sarwate	22	1	121	0				
Hazare	21·3	1	110	2				
AUSTRALIA								
Lindwall	21	6	61	1	16·5	4	38	7
Miller	9	1	39	2	9	3	13	1
McCool	28	2	102	1	4	0	26	0
Johnson	23·1	5	64	4	20	4	54	0
Toshack	18	2	66	1	25	8	73	1
Barnes	9	0	23	0	18	4	51	1
Bradman	1	0	4	0				

FALL OF WICKETS

	A	I	I
Wkt	1st	1st	2nd
1st	20	6	0
2nd	256	6	0
3rd	361	69	33
4th	503	124	99
5th	523	133	139
6th	576	321	139
7th	634	353	271
8th	640	359	273
9th	641	375	273
10th	674	381	277

Umpires: G. Borwick (24) and R. Wright (1).

Close: 1st day – A(1) 370-3 (Hassett 39, Miller 4); 2nd – I(1) 6-2 (Mankad 3); 3rd – I(1) 299-5 (Hazare 108, Phadkar 77); 4th – I(2) 188-6 (Hazare 102, Adhikari 18).

AUSTRALIA v INDIA 1947–48 (5th Test)

Played at Melbourne Cricket Ground on 6, 7, 9, 10 February.
Toss: Australia.   Result: AUSTRALIA won by an innings and 177 runs.
Debuts: Australia – L.J. Johnson, S.J.E. Loxton, D.T. Ring.

Although they rested Morris, Australia completed their third innings victory of the rubber with ease. Bradman, playing his last Test innings in Australia, tore a muscle under his left ribs and retired at 140. The left-handed Harvey became, at 19 years 121 days, the youngest to score a century for Australia. India lost their last 16 wickets of the rubber for 147 runs on the fourth day.

AUSTRALIA

S.G. Barnes	run out	33
W.A. Brown	run out	99
D.G. Bradman*	retired hurt	57
K.R. Miller	c Sen b Phadkar	14
R.N. Harvey	c Sen b Mankad	153
S.J.E. Loxton	c Sen b Amarnath	80
R.R. Lindwall	c Phadkar b Mankad	35
D. Tallon†	c Sen b Sarwate	37
L.J. Johnson	not out	25
D.T. Ring	c Kishenchand b Hazare	11
W.A. Johnston	not out	23
Extras	(B 4, LB 4)	8
Total	**(8 wickets declared)**	**575**

INDIA

M.H. Mankad	c Tallon b Loxton	111	c Tallon b Lindwall		0
C.T. Sarwate	b Lindwall	0	lbw b Johnston		10
H.R. Adhikari	c Tallon b Loxton	38	c Bradman b Loxton		17
V.S. Hazare	lbw b Lindwall	74	c and b Johnson		10
L. Amarnath*	c Barnes b Ring	12	(6) c Johnson b Ring		8
D.G. Phadkar	not out	56	(5) lbw b Johnston		0
Gul Mahomed	c Lindwall b Johnson	1	c Barnes b Ring		4
G. Kishenchand	b Ring	14	c Barnes b Johnson		0
C.S. Nayudu	c Bradman b Ring	2	c Brown b Ring		0
P. Sen†	b Johnson	13	b Johnson		10
C.R. Rangachari	b Johnson	0	not out		0
Extras	(B 6, LB 2, NB 2)	10	(B 6, LB 1, NB 1)		8
Total		**331**			**67**

INDIA	O	M	R	W	O	M	R	W
Phadkar	9	0	58	1				
Amarnath	23	1	79	1				
Rangachari	17	1	97	0				
Hazare	14	1	63	1				
Mankad	33	2	107	2				
Sarwate	18	1	82	1				
Nayudu	13	0	77	0				
Adhikari	1	0	4	0				
AUSTRALIA								
Lindwall	25	5	66	2	3	0	9	1
Johnson	30	8	66	3	5·2	2	8	3
Loxton	19	1	61	2	4	1	10	1
Johnston	8	4	14	0	7	0	15	2
Ring	36	8	103	3	5	1	17	3
Miller	3	0	10	0				
Barnes	2	1	1	0				

FALL OF WICKETS

	A	I	I
Wkt	1st	1st	2nd
1st	48	3	0
2nd	182	127	22
3rd	219	206	28
4th	378	231	35
5th	457	257	51
6th	497	260	51
7th	527	284	56
8th	544	286	56
9th	–	331	66
10th	–	331	67

Umpires: A.N. Barlow (5) and G.C. Cooper (1).

Close: 1st day – A(1) 336-3 (Harvey 78, Loxton 48); 2nd – I(1) 43-1 (Mankad 30, Adhikari 10); 3rd – I(1) 251-4 (Hazare 72, Phadkar 8).

WEST INDIES v ENGLAND 1947–48 (1st Test)

Played at Kensington Oval, Bridgetown, Barbados, on 21, 22, 23, 24, 26 January.
Toss: West Indies.   Result: MATCH DRAWN.
Debuts: West Indies – R.J. Christiani, W. Ferguson, B.B.M. Gaskin, J.D.C. Goddard, P.E. Jones,
C.L. Walcott, E. de C. Weekes; England – D. Brookes, J.C. Laker, W. Place, G.A. Smithson,
M.F. Tremlett.

Laker took 7 for 103 in his first Test innings, including a spell of 6 for 25 on the second morning. Williams hit
72 runs in 63 minutes in the second innings, including 6, 6, 4, 4 off his first four balls (from Laker). His fifty
took 30 minutes and is now the third-fastest in Test cricket and the fastest for West Indies. Christiani was the
second player after A.G. Chipperfield (*Test No. 233*) to score 99 in his first Test. Because of back strain Headley
batted last in the second innings. Needing 395 to win, England were 60 for 2 overnight. Tropical rain ended the
match after 63 minutes on the fifth day. Cranston deputised as captain in the absence of G.O.B. Allen (45), who
had pulled a calf muscle while skipping on the voyage out.

WEST INDIES

J.B. Stollmeyer	c Robertson b Ikin	78		c Evans b Howorth	31
C.L. Walcott†	b Laker	8		c Ikin b Howorth	16
E. de C. Weekes	c Evans b Tremlett	35		b Laker	25
G.E. Gomez	b Laker	86		st Evans b Howorth	0
G.A. Headley*	b Laker	29	(11)	not out	7
R.J. Christiani	lbw b Laker	1		lbw b Cranston	99
J.D.C. Goddard	b Howorth	28	(5)	c Ikin b Laker	18
E.A.V. Williams	c Ikin b Laker	2	(7)	c Evans b Howorth	72
W. Ferguson	b Laker	0		not out	56
P.E. Jones	not out	10	(8)	c Robertson b Howorth	7
B.B.M. Gaskin	c Ikin b Laker	10	(10)	c Brookes b Howorth	7
Extras	(LB 4, W 2, NB 3)	9		(B 6, LB 4, W 1, NB 2)	13
Total		**296**		(9 wickets declared)	**351**

ENGLAND

J.D.B. Robertson	lbw b Williams	80		not out	51
W. Place	c Gomez b Goddard	12	(6)	not out	1
D. Brookes	b Jones	10	(2)	c Walcott b Goddard	7
J. Hardstaff, jr	b Williams	98	(5)	c Gomez b Goddard	0
J.T. Ikin	c Walcott b Williams	3			
G.A. Smithson	c Gomez b Jones	0			
K. Cranston*	run out	2	(4)	lbw b Gaskin	8
R. Howorth	c Goddard b Ferguson	14	(3)	b Ferguson	16
T.G. Evans†	b Jones	26			
J.C. Laker	c Walcott b Jones	2			
M.F. Tremlett	not out	0			
Extras	(B 2, LB 2, W 1, NB 1)	6		(LB 3)	3
Total		**253**		(4 wickets)	**86**

ENGLAND	O	M	R	W	O	M	R	W
Tremlett	26	8	49	1	10	0	40	0
Cranston	15	4	29	0	13	3	31	1
Laker	37	9	103	7	30	12	95	2
Ikin	16	3	38	1	12	1	48	0
Howorth	30	8	68	1	41	8	124	6
WEST INDIES								
Jones	25·2	6	54	4	9	1	29	0
Gaskin	11	0	30	0	10	4	15	1
Williams	33	15	51	3	9	3	17	0
Goddard	21	6	49	1	14	4	18	2
Ferguson	14	1	52	1	3·4	1	4	1
Headley	6	1	11	0				

FALL OF WICKETS

	WI	E	WI	E
Wkt	*1st*	*1st*	*2nd*	*2nd*
1st	18	32	46	33
2nd	81	67	69	55
3rd	185	130	71	70
4th	245	153	87	71
5th	246	156	144	–
6th	271	176	240	–
7th	273	197	252	–
8th	273	250	301	–
9th	279	252	328	–
10th	296	253	–	–

Umpires: S.C. Foster (1) and J.H. Walcott (1).

Close: 1st day – WI(1) 244-3 (Gomez 85, Headley 29); 2nd – E(1) 150-3 (Hardstaff 42, Ikin 3); 3rd – WI(2)
117-4 (Goddard 9, Christiani 28); 4th – E(2) 60-2 (Robertson 35, Cranston 2).

WEST INDIES v ENGLAND 1947–48 (2nd Test)

Played at Queen's Park Oval, Port-of-Spain, Trinidad, on 11, 12, 13, 14, 16 February.
Toss: England.   Result: MATCH DRAWN.
Debuts: West Indies – A.G. Ganteaume, F.M.M. Worrell; England – S.C. Griffith, J.H. Wardle.

Pressed into service as an opening batsman because of injuries, Griffith, who batted for 354 minutes and hit 15 fours, became the only player to score his maiden first-class century in his first Test innings for England. All four openers scored hundreds, Ganteaume doing so in his only Test innings and Carew doing so from under a chocolate-brown felt hat. Exploiting the matting pitch skilfully with his leg-breaks, Ferguson recorded his best innings and match analyses in Test cricket. On the last day Allen pulled up lame when fielding off his own bowling and was unable to complete his fifth over.

ENGLAND

J.D.B. Robertson	run out	2	c Christiani b Ferguson		133
S.C. Griffith	lbw b Worrell	140	c Ferguson b Gomez		4
J.T. Ikin	b Ferguson	21	lbw b Ferguson		19
K. Cranston	c and b Ferguson	7	c Christiani b Williams		6
G.O.B. Allen*	c Walcott b Gaskin	36	(6) c Walcott b Williams		2
R. Howorth	b Ferguson	14	(7) b Ferguson		14
T.G. Evans†	c Walcott b Williams	30	(8) st Walcott b Ferguson		21
G.A. Smithson	c Goddard b Ferguson	35	(9) b Ferguson		35
J.C. Laker	c Gaskin b Goddard	55	(5) c Carew b Williams		24
J.H. Wardle	c Worrell b Ferguson	4	not out		2
H.J. Butler	not out	15	b Ferguson		0
Extras	(LB 1, NB 2)	3	(B 5, LB 3, NB 7)		15
Total		**362**			**275**

WEST INDIES

G.M. Carew	lbw b Laker	107	(5) not out		18
A.G. Ganteaume	c Ikin b Howorth	112			
E. de C. Weekes	b Butler	36	(1) c Evans b Butler		20
F.M.M. Worrell	c Evans b Cranston	97	not out		28
C.L. Walcott†	c Butler b Howorth	20	(2) lbw b Allen		2
G.E. Gomez*	lbw b Laker	62			
R.J. Christiani	c Robertson b Allen	7			
J.D.C. Goddard	not out	9			
E.A.V. Williams	c and b Allen	31	(3) b Butler		0
W. Ferguson	b Butler	5			
B.B.M. Gaskin	b Butler	0			
Extras	(B 2, LB 4, W 1, NB 4)	11	(LB 2, W 1, NB 1)		4
Total		**497**	(3 wickets)		**72**

WEST INDIES	O	M	R	W	O	M	R	W		FALL OF WICKETS			
Gaskin	37	14	72	1	21	6	41	0		E	WI	E	WI
Williams	21	8	31	1	27	7	64	3	*Wkt*	*1st*	*1st*	*2nd*	*2nd*
Ferguson	39	5	137	5	34·2	4	92	6	1st	5	173	18	3
Goddard	23·3	6	64	1	9	4	11	0	2nd	42	226	53	8
Worrell	23	4	55	1	14	2	30	0	3rd	54	306	62	41
Gomez					8	2	22	1	4th	126	341	97	–
									5th	158	440	122	–
ENGLAND									6th	201	447	149	–
Butler	32	4	122	3	8	2	27	2	7th	288	454	196	–
Allen	16	0	82	2	4·2	0	21	1	8th	296	488	270	–
Laker	36	10	108	2					9th	306	497	275	–
Cranston	7	1	29	1	3	0	18	0	10th	362	497	275	–
Ikin	20	5	60	0									
Howorth	32	3	76	2	1	0	2	0					
Wardle	3	0	9	0									

Umpires: V. Guillen (2) and B. Henderson (1).

Close: 1st day – E(1) 230-6 (Griffith 110, Smithson 7); 2nd – WI(1) 160-0 (Carew 101, Ganteaume 52); 3rd – WI(1) 447-6 (Christiani 2); 4th – E(2) 70-3 (Robertson 28, Laker 4).

WEST INDIES v ENGLAND 1947–48 (3rd Test)

Played at Bourda, Georgetown, British Guiana, on 3, 4, 5, 6 March.
Toss: West Indies.   Result: WEST INDIES won by seven wickets
Debuts: West Indies – L.R. Pierre, J. Trim.

Rain, which curtailed the first day when West Indies were 284 for 5 and delayed the start of the second, prompted Goddard's declaration. His off-breaks then achieved their only five-wicket analysis in Tests and led to a notable victory, with a day and a half to spare, in his first Test as captain. Hutton had joined the touring team after the 2nd Test. Allen pulled a leg muscle and was unable to complete his third over.

WEST INDIES

G.M. Carew	b Cranston	17	c Allen b Laker	8
J.D.C. Goddard*	b Allen	1	lbw b Laker	3
C.L. Walcott†	lbw b Cranston	11	not out	31
R.J. Christiani	c Hardstaff b Tremlett	51	lbw b Howorth	3
F.M.M. Worrell	not out	131		
G.E. Gomez	c Evans b Cranston	36	(5) not out	25
E. de C. Weekes	b Cranston	36		
E.A.V. Williams	b Laker	7		
W. Ferguson	c Allen b Laker	2		
J. Trim	) did not bat			
L.R. Pierre	)			
Extras	(LB 1, W 3, NB 1)	5	(LB 7, NB 1)	8
Total	(8 wickets declared)	**297**	(3 wickets)	**78**

ENGLAND

L. Hutton	c Williams b Goddard	31	b Ferguson	24
J.D.B. Robertson	c Ferguson b Goddard	23	lbw b Ferguson	9
W. Place	c Christiani b Goddard	1	b Ferguson	15
J. Hardstaff, jr	b Ferguson	3	c Christiani b Trim	63
J.T. Ikin	c Ferguson b Goddard	7	(8) run out	24
K. Cranston	st Walcott b Ferguson	24	c Christiani b Goddard	32
R. Howorth	c Ferguson b Goddard	4	(9) lbw b Ferguson	2
J.C. Laker	c Walcott b Ferguson	10	(10) c Goddard b Williams	6
T.G. Evans†	b Trim	1	(7) c Goddard b Williams	37
M.F. Tremlett	c Christiani b Trim	0	(11) not out	18
G.O.B. Allen*	not out	0	(5) lbw b Ferguson	20
Extras	(B 4, LB 1, NB 2)	7	(B 4, LB 5, W 1, NB 3)	13
Total		**111**		**263**

ENGLAND	O	M	R	W	O	M	R	W	FALL OF WICKETS				
										WI	E	E	WI
Allen	2·4	0	5	1					*Wkt*	*1st*	*1st*	*2nd*	*2nd*
Tremlett	14	4	35	1					1st	7	59	21	10
Cranston	25	5	78	4	2	0	11	0	2nd	26	61	51	23
Laker	36	11	94	2	9	1	34	2	3rd	48	64	52	26
Howorth	23	4	58	0	9	0	25	1	4th	127	64	137	–
Ikin	5	2	22	0					5th	224	94	145	–
WEST INDIES									6th	284	96	185	–
Trim	10	6	6	2	13	2	38	1	7th	295	109	226	–
Pierre	2	0	9	0	5	0	19	0	8th	297	110	233	–
Williams	6	0	21	0	24·4	12	34	2	9th	–	110	249	–
Goddard	14·2	5	31	5	24	8	43	1	10th	–	111	263	–
Worrell	2	0	5	0									
Ferguson	15	5	23	3	40	6	116	5					
Gomez	1	0	9	0									

Umpires: J. Da Silva (1) and E.S. Gillette (1).

Close: 1st day – WI(1) 284-5 (Worrell 127, Weekes 36); 2nd – E(1) 110-9 (Howorth 3); 3rd – E(2) 226-6 (Evans 37, Ikin 18).

WEST INDIES v ENGLAND 1947–48 (4th Test)

Played at Sabina Park, Kingston, Jamaica, on 27, 29, 30, 31 March, 1 April.
Toss: England.   Result: WEST INDIES won by ten wickets.
Debuts: West Indies – H.H.H. Johnson, E.S.M. Kentish, K.R. Rickards

Johnson marked his first appearance in Test cricket at the age of 37 by taking five wickets in each innings; his match analysis of 10 for 96 remains the best for any Test in Jamaica. Weekes scored the first of his record run of five hundreds in consecutive innings. After Place had completed his only Test century England lost their last six wickets for 20 runs. West Indies took only 34 minutes to complete their task, Goddard hitting a six and eight fours. At 45 years 245 days, Allen was the second oldest Test captain after W.G. Grace when the match and his career ended.

ENGLAND

L. Hutton	b Johnson	56	c sub (J.K. Holt) b Goddard	60
J.D.B. Robertson	lbw b Johnson	64	b Johnson	28
W. Place	st Walcott b Ferguson	8	st Walcott b Stollmeyer	107
J. Hardstaff, jr	c Gomez b Ferguson	9	b Johnson	64
K. Cranston	c Walcott b Johnson	13	b Kentish	36
G.O.B. Allen*	c Walcott b Kentish	23	lbw b Johnson	13
J.T. Ikin	run out	5	c Worrell b Stollmeyer	3
T.G. Evans†	c Weekes b Kentish	9	b Johnson	4
R. Howorth	not out	12	st Walcott b Stollmeyer	1
J.C. Laker	c Walcott b Johnson	6	not out	6
M.F. Tremlett	b Johnson	0	c Walcott b Johnson	2
Extras	(B 12, LB 8, NB 2)	22	(B 8, LB 2, NB 2)	12
Total		**227**		**336**

WEST INDIES

J.D.C. Goddard*	c Hutton b Howorth	17	not out	46
J.B. Stollmeyer	lbw b Howorth	30	not out	25
E. de C. Weekes	c Hutton b Ikin	141		
F.M.M. Worrell	lbw b Allen	38		
G.E. Gomez	b Tremlett	23		
K.R. Rickards	b Laker	67		
R.J. Christiani	c and b Laker	14		
C.L. Walcott†	c Hutton b Tremlett	45		
W. Ferguson	c Hardstaff b Laker	75		
H.H.H. Johnson	b Howorth	8		
E.S.M. Kentish	not out	1		
Extras	(B 11, LB 17, NB 3)	31	(LB 4, W 1)	5
Total		**490**	(0 wickets)	**76**

WEST INDIES	O	M	R	W	O	M	R	W		FALL OF WICKETS			
Johnson	34·5	13	41	5	31	11	55	5		E	WI	E	WI
Kentish	21	8	38	2	26	7	68	1	*Wkt*	*1st*	*1st*	*2nd*	*2nd*
Goddard	19	7	33	0	25	9	38	1	1st	129	39	69	–
Ferguson	38	14	53	2	32	7	90	0	2nd	132	62	101	–
Worrell	11	1	25	0	20	3	41	0	3rd	147	144	214	–
Stollmeyer	5	1	15	0	19	7	32	3	4th	150	204	291	–
									5th	173	320	316	–
ENGLAND									6th	185	351	316	–
Allen	20	1	83	1	2	0	14	0	7th	200	358	327	–
Tremlett	31	1	98	2	1	0	4	0	8th	205	455	327	–
Howorth	40	10	106	3	4	0	27	0	9th	221	482	329	–
Laker	36·4	5	103	3	2	0	11	0	10th	227	490	336	–
Ikin	19	0	69	1	2	0	15	0					

Umpires: S.C. Burke (2) and T.A. Ewart (1).

Close: 1st day – E(1) 183-5 (Allen 13, Ikin 5); 2nd – WI(1) 168-3 (Weekes 68, Gomez 5); 3rd – E(2) 21-0 (Hutton 11, Robertson 10); 4th – E(2) 258-3 (Place 88, Cranston 15).

ENGLAND v AUSTRALIA 1948 (1st Test)

Played at Trent Bridge, Nottingham, on 10, 11, 12, 14, 15 June.
Toss: England.   Result: AUSTRALIA won by eight wickets.
Debuts: Nil.

Bradman batted for 288 minutes for his 28th Test century, while Hassett (354 minutes) made his highest score against England. In a spell of 26–16–14–1 Young bowled 11 successive maiden overs. Lindwall (groin strain) was unable to bowl in the second innings. Compton's highest innings against Australia lasted 410 minutes, was spread over three days, and was interrupted nine times by rain, bad light or scheduled intervals.

ENGLAND

L. Hutton	b Miller	3	b Miller		74
C. Washbrook	c Brown b Lindwall	6	c Tallon b Miller		1
W.J. Edrich	b Johnston	18	c Tallon b Johnson		13
D.C.S. Compton	b Miller	19	hit wkt b Miller		184
J. Hardstaff, jr	c Miller b Johnston	0	c Hassett b Toshack		43
C.J. Barnett	b Johnston	8	c Miller b Johnston		6
N.W.D. Yardley*	lbw b Toshack	3	c and b Johnston		22
T.G. Evans†	c Morris b Johnston	12	c Tallon b Johnston		50
J.C. Laker	c Tallon b Miller	63	b Miller		4
A.V. Bedser	c Brown b Johnston	22	not out		3
J.A. Young	not out	1	b Johnston		9
Extras	(B 5, LB 5)	10	(B 12, LB 17, NB 3)		32
Total		**165**			**441**

AUSTRALIA

S.G. Barnes	c Evans b Laker	62	not out		64
A.R. Morris	b Laker	31	b Bedser		9
D.G. Bradman*	c Hutton b Bedser	138	c Hutton b Bedser		0
K.R. Miller	c Edrich b Laker	0			
W.A. Brown	lbw b Yardley	17			
A.L. Hassett	b Bedser	137	(4) not out		21
I.W. Johnson	b Laker	21			
D. Tallon†	c and b Young	10			
R.R. Lindwall	c Evans b Yardley	42			
W.A. Johnston	not out	17			
E.R.H. Toshack	lbw b Bedser	19			
Extras	(B 9, LB 4, W 1, NB 1)	15	(LB 2, W 1, NB 1)		4
Total		**509**	(2 wickets)		**98**

AUSTRALIA	O	M	R	W	O	M	R	W
Lindwall	13	5	30	1				
Miller	19	8	38	3	44	10	125	4
Johnston	25	11	36	5	59	12	147	4
Toshack	14	8	28	1	33	14	60	1
Johnson	5	1	19	0	42	15	66	1
Morris	3	1	4	0				
Barnes					5	2	11	0
ENGLAND								
Edrich	18	1	72	0	4	0	20	0
Bedser	44·2	12	113	3	14·3	4	46	2
Barnett	17	5	36	0				
Young	60	28	79	1	10	3	28	0
Laker	55	14	138	4				
Compton	5	0	24	0				
Yardley	17	6	32	2				

FALL OF WICKETS

	E	A	E	A
Wkt	1st	1st	2nd	2nd
1st	9	73	5	38
2nd	15	121	39	48
3rd	46	121	150	–
4th	46	185	243	–
5th	48	305	264	–
6th	60	338	321	–
7th	74	365	405	–
8th	74	472	413	–
9th	163	476	423	–
10th	165	509	441	–

Umpires: F. Chester (33) and E. Cooke (1).

Close: 1st day – A(1) 17-0 (Barnes 6, Morris 10); 2nd – A(1) 293-4 (Bradman 130, Hassett 41); 3rd – E(2) 121-2 (Hutton 63, Compton 36); 4th – E(2) 345-6 (Compton 154, Evans 10).

ENGLAND v AUSTRALIA 1948 (2nd Test)

Played at Lord's, London, on 24, 25, 26, 28, 29 June.
Toss: Australia.   Result: AUSTRALIA won by 409 runs.
Debuts: England – A. Coxon.

This was the 14th successive Test against England in which he had batted, that Bradman scored at least one fifty. At the end of it he had been dismissed by Bedser in five consecutive Test innings. An injured back prevented Miller from bowling. England needed 596 runs to win this 150th match between the two countries.

AUSTRALIA

S.G. Barnes	c Hutton b Coxon	0	c Washbrook b Yardley		141
A.R. Morris	c Hutton b Coxon	105	b Wright		62
D.G. Bradman*	c Hutton b Bedser	38	c Edrich b Bedser		89
A.L. Hassett	b Yardley	47	b Yardley		0
K.R. Miller	lbw b Bedser	4	c Bedser b Laker		74
W.A. Brown	lbw b Yardley	24	c Evans b Coxon		32
I.W. Johnson	c Evans b Edrich	4	(8) not out		9
D. Tallon†	c Yardley b Bedser	53			
R.R. Lindwall	b Bedser	15	(7) st Evans b Laker		25
W.A. Johnston	st Evans b Wright	29			
E.R.H. Toshack	not out	20			
Extras	(B 3, LB 7, NB 1)	11	(B 22, LB 5, NB 1)		28
Total		**350**	(7 wickets declared)		**460**

ENGLAND

L. Hutton	b Johnson	20	c Johnson b Lindwall		13
C. Washbrook	c Tallon b Lindwall	8	c Tallon b Toshack		37
W.J. Edrich	b Lindwall	5	c Johnson b Toshack		2
D.C.S. Compton	c Miller b Johnston	53	c Miller b Johnston		29
H.E. Dollery	b Lindwall	0	b Lindwall		37
N.W.D. Yardley*	b Lindwall	44	b Toshack		11
A. Coxon	c and b Johnson	19	lbw b Toshack		0
T.G. Evans†	c Miller b Johnston	9	not out		24
J.C. Laker	c Tallon b Johnson	28	b Lindwall		0
A.V. Bedser	b Lindwall	9	c Hassett b Johnston		9
D.V.P. Wright	not out	13	c Lindwall b Toshack		4
Extras	(LB 3, NB 4)	7	(B 16, LB 4)		20
Total		**215**			**186**

ENGLAND	O	M	R	W	O	M	R	W
Bedser	43	14	100	4	34	6	112	1
Coxon	35	10	90	2	28	3	82	1
Edrich	8	0	43	1	2	0	11	0
Wright	21·3	8	54	1	19	4	69	1
Laker	7	3	17	0	31·2	6	111	2
Yardley	15	4	35	2	13	4	36	2
Compton					3	0	11	0
AUSTRALIA								
Lindwall	27·4	7	70	5	23	9	61	3
Johnston	22	4	43	2	33	15	62	2
Johnson	35	13	72	3	2	1	3	0
Toshack	18	11	23	0	20·1	6	40	5

FALL OF WICKETS

	A	E	A	E
Wkt	1st	1st	2nd	2nd
1st	3	17	122	42
2nd	87	32	296	52
3rd	166	46	296	65
4th	173	46	329	106
5th	216	133	416	133
6th	225	134	445	133
7th	246	145	460	141
8th	275	186	–	141
9th	320	197	–	158
10th	350	215	–	186

Umpires: D. Davies (2) and C.N. Woolley (1).

Close: 1st day – A(1) 258-7 (Tallon 25, Lindwall 3); 2nd – E(1) 207-9 (Bedser 6, Wright 8); 3rd – A(2) 343-4 (Miller 22, Brown 7); 4th – E(2) 106-3 (Compton 29, Dollery 21).

ENGLAND v AUSTRALIA 1948 (3rd Test)

Played at Old Trafford, Manchester, on 8, 9, 10, 12 (*no play*), 13 July.
Toss: England.   Result: MATCH DRAWN.
Debuts: England – J.F. Crapp, G.M. Emmett.

This was the eighth successive Test at Old Trafford involving Australia since 1905 to be drawn or abandoned. The selectors omitted Hutton. Compton, when 4, mishooked a ball from Lindwall into his forehead and retired hurt at 33. He resumed his innings, stitched, at 119, batted 327 minutes and hit 16 fours. Barnes, fielding at silly mid-on, stopped a full-blooded pull-drive from Pollard under his ribs and was X-rayed. Surprisingly, after collapsing in the nets, he batted in great pain for half an hour before retiring and spending the next ten days under hospital observation. On the final day Morris and Bradman remained at the same batting ends for 100 minutes.

ENGLAND

C. Washbrook	b Johnston	11	not out		85
G.M. Emmett	c Barnes b Lindwall	10	c Tallon b Lindwall		0
W.J. Edrich	c Tallon b Lindwall	32	run out		53
D.C.S. Compton	not out	145	c Miller b Toshack		0
J.F. Crapp	lbw b Lindwall	37	not out		19
H.E. Dollery	b Johnston	1			
N.W.D. Yardley*	c Johnson b Toshack	22			
T.G. Evans†	c Johnston b Lindwall	34			
A.V. Bedser	run out	37			
R. Pollard	b Toshack	3			
J.A. Young	c Bradman b Johnston	4			
Extras	(B 7, LB 17, NB 3)	27	(B 9, LB 7, W 1)		17
Total		**363**	(3 wickets declared)		**174**

AUSTRALIA

A.R. Morris	c Compton b Bedser	51	not out		54
I.W. Johnson	c Evans b Bedser	1	c Crapp b Young		6
D.G. Bradman*	lbw b Pollard	7	not out		30
A.L. Hassett	c Washbrook b Young	38			
K.R. Miller	lbw b Pollard	31			
S.G. Barnes	retired hurt	1			
S.J.E. Loxton	b Pollard	36			
D. Tallon†	c Evans b Edrich	18			
R.R. Lindwall	c Washbrook b Bedser	23			
W.A. Johnston	c Crapp b Bedser	3			
E.R.H. Toshack	not out	0			
Extras	(B 5, LB 4, NB 3)	12	(NB 2)		2
Total		**221**	(1 wicket)		**92**

AUSTRALIA	O	M	R	W	O	M	R	W	FALL OF WICKETS				
Lindwall	40	8	99	4	14	4	37	1		E	A	E	A
Johnston	45·5	13	67	3	14	3	34	0	*Wkt*	*1st*	*1st*	*2nd*	*2nd*
Loxton	7	0	18	0	8	2	29	0	1st	22	3	1	10
Toshack	41	20	75	2	12	5	26	1	2nd	28	13	125	–
Johnson	38	16	77	0	7	3	16	0	3rd	96	82	129	–
Miller					14	7	15	0	4th	97	135	–	–
									5th	119	139	–	–
									6th	141	172	–	–
ENGLAND									7th	216	208	–	–
Bedser	36	12	81	4	19	12	27	0	8th	337	219	–	–
Pollard	32	9	53	3	10	8	6	0	9th	352	221	–	–
Edrich	7	3	27	1	2	0	8	0	10th	363	–	–	–
Yardley	4	0	12	0									
Young	14	5	36	1	21	12	31	1					
Compton					9	3	18	0					

Umpires: F. Chester (34) and D. Davies (3).

Close: 1st day – E(1) 231-7 (Compton 64, Bedser 4); 2nd – A(1) 126-3 (Morris 48, Miller 23); 3rd – E(2) 174-3 (Washbrook 85, Crapp 19); 4th – no play.

ENGLAND v AUSTRALIA 1948 (4th Test)

Played at Headingley, Leeds, on 22, 23, 24. 26, 27 July.
Toss: England.   Result: AUSTRALIA won by seven wickets.
Debuts: Australia – R.A. Saggers.

Harvey became the first Australian left-hander to score a hundred in his first Test against England. Loxton set a record for this series by hitting five sixes in his 93. Bradman's hundred was the last of his 29 in Test matches, 14 as captain, 19 against England, and four in six innings at Leeds – all records which remain unequalled. Set 404 runs in 344 minutes on a pitch taking spin, Australia's was the highest fourth innings total to win a Test match until 1975-76 when India scored 406 for 4 to beat West Indies (*Test No. 775*). Morris (291 minutes, 33 fours) and Bradman (255 minutes, 29 fours) put on 301 runs in 217 minutes. This is the only match in this series to be won against a third innings declaration.

ENGLAND

L. Hutton	b Lindwall	81		c Bradman b Johnson	57
C. Washbrook	c Lindwall b Johnston	143		c Harvey b Johnston	65
W.J. Edrich	c Morris b Johnson	111		lbw b Lindwall	54
A.V. Bedser	c and b Johnson	79	(9)	c Hassett b Miller	17
D.C.S. Compton	c Saggers b Lindwall	23	(4)	c Miller b Johnston	66
J.F. Crapp	b Toshack	5	(5)	b Lindwall	18
N.W.D. Yardley*	b Miller	25	(6)	c Harvey b Johnston	7
K. Cranston	b Loxton	10	(7)	c Saggers b Johnston	0
T.G. Evans†	c Hassett b Loxton	3	(8)	not out	47
J.C. Laker	c Saggers b Loxton	4		not out	15
R. Pollard	not out	0			
Extras	(B 2, LB 8, W 1, NB 1)	12		(B 4, LB 12, NB 3)	19
Total		**496**		(8 wickets declared)	**365**

AUSTRALIA

A.R. Morris	c Cranston b Bedser	6		c Pollard b Yardley	182
A.L. Hassett	c Crapp b Pollard	13		c and b Compton	17
D.G. Bradman*	b Pollard	33		not out	173
K.R. Miller	c Edrich b Yardley	58		lbw b Cranston	12
R.N. Harvey	b Laker	112		not out	4
S.J.E. Loxton	b Yardley	93			
I.W. Johnson	c Cranston b Laker	10			
R.R. Lindwall	c Crapp b Bedser	77			
R.A. Saggers†	st Evans b Laker	5			
W.A. Johnston	c Edrich b Bedser	13			
E.R.H. Toshack	not out	12			
Extras	(B 9, LB 14, NB 3)	26		(B 6, LB 9, NB 1)	16
Total		**458**		(3 wickets)	**404**

AUSTRALIA	O	M	R	W	O	M	R	W
Lindwall	38	10	79	2	26	6	84	2
Miller	17·1	2	43	1	21	5	53	1
Johnston	38	12	86	1	29	5	95	4
Toshack	35	6	112	1				
Loxton	26	4	55	3	10	2	29	0
Johnson	33	9	89	2	21	2	85	1
Morris	5	0	20	0				
ENGLAND								
Bedser	31·2	4	92	3	21	2	56	0
Pollard	38	6	104	2	22	6	55	0
Cranston	14	1	51	0	7·1	0	28	1
Edrich	3	0	19	0				
Laker	30	8	113	3	32	11	93	0
Yardley	17	6	38	2	13	1	44	1
Compton	3	0	15	0	15	3	82	1
Hutton					4	1	30	0

FALL OF WICKETS

	E	A	E	A
Wkt	1st	1st	2nd	2nd
1st	168	13	129	57
2nd	268	65	129	358
3rd	423	68	232	396
4th	426	189	260	–
5th	447	294	277	–
6th	473	329	278	–
7th	486	344	293	–
8th	490	355	330	–
9th	496	403	–	–
10th	496	458	–	–

Umpires: H.G. Baldwin (4) and F. Chester (35).

Close: 1st day – E(1) 268-2 (Edrich 41, Bedser 0); 2nd – A(1) 63-1 (Hassett 13, Bradman 31); 3rd – A(1) 457-9 (Lindwall 76, Toshack 12); 4th – E(2) 362-8 (Evans 47, Laker 14).

ENGLAND v AUSTRALIA 1948 (5th Test)

Played at Kennington Oval, London, on 14, 16, 17, 18 August.
Toss: England.   Result: AUSTRALIA won by an innings and 149 runs.
Debuts: England – J.G. Dewes, A.J. Watkins.

England were dismissed for their lowest total this century and second-lowest in all Tests. Bradman, playing in his last Test match, was bowled second ball; four runs would have taken his aggregate to 7,000 and his average to 100. Hutton, last out in the first innings, was on the field for all but the last 57 minutes of the match. Bradman retired having set five major batting records for this series: most runs (5,028); most hundreds (19); most double-centuries (8); most triple-centuries (2); and the highest average (89.78).

ENGLAND

L. Hutton	c Tallon b Lindwall	30	c Tallon b Miller		64
J.G. Dewes	b Miller	1	b Lindwall		10
W.J. Edrich	c Hassett b Johnston	3	b Lindwall		28
D.C.S. Compton	c Morris b Lindwall	4	c Lindwall b Johnston		39
J.F. Crapp	c Tallon b Miller	0	b Miller		9
N.W.D. Yardley*	b Lindwall	7	c Miller b Johnston		9
A.J. Watkins	lbw b Johnston	0	c Hassett b Ring		2
T.G. Evans†	b Lindwall	1	b Lindwall		8
A.V. Bedser	b Lindwall	0	b Johnston		0
J.A. Young	b Lindwall	0	not out		3
W.E. Hollies	not out	0	c Morris b Johnston		0
Extras	(B 6)	6	(B 9, LB 4, NB 3)		16
Total		**52**			**188**

AUSTRALIA

S.G. Barnes	c Evans b Hollies	61
A.R. Morris	run out	196
D.G. Bradman*	b Hollies	0
A.L. Hassett	lbw b Young	37
K.R. Miller	st Evans b Hollies	5
R.N. Harvey	c Young b Hollies	17
S.J.E. Loxton	c Evans b Edrich	15
R.R. Lindwall	c Edrich b Young	9
D. Tallon†	c Crapp b Hollies	31
D.T. Ring	c Crapp b Bedser	9
W.A. Johnston	not out	0
Extras	(B 4, LB 2, NB 3)	9
Total		**389**

AUSTRALIA	O	M	R	W	O	M	R	W	FALL OF WICKETS			
Lindwall	16·1	5	20	6	25	3	50	3		E	A	E
Miller	8	5	5	2	15	6	22	2	*Wkt*	*1st*	*1st*	*2nd*
Johnston	16	4	20	2	27·3	12	40	4	1st	2	117	20
Loxton	2	1	1	0	10	2	16	0	2nd	10	117	64
Ring					28	13	44	1	3rd	17	226	125
									4th	23	243	153
ENGLAND									5th	35	265	164
Bedser	31·2	9	61	1					6th	42	304	167
Watkins	4	1	19	0					7th	45	332	178
Young	51	16	118	2					8th	45	359	181
Hollies	56	14	131	5					9th	47	389	188
Compton	2	0	6	0					10th	52	389	188
Edrich	9	1	38	1								
Yardley	5	1	7	0								

Umpires: H.G. Baldwin (5) and D. Davies (4).

Close: 1st day – A(1) 153-2 (Morris 77, Hassett 10); 2nd – E(2) 54-1 (Hutton 19, Edrich 23); 3rd – E(2) 178-7 (Yardley 2).

INDIA v WEST INDIES 1948–49 (1st Test)

Played at Feroz Shah Kotla, Delhi, on 10, 11, 12, 13, 14 November.
Toss: West Indies.   Result: MATCH DRAWN.
Debuts: India – K.C. Ibrahim, K.K. Tarapore; West Indies – D. St E. Atkinson, F.J. Cameron, A.F. Rae.

This was the first match between India and West Indies, the first Test to be played at Delhi, and the first in India since 1933-34. West Indies equalled England's performance at Nottingham in 1938 (*Test No. 263*) by scoring four hundreds in their innings of 631 (their highest total until 1953-54). Weekes completed his second successive hundred in Tests. The fourth-wicket partnership of 267 (Walcott/Gomez) and ninth-wicket stand of 106 (Christiani/Atkinson) were then West Indies records; the former is still a record for this series.

WEST INDIES

A.F. Rae	c Sen b Rangachari	8
J.B. Stollmeyer	lbw b Rangachari	13
G.A. Headley	b Rangachari	2
C.L. Walcott†	run out	152
G.E. Gomez	st Sen b Amarnath	101
J.D.C. Goddard*	b Mankad	44
E. de C. Weekes	c Hazare b Mankad	128
R.J. Christiani	c Hazare b Rangachari	107
F.J. Cameron	lbw b Sarwate	2
D. St E. Atkinson	c Sen b Rangachari	45
P.E. Jones	not out	1
Extras	(B 20, LB 8)	28
Total		**631**

INDIA

M.H. Mankad	lbw b Jones	5	b Goddard	17
K.C. Ibrahim	lbw b Gomez	85	run out	44
R.S. Modi	c Rae b Cameron	63	b Christiani	36
L. Amarnath*	c Christiani b Jones	62	b Cameron	36
V.S. Hazare	c Atkinson b Gomez	18	b Christiani	7
D.G. Phadkar	c Weekes b Stollmeyer	41	c and b Christiani	5
H.R. Adhikari	not out	114	not out	29
C.T. Sarwate	st Walcott b Stollmeyer	37	not out	35
P. Sen†	c Walcott b Cameron	22		
C.R. Rangachari	c and b Goddard	0		
K.K. Tarapore	c Walcott b Jones	2		
Extras	(B 1, LB 3, NB 1)	5	(B 8, LB 3)	11
Total		**454**	(6 wickets)	**220**

INDIA	O	M	R	W	O	M	R	W
Phadkar	18	1	61	0				
Amarnath	25	3	73	1				
Rangachari	29·4	4	107	5				
Mankad	59	10	176	2				
Tarapore	19	2	72	0				
Hazare	17	1	62	0				
Sarwate	16	0	52	1				
WEST INDIES								
Jones	28·4	5	90	3	10	2	32	0
Gomez	39	14	76	2	10	4	17	0
Atkinson	13	3	27	0	5	0	11	0
Headley	2	0	13	0	1	0	5	0
Cameron	27	3	74	2	27	10	49	1
Stollmeyer	15	0	80	2	10	2	23	0
Goddard	30	7	83	1	15	7	18	1
Christiani	4	0	6	0	23	1	52	3
Weekes					1	0	2	0

FALL OF WICKETS

Wkt	WI 1st	I 1st	I 2nd
1st	15	8	44
2nd	22	129	102
3rd	27	181	111
4th	294	223	121
5th	302	249	142
6th	403	309	162
7th	521	388	–
8th	524	419	–
9th	630	438	–
10th	631	454	–

Umpires: D.K. Naik (1) and J.R. Patel (1).

Close: 1st day – WI(1) 294-3 (Walcott 152, Gomez 99); 2nd – WI(1) 623-8 (Christiani 103, Atkinson 42); 3rd – I(1) 223-3 (Amarnath 50, Hazare 18); 4th – I(1) 454 all out.

INDIA v WEST INDIES 1948–49 (2nd Test)

Played at Brabourne Stadium, Bombay, on 9, 10, 11, 12, 13 December.
Toss: West Indies.   Result: MATCH DRAWN.
Debuts: India – P.R. Umrigar.

West Indies recorded their second consecutive total of over 600, Weekes hit his third successive hundred, and India again saved the match after following on. Stollmeyer took over the captaincy in the closing stages when Goddard became ill with a fever. This was the first Test match to be staged at Bombay's second Test ground.

WEST INDIES

A.F. Rae	c and b Phadkar	104	
J.B. Stollmeyer	b Mankad	66	
C.L. Walcott†	run out	68	
E. de C. Weekes	c Sen b Mankad	194	
G.E. Gomez	c Sen b Hazare	7	
R.J. Christiani	lbw b Mankad	74	
F.J. Cameron	not out	75	
D. St E. Atkinson	not out	23	
J.D.C. Goddard*	)		
P.E. Jones	) did not bat		
W. Ferguson	)		
Extras	(B 5, LB 5, NB 4)	18	
Total	(6 wickets declared)	**629**	

INDIA

M.H. Mankad	run out	21	c Ferguson b Gomez	16	
K.C. Ibrahim	run out	9	c Goddard b Jones	0	
R.S. Modi	c Atkinson b Ferguson	1	c Gomez b Ferguson	112	
V.S. Hazare	lbw b Atkinson	26	not out	134	
H.R. Adhikari	lbw b Ferguson	34			
D.G. Phadkar	c Jones b Gomez	74			
L. Amarnath*	c and b Ferguson	24	(5) not out	58	
P.R. Umrigar	c Goddard b Ferguson	30			
P. Sen†	lbw b Goddard	19			
S.G. Shinde	st Walcott b Gomez	13			
C.R. Rangachari	not out	8			
Extras	(B 1, LB 5, NB 8)	14	(B 11, LB 1, NB 1)	13	
Total		**273**	(3 wickets)	**333**	

INDIA	O	M	R	W	O	M	R	W	FALL OF WICKETS			
Phadkar	16	5	35	1						WI	I	I
Rangachari	34	1	148	0					Wkt	1st	1st	2nd
Hazare	42	12	74	1					1st	134	27	1
Umrigar	15	2	51	0					2nd	206	28	33
Mankad	75	16	202	3					3rd	295	32	189
Shinde	16	0	68	0					4th	311	82	–
Amarnath	8	1	33	0					5th	481	116	–
WEST INDIES									6th	574	150	–
Jones	21	7	34	0	12	2	52	1	7th	–	229	–
Gomez	24	9	32	2	28	12	37	1	8th	–	233	–
Atkinson	14	5	21	1	13	4	26	0	9th	–	261	–
Ferguson	57	8	126	4	39	14	105	1	10th	–	273	–
Goddard	12·2	7	19	1	3	1	6	0				
Cameron	10	3	9	0	27	9	52	0				
Stollmeyer	4	0	18	0	4	0	12	0				
Christiani					6	0	30	0				

Umpires: T.A. Ramachandran (1) and P.K. Sinha (1).

Close: 1st day – WI(1) 255-2 (Walcott 47, Weekes 26); 2nd – WI(1) 557-5 (Weekes 183, Cameron 38); 3rd – I(1) 150-6 (Phadkar 27); 4th – I(2) 95-2 (Modi 56, Hazare 21).

INDIA v WEST INDIES 1948–49 (3rd Test)

Played at Eden Gardens, Calcutta, on 31 December, 1, 2, 3, 4 January.
Toss: West Indies. Result: MATCH DRAWN.
Debuts: India – S.A. Banerjee, Ghulam Ahmed.

By scoring a hundred in each innings, Weekes extended to five his run of consecutive Test centuries. His record remains unequalled. Christiani deputised as wicket-keeper when Walcott retired ill for a time with fever; he recovered sufficiently to score 108 in 175 minutes. Banerjee bowled Atkinson with his fifth ball in Test cricket.

WEST INDIES

A.F. Rae	lbw b Banerjee	15	run out	34
D. St E. Atkinson	b Banerjee	0	(10) not out	5
C.L. Walcott†	c Banerjee b Ghulam Ahmed	54	(6) c Amarnath b Mankad	108
E. de C. Weekes	c and b Ghulam Ahmed	162	c and b Ghulam Ahmed	101
G.E. Gomez	b Mankad	26	(7) b Ghulam Ahmed	29
G.M. Carew	lbw b Mankad	11	(2) b Banerjee	9
J.D.C. Goddard*	not out	39	(5) c Banerjee b Amarnath	9
R.J. Christiani	c and b Banerjee	23	b Amarnath	22
F.J. Cameron	c Mushtaq Ali b Banerjee	23	c and b Mankad	2
W. Ferguson	b Ghulam Ahmed	2	(3) lbw b Mankad	6
P.E. Jones	b Ghulam Ahmed	6		
Extras	(B 1, LB 4)	5	(B 6, LB 1, W 1, NB 3)	11
Total		**366**	(9 wickets declared)	**336**

INDIA

Mushtaq Ali	c Rae b Goddard	54	lbw b Atkinson	106
K.C. Ibrahim	b Gomez	1	c Atkinson b Gomez	25
R.S. Modi	b Jones	80	c Christiani b Goddard	87
V.S. Hazare	b Gomez	59	not out	58
L. Amarnath*	c Christiani b Gomez	3	not out	34
M.H. Mankad	c Ferguson b Goddard	29		
H.R. Adhikari	not out	31		
C.T. Sarwate	b Goddard	0		
P. Sen†	lbw b Ferguson	1		
Ghulam Ahmed	st Christiani b Ferguson	0		
S.A. Banerjee	st Christiani b Ferguson	0		
Extras	(B 5, LB 6, NB 3)	14	(B 12, NB 3)	15
Total		**272**	(3 wickets)	**325**

INDIA	O	M	R	W	O	M	R	W	FALL OF WICKETS				
										WI	I	WI	I
Banerjee	30	3	120	4	21	0	61	1	Wkt	1st	1st	2nd	2nd
Amarnath	20	6	34	0	23	4	75	2	1st	1	12	13	84
Hazare	5	0	33	0	11	3	33	0	2nd	28	77	32	154
Ghulam Ahmed	35·2	5	94	4	25	0	87	2	3rd	109	206	104	262
Mankad	23	5	74	2	24·3	5	68	3	4th	188	206	130	–
Sarwate	2	0	6	0	1	0	1	0	5th	238	210	181	–
									6th	284	267	244	–
WEST INDIES									7th	309	267	304	–
Jones	17	3	48	1	21	5	49	0	8th	340	268	321	–
Gomez	32	10	65	3	29	10	47	1	9th	342	269	336	–
Ferguson	29	8	66	3	9	0	35	0	10th	366	272	–	–
Goddard	13	3	34	3	23	11	41	1					
Cameron	7	2	12	0	30	7	67	0					
Atkinson	9	0	27	0	14	3	42	1					
Christiani	2	0	6	0	3	0	12	0					
Carew					3	2	2	0					
Walcott					3	0	12	0					
Weekes					1	0	3	0					

Umpires: A.R. Joshi (1) and B.J. Mohoni (1).

Close: 1st day – WI(1) 339-7 (Goddard 22, Cameron 22); 2nd – I(1) 204-2 (Modi 78, Hazare 59); 3rd – WI(2) 120-3 (Weekes 62, Goddard 6); 4th – I(2) 66-0 (Mushtaq Ali 45, Ibrahim 21).

INDIA v WEST INDIES 1948–49 (4th Test)

Played at Chepauk, Madras, on 27, 28, 29, 31 January.
Toss: West Indies.   Result: WEST INDIES won by an innings and 193 runs.
Debuts: India – N.R. Chowdhury, M.R. Rege.

The partnership of 239 by Rae and Stollmeyer was the highest opening West Indies stand in all Test matches. Weekes was run out when just ten runs short of his sixth successive Test hundred. Phadkar achieved his best analysis in Test cricket. India, following on for the third time in four Tests, suffered their only defeat of the rubber. On the fourth day India lost 14 wickets for 164 runs.

WEST INDIES

A.F. Rae	c Rege b Phadkar	109
J.B. Stollmeyer	c Sen b Chowdhury	160
C.L. Walcott†	lbw b Phadkar	43
E. de C. Weekes	run out	90
R.J. Christiani	c Modi b Phadkar	18
J.D.C. Goddard*	c Sen b Phadkar	24
G.E. Gomez	c Mankad b Phadkar	50
F.J. Cameron	c Hazare b Phadkar	48
P.E. Jones	c Ghulam Ahmed b Mankad	10
J.Trim	c Sen b Phadkar	9
W. Ferguson	not out	2
Extras	(B 10, LB 7, NB 2)	19
Total		**582**

INDIA

Mushtaq Ali	lbw b Trim	32	c Walcott b Jones	14
M.R. Rege	b Jones	15	c Walcott b Jones	0
R.S. Modi	b Ferguson	56	b Gomez	6
V.S. Hazare	c Goddard b Ferguson	27	c Stollmeyer b Trim	52
L. Amarnath*	hit wkt b Trim	13	b Jones	6
H.R. Adhikari	c Stollmeyer b Jones	32	c Walcott b Jones	1
D.G. Phadkar	c Jones b Goddard	48	c Rae b Trim	10
M.H. Mankad	b Trim	1	b Trim	21
P. Sen†	c Stollmeyer b Gomez	2	not out	19
Ghulam Ahmed	b Trim	5	c sub (D. St E. Atkinson) b Gomez	11
N.R. Chowdhury	not out	3	c Rae b Gomez	0
Extras	(B 5, LB 1, NB 5)	11	(LB 2, NB 2)	4
Total		**245**		**144**

INDIA	O	M	R	W	O	M	R	W
Phadkar	45·3	10	159	7				
Hazare	12	1	44	0				
Amarnath	16	4	39	0				
Chowdhury	37	6	130	1				
Mankad	33	4	93	1				
Ghulam Ahmed	32	3	88	0				
Adhikari	1	0	10	0				
WEST INDIES								
Jones	16	5	28	2	10	3	30	4
Gomez	28	10	60	1	20·3	12	35	3
Trim	27	7	48	4	16	5	28	3
Ferguson	20	2	72	2	11	1	39	0
Goddard	8	1	26	1	6	3	8	0

FALL OF WICKETS

Wkt	WI 1st	I 1st	I 2nd
1st	239	41	0
2nd	319	52	7
3rd	319	116	29
4th	339	136	42
5th	420	158	44
6th	472	220	61
7th	532	225	106
8th	551	228	119
9th	565	233	132
10th	582	245	144

Umpires: A.R. Joshi (2) and B.J. Mohoni (2).

Close: 1st day – WI(1) 315-1 (Stollmeyer 157, Walcott 42); 2nd – WI(1) 582 all out; 3rd – I(1) 225-6 (Phadkar 39, Mankad 1).

INDIA v WEST INDIES 1948–49 (5th Test)

Played at Brabourne Stadium, Bombay, on 4, 5, 6, 7, 8 February.
Toss: West Indies.   Result: MATCH DRAWN.
Debuts: India – S.N. Banerjee.

Weekes established a Test record by scoring his seventh consecutive fifty; it remains unequalled. Amarnath kept wicket after Sen was injured attempting a catch early in the first innings. Needing 361 runs to win in 395 minutes, India fell just six runs short with only one wicket – apart from that of the injured Sen – remaining. Jones accomplished the best bowling figures of his Test career. Goddard was the fourth captain to win all five tosses in a rubber.

WEST INDIES

A.F. Rae	c Mushtaq Ali b Phadkar	7		c Mankad b Phadkar	97
J.B. Stollmeyer	c Mankad b Ghulam Ahmed	85		b Mankad	18
C.L. Walcott†	b Phadkar	11		b Phadkar	16
E. de C. Weekes	c Mankad b Ghulam Ahmed	56		b Hazare	48
G.E. Gomez	c Modi b Mankad	19	(7)	c and b Mankad	24
R.J. Christiani	b Banerjee	40		lbw b Mankad	10
J.D.C. Goddard*	c Amarnath b Mankad	41	(8)	not out	33
F.J. Cameron	c Amarnath b Phadkar	0	(9)	lbw b Banerjee	1
D. St E. Atkinson	c Amarnath b Mankad	6	(5)	c Amarnath b Banerjee	0
P.E. Jones	lbw b Phadkar	3		c Amarnath b Banerjee	1
J. Trim	not out	0		lbw b Banerjee	12
Extras	(B 10, LB 5, NB 3)	18		(B 4, NB 3)	7
Total		**286**			**267**

INDIA

Mushtaq Ali	c Atkinson b Gomez	28		c Walcott b Jones	6
K.C. Ibrahim	c Atkinson b Gomez	4		b Gomez	1
R.S. Modi	c Trim b Atkinson	33		c Walcott b Goddard	86
V.S. Hazare	c Christiani b Atkinson	40	(5)	b Jones	122
H.R. Adhikari	c Walcott b Trim	5	(9)	c Trim b Jones	8
D.G. Phadkar	b Trim	25	(7)	not out	37
L. Amarnath*	b Trim	19	(4)	b Atkinson	39
M.H. Mankad	run out	19	(6)	c Walcott b Jones	14
S.N. Banerjee	b Jones	5	(8)	b Jones	8
Ghulam Ahmed	not out	6		not out	9
P. Sen†	absent hurt	–			
Extras	(B 6, LB 1, NB 2)	9		(B 13, LB 1, NB 11)	25
Total		**193**		(8 wickets)	**355**

INDIA	O	M	R	W	O	M	R	W					
Banerjee	21	2	73	1	24·3	6	54	4					
Phadkar	29·2	8	74	4	31	7	82	2					
Amarnath	4	2	9	0									
Ghulam Ahmed	23	4	58	2	14	3	34	0					
Mankad	26	4	54	3	32	8	77	3					
Hazare	1	1	0	0	6	1	13	1					
WEST INDIES													
Jones	14·4	4	31	1	41	8	85	5					
Gomez	21	8	30	2	26	5	55	1					
Trim	30	3	69	3	7	0	43	0					
Atkinson	23	2	54	2	3	0	16	1					
Cameron					3	0	15	0					
Goddard					27	1	116	1					

FALL OF WICKETS

Wkt	WI 1st	I 1st	WI 2nd	I 2nd
1st	11	10	47	2
2nd	27	37	68	9
3rd	137	109	148	81
4th	176	112	152	220
5th	190	122	166	275
6th	248	146	192	285
7th	253	180	228	303
8th	281	181	230	321
9th	284	193	240	–
10th	286	–	267	–

Umpires: A.R. Joshi (3) and B.J. Mohoni (3).

Close: 1st day – WI(1) 235-5 (Christiani 30, Goddard 14); 2nd – I(1) 132-5 (Phadkar 11, Amarnath 5); 3rd – WI(2) 152-3 (Rae 68, Atkinson 0); 4th – I(2) 90-3 (Modi 39, Hazare 1).

SOUTH AFRICA v ENGLAND 1948–49 (1st Test)

Played at Kingsmead, Durban, on 16, 17, 18, 20, December.
Toss: South Africa.   Result: ENGLAND won by two wickets.
Debuts: South Africa – D.W. Begbie, C.N. McCarthy, O.E. Wynne; England – R.O. Jenkins, F.G. Mann, R.T. Simpson.

Jenkins took Eric Rowan's wicket with his third ball in Test cricket. England needed eight runs to win from the last (8-ball) over, bowled by Tuckett, and won with a leg bye off the very last ball when Gladwin missed a vast heave and was hit on the thigh. McCarthy's second innings analysis remained his best for South Africa.

SOUTH AFRICA

E.A.B. Rowan	c Evans b Jenkins	7	c Compton b Jenkins	16
O.E. Wynne	c Compton b Bedser	5	c Watkins b Wright	4
B. Mitchell	c Evans b Bedser	27	b Wright	19
A.D. Nourse*	c Watkins b Wright	37	c and b Bedser	32
W.W. Wade†	run out	8	b Jenkins	63
D.W. Begbie	c Compton b Bedser	37	c Mann b Bedser	48
O.C. Dawson	b Gladwin	24	c Compton b Wright	3
A.M.B. Rowan	not out	5	b Wright	15
L. Tuckett	lbw b Gladwin	1	not out	3
N.B.F. Mann	c Evans b Gladwin	4	c Mann b Compton	10
C.N. McCarthy	b Bedser	0	b Jenkins	0
Extras	(B 3, LB 2, NB 1)	6	(B 1, LB 5)	6
Total		**161**		**219**

ENGLAND

L. Hutton	c McCarthy b A.M.B. Rowan	83	c Dawson b Tuckett	5
C. Washbrook	c Wade b Mann	35	lbw b Mann	25
R.T. Simpson	c Begbie b Mann	5	(6) c E.A.B. Rowan b McCarthy	0
D.C.S. Compton	c Wade b Mann	72	b McCarthy	28
A.J. Watkins	c Nourse b A.M.B. Rowan	9	b McCarthy	4
F.G. Mann*	c E.A.B. Rowan b A.M.B. Rowan	19	(3) c Mitchell b McCarthy	13
T.G. Evans†	c Wynne b A.M.B. Rowan	0	b McCarthy	4
R.O. Jenkins	c Mitchell b Mann	5	c Wade b McCarthy	22
A.V. Bedser	c Tuckett b Mann	11	not out	1
C. Gladwin	not out	0	not out	7
D.V.P. Wright	c Tuckett b Mann	0		
Extras	(B 2, LB 12)	14	(B 9, LB 10)	19
Total		**253**	(8 wickets)	**128**

ENGLAND	O	M	R	W	O	M	R	W		FALL OF WICKETS			
Bedser	13·5	2	39	4	18	5	51	2		SA	E	SA	E
Gladwin	12	3	21	3	7	3	15	0	*Wkt*	*1st*	*1st*	*2nd*	*2nd*
Jenkins	14	3	50	1	22·3	6	64	3	1st	9	84	22	25
Wright	9	3	29	1	26	3	72	4	2nd	18	104	22	49
Compton	2	0	5	0	16	11	11	1	3rd	69	146	67	52
Watkins	3	0	11	0					4th	80	172	89	64
									5th	99	212	174	64
SOUTH AFRICA									6th	148	212	179	70
McCarthy	9	2	20	0	12	2	43	6	7th	150	221	208	115
Dawson	3	0	16	0					8th	152	247	208	116
Tuckett	6	0	36	0	10	0	38	1	9th	160	253	219	–
A.M.B. Rowan	44	8	108	4	4	0	15	0	10th	161	253	219	–
Mann	37·4	14	59	6	2	0	13	1					

Umpires: R.G.A. Ashman (9) and G.L. Sickler (6).

Close: 1st day – SA(1) 161 all out; 2nd – E(1) 144-2 (Hutton 81, Compton 17); 3rd – SA (2) 90-4 (Wade 17, Begbie 0).

Test No. 310/71

SOUTH AFRICA v ENGLAND 1948–49 (2nd Test)

Played at Ellis Park, Johannesburg, on 27, 28, 29, 30 December.
Toss: England.   Result: MATCH DRAWN.
Debuts: Nil.

On the first day of Test cricket at Ellis Park (the Old Wanderers having been lost to the South African Railways), Hutton and Washbrook set a world Test record by scoring 359 in 310 minutes for the first wicket. It remains England's highest opening stand against all countries. The South African selectors dropped Eric Rowan from the team for the 3rd Test, which they announced at the end of the third day's play. Rowan responded by batting throughout the last day to save the match.

ENGLAND

L. Hutton	c Wade b McCarthy	158
C. Washbrook	c Begbie b McCarthy	195
J.F. Crapp	c and b Mitchell	56
D.C.S. Compton	c Mitchell b Mann	114
A.J. Watkins	c Wade b Mann	7
F.G. Mann*	c McCarthy b Mann	7
T.G. Evans†	run out	18
R.O. Jenkins	c Wade b A.M.B. Rowan	4
A.V. Bedser	b McCarthy	12
C. Gladwin	lbw b Dawson	23
D.V.P. Wright	not out	1
Extras	(B 3, LB 10)	13
Total		**608**

SOUTH AFRICA

E.A.B. Rowan	lbw b Bedser	8	not out	156
O.E. Wynne	lbw b Wright	4	lbw b Bedser	4
B. Mitchell	b Gladwin	86	c Hutton b Wright	40
A.D. Nourse*	lbw b Wright	32	not out	56
W.W. Wade†	c Evans b Compton	85		
D.W. Begbie	c Watkins b Jenkins	5		
O.C. Dawson	c Watkins b Jenkins	12		
A.M.B. Rowan	b Wright	8		
L. Tuckett	st Evans b Watkins	38		
N.B.F. Mann	st Evans b Jenkins	23		
C.N. McCarthy	not out	1		
Extras	(B 4, LB 7, NB 2)	13	(B 9, LB 4, NB 1)	14
Total		**315**	(2 wickets)	**270**

SOUTH AFRICA	O	M	R	W	O	M	R	W
McCarthy	26	1	102	3				
Dawson	16·5	3	59	1				
A.M.B. Rowan	41	4	155	1				
Tuckett	12	0	55	0				
Mann	30	2	107	3				
Begbie	6	0	38	0				
Mitchell	18	1	79	1				
ENGLAND								
Bedser	22	6	42	1	17	4	51	1
Gladwin	20	6	29	1	16	5	37	0
Jenkins	21·4	3	88	3	19	3	54	0
Wright	26	2	104	3	14	3	35	1
Compton	10	0	34	1	13	3	31	0
Watkins	5	2	5	1	12	2	48	0

FALL OF WICKETS

Wkt	E 1st	SA 1st	SA 2nd
1st	359	12	15
2nd	366	17	108
3rd	516	96	–
4th	540	191	–
5th	549	204	–
6th	550	220	–
7th	570	235	–
8th	576	273	–
9th	602	313	–
10th	608	315	–

Umpires: J.V. Hart-Davis (1) and G.L. Sickler (7).

Close: 1st day – E(1) 387-2 (Crapp 14, Compton 10); 2nd – SA(1) 95-2 (Mitchell 47, Nourse 32); 3rd – SA(2) 28-1 (E.A.B. Rowan 17, Mitchell 7).

SOUTH AFRICA v ENGLAND 1948–49 (3rd Test)

Played at Newlands, Cape Town, on 1, 3, 4, 5 January.
Toss: England.   Result: MATCH DRAWN.
Debuts: South Africa – M.A. Hanley.

Mitchell, who scored his seventh (and last) hundred against England to equal H.W. Taylor's record, and Nourse added 190 before eight wickets fell for 58 runs. Compton, bowling left-arm orthodox leg-breaks to the exclusion of his 'chinamen' and googlies, took five wickets for the only time in his 78 Test matches. South Africa were set a target of 229 runs in 125 minutes.

ENGLAND

L. Hutton	run out	41	b Rowan	87
C. Washbrook	b Rowan	74	c Mitchell b McCarthy	9
J.F. Crapp	c Wynne b Mitchell	35	c Wade b McCarthy	54
D.C.S. Compton	b Rowan	1	not out	51
A.J. Watkins	c Melville b Dawson	27	not out	64
F.G. Mann*	c Mitchell b Hanley	44		
T.G. Evans†	b Rowan	27		
R.O. Jenkins	c Wynne b Rowan	1		
A.V. Bedser	b McCarthy	16		
C. Gladwin	not out	17		
D.V.P. Wright	c Dawson b Rowan	11		
Extras	(B 7, LB 7)	14	(B 8, LB 3)	11
Total		**308**	(3 wickets declared)	**276**

SOUTH AFRICA

O.E. Wynne	c Crapp b Watkins	50	c Bedser b Jenkins	46
A. Melville	b Jenkins	15	st Evans b Jenkins	24
B. Mitchell	b Compton	120	(5) not out	20
A.D. Nourse*	c and b Compton	112	st Evans b Jenkins	34
W.W. Wade†	c Watkins b Compton	0	(3) c Evans b Jenkins	11
D.W. Begbie	run out	18		
O.C. Dawson	c Mann b Compton	25	(6) not out	5
A.M.B. Rowan	c Hutton b Gladwin	2		
N.B.F. Mann	not out	10		
M.A. Hanley	run out	0		
C.N. McCarthy	st Evans b Compton	1		
Extras	(B 1, NB 2)	3	(LB 1, NB 1)	2
Total		**356**	(4 wickets)	**142**

SOUTH AFRICA	O	M	R	W	O	M	R	W
McCarthy	26	2	95	1	20	2	75	2
Dawson	7	2	35	1	13	3	33	0
Rowan	31·2	3	80	5	30	5	65	1
Mann	3	0	18	0	15	5	27	0
Hanley	18	4	57	1	11	3	31	0
Mitchell	6	0	9	1	7	1	34	0
ENGLAND								
Bedser	34	5	92	0	7	0	40	0
Gladwin	30	7	51	1	10	2	27	0
Wright	9	0	58	0	2	0	18	0
Jenkins	11	1	46	1	9	0	48	4
Watkins	10	0	36	1				
Compton	25·2	3	70	5	3	1	7	0

FALL OF WICKETS

Wkt	E 1st	SA 1st	E 2nd	SA 2nd
1st	88	30	11	58
2nd	149	108	145	83
3rd	151	298	165	83
4th	152	298	–	132
5th	203	303	–	–
6th	249	342	–	–
7th	251	344	–	–
8th	263	349	–	–
9th	281	349	–	–
9th	281	349	–	–
10th	308	356	–	–

Umpires: R.G.A. Ashman (10) and J.V. Hart-Davis (2).

Close: 1st day – E(1) 294-9 (Gladwin 11, Wright 3); 2nd – SA(1) 223-2 (Mitchell 93, Nourse 64); 3rd – E(2) 85-1 (Hutton 45, Crapp 31).

SOUTH AFRICA v ENGLAND 1948–49 (4th Test)

Played at Ellis Park, Johannesburg. on 12, 14, 15, 16 February.
Toss: England.   Result: MATCH DRAWN.
Debuts: South Africa – L.A. Markham.

South Africa were set 376 runs to win in 270 minutes.

ENGLAND

L. Hutton	b Tuckett	2	b A.M.B. Rowan	123
C. Washbrook	c E.A.B. Rowan b McCarthy	97	lbw b A.M.B. Rowan	31
J.F. Crapp	b A.M.B. Rowan	51	(5) hit wkt b McCarthy	5
D.C.S. Compton	c A.M.B. Rowan b Tuckett	24	(3) b Markham	25
A.J. Watkins	hit wkt b McCarthy	111	(6) b A.M.B. Rowan	10
F.G. Mann*	c Wade b McCarthy	17	(4) lbw b A.M.B. Rowan	16
R.O. Jenkins	lbw b Mitchell	25		
A.V. Bedser	lbw b Tuckett	1	(7) b McCarthy	19
C. Gladwin	b McCarthy	19	(8) not out	7
S.C. Griffith†	c Mitchell b McCarthy	8		
J.A. Young	not out	10		
Extras	(B 2, LB 12)	14	(B 5, LB 11, NB 1)	17
Total		**379**	(7 wickets declared)	**253**

SOUTH AFRICA

B. Mitchell	c Griffith b Bedser	2	c Compton b Gladwin	6
E.A.B. Rowan	run out	6	not out	86
K.G. Viljoen	run out	0	b Watkins	63
A.D. Nourse*	not out	129	b Watkins	1
W.W. Wade†	lbw b Young	54	lbw b Bedser	27
T.A. Harris	b Bedser	6	not out	1
A.M.B. Rowan	b Gladwin	12		
L. Tuckett	b Young	0		
L.A. Markham	c Griffith b Jenkins	20		
N.B.F. Mann	c Griffith b Gladwin	14		
C.N. McCarthy	not out	0		
Extras	(B 4, LB 10)	14	(B 7, LB 1, NB 2)	10
Total	(9 wickets declared)	**257**	(4 wickets)	**194**

SOUTH AFRICA	O	M	R	W	O	M	R	W
McCarthy	35·7	3	114	5	12·2	2	50	2
Tuckett	29	2	109	3	10	0	43	0
A.M.B. Rowan	23	1	70	1	34	10	69	4
Markham	5	1	38	0	8	0	34	1
Mann	10	3	26	0	7	0	20	0
Mitchell	3	0	8	1	7	1	20	0
ENGLAND								
Bedser	24	3	81	2	17	0	54	1
Gladwin	24	7	43	2	16	6	39	1
Jenkins	8	1	39	1	9	2	26	0
Young	23	6	52	2	11	6	14	0
Watkins	2	0	9	0	3	0	16	2
Compton	4	0	19	0	9	2	35	0

FALL OF WICKETS

Wkt	E 1st	SA 1st	E 2nd	SA 2nd
1st	3	4	77	23
2nd	123	4	151	136
3rd	172	19	186	140
4th	180	125	204	182
5th	213	137	222	–
6th	282	156	237	–
7th	287	161	253	–
8th	316	192	–	–
9th	346	236	–	–
10th	379	–	–	–

Umpires: R.G.A. Ashman (11) and J.V. Hart-Davis (3).

Close: 1st day – E(1) 290-7 (Watkins 64, Gladwin 1); 2nd – SA(1) 161-7 (Nourse 75); 3rd – E(2) 196-3 (Hutton 111, Crapp 1).

SOUTH AFRICA v ENGLAND 1948–49 (5th Test)

Played at St. George's Park, Port Elizabeth, on 5, 7, 8, 9 March.
Toss: South Africa.   Result: ENGLAND won by three wickets.
Debuts: South Africa – J.E. Cheetham.

Set 172 runs to win in 95 minutes, England won with just one minute remaining for play. Hutton and Washbrook, who hit their first balls for four and six respectively, scored 58 in 27 minutes. The 100 arrived in 53 minutes, but wickets fell rapidly before Crapp won the match by making ten runs off three successive balls in Mann's final over. Earlier Wade, who scored South Africa's first hundred at Port Elizabeth, and F.G. Mann had completed their only Test centuries. Mitchell, having played in 42 consecutive matches, ended his career with what is still the record aggregate for South Africa: 3,471 runs, average 48·88.

SOUTH AFRICA

B. Mitchell	c Griffith b Bedser	99	c Griffith b Bedser		56
E.A.B. Rowan	c Watkins b Gladwin	3	c Jenkins b Young		37
K.G. Viljoen	b Bedser	2			
A.D. Nourse*	b Bedser	73	not out		30
W.W. Wade†	c Compton b Jenkins	125	not out		34
J.E. Cheetham	c and b Bedser	2	(3) c Compton b Young		18
O.C. Dawson	c Gladwin b Jenkins	20			
A.M.B. Rowan	not out	29			
L. Tuckett	b Jenkins	2			
N.B.F. Mann	c Compton b Gladwin	11			
C.N. McCarthy	b Gladwin	3			
Extras	(B 2, LB 5, NB 3)	10	(B 6, LB 5, NB 1)		12
Total		**379**	(3 wickets declared)		**187**

ENGLAND

L. Hutton	c Dawson b A.M.B. Rowan	46	st Wade b A.M.B. Rowan		32
C. Washbrook	c Dawson b A.M.B. Rowan	36	c A.M.B. Rowan b Mann		40
J.F. Crapp	b McCarthy	4	(6) not out		26
D.C.S. Compton	c Wade b Mann	49	(3) c Cheetham b A.M.B. Rowan		42
A.J. Watkins	c A.M.B. Rowan b Mann	14	(9) not out		5
F.G. Mann*	not out	136	(4) c Dawson b Mann		2
R.O. Jenkins	lbw b Mann	29			
A.V. Bedser	c Mitchell b A.M.B. Rowan	33	(5) c Nourse b A.M.B. Rowan		1
C. Gladwin	c Dawson b A.M.B. Rowan	10	(7) c Tuckett b Mann		15
S.C. Griffith†	c E.A.B. Rowan b A.M.B. Rowan	5	(8) b Mann		0
J.A. Young	c Wade b McCarthy	0			
Extras	(B 11, LB 18, NB 4)	33	(B 3, LB 8)		11
Total		**395**	(7 wickets)		**174**

ENGLAND	O	M	R	W	O	M	R	W
Bedser	38	9	61	4	16	3	43	1
Gladwin	30·5	6	70	3	6	2	14	0
Jenkins	15	2	53	3	4	0	27	0
Watkins	5	0	24	0				
Young	48	9	122	0	23	9	34	2
Compton	7	0	39	0	9	0	57	0
SOUTH AFRICA								
McCarthy	17·4	1	42	2	2	0	20	0
Dawson	3	0	10	0				
Tuckett	5	0	22	0	2	0	13	0
A.M.B. Rowan	60	9	167	5	10	0	65	3
Mann	51	18	95	3	9·7	0	65	4
Mitchell	5	0	26	0				

FALL OF WICKETS

Wkt	SA 1st	E 1st	SA 2nd	E 2nd
1st	10	78	101	58
2nd	13	82	101	104
3rd	114	96	127	124
4th	264	149	–	125
5th	282	168	–	125
6th	330	268	–	152
7th	336	341	–	153
8th	338	362	–	–
9th	375	390	–	–
10th	379	395	–	–

Umpires: R.G.A. Ashman (12) and D. Collins (1).

Close: 1st day – SA(1) 219-3 (Mitchell 73, Wade 63); 2nd – E(1) 80-1 (Hutton 37, Crapp 2); 3rd – E(1) 390-9 (Mann 131).

ENGLAND v NEW ZEALAND 1949 (1st Test)

Played at Headingley, Leeds, on 11, 13, 14 June.
Toss: England.   Result: MATCH DRAWN.
Debuts: England – T.E. Bailey, A. Wharton; New Zealand – H.B. Cave, F.L.H. Mooney, G.O. Rabone.

After an unsuccessful rest day search for the seaside in Harrogate, Bailey had Scott caught at fourth slip with his eighth ball in Test cricket and finished with six wickets on debut. Cowie pulled a leg muscle, finished his share of a record last-wicket partnership with a runner, but was unable to bowl in the second innings. Washbrook sustained a similar injury and completed his three-hour century with a runner. By declaring, Mann missed scoring the fastest Test fifty (28 minutes by J.T. Brown in *Test No. 46*); he had made his 49 in only 24 minutes with a six and nine fours. His decision set the touring side a target of 299 in 150 minutes.

ENGLAND

L. Hutton	c Sutcliffe b Cowie	101	c Mooney b Cave	0
C. Washbrook	c Sutcliffe b Cowie	10	not out	103
W.J. Edrich	c Donnelly b Cowie	36	b Cave	70
D.C.S. Compton	st Mooney b Burtt	114	c Mooney b Cave	26
A. Wharton	lbw b Cowie	7	b Sutcliffe	13
F.G. Mann*	c Scott b Burtt	38	not out	49
T.E. Bailey	c Scott b Cowie	12		
T.G. Evans†	c Mooney b Burtt	27		
A.V. Bedser	c Donnelly b Burtt	20		
J.A. Young	st Mooney b Burtt	0		
W.E. Hollies	not out	0		
Extras	(B 3, LB 4)	7	(B4, LB 2)	6
Total		**372**	(4 wickets declared)	**267**

NEW ZEALAND

B. Sutcliffe	c Evans b Young	32	c Bedser b Young	82
V.J. Scott	c Washbrook b Bailey	1	c Bedser b Young	43
W.A. Hadlee*	c Edrich b Bailey	34	(4) not out	13
W.M. Wallace	c Evans b Bailey	3		
M.P. Donnelly	c Young b Bailey	64		
F.B. Smith	c Compton b Edrich	96	(3) not out	54
G.O. Rabone	c Evans b Edrich	13		
F.L.H. Mooney†	c Edrich b Bailey	46		
T.B. Burtt	c Bedser b Compton	7		
H.B. Cave	c Edrich b Bailey	2		
J. Cowie	not out	26		
Extras	(B 2, LB 8, NB 7)	17	(B 1, LB 2)	3
Total		**341**	(2 wickets)	**195**

NEW ZEALAND	O	M	R	W	O	M	R	W	FALL OF WICKETS				
										E	NZ	E	NZ
Cowie	43	6	127	5					*Wkt*	*1st*	*1st*	*2nd*	*2nd*
Cave	27	5	85	0	26	3	103	3	1st	17	4	0	112
Rabone	18	7	56	0	17	4	56	0	2nd	92	64	118	147
Burtt	39·3	16	97	5	15	2	56	0	3rd	194	69	162	–
Donnelly					5	0	20	0	4th	214	80	201	–
Sutcliffe					4	1	17	1	5th	273	200	–	–
Scott					1	0	9	0	6th	322	251	–	–
									7th	330	254	–	–
ENGLAND									8th	353	273	–	–
Bailey	32·3	6	118	6	9	0	51	0	9th	367	284	–	–
Bedser	22	8	56	0	9	1	26	0	10th	372	341	–	–
Edrich	9	2	18	2	2	0	13	0					
Young	22	6	52	1	14	3	41	2					
Hollies	25	6	57	0	11	3	33	0					
Compton	8	2	23	1	1	0	5	0					
Hutton					3	0	23	0					

Umpires: W.H. Ashdown (1) and D. Davies (5).

Close: 1st day – E(1) 307-5 (Compton 103, Bailey 6); 2nd – NZ(1) 312-9 (Mooney 41, Cowie 6).

ENGLAND v NEW ZEALAND 1949 (2nd Test)

Played at Lord's, London, on 25, 27, 28 June.
Toss: England.   Result: MATCH DRAWN.
Debuts: Nil.

Mann created Test match history by declaring on the first day. His declaration was afterwards found to be incorrect as the current experimental law allowing a declaration on the first day of a three-day match did not apply to this Test rubber. No wicket fell in the last 15 minutes and so fortunately England gained no embarrassing advantage. Donnelly remains the only New Zealander to score a double-century against England. He batted 355 minutes, hit 26 fours, and completed a notable Lord's treble by scoring hundreds in a Test, the University match and in a Gentlemen v Players match.

ENGLAND

L. Hutton	b Burtt	23	c Cave b Rabone	66
J.D.B. Robertson	c Mooney b Cowie	26	c Cave b Rabone	121
W.J. Edrich	c Donnelly b Cowie	9	c Hadlee b Burtt	31
D.C.S. Compton	c Sutcliffe b Burtt	116	b Burtt	6
A.J. Watkins	c Wallace b Burtt	6	not out	49
F.G. Mann*	b Cave	18	c Donnelly b Rabone	17
T.E. Bailey	c Sutcliffe b Rabone	93	not out	6
T.G. Evans†	b Burtt	5		
C. Gladwin	run out	5		
J.A. Young	not out	1		
W.E. Hollies	did not bat			
Extras	(B 9, LB 2)	11	(B 9, LB 1)	10
Total	(9 wickets declared)	**313**	(5 wickets)	**306**

NEW ZEALAND

B. Sutcliffe	c Compton b Gladwin	57
V.J. Scott	c Edrich b Compton	42
W.A. Hadlee*	c Robertson b Hollies	43
W.M. Wallace	c Evans b Hollies	2
M.P. Donnelly	c Hutton b Young	206
F.B. Smith	b Hollies	23
G.O. Rabone	b Hollies	25
F.L.H. Mooney†	c Watkins b Young	33
T.B. Burtt	c Edrich b Hollies	23
H.B. Cave	c and b Young	6
J. Cowie	not out	1
Extras	(B 16, LB 3, W 3, NB 1)	23
Total		**484**

NEW ZEALAND	O	M	R	W	O	M	R	W		FALL OF WICKETS			
Cowie	26·1	5	64	2	14	3	39	0			E	NZ	E
Cave	27	2	79	1	7	1	23	0	*Wkt*	*1st*	*1st*	*2nd*
Rabone	14	5	56	1	28	6	116	3	1st	48	89	143
Burtt	35	7	102	4	37	12	58	2	2nd	59	124	216
Sutcliffe	1	0	1	0	16	1	55	0	3rd	72	137	226
Wallace					1	0	5	0	4th	83	160	226
									5th	112	197	252
ENGLAND									6th	301	273	–
Bailey	33	3	136	0					7th	307	351	–
Gladwin	28	5	67	1					8th	307	436	–
Edrich	4	0	16	0					9th	313	464	–
Hollies	58	18	133	5					10th	–	484	–
Compton	7	0	33	1								
Young	26·4	4	65	3								
Watkins	3	1	11	0								

Umpires: W.H. Ashdown (2) and F. Chester (36).

Close: 1st day – NZ(1) 20-0 (Sutcliffe 12, Scott 8); 2nd – NZ(1) 372-7 (Donnelly 126, Burtt 5).

ENGLAND v NEW ZEALAND 1949 (3rd Test)

Played at Old Trafford, Manchester, on 23, 25, 26 July.
Toss: England.   Result: MATCH DRAWN.
Debuts: England – D.B. Close, H.L. Jackson; New Zealand – J.R. Reid.

F.R. Brown's first gesture on being appointed captain and recalled to Test cricket after an absence of 12 years was to send New Zealand in to bat. Close made his debut at the age of 18 years 149 days and remains the youngest to play for England. Simpson scored a century in his first home Test, his last 53 runs coming in just 28 minutes.

NEW ZEALAND

Batsman	Dismissal	Score	Dismissal (2nd)	Score (2nd)
B. Sutcliffe	b Bailey	9	lbw b Compton	101
V.J. Scott	b Bailey	13	b Jackson	13
W.A. Hadlee*	b Bailey	34	c Brown b Hollies	22
W.M. Wallace	c Washbrook b Close	12	lbw b Hollies	14
M.P. Donnelly	lbw b Bailey	75	st Evans b Brown	80
J.R. Reid	lbw b Jackson	50	b Bailey	25
G.O. Rabone	c Brown b Bailey	33	not out	39
F.L.H. Mooney†	b Jackson	5	st Evans b Brown	15
T.B. Burtt	st Evans b Compton	32	not out	27
H.B. Cave	b Bailey	12		
J. Cowie	not out	3		
Extras	(B 3, LB 9, NB 3)	15	(B 2, LB 4, NB 6)	12
Total		293	(7 wickets)	348

ENGLAND

L. Hutton	st Mooney b Burtt	73
C. Washbrook	c Mooney b Cowie	44
W.J. Edrich	c Rabone b Burtt	78
D.C.S. Compton	b Cowie	25
R.T. Simpson	c Donnelly b Burtt	103
T.E. Bailey	not out	72
F.R. Brown*	c Wallace b Burtt	22
T.G. Evans†	c Mooney b Burtt	12
D.B. Close	c Rabone b Burtt	0
W.E. Hollies	c Mooney b Cowie	0
H.L. Jackson	not out	7
Extras	(B 2, LB 2)	4
Total	(9 wickets declared)	440

ENGLAND	O	M	R	W	O	M	R	W
Bailey	30·2	5	84	6	16	0	71	1
Jackson	27	11	47	2	12	3	25	1
Close	25	12	39	1	17	2	46	0
Hollies	18	8	29	0	26	6	52	2
Brown	18	4	43	0	21	3	71	2
Compton	6	0	28	1	8	0	28	1
Edrich	4	1	8	0	5	0	26	0
Simpson					2	1	9	0
Washbrook					2	0	8	0
Hutton					1	1	0	0
NEW ZEALAND								
Cowie	36	8	98	3				
Cave	30	4	97	0				
Burtt	45	11	162	6				
Rabone	10	0	43	0				
Sutcliffe	5	0	22	0				
Reid	2	0	14	0				

FALL OF WICKETS

	NZ	E	NZ
Wkt	1st	1st	2nd
1st	22	103	24
2nd	23	127	58
3rd	62	172	109
4th	82	258	187
5th	198	363	235
6th	205	404	295
7th	217	419	313
8th	269	419	–
9th	288	419	–
10th	293	–	–

Umpires: F. Chester (37) and F.S. Lee (1).

Close: 1st day – NZ(1) 276-8 (Rabone 27, Cave 6); 2nd – E(1) 363-5 (Bailey 36).

ENGLAND v NEW ZEALAND 1949 (4th Test)

Played at Kennington Oval, London, 13, 15, 16 August.
Toss: New Zealand. Result: MATCH DRAWN.
Debuts: New Zealand – G.F. Cresswell.

This rubber, in which all four matches were drawn, proved that three days was too short a period to decide Test matches on good pitches, even in an exceptionally dry summer like 1949. The stand of 147 between Hutton and Simpson was England's highest first-wicket partnership against New Zealand. Hutton's third fifty took 35 minutes.

NEW ZEALAND

B. Sutcliffe	c Bedser b Hollies	88	c Brown b Bedser	54
V.J. Scott	c Edrich b Bedser	60	c Evans b Bedser	6
J.R. Reid†	lbw b Wright	5	(5) c Wright b Laker	93
W.M. Wallace	c Edrich b Bedser	55	st Evans b Hollies	58
M.P. Donnelly	c Edrich b Bailey	27	(6) c Brown b Bedser	10
W.A. Hadlee*	c Evans b Bedser	25	(3) c Edrich b Hollies	22
G.O. Rabone	c Evans b Bailey	18	lbw b Laker	20
T.B. Burtt	c Evans b Bailey	36	c Compton b Laker	6
H.B. Cave	b Compton	10	not out	14
J. Cowie	c Hutton b Bedser	1	c Wright b Laker	4
G.F. Cresswell	not out	12	not out	0
Extras	(LB 1, W 1, NB 6)	8	(B 10, LB 5, NB 6)	21
Total		**345**	(9 wickets declared)	**308**

ENGLAND

L. Hutton	c Rabone b Cresswell	206
R.T. Simpson	c Donnelly b Cresswell	68
W.J. Edrich	c Cave b Cresswell	100
D.C.S. Compton	c Scott b Cresswell	13
T.E. Bailey	c Reid b Cowie	36
F.R. Brown*	c Hadlee b Cresswell	21
T.G. Evans†	c Donnelly b Cowie	17
J.C. Laker	c Scott b Cowie	0
A.V. Bedser	c Reid b Cowie	0
W.E. Hollies	not out	1
D.V.P. Wright	lbw b Cresswell	0
Extras	(B 6, LB 11, NB 3)	20
Total		**482**

ENGLAND	O	M	R	W	O	M	R	W
Bailey	26·1	7	72	3	11	1	67	0
Bedser	31	6	74	4	23	4	59	3
Edrich	3	0	16	0				
Wright	22	1	93	1	6	0	21	0
Laker	3	0	11	0	29	6	78	4
Hollies	20	7	51	1	17	6	30	2
Brown	5	1	14	0	10	0	29	0
Compton	2	0	6	1	1	0	3	0
NEW ZEALAND								
Cowie	28	1	123	4				
Cresswell	41·2	6	168	6				
Cave	24	4	78	0				
Burtt	24	2	93	0				

FALL OF WICKETS

Wkt	NZ 1st	E 1st	NZ 2nd
1st	121	147	24
2nd	134	365	68
3rd	170	396	115
4th	239	401	131
5th	239	436	188
6th	272	469	276
7th	287	470	283
8th	311	472	299
9th	320	481	308
10th	345	482	–

Umpires: D. Davies (6) and F.S. Lee (2).

Close: 1st day – NZ(1) 320-8 (Burtt 24, Cowie 1); 2nd – E(1) 432-4 (Bailey 10, Brown 21).

SOUTH AFRICA v AUSTRALIA 1949–50 (1st Test)

Played at Ellis Park, Johannesburg, on 24, 26, 27, 28 December.
Toss: Australia.   Result: AUSTRALIA won by an innings and 85 runs.
Debuts: South Africa – J.D. Nel, H.J. Tayfield, J.C. Watkins; Australia – J. Moroney (*not 'J.A.R.'*).

Australia entered the post-Bradman era with their fourth successive innings victory against South Africa, Hassett making a century in his first match as captain. Loxton scored his first hundred in Test matches in 135 minutes. Johnston achieved the best analysis of his 40-match Test career.

AUSTRALIA

A.R. Morris	c Tayfield b McCarthy	0
J. Moroney	run out	0
K.R. Miller	b Mann	21
A.L. Hassett*	b Watkins	112
R.N. Harvey	b Watkins	34
S.J.E. Loxton	st Wade b Tayfield	101
C.L. McCool	b Tayfield	31
I.W. Johnson	c Cheetham b Mann	66
R.A. Saggers†	lbw b McCarthy	14
R.R. Lindwall	c Nel b Tayfield	21
W.A. Johnston	not out	1
Extras	(B 5, LB 5, W 2)	12
Total		**413**

SOUTH AFRICA

E.A.B. Rowan	b Miller	60	lbw b McCool	32
O.E. Wynne	lbw b Johnston	3	c Saggers b Johnston	33
J.D. Nel	b Johnson	4	c Saggers b Johnston	14
A.D. Nourse*	c Hassett b Johnson	0	c Saggers b Johnson	36
W.W. Wade†	b Miller	2	b Johnston	11
J.E. Cheetham	lbw b Johnston	10	c Hassett b Johnston	35
J.C. Watkins	c Hassett b Miller	36	c Miller b Johnson	0
H.J. Tayfield	lbw b Miller	6	c Miller b Johnson	0
N.B.F. Mann	b Miller	0	lbw b Johnston	13
V.I. Smith	not out	1	c McCool b Johnston	1
C.N. McCarthy	b Johnson	0	not out	1
Extras	(LB 14, NB 1)	15	(B 9, LB 3, W 1, NB 2)	15
Total		**137**		**191**

SOUTH AFRICA	O	M	R	W	O	M	R	W				
McCarthy	25	2	90	2								
Watkins	19	3	56	2								
Smith	13	0	70	0								
Tayfield	28	3	93	3								
Mann	28·4	4	92	2								

FALL OF WICKETS

Wkt	A 1st	SA 1st	SA 2nd
1st	0	14	50
2nd	2	32	81
3rd	71	40	113
4th	163	47	133
5th	200	82	141
6th	283	112	142
7th	320	122	142
8th	372	122	184
9th	408	133	186
10th	413	137	191

AUSTRALIA	O	M	R	W	O	M	R	W
Lindwall	10	1	22	0	8	1	25	0
Johnston	12	4	21	2	20·1	5	44	6
Miller	15	3	40	5	11	1	27	0
Johnson	18·2	6	37	3	14	0	54	3
Loxton	1	0	2	0	3	0	11	0
McCool					9	3	15	1

Umpires: R.G.A. Ashman (13) and D. Collins (2).

Close: 1st day – A(1) 196-4 (Hassett 109, Loxton 16); 2nd – SA(1) 70-4 (Rowan 48, Cheetham 5); 3rd – SA(2) 84-2 (Nel 6, Nourse 2).

SOUTH AFRICA v AUSTRALIA 1949–50 (2nd Test)

Played at Newlands, Cape Town, on 31 December, 2, 3, 4 January.
Toss: Australia.   Result: AUSTRALIA won by eight wickets.
Debuts: Nil.

Harvey's highest Test innings so far was the first of four in successive matches in this rubber. Tayfield and Mann added 100 runs for the eighth wicket in just an hour.

AUSTRALIA

A.R. Morris	c Watkins b Tayfield	42	c and b Mann	24
J. Moroney	c Cheetham b Mann	87	lbw b Mann	19
K.R. Miller	b Watkins	58	(4) not out	16
A.L. Hassett*	c and b Mann	57		
R.N. Harvey	c Wade b Mann	178	(3) not out	23
S.J.E. Loxton	b Tayfield	35		
C.L. McCool	not out	49		
I.W. Johnson	c Watkins b Mann	0		
R.R. Lindwall	not out	8		
R.A. Saggers†	) did not bat			
W.A. Johnston	)			
Extras	(B 8, LB 4)	12	(B 5)	5
Total	(7 wickets declared)	**526**	(2 wickets)	**87**

SOUTH AFRICA

E.A.B. Rowan	lbw b McCool	67	c Harvey b Johnston	3
O.E. Wynne	c Johnson b Miller	13	c Saggers b Johnston	10
J.D. Nel	lbw b Johnson	38	c McCool b Johnston	19
A.D. Nourse*	c Johnston b Miller	65	lbw b McCool	114
W.W. Wade†	c Saggers b Loxton	4	b Johnston	11
J.E. Cheetham	c McCool b Miller	3	c Saggers b Lindwall	27
J.C. Watkins	st Saggers b McCool	35	c Saggers b Lindwall	9
H.J. Tayfield	st Saggers b McCool	15	b Lindwall	75
N.B.F. Mann	b McCool	16	b Lindwall	46
V.I. Smith	not out	11	lbw b Lindwall	4
C.N. McCarthy	st Saggers b McCool	0	not out	0
Extras	(B 2, LB 8, W 1)	11	(B 3, LB 10, NB 2)	15
Total		**278**		**333**

SOUTH AFRICA	O	M	R	W	O	M	R	W
McCarthy	24	2	98	0	4	1	18	0
Watkins	12	2	59	1	2	0	10	0
Mann	28	3	105	4	8	1	23	2
Tayfield	37	4	141	2	6	1	31	0
Smith	25	0	111	0				
AUSTRALIA								
Lindwall	12	2	33	0	15·4	2	32	5
Johnston	17	3	53	0	24	2	70	3
Johnson	12	1	61	1	24	5	91	1
Miller	17	3	54	3	11	0	43	0
McCool	11·4	1	41	5	21	3	71	1
Loxton	6	0	25	1	4	1	6	0
Harvey					3	1	5	0

FALL OF WICKETS

Wkt	A 1st	SA 1st	SA 2nd	A 2nd
1st	68	33	5	37
2nd	172	92	16	44
3rd	215	154	61	–
4th	276	169	80	–
5th	416	194	141	–
6th	502	203	159	–
7th	502	241	225	–
8th	–	250	327	–
9th	–	278	332	–
10th	–	278	333	–

Umpires: R.G.A. Ashman (14) and D. Collins (3).

Close: 1st day – A(1) 312-4 (Harvey 55, Loxton 7); 2nd – SA(1) 169-3 (Nourse 43, Wade 4); 3rd – SA(2) 120-4 (Nourse 55, Cheetham 16).

SOUTH AFRICA v AUSTRALIA 1949–50 (3rd Test)

Played at Kingsmead, Durban, on 20, 21, 23, 24 January.
Toss: South Africa.   Result: AUSTRALIA won by five wickets.
Debuts: Nil.

Having dismissed Australia for what remains their lowest total in this series of matches, South Africa did not enforce the follow-on. The pitch took spin from the second day when 18 wickets fell for 146 runs. Australia, needing 336 runs to win in 435 minutes, gained a remarkable victory with 25 minutes to spare. They were guided home by Harvey, who, batting totally out of character, displayed monumental patience for $5\frac{1}{2}$ hours in one of Test cricket's greatest innings. Tayfield's analysis of 7 for 23 is still the best by any bowler in Tests between South Africa and Australia.

SOUTH AFRICA

E.A.B. Rowan	c Johnston b Miller	143	c Saggers b Lindwall		4
O.E. Wynne	b Johnston	18	b Johnson		29
J.D. Nel	c and b Johnson	14	lbw b Johnston		20
A.D. Nourse*	c Saggers b Johnston	66	c McCool b Johnson		27
W.W. Wade†	b Lindwall	24	b Johnston		0
N.B.F. Mann	b Johnston	9	(9) lbw b Johnson		0
J.E. Cheetham	c Hassett b Johnston	4	(6) c Hassett b Johnson		1
J.C. Watkins	b Lindwall	5	(7) st Saggers b Johnson		2
H.J. Tayfield	run out	15	(8) b Johnston		3
V.I. Smith	b Lindwall	1	b Johnston		4
C.N. McCarthy	not out	0	not out		2
Extras	(B3, LB 7, NB 2)	12	(B 5, LB 1, NB 1)		7
Total		**311**			**99**

AUSTRALIA

A.R. Morris	c Smith b Tayfield	25	hit wkt b Tayfield		44
J. Moroney	b Tayfield	10	lbw b Tayfield		10
I.W. Johnson	lbw b Tayfield	2			
K.R. Miller	b Tayfield	2	(3) lbw b Mann		10
A.L. Hassett*	lbw b Tayfield	2	(4) lbw b Mann		11
R.A. Saggers†	c Cheetham b Mann	2			
C.L. McCool	lbw b Mann	1	not out		39
R.R. Lindwall	b Mann	7			
R.N. Harvey	c and b Tayfield	2	(5) not out		151
S.J.E. Loxton	c Cheetham b Tayfield	16	(6) b Mann		54
W.A. Johnston	not out	2			
Extras	(B 3, LB 1)	4	(B 7, LB 9, NB 1)		17
Total		**75**	(5 wickets)		**336**

AUSTRALIA	O	M	R	W	O	M	R	W		FALL OF WICKETS			
Lindwall	19	3	47	3	4	1	7	1		SA	A	SA	A
Miller	24	5	73	1	7	0	12	0	*Wkt*	*1st*	*1st*	*2nd*	*2nd*
McCool	13	3	35	0					1st	32	31	9	14
Johnston	31·2	5	75	4	18·2	6	39	4	2nd	75	35	51	33
Loxton	6	1	31	0					3rd	242	37	85	59
Johnson	16	5	38	1	17	2	34	5	4th	264	39	85	95
									5th	283	42	88	230
SOUTH AFRICA									6th	289	45	90	–
McCarthy	6	2	8	0	12	3	32	0	7th	293	46	93	–
Watkins	4	1	9	0	6	2	10	0	8th	304	53	93	–
Mann	10	1	31	3	51·6	13	101	3	9th	308	63	93	–
Tayfield	8·4	1	23	7	49	5	144	2	10th	311	75	99	–
Smith					5	0	32	0					

Umpires: J.V. Hart-Davis (4) and B.V. Malan (1).

Close: 1st day – SA(1) 240-2 (Rowan 133, Nourse 64); 2nd – A(1) 75 all out; 3rd – A(2) 80-3 (Morris 35, Harvey 12).

SOUTH AFRICA v AUSTRALIA 1949–50 (4th Test)

Played at Ellis Park, Johnnesburg, on 10, 11, 13, 14 February.
Toss: Australia.   Result: MATCH DRAWN.
Debuts: South Africa – R.G. Draper, M.G. Melle, P.L. Winslow.

Moroney remains the only player to score hundreds in both innings of a Test match between these two countries. Melle, a fast bowler aged 19 years 253 days, took five wickets in his first Test innings. He then dismissed Harvey immediately after he had completed his third hundred in consecutive Tests.

AUSTRALIA

A.R. Morris	c Fullerton b McCarthy	111	c Mann b McCarthy		19
J. Moroney	c Fullerton b Melle	118	not out		101
K.R. Miller	c Fullerton b Melle	84	(4) not out		33
R.R. Lindwall	b Melle	5			
A.L. Hassett*	b McCarthy	53			
R.N. Harvey	not out	56	(3) b Melle		100
S.J.E. Loxton	b Melle	6			
C.L. McCool	st Fullerton b Tayfield	8			
I.W. Johnson	c sub (J.B. Roothman) b Melle	3			
R.A. Saggers†	not out	5			
W.A. Johnston	did not bat				
Extras	(B 8, LB 7, NB 1)	16	(B 5, LB 1)		6
Total	(8 wickets declared)	**465**	(2 wickets)		**259**

SOUTH AFRICA

E.A.B. Rowan	b Lindwall	55
J.D. Nel	run out	25
R.G. Draper	c Saggers b Johnston	15
A.D. Nourse*	c Saggers b Lindwall	5
D.W. Begbie	c McCool b Miller	24
P.L. Winslow	c and b Miller	19
G.M. Fullerton†	c Hassett b McCool	88
H.J. Tayfield	c Johnson b Miller	40
N.B.F. Mann	b Lindwall	52
M.G. Melle	lbw b McCool	14
C.N. McCarthy	not out	2
Extras	(B 7, LB 5, NB 1)	13
Total		**352**

SOUTH AFRICA	O	M	R	W	O	M	R	W		FALL OF WICKETS		
McCarthy	31	4	113	2	13	1	56	1		A	SA	A
Melle	33	3	113	5	12	0	58	1	*Wkt*	*1st*	*1st*	*2nd*
Tayfield	31	4	103	1	14	2	88	0	1st	214	84	28
Mann	25	2	85	0	8	1	32	0	2nd	265	86	198
Begbie	7	0	35	0	3	0	19	0	3rd	273	96	–
Rowan					1	1	0	0	4th	382	115	–
Nourse					1	1	0	0	5th	392	145	–
									6th	418	148	–
AUSTRALIA									7th	437	213	–
Lindwall	26	3	82	3					8th	440	307	–
Johnston	29	5	68	1					9th	–	345	–
Miller	28	3	75	3					10th	–	352	–
Loxton	10	2	22	0								
Johnson	18	4	52	0								
McCool	7	0	29	2								
Hassett	1	0	5	0								
Harvey	3	0	6	0								

Umpires: D. Collins (4) and D.T. Drew (1).

Close: 1st day – A(1) 266-2 (Miller 25, Lindwall 0); 2nd – SA(1) 77-0 (Rowan 55, Nel 21); 3rd – SA(1) 275-7 (Fullerton 45, Mann 35).

SOUTH AFRICA v AUSTRALIA 1949–50 (5th Test)

Played at St George's Park, Port Elizabeth, on 3, 4, 6 March.
Toss: Australia.   Result: AUSTRALIA won by an innings and 259 runs.
Debuts: Australia – G. Noblet (*not 'G.J.'*).

Australia, having recorded what is still their highest total in South Africa, went on to achieve the largest margin of victory by either side in these matches. It extended South Africa's run of consecutive Tests without a win to 28 since 1935 (*Test No. 243*). Harvey, who scored hundreds in each of the last four Tests, established the present record aggregate for Australia in a rubber in South Africa: 660 runs, average 132.00.

AUSTRALIA

A.R. Morris	c Winslow b Melle	157
J. Moroney	c Nourse b Melle	7
K.R. Miller	c Nourse b Tayfield	22
R.N. Harvey	b Begbie	116
A.L. Hassett*	c McCarthy b Mann	167
S.J.E. Loxton	c Rowan b Mann	43
C.L. McCool	c Fullerton b Tayfield	6
I.W. Johnson	not out	26
R.A. Saggers†	not out	4
G. Noblet	) did not bat	
W.A. Johnston	)	
Extras	(B 1)	1
Total	(7 wickets declared)	**549**

SOUTH AFRICA

E.A.B. Rowan	b Johnson	40		c McCool b Miller	0
J.D. Nel	b Miller	0		lbw b Johnston	5
R.G. Draper	c Johnston b Miller	7		b Johnston	3
A.D. Nourse*	c McCool b Miller	37		b Johnson	55
D.W. Begbie	c Saggers b Noblet	1		b Johnston	5
P.L. Winslow	lbw b Noblet	0	(7)	st Saggers b Johnson	11
G.M. Fullerton†	st Saggers b McCool	18	(6)	c Saggers b Loxton	24
H.J. Tayfield	st Saggers b McCool	6		st Saggers b McCool	7
M.G. Melle	b Miller	1	(10)	c Harvey b McCool	6
N.B.F. Mann	b Noblet	41	(9)	lbw b Johnson	6
C.N. McCarthy	not out	1		not out	4
Extras	(B 5, NB 1)	6		(B 3, LB 3)	6
Total		**158**			**132**

SOUTH AFRICA	O	M	R	W	O	M	R	W		FALL OF WICKETS		
McCarthy	29	3	121	0						A	SA	SA
Melle	23	2	132	2					*Wkt*	*1st*	*1st*	*2nd*
Tayfield	25	1	103	2					1st	16	3	0
Mann	36	4	154	2					2nd	49	19	3
Begbie	4	0	38	1					3rd	236	71	12
									4th	350	84	24
AUSTRALIA									5th	449	84	63
Miller	14	3	42	4	8	0	24	1	6th	485	95	88
Johnston	3	0	12	0	6	1	10	3	7th	545	104	113
Noblet	17·1	7	21	3	9	2	16	0	8th	–	113	115
Johnson	11	1	48	1	7	1	21	3	9th	–	117	126
McCool	5	1	29	2	14·2	2	48	2	10th	–	158	132
Loxton					4	2	7	1				

Umpires: D. Collins (5) and B.V. Malan (2).

Close: 1st day – A(1) 380-4 (Hassett 68, Loxton 9); 2nd – SA(1) 104-7 (Fullerton 9, Melle 0).

ENGLAND v WEST INDIES 1950 (1st Test)

Played at Old Trafford, Manchester, on 8, 9, 10, 12 June.
Toss: England.   Result: ENGLAND won by 202 runs.
Debuts: England – R. Berry, G.H.G. Doggart. West Indies – S. Ramadhin, A.L. Valentine.

On a dry crumbling pitch favouring spin bowling, England completed a substantial victory after an hour's play on the fourth day. Two left-arm leg-break bowlers enjoyed remarkable debuts: Berry (9) and Valentine (11) shared half the wickets to fall in their first Test; the latter being the only bowler to take the first eight wickets to fall in his first Test innings. Hutton retired hurt at 22 after being struck on the hand by a ball from Johnson. He resumed at 249 and batted virtually one-handed. Evans batted for 140 minutes, hit 17 fours, and scored his first hundred in Tests and his first in major cricket in England, Walcott opened the bowling instead of Johnson (pulled side muscle) in the second innings while Christiani kept wicket.

ENGLAND

L. Hutton	b Valentine	39	(8) c and b Worrell		45
R.T. Simpson	c Goddard b Valentine	27	(1) c Weekes b Gomez		0
W.J. Edrich	c Gomez b Valentine	7	(2) c Weekes b Ramadhin		71
G.H.G. Doggart	c Rae b Valentine	29	(3) c Goddard b Valentine		22
H.E. Dollery	c Gomez b Valentine	8	(4) c Gomez b Valentine		0
N.W.D. Yardley*	c Gomez b Valentine	0	(5) lbw b Gomez		25
T.E. Bailey	not out	82	(6) run out		33
T.G. Evans†	c and b Valentine	104	(7) c Worrell b Ramadhin		15
J.C. Laker	b Valentine	4	c Stollmeyer b Valentine		40
W.E. Hollies	c Weekes b Ramadhin	0	c Walcott b Worrell		3
R. Berry	b Ramadhin	0	not out		4
Extras	(B 8, LB 3, NB 1)	12	(B 17, LB 12, NB 1)		30
Total		**312**			**288**

WEST INDIES

A.F. Rae	c Doggart b Berry	14	c Doggart b Hollies	10
J.B. Stollmeyer	lbw b Hollies	43	c sub (P. Hough) b Laker	78
F.M.M. Worrell	st Evans b Berry	15	st Evans b Hollies	28
E. de C. Weekes	c sub (P. Hough) b Bailey	52	lbw b Hollies	1
C.L. Walcott†	c Evans b Berry	13	b Berry	9
R.J. Christiani	lbw b Berry	17	c Yardley b Hollies	6
G.E. Gomez	c Berry b Hollies	35	st Evans b Berry	8
J.D.C. Goddard*	run out	7	not out	16
H.H.H. Johnson	c Dollery b Hollies	8	b Berry	22
S. Ramadhin	not out	4	b Berry	0
A.L. Valentine	c and b Berry	0	c Bailey b Hollies	0
Extras	(LB 6, NB 1)	7	(B 4, W 1)	5
Total		**215**		**183**

WEST INDIES	O	M	R	W	O	M	R	W	FALL OF WICKETS				
Johnson	10	3	18	0						E	WI	E	WI
Gomez	10	1	29	0	25	12	47	2	*Wkt*	*1st*	*1st*	*2nd*	*2nd*
Valentine	50	14	104	8	56	22	100	3	1st	31	52	0	32
Ramadhin	39·3	12	90	2	42	17	77	2	2nd	74	74	31	68
Goddard	15	1	46	0	9	3	42	0	3rd	79	74	43	80
Worrell	4	1	13	0	5·5	1	10	2	4th	83	94	106	113
Walcott					4	1	12	0	5th	88	146	131	126
									6th	249	178	151	141
ENGLAND									7th	293	201	200	146
Bailey	10	2	28	1	3	1	9	0	8th	301	211	266	178
Edrich	2	1	4	0	3	1	10	0	9th	308	211	284	178
Hollies	33	13	70	3	35·2	11	63	5	10th	312	215	288	183
Laker	17	5	43	0	14	4	43	1					
Berry	31·5	13	63	5	26	12	53	4					

Umpires: F. Chester (38) and D. Davies (7).

Close: 1st day – WI(1) 17-0 (Rae 8, Stollmeyer 8); 2nd – E(2) 108-4 (Edrich 56, Bailey 0); 3rd – WI(2) 122-4 (Stollmeyer 67, Christiani 2).

ENGLAND v WEST INDIES 1950 (2nd Test)

Played at Lord's, London, on 24, 26, 27, 28, 29 June.
Toss: West Indies.   Result: WEST INDIES won by 326 runs.
Debuts: England – W.G.A. Parkhouse.

Ramadhin and Valentine, who had each played only two first-class matches before this tour, bowled West Indies to their first win in England. This famous victory introduced Caribbean dancing and calypso singing to the playing area at Lord's. Wardle dismissed Stollmeyer with his first ball in Test cricket in England.

WEST INDIES

A.F. Rae	c and b Jenkins	106		b Jenkings	24
J.B. Stollmeyer	lbw b Wardle	20		b Jenkins	30
F.M.M. Worrell	b Bedser	52		c Doggart b Jenkins	45
E. de C. Weekes	b Bedser	63		run out	63
C.L. Walcott†	st Evans b Jenkins	14	(6)	not out	168
G.E. Gomez	st Evans b Jenkins	1	(7)	c Edrich b Bedser	70
R.J. Christiani	b Bedser	33	(8)	not out	5
J.D.C. Goddard*	b Wardle	14	(5)	c Evans b Jenkins	11
P.E. Jones	c Evans b Jenkins	0			
S. Ramadhin	not out	1			
A.L. Valentine	c Hutton b Jenkins	5			
Extras	(B 10, LB 5, W 1, NB 1)	17		(LB 8, NB 1)	9
Total		**326**		(6 wickets declared)	**425**

ENGLAND

L. Hutton	st Walcott b Valentine	35	b Valentine	10
C. Washbrook	st Walcott b Ramadhin	36	b Ramadhin	114
W.J. Edrich	c Walcott b Ramadhin	8	c Jones b Ramadhin	8
G.H.G. Doggart	lbw b Ramadhin	0	b Ramadhin	25
W.G.A. Parkhouse	b Valentine	0	c Goddard b Valentine	48
N.W.D. Yardley*	b Valentine	16	c Weekes b Valentine	19
T.G. Evans†	b Ramadhin	8	c Rae b Ramadhin	2
R.O. Jenkins	c Walcott b Valentine	4	b Ramadhin	4
J.H. Wardle	not out	33	lbw b Worrell	21
A.V. Bedser	b Ramadhin	5	b Ramadhin	0
R. Berry	c Goddard b Jones	2	not out	0
Extras	(B 2, LB 1, W 1)	4	(B 16, LB 7)	23
Total		**151**		**274**

ENGLAND	O	M	R	W	O	M	R	W	FALL OF WICKETS				
										WI	E	WI	E
Bedser	40	14	60	3	44	16	80	1	*Wkt*	*1st*	*1st*	*2nd*	*2nd*
Edrich	16	4	30	0	13	2	37	0	1st	37	62	48	28
Jenkins	35·2	6	116	5	59	13	174	4	2nd	128	74	75	57
Wardle	17	6	46	2	30	10	58	0	3rd	233	74	108	140
Berry	19	7	45	0	32	15	67	0	4th	262	75	146	218
Yardley	4	1	12	0					5th	273	86	199	228
									6th	274	102	410	238
WEST INDIES									7th	320	110	–	245
Jones	8.4	2	13	1	7	1	22	0	8th	320	113	–	248
Worrell	10	4	20	0	22.3	9	39	1	9th	320	122	–	258
Valentine	45	28	48	4	71	47	79	3	10th	326	151	–	274
Ramadhin	43	27	66	5	72	43	86	6					
Gomez					13	1	25	0					
Goddard					6	6	0	0					

Umpires: D. Davies (8) and F.S. Lee (3).

Close: 1st day – WI(1) 320-7 (Christiani 33, Jones 0); 2nd – WI(2) 45-0 (Rae 16, Stollmeyer 29); 3rd – WI(2) 386-5 (Walcott 148, Gomez 57); 4th – E(2) 218-4 (Washbrook 114, Yardley 0).

ENGLAND v WEST INDIES 1950 (3rd Test)

Played at Trent Bridge, Nottingham, on 20, 21, 22, 24, 25 July.
Toss: England.   Result: WEST INDIES won by ten wickets.
Debuts: England – D.J. Insole, D. Shackleton.

Worrell's 261 was then the highest score for West Indies in England, and the highest by any batsman in a Nottingham Test. With Weekes he shared a fourth-wicket partnership of 283 in 210 minutes. The partnership of 212 between Simpson and Washbrook remains the first-wicket record for this series. For the first time 11 different counties were represented in England's team. Harold Elliott of Lancashire, not to be confused with Harry Elliott of Derbyshire, made his first appearance as an umpire in Test cricket.

ENGLAND

R.T. Simpson	c Walcott b Johnson	4	run out	94
C. Washbrook	c Stollmeyer b Worrell	3	c Worrell b Valentine	102
W.G.A. Parkhouse	c Weekes b Johnson	13	lbw b Goddard	69
J.G. Dewes	c Gomez b Worrell	0	lbw b Valentine	67
N.W.D. Yardley*	c Goddard b Valentine	41	b Ramadhin	7
D.J. Insole	lbw b Ramadhin	21	st Walcott b Ramadhin	0
T.G. Evans†	b Ramadhin	32	c Stollmeyer b Ramadhin	63
D. Shackleton	b Worrell	42	c Weekes b Valentine	1
R.O. Jenkins	b Johnson	39	not out	6
A.V. Bedser	c Stollmeyer b Valentine	13	b Ramadhin	2
W.E. Hollies	not out	2	lbw b Ramadhin	0
Extras	(LB 12, NB 1)	13	(B 11, LB 10, W 2, NB 2)	25
Total		**223**		**436**

WEST INDIES

A.F. Rae	st Evans b Yardley	68	not out	46
J.B. Stollmeyer	c and b Jenkins	46	not out	52
R.J. Christiani	lbw b Shackleton	10		
F.M.M. Worrell	c Yardley b Bedser	261		
E. de C. Weekes	c and b Hollies	129		
C.L. Walcott†	b Bedser	8		
G.E. Gomez	not out	19		
J.D.C. Goddard*	c Yardley b Bedser	0		
H.H.H. Johnson	c Insole b Bedser	0		
S. Ramadhin	b Bedser	2		
A.L. Valentine	b Hollies	1		
Extras	(B 2, LB 10, NB 2)	14	(NB 5)	5
Total		**558**	(0 wickets)	**103**

WEST INDIES	O	M	R	W	O	M	R	W
Johnson	25·4	5	59	3	30	5	65	0
Worrell	17	4	40	3	19	8	30	0
Gomez	3	1	9	0	11	3	23	0
Goddard	6	3	10	0	12	6	18	1
Ramadhin	29	12	49	2	81·2	25	135	5
Valentine	18	6	43	2	92	49	140	3
ENGLAND								
Bedser	48	9	127	5	11	1	35	0
Shackleton	43	7	128	1	6	2	7	0
Yardley	27	3	82	1				
Jenkins	13	0	73	1	11	1	46	0
Hollies	43·4	8	134	2	7	6	1	0
Simpson					1·3	0	9	0

FALL OF WICKETS

Wkt	E 1st	WI 1st	E 2nd	WI 2nd
1st	6	77	212	–
2nd	18	95	220	–
3rd	23	238	326	–
4th	25	521	346	–
5th	75	535	350	–
6th	105	537	408	–
7th	147	538	410	–
8th	174	539	434	–
9th	191	551	436	–
10th	223	558	436	–

Umpires: F. Chester (39) and H. Elliott (1).

Close: 1st day – WI(1) 77-1 (Rae 31, Christiani 0); 2nd – WI(1) 479-3 (Worrell 239, Weekes 108); 3rd – E(2) 87-0 (Simpson 37, Washbrook 38); 4th – E(2) 350-5 (Dewes 55).

ENGLAND v WEST INDIES 1950 (4th Test)

Played at Kennington Oval, London, on 12, 14, 15, 16 August.
Toss: West Indies.   Result: WEST INDIES won by an innings and 56 runs.
Debuts: M.J. Hilton, A.J.W. McIntyre, D.S. Sheppard (later The Right Reverend D.S. Sheppard, Bishop of Liverpool).

Hutton scored England's first double-century in a home Test against West Indies and remains the only England player to carry his bat throughout a completed innings against that team. His is the highest score by an England player involved in this feat and he is the only one to achieve it twice for England (also Test No. 330). He batted for 470 minutes and hit 22 fours. Worrell retired hurt when 116 because of stomach trouble and giddiness, and resumed at 446. He did not field on the final day because of a groin strain. Valentine took 33 wickets in the rubber – the West Indies record against England until 1988. By making eight changes from the side defeated at Trent Bridge, the selectors brought their total of England representatives in this four-match rubber to 25.

WEST INDIES

A.F. Rae	b Bedser	109
J.B. Stollmeyer	lbw b Bailey	36
F.M.M. Worrell	lbw b Wright	138
E. de C. Weekes	c Hutton b Wright	30
C.L. Walcott†	b Wright	17
G.E. Gomez	c McIntyre b Brown	74
R.J. Christiani	c McIntyre b Bedser	11
J.D.C. Goddard*	not out	58
P.E. Jones	b Wright	1
S. Ramadhin	c McIntyre b Wright	3
A.L. Valentine	b Bailey	9
Extras	(B 5, LB 11, NB 1)	17
Total		**503**

ENGLAND

L. Hutton	not out	202	c Christiani b Goddard	2
R.T. Simpson	c Jones b Valentine	30	b Ramadhin	16
D.S. Sheppard	b Ramadhin	11	c Weekes b Valentine	29
D.C.S. Compton	run out	44	c Weekes b Valentine	11
J.G. Dewes	c Worrell b Valentine	17	c Christiani b Valentine	3
T.E. Bailey	c Weekes b Goddard	18	lbw b Ramadhin	12
F.R. Brown*	c Weekes b Valentine	0	c Stollmeyer b Valentine	15
A.J.W. McIntyre†	c and b Valentine	4	c sub (K.B. Trestrail) b Ramadhin	0
A.V. Bedser	lbw b Goddard	0	c Weekes b Valentine	0
M.J. Hilton	b Goddard	3	c sub (K.B. Trestrail) b Valentine	0
D.V.P. Wright	lbw b Goddard	4	not out	6
Extras	(B 5, LB 6)	11	(B 6, LB 3)	9
Total		**344**		**103**

ENGLAND	O	M	R	W	O	M	R	W
Bailey	34·2	9	84	2				
Bedser	38	9	75	2				
Brown	21	4	74	1				
Wright	53	16	141	5				
Hilton	41	12	91	0				
Compton	7	2	21	0				
WEST INDIES								
Jones	23	4	70	0				
Worrell	20	9	30	0				
Ramadhin	45	23	63	1	26	11	38	3
Valentine	64	21	121	4	26·3	10	39	6
Gomez	10	3	24	0	8	4	6	0
Goddard	17·4	6	25	4	9	4	11	1

FALL OF WICKETS

Wkt	WI 1st	E 1st	E 2nd
1st	72	73	2
2nd	244	120	39
3rd	295	229	50
4th	318	259	56
5th	337	310	79
6th	446	315	83
7th	480	321	83
8th	482	322	83
9th	490	326	85
10th	503	344	103

Umpires: W.H. Ashdown (3) and F.S. Lee (4).

Close: 1st day – WI(1) 295-3 (Worrell 110); 2nd – E(1) 29-0 (Hutton 14, Simpson 12); 3rd – E(1) 282-4 (Hutton 160, Bailey 9).

AUSTRALIA v ENGLAND 1950–51 (1st Test)

Played at Woolloongabba, Brisbane, on 1, 2 (*no play*), 4, 5 December.
Toss: Australia.   Result: AUSTRALIA won by 70 runs.
Debuts: Australia – J.B. Iverson.

Rain provided the traditional Brisbane 'sticky' after England had dismissed Australia on a good batting pitch for only 228. Twenty wickets fell for 102 runs after lunch on the third day, the start of which had been delayed until 1 pm. Hutton's innings on the last morning was one of the most remarkable in Test cricket.

AUSTRALIA

J. Moroney	c Hutton b Bailey	0	lbw b Bailey	0
A.R. Morris	lbw b Bedser	25	c Bailey b Bedser	0
R.N. Harvey	c Evans b Bedser	74	(6) c Simpson b Bedser	12
K.R. Miller	c McIntyre b Wright	15	(7) c Simpson b Bailey	8
A.L. Hassett*	b Bedser	8	lbw b Bailey	3
S.J.E. Loxton	c Evans b Brown	24	(4) c Bailey b Bedser	0
R.R. Lindwall	c Bedser b Bailey	41	(8) not out	0
D. Tallon†	c Simpson b Brown	5		
I.W. Johnson	c Simpson b Bailey	23	(3) lbw b Bailey	8
W.A. Johnston	c Hutton b Bedser	1		
J.B. Iverson	not out	1		
Extras	(B 5, LB 3, NB 3)	11	(NB 1)	1
Total		**228**	(7 wickets declared)	**32**

ENGLAND

R.T. Simpson	b Johnston	12	b Lindwall	0
C. Washbrook	c Hassett b Johnston	19	c Loxton b Lindwall	6
T.G. Evans†	c Iverson b Johnston	16	(6) c Loxton b Johnston	5
D.C.S. Compton	c Lindwall b Johnston	3	(9) c Loxton b Johnston	0
J.G. Dewes	c Loxton b Miller	1	(3) b Miller	9
L. Hutton	not out	8	(8) not out	62
A.J.W. McIntyre	b Johnston	1	run out	7
F.R. Brown*	c Tallon b Miller	4	(10) c Loxton b Iverson	17
T.E. Bailey	not out	1	(4) c Johnston b Iverson	7
A.V. Bedser			(5) c Harvey b Iverson	0
D.V.P. Wright			c Lindwall b Iverson	2
Extras	(LB 2, NB 1)	3	(B 6, NB 1)	7
Total	(7 wickets declared)	**68**		**122**

ENGLAND	O	M	R	W	O	M	R	W
Bailey	12	4	28	3	7	2	22	4
Bedser	16·5	4	45	4	6·5	2	9	3
Wright	16	0	81	1				
Brown	11	0	63	2				
AUSTRALIA								
Lindwall	1	0	1	0	7	3	21	2
Johnston	11	2	35	5	11	2	30	2
Miller	10	1	29	2	7	3	21	1
Iverson					13	3	43	4

FALL OF WICKETS

	A	E	A	E
Wkt	1st	1st	2nd	2nd
1st	0	28	0	0
2nd	69	49	0	16
3rd	116	52	0	22
4th	118	52	12	23
5th	129	56	19	23
6th	156	57	31	30
7th	172	67	32	46
8th	219	–	–	46
9th	226	–	–	77
10th	228	–	–	122

Umpires: A.N. Barlow (6) and H. Elphinston (2).

Close: 1st day – A(1) 228 all out; 2nd – no play; 3rd – E(2) 30-6 (Evans 0).

AUSTRALIA v ENGLAND 1950–51 (2nd Test)

Played at Melbourne Cricket Ground on 22, 23, 26, 27 December.
Toss: Australia.   Result: AUSTRALIA won by 28 runs.
Debuts: Australia – K.A. Archer.

This match, which included the unusual feature of a two-day interlude for Sunday and Christmas Day, produced a close and tense contest. England, needing to score 179 runs in just over three days to end Australia's long unbeaten run, eventually failed against a fine display by Lindwall, Johnston, and the 'mystery' slow bowler, Iverson. Close, aged 19 years 301 days, remains England's youngest representative in this series.

AUSTRALIA

K.A. Archer	c Bedser b Bailey	26	c Bailey b Bedser	46
A.R. Morris	c Hutton b Bedser	2	lbw b Wright	18
R.N. Harvey	c Evans b Bedser	42	run out	31
K.R. Miller	lbw b Brown	18	b Bailey	14
A.L. Hassett*	b Bailey	52	c Bailey b Brown	19
S.J.E. Loxton	c Evans b Close	32	c Evans b Brown	2
R.R. Lindwall	lbw b Bailey	8	c Evans b Brown	7
D. Tallon†	not out	7	lbw b Brown	0
I.W. Johnson	c Parkhouse b Bedser	0	c Close b Bedser	23
W.A. Johnston	c Hutton b Bedser	0	b Bailey	6
J.B. Iverson	b Bailey	1	not out	0
Extras	(B 4, LB 2)	6	(B 10, LB 5)	15
Total		**194**		**181**

ENGLAND

R.T. Simpson	c Johnson b Miller	4	b Lindwall	23
C. Washbrook	lbw b Lindwall	21	b Iverson	8
J.G. Dewes	c Miller b Johnston	8	(5) c Harvey b Iverson	5
L. Hutton	c Tallon b Iverson	12	c Lindwall b Johnston	40
W.G.A. Parkhouse	c Hassett b Miller	9	(6) lbw b Johnston	28
D.B. Close	c Loxton b Iverson	0	(7) lbw b Johnston	1
F.R. Brown*	c Johnson b Iverson	62	(8) b Lindwall	8
T.E. Bailey	b Lindwall	12	(3) b Johnson	0
T.G. Evans†	c Johnson b Iverson	49	b Lindwall	2
A.V. Bedser	not out	4	not out	14
D.V.P. Wright	lbw b Johnston	2	lbw b Johnston	2
Extras	(B 8, LB 6)	14	(B 17, LB 2)	19
Total		**197**		**150**

ENGLAND	O	M	R	W	O	M	R	W
Bailey	17·1	5	40	4	15	3	47	2
Bedser	19	3	37	4	16·3	2	43	2
Wright	8	0	63	0	9	0	42	1
Brown	9	0	28	1	12	2	26	4
Close	6	1	20	1	1	0	8	0
AUSTRALIA								
Lindwall	13	2	46	2	12	1	29	3
Miller	13	0	39	2	5	2	16	0
Johnston	9	1	28	2	13·7	1	26	4
Iverson	18	3	37	4	20	4	36	2
Johnson	5	1	19	0	13	3	24	1
Loxton	4	1	14	0				

FALL OF WICKETS

Wkt	A 1st	E 1st	A 2nd	E 2nd
1st	6	11	43	21
2nd	67	33	99	22
3rd	89	37	100	52
4th	93	54	126	82
5th	177	54	131	92
6th	177	61	151	95
7th	192	126	151	122
8th	193	153	156	124
9th	193	194	181	134
10th	194	197	181	150

Umpires: G.C. Cooper (2) and R. Wright (2).

Close: 1st day – A(1) 194 all out; 2nd – E(1) 197 all out; 3rd – E(2) 28-2 (Simpson 10, Hutton 2).

AUSTRALIA v ENGLAND 1950–51 (3rd Test)

Played at Sydney Cricket Ground on 5, 6, 8, 9 January.
Toss: England.   Result: AUSTRALIA won by an innings and 13 runs.
Debuts: England – J.J. Warr.

England were reduced to three main bowlers after Bailey had had his thumb fractured by a ball from Lindwall and Wright had torn a leg tendon when he was run out. On the third day, Brown bowled 22 eight-ball overs, while Bedser and Warr each sent down 20; all this in great heat and on a good batting pitch. After two close contests Australia retained the Ashes with remarkable ease. Compton made his highest score of the rubber and Brown won his only toss in seven Tests on the tour.

ENGLAND

L. Hutton	lbw b Miller	62		c Tallon b Iverson	9
C. Washbrook	c Miller b Johnson	18		b Iverson	34
R.T. Simpson	c Loxton b Miller	49		c Tallon b Iverson	0
D.C.S. Compton	b Miller	0		c Johnson b Johnston	23
W.G.A. Parkhouse	c Morris b Johnson	25		run out	15
F.R. Brown*	b Lindwall	79		b Iverson	18
T.E. Bailey	c Tallon b Johnson	15	(8)	not out	0
T.G. Evans†	not out	23	(7)	b Johnson	14
A.V. Bedser	b Lindwall	3		b Iverson	4
J.J. Warr	b Miller	4		b Iverson	0
D.V.P. Wright	run out	0		absent hurt	–
Extras	(LB 10, NB 2)	12		(B 1, LB 5)	6
Total		**290**			**123**

AUSTRALIA

K.A. Archer	c Evans b Bedser	48
A.R. Morris	b Bedser	0
A.L. Hassett*	c Bedser b Brown	70
R.N. Harvey	b Bedser	39
K.R. Miller	not out	145
S.J.E. Loxton	c Bedser b Brown	17
D. Tallon†	lbw b Bedser	18
I.W. Johnson	b Brown	77
R.R. Lindwall	lbw b Brown	1
W.A. Johnston	run out	0
J.B. Iverson	run out	1
Extras	(B 3, LB 7)	10
Total		**426**

AUSTRALIA	O	M	R	W	O	M	R	W
Lindwall	16	0	60	2	4	1	12	0
Miller	15·7	4	37	4	6	2	15	0
Johnson	31	8	94	3	10	2	32	1
Johnston	21	5	50	0	13	6	31	1
Iverson	10	1	25	0	19·4	8	27	6
Loxton	5	0	12	0				
ENGLAND								
Bedser	43	4	107	4				
Warr	36	4	142	0				
Brown	44	4	153	4				
Compton	6	1	14	0				

FALL OF WICKETS

Wkt	E 1st	A 1st	E 2nd
1st	34	1	32
2nd	128	122	40
3rd	128	122	45
4th	137	190	74
5th	187	223	91
6th	258	252	119
7th	267	402	119
8th	281	406	123
9th	286	418	123
10th	290	426	–

Umpires: A.N. Barlow (7) and H. Elphinston (3).

Close: 1st day – E(1) 211-5 (Brown 36, Bailey 9); 2nd – A(1) 110-1 (Archer 44, Hassett 62); 3rd – A(1) 362-6 (Miller 96, Johnson 64).

AUSTRALIA v ENGLAND 1950–51 (4th Test)

Played at Adelaide Oval on 2, 3, 5, 6, 7, 8 February.
Toss: Australia.   Result: AUSTRALIA won by 274 runs.
Debuts: Australia – J.W. Burke; England – R. Tattersall.

Hutton became the only England batsman to carry his bat through a complete Test innings twice and the second after R. Abel in 1891-92 (*Test No. 36*) to do so against Australia. Morris (206) batted 462 minutes for the then highest score by an Australian left-hander against England. Burke, aged 20 years 240 days, scored a hundred in his first Test match. Compton captained on the fifth day after Brown had been injured in a motoring accident the previous night. Warr ended his two-match career as the most expensive wicket-taker in Test cricket: 1 for 281.

AUSTRALIA

K.A. Archer	c Compton b Bedser	0	c Bedser b Tattersall	32
A.R. Morris	b Tattersall	206	run out	16
A.L. Hassett*	c Evans b Wright	43	lbw b Wright	31
R.N. Harvey	b Bedser	43	b Brown	68
K.R. Miller	c Brown b Wright	44	b Wright	99
J.W. Burke	b Tattersall	12	not out	101
I.W. Johnson	c Evans b Bedser	16	c Evans b Warr	3
R.R. Lindwall	lbw b Wright	1	run out	31
D. Tallon†	b Tattersall	1	c Hutton b Compton	5
W.A. Johnston	c Hutton b Wright	0	not out	9
J.B. Iverson	not out	0		
Extras	(B 2, LB 1, W 1, NB 1)	5	(B 7, LB 1)	8
Total		**371**	(8 wickets declared)	**403**

ENGLAND

L. Hutton	not out	156	c sub (S.J.E. Loxton) b Johnston	45
C. Washbrook	c Iverson b Lindwall	2	lbw b Johnston	31
R.T. Simpson	b Johnston	29	c Burke b Johnston	61
D.C.S. Compton	c Tallon b Lindwall	5	c sub (S.J.E. Loxton) b Johnston	0
D.S. Sheppard	b Iverson	9	lbw b Miller	41
F.R. Brown*	b Miller	16	absent hurt	–
T.G. Evans†	c Burke b Johnston	13	(6) c Johnson b Miller	21
A.V. Bedser	lbw b Iverson	7	(7) c Morris b Miller	0
R. Tattersall	c Harvey b Iverson	0	(8) c Morris b Johnson	6
J.J. Warr	b Johnston	0	(9) b Johnson	0
D.V.P. Wright	lbw b Lindwall	14	(10) not out	0
Extras	(B 15, LB 5, NB 1)	21	(B 15, LB 3, W 2, NB 3)	23
Total		**272**		**228**

ENGLAND	O	M	R	W	O	M	R	W
Bedser	26	4	74	3	25	6	62	0
Warr	16	2	63	0	21	0	76	1
Wright	25	1	99	4	21	2	109	2
Tattersall	25·5	5	95	3	27	2	116	1
Brown	3	0	24	0	3	1	14	1
Compton	1	0	11	0	4·6	1	18	1
AUSTRALIA								
Lindwall	13·3	0	51	3	10	2	35	0
Miller	13	2	36	1	13	4	27	3
Johnson	15	2	38	0	25·6	6	63	2
Iverson	26	4	68	3				
Johnston	25	4	58	3	27	4	73	4
Burke					3	1	7	0

FALL OF WICKETS

	A	E	A	E
Wkt	1st	1st	2nd	2nd
1st	0	7	26	74
2nd	95	80	79	90
3rd	205	96	95	90
4th	281	132	194	181
5th	310	161	281	221
6th	357	195	297	221
7th	363	206	367	228
8th	366	214	378	228
9th	367	219	–	228
10th	371	272	–	–

Umpires: A.N. Barlow (8) and A.F. Cocks (1).

Close: 1st day – A(1) 254-3 (Morris 140, Miller 24); 2nd – E(1) 96-2 (Hutton 56, Compton 5); 3rd – A(2) 34-1 (Archer 12, Hassett 5); 4th – A(2) 285-5 (Burke 37, Johnson 1); 5th – E(2) 114-3 (Simpson 23, Sheppard 6).

AUSTRALIA v ENGLAND 1950–51 (5th Test)

Played at Melbourne Cricket Ground on 23, 24 (*no play*), 26, 27, 28 February.
Toss: Australia.   Result: ENGLAND won by eight wickets.
Debuts: Australia – G.B. Hole.

England beat Australia for the first time since 1938 (*Test No. 266*) and ended their record run of 25 consecutive Test matches without defeat (20 wins, 5 draws). Simpson reached his only hundred against Australia on his 31st birthday and went on to score all but ten of a last-wicket partnership of 74 in 55 minutes with Tattersall. Bedser took 30 wickets, average 16·06, in the rubber, while Hutton averaged 88·83 with the bat – and Compton 7·57.

AUSTRALIA

J.W. Burke	c Tattersall b Bedser	11	c Hutton b Bedser	1
A.R. Morris	lbw b Brown	50	lbw b Bedser	4
A.L. Hassett*	c Hutton b Brown	92	b Wright	48
R.N. Harvey	c Evans b Brown	1	lbw b Wright	52
K.R. Miller	c and b Brown	7	c and b Brown	0
G.B. Hole	b Bedser	18	b Bailey	63
I.W. Johnson	lbw b Bedser	1	c Brown b Wright	0
R.R. Lindwall	c Compton b Bedser	21	b Bedser	14
D. Tallon†	c Hutton b Bedser	1	not out	2
W.A. Johnston	not out	12	b Bedser	1
J.B. Iverson	c Washbrook b Brown	0	c Compton b Bedser	0
Extras	(B 2, LB 1)	3	(B 2, LB 8, W 1, NB 1)	12
Total		**217**		**197**

ENGLAND

L. Hutton	b Hole	79	not out	60
C. Washbrook	c Tallon b Miller	27	c Lindwall b Johnston	7
R.T. Simpson	not out	156	run out	15
D.C.S. Compton	c Miller b Lindwall	11	not out	11
D.S. Sheppard	c Tallon b Miller	1		
F.R. Brown*	b Lindwall	6		
T.G. Evans†	b Miller	1		
A.V. Bedser	b Lindwall	11		
T.E. Bailey	c Johnson b Iverson	5		
D.V.P. Wright	lbw b Iverson	3		
R. Tattersall	b Miller	10		
Extras	(B 9, LB 1)	10	(LB 2)	2
Total		**320**	(2 wickets)	**95**

ENGLAND	O	M	R	W	O	M	R	W
Bedser	22	5	46	5	20·3	4	59	5
Bailey	9	1	29	0	15	3	32	1
Brown	18	4	49	5	9	1	32	1
Wright	9	1	50	0	15	2	56	3
Tattersall	11	3	40	0	5	2	6	0
AUSTRALIA								
Lindwall	21	1	77	3	2	0	12	0
Miller	21·7	5	76	4	2	0	5	0
Johnston	12	1	55	0	11	3	36	1
Iverson	20	4	52	2	12	2	32	0
Johnson	11	1	40	0	1	0	1	0
Hole	5	0	10	1	1	0	3	0
Hassett					0·6	0	4	0

FALL OF WICKETS

Wkt	A 1st	E 1st	A 2nd	E 2nd
1st	23	40	5	32
2nd	111	171	6	62
3rd	115	204	87	–
4th	123	205	89	–
5th	156	212	142	–
6th	166	213	142	–
7th	184	228	192	–
8th	187	236	196	–
9th	216	246	197	–
10th	217	320	197	–

Umpires: A.N. Barlow (9) and H. Elphinston (4).

Close: 1st day – A(1) 206-8 (Lindwall 18, Johnston 4); 2nd – no play; 3rd – E(1) 218-6 (Simpson 80, Bedser 4); 4th – A(2) 129-4 (Hassett 44, Hole 18).

NEW ZEALAND v ENGLAND 1950–51 (1st Test)

Played at Lancaster Park, Christchurch, on 17, 19, 20, 21 March.
Toss: New Zealand.   Result: MATCH DRAWN.
Debuts: New Zealand – J.A. Hayes, A.R. MacGibbon, A.M. Moir; England – J.B. Statham.

A lifeless pitch resulted in 1,013 runs being scored in 22 hours for the loss of 21 wickets. The match provided
Statham with the first of his 252 Test wickets and Bailey with his only hundred. Washbrook, given out 'lbw',
was recalled after Hadlee had told the umpire that the ball had hit bat before pad. Sutcliffe and Reid added 131
in what remains New Zealand's highest second-wicket partnership of this series. Moir, leg-breaks and googlies,
achieved his best analysis for New Zealand in his first match.

NEW ZEALAND

B. Sutcliffe	b Statham	116		
V.J. Scott	b Bailey	16	(5) not out	10
J.R. Reid	b Wright	50		
W.M. Wallace	c Brown b Bedser	66		
W.A. Hadlee*	c Brown b Bailey	50		
A.R. MacGibbon	lbw b Wright	4	(1) c Evans b Simpson	8
F.L.H. Mooney†	st Evans b Tattersall	39		
T.B. Burtt	b Brown	42		
A.M. Moir	not out	0	(4) not out	7
J.A. Hayes	⎫ did not bat		(2) lbw b Washbrook	19
G.F. Cresswell	⎭		(3) c Evans b Simpson	2
Extras	(B 16, LB 16, W 1, NB 1)	34		
Total	(8 wickets declared)	**417**	(3 wickets)	**46**

ENGLAND

L. Hutton	b Moir	28
C. Washbrook	c Mooney b Hayes	58
R.T. Simpson	c Wallace b Moir	81
D.C.S. Compton	b Burtt	79
T.E. Bailey	not out	134
F.R. Brown*	c Scott b Cresswell	62
T.G. Evans†	c Hayes b Moir	19
A.V. Bedser	c Hayes b Moir	5
R. Tattersall	b Moir	2
D.V.P. Wright	c MacGibbon b Cresswell	45
J.B. Statham	b Moir	9
Extras	(B 20, LB 8)	28
Total		**550**

ENGLAND	O	M	R	W	O	M	R	W
Bedser	41	10	83	1				
Bailey	30	9	51	2				
Statham	24	6	47	1				
Tattersall	16	3	48	1				
Wright	27	2	99	2				
Brown	15·2	3	34	1				
Compton	4	0	21	0	2	0	10	0
Washbrook					4	0	25	1
Simpson					4	1	4	2
Hutton					3	0	7	0
NEW ZEALAND								
Hayes	43	11	85	1				
Reid	10	2	29	0				
MacGibbon	27	6	74	0				
Cresswell	34	10	75	2				
Moir	56·3	16	155	6				
Burtt	49	23	99	1				
Scott	2	0	5	0				

FALL OF WICKETS

Wkt	NZ 1st	E 1st	NZ 2nd
1st	37	57	9
2nd	168	108	29
3rd	203	237	29
4th	297	264	–
5th	307	356	–
6th	335	388	–
7th	415	398	–
8th	417	406	–
9th	–	523	–
10th	–	550	–

Umpires: E.G. Brook (1) and S.B. Tonkinson (1).

Close: 1st day – NZ(1) 247-3 (Wallace 32, Hadlee 20); 2nd – E(1) 67-1 (Washbrook 31, Simpson 0); 3rd – E(1)
317-4 (Bailey 19, Brown 39).

NEW ZEALAND v ENGLAND 1950–51 (2nd Test)

Played at Basin Reserve, Wellington, on 24 (*no play*), 26, 27, 28 March.
Toss: New Zealand.   Result: ENGLAND won by six wickets.
Debuts: Nil.

Torrential rain prevented play until the second morning and an earthquake tested the ground shortly after lunch on the last day. Moir emulated W.W. Armstrong (*Test No. 143*) by bowling two consecutive overs – the last before tea on the fourth day and the first afterwards. Left to score 88 in 145 minutes, England won with 14 minutes to spare.

NEW ZEALAND

B. Sutcliffe	c and b Wright	20		b Tattersall	11
V.J. Scott	lbw b Bailey	0	(7)	c Sheppard b Bedser	60
J.R. Reid	b Brown	11		b Tattersall	11
W.M. Wallace	b Wright	15	(5)	c Brown b Bailey	1
W.A. Hadlee*	lbw b Wright	15	(4)	c Bailey b Tattersall	9
A.R. MacGibbon	c Brown b Wright	20		lbw b Tattersall	0
F.L.H. Mooney†	c Compton b Bailey	3	(8)	b Tattersall	0
T.B. Burtt	c Parkhouse b Wright	3	(2)	b Tattersall	31
A.M. Moir	not out	26		c Bedser b Bailey	26
J.A. Hayes	b Tattersall	0		b Bailey	5
G.F. Cresswell	run out	0		not out	0
Extras	(B 3, LB 5, NB 4)	12		(B 30, LB 2, NB 3)	35
Total		**125**			**189**

ENGLAND

L. Hutton	c Reid b Moir	57		c Hadlee b Cresswell	29
R.T. Simpson	b Moir	6		b Burtt	5
W.G.A. Parkhouse	b Burtt	2		c and b Burtt	20
D.S. Sheppard	b Hayes	3	(5)	not out	4
D.C.S. Compton	b Burtt	10	(4)	b Cresswell	18
F.R. Brown*	b Hayes	47		not out	10
T.E. Bailey	st Mooney b Burtt	29			
T.G. Evans†	b Cresswell	13			
A.V. Bedser	b Cresswell	28			
D.V.P. Wright	not out	9			
R. Tattersall	b Cresswell	1			
Extras	(B 11, LB 8, NB 3)	22		(B 1, LB 4)	5
Total		**227**		(4 wickets)	**91**

ENGLAND	O	M	R	W	O	M	R	W		FALL OF WICKETS			
Bailey	11	2	18	2	14·2	1	43	3		NZ	E	NZ	E
Bedser	19	6	21	0	24	10	34	1	*Wkt*	*1st*	*1st*	*2nd*	*2nd*
Brown	6	1	10	1	1	0	1	0	1st	1	10	25	16
Tattersall	15	9	16	1	21	6	44	6	2nd	25	31	62	56
Wright	19	3	48	5	12	2	32	0	3rd	37	40	76	60
									4th	68	69	82	80
NEW ZEALAND									5th	69	140	82	–
Hayes	20	2	44	2					6th	83	144	98	–
Cresswell	15	6	18	3	18	8	31	2	7th	94	173	105	–
Moir	28	5	65	2	6	0	19	0	8th	102	216	156	–
Burtt	27	14	46	3	21·2	10	36	2	9th	105	218	187	–
MacGibbon	7	0	32	0					10th	125	227	189	–

Umpires: J. McLellan (1) and M.F. Pengelly (3).

Close: 1st day – no play; 2nd – E(1) 42-3 (Hutton 18, Compton 0); 3rd – NZ(2) 32-1 (Burtt 17, Reid 0).

ENGLAND v SOUTH AFRICA 1951 (1st Test)

Played at Trent Bridge, Nottingham, on 7, 8, 9, 11, 12 June.
Toss: South Africa.   Result: SOUTH AFRICA won by 71 runs.
Debuts: England – W. Watson; South Africa – G.W.A. Chubb, D.J. McGlew, C.B. van Ryneveld, J.H.B. Waite.

South Africa ended their abortive run of 28 Tests without victory since 1935. Nourse batted in pain for 550 minutes and South Africa's first double-century against England – his thumb had been fractured three weeks earlier. His seventh hundred against England enabled him to equal the record shared by H.W. Taylor and B. Mitchell. He played no further part in the match after his innings, E.A.B. Rowan taking over as captain. Simpson remains the only Nottinghamshire player to score a hundred for England at Trent Bridge.

SOUTH AFRICA

E.A.B. Rowan	c Evans b Brown	17		c Ikin b Bedser	11
J.H.B. Waite†	run out	76		c Ikin b Tattersall	5
D.J. McGlew	b Brown	40		st Evans b Bedser	5
A.D. Nourse*	run out	208		absent hurt	–
J.E. Cheetham	c Ikin b Bedser	31		b Bedser	28
G.M. Fullerton	c Compton b Tattersall	54	(4)	c Brown b Tattersall	13
C.B. van Ryneveld	lbw b Bedser	32	(6)	c Hutton b Bedser	22
A.M.B. Rowan	b Bedser	2	(7)	c Evans b Bedser	5
N.B.F. Mann	c Tattersall b Wardle	1	(8)	b Tattersall	2
G.W.A. Chubb	not out	0	(9)	not out	11
C.N. McCarthy	not out	1	(10)	b Bedser	5
Extras	(B 3, LB 17, NB 1)	21		(B 4, LB 9, NB 1)	14
Total	(9 wickets declared)	**483**			**121**

ENGLAND

L.Hutton	c Waite b A.M.B. Rowan	63		c and b A.M.B. Rowan	11
J.T. Ikin	c McCarthy b Chubb	1		b Mann	33
R.T. Simpson	c Waite b McCarthy	137		c and b A.M.B. Rowan	7
D.C.S. Compton	c Waite b McCarthy	112		lbw b A.M.B. Rowan	5
W. Watson	lbw b McCarthy	57		lbw b Mann	5
F.R. Brown*	c Fullerton b Chubb	29	(7)	c McCarthy b A.M.B. Rowan	7
T.G. Evans†	c sub (R.A. McLean) b Chubb	5	(8)	c Van Ryneveld b Mann	0
J.H. Wardle	c Fullerton b Chubb	5	(9)	c sub (R.A.McLean) b A.M.B. Rowan	30
T.E. Bailey	c Fullerton b McCarthy	3	(6)	c Waite b Mann	11
A.V. Bedser	not out	0		b McCarthy	0
R. Tattersall	did not bat			not out	0
Extras	(B 4, LB 3)	7		(LB 5)	5
Total	(9 wickets declared)	**419**			**114**

ENGLAND	O	M	R	W	O	M	R	W
Bedser	63	18	122	3	22·4	8	37	6
Bailey	45	13	102	0	2	0	10	0
Brown	34	11	74	2				
Tattersall	47	20	80	1	23	6	56	3
Wardle	49	21	77	1	4	3	4	0
Compton	2	0	7	0				
SOUTH AFRICA								
McCarthy	48	10	104	4	8	1	8	1
Chubb	46·2	12	146	4	6	2	9	0
A.M.B. Rowan	46	10	101	1	27·2	4	68	5
Mann	20	5	51	0	24	16	24	4
Van Ryneveld	3	0	10	0				

FALL OF WICKETS

Wkt	SA 1st	E 1st	SA 2nd	E 2nd
1st	31	4	12	23
2nd	107	148	20	41
3rd	189	234	24	57
4th	273	375	52	63
5th	394	382	87	67
6th	465	395	98	80
7th	467	410	103	83
8th	476	419	106	84
9th	482	419	121	110
10th	–	–	–	114

Umpires: H.G. Baldwin (6) and F. Chester (40).

Close: 1st day – SA(1) 239-3 (Nourse 76, Cheetham 13); 2nd – E(1) 4-1 (Hutton 3); 3rd – E(1) 251-3 (Compton 46, Watson 4); 4th – SA(2) 95-5 (Van Ryneveld 20, A.M.B. Rowan 0).

ENGLAND v SOUTH AFRICA 1951 (2nd Test)

Played at Lord's, London, on 21, 22, 23 June.
Toss: England.   Result: ENGLAND won by ten wickets.
Debuts: Nil.

On a rain-affected pitch, Tattersall's off-spin accounted for nine of the 14 wickets which fell on the second day. He achieved the best innings and match figures of his Test career. England drew level in the rubber at 2.20 on the third afternoon.

ENGLAND

L. Hutton	lbw b McCarthy	12	not out	12
J.T. Ikin	b Mann	51	not out	4
R.T. Simpson	lbw b McCarthy	26		
D.C.S. Compton	lbw b McCarthy	79		
W. Watson	c McCarthy b Chubb	79		
F.R. Brown*	b Chubb	1		
T.G. Evans†	c Fullerton b McCarthy	0		
J.H. Wardle	lbw b Chubb	18		
A.V. Bedser	not out	26		
J.B. Statham	b Chubb	1		
R. Tattersall	b Chubb	1		
Extras	(B 8, LB 9)	17		
Total		**311**	(0 wickets)	**16**

SOUTH AFRICA

E.A.B. Rowan	c Ikin b Tattersall	24	c Ikin b Statham	10
J.H.B. Waite†	c Hutton b Wardle	15	c Compton b Tattersall	17
D.J. McGlew	c Evans b Tattersall	3	b Tattersall	2
A.D. Nourse*	c Watson b Tattersall	20	lbw b Wardle	3
J.E. Cheetham	c Hutton b Tattersall	15	b Statham	54
G.M. Fullerton	b Tattersall	12	lbw b Bedser	60
C.B. van Ryneveld	lbw b Wardle	0	c Ikin b Tattersall	18
A.M.B. Rowan	c Ikin b Tattersall	3	c Brown b Bedser	10
N.B.F. Mann	c Brown b Tattersall	14	c Brown b Tattersall	13
G.W.A. Chubb	c Tattersall b Wardle	5	b Tattersall	3
C.N. McCarthy	not out	1	not out	2
Extras	(LB 3)	3	(B 11, LB 8)	19
Total		**115**		**211**

SOUTH AFRICA	O	M	R	W	O	M	R	W
McCarthy	23	2	76	4				
Chubb	34·4	9	77	5				
A.M.B. Rowan	13	1	63	0				
Mann	32	12	51	1				
Van Ryneveld	5	0	27	0				
Nourse					2	0	9	0
E.A.B. Rowan					1·5	0	7	0
ENGLAND								
Bedser	8	5	7	0	24	8	53	2
Statham	6	3	7	0	18	6	33	2
Tattersall	28	10	52	7	32·2	14	49	5
Wardle	22·5	10	46	3	20	5	44	1
Compton					2	0	13	0

FALL OF WICKETS

Wkt	E 1st	SA 1st	SA 2nd	E 2nd
1st	20	25	21	–
2nd	89	38	29	–
3rd	103	47	32	–
4th	225	72	58	–
5th	226	88	152	–
6th	231	91	160	–
7th	265	91	178	–
8th	299	103	196	–
9th	301	112	200	–
10th	311	115	211	–

Umpires: H. Elliott (2) and F.S. Lee (5).

Close: 1st day – SA(1) 4-0 (E.A.B. Rowan 0, Waite 4); 2nd – SA(2) 137-4 (Cheetham 46, Fullerton 50).

ENGLAND v SOUTH AFRICA 1951 (3rd Test)

Played at Old Trafford, Manchester, on 5, 6 (*no play*), 7, 9, 10 July.
Toss: South Africa.   Result: ENGLAND won by nine wickets.
Debuts: England – T.W. Graveney; South Africa – R.A. McLean.

Although Bedser took full advantage of a pitch livened by heavy rain before the match, England had much the worst of batting conditions when play resumed on the third day. The medium-paced swing bowling of Chubb accounted for five or more wickets in an innings for the second successive Test. Aged 40 and playing in his only Test rubber, he bowled most overs and took most wickets on the South Africans' tour. Hutton narrowly missed becoming the first to score his 100th first-class hundred in a Test match.

SOUTH AFRICA

E.A.B. Rowan	c Brown b Bedser	0	c Ikin b Laker	57
J.H.B. Waite†	c Ikin b Bedser	1	b Statham	0
C.B. van Ryneveld	lbw b Tattersall	40	b Laker	7
A.D. Nourse*	c Ikin b Bedser	29	c Evans b Tattersall	20
J.E. Cheetham	c Hutton b Bedser	20	b Bedser	46
G.M. Fullerton	c Hutton b Bedser	0	c Tattersall b Laker	10
R.A. McLean	b Laker	20	c Ikin b Bedser	19
A.M.B. Rowan	b Statham	17	lbw b Bedser	3
N.B.F. Mann	b Bedser	0	b Bedser	4
G.W.A. Chubb	not out	15	b Bedser	1
C.N. McCarthy	c Ikin b Bedser	0	not out	0
Extras	(LB 14, NB 2)	16	(B 13, LB 10 NB 1)	24
Total		**158**		**191**

ENGLAND

L. Hutton	c Van Ryneveld b A.M.B. Rowan	27	not out	98
J.T. Ikin	c Cheetham b Chubb	22	b Mann	38
R.T. Simpson	st Waite b Mann	11	not out	4
T.W. Graveney	b A.M.B. Rowan	15		
W. Watson	b Chubb	21		
F.R. Brown*	c Van Ryneveld b A.M.B. Rowan	42		
T.G. Evans†	c Waite b Chubb	2		
J.C. Laker	c Nourse b Chubb	27		
A.V. Bedser	not out	30		
R. Tattersall	c Cheetham b Chubb	1		
J.B. Statham	c Cheetham b Chubb	1		
Extras	(B 4, LB 8)	12	(LB 1, NB 1)	2
Total		**211**	(1 wicket)	**142**

ENGLAND	O	M	R	W	O	M	R	W
Bedser	32·3	10	58	7	24·2	8	54	5
Statham	7	2	8	1	17	3	30	1
Laker	27	7	47	1	19	3	42	3
Tattersall	18	6	29	1	18	3	41	1
SOUTH AFRICA								
McCarthy	14	4	36	0	19	4	46	0
Chubb	26·3	7	51	6	23	6	72	0
A.M.B. Rowan	29	4	75	3	7	1	17	0
Mann	16	5	37	1	2·3	1	5	1

FALL OF WICKETS

Wkt	SA 1st	E 1st	SA 2nd	E 2nd
1st	0	30	4	121
2nd	12	58	19	–
3rd	66	70	60	–
4th	87	91	145	–
5th	88	127	155	–
6th	105	143	168	–
7th	129	147	181	–
8th	132	200	185	–
9th	143	207	190	–
10th	158	211	191	–

Umpires: H.G. Baldwin (7) and F.S. Lee (6).

Close: 1st day – E(1) 50-1 (Hutton 24, Simpson 3); 2nd – no play; 3rd – SA(2) 121-3 (E.A.B Rowan 44, Cheetham 35); 4th – E(2) 36-0 (Hutton 28, Ikin 8).

ENGLAND v SOUTH AFRICA 1951 (4th Test)

Played at Headingley, Leeds, on 26, 27, 28, 30, 31 (*no play*) July.
Toss: South Africa.   Result: MATCH DRAWN.
Debuts: England – D.V. Brennan, F.A. Lowson, P.B.H. May; South Africa – P.N.F. Mansell.

Eric Rowan's 236 remains South Africa's highest score against England (only E. Paynter with 243 at Durban in 1938-39 has scored more in this series), and his partnership of 198 with Van Ryneveld is still the South African second-wicket record in all Tests. Their total of 538 is the highest against England. May is the only England batsman to score a hundred in his first Test, that match being at home against South Africa.

SOUTH AFRICA

E.A.B. Rowan	c Bedser b Brown	236	not out	60
J.H.B. Waite†	lbw b Bedser	13	not out	25
C.B. van Ryneveld	c and b Hilton	83		
A.D. Nourse*	lbw b Brown	13		
J.E. Cheetham	b Bedser	7		
R.A. McLean	run out	67		
P.N.F. Mansell	c Tattersall b Hilton	90		
A.M.B. Rowan	b Brown	9		
N.B.F. Mann	b Tattersall	2		
G.W.A. Chubb	c Lowson b Hilton	11		
C.N. McCarthy	not out	0		
Extras	(B 1, LB 6)	7	(LB 2)	2
Total		**538**	(0 wickets)	**87**

ENGLAND

L. Hutton	b Van Ryneveld	100
F.A. Lowson	c Mansell b A.M.B. Rowan	58
P.B.H. May	b A.M.B. Rowan	138
D.C.S. Compton	lbw b A.M.B. Rowan	25
W. Watson	b Chubb	32
T.E. Bailey	b Mann	95
F.R. Brown*	c E.A.B. Rowan b A.M.B. Rowan	2
A.V. Bedser	b Mann	8
D.V. Brennan†	b Mann	16
R. Tattersall	c E.A.B. Rowan b A.M.B. Rowan	4
M.J. Hilton	not out	9
Extras	(B 10, LB 7, NB 1)	18
Total		**505**

ENGLAND	O	M	R	W	O	M	R	W
Bedser	58	14	113	2	4	1	5	0
Bailey	17	4	48	0	1	0	8	0
Brown	38	10	107	3	11	2	26	0
Tattersall	60	23	83	1	16	9	13	0
Hilton	61·3	18	176	3	10	5	17	0
Compton	1	0	4	0	7	1	16	0
SOUTH AFRICA								
McCarthy	41	10	81	0				
Chubb	43	12	99	1				
A.M.B. Rowan	68	17	174	5				
Mann	60·5	23	96	3				
Mansell	4	0	11	0				
Van Ryneveld	8	0	26	1				

FALL OF WICKETS

Wkt	SA 1st	E 1st	SA 2nd
1st	40	99	–
2nd	238	228	–
3rd	267	266	–
4th	286	345	–
5th	394	387	–
6th	480	391	–
7th	498	400	–
8th	505	432	–
9th	538	445	–
10th	538	505	–

Umpires: D. Davies (9) and H. Elliott (3).

Close: 1st day – SA(1) 282-3 (E.A.B. Rowan 160, Cheetham 7); 2nd – E(1) 37-0 (Hutton 9, Lowson 27); 3rd – E(1) 325-3 (May 110, Watson 21); 4th – SA(2) 87-0 (E.A.B. Rowan 60, Waite 25).

ENGLAND v SOUTH AFRICA 1951 (5th Test)

Played at Kennington Oval, London, on 16, 17, 18 August.
Toss: South Africa.   Result: ENGLAND won by four wickets.
Debuts: South Africa – W.R. Endean.

A close match on a pitch which took spin from the start brought England's first win at The Oval since 1938. It also provided Test cricket with its only instance of a batsman dismissed for obstructing the field; there had been only four previous instances in first-class cricket and none for 50 years. A ball from Athol Rowan ballooned up from the bat's top edge and Hutton, in fending it off his wicket with his bat, prevented Endean from making a catch. While Laker's off-breaks accounted for ten wickets, South Africa were deprived of the left-arm spin of 'Tufty' Mann, stricken by the illness from which he was to die 11 months later. This match marked the end of the Test careers of Nourse, McCarthy, Chubb and the brothers Rowan.

SOUTH AFRICA

E.A.B. Rowan	c Hutton b Brown	55	lbw b Laker	45
W.R. Endean†	c Brown b Laker	31	lbw b Bedser	7
C.B. van Ryneveld	st Brennan b Laker	10	lbw b Laker	5
A.D. Nourse*	lbw b Brown	4	b Laker	4
J.E. Cheetham	lbw b Laker	0	c Hutton b Tattersall	18
R.A. McLean	c May b Laker	14	c Lowson b Laker	18
P.N.F. Mansell	b Tattersall	8	lbw b Laker	0
A.M.B. Rowan	c Laker b Bedser	41	not out	15
G.W.A. Chubb	b Bedser	10	c Hutton b Bedser	7
M.G. Melle	b Shackleton	5	b Laker	17
C.N. McCarthy	not out	4	b Bedser	0
Extras	(B 11, LB 8, NB 1)	20	(B 11, LB 7)	18
Total		**202**		**154**

ENGLAND

L. Hutton	lbw b A.M.B. Rowan	28	obstructing the field	27
F.A. Lowson	c Endean b Melle	0	c Van Ryneveld b A.M.B. Rowan	37
P.B.H. May	b Chubb	33	c E.A.B. Rowan b A.M.B. Rowan	0
D.C.S. Compton	b McCarthy	73	c Van Ryneveld b Chubb	18
W. Watson	run out	31	c Endean b Chubb	15
F.R. Brown*	c Van Ryneveld b A.M.B. Rowan	1	lbw b Chubb	40
J.C. Laker	b Chubb	6	not out	13
D. Shackleton	c Van Ryneveld b Melle	14	not out	5
A.V. Bedser	c Endean b Melle	2		
D.V. Brennan†	lbw b Melle	0		
R. Tattersall	not out	0		
Extras	(LB 4, NB 2)	6	(B 5, LB 3, NB 1)	9
Total		**194**	(6 wickets)	**164**

ENGLAND	O	M	R	W	O	M	R	W		FALL OF WICKETS			
Bedser	19·3	6	36	2	19·5	6	32	3		SA	E	SA	E
Shackleton	15	5	20	1	10	2	19	0	Wkt	1st	1st	2nd	2nd
Tattersall	14	7	26	1	5	1	10	1	1st	66	2	15	53
Laker	37	12	64	4	28	8	55	6	2nd	106	51	35	53
Brown	20	10	31	2	13	5	20	0	3rd	106	79	57	84
Compton	1	0	5	0					4th	106	128	84	90
									5th	126	134	106	132
SOUTH AFRICA									6th	131	145	111	151
McCarthy	17	0	45	1	7	0	17	0	7th	146	173	116	–
Melle	10	6	9	4	3	0	8	0	8th	175	189	130	–
A.M.B. Rowan	27	9	44	2	24·1	2	77	2	9th	186	190	153	–
Chubb	30	5	70	2	28	10	53	3	10th	202	194	154	–
Van Ryneveld	3	0	20	0									

Umpires: F. Chester (41) and D. Davies (10).

Close: 1st day – E(1) 51-2 (May 22); 2nd – SA(2) 68-3 (E.A.B. Rowan 36, Cheetham 7).

INDIA v ENGLAND 1951–52 (1st Test)

Played at Feroz Shah Kotla, Delhi, on 2, 3, 4, 6, 7 November.
Toss: England.   Result: MATCH DRAWN.
Debuts: India – P.G. Joshi, Pankaj Roy; England – D.B. Carr, N.D. Howard, D. Kenyon,
F. Ridgway, R.T. Spooner. *Roy is given his full name to differentiate him from his son, Pranab, who made his debut in Test No. 916.*

An heroic rearguard action led by Watkins, who batted for nine hours and was the first England player to bat throughout a whole day's play in a Test in India, enabled England to draw a match which India should have won. Merchant and Hazare set a new India record for any wicket against England by adding 211 for the third wicket. Previously published scores of this match give Watkins 138 and Shackleton 20, but the official MCC Scorebook confirms the second innings scores shown here.

ENGLAND

J.D.B. Robertson	lbw b Shinde	50	c Phadkar b Mankad	22
F.A. Lowson	lbw b Phadkar	4	c Phadkar b Mankad	68
D. Kenyon	b Shinde	35	c Roy b Shinde	6
D.B. Carr	c Joshi b Shinde	14	(5) c Umrigar b Shinde	76
A.J. Watkins	c Joshi b Mankad	40	(4) not out	137
R.T. Spooner†	hit wkt b Shinde	11	b Mankad	1
N.D. Howard*	st Joshi b Mankad	13	lbw b Mankad	9
D. Shackleton	st Joshi b Mankad	10	not out	21
J.B. Statham	b Shinde	4		
R. Tattersall	not out	4		
F. Ridgway	b Shinde	15		
Extras	(LB 3)	3	(B 18, LB 7, W 1, NB 2)	28
Total		**203**	(6 wickets)	**368**

INDIA

V.M Merchant	b Statham	154
Pankaj Roy	lbw b Shackleton	12
P.R. Umrigar	run out	21
V.S. Hazare*	not out	164
D.G. Phadkar	run out	3
M.H. Mankad	c Spooner b Tattersall	4
R.S. Modi	lbw b Tattersall	7
H.R. Adhikari	not out	38
S.G. Shinde	)	
P.G. Joshi†	) did not bat	
N.R. Chowdhury	)	
Extras	(B 12, LB 2, NB 1)	15
Total	(6 wickets declared)	**418**

INDIA	O	M	R	W	O	M	R	W		FALL OF WICKETS		
										E	I	E
Phadkar	11	4	26	1	14	3	28	0				
Chowdhury	18	4	30	0	31	11	45	0	*Wkt*	*1st*	*1st*	*2nd*
Hazare	5	5	0	0	12	4	24	0	1st	9	18	61
Mankad	33	15	53	3	76	47	58	4	2nd	79	64	78
Shinde	35·3	9	91	6	73	26	162	2	3rd	102	275	116
Umrigar					6	1	8	0	4th	111	278	274
Modi					5	1	14	0	5th	153	292	275
Roy					4	3	1	0	6th	161	328	309
									7th	175	–	–
ENGLAND									8th	184	–	–
Statham	21	4	49	1					9th	184	–	–
Ridgway	20	1	55	0					10th	203	–	–
Watkins	31	7	60	0								
Shackleton	29	7	76	1								
Tattersall	53	17	95	2								
Carr	16	4	56	0								
Robertson	5	1	12	0								

Umpires: B.J. Mohoni (4) and M.G. Vijayasarathi (1).

Close: 1st day – E(1) 203 all out; 2nd – I(1) 186-2 (Merchant 106, Hazare 45); 3rd – I(1) 418-6 (Hazare 164, Adhikari 38); 4th – E(2) 202-3 (Watkins 51, Carr 44).

INDIA v ENGLAND 1951–52 (2nd Test)

Played at Brabourne Stadium, Bombay, on 14, 15, 16, 18, 19 December.
Toss: India.   Result: MATCH DRAWN.
Debuts: India – C.D. Gopinath, M.K. Mantri; England – E. Leadbeater.

Hazare scored his second consecutive Test hundred and took his aggregate against England to 325 before he was dismissed by a bowler. Edric Leadbeater, flown out as a replacement for A.E.G. Rhodes (hernia), played for England before being capped by his county; he played for Yorkshire and Warwickshire without winning a 1st XI cap. India's total of 485 was their highest against England. Graveney batted for $8\frac{1}{4}$ hours in compiling England's highest score in India until 1976-77 (*Test No. 788*).

INDIA

Pankaj Roy	c Kenyon b Statham	140	lbw b Ridgway		0
M.K. Mantri†	c Spooner b Statham	39	c Spooner b Ridgway		7
P.R. Umrigar	lbw b Leadbeater	8	c Watkins b Statham		38
V.S. Hazare*	run out	155	c sub (C.J. Poole) b Watkins		6
L. Amarnath	c Howard b Tattersall	32	c Howard b Watkins		4
C.T. Sarwate	b Tattersall	18	run out		16
H.R. Adhikari	c Spooner b Tattersall	25	c Howard b Tattersall		15
C.D. Gopinath	not out	50	c Leadbeater b Tattersall		42
S.W. Sohoni	c Robertson b Statham	6	(10) run out		28
M.H. Mankad	b Statham	0	(9) b Watkins		41
S.G. Shinde	not out	8	not out		3
Extras	(LB 4)	4	(B 6, LB 2)		8
Total	(9 wickets declared)	**485**			**208**

ENGLAND

F.A. Lowson	c Mantri b Sohoni	5	c Sohoni b Gopinath		22
J.D.B. Robertson	c Amarnath b Mankad	44			
T.W. Graveney	c Adhikari b Shinde	175	not out		25
R.T. Spooner†	lbw b Hazare	46	not out		5
D. Kenyon	lbw b Amarnath	21	(2) lbw b Sohoni		2
A.J. Watkins	c and b Mankad	80			
N.D. Howard*	c Umrigar b Mankad	20			
E. Leadbeater	lbw b Mankad	2			
J.B. Statham	c Mankad b Amarnath	27			
R. Tattersall	not out	10			
F. Ridgway	c and b Amarnath	5			
Extras	(B 10, LB 11)	21	(LB 1)		1
Total		**456**	(2 wickets)		**55**

ENGLAND	O	M	R	W	O	M	R	W		FALL OF WICKETS			
Statham	29	5	96	4	20	11	30	1		I	E	I	E
Ridgway	32	5	137	0	16	3	33	2	*Wkt*	*1st*	*1st*	*2nd*	*2nd*
Watkins	32	2	97	0	13	4	20	3	1st	75	18	2	3
Leadbeater	11	2	38	1	14·1	4	62	0	2nd	99	79	13	43
Tattersall	34	8	112	3	20	6	55	2	3rd	286	166	24	–
Robertson	1	0	1	0					4th	368	233	34	–
									5th	388	381	72	–
INDIA									6th	397	389	77	–
Sohoni	30	7	72	1	13	5	16	1	7th	460	407	88	–
Amarnath	34·1	9	61	3	5	1	6	0	8th	471	408	159	–
Shinde	53	13	151	1	5	0	11	0	9th	471	448	177	–
Mankad	57	22	91	4	5	1	10	0	10th	–	456	208	–
Sarwate	13	2	27	0									
Hazare	17	5	30	1									
Umrigar	3	1	3	0									
Gopinath					8	2	11	1					

Umpires: M.M. Naidu (1) and J.R. Patel (2).

Close: 1st day – E(1) 286-3 (Hazare 95); 2nd – E(1) 40-1 (Robertson 29, Graveney 2); 3rd – E(1) 263-4 (Graveney 120, Watkins 17); 4th – I(2) 42-4 (Umrigar 21, Sarwate 4).

INDIA v ENGLAND 1951–52 (3rd Test)

Played at Eden Gardens, Calcutta, on 30, 31 December, 1, 3, 4 January.
Toss: England.   Result: MATCH DRAWN.
Debuts: India – R.V. Divecha, S.P. Gupte, V.L. Manjrekar; England – C.J. Poole.

An uninterrupted match occupying $27\frac{1}{2}$ hours produced only 1,041 runs and, not surprisingly, a draw. On a lifeless pitch the second, third and fourth days produced 190, 192 and 185 runs respectively. Roy and Mankad achieved the first century opening partnership in any match against this touring team.

ENGLAND

J.D.B. Robertson	c Phadkar b Divecha	13	st Sen b Mankad	22
R.T. Spooner†	c Sen b Mankad	71	b Mankad	92
T.W. Graveney	c Amarnath b Divecha	24	c Sen b Divecha	21
A.J. Watkins	c Sen b Phadkar	68	b Divecha	2
D. Kenyon	c Manjrekar b Mankad	3	b Phadkar	0
C.J. Poole	c Divecha b Phadkar	55	not out	69
N.D. Howard*	c Amarnath b Mankad	23	not out	20
J.B. Statham	b Phadkar	1		
E. Leadbeater	run out	38		
F. Ridgway	st Sen b Mankad	24		
R. Tattersall	not out	5		
Extras	(B 4, LB 1, W 1, NB 11)	17	(B 13, LB 6, W 2, NB 5)	26
Total		**342**	(5 wickets declared)	**252**

INDIA

Pankaj Roy	c Spooner b Ridgway	42	not out	31
M.H. Mankad	c Tattersall b Leadbeater	59	not out	71
P.R. Umrigar	c Howard b Ridgway	10		
V.S. Hazare*	b Tattersall	2		
L. Amarnath	b Tattersall	0		
D.G. Phadkar	c Leadbeater b Ridgway	115		
V.L. Manjrekar	b Tattersall	48		
C.D. Gopinath	c Robertson b Ridgway	19		
R.V. Divecha	c Watkins b Tattersall	26		
S.P. Gupte	c Leadbeater b Statham	0		
P. Sen†	not out	7		
Extras	(B 3, LB 10, W 1, NB 2)	16	(B 1)	1
Total		**344**	(0 wickets)	**103**

INDIA	O	M	R	W	O	M	R	W
Phadkar	38	11	89	3	20	7	27	1
Divecha	33	9	60	2	25	7	55	2
Amarnath	20	5	35	0	22	5	43	0
Mankad	52·5	16	89	4	35	13	64	2
Gupte	13	0	43	0	5	0	14	0
Hazare	3	0	9	0	9	4	11	0
Umrigar					4	1	12	0
ENGLAND								
Statham	27	10	46	1	4	0	8	0
Ridgway	38·1	10	83	4	2	1	8	0
Tattersall	48	13	104	4	4	2	4	0
Leadbeater	15	2	64	1	8	0	54	0
Watkins	21	9	31	0				
Poole					5	1	9	0
Robertson					5	1	10	0
Graveney					1	0	9	0

FALL OF WICKETS

	E	I	E	I
Wkt	1st	1st	2nd	2nd
1st	22	72	52	–
2nd	76	90	93	–
3rd	133	93	99	–
4th	139	93	102	–
5th	246	144	184	–
6th	247	220	–	–
7th	259	272	–	–
8th	290	320	–	–
9th	332	327	–	–
10th	342	344	–	–

Umpires: A.R. Joshi (4) and B.J. Mohoni (5).

Close: 1st day – E(1) 214-4 (Watkins 53, Poole 43); 2nd – I(1) 65-0 (Roy 40, Mankad 20); 3rd – I(1) 257-6 (Phadkar 72, Gopinath 11); 4th – E(2) 98-2 (Spooner 39, Watkins 1).

INDIA v ENGLAND 1951–52 (4th Test)

Played at Green Park, Kanpur, on 12, 13, 14 January.
Toss: India.   Result: ENGLAND won by eight wickets.
Debuts: Nil.

On a spinners' pitch, England gained a convincing win in only three days through Hilton and Tattersall, the latter taking three wickets with his first eight balls in the Test, the first to be staged at Kanpur (formerly Cawnpore). In the second innings the spinners opened England's attack after rubbing the ball on the ground to remove the shine, Hilton taking the first five wickets to fall and recording his best figures for England.

INDIA

Pankaj Roy	b Tattersall	37		c Ridgway b Hilton	14
M.H. Mankad	b Tattersall	19		c Statham b Hilton	7
P.R. Umrigar	b Tattersall	0	(5)	c Spooner b Robertson	36
V.S. Hazare*	c Ridgway b Tattersall	0		b Hilton	0
D.G. Phadkar	b Tattersall	8	(6)	lbw b Hilton	2
H.R. Adhikari	b Hilton	6	(7)	c Lowson b Tattersall	60
V.L. Manjrekar	c Graveney b Hilton	6	(3)	c Ridgway b Hilton	20
C.S. Nayudu	st Spooner b Hilton	21		b Robertson	0
P.G. Joshi†	b Tattersall	4	(10)	run out	0
S.G. Shinde	not out	5	(9)	c Lowson b Tattersall	14
Ghulam Ahmed	c Poole b Hilton	6		not out	2
Extras	(B 8, LB 1)	9		(B 2)	2
Total		**121**			**157**

ENGLAND

F.A. Lowson	hit wkt b Mankad	26		c Adhikari b Ghulam Ahmed	12
R.T. Spooner†	b Shinde	21		b Mankad	0
T.W. Graveney	b Mankad	6		not out	48
J.D.B. Robertson	lbw b Mankad	21		not out	5
A.J. Watkins	c Joshi b Ghulam Ahmed	66			
M.J. Hilton	st Joshi b Ghulam Ahmed	10			
C.J. Poole	b Ghulam Ahmed	19			
N.D. Howard*	b Mankad	1			
J.B. Statham	not out	12			
F. Ridgway	b Ghulam Ahmed	5			
R. Tattersall	st Joshi b Ghulam Ahmed	2			
Extras	(B 13, LB 1)	14		(B 11)	11
Total		**203**		**(2 wickets)**	**76**

ENGLAND	O	M	R	W	O	M	R	W
Statham	6	3	10	0				
Ridgway	7	1	16	0				
Watkins	5	3	6	0				
Hilton	22·5	10	32	4	32	11	61	5
Tattersall	21	3	48	6	27·5	7	77	2
Robertson					7	1	17	2
INDIA								
Phadkar	2	2	0	0	2	0	11	0
Hazare	2	0	5	0				
Ghulam Ahmed	37·1	14	70	5	10	1	10	1
Mankad	35	13	54	4	7·2	0	44	1
Shinde	17	4	46	1				
Nayudu	2	0	14	0				

FALL OF WICKETS

	I	E	I	E
Wkt	1st	1st	2nd	2nd
1st	39	46	7	1
2nd	39	57	37	57
3rd	39	60	37	–
4th	49	103	42	–
5th	66	114	44	–
6th	76	174	102	–
7th	101	181	102	–
8th	106	181	142	–
9th	110	197	143	–
10th	121	203	157	–

Umpires: J.R. Patel (3) and M.G. Vijayasarathi (2).

Close: 1st day – E(1) 63-3 (Robertson 4, Watkins 0); 2nd – I(2) 125-7 (Adhikari 37, Shinde 7).

INDIA v ENGLAND 1951–52 (5th Test)

Played at Chepauk, Madras, on 6, 8, 9, 10 February.
Toss: England.   Result: INDIA won by an innings and 8 runs.
Debuts: Nil.

After waiting for almost 20 years India gained a most emphatic first victory in their 25th Test match. Mankad's innings and match analyses were the best in any Test at Madras and remain the records for India against England. Umrigar was omitted from the original selection in favour of Adhikari. When the latter damaged his wrist in a fall the reinstated Umrigar seized a last opportunity to score his maiden Test hundred. Because of the death of King George VI on 6 February, the following day was made the rest day.

ENGLAND

F.A. Lowson	b Phadkar	1	c Mankad b Phadkar	7
R.T. Spooner†	c Phadkar b Hazare	66	lbw b Divecha	6
T.W. Graveney	st Sen b Mankad	39	c Divecha b Ghulam Ahmed	25
J.D.B. Robertson	c and b Mankad	77	lbw b Ghulam Ahmed	56
A.J. Watkins	c Gopinath b Mankad	9	c and b Mankad	48
C.J. Poole	b Mankad	15	c Divecha b Ghulam Ahmed	3
D.B. Carr*	st Sen b Mankad	40	c Mankad b Ghulam Ahmed	5
M.J. Hilton	st Sen b Mankad	0	st Sen b Mankad	15
J.B. Statham	st Sen b Mankad	6	c Gopinath b Mankad	9
F. Ridgway	lbw b Mankad	0	b Mankad	0
R. Tattersall	not out	2	not out	0
Extras	(B 4, LB 4, NB 3)	11	(B 7, LB 2)	9
Total		**266**		**183**

INDIA

Mushtaq Ali	st Spooner b Carr	22
Pankaj Roy	c Watkins b Tattersall	111
V.S. Hazare*	b Hilton	20
M.H. Mankad	c Watkins b Carr	22
L. Amarnath	c Spooner b Statham	31
D.G. Phadkar	b Hilton	61
P.R. Umrigar	not out	130
C.D. Gopinath	b Tattersall	35
R.V. Divecha	c Spooner b Ridgway	12
P. Sen†	b Watkins	2
Ghulam Ahmed	not out	1
Extras	(B 8, LB 2)	10
Total	(9 wickets declared)	**457**

INDIA	O	M	R	W	O	M	R	W
Phadkar	16	2	49	1	9	2	17	1
Divecha	12	2	27	0	7	1	21	1
Amarnath	27	6	56	0	3	0	6	0
Ghulam Ahmed	18	5	53	0	26	6	77	4
Mankad	38·5	15	55	8	30·5	9	53	4
Hazare	10	5	15	1				
ENGLAND								
Statham	19	3	54	1				
Ridgway	17	2	47	1				
Tattersall	39	13	94	2				
Hilton	40	9	100	2				
Carr	19	2	84	2				
Watkins	14	1	50	1				
Robertson	5	1	18	0				

FALL OF WICKETS

Wkt	E 1st	I 1st	E 2nd
1st	3	53	12
2nd	71	97	15
3rd	131	157	68
4th	174	191	117
5th	197	216	135
6th	244	320	159
7th	252	413	159
8th	261	430	178
9th	261	448	178
10th	266	–	183

Umpires: B.J. Mohoni (6) and M.G. Vijayasarathi (3).

Close: 1st day – E(1) 224-5 (Robertson 71, Carr 12); 2nd – I(1) 206-4 (Amarnath 27, Phadkar 3); 3rd – E(2) 12-0 (Lowson 6, Spooner 6).

AUSTRALIA v WEST INDIES 1951–52 (1st Test)

Played at Woolloongabba, Brisbane, on 9, 10, 12, 13 November.
Toss: West Indies.   Result: AUSTRALIA won by three wickets.
Debuts: Australia – G.R.A. Langley; West Indies – R.E. Marshall.

Australia narrowly won an intriguing duel with Ramadhin and Valentine whom Goddard bowled for 129·7 overs out of 150·4 (86%) in the match. Walcott was dismissed for his only duck in 74 Test innings. Umpire Barlow warned Miller for intimidation when he released a succession of navel-high short balls at Marshall.

WEST INDIES

A.F. Rae	b Lindwall	0	lbw b Johnson	25
J.B. Stollmeyer	c Langley b Johnston	8	st Langley b Johnson	10
F.M.M. Worrell	b Johnston	37	st Langley b Ring	20
E. de C. Weekes	c Langley b Ring	35	c Hole b Johnston	70
R.J. Christiani	c Ring b Lindwall	22	(6) b Ring	6
C.L. Walcott†	lbw b Lindwall	0	(8) st Langley b Ring	4
R.E. Marshall	b Johnson	28	(9) c Hassett b Miller	30
G.E. Gomez	c Langley b Lindwall	22	(7) c Harvey b Ring	55
J.D.C. Goddard*	b Miller	45	(5) c and b Ring	0
S. Ramadhin	not out	16	not out	2
A.L. Valentine	st Langley b Ring	2	c Morris b Ring	13
Extras	(LB 1)	1	(B 8, LB 2)	10
Total		**216**		**245**

AUSTRALIA

K.A. Archer	c Goddard b Valentine	20	b Gomez	4
A.R. Morris	c Rae b Valentine	33	c Gomez b Ramadhin	48
A.L. Hassett*	b Ramadhin	6	lbw b Ramadhin	35
R.N. Harvey	lbw b Valentine	18	b Ramadhin	42
K.R. Miller	c and b Valentine	46	b Valentine	4
G.B. Hole	lbw b Valentine	20	not out	45
R.R. Lindwall	b Gomez	61	b Ramadhin	29
I.W. Johnson	not out	16	b Ramadhin	8
D.T. Ring	c Walcott b Gomez	0	not out	6
G.R.A. Langley†	lbw b Worrell	0		
W.A. Johnston	run out	2		
Extras	(B 4)	4	(B 3, LB 11, NB 1)	15
Total		**226**	(7 wickets)	**236**

AUSTRALIA	O	M	R	W	O	M	R	W		FALL OF WICKETS			
Lindwall	20	4	62	4	10	0	36	0		WI	A	WI	A
Miller	14	3	40	1	8	2	19	1	Wkt	1st	1st	2nd	2nd
Johnston	17	2	49	2	16	4	41	1	1st	0	30	23	8
Ring	14	2	52	2	16	2	80	6	2nd	18	53	50	69
Johnson	5	1	12	1	18	1	56	2	3rd	63	80	88	126
Hole					1	0	3	0	4th	92	85	88	143
									5th	95	129	96	149
WEST INDIES									6th	112	188	153	203
Worrell	8	0	38	1	2	1	2	0	7th	150	215	184	225
Gomez	7·5	2	10	2	3	0	12	1	8th	170	215	229	–
Valentine	25	4	99	5	40·7	6	117	1	9th	207	216	230	–
Ramadhin	24	5	75	1	40	9	90	5	10th	216	226	245	–

Umpires: A.N. Barlow (10) and H. Elphinston (5).

Close: 1st day – A(1) 16-0 (Archer 9, Morris 7); 2nd – WI(2) 88-4 (Weekes 25); 3rd – A(2) 108-2 (Morris 40, Harvey 18).

AUSTRALIA v WEST INDIES 1951–52 (2nd Test)

Played at Sydney Cricket Ground on 30 November, 1, 3, 4, 5 December.
Toss: Australia.   Result: AUSTRALIA won by seven wickets.
Debuts: Nil.

Lindwall, playing in his 26th Test, took his 100th wicket when he bowled Ramadhin. Hassett, dropped behind the wicket early in his innings, added 235 with Miller in Australia's highest stand against West Indies to date. Both Stollmeyer and Weekes were suffering from pulled leg muscles, the former employing a runner in the second innings.

WEST INDIES

A.F. Rae	c Johnson b Johnston	17	c Ring b Miller		9
J.B. Stollmeyer	c Johnson b Lindwall	36	b Johnson		35
F.M.M. Worrell	b Johnson	64	c Langley b Lindwall		20
E. de C. Weekes	b Lindwall	5	b Johnson		56
C.L. Walcott†	c Langley b Ring	60	st Langley b Johnson		10
R.J. Christiani	b Hole	76	c Hassett b Miller		30
G.E. Gomez	lbw b Johnston	54	c Miller b Lindwall		41
J.D.C. Goddard*	c Johnson b Johnston	33	not out		57
P.E. Jones	lbw b Lindwall	1	c Miller b Johnston		7
S. Ramadhin	b Lindwall	0	b Johnston		3
A.L. Valentine	not out	0	b Miller		1
Extras	(B 12, LB 3, NB 1)	16	(B 9, LB 12)		21
Total		**362**			**290**

AUSTRALIA

K.A. Archer	c Weekes b Gomez	11	lbw b Worrell		47
A.R. Morris	c Walcott b Jones	11	st Walcott b Ramadhin		30
A.L. Hassett*	c Christiani b Jones	132	not out		46
R.N. Harvey	c Gomez b Goddard	39	lbw b Worrell		1
K.R. Miller	b Valentine	129	not out		6
G.B. Hole	b Valentine	1			
R.R. Lindwall	run out	48			
I.W. Johnson	c Walcott b Jones	5			
D.T. Ring	c Ramadhin b Valentine	65			
G.R.A. Langley†	not out	15			
W.A. Johnston	b Valentine	28			
Extras	(B 12, LB 18, NB 3)	33	(B 6, LB 1)		7
Total		**517**	(3 wickets)		**137**

AUSTRALIA	O	M	R	W	O	M	R	W		FALL OF WICKETS			
Lindwall	26	2	66	4	17	3	59	2		WI	A	WI	A
Johnston	25·4	2	80	3	24	5	61	2	*Wkt*	*1st*	*1st*	*2nd*	*2nd*
Johnson	14	3	48	1	23	2	78	3	1st	33	19	19	49
Miller	21	3	72	0	13·2	2	50	3	2nd	84	27	52	123
Ring	17	1	71	1	7	0	21	0	3rd	99	106	102	125
Hole	4	1	9	1					4th	139	341	130	–
									5th	218	345	141	–
WEST INDIES									6th	286	348	210	–
Jones	27	5	68	3	5	1	16	0	7th	359	372	230	–
Gomez	18	2	47	1	5	1	9	0	8th	360	457	246	–
Worrell	11	0	60	0	2	0	7	2	9th	360	485	268	–
Valentine	30·5	3	111	4	10	0	45	0	10th	362	517	290	–
Ramadhin	41	7	143	0	12·3	1	53	1					
Goddard	24	6	55	1									

Umpires: A.N. Barlow (11) and H. Elphinston (6).

Close: 1st day – WI(1) 286-6 (Gomez 24); 2nd – A(1) 131-3 (Hassett 54, Miller 12); 3rd – WI(1) 451-7 (Lindwall 44, Ring 46); 4th – WI(2) 221-6 (Gomez 40, Goddard 6).

AUSTRALIA v WEST INDIES 1951–52 (3rd Test)

Played at Adelaide Oval on 22, 24, 25 December.
Toss: Australia.   Result: WEST INDIES won by six wickets.
Debuts: West Indies – S.C. Guillen.

Morris, who took over the captaincy for the first time when Hassett withdrew because of leg strain, decided to bat on a rain-affected pitch. Twenty wickets fell for 207 runs on the first day, Australia being dismissed for their lowest total against West Indies until 1984-85. Worrell bowled throughout that innings. Marshall pulled a leg muscle in the field but opened the second innings with Rae as his runner. Australia's second post-war defeat in 29 matches was completed midway through the first Christmas Day of Test cricket.

AUSTRALIA

J.W. Burke	c Stollmeyer b Worrell	3	(9) b Valentine	15
A.R. Morris*	b Worrell	1	(5) b Valentine	45
R.N. Harvey	c Guillen b Gomez	10	(6) c Guillen b Ramadhin	9
K.R. Miller	c Ramadhin b Worrell	4	(7) lbw b Gomez	35
G.B. Hole	c Worrell b Goddard	23	(8) c Weekes b Gomez	25
R.R. Lindwall	b Worrell	2	(10) not out	8
I.W. Johnson	c Stollmeyer b Worrell	11	(1) c Marshall b Valentine	16
D.T. Ring	c Christiani b Goddard	5	(4) run out	67
G.R.A. Langley†	b Worrell	5	(2) b Valentine	23
G. Noblet	b Goddard	8	(3) c Weekes b Valentine	0
W.A. Johnston	not out	7	lbw b Valentine	0
Extras	(LB 3)	3	(B 8, LB 4)	12
Total		**82**		**255**

WEST INDIES

R.E. Marshall	c Burke b Johnston	14	c Langley b Ring	29
J.B. Stollmeyer	b Johnston	17	c Miller b Ring	47
J.D.C. Goddard*	c Langley b Lindwall	0		
F.M.M. Worrell	b Miller	6	(3) c Noblet b Johnston	28
E. de C. Weekes	b Johnston	26	(4) c and b Ring	29
G.E. Gomez	c Langley b Johnston	4	(5) not out	46
R.J. Christiani	c Miller b Johnston	4	(6) not out	42
S.C. Guillen†	b Noblet	9		
D. St E. Atkinson	c Burke b Johnston	15		
S. Ramadhin	not out	5		
A.L. Valentine	b Noblet	0		
Extras	(LB 5)	5	(B 6, LB 5, W 1)	12
Total		**105**	(4 wickets)	**233**

WEST INDIES	O	M	R	W	O	M	R	W
Gomez	5	3	5	1	7	2	17	2
Worrell	12·7	3	38	6	9	2	29	0
Goddard	8	1	36	3	1	0	7	0
Valentine					27·5	6	102	6
Ramadhin					25	4	76	1
Marshall					5	1	12	0
AUSTRALIA								
Lindwall	4	0	18	1	13	1	40	0
Johnston	12	0	62	6	19	4	50	1
Miller	5	1	13	1	5	0	12	0
Noblet	3·5	0	7	2	13	1	30	0
Ring					16·5	3	62	3
Johnson					7	1	27	0

FALL OF WICKETS

Wkt	A 1st	WI 1st	A 2nd	WI 2nd
1st	4	25	16	72
2nd	5	26	20	85
3rd	15	34	81	141
4th	39	44	148	141
5th	41	51	162	–
6th	43	55	172	–
7th	58	85	227	–
8th	62	87	240	–
9th	72	101	255	–
10th	82	105	255	–

Umpires: M.J. McInnes (1) and R. Wright (3).

Close: 1st day – A(2) 20-2 (Langley 0, Ring 0); 2nd – WI(2) 54-0 (Marshall 18, Stollmeyer 33).

AUSTRALIA v WEST INDIES 1951–52 (4th Test)

Played at Melbourne Cricket Ground on 31 December, 1, 2, 3 January.
Toss: West Indies. Result: AUSTRALIA won by one wicket.
Debuts: Nil.

Australia's last-wicket pair, Ring and Johnston, scored 38 together to record the fifth one-wicket win in a Test match and secure the rubber for Australia. Worrell batted in considerable pain after being struck on the right hand by a ball from Miller and he completed his hundred virtually one-handed. Moroney retired hurt when 3 in the second innings.

WEST INDIES

K.R. Rickards	b Miller	15	(4) lbw b Johnston		22
J.B. Stollmeyer	c Langley b Miller	7	lbw b Miller		54
F.M.M. Worrell	b Lindwall	108	(8) b Johnston		30
E. de C. Weekes	c Johnson b Johnston	1	(5) lbw b Johnson		2
G.E. Gomez	c Langley b Miller	37	(7) b Johnston		52
R.J. Christiani	run out	37	b Miller		33
J.D.C. Goddard*	b Miller	21	(3) lbw b Lindwall		0
S.C. Guillen†	not out	22	(1) c Johnston b Lindwall		0
J. Trim	run out	0	run out		0
S. Ramadhin	c Langley b Johnston	1	run out		0
A.L. Valentine	c Lindwall b Miller	14	not out		1
Extras	(B 2, LB 6, W 1)	9	(B 4, LB 5)		9
Total		**272**			**203**

AUSTRALIA

J. Moroney	lbw b Ramadhin	26	lbw b Ramadhin		5
A.R. Morris	b Trim	6	lbw b Valentine		12
A.L. Hassett*	run out	15	lbw b Valentine		102
R.N. Harvey	c and b Ramadhin	83	b Valentine		33
K.R. Miller	b Trim	47	hit wkt b Valentine		2
G.B. Hole	b Valentine	2	c Gomez b Worrell		13
R.R. Lindwall	lbw b Trim	13	c Guillen b Ramadhin		29
I.W. Johnson	c Guillen b Trim	1	c Guillen b Ramadhin		6
D.T. Ring	b Trim	6	not out		32
G.R.A. Langley†	not out	0	lbw b Valentine		1
W.A. Johnston	b Gomez	1	not out		7
Extras	(B 12, LB 4)	16	(B 14, LB 4)		18
Total		**216**	(9 wickets)		**260**

AUSTRALIA	O	M	R	W	O	M	R	W
Lindwall	18	2	72	1	17	2	59	2
Miller	19·3	1	60	5	16	1	49	2
Johnston	20	1	59	2	14·3	2	51	3
Ring	9	0	43	0	7	1	17	0
Johnson	7	0	23	0	5	0	18	1
Hole	2	0	6	0				
WEST INDIES								
Trim	12	2	34	5	10	3	25	0
Gomez	13·3	7	25	1	9	1	18	0
Valentine	23	8	50	1	30	9	88	5
Ramadhin	17	4	63	2	39	15	93	3
Goddard	8	0	28	0				
Worrell					9	1	18	1

FALL OF WICKETS				
	WI	A	WI	A
Wkt	1st	1st	2nd	2nd
1st	16	17	0	27
2nd	29	48	0	93
3rd	30	49	53	106
4th	102	173	60	109
5th	194	176	97	147
6th	221	208	128	192
7th	237	209	190	218
8th	242	210	194	218
9th	248	215	194	222
10th	272	216	203	–

Umpires: M.J. McInnes (2) and R. Wright (4).

Close: 1st day – WI(1) 272 all out; 2nd – WI(2) 20-2 (Stollmeyer 9, Rickards 8); 3rd – A(2) 68-1 (Hassett 23, Harvey 21).

AUSTRALIA v WEST INDIES 1951–52 (5th Test)

Played at Sydney Cricket Ground on 25, 26, 28, 29 January.
Toss: Australia.   Result: AUSTRALIA won by 202 runs.
Debuts: Australia – R. Benaud, C.C. McDonald, G.R. Thoms.

On a perfect pitch and with the temperature 105 degrees in the shade, 19 wickets fell for 180 runs on the first day. West Indies were dismissed for what is still their lowest total against Australia, collapsing against a barrage of bouncers from Lindwall and Miller. Rae, who had influenza, left his sick-bed to open the second innings. His partner, who completed a brave and elegant hundred, led West Indies for the first time after Goddard had stood down at the last minute. Lindwall was allowed to bowl 15 bouncers within 40 deliveries to Weekes.

AUSTRALIA

C.C. McDonald	c Worrell b Gomez	32	b Ramadhin		62
G.R. Thoms	b Gomez	16	hit wkt b Worrell		28
A.L. Hassett*	c Guillen b Gomez	2	c Worrell b Valentine		64
R.N. Harvey	b Gomez	18	c Guillen b Worrell		8
K.R. Miller	c Rae b Worrell	20	c Weekes b Valentine		69
G.B. Hole	c Guillen b Worrell	1	b Worrell		62
R. Benaud	c Stollmeyer b Gomez	3	c sub (K.R. Rickards) b Worrell		19
R.R. Lindwall	c Worrell b Gomez	0	c Walcott b Gomez		21
D.T. Ring	c Atkinson b Gomez	4	b Gomez		12
G.R.A. Langley†	c Weekes b Worrell	6	b Gomez		8
W.A. Johnston	not out	13	not out		6
Extras	(LB 1)	1	(B 10, LB 8)		18
Total		**116**			**377**

WEST INDIES

A.F. Rae	c Langley b Johnston	11	c Harvey b Ring		25
J.B. Stollmeyer*	lbw b Johnston	10	lbw b Lindwall		104
C.L. Walcott	b Lindwall	1	c Langley b Miller		12
E. de C. Weekes	c Langley b Lindwall	0	c Langley b Lindwall		21
R.J. Christiani	c and b Miller	7	(6) c Johnston b Lindwall		4
F.M.M. Worrell	b Miller	6	(5) run out		18
G.E. Gomez	b Miller	11	b Miller		2
D. St E. Atkinson	b Miller	6	hit wkt b Lindwall		2
S.C. Guillen†	not out	13	b Lindwall		6
S. Ramadhin	b Johnston	0	not out		3
A.L. Valentine	c Langley b Miller	6	b Benaud		0
Extras	(B 3, LB 3, W 1)	7	(B 4, LB 11, W 1)		16
Total		**78**			**213**

WEST INDIES	O	M	R	W	O	M	R	W	FALL OF WICKETS				
Worrell	12·2	1	42	3	23	2	95	4		A	WI	A	WI
Gomez	18	3	55	7	18·2	3	58	3	*Wkt*	*1st*	*1st*	*2nd*	*2nd*
Atkinson	6	2	18	0	8	0	25	0	1st	39	17	55	48
Ramadhin					34	8	102	1	2nd	49	18	138	83
Valentine					30	6	79	2	3rd	54	18	152	147
									4th	77	34	216	191
AUSTRALIA									5th	78	34	287	192
Lindwall	8	1	20	2	21	4	52	5	6th	91	51	326	194
Johnston	14	3	25	3	10	2	30	0	7th	91	56	347	200
Miller	7·6	1	26	5	19	2	57	2	8th	97	59	353	205
Ring					13	1	44	1	9th	99	60	370	212
Benaud					4·3	0	14	1	10th	116	78	377	213

Umpires: H. Elphinston (7) and M.J. McInnes (3).

Close: 1st day – WI(1) 64-9 (Guillen 4, Valentine 2); 2nd – A(2) 216-4 (Miller 49, Hole 0); 3rd – WI(2) 112-2 (Stollmeyer 64, Weekes 5).

NEW ZEALAND v WEST INDIES 1951–52 (1st Test)

Played at Lancaster Park, Christchurch, on 8, 9, 11, 12 February.
Toss: New Zealand.   Result: WEST INDIES won by five wickets.
Debuts: New Zealand – D.D. Beard, R.W.G. Emery.

The initial meeting between these two sides brought a record Christchurch crowd of 18,000 on the second day. Guillen, who later played Test cricket for New Zealand, made the highest score of his first-class career to date; after preventing a hat-trick he scored 54 in 78 minutes.

NEW ZEALAND

Batsman	Dismissal 1	Score 1	Dismissal 2	Score 2
G.O. Rabone	c Christiani b Ramadhin	37	lbw b Goddard	18
R.W.G. Emery	lbw b Gomez	5	c Stollmeyer b Valentine	28
V.J. Scott	lbw b Ramadhin	45	b Ramadhin	29
B. Sutcliffe*	c Stollmeyer b Ramadhin	45	(5) b Ramadhin	36
J.R. Reid	b Ramadhin	0	(4) b Valentine	3
F.B. Smith	c Weekes b Valentine	9	b Gomez	37
F.L.H. Mooney†	not out	34	lbw b Gomez	1
T.B. Burtt	c Christiani b Valentine	1	(10) not out	9
A.M. Moir	c Worrell b Valentine	15	lbw b Ramadhin	5
D.D. Beard	run out	28	(8) c Christiani b Worrell	10
J.A. Hayes	st Guillen b Ramadhin	1	b Ramadhin	2
Extras	(B 15, LB 1)	16	(B 10, W 1)	11
Total		**236**		**189**

WEST INDIES

Batsman	Dismissal 1	Score 1	Dismissal 2	Score 2
R.E. Marshall	c Reid b Moir	16	c sub (E.W. Dempster) b Burtt	26
J.B. Stollmeyer	c Sutcliffe b Burtt	23	c Reid b Beard	13
F.M.M. Worrell	b Hayes	71	not out	62
E. de C. Weekes	b Burtt	7	(5) b Moir	2
C.L. Walcott	b Hayes	65	(4) lbw b Burtt	19
R.J. Christiani	c Scott b Beard	3	c Mooney b Hayes	3
J.D.C. Goddard*	c Reid b Burtt	26		
G.E. Gomez	c Mooney b Hayes	0	(7) not out	14
S.C. Guillen†	c and b Burtt	54		
S. Ramadhin	b Burtt	10		
A.L. Valentine	not out	0		
Extras	(B 2, LB 4, NB 6)	12	(NB 3)	3
Total		**287**	(5 wickets)	**142**

WEST INDIES	O	M	R	W	O	M	R	W
Gomez	28	12	47	1	12	3	25	2
Worrell	11	3	25	0	15	6	24	1
Ramadhin	36·4	11	86	5	38·2	21	39	4
Valentine	38	15	51	3	41	19	73	2
Goddard	4	1	8	0	8	3	17	1
Marshall	2	1	3	0				
NEW ZEALAND								
Hayes	12	2	52	3	12	2	28	1
Reid	9	2	25	0				
Burtt	29·2	7	69	5	16	3	37	2
Moir	20	1	70	1	18	4	49	1
Rabone	6	1	17	0				
Beard	21	5	42	1	13	4	25	1

FALL OF WICKETS

Wkt	NZ 1st	WI 1st	NZ 2nd	WI 2nd
1st	5	42	44	28
2nd	91	42	49	48
3rd	102	57	49	86
4th	102	186	118	91
5th	115	189	119	99
6th	153	189	148	–
7th	162	189	172	–
8th	181	240	172	–
9th	231	278	187	–
10th	236	287	189	–

Umpires: M.F. Pengelly (4) and B. Vine (1).

Close: 1st day – NZ(1) 236 all out; 2nd – NZ(2) 12-0 (Rabone 1, Emery 11); 3rd – WI(2) 24-0 (Marshall 9, Stollmeyer 13).

NEW ZEALAND v WEST INDIES 1951–52 (2nd Test)

Played at Eden Park, Auckland, on 15, 16, 18, 19 (*no play*) February.
Toss: New Zealand.   Result: MATCH DRAWN.
Debuts: New Zealand – J.G. Leggat.

After being put in to bat, West Indies recorded what is still their highest score in New Zealand. Moir made a memorably sporting gesture shortly after lunch on the first day when the score was 44 for 0. Rae (10) fell while backing up but Moir, who was bowling and had had the ball returned to him, allowed the batsman to regain his crease. The partnership of 189 in 138 minutes between Worrell and Walcott remains the record for the fifth wicket in this series. Rabone batted 83 minutes for his 9 runs while Valentine conceded just one single off 13 overs. Beard (injured ankle) batted with Sutcliffe as runner.

WEST INDIES

A.F. Rae	b Burtt	99
J.B. Stollmeyer	st Mooney b Beard	152
R.E. Marshall	b Beard	0
E. de C. Weekes	c Reid b Hayes	51
F.M.M. Worrell	c Sutcliffe b Emery	100
C.L. Walcott	lbw b Emery	115
D. St E. Atkinson	not out	8
J.D.C. Goddard*	)	
S.C. Guillen†	) did not bat	
S. Ramadhin	)	
A.L. Valentine	)	
Extras	(B 6, LB 9, NB 6)	21
Total	(6 wickets declared)	**546**

NEW ZEALAND

R.W.G. Emery	c Guillen b Atkinson	5	c Walcott b Atkinson	8
J.G. Leggat	b Worrell	0	not out	6
V.J. Scott	c Stollmeyer b Valentine	84		
B. Sutcliffe*	c Worrell b Ramadhin	20	(3) not out	2
J.R. Reid	st Guillen b Valentine	6		
G.O. Rabone	b Stollmeyer	9		
F.L.H. Mooney†	c Walcott b Stollmeyer	6		
A.M. Moir	b Ramadhin	20		
T.B. Burtt	c Goddard b Valentine	1		
D.D. Beard	c Weekes b Ramadhin	4		
J.A. Hayes	not out	0		
Extras	(B 4, LB 1)	5	(LB 1)	1
Total		**160**	(1 wicket)	**17**

NEW ZEALAND	O	M	R	W	O	M	R	W
Hayes	30	3	106	1				
Beard	40	8	96	2				
Reid	14	4	33	0				
Burtt	36	4	120	1				
Moir	16	2	69	0				
Rabone	15	1	48	0				
Sutcliffe	1	0	1	0				
Emery	7·4	0	52	2				
WEST INDIES								
Worrell	12	3	20	1	9	2	12	0
Atkinson	18	3	42	1	8	5	4	1
Valentine	34·4	21	29	3				
Ramadhin	25	12	41	3				
Stollmeyer	8	3	12	2				
Goddard	2	0	11	0				

FALL OF WICKETS

	WI	NZ	NZ
Wkt	*1st*	*1st*	*2nd*
1st	197	0	14
2nd	202	12	–
3rd	317	50	–
4th	321	61	–
5th	510	93	–
6th	546	101	–
7th	–	155	–
8th	–	155	–
9th	–	160	–
10th	–	160	–

Umpires: J.C. Harris (1) and T.M. Pearce (1).

Close: 1st day – WI(1) 288-2 (Stollmeyer 135, Weekes 36); 2nd – NZ(1) 76-4 (Scott 41, Rabone 4); 3rd – NZ(2) 17-1 (Leggat 6, Sutcliffe 2).

ENGLAND v INDIA 1952 (1st Test)

Played at Headingley, Leeds, on 5, 6, 7, 9, June.
Toss: India.   Result: ENGLAND won by seven wickets.
Debuts: England – F.S. Trueman; India – D.K. Gaekwad, G.S. Ramchand.

The England selectors broke with amateur tradition by appointing Hutton as captain. Hazare and Manjrekar (whose hundred was his first in first-class cricket) shared a partnership of 222 which is still India's highest in all Tests for the fourth wicket. India made Test history by losing four wickets for no runs to the first 14 balls of the second innings, three of them to eight balls from Trueman on his debut.

INDIA

Pankaj Roy	st Evans b Jenkins	19	c Compton b Trueman	0
D.K. Gaekwad	b Bedser	9	c Laker b Bedser	0
P.R. Umrigar	c Evans b Trueman	8	(4) c and b Jenkins	9
V.S. Hazare*	c Evans b Bedser	89	(6) b Trueman	56
V.L. Manjrekar	c Watkins b Trueman	133	b Trueman	0
D.G. Phadkar	c Watkins b Laker	12	(7) b Bedser	64
C.D. Gopinath	b Trueman	0	(8) lbw b Jenkins	8
M.K. Mantri†	not out	13	(3) b Trueman	0
G.S. Ramchand	c Watkins b Laker	0	st Evans b Jenkins	0
S.G. Shinde	c May b Laker	2	not out	7
Ghulam Ahmed	b Laker	0	st Evans b Jenkins	14
Extras	(B 1, LB 7)	8	(LB 5, W 1, NB 1)	7
Total		**293**		**165**

ENGLAND

L. Hutton*	c Ramchand b Ghulam Ahmed	10	b Phadkar	10
R.T. Simpson	c Ramchand b Ghulam Ahmed	23	c Mantri b Ghulam Ahmed	51
P.B.H. May	b Shinde	16	c Phadkar b Ghulam Ahmed	4
D.C.S. Compton	c Ramchand b Ghulam Ahmed	14	not out	35
T.W. Graveney	b Ghulam Ahmed	71	not out	20
A.J. Watkins	lbw b Ghulam Ahmed	48		
T.G. Evans†	lbw b Hazare	66		
R.O. Jenkins	c Mantri b Ramchand	38		
J.C. Laker	b Phadkar	15		
A.V. Bedser	b Ramchand	7		
F.S. Trueman	not out	0		
Extras	(B 15, LB 11)	26	(B 4, LB 3, NB 1)	8
Total		**334**	(3 wickets)	**128**

ENGLAND	O	M	R	W	O	M	R	W	FALL OF WICKETS				
Bedser	33	13	38	2	21	9	32	2		I	E	I	E
Trueman	26	6	89	3	9	1	27	4	*Wkt*	*1st*	*1st*	*2nd*	*2nd*
Laker	22·3	9	39	4	13	4	17	0	1st	18	21	0	16
Watkins	11	1	21	0	11	2	32	0	2nd	40	48	0	42
Jenkins	27	6	78	1	13	2	50	4	3rd	42	62	0	89
Compton	7	1	20	0					4th	264	92	0	–
									5th	264	182	26	–
INDIA									6th	264	211	131	–
Phadkar	24	7	54	1	11	2	21	1	7th	291	290	143	–
Ramchand	36·2	11	61	2	17	3	43	0	8th	291	325	143	–
Ghulam Ahmed	63	24	100	5	22	8	37	2	9th	293	329	143	–
Hazare	20	9	22	1	3	0	11	0	10th	293	334	165	–
Shinde	22	5	71	1	2	0	8	0					

Umpires: H.G. Baldwin (8) and H. Elliott (4).

Close: 1st day – I(1) 272-6 (Phadkar 3, Mantri 5); 2nd – E(1) 206-5 (Graveney 68, Evans 15); 3rd – I(2) 136-6 (Phadkar 62, Gopinath 3).

ENGLAND v INDIA 1952 (2nd Test)

Played at Lord's, London, on 19, 20, 21, 23, 24 June.
Toss: India.   Result: ENGLAND won by eight wickets.
Debuts: Nil.

Evans became the first England wicket-keeper to make a hundred dismissals and to complete the wicket-keepers' double when he stumped Shinde, and he narrowly missed scoring a century before lunch, being 98 at the interval on the third day. Mankad's 184 was then the highest innings for India in England; temporarily released from his duties as professional with the Lancashire League club, Haslingden, and making his first appearance for the touring side, he scored 256 runs and bowled 97 overs in the match. His partnership of 211 with Hazare equalled India's third-wicket record against England at that time. Queen Elizabeth II, in the first summer of her reign, visited Lord's on the fourth afternoon.

INDIA

M.H. Mankad	c Watkins b Trueman	72		b Laker	184
Pankaj Roy	c and b Bedser	35		b Bedser	0
P.R. Umrigar	b Trueman	5	(7)	b Trueman	14
V.S. Hazare*	not out	69		c Laker b Bedser	49
V.L. Manjrekar	lbw b Bedser	5		b Laker	1
D.G. Phadkar	b Watkins	8		b Laker	16
H.R. Adhikari	lbw b Watkins	0	(3)	b Trueman	16
G.S. Ramchand	b Trueman	18	(9)	b Trueman	42
M.K. Mantri†	b Trueman	1	(8)	c Compton b Laker	5
S.G. Shinde	st Evans b Watkins	5		c Hutton b Truemann	14
Ghulam Ahmed	b Jenkins	0		not out	1
Extras	(B 7, NB 10)	17		(B 29, LB 3, NB 4)	36
Total		**235**			**378**

ENGLAND

L. Hutton*	c Mantri b Hazare	150		not out	39
R.T. Simpson	b Mankad	53		run out	2
P.B.H. May	c Mantri b Mankad	74		c Roy b Ghulam Ahmed	26
D.C.S. Compton	lbw b Hazare	6		not out	4
T.W. Graveney	c Mantri b Ghulam Ahmed	73			
A.J. Watkins	b Mankad	0			
T.G. Evans†	c and b Ghulam Ahmed	104			
R.O. Jenkins	st Mantri b Mankad	21			
J.C. Laker	not out	23			
A.V. Bedser	c Ramchand b Mankad	3			
F.S. Trueman	b Ghulam Ahmed	17			
Extras	(B 8, LB 5)	13		(B 4, LB 4)	8
Total		**537**		(2 wickets)	**79**

ENGLAND	O	M	R	W	O	M	R	W	FALL OF WICKETS				
Bedser	33	8	62	2	36	13	60	2		I	E	I	E
Trueman	25	3	72	4	27	4	110	4	*Wkt*	*1st*	*1st*	*2nd*	*2nd*
Jenkins	7·3	1	26	1	10	1	40	0	1st	106	106	7	8
Laker	12	5	21	0	39	15	102	4	2nd	116	264	59	71
Watkins	17	7	37	3	8	0	20	0	3rd	118	272	270	–
Compton					2	0	10	0	4th	126	292	272	–
									5th	135	292	289	–
INDIA									6th	139	451	312	–
Phadkar	27	8	44	0					7th	167	468	314	–
Ramchand	29	8	67	0	1	0	5	0	8th	180	506	323	–
Hazare	24	4	53	2	1	1	0	0	9th	221	514	377	–
Mankad	73	24	196	5	24	12	35	0	10th	235	537	378	–
Ghulam Ahmed	43·4	12	106	3	23·2	9	31	1					
Shinde	6	0	43	0									
Umrigar	4	0	15	0									

Umpires: F. Chester (42) and F.S. Lee (7).

Close: 1st day – E(1) 8-0 (Hutton 6, Simpson 2); 2nd – E(1) 292-5 (Graveney 8); 3rd – I(2) 137-2 (Mankad 86, Hazare 24); 4th – E(2) 40-1 (Hutton 27, May 8).

ENGLAND v INDIA 1952 (3rd Test)

Played at Old Trafford, Manchester, on 17, 18, 19 July.
Toss: England.   Result: ENGLAND won by an innings and 207 runs.
Debuts: England – G.A.R. Lock.

India equalled their lowest Test score to date and became the first team to be dismissed twice in a day; 22 wickets fell on the third day. Trueman's analysis of 8 for 31 remains the best in Tests between England and India. When Lock held a stunning catch at short leg to dismiss Mankad it was the first time he had touched a ball in a Test match. Evans scored 71 out of 84 in 70 minutes.

ENGLAND

L. Hutton*	c Sen b Divecha	104
D.S. Sheppard	lbw b Ramchand	34
J.T. Ikin	c Divecha b Ghulam Ahmed	29
P.B.H. May	c Sen b Mankad	69
T.W. Graveney	lbw b Divecha	14
A.J. Watkins	c Phadkar b Mankad	4
T.G. Evans†	c and b Ghulam Ahmed	71
J.C. Laker	c Sen b Divecha	0
A.V. Bedser	c Phadkar b Ghulam Ahmed	17
G.A.R. Lock	not out	1
F.S. Trueman	did not bat	
Extras	(B 2, LB 2)	4
Total	(9 wickets declared)	**347**

INDIA

M.H. Mankad	c Lock b Bedser	4	lbw b Bedser	6
Pankaj Roy	c Hutton b Trueman	0	c Laker b Trueman	0
H.R. Adhikari	c Graveney b Trueman	0	c May b Lock	27
V.S. Hazare*	b Bedser	16	c Ikin b Lock	16
P.R. Umrigar	b Trueman	4	c Watkins b Bedser	3
D.G. Phadkar	c Sheppard b Trueman	0	b Bedser	5
V.L. Manjrekar	c Ikin b Trueman	22	c Evans b Bedser	0
R.V. Divecha	b Trueman	4	b Bedser	2
G.S. Ramchand	c Graveney b Trueman	2	c Watkins b Lock	1
P. Sen†	c Lock b Trueman	4	not out	13
Ghulam Ahmed	not out	1	c Ikin b Lock	0
Extras	(LB 1)	1	(B 8, NB 1)	9
Total		**58**		**82**

INDIA	O	M	R	W	O	M	R	W
Phadkar	22	10	30	0				
Divecha	45	12	102	3				
Ramchand	33	7	78	1				
Mankad	28	9	67	2				
Ghulam Ahmed	9	3	43	3				
Hazare	7	3	23	0				
ENGLAND								
Bedser	11	4	19	2	15	6	27	5
Trueman	8·4	2	31	8	8	5	9	1
Laker	2	0	7	0				
Watkins					4	3	1	0
Lock					9·3	2	36	4

FALL OF WICKETS

	E	I	I
Wkt	1st	1st	2nd
1st	78	4	7
2nd	133	4	7
3rd	214	5	55
4th	248	17	59
5th	252	17	66
6th	284	45	66
7th	292	51	66
8th	336	53	67
9th	347	53	77
10th	–	58	82

Umpires: D. Davies (11) and F.S. Lee (8).

Close: 1st day – E(1) 153-2 (Hutton 85, May 5); 2nd – E(1) 292-7 (Evans 35).

ENGLAND v INDIA 1952 (4th Test)

Played at Kennington Oval, London, on 14, 15, 16 (*no play*), 18, 19 (*no play*) August.
Toss: England.   Result: MATCH DRAWN.
Debuts: Nil.

Hutton and Sheppard shared England's highest opening partnership against India to date. Only 56 runs came before lunch on the first day, Mankad conceding just a single in his first 13 overs. India achieved another dismal Test record by losing their first five wickets for six runs. Rain reduced play by almost two-thirds, only 10 hours 35 minutes being possible. After he had enforced the follow-on, rain prevented Hutton from leading England to a fourth successive victory in his first season as captain.

ENGLAND

L. Hutton*	c Phadkar b Ramchand	86
D.S. Sheppard	lbw b Divecha	119
J.T. Ikin	c Sen b Phadkar	53
P.B.H. May	c Manjrekar b Mankad	17
T.W. Graveney	c Divecha b Ghulam Ahmed	13
W. Watson	not out	18
T.G. Evans†	c Phadkar b Mankad	1
J.C. Laker	not out	6
A.V. Bedser	)	
G.A.R. Lock	) did not bat	
F.S. Trueman	)	
Extras	(B 10, LB 2, NB 1)	13
Total	**(6 wickets declared)**	**326**

INDIA

M.H. Mankad	c Evans b Trueman	5
Pankaj Roy	c Lock b Trueman	0
H.R. Adhikari	c Trueman b Bedser	0
V.S. Hazare*	c May b Trueman	38
V.L. Manjrekar	c Ikin b Bedser	1
P.R. Umrigar	b Bedser	0
D.G. Phadkar	b Trueman	17
R.V. Divecha	b Bedser	16
G.S. Ramchand	c Hutton b Bedser	5
P. Sen†	b Trueman	9
Ghulam Ahmed	not out	2
Extras	(LB 3, NB 2)	5
Total		**98**

INDIA	O	M	R	W
Divecha	33	9	60	1
Phadkar	32	8	61	1
Ramchand	14	2	50	1
Mankad	48	23	88	2
Ghulam Ahmed	24	1	54	1
Hazare	3	3	0	0
ENGLAND				
Bedser	14·5	4	41	5
Trueman	16	4	48	5
Lock	6	5	1	0
Laker	2	0	3	0

FALL OF WICKETS

	E	I
Wkt	*1st*	*1st*
1st	143	0
2nd	261	5
3rd	273	5
4th	293	6
5th	304	6
6th	307	64
7th	–	71
8th	–	78
9th	–	94
10th	–	98

Umpires: F. Chester (43) and H. Elliott (5).

Close: 1st day – E(1) 264-2 (Ikin 53, May 0); 2nd – I(1) 49-5 (Hazare 27, Phadkar 12); 3rd – no play; 4th – I(1) 98 all out.

INDIA v PAKISTAN 1952–53 (1st Test)

Played at Feroz Shah Kotla, Delhi, on 16, 17, 18 October.
Toss: India.   Result: INDIA won by an innings and 70 runs.
Debuts: Pakistan – all except A.H. Kardar and Amir Elahi who had previously appeared for India, Kardar playing as 'Abdul Hafeez'.

Pakistan's first official Test established Hanif Mohammad (17 years 300 days) as the world's youngest Test wicket-keeper. Adhikari and Ghulam Ahmed added 109 in 80 minutes for the tenth wicket; it remains India's only three-figure last-wicket partnership. Mankad's innings (8 for 52) and match (13 for 131) analyses were then records for India in all Tests and remain the best performances in Tests at Delhi and for either country in this series.

INDIA

M.H. Mankad	b Khan	11
Pankaj Roy	b Khan	7
V.S. Hazare	b Amir Elahi	76
V.L. Manjrekar	c Nazar b Amir Elahi	23
L. Amarnath*	c Khan b Fazal	9
P.R. Umrigar	lbw b Kardar	25
Gul Mahomed	c Hanif b Amir Elahi	24
H.R. Adhikari	not out	81
G.S. Ramchand	c Imtiaz b Fazal	13
P. Sen†	c Nazar b Kardar	25
Ghulam Ahmed	b Amir Elahi	50
Extras	(B 28)	28
Total		**372**

PAKISTAN

Nazar Mohammad	run out	27	b Mankad	7
Hanif Mohammad†	c Ramchand b Mankad	51	b Amarnath	1
Israr Ali	b Mankad	1	lbw b Mankad	9
Imtiaz Ahmed	lbw b Mankad	0	lbw b Ghulam Ahmed	41
Maqsood Ahmed	c Roy b Mankad	15	c Adhikari b Mankad	5
A.H. Kardar*	c Roy b Mankad	4	not out	43
Anwar Hussain	c and b Mankad	4	lbw b Ghulam Ahmed	4
Waqar Hassan	lbw b Mankad	8	c Gul Mahomed b Ghulam Ahmed	5
Fazal Mahmood	not out	21	c and b Ghulam Ahmed	27
Khan Mohammad	c Ramchand b Mankad	0	st Sen b Mankad	5
Amir Elahi	c Gul Mahomed b Ghulam Ahmed	9	c Ramchand b Mankad	0
Extras	(B 9, LB 1)	10	(B 5)	5
Total		**150**		**152**

PAKISTAN	O	M	R	W	O	M	R	W
Khan	20	5	52	2				
Maqsood	6	1	13	0				
Fazal	40	13	92	2				
Amir Elahi	39·4	4	134	4				
Kardar	34	12	53	2				
INDIA								
Ramchand	14	7	24	0	6	1	21	0
Amarnath	13·	9	10	0	5	2	12	1
Mankad	47	27	52	8	24·2	3	79	5
Ghulam Ahmed	22·3	6	51	1	23	7	35	4
Hazare	6	5	3	0				
Gul Mahomed	2	2	0	0				

FALL OF WICKETS

Wkt	I 1st	P 1st	P 2nd
1st	19	64	2
2nd	26	65	17
3rd	67	65	42
4th	76	97	48
5th	110	102	73
6th	180	111	79
7th	195	112	87
8th	229	129	121
9th	263	129	152
10th	372	150	152

Umpires: B.J. Mohoni (7) and M.G. Vijayasarathi (4).

Close: 1st day – I(1) 217-7 (Adhikari 12, Ramchand 9); 2nd – P(1) 90-3 (Hanif 42, Maqsood 11).

INDIA v PAKISTAN 1952–53 (2nd Test)

Played at University Ground, Lucknow, on 23, 24, 25, 26 October.
Toss: India.   Result: PAKISTAN won by an innings and 43 runs.
Debuts: India – H.G. Gaekwad, S. Nyalchand; Pakistan – Mahmood Hussain, Zulfiqar Ahmed.

The only Test played at Lucknow (on jute matting) brought Pakistan's first victory in their second match. Nazar Mohammad scored Pakistan's first century, carried his bat through a completed innings (515 minutes), and became the first player to be on the field for an entire Test match. India's total of 106 remains their lowest in this series. Fazal's match figures of 12 for 94 are still the best for Pakistan against India, and his innings analysis of 7 for 42 remained the best of his Test career.

INDIA

Pankaj Roy	lbw b Fazal	30	c Imtiaz b Mahmood		2
D.K. Gaekwad	b Maqsood	6	c Nazar b Fazal		32
Gul Mahomed	lbw b Maqsood	0	(6) b Fazal		2
V.L. Manjrekar	b Fazal	3	lbw b Fazal		3
G. Kishenchand	lbw b Fazal	0	(3) c Nazar b Fazal		20
P.R. Umrigar	b Mahmood	15	(5) lbw b Fazal		32
L. Amarnath*	c Zulfiqar b Mahmood	10	not out		61
P.G. Joshi†	b Mahmood	9	(9) b Amir Elahi		15
H.G. Gaekwad	b Fazal	14	(8) b Fazal		8
S. Nyalchand	not out	6	(11) lbw b Fazal		1
Ghulam Ahmed	c Hanif b Fazal	8	(10) c sub (Israr Ali) b Amir Elahi		0
Extras	(B 5)	5	(B 5, NB 1)		6
Total		**106**			**182**

PAKISTAN

Nazar Mohammad	not out	124
Hanif Mohammad†	c Umrigar b Ghulam Ahmed	34
Waqar Hassan	lbw b Amarnath	23
Imtiaz Ahmed	lbw b Amarnath	0
Maqsood Ahmed	lbw b Nyalchand	41
A.H. Kardar*	c Ghulam Ahmed b Nyalchand	16
Anwar Hussain	b Nyalchand	5
Fazal Mahmood	c Joshi b Gul Mahomed	29
Zulfiqar Ahmed	lbw b Ghulam Ahmed	34
Mahmood Hussain	b Ghulam Ahmed	13
Amir Elahi	b Gul Mahomed	4
Extras	(B 4, LB 3, NB 1)	8
Total		**331**

PAKISTAN	O	M	R	W	O	M	R	W	FALL OF WICKETS			
Mahmood Hussain	23	7	35	3	19	5	57	1		I	P	I
Kardar	3	2	2	0	13	5	15	0	*Wkt*	*1st*	*1st*	*2nd*
Fazal	24·1	8	52	5	27·3	11	42	7	1st	17	63	4
Maqsood	5	1	12	2	5	0	25	0	2nd	17	118	27
Amir Elahi					7	1	20	2	3rd	20	120	43
Zulfiqar					5	1	17	0	4th	22	167	73
									5th	55	194	77
INDIA									6th	65	201	103
Amarnath	40	18	74	2					7th	68	239	115
Umrigar	1	0	1	0					8th	85	302	170
Nyalchand	64	33	97	3					9th	93	318	170
H.G. Gaekwad	37	21	47	0					10th	106	331	182
Ghulam Ahmed	45	19	83	3								
Gul Mahomed	7·3	2	21	2								

Umpires: B.J. Mohoni (8) and J.R. Patel (4).

Close: 1st day – P(1) 46-0 (Nazar 21, Hanif 25); 2nd – P(1) 239-7 (Nazar 87); 3rd – I(2) 170-9 (Amarnath 50).

INDIA v PAKISTAN 1952–53 (3rd Test)

Played at Brabourne Stadium, Bombay, on 13, 14, 15, 16 November.
Toss: Pakistan.   Result: INDIA won by ten wickets.
Debuts: India – M.L. Apte, H.T. Dani, Rajindernath; Pakistan – Wazir Mohammad.

Mankad completed the Test 'double' of 1,000 runs and 100 wickets in his 23rd match. This was the fastest Test double until 1979 when I.T. Botham achieved this feat in 21 matches (*Test No. 854*). Kardar elected to bat on a dew-laden pitch drying under a burning sun. Hazare and Umrigar added 183 to establish India's present fourth-wicket record for this series. Hanif, 'The Little Master', demonstrated his powers of concentration by batting for six hours in the second innings. Rajindernath, playing in his only Test match, ruined his chances of emulating J.C.W. McBryan (*Test No. 156*) by making four stumpings.

PAKISTAN

Nazar Mohammad	b Amarnath	4	c Umrigar b Dani	0
Hanif Mohammad†	b Mankad	15	c sub (G.S. Ramchand) b Mankad	96
A.H. Kardar*	c Dani b Amarnath	20	(5) lbw b Mankad	3
Imtiaz Ahmed	b Amarnath	0	c Adhikari b Gupte	28
Maqsood Ahmed	c Umrigar b Amarnath	6	(6) c Hazare b Mankad	9
Wazir Mohammad	c and b Mankad	8	(7) lbw b Mankad	4
Waqar Hassan	st Rajindernath b Mankad	81	(3) c Hazare b Mankad	65
Fazal Mahmood	c Amarnath b Hazare	33	st Rajindernath b Gupte	0
Israr Ali	b Gupte	10	st Rajindernath b Gupte	5
Mahmood Hussain	st Rajindernath b Gupte	2	not out	21
Amir Elahi	not out	0	run out	1
Extras	(B 5, LB 2)	7	(B 4, LB 6)	10
Total		**186**		**242**

INDIA

M.H. Mankad	c Nazar b Kardar	41	not out	35
M.L. Apte	c Imtiaz b Mahmood	30	not out	10
R.S. Modi	b Mahmood	32		
V.S. Hazare	not out	146		
P.R. Umrigar	b Mahmood	102		
H.R. Adhikari	not out	31		
L. Amarnath*	)			
H.T. Dani	)			
Rajindernath†	) did not bat			
S.P. Gupte	)			
Ghulam Ahmed	)			
Extras	(B 1, LB 4)	5		
Total	(4 wickets declared)	**387**	(0 wickets)	**45**

INDIA	O	M	R	W	O	M	R	W		FALL OF WICKETS			
										P	I	P	I
Amarnath	21	10	40	4	18	9	25	0	*Wkt*	*1st*	*1st*	*2nd*	*2nd*
Dani	4	2	10	0	6	3	9	1	1st	10	55	1	–
Hazare	7	1	21	1	6	2	13	0	2nd	40	103	166	–
Mankad	25	11	52	3	65	31	72	5	3rd	40	122	171	–
Ghulam Ahmed	7	1	14	0	21	8	36	0	4th	44	305	183	–
Gupte	9	1	42	2	33·2	10	77	3	5th	56	–	201	–
PAKISTAN									6th	60	–	215	–
Mahmood Hussain	35	5	121	3	6	2	21	0	7th	143	–	215	–
Fazal	39	10	111	0	7·2	2	22	0	8th	174	–	215	–
Maqsood	7	2	20	0					9th	182	–	232	–
Kardar	14	2	54	1	2	1	2	0	10th	186	–	242	–
Amir Elahi	14	0	65	0									
Israr Ali	3	1	11	0									

Umpires: J.R. Patel (5) and M.G. Vijayasarathi (5).

Close: 1st day – I(1) 90-1 (Apte 27, Modi 20); 2nd – P(2) 6-1 (Hanif 2, Waqar 4); 3rd – P(2) 176-3 (Imtiaz 7, Kardar 0).

INDIA v PAKISTAN 1952–53 (4th Test)

Played at Chepauk, Madras, on 28, 29, 30 (*no play*) November, 1 (*no play*) December.
Toss: Pakistan.   Result: MATCH DRAWN.
Debuts: India – E.S. Maka.

This was the first Test in India to be seriously interrupted by rain. Zulfiqar Ahmed and Amir Elahi added 104 in 85 minutes for the last wicket. It was the sixth century last-wicket partnership in Tests, the second of this rubber, and it remains the only one scored against India.

PAKISTAN

Nazar Mohammad	run out	13
Hanif Mohammad	lbw b Divecha	22
Waqar Hassan	st Maka b Mankad	49
Imtiaz Ahmed†	c Maka b Divecha	6
A.H. Kardar*	b Ramchand	79
Maqsood Ahmed	c sub (R.H. Shodhan) b Mankad	1
Anwar Hussain	run out	17
Fazal Mahmood	c Maka b Phadkar	30
Zulfiqar Ahmed	not out	63
Mahmood Hussain	b Phadkar	0
Amir Elahi	b Amarnath	47
Extras	(B 9, LB 7, NB 1)	17
Total		**344**

INDIA

M.H. Mankad	b Fazal	7
M.L. Apte	c Maqsood b Kardar	42
V.S. Hazare	c Zulfiqar b Mahmood	1
C.D. Gopinath	c Nazar b Mahmood	0
P.R. Umrigar	c Nazar b Fazal	62
L. Amarnath*	c Imtiaz b Kardar	14
D.G. Phadkar	not out	18
G.S. Ramchand	not out	25
R.V. Divecha	)	
E.S. Maka†	) did not bat	
S.P. Gupte	)	
Extras	(B 4, NB 2)	6
Total	(6 wickets)	**175**

INDIA	O	M	R	W
Phadkar	19	3	61	2
Divecha	19	4	36	2
Ramchand	20	3	66	1
Amarnath	6·5	3	9	1
Mankad	35	3	113	2
Gupte	5	2	14	0
Hazare	6	0	28	0
PAKISTAN				
Mahmood Hussain	22	4	70	2
Fazal	27	11	52	2
Maqsood	4	1	10	0
Kardar	21	7	37	2

FALL OF WICKETS

	P	I
Wkt	*1st*	*1st*
1st	26	21
2nd	46	28
3rd	73	30
4th	111	104
5th	115	132
6th	195	134
7th	195	–
8th	240	–
9th	240	–
10th	344	–

Umpires: N.D. Nagarwalla (1) and P.K. Sinha (2).

Close: 1st day – P(1) 273-9 (Zulfiqar 28, Amir 12); 2nd – I(1) 175-6 (Phadkar 18, Ramchand 25); 3rd – no play.

INDIA v PAKISTAN 1952–53 (5th Test)

Played at Eden Gardens, Calcutta, on 12, 13, 14, 15 December.
Toss: India.   Result: MATCH DRAWN.
Debuts: India – R.H. Shodhan.

Shodhan, a left-hander, became the first player to score a hundred in the first innings of his first Test for India, L. Amarnath having done so in the second innings (*Test No. 230*). The match ended with an intriguing declaration by Kardar which set India to score 97 runs in 15 minutes. India won their first rubber.

PAKISTAN

Nazar Mohammad	c Amarnath b Ghulam Ahmed	55	lbw b Mankad		47
Hanif Mohammad	c Ramchand b Phadkar	56	b Ramchand		12
Waqar Hassan	lbw b Phadkar	29	b Ramchand		97
Imtiaz Ahmed†	c Gaekwad b Phadkar	57	b Mankad		13
A.H. Kardar*	b Phadkar	7	c Ramchand b Ghulam Ahmed		1
Maqsood Ahmed	c Manjrekar b Amarnath	17	c Shodhan b Ghulam Ahmed		8
Anwar Hussain	lbw b Phadkar	9	c Mankad b Ghulam Ahmed		3
Fazal Mahmood	c Mankad b Ramchand	5	not out		28
Zulfiqar Ahmed	not out	6	not out		5
Mahmood Hussain	st Sen b Ramchand	5			
Amir Elahi	c Sen b Ramchand	4			
Extras	(B 3, LB 3, NB 1)	7	(B 14, LB 6, NB 2)		22
Total		**257**	(7 wickets declared)		**236**

INDIA

Pankaj Roy	c Zulfiqar b Amir Elahi	29	not out	8
D.K. Gaekwad	b Mahmood	21	not out	20
M.H. Mankad	lbw b Fazal	35		
V.L. Manjrekar	c Fazal b Mahmood	29		
P.R. Umrigar	c Kardar b Fazal	22		
D.G. Phadkar	c Imtiaz b Kardar	57		
L. Amarnath*	c Maqsood b Fazal	11		
R.H. Shodhan	c Imtiaz b Fazal	110		
G.S. Ramchand	b Mahmood	25		
P. Sen†	b Anwar	13		
Ghulam Ahmed	not out	20		
Extras	(B 7, LB 16, LB 2)	25		
Total		**397**	(0 wickets)	**28**

INDIA	O	M	R	W	O	M	R	W		FALL OF WICKETS			
Phadkar	32	10	72	5	21	8	30	0		P	I	P	I
Ramchand	13	6	20	3	16	3	43	2	*Wkt*	*1st*	*1st*	*2nd*	*2nd*
Amarnath	21	7	31	1	3	2	1	0	1st	94	37	18	–
Mankad	28	7	78	0	41	18	68	2	2nd	128	87	96	–
Ghulam Ahmed	22	6	49	1	33	11	56	3	3rd	169	99	126	–
Shodhan					2	1	6	0	4th	185	135	131	–
Roy					2	1	4	0	5th	215	157	141	–
Manjrekar					2	0	6	0	6th	233	179	152	–
									7th	240	265	216	–
PAKISTAN									8th	242	319	–	–
Mahmood Hussain	46	11	114	3					9th	253	357	–	–
Fazal	64	19	141	4					10th	257	397	–	–
Maqsood	8	2	20	0									
Amir Elahi	6	0	29	1									
Kardar	15	3	43	1									
Anwar	5	1	25	1	1	0	4	0					
Nazar					2	1	4	0					
Hanif					2	0	10	0					
Waqar					1	0	10	0					

Umpires: J.R. Patel (6) and M.G. Vijayasarathi (6).

Close: 1st day – P(1) 230-5 (Imtiaz 50, Anwar 9); 2nd – I(1) 173-5 (Phadkar 19, Amarnath 6); 3rd – P(2) 38-1 (Nazar 22, Waqar 4).

AUSTRALIA v SOUTH AFRICA 1952–53 (1st Test)

Played at Woolloongabba, Brisbane, on 5, 6, 8, 9, 10 December.
Toss: Australia.   Result: AUSTRALIA won by 96 runs.
Debuts: South Africa – K.J. Funston, A.R.A. Murray.

South Africa, without their established players and written off before the rubber began, fielded magnificently and held Australia until the final day. Harvey reached a chanceless hundred in 143 minutes; it was his fifth in consecutive Tests against South Africa. Melle (6 for 71) achieved his best figures in Test cricket. In a heatwave and bereft of his opening partner, Miller (throat infection), Lindwall decided the match with a prolonged spell of fast bowling.

AUSTRALIA

C.C. McDonald	c and b Watkins	27	st Waite b Tayfield		17
A.R. Morris	lbw b Watkins	29	c Melle b Tayfield		58
R.N. Harvey	c sub (G.A.S. Innes) b Melle	109	(4) run out		52
A.L. Hassett*	c Waite b Watkins	55	(3) c McGlew b Melle		17
K.R. Miller	b Watkins	3	lbw b Tayfield		3
G.B. Hole	c Tayfield b Melle	8	lbw b Melle		42
R.R. Lindwall	lbw b Melle	5	not out		38
G.R.A. Langley†	c Tayfield b Melle	17	b Watkins		27
D.T. Ring	c Mansell b Melle	13	b Melle		4
I.W. Johnson	lbw b Melle	7	lbw b Watkins		13
W.A. Johnston	not out	1	c McGlew b Tayfield		0
Extras	(B 1, LB 3, NB 2)	6	(B 2, LB 4)		6
Total		**280**			**277**

SOUTH AFRICA

D.J. McGlew	c Johnson b Miller	9	lbw b Lindwall		69
J.H.B. Waite†	lbw b Ring	39	st Langley b Johnson		14
W.R. Endean	c Langley b Ring	14	lbw b Lindwall		12
K.J. Funston	b Ring	33	c Langley b Johnston		65
R.A. McLean	c Miller b Johnson	13	b Lindwall		38
J.E. Cheetham*	c Langley b Lindwall	26	b Johnston		18
J.C. Watkins	c Miller b Ring	25	hit wkt b Johnson		1
P.N.F. Mansell	c Lindwall b Ring	31	b Lindwall		4
A.R.A. Murray	lbw b Johnston	18	not out		11
H.J. Tayfield	lbw b Ring	3	c Langley b Johnson		1
M.G. Melle	not out	7	b Lindwall		4
Extras	(B 3)	3	(B 2, NB 1)		3
Total		**221**			**240**

SOUTH AFRICA	O	M	R	W	O	M	R	W
Melle	20·5	0	71	6	26	2	95	3
Watkins	24	8	41	4	26	13	47	2
Murray	14	1	63	0	13	7	13	0
Tayfield	15	3	59	0	33·3	5	116	4
Mansell	8	0	40	0				
AUSTRALIA								
Lindwall	12	0	48	1	30	8	60	5
Miller	10	0	46	1				
Johnston	7·6	2	21	1	26	5	62	2
Ring	21	2	72	6	17	3	58	0
Johnson	12	3	31	1	30	7	52	3
Hole					3	0	5	0
Harvey					1	1	0	0

	FALL OF WICKETS			
	A	SA	A	SA
Wkt	1st	1st	2nd	2nd
1st	55	13	48	20
2nd	56	39	75	57
3rd	211	88	115	153
4th	216	103	123	170
5th	231	113	160	209
6th	237	153	198	210
7th	252	177	246	215
8th	272	195	251	226
9th	273	211	276	227
10th	280	221	277	240

Umpires: H. Elphinston (8) and R. Wright (5).

Close: 1st day – A(1) 273-8 (Langley 17, Johnson 1); 2nd – A(2) 2-0 (McDonald 1, Morris 1); 3rd – A(2) 242-6 (Lindwall 30, Langley 23); 4th – SA(2) 150-2 (McGlew 68, Funston 53).

AUSTRALIA v SOUTH AFRICA 1952–53 (2nd Test)

Played at Melbourne Cricket Ground on 24, 26, 27, 29, 30 December.
Toss: South Africa.   Result: SOUTH AFRICA won by 82 runs.
Debuts: Nil.

South Africa gained their first win against Australia since 1910-11; it was only their second in 31 Tests in this series. Tayfield's match analysis of 13 for 165 remains the best for South Africa in all Test matches, while his 7 for 81 is their best in Australia. He also dived to hold a most spectacular catch from Morris when the ball rebounded off a leaping silly mid-off. On the second day South Africa were without two main bowlers, Murray (fibrositis) and Watkins (strained back). Endean batted $7\frac{1}{2}$ hours and gave no chances; it was the first of his three Test hundreds and remained the highest. Miller completed the Test double in his 33rd Test when he dismissed Waite a second time.

SOUTH AFRICA

D.J. McGlew	b Lindwall	46	st Langley b Ring		13
J.H.B. Waite†	c Lindwall b Miller	0	c Hole b Miller		62
W.R. Endean	c Benaud b Lindwall	2	not out		162
K.J. Funston	c Ring b Miller	9	run out		26
R.A. McLean	c Lindwall b Ring	27	lbw b Miller		42
J.E. Cheetham*	c Johnston b Miller	15	lbw b Johnston		6
J.C. Watkins	c Langley b Benaud	19	b Johnston		3
P.N.F. Mansell	b Lindwall	24	b Miller		18
A.R.A. Murray	c Johnston b Benaud	51	st Langley b Ring		23
H.J. Tayfield	c Langley b Miller	23	lbw b Lindwall		22
M.G. Melle	not out	4	b Lindwall		0
Extras	(B 4, LB 3)	7	(B 1, LB 5, W 4, NB 1)		11
Total		227			388

AUSTRALIA

C.C. McDonald	c sub (E.R.H. Fuller) b Mansell	82	c Mansell b Murray		23
A.R. Morris	c and b Tayfield	43	c Watkins b Melle		1
R.N. Harvey	c Cheetham b Tayfield	11	(4) c Watkins b Tayfield		60
A.L. Hassett*	c Melle b Mansell	18	(3) lbw b Tayfield		21
K.R. Miller	c Endean b Tayfield	52	b Tayfield		31
G.B. Hole	c Waite b Mansell	13	(7) b Tayfield		25
R. Benaud	b Tayfield	5	(8) c Melle b Tayfield		45
R.R. Lindwall	run out	1	(9) b Melle		19
D.T. Ring	c McGlew b Tayfield	14	(10) c Melle b Tayfield		53
G.R.A. Langley†	not out	2	(6) b Tayfield		4
W.A. Johnston	lbw b Tayfield	0	not out		0
Extras	(NB 2)	2	(B 1, LB 6, NB 1)		8
Total		243			290

AUSTRALIA	O	M	R	W	O	M	R	W	FALL OF WICKETS				
Lindwall	14	2	29	3	31·5	4	87	2		SA	A	SA	A
Miller	21	3	62	4	22	5	51	3	Wkt	1st	1st	2nd	2nd
Johnston	12	2	37	0	31	9	77	2	1st	2	84	23	3
Ring	18	1	72	1	31	5	115	2	2nd	9	98	134	34
Benaud	6·6	1	20	2	6	0	23	0	3rd	27	155	196	76
Hole					7	0	24	0	4th	63	158	261	131
									5th	93	188	284	139
SOUTH AFRICA									6th	112	211	290	148
Melle	14	0	73	0	11	2	39	2	7th	126	219	317	181
Watkins	6	1	15	0	10	2	34	0	8th	156	239	353	216
Murray	3	1	11	0	23	7	59	1	9th	207	243	388	277
Tayfield	29·4	9	84	6	37·1	13	81	7	10th	227	243	388	290
Mansell	19	3	58	3	14	2	69	0					

Umpires: H. Elphinston (9) and M.J. McInnes (4).

Close: 1st day – A(1) 26-0 (McDonald 14, Morris 11); 2nd – SA(2) 6-0 (McGlew 4, Waite 2); 3rd – SA(2) 267-4 (Endean 115, Cheetham 2); 4th – A(2) 132-4 (Miller 23, Langley 0).

AUSTRALIA v SOUTH AFRICA 1952–53 (3rd Test)

Played at Sydney Cricket Ground on 9, 10, 12, 13 January.
Toss: South Africa.   Result: AUSTRALIA won by an innings and 38 runs.
Debuts: Nil.

Harvey became the first Australian to score 1,000 runs against South Africa; it was only his eighth Test against them. His stand of 168 with Miller remains Australia's highest for the fourth wicket in this series. During that partnership, Tayfield fractured his left thumb in stopping a ball driven by Miller.

SOUTH AFRICA

D.J. McGlew	run out	24		c Langley b Lindwall	9
J.H.B. Waite†	c Morris b Johnston	32		c Hole b Lindwall	0
W.R. Endean	b Lindwall	18		lbw b Miller	71
K.J. Funston	b Ring	56		c Hole b Miller	16
R.A. McLean	b Lindwall	0	(6)	c Benaud b Lindwall	65
J.E. Cheetham*	c Johnston b Miller	5	(5)	c Morris b Lindwall	5
A.R.A. Murray	c sub (J.H. de Courcy) b Miller	4		c Hole b Benaud	17
J.C. Watkins	c sub (J.H. de Courcy) b Miller	17		c Miller b Johnston	48
P.N.F. Mansell	b Lindwall	8		c Hole b Benaud	0
H.J. Tayfield	not out	3		absent hurt	–
M.G. Melle	c Langley b Lindwall	1	(10)	not out	0
Extras	(B 1, LB 3, W 1)	5		(LB 1)	1
Total		**173**			**232**

AUSTRALIA

C.C. McDonald	c Endean b Tayfield	67
A.R. Morris	b Watkins	18
A.L. Hassett*	c Funston b Murray	2
R.N. Harvey	c Watkins b Murray	190
K.R. Miller	lbw b Tayfield	55
G.B. Hole	run out	5
R. Benaud	lbw b Melle	0
D.T. Ring	b Tayfield	58
R.R. Lindwall	b Murray	1
G.R.A. Langley†	c Mansell b Murray	20
W.A. Johnston	not out	7
Extras	(B 3, LB 12, W 1, NB 4)	20
Total		**443**

AUSTRALIA	O	M	R	W	O	M	R	W
Lindwall	14·2	1	40	4	20	3	72	4
Miller	17	1	48	3	18	6	33	2
Johnston	18	5	46	1	14·6	0	51	1
Ring	12	4	23	1	12	1	54	0
Hole	2	0	11	0				
Benaud					5	1	21	2
SOUTH AFRICA								
Melle	23	3	98	1				
Watkins	12	5	16	1				
Murray	51·2	11	169	4				
Tayfield	38	9	94	3				
Mansell	7	0	46	0				

	FALL OF WICKETS		
	SA	A	SA
Wkt	1st	1st	2nd
1st	54	40	9
2nd	65	49	10
3rd	83	162	60
4th	83	330	68
5th	115	344	167
6th	142	350	167
7th	144	374	232
8th	156	379	232
9th	172	425	232
10th	173	443	–

Umpires: H. Elphinston (10) and M.J. McInnes (5).

Close: 1st day – SA(1) 173 all out; 2nd – A(1) 277-3 (Harvey 133, Miller 40); 3rd – SA(2) 77-4 (Endean 47, McLean 0).

AUSTRALIA v SOUTH AFRICA 1952–53 (4th Test)

Played at Adelaide Oval on 24, 26, 27, 28, 29 January.
Toss: Australia.   Result: MATCH DRAWN.
Debuts: South Africa – E.R.H. Fuller.

South Africa saved the follow-on by seven runs and, set 377 runs in $4\frac{1}{4}$ hours for victory, forced a draw. The second-wicket partnership of 275 between McDonald and Hassett remains Australia's highest for any wicket against South Africa. Harvey reached a chanceless hundred in only 106 minutes. Lindwall (damaged leg tendon) and Miller (pulled ligament in the back) were unable to bowl in the second innings.

AUSTRALIA

C.C. McDonald	st Waite b Tayfield	154	b Mansell		15
A.R. Morris	c Endean b Fuller	1	c Endean b Melle		77
A.L. Hassett*	c McGlew b Mansell	163			
R.N. Harvey	c Tayfield b Fuller	84	(3) c Endean b Watkins		116
K.R. Miller	c Waite b Tayfield	9			
G.B. Hole	c and b Mansell	59	(4) not out		6
R. Benaud	b Melle	6	(5) not out		18
D.T. Ring	c McLean b Tayfield	28			
R.R. Lindwall	lbw b Tayfield	2			
G.R.A. Langley†	not out	5			
W.A. Johnston	run out	11			
Extras	(B 1, LB 7)	8	(B 1)		1
Total		**530**	(3 wickets declared)		**233**

SOUTH AFRICA

D.J. McGlew	c Hole b Johnston	26	c Langley b Johnston		54
W.R. Endean	c Langley b Benaud	56	(4) b Harvey		17
R.A. McLean	c Hassett b Ring	11	c Hole b Benaud		17
J.H.B. Waite†	c Hole b Benaud	44	(2) b Hole		20
K.J. Funston	c and b Benaud	92	lbw b Johnston		17
J.C. Watkins	b Benaud	76	b Morris		21
J.E. Cheetham*	b Johnston	6	not out		13
P.N.F. Mansell	c Hole b Johnston	33	not out		2
H.J. Tayfield	b Johnston	16			
E.R.H. Fuller	c and b Johnston	0			
M.G. Melle	not out	9			
Extras	(B 12, LB 4, NB 2)	18	(B 16)		16
Total		**387**	(6 wickets)		**177**

SOUTH AFRICA	O	M	R	W	O	M	R	W
Melle	26	1	105	1	10	1	50	1
Fuller	25	2	119	2	3	0	12	0
Tayfield	44	6	142	4	14	1	65	0
Mansell	32	1	113	2	7	0	40	1
McGlew	2	0	9	0	1	0	7	0
Watkins	6	1	34	0	12	1	58	1
AUSTRALIA								
Lindwall	13	0	47	0				
Johnston	49·3	17	110	5	24	4	67	2
Miller	2·1	1	1	0				
Ring	30	8	88	1	11	3	25	0
Benaud	44	9	118	4	14	5	28	1
Hole	3	1	5	0	9	4	17	1
Harvey					7	2	9	1
Morris					5	0	11	1
Hassett					1	0	1	0
McDonald					1	0	3	0

FALL OF WICKETS

Wkt	A 1st	SA 1st	A 2nd	SA 2nd
1st	2	62	42	81
2nd	277	79	199	95
3rd	356	100	209	109
4th	387	208	–	127
5th	439	270	–	158
6th	448	296	–	166
7th	494	350	–	–
8th	505	374	–	–
9th	517	378	–	–
10th	530	387	–	–

Umpires: M.J. McInnes (6) and R. Wright (6).

Close: 1st day – A(1) 182-1 (McDonald 107, Hassett 71); 2nd – SA(1) 4-0 (McGlew 4, Endean 0); 3rd – SA(1) 224-4 (Funston 71, Watkins 4); 4th – A(2) 144-1 (Morris 58, Harvey 70).

AUSTRALIA v SOUTH AFRICA 1952–53 (5th Test)

Played at Melbourne Cricket Ground on 6, 7, 9, 10, 11, 12 February.
Toss: Australia.   Result: SOUTH AFRICA won by six wickets.
Debuts: Australia – R.G. Archer, I.D. Craig; South Africa – H.J. Keith.

At 17 years 239 days Craig became the youngest Australian to play Test cricket – a record he still holds. South Africa achieved the third instance in Test cricket of a side winning in face of a first innings total of over 500, and so squared a rubber against Australia for the first time. Harvey's 205, his eighth hundred in ten Tests against South Africa, remained his highest score for Australia. His final aggregate for this rubber of 834 runs is the highest for either country in the series. Tayfield's total of 30 wickets in the rubber is the highest by a South African bowler against Australia and in any rubber played overseas. McLean, dropped first ball, brought the match to a rousing conclusion by scoring 76 out of 106 in 80 minutes and hitting 14 fours.

AUSTRALIA

C.C. McDonald	c McLean b Mansell	41	c Watkins b Fuller	11	
A.R. Morris	run out	99	lbw b Tayfield	44	
R.N. Harvey	c Cheetham b Fuller	205	b Fuller	7	
A.L. Hassett*	run out	40	c Endean b Mansell	30	
I.D. Craig	c Keith b Fuller	53	c Endean b Tayfield	47	
R.G. Archer	c Waite b Fuller	18	c Watkins b Tayfield	0	
R. Benaud	c and b Tayfield	20	c Watkins b Fuller	30	
D.T. Ring	b Tayfield	14	c Endean b Mansell	0	
G.R.A. Langley†	b Murray	2	not out	26	
W.A. Johnston	c Endean b Tayfield	12	c Cheetham b Fuller	5	
G. Noblet	not out	13	b Fuller	1	
Extras	(LB 3)	3	(B 7, LB 1)	8	
Total		**520**		**209**	

SOUTH AFRICA

W.R. Endean	c Langley b Johnston	16	b Johnston	70	
J.H.B. Waite†	run out	64	c Archer b Noblet	18	
J.C. Watkins	b Archer	92	b Ring	50	
K.J. Funston	lbw b Johnston	16	b Benaud	35	
H.J. Keith	b Johnston	10	not out	40	
R.A. McLean	lbw b Noblet	81	not out	76	
J.E. Cheetham*	c McDonald b Johnston	66			
P.N.F. Mansell	lbw b Johnston	52			
A.R.A. Murray	c and b Johnston	17			
H.J. Tayfield	c Benaud b Ring	17			
E.R.H. Fuller	not out	0			
Extras	(B 1, LB 3)	4	(B 2, LB 6)	8	
Total		**435**	(4 wickets)	**297**	

SOUTH AFRICA	O	M	R	W	O	M	R	W
Fuller	19	4	74	3	30·2	4	66	5
Watkins	23	3	72	0	14	4	33	0
Tayfield	35·4	4	129	3	32	8	73	3
Murray	25	3	84	1				
Mansell	22	0	114	1	8	3	29	2
Keith	9	0	44	0				
AUSTRALIA								
Noblet	30	6	65	1	24	9	44	1
Archer	33	4	97	1	5	0	23	0
Johnston	46	8	152	6	38	7	114	1
Ring	19·1	1	62	1	13	2	55	1
Benaud	15	3	55	0	15	4	41	1
Hassett					0·5	0	12	0

FALL OF WICKETS

	A	SA	A	SA
Wkt	1st	1st	2nd	2nd
1st	122	31	36	42
2nd	166	129	44	124
3rd	269	189	70	174
4th	417	189	128	191
5th	450	239	129	–
6th	459	290	152	–
7th	490	401	152	–
8th	493	402	187	–
9th	495	435	193	–
10th	520	435	209	–

Umpires: M.J. McInnes (7) and R. Wright (7).

Close: 1st day – A(1) 243-2 (Harvey 71, Hassett 30); 2nd – SA(1) 48-1 (Waite 29, Watkins 3); 3rd – SA(1) 325-6 (Cheetham 27, Mansell 16); 4th – A(2) 89-3 (Hassett 17, Craig 7); 5th – SA(2) 94-1 (Endean 57, Watkins 17).

WEST INDIES v INDIA 1952–53 (1st Test)

Played at Queen's Park Oval, Port-of-Spain, Trinidad, on 21, 22, 23, 24, 27, 28 January.
Toss: India. Result: MATCH DRAWN.
Debuts: West Indies – A.P. Binns, F.M. King, B.H. Pairaudeau; India – C.V. Gadkari.

Played on an easy-paced jute matting pitch, this match had reached only the halfway stage at the end of the fourth day. Needing 274 to win in 160 minutes West Indies settled for batting practice. Weekes scored the first double-century for West Indies in this series of Tests, Pairaudeau scored a hundred on debut, and they shared together a partnership of 219 which was a fifth-wicket record for West Indies in all Tests to date and remains the record against India. Gupte's analysis of 7 for 162 is the best for India in the West Indies. A crowd of 22,000 – then a record for a cricket match – watched the third day.

INDIA

M.H. Mankad	lbw b King	2	(9) b Ramadhin		10
M.L. Apte	c Binns b Stollmeyer	64	b Valentine		52
G.S. Ramchand	c Stollmeyer b Ramadhin	61	c Binns b Walcott		17
V.S. Hazare*	c Worrell b Valentine	29	c and b Walcott		0
P.R. Umrigar	c Binns b Valentine	130	b Worrell		69
D.G. Phadkar	b Gomez	30	c Walcott b Worrell		65
D.K. Gaekwad	c Worrell b Stollmeyer	43	lbw b King		24
R.H. Shodhan	c Worrell b Gomez	45	b Ramadhin		11
C.V. Gadkari	c Walcott b Gomes	7	(10) not out		11
P.G. Joshi†	c Binns b King	3	(1) run out		32
S.P. Gupte	not out	0	c Rae b Ramadhin		1
Extras	(LB 2, NB 1)	3	(LB 1, NB 1)		2
Total		**417**			**294**

WEST INDIES

A.F. Rae	b Ramchand	1	not out	63
J.B. Stollmeyer*	c Phadkar b Gupte	33	not out	76
F.M.M. Worrell	b Gupte	18		
E. de C. Weekes	c Gadkari b Gupte	207		
C.L. Walcott	c Ramchand b Mankad	47		
B.H. Pairaudeau	st Joshi b Gupte	115		
G.E. Gomez	c Mankad b Gupte	0		
A.P. Binns†	run out	2		
F.M. King	lbw b Gupte	0		
S. Ramadhin	not out	5		
A.L. Valentine	st Joshi b Gupte	0		
Extras	(B 5, LB 1, W 2, NB 2)	10	(B 1, LB 1 W 1)	3
Total		**438**	(0 wickets)	**142**

WEST INDIES	O	M	R	W	O	M	R	W	FALL OF WICKETS				
										I	WI	I	WI
King	41·1	10	75	2	24	12	35	1	*Wkt*	*1st*	*1st*	*2nd*	*2nd*
Gomez	42	12	84	3	18	5	51	0	1st	16	3	55	–
Ramadhin	37	13	107	1	24·5	7	58	3	2nd	110	36	90	–
Valentine	56	28	92	2	28	13	47	1	3rd	157	89	90	–
Stollmeyer	16	2	56	2	11	1	47	0	4th	158	190	106	–
Worrell					20	4	32	2	5th	210	409	237	–
Walcott					16	10	12	2	6th	328	409	238	–
Weekes					2	0	10	0	7th	379	413	257	–
INDIA									8th	412	419	273	–
Phadkar	13	4	38	0	9	4	12	0	9th	417	438	291	–
Ramchand	22	7	56	1	13	2	31	0	10th	417	438	294	–
Gupte	66	15	162	7	2	1	2	0					
Mankad	63	16	129	1	12	1	32	0					
Hazare	12	1	30	0									
Shodhan	1	0	1	0	7	2	19	0					
Gadkari	5	0	12	0	9	3	25	0					
Umrigar					2	0	14	0					
Gaekwad					1	0	4	0					

Umpires: C. John (1) and E.N. Lee Kow (1).

Close: 1st day – I(1) 208-4 (Umrigar 22, Phadkar 28): 2nd – I(1) 417 all out; 3rd – WI(1) 205-4 (Weekes 92, Pairaudeau 8); 4th – WI(1) 438 all out; 5th – I(2) 179-4 (Umrigar 30, Phadkar 46).

WEST INDIES v INDIA 1952–53 (2nd Test)

Played at Kensington Oval, Bridgetown, Barbados, on 7, 9, 10, 11, 12 February.
Toss: West Indies.   Result: WEST INDIES won by 142 runs.
Debuts: West Indies – R.A. Legall.

Set 272 to win, India were shackled and dismissed by Ramadhin who took 5 for 26 in 24·5 overs. Gaekwad was carried from the field after colliding with Hazare while attempting to catch King in the second innings.

WEST INDIES

B.H. Pairaudeau	c Joshi b Hazare	43		lbw b Phadkar	0
J.B. Stollmeyer*	c Mankad b Gupte	32		c Gupte b Mankad	54
F.M.M. Worrell	lbw b Mankad	24		b Phadkar	7
E. de C. Weekes	c Joshi b Hazare	47		b Mankad	15
C.L. Walcott	lbw b Phadkar	98	(6)	b Phadkar	34
R.J. Christiani	st Joshi b Gupte	4	(7)	st Joshi b Gupte	33
G.E. Gomez	c Gaekwad b Gupte	0	(5)	lbw b Phadkar	35
R.A. Legall†	c Ramchand b Mankad	23		b Gupte	1
F.M. King	lbw b Mankad	0		c Manjrekar b Ramchand	19
S. Ramadhin	not out	16		b Phadkar	12
A.L. Valentine	b Phadkar	6		not out	0
Extras	(LB 3)	3		(B 6, LB 11, W 1)	18
Total		**296**			**228**

INDIA

Pankaj Roy	c Worrell b King	1	(3)	c Legall b Valentine	22
M.L. Apte	c Worrell b Valentine	64		b King	9
V.L. Manjrekar	lbw b Ramadhin	25	(6)	not out	32
V.S. Hazare*	c Weekes b King	63	(7)	b Ramadhin	0
P.R. Umrigar	c Christiani b Valentine	56		b Ramadhin	6
G.S. Ramchand	b Ramadhin	17	(4)	b Ramadhin	34
D.K. Gaekwad	c and b Valentine	0		absent hurt	–
D.G. Phadkar	b Worrell	17		c Valentine b Ramadhin	8
P.G. Joshi†	c Worrell b Valentine	0		c Worrell b Valentine	0
S.P. Gupte	run out	2		lbw b Ramadhin	5
M.H. Mankad	not out	0	(1)	b Gomez	3
Extras	(B 2, LB 5, NB 1)	8		(B 8, LB 2)	10
Total		**253**			**129**

INDIA	O	M	R	W	O	M	R	W	FALL OF WICKETS				
Phadkar	11·4	2	24	2	29·3	4	64	5		WI	I	WI	I
Ramchand	9	1	32	0	4	1	9	1	*Wkt*	*1st*	*1st*	*2nd*	*2nd*
Gupte	41	10	99	3	36	12	82	2	1st	52	6	0	9
Mankad	46	15	125	3	19	3	54	2	2nd	81	44	25	13
Hazare	9	2	13	2	2	1	1	0	3rd	123	156	47	70
									4th	168	164	105	72
WEST INDIES									5th	173	204	138	89
King	28	7	66	2	9	3	18	1	6th	177	205	175	89
Gomez	17	9	27	0	5	2	9	1	7th	222	242	190	107
Ramadhin	30	13	59	2	24·5	11	26	5	8th	222	243	205	110
Worrell	13	4	25	1	6	0	13	0	9th	280	251	228	129
Valentine	41	21	58	4	35	16	53	2	10th	296	253	228	–
Stollmeyer	5	2	10	0									

Umpires: H.B. de C. Jordan (1) and J.H. Walcott (2).

Close: 1st day – WI(1) 262-8 (Walcott 82, Ramadhin 4); 2nd – I(1) 155-2 (Apte 63, Hazare 63); 3rd – WI(2) 91-3 (Stollmeyer 37, Gomez 24); 4th – I(2) 54-2 (Roy 9, Ramchand 31).

WEST INDIES v INDIA 1952–53 (3rd Test)

Played at Queen's Park Oval, Port-of-Spain, Trinidad, on 19, 20, 21, 23, 24, 25 February.
Toss: India.   Result: MATCH DRAWN.
Debuts: India – J.M. Ghorpade.

Originally scheduled for Georgetown, this Test had to be transferred because of serious flooding in British Guiana. Weekes scored his sixth hundred in eight Tests against India. Manjrekar kept wicket in both innings after Maka, at 275, had fractured two bones in his left hand while batting against King – he took no further part in the tour. Apte's tenacious innings was then the highest for India in the Caribbean. West Indies were set 327 runs in 165 minutes. Stollmeyer had dropped down the order because of a bruised thumb but he opened in the second innings after Rae had been caught via his eye.

INDIA

Pankaj Roy	c Weekes b Worrell	49	c sub (N.S. Asgarali) b Gomez	0
M.L. Apte	b Gomez	0	not out	163
G.S. Ramchand	c Legall b King	62	c Weekes b King	1
V.S. Hazare*	c Rae b Worrell	11	(6) lbw b Worrell	24
P.R. Umrigar	c Gomez b King	61	st Legall b Valentine	67
V.L. Manjrekar	c Weekes b King	3	(4) Legall b Worrell	2
M.H. Mankad	lbw b King	17	(8) run out	96
D.G. Phadkar	c Pairaudeau b King	13		
J.M. Ghorpade	c Walcott b Valentine	35	(7) run out	0
E.S. Maka†	retired hurt	2		
S.P. Gupte	not out	17		
Extras	(LB 5, W 2, NB 2)	9	(LB 4, W 3, NB 2)	9
Total		**279**	(7 wickets declared)	**362**

WEST INDIES

A.F. Rae	c sub (C.V. Gadkari) b Gupte	15		
B.H. Pairaudeau	b Ramchand	8	c Ghorpade b Gupte	29
C.L. Walcott	st Manjrekar b Gupte	30		
E. de C. Weekes	run out	161	not out	55
F.M.M. Worrell	b Gupte	31	(3) c Manjrekar b Ramchand	2
G.E. Gomez	c Hazare b Phadkar	15		
R.A. Legall†	run out	17		
J.B. Stollmeyer*	not out	20	(1) not out	104
F.M. King	c sub (C.V. Gadkari) b Gupte	12		
S. Ramadhin	c Manjrekar b Phadkar	1		
A.L. Valentine	c Ghorpade b Gupte	0		
Extras	(B 3, W 2)	5	(B 1, LB 1)	2
Total		**315**	(2 wickets)	**192**

WEST INDIES	O	M	R	W	O	M	R	W		FALL OF WICKETS			
King	31	9	74	5	22	9	29	1			I	WI	I	WI
Gomez	16	5	26	1	46·1	20	42	1	*Wkt*	*1st*	*1st*	*2nd*	*2nd*
Worrell	26	9	47	2	31	7	62	2	1st	6	12	1	47
Valentine	37·2	18	62	1	50	17	105	1	2nd	87	41	4	65
Ramadhin	21	7	61	0	28	13	47	0	3rd	117	82	10	–
Stollmeyer					15	3	54	0	4th	124	178	145	–
Walcott					7	2	13	0	5th	136	215	209	–
Weekes					1	0	1	0	6th	177	281	209	–
INDIA									7th	211	286	362	–
Phadkar	43	14	85	2	7	5	7	0	8th	225	299	–	–
Ramchand	15	3	48	1	20	3	61	1	9th	279	304	–	–
Gupte	48	14	107	5	7	0	19	1	10th	–	315	–	–
Mankad	33	16	47	0									
Hazare	2	0	6	0	2	0	12	0					
Ghorpade	5	0	17	0	11	0	53	0					
Roy					6	0	35	0					
Apte					1	0	3	0					

Umpires: C. John (2) and E.N. Lee Kow (2).

Close: 1st day – I(1) 167-5 (Umrigar 27, Mankad 12); 2nd – WI(1) 78-2 (Walcott 30, Weekes 23); 3rd – WI(1) 280-5 (Weekes 159, Legall 17); 4th – I(2) 118-3 (Apte 60, Umrigar 49); 5th – I(2) 287-6 (Apte 141, Mankad 43).

WEST INDIES v INDIA 1952–53 (4th Test)

Played at Bourda, Georgetown, British Guiana, on 11, 12, 13, 14, 16, 17 March.
Toss: India.   Result: MATCH DRAWN.
Debuts: West Indies – R. Miller, G.L. Wight.

Another slow-scoring match much interrupted by rain produced only 793 runs from over 19 hours of cricket. Although the umpires ruled that play was impossible on the second day, a crowd demonstration resulted in the officials ordering the restart of play for the final hour. Walcott's fifth Test hundred was his first in a home match. Miller was unable to bowl after straining his back attempting a vast hit.

INDIA

Pankaj Roy	lbw b Valentine	28	c Worrell b Valentine		48
M.L. Apte	lbw b Ramadhin	30	hit wkt b Stollmeyer		30
G.S. Ramchand	run out	0	b Valentine		2
V.L. Manjrekar	run out	0	(6) b Valentine		31
P.R. Umrigar	c Walcott b Valentine	1	not out		40
V.S. Hazare*	c Walcott b Valentine	30	(4) lbw b King		9
M.H. Mankad	c Legall b Valentine	66	not out		20
D.G. Phadkar	c Legall b Valentine	30			
C.V. Gadkari	not out	50			
P.G. Joshi†	lbw b Ramadhin	7			
S.P. Gupte	run out	12			
Extras	(B 4, LB 2, NB 2)	8	(B 4, LB 5, W 1)		10
Total		**262**	(5 wickets)		**190**

WEST INDIES

B.H. Pairaudeau	b Ramchand	2
J.B. Stollmeyer*	lbw b Mankad	13
F.M.M. Worrell	b Mankad	56
E. de C. Weekes	lbw b Ramchand	86
C.L. Walcott	lbw b Hazare	125
G.L. Wight	b Mankad	21
R.A. Legall†	lbw b Gupte	8
R. Miller	c Apte b Gupte	23
F.M. King	b Gupte	2
S. Ramadhin	not out	6
A.L. Valentine	c Hazare b Gupte	13
Extras	(B 4, LB 4, W 1)	9
Total		**364**

WEST INDIES	O	M	R	W	O	M	R	W	FALL OF WICKETS			
King	6	3	4	0	17	6	32	1		I	WI	I
Miller	16	8	28	0					*Wkt*	*1st*	*1st*	*2nd*
Valentine	53·5	20	127	5	34	14	71	3	1st	47	2	66
Ramadhin	41	18	74	2	26	14	39	0	2nd	47	44	72
Stollmeyer	1	0	1	0	8	2	15	1	3rd	56	101	91
Walcott	3	0	8	0					4th	62	231	117
Worrell	4	1	12	0	13	2	23	0	5th	64	302	161
									6th	120	311	–
INDIA									7th	183	343	–
Ramchand	17	4	48	2					8th	211	345	–
Hazare	12	3	22	1					9th	236	345	–
Gadkari	3	1	8	0					10th	262	364	–
Gupte	56·2	19	122	4								
Mankad	68	23	155	3								

Umpires: E.S. Gillette (2) and A.B. Rollox (1).

Close: 1st day – I(1) 182-6 (Mankad 65, Phadkar 25); 2nd – I(1) 237-9 (Gadkari 37, Gupte 0); 3rd – WI(1) 109-3 (Weekes 30, Walcott 5); 4th – I(2) 23-0 (Roy 3, Apte 14); 5th – I(2) 167-5 (Umrigar 37, Mankad 1).

WEST INDIES v INDIA 1952–53 (5th Test)

Played at Sabina Park, Kingston, Jamaica, on 28, 30, 31 March, 1, 2, 4 April.
Toss: India.   Result: MATCH DRAWN.
Debuts: West Indies – A.P.H. Scott.

Needing 181 runs in 145 minutes for victory, West Indies settled for a draw after losing both openers cheaply. Worrell's 237 remains the highest score for West Indies in a home Test against India. For the first time Worrell, Weekes and Walcott scored hundreds in the same innings. Roy and Manjrekar added 237 in 255 minutes for India's highest second-wicket partnership in all Tests so far. West Indies needed 181 runs in 145 minutes.

INDIA

Pankaj Roy	c Legall b King	85	lbw b Valentine	150
M.L. Apte	run out	15	lbw b Valentine	33
G.S. Ramchand	lbw b Valentine	22	(7) c Pairaudeau b Valentine	33
V.S. Hazare*	c Valentine b King	16	c Weekes b Valentine	12
P.R. Umrigar	b Valentine	117	c Weekes b King	13
V.L. Manjrekar†	c Weekes b Valentine	43	(3) c Weekes b Gomez	118
M.H. Mankad	lbw b Valentine	6	(6) c Weekes b Gomez	9
C.V. Gadkari	c Legall b Valentine	0	c Stollmeyer b Gomez	0
J.M. Ghorpade	c Legall b Gomez	4	b King	24
S.P. Gupte	not out	0	(11) b Gomez	8
R.H. Shodhan	absent ill	–	(10) not out	15
Extras	(B 1, W 3)	4	(B 18, LB 10, W 1)	29
Total		**312**		**444**

WEST INDIES

B.H. Pairaudeau	b Gupte	58	run out	2
J.B. Stollmeyer*	b Mankad	13	b Ramchand	9
F.M.M. Worrell	c Hazare b Mankad	237	c Apte b Mankad	23
E. de C. Weekes	c Gadkari b Gupte	109	c Ghorpade b Ramchand	36
C.L. Walcott	c Gadkari b Mankad	118	not out	5
R.J. Christiani	lbw b Mankad	4	not out	1
G.E. Gomez	c Hazare b Mankad	12		
R.A. Legall†	c sub (D.K. Gaekwad) b Gupte	1		
F.M. King	st Manjrekar b Gupte	0		
A.P.H. Scott	c and b Gupte	5		
A.L. Valentine	not out	4		
Extras	(B 7, LB 4, W 4)	15	(B 15, W 1)	16
Total		**576**	(4 wickets)	**92**

WEST INDIES	O	M	R	W	O	M	R	W
King	34	13	64	2	26	6	83	2
Gomez	28	13	40	1	47	25	72	4
Worrell	16	6	31	0	6	2	17	0
Scott	31	7	88	0	13	2	52	0
Valentine	27·5	9	64	5	67	22	149	4
Stollmeyer	4	0	20	0	11	3	28	0
Walcott	1	0	1	0	8	2	14	0
INDIA								
Ramchand	36	9	84	0	15	6	33	2
Hazare	17	2	47	0	2	1	1	0
Gupte	65·1	14	180	5	8	2	16	0
Mankad	82	17	228	5	22	11	26	1
Ghorpade	6	1	22	0				

FALL OF WICKETS

	I	WI	I	WI
Wkt	1st	1st	2nd	2nd
1st	30	36	80	11
2nd	57	133	317	15
3rd	80	330	327	82
4th	230	543	346	91
5th	277	554	360	–
6th	295	554	360	–
7th	295	567	368	–
8th	312	567	408	–
9th	312	569	431	–
10th	–	576	444	–

Umpires: S.C. Burke (3) and T.A. Ewart (2).

Close: 1st day – I(1) 216-3 (Roy 81, Umrigar 80); 2nd – WI(1) 103-1 (Pairaudeau 47, Worrell 39); 3rd – WI(1) 400-3 (Worrell 171, Walcott 36); 4th – I(2) 63-0 (Roy 30, Apte 26); 5th – I(2) 327-3 (Hazare 1).

NEW ZEALAND v SOUTH AFRICA 1952–53 (1st Test)

Played at Basin Reserve, Wellington, on 6, 7, 9, 10 March.
Toss: South Africa.   Result: SOUTH AFRICA won by an innings and 180 runs.
Debuts: New Zealand – R.W. Blair, F.E. Fisher, E.M. Meuli, L.S.M. Miller.

McGlew, whose 255 not out was then the highest score for South Africa in Tests, became the second player after Nazar Mohammad to be on the field throughout a Test match. The Pakistani had achieved this feat in the previous October (*Test No. 356*). The partnership of 246 in 219 minutes between McGlew and Murray established a new seventh-wicket record, since beaten, for all Test cricket; it remains South Africa's highest. It was McGlew's first three-figure score in Tests; he batted 534 minutes and hit a five and 19 fours. South Africa's total is their highest against New Zealand. When he had scored 33, Waite strained muscles in his neck and retired, returning at 187. New Zealand provided the first instance of a side scoring identical totals in both innings of a Test match.

SOUTH AFRICA

D.J. McGlew	not out	255
J.H.B. Waite†	c Mooney b Blair	35
J.C. Watkins	c Reid b Blair	14
K.J. Funston	b Fisher	2
W.R. Endean	c Mooney b Blair	41
R.A. McLean	b Blair	5
J.E. Cheetham*	b Burtt	17
A.R.A. Murray	st Mooney b Burtt	109
P.N.F. Mansell	run out	10
H.J. Tayfield	not out	27
E.R.H. Fuller	did not bat	
Extras	(B 5, LB 4)	9
Total	**(8 wickets declared)**	**524**

NEW ZEALAND

B. Sutcliffe	c McGlew b Watkins	62		b Murray	33
J.G. Leggat	c Fuller b Tayfield	22		c Endean b Watkins	47
F.E. Fisher	b Fuller	9	(9)	c Waite b Watkins	14
W.M. Wallace*	c Waite b Murray	4	(3)	b Tayfield	2
E.M. Meuli	c Endean b Murray	15	(4)	b Fuller	23
L.S.M. Miller	c Endean b Tayfield	17	(5)	c Waite b Watkins	13
J.R. Reid	b Murray	1	(6)	c Waite b Murray	9
F.L.H. Mooney†	not out	27	(7)	b Tayfield	9
A.M. Moir	run out	1	(8)	c Fuller b Watkins	0
T.B. Burtt	lbw b Fuller	10		lbw b Tayfield	0
R.W. Blair	b Fuller	0		not out	6
Extras	(B 3, NB 1)	4		(B 16)	16
Total		**172**			**172**

NEW ZEALAND	O	M	R	W	O	M	R	W		FALL OF WICKETS		
Blair	36	4	98	4						SA	NZ	NZ
Fisher	34	6	78	1					*Wkt*	*1st*	*1st*	*2nd*
Reid	24	8	36	0					1st	83	71	43
Burtt	44	7	140	2					2nd	92	91	46
Moir	35	4	159	0					3rd	177	96	109
Sutcliffe	1	0	4	0					4th	187	98	121
									5th	189	127	137
SOUTH AFRICA									6th	238	131	141
Fuller	19·4	7	29	3	27	8	43	1	7th	484	134	142
Watkins	27	17	29	1	23·5	14	22	4	8th	494	135	162
Tayfield	38	15	53	2	32	12	42	3	9th	–	172	162
Mansell	11	3	27	0	13	2	30	0	10th	–	172	172
Murray	28	15	30	3	23	16	19	2				

Umpires: R.G. Currie (1) and J. McLellan (2).

Close: 1st day – SA(1) 300-6 (McGlew 151, Murray 29); 2nd – NZ(1) 80-1 (Sutcliffe 57, Fisher 0); 3rd – NZ(2) 58-2 (Leggat 13, Meuli 6).

NEW ZEALAND v SOUTH AFRICA 1952–53 (2nd Test)

Played at Eden Park, Auckland, on 13, 14, 16, 17 March.
Toss: South Africa.   Result: MATCH DRAWN.
Debuts: New Zealand – M.E. Chapple, E.W. Dempster, M.B. Poore.

Endean and Cheetham established South Africa's present record fifth-wicket partnership for this series (130).
Tayfield bowled eight successive maiden overs on the third day. Cheetham declared 332 runs ahead when 90
minutes of playing time were left.

SOUTH AFRICA

D.J. McGlew	c Chapple b Dempster	18	b Reid	50
J.H.B. Waite†	c Mooney b Blair	72	b Poore	26
J.C. Watkins	c Reid b Blair	30	c Sutcliffe b Poore	12
K.J. Funston	c Dempster b Poore	13	(5) b Rabone	17
W.R. Endean	st Mooney b Rabone	116	(6) not out	47
J.E. Cheetham*	run out	54	(7) not out	10
R.A. McLean	c Reid b Rabone	0	(4) c Rabone b MacGibbon	20
A.R.A. Murray	b Reid	6		
P.N.F. Mansell	not out	30		
H.J. Tayfield	b Rabone	9		
E.R.H. Fuller	c Mooney b Poore	17		
Extras	(B 7, LB 2, NB 3)	12	(B 6, LB 6, W 4, NB 2)	18
Total		**377**	(5 wickets declared)	**200**

NEW ZEALAND

B. Sutcliffe	c Waite b Tayfield	45	run out	10
M.E. Chapple	c Cheetham b Tayfield	22	c McGlew b Watkins	7
G.O. Rabone	run out	29	not out	6
M.B. Poore	b Mansell	45	not out	8
W.M. Wallace*	c Mansell b Tayfield	23		
L.S.M. Miller	c Waite b Murray	44		
F.L.H. Mooney†	c Endean b Tayfield	2		
J.R. Reid	c Waite b Watkins	7		
A.R. MacGibbon	c Murray b Watkins	2		
E.W. Dempster	c Funston b Tayfield	14		
R.W. Blair	not out	0		
Extras	(B 7, LB 5)	12		
Total		**245**	(2 wickets)	**31**

NEW ZEALAND	O	M	R	W	O	M	R	W		FALL OF WICKETS			
										SA	NZ	SA	NZ
Blair	30	6	64	2	11	3	26	0	*Wkt*	*1st*	*1st*	*2nd*	*2nd*
MacGibbon	28	6	72	0	16	6	17	1	1st	39	54	62	16
Reid	22	3	55	1	13	5	21	1	2nd	78	70	80	20
Dempster	39	9	84	1	13	4	29	0	3rd	124	141	116	–
Rabone	24	4	62	3	17	4	46	1	4th	139	152	124	–
Poore	19	8	28	2	8	1	43	2	5th	269	175	173	–
SOUTH AFRICA									6th	274	185	–	–
Fuller	37	13	60	0	8	1	14	0	7th	308	203	–	–
Watkins	38	20	51	2	8	3	12	1	8th	330	207	–	–
Murray	31	16	29	1					9th	340	245	–	–
Tayfield	46·2	19	62	5	2·3	0	5	0	10th	377	245	–	–
Mansell	18	9	29	1	1	1	0	0					
Cheetham	1	0	2	0									

Umpires: J.C. Harris (2) and T.M. Pearce (2).

Close: 1st day – SA(1) 230-4 (Endean 50, Cheetham 38); 2nd – NZ(1) 74-2 (Rabone 6, Poore 1); 3rd – NZ(1)
245 all out.

ENGLAND v AUSTRALIA 1953 (1st Test)

Played at Trent Bridge, Nottingham, on 11, 12, 13, 15 (*no play*), 16 June.
Toss: Australia.   Result: MATCH DRAWN.
Debuts: Australia – A.K. Davidson, J.C. Hill.

Australia lost their last seven first innings wickets for 12 runs to Bedser, Bailey and the new ball. Bedser's match analysis of 14 for 99, still the record for a Nottingham Test, was the best by an England bowler since 1934. With two days left, England needed 187 to win with nine wickets in hand, but rain prevented further play until 4.30 on the final afternoon. Hassett batted for 394 minutes, hit nine fours and gave no chances during an innings played in heavy atmosphere, poor light and on a damp pitch. Hutton was the first professional to captain England in a home Test against Australia, and the first to do so in either country since A. Shrewsbury in 1886-87.

AUSTRALIA

G.B. Hole	b Bedser	0	b Bedser		5
A.R. Morris	lbw b Bedser	67	b Tattersall		60
A.L. Hassett*	b Bedser	115	c Hutton b Bedser		5
R.N. Harvey	c Compton b Bedser	0	c Graveney b Bedser		2
K.R. Miller	c Bailey b Wardle	55	c Kenyon b Bedser		5
R. Benaud	c Evans b Bailey	3	b Bedser		0
A.K. Davidson	b Bedser	4	c Graveney b Tattersall		6
D. Tallon†	b Bedser	0	c Simpson b Tattersall		15
R.R. Lindwall	c Evans b Bailey	0	c Tattersall b Bedser		12
J.C. Hill	b Bedser	0	c Tattersall b Bedser		4
W.A. Johnston	not out	0	not out		4
Extras	(B 2, LB 2, NB 1)	5	(LB 5)		5
Total		**249**			**123**

ENGLAND

L. Hutton*	c Benaud b Davidson	43	not out	60
D. Kenyon	c Hill b Lindwall	8	c Hassett b Hill	16
R.T. Simpson	lbw b Lindwall	0	not out	28
D.C.S. Compton	c Morris b Lindwall	0		
T.W. Graveney	c Benaud b Hill	22		
P.B.H. May	c Tallon b Hill	9		
T.E. Bailey	lbw b Hill	13		
T.G. Evans†	c Tallon b Davidson	8		
J.H. Wardle	not out	29		
A.V. Bedser	lbw b Lindwall	2		
R. Tattersall	b Lindwall	2		
Extras	(B 5, LB 3)	8	(B 8, LB 4, W 2, NB 2)	16
Total		**144**	(1 wicket)	**120**

ENGLAND	O	M	R	W	O	M	R	W
Bedser	38·3	16	55	7	17·2	7	44	7
Bailey	44	14	75	2	5	1	28	0
Wardle	35	16	55	1	12	3	24	0
Tattersall	23	5	59	0	5	0	22	3
AUSTRALIA								
Lindwall	20·4	2	57	5	16	4	37	0
Johnston	18	7	22	0	18	9	14	0
Hill	19	8	35	3	12	3	26	1
Davidson	15	7	22	2	5	1	7	0
Benaud					5	0	15	0
Morris					2	0	5	0

FALL OF WICKETS

	A	E	A	E
Wkt	1st	1st	2nd	2nd
1st	2	17	28	26
2nd	124	17	44	–
3rd	128	17	50	–
4th	237	76	64	–
5th	244	82	68	–
6th	244	92	81	–
7th	246	107	92	–
8th	247	121	106	–
9th	248	136	115	–
10th	249	144	123	–

Umpires: D. Davies (12) and H. Elliott (6).

Close: 1st day – A(1) 157-3 (Hassett 67, Miller 19); 2nd – E(1) 92-6 (Bailey 2, Evans 0); 3rd – E(2) 42-1 (Hutton 10, Simpson 8); 4th – no play.

ENGLAND v AUSTRALIA 1953 (2nd Test)

Played at Lord's, London, on 25, 26, 27, 29, 30 June.
Toss: Australia.   Result: MATCH DRAWN.
Debuts: Nil.

Hassett, who scored his second hundred in successive Tests, retired at 201 with cramp when 101, and resumed at 280. The final day saw one of the classic rearguard actions of Test cricket, with Watson (109 in 346 minutes on debut against Australia) and Bailey (71 in 257 minutes) saving England from defeat with a fifth-wicket partnership of 163 which lasted from 12.42 pm to 5.50 pm (40 minutes before the close). Bailey later confessed to eating his partner's lunch as well as his own. Brown (42), then chairman of selectors, was persuaded to make his first Test appearance for two years. He ended his career with four wickets and a robust innings of 28 in the final 35 minutes of the match. Earlier, Hutton had made his fifth and final hundred of this series; a chanceless innings, it has been rated as his best. Bedser became the first to take 200 Test wickets for England when he dismissed Davidson.

AUSTRALIA

A.L. Hassett*	c Bailey b Bedser	104		c Evans b Statham	3
A.R. Morris	st Evans b Bedser	30		c Statham b Compton	89
R.N. Harvey	lbw b Bedser	59	(4)	b Bedser	21
K.R. Miller	b Wardle	25	(3)	b Wardle	109
G.B. Hole	c Compton b Wardle	13		lbw b Brown	47
R. Benaud	lbw b Wardle	0		c Graveney b Bedser	5
A.K. Davidson	c Statham b Bedser	76		c and b Brown	15
D.T. Ring	lbw b Wardle	18		lbw b Brown	7
R.R. Lindwall	b Statham	9		b Bedser	50
G.R.A. Langley†	c Watson b Bedser	1		b Brown	9
W.A. Johnston	not out	3		not out	0
Extras	(B 4, LB 4)	8		(B 8, LB 5)	13
Total		**346**			**368**

ENGLAND

L. Hutton*	c Hole b Johnston	145	c Hole b Lindwall	5
D. Kenyon	c Davidson b Lindwall	3	c Hassett b Lindwall	2
T.W. Graveney	b Lindwall	78	c Langley b Johnston	2
D.C.S. Compton	c Hole b Benaud	57	lbw b Johnston	33
W. Watson	st Langley b Johnston	4	c Hole b Ring	109
T.E. Bailey	c and b Miller	2	c Benaud b Ring	71
F.R. Brown	c Langley b Lindwall	22	c Hole b Benaud	28
T.G. Evans†	b Lindwall	0	not out	11
J.H. Wardle	b Davidson	23	not out	0
A.V. Bedser	b Lindwall	1		
J.B. Statham	not out	17		
Extras	(B 11, LB 1, W 1, NB 7)	20	(B 7, LB 6, W 2, NB 6)	21
Total		**372**	(7 wickets)	**282**

ENGLAND	O	M	R	W	O	M	R	W
Bedser	42·4	8	105	5	31·5	8	77	3
Statham	28	7	48	1	15	3	40	1
Brown	25	7	53	0	27	4	82	4
Bailey	16	2	55	0	10	4	24	0
Wardle	29	8	77	4	46	18	111	1
Compton					3	0	21	1
AUSTRALIA								
Lindwall	23	4	66	5	19	3	26	2
Miller	25	6	57	1	17	8	17	0
Johnston	35	11	91	2	29	10	70	2
Ring	14	2	43	0	29	5	84	2
Benaud	19	4	70	1	17	6	51	1
Davidson	10·5	2	25	1	14	5	13	0
Hole					1	1	0	0

FALL OF WICKETS

Wkt	A 1st	E 1st	A 2nd	E 2nd
1st	65	9	3	6
2nd	190	177	168	10
3rd	225	279	227	12
4th	229	291	235	73
5th	240	301	248	236
6th	280	328	296	246
7th	291	328	305	282
8th	330	332	308	–
9th	331	341	362	–
10th	346	372	368	–

Umpires: H.G. Baldwin (9) and F.S. Lee (9).

Close: 1st day – A(1) 263-5 (Davidson 17, Ring 10); 2nd – E(1) 177-1 (Hutton 83, Graveney 78); 3rd – A(2) 96-1 (Morris 35, Miller 58); 4th – E(2) 20-3 (Compton 5, Watson 3).

ENGLAND v AUSTRALIA 1953 (3rd Test)

Played at Old Trafford, Manchester, on 9, 10, 11, 13 (*no play*), 14 July.
Toss: Australia.   Result: MATCH DRAWN.
Debuts: Australia – J.H. de Courcy.

Rain restricted playing time to 13 hours 50 minutes, the last half hour of which saw Wardle induce a startling collapse against the turning ball. This was the ninth successive Test between England and Australia at Old Trafford to be drawn or abandoned (1938). During that sequence play was totally abandoned on nine days.

AUSTRALIA

A.L. Hassett*	b Bailey	26		c Bailey b Bedser	8
A.R. Morris	b Bedser	1		c Hutton b Laker	0
K.R. Miller	b Bedser	17		st Evans b Laker	6
R.N. Harvey	c Evans b Bedser	122	(7)	b Wardle	0
G.B. Hole	c Evans b Bedser	66	(4)	c Evans b Bedser	2
J.H. de Courcy	lbw b Wardle	41	(5)	st Evans b Wardle	8
A.K. Davidson	st Evans b Laker	15	(6)	not out	4
R.G. Archer	c Compton b Bedser	5		lbw b Wardle	0
R.R. Lindwall	c Edrich b Wardle	1		b Wardle	4
J.C. Hill	not out	8		not out	0
G.R.A. Langley†	c Edrich b Wardle	8			
Extras	(B 6, LB 1, NB 1)	8		(LB 3)	3
Total		**318**		(8 wickets)	**35**

ENGLAND

L. Hutton*	lbw b Lindwall	66
W.J. Edrich	c Hole b Hill	6
T.W. Graveney	c De Courcy b Miller	5
D.C.S. Compton	c Langley b Archer	45
J.H. Wardle	b Lindwall	5
W. Watson	b Davidson	16
R.T. Simpson	c Langley b Davidson	31
T.E. Bailey	c Hole b Hill	27
T.G. Evans†	not out	44
J.C. Laker	lbw b Hill	5
A.V. Bedser	b Morris	10
Extras	(B 8, LB 8)	16
Total		**276**

ENGLAND	O	M	R	W	O	M	R	W		FALL OF WICKETS		
Bedser	45	10	115	5	4	1	14	2		A	E	A
Bailey	26	4	83	1					*Wkt*	*1st*	*1st*	*2nd*
Wardle	28·3	10	70	3	5	2	7	4	1st	15	19	8
Laker	17	3	42	1	9	5	11	2	2nd	48	32	12
									3rd	48	126	18
AUSTRALIA									4th	221	126	18
Lindwall	20	8	30	2					5th	256	149	31
Archer	15	8	12	1					6th	285	149	31
Hill	35	7	97	3					7th	290	209	31
Miller	24	11	38	1					8th	291	231	35
Davidson	20	4	60	2					9th	302	243	–
Harvey	3	2	2	0					10th	318	276	–
Hole	2	0	16	0								
Morris	1	0	5	1								

Umpires: D. Davies (13) and H. Elliott (7).

Close: 1st day – A(1) 151-3 (Harvey 60, Hole 41); 2nd – A(1) 221-3 (Harvey 105, Hole 66); 3rd – E(1) 126-4 (Wardle 0, Watson 0); 4th – no play.

ENGLAND v AUSTRALIA 1953 (4th Test)

Played at Headingley, Leeds, on 23, 24, 25, 27, 28 July.
Toss: Australia.   Result: MATCH DRAWN.
Debuts: Nil.

England, put in to bat by Australia for the first time since 1909, scored only 142 runs off 96 overs on the opening day, which rain shortened by 25 minutes. Simpson retired hurt with a severely bruised elbow in the first innings, resuming at the fall of the eighth wicket. Bedser set a world Test record when he dismissed Langley and passed C.V. Grimmett's total of 216 wickets. Lock opened the bowling with Bedser in the second innings when Australia needed 177 runs in 115 minutes. Bailey defended for 262 minutes in the second innings; later he seized the ball and bowled leg theory when Australia were heading for victory.

ENGLAND

L. Hutton*	b Lindwall	0	c Langley b Archer	25
W.J. Edrich	lbw b Miller	10	c De Courcy b Lindwall	64
T.W. Graveney	c Benaud b Miller	55	b Lindwall	3
D.C.S. Compton	c Davidson b Lindwall	0	lbw b Lindwall	61
W. Watson	b Lindwall	24	c Davidson b Miller	15
R.T. Simpson	c Langley b Lindwall	15	c De Courcy b Miller	0
T.E. Bailey	run out	7	c Hole b Davidson	38
T.G. Evans†	lbw b Lindwall	25	c Lindwall b Miller	1
J.C. Laker	c Lindwall b Archer	10	c Benaud b Davidson	48
G.A.R. Lock	b Davidson	9	c Morris b Miller	8
A.V. Bedser	not out	0	not out	3
Extras	(B 8, LB 4)	12	(B 1, LB 8)	9
Total		**167**		**275**

AUSTRALIA

A.L. Hassett*	c Lock b Bedser	37	b Lock	4
A.R. Morris	c Lock b Bedser	10	st Evans b Laker	38
R.N. Harvey	lbw b Bailey	71	(4) lbw b Bedser	34
K.R. Miller	c Edrich b Bailey	5		
G.B. Hole	c Lock b Bedser	53	(3) c Graveney b Bailey	33
J.H. de Courcy	lbw b Lock	10	not out	13
R. Benaud	b Bailey	7		
A.K. Davidson	c Evans b Bedser	2	(5) not out	17
R.G. Archer	not out	31		
R.R. Lindwall	b Bedser	9		
G.R.A. Langley†	c Hutton b Bedser	17		
Extras	(B 4, LB 8, W 2)	14	(B 3, LB 4, W 1)	8
Total		**266**	(4 wickets)	**147**

AUSTRALIA	O	M	R	W	O	M	R	W	FALL OF WICKETS				
Lindwall	35	10	54	5	54	19	104	3		E	A	E	A
Miller	28	13	39	2	47	19	63	4	*Wkt*	*1st*	*1st*	*2nd*	*2nd*
Davidson	20·4	7	23	1	29·3	15	36	2	1st	0	27	57	27
Archer	18	4	27	1	25	12	31	1	2nd	33	70	62	54
Benaud	8	1	12	0	19	8	26	0	3rd	36	84	139	111
Hole					3	1	6	0	4th	98	168	167	117
									5th	108	183	171	–
ENGLAND									6th	110	203	182	–
Bedser	28·5	2	95	6	17	1	65	1	7th	133	203	239	–
Bailey	22	4	71	3	6	1	9	1	8th	149	208	244	–
Lock	23	9	53	1	8	1	48	1	9th	167	218	258	–
Laker	9	1	33	0	2	0	17	1	10th	167	266	275	–

Umpires: F. Chester (44) and F.S. Lee (10).

Close: 1st day – E(1) 142-7 (Evans 18, Lock 5); 2nd – A(1) 266 all out; 3rd – E(2) 62-1 (Edrich 33, Graveney 3); 4th – E(2) 177-5 (Compton 60, Bailey 4).

ENGLAND v AUSTRALIA 1953 (5th Test)

Played at Kennington Oval, London, on 15, 17, 18, 19 August.
Toss: Australia.   Result: ENGLAND won by eight wickets.
Debuts: Nil.

By winning this six-day Test, England regained the Ashes after Australia had held them for the record period of 18 years 362 days. Hutton became the first captain to win a rubber after losing the toss in all five Tests. Bedser, who dismissed Morris for the 18th time in 20 Tests, beat M.W. Tate's record by taking 39 wickets in a rubber against Australia. When his score reached 52, Lindwall became the fourth to complete the double for Australia. The rubber attracted a total attendance of 549,650 – the record for England.

AUSTRALIA

A.L. Hassett*	c Evans b Bedser	53	lbw b Laker	10
A.R. Morris	lbw b Bedser	16	lbw b Lock	26
K.R. Miller	lbw b Bailey	1	(5) c Trueman b Laker	0
R.N. Harvey	c Hutton b Trueman	36	b Lock	1
G.B. Hole	c Evans b Trueman	37	(3) lbw b Laker	17
J.H. de Courcy	c Evans b Trueman	5	run out	4
R.G. Archer	c and b Bedser	10	c Edrich b Lock	49
A.K. Davidson	c Edrich b Laker	22	b Lock	21
R.R. Lindwall	c Evans b Trueman	62	c Compton b Laker	12
G.R.A. Langley†	c Edrich b Lock	18	c Trueman b Lock	2
W.A. Johnston	not out	9	not out	6
Extras	(B 4, NB 2)	6	(B 11, LB 3)	14
Total		**275**		**162**

ENGLAND

L. Hutton*	b Johnston	82	run out	17
W.J. Edrich	lbw b Lindwall	21	not out	55
P.B.H. May	c Archer b Johnston	39	c Davidson b Miller	37
D.C.S. Compton	c Langley b Lindwall	16	not out	22
T.W. Graveney	c Miller b Lindwall	4		
T.E. Bailey	b Archer	64		
T.G. Evans†	run out	28		
J.C. Laker	c Langley b Miller	1		
G.A.R. Lock	c Davidson b Lindwall	4		
F.S. Trueman	b Johnston	10		
A.V. Bedser	not out	22		
Extras	(B 9, LB 5, W 1)	15	(LB 1)	1
Total		**306**	(2 wickets)	**132**

ENGLAND	O	M	R	W	O	M	R	W		FALL OF WICKETS			
Bedser	29	3	88	3	11	2	24	0		A	E	A	E
Trueman	24·3	3	86	4	2	1	4	0	Wkt	1st	1st	2nd	2nd
Bailey	14	3	42	1					1st	38	37	23	24
Lock	9	2	19	1	21	9	45	5	2nd	41	137	59	88
Laker	5	0	34	1	16·5	2	75	4	3rd	107	154	60	–
									4th	107	167	61	–
AUSTRALIA									5th	118	170	61	–
Lindwall	32	7	70	4	21	5	46	0	6th	160	210	85	–
Miller	34	12	65	1	11	3	24	1	7th	160	225	135	–
Johnston	45	16	94	3	29	14	52	0	8th	207	237	140	–
Davidson	10	1	26	0					9th	245	262	144	–
Archer	10·3	2	25	1	1	1	0	0	10th	275	306	162	–
Hole	11	6	11	0									
Hassett					1	0	4	0					
Morris					0·5	0	5	0					

Umpires: D. Davies (14) and F.S. Lee (11).

Close: 1st day – E(1) 1-0 (Hutton 0, Edrich 1); 2nd – E(1) 235-7 (Bailey 33, Lock 4); 3rd – E(2) 38-1 (Edrich 15, May 6).

SOUTH AFRICA v NEW ZEALAND 1953–54 (1st Test)

Played at Kingsmead, Durban, on 11, 12, 14, 15 December.
Toss: South Africa.   Result: SOUTH AFRICA won by an innings and 58 runs.
Debuts: South Africa – N.A.T. Adcock; New Zealand – G.W.F. Overton.

New Zealand's first Test match in the Union resulted in South Africa's first home win for 23 years. McLean reached his first Test hundred in 138 minutes, his partnership of 135 with Funston being South Africa's highest for the fourth wicket in this series. Rabone batted 361 minutes for his only century in Tests, before resisting a further 151 minutes when his side followed on.

SOUTH AFRICA

D.J. McGlew	b MacGibbon	84
J.H.B. Waite†	b Overton	43
W.R. Endean	b MacGibbon	6
K.J. Funston	lbw b Reid	39
R.A. McLean	c Chapple b Blair	101
J.C. Watkins	c Mooney b MacGibbon	29
J.E. Cheetham*	b Rabone	17
C.B. van Ryneveld	not out	68
H.J. Tayfield	b Overton	28
A.R.A. Murray	b Blair	0
N.A.T. Adcock	did not bat	
Extras	(B 10, LB 8, W 1, NB 3)	22
Total	(9 wickets declared)	**437**

NEW ZEALAND

B. Sutcliffe	c Waite b Tayfield	20		c Endean b Tayfield	16
G.O. Rabone*	lbw b Tayfield	107	(5)	b Adcock	68
M.E. Chapple	b Tayfield	1	(2)	c Funston b Watkins	1
J.R. Reid	b Tayfield	6	(3)	c Funston b Watkins	0
L.S.M. Miller	lbw b Van Ryneveld	13	(6)	lbw b Murray	18
M.B. Poore	c Cheetham b Tayfield	32	(7)	st Waite b Van Ryneveld	1
F.L.H. Mooney†	b Watkins	9	(4)	c Waite b Adcock	7
A.R. MacGibbon	st Waite b Van Ryneveld	21		c Watkins b Tayfield	19
E.W. Dempster	not out	7		c McGlew b Adcock	0
R.W. Blair	b Tayfield	2		st Waite b Tayfield	6
G.W.F. Overton	b Van Ryneveld	2		not out	3
Extras	(B 9, LB 1)	10		(B 6, LB 3, NB 1)	10
Total		**230**			**149**

NEW ZEALAND	O	M	R	W	O	M	R	W
Blair	22	2	104	2				
Reid	16	2	49	1				
Overton	27	8	92	2				
MacGibbon	27	4	73	3				
Poore	5	0	30	0				
Dempster	10	1	36	0				
Rabone	8	0	31	1				
SOUTH AFRICA								
Adcock	19	3	52	0	14	4	38	3
Watkins	15	5	28	1	14	7	16	2
Murray	7	5	9	0	7	4	8	1
Tayfield	36	17	62	6	26·1	12	35	3
Van Ryneveld	28·6	6	69	3	21	9	42	1

FALL OF WICKETS

Wkt	SA 1st	NZ 1st	NZ 2nd
1st	113	39	6
2nd	140	53	15
3rd	143	75	24
4th	278	100	36
5th	294	162	85
6th	335	181	103
7th	337	215	125
8th	422	215	125
9th	437	219	146
10th	–	230	149

Umpires: A.N. McCabe (1) and B.V. Malan (3).

Close: 1st day – SA(1) 278-3 (Funston 39, McLean 93); 2nd – NZ(1) 70-2 (Rabone 40, Reid 5); 3rd – NZ(2) 22-2 (Sutcliffe 15, Mooney 5).

SOUTH AFRICA v NEW ZEALAND 1953–54 (2nd Test)

Played at Ellis Park, Johannesburg, on 24, 26, 28, 29 December.
Toss: South Africa.   Result: SOUTH AFRICA won by 132 runs.
Debuts: South Africa – D.E.J. Ironside; New Zealand – J.E.F. Beck.

Adcock produced one of Test cricket's most lethal spells on the second day. Chapple and Poore were bowled via their chests and Sutcliffe and Miller were put in hospital. Sutcliffe (0) was struck on the head, retired at 9 and resumed at 81. He proceeded to hit seven sixes and four fours, scoring 80 out of 106 in 112 minutes, and became the first New Zealander to reach 1,000 runs in Tests. Miller (1) retired at 24 after being struck on the chest, and returned at 57. Blair, who had learnt on Christmas Day of the death of his fiancée in the Tangiwai train disaster, surprisingly appeared at the fall of the ninth wicket, walking slowly as the entire crowd stood in silence. He helped Sutcliffe score 33 runs in ten minutes, 25 of them coming from Tayfield's eighth over (66061060).

SOUTH AFRICA

D.J. McGlew	c Reid b MacGibbon	13	b MacGibbon	8
A.R.A. Murray	c Chapple b Blair	7	(9) c Blair b Overton	13
W.R. Endean	c Sutcliffe b Reid	93	c sub (I.B. Leggat) b Reid	1
K.J. Funston	lbw b Overton	0	c Overton b MacGibbon	11
R.A. McLean	c Blair b Overton	27	(7) lbw b Reid	36
C.B. van Ryneveld	b Blair	65	(8) c Reid b MacGibbon	17
J.E. Cheetham*	c Mooney b MacGibbon	20	(6) c Sutcliffe b Reid	1
H.J. Tayfield	not out	20	(5) b Reid	34
J.H.B. Waite†	c Mooney b MacGibbon	0	(2) c Reid b MacGibbon	5
D.E.J. Ironside	b Reid	13	not out	11
N.A.T. Adcock	run out	0	c Poore b Overton	6
Extras	(B 3, LB 2, NB 8)	13	(LB 3, NB 2)	5
Total		**271**		**148**

NEW ZEALAND

G.O. Rabone*	c Endean b Ironside	1	c Van Ryneveld b Adcock	22
M.E. Chapple	b Adcock	8	c Waite b Ironside	22
M.B. Poore	b Adcock	15	b Adcock	1
B. Sutcliffe	not out	80	c Endean b Murray	10
J.R. Reid	c Endean b Adcock	3	(6) c Funston b Ironside	1
L.S.M. Miller	b Ironside	14	(7) c Waite b Adcock	0
J.E.F. Beck	c Waite b Murray	16	(8) c Endean b Ironside	7
F.L.H. Mooney†	b Ironside	35	(5) c Funston b Adcock	10
A.R. MacGibbon	c Endean b Ironside	0	not out	11
G.W.F. Overton	c Murray b Ironside	0	(11) run out	2
R.W. Blair	st Waite b Tayfield	6	(10) b Adcock	4
Extras	(B 3, LB 4, NB 2)	9	(B 3, LB 5, NB 2)	10
Total		**187**		**100**

NEW ZEALAND	O	M	R	W	O	M	R	W
Blair	17	4	50	2	5	0	14	0
Reid	18	3	63	2	16	5	34	4
Overton	20	4	68	2	12·1	1	33	2
MacGibbon	22	5	61	3	20	2	62	4
Rabone	3	0	16	0				
SOUTH AFRICA								
Adcock	14	2	44	3	19	4	43	5
Ironside	19	4	51	5	20·5	10	37	3
Murray	12	3	30	1	8	3	10	1
Tayfield	8·2	2	53	1				

FALL OF WICKETS

	SA	NZ	SA	NZ
Wkt	1st	1st	2nd	2nd
1st	13	5	11	35
2nd	37	9	13	38
3rd	43	23	24	58
4th	100	35	37	75
5th	168	57	44	75
6th	226	81	67	76
7th	244	138	112	76
8th	244	146	122	84
9th	271	154	138	89
10th	271	187	148	100

Umpires: C.D. Coote (1) and D.T. Drew (2).

Close: 1st day – SA(1) 259-8 (Tayfield 16, Ironside 6); 2nd – SA(2) 35-3 (Waite 4, Tayfield 9); 3rd – NZ(2) 68-3 (Rabone 19, Mooney 6).

SOUTH AFRICA v NEW ZEALAND 1953–54 (3rd Test)

Played at Newlands, Cape Town, on 1, 2, 4, 5 January.
Toss: New Zealand.   Result: MATCH DRAWN.
Debuts: South Africa – R.J. Westcott; New Zealand – W. Bell, I.B. Leggat.

New Zealand recorded their highest total and enforced the follow-on for the first time in any Test match. The partnership of 176 between Reid, who batted 196 minutes, and Beck, a 19-year-old who batted 224 minutes, set a record, subsequently beaten, for New Zealand's fifth wicket, and is their highest for any wicket against South Africa. Rabone's figures of 6 for 68 remain New Zealand's best analysis in a Test in South Africa. For the first time brothers umpired a Test match.

NEW ZEALAND

G.O. Rabone*	lbw b Van Ryneveld	56
M.E. Chapple	c Waite b Van Ryneveld	76
M.B. Poore	c McGlew b Adcock	44
B. Sutcliffe	c Waite b Ironside	66
J.R. Reid	b Murray	135
J.E.F. Beck	run out	99
F.L.H. Mooney†	b Ironside	4
A.R. MacGibbon	c McGlew b Ironside	8
E.W. Dempster	c Endean b Ironside	0
I.B. Leggat	c McGlew b Tayfield	0
W. Bell	not out	0
Extras	(B 14, LB 3)	17
Total		**505**

SOUTH AFRICA

D.J. McGlew	c Sutcliffe b MacGibbon	86	c Chapple b Poore	28
J.H.B. Waite†	lbw b MacGibbon	8	st Mooney b Rabone	16
R.J. Westcott	c Leggat b MacGibbon	2	b Dempster	62
W.R. Endean	c Sutcliffe b MacGibbon	33	not out	34
R.A. McLean	c Mooney b Rabone	9	not out	18
C.B. van Ryneveld	c Mooney b Rabone	23		
J.E. Cheetham*	b Rabone	89		
A.R.A. Murray	lbw b Rabone	6		
H.J. Tayfield	c Leggat b Rabone	34		
D.E.J. Ironside	c MacGibbon b Rabone	10		
N.A.T. Adcock	not out	8		
Extras	(B 6, LB 6, NB 6)	18	(B 1)	1
Total		**326**	(3 wickets)	**159**

SOUTH AFRICA	O	M	R	W	O	M	R	W		FALL OF WICKETS		
Adcock	29	3	105	1						NZ	SA	SA
Ironside	46·3	16	117	4					*Wkt*	*1st*	*1st*	*2nd*
Murray	34	8	93	1					1st	126	17	26
Tayfield	33	10	80	1					2nd	145	23	57
Van Ryneveld	23	1	93	2					3rd	239	82	139
									4th	271	101	–
NEW ZEALAND									5th	447	172	–
MacGibbon	33	13	71	4	8	4	15	0	6th	472	180	–
Reid	20	7	48	0	4	1	8	0	7th	490	204	–
Leggat	3	0	6	0					8th	505	299	–
Bell	18	5	77	0	6	2	22	0	9th	505	313	–
Rabone	38·7	10	68	6	10	6	16	1	10th	505	326	–
Dempster	8	3	19	0	6	0	24	1				
Sutcliffe	5	1	13	0	7	0	33	0				
Poore	2	0	6	0	12	1	39	1				
Chapple					1	0	1	0				

Umpires: D. Collins (6) and S. Collins (1).

Close: 1st day – NZ(1) 212-2 (Poore 31, Sutcliffe 37); 2nd – SA(1) 5-0 (McGlew 1, Waite 3); 3rd – SA(1) 206-7 (Cheetham 25, Tayfield 2).

SOUTH AFRICA v NEW ZEALAND 1953–54 (4th Test)

Played at Ellis Park, Johannesburg, on 29, 30 January, 1, 2 February.
Toss: New Zealand.   Result: SOUTH AFRICA won by nine wickets.
Debuts: Nil.

South Africa won their first home rubber since beating England one-nil in 1930-31. In one first innings spell, Tayfield's off-spin accounted for five wickets for no runs in 32 balls. New Zealand's 79 remains the lowest score by either country in this series. Sutcliffe elected to field for the second time in his three Tests as captain – Rabone having fractured a bone in his right foot while batting against Border immediately before this match.

SOUTH AFRICA

D.J. McGlew	lbw b MacGibbon	61	not out	6
R.J. Westcott	c Chapple b Overton	43	lbw b MacGibbon	1
J.C. Watkins	c Mooney b MacGibbon	6		
W.R. Endean	c Sutcliffe b Overton	7		
R.A. McLean	c Sutcliffe b Overton	0		
C.B. van Ryneveld	c Mooney b Blair	11		
J.E. Cheetham*	run out	29	(3) not out	16
J.H.B. Waite†	run out	52		
H.J. Tayfield	c Reid b Blair	19		
D.E.J. Ironside	not out	3		
N.A.T. Adcock	b Blair	0		
Extras	(B 4, LB 4, NB 4)	12	(NB 2)	2
Total		**243**	(1 wicket)	**25**

NEW ZEALAND

F.L.H. Mooney†	run out	23	(2) b Adcock	2
M.E. Chapple	c Waite b Ironside	4	(4) c sub (K.J. Funston) b Watkins	42
M.B. Poore	c and b Tayfield	18	c Endean b Adcock	0
B. Sutcliffe*	c McLean b Tayfield	0	(6) b Adcock	23
J.R. Reid	c Waite b Tayfield	0	c Ironside b Tayfield	26
L.S.M. Miller	b Tayfield	0	(7) c Waite b Tayfield	0
J.E.F. Beck	b Tayfield	0	(8) b Adcock	21
E.W. Dempster	not out	21	(1) c Waite b Watkins	47
A.R. MacGibbon	st Waite b Ironside	10	b Adcock	8
R.W. Blair	b Tayfield	1	not out	5
G.W.F. Overton	b Adcock	0	c Van Ryneveld b Ironside	1
Extras	(LB 1, NB 1)	2	(B 5, LB 6, NB 2)	13
Total		**79**		**188**

NEW ZEALAND	O	M	R	W	O	M	R	W		FALL OF WICKETS			
Blair	19	4	42	3	3	0	6	0		SA	NZ	NZ	SA
Reid	21	3	67	0					*Wkt*	*1st*	*1st*	*2nd*	*2nd*
MacGibbon	26	6	57	2	3	0	16	1	1st	104	14	4	4
Overton	32	10	65	3					2nd	112	34	8	–
Miller					0·2	0	1	0	3rd	122	34	79	–
									4th	122	34	113	–
SOUTH AFRICA									5th	125	40	139	–
Adcock	11·3	1	27	1	26	8	45	5	6th	139	40	141	–
Ironside	14	5	20	2	23·2	6	50	1	7th	174	46	168	–
Watkins	7	1	17	0	12	4	13	2	8th	228	69	182	–
Tayfield	14	7	13	6	29	12	48	2	9th	243	76	183	–
Van Ryneveld					2	0	19	0	10th	243	79	188	–

Umpires: D.T. Drew (3) and B.V. Malan (4).

Close: 1st day – SA(1) 200-7 (Waite 24, Tayfield 10); 2nd – NZ(2) 8-1 (Dempster 5, Poore 0); 3rd – NZ(2) 148-6 (Sutcliffe 13, Beck 6).

SOUTH AFRICA v NEW ZEALAND 1953–54 (5th Test)

Played at St George's Park, Port Elizabeth, on 5, 6, 8, 9 February.
Toss: New Zealand.   Result: SOUTH AFRICA won by five wickets.
Debuts: Nil.

The selectors caused a major surprise by omitting McLean, who had scored a rapid maiden hundred in the 1st Test.

NEW ZEALAND

F.L.H. Mooney†	c Tayfield b Murray	24	c Van Ryneveld b Adcock	9
M.E. Chapple	c Waite b Watkins	18	lbw b Murray	8
M.B. Poore	c Waite b Adcock	41	c Waite b Van Ryneveld	18
B. Sutcliffe*	c Waite b Watkins	38	c and b Van Ryneveld	52
J.R. Reid	b Adcock	19	run out	73
L.S.M. Miller	c Endean b Adcock	0	(9) c Waite b Adcock	2
J.E.F. Beck	b Adcock	48	(6) b Tayfield	12
E.W. Dempster	c and b Watkins	16	(7) st Waite b Van Ryneveld	1
A.R. MacGibbon	b Watkins	7	(8) c Adcock b Watkins	14
R.W. Blair	c Murray b Tayfield	8	st Waite b Van Ryneveld	8
W. Bell	not out	0	not out	21
Extras	(LB 1, W 1, NB 5)	7	(LB 3, NB 1)	4
Total		**226**		**222**

SOUTH AFRICA

D.J. McGlew	b Bell	27	run out	38
R.J. Westcott	lbw b Reid	29	b MacGibbon	11
J.E. Cheetham*	c Sutcliffe b MacGibbon	42	(7) not out	13
K.J. Funston	lbw b Reid	10	(3) c Mooney b MacGibbon	0
W.R. Endean	c Reid b MacGibbon	32	(4) c and b Bell	87
J.C. Watkins	b Reid	13	(5) b Reid	45
C.B. van Ryneveld	lbw b Blair	40	(6) not out	10
J.H.B. Waite†	not out	20		
H.J. Tayfield	c Sutcliffe b Blair	2		
A.R.A. Murray	lbw b Reid	7		
N.A.T. Adcock	b MacGibbon	5		
Extras	(B 3, LB 1, NB 6)	10	(B 5, LB 4, NB 2)	11
Total		**237**	(5 wickets)	**215**

SOUTH AFRICA	O	M	R	W	O	M	R	W		FALL OF WICKETS			
										NZ	SA	NZ	SA
Adcock	19	1	86	4	19	1	45	2	*Wkt*	*1st*	*1st*	*2nd*	*2nd*
Watkins	16	6	34	4	14	6	21	1	1st	24	40	13	44
Tayfield	29·3	15	35	1	17	5	51	1	2nd	64	69	17	46
Van Ryneveld	7	1	15	0	20·6	1	67	4	3rd	99	89	77	81
Murray	21	4	49	1	17	7	34	1	4th	141	140	122	188
									5th	146	146	161	198
NEW ZEALAND									6th	146	173	166	–
Blair	16	4	39	2	7	0	15	0	7th	176	207	181	–
MacGibbon	22·1	2	55	3	10	0	44	2	8th	188	209	189	–
Reid	32	16	51	4	15	2	64	1	9th	226	224	193	–
Bell	28	6	82	1	9·3	0	54	1	10th	226	237	222	–
Dempster					5	0	27	0					
Mooney					1	1	0	0					

Umpires: D. Collins (7) and F.R.W. Payne (1).

Close: 1st day – NZ(1) 218-8 (Beck 42, Blair 6); 2nd – SA(1) 194-6 (Van Ryneveld 30, Waite 6); 3rd – NZ(2) 141-4 (Reid 42, Beck 10).

WEST INDIES v ENGLAND 1953–54 (1st Test)

Played at Sabina Park, Kingston, Jamaica, on 15, 16, 18, 19, 20, 21 January.
Toss: West Indies.   Result: WEST INDIES won by 140 runs.
Debuts: West Indies – M.C. Frederick, J.K. Holt, jr (*Holt's father, also 'J.K.', represented Jamaica 1905-06 to 1929-30 and toured England with the 1923 West Indies team*), C.A. McWatt; England – A.E. Moss.

Stollmeyer evoked much criticism for not enforcing the follow-on. Lock became the second bowler after E. Jones in 1897-98 (*Test No. 54*) to be no-balled for throwing in a Test match; he was no-balled once in the second innings. Physical attacks were made on the wife and son of umpire Burke who upheld an appeal against Holt when the local player was six runs short of a century in his first Test. England were left 9½ hours in which to score 457 and were 227 for 2 at the start of the last day.

WEST INDIES

M.C. Frederick	c Graveney b Statham	0	lbw b Statham		30
J.B. Stollmeyer*	lbw b Statham	60	c Evans b Bailey		8
J.K. Holt	lbw b Statham	94	lbw b Moss		1
E. de C. Weekes	b Moss	55	not out		90
C.L. Walcott	b Lock	65	c Bailey b Lock		25
G.A. Headley	c Graveney b Lock	16	b Lock		1
G.E. Gomez	not out	47	lbw b Statham		3
C.A. McWatt†	b Lock	54	not out		36
S. Ramadhin	lbw b Trueman	7			
E.S.M. Kentish	b Statham	0			
A.L. Valentine	b Trueman	0			
Extras	(B 9, LB 4, W 1, NB 5)	19	(B 10, LB 4, NB 1)		15
Total		**417**	(6 wickets declared)		**209**

ENGLAND

W. Watson	b Gomez	3	c and b Stollmeyer		116
L. Hutton*	b Valentine	24	lbw b Gomez		56
P.B.H. May	c Headley b Ramadhin	31	c McWatt b Kentish		69
D.C.S. Compton	lbw b Valentine	12	(5) b Ramadhin		2
T.W. Graveney	lbw b Ramadhin	16	(4) c Weekes b Kentish		34
T.E. Bailey	not out	28	not out		15
T.G. Evans†	c Kentish b Valentine	10	b Kentish		0
G.A.R. Lock	b Ramadhin	4	b Kentish		0
J.B. Statham	b Ramadhin	8	lbw b Ramadhin		1
F.S. Trueman	c McWatt b Gomez	18	b Kentish		1
A.E. Moss	b Gomez	0	run out		16
Extras	(B 9, LB 2, W 1, NB 4)	16	(B 4, LB 1, NB 1)		6
Total		**170**			**316**

ENGLAND	O	M	R	W	O	M	R	W
Statham	36	6	90	4	17	2	50	2
Trueman	34·4	8	107	2	6	0	32	0
Moss	26	5	84	1	10	0	30	1
Bailey	16	4	36	0	20	4	46	1
Lock	41	14	76	3	14	2	36	2
Compton	2	1	5	0				
WEST INDIES								
Kentish	14	5	23	0	29	11	49	5
Gomez	9·2	3	16	3	30	9	63	1
Ramadhin	35	14	65	4	35·3	12	88	2
Valentine	31	10	50	3	25	6	71	0
Headley					5	0	23	0
Walcott					2	1	4	0
Stollmeyer					3	0	12	1

FALL OF WICKETS

Wkt	WI 1st	E 1st	WI 2nd	E 2nd
1st	6	4	28	130
2nd	140	49	31	220
3rd	216	73	46	277
4th	234	79	92	282
5th	286	94	94	282
6th	316	105	119	282
7th	404	117	–	282
8th	415	135	–	283
9th	416	165	–	285
10th	417	170	–	316

Umpires: P. Burke (1) and T.A. Ewart (3).

Close: 1st day – WI(1) 168-2 (Holt 76, Weekes 21); 2nd – WI(1) 408-7 (Gomez 41, Ramadhin 4); 3rd – E(1) 168-9 (Bailey 26, Moss 0); 4th – WI(2) 203-6 (Weekes 86, McWatt 34); 5th – E(2) 227-2 (May 50, Graveney 1).

WEST INDIES v ENGLAND 1953–54 (2nd Test)

Played at Kensington Oval, Bridgetown, Barbados, on 6, 8, 9, 10, 11, 12 February.
Toss: West Indies.   Result: WEST INDIES won by 181 runs.
Debuts: England – C.H. Palmer.

Walcott recorded his only double-century in Tests in an innings lasting 6½ hours. On the third day England scored only 128 runs from 114 overs. Hutton lost the toss for the seventh consecutive time. England required 495 runs to win in 9½ hours and were 259 for 3 soon after lunch on the final day when Compton was adjudged 'lbw' stretching forward to a googly. Ninety minutes later the match had ended.

WEST INDIES

J.K. Holt	c Graveney b Bailey	11	c and b Statham	166
J.B. Stollmeyer*	run out	0	run out	28
F.M.M. Worrell	b Statham	0	not out	76
C.L. Walcott	st Evans b Laker	220	not out	17
B.H. Pairaudeau	c Hutton b Laker	71		
G.E. Gomez	lbw b Statham	7		
D. St E. Atkinson	c Evans b Laker	53		
C.A. McWatt†	lbw b Lock	11		
S. Ramadhin	b Statham	1		
F.M. King	b Laker	5		
A.L. Valentine	not out	0		
Extras	(LB 2, NB 2)	4	(B 4, NB 1)	5
Total		**383**	(2 wickets declared)	**292**

ENGLAND

L. Hutton*	c Ramadhin b Valentine	72	c Worrell b Ramadhin	77
W. Watson	st McWatt b Ramadhin	6	c McWatt b King	0
P.B.H. May	c King b Ramadhin	7	c Walcott b Gomez	62
D.C.S. Compton	c King b Valentine	13	lbw b Stollmeyer	93
T.W. Graveney	c and b Ramadhin	15	not out	64
C.H. Palmer	c Walcott b Ramadhin	22	c Gomez b Atkinson	0
T.E. Bailey	c McWatt b Atkinson	28	c sub (C.C. Hunte) b Stollmeyer	4
T.G. Evans†	b Gomez	10	b Ramadhin	5
J.C. Laker	c Gomez b Atkinson	1	lbw b Ramadhin	0
G.A.R. Lock	not out	0	b King	0
J.B. Statham	c Holt b Valentine	3	b Gomez	0
Extras	(B 2, LB 1, NB 1)	4	(B 6, LB 1, W 1)	8
Total		**181**		**313**

ENGLAND	O	M	R	W	O	M	R	W
Statham	27	6	90	3	15	1	49	1
Bailey	22	6	63	1	12	1	48	0
Lock	41	9	116	1	33	7	100	0
Laker	30·1	6	81	4	30	13	62	0
Compton	5	0	29	0	1	0	13	0
Palmer					5	1	15	0
WEST INDIES								
King	14	6	28	0	18	6	56	2
Gomez	13	8	10	1	13·4	3	28	2
Worrell	9	2	21	0	1	0	10	0
Atkinson	9	7	5	2	23	10	35	1
Ramadhin	53	30	50	4	37	17	71	3
Valentine	51·5	30	61	3	39	18	87	0
Stollmeyer	1	0	2	0	6	1	14	2
Walcott					2	0	4	0

FALL OF WICKETS

Wkt	WI 1st	E 1st	WI 2nd	E 2nd
1st	11	35	51	1
2nd	11	45	273	108
3rd	25	70	–	181
4th	190	107	–	258
5th	226	119	–	259
6th	319	158	–	264
7th	352	176	–	281
8th	372	176	–	281
9th	378	177	–	300
10th	383	181	–	313

Umpires: H.B. de C. Jordan (2) and J.H. Walcott (3).

Close: 1st day – WI(1) 258-5 (Walcott 147, Atkinson 18); 2nd – E(1) 53-2 (Hutton 34, Compton 5); 3rd – E(1) 181-9 (Lock 0, Statham 3); 4th – WI(2) 272-1 (Holt 166, Worrell 74); 5th – E(2) 214-3 (Compton 65, Graveney 5).

WEST INDIES v ENGLAND 1953–54 (3rd Test)

Played at Bourda, Georgetown, British Guiana, on 24, 25, 26, 27 February, 1, 2 March.
Toss: England.   Result: ENGLAND won by nine wickets.
Debuts: Nil.

Valentine took his hundredth Test wicket at the age of 23 years 302 days. The partnership of 99 between McWatt and Holt remains the West Indies record for the eighth wicket against England. When it was ended with a run out, sections of the crowd hurled bottles and other missiles on to the playing area. Watson completed England's victory with a six.

ENGLAND

W. Watson	b Ramadhin	12	(3) not out		27
L. Hutton*	c Worrell b Ramadhin	169			
P.B.H. May	lbw b Atkinson	12	(2) b Atkinson		12
D.C.S. Compton	c Stollmeyer b Atkinson	64			
T.W. Graveney	b Ramadhin	0	(1) not out		33
J.H. Wardle	b Ramadhin	38			
T.E. Bailey	c Weekes b Ramadhin	49			
T.G. Evans†	lbw b Atkinson	19			
J.C. Laker	b Valentine	27			
G.A.R. Lock	b Ramadhin	13			
J.B. Statham	not out	10			
Extras	(B 20, NB 2)	22	(B 3)		3
Total		**435**	(1 wicket)		**75**

WEST INDIES

F.M.M. Worrell	c Evans b Statham	0	(3) c Evans b Statham		2
J.B. Stollmeyer*	b Statham	2	c Compton b Laker		44
E. de C. Weekes	b Lock	94	(4) c Graveney b Bailey		38
C.L. Walcott	b Statham	4	(5) lbw b Laker		26
R.J. Christiani	c Watson b Laker	25	(6) b Bailey		11
G.E. Gomez	b Statham	8	(7) c Graveney b Wardle		35
D. St E. Atkinson	c and b Lock	0	(8) b Wardle		18
C.A. McWatt†	run out	54	(9) not out		9
J.K. Holt	not out	48	(1) b Lock		64
S. Ramadhin	b Laker	0	b Statham		1
A.L. Valentine	run out	0	b Wardle		0
Extras	(B 8, LB 7, W 1)	16	(B 2, LB 4, NB 2)		8
Total		**251**			**256**

WEST INDIES	O	M	R	W	O	M	R	W	FALL OF WICKETS				
Gomez	32	6	75	0	5	1	15	0		E	WI	WI	E
Worrell	15	4	33	0					Wkt	1st	1st	2nd	2nd
Ramadhin	67	34	113	6	4	0	7	0	1st	33	1	79	18
Valentine	44	18	109	1					2nd	76	12	96	–
Atkinson	58	27	78	3	7	0	34	1	3rd	226	16	120	–
Stollmeyer	2	1	3	0					4th	227	78	168	–
Walcott	2	0	2	0	2	0	6	0	5th	306	132	186	–
Weekes					1·1	0	8	0	6th	321	134	200	–
Christiani					1	0	2	0	7th	350	139	245	–
ENGLAND									8th	390	238	246	–
Statham	27	6	64	4	22	3	86	2	9th	412	240	251	–
Bailey	5	0	13	0	22	9	41	2	10th	435	251	256	–
Laker	21	11	32	2	36	18	56	2					
Wardle	22	4	60	0	12·3	4	24	3					
Compton	3	1	6	0									
Lock	27·5	7	60	2	25	11	41	1					

Umpires: E.S. Gillette (3) and B. Menzies (1).

Close: 1st day – E(1) 153-2 (Hutton 84, Compton 37); 2nd – E(1) 401-8 (Bailey 40, Lock 0); 3rd – WI(1) 31-3 (Weekes 21, Christiani 3); 4th – WI(1) 241-9 (Holt 38, Valentine 0); 5th – WI(2) 205-6 (Gomez 13, Atkinson 0).

WEST INDIES v ENGLAND 1953–54 (4th Test)

Played at Queen's Park Oval, Port-of-Spain, Trinidad, on 17, 18, 19, 20, 22, 23 March.
Toss: West Indies.   Result: MATCH DRAWN.
Debuts: Nil.

Batsmen averaged nearly 64 runs per wicket (1,528 runs for 24 wickets) in this Test played on a jute matting pitch – the highest scoring ratio in this series. Statham pulled a rib muscle on the first day and was unable to bowl again on the tour. The West Indies total of 681 remains their highest at home against England and the record for any Trinidad Test. For the second and last time, all three 'W's scored hundreds in the same innings (also *Test No. 369*). The stand of 338 between Weekes and Worrell is still the West Indies third-wicket record in all Tests. Laker retired at 515 after being hit in his right eye by a bouncer from King. Ferguson kept wicket in the second innings and held two catches.

WEST INDIES

J.K. Holt	c Compton b Trueman	40		
J.B. Stollmeyer*	c and b Compton	41		
E. de C. Weekes	c Bailey b Lock	206	c sub (K.G. Suttle) b Trueman	1
F.M.M. Worrell	b Lock	167	c sub (A.E. Moss) b Lock	56
C.L. Walcott	c and b Laker	124	not out	51
B.H. Pairaudeau	run out	0	(1) hit wkt b Bailey	5
D. St E. Atkinson	c Graveney b Compton	74	(6) not out	53
C.A. McWatt†	b Laker	4		
W. Ferguson	not out	8	(2) b Bailey	44
S. Ramadhin	) did not bat			
F.M. King	)			
Extras	(B 6, LB 4, W 4, NB 3)	17	(LB 2)	2
Total	(8 wickets declared)	**681**	(4 wickets declared)	**212**

ENGLAND

L. Hutton*	c Ferguson b King	44	(4) not out	30
T.E. Bailey	c Weekes b Ferguson	46		
P.B.H. May	c Pairaudeau b King	135	c Worrell b McWatt	16
D.C.S. Compton	c and b Ramadhin	133		
W. Watson	c Atkinson b Walcott	4	(1) c Ferguson b Worrell	32
T.W. Graveney	c and b Walcott	92	(5) not out	0
R.T. Spooner†	b Walcott	19	(2) c Ferguson b Ramadhin	16
J.C. Laker	retired hurt	7		
G.A.R. Lock	lbw b Worrell	10		
F.S. Trueman	lbw b King	19		
J.B. Statham	not out	6		
Extras	(B 10, LB 5, W 7)	22	(LB 4)	4
Total		**537**	(3 wickets)	**98**

ENGLAND	O	M	R	W	O	M	R	W
Statham	9	0	31	0				
Trueman	33	3	131	1	15	5	23	1
Bailey	32	7	104	0	12	2	20	2
Laker	50	8	154	2				
Lock	63	14	178	2	10	2	40	1
Compton	8·4	1	40	2	7	0	51	0
Graveney	3	0	26	0	5	0	33	0
Hutton					6	0	43	0
WEST INDIES								
King	48·2	16	97	3				
Worrell	20	2	58	1	9	1	29	1
Ramadhin	34	13	74	1	7	4	6	1
Atkinson	32	12	60	0	4	0	12	0
Ferguson	47	7	155	1				
Stollmeyer	6	2	19	0				
Walcott	34	18	52	3				
Weekes					5	1	28	0
McWatt					4	2	16	1
Pairaudeau					1	0	3	0

FALL OF WICKETS

Wkt	WI 1st	E 1st	WI 2nd	E 2nd
1st	78	73	19	52
2nd	92	135	20	52
3rd	430	301	72	83
4th	517	314	111	–
5th	540	424	–	–
6th	627	493	–	–
7th	641	496	–	–
8th	681	510	–	–
9th	–	537	–	–
10th	–	–	–	–

Umpires: E.E. Achong (1) and K. Woods (1).

Close: 1st day – WI(1) 294-2 (Weekes 130, Worrell 76); 2nd – WI(1) 546-5 (Walcott 70, Atkinson 5); 3rd – E(1) 130-1 (Bailey 46, May 38); 4th – E(1) 332-4 (Compton 81, Graveney 6); 5th – WI(2) 5-0 (Pairaudeau 1, Ferguson 4).

WEST INDIES v ENGLAND 1953–54 (5th Test)

Played at Sabina Park, Kingston, Jamaica, on 30, 31 March, 1, 2, 3 April.
Toss: West Indies.   Result: ENGLAND won by nine wickets.
Debuts: West Indies – G. St A. Sobers.

West Indies suffered their first defeat at Sabina Park after Hutton had scored the first double-century by an England captain in an overseas Test, and Bailey had returned what was then England's best analysis against West Indies. England thus squared the rubber after being two matches down and in spite of losing the toss four times. Sobers took the first of his 235 Test wickets when he dismissed his eventual biographer.

WEST INDIES

J.K. Holt	c Lock b Bailey	0	c Lock b Trueman		8
J.B. Stollmeyer*	c Evans b Bailey	9	lbw b Trueman		64
E. de C. Weekes	b Bailey	0	b Wardle		3
F.M.M. Worrell	c Wardle b Trueman	4	c Graveney b Trueman		29
C.L. Walcott	c Laker b Lock	50	c Graveney b Laker		116
D. St E. Atkinson	lbw b Bailey	21	(7) c Watson b Bailey		40
G.E. Gomez	c Watson b Bailey	4	(6) lbw b Laker		22
C.A. McWatt†	c Lock b Bailey	22	c Wardle b Laker		8
G. St A. Sobers	not out	14	c Compton b Lock		26
F.M. King	b Bailey	9	(11) not out		10
S. Ramadhin	lbw b Trueman	4	(10) c and b Laker		10
Extras	(LB 1, NB 1)	2	(B 4, LB 3, W 1, NB 2)		10
Total		**139**			**346**

ENGLAND

L. Hutton*	c McWatt b Walcott	205		
T.E. Bailey	c McWatt b Sobers	23		
P.B.H. May	c sub (B.H. Pairaudeau) b Ramadhin	30	not out	40
D.C.S. Compton	hit wkt b King	31		
W. Watson	c McWatt b King	4	(2) not out	20
T.W. Graveney	lbw b Atkinson	11	(1) b King	0
T.G. Evans†	c Worrell b Ramadhin	28		
J.H. Wardle	c Holt b Sobers	66		
G.A.R. Lock	b Sobers	4		
J.C. Laker	b Sobers	9		
F.S. Trueman	not out	0		
Extras	(LB 3)	3	(B 12)	12
Total		**414**	(1 wicket)	**72**

ENGLAND	O	M	R	W	O	M	R	W		FALL OF WICKETS			
										WI	E	WI	E
Bailey	16	7	34	7	25	11	54	1	*Wkt*	*1st*	*1st*	*2nd*	*2nd*
Trueman	15·4	4	39	2	29	7	88	3	1st	0	43	26	0
Wardle	10	1	20	0	39	14	83	1	2nd	2	104	38	–
Lock	15	6	31	1	27	16	40	1	3rd	13	152	102	–
Laker	4	1	13	0	50	27	71	4	4th	13	160	123	–
									5th	65	179	191	–
WEST INDIES									6th	75	287	273	–
King	26	12	45	2	4	1	21	1	7th	110	392	293	–
Gomez	25	8	56	0					8th	115	401	306	–
Atkinson	41	15	82	1	3	0	8	0	9th	133	406	326	–
Ramadhin	29	9	71	2	3	0	14	0	10th	139	414	346	–
Sobers	28·5	9	75	4	1	0	6	0					
Walcott	11	5	26	1									
Worrell	11	0	34	0	4	0	8	0					
Stollmeyer	5	0	22	0									
Weekes					0·5	0	3	0					

Umpires: P. Burke (2) and T.A. Ewart (4).

Close: 1st day – E(1) 17-0 (Hutton 8, Bailey 9); 2nd – E(1) 194-5 (Hutton 93, Evans 0); 3rd – WI(2) 20-0 (Holt 7, Stollmeyer 12); 4th – WI(2) 184-4 (Walcott 51, Gomez 21).

ENGLAND v PAKISTAN 1954 (1st Test)

Played at Lord's, London, on 10 (*no play*), 11 (*no play*), 12 (*no play*), 14, 15 June.
Toss: England.   Result: MATCH DRAWN.
Debuts: Pakistan – Alimuddin, Khalid Wazir, Shujauddin.

Play in Pakistan's first official Test against England could not begin until 3.45 pm on the fourth day. Pakistan's total of 87 was their lowest in any Test until 1981-82 (*Test No. 909*) and occupied 235 minutes. Hanif took 340 minutes to score 59 runs in the match. Khan Mohammad bowled all five of his victims, including Hutton with his first ball.

PAKISTAN

Batsman	Dismissal	Runs	Dismissal (2nd)	Runs
Hanif Mohammad	b Tattersall	20	lbw b Laker	39
Alimuddin	c Edrich b Wardle	19	b Bailey	0
Waqar Hassan	c Compton b Wardle	9	c Statham b Compton	53
Maqsood Ahmed	st Evans b Wardle	0	not out	29
Imtiaz Ahmed†	b Laker	12		
A.H. Kardar*	b Statham	2		
Fazal Mahmood	b Wardle	5		
Khalid Wazir	b Statham	3		
Khan Mohammad	b Statham	0		
Zulfiqar Ahmed	b Statham	11		
Shujauddin	not out	0		
Extras	(B 4, LB 1, NB 1)	6		
Total		**87**	(3 wickets)	**121**

ENGLAND

L. Hutton*	b Khan	0
R.T. Simpson	lbw b Fazal	40
P.B.H. May	b Khan	27
D.C.S. Compton	b Fazal	0
W.J. Edrich	b Khan	4
J.H. Wardle	c Maqsood b Fazal	3
T.G. Evans†	b Khan	25
T.E. Bailey	b Khan	3
J.C. Laker	not out	13
J.B. Statham	b Fazal	0
R. Tattersall	did not bat	
Extras	(B 2)	2
Total	(9 wickets declared)	**117**

ENGLAND	O	M	R	W	O	M	R	W
Statham	13	6	18	4	5	2	17	0
Bailey	3	2	1	0	6	2	13	1
Wardle	30·5	22	33	4	8	6	6	0
Tattersall	15	8	12	1	10	1	27	0
Laker	22	12	17	1	10·2	5	22	1
Compton					13	2	36	1
PAKISTAN								
Fazal	16	2	54	4				
Khan	15	3	61	5				

FALL OF WICKETS

	P	E	P
Wkt	1st	1st	2nd
1st	24	9	0
2nd	42	55	71
3rd	43	59	121
4th	57	72	–
5th	67	75	–
6th	67	79	–
7th	71	85	–
8th	71	110	–
9th	87	117	–
10th	87	–	–

Umpires: T.J. Bartley (1) and D. Davies (15).

Close: 1st day – no play; 2nd – no play; 3rd – no play; 4th – P(1) 50-3 (Hanif 11, Imtiaz 6).

ENGLAND v PAKISTAN 1954 (2nd Test)

Played at Trent Bridge, Nottingham, on 1, 2, 3, 5 July.
Toss: Pakistan.   Result: ENGLAND won by an innings and 129 runs.
Debuts: England – R. Appleyard; Pakistan – M.E.Z. Ghazali, Khalid Hassan, Mohammad Aslam.

England recorded their highest total against Pakistan. Compton reached his 200 in 245 minutes and batted 290 minutes for his highest Test innings, which included a six and 33 fours; it remains the Test record for Trent Bridge and the highest innings for either country in this series. His stand of 192 in 105 minutes with Bailey is still England's highest for the fifth wicket against Pakistan. Appleyard took a wicket with his second ball in Test cricket. The last of Simpson's four Test hundreds was his second at Trent Bridge; no other Nottinghamshire player has scored one there for England. Khalid Hassan, playing in his only Test, was then the world's youngest Test cricketer at 16 years 352 days. Sheppard deputised as captain and opening batsman while Hutton convalesced.

PAKISTAN

Hanif Mohammad	lbw b Appleyard	19	c Evans b Bedser	51
Alimuddin	b Statham	4	b Statham	18
Waqar Hassan	b Appleyard	7	c Evans b Statham	7
Maqsood Ahmed	c Evans b Appleyard	6	c Statham b Appleyard	69
Imtiaz Ahmed†	b Appleyard	11	lbw b Wardle	33
A.H. Kardar*	c Compton b Bedser	28	c Graveney b Wardle	4
Fazal Mahmood	c Sheppard b Bedser	14	b Statham	36
M.E.Z. Ghazali	b Statham	18	c Statham b Bedser	14
Mohammad Aslam	b Wardle	16	c Sheppard b Appleyard	18
Khalid Hassan	c May b Appleyard	10	(11) not out	7
Khan Mohammad	not out	13	(10) c Compton b Wardle	8
Extras	(B 9, LB 1, NB 1)	11	(B 4, LB 3)	7
Total		**157**		**272**

ENGLAND

D.S. Sheppard*	c Imtiaz b Khan	37
R.T. Simpson	b Khalid	101
P.B.H. May	b Khan	0
D.C.S. Compton	b Khalid	278
T.W. Graveney	c Maqsood b Kardar	84
T.E. Bailey	not out	36
T.G. Evans†	b Khan	4
J.H. Wardle	not out	14
A.V. Bedser	)	
J.B. Statham	) did not bat	
R. Appleyard	)	
Extras	(B 2, LB 1, NB 1)	4
Total	(6 wickets declared)	**558**

ENGLAND	O	M	R	W	O	M	R	W		FALL OF WICKETS		
Bedser	21	8	30	2	30	11	83	2		P	E	P
Statham	18	3	38	2	20	3	66	3	*Wkt*	*1st*	*1st*	*2nd*
Appleyard	17	5	51	5	30·4	8	72	2	1st	26	98	69
Bailey	3	0	18	0					2nd	37	102	70
Wardle	6	3	9	1	32	17	44	3	3rd	43	185	95
									4th	50	339	164
PAKISTAN									5th	55	531	168
Fazal	47	7	148	0					6th	86	536	189
Khan	40	3	155	3					7th	111	–	216
Kardar	28	4	110	1					8th	121	–	242
Khalid	21	1	116	2					9th	138	–	254
Maqsood	3	0	25	0					10th	157	–	272

Umpires: F. Chester (45) and T.W. Spencer (1).

Close: 1st day – E(1) 121-2 (Simpson 79, Compton 5); 2nd – P(2) 59-0 (Hanif 46, Alimuddin 13); 3rd – P(2) 189-6 (Fazal 5, Ghazali 0).

ENGLAND v PAKISTAN 1954 (3rd Test)

Played at Old Trafford, Manchester, on 22, 23 (*no play*), 24, 26 (*no play*), 27 (*no play*) July.
Toss: England.   Result: MATCH DRAWN.
Debuts: England – J.E. McConnon, J.M. Parks.

Rain allowed play on only two days – 10¾ hours in all. McConnon began his short Test career with 3 for 12 in six overs and held four outstanding catches. Ghazali was out without scoring twice within two hours on the third afternoon – probably the quickest 'pair' in Test cricket.

ENGLAND

D.S. Sheppard*	b Fazal	13	
T.E. Bailey	run out	42	
P.B.H. May	c Imtiaz b Shujauddin	14	
D.C.S. Compton	c Imtiaz b Shujauddin	93	
T.W. Graveney	st Imtiaz b Shujauddin	65	
J.M. Parks	b Fazal	15	
T.G. Evans†	c Hanif b Fazal	31	
J.H. Wardle	c Waqar b Fazal	54	
A.V. Bedser	not out	22	
J.E. McConnon	not out	5	
J.B. Statham	did not bat		
Extras	(B 1, LB 4)	5	
Total	(8 wickets declared)	**359**	

PAKISTAN

Hanif Mohammad	c Wardle b McConnon	32	c Sheppard b Wardle		1
Imtiaz Ahmed†	c McConnon b Wardle	13			
Waqar Hassan	c and b McConnon	11			
Maqsood Ahmed	c Wardle b McConnon	4			
A.H. Kardar*	b Wardle	9	(4) not out		0
M.E.Z. Ghazali	c Sheppard b Wardle	0	(5) c Wardle b Bedser		0
Wazir Mohammad	c McConnon b Bedser	5	(3) c Parks b Bedser		7
Fazal Mahmood	c Compton b Bedser	9			
Khalid Wazir	c McConnon b Wardle	2	(6) not out		9
Shujauddin	not out	0	(2) c Graveney b Bedser		1
Mahmood Hussain	b Bedser	0			
Extras	(B 4, NB 1)	5	(B 2, LB 4, NB 1)		7
Total		**90**	(4 wickets)		**25**

PAKISTAN	O	M	R	W	O	M	R	W
Fazal	42	·14	107	4				
Mahmood Hussain	27	5	88	0				
Shujauddin	48	12	127	3				
Ghazali	8	1	18	0				
Maqsood	4	0	14	0				
ENGLAND								
Statham	4	0	11	0				
Bedser	15·5	4	36	3	8	5	9	3
Wardle	24	16	19	4	7	2	9	1
McConnon	13	5	19	3				

FALL OF WICKETS

Wkt	E 1st	P 1st	P 2nd
1st	20	26	1
2nd	57	58	8
3rd	97	63	10
4th	190	66	10
5th	217	66	–
6th	261	77	–
7th	293	80	–
8th	348	87	–
9th	–	89	–
10th	–	90	–

Umpires: F. Chester (46) and F.S. Lee (12).

Close: 1st day – E(1) 293-6 (Evans 31, Wardle 19); 2nd – no play; 3rd – P(2) 25-4 (Kardar 0, Khalid 9); 4th – no play.

ENGLAND v PAKISTAN 1954 (4th Test)

Played at Kennington Oval, London, on 12, 13 (*no play*), 14, 16, 17 August.
Toss: Pakistan.   Result: PAKISTAN won by 24 runs.
Debuts: England – P.J. Loader, F.H. Tyson.

Pakistan gained their first victory against England and so squared the rubber. In doing so they became the first country to win a Test in their first rubber in England. Evans beat W.A.S. Oldfield's world record of 130 dismissals when he caught Kardar. England's total of 130 remains their lowest against Pakistan (equalled in 1987-88 – *Test No. 1084*). Fazal Mahmood's match analysis of 12 for 99 remains the best for Pakistan in England.

PAKISTAN

Hanif Mohammad	lbw b Statham	0	c Graveney b Wardle	19
Alimuddin	b Tyson	10	(7) lbw b Wardle	0
Waqar Hassan	b Loader	7	run out	9
Maqsood Ahmed	b Tyson	0	c Wardle b McConnon	4
Imtiaz Ahmed†	c Evans b Tyson	23	c Wardle b Tyson	12
A.H. Kardar*	c Evans b Statham	36	c and b Wardle	17
Wazir Mohammad	run out	0	(8) not out	42
Fazal Mahmood	c Evans b Loader	0	(9) b Wardle	6
Shujauddin	not out	16	(2) c May b Wardle	12
Zulfiqar Ahmed	c Compton b Loader	16	c May b Wardle	34
Mahmood Hussain	b Tyson	23	c Statham b Wardle	6
Extras	(NB 2)	2	(B 3)	3
Total		**133**		**164**

ENGLAND

L. Hutton*	c Imtiaz b Fazal	14	c Imtiaz b Fazal	5
R.T. Simpson	c Kardar b Mahmood	2	c and b Zulfiqar	27
P.B.H. May	c Kardar b Fazal	26	c Kardar b Fazal	53
D.C.S. Compton	c Imtiaz b Fazal	53	c Imtiaz b Fazal	29
T.W. Graveney	c Hanif b Fazal	1	(6) lbw b Shujauddin	0
T.G. Evans†	c Maqsood b Mahmood	0	(5) b Fazal	3
J.H. Wardle	c Imtiaz b Fazal	8	c Shujauddin b Fazal	9
F.H. Tyson	c Imtiaz b Fazal	3	c Imtiaz b Fazal	3
J.E. McConnon	c Fazal b Mahmood	11	(10) run out	2
J.B. Statham	c Shujauddin b Mahmood	1	(11) not out	2
P.J Loader	not out	8	(9) c Waqar b Mahmood	5
Extras	(LB 1, W 1, NB 1)	3	(LB 2, NB 3)	5
Total		**130**		**143**

ENGLAND	O	M	R	W	O	M	R	W		FALL OF WICKETS			
Statham	11	5	26	2	18	7	37	0		P	E	P	E
Tyson	13·4	3	35	4	9	2	22	1	*Wkt*	*1st*	*1st*	*2nd*	*2nd*
Loader	18	5	35	3	16	6	26	0	1st	0	6	19	15
McConnon	9	2	35	0	14	5	20	1	2nd	10	26	38	66
Wardle					35	16	56	7	3rd	10	56	43	109
									4th	26	63	54	115
PAKISTAN									5th	51	69	63	116
Fazal	30	16	53	6	30	11	46	6	6th	51	92	73	121
Mahmood Hussain	21·3	6	58	4	14	4	32	1	7th	51	106	76	131
Zulfiqar	5	2	8	0	14	2	35	1	8th	77	115	82	138
Shujauddin	3	0	8	0	10	1	25	1	9th	106	116	140	138
									10th	133	130	164	143

Umpires: D. Davies (16) and F.S. Lee (13).

Close: 1st day – E(1) 1-0 (Hutton 0, Simpson 1); 2nd – no play; 3rd – P(2) 63-4 (Imtiaz 12, Kardar 4); 4th – E(2) 125-6 (Wardle 5, Tyson 0).

AUSTRALIA v ENGLAND 1954–55 (1st Test)

Played at Woolloongabba, Brisbane, on 26, 27, 29, 30 November, 1 December.
Toss: England.   Result: AUSTRALIA won by an innings and 154 runs.
Debuts: Australia – L.E. Favell; England – K.V. Andrew, M.C. Cowdrey.

Granted complete covering of the pitch for the first time in Australia and expecting that surface to be at its liveliest on the first day, Hutton became the first England captain to put the opposition in to bat in Australia since J.W.H.T. Douglas (1911-12) and Australia's total was the highest in response to this action in a Test match. England took the field without a specialist slow bowler for only the second time (also *Test No. 221*). Compton fractured a bone in his left hand on the fencing while fielding. Morris and Harvey added 202 in 249 minutes. Australia were to wait 11 Tests for their next century against England.

AUSTRALIA

L.E. Favell	c Cowdrey b Statham	23
A.R. Morris	c Cowdrey b Bailey	153
K.R. Miller	b Bailey	49
R.N. Harvey	c Bailey b Bedser	162
G.B. Hole	run out	57
R. Benaud	c May b Tyson	34
R.G. Archer	c Bedser b Statham	0
R.R. Lindwall	not out	64
G.R.A. Langley†	b Bailey	16
I.W. Johnson*	not out	24
W.A. Johnston	did not bat	
Extras	(B 11, LB 7, NB 1)	19
Total	**(8 wickets declared)**	**601**

ENGLAND

L. Hutton*	c Langley b Lindwall	4	lbw b Miller		13
R.T. Simpson	b Miller	2	run out		9
W.J Edrich	c Langley b Archer	15	b Johnston		88
P.B.H May	b Lindwall	1	lbw b Lindwall		44
M.C. Cowdrey	c Hole b Johnston	40	b Benaud		10
T.E. Bailey	b Johnston	88	c Langley b Lindwall		23
F.H. Tyson	b Johnson	7	not out		37
A.V. Bedser	b Johnson	5	c Archer b Johnson		5
K.V. Andrew†	b Lindwall	6	b Johnson		5
J.B. Statham	b Johnson	11	(11) c Harvey b Benaud		14
D.C.S. Compton	not out	2	(10) c Langley b Benaud		0
Extras	(B 3, LB 6)	9	(B 7, LB 2)		9
Total		**190**			**257**

ENGLAND	O	M	R	W	O	M	R	W	FALL OF WICKETS			
										A	E	E
Bedser	37	4	131	1					*Wkt*	*1st*	*1st*	*2nd*
Statham	34	2	123	2					1st	51	4	22
Tyson	29	1	160	1					2nd	123	10	23
Bailey	26	1	140	3					3rd	325	11	147
Edrich	3	0	28	0					4th	456	25	163
									5th	463	107	181
AUSTRALIA									6th	464	132	220
Lindwall	14	4	27	3	17	3	50	2	7th	545	141	231
Miller	11	5	19	1	12	2	30	1	8th	572	156	242
Archer	4	1	14	1	15	4	28	0	9th	–	181	243
Johnson	19	5	46	3	17	5	38	2	10th	–	190	257
Benaud	12	5	28	0	8·1	1	43	3				
Johnston	16·1	5	47	2	21	8	59	1				

Umpires: C. Hoy (1) and M.J. McInnes (8).

Close: 1st day – A(1) 208-2 (Morris 82, Harvey 41); 2nd – A(1) 503-6 (Benaud 14, Lindwall 27); 3rd – E(1) 107-5 (Bailey 38, Tyson 0); 4th – E(2) 130-2 (Edrich 68, May 39).

AUSTRALIA v ENGLAND 1954–55 (2nd Test)

Played at Sydney Cricket Ground on 17, 18, 20, 21, 22 December.
Toss: Australia. Result: ENGLAND won by 38 runs.
Debuts: Nil.

Tyson, having been knocked unconscious by a Lindwall bouncer, bowled with great speed and stamina to win
a palpitating victory for England. Statham, bowling into a very strong wind, gave him splendid support. May's
first hundred against Australia, an innings lasting 298 minutes, and his partnership of 116 with Cowdrey, made
England's victory possible and had a vital effect on the outcome of the rubber.

ENGLAND

L. Hutton*	c Davidson b Johnston	30	c Benaud b Johnston	28
T.E. Bailey	b Lindwall	0	c Langley b Archer	6
P.B.H. May	c Johnston b Archer	5	b Lindwall	104
T.W. Graveney	c Favell b Johnston	21	c Langley b Johnston	0
M.C. Cowdrey	c Langley b Davidson	23	c Archer b Benaud	54
W.J. Edrich	c Benaud b Archer	10	b Archer	29
F.H. Tyson	b Lindwall	0	b Lindwall	9
T.G. Evans†	c Langley b Archer	3	c Lindwall b Archer	4
J.H. Wardle	c Burke b Johnson	35	lbw b Lindwall	8
R. Appleyard	c Hole b Davidson	8	not out	19
J.B. Statham	not out	14	c Langley b Johnston	25
Extras	(LB 5)	5	(LB 6, NB 4)	10
Total		**154**		**296**

AUSTRALIA

L.E. Favell	c Graveney b Bailey	26	c Edrich b Tyson	16
A.R. Morris*	c Hutton b Bailey	12	lbw b Statham	10
J.W. Burke	c Graveney b Bailey	44	b Tyson	14
R.N. Harvey	c Cowdrey b Tyson	12	not out	92
G.B. Hole	b Tyson	12	b Tyson	0
R. Benaud	lbw b Statham	20	c Tyson b Appleyard	12
R.G. Archer	c Hutton b Tyson	49	b Tyson	6
A.K. Davidson	b Statham	20	c Evans b Statham	5
R.R. Lindwall	c Evans b Tyson	19	b Tyson	8
G.R.A. Langley†	b Bailey	5	b Statham	0
W.A. Johnston	not out	0	c Evans b Tyson	11
Extras	(B 5, LB 2, NB 2)	9	(LB 7, NB 3)	10
Total		**228**		**184**

AUSTRALIA	O	M	R	W	O	M	R	W
Lindwall	17	3	47	2	31	10	69	3
Archer	12	7	12	3	22	9	53	3
Davidson	12	3	34	2	13	2	52	0
Johnston	13·3	1	56	3	19·3	2	70	3
Benaud					19	3	42	1
ENGLAND								
Statham	18	1	83	2	19	6	45	3
Bailey	17·4	3	59	4	6	0	21	0
Tyson	13	2	45	4	18·4	1	85	6
Appleyard	7	1	32	0	6	1	12	1
Wardle					4	2	11	0

FALL OF WICKETS

	E	A	E	A
Wkt	1st	1st	2nd	2nd
1st	14	18	18	27
2nd	19	65	55	34
3rd	58	100	55	77
4th	63	104	171	77
5th	84	122	222	102
6th	85	141	232	122
7th	88	193	239	127
8th	99	213	249	136
9th	111	224	250	145
10th	154	228	296	184

Umpires: M.J. McInnes (9) and R. Wright (8).

Close: 1st day – A(1) 18-1 (Favell 6); 2nd – A(1) 228 all out; 3rd – E(2) 204-4 (May 98, Edrich 16); 4th – A(2)
72-2 (Burke 13, Harvey 26).

AUSTRALIA v ENGLAND 1954–55 (3rd Test)

Played at Melbourne Cricket Ground on 31 December, 1, 3, 4, 5 January.
Toss: England.   Result: ENGLAND won by 128 runs.
Debuts: Australia – L.V. Maddocks.

Cowdrey, the fiftieth England batsman to score a hundred against Australia, made his runs out of the lowest total to contain a century in this series to share that record with Bradman (103 out of 191 in 1932-33 – *Test No. 221*). Australia's last eight second-innings wickets fell for 34 runs, Tyson taking 6 for 16 in 51 balls to finish with an exceptional analysis for a fast bowler in this long series. Miller began the match with a pre-lunch spell of 9-8-5-3. The deteriorating pitch was illegally watered on the rest day.

ENGLAND

L. Hutton*	c Hole b Miller	12	lbw b Archer		42
W.J. Edrich	c Lindwall b Miller	4	b Johnston		13
P.B.H. May	c Benaud b Lindwall	0	b Johnston		91
M.C. Cowdrey	b Johnson	102	b Benaud		7
D.C.S. Compton	c Harvey b Miller	4	c Maddocks b Archer		23
T.E. Bailey	c Maddocks b Johnston	30	not out		24
T.G. Evans†	lbw b Archer	20	c Maddocks b Miller		22
J.H. Wardle	b Archer	0	b Johnson		38
F.H. Tyson	b Archer	6	c Harvey b Johnston		6
J.B. Statham	b Archer	3	c Favell b Johnston		0
R. Appleyard	not out	1	b Johnston		6
Extras	(B 9)	9	(B 2, LB 4, W 1)		7
Total		**191**			**279**

AUSTRALIA

L.E. Favell	lbw b Statham	25	b Appleyard		30
A.R. Morris	lbw b Tyson	3	c Cowdrey b Tyson		4
K.R. Miller	c Evans b Statham	7	(5) c Edrich b Tyson		6
R.N. Harvey	b Appleyard	31	c Evans b Tyson		11
G.B. Hole	b Tyson	11	(6) c Evans b Statham		5
R. Benaud	c sub (J.V. Wilson) b Appleyard	15	(3) b Tyson		22
R.G. Archer	b Wardle	23	b Statham		15
L.V. Maddocks†	c Evans b Statham	47	b Tyson		0
R.R. Lindwall	b Statham	13	lbw b Tyson		0
I.W. Johnson*	not out	33	not out		4
W.A. Johnston	b Statham	11	c Evans b Tyson		0
Extras	(B 7, LB 3, NB 2)	12	(B 1, LB 13)		14
Total		**231**			**111**

AUSTRALIA	O	M	R	W	O	M	R	W		FALL OF WICKETS			
Lindwall	13	0	59	1	18	3	52	0		E	A	E	A
Miller	11	8	14	3	18	6	35	1	*Wkt*	*1st*	*1st*	*2nd*	*2nd*
Archer	13·6	4	33	4	24	7	50	2	1st	14	15	40	23
Benaud	7	0	30	0	8	2	25	1	2nd	21	38	96	57
Johnston	12	6	26	1	24·5	2	85	5	3rd	29	43	128	77
Johnson	11	3	20	1	8	2	25	1	4th	41	65	173	86
									5th	115	92	185	87
ENGLAND									6th	169	115	211	97
Tyson	21	2	68	2	12·3	1	27	7	7th	181	134	257	98
Statham	16·3	0	60	5	11	1	38	2	8th	181	151	273	98
Bailey	9	1	33	0	3	0	14	0	9th	190	205	273	110
Appleyard	11	3	38	2	4	1	17	1	10th	191	231	279	111
Wardle	6	0	20	1	1	0	1	0					

Umpires: C. Hoy (2) and M.J. McInnes (10).

Close: 1st day – E(1) 191 all out; 2nd – A(1) 188-8 (Maddocks 36, Johnson 12); 3rd – E(2) 159-3 (May 83, Compton 10); 4th – A(2) 75-2 (Benaud 19, Harvey 9).

AUSTRALIA v ENGLAND 1954–55 (4th Test)

Played at Adelaide Oval on 28, 29, 31 January, 1, 2 February.
Toss: Australia.   Result: ENGLAND won by five wickets.
Debuts: Nil.

England won their first rubber in Australia since the 'bodyline' tour of 1932-33 and so retained the Ashes. Hutton was the first England captain to regain the Ashes and to lead a successful campaign in their defence. To the delight of cricket's more superstitious observers, 'Nelson' appeared to control Australia's last innings for the second match in succession.

AUSTRALIA

C.C. McDonald	c May b Appleyard	48	b Statham		29
A.R. Morris	c Evans b Tyson	25	c and b Appleyard		16
J.W. Burke	c May b Tyson	18	b Appleyard		5
R.N. Harvey	c Edrich b Bailey	25	b Appleyard		7
K.R. Miller	c Bailey b Appleyard	44	b Statham		14
R. Benaud	c May b Appleyard	15	(7) lbw b Tyson		1
L.V. Maddocks†	run out	69	(6) lbw b Statham		2
R.G. Archer	c May b Tyson	21	c Evans b Tyson		3
A.K. Davidson	c Evans b Bailey	5	lbw b Wardle		23
I.W. Johnson*	c Statham b Bailey	41	(11) not out		3
W.A. Johnston	not out	0	(10) c Appleyard b Tyson		3
Extras	(B 3, LB 7, NB 2)	12	(B 4, LB 1)		5
Total		**323**			**111**

ENGLAND

L. Hutton*	c Davidson b Johnston	80	c Davidson b Miller		5
W.J. Edrich	b Johnson	21	b Miller		0
P.B.H. May	c Archer b Benaud	1	c Miller b Johnston		26
M.C. Cowdrey	c Maddocks b Davison	79	c Archer b Miller		4
D.C.S. Compton	lbw b Miller	44	not out		34
T.E. Bailey	c Davidson b Johnston	38	lbw b Johnston		15
T.G. Evans†	c Maddocks b Benaud	37	not out		6
J.H. Wardle	c and b Johnson	23			
F.H. Tyson	c Burke b Benaud	1			
R. Appleyard	not out	10			
J.B. Statham	c Maddocks b Benaud	0			
Extras	(B 1, LB 2, NB 4)	7	(B 3, LB 4)		7
Total		**341**	(5 wickets)		**97**

ENGLAND	O	M	R	W	O	M	R	W
Tyson	26·1	4	85	3	15	2	47	3
Statham	19	4	70	0	12	1	38	3
Bailey	12	3	39	3				
Appleyard	23	7	58	3	12	7	13	3
Wardle	19	5	59	0	4·2	1	8	1
AUSTRALIA								
Miller	11	4	34	1	10·4	2	40	3
Archer	3	0	12	0	4	0	13	0
Johnson	36	17	46	2				
Davidson	25	8	55	1	2	0	7	0
Johnston	27	11	60	2	8	2	20	2
Benaud	36·6	6	120	4	6	2	10	0
Burke	2	0	7	0				

FALL OF WICKETS

	A	E	A	E
Wkt	*1st*	*1st*	*2nd*	*2nd*
1st	59	60	24	3
2nd	86	63	40	10
3rd	115	162	54	18
4th	129	232	69	49
5th	175	232	76	90
6th	182	283	77	–
7th	212	321	79	–
8th	229	323	83	–
9th	321	336	101	–
10th	323	341	111	–

Umpires: M.J. McInnes (11) and R. Wright (9).

Close: 1st day – A(1) 161-4 (Miller 26, Benaud 11); 2nd – E(1) 57-0 (Hutton 34, Edrich 21); 3rd – E(1) 230-3 (Cowdrey 37, Compton 44); 4th – A(2) 69-3 (McDonald 29, Miller 12).

AUSTRALIA v ENGLAND 1954–55 (5th Test)

Played at Sydney Cricket Ground on 25 (*no play*), 26(*no play*), 28 (*no play*) February, 1, 2, 3 March.
Toss: Australia. Result: MATCH DRAWN.
Debuts: Australia - P.J.P. Burge, W.J. Watson.

Incessant heavy rain wrought havoc in New South Wales and delayed the start of this match until 2 pm on the fourth day. Graveney became the hundredth player to score a century in this series of Tests. Bailey allowed himself to be bowled to give Lindwall 100 wickets in Australia-England Tests. Lindwall acknowledged this gesture by dismissing Bailey for a 'pair' four years later in the latter's last Test (*No. 468*). Hutton's final innings against Australia lasted only four balls. Australia failed to avoid the follow on by a single run.

ENGLAND

L. Hutton*	c Burge b Lindwall	6
T.W. Graveney	c and b Johnson	111
P.B.H. May	c Davidson b Benaud	79
M.C. Cowdrey	c Maddocks b Johnson	0
D.C.S. Compton	c and b Johnson	84
T.E. Bailey	b Lindwall	72
T.G. Evans†	c McDonald b Lindwall	10
J.H. Wardle	not out	5
F.H. Tyson	)	
R. Appleyard	) did not bat	
J.B. Statham	)	
Extras	(B 1, LB 3)	4
Total	(7 wickets declared)	**371**

AUSTRALIA

W.J. Watson	b Wardle	18	c Graveney b Statham	3
C.C. McDonald	c May b Appleyard	72	c Evans b Graveney	37
L.E. Favell	b Tyson	1	c Graveney b Wardle	9
R.N. Harvey	c and b Tyson	13	c and b Wardle	1
K.R. Miller	run out	19	b Wardle	28
P.J.P. Burge	c Appleyard b Wardle	17	not out	18
R. Benaud	b Wardle	7	b Hutton	22
L.V. Maddocks†	c Appleyard b Wardle	32		
A.K. Davidson	c Evans b Wardle	18		
I.W. Johnson*	run out	11		
R.R. Lindwall	not out	2		
Extras	(B 10, LB 1)	11		
Total		**221**	(6 wickets)	**118**

AUSTRALIA	O	M	R	W	O	M	R	W
Lindwall	20·6	5	77	3				
Miller	15	1	71	0				
Davidson	19	3	72	0				
Johnson	20	5	68	3				
Benaud	20	4	79	1				
ENGLAND								
Tyson	11	1	46	2	5	2	20	0
Statham	9	1	31	0	5	0	11	1
Appleyard	16	2	54	1				
Wardle	24·4	6	79	5	12	1	51	3
Graveney					6	0	34	1
Hutton					0·6	0	2	1

FALL OF WICKETS

Wkt	E 1st	A 1st	A 2nd
1st	6	52	14
2nd	188	53	27
3rd	188	85	29
4th	196	129	67
5th	330	138	87
6th	359	147	118
7th	371	157	–
8th	–	202	–
9th	–	217	–
10th	–	221	–

Umpires: M.J. McInnes (12) and R. Wright (10).

Close: 1st day – no play; 2nd – no play; 3rd – no play; 4th – E(1) 196-4 (Compton 0); 5th – A(1) 82-2 (McDonald 45, Harvey 12).

PAKISTAN v INDIA 1954–55 (1st Test)

Played at Dacca Stadium on 1, 2, 3, 4 January.
Toss: Pakistan. Result: MATCH DRAWN.
Debuts: India – P.H. Punjabi, N.S. Tamhane.

The first official Test in Pakistan established the defensive nature of the cricket played in this series. At the end of four days only 710 runs had been scored from 387·3 overs; a scoring rate of 1·83 runs per over. Pakistan's 158 remains their lowest total in a home Test against India.

PAKISTAN

Hanif Mohammad	c Tamhane b Ghulam Ahmed	41		c Umrigar b Phadkar	14
Alimuddin	c Phadkar b Ghulam Ahmed	7		c sub (P. Bhandari) b Gupte	51
Waqar Hassan	c and b Ghulam Ahmed	52		st Tamhane b Gupte	51
Maqsood Ahmed	c Tamhane b Ghulam Ahmed	11		c Mantri b Gupte	16
Wazir Mohammad	c Phadkar b Gupte	23	(8)	run out	0
Imtiaz Ahmed†	b Phadkar	54	(5)	c Umrigar b Gupte	5
A.H. Kardar*	b Ramchand	29	(6)	c Mantri b Phadkar	3
Shujauddin	st Tamhane b Mankad	25	(7)	run out	1
Fazal Mahmood	c Tamhane b Ramchand	0		not out	15
Mahmood Hussain	b Ghulam Ahmed	9		c Punjabi b Gupte	0
Khan Mohammad	not out	4		run out	0
Extras	(LB 2)	2		(LB 2)	2
Total		**257**			**158**

INDIA

Pankaj Roy	b Mahmood	0		not out	67
P.H. Punjabi	b Khan	26		lbw b Khan	3
M.K. Mantri	b Mahmood	0		c Imtiaz b Khan	2
V.L. Manjrekar	b Khan	18		not out	74
P.R. Umrigar	c Kardar b Mahmood	32			
G.S. Ramchand	c Imtiaz b Mahmood	37			
D.G. Phadkar	c Imtiaz b Mahmood	11			
M.H. Mankad*	c Imtiaz b Mahmood	2			
N.S. Tamhane†	b Khan	5			
Ghulam Ahmed	b Khan	2			
S.P. Gupte	not out	1			
Extras	(B 7, LB 5, NB 2)	14		(B 1)	1
Total		**148**		(2 wickets)	**147**

INDIA	O	M	R	W	O	M	R	W		FALL OF WICKETS			
Phadkar	18	11	24	1	28·2	11	57	2		P	I	P	I
Ramchand	15	7	19	2	19	10	30	0	*Wkt*	*1st*	*1st*	*2nd*	*2nd*
Gupte	46	14	79	1	6	0	18	5	1st	21	17	24	15
Ghulam Ahmed	45	8	109	5					2nd	74	19	116	17
Mankad	12·2	3	24	1	18	6	34	0	3rd	88	45	122	–
Umrigar					15	8	17	0	4th	125	56	137	–
									5th	157	115	139	–
PAKISTAN									6th	207	129	140	–
Fazal	25	19	18	0	23	11	34	0	7th	227	131	140	–
Mahmood Hussain	27	6	67	6	7	2	21	0	8th	227	143	148	–
Khan	26·5	12	42	4	12	5	18	2	9th	240	145	156	–
Shujauddin	4	2	7	0	14	6	25	0	10th	257	148	158	–
Maqsood					3	1	4	0					
Kardar					12	3	17	0					
Hanif					5	1	15	0					
Alimuddin					5	0	12	0					
Imtiaz					1	1	0	0					

Umpires: Daud Khan (1) and Idris Beg (1).

Close: 1st day – P(1) 207-5 (Imtiaz 54, Kardar 17); 2nd – I(1) 115-5 (Umrigar 24, Phadkar 0); 3rd – P(2) 97-1 (Alimuddin 45, Waqar 38).

PAKISTAN v INDIA 1954–55 (2nd Test)

Played at Dring Stadium, Bahawalpur, on 15, 16, 17, 18 January.
Toss: India.   Result: MATCH DRAWN.
Debuts: Nil.

Bahawalpur's only Test match produced the first of Hanif's 12 Test centuries, Pakistan's first three-figure opening partnership, and Umrigar's best bowling analysis for India. A run rate of under two per over resulted in only two innings being completed in the four days.

INDIA

Pankaj Roy	b Fazal	0	c Kardar b Khan	78
P.H. Punjabi	b Khan	18	c Maqsood b Mahmood	33
M.H. Mankad*	c Imtiaz b Fazal	6	c Imtiaz b Fazal	1
V.L. Manjrekar	c Mahmood b Khan	50	c Imtiaz b Fazal	59
P.R. Umrigar	b Khan	20		
G.S. Ramchand	b Mahmood	53		
C.V. Gadkari	lbw b Khan	2	(6) not out	4
C.D. Gopinath	c Waqar b Fazal	0	(5) c Maqsood b Khan	8
N.S. Tamhane†	not out	54	(7) not out	12
S.P. Gupte	b Khan	15		
Ghulam Ahmed	b Fazal	8		
Extras	(LB 4, NB 5)	9	(B 12, LB 1, NB 1)	14
Total		235	(5 wickets)	209

PAKISTAN

Hanif Mohammad	c Gadkari b Umrigar	142
Alimuddin	b Ghulam Ahmed	64
Waqar Hassan	c Gupte b Umrigar	48
Maqsood Ahmed	c Gadkari b Umrigar	10
Imtiaz Ahmed†	st Tamhane b Gupte	3
A.H. Kardar*	c Punjabi b Umrigar	13
Fazal Mahmood	b Umrigar	9
Mahmood Hussain	c Gadkari b Umrigar	0
Shujauddin	run out	7
Wazir Mohammad	not out	4
Khan Mohammad	not out	1
Extras	(B 6, LB 5)	11
Total	(9 wickets declared)	312

PAKISTAN	O	M	R	W	O	M	R	W
Fazal	52·5	23	86	4	28	6	58	2
Mahmood Hussain	25	6	56	1	17	3	47	1
Khan	33	7	74	5	22	6	50	2
Shujauddin	9	4	10	0	8	6	2	0
Maqsood					7	3	19	0
Kardar					7	0	19	0
INDIA								
Ramchand	13	5	26	0				
Umrigar	58	25	74	6				
Gupte	17	8	49	1				
Ghulam Ahmed	36	4	63	1				
Mankad	40	19	89	0				

FALL OF WICKETS

Wkt	I 1st	P 1st	I 2nd
1st	0	127	58
2nd	16	220	62
3rd	61	226	185
4th	93	229	189
5th	95	250	193
6th	100	286	–
7th	107	286	–
8th	189	301	–
9th	205	307	–
10th	235	–	–

Umpires: Idris Beg (2) and Shujauddin (1).

Close: 1st day – I(1) 157-7 (Ramchand 36, Tamhane 17); 2nd – P(1) 90-0 (Hanif 40, Alimuddin 45); 3rd – P(1) 312-9 (Wazir 4, Khan 1).

PAKISTAN v INDIA 1954–55 (3rd Test)

Played at Bagh-i-Jinnah, Lahore, on 29, 30, 31 January, 1 February.
Toss: Pakistan.   Result: MATCH DRAWN.
Debuts: Pakistan – Miran Bux.

Miran Bux, aged 47 years 284 days, became the second-oldest player to make his Test debut; J. Southerton was 49 years 119 days when he appeared in the very first Test of all. This match was the first played on the ground formerly known as Lawrence Gardens. Pakistan achieved the highest Test match total without an extra.

PAKISTAN

Hanif Mohammad	c Tamhane b Gupte	12	(6) not out	0
Alimuddin	run out	38	b Mankad	58
Waqar Hassan	c Mankad b Gupte	9	c Tamhane b Mankad	12
Maqsood Ahmed	st Tamhane b Gupte	99	c Punjabi b Mankad	15
A.H. Kardar*	c Ramchand b Mankad	44		
Wazir Mohammad	lbw b Mankad	55		
Imtiaz Ahmed†	run out	55	(5) c Tamhane b Gupte	9
Shujauddin	c Mankad b Ghulam Ahmed	3	(1) c sub (P. Bhandari) b Gupte	40
Fazal Mahmood	st Tamhane b Gupte	12		
Mahmood Hussain	b Gupte	0		
Miran Bux	not out	1		
Extras		–	(B 2)	2
Total		**328**	(5 wickets declared)	**136**

INDIA

Pankaj Roy	b Mahmood	23	c Imtiaz b Kardar	23
P.H. Punjabi	b Miran Bux	27	c Maqsood b Kardar	1
C.V. Gadkari	b Fazal	13	not out	27
V.L. Manjrekar	b Miran Bux	0	not out	22
P.R. Umrigar	c Hanif b Mahmood	78		
G.S. Ramchand	c Maqsood b Fazal	12		
C.D. Gopinath	c Fazal b Shujauddin	41		
M.H. Mankad*	c Imtiaz b Mahmood	33		
N.S. Tamhane†	c Imtiaz b Mahmood	0		
Ghulam Ahmed	c Imtiaz b Fazal	0		
S.P. Gupte	not out	0		
Extras	(B 12, LB 10, NB 2)	24	(NB 1)	1
Total		**251**	(2 wickets)	**74**

INDIA	O	M	R	W	O	M	R	W		FALL OF WICKETS			
										P	I	P	I
Umrigar	14	4	23	0					*Wkt*	*1st*	*1st*	*2nd*	*2nd*
Ramchand	10	5	12	0	6	1	20	0	1st	32	52	83	3
Ghulam Ahmed	46	11	95	1	14	2	47	0	2nd	55	56	109	40
Gupte	73·5	32	133	5	36·3	22	34	2	3rd	62	58	112	–
Mankad	44	25	65	2	28	17	33	3	4th	198	91	135	–
									5th	202	117	136	–
PAKISTAN									6th	286	179	–	–
Mahmood Hussain	26·1	6	70	4	1	0	1	0	7th	302	243	–	–
Fazal	47	24	62	3	1	0	2	0	8th	327	243	–	–
Miran Bux	48	20	82	2					9th	327	251	–	–
Shujauddin	7	1	13	1	6	1	20	0	10th	328	251	–	–
Maqsood					4	2	4	0					
Kardar					12	3	20	2					
Alimuddin					3	0	12	0					
Hanif					3	0	9	0					
Wazir					2	0	5	0					

Umpires: Idris Beg (3) and Shujauddin (2).

Close: 1st day – P(1) 202-5 (Wazir 0, Imtiaz 0); 2nd – I(1) 80-3 (Gadkari 11, Umrigar 12); 3rd – P(2) 9-0 (Shujauddin 0, Alimuddin 9).

PAKISTAN v INDIA 1954–55 (4th Test)

Played at Club Ground, Peshawar, on 12, 13, 14, 15 February
Toss: Pakistan.   Result: MATCH DRAWN.
Debuts: Nil

The run rate declined to 1.61 per over, with 638 runs accruing from 395.3 overs. India never threatened to score the 126 runs needed for victory in the final hour of the first Test match to be played at Peshawar.

PAKISTAN

Hanif Mohammad	c Phadkar b Gupte	13		c and b Mankad	21
Alimuddin	b Ramchand	0		lbw b Ghulam Ahmed	4
Waqar Hassan	c and b Gupte	43		lbw b Gupte	16
Maqsood Ahmed	c Punjabi b Phadkar	31	(5)	c and b Mankad	44
Imtiaz Ahmed†	b Phadkar	0	(6)	c Punjabi b Mankad	69
Wazir Mohammad	hit wkt b Mankad	34	(4)	b Mankad	0
A.H. Kardar*	b Gupte	11		b Phadkar	0
Shujauddin	c Tamhane b Gupte	37		run out	11
Khan Mohammad	c Mankad b Ghulam Ahmed	4		c sub (P. Bhandari) b Mankad	3
Mahmood Hussain	not out	5		st Tamhane b Phadkar	2
Miran Bux	lbw b Gupte	0		not out	0
Extras	(B 5, LB 4, NB 1)	10		(B 8, LB 4)	12
Total		**188**			**182**

INDIA

Pankaj Roy	run out	16		not out	13
P.H. Punjabi	b Khan	16		b Hanif	6
P.R. Umrigar	run out	108		not out	3
V.L. Manjrekar	run out	32			
C.V. Gadkari	c Maqsood b Mahmood	15			
G.S. Ramchand	c Shujauddin b Khan	18			
M.H. Mankad*	not out	3			
N.S. Tamhane†	run out	0			
D.G. Phadkar	b Khan	13			
S.P. Gupte	c Waqar b Mahmood	2			
Ghulam Ahmed	b Khan	8			
Extras	(B 5, LB 4, W 1, NB 4)	14		(NB 1)	1
Total		**245**		(1 wicket)	**23**

INDIA	O	M	R	W	O	M	R	W
Phadkar	24	14	19	2	18	2	42	2
Ramchand	7	2	13	1	2	1	3	0
Gupte	41·3	22	63	5	35	16	52	1
Mankad	61	34	71	1	54	26	64	5
Ghulam Ahmed	13	7	12	1	13	9	9	1
PAKISTAN								
Khan	36	14	79	4	4	0	10	0
Mahmood Hussain	38	11	78	2	2	1	2	0
Miran Bux	8	2	30	0	2	0	3	0
Kardar	19	6	34	0	1	1	0	0
Maqsood	7	3	10	0	6	2	6	0
Hanif					4	3	1	1

FALL OF WICKETS

	P	I	P	I
Wkt	1st	1st	2nd	2nd
1st	2	30	10	19
2nd	31	44	50	–
3rd	81	135	68	–
4th	81	182	70	–
5th	96	210	153	–
6th	111	218	156	–
7th	171	219	176	–
8th	176	232	177	–
9th	188	235	182	–
10th	188	245	182	–

Umpires: Idris Beg (4) and Shujauddin (3).

Close: 1st day – P(1) 129-6 (Wazir 20, Shujauddin 5); 2nd – I(1) 162-3 (Umrigar 94, Gadkari 2); 3rd – P(2) 44-1 (Hanif 13, Waqar 15).

PAKISTAN v INDIA 1954–55 (5th Test)

Played at National Stadium, Karachi, on 26, 27, 28 February, 1 March.
Toss: Pakistan.   Result: MATCH DRAWN.
Debuts: India – P. Bhandari, J.M. Patel.

A heavy thunderstorm restricted play to less than two hours on the third day. The first Test to be staged at Karachi produced what is still India's lowest total in Pakistan (145). Fazal became the first bowler to take 50 wickets for Pakistan when he bowled Umrigar. Alimuddin and Kardar shared a fifth-wicket partnership of 155 in even time – it provided the fastest scoring of the rubber and was then Pakistan's record for that wicket against India. Kardar accomplished his highest innings in Tests for either India (3) or Pakistan (23). This was the first rubber to produce a stalemate of five drawn matches.

PAKISTAN

Hanif Mohammad	c Tamhane b Phadkar	2	(3) c Tamhane b Umrigar		28
Alimuddin	c Tamhane b Ramchand	7	not out		103
Waqar Hassan	c Umrigar b Ramchand	12	(7) not out		1
Maqsood Ahmed	c Tamhane b Ramchand	22	c Bhandari b Umrigar		2
Imtiaz Ahmed†	c Ramchand b Patel	37	run out		1
Wazir Mohammad	c Phadkar b Patel	23			
A.H. Kardar*	c Tamhane b Ramchand	14	(6) st Tamhane b Gupte		93
Shujauddin	c Mankad b Ramchand	0	(1) b Ramchand		8
Fazal Mahmood	lbw b Patel	3			
Khan Mohammad	not out	15			
Mahmood Hussain	c Phadkar b Ramchand	14			
Extras	(B 10, NB 3)	13	(B 1, LB 3, NB 1)		5
Total		**162**	(5 wickets declared)		**241**

INDIA

Pankaj Roy	c Kardar b Khan	37	lbw b Maqsood		16
P.H. Punjabi	lbw b Khan	12	c Imtiaz b Fazal		22
P.R. Umrigar	b Fazal	16	not out		14
V.L. Manjrekar	c Kardar b Khan	14			
M.H. Mankad*	c Maqsood b Fazal	6			
G.S. Ramchand	c Hanif b Fazal	15	(4) not out		12
N.S. Tamhane†	b Fazal	9			
P. Bhandari	b Khan	19			
D.G. Phadkar	not out	6			
J.M. Patel	lbw b Khan	0			
S.P. Gupte	c Shujauddin b Fazal	1			
Extras	(LB 7, NB 3)	10	(B 1, LB 1, NB 3)		5
Total		**145**	(2 wickets)		**69**

INDIA	O	M	R	W	O	M	R	W		FALL OF WICKETS			
Phadkar	10	6	7	1	34	6	95	0			P	I	P	I
Ramchand	28	10	49	6	11	4	27	1	*Wkt*	*1st*	*1st*	*2nd*	*2nd*
Patel	33	12	49	3	7	1	23	0	1st	2	22	25	34
Gupte	15	4	24	0	6	0	24	1	2nd	19	45	69	49
Mankad	5	0	16	0	1	0	3	0	3rd	37	68	77	–
Umrigar	5	3	4	0	27	6	64	2	4th	66	89	81	–
									5th	88	95	236	–
PAKISTAN									6th	119	110	–	–
Khan	28	5	73	5	7	5	4	0	7th	119	131	–	–
Mahmood Hussain	7	0	14	0	3	0	16	0	8th	122	144	–	–
Fazal	28·3	7	48	5	11	4	21	1	9th	135	144	–	–
Hanif					6	1	18	0	10th	162	145	–	–
Maqsood					5	2	5	1					

Umpires: Daud Khan (2) and Masood Salahuddin (1).

Close: 1st day – P(1) 162-9 (Khan 15, Mahmood Hussain 14); 2nd – I(1) 145 all out; 3rd – P(2) 69-1 (Alimuddin 30, Hanif 28).

NEW ZEALAND v ENGLAND 1954–55 (1st Test)

Played at Carisbrook, Dunedin, on 11, 12, 14 (*no play*), 15 (*no play*), 16 March.
Toss: England.   Result: ENGLAND won by eight wickets.
Debuts: New Zealand – I.A. Colquhoun, S.N. McGregor, L. Watt (*not 'L.A.'*).

Although the first day of Test cricket in Dunedin produced only 125 runs, the fewest in New Zealand's Test history, a record crowd of 16,000 was attracted to the Carisbrook Ground on the next day. Sent in on a damp pitch surrounded by a sluggish outfield, the New Zealand batsmen found scoring extremely difficult against the attack that had just demolished Australia. Heavy rain saturated the pitch and prevented play on the next two days. England required only 50 of the final 90 minutes to complete their victory.

NEW ZEALAND

G.O. Rabone*	st Evans b Wardle	18	lbw b Wardle	7
M.E. Chapple	b Statham	0	(3) b Statham	20
B. Sutcliffe	c Statham b Bailey	74	(2) run out	35
J.R. Reid	b Statham	4	b Tyson	28
S.N. McGregor	b Tyson	2	c Cowdrey b Appleyard	8
L. Watt	b Tyson	0	b Appleyard	2
H.B. Cave	b Tyson	1	b Tyson	1
A.M. Moir	b Statham	7	(9) lbw b Tyson	10
R.W. Blair	b Statham	0	(10) b Wardle	3
A.R. MacGibbon	c Evans b Bailey	7	(8) b Tyson	0
I.A. Colquhoun†	not out	0	not out	1
Extras	(B 5, LB 4, NB 3)	12	(B 7, LB 10)	17
Total		**125**		**132**

ENGLAND

L. Hutton*	c Colquhoun b Reid	11	c Colquhoun b Blair	3
T.W. Graveney	b Cave	41	not out	32
P.B.H. May	b MacGibbon	10	b MacGibbon	13
M.C. Cowdrey	lbw b Reid	42	not out	0
R.T. Simpson	b Cave	21		
T.E. Bailey	lbw b Reid	0		
T.G. Evans†	b Reid	0		
J.H. Wardle	not out	32		
F.H. Tyson	c McGregor b MacGibbon	16		
R. Appleyard	not out	0		
J.B. Statham	did not bat			
Extras	(B 13, LB 17, NB 6)	36	(LB 1)	1
Total	(8 wickets declared)	**209**	(2 wickets)	**49**

ENGLAND	O	M	R	W	O	M	R	W	FALL OF WICKETS				
Tyson	19	7	23	3	12	6	16	4		NZ	E	NZ	E
Statham	17	9	24	4	15	5	30	1	*Wkt*	*1st*	*1st*	*2nd*	*2nd*
Bailey	12·2	6	19	2	8	4	9	0	1st	3	60	24	22
Wardle	26	15	31	1	14·3	4	41	2	2nd	63	71	68	47
Appleyard	7	3	16	0	7	2	19	2	3rd	68	101	75	–
									4th	72	150	96	–
NEW ZEALAND									5th	76	152	98	–
Blair	8	1	29	0	4	0	20	1	6th	86	152	103	–
MacGibbon	24·5	11	39	2	7·2	2	16	1	7th	103	156	103	–
Reid	27	11	36	4	4	2	12	0	8th	113	208	123	–
Cave	24	15	27	2					9th	122	–	126	–
Moir	9	1	42	0					10th	125	–	132	–

Umpires: R.G. Currie (2) and S.B. Tonkinson (2).

Close: 1st day – NZ(1) 125 all out; 2nd – E(1) 209-8 (Wardle 32, Appleyard 0); 3rd – no play; 4th – no play.

NEW ZEALAND v ENGLAND 1954–55 (2nd Test)

Played at Eden Park, Auckland, on 25, 26, 28 March.
Toss: New Zealand.   Result: ENGLAND won by an innings and 20 runs.
Debuts: Nil.

England dismissed New Zealand in 106 minutes for the lowest total in all Test cricket. The previous lowest was 30 – inflicted twice by England upon South Africa (*Tests No. 47 and 153*). Tyson and Statham brought their aggregate of Test wickets for the tour of Australasia to 69 (Tyson 39, Statham 30). Appleyard took three wickets in four balls in the second innings and twice during the match was on a hat-trick. Hutton was top-scorer in his last innings for England.

NEW ZEALAND

B. Sutcliffe	c Bailey b Statham	49	b Wardle	11
J.G. Leggat	lbw b Tyson	4	c Hutton b Tyson	1
M.B. Poore	c Evans b Tyson	0	b Tyson	0
J.R. Reid	c Statham b Wardle	73	b Statham	1
G.O. Rabone*	c Evans b Statham	29	(6) lbw b Statham	7
S.N. McGregor	not out	15	(5) c May b Appleyard	1
H.B. Cave	c Bailey b Appleyard	6	c Graveney b Appleyard	5
A.R. MacGibbon	b Appleyard	9	lbw b Appleyard	0
I.A. Colquhoun†	c sub (J.V. Wilson) b Appleyard	0	c Graveney b Appleyard	0
A.M. Moir	lbw b Statham	0	not out	0
J.A. Hayes	b Statham	0	b Statham	0
Extras	(B 3, LB 6, W 4, NB 2)	15		–
Total		**200**		**26**

ENGLAND

R.T. Simpson	c and b Moir	23
T.W. Graveney	c Rabone b Hayes	13
P.B.H. May	b Hayes	48
M.C. Cowdrey	b Moir	22
L. Hutton*	b MacGibbon	53
T.E. Bailey	c Colquhoun b Cave	18
T.G. Evans†	c Reid b Moir	0
J.H. Wardle	c Reid b Moir	0
F.H. Tyson	not out	27
R. Appleyard	c Colquhoun b Hayes	6
J.B. Statham	c Reid b Moir	13
Extras	(B 12, LB 3, NB 8)	23
Total		**246**

ENGLAND	O	M	R	W	O	M	R	W
Tyson	11	2	41	2	7	2	10	2
Statham	17·4	7	28	4	9	3	9	3
Bailey	13	2	34	0				
Appleyard	16	4	38	3	6	3	7	4
Wardle	31	19	44	1	5	5	0	1
NEW ZEALAND								
Hayes	23	7	71	3				
MacGibbon	20	7	33	1				
Reid	25	15	28	0				
Cave	24	10	25	1				
Moir	25·1	3	62	5				
Rabone	2	0	4	0				

FALL OF WICKETS

Wkt	NZ 1st	E 1st	NZ 2nd
1st	13	21	6
2nd	13	56	8
3rd	76	112	9
4th	154	112	14
5th	171	163	14
6th	189	164	22
7th	199	164	22
8th	199	201	22
9th	200	218	26
10th	200	246	26

Umpires: J.C. Harris (3) and J. McLellan (3).

Close: 1st day – NZ(1) 199-8 (McGregor 15); 2nd – E(1) 148-4 (Hutton 19, Bailey 13).

WEST INDIES v AUSTRALIA 1954–55 (1st Test)

Played at Sabina Park, Kingston, Jamaica, on 26, 28, 29, 30, 31 March.
Toss: Australia.   Result: AUSTRALIA won by nine wickets.
Debuts: West Indies – G.L. Gibbs, O.G. Smith.

Australia won their first Test match in the Caribbean with a day to spare. O.G. 'Collie' Smith scored a hundred on Test debut batting for 220 minutes and hitting 14 fours. Miller led Australia after Johnson had injured his foot while batting.

AUSTRALIA

C.C. McDonald	st Binns b Valentine	50	(3) not out	7
A.R. Morris	lbw b Valentine	65	c Gibbs b Weekes	1
R.N. Harvey	b Walcott	133		
K.R. Miller	lbw b Walcott	147		
R.R. Lindwall	lbw b Ramadhin	10		
P.J.P. Burge	c and b Atkinson	14		
L.V. Maddocks†	b Valentine	1	(1) not not	12
R. Benaud	b Walcott	46		
R.G. Archer	c Walcott b Holt	24		
I.W. Johnson*	not out	18		
W.A. Johnston	not out	0		
Extras	(B 3, LB 3, W 1)	7		
Total	(9 wickets declared)	**515**	(1 wicket)	**20**

WEST INDIES

J.K. Holt	c Benaud b Lindwall	31	c Maddocks b Benaud	60
G.L. Gibbs	lbw b Archer	12	b Johnston	0
A.P. Binns†	c Burge b Archer	0	(7) lbw b Miller	0
E. de C. Weekes	run out	19	c and b Benaud	1
C.L. Walcott	c Benaud b Miller	108	c Archer b Lindwall	39
F.M.M. Worrell	b Johnston	9	(8) b Archer	9
O.G. Smith	lbw b Lindwall	44	(3) c Harvey b Miller	104
D. St E. Atkinson*	c Harvey b Miller	1	(6) c Benaud b Miller	30
F.M. King	c Maddocks b Lindwall	4	b Lindwall	21
S. Ramadhin	not out	12	c Lindwall b Archer	3
A.L. Valentine	b Lindwall	0	not out	2
Extras	(B 14, LB 2, NB 3)	19	(B 5, NB 1)	6
Total		**259**		**275**

WEST INDIES	O	M	R	W	O	M	R	W
King	28	7	122	0	2	0	10	0
Worrell	7	2	13	0				
Atkinson	23	9	46	1				
Ramadhin	46	12	112	1				
Valentine	54	20	113	3				
Smith	11	0	27	0				
Walcott	26	9	50	3				
Gibbs	3	1	5	0	1	0	2	0
Holt	3	0	20	1				
Weekes					2·2	0	8	1
AUSTRALIA								
Lindwall	24	6	61	4	16·1	3	63	2
Archer	19	8	39	2	12	3	44	2
Johnston	23	4	75	1	16	3	54	1
Benaud	19	7	29	0	23	7	44	2
Miller	16	5	36	2	28	9	62	3
Harvey					1	0	2	0

FALL OF WICKETS

Wkt	A 1st	WI 1st	WI 2nd	A 2nd
1st	102	27	20	6
2nd	137	27	122	–
3rd	361	56	132	–
4th	391	75	209	–
5th	417	101	213	–
6th	430	239	213	–
7th	435	240	239	–
8th	475	243	253	–
9th	506	253	270	–
10th	–	259	275	–

Umpires: P. Burke (3) and T.A. Ewart (5).

Close: 1st day – A(1) 266-2 (Harvey 84, Miller 64); 2nd – A (1) 515-9 (Johnson 18, Johnston 0); 3rd – WI(1) 221-5 (Walcott 95, Smith 37); 4th – WI(2) 186-3 (Smith 92, Walcott 28).

WEST INDIES v AUSTRALIA 1954–55 (2nd Test)

Played at Queen's Park Oval, Port-of-Spain, Trinidad, on 11, 12, 13, 14, 15, 16 April.
Toss: West Indies.   Result: MATCH DRAWN.
Debuts: West Indies – L.S. Butler.

This was the first Trinidad Test match to be played on a turf pitch and it yielded 1,255 runs and only 23 wickets. A record crowd for any cricket match in the West Indies, estimated at 28,000, attended the first day's play, which rain reduced to 85 minutes. Walcott became the third West Indian after G.A. Headley and E. de C. Weekes to score a hundred in both innings of a Test. His partnership of 242 with Weekes set a record, since beaten, for any West Indies wicket against Australia.

WEST INDIES

J.K. Holt	c Johnston b Lindwall	25	lbw b Archer		21
J.B. Stollmeyer*	b Lindwall	14	b Johnson		42
C.L. Walcott	st Langley b Benaud	126	c Watson b Archer		110
E. de C. Weekes	c Johnson b Benaud	139	not out		87
O.G. Smith	b Benaud	0	c Langley b Archer		0
G. St A. Sobers	c Langley b Lindwall	47	not out		8
C.A. McWatt†	c Benaud b Miller	4			
F.M. King	b Lindwall	2			
S. Ramadhin	b Lindwall	0			
L.S. Butler	c Johnson b Lindwall	16			
A.L. Valentine	not out	4			
Extras	(B 1, LB 3, NB 1)	5	(LB 3, NB 2)		5
Total		**382**	(4 wickets)		**273**

AUSTRALIA

C.C. McDonald	c Walcott b Valentine	110
A.R. Morris	c King b Butler	111
R.N. Harvey	lbw b King	133
W.J. Watson	lbw b Ramadhin	27
R. Benaud	c Walcott b Ramadhin	5
K.R. Miller	run out	3
R.G. Archer	c McWatt b Valentine	84
I.W. Johnson*	c McWatt b Butler	66
R.R. Lindwall	not out	37
G.R.A. Langley†	c King b Walcott	9
W.A. Johnston	not out	1
Extras	(B 5, LB 6, W 1, NB 2)	14
Total	(9 wickets declared)	**600**

AUSTRALIA	O	M	R	W	O	M	R	W
Lindwall	24·5	3	95	6	17	0	70	0
Miller	28	8	96	1	11	0	52	0
Archer	9	0	42	0	8	1	37	3
Johnston	7	2	29	0	7	0	31	0
Johnson	19	5	72	0	7	2	26	1
Benaud	17	3	43	3	12	2	52	0

WEST INDIES	O	M	R	W
Butler	40	7	151	2
King	37	7	98	1
Holt	1	1	0	0
Ramadhin	32	8	90	2
Valentine	49	12	133	2
Walcott	19	5	45	1
Sobers	3	1	10	0
Smith	15	1	48	0
Stollmeyer	5	0	11	0

FALL OF WICKETS

	WI	A	WI
Wkt	1st	1st	2nd
1st	39	191	40
2nd	40	259	103
3rd	282	328	230
4th	282	336	236
5th	323	345	–
6th	355	439	–
7th	360	529	–
8th	360	570	–
9th	361	594	–
10th	382	–	–

Umpires: H.B. de C. Jordan (3) and E.N. Lee Kow (3).

Close: 1st day – WI(1) 73-2 (Walcott 7, Weekes 27); 2nd – WI(1) 355-5 (Sobers 43, McWatt 4); 3rd – A(1) 147-0 (McDonald 90, Morris 50); 4th – A(1) 447-6 (Archer 47, Johnson 0); 5th – WI(2) 40-1 (Stollmeyer 17).

WEST INDIES v AUSTRALIA 1954–55 (3rd Test)

Played at Bourda, Georgetown, British Guiana, on 26, 27, 28, 29 April.
Toss: West Indies.   Result: AUSTRALIA won by eight wickets.
Debuts: West Indies – C.C. Depeiza, N.E. Marshall.

Australia won in the first over after lunch on the fourth day after Johnson's off-breaks had established a record innings analysis for a Georgetown Test. Benaud became the first bowler to take three wickets in four balls in the West Indies. In the second innings, Langley equalled W.A.S. Oldfield's world Test record, set in 1924-25 (*Test No. 161*), by making five dismissals.

WEST INDIES

J.K. Holt	c and b Miller	12	c Langley b Miller	6
J.B. Stollmeyer*	c Archer b Miller	16	c and b Johnson	17
C.L. Walcott	c and b Archer	8	hit wkt b Lindwall	73
E. de C. Weekes	c Archer b Benaud	81	c Langley b Johnson	0
F.M.M. Worrell	c Johnson b Archer	9	hit wkt b Benaud	56
G. St A. Sobers	c Watson b Johnson	12	(8) b Johnson	11
D. St E. Atkinson	b Lindwall	13	st Langley b Johnson	16
C.C. Depeiza†	not out	16	(6) st Langley b Johnson	13
N.E. Marshall	b Benaud	0	c sub (L.E. Favell) b Johnson	8
S. Ramadhin	c Archer b Benaud	0	st Langley b Johnson	2
F.M. King	c Langley b Benaud	13	not out	0
Extras	(B 1, LB 1)	2	(B 1, LB 2, NB 2)	5
Total		**182**		**207**

AUSTRALIA

C.C. McDonald	b Atkinson	61	b Atkinson	31
A.R. Morris	c Sobers b Atkinson	44	c Walcott b Marshall	38
R.N. Harvey	c Holt b Ramadhin	38	not out	41
W.J. Watson	c and b Ramadhin	6	not out	22
K.R. Miller	c Depeiza b Sobers	33		
R. Benaud	c sub (O.G. Smith) b Marshall	68		
R.G. Archer	st Depeiza b Sobers	2		
I.W. Johnson*	c Stollmeyer b Sobers	0		
R.R. Lindwall	b Atkinson	2		
G.R.A. Langley†	not out	1		
W.A. Johnston	absent hurt	–		
Extras	(LB 2)	2	(NB 1)	1
Total		**257**	(2 wickets)	**133**

AUSTRALIA	O	M	R	W	O	M	R	W		FALL OF WICKETS			
										WI	A	WI	A
Lindwall	12	0	44	1	18	1	54	1	*Wkt*	*1st*	*1st*	*2nd*	*2nd*
Miller	9	1	33	2	9	3	18	1	1st	23	71	25	70
Archer	10	0	46	2	12	3	43	0	2nd	30	135	25	70
Johnson	9	1	42	1	22·2	10	44	7	3rd	42	147	25	–
Benaud	3·5	1	15	4	14	3	43	1	4th	52	161	150	–
WEST INDIES									5th	83	215	162	–
King	12	1	37	0	3	0	10	0	6th	124	231	175	–
Worrell	9	2	17	0	7	2	20	0	7th	156	231	186	–
Ramadhin	26	9	55	2	9	1	29	0	8th	156	238	204	–
Atkinson	37	13	85	3	15·5	5	32	1	9th	160	257	204	–
Marshall	33·3	16	40	1	13	6	22	1	10th	182	–	207	–
Stollmeyer	1	0	1	0									
Sobers	16	10	20	3	11	4	19	0					

Umpires: E.S. Gillette (4) and E.N. Lee Kow (4).

Close: 1st day – A(1) 83-1 (McDonald 32, Harvey 6); 2nd – WI(2) 17-0 (Holt 5, Stollmeyer 11); 3rd – A(2) 40-0 (McDonald 20, Morris 19).

WEST INDIES v AUSTRALIA 1954–55 (4th Test)

Played at Kensington Oval, Bridgetown, Bardados, on 14, 16, 17, 18, 19, 20 May.
Toss: Australia.   Result: MATCH DRAWN.
Debuts: West Indies – D.T. Dewdney.

Australia's total of 668 remains the highest of any Barbados Test match and the partnership of 206 between Miller and Archer is still the highest for the sixth wicket in this series. Both records were overshadowed by the batting of Atkinson and Depeiza, who set a new world first-class record of 347 for the seventh wicket after six wickets had fallen for 147. On the fourth day they became the second pair of batsmen after J.B. Hobbs and H. Sutcliffe (*Test No. 159*) to bat throughout a complete day's play. Depeiza scored his only hundred in first-class cricket. Atkinson was the first to score a double century and take five wickets in an innings of the same Test. Opening bowlers Miller and Lindwall contributed centuries to the draw that gained Australia the rubber.

AUSTRALIA

C.C. McDonald	run out	46	b Smith		17
L.E. Favell	c Weekes b Atkinson	72	run out		53
R.N. Harvey	c Smith b Worrell	74	c Valentine b Smith		27
W.J. Watson	c Depeiza b Dewdney	30	b Atkinson		0
K.R. Miller	c Depeiza b Dewdney	137	lbw b Atkinson		10
R. Benaud	c Walcott b Dewdney	1	b Sobers		5
R.G. Archer	b Worrell	98	lbw b Atkinson		28
R.R. Lindwall	c Valentine b Atkinson	118	(9) b Atkinson		10
I.W. Johnson*	b Dewdney	23	(8) c Holt b Smith		57
G.R.A. Langley†	b Sobers	53	not out		28
J.C. Hill	not out	8	c Weekes b Atkinson		1
Extras	(B 1, LB 2, W 4, NB 1)	8	(B 9, LB 4)		13
Total		**668**			**249**

WEST INDIES

J.K. Holt	b Lindwall	22	lbw b Hill		49
G. St A. Sobers	c Hill b Johnson	43	lbw b Archer		11
C.L. Walcott	c Langley b Benaud	15	b Benaud		83
E. de C. Weekes	c Langley b Miller	44	run out		6
F.M.M. Worrell	run out	16	c Archer b Miller		34
O.G. Smith	c Langley b Miller	2	b Lindwall		11
D. St E. Atkinson*	c Archer b Johnson	219	not out		20
C.C. Depeiza†	b Benaud	122	not out		11
S. Ramadhin	c and b Benaud	10			
D.T. Dewdney	b Johnson	0			
A.L. Valentine	not out	2			
Extras	(B 5, LB 4, W 2, NB 4)	15	(B 6, LB 2, W 1)		9
Total		**510**	(6 wickets)		**234**

WEST INDIES	O	M	R	W	O	M	R	W
Worrell	40	7	120	2	7	0	25	0
Dewdney	33	5	125	4	10	4	23	0
Walcott	26	10	57	0				
Valentine	31	9	87	0	6	1	16	0
Ramadhin	24	3	84	0	2	0	10	0
Atkinson	48	14	108	2	36·2	16	56	5
Smith	22	8	49	0	34	12	71	3
Sobers	11·5	6	30	1	14	3	35	1
AUSTRALIA								
Lindwall	25	3	96	1	8	1	39	1
Miller	22	2	113	2	21	3	66	1
Archer	15	4	44	0	7	1	11	1
Johnson	35	13	77	3	14	4	30	0
Hill	24	9	71	0	11	2	44	1
Benaud	31·1	6	73	3	11	3	35	1
Harvey	4	0	16	0				
Watson	1	0	5	0				

FALL OF WICKETS

Wkt	A 1st	WI 1st	A 2nd	WI 2nd
1st	108	52	71	38
2nd	126	69	72	67
3rd	226	105	73	81
4th	226	142	87	154
5th	233	143	107	193
6th	439	147	119	207
7th	483	494	151	–
8th	562	504	177	–
9th	623	504	241	–
10th	668	510	249	–

Umpires: H.B. de C. Jordan (4) and E.N. Lee Kow (5).

Close: 1st day – A(1) 243-5 (Miller 9, Archer 6); 2nd – A(1) 569-8 (Lindwall 80, Langley 2); 3rd – WI(1) 187-6 (Atkinson 19, Depeiza 22); 4th – WI(1) 494-6 (Atkinson 215, Depeiza 122); 5th – A(2) 184-8 (Johnson 25, Langley 0).

WEST INDIES v AUSTRALIA 1954-55 (5th Test)

Played at Sabina Park, Kingston, Jamaica, on 11, 13, 14, 15, 16, 17 June.
Toss: West Indies.   Result: AUSTRALIA won by an innings and 82 runs.
Debuts: West Indies – H.A. Furlonge.

Australia's total was then the highest by a country other than England and remains unique in including five centuries, Benaud's taking only 78 minutes. Walcott is the only batsman to score a hundred in each innings of a Test twice in the same rubber; nor has any batsman equalled his feat of scoring five centuries in a Test rubber. A twisted knee, sustained while attempting a catch on the first morning, prevented Johnston from bowling in his final Test. The stand of 295 between McDonald and Harvey remains Australia's highest for the third wicket in all Tests. Benaud scored his first fifty in 38 minutes. For the first time in Test cricket, five bowlers conceded a hundred or more runs in the same innings – and a sixth missed joining them by the narrowest margin.

WEST INDIES

J.K. Holt	c Langley b Miller	4		c Langley b Benaud	21
H.A. Furlonge	c Benaud b Lindwall	4		c sub (A.K. Davidson) b Miller	28
C.L. Walcott	c Langley b Miller	155	(4)	c Langley b Lindwall	110
E. de C. Weekes	b Benaud	56	(9)	not out	36
F.M.M. Worrell	c Langley b Lindwall	61	(7)	b Johnson	12
O.G. Smith	c Langley b Miller	29		c and b Benaud	16
G. St A. Sobers	not out	35	(5)	c Favell b Lindwall	64
D. St E. Atkinson*	run out	8		c Langley b Archer	4
C.C. Depeiza†	c Langley b Miller	0	(3)	b Miller	7
F.M. King	b Miller	0		c Archer b Johnson	6
D.T. Dewdney	b Miller	2		lbw b Benaud	0
Extras	(LB 2, W 1)	3		(B 8, LB 6, W 1)	15
Total		**357**			**319**

AUSTRALIA

C.C. McDonald	b Worrell	127
L.E. Favell	c Weekes b King	0
A.R. Morris	lbw b Dewdney	7
R.N. Harvey	c Atkinson b Smith	204
K.R. Miller	c Worrell b Atkinson	109
R.G. Archer	c Depeiza b Sobers	128
R.R. Lindwall	c Depeiza b King	10
R. Benaud	c Worrell b Smith	121
I.W. Johnson*	not out	27
G.R.A. Langley†	} did not bat	
W.A. Johnston		
Extras	(B 8, LB 7, W 9, NB 1)	25
Total	(8 wickets declared)	**758**

AUSTRALIA	O	M	R	W	O	M	R	W		FALL OF WICKETS		
										WI	A	WI
Lindwall	12	2	64	2	19	6	51	2	*Wkt*	*1st*	*1st*	*2nd*
Miller	25·2	3	107	6	19	3	58	2	1st	5	0	47
Archer	11	1	39	0	27	6	73	1	2nd	13	7	60
Benaud	24	5	75	1	29·5	10	76	3	3rd	95	302	65
Johnson	22	7	69	0	23	10	46	2	4th	204	373	244
									5th	268	593	244
WEST INDIES									6th	327	597	268
Dewdney	24	4	115	1					7th	341	621	273
King	31	1	126	2					8th	347	758	283
Atkinson	55	20	132	1					9th	347	–	289
Smith	52·4	17	145	2					10th	357	–	319
Worrell	45	10	116	1								
Sobers	38	12	99	1								

Umpires: P. Burke (4) and T.A. Ewart (6).

Close: 1st day – WI(1) 327-6 (Sobers 15); 2nd – A(1) 258-2 (McDonald 115, Harvey 121); 3rd – A(1) 480-4 (Miller 70, Archer 57); 4th – WI(2) 60-1 (Furlonge 28, Depeiza 7); 5th – WI(2) 293-9 (Weekes 19, Dewdney 0).

ENGLAND v SOUTH AFRICA 1955 (1st Test)

Played at Trent Bridge, Nottingham, on 9, 10, 11, 13 June.
Toss: England.   Result: ENGLAND won by an innings and 5 runs.
Debuts: England – K.F. Barrington; South Africa – T.L. Goddard.

Hutton, chosen as captain for all five Tests, stood down because of lumbago. May began his record reign of 41 matches as captain of England. South Africa scored only 144 runs in 345 minutes on the third day. McGlew's match aggregate of 119 runs took him over nine hours. Evans became the first wicket-keeper to make 150 dismissals in Test matches when he caught Fuller. Tyson ended the match with a spell of 5 for 5 in 7·3 overs; it brought his tally of Test wickets to 52 from nine matches.

ENGLAND

D. Kenyon	lbw b Goddard	87
T.W. Graveney	c Waite b Adcock	42
P.B.H. May*	c McGlew b Smith	83
D.C.S. Compton	lbw b Adcock	27
K.F. Barrington	c Waite b Fuller	0
T.E. Bailey	lbw b Goddard	49
T.G. Evans†	c Goddard b Fuller	12
J.H. Wardle	lbw b Tayfield	2
F.H. Tyson	c McLean b Tayfield	0
J.B. Statham	c Waite b Fuller	20
R. Appleyard	not out	0
Extras	(B 6, LB 6)	12
Total		**334**

SOUTH AFRICA

D.J. McGlew	c Evans b Wardle	68	c May b Bailey	51
T.L. Goddard	lbw b Statham	12	run out	32
J.H.B. Waite†	run out	0	c Compton b Tyson	3
W.R. Endean	lbw b Tyson	0	c Graveney b Bailey	6
R.A. McLean	b Tyson	13	c Graveney b Tyson	16
P.L. Winslow	c May b Appleyard	2	(7) b Tyson	3
J.E. Cheetham*	c Graveney b Wardle	54	(6) b Tyson	5
H.J. Tayfield	c Bailey b Appleyard	11	b Tyson	0
E.R.H. Fuller	b Wardle	15	c Evans b Wardle	6
V.I. Smith	c May b Wardle	0	not out	2
N.A.T. Adcock	not out	1	b Tyson	6
Extras	(B 1, LB 2, NB 2)	5	(B 8, LB 4, W 4, NB 2)	18
Total		**181**		**148**

SOUTH AFRICA	O	M	R	W	O	M	R	W
Adcock	36	9	74	2				
Goddard	36·4	18	61	2				
Fuller	29	5	59	3				
Tayfield	37	11	66	2				
Smith	30	9	62	1				
ENGLAND								
Statham	25	5	47	1	10	4	16	0
Tyson	24	5	51	2	21·3	7	28	6
Bailey	5	2	8	0	17	8	21	2
Appleyard	28	9	46	2	19	4	32	0
Wardle	32	23	24	4	29	17	33	1

FALL OF WICKETS

Wkt	E 1st	SA 1st	SA 2nd
1st	91	15	73
2nd	166	17	83
3rd	228	19	101
4th	233	35	108
5th	252	55	131
6th	285	149	132
7th	294	156	132
8th	298	174	135
9th	334	180	141
10th	334	181	148

Umpires: T.J. Bartley (2) and F.S. Lee (14).

Close: 1st day – E(1) 244-4 (May 81, Bailey 1); 2nd – SA(1) 83-5 (McGlew 38, Cheetham 17); 3rd – SA(2) 46-0 (McGlew 24, Goddard 21).

ENGLAND v SOUTH AFRICA 1955 (2nd Test)

Played at Lord's, London, on 23, 24, 25, 27 June.
Toss: England.   Result: ENGLAND won by 71 runs.
Debuts: England – F.J. Titmus; South Africa – P.S. Heine.

Compton emulated Hobbs, Bradman, Hammond and Hutton by scoring his 5,000th run in Test cricket. Tayfield overtook C.L. Vincent's South African Test record of 84 wickets. May scored a hundred on his first appearance as England's captain at Lord's. The only serious casualty on a lively, well-grassed pitch was Cheetham, who sustained a chipped left elbow when he was hit by the last ball of the third day's play (South Africa 17 for 2), and missed the next two Tests. Statham, who dismissed McGlew twice in three balls for a 'pair', bowled unchanged for $3\frac{3}{4}$ hours, a magnificent feat of endurance that brought England victory, the bowler his best England analysis, and 'Nelson' his third last-innings success of the year.

ENGLAND

D. Kenyon	b Adcock	1		lbw b Goddard	2
T.W. Graveney	c Waite b Heine	15		c Heine b Goddard	60
P.B.H. May*	c Tayfield b Heine	0		hit wkt b Heine	112
D.C.S. Compton	c Keith b Heine	20		c Mansell b Goddard	69
K.F. Barrington	b Heine	34		c McLean b Tayfield	18
T.E. Bailey	lbw b Goddard	13		c Adcock b Tayfield	22
T.G. Evans†	c Waite b Heine	20		c and b Tayfield	14
F.J. Titmus	lbw b Goddard	4	(9)	c Waite b Adcock	16
J.H. Wardle	c Tayfield b Goddard	20	(8)	c Heine b Tayfield	4
J.B. Statham	c McLean b Goddard	0		b Tayfield	11
F.S. Trueman	not out	2		not out	6
Extras	(B 2, LB 2)	4		(B 15, LB 2, NB 2)	19
Total		**133**			**353**

SOUTH AFRICA

D.J. McGlew	c Evans b Statham	0		lbw b Statham	0
T.L. Goddard	c Evans b Trueman	0		c Evans b Statham	10
J.E. Cheetham*	lbw b Bailey	13		retired hurt	3
W.R. Endean	lbw b Wardle	48	(5)	c Evans b Statham	28
R.A. McLean	b Statham	142	(6)	b Statham	8
J.H.B. Waite†	c Evans b Trueman	8	(8)	lbw b Statham	9
H.J. Keith	c Titmus b Wardle	57		c Graveney b Statham	5
P.N.F. Mansell	c Graveney b Wardle	2	(9)	c Kenyon b Wardle	16
H.J. Tayfield	b Titmus	21	(4)	c Evans b Statham	3
P.S. Heine	st Evans b Wardle	2		c Kenyon b Wardle	14
N.A.T. Adcock	not out	0		not out	0
Extras	(B 6, LB 1, NB 4)	11		(B 11, LB 3, NB 1)	15
Total		**304**			**111**

SOUTH AFRICA	O	M	R	W	O	M	R	W
Heine	25	7	60	5	29	5	87	1
Adcock	8	3	10	1	25	5	64	1
Goddard	21·2	8	59	4	55	23	96	3
Tayfield					38·5	12	80	5
Mansell					2	0	7	0
ENGLAND								
Statham	27	9	49	2	29	12	39	7
Trueman	16	2	73	2	19	2	39	0
Bailey	16	2	56	1				
Wardle	29	10	65	4	9·4	4	18	2
Titmus	14	3	50	1				

FALL OF WICKETS

	E	SA	E	SA
Wkt	1st	1st	2nd	2nd
1st	7	0	9	0
2nd	8	7	141	17
3rd	30	51	237	40
4th	45	101	277	54
5th	82	138	285	63
6th	98	247	302	75
7th	111	259	306	78
8th	111	302	336	111
9th	111	304	336	111
10th	133	304	353	–

Umpires: F. Chester (47) and L.H. Gray (1).

Close: 1st day – SA(1) 142-5 (McLean 62, Keith 0); 2nd – E(2) 108-1 (Graveney 53, May 50); 3rd – SA(2) 17-2 (Cheetham 3, Tayfield 0).

ENGLAND v SOUTH AFRICA 1955 (3rd Test)

Played at Old Trafford, Manchester, on 7, 8, 9, 11, 12 July.
Toss: England.   Result: SOUTH AFRICA won by three wickets.
Debuts: Nil.

Needing 145 runs to win in 135 minutes, South Africa gained their third victory in England with nine balls to spare. It was England's first defeat at Manchester since 1902. Evans fractured his right-hand little finger in two places (Graveney deputised as wicket-keeper) but hit powerfully in a last-wicket stand of 48 with Bailey which almost saved the match for England. Winslow reached his maiden first-class hundred with a straight drive over the sight-screen off Lock, and added a record 171 for the sixth wicket with Waite. McGlew retired with a damaged hand when 77 at 147, and resumed at 457. Bedser ended a most distinguished 51-match career with the then world record total of 236 Test wickets.

ENGLAND

D. Kenyon	c Waite b Heine	5	c Waite b Heine	1
T.W. Graveney	c Tayfield b Adcock	0	b Adcock	1
P.B.H. May*	c Mansell b Goddard	34	b Mansell	117
D.C.S. Compton	c Waite b Adcock	158	c Mansell b Heine	71
M.C. Cowdrey	c Mansell b Tayfield	1	c Goddard b Heine	50
T.E. Bailey	c Waite b Adcock	44	(7) not out	38
F.J. Titmus	lbw b Heine	0	(8) c Mansell b Adcock	19
T.G. Evans†	c Keith b Heine	0	(11) c McLean b Tayfield	36
G.A.R. Lock	not out	19	(6) c McGlew b Adcock	17
F.H. Tyson	b Goddard	2	(9) b Heine	8
A.V. Bedser	lbw b Goddard	1	(10) c Waite b Heine	3
Extras	(B 13, LB 6, W 1)	20	(B 13, LB 5, W 2)	20
Total		**284**		**381**

SOUTH AFRICA

D.J. McGlew*	not out	104	b Tyson	48
T.L. Goddard	c Graveney b Tyson	62	c May b Bedser	8
H.J. Keith	c Graveney b Bailey	38	b Bedser	0
P.N.F. Mansell	lbw b Lock	7	(6) lbw b Tyson	4
W.R. Endean	c Evans b Lock	5	(8) c Titmus b Lock	2
R.A. McLean	b Tyson	3	(4) run out	50
J.H.B. Waite†	c Kenyon b Bedser	113	not out	10
P.L. Winslow	lbw b Bedser	108	(5) b Tyson	16
H.J. Tayfield	b Tyson	28	not out	1
P.S. Heine	not out	22		
N.A.T. Adcock	did not bat			
Extras	(B 15, LB 12, W 1, NB 3)	31	(B 2, LB 2, W 1, NB 1)	6
Total	(8 wickets declared)	**521**	(7 wickets)	**145**

SOUTH AFRICA	O	M	R	W	O	M	R	W		FALL OF WICKETS			
										E	SA	E	SA
Heine	24	4	71	3	32	8	86	5	*Wkt*	*1st*	*1st*	*2nd*	*2nd*
Adcock	28	5	52	3	28	12	48	3	1st	2	147	2	18
Tayfield	35	15	57	1	51·5	21	102	1	2nd	22	171	2	23
Goddard	27	10	52	3	47	21	92	0	3rd	70	179	95	95
Mansell	6	2	13	0	15	3	33	1	4th	75	182	234	112
Keith	6	2	19	0					5th	219	245	270	129
									6th	234	416	274	132
ENGLAND									7th	242	457	304	135
Bedser	31	2	92	2	10	1	61	2	8th	271	494	325	–
Tyson	44	5	124	3	13·3	2	55	3	9th	280	–	333	–
Bailey	37	8	102	1					10th	284	–	381	–
Lock	64	24	121	2	7	2	23	1					
Titmus	19	7	51	0									

Umpires: D. Davies (17) and F.S. Lee (15).

Close: 1st day – E(1) 264-7 (Compton 155, Lock 6); 2nd – SA(1) 199-4 (Keith 22, Waite 14); 3rd – SA(1) 482-7 (McGlew 89, Tayfield 26); 4th – E(2) 250-4 (Cowdrey 42, Lock 3).

ENGLAND v SOUTH AFRICA 1955 (4th Test)

Played at Headingley, Leeds, on 21, 22, 23, 25, 26 July.
Toss: South Africa.   Result: SOUTH AFRICA won by 224 runs.
Debuts: Nil.

Despite losing Adcock with a broken bone in his left foot, South Africa gained an unprecedented second victory in a rubber in England. McGlew and Goddard shared a record opening partnership for South Africa in England. Bailey batted two hours for eight runs in the second innings, including a period of 79 minutes without scoring. On the last day, Goddard bowled unchanged from 11.30 am until 4.15 pm when his major contribution saw South Africa square the rubber. Frank Chester ended his career as an international umpire after officiating in a record number of Tests (48). Six batsmen were given out 'lbw' in England's first innings – a Test record subsequently equalled.

SOUTH AFRICA

D.J. McGlew*	c McIntyre b Loader	23		c May b Wardle	133
T.L. Goddard	b Loader	9		c McIntyre b Wardle	74
H.J. Keith	c McIntyre b Loader	0		b Wardle	73
P.N.F. Mansell	b Bailey	0	(8)	lbw b Bailey	1
R.A. McLean	c May b Loader	41	(4)	c Lowson b Wardle	3
J.H.B. Waite†	run out	2	(7)	c McIntyre b Lock	32
P.L. Winslow	b Statham	8	(5)	c Lock b Statham	19
W.R. Endean	b Statham	41	(6)	not out	116
H.J. Tayfield	not out	25		lbw b Statham	14
P.S. Heine	b Lock	14		b Bailey	10
N.A.T. Adcock	lbw b Statham	0		b Bailey	6
Extras	(LB 4, NB 4)	8		(B 8, LB 6, W 1, NB 4)	19
Total		**171**			**500**

ENGLAND

T.E. Bailey	lbw b Heine	9	(6)	c and b Tayfield	8
F.A. Lowson	lbw b Goddard	5		b Goddard	0
P.B.H. May*	b Tayfield	47		lbw b Tayfield	97
G.A.R. Lock	lbw b Goddard	17	(9)	c Mansell b Goddard	7
D.C.S. Compton	c Mansell b Tayfield	61		c Waite b Goddard	26
T.W. Graveney	lbw b Heine	10	(1)	c McLean b Tayfield	36
D.J. Insole	lbw b Heine	3	(4)	c Keith b Goddard	47
A.J.W. McIntyre†	lbw b Heine	3	(7)	c Heine b Tayfield	4
J.H. Wardle	c Goddard b Tayfield	24	(8)	c Heine b Tayfield	21
J.B. Statham	b Tayfield	4		hit wkt b Goddard	3
P.J. Loader	not out	0		not out	0
Extras	(B 5, LB 2, W 1)	8		(B 1, LB 6)	7
Total		**191**			**256**

ENGLAND	O	M	R	W	O	M	R	W		FALL OF WICKETS			
Statham	20·2	7	35	3	40	10	129	2		SA	E	SA	E
Loader	19	7	52	4	29	9	67	0	*Wkt*	*1st*	*1st*	*2nd*	*2nd*
Bailey	16	7	23	1	40·5	11	97	3	1st	33	15	176	3
Wardle	9	1	33	0	57	22	100	4	2nd	33	23	265	59
Lock	6	1	20	1	42	13	88	1	3rd	34	53	269	160
									4th	34	117	303	204
SOUTH AFRICA									5th	38	152	311	210
Heine	29·5	11	70	4	14	2	33	0	6th	63	152	387	215
Adcock	4	3	4	0					7th	98	161	400	239
Goddard	25	12	39	2	62	37	69	5	8th	154	186	439	246
Tayfield	31	14	70	4	47·1	15	94	5	9th	170	191	468	256
Mansell					19	2	53	0	10th	171	191	500	256

Umpires: T.J. Bartley (3) and F. Chester (48).

Close: 1st day – E(1) 25-2 (May 7, Lock 2); 2nd – SA(2) 107-0 (McGlew 59, Goddard 46); 3rd – SA(2) 341-5 (Endean 18, Waite 8); 4th – E(2) 115-2 (May 47, Insole 30).

ENGLAND v SOUTH AFRICA 1955 (5th Test)

Played at Kennington Oval, London, on 13, 15, 16, 17 August.
Toss: England.   Result: ENGLAND won by 92 runs.
Debuts: Nil.

This was the first rubber in England to produce five definite results, England winning this deciding match at 5.15 pm on the fourth day. On the third day Tayfield had bowled unchanged from 12.30 to 6.30 pm, five hours of play during which he bowled 52 overs for 54 runs and four wickets. He became the first bowler to take 100 Test wickets for South Africa when he bowled Graveney. His 26 wickets in the rubber is the record, subsequently equalled, for a South African bowler in England.

ENGLAND

J.T. Ikin	c Waite b Heine	17	c Goddard b Heine	0
D.B. Close	c Mansell b Goddard	32	b Goddard	15
P.B.H. May*	c Goddard b Fuller	3	(4) not out	89
D.C.S. Compton	c Waite b Goddard	30	(5) c Waite b Fuller	30
W. Watson	c Mansell b Tayfield	25	(6) b Fuller	3
T.W. Graveney	c Fuller b Goddard	13	(3) b Tayfield	42
T.E. Bailey	c Heine b Tayfield	0	lbw b Tayfield	1
R.T. Spooner†	b Tayfield	0	b Tayfield	0
J.C. Laker	c and b Goddard	2	b Tayfield	12
G.A.R. Lock	c McLean b Goddard	18	lbw b Heine	1
J.B. Statham	not out	4	lbw b Tayfield	0
Extras	(B 2, LB 5)	7	(B 4, LB 6, NB 1)	11
Total		**151**		**204**

SOUTH AFRICA

D.J. McGlew	c Spooner b Statham	30	lbw b Lock	19
T.L. Goddard	lbw b Bailey	8	c Graveney b Lock	20
H.J. Keith	b Lock	5	c May b Lock	0
W.R. Endean	c Ikin b Lock	0	lbw b Laker	0
R.A. McLean	b Lock	1	lbw b Laker	0
J.H.B. Waite†	c Lock b Laker	28	b Laker	60
J.E. Cheetham*	not out	12	lbw b Laker	9
P.N.F. Mansell	lbw b Laker	6	c Watson b Lock	9
H.J. Tayfield	b Statham	4	not out	10
E.R.H. Fuller	c Spooner b Lock	5	run out	16
P.S. Heine	run out	5	c Graveney b Laker	7
Extras	(LB 7, NB 1)	8	(LB 1)	1
Total		**112**		**151**

SOUTH AFRICA	O	M	R	W	O	M	R	W	FALL OF WICKETS				
Heine	21	3	43	1	25	6	44	2		E	SA	E	SA
Goddard	22·4	9	31	5	19	10	29	1	*Wkt*	*1st*	*1st*	*2nd*	*2nd*
Fuller	27	11	31	1	20	3	36	2	1st	51	22	5	28
Tayfield	19	7	39	3	53·4	29	60	5	2nd	59	29	30	28
Mansell					6	0	24	0	3rd	69	31	95	29
									4th	105	33	157	33
ENGLAND									5th	117	77	165	59
Statham	15	3	31	2	11	4	17	0	6th	117	77	166	88
Bailey	5	1	6	1	6	1	15	0	7th	118	86	170	118
Lock	22	11	39	4	33	14	62	4	8th	123	91	188	118
Laker	23	13	28	2	37·4	18	56	5	9th	130	98	197	144
									10th	151	112	204	151

Umpires: T.J. Bartley (4) and D. Davies (18).

Close: 1st day – E(1) 70-3 (Compton 12, Watson 1); 2nd – SA(1) 112 all out; 3rd – E(2) 195-8 (May 81, Lock 0).

PAKISTAN v NEW ZEALAND 1955–56 (1st Test)

Played at National Stadium, Karachi, on 13, 14, 16, 17 October.
Toss: New Zealand.   Result: PAKISTAN won by an innings and 1 run.
Debuts: New Zealand – J.C. Alabaster, P.G.Z. Harris, T.G. McMahon.

Zulfiqar Ahmed's off-spin on a matting pitch laid on grass provided – at the earliest possible opportunity – the first instance of a bowler taking ten wickets in a Test match between these two countries. His match analysis of 11 for 79 remains the record for either country in this series.

NEW ZEALAND

J.G. Leggat	c Imtiaz b Fazal	16	lbw b Zulfiqar	39
B. Sutcliffe	c Kardar b Zulfiqar	15	b Shujauddin	17
M.B. Poore	st Imtiaz b Zulfiqar	43	b Shujauddin	0
J.R. Reid	c Khan b Kardar	10	(5) c Waqar b Zulfiqar	11
P.G.Z. Harris	c Wazir b Kardar	7	(6) run out	21
S.N. McGregor	c Alimuddin b Shujauddin	10	(4) lbw b Shujauddin	0
H.B. Cave*	b Kardar	0	c sub (Agha Saadat) b Zulfiqar	21
J.C. Alabaster	c sub (Agha Saadat) b Zulfiqar	14	b Zulfiqar	8
A.R. MacGibbon	b Zulfiqar	33	c Hanif b Zulfiqar	0
A.M. Moir	c Khan b Zulfiqar	10	c Alimuddin b Zulfiqar	2
T.G. McMahon†	not out	0	not out	0
Extras	(B 4, LB 2)	6	(B 1, LB 4)	5
Total		**164**		**124**

PAKISTAN

Hanif Mohammad	c McGregor b Cave	5
Alimuddin	c MacGibbon b Moir	28
Waqar Hassan	c McMahon b Cave	17
Maqsood Ahmed	b MacGibbon	2
Imtiaz Ahmed†	c McMahon b MacGibbon	64
A.H. Kardar*	run out	22
Wazir Mohammad	c and b Cave	43
Shujauddin	b MacGibbon	47
Zulfiqar Ahmed	b MacGibbon	10
Fazal Mahmood	not out	34
Khan Mohammad	run out	5
Extras	(B 4, LB 1, NB 7)	12
Total		**289**

PAKISTAN	O	M	R	W	O	M	R	W	FALL OF WICKETS			
										NZ	P	NZ
Fazal	31	12	46	1					*Wkt*	*1st*	*1st*	*2nd*
Khan	23	9	27	0	13	3	33	0	1st	18	7	27
Zulfiqar	37·2	19	37	5	46·3	21	42	6	2nd	50	25	27
Kardar	31	10	35	3	27	15	22	0	3rd	71	34	27
Shujauddin	11	7	13	1	22	12	22	3	4th	95	74	42
NEW ZEALAND									5th	95	140	79
MacGibbon	37·1	8	98	4					6th	95	144	109
Cave	24	6	56	3					7th	114	222	118
Reid	30	17	34	0					8th	129	240	120
Moir	37	9	87	1					9th	163	251	122
Poore	2	0	2	0					10th	164	289	124

Umpires: Idris Beg (5) and Shujauddin (4).

Close: 1st day – NZ(1) 145-8 (MacGibbon 19, Moir 5); 2nd – P(1) 178-6 (Wazir 25, Shujauddin 13); 3rd – NZ(2) 79-4 (Leggat 39, Harris 9).

PAKISTAN v NEW ZEALAND 1955–56 (2nd Test)

Played at Bagh-i-Jinnah, Lahore, on 26, 27, 29, 30, 31 October.
Toss: New Zealand.   Result: PAKISTAN won by four wickets.
Debuts: New Zealand – N.S. Harford, E.C. Petrie.

Pakistan won with 18 minutes to spare after compiling their highest total in any Test so far. First Waqar Hassan and then Imtiaz Ahmed established a new record score for their country, Imtiaz hitting Pakistan's first double-century in an innings lasting 680 minutes and containing 28 fours. His partnership of 308 with Waqar remains Pakistan's highest for the seventh wicket in all Tests. His score of 209 remains the highest by a number eight batsman in Test cricket and, until *Test No. 878*, was the highest by a wicket-keeper at this level. This victory gained Pakistan their first rubber. McGregor's hundred was his first in first-class cricket.

NEW ZEALAND

B. Sutcliffe	c Waqar b Khan	4		lbw b Shujauddin	25
M.B. Poore	c Alimuddin b Khan	6		c Imtiaz b Zulfiqar	9
P.G.Z. Harris	run out	28		b Shujauddin	11
S.N. McGregor	lbw b Kardar	111		c Imtiaz b Khan	43
J.R. Reid	c Maqsood b Khan	5		b Kardar	86
N.S. Harford	c Maqsood b Khan	93	(7)	c Khan b Zulfiqar	64
A.R. MacGibbon	lbw b Zulfiqar	61	(6)	c Wazir b Kardar	40
E.C. Petrie†	b Kardar	0		c Hanif b Kardar	7
H.B. Cave*	c and b Zulfiqar	14		c Alimuddin b Zulfiqar	17
A.M. Moir	b Mahmood	8		not out	11
J.A. Hayes	not out	0		lbw b Zulfiqar	0
Extras	(B 4, LB 10, NB 4)	18		(B 6, LB 5, NB 4)	15
Total		**348**			**328**

PAKISTAN

Hanif Mohammad	hit wkt b Hayes	10		lbw b Reid	33
Alimuddin	c Sutcliffe b MacGibbon	4		c MacGibbon b Reid	37
Shujauddin	b Moir	29	(7)	not out	1
Waqar Hassan	c Petrie b MacGibbon	189	(5)	c MacGibbon b Hayes	17
Wazir Mohammad	lbw b Moir	0	(8)	not out	2
A.H. Kardar*	b Moir	2		c Reid b Hayes	11
Khan Mohammad	run out	10			
Imtiaz Ahmed†	b Moir	209	(3)	c Cave b Reid	0
Maqsood Ahmed	c Cave b Reid	33	(4)	c McGregor b Reid	8
Zulfiqar Ahmed	not out	21			
Mahmood Hussain	c MacGibbon b Sutcliffe	32			
Extras	(B 3, LB 7, NB 12)	22		(B 2, LB 4, NB 2)	8
Total		**561**		(6 wickets)	**117**

PAKISTAN	O	M	R	W	O	M	R	W		FALL OF WICKETS			
Khan	34	10	78	4	18	6	26	1		NZ	P	NZ	P
Mahmood Hussain	31·5	4	67	1	21	6	47	0	*Wkt*	*1st*	*1st*	*2nd*	*2nd*
Shujauddin	43	11	84	0	38	12	79	2	1st	8	11	34	45
Zulfiqar	35	13	71	2	43·2	10	114	4	2nd	13	23	43	49
Maqsood	3	1	4	0					3rd	48	84	60	80
Kardar	14	5	26	2	38	15	47	3	4th	76	84	148	93
									5th	226	87	224	107
NEW ZEALAND									6th	267	111	237	115
Hayes	37	12	107	1	8·5	2	25	2	7th	267	419	252	–
MacGibbon	40	7	135	2	5	0	20	0	8th	333	482	293	–
Reid	35	13	82	1	8	2	38	4	9th	348	517	324	–
Cave	30	6	84	0	5	0	26	0	10th	348	561	328	–
Moir	39	13	114	4									
Poore	3	0	13	0									
Sutcliffe	1·3	0	4	1									

Umpires: Daud Khan (3) and Idris Beg (6).

Close: 1st day – NZ(1) 206-4 (McGregor 72, Harford 81); 2nd – P(1) 87-5 (Waqar 35); 3rd – P(1) 419-7 (Imtiaz 158); 4th – NZ(2) 166-4 (Reid 58, MacGibbon 11).

PAKISTAN v NEW ZEALAND 1955–56 (3rd Test)

Played at Dacca Stadium on 7 (*no play*), 8 (*no play*), 9, 11, 12 (*no play*) November.
Toss: New Zealand.   Result: MATCH DRAWN.
Debuts: Pakistan – Agha Saadat Ali, Wallis Mathias; New Zealand – J.W. Guy.

Incessant drizzle prevented play until the third day. On a wet coir matting pitch laid on grass, New Zealand were bowled out in a humid atmosphere for the lowest total by any country against Pakistan until 1986-87. Khan Mohammad's analysis of 6 for 21 is the best in any Test at Dacca.

NEW ZEALAND

J.G. Leggat	b Khan	1	c Agha Saadat b Fazal		1
B. Sutcliffe	b Fazal	3	c Imtiaz b Khan		17
M.B. Poore	b Fazal	0	c Agha Saadat b Kardar		18
S.N. McGregor	b Khan	7	c Imtiaz b Zulfiqar		4
J.R. Reid	c Imtiaz b Khan	9	b Kardar		12
N.S. Harford	c Imtiaz b Fazal	0	c Hanif b Khan		1
J.W. Guy	st Imtiaz b Zulfiqar	11	not out		8
A.R. MacGibbon	not out	29	not out		7
E.C. Petrie†	lbw b Khan	6			
H.B. Cave*	c Agha Saadat b Khan	0			
A.M. Moir	c Shujauddin b Khan	0			
Extras	(LB 4)	4	(LB 1)		1
Total		**70**	(6 wickets)		**69**

PAKISTAN

Alimuddin	b Reid	5
Hanif Mohammad	c Reid b Cave	103
Waqar Hassan	lbw b Reid	8
Shujauddin	c Guy b Cave	3
Imtiaz Ahmed†	b Cave	11
A.H. Kardar*	b MacGibbon	14
W. Mathias	not out	41
Agha Saadat Ali	not out	8
Fazal Mahmood	)	
Zulfiqar Ahmed	) did not bat	
Khan Mohammad	)	
Extras	(LB 1, NB 1)	2
Total	(6 wickets declared)	**195**

PAKISTAN	O	M	R	W	O	M	R	W	FALL OF WICKETS			
										NZ	P	NZ
Fazal	20	7	34	3	6	3	12	1	*Wkt*	*1st*	*1st*	*2nd*
Khan	16·2	6	21	6	30	19	20	2	1st	1	22	12
Zulfiqar	3	1	11	1	16	8	13	1	2nd	4	30	22
Kardar					28	17	21	2	3rd	9	37	32
Shujauddin					9	8	1	0	4th	15	55	51
Hanif					1	0	1	0	5th	20	86	52
									6th	26	182	56
NEW ZEALAND									7th	54	–	–
MacGibbon	20	4	64	1					8th	64	–	–
Cave	20	4	45	3					9th	68	–	–
Reid	30	10	67	2					10th	70	–	–
Moir	6	1	17	0								

Umpires: Daud Khan (4) and Idris Beg (7).

Close: 1st day – no play; 2nd – no play; 3rd – P(1) 113-5 (Hanif 68, Mathias 4); 4th – NZ (2) 69-6 (Guy 8, MacGibbon 7).

INDIA v NEW ZEALAND 1955–56 (1st Test)

Played at Fateh Maidan, Hyderabad, on 19, 20, 22, 23, 24 November.
Toss: India.   Result: MATCH DRAWN.
Debuts: India – A.G. Kripal Singh, V.N. Swamy.

The first Test between these two countries was also the first to be staged at Hyderabad where a turf pitch had recently been laid. It proved a perfect batting surface as India made their highest Test total so far and Umrigar reached India's first double-century; his partnership of 238 with Manjrekar was India's third-wicket record in all Tests and it remains the record for this series, as does his fourth-wicket stand of 171 with Kripal Singh, who became the second to score a century in his first Test innings for India.

INDIA

M.H. Mankad	c Alabaster b MacGibbon	30
Pankaj Roy	c Petrie b Hayes	0
P.R. Umrigar	c Petrie b Hayes	223
V.L. Manjrekar	c MacGibbon b Hayes	118
A.G. Kripal Singh	not out	100
G.S. Ramchand	not out	12
D.G. Phadkar	)	
V.N. Swamy	)	
N.S. Tamhane†	) did not bat	
S.P. Gupte	)	
Ghulam Ahmed*	)	
Extras	(B 8, LB 4, NB 3)	15
Total	**(4 wickets declared)**	**498**

NEW ZEALAND

B. Sutcliffe	c Umrigar b Gupte	17	not out	137
E.C. Petrie†	b Gupte	15	lbw b Gupte	4
J.W. Guy	c Ghulam Ahmed b Mankad	102	c Ghulam Ahmed b Mankad	21
J.R. Reid	lbw b Ramchand	54	not out	45
S.N. McGregor	st Tamhane b Gupte	19		
N.S. Harford	lbw b Gupte	4		
A.R. MacGibbon	c Kripal Singh b Ghulam Ahmed	59		
M.B. Poore	lbw b Gupte	23		
H.B. Cave*	st Tamhane b Gupte	14		
J.C. Alabaster	lbw b Gupte	11		
J.A. Hayes	not out	1		
Extras	(B 2, LB 5)	7	(B 2, LB 2, NB 1)	5
Total		326	(2 wickets)	212

NEW ZEALAND	O	M	R	W	O	M	R	W
Hayes	26	5	91	3				
MacGibbon	43·1	15	102	1				
Reid	16	2	63	0				
Cave	41	20	59	0				
Alabaster	31	5	96	0				
Poore	9	2	36	0				
Sutcliffe	9	1	36	0				
INDIA								
Phadkar	25	11	34	0	12	5	24	0
Swamy	8	2	15	0	10	3	30	0
Gupte	76·4	35	128	7	18	7	28	1
Ghulam Ahmed	39	15	56	1	13	2	36	0
Mankad	36	16	48	1	25	7	75	1
Ramchand	20	12	33	1	14	7	14	0
Kripal Singh	1	0	5	0				
Umrigar	4	4	0	0				

FALL OF WICKETS

	I	NZ	NZ
Wkt	1st	1st	2nd
1st	1	27	42
2nd	48	36	104
3rd	286	119	–
4th	457	154	–
5th	–	166	–
6th	–	253	–
7th	–	292	–
8th	–	305	–
9th	–	325	–
10th	–	326	–

Umpires: J.R. Patel (7) and M.G. Vijayasarathi (7).

Close: 1st day – I(1) 250-2 (Umrigar 112, Manjrekar 102); 2nd – NZ(1) 1-0 (Sutcliffe 1, Petrie 0); 3rd – NZ(1) 170-5 (Guy 57, MacGibbon 2); 4th – NZ(1) 326 all out.

INDIA v NEW ZEALAND 1955–56 (2nd Test)

Played at Brabourne Stadium, Bombay, on 2, 3, 4, 6, 7 December.
Toss: India.   Result: INDIA won by an innings and 27 runs.
Debuts: India – N.J. Contractor, V.L. Mehra, S.R. Patil.

Mankad scored India's second double-century and equalled Umrigar's record score set in the previous Test. Reid (bruised ankle) batted with a runner in both innings. India gained the first victory of this series after 55 minutes of play on the fifth day.

INDIA

M.H. Mankad	c sub (T.G. McMahon) b Poore	223
V.L. Mehra	c Harris b Hayes	10
P.R. Umrigar*	b Cave	15
V.L. Manjrekar	c Alabaster b Cave	0
A.G. Kripal Singh	b Cave	63
G.S. Ramchand	b MacGibbon	22
N.J. Contractor	c Petrie b MacGibbon	16
D.G. Phadkar	not out	37
N.S. Tamhane†	b Poore	10
S.R. Patil	not out	14
S.P. Gupte	did not bat	
Extras	(LB 3, NB 8)	11
Total	(8 wickets declared)	**421**

NEW ZEALAND

B. Sutcliffe	c Gupte b Ramchand	73	c Mankad b Gupte	37
E.C. Petrie†	lbw b Gupte	4	c Gupte b Phadkar	4
J.W. Guy	c Gupte b Ramchand	23	lbw b Gupte	2
J.R. Reid	lbw b Patil	39	c Phadkar b Patil	4
P.G.Z. Harris	lbw b Gupte	19	c Tamhane b Mankad	7
A.R. MacGibbon	c Mankad b Phadkar	46	c Patil b Gupte	24
M.B. Poore	c Umrigar b Phadkar	17	b Mankad	0
H.B. Cave*	run out	12	c Umrigar b Mankad	21
A.M. Moir	lbw b Gupte	0	c Manjrekar b Gupte	28
J.C. Alabaster	b Mankad	16	b Gupte	4
J.A. Hayes	not out	0	not out	0
Extras	(B 3, LB 2, W 4)	9	(B 1, LB 4)	5
Total		**258**		**136**

NEW ZEALAND	O	M	R	W	O	M	R	W
Hayes	26	4	79	1				
MacGibbon	23	6	56	2				
Cave	48	23	77	3				
Reid	3	1	6	0				
Alabaster	25	4	83	0				
Moir	12	2	51	0				
Poore	19	3	49	2				
Sutcliffe	2	0	9	0				
INDIA								
Phadkar	28	10	53	2	6	4	5	1
Patil	14	3	36	1	9	4	15	1
Gupte	51	26	83	3	32·4	19	45	5
Ramchand	31	15	48	2	6	4	9	0
Mankad	10·1	3	29	1	24	8	57	3

FALL OF WICKETS

Wkt	I 1st	NZ 1st	NZ 2nd
1st	36	21	13
2nd	61	94	22
3rd	63	133	33
4th	230	156	45
5th	281	166	67
6th	347	218	68
7th	365	231	86
8th	377	232	117
9th	–	258	136
10th	–	258	136

Umpires: B.J. Mohoni (9) and M.G. Vijayasarathi (8).

Close: 1st day – I(1) 223-3 (Mankad 132, Kripal Singh 59); 2nd – NZ(1) 21-1 (Sutcliffe 13, Guy 0); 3rd – NZ(1) 208-5 (MacGibbon 28, Poore 15); 4th – NZ(2) 99-7 (Cave 14, Moir 3).

INDIA v NEW ZEALAND 1955–56 (3rd Test)

Played at Feroz Shah Kotla, Delhi, on 16, 17, 18, 20, 21 December.
Toss: New Zealand.   Result: MATCH DRAWN.
Debuts: India – R.G. Nadkarni, G.R. Sunderam.

Sutcliffe's 230 not out remains the record score in a Test at Delhi and was then the highest for New Zealand in any Test. His unfinished partnership of 222 with Reid was New Zealand's highest for the third wicket until 1986-87. India reached a total of 500 for the first time in Test cricket. In 25 hours only ten wickets fell for 1,093 runs; it remains the only Test in which batsmen averaged over 100 runs per wicket.

NEW ZEALAND

J.G. Leggat	c Manjrekar b Gupte	37	not out		50
B. Sutcliffe	not out	230			
J.W. Guy	c Mehra b Sunderam	52	not out		10
J.R. Reid	not out	119			
S.N. McGregor	)		(2) c Tamhane b Manjrekar		49
A.R. MacGibbon	)				
M.B. Poore	)				
H.B. Cave*	) did not bat				
J.C. Alabaster	)				
T.G. McMahon†	)				
J.A. Hayes	)				
Extras	(B 7, LB 5)	12	(LB 2, NB 1)		3
Total	(2 wickets declared)	**450**	(1 wicket)		**112**

INDIA

V.L. Mehra	c McMahon b Hayes	32
N.J. Contractor	b Reid	62
P.R. Umrigar*	b MacGibbon	18
V.L. Manjrekar	c McMahon b Cave	177
A.G. Kripal Singh	b Hayes	36
G.S. Ramchand	st McMahon b Poore	72
R.G. Nadkarni	not out	68
P. Bhandari	b MacGibbon	39
N.S. Tamhane†	)	
G.R. Sunderam	) did not bat	
S.P. Gupte	)	
Extras	(B 16, LB 4, NB 7)	27
Total	(7 wickets declared)	**531**

INDIA	O	M	R	W	O	M	R	W	FALL OF WICKETS			
										NZ	I	NZ
Sunderam	39	5	99	1	3	0	8	0	*Wkt*	*1st*	*1st*	*2nd*
Ramchand	38	11	82	0	3	0	11	0	1st	98	68	101
Gupte	39	10	98	1	6	1	22	0	2nd	228	111	–
Nadkarni	54	13	132	0	3	1	10	0	3rd	–	119	–
Bhandari	6	0	27	0	7	2	12	0	4th	–	208	–
Manjrekar					20	13	16	1	5th	–	335	–
Kripal Singh					7	3	10	0	6th	–	458	–
Contractor					6	1	17	0	7th	–	531	–
Mehra					3	0	3	0	8th	–	–	–
									9th	–	–	–
NEW ZEALAND									10th	–	–	–
MacGibbon	59·5	16	121	2								
Cave	50	28	68	1								
Hayes	44	9	105	2								
Reid	41	14	86	1								
Alabaster	29	9	90	0								
Poore	15	4	26	1								
Sutcliffe	3	0	8	0								

Umpires: D.D. Desai (1) and N.D. Nagarwalla (2).

Close: 1st day – NZ(1) 218-1 (Sutcliffe 134, Guy 44); 2nd – I(1) 24-0 (Mehra 10, Contractor 14); 3rd – I(1) 187-3 (Manjrekar 30, Kripal Singh 31); 4th – I(1) 393-5 (Manjrekar 140, Nadkarni 11).

INDIA v NEW ZEALAND 1955–56 (4th Test)

Played at Eden Gardens, Calcutta, on 28, 29, 31 December, 1, 2 January.
Toss: India.   Result: MATCH DRAWN.
Debuts: India – C.T. Patankar.

India's total of 132 was then the lowest by any country against New Zealand. Umrigar's declaration left New Zealand 90 minutes in which to score 235 runs.

INDIA

M.H. Mankad	c McMahon b Reid	25	c MacGibbon b Reid	17
N.J. Contractor	b Hayes	6	b Hayes	61
Pankaj Roy	b Hayes	28	lbw b Cave	100
V.L. Manjrekar	c Reid b Cave	1	c MacGibbon b Reid	90
P.R. Umrigar*	run out	1	b MacGibbon	15
G.S. Ramchand	b Reid	1	not out	106
J.M. Ghorpade	b Alabaster	39	c Sutcliffe b Cave	4
D.G. Phadkar	run out	0	b Hayes	17
C.T. Patankar†	b Reid	13	not out	1
G.R. Sunderam	not out	3		
S.P. Gupte	b Alabaster	4		
Extras	(B 4, LB 2, NB 5)	11	(B 9, LB 10, NB 8)	27
Total		**132**	(7 wickets declared)	**438**

NEW ZEALAND

J.G. Leggat	c Patankar b Sunderam	8	c Mankad b Phadkar	7
B. Sutcliffe	c Patankar b Ramchand	25	lbw b Gupte	5
J.W. Guy	lbw b Gupte	91	b Phadkar	0
J.R. Reid	b Sunderam	120	(5) b Mankad	5
S.N. McGregor	b Gupte	6	(4) b Mankad	29
A.R. MacGibbon	st Patankar b Gupte	23	(7) not out	21
N.S. Harford	c Mankad b Ramchand	25	(6) c Phadkar b Gupte	1
H.B. Cave*	c Umrigar b Gupte	5	not out	4
J.C. Alabaster	c Patankar b Gupte	18		
J.A. Hayes	b Gupte	1		
T.G. McMahon†	not out	1		
Extras	(B 7, LB 3, NB 3)	13	(LB 2, NB 1)	3
Total		**336**	(6 wickets)	**75**

NEW ZEALAND	O	M	R	W	O	M	R	W
Hayes	14	3	38	2	30	4	67	2
MacGibbon	13	3	27	0	43	16	92	1
Cave	14	6	29	1	57	26	85	2
Reid	16	9	19	3	45	21	87	2
Alabaster	2·3	0	8	2	27	7	52	0
Sutcliffe					7	0	28	0
INDIA								
Phadkar	35	9	76	0	4	1	11	2
Sunderam	21	6	46	2	3	1	13	0
Gupte	33·5	7	90	6	14	7	30	2
Ramchand	37	15	64	2	1	0	4	0
Mankad	1	0	9	0	12	8	14	2
Ghorpade	1	0	17	0				
Umrigar	17	7	21	0				

FALL OF WICKETS

	I	NZ	I	NZ
Wkt	1st	1st	2nd	2nd
1st	13	25	40	8
2nd	41	55	119	9
3rd	42	239	263	37
4th	47	255	287	42
5th	49	262	331	47
6th	87	300	370	55
7th	88	310	424	–
8th	125	318	–	–
9th	125	333	–	–
10th	132	336	–	–

Umpires: D.D. Desai (2) and S.K. Ganguli (1).

Close: 1st day – NZ(1) 35-1 (Sutcliffe 14, Guy 9); 2nd – NZ(1) 262-4 (Reid 120, MacGibbon 2); 3rd – I(2) 107-1 (Contractor 54, Roy 23); 4th – I(2) 301-4 (Manjrekar 76, Ramchand 10).

INDIA v NEW ZEALAND 1955–56 (5th Test)

Played at Corporation Stadium, Madras, on 6, 7, 8, 10, 11 January.
Toss: India.   Result: INDIA won by an innings and 109 runs.
Debuts: Nil.

The first Madras Test to be staged at the Corporation Stadium produced the world record opening partnership for all Test cricket: 413 in 472 minutes between Mankad and Roy. It eclipsed the stand of 359 by Hutton and Washbrook in 1948-49 (*Test No. 310*) and, until 1977-78, was the highest first-wicket partnership in Indian first-class cricket. They were the third pair of batsmen – the first for India – to bat throughout a complete day's play in a Test. Mankad's second double-century of the rubber was then the highest score in a Madras Test and the record score for India. Their score of 537 for 3 was their highest in Tests – the third time in this rubber that that record had been broken. India won the match with 105 minutes to spare.

INDIA

M.H. Mankad	c Cave b Moir	231
Pankaj Roy	b Poore	173
P.R. Umrigar*	not out	79
G.S. Ramchand	lbw b MacGibbon	21
V.L. Manjrekar	not out	0
A.G. Kripal Singh	)	
N.J. Contractor	)	
D.G. Phadkar	) did not bat	
N.S. Tamhane†	)	
J.M. Patel	)	
S.P. Gupte	)	
Extras	(B 18, LB 11, NB 4)	33
Total	(3 wickets declared)	**537**

NEW ZEALAND

J.G. Leggat	lbw b Phadkar	31		c Tamhane b Mankad	61
B. Sutcliffe	c Umrigar b Patel	47		c and b Gupte	40
J.R. Reid	b Patel	44	(4)	c Umrigar b Gupte	63
J.W. Guy	c Umrigar b Gupte	3	(3)	st Tamhane b Gupte	9
S.N. McGregor	c Phadkar b Gupte	10	(6)	c Gupte b Mankad	12
A.R. MacGibbon	c Phadkar b Gupte	0	(7)	lbw b Patel	0
M.B. Poore	lbw b Gupte	15	(5)	b Mankad	1
A.M. Moir	c Umrigar b Patel	30		c Ramchand b Mankad	1
H.B. Cave*	c Roy b Gupte	9		not out	22
T.G. McMahon†	not out	4		b Gupte	0
J.A. Hayes	absent ill	–		absent ill	–
Extras	(B 4, LB 10, NB 2)	16		(B 1, LB 8, NB 1)	10
Total		**209**			**219**

NEW ZEALAND	O	M	R	W	O	M	R	W
Hayes	31	2	94	0				
MacGibbon	38	9	97	1				
Cave	44	16	94	0				
Reid	7	3	10	0				
Moir	26	1	114	1				
Poore	31	5	95	1				
INDIA								
Phadkar	15	4	25	1	28	13	33	0
Ramchand	4	3	1	0	8	5	10	0
Gupte	49	26	72	5	36·3	14	73	4
Patel	45	23	63	3	18	7	28	1
Mankad	19	10	32	0	40	14	65	4

FALL OF WICKETS

Wkt	I 1st	NZ 1st	NZ 2nd
1st	413	75	89
2nd	449	109	114
3rd	537	121	116
4th	–	141	117
5th	–	144	147
6th	–	145	148
7th	–	190	151
8th	–	201	219
9th	–	209	219
10th	–	–	–

Umpires: A.R. Joshi (5) and M.G. Vijayasarathi (9).

Close: 1st day – I(1) 234-0 (Mankad 109, Roy 114); 2nd – I(1) 537-3 (Umrigar 79, Manjrekar 0); 3rd – NZ(1) 158-6 (Poore 6, Moir 6); 4th – NZ(2) 114-1 (Leggat 61, Guy 8).

NEW ZEALAND v WEST INDIES 1955–56 (1st Test)

Played at Carisbrook, Dunedin, on 3, 4, 6 February.
Toss: New Zealand.   Result: WEST INDIES won by an innings and 71 runs.
Debuts: New Zealand – A.F. Lissette.

New Zealand were dismissed for what is still the lowest score in this series of Tests. Ramadhin took his hundredth Test wicket when he dismissed Leggat. When King pulled a muscle as he ran in to bowl the first ball of his ninth over, the umpire ruled that the over had not begun and the bowling was continued from the same end. Weekes, who reached his century in 132 minutes, and Smith added 162 in 112 minutes for the highest West Indies fourth-wicket partnership (since equalled) against New Zealand. Ramadhin's match analysis of 9 for 81 is the best by a West Indies bowler in New Zealand.

NEW ZEALAND

J.G. Leggat	c Sobers b Atkinson	3	lbw b Ramadhin		17
B. Sutcliffe	b Valentine	9	c Binns b Valentine		48
J.W. Guy	c Goddard b Ramadhin	23	st Binns b Smith		0
J.R. Reid	b Ramadhin	10	run out		23
S.N. McGregor	run out	0	b Smith		11
J.E.F. Beck	b Valentine	7	lbw b Atkinson		66
R.W. Blair	c Binns b Ramadhin	0	c Depeiza b Smith		0
A.M. Moir	not out	15	c Binns b Ramadhin		20
H.B. Cave*	b Ramadhin	0	c Pairaudeau b Valentine		0
T.G. McMahon†	c Binns b Ramadhin	0	b Ramadhin		2
A.F. Lissette	lbw b Ramadhin	0	not out		1
Extras	(B 5, LB 2)	7	(B 19, LB 1)		20
Total		**74**			**208**

WEST INDIES

B.H. Pairaudeau	c Lissette b Blair	0
A.P. Binns†	b Lissette	10
G. St A. Sobers	run out	27
E. de C. Weekes	c McMahon b Cave	123
O.G. Smith	b Blair	64
D. St E. Atkinson*	c McMahon b Cave	0
C.C. Depeiza	b Lissette	14
J.D.C. Goddard	not out	48
S. Ramadhin	b Blair	44
A.L. Valentine	lbw b Blair	2
F.M. King	absent hurt	–
Extras	(B 9, LB 10, NB 2)	21
Total		**353**

WEST INDIES	O	M	R	W	O	M	R	W		FALL OF WICKETS		
										NZ	WI	NZ
King	8	2	11	0					*Wkt*	*1st*	*1st*	*2nd*
Atkinson	7	5	2	1	13	5	25	1	1st	3	0	61
Depeiza	2	0	3	0	3	0	12	0	2nd	36	30	65
Valentine	24	13	28	2	36	17	51	2	3rd	36	72	73
Ramadhin	21·2	13	23	6	36·2	17	58	3	4th	43	234	108
Smith					18	7	42	3	5th	54	234	108
Sobers					4	4	0	0	6th	54	236	108
									7th	54	272	198
NEW ZEALAND									8th	62	347	201
Blair	22·5	5	90	4					9th	70	353	207
Cave	26	12	47	2					10th	74	–	208
Reid	17	3	43	0								
Lissette	28	11	73	2								
Moir	19	3	79	0								

Umpires: L.G. Clark (1) and A.E. Jelley (1).

Close: 1st day – WI(1) 234-3 (Weekes 123, Smith 63); 2nd – NZ(2) 158-6 (Beck 36, Moir 7).

NEW ZEALAND v WEST INDIES 1955–56 (2nd Test)

Played at Lancaster Park, Christchurch, on 18, 20, 21 February.
Toss: West Indies.   Result: WEST INDIES won by an innings and 64 runs.
Debuts: New Zealand – I.M. Sinclair. *S.C. Guillen was making his debut for New Zealand after appearing in five Tests for West Indies.*

Weekes scored his second consecutive Test hundred to bring his run in first-class matches on the tour to five centuries in successive innings. He was out for 43 and 56 against Central Districts in the tourists' next match. Reid began a record run of 34 Tests as New Zealand's captain but was unable to prevent a second successive innings defeat with over a day to spare.

WEST INDIES

H.A. Furlonge	lbw b Blair	0
B.H. Pairaudeau	b Reid	13
G. St A. Sobers	b Lissette	25
E. de C. Weekes	b Sinclair	103
O.G. Smith	c Reid b MacGibbon	11
C.C. Depeiza†	b Reid	4
D. St E. Atkinson*	c and b Reid	85
J.D.C. Goddard	not out	83
S. Ramadhin	b MacGibbon	33
D.T. Dewdney	run out	3
A.L. Valentine	run out	1
Extras	(B 9, LB 8, W 1, NB 7)	25
Total		**386**

NEW ZEALAND

B. Sutcliffe	st Depeiza b Ramadhin	26	st Depeiza b Smith	10
S.N. McGregor	b Dewdney	19	c Depeiza b Valentine	17
L.S.M. Miller	c Goddard b Ramadhin	7	c Weekes b Ramadhin	31
J.R. Reid*	b Valentine	28	(5) b Smith	40
J.W. Guy	c and b Ramadhin	3	(6) b Valentine	4
J.E.F. Beck	lbw b Ramadhin	4	(4) st Depeiza b Smith	13
S.C. Guillen†	b Valentine	15	c and b Smith	0
A.R. MacGibbon	not out	31	hit wkt b Valentine	34
I.M. Sinclair	b Ramadhin	7	c Goddard b Valentine	0
R.W. Blair	b Smith	2	c Sobers b Valentine	9
A.F. Lissette	b Smith	0	not out	1
Extras	(B 14, LB 2)	16	(B 4, LB 1)	5
Total		**158**		**164**

NEW ZEALAND	O	M	R	W	O	M	R	W
Blair	27	5	66	1				
MacGibbon	33	9	81	2				
Reid	24	7	68	3				
Lissette	20	5	51	1				
Sinclair	30·5	9	79	1				
Sutcliffe	2	0	16	0				
WEST INDIES								
Dewdney	16	5	31	1	8	2	20	0
Atkinson	10	3	16	0	3	0	6	0
Ramadhin	26	10	46	5	9	1	26	1
Valentine	22	9	48	2	22·4	11	32	5
Smith	1·5	1	1	2	18	4	75	4

FALL OF WICKETS

	WI	NZ	NZ
Wkt	1st	1st	2nd
1st	0	39	22
2nd	28	50	62
3rd	72	67	62
4th	109	85	115
5th	163	90	120
6th	169	113	120
7th	312	121	120
8th	361	140	121
9th	368	156	133
10th	386	158	164

Umpires: J. Cowie (1) and W.J.C. Gwynne (1).

Close: 1st day – WI(1) 349-7 (Goddard 63, Ramadhin 26); 2nd – NZ(1) 93-5 (Guy 0, Guillen 0).

NEW ZEALAND v WEST INDIES 1955–56 (3rd Test)

Played at Basin Reserve, Wellington, on 3, 5, 6, 7 March.
Toss: West Indies.   Result: WEST INDIES won by nine wickets.
Debuts: New Zealand – R.T. Barber.

Weekes scored his third hundred in consecutive Test innings. New Zealand narrowly averted a third successive innings defeat thanks to some enterprising batting by Taylor who had been recalled to Test cricket after an interval of nine years.

WEST INDIES

B.H. Pairaudeau	c MacGibbon b Cave	68	c Sinclair b MacGibbon	8
G. St A. Sobers	c Barber b Reid	27		
J.D.C. Goddard	c Beard b MacGibbon	16	not out	0
E. de C. Weekes	c Guillen b Cave	156		
O.G. Smith	lbw b MacGibbon	1		
D. St E. Atkinson*	run out	60		
A.P. Binns†	lbw b Beard	27	(2) not out	5
S. Ramadhin	c Beard b Reid	15		
F.M. King	not out	13		
D.T. Dewdney	run out	2		
A.L. Valentine	c McGregor b Reid	2		
Extras	(B 9, LB 3, NB 5)	17		
Total		**404**	(1 wicket)	**13**

NEW ZEALAND

L.S.M. Miller	c and b King	16	c Binns b Dewdney	7
S.N. McGregor	c Weekes b Smith	5	c Binns b Atkinson	41
A.R. MacGibbon	c Goddard b Valentine	3	b Atkinson	36
D.D. Taylor	run out	43	c Pairaudeau b Atkinson	77
J.R. Reid*	b Ramadhin	1	b Atkinson	5
J.E.F. Beck	lbw b Sobers	55	b Smith	6
R.T. Barber	b Ramadhin	12	c Goddard b Ramadhin	5
S.C. Guillen†	b Smith	36	c Goddard b Dewdney	0
D.D. Beard	not out	17	c Binns b Atkinson	5
H.B. Cave	b Atkinson	0	c and b Sobers	5
I.M. Sinclair	lbw b Atkinson	0	not out	18
Extras	(B 11, LB 9)	20	(B 2, NB 1)	3
Total		**208**		**208**

NEW ZEALAND	O	M	R	W	O	M	R	W	FALL OF WICKETS				
MacGibbon	24	4	75	2	3	1	6	1		WI	NZ	NZ	WI
Cave	37	10	96	2					*Wkt*	*1st*	*1st*	*2nd*	*2nd*
Beard	34	9	90	1	2·2	0	7	0	1st	72	23	16	12
Reid	32·5	8	85	3					2nd	117	23	82	–
Sinclair	8	0	41	0					3rd	117	27	93	–
									4th	119	28	99	–
WEST INDIES									5th	239	104	121	–
Dewdney	11	3	26	0	17	3	54	2	6th	345	116	141	–
King	8·4	3	18	1					7th	387	176	142	–
Smith	29	15	27	2	14	7	23	1	8th	387	205	180	–
Valentine	35	20	31	1	15	9	18	0	9th	391	208	185	–
Ramadhin	30	11	63	2	21	10	33	1	10th	404	208	208	–
Atkinson	12·2	2	20	2	31	12	66	5					
Sobers	14	11	3	1	8·5	4	11	1					

Umpires: L.G. Clark (2) and W.J.C. Gwynne (2).

Close: 1st day – WI(1) 361-6 (Weekes 145, Ramadhin 5); 2nd – NZ(1) 140-6 (Beck 29, Guillen 19); 3rd – NZ(2) 141-5 (Taylor 38, Barber 5).

NEW ZEALAND v WEST INDIES 1955–56 (4th Test)

Played at Eden Park, Auckland, on 9, 10, 12, 13 March.
Toss: New Zealand.   Result: NEW ZEALAND won by 190 runs.
Debuts: West Indies – A.T. Roberts.

Shortly after tea on the fourth day, Guillen stumped Valentine off Cave's bowling to dismiss West Indies for their (then) lowest total, and to bring New Zealand their first win in any official Test match. They had waited 26 years and 45 matches for this success. Roberts was the first St Vincent Islander to represent West Indies. Atkinson's analysis of 7 for 53 remained his career-best in Tests and the record for either country in this series. The match aggregate of 634 runs is the lowest for a completed Test between West Indies and New Zealand.

NEW ZEALAND

L.S.M. Miller	c Weekes b Valentine	47	c Weekes b Atkinson		25
S.N. McGregor	c Smith b Dewdney	2	c Binns b Atkinson		5
A.R. MacGibbon	b Smith	9	c Weekes b Atkinson		35
D.D. Taylor	lbw b Valentine	11	c Valentine b Atkinson		16
J.R. Reid*	hit wkt b Dewdney	84	c Binns b Atkinson		12
J.E.F. Beck	c Sobers b Ramadhin	38	lbw b Atkinson		2
S.C. Guillen†	run out	6	st Binns b Valentine		41
M.E. Chapple	c Atkinson b Dewdney	3	lbw b Ramadhin		1
D.D. Beard	c Binns b Dewdney	31	not out		6
H.B. Cave	c Smith b Dewdney	11	(11) not out		0
J.C. Alabaster	not out	1	(10) b Atkinson		5
Extras	(B 7, LB 5)	12	(B 4, LB 5)		9
Total		**255**	(9 wickets declared)		**157**

WEST INDIES

H.A. Furlonge	c Guillen b Cave	64	c MacGibbon b Beard		3
B.H. Pairaudeau	c MacGibbon b Cave	9	b Cave		3
G. St A. Sobers	c Guillen b MacGibbon	1	(6) run out		1
E. de C. Weekes	c Guillen b MacGibbon	5	c McGregor b Alabaster		31
O.G. Smith	b Beard	2	b Cave		0
D. St E. Atkinson*	b Reid	28	(3) c Chapple b Cave		10
A.T. Roberts	b MacGibbon	28	b Beard		0
A.P. Binns†	lbw b MacGibbon	0	b Alabaster		20
S. Ramadhin	b Cave	3	c Miller b Beard		0
A.L. Valentine	c Taylor b Cave	0	st Guillen b Cave		5
D.T. Dewdney	not out	0	not out		4
Extras	(B 1, LB 3, NB 1)	5			—
Total		**145**			**77**

WEST INDIES	O	M	R	W	O	M	R	W		FALL OF WICKETS			
Dewdney	19·5	11	21	5	12	5	22	0		NZ	WI	NZ	WI
Atkinson	32	14	45	0	40	21	53	7	*Wkt*	*1st*	*1st*	*2nd*	*2nd*
Valentine	41	20	46	2	6	0	29	1	1st	9	25	14	4
Ramadhin	23	8	41	1	18	6	26	1	2nd	45	32	61	16
Smith	31	19	55	1	4	0	18	0	3rd	66	46	66	16
Sobers	20	7	35	0					4th	87	59	91	16
									5th	191	94	100	18
NEW ZEALAND									6th	203	139	102	22
MacGibbon	21	5	44	4	6	1	16	0	7th	205	140	109	68
Cave	27·3	17	22	4	13·1	9	21	4	8th	210	145	146	68
Reid	18	5	48	1	6	2	14	0	9th	250	145	155	68
Beard	9	4	20	1	15	7	22	3	10th	255	145	—	77
Alabaster	3	1	6	0	5	4	4	2					

Umpires: J.C. Harris (4) and T.M. Pearce (3).

Close: 1st day – NZ(1) 203-6 (Reid 82); 2nd – WI(1) 96-5 (Furlonge 48, Roberts 1); 3rd – NZ(2) 61-2 (MacGibbon 30).

ENGLAND v AUSTRALIA 1956 (1st Test)

Played at Trent Bridge, Nottingham, on 7, 8 (*no play*), 9, 11, 12 June.
Toss: England.   Result: MATCH DRAWN.
Debuts: England – P.E. Richardson.

More than 12 hours of play were lost to rain and even two declarations by England could not force a result. Left 258 runs to win in four hours on the final day, Australia settled for survival. Richardson was the first batsman to score fifty in each innings of his first England–Australia Test without reaching a hundred in either of them. Davidson fell while bowling his tenth over and was carried off with a chipped ankle bone.

ENGLAND

P.E. Richardson	c Langley b Miller	81	c Langley b Archer		73
M.C. Cowdrey	c Miller b Davidson	25	c Langley b Miller		81
T.W. Graveney	c Archer b Johnson	8	(4) not out		10
P.B.H. May*	c Langley b Miller	73			
W. Watson	lbw b Archer	0	(3) c Langley b Miller		8
T.E. Bailey	c Miller b Archer	14			
T.G. Evans†	c Langley b Miller	0	(5) not out		8
J.C. Laker	not out	9			
G.A.R. Lock	lbw b Miller	0			
R. Appleyard	not out	1			
A.E. Moss	did not bat				
Extras	(B 5, LB 1)	6	(B 4, LB 1, W 2, NB 1)		8
Total	(8 wickets declared)	**217**	(3 wickets declared)		**188**

AUSTRALIA

C.C. McDonald	lbw b Lock	1	c Lock b Laker		6
J.W. Burke	c Lock b Laker	11	not out		58
R.N. Harvey	lbw b Lock	64	b Lock		3
P.J.P. Burge	c sub (J.M. Parks) b Lock	7	(5) not out		35
K.R. Miller	lbw b Laker	0	(4) lbw b Laker		4
R.G. Archer	c Lock b Appleyard	33			
R. Benaud	b Appleyard	17			
I. W. Johnson*	c Bailey b Laker	12			
R.R. Lindwall	c Bailey b Laker	0			
G.R.A. Langley†	not out	0			
A.K. Davidson	absent hurt	–			
Extras	(LB 3)	3	(B 10, LB 3, NB 1)		14
Total		**148**	(3 wickets)		**120**

AUSTRALIA	O	M	R	W	O	M	R	W	FALL OF WICKETS				
										E	A	E	A
Lindwall	15	4	43	0					*Wkt*	*1st*	*1st*	*2nd*	*2nd*
Miller	33	5	69	4	19	2	58	2	1st	53	10	151	13
Davidson	9·4	1	22	1					2nd	72	12	163	18
Archer	31	10	51	2	9	0	46	1	3rd	180	33	178	41
Johnson	14	7	26	1	12	2	29	0	4th	181	36	–	–
Burke	1	1	0	0	3	1	6	0	5th	201	90	–	–
Benaud					18	4	41	0	6th	203	110	–	–
ENGLAND									7th	213	148	–	–
Moss	4	3	1	0					8th	214	148	–	–
Bailey	3	1	8	0	9	3	16	0	9th	–	148	–	–
Laker	29·1	11	58	4	30	19	29	2	10th	–	–	–	–
Lock	36	16	61	3	22	11	23	1					
Appleyard	11	4	17	2	19	6	32	0					
Graveney					6	3	6	0					

Umpires: T.J. Bartley (5) and J.S. Buller (1).

Close: 1st day – E(1) 134-2 (Richardson 65, May 31); 2nd – no play; 3rd – A(1) 19-2 (Harvey 5, Burge 2); 4th – E(2) 129-0 (Richardson 56, Cowdrey 67).

ENGLAND v AUSTRALIA 1956 (2nd Test)

Played at Lord's, London, on 21, 22, 23, 25, 26 June.
Toss: Australia.   Result: AUSTRALIA won by 185 runs.
Debuts: Australia – W.P.A. Crawford, K.D. Mackay.

Australia gained their first victory in England since 1948. McDonald and Burke's opening partnership of 137 was the highest by Australia against England since 1930. Langley established a world Test record (which stood until *Test No. 876*) when he made his ninth dismissal of the match. Miller (36) took ten wickets in the Test for the only time in his 55-match career. Crawford pulled a muscle behind his thigh and was unable to complete his first spell in Test cricket.

AUSTRALIA

C.C. McDonald	c Trueman b Bailey	78	c Cowdrey b Bailey	26
J.W. Burke	st Evans b Laker	65	c Graveney b Trueman	16
R.N. Harvey	c Evans b Bailey	0	c Bailey b Trueman	10
P.J.P. Burge	b Statham	21	b Trueman	14
K.R. Miller	b Trueman	28	(7) c Evans b Trueman	30
K.D. Mackay	c Bailey b Laker	38	(5) c Evans b Statham	31
R.G. Archer	b Wardle	28	(6) c Evans b Bailey	1
R. Benaud	b Statham	5	c Evans b Trueman	97
I.W. Johnson*	c Evans b Trueman	6	lbw b Bailey	17
G.R.A. Langley†	c Bailey b Laker	14	not out	7
W.P.A. Crawford	not out	0	lbw b Bailey	0
Extras	(LB 2)	2	(B 2, LB 2, NB 4)	8
Total		**285**		**257**

ENGLAND

P.E. Richardson	c Langley b Miller	9	c Langley b Archer	21
M.C. Cowdrey	c Benaud b Mackay	23	lbw b Benaud	27
T.W. Graveney	b Miller	5	c Langley b Miller	18
P.B.H. May*	b Benaud	63	(5) c Langley b Miller	53
W. Watson	c Benaud b Miller	6	(4) b Miller	18
T.E. Bailey	b Miller	32	c Harvey b Archer	18
T.G. Evans†	st Langley b Benaud	0	c Langley b Miller	20
J.C. Laker	b Archer	12	c Langley b Archer	4
J.H. Wardle	c Langley b Archer	0	b Miller	0
F.S. Trueman	c Langley b Miller	7	b Archer	2
J.B. Statham	not out	0	not out	0
Extras	(LB 14)	14	(LB 5)	5
Total		**171**		**186**

ENGLAND	O	M	R	W	O	M	R	W		FALL OF WICKETS			
Statham	35	9	70	2	26	5	59	1		A	E	A	E
Trueman	28	6	54	2	28	2	90	5	*Wkt*	*1st*	*1st*	*2nd*	*2nd*
Bailey	34	12	72	2	24·5	8	64	4	1st	137	22	36	35
Laker	29·1	10	47	3	7	3	17	0	2nd	137	32	47	59
Wardle	20	7	40	1	7	2	19	0	3rd	151	60	69	89
									4th	185	87	70	91
AUSTRALIA									5th	196	128	79	142
Miller	34·1	9	72	5	36	12	80	5	6th	249	128	112	175
Crawford	4·5	2	4	0					7th	255	161	229	180
Archer	23	9	47	2	31·2	8	71	4	8th	265	161	243	184
Mackay	11	3	15	1					9th	285	170	257	184
Benaud	9	2	19	2	28	14	27	1	10th	285	171	257	186
Johnson					4	2	3	0					

Umpires: D.E. Davies (1) and F.S. Lee (16).

Close: 1st day – A(1) 180-3 (Burge 18, Miller 19); 2nd – E(1) 74-3 (May 23, Watson 4); 3rd – A(2) 115-3 (Mackay 9, Benaud 3); 4th – E(2) 72-2 (Cowdrey 21, Watson 9).

ENGLAND v AUSTRALIA 1956 (3rd Test)

Played at Headingley, Leeds, on 12, 13, 14 (*no play*), 16, 17 July.
Toss: England.   Result: ENGLAND won by an innings and 42 runs.
Debuts: England – A.S.M. Oakman.

Washbrook, who had not played Test cricket since the 1950-51 Australasian tour, was recalled to the England team at the age of 41 and whilst a selector. He joined May with the score 17 for 3 and their partnership of 187 in 287 minutes proved to be the turning point of the rubber. May became the first England batsman to score five consecutive fifties against Australia. This was England's first victory against Australia at Headingley.

ENGLAND

P.E. Richardson	c Maddocks b Archer	5
M.C. Cowdrey	c Maddocks b Archer	0
A.S.M. Oakman	b Archer	4
P.B.H. May*	c Lindwall b Johnson	101
C. Washbrook	lbw b Benaud	98
G.A.R. Lock	c Miller b Benaud	21
D.J. Insole	c Mackay b Benaud	5
T.E. Bailey	not out	33
T.G. Evans†	b Lindwall	40
J.C. Laker	b Lindwall	5
F.S. Trueman	c and b Lindwall	0
Extras	(B 4, LB 9)	13
Total		**325**

AUSTRALIA

C.C. McDonald	c Evans b Trueman	2		b Trueman	6
J.W. Burke	lbw b Lock	41		b Laker	16
R.N. Harvey	c Trueman b Lock	11		c and b Lock	69
P.J.P. Burge	lbw b Laker	2	(5)	lbw b Laker	5
K.D. Mackay	c Bailey b Laker	2	(8)	b Laker	2
K.R. Miller	b Laker	41	(4)	c Trueman b Laker	26
R.G. Archer	b Laker	4	(9)	c Washbrook b Lock	1
R. Benaud	c Oakman b Laker	30	(6)	b Laker	1
L.V. Maddocks†	c Trueman b Lock	0	(10)	lbw b Lock	0
I.W. Johnson*	c Richardson b Lock	0	(7)	c Oakman b Laker	3
R.R. Lindwall	not out	0		not out	0
Extras	(B 4, LB 6)	10		(B 7, LB 4)	11
Total		**143**			**140**

AUSTRALIA	O	M	R	W	O	M	R	W
Lindwall	33·4	11	67	3				
Archer	50	24	68	3				
Mackay	13	3	29	0				
Benaud	42	9	89	3				
Johnson	29	8	59	1				
ENGLAND								
Trueman	8	2	19	1	11	3	21	1
Bailey	7	2	15	0	7	2	13	0
Laker	29	10	58	5	41·3	21	55	6
Lock	27·1	11	41	4	40	23	40	3

FALL OF WICKETS

Wkt	E 1st	A 1st	A 2nd
1st	2	2	10
2nd	8	40	45
3rd	17	59	108
4th	204	59	120
5th	226	63	128
6th	243	69	136
7th	248	142	138
8th	301	143	140
9th	321	143	140
10th	325	143	140

Umpires: J.S. Buller (2) and D. Davies (19).

Close: 1st day – E(1) 204-4 (Washbrook 90, Lock 0); 2nd – A(1) 81-6 (Miller 8, Benaud 8); 3rd – no play; 4th – A(2) 93-2 (Harvey 40, Miller 24).

ENGLAND v AUSTRALIA 1956 (4th Test)

Played at Old Trafford, Manchester, on 26, 27, 28, 30, 31 July.
Toss: England.   Result: ENGLAND won by an innings and 170 runs.
Debuts: Nil.

'Laker's Match', in which the Yorkshire-born Surrey offspinner broke several major bowling records with his match analysis of 19 for 90, all taken from the Stretford End: most wickets in any first-class match; only instance of ten wickets in a Test innings; only instance of ten wickets in a season twice – also 10 for 88 for Surrey v Australians; 39 wickets in the rubber equalling A.V. Bedser's record for England–Australia matches with a game to play. Not since 1905 had England twice beaten Australia in a home rubber, nor indeed finished a Test against them at Manchester. Astonishingly, on a pitch favouring spin, Lock took only one wicket in the match – the third one to fall. Laker tidied up the first innings with a spell of 7 for 8 in 22 balls. Harvey was dismissed twice without scoring on the second day. McDonald (11) retired because of a jarred knee at 28 in the second innings, returning at 55 to extend his defiant and much-interrupted innings to 337 minutes.

ENGLAND

P.E. Richardson	c Maddocks b Benaud	104
M.C. Cowdrey	c Maddocks b Lindwall	80
Rev. D.S. Sheppard	b Archer	113
P.B.H. May*	c Archer b Benaud	43
T.E. Bailey	b Johnson	20
C. Washbrook	lbw b Johnson	6
A.S.M. Oakman	c Archer b Johnson	10
T.G. Evans†	st Maddocks b Johnson	47
J.C. Laker	run out	3
G.A.R. Lock	not out	25
J.B. Statham	c Maddocks b Lindwall	0
Extras	(B 2, LB 5, W 1)	8
Total		**459**

AUSTRALIA

C.C. McDonald	c Lock b Laker	32	c Oakman b Laker	89
J.W. Burke	c Cowdrey b Lock	22	c Lock b Laker	33
R.N. Harvey	b Laker	0	c Cowdrey b Laker	0
I.D. Craig	lbw b Laker	8	lbw b Laker	38
K.R. Miller	c Oakman b Laker	6	(6) b Laker	0
K.D. Mackay	c Oakman b Laker	0	(5) c Oakman b Laker	0
R.G. Archer	st Evans b Laker	6	c Oakman b Laker	0
R. Benaud	c Statham b Laker	0	b Laker	18
R.R. Lindwall	not out	6	c Lock b Laker	8
L.V. Maddocks†	b Laker	4	(11) lbw b Laker	2
I.W. Johnson*	b Laker	0	(10) not out	1
Extras		–	(B 12, LB 4)	16
Total		**84**		**205**

AUSTRALIA	O	M	R	W	O	M	R	W
Lindwall	21·3	6	63	2				
Miller	21	6	41	0				
Archer	22	6	73	1				
Johnson	47	10	151	4				
Benaud	47	17	123	2				
ENGLAND								
Statham	6	3	6	0	16	10	15	0
Bailey	4	3	4	0	20	8	31	0
Laker	16·4	4	37	9	51·2	23	53	10
Lock	14	3	37	1	55	30	69	0
Oakman					8	3	21	0

FALL OF WICKETS

	E	A	A
Wkt	1st	1st	2nd
1st	174	48	28
2nd	195	48	55
3rd	288	62	114
4th	321	62	124
5th	327	62	130
6th	339	73	130
7th	401	73	181
8th	417	78	198
9th	458	84	203
10th	459	84	205

Umpires: D.E. Davies (2) and F.S. Lee (17).

Close: 1st day – E(1) 307-3 (Sheppard 59, Bailey 14); 2nd – A(2) 53-1 (Burke 33, Craig 8); 3rd – A(2) 59-2 (McDonald 15, Craig 10); 4th – A(2) 84-2 (McDonald 25, Craig 24).

ENGLAND v AUSTRALIA 1956 (5th Test)

Played at Kennington Oval, London, on 23, 24, 25, 27 (*no play*), 28 August.
Toss: England.   Result: MATCH DRAWN.
Debuts: Nil.

Exactly the same amount of time, 12 hours 20 minutes, was lost to rain as in the 1st Test–with the same result.
The selectors completed their hat-trick of successful recalls, Compton, minus his right knee-cap, top-scoring with
94 to follow the achievements of Washbrook and Sheppard in the previous two Tests. Laker extended his record
haul to 46 wickets in the rubber. Harvey kept wicket when Langley retired to hospital after being struck on the
forehead by a ball from Archer.

ENGLAND

P.E. Richardson	c Langley b Miller	37	c Langley b Lindwall	34
M.C. Cowdrey	c Langley b Lindwall	0	c Benaud b Davidson	8
Rev. D.S. Sheppard	c Archer b Miller	24	c Archer b Miller	62
P.B.H. May*	not out	83	not out	37
D.C.S. Compton	c Davidson b Archer	94	not out	35
G.A.R. Lock	c Langley b Archer	0		
C. Washbrook	lbw b Archer	0		
T.G. Evans†	lbw b Miller	0		
J.C. Laker	c Archer b Miller	4		
F.H. Tyson	c Davidson b Archer	3		
J.B. Statham	b Archer	0		
Extras	(W2)	2	(B 3, LB 3)	6
Total		**247**	(3 wickets declared)	**182**

AUSTRALIA

C.C. McDonald	c Lock b Tyson	3	lbw b Statham	0
J.W. Burke	b Laker	8	lbw b Laker	1
R.N. Harvey	c May b Lock	39	c May b Lock	1
I.D. Craig	c Statham b Lock	2	c Lock b Laker	7
I.W. Johnson*	b Laker	12	(6) c Lock b Laker	10
A.K. Davidson	c May b Laker	8		
K.R. Miller	c Washbrook b Statham	61	(5) not out	7
R.G. Archer	c Tyson b Laker	9		
R. Benaud	b Statham	32	(7) not out	0
R.R. Lindwall	not out	22		
G.R.A. Langley†	lbw b Statham	0		
Extras	(B 6)	6	(B 1)	1
Total		**202**	(5 wickets)	**27**

AUSTRALIA	O	M	R	W	O	M	R	W
Lindwall	18	5	36	1	12	3	29	1
Miller	40	7	91	4	22	3	56	1
Davidson	5	1	16	0	5	0	18	1
Archer	28·2	7	53	5	13	3	42	0
Johnson	9	2	28	0	4	1	7	0
Benaud	9	2	21	0	1	0	10	0
Burke					4	2	14	0
ENGLAND								
Statham	21	8	33	3	2	1	1	1
Tyson	14	5	34	1				
Laker	32	12	80	4	18	14	8	3
Lock	25	10	49	2	18·1	11	17	1

FALL OF WICKETS

	E	A	E	A
Wkt	*1st*	*1st*	*2nd*	*2nd*
1st	1	3	17	0
2nd	53	17	100	1
3rd	66	20	108	5
4th	222	35	–	10
5th	222	47	–	27
6th	222	90	–	–
7th	223	111	–	–
8th	231	154	–	–
9th	243	202	–	–
10th	247	202	–	–

Umpires: T.J. Bartley (6) and D. Davies (20).

Close: 1st day – E(1) 223-7 (May 67, Laker 0); 2nd – A(1) 198-8 (Miller 57, Lindwall 22); 3rd – E(2) 76-1
(Richardson 28, Sheppard 40); 4th – no play.

PAKISTAN v AUSTRALIA 1956–57 (Only Test)

Played at National Stadium, Karachi, on 11, 12, 13, 15, 17 October.
Toss: Australia.   Result: PAKISTAN won by nine wickets.
Debuts: Nil. *Gul Mahomed made his only appearance for Pakistan after playing in eight Tests for India.*

Pakistan gained their first victory against Australia at the earliest possible opportunity. Played on matting, this match produced the slowest day of Test cricket, the two sides combining to score only 95 runs on the first day. Australia's total of 80 is their lowest against Pakistan and the lowest in any Karachi Test. That innings provided the last instance of two bowlers bowling unchanged through a completed innings of a Test match, and the only one for Pakistan. Fazal Mahmood's match analysis of 13 for 114 included three wickets in four balls in the second innings, was a national record, and remains the best in this series and in any Test on that ground. Lindwall, playing in his 52nd match, took his 200th Test wicket when he dismissed Zulfiqar. The match aggregate of 535 is the lowest for a finished match in this series.

AUSTRALIA

C.C. McDonald	c Imtiaz b Fazal	17	b Fazal		3
J.W. Burke	c Mathias b Fazal	4	c Mathias b Fazal		10
R.N. Harvey	lbw b Fazal	2	b Fazal		4
I.D. Craig	c Imtiaz b Fazal	0	lbw b Fazal		18
K.R. Miller	c Wazir b Fazal	21	b Khan		11
R.G. Archer	c Imtiaz b Khan	10	c Fazal b Khan		27
R. Benaud	c Waqar b Fazal	4	b Fazal		56
A.K. Davidson	c Kardar b Khan	3	c Imtiaz b Khan		37
R.R. Lindwall	c Mathias b Khan	2	lbw b Fazal		0
I.W. Johnson*	not out	13	b Fazal		0
G.R.A. Langley†	c Waqar b Khan	1	not out		13
Extras	(LB 2, NB 1)	3	(LB 2, NB 6)		8
Total		**80**			**187**

PAKISTAN

Hanif Mohammad	c Langley b Miller	0	c Harvey b Davidson		5
Alimuddin	c Lindwall b Archer	10	not out		34
Gul Mahomed	b Davidson	12	not out		27
Imtiaz Ahmed†	c McDonald b Benaud	15			
Waqar Hassan	c Langley b Miller	6			
Wazir Mohammad	c and b Johnson	67			
A.H. Kardar*	lbw b Johnson	69			
W. Mathias	b Johnson	0			
Fazal Mahmood	not out	10			
Zulfiqar Ahmed	c Langley b Lindwall	0			
Khan Mohammad	b Johnson	3			
Extras	(B 5, LB 2)	7	(LB 1, NB 2)		3
Total		**199**	(1 wicket)		**69**

PAKISTAN	O	M	R	W	O	M	R	W	FALL OF WICKETS				
Fazal	27	11	34	6	48	17	80	7		A	P	A	P
Khan	26·1	9	43	4	40·5	13	69	3	*Wkt*	*1st*	*1st*	*2nd*	*2nd*
Zulfiqar					9	1	18	0	1st	19	3	6	7
Kardar					12	5	12	0	2nd	23	15	10	–
									3rd	24	25	23	–
AUSTRALIA									4th	43	35	46	–
Lindwall	27	8	42	1	16	8	22	0	5th	48	70	47	–
Miller	17	5	40	2	12	4	18	0	6th	52	174	111	–
Archer	4	0	18	1	3·5	3	1	0	7th	56	174	141	–
Davidson	6	4	6	1	9	5	9	1	8th	65	189	141	–
Benaud	17	5	36	1					9th	76	190	143	–
Johnson	20·3	3	50	4	7·5	2	16	0	10th	80	199	187	–

Umpires: Daud Khan (5) and Idris Beg (8).

Close: 1st day – P(1) 15-2 (Gul Mahomed 5); 2nd – P(1) 199 all out; 3rd – A(2) 138-6 (Benaud 53, Davidson 9); 4th – P(2) 63-1 (Alimuddin 31, Gul Mahomed 24).

INDIA v AUSTRALIA 1956–57 (1st Test)

Played at Corporation Stadium, Madras, on 19, 20, 22, 23 October.
Toss: India.   Result: AUSTRALIA won by an innings and 5 runs.
Debuts: Nil.

Returning to a turf pitch, Australia won their first Test in India with more than a day to spare. Lindwall, who retired with a stomach complaint in the first innings, returned Australia's best analysis in India in the second. The stand of 87 for the ninth wicket between Johnson and Crawford is still the highest between these two countries.

INDIA

M.H. Mankad	c McDonald b Benaud	27	c Langley b Lindwall	11
Pankaj Roy	c Harvey b Benaud	13	c Harvey b Lindwall	9
P.R. Umrigar*	c Craig b Benaud	31	c Langley b Lindwall	25
V.L. Manjrekar	lbw b Benaud	41	(5) b Crawford	16
G.S. Ramchand	b Crawford	0	(6) lbw b Johnson	28
H.R. Adhikari	c Burke b Crawford	5	(7) lbw b Lindwall	0
A.G. Kripal Singh	c Harvey b Crawford	13	(8) not out	20
N.S. Tamhane†	not out	9	(4) c Crawford b Benaud	5
J.M. Patel	c Johnson b Benaud	3	b Lindwall	0
Ghulam Ahmed	c Harvey b Benaud	11	c Burge b Lindwall	13
S.P. Gupte	c McDonald b Benaud	4	b Lindwall	8
Extras	(LB 4)	4	(B 10, LB 5, NB 3)	18
Total		**161**		**153**

AUSTRALIA

C.C. McDonald	st Tamhane b Mankad	29
J.W. Burke	c Tamhane b Gupte	10
R.N. Harvey	b Mankad	37
I.D. Craig	c Ramchand b Mankad	40
P.J.P. Burge	lbw b Patel	35
K.D. Mackay	c Tamhane b Ghulam Ahmed	29
R. Benaud	b Ghulam Ahmed	6
R.R. Lindwall	c Adhikari b Gupte	8
I.W. Johnson*	c Roy b Gupte	73
W.P.A. Crawford	st Tamhane b Mankad	34
G.R.A. Langley†	not out	10
Extras	(B 5, LB 3)	8
Total		**319**

AUSTRALIA	O	M	R	W	O	M	R	W	FALL OF WICKETS			
Lindwall	9	1	15	0	22·5	9	43	7		I	A	I
Crawford	26	8	32	3	12	6	18	1	*Wkt*	*1st*	*1st*	*2nd*
Benaud	29·3	10	72	7	20	5	59	1	1st	41	12	18
Mackay	20	9	25	0					2nd	44	58	22
Johnson	15	10	13	0	9	5	15	1	3rd	97	97	39
									4th	98	152	63
INDIA									5th	106	186	99
Ramchand	5	1	12	0					6th	134	186	100
Umrigar	4	0	17	0					7th	134	198	113
Gupte	28·3	6	89	3					8th	137	200	119
Ghulam Ahmed	38	17	67	2					9th	151	287	143
Mankad	45	15	90	4					10th	161	319	153
Patel	14	3	36	1								

Umpires: D.D. Desai (3) and M.G. Vijayasarathi (10).

Close: 1st day – I(1) 117-5 (Manjrekar 33, Kripal Singh 4); 2nd – A(1) 120-3 (Craig 30, Burge 12); 3rd – I(2) 29-2 (Umrigar 0, Tamhane 3).

INDIA v AUSTRALIA 1956–57 (2nd Test)

Played at Brabourne Stadium, Bombay, on 26, 27, 29, 30, 31 October.
Toss: India.   Result: MATCH DRAWN.
Debuts: Australia – J.W. Rutherford, J.W. Wilson.

Crawford retired because of a muscular injury on the first day. Umrigar batted six hours for 78 in India's successful rearguard action after Harvey had scored 140 in just over four hours (73 overs). Having completed his hundred in 368 minutes, Burke went on to contribute 161 runs in 504 minutes off 154·3 overs towards Australia's highest total in India until 1986-87.

INDIA

M.H. Mankad	c Burge b Lindwall	0	c Burke b Benaud		16
Pankaj Roy	c Burge b Crawford	31	c Maddocks b Benaud		79
P.R. Umrigar*	b Crawford	8	c and b Lindwall		78
V.L. Manjrekar	c Harvey b Benaud	55	b Rutherford		30
J.M. Ghorpade	b Crawford	0			
G.S. Ramchand	c sub (C.C. McDonald) b Mackay	109	c Maddocks b Wilson		16
D.G. Phadkar	c Maddocks b Benaud	1	not out		3
H.R. Adhikari	c Davidson b Mackay	33	(5) not out		22
N.S. Tamhane†	c Harvey b Davidson	5			
J.M. Patel	c Maddocks b Mackay	6			
S.P. Gupte	not out	0			
Extras	(LB 1, NB 2)	3	(B 1, LB 1, NB 4)		6
Total		**251**	(5 wickets)		**250**

AUSTRALIA

J.W. Burke	c Umrigar b Mankad	161
J.W. Rutherford	c Tamhane b Gupte	30
R.N. Harvey	c sub (R.G. Nadkarni) b Patel	140
P.J.P. Burge	c Patel b Gupte	83
K.D. Mackay	c Roy b Patel	26
A.K. Davidson	lbw b Ramchand	16
R. Benaud	c sub (R.G. Nadkarni) b Gupte	2
R.R. Lindwall*	not out	48
L.V. Maddocks†	not out	8
W.P.A. Crawford	) did not bat	
J.W. Wilson	)	
Extras	(B 2, LB 4, NB 3)	9
Total	(7 wickets declared)	**523**

AUSTRALIA	O	M	R	W	O	M	R	W
Lindwall	22	7	60	1	23	9	40	1
Crawford	12	3	28	3	13	4	24	0
Davidson	9	1	24	1	14	9	18	0
Benaud	25	6	54	2	42	15	98	2
Mackay	14·2	5	27	3	17	6	22	0
Wilson	15	6	39	0	21	11	25	1
Burke	2	0	12	0	2	0	6	0
Rutherford	1	0	4	0	5	2	11	1

INDIA	O	M	R	W
Phadkar	39	9	92	0
Ramchand	18	2	78	1
Patel	39	10	111	2
Gupte	38	13	115	3
Mankad	46	9	118	1

FALL OF WICKETS

Wkt	I 1st	A 1st	I 2nd
1st	·0	57	31
2nd	18	261	121
3rd	74	398	191
4th	74	432	217
5th	130	459	242
6th	140	462	–
7th	235	470	–
8th	240	–	–
9th	251	–	–
10th	251	–	–

Umpires: A.R. Joshi (6) and B.J. Mohoni (10).

Close: 1st day – I(1) 169-6 (Ramchand 65, Adhikari 6); 2nd – A(1) 134-1 (Burke 42, Harvey 57); 3rd – A(1) 386-2 (Burke 156, Burge 52); 4th – I(2) 92-1 (Roy 57, Umrigar 19).

INDIA v AUSTRALIA 1956–57 (3rd Test)

Played at Eden Gardens, Calcutta, on 2, 3, 5, 6 November.
Toss: India.   Result: AUSTRALIA won by 94 runs.
Debuts: Nil.

Spin bowlers took all but four of the 39 wickets which fell on a pitch that encouraged them from the start, and enabled Australia to win a low-scoring match with a day and a half to spare. Benaud's match analysis of 11 for 105 remains the best in any Test match in Calcutta. Johnson led Australia to victory in the last of his 17 Tests as captain and, taking his aggregate to exactly 1,000 runs, neatly completed the double in his 45th and final match.

AUSTRALIA

C.C. McDonald	b Ghulam Ahmed	3	lbw b Ramchand	0
J.W. Burke	c Manjrekar b Ghulam Ahmed	10	c Contractor b Ghulam Ahmed	2
R.N. Harvey	c Tamhane b Ghulam Ahmed	7	c Umrigar b Mankad	69
I.D. Craig	c Tamhane b Gupte	36	b Ghulam Ahmed	6
P.J.P. Burge	c Ramchand b Ghulam Ahmed	58	c Ramchand b Ghulam Ahmed	22
K.D. Mackay	lbw b Mankad	5	hit wkt b Mankad	27
R. Benaud	b Ghulam Ahmed	24	b Gupte	21
R.R. Lindwall	b Ghulam Ahmed	8	c Tamhane b Mankad	28
I.W. Johnson*	c Ghulam Ahmed b Mankad	1	st Tamhane b Mankad	5
W.P.A. Crawford	c Contractor b Ghulam Ahmed	18	not out	1
G.R.A. Langley†	not out	1		
Extras	(B 6)	6	(B 6, LB 2)	8
Total		**177**	(9 wickets declared)	**189**

INDIA

Pankaj Roy	b Lindwall	13	lbw b Burke	24
N.J. Contractor	lbw b Benaud	22	b Johnson	20
P.R. Umrigar*	c Burge b Johnson	5	c Burke b Benaud	28
V.L. Manjrekar	c Harvey b Benaud	33	c Harvey b Benaud	22
M.H. Mankad	lbw b Benaud	4	c Harvey b Benaud	24
G.S. Ramchand	st Langley b Benaud	2	b Burke	3
A.G. Kripal Singh	c Mackay b Benaud	14	b Benaud	0
P. Bhandari	lbw b Lindwall	17	c Harvey b Burke	2
N.S. Tamhane†	b Benaud	5	b Benaud	0
Ghulam Ahmed	c Mackay b Lindwall	10	b Burke	0
S.P. Gupte	not out	1	not out	0
Extras	(B 7, LB 1, NB 2)	10	(B 5, LB 5, NB 3)	13
Total		**136**		**136**

INDIA	O	M	R	W	O	M	R	W		FALL OF WICKETS			
Ramchand	2	1	1	0	2	1	6	1		A	I	A	I
Umrigar	16	3	30	0	20	9	21	0	*Wkt*	*1st*	*1st*	*2nd*	*2nd*
Ghulam Ahmed	20·3	6	49	7	29	5	81	3	1st	6	15	0	44
Gupte	23	11	35	1	7	1	24	1	2nd	22	20	9	50
Mankad	25	4	56	2	9·4	1	49	4	3rd	25	76	27	94
									4th	93	80	59	99
AUSTRALIA									5th	106	82	122	102
Lindwall	25·2	12	32	3	12	7	9	0	6th	141	98	149	121
Crawford	3	3	0	0	2	1	1	0	7th	152	99	159	134
Johnson	12	2	27	1	14	5	23	1	8th	157	115	188	136
Benaud	29	10	52	6	24·2	6	53	5	9th	163	135	189	136
Harvey	1	1	0	0					10th	177	136	–	136
Burke	8	3	15	0	17	4	37	4					

Umpires: G. Ayling (1) and B.J. Mohoni (11).

Close: 1st day – I(1) 15-0 (Roy 13, Contractor 0); 2nd – I(1) 135-8 (Bhandari 17, Ghulam Ahmed 10); 3rd – I(2) 12-0 (Roy 5, Contractor 5).

SOUTH AFRICA v ENGLAND 1956–57 (1st Test)

Played at New Wanderers, Johannesburg, on 24, 26, 27, 28, 29 December.
Toss: England.   Result: ENGLAND won by 131 runs.
Debuts: South Africa – A.I. Taylor.

This was the first Test match to be played on the New Wanderers ground and it attracted the highest attendance (100,000) for any match in South Africa so far. Richardson took 488 minutes to reach what was then the slowest century in Test cricket. South Africa's total of 72 was their lowest in a home Test since 1898-99. D.J. McGlew, South Africa's appointed captain for the rubber, withdrew because of a shoulder injury.

ENGLAND

P.E. Richardson	lbw b Goddard	117	lbw b Adcock	10
T.E. Bailey	c Waite b Heine	16	c Endean b Heine	10
D.C.S. Compton	c Keith b Goddard	5	c and b Tayfield	32
P.B.H. May*	c Goddard b Adcock	6	(6) c Endean b Heine	14
M.C. Cowdrey	c Goddard b Heine	59	(7) c Goddard b Adcock	6
D.J. Insole	c Waite b Van Ryneveld	1	(5) c Waite b Goddard	29
T.G. Evans†	c Keith b Adcock	20	(8) c Heine b Tayfield	30
F.H. Tyson	b Adcock	22	(9) c Watkins b Adcock	2
J.H. Wardle	not out	6	(4) lbw b Heine	0
J.C. Laker	c Goddard b Adcock	0	not out	3
J.B. Statham	c Waite b Goddard	0	lbw b Tayfield	2
Extras	(B 4, LB 9, NB 3)	16	(B 8, LB 1, NB 3)	12
Total		**268**		**150**

SOUTH AFRICA

A.I. Taylor	st Evans b Wardle	12	c Insole b Bailey	6
T.L. Goddard	c Cowdrey b Statham	49	c Insole b Bailey	5
H.J. Keith	c Cowdrey b Bailey	42	c Evans b Bailey	2
W.R. Endean	c Cowdrey b Laker	18	(5) b Statham	3
R.A. McLean	lbw b Bailey	0	(6) c Insole b Bailey	6
J.C. Watkins	c Insole b Wardle	9	(7) b Laker	8
C.B. van Ryneveld*	c Bailey b Statham	10	(8) run out	16
J.H.B. Waite†	c Evans b Bailey	17	(4) b Statham	0
H.J. Tayfield	b Wardle	24	c Evans b Bailey	2
P.S. Heine	not out	13	run out	17
N.A.T. Adcock	b Statham	17	not out	0
Extras	(B 1, LB 3)	4	(B 2, LB 3, NB 2)	7
Total		**215**		**72**

SOUTH AFRICA	O	M	R	W	O	M	R	W		FALL OF WICKETS			
Heine	31	5	89	2	19	7	41	3		E	SA	E	SA
Adcock	20	6	36	4	13	1	33	3	*Wkt*	*1st*	*1st*	*2nd*	*2nd*
Goddard	28·5	9	51	3	14	7	14	1	1st	28	54	11	6
Watkins	11	3	23	0	3	0	10	0	2nd	37	92	37	10
Tayfield	20	4	30	0	17·6	5	40	3	3rd	48	112	37	11
Van Ryneveld	8	2	23	1					4th	169	112	84	20
									5th	170	126	100	25
ENGLAND									6th	205	141	107	36
Statham	24·1	4	71	3	13	4	22	2	7th	259	141	126	40
Tyson	9	1	22	0					8th	263	176	145	44
Wardle	20	4	52	3	3	0	18	0	9th	263	194	147	71
Laker	21	10	33	1	2	1	5	1	10th	268	215	150	72
Bailey	15	5	33	3	15·4	6	20	5					

Umpires: J.H. McMenamin (1) and W. Marais (1).

Close: 1st day – E(1) 157-3 (Richardson 69, Cowdrey 51); 2nd – SA(1) 91-1 (Goddard 49, Keith 29); 3rd – E(2) 42-3 (Compton 17, Insole 0); 4th – SA(2) 40-7 (Van Ryneveld 4).

SOUTH AFRICA v ENGLAND 1956–57 (2nd Test)

Played at Newlands, Cape Town, on 1, 2, 3, 4, 5 January.
Toss: England.   Result: ENGLAND won by 312 runs.
Debuts: Nil.

The first 'handled the ball' dismissal in Test cricket occurred on the fifth day; Endean padded away a ball from Laker pitched outside the off stump and, as it deflected upwards and towards the stumps, he diverted it with his hand. Endean was also involved when Hutton was given out 'obstructing the field' in 1951 (*Test No. 338*). South Africa were bowled out for 72 for the second Test in succession. McGlew aggravated his shoulder injury and withdrew from the remainder of the rubber for surgery. Wardle's innings and match analyses remained the best of his career.

ENGLAND

P.E. Richardson	lbw b Heine	45	c Endean b Goddard	44
T.E. Bailey	c Waite b Tayfield	34	b Heine	28
D.C.S. Compton	c McLean b Tayfield	58	c and b Goddard	64
P.B.H. May*	c Waite b Tayfield	8	c Waite b Heine	15
M.C. Cowdrey	lbw b Adcock	101	c Waite b Tayfield	61
D.J. Insole	c Goddard b Adcock	29	(7) not out	3
T.G. Evans†	c McGlew b Goddard	62	(6) c Endean b Goddard	1
J.H. Wardle	st Waite b Tayfield	3		
J.C. Laker	b Adcock	0		
P.J. Loader	c Keith b Tayfield	10		
J.B. Statham	not out	2		
Extras	(B 6, LB 6, NB 5)	17	(LB 2, NB 2)	4
Total		**369**	(6 wickets declared)	**220**

SOUTH AFRICA

D.J. McGlew*	c Cowdrey b Laker	14	b Wardle	7
T.L. Goddard	c Evans b Loader	18	c Bailey b Wardle	26
H.J. Keith	c Evans b Loader	14	c May b Wardle	4
C.B. van Ryneveld	b Wardle	25	(7) not out	0
H.J. Tayfield	run out	5	(10) c Evans b Wardle	4
R.A. McLean	c May b Statham	42	(5) lbw b Laker	22
J.H.B. Waite†	c Evans b Wardle	49	(6) c Cowdrey b Wardle	2
W.R. Endean	b Wardle	17	(4) handled the ball	3
J.C. Watkins	not out	7	(8) c and b Wardle	0
P.S. Heine	b Wardle	0	(9) b Wardle	0
N.A.T. Adcock	c Evans b Wardle	11	b Laker	1
Extras	(B 1, LB 1, NB 1)	3	(LB 2, NB 1)	3
Total		**205**		**72**

SOUTH AFRICA	O	M	R	W	O	M	R	W
Heine	19	0	78	1	21	1	67	2
Adcock	22·2	2	54	3	3	0	8	0
Tayfield	53	21	130	5	12	4	33	1
Goddard	38	12	74	1	17·5	1	62	3
Van Ryneveld	3	0	16	0				
Watkins					10	2	46	0
ENGLAND								
Statham	16	0	38	1	8	2	12	0
Loader	21	5	33	2	7	2	11	0
Laker	28	8	65	1	14·1	9	7	2
Bailey	11	5	13	0				
Wardle	23·6	9	53	5	19	3	36	7
Compton					2	1	3	0

FALL OF WICKETS

Wkt	E 1st	SA 1st	E 2nd	SA 2nd
1st	76	23	74	21
2nd	88	39	74	28
3rd	116	48	109	42
4th	183	63	196	56
5th	233	110	208	67
6th	326	126	220	67
7th	334	178	–	67
8th	335	191	–	67
9th	346	191	–	71
10th	369	205	–	72

Umpires: D. Collins (8) and V. Costello (1).

Close: 1st day – E(1) 214-4 (Cowdrey 43, Insole 21); 2nd – SA(1) 51-3 (Van Ryneveld 4, Tayfield 1); 3rd – E(2) 21-0 (Richardson 17, Bailey 3); 4th – SA(2) 41-2 (Goddard 26, Endean 3).

SOUTH AFRICA v ENGLAND 1956–57 (3rd Test)

Played at Kingsmead, Durban, on 25, 26, 28, 29, 30 January.
Toss: England.   Result: MATCH DRAWN.
Debuts: South Africa – A.J. Pithey.

In the second innings, Bailey retired hurt at 48, a bone in his right hand fractured by a short ball from Heine. He resumed at 167 with his hand in plaster and scored three more runs in 55 minutes. Tayfield's analysis of 8 for 69 was the best by a South African bowler in Tests and his first innings spell of 137 balls without conceding a run remains a record for all first-class cricket. South Africa were left 250 minutes in which to score 190 runs for victory.

ENGLAND

P.E. Richardson	lbw b Adcock	68		b Van Ryneveld	32
T.E. Bailey	c Keith b Adcock	80		c Van Ryneveld b Tayfield	18
D.C.S. Compton	b Heine	16		c Keith b Tayfield	19
P.B.H. May*	c Goddard b Tayfield	2	(5)	lbw b Tayfield	2
M.C. Cowdrey	lbw b Goddard	6	(6)	lbw b Heine	24
D.J. Insole	b Van Ryneveld	13	(4)	not out	110
T.G. Evans†	st Waite b Van Ryneveld	0		c Waite b Tayfield	10
J.H. Wardle	b Heine	13		c Waite b Tayfield	8
J.C. Laker	not out	0		c Goddard b Tayfield	6
P.J. Loader	c Waite b Adcock	1		lbw b Tayfield	3
J.B. Statham	b Adcock	6		c Van Ryneveld b Tayfield	9
Extras	(B 2, LB 4, W 5, NB 2)	13		(B 8, LB 4, NB 1)	13
Total		**218**			**254**

SOUTH AFRICA

A.J. Pithey	st Evans b Wardle	25		b Statham	0
T.L. Goddard	lbw b Statham	69		c Cowdrey b Wardle	18
H.J. Keith	c Evans b Loader	6		c sub (G.A.R. Lock) b Laker	22
W.R. Endean	c sub (G.A.R. Lock) b Wardle	5		c and b Laker	26
R.A. McLean	c Insole b Bailey	100		b Wardle	4
K.J. Funston	b Wardle	19		b Loader	44
J.H.B. Waite†	b Statham	12	(8)	not out	1
C.B. van Ryneveld*	c Cowdrey b Loader	16	(7)	not out	14
H.J. Tayfield	not out	20			
P.S. Heine	b Wardle	6			
N.A.T. Adcock	lbw b Wardle	3			
Extras	(LB 2)	2		(B 5, LB 6, NB 2)	13
Total		**283**		(6 wickets)	**142**

SOUTH AFRICA	O	M	R	W	O	M	R	W		FALL OF WICKETS			
Heine	16	2	65	2	22	3	58	1		E	SA	E	SA
Adcock	15·3	3	39	4	21	8	39	0	*Wkt*	*1st*	*1st*	*2nd*	*2nd*
Goddard	25	11	42	1	13	5	26	0	1st	115	65	45	0
Tayfield	24	17	21	1	37·7	14	69	8	2nd	148	76	77	39
Van Ryneveld	14	4	38	2	14	2	49	1	3rd	151	81	79	45
									4th	163	145	144	49
ENGLAND									5th	186	199	167	124
Statham	22	4	56	2	11	0	32	1	6th	186	225	192	124
Loader	25	6	79	2	8	2	21	1	7th	202	241	203	–
Bailey	17	3	38	1					8th	210	264	220	–
Wardle	20·2	6	61	5	20	7	42	2	9th	212	279	230	–
Laker	12	1	47	0	18	7	29	2	10th	218	283	254	–
Compton					1	0	5	0					

Umpires: B.V. Malan (5) and W. Marais (2).

Close: 1st day – E(1) 184-4 (Bailey 71, Insole 11); 2nd – SA(1) 140-3 (Goddard 67, McLean 35); 3rd – E(2) 48-1 (Bailey 13, Compton 1); 4th – E(2) 192-6 (Insole 77).

SOUTH AFRICA v ENGLAND 1956–57 (4th Test)

Played at New Wanderers, Johannesburg, on 15, 16, 18, 19, 20 February.
Toss: South Africa.   Result: SOUTH AFRICA won by 17 runs.
Debuts: South Africa – C.A.R. Duckworth.

South Africa gained their first win against England at home since 1930-31 (*Test No. 204*); it was their first home win on a turf pitch in this series. Tayfield remains the only South African to take nine wickets in a Test innings, or 13 in a match. He bowled throughout the last day, sending down 35 eight-ball overs in 4 hours 50 minutes, and finally had Loader caught by his brother, Arthur, who was substituting for Funston. Bailey completed the Test double in his 47th match.

SOUTH AFRICA

A.J. Pithey	c Wardle b Bailey	10		b Laker	18
T.L. Goddard	b Bailey	67		c Evans b Bailey	49
J.H.B. Waite†	c Evans b Statham	61	(7)	c Cowdrey b Statham	17
K.J. Funston	c Evans b Bailey	20	(3)	run out	23
R.A. McLean	run out	93	(4)	c Cowdrey b Statham	0
C.A.R. Duckworth	c Wardle b Loader	13		b Wardle	3
W.R. Endean	b Statham	13	(5)	c Insole b Bailey	2
C.B. van Ryneveld*	c Cowdrey b Laker	36		c and b Statham	12
H.J. Tayfield	c Bailey b Wardle	10		not out	12
P.S. Heine	not out	1		c Insole b Wardle	0
N.A.T. Adcock	lbw b Wardle	6		run out	1
Extras	(LB 8, W 1, NB 1)	10		(B 4, LB 1)	5
Total		**340**			**142**

ENGLAND

P.E. Richardson	c Tayfield b Heine	11		b Tayfield	39
T.E. Bailey	c Waite b Adcock	13		c Endean b Tayfield	1
D.J. Insole	run out	47		c Tayfield b Goddard	68
P.B.H. May*	b Adcock	61	(5)	c Endean b Tayfield	0
D.C.S. Compton	c Pithey b Heine	42	(6)	c Goddard b Tayfield	1
M.C. Cowdrey	c Goddard b Tayfield	8	(4)	c and b Tayfield	55
T.G. Evans†	c Endean b Tayfield	7	(8)	b Tayfield	8
J.H. Wardle	c Goddard b Tayfield	16	(7)	c Waite b Tayfield	22
J.C. Laker	lbw b Tayfield	17		c Duckworth b Tayfield	5
P.J. Loader	c Endean b Goddard	13		c sub (A. Tayfield) b Tayfield	7
J.B. Statham	not out	12		not out	4
Extras	(LB 1, NB 3)	4		(B 1, LB 3)	4
Total		**251**			**214**

ENGLAND	O	M	R	W	O	M	R	W
Statham	23	5	81	2	13	1	37	3
Loader	23	3	78	1	13	3	33	0
Bailey	21	3	54	3	13	4	12	2
Wardle	19·6	4	68	2	14	4	29	2
Laker	15	3	49	1	7	1	26	1
SOUTH AFRICA								
Adcock	21	5	52	2	8	1	22	0
Heine	23	6	54	2	8	1	21	0
Goddard	25·2	15	22	1	25	5	54	1
Tayfield	37	15	79	4	37	11	113	9
Van Ryneveld	8	0	40	0				

FALL OF WICKETS

	SA	E	SA	E
Wkt	1st	1st	2nd	2nd
1st	22	25	62	10
2nd	134	40	91	65
3rd	151	131	94	147
4th	172	135	95	148
5th	238	152	97	156
6th	251	160	104	186
7th	309	176	129	196
8th	328	213	130	199
9th	333	227	131	208
10th	340	251	142	214

Umpires: J.H. McMenamin (2) and B.V. Malan (6).

Close: 1st day – SA(1) 234-4 (McLean 56, Duckworth 13); 2nd – E(1) 87-2 (Insole 30, May 30); 3rd – SA(2) 0-0 (Pithey 0, Goddard 0); 4th – E(2) 19-1 (Richardson 11, Insole 6).

SOUTH AFRICA v ENGLAND 1956–57 (5th Test)

Played at St. George's Park, Port Elizabeth, on 1, 2, 4, 5 March.
Toss: South Africa.　Result: SOUTH AFRICA won by 58 runs.
Debuts: Nil.

Evans conceded only one bye on a recently relaid pitch where the ball frequently kept low or 'shot'. Waite tore fibres in his shoulder diving to stop a 'shooter' towards the end of the first innings and Endean took over as wicket-keeper after the first few overs of the second innings. Tayfield's 37 wickets in this rubber still stands as the South African record against any country. Only 122 runs were scored on the third day – the fewest in a day of Test cricket in South Africa. After starting the tour with scores of 162, 118, 124 not out and 206, May averaged only 15.30 in the Tests.

SOUTH AFRICA

A.J. Pithey	c Evans b Bailey	15		b Laker	6
T.L. Goddard	lbw b Bailey	2		c Evans b Tyson	30
J.H.B. Waite†	c Evans b Loader	3	(9)	not out	7
K.J. Funston	b Bailey	3		b Lock	24
W.R. Endean	lbw b Tyson	70	(3)	b Tyson	1
R.A. McLean	c Evans b Lock	23		b Bailey	19
C.B. van Ryneveld*	c Tyson b Loader	24	(5)	lbw b Tyson	13
C.A.R. Duckworth	lbw b Laker	6	(7)	b Tyson	6
H.J. Tayfield	b Loader	4	(8)	c Evans b Tyson	10
P.S. Heine	b Tyson	4		c Evans b Tyson	4
N.A.T. Adcock	not out	0		b Bailey	3
Extras	(LB 1, NB 9)	10		(B 1, LB 7, NB 3)	11
Total		**164**			**134**

ENGLAND

P.E. Richardson	lbw b Adcock	0		b Adcock	3
T.E. Bailey	b Heine	41		c McLean b Tayfield	18
D.C.S. Compton	b Adcock	0	(6)	c Endean b Tayfield	5
P.B.H. May*	c Duckworth b Goddard	24	(3)	lbw b Goddard	21
D.J. Insole	lbw b Heine	4		c Duckworth b Tayfield	8
M.C. Cowdrey	c Waite b Adcock	3	(4)	c Van Ryneveld b Tayfield	8
T.G. Evans†	b Heine	5		c Endean b Heine	21
G.A.R. Lock	b Adcock	14		c Goddard b Tayfield	12
F.H. Tyson	c and b Heine	1		c Tayfield b Goddard	23
J.C. Laker	b Goddard	6		not out	3
P.J. Loader	not out	0		c McLean b Tayfield	0
Extras	(B 8, LB 4)	12		(B 5, LB 3)	8
Total		**110**			**130**

ENGLAND	O	M	R	W	O	M	R	W		FALL OF WICKETS			
Loader	20	3	35	3	4	3	1	0		SA	E	SA	E
Bailey	25	12	23	3	24·7	5	39	2	*Wkt*	*1st*	*1st*	*2nd*	*2nd*
Tyson	17	6	38	2	23	7	40	6	1st	4	1	20	15
Laker	14	1	37	1	14	5	26	1	2nd	15	1	21	41
Lock	11	5	21	1	15	6	17	1	3rd	21	55	65	53
									4th	41	77	98	57
SOUTH AFRICA									5th	78	78	99	71
Heine	15	6	22	4	11	3	22	1	6th	143	86	105	72
Adcock	11·3	4	20	4	7	2	10	1	7th	155	89	111	99
Tayfield	22	8	43	0	24·3	6	78	6	8th	155	97	123	127
Goddard	13	8	13	2	16	8	12	2	9th	163	110	129	129
									10th	164	110	134	130

Umpires: V. Costello (2) and W. Marais (3).

Close: 1st day – SA(1) 138-5 (Endean 68, Van Ryneveld 17); 2nd – E(1) 110-9 (Lock 14, Loader 0); 3rd – SA(2) 122-7 (Tayfield 9, Waite 4).

ENGLAND v WEST INDIES 1957 (1st Test)

Played at Edgbaston, Birmingham, on 30, 31 May, 1, 3, 4 June.
Toss: England.   Result: MATCH DRAWN.
Debuts: West Indies – R. Gilchrist, R.B. Kanhai.

Birmingham's first Test for 28 years brought a host of records. May's 285 not out remains the highest score by an England captain and the highest in any Edgbaston Test. His stand of 411 with Cowdrey is still England's highest for any wicket and the Test record for the fourth wicket. Ramadhin bowled most balls (588) in any first-class innings and the most in any Test match (774); both records still stand. Smith scored a hundred in his first Test against England.

ENGLAND

P.E. Richardson	c Walcott b Ramadhin	47	c sub (N.S. Asgarali) b Ramadhin	34
D.B. Close	c Kanhai b Gilchrist	15	c Weekes b Gilchrist	42
D.J. Insole	b Ramadhin	20	b Ramadhin	0
P.B.H. May*	c Weekes b Ramadhin	30	not out	285
M.C. Cowdrey	c Gilchrist b Ramadhin	4	c sub (N.S. Asgarali) b Smith	154
T.E. Bailey	b Ramadhin	1		
G.A.R. Lock	b Ramadhin	0		
T.G. Evans†	b Gilchrist	14	(6) not out	29
J.C. Laker	b Ramadhin	7		
F.S. Trueman	not out	29		
J.B. Statham	b Atkinson	13		
Extras	(B 3, LB 3)	6	(B 23, LB 16)	39
Total		**186**	(4 wickets declared)	**583**

WEST INDIES

B.H. Pairaudeau	b Trueman	1	b Trueman	7
R.B. Kanhai†	lbw b Statham	42	c Close b Trueman	1
C.L. Walcott	c Evans b Laker	90	(6) c Lock b Laker	1
E. de C. Weekes	b Trueman	9	c Trueman b Lock	33
G. St A. Sobers	c Bailey b Statham	53	(3) c Cowdrey b Lock	14
O.G. Smith	lbw b Laker	161	(7) lbw b Laker	5
F.M.M. Worrell	b Statham	81	(5) c May b Lock	0
J.D.C. Goddard*	c Lock b Laker	24	not out	0
D. St E. Atkinson	c Statham b Laker	1	not out	4
S. Ramadhin	not out	5		
R. Gilchrist	run out	0		
Extras	(B 1, LB 6)	7	(B 7)	7
Total		**474**	(7 wickets)	**72**

WEST INDIES	O	M	R	W	O	M	R	W
Worrell	9	1	27	0				
Gilchrist	27	4	74	2	26	2	67	1
Ramadhin	31	16	49	7	98	35	179	2
Atkinson	12·4	3	30	1	72	29	137	0
Sobers					30	4	77	0
Smith					26	4	72	1
Goddard					6	2	12	0
ENGLAND								
Statham	39	4	114	3	2	0	6	0
Trueman	30	4	99	2	5	3	7	2
Bailey	34	11	80	0				
Laker	54	17	119	4	24	20	13	2
Lock	34·4	15	55	0	27	19	31	3
Close					2	1	8	0

FALL OF WICKETS

	E	WI	E	WI
Wkt	*1st*	*1st*	*2nd*	*2nd*
1st	32	4	63	1
2nd	61	83	65	9
3rd	104	120	113	25
4th	115	183	524	27
5th	116	197	–	43
6th	118	387	–	66
7th	121	466	–	68
8th	130	469	–	–
9th	150	474	–	–
10th	186	474	–	–

Umpires: D.E. Davies (3) and C.S. Elliott (1).

Close: 1st day – WI(1) 83-1 (Kanhai 42, Walcott 40); 2nd – WI(1) 316-5 (Smith 70, Worrell 48); 3rd – E(2) 102-2 (Close 34, May 21); 4th – E(2) 378-3 (May 193, Cowdrey 78).

ENGLAND v WEST INDIES 1957 (2nd Test)

Played at Lord's, London, on 20, 21, 22 June.
Toss: West Indies.   Result: ENGLAND won by an innings and 36 runs.
Debuts: England – D.V. Smith; West Indies – N.S. Asgarali.

Bailey's analysis for 7 for 44, returned in his 50th Test match, was then the best for England in a home Test against West Indies. Bailey's 11 wickets equalled England's match record for any West Indies Test so far. Cowdrey reached 150 for the second innings in succession.

WEST INDIES

N.S. Asgarali	lbw b Trueman	0	(4) c Trueman b Wardle	26
R.B. Kanhai†	c Cowdrey b Bailey	34	(1) c Bailey b Statham	0
C.L. Walcott	lbw b Bailey	14	c Trueman b Bailey	21
G. St A. Sobers	c May b Statham	17	(5) c May b Bailey	66
E. de C.Weekes	c Evans b Bailey	13	(6) c Evans b Bailey	90
F.M.M. Worrell	c Close b Bailey	12	(7) c Evans b Trueman	10
O.G. Smith	c Graveney b Bailey	25	(2) lbw b Statham	5
J.D.C. Goddard*	c Cowdrey b Bailey	1	c Evans b Trueman	21
S. Ramadhin	b Trueman	0	c Statham b Bailey	0
R. Gilchrist	c and b Bailey	4	not out	11
A.L. Valentine	not out	0	b Statham	1
Extras	(B 2, LB 1, W 4)	7	(B 4, LB 6)	10
Total		**127**		**261**

ENGLAND

P.E. Richardson	b Gilchrist	76
D.V. Smith	lbw b Worrell	8
T.W. Graveney	lbw b Gilchrist	0
P.B.H. May*	c Kanhai b Gilchrist	0
M.C. Cowdrey	c Walcott b Sobers	152
T.E. Bailey	b Worrell	1
D.B. Close	c Kanhai b Goddard	32
T.G. Evans†	b Sobers	82
J.H. Wardle	c Sobers b Ramadhin	11
F.S. Trueman	not out	36
J.B. Statham	b Gilchrist	7
Extras	(B 7, LB 11, W 1)	19
Total		**424**

ENGLAND	O	M	R	W	O	M	R	W		FALL OF WICKETS		
										WI	E	WI
Statham	18	3	46	1	29·1	9	71	3	*Wkt*	*1st*	*1st*	*2nd*
Trueman	12·3	2	30	2	23	5	73	2	1st	7	25	0
Bailey	21	8	44	7	22	6	54	4	2nd	34	34	17
Wardle					22	5	53	1	3rd	55	34	32
									4th	79	129	80
WEST INDIES									5th	85	134	180
Worrell	42	7	114	2					6th	118	192	203
Gilchrist	36·3	7	115	4					7th	120	366	233
Ramadhin	22	5	83	1					8th	123	379	241
Valentine	3	0	20	0					9th	127	387	256
Goddard	13	1	45	1					10th	127	424	261
Sobers	7	0	28	2								

Umpires: D.E. Davies (4) and C.S. Elliott (2).

Close: 1st day – E(1) 134-4 (Cowdrey 39, Bailey 1); 2nd – WI(2) 45-3 (Asgarali 12, Sobers 7).

ENGLAND v WEST INDIES 1957 (3rd Test)

Played at Trent Bridge, Nottingham, on 4, 5, 6, 8, 9 July.
Toss: England.   Result: MATCH DRAWN.
Debuts: England – D.W. Richardson.

England's partnership of 266 between Richardson and Graveney, whose highest first-class score took 475 minutes and included 30 fours, remains their highest for the second wicket against West Indies. Worrell was the first to carry his bat through a completed West Indies innings and his stand of 55 with Ramadhin, who batted with a runner, was then the West Indies tenth-wicket record against England. Worrell was on the field for the first $20\frac{1}{2}$ hours of the match. Peter and Dick Richardson, playing their only Test together, were the first pair of brothers to appear for England since 1891-92 (*Test No. 38*), when Alec and George Hearne represented England against a South African team which included a third brother, Frank. They contributed a quarter of England's highest total against West Indies in a home Test.

ENGLAND

P.E. Richardson	c Walcott b Atkinson	126	c Kanhai b Gilchrist	11
D.V. Smith	c Kanhai b Worrell	1	not out	16
T.W. Graveney	b Smith	258	not out	28
P.B.H. May*	lbw b Smith	104		
M.C. Cowdrey	run out	55		
D.W. Richardson	b Sobers	33		
T.G. Evans†	not out	26		
T.E. Bailey	not out	3		
J.C. Laker	)			
F.S. Trueman	) did not bat			
J.B. Statham	)			
Extras	(B 1, LB 10, W 1, NB 1)	13	(B 7, LB 2)	9
Total	(6 wickets declared)	**619**	(1 wicket)	**64**

WEST INDIES

F.M.M. Worrell	not out	191	b Statham	16
G. St A. Sobers	b Laker	47	lbw b Trueman	9
C.L. Walcott	c and b Laker	17	c Evans b Laker	7
R.B. Kanhai†	c Evans b Bailey	42	c Evans b Trueman	28
E. de C. Weekes	b Trueman	33	b Statham	3
O.G. Smith	c Evans b Trueman	2	b Trueman	168
D. St E. Atkinson	c Evans b Trueman	4	c Evans b Statham	46
J.D.C. Goddard*	c May b Trueman	0	c Evans b Statham	61
R. Gilchrist	c D.W. Richardson b Laker	1	(10) b Statham	0
A.L. Valentine	b Trueman	1	(11) not out	2
S. Ramadhin	b Statham	19	(9) b Trueman	15
Extras	(B 5, LB 10)	15	(B 2, LB 10)	12
Total		**372**		**367**

WEST INDIES	O	M	R	W	O	M	R	W	FALL OF WICKETS				
Worrell	21	4	79	1	7	1	27	0		E	WI	WI	E
Gilchrist	29	3	118	0	7	0	21	1	*Wkt*	*1st*	*1st*	*2nd*	*2nd*
Atkinson	40	7	99	1	1	0	1	0	1st	14	87	22	13
Ramadhin	38	5	95	0					2nd	280	120	30	–
Valentine	23	4	68	0					3rd	487	229	39	–
Sobers	21	6	60	1					4th	510	295	56	–
Goddard	15	5	26	0	1	0	2	0	5th	573	297	89	–
Smith	25	5	61	2					6th	609	305	194	–
Walcott					1	0	4	0	7th	–	305	348	–
ENGLAND									8th	–	314	352	–
Statham	28·4	9	78	1	41·2	12	118	5	9th	–	317	365	–
Trueman	30	8	63	5	35	5	80	4	10th	–	372	367	–
Laker	62	27	101	3	43	14	98	1					
Bailey	28	9	77	1	12	3	22	0					
Smith	12	1	38	0	12	5	23	0					
Graveney					5	2	14	0					

Umpires: J.S. Buller (3) and F.S. Lee (18).

Close: 1st day – E(1) 360-2 (Graveney 188, May 40); 2nd – WI(1) 59-0 (Worrell 29, Sobers 24); 3rd – WI(1) 295-3 (Worrell 145, Weekes 33); 4th – WI(2) 175-5 (Smith 67, Atkinson 36).

ENGLAND v WEST INDIES 1957 (4th Test)

Played at Headingley, Leeds, on 25, 26, 27 July.
Toss: West Indies.   Result: ENGLAND won by an innings and 5 runs.
Debuts: West Indies – F.C.M. Alexander.

West Indies last four first-innings wickets fell in consecutive balls, Trueman bowling Smith with the last ball of an over before Loader dismissed Goddard, Ramadhin and Gilchrist to complete the first hat-trick for England in a home Test since 1899 (*Test No. 62*). Evans became the first wicket-keeper to make 200 dismissals in Tests when he caught Smith. Prompted by the non-striker, Walcott, umpire Davies warned Trueman for intimidation when he unleashed four bouncers in one over at Kanhai. This victory gave England their first rubber in this series since 1939.

WEST INDIES

F.M.M. Worrell	b Loader	29	c Cowdrey b Trueman	7
G. St A. Sobers	c Lock b Loader	4	run out	29
R.B. Kanhai	lbw b Laker	47	lbw b Loader	0
E. de C. Weekes	b Loader	0	c Cowdrey b Trueman	14
C.L. Walcott	c Cowdrey b Laker	38	c Sheppard b Loader	35
O.G. Smith	b Trueman	15	c Evans b Smith	8
B.H. Pairaudeau	b Trueman	6	c Trueman b Loader	6
J.D.C. Goddard*	b Loader	1	c Loader b Lock	4
F.C.M. Alexander†	not out	0	b Laker	11
S. Ramadhin	c Trueman b Loader	0	run out	6
R. Gilchrist	b Loader	0	not out	6
Extras	(LB 2)	2	(LB 5, NB 1)	6
Total		**142**		**132**

ENGLAND

P.E. Richardson	c Alexander b Worrell	10
D.V. Smith	b Worrell	0
T.W. Graveney	b Gilchrist	22
P.B.H. May*	c Alexander b Sobers	69
M.C. Cowdrey	c Weekes b Worrell	68
Rev. D.S. Sheppard	c Walcott b Worrell	68
T.G. Evans†	b Worrell	10
G.A.R. Lock	b Gilchrist	20
J.C. Laker	c Alexander b Worrell	1
F.S. Trueman	not out	2
P.J. Loader	c Pairaudeau b Worrell	1
Extras	(B 2, LB 5, W 1)	8
Total		**279**

ENGLAND	O	M	R	W	O	M	R	W	FALL OF WICKETS			
Trueman	17	4	33	2	11	0	42	2		WI	E	WI
Loader	20·3	9	36	6	14	2	50	3	*Wkt*	*1st*	*1st*	*2nd*
Smith	17	6	24	0	4	1	12	1	1st	16	1	40
Laker	17	4	24	2	6·2	1	16	1	2nd	42	12	40
Lock	14	6	23	0	1	0	6	1	3rd	42	42	49
									4th	112	136	56
WEST INDIES									5th	125	227	71
Worrell	38·2	9	70	7					6th	139	239	92
Gilchrist	27	3	71	2					7th	142	264	103
Sobers	32	9	79	1					8th	142	272	113
Ramadhin	19	5	34	0					9th	142	278	123
Smith	8	1	17	0					10th	142	279	132

Umpires: J.S. Buller (4) and D. Davies (21).

Close: 1st day – E(1) 11-1 (Richardson 10, Graveney 1); 2nd – E(1) 279 all out.

ENGLAND v WEST INDIES 1957 (5th Test)

Played at Kennington Oval, London, on 22, 23, 24 August.
Toss: England.   Result: ENGLAND won by an innings and 237 runs.
Debuts: Nil.

Dismissed for what are still their two lowest totals against England, West Indies were beaten in three days for the third time in this rubber, the match ending at 2.30 pm. Walcott took over the captaincy when Goddard was taken ill with influenza at the end of the first day. Lock's match analysis (11 for 48) was then the record for either side in this series.

ENGLAND

P.E. Richardson	b Smith	107
Rev. D.S. Sheppard	c and b Goddard	40
T.W. Graveney	b Ramadhin	164
P.B.H. May*	c Worrell b Smith	1
M.C. Cowdrey	b Ramadhin	2
T.E. Bailey	run out	0
T.G. Evans†	c Weekes b Dewdney	40
G.A.R. Lock	c Alexander b Sobers	17
F.S. Trueman	b Ramadhin	22
J.C. Laker	not out	10
P.J. Loader	lbw b Ramadhin	0
Extras	(B 1, LB 8)	9
Total		**412**

WEST INDIES

F.M.M. Worrell	c Lock b Loader	4	(4) c Cowdrey b Lock		0
N.S. Asgarali	c Cowdrey b Lock	29	b Lock		7
G. St A. Sobers	b Lock	39	b Lock		42
C.L. Walcott	b Laker	5	(5) not out		19
E. de C. Weekes	c Trueman b Laker	0	(6) b Lock		0
O.G. Smith	c May b Laker	7	(7) c Sheppard b Lock		0
R.B. Kanhai	not out	4	(1) c Evans b Trueman		8
F.C.M. Alexander†	b Lock	0	b Laker		0
D.T. Dewdney	b Lock	0	st Evans b Lock		1
S. Ramadhin	c Trueman b Lock	0	b Laker		2
J.D.C. Goddard*	absent ill	–	absent ill		–
Extras	(NB 1)	1	(B 4, LB 2, NB 1)		7
Total		**89**			**86**

WEST INDIES	O	M	R	W	O	M	R	W
Worrell	11	3	26	0				
Dewdney	15	2	43	1				
Ramadhin	53·3	12	107	4				
Sobers	44	6	111	1				
Goddard	23	10	43	1				
Smith	30	4	73	2				
ENGLAND								
Trueman	5	1	9	0	5	2	19	1
Loader	7	4	12	1	3	2	2	0
Laker	23	12	39	3	17	4	38	2
Lock	21·4	12	28	5	16	7	20	6

FALL OF WICKETS

Wkt	E 1st	WI 1st	WI 2nd
1st	92	7	10
2nd	238	68	39
3rd	242	73	43
4th	255	73	69
5th	256	85	69
6th	322	89	69
7th	366	89	70
8th	399	89	75
9th	412	89	86
10th	412	–	–

Umpires: D.E. Davies (5) and F.S. Lee (19).

Close: 1st day – E(1) 283-5 (Graveney 113, Evans 15); 2nd – WI(1) 89 all out.

SOUTH AFRICA v AUSTRALIA 1957–58 (1st Test)

Played at New Wanderers, Johannesburg, on 23, 24, 26, 27, 28 December.
Toss: South Africa.   Result: MATCH DRAWN.
Debuts: Australia – A.T.W. Grout, L.F. Kline, I. Meckiff, R.B. Simpson.

At 22 years 194 days, Craig was the youngest Test captain until 1961-62 (*Test No. 527*). C.B. van Ryneveld, South Africa's appointed captain, withdrew after splitting his hand fielding for Western Province against the Australians a week earlier. The partnership of 176 between McGlew and Goddard remains South Africa's highest for the first wicket against Australia, as does that of 129 between Waite and Endean for the fifth wicket in the second innings. Heine (6 for 58) achieved the best analysis of his Test career. In his first Test, Grout set what was then a world record by holding six catches in an innings. Australia, left 268 minutes to score 304, were soon deprived of Burke when he was hit on the hand. On Boxing Day, a record crowd of 36,057 caused the gates to be closed at a cricket match for the first time in the Union.

SOUTH AFRICA

D.J. McGlew*	c Simpson b Meckiff	108		c Simpson b Meckiff	6
T.L. Goddard	b Meckiff	90		c Grout b Davidson	5
J.D. Nel	b Meckiff	4		c Grout b Davidson	7
J.H.B. Waite†	c Burge b Benaud	115		c Grout b Burke	59
W.R. Endean	lbw b Meckiff	50	(6)	c Meckiff b Davidson	77
R.A. McLean	b Meckiff	50	(5)	c Grout b Davidson	0
K.J. Funston	lbw b Mackay	12		b Meckiff	27
H.J. Tayfield	b Davidson	18		c Grout b Meckiff	3
P.S. Heine	b Mackay	7		c Grout b Davidson	2
V.J. Smith	not out	2		not out	1
N.A.T. Adcock	did not bat			c Simpson b Davidson	0
Extras	(B 8, LB 4, W 1, NB 1)	14		(B 5, LB 7, W 1, NB 1)	14
Total	(9 wickets declared)	**470**			**201**

AUSTRALIA

C.C. McDonald	c Tayfield b Smith	75		st Waite b Smith	25
J.W. Burke	c Waite b Heine	16		retired hurt	10
K.D. Mackay	c Waite b Heine	3		not out	65
I.D. Craig*	b Heine	14		b Tayfield	17
P.J.P. Burge	c Waite b Heine	0		b Tayfield	14
R.B. Simpson	lbw b Tayfield	60		not out	23
R. Benaud	c Heine b Adcock	122			
A.K. Davidson	c sub (E.R.H. Fuller) b Heine	24			
A.T.W. Grout†	c Endean b Tayfield	21			
I. Meckiff	c Smith b Heine	11			
L.F. Kline	not out	6			
Extras	(B 4, LB 11, NB 1)	16		(B 6, LB 2)	8
Total		**368**		(3 wickets)	**162**

AUSTRALIA	O	M	R	W	O	M	R	W		FALL OF WICKETS			
Davidson	32	4	115	1	17·4	4	34	6		SA	A	SA	A
Meckiff	31	3	125	5	26	3	52	3	*Wkt*	*1st*	*1st*	*2nd*	*2nd*
Mackay	20·6	3	54	2	11	1	29	0	1st	176	34	6	44
Benaud	27	7	115	1	2	0	15	0	2nd	182	40	19	85
Kline	20	6	47	0	8	2	18	0	3rd	237	56	19	118
Burke					14	3	39	1	4th	341	62	19	–
									5th	412	151	148	–
SOUTH AFRICA									6th	436	177	193	–
Heine	14·2	3	58	6	8	2	17	0	7th	461	244	196	–
Adcock	23	3	106	1	3	0	11	0	8th	465	313	199	–
Goddard	16	5	57	0	12	6	24	0	9th	470	355	199	–
Tayfield	29	9	101	2	33	12	70	2	10th	–	368	201	–
Smith	9	2	30	1	16	8	25	1					
McGlew					1	0	7	0					

Umpires: A. Birkett (1) and J.H. McMenamin (3).

Close: 1st day – SA(1) 222-2 (McGlew 100, Waite 19); 2nd – A(1) 15-0 (McDonald 10, Burke 5); 3rd – A(1) 307-7 (Benaud 80, Grout 21); 4th – SA(2) 176-5 (Endean 68, Funston 18).

SOUTH AFRICA v AUSTRALIA 1957–58 (2nd Test)

Played at Newlands, Cape Town, on 31 December, 1, 2, 3 January.
Toss: Australia.   Result: AUSTRALIA won by an innings and 141 runs.
Debuts: Nil.

Burke batted 578 minutes for his highest Test score. Meckiff left the field with a pulled shoulder muscle after bowling four balls on the third day. Kline (slow left-arm unorthodox) ended the match soon after lunch on the fourth day when he did the hat-trick, dismissing Fuller, Tayfield and Adcock. Goddard became the third player to carry his bat through a completed innings for South Africa; all three instances occurred at Newlands.

AUSTRALIA

C.C. McDonald	c Waite b Fuller	99
J.W. Burke	b Tayfield	189
R.N. Harvey	c Goddard b Adcock	15
I.D. Craig*	b Goddard	0
K.D. Mackay	lbw b Tayfield	63
R. Benaud	c McGlew b Tayfield	33
A.K. Davidson	c and b Tayfield	21
R.B. Simpson	c Funston b Tayfield	3
A.T.W. Grout†	run out	0
I. Meckiff	not out	11
L.F. Kline	lbw b Fuller	5
Extras	(B 1, LB 6, NB 3)	10
Total		**449**

SOUTH AFRICA

D.J. McGlew	c Mackay b Davidson	30	c McDonald b Davidson	0
T.L. Goddard	lbw b Benaud	29	not out	56
R.J. Westcott	c Simpson b Davidson	0	c Davidson b Benaud	18
J.H.B. Waite†	c Simpson b Kline	7	c Benaud b Davidson	8
R.A. McLean	c Harvey b Kline	38	c Burke b Benaud	2
W.R. Endean	c Davidson b Burke	21	b Benaud	5
K.J. Funston	c and b Benaud	2	b Benaud	8
C.B. van Ryneveld*	b Benaud	43	c Burke b Benaud	1
E.R.H. Fuller	c Harvey b Benaud	5	c Benaud b Kline	0
H.J. Tayfield	c Benaud b Kline	21	lbw b Kline	0
N.A.T. Adcock	not out	0	c Simpson b Kline	0
Extras	(B 6, LB 5, W 1, NB 1)	13	(LB 1)	1
Total		**209**		**99**

SOUTH AFRICA	O	M	R	W	O	M	R	W		FALL OF WICKETS			
Adcock	27	5	80	1							A	SA	SA
Goddard	29	9	57	1					*Wkt*	*1st*	*1st*	*2nd*
Fuller	34·2	3	125	2					1st	190	61	0
Tayfield	51	18	120	5					2nd	215	61	56
Westcott	4	0	22	0					3rd	220	70	69
Van Ryneveld	7	0	35	0					4th	350	103	74
									5th	399	118	80
AUSTRALIA									6th	408	121	88
Meckiff	5·4	1	18	0					7th	412	146	98
Davidson	18	5	31	2	15	6	18	2	8th	412	164	99
Benaud	35	6	95	4	21	6	49	5	9th	434	209	99
Kline	19·1	5	29	3	10·4	2	18	3	10th	449	209	99
Burke	9	2	23	1	6	4	7	0				
Mackay					5	3	6	0				

Umpires: D. Collins (9) and V. Costello (3).

Close: 1st day – A(1) 234-3 (Burke 114, Mackay 3); 2nd – SA(1) 46-0 (McGlew 25, Goddard 20); 3rd – SA(2) 17-1 (Goddard 12, Westcott 5).

SOUTH AFRICA v AUSTRALIA 1957–58 (3rd Test)

Played at Kingsmead, Durban, on 24, 25, 27, 28, 29 January.
Toss: Australia.   Result: MATCH DRAWN.
Debuts: Australia – R.A. Gaunt.

Gaunt bowled Westcott with his seventh ball in Test cricket. McGlew took nine hours five minutes to reach the slowest century then in Test cricket, his 105 lasting a further 30 minutes. His third-wicket partnership of 231 with Waite was the highest so far for any South African wicket against Australia. Adcock's analysis of 6 for 43 remained his best in Tests.

AUSTRALIA

C.C. McDonald	c Goddard b Adcock	28	lbw b Tayfield	33
J.W. Burke	c Waite b Adcock	2	b Goddard	83
R.N. Harvey	c Waite b Adcock	6	b Adcock	68
I.D. Craig*	b Goddard	52	c Goddard b Tayfield	0
R.B. Simpson	b Goddard	17	(8) c Tayfield b Van Ryneveld	4
K.D. Mackay	hit wkt b Adcock	32	(5) not out	52
R. Benaud	lbw b Adcock	5	(6) b Van Ryneveld	20
A.K. Davidson	c Waite b Heine	12	(7) c McGlew b Tayfield	4
A.T.W. Grout†	b Heine	2	not out	3
L.F. Kline	c Goddard b Adcock	0		
R.A. Gaunt	not out	0		
Extras	(NB 7)	7	(B 19, LB 5, NB 1)	25
Total		**163**	(7 wickets)	**292**

SOUTH AFRICA

D.J. McGlew	c Grout b Gaunt	105
R.J. Westcott	b Gaunt	0
W.R. Endean	c Simpson b Benaud	15
J.H.B. Waite†	b Davidson	134
T.L. Goddard	lbw b Davidson	45
K.J. Funston	c Grout b Mackay	27
C.B. van Ryneveld*	not out	32
R.A. McLean	c Grout b Benaud	11
H.J. Tayfield	st Grout b Benaud	0
P.S. Heine	c Burke b Benaud	7
N.A.T. Adcock	c Grout b Benaud	0
Extras	(B 2, LB 5, NB 1)	8
Total		**384**

SOUTH AFRICA	O	M	R	W	O	M	R	W	FALL OF WICKETS			
										A	SA	A
Heine	17·4	4	30	2	14	1	40	0	*Wkt*	*1st*	*1st*	*2nd*
Adcock	18	2	43	6	15	1	34	1	1st	13	6	92
Goddard	23	12	25	2	42	18	62	1	2nd	19	28	170
Tayfield	21	7	41	0	59	24	94	3	3rd	54	259	179
Van Ryneveld	3	0	17	0	17	1	37	2	4th	87	259	221
AUSTRALIA									5th	131	313	261
Davidson	34	8	62	2					6th	142	356	274
Gaunt	27	2	87	2					7th	161	371	289
Mackay	35	5	77	1					8th	163	371	–
Benaud	50·7	13	114	5					9th	163	383	–
Kline	17	6	36	0					10th	163	384	–

Umpires: V. Costello (4) and W. Marais (4).

Close: 1st day – A(1) 155-6 (Mackay 27, Davidson 11); 2nd – SA(1) 150-2 (McGlew 64, Waite 68); 3rd – SA(1) 318-5 (Goddard 25, Van Ryneveld 4); 4th – A(2) 117-1 (Burke 64, Harvey 13).

SOUTH AFRICA v AUSTRALIA 1957–58 (4th Test)

Played at New Wanderers, Johannesburg, on 7, 8, 10, 11, 12 February.
Toss: Australia.   Result: AUSTRALIA won by ten wickets.
Debuts: South Africa – C.G. de V. Burger.

Australia won immediately after lunch on the fifth day, South Africa being handicapped on the first day when Adcock retired at lunch with influenza and Heine's bowling was restricted by a damaged ankle. McGlew needed 313 minutes to reach the slowest Test fifty so far. For the second time in two months, Van Ryneveld badly split his hand fielding.

AUSTRALIA

C.C. McDonald	lbw b Tayfield	26	not out	1
J.W. Burke	c Waite b Heine	81	not out	0
R.N. Harvey	c Waite b Goddard	5		
R. Benaud	c Endean b Heine	100		
I.D. Craig*	b Heine	3		
A.T.W. Grout†	lbw b Adcock	7		
K.D. Mackay	not out	83		
R.B. Simpson	c Waite b Adcock	6		
A.K. Davidson	c Burger b Heine	62		
I. Meckiff	c Endean b Heine	26		
L.F. Kline	c Waite b Heine	1		
Extras	(LB 1)	1		
Total		**401**	(0 wickets)	**1**

SOUTH AFRICA

D.J. McGlew	c Grout b Meckiff	1	c Simpson b Benaud	70
W.R. Endean	lbw b Davidson	22	c Simpson b Benaud	38
H.J. Tayfield	lbw b Benaud	27	(9) st Grout b Kline	0
T.L. Goddard	c and b Meckiff	9	(3) c Simpson b Benaud	0
K.J. Funston	c Craig b Kline	70	(4) not out	64
R.A. McLean	c Grout b Davidson	9	(5) c Grout b Davidson	0
C.G. de V. Burger	st Grout b Kline	21	c McDonald b Kline	1
J.H.B. Waite†	lbw b Benaud	12	(6) c Grout b Benaud	10
P.S. Heine	c and b Benaud	24	(10) c Meckiff b Benaud	1
N.A.T. Adcock	b Benaud	0	(11) run out	3
C.B. van Ryneveld*	not out	0	(8) lbw b Kline	0
Extras	(B 3, W 2, NB 3)	8	(LB 8, W 2, NB 1)	11
Total		**203**		**198**

SOUTH AFRICA	O	M	R	W	O	M	R	W
Heine	37·5	6	96	6				
Adcock	17	3	37	2				
Goddard	43	10	136	1				
Tayfield	49	17	107	1				
Van Ryneveld	3	0	24	0				
McLean					0·4	0	1	0
AUSTRALIA								
Meckiff	21	3	38	2	13	2	24	0
Davidson	19	2	39	2	20	4	44	1
Mackay	11	5	11	0				
Benaud	20·2	0	70	4	41	8	84	5
Kline	9	1	37	2	16	6	27	3
Burke					15	10	8	0

FALL OF WICKETS

	A	SA	SA	A
Wkt	1st	1st	2nd	2nd
1st	43	17	78	–
2nd	52	27	78	–
3rd	210	46	147	–
4th	213	104	148	–
5th	222	115	161	–
6th	222	166	180	–
7th	234	166	180	–
8th	315	186	182	–
9th	393	194	183	–
10th	401	203	198	–

Umpires: A. Birkett (2) and J.H. McMenamin (4).

Close: 1st day – A(1) 217-4 (Burke 79, Grout 4); 2nd – SA(1) 19-1 (Endean 17, Tayfield 0); 3rd – SA(2) 7-0 (McGlew 1, Endean 5); 4th – SA(2) 126-2 (McGlew 57, Funston 20).

Test No. 448/39

SOUTH AFRICA v AUSTRALIA 1957–58 (5th Test)

Played at St George's Park, Port Elizabeth, on 28 February, 1, 3, 4 March.
Toss: South Africa.   Result: AUSTRALIA won by eight wickets.
Debuts: South Africa – P.R. Carlstein.

Australia won their third victory of the rubber and with a day to spare. It extended their unbeaten run of Test matches in the Union to 21. Benaud took his hundredth Test wicket to complete the Test 'double' in his 32nd match. Heine and Adcock were allowed to bowl an excessive number of short-pitched balls in this match – both Burke and Benaud were felled by them, while Craig retired at lunch on the second day for an X-ray, returning at 199.

SOUTH AFRICA

D.J. McGlew	c Simpson b Davidson	14	(7) b Benaud	20
T.L. Goddard	c Harvey b Meckiff	17	lbw b Benaud	33
W.R. Endean	c McDonald b Davidson	2	(1) c Simpson b Davidson	23
J.H.B. Waite†	c Harvey b Davidson	17	(3) b Davidson	0
K.J. Funston	c Grout b Davidson	20	(4) c Simpson b Davidson	4
C.B. van Ryneveld*	c Burke b Kline	26	b Benaud	5
C.G. de V. Burger	lbw b Kline	3	(8) not out	37
P.R. Carlstein	c and b Kline	32	(9) lbw b Benaud	1
H.J. Tayfield	c Burke b Kline	66	(5) c Grout b Davidson	2
P.S. Heine	lbw b Benaud	3	lbw b Benaud	15
N.A.T. Adcock	not out	3	b Davidson	0
Extras	(B 4, LB 5, NB 2)	11	(B 2, LB 2)	4
Total		**214**		**144**

AUSTRALIA

C.C. McDonald	c Waite b Adcock	58	c Tayfield b Adcock	4
J.W. Burke	c Endean b Adcock	8		
R.N. Harvey	lbw b Heine	15	c and b Tayfield	22
I.D. Craig*	c Endean b Tayfield	17		
R. Benaud	c and b Goddard	43	(4) not out	6
R.B. Simpson	c Carlstein b Tayfield	23		
K.D. Mackay	not out	77		
A.K. Davidson	lbw b Heine	4		
A.T.W. Grout†	c Endean b Goddard	25	(2) not out	35
I. Meckiff	c Waite b Heine	8		
L.F. Kline	c Goddard b Tayfield	0		
Extras	(B 2, LB 4, NB 7)	13	(B 1)	1
Total		**291**	(2 wickets)	**68**

AUSTRALIA	O	M	R	W	O	M	R	W
Davidson	20	6	44	4	26·1	8	38	5
Meckiff	18	4	76	1	16	8	20	0
Benaud	12	2	34	1	33	14	82	5
Mackay	11	3	16	0				
Kline	13·6	3	33	4				
SOUTH AFRICA								
Heine	30	3	68	3	3	0	12	0
Adcock	24	1	81	2	4	0	18	1
Goddard	23	9	48	2	1	0	8	0
Tayfield	30·3	12	81	3	4	1	25	1
Van Ryneveld					0·4	0	4	0

FALL OF WICKETS

Wkt	SA 1st	A 1st	SA 2nd	A 2nd
1st	28	13	55	4
2nd	30	37	55	53
3rd	36	124	63	–
4th	57	145	63	–
5th	86	194	70	–
6th	96	199	70	–
7th	105	239	97	–
8th	191	265	99	–
9th	198	278	131	–
10th	214	291	144	–

Umpires: V. Costello (5) and W. Marais (5).

Close: 1st day – SA(1) 214 all out; 2nd – A(1) 208-6 (Mackay 40, Grout 2); 3rd – SA(2) 68-4 (Tayfield 0, Van Ryneveld 5).

WEST INDIES v PAKISTAN 1957–58 (1st Test)

Played at Kensington Oval, Bridgetown, Barbados, on 17, 18, 20, 21, 22, 23 January.
Toss: West Indies. Result: MATCH DRAWN.
Debuts: West Indies – E. St E. Atkinson, C.C. Hunte; Pakistan – Haseeb Ahsan, Nasim-ul-Ghani,
Saeed Ahmed.

In the first meeting of these teams, Nasim-ul-Ghani, aged 16 years 248 days, became the youngest Test player
so far. Hanif, in what remains the longest first-class innings (16 hours 10 minutes), compiled the then
second-highest score in Test cricket. Hutton had scored 27 more runs in 173 fewer minutes in 1938. Hanif shared
in four century-partnerships during the innings which was, until 1984-85, Pakistan's highest in all Test matches.
It remains the highest second innings total and the highest total after following on in Test cricket; it is also the
longest Test innings – 16 hours 53 minutes. Hunte scored a hundred on debut.

WEST INDIES

C.C. Hunte	c Imtiaz b Fazal	142	not out	11
R.B. Kanhai	c Mathias b Fazal	27	not out	17
G. St A. Sobers	c Mathias b Mahmood	52		
E. de C. Weekes	c Imtiaz b Mahmood	197		
C.L. Walcott	c Mathias b Kardar	43		
O.G. Smith	c Mathias b Alimuddin	78		
D. St E. Atkinson	b Mahmood	4		
E. St E. Atkinson	b Fazal	0		
F.C.M. Alexander*†	b Mahmood	9		
A.L. Valentine	not out	5		
R. Gilchrist	did not bat			
Extras	(B 9, LB 4, W 3, NB 6)	22		
Total	(9 wickets declared)	**579**	(0 wickets)	**28**

PAKISTAN

Hanif Mohammad	b E. St E. Atkinson	17	c Alexander b D. St E. Atkinson	337
Imtiaz Ahmed†	lbw b Gilchrist	20	lbw b Gilchrist	91
Alimuddin	c Weekes b Gilchrist	3	c Alexander b Sobers	37
Saeed Ahmed	st Alexander b Smith	13	c Alexander b Smith	65
Wazir Mohammad	lbw b Valentine	4	c Alexander b E. St E. Atkinson	35
W. Mathias	c Alexander b Smith	17	lbw b E. St E. Atkinson	17
A.H. Kardar*	c D. St E. Atkinson b Smith	4	not out	23
Fazal Mahmood	b Gilchrist	4	b Valentine	19
Nasim-ul-Ghani	run out	11	b Valentine	0
Mahmood Hussain	b Gilchrist	3	not out	0
Haseeb Ahsan	not out	1		
Extras	(B 4, LB 5)	9	(B 19, LB 7, NB 7)	33
Total		**106**	(8 wickets declared)	**657**

PAKISTAN	O	M	R	W	O	M	R	W	FALL OF WICKETS				
										WI	P	P	WI
Fazal	62	21	145	3	2	1	3	0	Wkt	1st	1st	2nd	2nd
Mahmood Hussain	41·2	4	153	4					1st	122	35	152	–
Kardar	32	4	107	1	3	1	13	0	2nd	209	39	264	–
Haseeb	21	0	84	0					3rd	266	44	418	–
Nasim	14	1	51	0					4th	356	53	539	–
Alimuddin	2	0	17	1					5th	541	81	598	–
Hanif					3	1	10	0	6th	551	84	626	–
Saeed					2	2	0	0	7th	556	91	649	–
Wazir					1	0	2	0	8th	570	93	649	–
WEST INDIES									9th	579	96	–	–
Gilchrist	15	4	32	4	41	5	121	1	10th	–	106	–	–
E. St E. Atkinson	8	0	27	1	49	5	136	2					
Smith	13	4	23	3	61	30	93	1					
Valentine	6·2	1	15	1	39	8	109	2					
D. St E. Atkinson					62	35	61	1					
Sobers					57	25	94	1					
Walcott					10	5	10	0					

Umpires: H.B. de C. Jordan (5) and J.H. Walcott (4).

Close: 1st day – WI(1) 266-2 (Hunte 142, Weekes 40); 2nd – P(1) 6-0 (Hanif 5, Imtiaz 1); 3rd – P(2) 162-1
(Hanif 61, Alimuddin 1); 4th – P(2) 239-2 (Hanif 161, Saeed 26); 5th – P(2) 525-3 (Hanif 270, Wazir 31).

WEST INDIES v PAKISTAN 1957–58 (2nd Test)

Played at Queen's Park Oval, Port-of-Spain, Trinidad, on 5, 6, 7, 8, 10, 11 February.
Toss: West Indies.   Result: WEST INDIES won by 120 runs.
Debuts: West Indies – L.R. Gibbs, E.D.A. St J. McMorris, I.S. Madray.

West Indies gained the first victory in this new series. Waqar Hassan was the first of 309 wickets to fall to the off-spin of Gibbs. Fazal Mahmood set the present Pakistan record by bowling 606 balls in the match.

WEST INDIES

C.C. Hunte	c Imtiaz b Fazal	8	c Kardar b Nasim	37
E.D.A. St J. McMorris	b Kardar	13	lbw b Fazal	16
G. St A. Sobers	b Nasim	52	(6) lbw b Fazal	80
E. de C. Weekes	run out	78	(5) b Nasim	24
R.B. Kanhai	c Mathias b Mahmood	96	(3) c Mathias b Mahmood	5
O.G. Smith	c Kardar b Mahmood	41	(7) c Waqar b Fazal	51
F.C.M. Alexander*†	c Imtiaz b Nasim	26	(4) run out	57
I.S. Madray	lbw b Fazal	1	lbw b Mahmood	0
L.R. Gibbs	c Kardar b Nasim	2	b Nasim	22
R. Gilchrist	run out	0	b Fazal	7
D.T. Dewdney	not out	0	not out	5
Extras	(B 5, LB 2, NB 1)	8	(B 4, LB 2, NB 2)	8
Total		**325**		**312**

PAKISTAN

Hanif Mohammad	c Gibbs b Smith	30	c Sobers b Gilchrist	81
Alimuddin	b Gilchrist	9	b Gilchrist	0
Imtiaz Ahmed†	lbw b Smith	39	(4) b Sobers	18
Saeed Ahmed	lbw b Smith	11	(3) c Alexander b Sobers	64
W. Mathias	b Dewdney	73	(6) c Weekes b Dewdney	10
Nasim-ul-Ghani	c Alexander b Gilchrist	0	(11) b Gibbs	0
Wazir Mohammad	c Weekes b Gilchrist	0	(5) b Gilchrist	0
Waqar Hassan	c Weekes b Gibbs	17	(7) st Alexander b Gibbs	28
A.H. Kardar*	st Alexander b Smith	4	b Gibbs	24
Fazal Mahmood	c Madray b Sobers	60	(8) b Gilchrist	0
Mahmood Hussain	not out	19	(10) not out	1
Extras	(B 13, LB 5, NB 2)	20	(B 1, LB 5, NB 3)	9
Total		**282**		**235**

PAKISTAN	O	M	R	W	O	M	R	W		FALL OF WICKETS			
Mahmood Hussain	36	6	128	2	37	4	132	2		WI	P	WI	P
Fazal	50	24	76	2	51	21	89	4	*Wkt*	*1st*	*1st*	*2nd*	*2nd*
Kardar	32	13	71	1	9	2	19	0	1st	11	21	38	1
Nasim	13·1	3	42	3	33·2	11	64	3	2nd	51	66	51	131
									3rd	129	90	71	159
WEST INDIES									4th	177	91	105	161
Gilchrist	21	4	67	3	19	5	61	4	5th	276	104	206	180
Dewdney	17	3	50	1	18	8	29	1	6th	302	116	255	180
Smith	25	7	71	4	19	7	31	0	7th	307	150	277	180
Sobers	5·3	1	14	1	22	8	41	2	8th	325	155	277	222
Madray	6	0	22	0	13	5	32	0	9th	325	226	288	235
Gibbs	12	2	38	1	13·5	6	32	3	10th	325	282	312	235

Umpires: E.N. Lee Kow (6) and E.L. Lloyd (1).

Close: 1st day – WI(1) 236-4 (Kanhai 60, Smith 19); 2nd – P(1) 91-4 (Mathias 0, Nasim 0); 3rd – WI(2) 56-2 (Hunte 34, Alexander 0); 4th – WI(2) 255-6 (Smith 31); 5th – P(2) 161-3 (Hanif 73, Wazir 0).

WEST INDIES v PAKISTAN 1957–58 (3rd Test)

Played at Sabina Park, Kingston, Jamaica, on 26, 27, 28, February, 1, 3, 4 March.
Toss: Pakistan.   Result: WEST INDIES won by an innings and 174 runs.
Debuts: Nil.

Garfield St Aubrun Sobers, aged 21, recorded the highest score in Test cricket, hitting 38 fours and batting for 10 hours 14 minutes (3 hours 3 minutes less than Hutton, whose record he beat by one run). His stand of 446 with Hunte for the second wicket was then the second-highest for any wicket in Test matches. They were the fourth pair to bat throughout a complete day's Test cricket. It was Sobers' first three-figure score in a Test. West Indies compiled the third-highest total in a Test against an attack containing only two uninjured specialist bowlers. The retirement of Nasim (fractured thumb) and Hussain (pulled thigh muscle) led to Fazal (most overs) and Khan (most runs conceded) setting the present Pakistan records.

PAKISTAN

Hanif Mohammad	c Alexander b Gilchrist	3	b Gilchrist		13
Imtiaz Ahmed†	c Alexander b Gilchrist	122	lbw b Dewdney		0
Saeed Ahmed	c Weekes b Smith	52	c Gilchrist b Gibbs		44
W. Mathias	b Dewdney	77	c Alexander b Atkinson		19
Alimuddin	c Alexander b Atkinson	15	b Gibbs		30
A.H. Kardar*	c Sobers b Atkinson	15	(7) lbw b Dewdney		57
Wazir Mohammad	c Walcott b Dewdney	2	(6) lbw b Atkinson		106
Fazal Mahmood	c Alexander b Atkinson	6	c Alexander b Atkinson		0
Nasim-ul-Ghani	b Atkinson	5	absent hurt		–
Mahmood Hussain	b Atkinson	20	absent hurt		–
Khan Mohammad	not out	3	(9) not out		0
Extras	(LB 5, NB 3)	8	(B 16, LB 3)		19
Total		**328**			**288**

WEST INDIES

C.C. Hunte	run out	260
R.B. Kanhai	c Imtiaz b Fazal	25
G. St A. Sobers	not out	365
E. de C.Weekes	c Hanif b Fazal	39
C.L. Walcott	not out	88
O.G. Smith	)	
F.C.M. Alexander*†	)	
L.R. Gibbs	) did not bat	
E. St E. Atkinson	)	
R. Gilchrist	)	
D.T. Dewdney·	)	
Extras	(B 2, LB 7, W 4)	13
Total	(3 wickets declared)	**790**

WEST INDIES	O	M	R	W	O	M	R	W
Gilchrist	25	3	106	2	12	3	65	1
Dewdney	26	4	88	2	19·3	2	51	2
Atkinson	21	7	42	5	18	6	36	3
Gibbs	7	0	32	0	21	6	46	2
Smith	18	3	39	1	8	2	20	0
Sobers	5	1	13	0	15	4	41	0
Weekes					3	1	10	0

PAKISTAN	O	M	R	W
Mahmood Hussain	0·5	0	2	0
Fazal	85·2	20	247	2
Khan	54	5	259	0
Nasim	15	3	39	0
Kardar	37	2	141	0
Mathias	4	0	20	0
Alimuddin	4	0	34	0
Hanif	2	0	11	0
Saeed	6	0	24	0

FALL OF WICKETS

	P	WI	P
Wkt	1st	1st	2nd
1st	4	87	8
2nd	122	533	20
3rd	223	602	57
4th	249	–	105
5th	287	–	120
6th	291	–	286
7th	299	–	286
8th	301	–	288
9th	317	–	–
10th	328	–	–

Umpires: P. Burke (5) and T.A. Ewart (7).

Close: 1st day – P(1) 274-4 (Mathias 70, Kardar 5); 2nd – WI(1) 147-1 (Hunte 100, Sobers 20); 3rd – WI(1) 504-1 (Hunte 242, Sobers 228); 4th – WI(1) 790-3 dec; 5th – P(2) 273-5 (Wazir 102, Kardar 46).

WEST INDIES v PAKISTAN 1957–58 (4th Test)

Played at Bourda, Georgetown, British Guiana, on 13, 14, 15, 17, 18, 19 March.
Toss: Pakistan.   Result: WEST INDIES won by eight wickets.
Debuts: Pakistan – S.F. Rehman.

Sobers scored a hundred in each innings to bring his aggregate in his last three innings against Pakistan to 599 runs for once out. He put on 269 for the second wicket with Walcott. Fazal, struck on the knee while batting, broke down after four overs in the final innings. The match aggregate of 1,453 runs is the highest for this series.

PAKISTAN

Alimuddin	b Smith	30	lbw b Smith		41
Imtiaz Ahmed†	c Walcott b Smith	32	b Gibbs		7
Saeed Ahmed	b Gibbs	150	run out		12
Hanif Mohammad	b Gilchrist	79	c Madray b Gilchrist		14
Wazir Mohammad	lbw b Gilchrist	7	not out		97
W. Mathias	b Gilchrist	16	lbw b Gibbs		18
A.H. Kardar*	b Smith	26	c Smith b Gibbs		56
Fazal Mahmood	c Gibbs b Gilchrist	39	c Alexander b Gibbs		31
S.F. Rehman	b Gibbs	8	run out		2
Nasim-ul-Ghani	b Dewdney	13	c and b Gibbs		22
Haseeb Ahsan	not out	0	b Gilchrist		0
Extras	(B 2, LB 2, W 2, NB 2)	8	(B 8, LB 4, W 1, NB 5)		18
Total		**408**			**318**

WEST INDIES

C.C. Hunte	b Fazal	5	b Rehman		114
G. St A. Sobers	b Nasim	125	(3) not out		109
C.L. Walcott	run out	145			
E. de C. Weekes	c Rehman b Nasim	41	not out		16
O.G. Smith	c sub (Ijaz Butt) b Haseeb	27			
R.B. Kanhai	st Imtiaz b Nasim	24	(2) c Mathias b Haseeb		62
F.C.M. Alexander*†	c Mathias b Haseeb	2			
I.S. Madray	c Fazal b Nasim	2			
L.R. Gibbs	run out	11			
R. Gilchrist	c Alimuddin b Nasim	12			
D.T. Dewdney	not out	0			
Extras	(B 4, LB 9, W 1, NB 2)	16	(B 12, LB 1, W 2, NB 1)		16
Total		**410**	(2 wickets)		**317**

WEST INDIES	O	M	R	W	O	M	R	W		FALL OF WICKETS			
Gilchrist	28	3	102	4	19·1	3	66	2		P	WI	P	WI
Dewdney	16·1	1	79	1	11	3	30	0	*Wkt*	*1st*	*1st*	*2nd*	*2nd*
Gibbs	30	12	56	2	42	12	80	5	1st	60	11	22	125
Sobers	16	2	47	0	17	6	32	0	2nd	69	280	44	260
Smith	25	2	74	3	44	12	80	1	3rd	205	297	62	–
Madray	10	0	42	0	6	1	12	0	4th	221	336	102	–
									5th	249	361	130	–
PAKISTAN									6th	337	370	224	–
Fazal	25	5	74	1	4	2	12	0	7th	349	384	263	–
Kardar	6	1	24	0	2	0	10	0	8th	365	389	265	–
Nasim	41·4	11	116	5	28	4	76	0	9th	408	410	304	–
Haseeb	44	10	124	2	41	7	151	1	10th	408	410	318	–
Rehman	17	1	56	0	17	2	43	1					
Wazir					1	0	8	0					
Saeed					0·1	0	1	0					

Umpires: E.S. Gillette (5) and C.P. Kippins (1).

Close: 1st day – P(1) 259-5 (Saeed 83, Kardar 7); 2nd – WI(1) 164-1 (Sobers 63, Walcott 87); 3rd – WI(1) 391-8 (Gibbs 6, Gilchrist 0); 4th – P(2) 196-5 (Wazir 54, Kardar 35); 5th – WI(2) 99-0 (Hunte 39, Kanhai 52).

WEST INDIES v PAKISTAN 1957–58 (5th Test)

Played at Queen's Park Oval, Port-of-Spain, Trinidad, on 26, 27, 28, 29, 31 March.
Toss: West Indies.   Result: PAKISTAN won by an innings and 1 run.
Debuts: West Indies – J. Taylor.

Pakistan completed their first win against West Indies before lunch on the penultimate day. Gilchrist sprained an ankle early in the Pakistan innings but his fellow fast bowler, Taylor, took five wickets in his first match. Wazir shared in two record partnerships for this series: 169 for the third wicket with Saeed and 154 for the fourth with Hanif. Nasim's career-best analysis of 6 for 67 was then the best for Pakistan in the Caribbean. Hunte was the first West Indies batsman to be out to the first ball of a Test match.

WEST INDIES

C.C. Hunte	c Hanif b Fazal	0	c Fazal b Nasim		45
R.B. Kanhai	c Imtiaz b Khan	0	b Haseeb		43
G. St A. Sobers	c Kardar b Fazal	14	b Nasim		27
E. de C. Weekes	c Imtiaz b Khan	51	b Haseeb		9
C.L. Walcott	st Imtiaz b Nasim	47	c Wazir b Nasim		62
O.G. Smith	lbw b Fazal	86	st Imtiaz b Nasim		0
F.C.M. Alexander*†	b Fazal	38	b Nasim		1
E. St E. Atkinson	c Hanif b Fazal	0	b Fazal		19
L.R. Gibbs	lbw b Fazal	14	c Mathias b Fazal		2
J. Taylor	not out	4	st Imtiaz b Nasim		0
R. Gilchrist	c Kardar b Nasim	9	not out		2
Extras	(B 5)	5	(B 12, LB 4, NB 1)		17
Total		**268**			**227**

PAKISTAN

Imtiaz Ahmed†	b Taylor	15
Alimuddin	b Gibbs	21
Saeed Ahmed	c Alexander b Taylor	97
Wazir Mohammad	b Gibbs	189
Hanif Mohammad	b Taylor	54
W. Mathias	b Atkinson	4
A.H. Kardar*	c Walcott b Gibbs	44
Fazal Mahmood	b Taylor	0
Nasim-ul-Ghani	c Alexander b Gibbs	15
Khan Mohammad	not out	26
Haseeb Ahsan	b Taylor	2
Extras	(B 14, LB 10, W 1, NB 4)	29
Total		**496**

PAKISTAN	O	M	R	W	O	M	R	W
Fazal	32	10	83	6	9	1	35	2
Khan	25	8	79	2	2	0	19	0
Nasim	22·1	6	53	2	30·5	9	67	6
Haseeb	14	2	48	0	24	3	89	2
WEST INDIES								
Gilchrist	7	2	16	0				
Taylor	36·5	6	109	5				
Atkinson	31	3	66	1				
Smith	23	4	63	0				
Gibbs	41	9	108	4				
Sobers	34	6	95	0				
Walcott	2	0	6	0				
Weekes	3	1	4	0				

FALL OF WICKETS

	WI	P	WI
Wkt	*1st*	*1st*	*2nd*
1st	0	22	71
2nd	2	69	115
3rd	48	238	130
4th	78	392	140
5th	141	407	141
6th	219	407	162
7th	219	408	219
8th	249	463	223
9th	254	478	225
10th	268	496	227

Umpires: E.L. Lloyd (2) and G. Williams (1).

Close: 1st day – WI(1) 234-7 (Alexander 28, Gibbs 4); 2nd – P(1) 186-2 (Saeed 78, Wazir 56); 3rd – P(1) 407-4 (Hanif 54, Mathias 4); 4th – WI(2) 153-5 (Walcott 16, Alexander 1).

ENGLAND v NEW ZEALAND 1958 (1st Test)

Played at Edgbaston, Birmingham, on 5, 6, 7, 9 June.
Toss: England.   Result: ENGLAND won by 205 runs.
Debuts: England – M.J.K. Smith; New Zealand – J.W. D'Arcy, T. Meale, W.R. Playle.

England won at 2.48 pm on the fourth day. Harford was struck in the face by a lifting ball from Trueman in the second innings and retired hurt for a time; resuming at 93, he failed to add to his score. Richardson scored the last of his five Test hundreds in his first match against New Zealand.

ENGLAND

P.E. Richardson	lbw b MacGibbon	4	c Cave b MacGibbon	100
M.J.K. Smith	lbw b MacGibbon	0	c Petrie b MacGibbon	7
T.W. Graveney	c Alabaster b Hayes	7	c Petrie b Cave	19
P.B.H. May*	c Petrie b MacGibbon	84	c Petrie b MacGibbon	11
M.C. Cowdrey	b MacGibbon	81	c Reid b Hayes	70
T.E. Bailey	c Petrie b Alabaster	2	not out	6
T.G. Evans†	c Petrie b MacGibbon	2	c Reid b Cave	0
G.A.R. Lock	lbw b Alabaster	4		
F.S. Trueman	b Alabaster	0		
J.C. Laker	not out	11		
P.J. Loader	b Alabaster	17		
Extras	(LB 3, W 4, NB 2)	9	(B 1, LB 1)	2
Total		**221**	(6 wickets declared)	**215**

NEW ZEALAND

L.S.M. Miller	lbw b Trueman	7	b Trueman	8
J.W. D'Arcy	c Evans b Trueman	19	c Trueman b Loader	25
N.S. Harford	b Bailey	9	(4) c Graveney b Loader	23
J.R. Reid*	b Bailey	7	(6) b Bailey	13
W.R. Playle	b Trueman	4	(3) c Bailey b Loader	8
T. Meale	lbw b Trueman	7	(5) c Smith b Lock	10
A.R. MacGibbon	c Evans b Laker	5	(8) c Cowdrey b Laker	26
E.C. Petrie†	lbw b Loader	1	(10) not out	5
J.C. Alabaster	b Trueman	9	c Laker b Lock	11
H.B. Cave	not out	12	(7) b Bailey	1
J.A. Hayes	run out	14	c Bailey b Lock	5
Extras		–	(LB 1, W 1)	2
Total		**94**		**137**

NEW ZEALAND	O	M	R	W	O	M	R	W		FALL OF WICKETS			
Hayes	15	2	57	1	20	3	51	1		E	NZ	E	NZ
MacGibbon	27	11	64	5	24	8	41	3	*Wkt*	*1st*	*1st*	*2nd*	*2nd*
Cave	12	2	29	0	28·2	9	70	2	1st	4	12	24	19
Reid	6	3	16	0	9	2	18	0	2nd	11	21	71	42
Alabaster	15·5	4	46	4	15	7	33	0	3rd	29	39	94	49
ENGLAND									4th	150	43	198	64
									5th	153	46	214	93
Trueman	21	8	31	5	17	5	33	1	6th	172	54	215	94
Loader	21·3	6	37	1	23	11	40	3	7th	185	59	–	95
Bailey	20	9	17	2	20	9	23	2	8th	191	67	–	123
Lock	2	2	0	0	8·3	3	25	3	9th	191	68	–	131
Laker	5	2	9	1	9	4	14	1	10th	221	94	–	137

Umpires: J.S. Buller (5) and C.S. Elliott (3).

Close: 1st day – NZ(1) 41-3 (D'Arcy 18, Playle 0); 2nd – E(2) 131-3 (Richardson 71, Cowdrey 21); 3rd – NZ(2) 69-4 (Harford 15, Reid 1).

ENGLAND v NEW ZEALAND 1958 (2nd Test)

Played at Lord's, London, on 19, 20, 21 June.
Toss: England.   Result: ENGLAND won by an innings and 148 runs.
Debuts: Nil.

New Zealand, trapped on a pitch affected by rain after England's innings, were dismissed in 110 minutes for their lowest total in England; it was then the lowest total in a Lord's Test. The match, involving only $11\frac{1}{2}$ hours of play, ended at 3.30 on the third afternoon. Flags were flown at half-mast on the first day in tribute to the memory of D.R. Jardine who had died in Switzerland.

ENGLAND

P.E. Richardson	c Petrie b Hayes	36
M.J.K. Smith	c Petrie b Hayes	47
T.W. Graveney	c Petrie b Alabaster	37
P.B.H. May*	c Alabaster b MacGibbon	19
M.C. Cowdrey	b Hayes	65
T.E. Bailey	c Petrie b Reid	17
T.G. Evans†	c Hayes b MacGibbon	11
G.A.R. Lock	not out	23
F.S. Trueman	b Hayes	8
J.C. Laker	c Blair b MacGibbon	1
P.J. Loader	c Playle b MacGibbon	4
Extras	(LB 1)	1
Total		**269**

NEW ZEALAND

L.S.M. Miller	lbw b Trueman	4	c Trueman b Loader	0
J.W. D'Arcy	c Trueman b Laker	14	c Bailey b Trueman	33
W.R. Playle	c Graveney b Laker	1	b Loader	3
N.S. Harford	c and b Laker	0	c May b Lock	3
J.R. Reid*	c Loader b Lock	6	c Cowdrey b Trueman	5
B. Sutcliffe	b Lock	18	b Bailey	0
A.R. MacGibbon	c May b Lock	2	c May b Lock	7
J.C. Alabaster	c and b Lock	0	b Laker	5
E.C. Petrie†	c Trueman b Laker	0	not out	4
R.W. Blair	not out	0	b Lock	0
J.A. Hayes	c Cowdrey b Lock	1	c and b Lock	14
Extras	(LB 1)	1		–
Total		**47**		**74**

NEW ZEALAND	O	M	R	W	O	M	R	W	FALL OF WICKETS			
										E	NZ	NZ
Hayes	22	5	36	4					*Wkt*	*1st*	*1st*	*2nd*
MacGibbon	36·4	11	86	4					1st	54	4	11
Blair	25	6	57	0					2nd	113	12	21
Reid	24	12	41	1					3rd	139	12	34
Alabaster	16	6	48	1					4th	141	19	41
ENGLAND									5th	201	25	44
Trueman	4	1	6	1	11	6	24	2	6th	222	31	44
Loader	4	2	6	0	9	6	7	2	7th	237	34	56
Laker	12	6	13	4	13	8	24	1	8th	259	46	56
Lock	11·3	7	17	5	12·3	8	12	4	9th	260	46	56
Bailey	1	0	4	0	5	1	7	1	10th	269	47	74

Umpires: D. Davies (22) and C.S. Elliott (4).

Close: 1st day – E(1) 237-7 (Lock 4); 2nd – NZ(2) 0-0 (Miller 0, D'Arcy 0).

ENGLAND v NEW ZEALAND 1958 (3rd Test)

Played at Headingley, Leeds, on 3 (*no play*), 4 (*no play*), 5, 7, 8 July.
Toss: New Zealand.   Result: ENGLAND won by an innings and 71 runs.
Debuts: England – C.A. Milton; New Zealand – J.T. Sparling.

England again won inside three days, there being no play on the first two. They omitted Richardson to try out possible opening partners for him on the forthcoming tour to Australia. Milton (Association Football) opened with his fellow double-international Smith (Rugby Union) and became the first Gloucestershire player since W.G. Grace in 1880 to score a hundred for England in his first Test. He was the first England player to be on the field throughout a Test match and was alone in achieving this feat on debut until 1986-87. Lock's match analysis of 11 for 65 was then the best recorded in any Test against New Zealand. Playle batted 194 minutes for 18 runs, including 63 minutes without scoring. This was the second of only three instances, all by England, of a side winning a Test after losing only two wickets in the match (also *Tests No. 154 and 741*).

NEW ZEALAND

L.S.M. Miller	c Smith b Laker	26	lbw b Lock		18
J.W. D'Arcy	c Smith b Trueman	11	b Lock		6
N.S. Harford	c Cowdrey b Laker	0	lbw b Lock		0
B. Sutcliffe	b Laker	6	lbw b Lock		0
J.R. Reid*	b Lock	3	c Trueman b Laker		13
W.R. Playle	c Milton b Lock	0	b Laker		18
A.R. MacGibbon	b Laker	3	lbw b Lock		39
J.T. Sparling	not out	9	c May b Lock		18
E.C. Petrie†	c Cowdrey b Lock	5	b Lock		3
H.B. Cave	c Milton b Laker	2	c Cowdrey b Laker		2
J.A. Hayes	c Evans b Lock	1	not out		0
Extras	(LB 1)	1	(B 6, LB 6)		12
Total		**67**			**129**

ENGLAND

M.J.K. Smith	c Reid b MacGibbon	3
C.A. Milton	not out	104
T.W. Graveney	c and b Sparling	31
P.B.H. May*	not out	113
M.C. Cowdrey	)	
T.E. Bailey	)	
T.G. Evans†	)	
G.A.R. Lock	) did not bat	
F.S. Trueman	)	
J.C. Laker	)	
P.J. Loader	)	
Extras	(B 5, LB 8, W 1, NB 2)	16
Total	(2 wickets declared)	**267**

ENGLAND	O	M	R	W	O	M	R	W		FALL OF WICKETS		
Trueman	11	5	18	1	14	6	22	0		NZ	E	NZ
Loader	5	2	10	0	13	7	14	0	Wkt	1st	1st	2nd
Bailey	3	0	7	0	3	2	3	0	1st	37	7	23
Laker	22	11	17	5	36	23	27	3	2nd	37	73	23
Lock	18·1	13	14	4	35·2	20	51	7	3rd	37	–	24
									4th	40	–	32
NEW ZEALAND									5th	46	–	42
Hayes	13	4	30	0					6th	46	–	88
MacGibbon	27	8	47	1					7th	49	–	121
Reid	26	7	54	0					8th	59	–	124
Sparling	23	2	78	1					9th	66	–	129
Cave	13	4	42	0					10th	67	–	129

Umpires: J.S. Buller (6) and F.S. Lee (20).

Close: 1st day – no play; 2nd – no play; 3rd – E(1) 14-1 (Milton 5, Graveney 4); 4th – NZ(2) 32-3 (Sutcliffe 0, Reid 4).

ENGLAND v NEW ZEALAND 1958 (4th Test)

Played at Old Trafford, Manchester, on 24, 25, 26, 28, 29 July.
Toss: New Zealand.   Result: ENGLAND won by an innings and 13 runs.
Debuts: England – E.R. Dexter, R. Illingworth, R. Subba Row.

England became the first team to win the first four Tests of a rubber in England – in spite of the loss of over eight hours to rain on the third and fourth days. Reid kept wicket on Friday and Saturday after Petrie had edged a hook on to his left ear while batting against Trueman. Lock took his 100th Test wicket when he dismissed Sparling and went on to record his best analysis for England.

NEW ZEALAND

B. Sutcliffe	b Statham	41	b Statham		28
J.W. D'Arcy	lbw b Trueman	1	c Subba Row b Lock		8
N.S. Harford	lbw b Statham	2	b Illingworth		4
J.R. Reid*	c Trueman b Lock	14	c Watson b Lock		8
W.R. Playle	lbw b Illingworth	15	lbw b Lock		1
A.R. MacGibbon	c Evans b Statham	66	lbw b Lock		1
J.T. Sparling	c Evans b Statham	50	c and b Lock		2
E.C. Petrie†	retired hurt	45	c Statham b Illingworth		9
A.M. Moir	not out	21	c Evans b Lock		12
J.A. Hayes	b Trueman	4	not out		5
R.W. Blair	b Trueman	2	b Lock		0
Extras	(B 4, LB 2)	6	(B 5, LB 2)		7
Total		**267**			**85**

ENGLAND

P.E. Richardson	st Reid b Sparling	74
W. Watson	c MacGibbon b Moir	66
T.W. Graveney	c sub (J.C. Alabaster)	
	b MacGibbon	25
P.B.H. May*	c Playle b MacGibbon	101
R. Subba Row	c Petrie b Blair	9
E.R. Dexter	lbw b Reid	52
T.G. Evans†	c Blair b Reid	3
R. Illingworth	not out	3
G.A.R. Lock	lbw b MacGibbon	7
F.S. Trueman	b Reid	5
J.B. Statham	did not bat	
Extras	(B 13, LB 4, W 1, NB 2)	20
Total	(9 wickets declared)	**365**

ENGLAND	O	M	R	W	O	M	R	W		FALL OF WICKETS		
Trueman	29·5	4	67	3	2	1	11	0		NZ	E	NZ
Statham	33	10	71	4	9	4	12	1	*Wkt*	*1st*	*1st*	*2nd*
Dexter	5	0	23	0					1st	15	126	36
Lock	33	12	61	1	24	11	35	7	2nd	22	180	36
Illingworth	28	9	39	1	17	9	20	2	3rd	62	193	46
NEW ZEALAND									4th	62	248	49
Hayes	19	4	51	0					5th	117	330	49
MacGibbon	34	8	86	3					6th	166	337	51
Blair	27	5	68	1					7th	227	351	60
Moir	17	3	47	1					8th	257	360	78
Sparling	21	7	46	1					9th	267	365	80
Reid	11·3	2	47	3					10th	–	–	85

Umpires: D.E. Davies (6) and W.E. Phillipson (1).

Close: 1st day – NZ(1) 220-6 (Sparling 45, Petrie 32); 2nd – E(1) 192-2 (Graveney 25, May 10); 3rd – E(1) 206-3 (May 23, Subba Row 1); 4th – NZ(2) 30-0 (Sutcliffe 28, D'Arcy 2).

ENGLAND v NEW ZEALAND 1958 (5th Test)

Played at Kennington Oval, London, on 21, 22, 23 (*no play*), 25 (*no play*), 26 August.
Toss: New Zealand.   Result: MATCH DRAWN.
Debuts: Nil.

Rain frustrated England's attempt to win all five Tests of a rubber in England for the first time – only 12 hours of play were possible over the five days, the second of which produced just five maiden overs. Sparling ducked into a short-pitched ball from Trueman which bounced lower than he expected and he took no further part in the match. Lock's figures of 34 wickets at 7·47 runs each for the rubber are easily the record for this series. Both Moir and Trueman recorded their highest scores in Test cricket, England's fiery fast bowler clubbing three sixes off the New Zealand leg-spinner.

NEW ZEALAND

L.S.M. Miller	c Lock b Laker	25	c Evans b Statham		4
J.W. D'Arcy	c Milton b Bailey	9	c and b Lock		10
T. Meale	c Lock b Trueman	1	c Cowdrey b Laker		3
B. Sutcliffe	c Watson b Trueman	11	not out		18
J.R. Reid*	b Lock	27	not out		51
W.R. Playle	b Statham	6			
A.R. MacGibbon	b Bailey	26			
J.T. Sparling	retired hurt	0			
E.C. Petrie†	c Milton b Lock	8			
A.M. Moir	not out	41			
R.W. Blair	run out	3			
Extras	(LB 4)	4	(B 2, LB 3)		5
Total		**161**	(3 wickets)		**91**

ENGLAND

P.E. Richardson	b Blair	28
C.A. Milton	lbw b MacGibbon	36
W. Watson	b MacGibbon	10
P.B.H. May*	c Petrie b Blair	9
M.C. Cowdrey	c Playle b Reid	25
T.E. Bailey	c Petrie b MacGibbon	14
T.G. Evans†	c Petrie b MacGibbon	12
G.A.R. Lock	c Reid b Moir	25
J.C. Laker	c Blair b Reid	15
F.S. Trueman	not out	39
J.B. Statham	did not bat	
Extras	(B 2, LB 4)	6
Total	(9 wickets declared)	**219**

ENGLAND	O	M	R	W	O	M	R	W
Trueman	16	3	41	2	6	5	3	0
Statham	18	6	21	1	7	0	26	1
Bailey	14	3	32	2				
Laker	14	3	44	1	20	10	25	1
Lock	13	6	19	2	18	11	20	1
Milton					4	2	12	0
NEW ZEALAND								
Blair	26	5	85	2				
MacGibbon	27	4	65	4				
Reid	7·5	2	11	2				
Moir	8	1	52	1				

FALL OF WICKETS			
	NZ	E	NZ
Wkt	*1st*	*1st*	*2nd*
1st	19	39	9
2nd	24	62	17
3rd	40	85	21
4th	46	87	–
5th	55	109	–
6th	93	125	–
7th	105	162	–
8th	132	162	–
9th	161	219	–
10th	–	–	–

Umpires: D.E. Davies (7) and F.S. Lee (21).

Close: 1st day – E(1) 30-0 (Richardson 20, Milton 10); 2nd – E(1) 30-0 (Richardson 20, Milton 10); 3rd – no play; 4th – no play.

INDIA v WEST INDIES 1958–59 (1st Test)

Played at Brabourne Stadium, Bombay, on 28, 29, 30 November, 2, 3 December.
Toss: West Indies.   Result: MATCH DRAWN.
Debuts: India – C.G. Borde, G.M. Guard, M.S. Hardikar; West Indies – B.F. Butcher, W.W. Hall.

Sobers and Butcher each had leg injuries and batted with a runner during their unfinished fifth-wicket partnership of 134. Gupte's leg-breaks acquired their hundredth wicket in Test matches. Kanhai's two catches were taken while keeping wicket in the second innings. When India were left $9\frac{1}{2}$ hours in which to score 399 runs for victory, Roy batted 444 minutes for 90. Hardikar took his only Test wicket with his third ball.

WEST INDIES

J.K. Holt	c Tamhane b Ramchand	16	c Hardikar b Guard	24
C.C. Hunte	c Guard b Ramchand	0	c Nadkarni b Guard	10
G. St A. Sobers	c and b Guard	25	not out	142
R.B. Kanhai	lbw b Hardikar	66	c Roy b Gupte	22
O.G. Smith	c Ramchand b Nadkarni	63	c Roy b Gupte	58
B.F. Butcher	lbw b Gupte	28	not out	64
F.C.M. Alexander*†	st Tamhane b Gupte	5		
E. St E. Atkinson	b Gupte	1		
S. Ramadhin	c Nadkarni b Gupte	9		
W.W. Hall	not out	12		
R. Gilchrist	b Nadkarni	1		
Extras	(B 1)	1	(LB 3)	3
Total		**227**	(4 wickets declared)	**323**

INDIA

Pankaj Roy	b Hall	18	c and b Hall	90
N.J. Contractor	c Atkinson b Hall	0	run out	6
P.R. Umrigar*	b Gilchrist	55	b Gilchrist	36
V.L. Manjrekar	c Sobers b Hall	0	c Kanhai b Gilchrist	23
R.G. Nadkarni	b Atkinson	2	c Kanhai b Atkinson	7
G.S. Ramchand	c Alexander b Atkinson	48	not out	67
M.S. Hardikar	lbw b Gilchrist	0	not out	32
C.G. Borde	run out	7		
N.S. Tamhane†	not out	9		
G.M. Guard	b Gilchrist	4		
S.P. Gupte	c Sobers b Gilchrist	1		
Extras	(B 3, LB 5)	8	(B 19, LB 2, NB 7)	28
Total		**152**	(5 wickets)	**289**

INDIA	O	M	R	W	O	M	R	W
Guard	15	7	19	1	17	2	69	2
Ramchand	12	2	31	2	10	3	22	0
Umrigar	3	0	12	0	9	0	22	0
Gupte	33	9	86	4	35	4	111	2
Borde	10	1	29	0	16	3	31	0
Nadkarni	21·1	7	40	2	15	3	29	0
Hardikar	7	5	9	1	10	2	36	0
WEST INDIES								
Gilchrist	23·2	8	39	4	41	13	75	2
Hall	14	4	35	3	30	10	72	1
Atkinson	19	10	21	2	29	11	56	1
Ramadhin	9	0	30	0	11	4	20	0
Sobers	3	0	19	0	3	0	8	0
Smith					18	4	30	0

FALL OF WICKETS

Wkt	WI 1st	I 1st	WI 2nd	I 2nd
1st	2	0	27	27
2nd	36	37	37	88
3rd	50	37	70	136
4th	118	40	189	159
5th	172	120	–	204
6th	200	120	–	–
7th	202	132	–	–
8th	206	138	–	–
9th	226	148	–	–
10th	227	152	–	–

Umpires: J.R. Patel (8) and M.G. Vijayasarathi (11).

Close: 1st day – WI(1) 227 all out; 2nd – I(1) 152 all out; 3rd – WI(2) 253-4 (Sobers 95, Butcher 41); 4th – I(2) 117-2 (Roy 54, Manjrekar 17).

INDIA v WEST INDIES 1958–59 (2nd Test)

Played at Green Park, Kanpur, on 12, 13, 14, 16, 17 December.
Toss: West Indies.   Result: WEST INDIES won by 203 runs.
Debuts: India – V.B. Ranjane; West Indies – J.S. Solomon.

Gupte (leg-breaks) became the first Indian to take nine wickets in an innings of a Test match; he was also the first to accomplish this feat and finish on the losing side. West Indies won with 78 minutes to spare after Hall had taken eleven wickets in his second Test and Sobers had scored his fifth hundred in five matches. Run out for 198 after batting for 340 minutes and hitting 28 fours, Sobers set a sixth-wicket partnership record for this series by adding 163 with Solomon. This match produced the second instance of a tie on first innings at this level (also *Test No. 107*).

WEST INDIES

J.K. Holt	lbw b Gupte	31	c Borde b Ramchand		0
C.C. Hunte	c Borde b Gupte	29	c and b Umrigar		0
G. St A. Sobers	c Hardikar b Gupte	4	(4) run out		198
R.B. Kanhai	b Gupte	0	(3) c Tamhane b Gupte		41
O.G. Smith	c and b Gupte	20	run out		7
B.F. Butcher	b Gupte	2	c Tamhane b Ramchand		60
J.S. Solomon	lbw b Gupte	45	run out		86
F.C.M. Alexander*†	c Hardikar b Gupte	70	not out		45
L.R. Gibbs	b Ranjane	16			
W.W. Hall	c Tamhane b Gupte	0			
J. Taylor	not out	0			
Extras	(B 1, LB 2, NB 2)	5	(LB 6)		6
Total		**222**	(7 wickets declared)		**443**

INDIA

Pankaj Roy	lbw b Sobers	46	run out	45
N.J. Contractor	lbw b Sobers	41	b Taylor	50
P.R. Umrigar	c Holt b Hall	57	c Smith b Hall	34
V.L. Manjrekar	lbw b Taylor	30	run out	31
C.G. Borde	c Alexander b Hall	0	c Alexander b Taylor	13
G.S. Ramchand	c Alexander b Hall	4	b Hall	0
M.S. Hardikar	b Hall	13	b Hall	11
N.S. Tamhane†	c Holt b Hall	0	c Solomon b Hall	20
V.B. Ranjane	b Taylor	3	b Taylor	12
Ghulam Ahmed*	not out	0	b Hall	0
S.P. Gupte	b Hall	0	not out	8
Extras	(LB 17, NB 11)	28	(B 4, LB 1, NB 11)	16
Total		**222**		**240**

INDIA	O	M	R	W	O	M	R	W	FALL OF WICKETS				
										WI	I	WI	I
Ranjane	18	6	35	1					Wkt	1st	1st	2nd	2nd
Ramchand	10	3	22	0	40	6	114	2	1st	55	93	0	99
Gupte	34·3	11	102	9	23	2	121	1	2nd	63	118	0	107
Ghulam Ahmed	10	3	29	0	30	8	81	0	3rd	65	182	73	173
Borde	13	4	29	0	5	0	15	0	4th	74	184	83	178
Umrigar					28	4	96	1	5th	76	191	197	182
Hardikar					1	0	10	0	6th	88	210	360	194
									7th	188	211	443	204
WEST INDIES									8th	220	222	–	227
Hall	28·4	4	50	6	32	12	76	5	9th	222	222	–	227
Taylor	18	7	38	2	30·1	11	68	3	10th	222	222	–	240
Gibbs	21	8	28	0	9	4	33	0					
Sobers	24	4	62	2	21	10	29	0					
Smith	8	1	14	0	6	0	12	0					
Solomon	2	1	2	0	3	2	6	0					

Umpires: Mahomed Yunus (1) and J.R. Patel (9).

Close: 1st day – I(1) 24-0 (Roy 11, Contractor 12); 2nd – I(1) 209-5 (Manjrekar 29, Hardikar 8); 3rd – WI(2) 261-5 (Sobers 136, Solomon 13); 4th – I(2) 76-0 (Roy 31, Contractor 39).

INDIA v WEST INDIES 1958–59 (3rd Test)

Played at Eden Gardens, Calcutta, on 31 December, 1, 3, 4 January.
Toss: West Indies.   Result: WEST INDIES won by an innings and 336 runs.
Debuts: India – R.B. Kenny, Surendranath.

Kanhai scored his maiden Test century and went on to record what is still the highest score in any Test in India in $6\frac{1}{2}$ hours with 42 fours. Sobers' hundred was his sixth in ten innings in six Tests, and his third of this rubber. West Indies achieved their victory with a day and a half to spare and by the second-largest margin in Test cricket.

WEST INDIES

J.K. Holt	c Contractor b Surendranath	5
C.C. Hunte	c Surendranath b Gupte	23
R.B. Kanhai	c Umrigar b Surendranath	256
O.G. Smith	b Umrigar	34
B.F. Butcher	lbw b Ghulam Ahmed	103
G. St A. Sobers	not out	106
J.S. Solomon	not out	69
F.C.M. Alexander*†	)	
S. Ramadhin	) did not bat	
W.W. Hall	)	
R. Gilchrist	)	
Extras	(B 8, LB 9, NB 1)	18
Total	(5 wickets declared)	**614**

INDIA

Pankaj Roy	c Solomon b Gilchrist	11	c Alexander b Hall	0
N.J. Contractor	lbw b Ramadhin	4	b Gilchrist	6
J.M. Ghorpade	c Alexander b Gilchrist	7	(6) b Sobers	16
R.B. Kenny	c Alexander b Hall	16	(5) b Hall	0
P.R. Umrigar	not out	44	(3) c Alexander b Hall	2
V.L. Manjrekar	b Hall	0	(4) not out	58
D.G. Phadkar	c Sobers b Gilchrist	3	b Gilchrist	35
N.S. Tamhane†	c Sobers b Hall	0	(9) b Gilchrist	0
Surendranath	run out	8	(8) c Alexander b Gilchrist	3
Ghulam Ahmed*	lbw b Sobers	4	b Gilchrist	0
S.P. Gupte	b Ramadhin	12	b Gilchrist	15
Extras	(B 2, LB 8, W 1, NB 4)	15	(B 3, NB 16)	19
Total		**124**		**154**

INDIA	O	M	R	W	O	M	R	W
Phadkar	43	6	173	0				
Surendranath	46	8	168	2				
Gupte	39	8	119	1				
Ghulam Ahmed	16·1	1	52	1				
Umrigar	16	1	62	1				
Ghorpade	2	0	22	0				
WEST INDIES								
Gilchrist	23	13	18	3	21	7	55	6
Hall	15	6	31	3	18	5	55	3
Ramadhin	16·5	8	27	2	8	3	14	0
Smith	2	1	1	0				
Sobers	6	0	32	1	2	0	11	1

FALL OF WICKETS

	WI	I	I
Wkt	1st	1st	2nd
1st	12	24	5
2nd	72	26	7
3rd	180	52	10
4th	397	52	17
5th	454	52	44
6th	–	57	115
7th	–	58	131
8th	–	89	131
9th	–	99	131
10th	–	124	154

Umpires: Mahomed Yunus (2) and N.D. Nagarwalla (3).

Close: 1st day – WI(1) 359-3 (Kanhai 203, Butcher 87); 2nd – I(1) 29-2 (Ghorpade 0, Kenny 3); 3rd – I(2) 69-5 (Manjrekar 20, Phadkar 14).

Test No. 462/14

INDIA v WEST INDIES 1958–59 (4th Test)

Played at Corporation Stadium, Madras, on 21, 22, 24, 25, 26 January.
Toss: West Indies.   Result: WEST INDIES won by 295 runs.
Debuts: India – A.K. Sengupta.

Umrigar resigned the captaincy shortly before the start of this match following a disagreement with the Indian selectors. Mankad was appointed in his place but illness prevented him from taking part after the first innings. Butcher scored his second consecutive hundred and Kanhai missed his by a fraction of a run.

WEST INDIES

C.C. Hunte	b Mankad	32	c Surendranath b Gupte	30
J.K. Holt	lbw b Gupte	63	not out	81
R.B. Kanhai	run out	99	lbw b Gupte	14
G. St A. Sobers	c Gupte b Mankad	29	c Joshi b Borde	9
O.G. Smith	b Mankad	0	c Joshi b Gupte	5
B.F. Butcher	b Ramchand	142	lbw b Gupte	16
J.S. Solomon	lbw b Borde	43	not out	8
F.C.M. Alexander*†	run out	11		
E. St E. Atkinson	not out	29		
W.W. Hall	lbw b Mankad	25		
R. Gilchrist	c Roy b Borde	7		
Extras	(B 8, LB 11, NB 1)	20	(B 5)	5
Total		**500**	(5 wickets declared)	**168**

INDIA

Pankaj Roy	b Sobers	49	c Kanhai b Hall	16
A.K. Sengupta	c Sobers b Hall	1	(4) c Alexander b Gilchrist	8
P.G. Joshi†	c Alexander b Gilchrist	17	(8) c Alexander b Hall	3
N.J. Contractor	run out	22	(2) c Alexander b Gilchrist	3
P.R. Umrigar	c Alexander b Hall	4	(3) b Sobers	29
G.S. Ramchand	c Gilchrist b Atkinson	30	b Gilchrist	1
A.G. Kripal Singh	c Hall b Sobers	53	c Alexander b Hall	9
M.H. Mankad*	b Gilchrist	4	absent ill	–
C.G. Borde	c Smith b Sobers	0	(5) c Butcher b Sobers	56
Surendranath	lbw b Sobers	0	(9) c Hunte b Smith	8
S.P. Gupte	not out	0	(10) not out	2
Extras	(B 14, LB 5, NB 23)	42	(B 5, LB 4, NB 7)	16
Total		**222**		**151**

INDIA	O	M	R	W	O	M	R	W
Ramchand	22	5	45	1	6	2	13	0
Surendranath	26	5	77	0	7	3	13	0
Umrigar	8	2	16	0	11	3	25	0
Gupte	58	15	166	1	30	6	78	4
Mankad	38	6	95	4				
Borde	27	2	80	2	22	11	34	1
Kripal Singh	2	1	1	0				
WEST INDIES								
Gilchrist	18	9	44	2	17	9	36	3
Hall	22	7	57	2	23	8	49	3
Atkinson	15	6	31	1	9	5	7	0
Sobers	18·1	8	26	4	18	8	39	2
Smith	5	0	22	0	3	1	4	1

FALL OF WICKETS

Wkt	WI 1st	I 1st	WI 2nd	I 2nd
1st	61	11	70	11
2nd	152	60	108	19
3rd	206	102	123	45
4th	206	121	130	97
5th	248	131	150	98
6th	349	135	–	114
7th	384	147	–	118
8th	453	221	–	149
9th	489	222	–	151
10th	500	222	–	–

Umpires: A.R. Joshi (7) and M.G. Vijayasarathi (12).

Close: 1st day – WI(1) 283-5 (Butcher 32, Solomon 14); 2nd – I(1) 27-1 (Roy 16, Joshi 2); 3rd – WI(2) 8-0 (Hunte 3, Holt 4); 4th – I(2) 48-3 (Umrigar 13, Borde 3).

INDIA v WEST INDIES 1958–59 (5th Test)

Played at Feroz Shah Kotla, Delhi, on 6, 7, 8, 10, 11 February.
Toss: India.   Result: MATCH DRAWN.
Debuts: India – R.B. Desai.

Adhikari became India's fourth captain in this rubber but, although he took three important wickets, he was unable to prevent West Indies from amassing the record total for a Test in India. This was equalled – and avenged – by India in 1978-79 (*Test No. 845*). West Indies would have needed only 47 runs to gain their fourth successive win in this rubber, but Borde batted until the last possible over before hitting his wicket when just four runs short of becoming the second Indian to score a hundred in each innings of a Test. 'Vinoo' Mankad ended his 44-match Test career having made a magnificent all-round contribution to Indian cricket: 2,109 runs, including five centuries; 162 wickets; and 33 catches.

INDIA

Pankaj Roy	c Solomon b Gilchrist	1		c Holt b Smith	58
N.J. Contractor	lbw b Hall	92		run out	4
P.R. Umrigar	b Hall	76		absent hurt	–
V.L. Manjrekar	c Alexander b Hall	6	(10)	not out	0
C.G. Borde	c Alexander b Smith	109	(4)	hit wkt b Gilchrist	96
D.K. Gaekwad	c Holt b Gilchrist	6	(3)	c Hunte b Smith	52
H.R. Adhikari*	c Alexander b Smith	63	(5)	c sub (J. Taylor) b Smith	40
M.H. Mankad	c sub (L.R. Gibbs) b Gilchrist	21	(6)	b Smith	0
N.S. Tamhane†	c Gilchrist b Smith	3	(7)	hit wkt b Smith	5
S.P. Gupte	b Hall	5	(8)	b Gilchrist	0
R.B. Desai	not out	2	(9)	b Gilchrist	5
Extras	(B 6, LB 15, NB 10)	31		(B 2, LB 6, NB 7)	15
Total		**415**			**275**

WEST INDIES

C.C. Hunte	lbw b Adhikari	92
J.K. Holt	c Roy b Desai	123
R.B. Kanhai	lbw b Desai	40
B.F. Butcher	lbw b Adhikari	71
O.G. Smith	c Tamhane b Desai	100
J.S. Solomon	not out	100
G. St A. Sobers	c Tamhane b Desai	44
F.C.M. Alexander*†	run out	25
E. St E. Atkinson	c and b Adhikari	37
W.W. Hall	not out	0
R. Gilchrist	did not bat	
Extras	(B 2, LB 8, W 1, NB 1)	12
Total	(8 wickets declared)	**644**

WEST INDIES	O	M	R	W	O	M	R	W	FALL OF WICKETS			
										I	WI	I
Gilchrist	30·3	8	90	3	24·2	6	62	3	*Wkt*	*1st*	*1st*	*2nd*
Hall	26	4	66	4	13	5	39	0	1st	6	159	5
Atkinson	14	4	44	0	1	0	4	0	2nd	143	244	98
Smith	40	7	94	3	42	19	90	5	3rd	170	263	135
Sobers	24	3	66	0					4th	208	390	243
Solomon	7	2	24	0	21	9	44	0	5th	242	455	247
Butcher					6	1	17	0	6th	376	524	260
Hunte					4	2	4	0	7th	399	565	264
									8th	407	635	274
INDIA									9th	413	–	275
Desai	49	10	169	4					10th	415	–	–
Roy	2	0	12	0								
Mankad	55	12	167	0								
Gupte	60	16	144	0								
Adhikari	26	2	68	3								
Gaekwad	1	0	8	0								
Contractor	4	1	11	0								
Borde	17	3	53	0								

Umpires: S.K. Ganguli (2) and N.D. Nagarwalla (4).

Close: 1st day – I(1) 236-4 (Borde 34, Gaekwad 6); 2nd – WI(1) 64-0 (Hunte 44, Holt 20); 3rd – WI(1) 408-4 (Smith 70, Solomon 4); 4th – I(2) 31-1 (Roy 9, Gaekwad 16).

AUSTRALIA v ENGLAND 1958–59 (1st Test)

Played at Woolloongabba, Brisbane, on 5, 6, 8, 9, 10 December.
Toss: England.   Result: AUSTRALIA won by eight wickets.
Debuts: Australia – N.C. O'Neill.

This was the first Test in Australia to be televised. Viewers were able to absorb one of cricket's more bizarre records: Bailey batted 357 minutes before reaching his fifty and this remains the slowest recorded half-century in all first-class cricket. His innings of 68 endured for 458 minutes at an average of slightly less than nine runs per hour. Out of 425 balls bowled to him, Bailey scored off 40: 4 fours, 3 threes, 10 twos and 23 singles. He also ran out Graveney. On the final day, Burke managed an even slower scoring rate by making 28 runs in 250 minutes. The fourth day produced only 106 runs (England 92 for 2 to 198 all out), the fewest ever scored in a day of Test cricket in Australia. May overtook W.M. Woodfull's record by leading his country for the 26th match in succession.

ENGLAND

P.E. Richardson	c Mackay b Davidson	11	c and b Benaud	8
C.A. Milton	b Meckiff	5	c Grout b Davidson	17
T.W. Graveney	c Grout b Davidson	19	(4) run out	36
P.B.H. May*	c Grout b Meckiff	26	(5) lbw b Benaud	4
M.C. Cowdrey	c Kline b Meckiff	13	(6) c Kline b Meckiff	28
T.E. Bailey	st Grout b Benaud	27	(3) b Mackay	68
T.G. Evans†	c Burge b Davidson	4	lbw b Davidson	4
G.A.R. Lock	c Davidson b Benaud	5	b Meckiff	1
J.C. Laker	c Burke b Benaud	13	b Benaud	15
J.B. Statham	c Grout b Mackay	2	c McDonald b Benaud	3
P.J. Loader	not out	6	not out	0
Extras	(LB 1, W 1, NB 1)	3	(B 10, LB 4)	14
Total		**134**		**198**

AUSTRALIA

C.C. McDonald	c Graveney b Bailey	42	c Statham b Laker	15
J.W. Burke	c Evans b Loader	20	not out	28
R.N. Harvey	lbw b Loader	14	c Milton b Lock	23
N.C. O'Neill	c Graveney b Bailey	34	not out	71
P.J.P. Burge	c Cowdrey b Bailey	2		
K.D. Mackay	c Evans b Laker	16		
R. Benaud*	lbw b Loader	16		
A.K. Davidson	lbw b Laker	25		
A.T.W. Grout†	b Statham	2		
I. Meckiff	b Loader	5		
L.F. Kline	not out	4		
Extras	(B 4, LB 1, NB 1)	6	(B 2, LB 3, NB 5)	10
Total		**186**	(2 wickets)	**147**

AUSTRALIA	O	M	R	W	O	M	R	W				
Davidson	16	4	36	3	28	12	30	2				
Meckiff	17	5	33	3	19	7	30	2				
Mackay	8	1	16	1	9	6	7	1				
Benaud	18·4	9	46	3	39·2	10	66	4				
Kline					14	4	34	0				
Burke					10	5	17	0				

FALL OF WICKETS

Wkt	E 1st	A 1st	E 2nd	A 2nd
1st	16	55	28	20
2nd	16	65	34	58
3rd	62	88	96	–
4th	75	94	102	–
5th	79	122	153	–
6th	83	136	161	–
7th	92	162	169	–
8th	112	165	190	–
9th	116	178	198	–
10th	134	186	198	–

ENGLAND	O	M	R	W	O	M	R	W
Statham	20	2	57	1	6	1	13	0
Loader	19	4	56	4	9	1	27	0
Bailey	13	2	35	3	5	1	21	0
Laker	10·1	3	15	2	17	3	39	1
Lock	10	4	17	0	14·7	5	37	1

Umpires: C. Hoy (3) and M.J. McInnes (13).

Close: 1st day – A(1) 8-0 (McDonald 5, Burke 3); 2nd – A(1) 156-6 (Benaud 15, Davidson 7); 3rd – E(2) 92-2 (Bailey 27, Graveney 33); 4th – E(2) 198 all out.

AUSTRALIA v ENGLAND 1958–59 (2nd Test)

Played at Melbourne Cricket Ground on 31 December, 1, 2, 3, 5 January.
Toss: England.   Result: AUSTRALIA won by eight wickets.
Debuts: Nil.

Davidson took the wickets of Richardson, Watson and Graveney with the first, fourth and fifth balls of his second over. May scored the first hundred by an England captain in Australia since A.C. MacLaren in 1901-02 (*Test No. 65*), and Harvey scored Australia's first hundred against England for eleven Tests. England's total of 87 was their lowest in Australia since 1903-04.

ENGLAND

P.E. Richardson	c Grout b Davidson	3	c Harvey b Meckiff		2
T.E. Bailey	c Benaud b Meckiff	48	c Burke b Meckiff		14
W. Watson	b Davidson	0	b Davidson		7
T.W. Graveney	lbw b Davidson	0	c Davidson b Meckiff		3
P.B.H. May*	b Meckiff	113	c Davidson b Meckiff		17
M.C. Cowdrey	c Grout b Davidson	44	c Grout b Meckiff		12
T.G. Evans†	c Davidson b Meckiff	4	run out		11
G.A.R. Lock	st Grout b Benaud	5	c and b Davidson		6
J.C. Laker	not out	22	c Harvey b Davidson		3
J.B. Statham	b Davidson	13	not out		8
P.J. Loader	b Davidson	1	b Meckiff		0
Extras	(B 1, LB 2, W 3)	6	(B 1, LB 1, NB 2)		4
Total		**259**			**87**

AUSTRALIA

C.C. McDonald	c Graveney b Statham	47	lbw b Statham	5
J.W. Burke	b Statham	3	not out	18
R.N. Harvey	b Loader	167	(4) not out	7
N.C. O'Neill	c Evans b Statham	37		
K.D. Mackay	c Evans b Statham	18		
R.B. Simpson	lbw b Loader	0		
R. Benaud*	lbw b Statham	0		
A.K. Davidson	b Statham	24		
A.T.W. Grout†	c May b Loader	8	(3) st Evans b Laker	12
I. Meckiff	b Statham	0		
L.F. Kline	not out	1		
Extras	(LB 3)	3		
Total		**308**	(2 wickets)	**42**

AUSTRALIA	O	M	R	W	O	M	R	W		FALL OF WICKETS			
										E	A	E	A
Davidson	25·5	7	64	6	15	2	41	3	*Wkt*	*1st*	*1st*	*2nd*	*2nd*
Meckiff	24	4	69	3	15·2	3	38	6	1st	7	11	3	6
Mackay	9	2	16	0					2nd	7	137	14	26
Benaud	29	7	61	1	1	0	4	0	3rd	7	255	21	–
Kline	11	2	43	0					4th	92	257	27	–
									5th	210	261	44	–
ENGLAND									6th	218	262	57	–
Statham	28	6	57	7	5	1	11	1	7th	218	295	71	–
Loader	27·2	4	97	3	5	1	13	0	8th	233	300	75	–
Bailey	16	0	50	0					9th	253	300	80	–
Laker	12	1	47	0	4	1	7	1	10th	259	308	87	–
Lock	17	2	54	0	3·1	1	11	0					

Umpires: M.J. McInnes (14) and R. Wright (11).

Close: 1st day – E(1) 173-4 (May 89, Cowdrey 28); 2nd – A(1) 96-1 (McDonald 32, Harvey 60); 3rd – A(1) 282-6 (Mackay 14, Davidson 12); 4th – A(2) 9-1 (Burke 2, Grout 2).

AUSTRALIA v ENGLAND 1958–59 (3rd Test)

Played at Sydney Cricket Ground on 9, 10, 12, 13, 14, 15 January.
Toss: England.   Result: MATCH DRAWN.
Debuts: Australia – K.N. Slater; England – R. Swetman.

Set to score 150 runs in 110 minutes on a wearing pitch, Australia were content to draw. Cowdrey's hundred took 362 minutes and was the slowest for either country in Australia-England Tests until R.A. Woolmer took 394 minutes to reach his century at The Oval in 1975 (*Test No. 763*). Rain delayed the start of play on the second day until 4.15 pm.

ENGLAND

T.E. Bailey	lbw b Meckiff	8		c sub (R.B. Simpson) b Benaud	25
C.A. Milton	c Meckiff b Davidson	8		c Davidson b Benaud	8
T.W. Graveney	c Harvey b Benaud	33		lbw b Davidson	22
P.B.H. May*	c Mackay b Slater	42		b Burke	92
M.C. Cowdrey	c Harvey b Benaud	34		not out	100
E.R. Dexter	lbw b Slater	1		c Grout b Benaud	11
R. Swetman†	c Mackay b Benaud	41		lbw b Burke	5
G.A.R. Lock	lbw b Mackay	21	(9)	not out	11
F.S. Trueman	c Burke b Benaud	18	(8)	st Grout b Benaud	0
J.C. Laker	c Harvey b Benaud	2			
J.B. Statham	not out	0			
Extras	(B 4, LB 5, W 2)	11		(B 11, LB 1, W 1)	13
Total		**219**		(7 wickets declared)	**287**

AUSTRALIA

C.C. McDonald	c Graveney b Lock	40		b Laker	16
J.W. Burke	c Lock b Laker	12		b Laker	7
R.N. Harvey	b Laker	7		not out	18
N.C. O'Neill	c Swetman b Laker	77		not out	7
L.E. Favell	c Cowdrey b Lock	54			
K.D. Mackay	b Trueman	57			
R. Benaud*	b Laker	6			
A.K. Davidson	lbw b Lock	71			
A.T.W. Grout†	c Statham b Laker	14			
K.N. Slater	not out	1			
I. Meckiff	b Lock	2			
Extras	(B 5, LB 10, NB 1)	16		(B 6)	6
Total		**357**		(2 wickets)	**54**

AUSTRALIA	O	M	R	W	O	M	R	W	FALL OF WICKETS				
Davidson	12	3	21	1	33	11	65	1		E	A	E	A
Meckiff	15	2	45	1	3	1	7	0	*Wkt*	*1st*	*1st*	*2nd*	*2nd*
Benaud	33·4	10	83	5	33	7	94	4	1st	19	26	30	22
Slater	14	4	40	2	18	5	61	0	2nd	23	52	37	33
Mackay	8	3	19	1	11	2	21	0	3rd	91	87	64	–
Burke					11	3	26	2	4th	97	197	246	–
									5th	98	199	262	–
ENGLAND									6th	155	208	269	–
Statham	16	2	48	0	2	0	6	0	7th	194	323	270	–
Trueman	18	3	37	1	4	1	9	0	8th	200	353	–	–
Lock	43·2	9	130	4	11	4	23	0	9th	202	355	–	–
Laker	46	9	107	5	8	3	10	2	10th	219	357	–	–
Bailey	5	1	19	0									

Umpires: C. Hoy (4) and M.J. McInnes (15).

Close: 1st day – E(1) 190-6 (Swetman 36, Lock 17); 2nd – A(1) 3-0 (McDonald 1, Burke 2); 3rd – A(1) 184-3 (O'Neill 66, Favell 50); 4th – E(2) 1-0 (Bailey 1, Milton 0); 5th – E(2) 178-3 (May 53, Cowdrey 50).

AUSTRALIA v ENGLAND 1958–59 (4th Test)

Played at Adelaide Oval on 30, 31 January, 2, 3, 4, 5 February.
Toss: England.   Result: AUSTRALIA won by ten wickets.
Debuts: Australia – G.F. Rorke.

McDonald, almost bowled first ball of the match by Statham, became the fiftieth Australian to score a hundred against England. He pulled a thigh muscle when 137, retired hurt 149 at lunch with Australia 268 for 1, and resumed his innings with a runner at 407. Evans re-fractured a little finger and, after continuing to keep wicket throughout the first day, handed over to Graveney for the rest of the match. Australia regained the Ashes after a period of five years 170 days.

AUSTRALIA

C.C. McDonald	b Trueman	170			
J.W. Burke	c Cowdrey b Bailey	66	not out		16
R.N. Harvey	run out	41			
N.C. O'Neill	b Statham	56			
L.E. Favell	b Statham	4	(1) not out		15
K.D. Mackay	c Evans b Statham	4			
R. Benaud*	b Trueman	46			
A.K. Davidson	c Bailey b Tyson	43			
A.T.W. Grout†	lbw b Trueman	9			
R.R. Lindwall	b Trueman	19			
G.F. Rorke	not out	2			
Extras	(B 2, LB 8, W 4, NB 2)	16	(B 4, LB 1)		5
Total		**476**	(0 wickets)		**36**

ENGLAND

P.E. Richardson	lbw b Lindwall	4	lbw b Benaud		43
T.E. Bailey	b Davidson	4	(6) c Grout b Lindwall		6
P.B.H. May*	b Benaud	37	lbw b Rorke		59
M.C. Cowdrey	b Rorke	84	b Lindwall		8
T.W. Graveney	c Benaud b Rorke	41	not out		53
W. Watson	b Rorke	25	(2) c Favell b Benaud		40
F.S. Trueman	c Grout b Benaud	0	c Grout b Davidson		0
G.A.R. Lock	c Grout b Benaud	2	b Rorke		9
F.H. Tyson	c and b Benaud	0	c Grout b Benaud		33
T.G. Evans†	c Burke b Benaud	4	(11) c Benaud b Davidson		0
J.B. Statham	not out	36	(10) c O'Neill b Benaud		2
Extras	(LB 2, NB 1)	3	(B 5, LB 5, W 3, NB 4)		17
Total		**240**			**270**

ENGLAND	O	M	R	W	O	M	R	W	FALL OF WICKETS				
Statham	23	0	83	3	4	0	11	0		A	E	E	A
Trueman	30·1	6	90	4	3	1	3	0	*Wkt*	*1st*	*1st*	*2nd*	*2nd*
Tyson	28	1	100	1					1st	171	7	89	–
Bailey	22	2	91	1					2nd	276	11	110	–
Lock	25	0	96	0	2	0	8	0	3rd	286	74	125	–
Cowdrey					1·3	0	9	0	4th	294	170	177	–
									5th	369	173	198	–
AUSTRALIA									6th	388	180	199	–
Davidson	12	0	49	1	8·3	3	17	2	7th	407	184	222	–
Lindwall	15	0	66	1	26	6	70	2	8th	445	184	268	–
Rorke	18·1	7	23	3	34	7	78	2	9th	473	188	270	–
Benaud	27	6	91	5	29	10	82	4	10th	476	240	270	–
O'Neill	2	1	8	0									
Burke					4	2	6	0					

Umpires: M.J. McInnes (16) and R. Wright (12).

Close: 1st day – A(1) 200-1 (McDonald 112, Harvey 11); 2nd – A(1) 403-6 (Davidson 16, Grout 7); 3rd – E(1) 115-3 (Cowdrey 53, Graveney 16); 4th – E(2) 43-0 (Richardson 28, Watson 10); 5th – E(2) 198-5 (Graveney 28).

AUSTRALIA v ENGLAND 1958–59 (5th Test)

Played at Melbourne Cricket Ground on 13, 14, 16, 17, 18 February.
Toss: Australia.   Result: AUSTRALIA won by nine wickets.
Debuts: England – J.B. Mortimore.

McDonald scored his second consecutive hundred after being given not out when 12 after a bail had been dislodged as he glanced Trueman to the boundary. Bailey, playing in his final Test match, was dismissed for a 'pair' by the bowler to whom he had sacrificed his wicket (Lindwall's 100th against England) four years earlier (*Test No. 395*). During this match Lindwall broke C.V. Grimmett's Australian record of 216 Test wickets.

ENGLAND

P.E. Richardson	c and b Benaud	68	lbw b Benaud	23
T.E. Bailey	c Davidson b Lindwall	0	b Lindwall	0
P.B.H. May*	c Benaud b Meckiff	11	c Harvey b Lindwall	4
M.C. Cowdrey	c Lindwall b Davidson	22	run out	46
T.W. Graveney	c McDonald b Benaud	19	c Harvey b Davidson	54
E.R. Dexter	c Lindwall b Meckiff	0	c Grout b Davidson	6
R. Swetman†	c Grout b Davidson	1	lbw b Lindwall	9
J.B. Mortimore	not out	44	b Rorke	11
F.S Trueman	c and b Benaud	21	b Rorke	36
F.H. Tyson	c Grout b Benaud	9	c Grout b Rorke	6
J.C. Laker	c Harvey b Davidson	2	not out	5
Extras	(B 4, W 4)	8	(B 9, LB 3, W 2)	14
Total		**205**		**214**

AUSTRALIA

C.C. McDonald	c Cowdrey b Laker	133	not out	51
J.W. Burke	c Trueman b Tyson	16	lbw b Tyson	13
R.N. Harvey	c Swetman b Trueman	13	not out	1
N.C. O'Neill	c Cowdrey b Trueman	0		
K.D. Mackay	c Graveney b Laker	23		
A.K. Davidson	b Mortimore	17		
R. Benaud*	c Swetman b Laker	64		
A.T.W. Grout†	c Trueman b Laker	74		
R.R. Lindwall	c Cowdrey b Trueman	0		
I. Meckiff	c and b Trueman	2		
G.F. Rorke	not out	0		
Extras	(B 5, LB 4)	9	(LB 4)	4
Total		**351**	(1 wicket)	**69**

AUSTRALIA	O	M	R	W	O	M	R	W		FALL OF WICKETS			
Davidson	12·5	2	38	3	21	1	95	2		E	A	E	A
Lindwall	14	2	36	1	11	2	37	3	*Wkt*	*1st*	*1st*	*2nd*	*2nd*
Meckiff	15	2	57	2	4	0	13	0	1st	0	41	0	66
Rorke	6	1	23	0	12·4	2	41	3	2nd	13	83	12	–
Benaud	17	5	43	4	6	1	14	1	3rd	61	83	78	–
									4th	109	154	105	–
ENGLAND									5th	112	207	131	–
Trueman	25	0	92	4	6·7	0	45	0	6th	124	209	142	–
Tyson	20	1	73	1	6	0	20	1	7th	128	324	158	–
Bailey	14	2	43	0					8th	191	327	172	–
Laker	30·5	4	93	4					9th	203	329	182	–
Mortimore	11	1	41	1					10th	205	351	214	–

Umpires: L. Townsend (1) and R. Wright (13).

Close: 1st day – E(1) 191-7 (Mortimore 41, Trueman 21); 2nd – A(1) 150-3 (McDonald 98, Mackay 22); 3rd – E(2) 22-2 (Richardson 6, Cowdrey 4); 4th – A(2) 15-0 (McDonald 15, Burke 0).

PAKISTAN v WEST INDIES 1958–59 (1st Test)

Played at National Stadium, Karachi, on 20, 21, 22, 24, 25 February.
Toss: Pakistan.   Result: PAKISTAN won by ten wickets.
Debuts: Pakistan – Antao D'Souza, Ijaz Butt.

Fazal Mahmood began his Test captaincy by putting Pakistan's newest visitors in to bat on a matting pitch and leading his country to their second win in successive matches against this powerful combination. The partnership of 178 between Hanif and Saeed for the second wicket is still a record against West Indies. Fazal became the first bowler to take 100 wickets for Pakistan when he had Sobers 'lbw' for the second time in the match. Hanif took no further part in the rubber after injuring his knee in the second innings and retiring at 27; he had played in Pakistan's first 24 Test matches.

WEST INDIES

C.C. Hunte	c Imtiaz b Fazal	0	lbw b Fazal	21
J.K. Holt	lbw b Nasim	29	c Ijaz Butt b Fazal	2
R.B. Kanhai	c Hanif b Nasim	33	c Imtiaz b Mahmood	12
G. St A. Sobers	lbw b Fazal	0	(6) lbw b Fazal	14
O.G. Smith	st Imtiaz b Nasim	0	lbw b Mahmood	11
B.F. Butcher	not out	45	(4) c Imtiaz b Nasim	61
J.S. Solomon	c Hanif b D'Souza	14	run out	66
F.C.M. Alexander*†	b D'Souza	0	lbw b Shujauddin	16
L.R. Gibbs	b Nasim	5	b Shujauddin	21
W.W. Hall	b Fazal	7	st Imtiaz b Shujauddin	4
J. Taylor	b Fazal	0	not out	0
Extras	(B 3, NB 10)	13	(LB 7, NB 10)	17
Total		**146**		**245**

PAKISTAN

Hanif Mohammad	c Alexander b Smith	103	retired hurt	5
Ijaz Butt	c Alexander b Hall	14	not out	41
Saeed Ahmed	run out	78	not out	33
Imtiaz Ahmed†	lbw b Smith	31		
Wazir Mohammad	st Alexander b Gibbs	23		
W. Mathias	b Hall	16		
Fazal Mahmood*	c Alexander b Hall	0		
Shujauddin	run out	1		
Nasim-ul-Ghani	b Gibbs	11		
Mahmood Hussain	b Gibbs	1		
A. D'Souza	not out	3		
Extras	(B 9, LB 3, W 1, NB 10)	23	(NB 9)	9
Total		**304**	**(0 wickets)**	**88**

PAKISTAN	O	M	R	W	O	M	R	W		FALL OF WICKETS			
										WI	P	WI	P
Fazal	22	9	35	4	36	9	89	3	*Wkt*	*1st*	*1st*	*2nd*	*2nd*
Mahmood Hussain	8	3	13	0	26	10	59	2	1st	0	33	12	–
D'Souza	14	0	50	2	13	5	28	0	2nd	62	211	34	–
Nasim	16	5	35	4	25	16	34	1	3rd	64	214	55	–
Shujauddin					13	7	18	3	4th	65	263	84	–
									5th	69	284	109	–
WEST INDIES									6th	104	287	140	–
Hall	30	7	57	3	8	1	35	0	7th	104	289	189	–
Taylor	21	7	43	0	6	2	15	0	8th	117	290	233	–
Gibbs	38·2	13	92	3	7	4	8	0	9th	145	291	241	–
Sobers	40	24	45	0	9	5	12	0	10th	146	304	245	–
Smith	27	14	36	2	3	2	9	0					
Solomon	4	1	8	0									
Holt					1	1	0	0					

Umpires: Daud Khan (6) and Syed Murawwat Hussain (1).

Close: 1st day – P(1) 54-1 (Hanif 26, Saeed 9); 2nd – P(1) 227-3 (Imtiaz 6, Wazir 6); 3rd – WI(2) 84-4 (Butcher 28); 4th – P(2) 27-0 (Hanif 5, Ijaz 18).

PAKISTAN v WEST INDIES 1958–59 (2nd Test)

Played at Dacca Stadium on 6, 7, 8 March.
Toss: West Indies.   Result: PAKISTAN won by 41 runs.
Debuts: Nil.

Fazal Mahmood's first innings analysis of 6 for 34 remains the best for either country in this series in Pakistan, and he was the first bowler to take ten wickets in Tests between these two countries. His match analysis of 12 for 100 is the record for any Test at Dacca. The match aggregate of 537 runs is the lowest for any completed West Indies-Pakistan Test. The West Indies total of 76 was their lowest in all Test cricket. Pakistan were to wait 20 years before they repeated this run of three successive victories.

PAKISTAN

Ijaz Butt	b Hall	2	b Ramadhin	21
Alimuddin	c and b Hall	6	c Smith b Atkinson	0
Saeed Ahmed	c Alexander b Hall	6	lbw b Ramadhin	22
Imtiaz Ahmed†	b Ramadhin	3	c Smith b Atkinson	4
Wazir Mohammad	b Hall	1	c Alexander b Atkinson	4
W. Mathias	c Atkinson b Gibbs	64	b Atkinson	45
Shujauddin	b Atkinson	26	b Hall	17
Fazal Mahmood*	c Alexander b Ramadhin	12	(9) not out	7
Nasim-ul-Ghani	run out	7	(8) b Hall	0
Mahmood Hussain	b Ramadhin	4	b Hall	2
Haseeb Ahsan	not out	4	b Hall	0
Extras	(B 5, LB 2, NB 3)	10	(B 9, LB 4, W 1, NB 8)	22
Total		**145**		**144**

WEST INDIES

J.K. Holt	b Mahmood	4	c Imtiaz b Fazal	5
R.B. Kanhai	c Wazir b Fazal	4	(3) lbw b Fazal	8
G. St A. Sobers	lbw b Fazal	29	(5) c Fazal b Mahmood	45
F.C.M. Alexander*†	st Imtiaz b Nasim	14	(2) c Imtiaz b Fazal	18
B.F. Butcher	c Shujauddin b Fazal	11	(4) b Fazal	8
O.G. Smith	c Nasim b Fazal	0	b Fazal	39
J.S. Solomon	c Imtiaz b Nasim	0	c Mahmood b Fazal	8
E. St E. Atkinson	c Mathias b Fazal	0	(9) lbw b Mahmood	20
L.R. Gibbs	st Imtiaz b Nasim	0	(8) b Mahmood	0
W.W. Hall	c Mathias b Fazal	0	lbw b Mahmood	6
S. Ramadhin	not out	0	not out	4
Extras	(B 5, LB 3, NB 6)	14	(LB 5, NB 6)	11
Total		**76**		**172**

WEST INDIES	O	M	R	W	O	M	R	W	FALL OF WICKETS				
Hall	13	5	28	4	16·5	2	49	4		P	WI	P	WI
Atkinson	10	2	22	1	22	9	42	4	*Wkt*	*1st*	*1st*	*2nd*	*2nd*
Ramadhin	23·3	6	45	3	15	9	10	2	1st	6	4	2	12
Gibbs	21	8	33	1	6	0	17	0	2nd	15	19	33	31
Sobers	8	4	7	0	3	2	4	0	3rd	18	56	40	35
									4th	22	65	54	48
PAKISTAN									5th	22	68	71	113
Fazal	18·3	9	34	6	27	10	66	6	6th	108	71	130	134
Mahmood Hussain	10	1	21	1	19·5	1	48	4	7th	126	72	130	141
Nasim	7	5	4	3	8	2	34	0	8th	130	74	131	150
Haseeb	1	0	3	0					9th	139	74	139	159
Shujauddin					6	2	13	0	10th	145	76	144	172

Umpires: Khwaja Saeed Ahmed (1) and Munawar Hussain (1).

Close: 1st day – WI(1) 46-2 (Sobers 22, Alexander 9); 2nd – P(2) 120-5 (Mathias 36, Shujauddin 16).

PAKISTAN v WEST INDIES 1958–59 (3rd Test)

Played at Bagh-i-Jinnah, Lahore, 26, 28, 29, 30, 31 March.
Toss: West Indies.   Result: WEST INDIES won by an innings and 156 runs.
Debuts: Pakistan – Mushtaq Mohammad; West Indies – M.R. Bynoe.

This was Pakistan's first defeat in a Test at home. Mushtaq Mohammad made his first appearance in Test cricket at the age of 15 years 124 days and remains the youngest ever to do so. Kanhai's 217 is still the highest score for either side in this series in Pakistan, and his partnership of 162 with Sobers remains the best West Indies third-wicket stand against Pakistan. Hall became the first West Indies bowler to take a Test hat-trick when he dismissed Mushtaq, Fazal and Nasim in the first innings. Kanhai kept wicket in the second innings, Alexander's three catches being taken in the field. In the first innings, Ijaz Butt retired hurt at 0 after being hit by a short ball from Hall; he resumed at 105. Pakistan's total of 104 was their lowest in any home Test.

WEST INDIES

F.C.M. Alexander*†	lbw b Fazal	21
M.R. Bynoe	c Mahmood b Fazal	1
R.B. Kanhai	c and b Shujauddin	217
G. St A. Sobers	b Nasim	72
O.G. Smith	c Waqar b Saeed	31
B.F. Butcher	run out	8
J.S. Solomon	c Mathias b Mahmood	56
E. St E. Atkinson	c Mathias b Nasim	20
L.R. Gibbs	c Saeed b Nasim	18
S. Ramadhin	not out	4
W.W. Hall	b Shujauddin	0
Extras	(B 7, LB 8, NB 6)	21
Total		**469**

PAKISTAN

Ijaz Butt	not out	47	c Gibbs b Atkinson	2
Imtiaz Ahmed†	run out	40	c Gibbs b Atkinson	1
Saeed Ahmed	c Gibbs b Smith	27	c Kanhai b Atkinson	33
Waqar Hassan	b Gibbs	41	c Alexander b Gibbs	28
W. Mathias	b Hall	14	c Alexander b Ramadhin	9
Shujauddin	b Hall	1	(7) c and b Ramadhin	0
Wazir Mohammad	run out	11	(6) c Alexander b Ramadhin	0
Mushtaq Mohammad	lbw b Hall	14	b Ramadhin	4
Fazal Mahmood*	c Sobers b Hall	0	b Gibbs	14
Nasim-ul-Ghani	b Hall	0	not out	6
Mahmood Hussain	c Sobers b Atkinson	0	c Bynoe b Gibbs	1
Extras	(B 1, LB 3, NB 10)	14	(B 2, LB 2, NB 2)	6
Total		**209**		**104**

PAKISTAN	O	M	R	W	O	M	R	W		FALL OF WICKETS		
Fazal	40	10	109	2						WI	P	P
Mahmood Hussain	28	4	99	1					*Wkt*	*1st*	*1st*	*2nd*
Nasim	30	6	106	3					1st	11	70	4
Shujauddin	34·3	7	81	2					2nd	38	75	5
Mushtaq	6	0	34	0					3rd	200	98	55
Saeed	11	1	19	1					4th	290	105	72
									5th	307	160	73
WEST INDIES									6th	407	180	73
Hall	24	2	87	5	9	1	31	0	7th	426	208	78
Atkinson	14·2	1	40	1	12	8	15	3	8th	463	208	97
Ramadhin	22	9	41	0	10	4	25	4	9th	464	208	97
Smith	7	3	11	1	2	1	4	0	10th	469	209	104
Gibbs	12	5	16	1	9·5	3	14	3				
Sobers					6	1	9	0				

Umpires: Akhtar Hussain (1) and Munawar Hussain (2).

Close: 1st day – WI(1) 325-5 (Butcher 8, Solomon 8); 2nd – P(1) 86-2 (Waqar 4, Mathias 6); 3rd – P(2) 55-2 (Saeed 33, Waqar 16); 4th – P(2) 64-3 (Waqar 24, Mathias 0).

NEW ZEALAND v ENGLAND 1958–59 (1st Test)

Played at Lancaster Park, Christchurch, on 27, 28 February, 2 March.
Toss: England.   Result: ENGLAND won by an innings and 99 runs.
Debuts: New Zealand – B.A. Bolton, R.M. Harris, K.W. Hough.

Dexter, who batted for 257 minutes and hit a five and 24 fours, registered the first of his nine hundreds for England. Petrie was hit in the face by a ball from Moir and handed over the gloves to Reid for a period. The New Zealand wicket-keeper later became Trueman's 100th victim in 25 Tests. Lock secured England's decisive victory at 2.57 on the third afternoon by taking the last five wickets for 14 runs in 11.2 overs. A record ground attendance of 20,000 watched the second day.

ENGLAND

P.E. Richardson	c Petrie b Blair	8
W. Watson	c Petrie b Blair	10
T.W. Graveney	lbw b Hough	42
P.B.H. May*	c Hough b Moir	71
M.C. Cowdrey	b Hough	15
E.R. Dexter	b Reid	141
J.B. Mortimore	c and b Moir	11
R. Swetman†	b Hough	9
F.S. Trueman	lbw b Reid	21
G.A.R. Lock	b Reid	15
F.H. Tyson	not out	6
Extras	(B 12, LB 13)	25
Total		**374**

NEW ZEALAND

B.A. Bolton	c Swetman b Lock	33	c May b Mortimore	26
R.M. Harris	c Lock b Tyson	6	b Truman	13
J.W. Guy	c Trueman b Lock	3	c Lock b Tyson	56
J.R. Reid*	b Tyson	40	c Cowdrey b Lock	1
B. Sutcliffe	c Lock b Tyson	0	c Trueman b Lock	12
S.N. McGregor	c Lock b Mortimore	0	lbw b Lock	6
J.T. Sparling	st Swetman b Lock	12	b Tyson	0
A.M. Moir	c Graveney b Lock	0	c Swetman b Lock	1
E.C. Petrie†	lbw b Trueman	8	not out	2
R.W. Blair	lbw b Lock	0	c Trueman b Lock	2
K.W. Hough	not out	31	b Lock	7
Extras	(B 5, LB 4)	9	(B 1, LB 5, NB 1)	7
Total		**142**		**133**

NEW ZEALAND	O	M	R	W	O	M	R	W		FALL OF WICKETS		
Blair	31	5	89	2						E	NZ	NZ
Hough	39	11	96	3					*Wkt*	*1st*	*1st*	*2nd*
Moir	36	9	83	2					1st	13	22	37
Reid	18·1	9	34	3					2nd	30	33	68
Sparling	16	7	38	0					3rd	98	83	79
Sutcliffe	2	0	9	0					4th	126	83	101
									5th	171	86	117
ENGLAND									6th	197	101	119
Trueman	10·5	3	39	1	8	2	20	1	7th	224	101	120
Tyson	14	4	23	3	14	6	23	2	8th	305	102	121
Lock	26	15	31	5	28·2	13	53	6	9th	367	102	123
Mortimore	22	8	40	1	21	10	27	1	10th	374	142	133
Dexter					1	0	3	0				

Umpires: J. Cowie (2) and E.W.T. Tindill (1).

Close: 1st day – E(1) 336-8 (Dexter 123, Lock 8); 2nd – NZ(2) 28-0 (Bolton 18, Harris 9).

NEW ZEALAND v ENGLAND 1958–59 (2nd Test)

Played at Eden Park, Auckland, on 14, 16, 17 (*no play*), 18 (*no play*) March.
Toss: New Zealand.   Result: MATCH DRAWN.
Debuts: Nil.

The first two days were played in blustery conditions with the bails frequently being blown off, and the last two were completely ruined by rain. The first hour brought warnings of cyclones, eight runs, two wickets, and seven maiden overs from Trueman. The outstanding feature of this truncated contest was May's unfinished 12th century.

NEW ZEALAND

B.A. Bolton	run out	0
R.M. Harris	c Swetman b Dexter	12
S.N. McGregor	hit wkt b Trueman	1
J.W. Guy	b Dexter	1
B. Sutcliffe	b Lock	61
J.R. Reid*	b Dexter	3
J.T. Sparling	c Swetman b Trueman	25
A.M. Moir	c Graveney b Trueman	10
E.C. Petrie†	c Trueman b Lock	13
R.W. Blair	c Cowdrey b Tyson	22
K.W. Hough	not out	24
Extras	(B 7, LB 1, NB 1)	9
Total		**181**

ENGLAND

P.E. Richardson	c Bolton b Moir	67
W. Watson	b Hough	11
T.W. Graveney	b Moir	46
P.B.H. May*	not out	124
M.C. Cowdrey	b Hough	5
E.R. Dexter	c Petrie b Moir	1
J.B. Mortimore	b Hough	9
R. Swetman†	run out	17
F.S. Trueman	not out	21
G.A.R. Lock	} did not bat	
F.H. Tyson	}	
Extras	(B 4, LB 6)	10
Total	(7 wickets)	**311**

ENGLAND	O	M	R	W
Trueman	26	12	46	3
Tyson	20	9	50	1
Dexter	19	8	23	3
Lock	20·3	12	29	2
Mortimore	4	1	24	0
NEW ZEALAND				
Blair	27	6	69	0
Hough	38	12	79	3
Reid	4	1	19	0
Sparling	20	7	48	0
Moir	28	4	84	3
Sutcliffe	1	0	2	0

FALL OF WICKETS

	NZ	E
Wkt	1st	1st
1st	3	26
2nd	6	94
3rd	11	165
4th	16	182
5th	41	183
6th	98	223
7th	116	261
8th	125	–
9th	157	–
10th	181	–

Umpires: J. Cowie (3) and R.W.R. Shortt (1).

Close: 1st day – E(1) 0-0 (Richardson 0, Watson 0); 2nd – E(1) 311-7 (May 24, Trueman 21); 3rd – no play.

ENGLAND v INDIA 1959 (1st Test)

Played at Trent Bridge, Nottingham, on 4, 5, 6, 8 June.
Toss: England.   Result: ENGLAND won by an innings and 59 runs.
Debuts: England – T. Greenhough, M.J. Horton, K. Taylor.

Borde's left-hand little finger was fractured by a ball from Trueman. England won at 3.30 on the fourth afternoon. Nadkarni was unable to complete his 29th over after a drive from Statham had severely bruised his left hand. May gave no chances in scoring the last of his 13 Test hundreds.

ENGLAND

C.A. Milton	b Surendranath	9
K. Taylor	lbw b Gupte	24
M.C. Cowdrey	c Borde b Surendranath	5
P.B.H. May*	c Joshi b Gupte	106
K.F. Barrington	b Nadkarni	56
M.J. Horton	c Nadkarni b Desai	58
T.G. Evans†	c Umrigar b Nadkarni	73
F.S. Trueman	b Borde	28
J.B. Statham	not out	29
T. Greenhough	c Gaekwad b Gupte	0
A.E. Moss	c Roy b Gupte	11
Extras	(B 15, LB 7, W 1)	23
Total		**422**

INDIA

Pankaj Roy	b Trueman	54	c Trueman b Greenhough		49
N.J. Contractor	c Barrington b Greenhough	15	c Cowdrey b Statham		0
P.R. Umrigar	b Trueman	21	b Statham		20
V.L. Manjrekar	lbw b Trueman	17	lbw b Greenhough		44
C.G. Borde	retired hurt	15	absent hurt		–
D.K. Gaekwad*	c Evans b Statham	33	(5) c Horton b Statham		31
R.G. Nadkarni	lbw b Trueman	15	(6) b Statham		1
P.G. Joshi†	lbw b Moss	21	(7) lbw b Trueman		1
S.P. Gupte	c Taylor b Moss	2	(8) c May b Statham		8
Surendranath	not out	4	(9) not out		1
R.B. Desai	b Statham	0	(10) c May b Trueman		1
Extras	(B 5, NB 4)	9	(NB 1)		1
Total		**206**			**157**

INDIA	O	M	R	W	O	M	R	W
Desai	33	7	127	1				
Surendranath	24	8	59	2				
Gupte	38·1	11	102	4				
Nadkarni	28·1	15	48	2				
Borde	20	4	63	1				
ENGLAND								
Statham	23·5	11	46	2	21	10	31	5
Trueman	24	9	45	4	22·3	10	44	2
Moss	24	11	33	2	12	7	13	0
Greenhough	26	7	58	1	23	5	48	2
Horton	5	0	15	0	19	11	20	0

FALL OF WICKETS

Wkt	E 1st	I 1st	I 2nd
1st	17	34	8
2nd	29	85	52
3rd	60	95	85
4th	185	126	124
5th	221	158	140
6th	327	190	143
7th	358	198	147
8th	389	206	156
9th	390	206	157
10th	422	–	–

Umpires: J.S. Buller (7) and W.E. Phillipson (2).

Close: 1st day – E(1) 358-6 (Horton 58, Trueman 11); 2nd – I(1) 116-3 (Manjrekar 13, Borde 11); 3rd – I(2) 96-3 (Manjrekar 23, Gaekwad 3).

ENGLAND v INDIA 1959 (2nd Test)

Played at Lord's, London, on 18, 19, 20 June.
Toss: India.   Result: ENGLAND won by eight wickets.
Debuts: India – M.L. Jaisimha.

England won shortly after tea on the third day. Contractor played the highest innings of the match, batting part of the time with a runner after a ball from Statham had fractured one of his ribs. Roy, captain in the absence of Gaekwad through bronchitis, became Statham's 150th Test wicket. In the last of his 91 Test appearances, Evans took his record total of dismissals to 219, including the surviving England record of 46 stumpings.

INDIA

Pankaj Roy*	c Evans b Statham	15	c May b Trueman	0
N.J. Contractor	b Greenhough	81	(8) not out	11
P.R. Umrigar	b Statham	1	c Horton b Trueman	0
V.L. Manjrekar	lbw b Trueman	12	(5) lbw b Statham	61
J.M. Ghorpade	lbw b Greenhough	41	(4) c Evans b Statham	22
A.G. Kripal Singh	b Greenhough	0	b Statham	41
M.L. Jaisimha	lbw b Greenhough	1	(2) lbw b Moss	8
P.G. Joshi†	b Horton	4	(7) b Moss	6
Surendranath	b Greenhough	0	run out	0
S.P. Gupte	c May b Horton	0	st Evans b Greenhough	7
R.B. Desai	not out	2	b Greenhough	5
Extras	(LB 11)	11	(LB 4)	4
Total		**168**		**165**

ENGLAND

C.A. Milton	c Surendranath b Desai	14	c Joshi b Desai	3
K. Taylor	c Gupte b Desai	6	lbw b Surendranath	3
M.C. Cowdrey	c Joshi b Desai	34	not out	63
P.B.H. May*	b Surendranath	9	not out	33
K.F. Barrington	c sub (V.M. Muddiah) b Desai	80		
M.J. Horton	b Desai	2		
T.G. Evans†	b Surendranath	0		
F.S. Trueman	lbw b Gupte	7		
J.B. Statham	c Surendranath b Gupte	38		
A.E. Moss	b Surendranath	26		
T. Greenhough	not out	0		
Extras	(B 5, LB 4, W 1)	10	(B 5, LB 1)	6
Total		**226**	(2 wickets)	**108**

ENGLAND	O	M	R	W	O	M	R	W		FALL OF WICKETS			
Trueman	16	4	40	1	21	3	55	2		I	E	I	E
Statham	16	6	27	2	17	7	45	3	Wkt	1st	1st	2nd	2nd
Moss	14	5	31	0	23	10	30	2	1st	32	9	0	8
Greenhough	16	4	35	5	18·1	8	31	2	2nd	40	26	0	12
Horton	15·4	7	24	2					3rd	61	35	22	–
									4th	144	69	42	–
INDIA									5th	152	79	131	–
Desai	31·4	8	89	5	7	1	29	1	6th	158	80	140	–
Surendranath	30	17	46	3	11	2	32	1	7th	163	100	147	–
Umrigar	1	1	0	0	1	0	8	0	8th	163	184	147	–
Gupte	19	2	62	2	6	2	21	0	9th	164	226	159	–
Kripal Singh	3	0	19	0	1	1	0	0	10th	168	226	165	–
Jaisimha					1	0	8	0					
Roy					0·2	0	4	0					

Umpires: D.E. Davies (8) and C.S. Elliott (5).

Close: 1st day – E(1) 50-3 (Cowdrey 19, Barrington 1); 2nd – I(2) 108-4 (Manjrekar 46, Kripal Singh 28).

ENGLAND v INDIA 1959 (3rd Test)

Played at Headingley, Leeds, on 2, 3, 4 July.
Toss: India. Result: ENGLAND won by an innings and 173 runs.
Debuts: England – G. Pullar, H.J. Rhodes; India – A.L. Apte.

May, who missed the next match, equalled F.E. Woolley's world record of 52 consecutive Test appearances. Rhodes dismissed Roy and Borde with his fourth and twelfth balls in Test cricket. The opening partnership of 146 between Parkhouse, recalled after eight years, and Pullar set a new England record against India (subsequently beaten). Cowdrey's innings, then his highest in Tests, occupied only 280 minutes and included four sixes. After making six changes from the team that won at Lord's, England still achieved their second consecutive three-day victory.

INDIA

Pankaj Roy	c Swetman b Rhodes	2	c Swetman b Trueman		20
A.L. Apte	b Moss	8	c Close b Moss		7
J.M. Ghorpade	c Swetman b Trueman	8	lbw b Trueman		0
C.G. Borde	c Swetman b Rhodes	0	c May b Close		41
P.R. Umrigar	c Trueman b Moss	29	c Trueman b Mortimore		39
D.K. Gaekwad*	c Cowdrey b Rhodes	25	c and b Close		8
R.G. Nadkarni	c Parkhouse b Rhodes	27	c Barrington b Close		11
N.S. Tamhane†	c Moss b Trueman	20	not out		9
Surendranath	c Close b Trueman	5	c Cowdrey b Mortimore		1
S.P. Gupte	c Swetman b Close	21	c and b Close		1
R.B. Desai	not out	7	c Cowdrey b Mortimore		8
Extras	(LB 4, NB 5)	9	(LB 4)		4
Total		**161**			**149**

ENGLAND

W.G.A. Parkhouse	c Tamhane b Desai	78
G. Pullar	c Borde b Nadkarni	75
M.C. Cowdrey	c Ghorpade b Gupte	160
P.B.H. May*	b Desai	2
K.F. Barrington	c Tamhane b Nadkarni	80
D.B. Close	b Gupte	27
J.B. Mortimore	b Gupte	7
R. Swetman†	not out	19
F.S. Trueman	c Desai b Gupte	17
A.E. Moss	) did not bat	
H.J. Rhodes	)	
Extras	(B 13, LB 5)	18
Total	(8 wickets declared)	**483**

ENGLAND	O	M	R	W	O	M	R	W	FALL OF WICKETS			
Trueman	15	6	30	3	10	1	29	2		I	E	I
Moss	22	11	30	2	6	3	10	1	*Wkt*	*1st*	*1st*	*2nd*
Rhodes	18·5	3	50	4	10	2	35	0	1st	10	146	16
Mortimore	8	3	24	0	18·4	6	36	3	2nd	10	180	19
Close	5	1	18	1	11	0	35	4	3rd	11	186	38
									4th	23	379	107
INDIA									5th	75	432	115
Desai	38	10	111	2					6th	75	439	121
Surendranath	32	11	84	0					7th	103	453	138
Gupte	44·3	13	111	4					8th	112	483	139
Umrigar	24	8	44	0					9th	141	–	140
Borde	14	1	51	0					10th	161	–	149
Nadkarni	22	2	64	2								

Umpires: F.S. Lee (22) and W.E. Phillipson (3).

Close: 1st day – E(1) 61-0 (Parkhouse 38, Pullar 23); 2nd – E(1) 408-4 (Cowdrey 148, Close 12).

ENGLAND v INDIA 1959 (4th Test)

Played at Old Trafford, Manchester, on 23, 24, 25, 27, 28 July
Toss: England.   Result: ENGLAND won by 171 runs.
Debuts: India – A.A. Baig.

Abbas Ali Baig, an Oxford University Freshman who had scored a hundred against Middlesex on his first appearance for the tourists in their previous match, remains the only Indian to score a hundred in his first Test, that match being in England. At 20 years 131 days he was then the youngest to score a hundred for India. He retired hurt when he had scored 85 (at 173) and resumed at 180. Pullar was the first Lancashire player to score a hundred for England at Old Trafford. In the absence of May (surgery), Cowdrey made the first of his 27 appearances as England's captain. For the second year in succession, England won the first four Tests of a home rubber.

ENGLAND

W.G.A. Parkhouse	c Roy b Surendranath	17	c Contractor b Nadkarni	49
G. Pullar	c Joshi b Surendranath	131	c Joshi b Gupte	14
M.C. Cowdrey*	c Joshi b Nadkarni	67	(5) c Borde b Gupte	9
M.J.K. Smith	c Desai b Borde	100	c Desai b Gupte	9
K.F. Barrington	lbw b Surendranath	87	(6) lbw b Nadkarni	46
E.R. Dexter	c Roy b Surendranath	13	(3) c Umrigar b Gupte	45
R. Illingworth	c Gaekwad b Desai	21	not out	47
J.B. Mortimore	c Contractor b Gupte	29	(9) c Nadkarni b Borde	7
R. Swetman†	c Joshi b Gupte	9	(10) not out	21
F.S. Trueman	b Surendranath	0	(8) c Baig b Borde	8
H.J. Rhodes	not out	0		
Extras	(B 7, LB 7, W 2)	16	(B 9, LB 1)	10
Total		**490**	(8 wickets declared)	**265**

INDIA

Pankaj Roy	c Smith b Rhodes	15	c Illingworth b Dexter	21
N.J. Contractor	c Swetman b Rhodes	23	c Barrington b Rhodes	56
A.A. Baig	c Cowdrey b Illingworth	26	run out	112
D.K. Gaekwad*	lbw b Trueman	5	c Illingworth b Rhodes	0
P.R. Umrigar	b Rhodes	2	c Illingworth b Barrington	118
C.G. Borde	c and b Barrington	75	c Swetman b Mortimore	3
R.G. Nadkarni	b Barrington	31	lbw b Trueman	28
P.G. Joshi†	run out	5	b Illingworth	5
Surendranath	b Illingworth	11	c Trueman b Barrington	4
S.P. Gupte	not out	4	b Trueman	8
R.B. Desai	b Barrington	5	not out	7
Extras	(LB 1, W 4, NB 1)	6	(B 8, LB 5, NB 1)	14
Total		**208**		**376**

INDIA	O	M	R	W	O	M	R	W		FALL OF WICKETS			
Desai	39	7	129	1	8	2	14	0		E	I	E	I
Surendranath	47·1	17	115	5	8	5	15	0	*Wkt*	*1st*	*1st*	*2nd*	*2nd*
Umrigar	19	3	47	0	7	3	4	0	1st	33	23	44	35
Gupte	28	8	98	2	26	6	76	4	2nd	164	54	100	144
Nadkarni	28	14	47	1	30	6	93	2	3rd	262	70	117	146
Borde	13	1	38	1	11	1	53	2	4th	371	72	132	180
									5th	417	78	136	243
ENGLAND									6th	440	124	196	321
Trueman	15	4	29	1	23·1	6	75	2	7th	454	154	209	334
Rhodes	18	3	72	3	28	2	87	2	8th	490	199	219	358
Dexter	3	0	3	0	12	2	33	1	9th	490	199	–	361
Illingworth	16	10	16	2	39	13	63	1	10th	490	208	–	376
Mortimore	13	6	46	0	16	6	29	1					
Barrington	14	3	36	3	27	4	75	2					

Umpires: J.S. Buller (8) and C.S. Elliott (6).

Close: 1st day – E(1) 304-3 (Smith 55, Barrington 22); 2nd – I(1) 127-6 (Borde 22, Joshi 2); 3rd – E(2) 265-8 (Illingworth 47, Swetman 21); 4th – I(2) 236-4 (Umrigar 37, Nadkarni 2).

ENGLAND v INDIA 1959 (5th Test)

Played at Kennington Oval, London, on 20, 21, 22, 24 August.
Toss: India.   Result: ENGLAND won by an innings and 27 runs.
Debuts: Nil.

England won before lunch on the fourth day and for the first time gained five victories in a rubber. It was also the first time that this had been achieved in England, the only other instances so far being by Australia at home – against England in 1920-21 and against South Africa in 1931-32. The partnership of 169 between Subba Row and Smith remains England's highest for the third wicket against India. Remarkably, Gupte's total of 17 wickets in the rubber remains India's best in England.

INDIA

Pankaj Roy	b Statham	3	lbw b Statham		0
N.J. Contractor	c Illingworth b Dexter	22	c Trueman b Statham		25
A.A. Baig	c Cowdrey b Trueman	23	c Cowdrey b Statham		4
R.G. Nadkarni	c Swetman b Trueman	6	lbw b Illingworth		76
C.G. Borde	b Greenhough	0	run out		6
D.K. Gaekwad*	c Barrington b Dexter	11	c Swetman b Greenhough		15
J.M. Ghorpade	b Greenhough	5	b Greenhough		24
N.S. Tamhane†	c Swetman b Statham	32	b Trueman		9
Surendranath	c Illingworth b Trueman	27	not out		17
S.P. Gupte	b Trueman	2	c Greenhough b Trueman		5
R.B. Desai	not out	3	c Swetman b Trueman		0
Extras	(B 1, LB 4, NB 1)	6	(B 4, LB 6, NB 3)		13
Total		**140**			**194**

ENGLAND

G. Pullar	c Tamhane b Surendranath	22
R. Subba Row	c Tamhane b Desai	94
M.C. Cowdrey*	c Borde b Surendranath	6
M.J.K. Smith	b Desai	98
K.F. Barrington	c sub (M.L. Jaisimha) b Gupte	8
E.R. Dexter	c Tamhane b Surendranath	0
R. Illingworth	c Gaekwad b Nadkarni	50
R. Swetman†	c Baig b Surendranath	65
F.S. Trueman	st Tamhane b Nadkarni	1
J.B. Statham	not out	3
T. Greenhough	c Contractor b Surendranath	2
Extras	(B 3, LB 8, W 1)	12
Total		**361**

ENGLAND	O	M	R	W	O	M	R	W		FALL OF WICKETS		
Trueman	17	6	24	4	14	4	30	3		I	E	I
Statham	16·3	6	24	2	18	4	50	3	*Wkt*	*1st*	*1st*	*2nd*
Dexter	16	7	24	2	7	1	11	0	1st	12	38	5
Greenhough	29	11	36	2	27	12	47	2	2nd	43	52	17
Illingworth	1	0	2	0	29	10	43	1	3rd	49	221	44
Barrington	6	0	24	0					4th	50	232	70
									5th	67	233	106
INDIA									6th	72	235	159
Desai	33	5	103	2					7th	74	337	163
Surendranath	51·3	25	75	5					8th	132	347	173
Gupte	38	9	119	1					9th	134	358	188
Nadkarni	25	11	52	2					10th	140	361	194

Umpires: D.E. Davies (9) and F.S. Lee (23).

Close: 1st day – E(1) 35-0 (Pullar 20, Subba Row 15); 2nd – E(1) 289-6 (Illingworth 20, Swetman 33); 3rd – I(2) 146-5 (Nadkarni 69, Ghorpade 15).

PAKISTAN v AUSTRALIA 1959–60 (1st Test)

Played at Dacca Stadium on 13, 14, 15, 17, 18 November.
Toss: Australia. Result: AUSTRALIA won by eight wickets.
Debuts: Pakistan – D. Sharpe.

Australia gained their first win in Pakistan. The match was played on matting after heavy rain had made it impossible to use the new grass pitch. Israr Ali was recalled after an hiatus of exactly seven years. Wazir, eldest of the Mohammad brethren, made the last of his 20 Test appearances. Mackay achieved his best analysis in Tests. Pakistan's total of 134 is still their lowest against Australia in a home Test.

PAKISTAN

Hanif Mohammad	b Mackay	66	b Benaud		19
Ijaz Butt	c Grout b Davidson	0	b Mackay		20
Saeed Ahmed	c Harvey b Davidson	37	b Mackay		15
W. Mathias	c and b Benaud	4	lbw b Mackay		1
D. Sharpe	run out	56	lbw b Mackay		35
Wazir Mohammad	c Meckiff b Benaud	0	lbw b Benaud		5
Imtiaz Ahmed†	b Davidson	13	b Mackay		4
Israr Ali	st Grout b Benaud	7	(9) b Benaud		1
Shujauddin	not out	2	(8) not out		16
Fazal Mahmood*	b Benaud	1	c and b Mackay		4
Nasim-ul-Ghani	b Davidson	5	c McDonald b Benaud		0
Extras	(B 5, LB 1, NB 3)	9	(B 7, LB 5, NB 2)		14
Total		**200**			**134**

AUSTRALIA

C.C. McDonald	lbw b Fazal	19	not out	44
L.E. Favell	b Israr Ali	0	c and b Israr Ali	4
R.N. Harvey	b Fazal	96	b Fazal	30
N.C. O'Neill	b Nasim	2	not out	26
P.J.P. Burge	c Imtiaz b Nasim	0		
R. Benaud*	lbw b Nasim	16		
K.D. Mackay	b Fazal	7		
A.K. Davidson	lbw b Israr Ali	4		
A.T.W. Grout†	not out	66		
R.R. Lindwall	lbw b Fazal	4		
I. Meckiff	b Fazal	2		
Extras	(LB 9)	9	(B 3, LB 3, NB 2)	8
Total		**225**	(2 wickets)	**112**

AUSTRALIA	O	M	R	W	O	M	R	W
Davidson	23·5	7	42	4	11	3	23	0
Meckiff	10	2	33	0	3	1	8	0
Lindwall	15	1	31	0	2	0	5	0
Benaud	38	10	69	4	39·3	26	42	4
Mackay	19	12	16	1	45	27	42	6
PAKISTAN								
Fazal	35·5	11	71	5	20·1	4	52	1
Israr Ali	23	5	85	2	9	0	20	1
Nasim	17	4	51	3	10	2	16	0
Shujauddin	3	0	9	0	8	4	12	0
Saeed					1	0	4	0

FALL OF WICKETS

Wkt	P 1st	A 1st	P 2nd	A 2nd
1st	3	0	32	12
2nd	75	51	57	65
3rd	82	53	62	–
4th	145	53	68	–
5th	146	112	81	–
6th	170	134	94	–
7th	184	143	117	–
8th	191	151	128	–
9th	193	189	133	–
10th	200	225	134	–

Umpires: Khwaja Saeed Ahmed (2) and A.A. Qureshi (1).

Close: 1st day – P(1) 146-4 (Sharpe 35, Wazir 0); 2nd – A(1) 125-5 (Harvey 80, Mackay 4); 3rd – P(2) 74-4 (Sharpe 8, Wazir 3); 4th – A(2) 64-1 (McDonald 28, Harvey 29).

PAKISTAN v AUSTRALIA 1959–60 (2nd Test)

Played at Lahore (*now Gaddafi*) Stadium on 21, 22, 23, 25, 26 November.
Toss: Pakistan.   Result: AUSTRALIA won by seven wickets.
Debuts: Pakistan – Mohammad Munaf; Australia – G.B. Stevens.

This was the first Test match to be played at the Lahore Stadium; previous Tests in that city had been staged at the Bagh-i-Jinnah Ground (formerly Lawrence Gardens). Australia required 122 runs in just under even time and, with just 12 minutes to spare, became the first visiting country to win a rubber in Pakistan. Shujauddin spent 318 minutes over his 45 runs. Kline's only five-wicket analysis in Tests remains Australia's best in Pakistan.

PAKISTAN

Hanif Mohammad	c Grout b Meckiff	49	(5) b Kline		18
Imtiaz Ahmed*†	b Davidson	18	c O'Neill b Kline		54
Saeed Ahmed	c Grout b Meckiff	17	st Grout b Kline		166
Alimuddin	b Meckiff	8	(1) b Kline		7
D. Sharpe	c Grout b Kline	12	(6) st Grout b Kline		1
Waqar Hassan	c Grout b Davidson	12	(7) b Kline		4
Shujauddin	b Benaud	17	(4) lbw b O'Neill		45
Israr Ali	lbw b Benaud	0	(10) not out		0
Nasim-ul-Ghani	c Stevens b Davidson	6	(8) b Benaud		15
Mohammad Munaf	c Grout b Davidson	5	(9) c Davidson b Kline		19
Haseeb Ahsan	not out	0	c Grout b Benaud		4
Extras	(B 1, LB 1)	2	(B 31, LB 2)		33
Total		**146**			**366**

AUSTRALIA

C.C. McDonald	c Imtiaz b Haseeb	42			
G.B. Stevens	c Imtiaz b Munaf	9	c Alimuddin b Munaf		8
R.N. Harvey	lbw b Munaf	43	b Munaf		37
N.C. O'Neill	st Imtiaz b Shujauddin	134	not out		43
L.E. Favell	b Israr Ali	32	(1) b Israr Ali		4
A.T.W. Grout†	lbw b Nasim	12			
R. Benaud*	b Haseeb	29	(5) not out		21
A.K. Davidson	c Imtiaz b Israr Ali	47			
K.D. Mackay	c Imtiaz b Haseeb	26			
L.F. Kline	not out	0			
I. Meckiff	did not bat				
Extras	(B 5, LB 5, NB 7)	17	(B 6, LB 4)		10
Total	(9 wickets declared)	**391**	(3 wickets)		**123**

AUSTRALIA	O	M	R	W	O	M	R	W	FALL OF WICKETS				
Davidson	19	2	48	4	35	9	56	0		P	A	P	A
Meckiff	19	7	45	3	22	4	44	0	*Wkt*	*1st*	*1st*	*2nd*	*2nd*
Benaud	16	6	36	2	54·4	22	92	2	1st	39	27	45	13
Kline	12	6	15	1	44	21	75	7	2nd	56	83	87	15
O'Neill					13	5	37	1	3rd	92	114	256	77
Mackay					6	1	21	0	4th	109	213	312	–
Harvey					5	2	8	0	5th	115	247	319	–
									6th	120	310	324	–
PAKISTAN									7th	121	311	325	–
Munaf	31	8	100	2	10	2	38	2	8th	126	391	362	–
Israr Ali	13	5	29	2	5	1	20	1	9th	142	391	362	–
Nasim	21	3	72	1	3·3	0	18	0	10th	146	–	366	
Shujauddin	20	2	58	1	3	0	16	0					
Haseeb	33·3	8	115	3	4	0	21	0					

Umpires: Khwaja Saeed Ahmed (3) and A.A. Qureshi (2).

Close: 1st day – A(1) 27-1 (McDonald 15); 2nd – A(1) 311-6 (Benaud 29, Davidson 1); 3rd – P(2) 138-2 (Saeed 58, Shujauddin 9); 4th – P(2) 288-3 (Saeed 152, Hanif 10).

PAKISTAN v AUSTRALIA 1959–60 (3rd Test)

Played at National Stadium, Karachi, on 4, 5, 6, 8, 9 December.
Toss: Pakistan.   Result: MATCH DRAWN.
Debuts: Pakistan – Intikhab Alam, Munir Malik.

Dwight D. Eisenhower became the first President of the United States of America to see Test cricket when he attended the fourth day of this match. It remains the second slowest day's play in Test history with Pakistan scoring 104 for 5. On a similar matting pitch on the same ground three years earlier, these countries had combined to produce only 95 runs in a full day. Intikhab became the first Pakistan bowler to take a wicket with his first ball in Test cricket when he bowled McDonald on the second day. No other bowler accomplished this feat in the next quarter-century of Test cricket involving over 500 matches. Ijaz Butt needed 367 minutes to make his highest Test score of 58.

PAKISTAN

Hanif Mohammad	lbw b Lindwall	51	(4) not out	101
Imtiaz Ahmed†	b Davidson	18	c Harvey b Davidson	9
Saeed Ahmed	c Harvey b Lindwall	91	c Harvey b Davidson	8
Shujauddin	c O'Neill b Benaud	5	(6) c Favell b Mackay	4
D. Sharpe	c Burge b Benaud	4	c Mackay b Lindwall	26
Ijaz Butt	c Grout b Benaud	58	(1) run out	8
W. Mathias	c Favell b Mackay	43	c Davidson b Benaud	13
Intikhab Alam	run out	0	c Burge b Mackay	6
Fazal Mahmood*	c Harvey b Benaud	7	c Benaud b Davidson	11
Mohammad Munaf	not out	4	not out	4
Munir Malik	st Grout b Benaud	0		
Extras	(LB 3, NB 3)	6	(LB 2, NB 2)	4
Total		**287**	(8 wickets declared)	**194**

AUSTRALIA

C.C. McDonald	b Intikhab	19	lbw b Munir	30
G.B. Stevens	c Mathias b Fazal	13	c Imtiaz b Intikhab	28
A.T.W. Grout†	c and b Intikhab	20		
K.D. Mackay	c Ijaz Butt b Fazal	40		
R.N. Harvey	c Imtiaz b Fazal	54	(3) not out	13
N.C. O'Neill	b Munir	6	(4) not out	7
L.E. Favell	c Sharpe b Fazal	10		
P.J.P. Burge	c Sharpe b Munaf	12		
R. Benaud*	c Imtiaz b Munir	18		
A.K. Davidson	not out	39		
R.R. Lindwall	c Imtiaz b Fazal	23		
Extras	(LB 1, NB 2)	3	(LB 3, NB 2)	5
Total		**257**	(2 wickets)	**83**

AUSTRALIA	O	M	R	W	O	M	R	W		FALL OF WICKETS			
										P	A	P	A
Davidson	26	5	59	1	34	8	70	3	*Wkt*	*1st*	*1st*	*2nd*	*2nd*
Lindwall	25	6	72	2	17	10	14	1	1st	36	29	11	54
Benaud	49·5	17	93	5	26	13	48	1	2nd	124	33	25	76
Mackay	27	8	53	1	32·4	11	58	2	3rd	143	82	25	–
O'Neill	4	1	4	0					4th	149	106	78	–
									5th	181	122	91	–
PAKISTAN									6th	265	145	124	–
Fazal	30·2	12	74	5	10	5	16	0	7th	267	174	159	–
Munaf	8	0	42	1	3	0	10	0	8th	276	184	179	–
Intikhab	19	4	49	2	6	1	13	1	9th	287	207	–	–
Munir	22	5	76	2	9	1	24	1	10th	287	257	–	–
Shujauddin	3	0	13	0	2	1	9	0					
Saeed					3	0	6	0					

Umpires: Khwaja Saeed Ahmed (4) and Munawar Hussain (3).

Close: 1st day – P(1) 157-4 (Saeed 72, Ijaz 2); 2nd – A(1) 36-2 (Grout 1, Mackay 3); 3rd – P(2) 0-0 (Ijaz 0, Imtiaz 0); 4th – P(2) 104-5 (Hanif 40, Mathias 5).

INDIA v AUSTRALIA 1959–60 (1st Test)

Played at Feroz Shah Kotla, Delhi, on 12, 13, 14, 16 December.
Toss: India.   Result: AUSTRALIA won by an innings and 127 runs.
Debuts: India – V.M. Muddiah.

Spectators reacted to Australia's comprehensive win with more than a day to spare by throwing bottles on to the field and jostling the umpires. It was only the second Test to be finished in six matches played at Delhi. Benaud achieved the unique Test analysis of 3 for 0 as India recorded their lowest total in a home Test against Australia. Desai jarred his ankle in mid-over and left the field.

INDIA

Pankaj Roy	c Grout b Davidson	0		c Benaud b Kline	99
N.J. Contractor	b Davidson	41		c Favell b Benaud	34
P.R. Umrigar	c Grout b Davidson	0	(5)	c Favell b Kline	32
A.A. Baig	b Rorke	9	(3)	run out	5
C.G. Borde	c Grout b Meckiff	14	(4)	c Davidson b Benaud	0
G.S. Ramchand*	c Grout b Kline	20		c Davidson b Kline	6
R.G. Nadkarni	b Rorke	1		lbw b Benaud	7
P.G. Joshi†	b Benaud	15		c Davidson b Kline	8
Surendranath	not out	24		c Davidson b Benaud	0
V.M. Muddiah	lbw b Benaud	0		not out	0
R.B. Desai	c O'Neill b Benaud	0		c Meckiff b Benaud	0
Extras	(B 6, LB 2, NB 3)	11		(B 8, LB 5, NB 2)	15
Total		**135**			**206**

AUSTRALIA

C.C. McDonald	b Surendranath	20
L.E. Favell	b Surendranath	39
R.N. Harvey	lbw b Nadkarni	114
N.C. O'Neill	run out	39
K.D. Mackay	c Joshi b Umrigar	78
A.K. Davidson	c Baig b Desai	25
R. Benaud*	c Borde b Umrigar	20
A.T.W. Grout†	b Umrigar	42
L.F. Kline	c and b Ramchand	14
I. Meckiff	not out	45
G.F. Rorke	c sub (B.K. Kunderan) b Umrigar	7
Extras	(B 11, LB 13, NB 1)	25
Total		**468**

AUSTRALIA	O	M	R	W	O	M	R	W		FALL OF WICKETS		
Davidson	14	9	22	3	14	5	16	0		I	A	I
Meckiff	17	4	52	1	14	3	33	0	*Wkt*	*1st*	*1st*	*2nd*
Rorke	14	5	30	2	7	3	5	0	1st	4	53	121
Kline	9	3	15	1	24	12	42	4	2nd	8	64	132
Benaud	3·4	3	0	3	46	18	76	5	3rd	32	143	132
Mackay	1	0	1	0					4th	66	275	172
O'Neill	1	0	4	0	5	0	19	0	5th	69	318	187
Harvey					1	1	0	0	6th	70	353	192
INDIA									7th	100	398	202
Desai	34·3	3	123	1					8th	131	402	206
Surendranath	38	8	101	2					9th	135	443	206
Borde	15	3	49	0					10th	135	468	206
Muddiah	13	4	32	0								
Nadkarni	20	6	62	1								
Ramchand	7	1	27	1								
Umrigar	15·3	1	49	4								

Umpires: S.K. Ganguli (3) and Mahomed Yunus (3).

Close: 1st day – A(1) 22-0 (McDonald 9, Favell 13); 2nd – A(1) 293-4 (Mackay 50, Davidson 12); 3rd – I(2) 46-0 (Roy 25, Contractor 12).

INDIA v AUSTRALIA 1959–60 (2nd Test)

Played at Green Park, Kanpur, on 19, 20, 21, 23, 24 December.
Toss: India.   Result: INDIA won by 119 runs.
Debuts: Australia – B.N. Jarman.

Jasu Patel exploited a newly-laid turf pitch with his off-spin to return what is still India's best analysis in Test cricket. S.P. Gupte had taken 9 for 102 against West Indies on the same ground the previous season (*Test No. 460*). Rorke was taken ill with severe stomach problems soon after the start. Davidson's match analysis is the best for Australia against India. Patel was the first Indian bowler to take 14 wickets in a Test match. This was India's first success in 10 Tests against Australia since 1947. Australia's second innings total is their lowest in any Test in India.

INDIA

Pankaj Roy	c Harvey b Benaud	17	c Benaud b Davidson	8
N.J. Contractor	c Jarman b Benaud	24	c Harvey b Davidson	74
P.R. Umrigar	c Davidson b Kline	6	c Rorke b Davidson	14
A.A. Baig	b Davidson	19	c Harvey b Benaud	36
C.G. Borde	c Kline b Davidson	20	c O'Neill b Meckiff	44
G.S. Ramchand*	c Mackay b Benaud	24	b Harvey	5
R.B. Kenny	b Davidson	0	c Jarman b Davidson	51
R.G. Nadkarni	c Harvey b Davidson	25	lbw b Davidson	46
N.S. Tamhane†	b Benaud	1	c Harvey b Davidson	0
J.M. Patel	c Kline b Davidson	4	(11) b Davidson	0
Surendranath	not out	8	(10) not out	4
Extras	(LB 2, NB 2)	4	(B 7, LB 2)	9
Total		**152**		**291**

AUSTRALIA

C.C. McDonald	b Patel	53	st Tamhane b Patel	34
G.B. Stevens	c and b Patel	25	c Kenny b Patel	7
R.N. Harvey	b Patel	51	c Nadkarni b Umrigar	25
N.C. O'Neill	b Borde	16	c Nadkarni b Umrigar	5
K.D. Mackay	lbw b Patel	0	lbw b Umrigar	0
A.K. Davidson	b Patel	41	b Patel	8
R. Benaud*	b Patel	7	c Ramchand b Patel	0
B.N. Jarman†	lbw b Patel	1	b Umrigar	0
L.F. Kline	b Patel	9	b Patel	0
I. Meckiff	not out	1	not out	14
G.F. Rorke	c Baig b Patel	0	absent ill	–
Extras	(B 9, LB 2, NB 4)	15	(B 5, LB 7)	12
Total		**219**		**105**

AUSTRALIA	O	M	R	W	O	M	R	W					
Davidson	20·1	7	31	5	57·3	23	93	7					
Meckiff	8	2	15	0	18	4	37	1					
Benaud	25	8	63	4	38	15	81	1					
Rorke	2	1	3	0									
Kline	15	7	36	1	7	3	14	0					
Mackay					10	5	14	0					
Harvey					12	3	31	1					
O'Neill					2	0	12	0					

FALL OF WICKETS				
	I	A	I	A
Wkt	1st	1st	2nd	2nd
1st	38	71	32	12
2nd	47	128	72	49
3rd	51	149	121	59
4th	77	159	147	61
5th	112	159	153	78
6th	112	174	214	78
7th	126	186	286	79
8th	128	216	286	84
9th	141	219	291	105
10th	152	219	291	–

INDIA	O	M	R	W	O	M	R	W
Surendranath	4	0	13	0	4	2	4	0
Ramchand	6	3	14	0	3	0	7	0
Patel	35·5	16	69	9	25·4	7	55	5
Umrigar	15	1	40	0	25	11	27	4
Borde	15	1	61	1				
Nadkarni	2	0	7	0				

Umpires: S.K. Ganguli (4) and A.R. Joshi (8).

Close: 1st day – A(1) 23-0 (McDonald 14, Stevens 9); 2nd – I(2) 31-0 (Roy 8, Contractor 23); 3rd – I(2) 226-6 (Kenny 29, Nadkarni 8); 4th – A(2) 59-2 (McDonald 16, O'Neill 5).

INDIA v AUSTRALIA 1959–60 (3rd Test)

Played at Brabourne Stadium, Bombay, on 1, 2, 3, 5, 6 January.
Toss: India.   Result: MATCH DRAWN.
Debuts: India – S.A. Durani (*not A.S. Durrani*), B.K. Kunderan.

Patel, hero of the previous Test, was taken ill on the morning of the match and his replacement, Durani, was unable to bowl because of a cut finger. Umrigar (back strain) took no part in the last two days' play. India declared leaving Australia 25 minutes in which to score 129 runs. The partnership of 207 between Harvey and O'Neill was then the highest for the third-wicket by either country in this series. Earlier, Contractor had scored his only hundred in an aggregate of 1,611 runs from 52 Test innings.

INDIA

Pankaj Roy	b Davidson	6	b Meckiff	57
N.J. Contractor	c Benaud b Meckiff	108	b Lindwall	43
P.R. Umrigar	c Harvey b Davidson	0		
A.A. Baig	c Grout b Davidson	50	(5) c Mackay b Lindwall	58
C.G. Borde	b Meckiff	26	(4) b Meckiff	1
G.S. Ramchand*	lbw b Meckiff	0		
R.B. Kenny	b Meckiff	20	(6) not out	55
B.K. Kunderan†	lbw b Lindwall	19	(3) hit wkt b Meckiff	2
R.G. Nadkarni	not out	18	(7) not out	1
S.A. Durani	c Stevens b Benaud	18		
G.M. Guard	c Benaud b Davidson	7		
Extras	(B 9, LB 4, NB 4)	17	(LB 9)	9
Total		**289**	(5 wickets declared)	**226**

AUSTRALIA

C.C. McDonald	b Nadkarni	36		
G.B. Stevens	b Nadkarni	22		
R.N. Harvey	b Nadkarni	102		
N.C. O'Neill	c sub (M.M. Sood) b Borde	163		
L.E. Favell	b Nadkarni	1		
A.T.W. Grout†	b Nadkarni	31	(1) not out	22
R. Benaud*	lbw b Nadkarni	14	(3) not out	12
A.K. Davidson	not out	9		
K.D. Mackay	b Borde	1		
R.R. Lindwall	not out	1		
I. Meckiff	did not bat	–	(2) b Roy	0
Extras	(B 4, LB 3)	7		
Total	(8 wickets declared)	**387**	(1 wicket)	**34**

AUSTRALIA	O	M	R	W	O	M	R	W
Davidson	34·5	9	62	4	14	4	25	0
Lindwall	23	7	56	1	23	7	56	2
Mackay	6	3	11	0	6	4	6	0
Meckiff	38	12	79	4	28	8	67	3
Benaud	41	24	64	1	24	10	36	0
O'Neill					3	1	16	0
Harvey					3	1	11	0
INDIA								
Guard	33	7	93	0	1	0	1	0
Ramchand	35	13	85	0				
Umrigar	8	2	19	0				
Nadkarni	51	11	105	6				
Borde	13	1	78	2				
Roy					2	0	6	1
Contractor					2	1	5	0
Baig					2	0	13	0
Durani					1	0	9	0

FALL OF WICKETS

	I	A	I	A
Wkt	1st	1st	2nd	2nd
1st	21	60	95	4
2nd	21	63	99	–
3rd	154	270	111	–
4th	199	282	112	–
5th	199	358	221	–
6th	203	376	–	–
7th	229	379	–	–
8th	246	380	–	–
9th	272	–	–	–
10th	289	–	–	–

Umpires: H.E. Choudhury (1) and N.D. Nagarwalla (5).

Close: 1st day – I(1) 153-2 (Contractor 86, Baig 50); 2nd – A(1) 17-0 (McDonald 9, Stevens 4); 3rd – A(1) 229-2 (Harvey 85, O'Neill 80); 4th – I(2) 92-0 (Roy 55, Contractor 32).

INDIA v AUSTRALIA 1959–60 (4th Test)

Played at Corporation Stadium, Madras, on 13, 14, 15, 17 January.
Toss: Australia.   Result: AUSTRALIA won by an innings and 55 runs.
Debuts: India – A.G. Milkha Singh, M.M. Sood.

Australia's second victory by an innings in the rubber was completed with 40 minutes of the penultimate day to spare. Davidson took his hundredth Test wicket when he bowled Sood. Favell batted throughout the first day for his only Test century before Mackay took $3\frac{1}{2}$ hours for his highest score for Australia.

AUSTRALIA

C.C. McDonald	b Patel	16
L.E. Favell	st Kunderan b Nadkarni	101
R.N. Harvey	b Desai	11
N.C. O'Neill	b Desai	40
P.J.P. Burge	b Desai	35
K.D. Mackay	st Kunderan b Patel	89
A.K. Davidson	lbw b Nadkarni	6
A.T.W. Grout†	c Milkha Singh b Nadkarni	2
R. Benaud*	b Borde	25
I. Meckiff	c Roy b Desai	8
L.F. Kline	not out	0
Extras	(B 3, LB 5, NB 1)	9
Total		**342**

INDIA

Pankaj Roy	c Grout b Davidson	1	c O'Neill b Meckiff	3
B.K. Kunderan†	b Benaud	71	(4) b Benaud	33
R.B. Kenny	b Mackay	33	c Grout b Meckiff	1
N.J. Contractor	c Kline b Benaud	7	(2) c Meckiff b Kline	41
C.G. Borde	c Grout b Kline	3	c Davidson b Benaud	1
G.S. Ramchand*	c Harvey b Benaud	13	(8) st Grout b Benaud	22
A.G. Milkha Singh	b Davidson	16	(6) b Harvey	9
R.G. Nadkarni	c Kline b Benaud	3	(7) run out	18
M.M. Sood	st Grout b Davidson	0	b Davidson	3
R.B. Desai	c McDonald b Benaud	0	not out	0
J.M. Patel	not out	0	c Kline b Davidson	0
Extras	(B 1, NB 1)	2	(B 4, LB 2, NB 1)	7
Total		**149**		**138**

INDIA	O	M	R	W	O	M	R	W		FALL OF WICKETS		
Desai	41	10	93	4						A	I	I
Ramchand	15	6	26	0					Wkt	1st	1st	2nd
Nadkarni	44	15	75	3					1st	58	20	7
Patel	37	12	84	2					2nd	77	95	11
Borde	16	1	55	1					3rd	147	111	54
									4th	197	114	62
AUSTRALIA									5th	216	130	78
Davidson	19	6	36	3	19	7	33	2	6th	239	130	100
Meckiff	7	4	21	0	22	10	33	2	7th	249	145	127
Benaud	32·1	14	43	5	35	19	43	3	8th	308	148	138
Kline	15	8	21	1	12	5	13	1	9th	329	149	138
Harvey	1	0	9	0	13	7	8	1	10th	342	149	138
Mackay	3	0	17	1	4	3	1	0				

Umpires: N.D. Sane (1) and M.G. Vijayasarathi (13).

Close: 1st day – A(1) 183-3 (Favell 100, Burge 13); 2nd – I(1) 46-1 (Kunderan 33, Kenny 11); 3rd – I(2) 26-2 (Contractor 11, Kunderan 10).

INDIA v AUSTRALIA 1959–60 (5th Test)

Played at Eden Gardens, Calcutta, on 23, 24, 25, 27, 28 January.
Toss: India.   Result: MATCH DRAWN.
Debuts: Nil.

Left to score 203 runs in 150 minutes, Australia were content to draw and take the rubber by two matches to one. After O'Neill had scored Australia's first century in a Calcutta Test, Lindwall, in his final match, took his record Australian total of Test wickets to 228 – just eight short of the then world record held by A.V. Bedser. Jaisimha was the first to bat on each day of a five-day Test.

INDIA

B.K. Kunderan†	b Mackay	12	b Davidson		0
N.J. Contractor	b Benaud	36	c Davidson b Benaud		30
Pankaj Roy	c Grout b Davidson	33	lbw b Benaud		39
R.G. Nadkarni	c Burge b Lindwall	2	(6) c Grout b Lindwall		29
R.B. Kenny	c Grout b Lindwall	7	(8) c Grout b Mackay		62
C.D. Gopinath	b Benaud	39	(5) c Grout b Benaud		0
C.G. Borde	b Benaud	6	b Meckiff		50
G.S. Ramchand*	b Davidson	12	(9) b Benaud		9
M.L. Jaisimha	not out	20	(4) b Mackay		74
R.B. Desai	c Grout b Davidson	17	not out		17
J.M. Patel	run out	0	c Benaud b Davidson		12
Extras	(B 5, LB 1, W 1, NB 3)	10	(B 11, LB 4, NB 2)		17
Total		**194**			**339**

AUSTRALIA

L.E. Favell	b Desai	26	not out		62
A.T.W. Grout†	b Patel	50			
R.N. Harvey	c Jaisimha b Patel	17	c and b Contractor		36
N.C. O'Neill	c Kunderan b Desai	113			
P.J.P. Burge	b Desai	60			
C.C. McDonald	lbw b Borde	27	(2) run out		6
K.D. Mackay	b Patel	18			
R.R. Lindwall	c Kunderan b Desai	10			
A.K. Davidson	b Borde	4			
R. Benaud*	c and b Borde	3	(4) not out		10
I. Meckiff	not out	0			
Extras	(LB 3)	3	(B 1, LB 5, NB 1)		7
Total		**331**	(2 wickets)		**121**

AUSTRALIA	O	M	R	W	O	M	R	W		FALL OF WICKETS			
Davidson	16	2	37	3	36·2	13	76	2		I	A	I	A
Meckiff	17	5	28	0	21	2	41	1	*Wkt*	*1st*	*1st*	*2nd*	*2nd*
Mackay	11	5	16	1	21	7	36	2	1st	30	76	0	20
Lindwall	16	6	44	2	20	3	66	1	2nd	59	76	67	104
Benaud	29·3	12	59	3	48	23	103	4	3rd	71	116	78	–
									4th	83	266	78	–
INDIA									5th	112	273	123	–
Desai	36	4	111	4	11	4	18	0	6th	131	299	206	–
Ramchand	10	1	37	0	3	2	4	0	7th	142	323	289	–
Patel	26	2	104	3	7	1	15	0	8th	158	325	294	–
Nadkarni	22	10	36	0	7	4	10	0	9th	194	328	316	–
Borde	13·1	4	23	3	13	1	45	0	10th	194	331	339	–
Jaisimha	4	0	17	0	6	2	13	0					
Contractor					5	1	9	1					

Umpires: S.K. Ganguli (5) and N.D. Sane (2).

Close: 1st day – I(1) 158-7 (Ramchand 12, Jaisimha 2); 2nd – A(1) 229-3 (O'Neill 93, Burge 43); 3rd – I(2) 67-2 (Roy 31, Jaisimha 0); 4th – I(2) 243-6 (Jaisimha 59, Kenny 26).

WEST INDIES v ENGLAND 1959–60 (1st Test)

Played at Kensington Oval, Bridgetown, Barbados, on 6, 7, 8, 9, 11, 12 January.
Toss: England.   Result: MATCH DRAWN.
Debuts: West Indies – R.O. Scarlett, C.D. Watson; England – D.A. Allen.

Worrell (682 minutes) and Sobers (647 minutes) played the two then longest innings against England and their partnership of 399 in 579 minutes remains the West Indies record for any wicket against England, the West Indies fourth-wicket record in all Tests, the highest fourth-wicket stand by any country against England, and the longest partnership in Test cricket. Worrell's innings remains the longest for West Indies. They are the only pair to bat throughout two consecutive days of a Test match, although a rest day intervened and the final hour of their first day together was lost to rain. Earlier Alexander had set a West Indies record by holding five catches in an innings and McMorris had been run out off a no-ball.

ENGLAND

G. Pullar	run out	65	not out	46
M.C. Cowdrey	c Sobers b Watson	30	not out	16
K.F. Barrington	c Alexander b Ramadhin	128		
P.B.H. May*	c Alexander b Hall	1		
M.J.K. Smith	c Alexander b Scarlett	39		
E.R. Dexter	not out	136		
R. Illingworth	b Ramadhin	5		
R. Swetman†	c Alexander b Worrell	45		
F.S. Trueman	c Alexander b Ramadhin	3		
D.A. Allen	lbw b Watson	10		
A.E. Moss	b Watson	4		
Extras	(B 4, LB 6, NB 6)	16	(B 7, LB 1, W 1)	9
Total		**482**	(0 wickets)	**71**

WEST INDIES

C.C. Hunte	c Swetman b Barrington	42
E.D.A. St J. McMorris	run out	0
R.B. Kanhai	b Trueman	40
G. St A. Sobers	b Trueman	226
F.M.M. Worrell	not out	197
B.F. Butcher	c Trueman b Dexter	13
W.W. Hall	lbw b Trueman	14
F.C.M. Alexander*†	c Smith b Trueman	3
R.O. Scarlett	lbw b Dexter	7
C.D. Watson	} did not bat	
S. Ramadhin	}	
Extras	(B 8, LB 7, W 1, NB 5)	21
Total	(8 wickets declared)	**563**

WEST INDIES	O	M	R	W	O	M	R	W		FALL OF WICKETS		
Hall	40	9	98	1	6	2	9	0		E	WI	E
Watson	32·4	6	121	3	8	1	19	0	*Wkt*	*1st*	*1st*	*2nd*
Worrell	15	2	39	1					1st	50	6	–
Ramadhin	54	22	109	3	7	2	11	0	2nd	153	68	–
Scarlett	26	9	46	1	10	4	12	0	3rd	162	102	–
Sobers	21	3	53	0					4th	251	501	–
Hunte					7	2	9	0	5th	291	521	–
Kanhai					4	3	2	0	6th	303	544	–
									7th	426	556	–
ENGLAND									8th	439	563	–
Trueman	47	15	93	4					9th	478	–	–
Moss	47	14	116	0					10th	482	–	–
Dexter	37·4	11	85	2								
Illingworth	47	9	106	0								
Allen	43	12	82	0								
Barrington	18	3	60	1								

Umpires: H.B. de C. Jordan (6) and J. Roberts (1).

Close: 1st day – E(1) 188-3 (Barrington 73, Smith 9); 2nd – E(1) 430-7 (Dexter 103, Trueman 0); 3rd – WI(1)114-3 (Sobers 21, Worrell 8); 4th – WI(1) 279-3 (Sobers 100, Worrell 91); 5th – WI(1) 486-3 (Sobers 216, Worrell 177).

WEST INDIES v ENGLAND 1959–60 (2nd Test)

Played at Queen's Park Oval, Port-of-Spain, Trinidad, on 28, 29, 30 January, 1, 2, 3 February.
Toss: England.   Result: ENGLAND won by 256 runs.
Debuts: West Indies – C.K. Singh.

A dramatic match which was marred when sections of the crowd of 30,000 – a record for any sporting event in the West Indies – threw bottles, rioted, and brought play to a premature close when Singh was run out soon after tea on the third day. Earlier Hall and Watson had been warned by umpires Lloyd and Lee Kow respectively for intimidatory bowling. Barrington scored his second hundred in only his second innings against West Indies. England won with 110 minutes to spare after setting West Indies 501 runs to win in 10 hours.

ENGLAND

G. Pullar	c Alexander b Watson	17	c Worrell b Ramadhin	28
M.C. Cowdrey	b Hall	18	c Alexander b Watson	5
K.F. Barrington	c Alexander b Hall	121	c Alexander b Hall	49
P.B.H. May*	c Kanhai b Watson	0	c and b Singh	28
E.R. Dexter	c and b Singh	77	b Hall	0
M.J.K. Smith	c Worrell b Ramadhin	108	lbw b Watson	12
R. Illingworth	b Ramadhin	10	not out	41
R. Swetman†	lbw b Watson	1	lbw b Singh	0
F.S. Trueman	lbw b Ramadhin	7	c Alexander b Watson	37
D.A. Allen	not out	10	c Alexander b Hall	16
J.B. Statham	b Worrell	1		
Extras	(LB 3, W 1, NB 8)	12	(B 6, LB 2, W 4, NB 2)	14
Total		**382**	(9 wickets declared)	**230**

WEST INDIES

C.C. Hunte	c Trueman b Statham	8	c Swetman b Allen	47
J.S. Solomon	run out	23	c Swetman b Allen	9
R.B. Kanhai	lbw b Trueman	5	c Smith b Dexter	110
G. St A. Sobers	c Barrington b Trueman	0	lbw b Trueman	31
F.M.M. Worrell	c Swetman b Trueman	9	lbw b Statham	0
B.F. Butcher	lbw b Statham	9	lbw b Statham	9
F.C.M. Alexander*†	lbw b Trueman	28	c Trueman b Allen	7
S. Ramadhin	b Trueman	23	lbw b Dexter	0
C.K. Singh	run out	0	c and b Barrington	11
W.W. Hall	b Statham	4	not out	0
C.D. Watson	not out	0	c Allen b Barrington	0
Extras	(LB 2, W 1)	3	(B 11, LB 6, W 2, NB 1)	20
Total		**112**		**244**

WEST INDIES	O	M	R	W	O	M	R	W		FALL OF WICKETS			
Hall	33	9	92	2	23·4	4	50	3		E	WI	E	WI
Watson	31	5	100	3	19	6	57	3	*Wkt*	*1st*	*1st*	*2nd*	*2nd*
Worrell	11·5	3	23	1	12	5	27	0	1st	37	22	18	29
Singh	23	6	59	1	8	3	28	2	2nd	42	31	79	107
Ramadhin	35	12	61	3	28	8	54	1	3rd	57	31	97	158
Sobers	3	0	16	0					4th	199	45	101	159
Solomon	7	0	19	0					5th	276	45	122	188
									6th	307	73	133	222
ENGLAND									7th	308	94	133	222
Trueman	21	11	35	5	19	9	44	1	8th	343	98	201	244
Statham	19·3	8	42	3	25	12	44	2	9th	378	108	230	244
Allen	5	0	9	0	31	13	57	3	10th	382	112	–	244
Barrington	16	10	15	0	25·5	13	34	2					
Illingworth	7	3	8	0	28	14	38	0					
Dexter					6	3	7	2					

Umpires: E.N. Lee Kow (7) and E.L. Lloyd (3).

Close: 1st day – E(1) 220-4 (Barrington 93, Smith 9); 2nd – WI(1) 22-0 (Hunte 8, Solomon 14); 3rd – WI(1) 98-8 (Ramadhin 13); 4th – E(2) 196-7 (Illingworth 28, Trueman 31); 5th – WI(2) 134-2 (Kanhai 55, Sobers 19).

WEST INDIES v ENGLAND 1959–60 (3rd Test)

Played at Sabina Park, Kingston, Jamaica, on 17, 18, 19, 20, 22, 23 February.
Toss: England.   Result: MATCH DRAWN.
Debuts: West Indies – S.M. Nurse.

England failed to take a wicket on the third day, McMorris (65) retiring with a contused lung at 189 after being hit on the chest by a ball from Statham; he resumed his innings at 329. After England's last wicket had survived for 45 minutes on the final morning, West Indies required 230 to square the rubber in 245 minutes. At tea their target had become 115 in 90 minutes with six wickets left. They gave up the chase when Kanhai was sixth out three quarters of an hour before the close. Six England batsmen were 'lbw' in the second innings, equalling the Test record which they had set in 1955 (*Test No. 411*).

ENGLAND

G. Pullar	c Sobers b Hall	19	lbw b Ramadhin	66
M.C. Cowdrey	c Scarlett b Ramadhin	114	c Alexander b Scarlett	97
K.F. Barrington	c Alexander b Watson	16	lbw b Solomon	4
P.B.H. May*	c Hunte b Hall	9	b Hall	45
E.R. Dexter	c Alexander b Hall	25	b Watson	16
M.J.K. Smith	b Hall	0	lbw b Watson	10
R. Illingworth	c Alexander b Hall	17	b Ramadhin	6
R. Swetman†	b Hall	0	lbw b Watson	5
F.S. Trueman	c Solomon b Ramadhin	17	lbw b Watson	4
D.A. Allen	not out	30	not out	17
J.B. Statham	b Hall	13	lbw b Ramadhin	12
Extras	(LB 4, W 10, NB 3)	17	(B 8, LB 10, W 3, NB 2)	23
Total		**277**		**305**

WEST INDIES

C.C. Hunte	c Illingworth b Statham	7	b Trueman	40
E.D.A. St J. McMorris	b Barrington	73	b Trueman	1
R.B. Kanhai	run out	18	b Trueman	57
G. St A. Sobers	lbw b Trueman	147	run out	19
S.M. Nurse	c Smith b Illingworth	70	b Trueman	11
J.S. Solomon	c Swetman b Allen	8	(8) not out	10
R.O. Scarlett	c Statham b Illingworth	6	(6) lbw b Statham	12
F.C.M. Alexander*†	b Trueman	0	(7) not out	7
S. Ramadhin	b Statham	5		
C.D. Watson	b Statham	3		
W.W. Hall	not out	0		
Extras	(B 6, LB 7, W 1, NB 2)	16	(B 9, LB 3, W 6)	18
Total		**353**	(6 wickets)	**175**

WEST INDIES	O	M	R	W	O	M	R	W	FALL OF WICKETS				
										E	WI	E	WI
Hall	31·2	8	69	7	26	5	93	1	*Wkt*	*1st*	*1st*	*2nd*	*2nd*
Watson	29	7	74	1	27	8	62	4	1st	28	12	177	11
Ramadhin	28	3	78	2	28·3	14	38	3	2nd	54	56	177	48
Scarlett	10	4	13	0	28	12	51	1	3rd	68	299	190	86
Sobers	2	0	14	0	8	2	18	0	4th	113	329	211	111
Solomon	4	1	12	0	6	1	20	1	5th	113	329	239	140
ENGLAND									6th	165	329	258	152
Statham	32·1	8	76	3	18	6	45	1	7th	170	341	269	–
Trueman	33	10	82	2	18	4	54	4	8th	215	347	269	–
Dexter	12	3	38	0					9th	245	350	280	–
Allen	28	10	57	1	9	4	19	0	10th	277	353	305	–
Barrington	21	7	38	1	4	4	0	0					
Illingworth	30	13	46	2	13	4	35	0					
Cowdrey					1	0	4	0					

Umpires: P. Burke (6) and E.N. Lee Kow (8).

Close: 1st day – E(1) 165-6 (Cowdrey 75); 2nd – WI(1) 81-2 (McMorris 31, Sobers 17); 3rd – WI(1) 291-2 (Sobers 142, Nurse 46); 4th – E(2) 65-0 (Pullar 40, Cowdrey 17); 5th – E(2) 280-9 (Allen 7, Statham 0).

WEST INDIES v ENGLAND 1959–60 (4th Test)

Played at Bourda, Georgetown, British Guiana, on 9, 10, 11, 12, 14, 15 March.
Toss: England.   Result: MATCH DRAWN.
Debuts: Nil.

Rain delayed the start by 75 minutes. Barrington, struck above the elbow by Hall on the first day, retired at 161 after 20 minutes' batting on the second, and resumed at 219. After Sobers had scored his third hundred of the rubber, West Indies declared with a lead of 107, eight hours of play left, and Watson (torn ankle ligaments) unable to bowl. Subba Row scored his first Test hundred under the handicap of a chipped knuckle and in his first match against West Indies.

ENGLAND

G. Pullar	c Alexander b Hall	33	lbw b Worrell	47
M.C. Cowdrey*	c Alexander b Hall	65	st Alexander b Singh	27
R. Subba Row	c Alexander b Sobers	27	(4) lbw b Worrell	100
K.F. Barrington	c Walcott b Sobers	27	(7) c Walcott b Worrell	0
E.R. Dexter	c Hunte b Hall	39	(3) c Worrell b Walcott	110
M.J.K. Smith	b Hall	0	(5) c Scarlett b Sobers	23
R. Illingworth	b Sobers	4	(6) c Kanhai b Worrell	9
R. Swetman†	lbw b Watson	4	(9) c Hall b Singh	3
D.A. Allen	c Alexander b Hall	55	(8) not out	1
F.S. Trueman	b Hall	6		
J.B. Statham	not out	20		
Extras	(B 5, LB 2, W 2, NB 6)	15	(B 6, LB 4, NB 4)	14
Total		**295**	(8 wickets)	**334**

WEST INDIES

C.C. Hunte	c Trueman b Allen	39
E.D.A. St J. McMorris	c Swetman b Statham	35
R.B. Kanhai	c Dexter b Trueman	55
G. St A. Sobers	st Swetman b Allen	145
C.L. Walcott	b Trueman	9
F.M.M. Worrell	b Allen	38
F.C.M. Alexander*†	run out	33
R.O. Scarlett	not out	29
C.K. Singh	b Trueman	0
W.W. Hall	not out	1
C.D. Watson	did not bat	
Extras	(B 4, LB 12, NB 2)	18
Total	(8 wickets declared)	**402**

WEST INDIES	O	M	R	W	O	M	R	W
Hall	30·2	8	90	6	18	1	79	0
Watson	20	2	56	1				
Worrell	16	9	22	0	31	12	49	4
Scarlett	22	11	24	0	38	13	63	0
Singh	12	4	29	0	41·2	22	50	2
Sobers	19	1	59	3	12	1	36	1
Walcott					9	0	43	1
ENGLAND								
Trueman	40	6	116	3				
Statham	36	8	79	1				
Illingworth	43	11	72	0				
Barrington	6	2	22	0				
Allen	42	11	75	3				
Dexter	5	0	20	0				

FALL OF WICKETS

Wkt	E 1st	WI 1st	E 2nd
1st	73	67	40
2nd	121	77	110
3rd	152	192	258
4th	161	212	320
5th	169	333	322
6th	175	338	322
7th	219	393	331
8th	258	398	334
9th	268	–	–
10th	295	–	–

Umpires: C.P. Kippins (2) and E.N. Lee Kow (9).

Close: 1st day – E(1) 152-2 (Cowdrey 65, Barrington 22); 2nd – WI(1) 32-0 (Hunte 22, McMorris 9); 3rd – WI(1) 139-2 (Kanhai 31, Sobers 33); 4th – WI(1) 332-4 (Sobers 142, Worrell 38); 5th – E(2) 110-2 (Dexter 30).

WEST INDIES v ENGLAND 1959–60 (5th Test)

Played at Queen's Park Oval, Port-of-Spain, Trinidad, on 25, 26, 28, 29, 30, 31 March.
Toss: England.   Result: MATCH DRAWN.
Debuts: West Indies – C.C. Griffith.

England won their fifth toss of the rubber – the only time that this has been achieved by a side with a change of captain. Barrington (23) retired hurt at 256 in the last over of the first day after twice being hit on the knuckles by Hall. Although fit to resume immediately the next morning, he had to wait until the fall of the fourth wicket as the umpires ruled, quite correctly, that a new batsman must go in. Hunte (12) retired hurt at 24 when he edged a hook at Trueman into his ear; he resumed two days later at 227. Smith and Parks (a late addition to the touring party) added 197 to set the present record for England's seventh wicket. West Indies were set 406 to win at 140 runs per hour. Pullar had Worrell caught on the boundary with his sixth ball in Test cricket.

ENGLAND

G. Pullar	c Sobers b Griffith	10	c and b Sobers	54
M.C. Cowdrey*	c Alexander b Sobers	119	c Worrell b Hall	0
E.R. Dexter	c and b Sobers	76	(4) run out	47
R. Subba Row	c Hunte b Hall	22	(5) lbw b Ramadhin	13
K.F. Barrington	c Alexander b Ramadhin	69	(6) c McMorris b Sobers	6
M.J.K. Smith	b Ramadhin	20	(7) c Alexander b Hunte	96
J.M. Parks†	c and b Sobers	43	(8) not out	101
R. Illingworth	c Sobers b Ramadhin	0		
D.A. Allen	c sub (S.M. Nurse) b Ramadhin	7	(3) run out	25
F.S. Trueman	not out	10	(9) not out	2
A.E. Moss	b Watson	1		
Extras	(B 7, NB 9)	16	(B 2, LB 3, NB 1)	6
Total		**393**	(7 wickets declared)	**350**

WEST INDIES

C.C. Hunte	not out	72	st Parks b Illingworth	36
E.D.A. St J. McMorris	run out	13	lbw b Moss	2
F.C.M. Alexander*†	b Allen	26	(7) not out	4
G. St A. Sobers	b Moss	92	(6) not out	49
C.L. Walcott	st Parks b Allen	53	(4) c Parks b Barrington	22
F.M.M. Worrell	b Trueman	15	(5) c Trueman b Pullar	61
R.B. Kanhai	b Moss	6	(3) c Trueman b Illingworth	34
S. Ramadhin	c Cowdrey b Dexter	13		
W.W. Hall	b Trueman	29		
C.C. Griffith	not out	5		
C.D. Watson	did not bat			
Extras	(B 6, LB 4, NB 4)	14	(LB 1)	1
Total	(8 wickets declared)	**338**	(5 wickets)	**209**

WEST INDIES	O	M	R	W	O	M	R	W		FALL OF WICKETS			
Hall	24	3	83	1	4	0	16	1		E	WI	E	WI
Griffith	15	2	62	1	9	1	40	0	*Wkt*	*1st*	*1st*	*2nd*	*2nd*
Watson	18·2	3	52	1	14	1	52	0	1st	19	26	3	11
Ramadhin	34	13	73	4	34	9	67	1	2nd	210	103	69	72
Worrell	8	1	29	0	22	5	44	0	3rd	215	190	102	75
Sobers	20	1	75	3	29	6	84	2	4th	268	216	136	107
Walcott	4	2	3	0	7	2	24	0	5th	317	227	145	194
Hunte					5	1	17	1	6th	350	230	148	–
ENGLAND									7th	350	263	345	–
Trueman	37·3	6	103	2	5	1	22	0	8th	374	328	–	–
Moss	34	3	94	2	4	0	16	1	9th	388	–	–	–
Allen	24	1	61	2	15	2	57	0	10th	393	–	–	–
Illingworth	12	4	25	0	16	3	53	2					
Dexter	4	1	20	1									
Barrington	8	0	21	0	8	2	27	1					
Subba Row					1	0	2	0					
Smith					1	0	15	0					
Pullar					1	0	1	1					
Cowdrey					1	0	15	0					

Umpires: H.B. de C. Jordan (7) and C.P. Kippins (3).

Close: 1st day – E(1) 256-3 (Subba Row 18, Barrington 23); 2nd – WI(1) 49-1 (Alexander 15, Sobers 9); 3rd – WI(1) 150-2 (Sobers 61, Walcott 34); 4th – E(2) 18-1 (Pullar 12, Allen 5); 5th – E(2) 238-6 (Smith 35, Parks 55).

ENGLAND v SOUTH AFRICA 1960 (1st Test)

Played at Edgbaston, Birmingham, on 9, 10, 11, 13, 14 June.
Toss: England.   Result: ENGLAND won by 100 runs.
Debuts: England – R.W. Barber, P.M. Walker; South Africa – J.P. Fellows-Smith, G.M. Griffin, S.O'Linn.

England included five county captains in Cowdrey, Dexter, Subba Row, Smith and Barber, but no Surrey player for the first time in a home Test since 1949 (*Test No. 316*). Pullar cracked a bone in his left wrist when he fended off an Adcock bouncer in the first innings. He came in last and played one ball single-handed in the second innings. England won with four hours to spare. John George Langridge, younger brother of James who played eight times for England between 1933 and 1946, made the first of seven Test appearances as an umpire in this match.

ENGLAND

G. Pullar	c McLean b Goddard	37	(11) not out	1
M.C. Cowdrey*	c Waite b Adcock	3	(1) b Adcock	0
E.R. Dexter	b Tayfield	52	b Adcock	26
R. Subba Row	c Waite b Griffin	56	(2) c Waite b Tayfield	32
M.J.K. Smith	c Waite b Adcock	54	(4) c O'Linn b Tayfield	28
J.M. Parks†	c Waite b Adcock	35	(5) b Griffin	4
R. Illingworth	b Tayfield	1	(6) c Waite b Adcock	16
R.W. Barber	lbw b Adcock	5	(7) c McLean b Tayfield	4
P.M. Walker	c Goddard b Adcock	9	(8) c Goddard b Griffin	37
F.S. Trueman	b Tayfield	11	(9) b Tayfield	25
J.B. Statham	not out	14	(10) c McLean b Griffin	22
Extras	(B 4, LB 9, NB 2)	15	(B 2, LB 4, NB 2)	8
Total		**292**		**203**

SOUTH AFRICA

D.J. McGlew*	c Parks b Trueman	11	c Parks b Statham	5
T.L. Goddard	c Smith b Statham	10	c Walker b Statham	0
A.J. Pithey	lbw b Statham	6	b Illingworth	17
R.A. McLean	c Statham b Trueman	21	lbw b Trueman	68
J.H.B. Waite†	b Illingworth	58	not out	56
P.R. Carstein	lbw b Trueman	4	b Trueman	10
S. O'Linn	c Cowdrey b Illingworth	42	lbw b Barber	12
J.P. Fellows-Smith	lbw b Illingworth	18	lbw b Illingworth	5
G.M. Griffin	b Trueman	6	(10) c Walker b Trueman	14
H.J. Tayfield	run out	6	(9) b Illingworth	3
N.A.T. Adcock	not out	1	b Statham	7
Extras	(B 2, NB 1)	3	(B 7, LB 5)	12
Total		**186**		**209**

SOUTH AFRICA	O	M	R	W	O	M	R	W	FALL OF WICKETS				
										E	SA	E	SA
Adcock	41·5	14	62	5	28	8	57	3	*Wkt*	*1st*	*1st*	*2nd*	*2nd*
Griffin	21	3	61	1	21	4	44	3	1st	19	11	0	4
Goddard	33	17	47	1	10	5	32	0	2nd	80	21	42	5
Tayfield	50	19	93	3	27	12	62	4	3rd	100	40	69	58
Fellows-Smith	5	1	14	0					4th	196	52	74	120
									5th	225	61	112	132
ENGLAND									6th	234	146	112	156
Statham	28	8	67	2	18	5	41	3	7th	255	168	118	161
Trueman	24·5	4	58	4	22	4	58	3	8th	262	179	163	167
Dexter	1	0	4	0	6	4	4	0	9th	275	179	202	200
Barber	6	0	26	0	10	2	29	1	10th	292	186	203	209
Illingworth	17	11	15	3	24	6	57	3					
Walker	6	1	13	0	4	2	8	0					

Umpires: J.G. Langridge (1) and W.E. Phillipson (4).

Close: 1st day – E(1) 175-3 (Subba Row 32, Smith 42); 2nd – SA(1) 114-5 (Waite 42, O'Linn 18); 3rd – E(2) 89-4 (Smith 18, Illingworth 6); 4th – SA(2) 120-3 (McLean 68, Waite 21).

ENGLAND v SOUTH AFRICA 1960 (2nd Test)

Played at Lord's, London, on 23, 24, 25, 27 June.
Toss: England.   Result: ENGLAND won by an innings and 73 runs.
Debuts: South Africa – C. Wesley.

Griffin became the only bowler to take a hat-trick for South Africa when he dismissed Smith with the last ball of one over and Walker and Trueman with the first two balls of his next. It was also the first hat-trick in a Test at Lord's. Griffin was called 11 times by umpire Lee for throwing during England's innings; it was the first instance in a Test in England and only the third in all Tests. He had already been no-balled 17 times for throwing during matches against MCC, Nottinghamshire and Hampshire – the first instances of a bowler touring England being called for throwing in first-class cricket. Griffin played no further Test cricket, did not bowl again on the tour, and retired after a further three seasons in South African first-class cricket. Statham's match analysis remained his best in Tests and was the first ten-wicket yield by a fast, as opposed to fast-medium, bowler for England in a post-war home Test.

ENGLAND

M.C. Cowdrey*	c McLean b Griffin	4
R. Subba Row	lbw b Adcock	90
E.R. Dexter	c McLean b Adcock	56
K.F. Barrington	lbw b Goddard	24
M.J.K. Smith	c Waite b Griffin	99
J.M. Parks†	c Fellows-Smith b Adcock	3
P.M. Walker	b Griffin	52
R. Illingworth	not out	0
F.S. Trueman	b Griffin	0
J.B. Statham	not out	2
A.E.Moss	did not bat	
Extras	(B 6, LB 14, W 1, NB 11)	32
Total	(8 wickets declared)	**362**

SOUTH AFRICA

D.J. McGlew*	lbw b Statham	15	b Statham		17
T.L. Goddard	b Statham	19	c Parks b Statham		24
S. O'Linn	c Walker b Moss	18	lbw b Trueman		8
R.A. McLean	c Cowdrey b Statham	15	c Parks b Trueman		13
J.H.B. Waite†	c Parks b Statham	3	lbw b Statham		0
P.R. Carlstein	c Cowdrey b Moss	12	c Parks b Moss		6
C. Wesley	c Parks b Statham	11	b Dexter		35
J.P. Fellows-Smith	c Parks b Moss	29	not out		27
H.J. Tayfield	c Smith b Moss	12	b Dexter		4
G.M. Griffin	b Statham	5	b Statham		0
N.A.T. Adcock	not out	8	b Statham		2
Extras	(LB 4, NB 1)	5	(NB 1)		1
Total		**152**			**137**

SOUTH AFRICA	O	M	R	W	O	M	R	W	FALL OF WICKETS			
										E	SA	SA
Adcock	36	11	70	3					*Wkt*	*1st*	*1st*	*2nd*
Griffin	30	7	87	4					1st	7	33	26
Goddard	31	6	96	1					2nd	103	48	49
Tayfield	27	9	64	0					3rd	165	56	49
Fellows-Smith	5	0	13	0					4th	220	69	50
ENGLAND									5th	227	78	63
Statham	20	5	63	6	21	6	34	5	6th	347	88	72
Trueman	13	2	49	0	17	5	44	2	7th	360	112	126
Moss	10·3	0	35	4	14	1	41	1	8th	360	132	132
Illingworth					1	1	0	0	9th	–	138	133
Dexter					4	0	17	2	10th	–	152	137

Umpires: J.S. Buller (9) and F.S. Lee (24).

Close: 1st day – E(1) 114-2 (Subba Row 36, Barrington 5); 2nd – E(1) 362-8 (Illingworth 0, Statham 2); 3rd – SA(2) 34-1 (Goddard 11, O'Linn 6).

ENGLAND v SOUTH AFRICA 1960 (3rd Test)

Played at Trent Bridge, Nottingham, on 7, 8, 9, 11 July.
Toss: England.   Result: ENGLAND won by eight wickets.
Debuts: South Africa – J.E. Pothecary.

Waite dislocated his left-hand little finger during England's first innings and O'Linn took over as wicket-keeper, in which position he caught Barrington and Walker. South Africa's total of 88 remains the lowest in any Test at Trent Bridge. McGlew, run out after colliding with the bowler (Moss), was recalled by Cowdrey but umpire Elliott refused to change his decision. Wesley was dismissed first ball in both innings.

ENGLAND

R. Subba Row	b Tayfield	30	not out	16
M.C. Cowdrey*	c Fellows-Smith b Goddard	67	lbw b Goddard	27
E.R. Dexter	b Adcock	3	c Adcock b Goddard	0
K.F. Barrington	c O'Linn b Goddard	80	not out	1
M.J.K. Smith	lbw b Goddard	0		
J.M. Parks†	run out	16		
R. Illingworth	c and b Tayfield	37		
P.M. Walker	c O'Linn b Tayfield	30		
F.S. Trueman	b Goddard	15		
J.B. Statham	b Goddard	2		
A.E. Moss	not out	3		
Extras	(B 2, LB 2)	4	(B 4, LB 1)	5
Total		**287**	(2 wickets)	**49**

SOUTH AFRICA

D.J. McGlew*	c Parks b Trueman	0	run out	45
T.L. Goddard	run out	16	b Trueman	0
S. O'Linn	c Walker b Trueman	1	(5) c Cowdrey b Moss	98
R.A. McLean	b Statham	11	c Parks b Trueman	0
P.R. Carlstein	c Walker b Statham	2	(6) c Cowdrey b Statham	19
C. Wesley	c Subba Row b Statham	0	(7) c Parks b Statham	0
J.P. Fellows-Smith	not out	31	(3) c Illingworth b Trueman	15
J.H.B. Waite†	c Trueman b Moss	1	lbw b Moss	60
H.J. Tayfield	b Trueman	11	c Parks b Moss	6
J.E. Pothecary	b Trueman	7	c Parks b Trueman	3
N.A.T. Adcock	b Trueman	0	not out	1
Extras	(B 4, LB 4)	8		–
Total		**88**		**247**

SOUTH AFRICA	O	M	R	W	O	M	R	W	FALL OF WICKETS				
Adcock	30	2	86	1	7·4	2	16	0		E	SA	SA	E
Pothecary	20	5	42	0	2	0	15	0	*Wkt*	*1st*	*1st*	*2nd*	*2nd*
Fellows-Smith	5	0	17	0					1st	57	0	1	48
Goddard	42	17	80	5	5	1	13	2	2nd	82	12	23	48
Tayfield	28·3	11	58	3					3rd	129	31	23	–
									4th	129	33	91	–
ENGLAND									5th	154	33	122	–
Trueman	14·3	6	27	5	22	3	77	4	6th	229	44	122	–
Statham	14	5	27	3	26	3	71	2	7th	241	49	231	–
Moss	10	3	26	1	15·4	3	36	3	8th	261	68	242	–
Illingworth					19	9	33	0	9th	267	82	245	–
Barrington					3	1	5	0	10th	287	88	247	–
Dexter					6	2	12	0					
Walker					3	0	13	0					

Umpires: C.S. Elliott (7) and F.S. Lee (25).

Close: 1st day – E(1) 242-7 (Walker 5, Trueman 0); 2nd – SA(2) 34-3 (McGlew 12, O'Linn 7); 3rd – E(2) 25-0 (Subba Row 3, Cowdrey 18).

ENGLAND v SOUTH AFRICA 1960 (4th Test)

Played at Old Trafford, Manchester, on 21 (*no play*), 22 (*no play*), 23, 25, 26 July.
Toss: England.   Result: MATCH DRAWN.
Debuts: England – D.E.V. Padgett.

Manchester's total of blank days of Test cricket was brought to 23 (out of 48 lost on all English grounds) when rain prevented a start until the third day. Goddard ended England's first innings with a spell of 3 for 0 in 56 balls. McLean batted for 160 minutes in compiling his last three-figure score against England. Cowdrey left South Africa 105 minutes in which to make 185 runs. On the final afternoon England fielded substitutes for Subba Row (fractured thumb), Barrington (pulled thigh muscle) and Statham (tonsillitis). This was England's 16th consecutive Test without a defeat – then their longest unbeaten run.

ENGLAND

Batsman	Dismissal 1	Score 1	Dismissal 2	Score 2
G. Pullar	b Pothecary	12	c and b Pothecary	9
R. Subba Row	lbw b Adcock	27		
E.R. Dexter	b Pothecary	38	c McLean b Pothecary	22
M.C. Cowdrey*	c Waite b Adcock	20	(2) b Adcock	25
K.F. Barrington	b Goddard	76	(7) c Waite b Goddard	35
D.E.V. Padgett	c Wesley b Pothecary	5	(5) c Waite b Adcock	2
J.M. Parks†	lbw b Goddard	36	(6) c and b Goddard	20
R. Illingworth	not out	22	(4) c McLean b Adcock	5
D.A. Allen	lbw b Goddard	0	(8) not out	14
F.S. Trueman	c Tayfield b Adcock	10	(9) not out	14
J.B. Statham	b Adcock	0		
Extras	(B 8, LB 6)	14	(B 1, LB 5, NB 1)	7
Total		**260**	(7 wickets declared)	**153**

SOUTH AFRICA

Batsman	Dismissal 1	Score 1	Dismissal 2	Score 2
D.J. McGlew*	c Subba Row b Trueman	32	not out	26
T.L. Goddard	c Parks b Statham	8	not out	16
A.J. Pithey	c Parks b Statham	7		
P.R. Carlstein	b Trueman	11		
R.A. McLean	b Allen	109		
J.H.B. Waite†	b Statham	11		
S. O'Linn	c sub (M.J. Hilton) b Allen	27		
C. Wesley	c Trueman b Allen	3		
H.J. Tayfield	c Trueman b Allen	4		
J.E. Pothecary	b Trueman	12		
N.A.T. Adcock	not out	0		
Extras	(B 1, LB 4)	5	(B 3, NB 1)	4
Total		**229**	(0 wickets)	**46**

SOUTH AFRICA	O	M	R	W	O	M	R	W		FALL OF WICKETS			
										E	SA	E	SA
Adcock	23	5	66	4	27	9	59	3	*Wkt*	*1st*	*1st*	*2nd*	*2nd*
Pothecary	28	3	85	3	32	10	61	2	1st	27	25	23	–
Goddard	24	16	26	3	16	5	26	2	2nd	85	33	41	–
Tayfield	18	3	69	0					3rd	108	57	63	–
									4th	113	62	65	–
ENGLAND									5th	134	92	71	–
Statham	22	11	32	3	4	2	3	0	6th	197	194	101	–
Trueman	20	2	58	3	6	1	10	0	7th	239	198	134	–
Dexter	17	5	41	0					8th	239	202	–	–
Allen	19·5	6	58	4	7	4	5	0	9th	260	225	–	–
Illingworth	11	2	35	0	5	3	6	0	10th	260	229	–	–
Pullar					1	0	6	0					
Padgett					2	0	8	0					
Cowdrey					1	0	4	0					

Umpires: J.G. Langridge (2) and N. Oldfield (1).

Close: 1st day – no play; 2nd – no play; 3rd – SA(1) 17-0 (McGlew 13, Goddard 4); 4th – E(2) 50-2 (Dexter 12, Illingworth 3).

ENGLAND v SOUTH AFRICA 1960 (5th Test)

Played at Kennington Oval, London, on 18, 19, 20, 22, 23 August.
Toss: England.   Result: MATCH DRAWN.
Debuts: South Africa – A.H. McKinnon.

For the second consecutive rubber England won all five tosses – a unique run. When he stumped Pullar, Waite became the first South African to complete the wicket-keeper's double of 1,000 runs and 100 dismissals in Test cricket; W.A.S. Oldfield (Australia) and T.G. Evans (England) were then the only others to achieve this feat. The opening partnership of 290 between Pullar and Cowdrey was England's third-highest in all Tests and the fourth-highest by all countries. A lunchtime declaration left South Africa three hours to make 216 runs but rain intervened. Adcock equalled Tayfield's 1955 record by taking 26 wickets in the rubber.

ENGLAND

G. Pullar	c Goddard b Pothecary	59	st Waite b McKinnon		175
M.C. Cowdrey*	b Adcock	11	lbw b Goddard		155
E.R. Dexter	b Adcock	28	b Tayfield		16
K.F. Barrington	lbw b Pothecary	1	c Carlstein b McKinnon		10
M.J.K. Smith	b Adcock	0	(6) c Goddard b Tayfield		11
D.E.V. Padgett	c Waite b Pothecary	13	(7) run out		31
J.M. Parks†	c Waite b Pothecary	23	(5) c Waite b Adcock		17
D.A. Allen	lbw b Adcock	0	not out		12
F.S. Trueman	lbw b Adcock	0	b Goddard		24
J.B. Statham	not out	13	c Pothecary b Goddard		4
T. Greenhough	b Adcock	2			
Extras	(B 3, LB 2)	5	(B 14, LB 9, W 1)		24
Total		**155**	(9 wickets declared)		**479**

SOUTH AFRICA

D.J. McGlew*	c Smith b Greenhough	22	c Allen b Statham		16
T.L. Goddard	c Cowdrey b Statham	99	c Cowdrey b Statham		28
J.P. Fellows-Smith	c Smith b Dexter	35	c Parks b Trueman		6
R.A. McLean	lbw b Dexter	0	(5) not out		32
J.H.B. Waite†	c Trueman b Dexter	77	(6) not out		1
S. O'Linn	b Trueman	55			
P.R. Carlstein	b Greenhough	42	(4) lbw b Trueman		13
J.E. Pothecary	run out	4			
H.J. Tayfield	not out	46			
A.H. McKinnon	run out	22			
N.A.T. Adcock	b Trueman	1			
Extras	(B 6, LB 7, NB 3)	16	(W 1)		1
Total		**419**	(4 wickets)		**97**

SOUTH AFRICA	O	M	R	W	O	M	R	W		FALL OF WICKETS			
Adcock	31·3	10	65	6	38	8	106	1		E	SA	E	SA
Pothecary	29	9	58	4	27	5	93	0	*Wkt*	*1st*	*1st*	*2nd*	*2nd*
Goddard	14	6	25	0	27	6	69	3	1st	27	44	290	21
McKinnon	2	1	2	0	24	7	62	2	2nd	89	107	339	30
Tayfield					37	14	108	2	3rd	90	107	362	52
Fellows-Smith					4	0	17	0	4th	95	222	373	89
									5th	107	252	387	–
ENGLAND									6th	125	326	412	–
Trueman	31·1	4	93	2	10	0	34	2	7th	130	330	447	–
Statham	38	8	96	1	12	1	57	2	8th	130	374	475	–
Dexter	30	5	79	3	0·2	0	0	0	9th	142	412	479	–
Greenhough	44	17	99	2	5	2	3	0	10th	155	419	–	–
Allen	28	15	36	0	2	1	2	0					

Umpires: C.S. Elliott (8) and W.E. Phillipson (5).

Close: 1st day – E(1) 131-8 (Parks 13, Statham 1); 2nd – SA(1) 167-3 (Goddard 81, Waite 22); 3rd – E(1) 0-0 (Pullar 0, Cowdrey 0); 4th – E(2) 380-4 (Parks 11, Smith 1).

INDIA v PAKISTAN 1960–61 (1st Test)

Played at Brabourne Stadium, Bombay, on 2, 3, 4, 6, 7 December.
Toss: Pakistan.   Result: MATCH DRAWN.
Debuts: India – R.F. Surti; Pakistan – Javed Burki, Mohammad Farooq.

The partnership of 246 between Hanif and Saeed was a Pakistan second-wicket record in all Tests (since beaten). Hanif's 160 is Pakistan's highest innings in India and, when his score reached 63, he became the first to score 2,000 runs for his country. Mohammad Farooq took the wickets of Roy and Baig in his second over in Test cricket. Joshi and Desai added 149 to establish the present ninth-wicket record for India in all Tests.

PAKISTAN

Hanif Mohammad	run out	160	c Umrigar b Desai		0
Imtiaz Ahmed†	b Desai	19	c Roy b Nadkarni		69
Saeed Ahmed	st Joshi b Gupte	121	c and b Gupte		41
Mushtaq Mohammad	lbw b Gupte	6	lbw b Nadkarni		19
W. Mathias	c Nadkarni b Desai	0	not out		6
Javed Burki	lbw b Gupte	7	not out		13
Nasim-ul-Ghani	c Joshi b Desai	4			
Fazal Mahmood*	c Joshi b Gupte	1			
Mahmood Hussain	c Desai b Nadkarni	23			
Mohammad Farooq	not out	2			
Haseeb Ahsan	c Contractor b Nadkarni	0			
Extras	(B 6, LB 1)	7	(B 16, LB 1, NB 1)		18
Total		**350**	(4 wickets)		**166**

INDIA

Pankaj Roy	c Mahmood b Farooq	23
N.J. Contractor*	c Burki b Farooq	62
A.A. Baig	c Hanif b Farooq	1
V.L. Manjrekar	b Mahmood	73
P.R. Umrigar	c sub (Zafar Altaf) b Mahmood	33
C.G. Borde	lbw b Mahmood	41
R.G. Nadkarni	c Burki b Mahmood	34
R.F. Surti	c Nasim b Farooq	11
P.G. Joshi†	not out	52
R.B. Desai	b Mahmood	85
S.P. Gupte	did not bat	
Extras	(B 14, LB 11, NB 9)	34
Total	(9 wickets declared)	**449**

INDIA	O	M	R	W	O	M	R	W	FALL OF WICKETS			
										P	I	P
Desai	36	6	116	3	8	2	27	1	Wkt	1st	1st	2nd
Surti	9	0	37	0	8	1	21	0	1st	55	56	0
Umrigar	17	2	46	0					2nd	301	58	80
Nadkarni	37·4	14	75	2	15	10	9	2	3rd	302	121	142
Gupte	31	15	43	4	25	10	46	1	4th	303	206	147
Borde	6	1	26	0	16	4	25	0	5th	318	207	–
Contractor	1	1	0	0	7	2	16	0	6th	319	289	–
Roy					1	0	4	0	7th	321	296	–
PAKISTAN									8th	331	300	–
Mahmood Hussain	51·4	10	129	5					9th	349	449	–
Fazal	6	2	5	0					10th	350	–	–
Farooq	46	7	139	4								
Nasim	41	19	74	0								
Haseeb	31	10	68	0								
Mushtaq	1	1	0	0								

Umpires: S.K. Ganguli (6) and A.R. Joshi (9).

Close: 1st day – P(1) 241-1 (Hanif 128, Saeed 94); 2nd – I(1) 50-0 (Roy 21, Contractor 22); 3rd – I(1) 205-3 (Manjrekar 72, Umrigar 33); 4th – I(1) 396-8 (Joshi 29, Desai 60).

INDIA v PAKISTAN 1960–61 (2nd Test)

Played at Green Park, Kanpur, on 16, 17, 18, 20, 21 December.
Toss: Pakistan.   Result: MATCH DRAWN.
Debuts: Nil.

This match produced a daily average aggregate of 155 and India did not complete their first innings until just before lunch on the fifth day. Jaisimha batted 500 minutes for 99 and made only five scoring strokes in the entire pre-lunch session on the third day.

PAKISTAN

Hanif Mohammad	c Contractor b Umrigar	5	c Jaisimha b Muddiah		19
Imtiaz Ahmed†	b Gupte	20	c Contractor b Muddiah		16
Saeed Ahmed	c Tamhane b Desai	32	b Gupte		4
Javed Burki	run out	79	not out		48
W. Mathias	lbw b Desai	37	not out		46
Alimuddin	c Nadkarni b Umrigar	24			
Mushtaq Mohammad	c Umrigar b Muddiah	13			
Nasim-ul-Ghani	not out	70			
Fazal Mahmood*	lbw b Umrigar	16			
Mahmood Hussain	c Borde b Umrigar	7			
Haseeb Ahsan	c Tamhane b Gupte	13			
Extras	(B 13, LB 6)	19	(B 2, LB 5)		7
Total		**335**	(3 wickets)		**140**

INDIA

N.J. Contractor*	b Haseeb	47
M.L. Jaisimha	run out	99
A.A. Baig	b Haseeb	13
V.L. Manjrekar	c Nasim b Fazal	52
P.R. Umrigar	c Burki b Mahmood	115
C.G. Borde	c Fazal b Nasim	0
R.G. Nadkarni	b Haseeb	16
R.B. Desai	b Haseeb	14
N.S. Tamhane†	c Mathias b Haseeb	3
V.M. Muddiah	b Mahmood	11
S.P. Gupte	not out	1
Extras	(B 20, LB 1, NB 12)	33
Total		**404**

INDIA	O	M	R	W	O	M	R	W	FALL OF WICKETS			
Desai	30	6	54	2	4	1	3	0		P	I	P
Umrigar	55	23	71	4	3	0	10	0	Wkt	1st	1st	2nd
Gupte	42·4	14	84	2	17	6	29	1	1st	21	71	31
Muddiah	22	6	62	1	18	7	40	2	2nd	29	92	42
Nadkarni	32	24	23	0	7	4	6	0	3rd	93	182	42
Borde	6	2	16	0	10	0	36	0	4th	174	258	–
Contractor	1	0	6	0					5th	177	263	–
Jaisimha					3	0	5	0	6th	214	294	–
Manjrekar					1	0	2	0	7th	240	334	–
Baig					1	0	2	0	8th	293	342	–
PAKISTAN									9th	305	403	–
Mahmood Hussain	44·5	13	101	2					10th	335	404	–
Fazal	36	14	37	1								
Nasim	55	17	109	1								
Haseeb	56	15	121	5								
Mushtaq	2	1	3	0								

Umpires: S.K. Ganguli (7) and A.R. Joshi (10).

Close: 1st day – P(1) 170-3 (Burki 77, Mathias 33); 2nd – I(1) 10-0 (Contractor 10, Jaisimha 0); 3rd – I(1) 159-2 (Jaisimha 54, Manjrekar 36); 4th – I(1) 335-7 (Umrigar 68, Tamhane 1).

INDIA v PAKISTAN 1960–61 (3rd Test)

Played at Eden Gardens, Calcutta, on 30, 31 December, 1, 3, 4, January.
Toss: Pakistan.   Result: MATCH DRAWN.
Debuts: Nil.

Rain on the third day and drying operations on the fourth reduced play by $4\frac{1}{2}$ hours. Pakistan set India 267 to win in three hours. The partnership of 88 between Mushtaq and Intikhab was Pakistan's highest for the seventh wicket against India until 1984-85.

PAKISTAN

Hanif Mohammad	c Baig b Desai	56	not out	63
Imtiaz Ahmed†	b Surendranath	9	b Desai	9
Saeed Ahmed	c Nadkarni b Surendranath	41	lbw b Surendranath	13
Javed Burki	lbw b Borde	48	run out	42
W. Mathias	c Umrigar b Desai	8		
Mushtaq Mohammad	c Jaisimha b Borde	61		
Nasim-ul-Ghani	b Surendranath	0		
Intikhab Alam	c Tamhane b Surendranath	56	(5) not out	11
Fazal Mahmood*	lbw b Borde	8		
Mahmood Hussain	b Borde	4		
Haseeb Ahsan	not out	1		
Extras	(B 6, LB 3)	9	(B 3, LB 5)	8
Total		**301**	(3 wickets declared)	**146**

INDIA

N.J. Contractor*	b Intikhab	25	c Fazal b Haseeb	12
M.L. Jaisimha	c Mathias b Mahmood	28	c Mathias b Intikhab	26
A.A. Baig	b Intikhab	19	b Haseeb	1
P.R. Umrigar	c Imtiaz b Mahmood	1	(5) b Intikhab	4
V.L. Manjrekar	b Fazal	29	(4) not out	45
C.G. Borde	c Imtiaz b Fazal	44	not out	23
R.G. Nadkarni	c Imtiaz b Fazal	1		
R.B. Desai	b Haseeb	14		
N.S. Tamhane†	c Intikhab b Fazal	0		
Surendranath	not out	5		
S.P. Gupte	b Fazal	0		
Extras	(B 10, LB 3, NB 1)	14	(B 3, LB 9, NB 4)	16
Total		**180**	(4 wickets)	**127**

INDIA	O	M	R	W	O	M	R	W		FALL OF WICKETS			
Desai	35	3	118	2	16	4	37	1		P	I	P	I
Surendranath	46	19	93	4	18	2	51	1	*Wkt*	*1st*	*1st*	*2nd*	*2nd*
Umrigar	6	2	15	0	7	2	14	0	1st	12	59	15	47
Gupte	18	5	41	0	1	1	0	0	2nd	84	83	34	47
Borde	16·2	7	21	4					3rd	135	83	116	48
Nadkarni	6	5	4	0	7	0	36	0	4th	164	85	–	65
									5th	185	145	–	–
PAKISTAN									6th	186	147	–	–
Mahmood Hussain	31	12	56	2	8	3	9	0	7th	274	174	–	–
Fazal	25·3	12	26	5	12	2	19	0	8th	296	175	–	–
Intikhab	24	11	35	2	15	2	33	2	9th	296	180	–	–
Nasim	12	5	32	0	2	1	5	0	10th	301	180	–	–
Haseeb	7	1	17	1	14	6	25	2					
Saeed					1	0	2	0					
Mushtaq					3	1	9	0					
Hanif					1	0	6	0					
Burki					1	0	3	0					

Umpires: S.K. Ganguli (8) and B. Satyaji Rao (1).

Close: 1st day – P(1) 201-6 (Mushtaq 28, Intikhab 3); 2nd – I(1) 83-2 (Jaisimha 28); 3rd – I(1) 147-6 (Borde 33, Desai 0); 4th – P(2) 30-1 (Hanif 9, Saeed 11).

INDIA v PAKISTAN 1960–61 (4th Test)

Played at Corporation Stadium, Madras, on 13, 14, 15, 17, 18 January.
Toss: Pakistan.   Result: MATCH DRAWN.
Debuts: India – B.P. Gupte.

Both countries recorded their highest totals for this series, India's 539 being at that time their best against all countries. Borde, whose innings was then the highest played in these Tests, and Umrigar added 177 to set India's fifth-wicket record against Pakistan. The opening partnership of 162 between Hanif and Imtiaz is still Pakistan's best against India. Haseeb was the third bowler to concede over 200 runs for Pakistan, Fazal Mahmood and Khan Mohammad suffering this fate in *Test No. 451*. A fire gutted the eastern section of the stands and ended play 20 minutes prematurely on the fourth day.

PAKISTAN

Hanif Mohammad	c Kunderan b Surendranath	62		
Imtiaz Ahmed†	b Desai	135	not out	20
Saeed Ahmed	c Kunderan b Desai	103	(1) not out	38
Javed Burki	c Contractor b Borde	19		
W. Mathias	lbw b Umrigar	49		
Mushtaq Mohammad	not out	41		
Nasim-ul-Ghani	c Kunderan b Umrigar	5		
Intikhab Alam	c Kunderan b Desai	13		
Fazal Mahmood*	lbw b Desai	4		
Mahmood Hussain	} did not bat			
Haseeb Ahsan	}			
Extras	(B 12, LB 3, NB 2)	17	(NB 1)	1
Total	(8 wickets declared)	**448**	(0 wickets)	**59**

INDIA

M.L. Jaisimha	c Intikhab b Mahmood	32
N.J. Contractor*	c Intikhab b Haseeb	81
D.K. Gaekwad	c and b Haseeb	9
V.L. Manjrekar	b Haseeb	30
P.R. Umrigar	b Haseeb	117
C.G. Borde	not out	177
A.G. Milkha Singh	c Fazal b Haseeb	18
B.K. Kunderan†	b Haseeb	12
R.B. Desai	st Imtiaz b Nasim	18
Surendranath	st Imtiaz b Nasim	6
B.P. Gupte	not out	17
Extras	(B 10, LB 7, NB 5)	22
Total	(9 wickets declared)	**539**

INDIA	O	M	R	W	O	M	R	W
Desai	28·5	4	66	4	3	0	14	0
Surendranath	38	10	99	1	3	2	8	0
Gupte	30	9	97	0	5	0	19	0
Umrigar	53	24	64	2				
Borde	33	4	105	1				
Jaisimha					3	0	8	0
Manjrekar					2	0	6	0
Contractor					1	0	1	0
Milkha Singh					1	0	2	0
PAKISTAN								
Mahmood Hussain	37	12	86	1				
Fazal	43	22	66	0				
Haseeb	84	19	202	6				
Intikhab	17	5	40	0				
Nasim	46	12	123	2				

FALL OF WICKETS

	P	I	P
Wkt	1st	1st	2nd
1st	162	84	–
2nd	252	102	–
3rd	322	146	–
4th	338	164	–
5th	408	341	–
6th	420	396	–
7th	444	416	–
8th	448	447	–
9th	–	476	–
10th	–	–	–

Umpires: S.P. Pan (1) and S.K. Raghunatha Rao (1).

Close: 1st day – P(1) 235-1 (Imtiaz 123, Saeed 40); 2nd – P(1) 448-8 (Mushtaq 41); 3rd – I(1) 177-4 (Umrigar 11, Borde 4); 4th – I(1) 345-5 (Borde 58, Milkha Singh 3).

INDIA v PAKISTAN 1960–61 (5th Test)

Played at Feroz Shah Kotla, Delhi, on 8, 9, 11, 12, 13 February.
Toss: India.   Result: MATCH DRAWN.
Debuts: India – V.V. Kumar.

India and Pakistan achieved their twelfth successive draw in their last match for more than 17 years. Umrigar was the first batsman to score five hundreds for any country against Pakistan. At 17 years 82 days, Mushtaq Mohammad remains Test cricket's youngest century-maker. Saeed's aggregate of 460 runs is Pakistan's highest for any rubber in India. Kumar bowled Imtiaz with his sixth ball in Test cricket.

INDIA

M.L. Jaisimha	b Farooq	27	not out	14
N.J. Contractor*	c and b Intikhab	92		
R.F. Surti	c Imtiaz b Fazal	64		
V.L. Manjrekar	c Mathias b Haseeb	18		
P.R. Umrigar	b Fazal	112		
C.G. Borde	c Imtiaz b Farooq	45		
A.G. Milkha Singh	b Mahmood	35		
R.G. Nadkarni	b Fazal	21		
B.K. Kunderan†	not out	12	(2) not out	1
R.B. Desai	b Mahmood	3		
V.V. Kumar	b Mahmood	6		
Extras	(B 6, LB 13, NB 9)	28	(NB 1)	1
Total		**463**	(0 wickets)	**16**

PAKISTAN

Hanif Mohammad	c Milkha Singh b Desai	1	b Desai	44
Imtiaz Ahmed†	b Kumar	25	lbw b Nadkarni	53
Saeed Ahmed	c Umrigar b Nadkarni	36	c sub (D.N. Sardesai) b Nadkarni	31
Javed Burki	c Manjrekar b Desai	61	c and b Kumar	8
W. Mathias	c Nadkarni b Kumar	10	c Borde b Nadkarni	2
Mushtaq Mohammad	c Kumar b Desai	101	lbw b Desai	22
Intikhab Alam	b Desai	0	b Kumar	10
Fazal Mahmood*⌐	c Nadkarni b Kumar	13	lbw b Desai	18
Mahmood Hussain	lbw b Kumar	20	b Nadkarni	35
Haseeb Ahsan	b Kumar	5	b Desai	6
Mohammad Farooq	not out	0	not out	14
Extras	(B 8, LB 1, W 1, NB 4)	14	(B 2, LB 5)	7
Total		**286**		**250**

PAKISTAN	O	M	R	W	O	M	R	W
Mahmood Hussain	40	9	115	3	1	0	7	0
Fazal	38	8	86	3				
Farooq	29	2	101	2	1	0	8	0
Haseeb	17	5	57	1				
Intikhab	34	6	76	1				
INDIA								
Desai	28	5	102	4	27	3	88	4
Surti	11	1	38	0	7	0	34	0
Nadkarni	34	24	24	1	52·4	38	43	4
Kumar	37·5	21	64	5	36	17	68	2
Borde	10	3	30	0	2	0	2	0
Umrigar	5	1	14	0	3	2	8	0

FALL OF WICKETS

Wkt	I 1st	P 1st	P 2nd	I 2nd
1st	43	10	83	–
2nd	150	60	107	–
3rd	201	78	126	–
4th	324	89	131	–
5th	338	225	142	–
6th	401	229	165	–
7th	439	254	189	–
8th	441	265	196	–
9th	453	281	212	–
10th	463	286	250	–

Umpires: I. Gopalakrishnan (1) and S.K. Raghunatha Rao (2).

Close: 1st day – I(1) 164-2 (Contractor 54, Manjrekar 6); 2nd – I(1) 393-5 (Umrigar 105, Milkha Singh 19); 3rd – P(1) 160-4 (Burki 42, Mushtaq 38); 4th – P(2) 57-0 (Hanif 31, Imtiaz 26).

AUSTRALIA v WEST INDIES 1960–61 (1st Test)

Played at Woolloongabba, Brisbane, on 9, 10, 12, 13, 14 December.
Toss: West Indies.   Result: MATCH TIED.
Debuts: West Indies – P.D. Lashley, C.W. Smith.

This match resulted, after some scoring confusion, in the first tie in Test cricket. Australia, requiring 233 runs to win in 310 minutes, lost their last wicket to a run out off the seventh ball of the final over and with the scores level. Davidson became the first player to complete the match double of 100 runs and ten wickets in a Test. Sobers, who hit his tenth hundred, scored his 3,000th run in Tests and took only 57 minutes to reach his fifty. The partnership of 134 between Davidson and Benaud is Australia's highest for the seventh wicket against West Indies.

WEST INDIES

C.C. Hunte	c Benaud b Davidson	24	c Simpson b Mackay	39
C.W. Smith	c Grout b Davidson	7	c O'Neill b Davidson	6
R.B. Kanhai	c Grout b Davidson	15	c Grout b Davidson	54
G. St A. Sobers	c Kline b Meckiff	132	b Davidson	14
F.M.M. Worrell*	c Grout b Davidson	65	c Grout b Davidson	65
J.S. Solomon	hit wkt b Simpson	65	lbw b Simpson	47
P.D. Lashley	c Grout b Kline	19	b Davidson	0
F.C.M. Alexander†	c Davidson b Kline	60	b Benaud	5
S. Ramadhin	c Harvey b Davidson	12	c Harvey b Simpson	6
W.W. Hall	st Grout b Kline	50	b Davidson	18
A.L. Valentine	not out	0	not out	7
Extras	(LB 3, W 1)	4	(B 14, LB 7, W 2)	23
Total		**453**		**284**

AUSTRALIA

C.C. McDonald	c Hunte b Sobers	57	b Worrell	16
R.B. Simpson	b Ramadhin	92	c sub (L.R. Gibbs) b Hall	0
R.N. Harvey	b Valentine	15	c Sobers b Hall	5
N.C. O'Neill	c Valentine b Hall	181	c Alexander b Hall	26
L.E. Favell	run out	45	c Solomon b Hall	7
K.D. Mackay	b Sobers	35	b Ramadhin	28
A.K. Davidson	c Alexander b Hall	44	run out	80
R. Benaud*	lbw b Hall	10	c Alexander b Hall	52
A.T.W. Grout†	lbw b Hall	4	run out	2
I. Meckiff	run out	4	run out	2
L.F. Kline	not out	3	not out	0
Extras	(B 2, LB 8, W 1, NB 4)	15	(B 2, LB 9, NB 3)	14
Total		**505**		**232**

AUSTRALIA	O	M	R	W	O	M	R	W					
Davidson	30	2	135	5	24·6	4	87	6					
Meckiff	18	0	129	1	4	1	19	0					
Mackay	3	0	15	0	21	7	52	1					
Benaud	24	3	93	0	31	6	69	1					
Simpson	8	0	25	1	7	2	18	2					
Kline	17·6	6	52	3	4	0	14	0					
O'Neill					1	0	2	0					

	O	M	R	W	O	M	R	W
WEST INDIES								
Hall	29·3	1	140	4	17·7	3	63	5
Worrell	30	0	93	0	16	3	41	1
Sobers	32	0	115	2	8	0	30	0
Valentine	24	6	82	1	10	4	27	0
Ramadhin	15	1	60	1	17	3	57	1

FALL OF WICKETS

	WI	A	WI	A
Wkt	1st	1st	2nd	2nd
1st	23	84	13	1
2nd	42	138	88	7
3rd	65	194	114	49
4th	239	278	127	49
5th	243	381	210	57
6th	283	469	210	92
7th	347	484	241	226
8th	366	489	250	228
9th	452	496	253	232
10th	453	505	284	232

Umpires: C.J. Egar (1) and C. Hoy (5).

Close: 1st day – WI(1) 359-7 (Alexander 21, Ramadhin 9); 2nd – A(1) 196-3 (O'Neill 28, Favell 1); 3rd – WI(2) 0-0 (Hunte 0, Smith 0); 4th – WI(2) 259-9 (Hall 0, Valentine 0).

AUSTRALIA v WEST INDIES 1960–61 (2nd Test)

Played at Melbourne Cricket Ground on 30, 31 December, 2, 3 January.
Toss: Australia.   Result: AUSTRALIA won by seven wickets.
Debuts: Australia – J.W. Martin, F.M. Misson.

Chronologically, this was the 500th official Test match (it began a few hours before *Test No. 499*). Although rain ended the second day's play shortly after lunch, Australia won with over a day to spare. Misson took Hunte's wicket with his second ball in Test cricket. In the second innings, Solomon was out when his cap fell on to the wicket as he was playing defensively. Martin, playing in his first Test, took the wickets of Kanhai, Sobers and Worrell in four balls, having already contributed an invaluable fifty and shared in a (then) record ninth-wicket stand of 97 with Mackay. Hall was twice warned for intimidatory bowling by umpire Egar.

AUSTRALIA

C.C. McDonald	c Watson b Hall	15	c Sobers b Hall		13
R.B. Simpson	c Alexander b Hall	49	not out		27
R.N. Harvey	c Sobers b Worrell	12	c Alexander b Hall		0
N.C. O'Neill	c Sobers b Worrell	40	lbw b Watson		0
L.E. Favell	c Nurse b Sobers	51	not out		24
K.D. Mackay	b Ramadhin	74			
A.K. Davidson	b Hall	35			
R. Benaud*	b Hall	2			
A.T.W. Grout†	b Watson	5			
J.W. Martin	b Valentine	55			
F.M. Misson	not out	0			
Extras	(LB 7, W 1, NB 2)	10	(B 4, LB 1, NB 1)		6
Total		**348**	(3 wickets)		**70**

WEST INDIES

C.C. Hunte	c Simpson b Misson	1	c Grout b O'Neill		110
J.S. Solomon	c Grout b Davidson	0	hit wkt b Benaud		4
S.M. Nurse	c Grout b Davidson	70	run out		3
R.B. Kanhai	c Harvey b Davidson	84	c Misson b Martin		25
G. St A. Sobers	c Simpson b Benaud	9	c Simpson b Martin		0
F.M.M. Worrell*	b Misson	0	c Simpson b Martin		0
F.C.M. Alexander†	c Favell b Davidson	5	c Grout b Davidson		72
S. Ramadhin	b Davidson	0	st Grout b Benaud		3
W.W. Hall	b Davidson	5	b Davidson		4
C.D. Watson	c McDonald b Benaud	4	run out		5
A.L. Valentine	not out	1	not out		0
Extras	(NB 2)	2	(B 2, LB 2, W 1, NB 2)		7
Total		**181**			**233**

WEST INDIES	O	M	R	W	O	M	R	W
Hall	12	2	51	4	9·4	0	32	2
Watson	12	1	73	1	9	1	32	1
Sobers	17	1	88	1				
Worrell	9	0	50	2				
Valentine	11·1	1	55	1				
Ramadhin	5	0	21	1				
AUSTRALIA								
Davidson	22	4	53	6	15·4	2	51	2
Misson	11	0	36	2	12	3	36	0
Benaud	27·2	10	58	2	20	3	49	2
Martin	8	1	32	0	20	3	56	3
Simpson	1	1	0	0	8	0	24	0
O'Neill					5	1	10	1

FALL OF WICKETS

Wkt	A 1st	WI 1st	WI 2nd	A 2nd
1st	35	1	40	27
2nd	60	1	51	27
3rd	105	124	97	30
4th	155	139	99	–
5th	189	142	99	–
6th	242	160	186	–
7th	244	160	193	–
8th	251	166	206	–
9th	348	177	222	–
10th	348	181	233	–

Umpires: C.J. Egar (2) and C. Hoy (6).

Close: 1st day – WI(1) 1-1 (Hunte 1); 2nd – WI(1) 108-2 (Nurse 35, Kanhai 70); 3rd – WI(2) 129-5 (Hunte 74, Alexander 19).

AUSTRALIA v WEST INDIES 1960–61 (3rd Test)

Played at Sydney Cricket Ground on 13, 14, 16, 17, 18 January.
Toss: West Indies.   Result: WEST INDIES won by 222 runs.
Debuts: Nil.

West Indies drew level in the rubber before lunch on the fifth day. Gibbs took the wickets of Mackay, Martin and Grout in four balls. Alexander's hundred remained the only one of his first-class career. It followed a fourth-wicket partnership of 101 between Smith and Worrell in only 67 minutes when Australia were without Davidson (leg strain) and Meckiff (back damage).

WEST INDIES

C.C. Hunte	c Simpson b Meckiff	34	c O'Neill b Davidson	1
C.W. Smith	c Simpson b Davidson	16	c Simpson b Benaud	55
R.B. Kanhai	c Grout b Davidson	21	c Martin b Davidson	3
G. St A. Sobers	c and b Davidson	168	c Grout b Davidson	1
F.M.M. Worrell*	c Davidson b Benaud	22	lbw b Benaud	82
S.M. Nurse	c Simpson b Benaud	43	c and b Mackay	11
J.S. Solomon	c Simpson b Benaud	14	c Harvey b Benaud	1
F.C.M. Alexander†	c Harvey b Benaud	0	lbw b Mackay	108
L.R. Gibbs	c Grout b Davidson	0	st Grout b Benaud	18
W.W. Hall	c Grout b Davidson	10	b Mackay	24
A.L. Valentine	not out	0	not out	10
Extras	(B 6, LB 4, W 1)	11	(B 4, LB 7, W 1)	12
Total		**339**		**326**

AUSTRALIA

C.C. McDonald	b Valentine	34	c Alexander b Valentine	27
R.B. Simpson	c Kanhai b Hall	10	b Sobers	12
R.N. Harvey	c Sobers b Hall	9	c Sobers b Gibbs	85
N.C. O'Neill	b Sobers	71	c Sobers b Gibbs	70
L.E. Favell	c Worrell b Valentine	16	b Gibbs	2
K.D. Mackay	c Solomon b Gibbs	39	c Nurse b Gibbs	0
A.K. Davidson	c Worrell b Valentine	16	(10) b Valentine	1
R. Benaud*	c and b Valentine	3	(7) c and b Valentine	24
J.W. Martin	c Solomon b Gibbs	0	(8) b Valentine	5
A.T.W. Grout†	c Hunte b Gibbs	0	(9) b Gibbs	0
I. Meckiff	not out	0	not out	6
Extras	(B 1, LB 2, NB 1)	4	(B 3, LB 6)	9
Total		**202**		**241**

AUSTRALIA	O	M	R	W	O	M	R	W		FALL OF WICKETS			
										WI	A	WI	A
Davidson	21·6	4	80	5	8	1	33	3	*Wkt*	*1st*	*1st*	*2nd*	*2nd*
Meckiff	13	1	74	1	5	2	12	0	1st	48	17	10	27
Mackay	14	1	40	0	31·4	5	75	3	2nd	68	40	20	83
Benaud	23	3	86	4	44	14	113	4	3rd	89	65	22	191
Martin	8	1	37	0	10	0	65	0	4th	152	105	123	197
Simpson	2	0	11	0	4	0	16	0	5th	280	155	144	197
									6th	329	194	159	202
WEST INDIES									7th	329	200	166	209
Hall	13	0	53	2	8	0	35	0	8th	329	200	240	220
Worrell	9	4	18	0	4	0	7	0	9th	329	202	309	234
Gibbs	23	6	46	3	26	5	66	5	10th	339	202	326	241
Valentine	24·2	6	67	4	25·2	7	86	4					
Sobers	5	2	14	1	9	1	38	1					

Umpires: C.J. Egar (3) and C. Hoy (7).

Close: 1st day – WI(1) 303-5 (Sobers 152, Solomon 4); 2nd – A(1) 172-5 (Mackay 27, Davidson 3); 3rd – WI(2) 179-7 (Alexander 11, Gibbs 4); 4th – A(2) 182-2 (Harvey 84, O'Neill 53).

AUSTRALIA v WEST INDIES 1960–61 (4th Test)

Played at Adelaide Oval on 27, 28, 30, 31 January, 1 February.
Toss: West Indies.   Result: MATCH DRAWN.
Debuts: Australia – D.E. Hoare.

After Hoare had taken Hunte's wicket in his second over of Test cricket, Kanhai scored a century in 126 minutes. Gibbs achieved the first hat-trick in this series when he dismissed Mackay, Grout and Misson; it remains the only hat-trick in an Adelaide Test. Kanhai became the first West Indian to score a hundred in each innings of a Test in Australia, his second hundred taking 150 minutes, before providing Benaud's 200th Test wicket. Mackay and Kline earned Australia a draw when their tenth-wicket partnership survived the final 100 minutes of the match.

WEST INDIES

C.C. Hunte	lbw b Hoare	6	run out		79
C.W. Smith	c and b Benaud	28	c Hoare b Mackay		46
R.B. Kanhai	c Simpson b Benaud	117	lbw b Benaud		115
G. St A. Sobers	b Benaud	1	run out		20
F.M.M. Worrell*	c Misson b Hoare	71	c Burge b Mackay		53
S.M. Nurse	c and b Misson	49	c Simpson b Benaud		5
J.S. Solomon	c and b Benaud	22	(8) not out		16
F.C.M. Alexander†	not out	63	(7) not out		87
L.R. Gibbs	b Misson	18			
W.W. Hall	c Hoare b Benaud	5			
A.L. Valentine	lbw b Misson	0			
Extras	(B 3, LB 3, W 5, NB 2)	13	(B 2, LB 6, W 2, NB 1)		11
Total		**393**	(6 wickets declared)		**432**

AUSTRALIA

C.C. McDonald	c Hunte b Gibbs	71	run out		2
L.E. Favell	c Alexander b Worrell	1	c Alexander b Hall		4
N.C. O'Neill	c Alexander b Sobers	11	c and b Sobers		65
R.B. Simpson	c Alexander b Hall	85	c Alexander b Hall		3
P.J.P. Burge	b Sobers	45	c Alexander b Valentine		49
R. Benaud*	c Solomon b Gibbs	77	c and b Sobers		17
K.D. Mackay	lbw b Gibbs	29	not out		62
A.T.W. Grout†	c Sobers b Gibbs	0	lbw b Worrell		42
F.M. Misson	b Gibbs	0	c Solomon b Worrell		1
D.E. Hoare	b Sobers	35	b Worrell		0
L.F. Kline	not out	0	not out		15
Extras	(B 2, LB 3, NB 7)	12	(B 9, LB 1, NB 3)		13
Total		**366**	(9 wickets)		**273**

AUSTRALIA	O	M	R	W	O	M	R	W	FALL OF WICKETS				
										WI	A	WI	A
Hoare	16	0	68	2	13	0	88	0	*Wkt*	*1st*	*1st*	*2nd*	*2nd*
Misson	17·5	2	79	3	28	3	106	0	1st	12	9	66	6
Mackay	2	0	11	0	12	0	72	2	2nd	83	45	229	7
Benaud	27	5	96	5	27	3	107	2	3rd	91	119	263	31
Kline	21	3	109	0	12	2	48	0	4th	198	213	270	113
Simpson	5	0	17	0					5th	271	221	275	129
WEST INDIES									6th	288	281	388	144
Hall	22	3	85	1	13	4	61	2	7th	316	281	–	203
Worrell	7	0	34	1	17	9	27	3	8th	375	281	–	207
Sobers	24	3	64	3	39	11	87	2	9th	392	366	–	207
Gibbs	35·6	4	97	5	28	13	44	0	10th	393	366	–	–
Valentine	21	4	74	0	20	7	40	1					
Solomon					3	2	1	0					

Umpires: C.J. Egar (4) and C. Hoy (8).

Close: 1st day – WI(1) 348-7 (Alexander 38, Gibbs 3); 2nd – A(1) 221-4 (Simpson 85, Benaud 1); 3rd – WI(2) 150-1 (Hunte 44, Kanhai 59); 4th – A(2) 31-3 (O'Neill 21).

AUSTRALIA v WEST INDIES 1960–61 (5th Test)

Played at Melbourne Cricket Ground on 10, 11, 13, 14, 15 February.
Toss: Australia.   Result: AUSTRALIA won by two wickets.
Debuts: Nil.

The most enterprising and exciting rubber of recent times ended late on the penultimate day (it was a six-day match) when Australia's ninth-wicket pair scampered a bye. The second day was watched by 90,800 – the world record attendance for any day's cricket. Sobers bowled unchanged for 41 eight-ball overs in the first innings, during the course of which Davidson scored his 1,000th run and completed the Test 'double' in his 34th match – the last player to accomplish this feat for Australia. Two record aggregates were reached in this rubber: Kanhai scored 503 runs and Davidson equalled C.V. Grimmett's 1930-31 total of 33 wickets.

WEST INDIES

C.W. Smith	c O'Neill b Misson	11	lbw b Davidson	37
C.C. Hunte	c Simpson b Davidson	31	c Grout b Davidson	52
R.B. Kanhai	c Harvey b Benaud	38	c Misson b Benaud	31
G. St A. Sobers	c Grout b Simpson	64	(5) c Grout b Simpson	21
F.M.M. Worrell*	c Grout b Martin	10	(7) c Grout b Davidson	7
P.D. Lashley	c Misson b Benaud	41	(8) lbw b Martin	18
F.C.M. Alexander†	c McDonald b Misson	11	(6) c Mackay b Davidson	73
J.S. Solomon	run out	45	(4) run out	36
L.R. Gibbs	c Burge b Misson	11	c O'Neill b Simpson	8
W.W. Hall	b Misson	21	c Grout b Davidson	21
A.L. Valentine	not out	0	not out	3
Extras	(B 4, LB 4, W 1)	9	(B 5, LB 8, W 1)	14
Total		**292**		**321**

AUSTRALIA

R.B. Simpson	c Gibbs b Sobers	75	b Gibbs	92
C.C. McDonald	lbw b Sobers	91	c Smith b Gibbs	11
N.C. O'Neill	b Gibbs	10	(4) c Alexander b Worrell	48
P.J.P. Burge	c Sobers b Gibbs	68	(5) b Valentine	53
K.D. Mackay	c Alexander b Hall	19	(8) not out	3
R.N. Harvey	c Alexander b Sobers	5	c Smith b Worrell	12
A.K. Davidson	c Alexander b Sobers	24	c Sobers b Worrell	12
R. Benaud*	b Gibbs	3	(3) b Valentine	6
J.W. Martin	c Kanhai b Sobers	15	(10) not out	1
F.M. Misson	not out	12		
A.T.W. Grout†	c Hunte b Gibbs	14	(9) c Smith b Valentine	5
Extras	(B 4, LB 8, NB 8)	20	(B 3, LB 9, NB 3)	15
Total		**356**	(8 wickets)	**258**

AUSTRALIA	O	M	R	W	O	M	R	W		FALL OF WICKETS			
										WI	A	WI	A
Davidson	27	4	89	1	24·7	4	84	5	*Wkt*	*1st*	*1st*	*2nd*	*2nd*
Misson	14	3	58	4	10	1	58	0	1st	18	146	54	50
Mackay	1	0	1	0	10	2	21	0	2nd	75	181	103	75
Benaud	21·7	5	55	2	23	4	53	1	3rd	81	181	135	154
Martin	8	0	29	1	10	1	36	1	4th	107	244	173	176
Simpson	18	3	51	1	18	4	55	2	5th	200	260	201	200
									6th	204	309	218	236
WEST INDIES									7th	221	309	262	248
Hall	15	1	56	1	5	0	40	0	8th	235	319	295	256
Worrell	11	2	44	0	31	16	43	3	9th	290	335	304	–
Sobers	44	7	120	5	13	2	32	0	10th	292	356	321	–
Gibbs	38·4	18	74	4	41	19	68	2					
Valentine	13	3	42	0	21·7	4	60	3					

Umpires: C.J. Egar (5) and C. Hoy (9).

Close: 1st day – WI(1) 252-8 (Solomon 21, Hall 5); 2nd – A(1) 236-3 (Burge 37, Mackay 16); 3rd – WI(2) 126-2 (Hunte 46, Solomon 9); 4th – A(2) 57-1 (Simpson 44, Benaud 1).

ENGLAND v AUSTRALIA 1961 (1st Test)

Played at Edgbaston, Birmingham, on 8, 9, 10, 12, 13 June.
Toss: England.   Result: MATCH DRAWN.
Debuts: England – J.T. Murray; Australia – W.M. Lawry.

Harvey's 20th hundred in Test matches was Australia's first at Birmingham, their only previous Tests there being in 1902 and 1909. Earlier Mackay had taken the wickets of Barrington, Smith and Subba Row in four balls. On the final day Subba Row became the twelfth England player to score a hundred in his first Test against Australia. Curiously this list includes the first four batsmen of Indian descent to play for England. Although over six hours were lost to rain on the third and fourth days, England began the final one with their score 106 for 1, still 215 behind. Dexter, who had scored 5 in 22 minutes overnight, batted in all for 344 minutes, hit 31 fours, and gave a superb exhibition of strokeplay in earning England a commendable draw with his highest innings against Australia.

ENGLAND

G. Pullar	b Davidson	17	c Grout b Misson	28
R. Subba Row	c Simpson b Mackay	59	b Misson	112
E.R. Dexter	c Davidson b Mackay	10	st Grout b Simpson	180
M.C. Cowdrey*	b Misson	13	b Mackay	14
K.F. Barrington	c Misson b Mackay	21	not out	48
M.J.K. Smith	c Lawry b Mackay	0	not out	1
R. Illingworth	c Grout b Benaud	15		
J.T. Murray†	c Davidson b Benaud	16		
D.A. Allen	run out	11		
F.S. Trueman	c Burge b Benaud	20		
J.B. Statham	not out	7		
Extras	(B 3, LB 3)	6	(LB 18)	18
Total		**195**	(4 wickets)	**401**

AUSTRALIA

W.M. Lawry	c Murray b Illingworth	57
C.C. McDonald	c Illingworth b Statham	22
R.N. Harvey	lbw b Allen	114
N.C. O'Neill	b Statham	82
P.J.P. Burge	lbw b Allen	25
R.B. Simpson	c and b Trueman	76
A.K. Davidson	c and b Illingworth	22
K.D. Mackay	c Barrington b Statham	64
R. Benaud*	not out	36
A.T.W. Grout†	c Dexter b Trueman	5
F.M. Misson	did not bat	
Extras	(B 8, LB 4, NB 1)	13
Total	(9 wickets declared)	**516**

AUSTRALIA	O	M	R	W	O	M	R	W
Davidson	26	6	70	1	31	10	60	0
Misson	15	6	47	1	28	6	82	2
Mackay	29	10	57	4	41	13	87	1
Benaud	14·3	8	15	3	20	4	67	0
Simpson					34	12	87	1
ENGLAND								
Trueman	36·5	1	136	2				
Statham	43	6	147	3				
Illingworth	44	12	110	2				
Allen	24	4	88	2				
Dexter	5	1	22	0				

FALL OF WICKETS

	E	A	E
Wkt	1st	1st	2nd
1st	36	47	93
2nd	53	106	202
3rd	88	252	239
4th	121	299	400
5th	121	322	–
6th	122	381	–
7th	153	469	–
8th	156	501	–
9th	181	516	–
10th	195	–	–

Umpires: J.S. Buller (10) and F.S. Lee (26).

Close: 1st day – E(1) 180-8 (Allen 11, Trueman 14); 2nd – A(1) 359-5 (Simpson 36, Davidson 16); 3rd – E(2) 5-0 (Pullar 0, Subba Row 5); 4th – E(2) 106-1 (Subba Row 68, Dexter 5).

ENGLAND v AUSTRALIA 1961 (2nd Test)

Played at Lord's, London, on 22, 23, 24, 26 June.
Toss: England.   Result: AUSTRALIA won by five wickets.
Debuts: Australia – G.D. McKenzie.

England won their twelfth consecutive toss, Cowdrey setting a Test record by winning nine in succession. Statham took his 200th wicket for England when he bowled McDonald. Grout made his hundredth dismissal when he caught Murray. Australia's win, completed at 2.50 on the fourth afternoon, ended England's then longest unbeaten run of 18 matches starting with the Christchurch Test of 1958-59 (*No. 472*). It was England's first defeat at home since the corresponding fixture in 1956 (*Test No. 426*). Lawry, playing in his second Test match, compiled the first of seven hundreds against England, batting with great courage for 369 minutes on a lively pitch which had a suspected 'ridge' at the Nursery End. Benaud's damaged shoulder allowed Harvey his only taste of Test match captaincy.

ENGLAND

G. Pullar	b Davidson	11	c Grout b Misson		42
R. Subba Row	lbw b Mackay	48	c Grout b Davidson		8
E.R. Dexter	c McKenzie b Misson	27	b McKenzie		17
M.C. Cowdrey*	c Grout b McKenzie	16	c Mackay b Misson		7
P.B.H. May	c Grout b Davidson	17	c Grout b McKenzie		22
K.F. Barrington	c Mackay b Davidson	4	lbw b Davidson		66
R. Illingworth	b Misson	13	c Harvey b Simpson		0
J.T. Murray†	lbw b Mackay	18	c Grout b McKenzie		25
G.A.R. Lock	c Grout b Davidson	5	b McKenzie		1
F.S. Trueman	b Davidson	25	c Grout b McKenzie		0
J.B. Statham	not out	11	not out		2
Extras	(LB 9, W 2)	11	(B 1, LB 10, W 1)		12
Total		**206**			**202**

AUSTRALIA

W.M. Lawry	c Murray b Dexter	130	c Murray b Statham		1
C.C. McDonald	b Statham	4	c Illingworth b Trueman		14
R.B. Simpson	c Illingworth b Trueman	0	(6) c Illingworth b Statham		15
R.N. Harvey*	c Barrington b Trueman	27	(3) c Murray b Trueman		4
N.C. O'Neill	b Dexter	1	(4) b Statham		0
P.J.P. Burge	c Murray b Statham	46	(5) not out		37
A.K. Davidson	lbw b Trueman	6	not out		0
K.D. Mackay	c Barrington b Illingworth	54			
A.T.W. Grout†	lbw b Dexter	0			
G.D. McKenzie	b Trueman	34			
F.M. Misson	not out	25			
Extras	(B 1, LB 12)	13			
Total		**340**	(5 wickets)		**71**

AUSTRALIA	O	M	R	W	O	M	R	W
Davidson	24·3	6	42	5	24	8	50	2
McKenzie	26	7	81	1	29	13	37	5
Misson	16	4	48	2	17	2	66	2
Mackay	12	3	24	2	8	6	5	0
Simpson					19	10	32	1
ENGLAND								
Statham	44	10	89	2	10·5	3	31	3
Trueman	34	3	118	4	10	0	40	2
Dexter	24	7	56	3				
Lock	26	13	48	0				
Illingworth	11·3	5	16	1				

FALL OF WICKETS

	E	A	E	A
Wkt	1st	1st	2nd	2nd
1st	26	5	33	15
2nd	87	6	63	15
3rd	87	81	67	19
4th	111	88	80	19
5th	115	183	127	58
6th	127	194	144	–
7th	156	238	191	–
8th	164	238	199	–
9th	167	291	199	–
10th	206	340	202	–

Umpires: C.S. Elliott (9) and W.E. Phillipson (6).

Close: 1st day – A(1) 42-2 (Lawry 32, Harvey 6); 2nd – A(1) 286-8 (Mackay 32, McKenzie 29); 3rd – E(2) 178-6 (Barrington 59, Murray 14).

ENGLAND v AUSTRALIA 1961 (3rd Test)

Played at Headingley, Leeds, on 6, 7, 8, July.
Toss: Australia.   Result: ENGLAND won by eight wickets.
Debuts: Nil.

England recalled Jackson for his first Test for 12 years and lost the toss for the first time in 13 matches. Australia bowled 70 balls while England's total stayed at 239, before Lock scored 30 off 20 balls with seven fours in 19 minutes. Trueman had a spell of 5 for 0 in 24 balls in the second innings, bowling off-cutters at a reduced pace.

AUSTRALIA

C.C. McDonald	st Murray b Lock	54	b Jackson	1
W.M. Lawry	lbw b Lock	28	c Murray b Allen	28
R.N. Harvey	c Lock b Trueman	73	c Dexter b Trueman	53
N.C. O'Neill	c Cowdrey b Trueman	27	c Cowdrey b Trueman	19
P.J.P. Burge	c Cowdrey b Jackson	5	lbw b Allen	0
K.D. Mackay	lbw b Jackson	6	(9) c Murray b Trueman	0
R.B. Simpson	lbw b Trueman	2	(6) b Trueman	3
A.K. Davidson	not out	22	(7) c Cowdrey b Trueman	7
R. Benaud*	b Trueman	0	(8) b Trueman	0
A.T.W. Grout†	c Murray b Trueman	3	c and b Jackson	7
G.D. McKenzie	b Allen	8	not out	0
Extras	(B 7, LB 2)	9	(LB 2)	2
Total		**237**		**120**

ENGLAND

G. Pullar	b Benaud	53	not out	26
R. Subba Row	lbw b Davidson	35	b Davidson	6
M.C. Cowdrey	c Grout b McKenzie	93	c Grout b Benaud	22
P.B.H. May*	c and b Davidson	26	not out	8
E.R. Dexter	b Davidson	28		
K.F. Barrington	c Simpson b Davidson	6		
J.T. Murray†	b McKenzie	6		
F.S. Trueman	c Burge b Davidson	4		
G.A.R. Lock	lbw b McKenzie	30		
D.A. Allen	not out	5		
H.L. Jackson	run out	8		
Extras	(LB 5)	5		
Total		**299**	(2 wickets)	**62**

ENGLAND	O	M	R	W	O	M	R	W
Trueman	22	5	58	5	15·5	5	30	6
Jackson	31	11	57	2	13	5	26	2
Allen	28	12	45	1	14	6	30	2
Lock	29	5	68	2	10	1	32	0
AUSTRALIA								
Davidson	47	23	63	5	11	6	17	1
McKenzie	27	4	64	3	5	0	15	0
Mackay	22	4	34	0	1	0	8	0
Benaud	39	15	86	1	6	1	22	1
Simpson	14	5	47	0				

FALL OF WICKETS

Wkt	A 1st	E 1st	A 2nd	E 2nd
1st	65	59	4	14
2nd	113	145	49	45
3rd	187	190	99	–
4th	192	223	102	–
5th	196	239	102	–
6th	203	248	105	–
7th	203	252	109	–
8th	204	286	109	–
9th	208	291	120	–
10th	237	299	120	–

Umpires: J.S. Buller (11) and J.G. Langridge (3).

Close: 1st day – E(1) 9-0 (Pullar 5, Subba Row 3); 2nd – E(1) 238-4 (Dexter 22, Barrington 5).

ENGLAND v AUSTRALIA 1961 (4th Test)

Played at Old Trafford, Manchester, on 27, 28, 29, 31 July, 1 August.
Toss: Australia.   Result: AUSTRALIA won by 54 runs.
Debuts: England – J.A. Flavell; Australia - B.C. Booth.

Rain prevented play after 2.40 pm on the first day and brought the total of time lost in post-war Tests at Manchester to 103 hours. Simpson ended England's first innings with a spell of 4 for 2 in 26 balls. Davidson scored 20 runs (604046) off one over from Allen and shared in a last-wicket partnership of 98 with McKenzie. Murray took seven catches to equal T.G. Evans' England record against Australia set in 1956 at Lord's. Benaud bowled his side to victory on the last afternoon with a spell of 5 for 12 in 25 balls, when England appeared certain to achieve their target of scoring 256 runs in 230 minutes. Even another glorious display by Dexter, who hit 76 in 84 minutes, could not prevent Australia from retaining the Ashes.

AUSTRALIA

W.M. Lawry	lbw b Statham	74	c Trueman b Allen	102
R.B. Simpson	c Murray b Statham	4	c Murray b Flavell	51
R.N. Harvey	c Subba Row b Statham	19	c Murray b Dexter	35
N.C. O'Neill	hit wkt b Trueman	11	c Murray b Statham	67
P.J.P. Burge	b Flavell	15	c Murray b Dexter	23
B.C. Booth	c Close b Statham	46	lbw b Dexter	9
K.D. Mackay	c Murray b Statham	11	c Close b Allen	18
A.K. Davidson	c Barrington b Dexter	0	not out	77
R. Benaud*	b Dexter	2	lbw b Allen	1
A.T.W. Grout†	c Murray b Dexter	2	c Statham b Allen	0
G.D. McKenzie	not out	1	b Flavell	32
Extras	(B 4, LB 1)	5	(B 6, LB 9, W 2)	17
Total		**190**		**432**

ENGLAND

G. Pullar	b Davidson	63	c O'Neill b Davidson	26
R. Subba Row	c Simpson b Davidson	2	b Benaud	49
E.R. Dexter	c Davidson b McKenzie	16	c Grout b Benaud	76
P.B.H. May*	c Simpson b Davidson	95	b Benaud	0
D.B. Close	lbw b McKenzie	33	c O'Neill b Benaud	8
K.F. Barrington	c O'Neill b Simpson	78	lbw b Mackay	5
J.T. Murray†	c Grout b Mackay	24	c Simpson b Benaud	4
D.A. Allen	c Booth b Simpson	42	c Simpson b Benaud	10
F.S. Trueman	c Harvey b Simpson	3	c Benaud b Simpson	8
J.B. Statham	c Mackay b Simpson	4	b Davidson	8
J.A. Flavell	not out	0	not out	0
Extras	(B 2, LB 4, W 1)	7	(B 5. W 2)	7
Total		**367**		**201**

ENGLAND	O	M	R	W	O	M	R	W		FALL OF WICKETS			
Trueman	14	1	55	1	32	6	92	0		A	E	A	E
Statham	21	3	53	5	44	9	106	1	*Wkt*	*1st*	*1st*	*2nd*	*2nd*
Flavell	22	8	61	1	29·4	4	65	2	1st	8	3	113	40
Dexter	6·4	2	16	3	20	4	61	3	2nd	51	43	175	150
Allen					38	25	58	4	3rd	89	154	210	150
Close					8	1	33	0	4th	106	212	274	158
									5th	150	212	290	163
AUSTRALIA									6th	174	272	296	171
Davidson	39	11	70	3	14·4	1	50	2	7th	185	358	332	171
McKenzie	38	11	106	2	4	1	20	0	8th	185	362	334	189
Mackay	40	9	81	1	13	7	33	1	9th	189	367	334	193
Benaud	35	15	80	0	32	11	70	6	10th	190	367	432	201
Simpson	11·4	4	23	4	8	4	21	1					

Umpires: J.G. Langridge (4) and W.E. Phillipson (7).

Close: 1st day – A(1) 124-4 (Lawry 64, Booth 6); 2nd – E(1) 187-3 (May 90, Close 14); 3rd – A(2) 63-0 (Lawry 33, Simpson 29); 4th – A(2) 331-6 (Mackay 18, Davidson 18).

ENGLAND v AUSTRALIA 1961 (5th Test)

Played at Kennington Oval, London, on 17, 18, 19, 21, 22 August.
Toss: England.   Result: MATCH DRAWN.
Debuts: Nil.

Rain interrupted play on the third and fourth days. Subba Row scored a hundred in his last Test against Australia, having also scored one in his first (*Test No. 507*). He scored his last 98 runs with a runner after pulling a muscle in his leg. Burge, whose previous highest score in nine Tests against England was only 46, and O'Neill registered their first hundreds in this series. In a chanceless innings lasting 411 minutes, Burge hit 22 fours. Peter May ended his 66-match England career at the sadly early age of 31. He scored 4,537 runs, average 46·77, made 13 hundreds, and led England a record 41 times. Murray's total of 18 dismissals was a new England record for a home rubber and Grout's 21 dismissals set a new record for a rubber in this series.

ENGLAND

G. Pullar	b Davidson	8	c Grout b Mackay	13
R. Subba Row	lbw b Gaunt	12	c and b Benaud	137
M.C. Cowdrey	c Grout b Davidson	0	(5) c Benaud b Mackay	3
P.B.H. May*	c Lawry b Benaud	71	c O'Neill b Mackay	33
E.R. Dexter	c Grout b Gaunt	24	(3) c Gaunt b Mackay	0
K.F. Barrington	c Grout b Gaunt	53	c O'Neill b Benaud	83
J.T. Murray†	c O'Neill b Mackay	27	c Grout b Benaud	40
G.A.R. Lock	c Grout b Mackay	3	c Benaud b Mackay	0
D.A. Allen	not out	22	not out	42
J.B. Statham	b Davidson	18	not out	9
J.A. Flavell	c Simpson b Davidson	14		
Extras	(B 1, LB 2, W 1)	4	(B 6, LB 3, W 1)	10
Total		**256**	(8 wickets)	**370**

AUSTRALIA

W.M. Lawry	c Murray b Statham	0
R.B. Simpson	b Allen	40
R.N. Harvey	lbw b Flavell	13
N.C. O'Neill	c sub (M.J. Stewart) b Allen	117
P.J.P. Burge	b Allen	181
B.C. Booth	c Subba Row b Lock	71
K.D. Mackay	c Murray b Flavell	5
A.K. Davidson	lbw b Statham	17
R. Benaud*	b Allen	6
A.T.W. Grout†	not out	30
R.A. Gaunt	b Statham	3
Extras	(B 10, LB 1)	11
Total		**494**

AUSTRALIA	O	M	R	W	O	M	R	W
Davidson	34·1	8	83	4	29	7	67	0
Gaunt	24	3	53	3	22	7	33	0
Benaud	17	4	35	1	51	18	113	3
Mackay	39	14	75	2	68	21	121	5
Simpson	4	2	6	0	2	0	13	0
O'Neill					4	1	13	0
Harvey					1	1	0	0
ENGLAND								
Statham	38·5	10	75	3				
Flavell	31	5	105	2				
Dexter	24	2	68	0				
Allen	30	6	133	4				
Lock	42	14	102	1				

FALL OF WICKETS

	E	A	E
Wkt	*1st*	*1st*	*2nd*
1st	18	0	33
2nd	20	15	33
3rd	20	88	83
4th	67	211	90
5th	147	396	262
6th	193	401	283
7th	199	441	283
8th	202	455	355
9th	238	472	–
10th	256	494	–

Umpires: C.S. Elliott (10) and F.S. Lee (27).

Close: 1st day – E(1) 210-8 (Allen 7, Statham 2); 2nd – A(1) 290-4 (Burge 86, Booth 33); 3rd – E(2) 32-0 (Pullar 13, Subba Row 19); 4th – E(2) 155-4 (Subba Row 69, Barrington 35).

PAKISTAN v ENGLAND 1961–62 (1st Test)

Played at Lahore Stadium on 21, 22, 24, 25, 26 October.
Toss: Pakistan.   Result: ENGLAND won by 5 wickets.
Debuts: Pakistan – Afaq Hussain; England – A. Brown, W.E. Russell, D.W. White.

England's first official Test in Pakistan – and the first match between the two countries since Pakistan's memorable win at The Oval in 1954 – brought the only result in 12 such contests in Pakistan before 1984. Barrington and Burki both scored hundreds on debut in this particular series. White took the wickets of Imtiaz and Hanif with his 11th and 16th balls in Test cricket. Javed Burki and Mushtaq shared a partnership of 153 which was Pakistan's highest for the fourth wicket against England until 1987. England continued this three-match rubber after playing five Tests in India.

PAKISTAN

Hanif Mohammad	b White	19	c Murray b Brown		17
Imtiaz Ahmed*†	c Murray b White	4	b Dexter		12
Saeed Ahmed	c Murray b Barber	74	c Murray b Brown		0
Javed Burki	c Murray b Allen	138	c Allen b Barber		15
Mushtaq Mohammad	run out	76	c Pullar b Allen		23
W. Mathias	c Smith b Barber	3	lbw b Allen		32
Intikhab Alam	b Barber	24	b Barber		17
Mohammad Munaf	b Allen	7	c Dexter b Brown		12
Mahmood Hussain	b White	14	b Allen		7
Afaq Hussain	not out	10	not out		35
Haseeb Ahsan	not out	7	c Smith b Barber		14
Extras	(B 4, LB 3, NB 4)	11	(B 9, LB 2, NB 5)		16
Total	(9 wickets declared)	**387**			**200**

ENGLAND

P.E. Richardson	c Afaq b Munaf	4	c Imtiaz b Intikhab		48
G. Pullar	c Mahmood b Munaf	0	b Munaf		0
K.F. Barrington	run out	139	lbw b Mahmood		6
M.J.K. Smith	run out	99	c Afaq b Haseeb		34
E.R. Dexter*	hit wkt b Afaq	20	not out		66
W.E. Russell	b Intikhab	34	b Intikhab		0
R.W. Barber	st Imtiaz b Haseeb	6	not out		39
J.T. Murray†	b Munaf	4			
D.A. Allen	lbw b Munaf	40			
D.W. White	b Saeed	0			
A. Brown	not out	3			
Extras	(B 21, LB 1, NB 9)	31	(B 10, LB 4, NB 2)		16
Total		**380**	(5 wickets)		**209**

ENGLAND	O	M	R	W	O	M	R	W		FALL OF WICKETS			
										P	E	P	E
White	22	3	65	3	12	2	42	0	Wkt	1st	1st	2nd	2nd
Brown	15·5	3	44	0	14	4	27	3	1st	17	2	33	1
Dexter	7	1	26	0	7	2	10	1	2nd	24	21	33	17
Barber	40	4	124	3	20·5	6	54	3	3rd	162	213	33	86
Allen	33	14	67	2	22	13	51	3	4th	315	275	69	108
Russell	19	9	25	0					5th	324	294	93	108
Barrington	6	0	25	0					6th	324	306	113	–
PAKISTAN									7th	327	322	138	–
Mahmood Hussain	25	8	35	0	12	3	30	1	8th	365	361	146	–
Munaf	31·1	15	42	4	15	1	54	1	9th	369	362	148	–
Intikhab	48	6	118	1	16	3	37	2	10th	–	380	200	–
Afaq	23	6	40	1	5	0	21	0					
Haseeb	36	7	95	1	9	0	42	1					
Saeed	11	3	19	1	2	0	9	0					

Umpires: Khwaja Saeed Ahmed (5) and Shujauddin (5).

Close: 1st day – P(1) 254-3 (Burki 103, Mushtaq 46); 2nd – E(1) 109-2 (Barrington 51, Smith 45); 3rd – E(1) 321-6 (Russell 22, Murray 4); 4th – P(2) 149-9 (Afaq 2, Haseeb 0).

INDIA v ENGLAND 1961–62 (1st Test)

Played at Brabourne Stadium, Bombay on 11, 12, 14, 15, 16 November.
Toss: England.   Result: MATCH DRAWN.
Debuts: England – D.R. Smith.

The partnership of 159 in 170 minutes between Richardson and Pullar was England's highest for the first wicket against India until 1984–85. Kunderan became Lock's 2,000th wicket in first-class matches. India were set 297 runs to win in 245 minutes. Barrington batted for over nine hours in the match without being dismissed. Jaisimha retired after being struck on the head by a bouncer from Brown and returned two days later when the first wicket fell.

ENGLAND

P.E. Richardson	c Kunderan b Borde	71	c Kripal Singh b Durani		43
G. Pullar	st Kunderan b Borde	83			
K.F. Barrington	not out	151	not out		52
M.J.K. Smith	c Kunderan b Ranjane	36	b Durani		0
E.R. Dexter*	b Durani	85	c sub (D.N. Sardesai) b Ranjane		27
R.W. Barber	st Kunderan b Borde	19	(2) run out		31
J.T. Murray†	c sub (D.N. Sardesai) b Ranjane	8	(6) b Desai		2
D.A. Allen	c Kunderan b Ranjane	0			
G.A.R. Lock	b Ranjane	23	(7) not out		22
D.R. Smith	⎫ did not bat				
A. Brown	⎭				
Extras	(B 7, LB 15, NB 2)	24	(B 3, LB 4)		7
Total	(8 wickets declared)	**500**	(5 wickets declared)		**184**

INDIA

N.J. Contractor*	b Allen	19	c Allen b D.R. Smith		1
M.L. Jaisimha	c Barrington b Dexter	56	c Barber b M.J.K. Smith		51
V.L. Manjrekar	c Lock b Barber	68	lbw b Lock		84
A.G. Milkha Singh	c Brown b Allen	2	c Allen b Richardson		12
C.G. Borde	b D.R. Smith	69	not out		12
S.A. Durani	c Barber b Allen	71	c and b Richardson		0
A.G. Kripal Singh	not out	38	not out		13
B.K. Kunderan†	lbw b Lock	5			
R.B. Desai	c Richardson b Lock	1			
V.B. Ranjane	c Barber b Lock	16			
V.V. Kumar	b Lock	0			
Extras	(B 33, LB 4, NB 8)	45	(B 4 LB 2, NB 1)		7
Total		**390**	(5 wickets)		**180**

INDIA	O	M	R	W	O	M	R	W
Desai	32	4	85	0	13	2	39	1
Ranjane	21	2	76	4	13	1	53	1
Kripal Singh	33	9	64	0	14	3	33	0
Kumar	27	8	70	0				
Durani	30	5	91	1	11	1	28	2
Borde	30	5	90	3	7	1	24	0
ENGLAND								
D.R. Smith	31	12	54	1	7	2	18	1
Brown	19	2	64	0	5	0	15	0
Dexter	12	4	25	1	4	0	15	0
Barber	22	5	74	1	13	2	42	0
Lock	45	22	74	4	16	9	33	1
Allen	39	21	54	3	11	5	12	0
Barrington					3	0	18	0
M.J.K. Smith					8	3	10	1
Richardson					6	3	10	2

FALL OF WICKETS

	E	I	E	I
Wkt	1st	1st	2nd	2nd
1st	159	80	74	5
2nd	164	121	93	136
3rd	228	140	93	140
4th	389	173	144	162
5th	434	315	147	162
6th	458	341	–	–
7th	458	356	–	–
8th	500	358	–	–
9th	–	383	–	–
10th	–	390	–	–

Umpires: S.K. Ganguli (9) and A.R. Joshi (11).

Close: 1st day – E(1) 288-3 (Barrington 52, Dexter 30); 2nd – I(1) 42-0 (Contractor 9, Manjrekar 18); 3rd – I(1) 255-4 (Borde 42, Durani 41); 4th – E(2) 127-3 (Barrington 34, Dexter 16).

INDIA v ENGLAND 1961–62 (2nd Test)

Played at Green Park, Kanpur, on 1, 2, 3, 5, 6 December.
Toss: India.   Result: MATCH DRAWN.
Debuts: India – F.M. Engineer, D.N. Sardesai; England – B.R. Knight.

During his third hundred in successive Test innings, Umrigar became the first to score 3,000 runs for India.
England followed-on for the first time in this series after a spell of 4 for 6 in 18 balls by leg-spinner Gupte.

INDIA

M.L. Jaisimha	c Richardson b Lock	70
N.J. Contractor*	b Knight	17
V.L. Manjrekar	c Knight b Allen	96
S.A. Durani	c Lock b Dexter	37
P.R. Umrigar	not out	147
C.G. Borde	b Dexter	21
D.N. Sardesai	hit wkt b Lock	28
A.G. Kripal Singh	b Knight	7
F.M. Engineer†	st Murray b Lock	33
V.B. Ranjane	) did not bat	
S.P. Gupte	)	
Extras	(B 2, LB 7, NB 2)	11
Total	(8 wickets declared)	**467**

ENGLAND

P.E. Richardson	c Engineer b Gupte	22	c Umrigar b Borde	48
G. Pullar	c Sardesai b Gupte	46	c Contractor b Durani	119
K.F. Barrington	b Gupte	21	run out	172
M.J.K. Smith	c and b Gupte	0	lbw b Gupte	0
E.R. Dexter*	c Kripal Singh b Gupte	2	not out	126
R.W. Barber	not out	69	run out	10
J.T. Murray†	b Borde	2	not out	9
B.R. Knight	c and b Borde	12		
D.A. Allen	c Engineer b Borde	12		
G.A.R. Lock	c and b Durani	49		
D.R. Smith	lbw b Ranjane	0		
Extras	(B 6, LB 2, NB 1)	9	(B 4, LB 7, NB 2)	13
Total		**244**	(5 wickets)	**497**

ENGLAND	O	M	R	W	O	M	R	W				
D.R. Smith	44	11	111	0								
Knight	36	11	80	2								
Dexter	31	5	84	2								
Lock	44	15	93	3								
Allen	43	17	88	1								

INDIA	O	M	R	W	O	M	R	W
Ranjane	21·3	9	38	1	18	1	61	0
Umrigar	6	1	11	0	19	6	53	0
Gupte	40	12	90	5	33	8	89	1
Kripal Singh	1	0	5	0	36	7	78	0
Durani	16	6	36	1	53	15	139	1
Borde	22	6	55	3	16	4	44	1
Jaisimha					6	1	8	0
Contractor					2	0	9	0
Sardesai					1	0	3	0

FALL OF WICKETS

	I	E	E
Wkt	1st	1st	2nd
1st	41	29	94
2nd	150	87	233
3rd	193	87	234
4th	261	95	440
5th	293	100	459
6th	368	104	–
7th	414	128	–
8th	467	162	–
9th	–	243	–
10th	–	244	–

Umpires: Mahomed Yunus (4) and S. Roy (1).

Close: 1st day – I(1) 209-3 (Durani 9, Umrigar 12); 2nd – I(1) 437-7 (Umrigar 132, Engineer 18); 3rd – E(1) 165-8 (Barber 41, Lock 0); 4th – E(2) 200-1 (Pullar 101, Barrington 47).

INDIA v ENGLAND 1961–62 (3rd Test)

Played at Feroz Shah Kotla, Delhi, on 13, 14, 16, 17 (*no play*), 18 (*no play*) December.
Toss: India.   Result: MATCH DRAWN.
Debuts: India – The Nawab Mansur Ali of Pataudi. *After the Indian Government abolished royal titles, Pataudi assumed the name of 'Mansur Ali Khan'. He is shown throughout these volumes as 'Nawab of Pataudi, jr'.*

For only the second time in India, rain seriously interrupted a Test match and, as had happened when Pakistan played at Madras in 1952-53 (*Test No. 358*), the last two days were abandoned. Barrington scored his fourth hundred in consecutive Tests and his partnership of 164 with Pullar was England's highest for the second wicket in India until 1984–85. Manjrekar's 189 not out was India's highest score against England so far; he batted for 440 minutes and hit 29 fours.

INDIA

M.L. Jaisimha	c and b D.R. Smith	127
N.J. Contractor*	c Pullar b Lock	39
V.L. Manjrekar	not out	189
Nawab of Pataudi, jr	c Richardson b Allen	13
P.R. Umrigar	lbw b Allen	22
C.G. Borde	b Barber	45
S.A. Durani	b Allen	18
F.M. Engineer†	lbw b Allen	1
A.G. Kripal Singh	run out	2
R.B. Desai	lbw b Knight	5
S.P. Gupte	b Knight	0
Extras	(B 2, LB 2, NB 1)	5
Total		**466**

ENGLAND

P.E. Richardson	lbw b Desai	1
G. Pullar	c Manjrekar b Kripal Singh	89
K.F. Barrington	not out	113
M.J.K. Smith	b Gupte	2
E.R. Dexter*	not out	45
R.W. Barber	)	
J.T. Murray†	)	
B.R. Knight	) did not bat	
D.A. Allen	)	
G.A.R. Lock	)	
D.R. Smith	)	
Extras	(B 5, NB 1)	6
Total	(3 wickets)	**256**

ENGLAND	O	M	R	W
D.R. Smith	30	11	66	1
Knight	24·3	5	72	2
Allen	47	18	87	4
Barber	25	3	103	1
Dexter	2	0	11	0
Lock	40	15	83	1
Barrington	9	1	39	0
INDIA				
Desai	28	5	57	1
Jaisimha	11	2	28	0
Gupte	36	14	78	1
Durani	13	3	38	0
Kripal Singh	12	4	27	1
Borde	10	4	19	0
Umrigar	4	1	3	0

FALL OF WICKETS

	I	E
Wkt	1st	1st
1st	121	2
2nd	199	166
3rd	244	177
4th	276	–
5th	408	–
6th	443	–
7th	451	–
8th	455	–
9th	462	–
10th	466	–

Umpires: S. Kumaraswamy (1) and B. Satyaji Rao (2).

Close: 1st day – I(1) 253-3 (Manjrekar 61, Umrigar 8); 2nd – E(1) 21-1 (Pullar 7, Barrington 13); 3rd – E(1) 256-3 (Barrington 113, Dexter 45); 4th – no play.

INDIA v ENGLAND 1961–62 (4th Test)

Played at Eden Gardens, Calcutta, on 30, 31 December, 1, 3, 4 January.
Toss: India.   Result: INDIA won by 187 runs.
Debuts: England – G. Millman, P.H. Parfitt.

India gained their second win against England in 28 matches and ended a sequence of nine drawn Tests in India when England failed to score 421 runs in 490 minutes. Mehra continued batting after fracturing his right thumb on the first morning.

INDIA

N.J. Contractor*	b Smith	4	st Millman b Allen	11
V.L. Mehra	c Parfitt b Lock	62	(11) not out	7
V.L. Manjrekar	b Allen	24	st Millman b Lock	27
Nawab of Pataudi, jr	c Lock b Allen	64	c Millman b Lock	32
P.R. Umrigar	c Smith b Allen	36	(6) b Allen	36
M.L. Jaisimha	c Millman b Smith	37	(2) b Lock	36
C.G. Borde	run out	68	(8) c Barrington b Allen	61
S.A. Durani	b Allen	43	(7) c Parfitt b Lock	0
F.M. Engineer†	c Parfitt b Lock	12	(5) c Millman b Allen	9
R.B. Desai	not out	13	(9) c Parfitt b Knight	29
V.B. Ranjane	c Barber b Allen	7	(10) c Lock b Knight	0
Extras	(B 2, LB 6, NB 2)	10	(LB 3, NB 1)	4
Total		**380**		**252**

ENGLAND

P.E. Richardson	c Contractor b Borde	62	b Umrigar	42
W.E. Russell	b Ranjane	10	b Ranjane	9
K.F. Barrington	b Durani	14	c Durani b Desai	3
P.H. Parfitt	c sub (G. Kasturirangan) b Borde	21	(6) lbw b Umrigar	46
E.R. Dexter*	b Borde	57	(4) lbw b Durani	62
R.W. Barber	b Borde	12	(5) c Jaisimha b Durani	6
B.R. Knight	st Engineer b Durani	12	not out	39
D.A. Allen	b Durani	15	c Manjrekar b Desai	7
G. Millman†	c Engineer b Durani	0	b Ranjane	4
G.A.R. Lock	not out	2	run out	1
D.R. Smith	b Durani	0	c Manjrekar b Durani	2
Extras	(B 1, LB 2, NB 4)	7	(B 1, LB 11)	12
Total		**212**		**233**

ENGLAND	O	M	R	W	O	M	R	W
Smith	31	10	60	2	3	0	15	0
Knight	18	3	61	0	7	2	18	2
Dexter	29	7	83	0				
Allen	34	13	67	5	43·2	16	95	4
Lock	36	19	63	2	46	15	111	4
Barber	3	0	17	0	2	0	9	0
Russell	5	0	19	0				
INDIA								
Desai	10	1	34	0	17	4	32	2
Ranjane	21	3	59	1	14	3	31	2
Durani	23·2	8	47	5	33·2	12	66	3
Borde	25	8	65	4	22	10	46	0
Umrigar					30	10	46	2

FALL OF WICKETS

	I	E	I	E
Wkt	1st	1st	2nd	2nd
1st	6	26	39	20
2nd	50	69	55	27
3rd	145	91	102	92
4th	185	130	119	101
5th	194	155	119	129
6th	259	181	119	195
7th	314	208	192	208
8th	355	209	233	217
9th	357	212	233	224
10th	380	212	252	233

Umpires: H.E. Choudhury (2) and S.K. Raghunatha Rao (3).

Close: 1st day – I(1) 221-5 (Jaisimha 12, Borde 15); 2nd – E(1) 107-3 (Parfitt 10, Dexter 11); 3rd – I(2) 106-3 (Pataudi 24, Engineer 4); 4th – E(2) 125-4 (Dexter 61, Parfitt 3).

INDIA v ENGLAND 1961–62 (5th Test)

Played at Corporation Stadium, Madras, on 10, 11, 13, 14, 15 January.
Toss: India.   Result: INDIA won by 128 runs.
Debuts: India – E.A.S. Prasanna.

India won their first rubber against England and only their third against any country with this second victory in successive matches. Engineer, who began the second day's play by scoring 16 (404224) off Knight's opening over, and Nadkarni shared India's first century partnership for the eighth wicket. India had scored 296 runs on the first day, Pataudi reaching his first Test hundred in 155 minutes. Durani achieved his best match analysis in 29 Tests. Barrington (594) and Manjrekar (586) set the present record aggregates for a rubber between these two countries.

INDIA

M.L. Jaisimha	b Knight	12		c Millman b Lock	10
N.J. Contractor*	b Barber	86		c Parfitt b D.R. Smith	3
V.L. Manjrekar	c Lock b Parfitt	13		run out	85
Nawab of Pataudi, jr	c Lock b Knight	103		c M.J.K. Smith b Lock	10
P.R. Umrigar	c Millman b Allen	2		c and b Allen	11
C.G. Borde	b Lock	31	(7)	c Dexter b Parfitt	7
S.A. Durani	b Allen	21	(8)	c Millman b Lock	9
R.G. Nadkarni	b Allen	63	(9)	c Parfitt b Lock	1
F.M. Engineer†	b Dexter	65	(10)	not out	15
R.B. Desai	lbw b Barber	13	(6)	c Parfitt b Lock	12
E.A.S. Prasanna	not out	9		c Dexter b Lock	17
Extras	(B 4, LB 6)	10		(B 6, LB 4)	10
Total		**428**			**190**

ENGLAND

P.E. Richardson	c Contractor b Desai	13	c Jaisimha b Desai	2
R.W. Barber	lbw b Borde	16	b Durani	21
K.F. Barrington	c Manjrekar b Durani	20	lbw b Nadkarni	48
E.R. Dexter*	b Borde	2	c Nadkarni b Borde	3
M.J.K. Smith	c Umrigar b Durani	73	c Borde b Durani	15
P.H. Parfitt	c Prasanna b Durani	25	c Contractor b Durani	33
B.R. Knight	c Nadkarni b Durani	19	c Engineer b Durani	33
D.A. Allen	b Durani	34	c Umrigar b Borde	21
G. Millman†	not out	32	c Contractor b Prasanna	14
G.A.R. Lock	c Borde b Durani	0	c Nadkarni b Borde	11
D.R. Smith	b Nadkarni	34	not out	2
Extras	(B 1, LB 12)	13	(B 2, LB 4)	6
Total		**281**		**209**

ENGLAND	O	M	R	W	O	M	R	W		FALL OF WICKETS			
D.R. Smith	9	1	20	0	7	0	15	1		I	E	I	E
Knight	14	2	62	2	4	0	12	0	*Wkt*	*1st*	*1st*	*2nd*	*2nd*
Lock	40	13	106	1	39·3	16	65	6	1st	27	18	15	2
Allen	51·3	20	116	3	33	11	64	1	2nd	74	41	30	32
Parfitt	11	2	22	1	11	3	24	1	3rd	178	45	50	41
Barber	14	0	70	2					4th	193	54	80	86
Dexter	5	0	22	1					5th	245	134	99	90
INDIA									6th	273	180	122	155
Desai	12	1	56	1	4	0	16	1	7th	277	189	146	164
Jaisimha	5	0	18	0					8th	378	226	150	194
Durani	36	9	105	6	34	12	72	4	9th	398	226	158	202
Borde	30	9	58	2	25·3	8	59	3	10th	428	281	190	209
Prasanna	9	2	20	0	11	3	19	1					
Umrigar	12	6	11	0	6	1	12	0					
Nadkarni	6·1	6	0	1	12	3	25	1					

Umpires: I. Gopalakrishnan (2) and S.P. Pan (2).

Close: 1st day – I(1) 295-7 (Nadkarni 12, Engineer 7); 2nd – E(1) 108-4 (Smith 29, Parfitt 16); 3rd – I(2) 65-3 (Manjrekar 31, Umrigar 7); 4th – E(2) 122-5 (Parfitt 18, Knight 14).

PAKISTAN v ENGLAND 1961–62 (2nd Test)

Played at Dacca Stadium, on 19, 20, 21, 23, 24 January.
Toss: Pakistan.   Result: MATCH DRAWN.
Debuts: Nil.

Hanif, who batted for 893 minutes in the match, became the first Pakistan batsman to score a hundred in each innings of a Test match. Only 175 runs were scored from 111 overs on the first day. The opening partnerships of 198 by Pullar and Barber and 122 by Hanif and Alimuddin established new records for this series; although England's has survived, Pakistan's was surpassed by Hanif's son, Shoaib, and Mohsin Khan in 1983-84 (*Test No. 980*).

PAKISTAN

Hanif Mohammad	c Lock b Allen	111	b Allen	104
Alimuddin	c Smith b Lock	7	c Dexter b Richardson	50
Saeed Ahmed	b Knight	69	c Parfitt b Lock	13
Javed Burki	c and b Lock	140	c Knight b Lock	0
Intikhab Alam	c Barrington b Lock	18	(9) b Lock	5
Mushtaq Mohammad	b Allen	26	(5) c and b Allen	6
Imtiaz Ahmed*†	b Lock	0	(6) hit wkt b Allen	0
Nasim-ul-Ghani	not out	15	c Richardson b Allen	12
Shujauddin	)		(7) b Lock	0
Mohammad Munaf	) did not bat		b Allen	12
A. D'Souza	)		not out	7
Extras	(B 4, LB 3)	7	(B 5, LB 1, NB 1)	7
Total	(7 wickets declared)	**393**		**216**

ENGLAND

G. Pullar	c and b D'Souza	165	not out	8
R.W. Barber	lbw b Nasim	86		
K.F. Barrington	b D'Souza	84		
M.J.K. Smith	lbw b D'Souza	10		
E.R. Dexter*	b Munaf	12		
P.E. Richardson	c D'Souza b Nasim	19	(2) not out	21
P.H. Parfitt	c and b Shujauddin	9		
B.R. Knight	b D'Souza	10		
D.A. Allen	b Shujauddin	0		
G. Millman†	not out	3		
G.A.R. Lock	c Hanif b Shujauddin	4		
Extras	(B 16, LB 15, NB 6)	37	(B 2, LB 6, NB 1)	9
Total		**439**	(0 wickets)	**38**

ENGLAND	O	M	R	W	O	M	R	W	FALL OF WICKETS				
Knight	29	13	52	1	14	6	19	0		P	E	P	E
Dexter	28	12	34	0	5	4	1	0	*Wkt*	*1st*	*1st*	*2nd*	*2nd*
Lock	73	24	155	4	42	23	70	4	1st	14	198	122	–
Allen	40·3	13	94	2	23·1	11	30	5	2nd	127	345	137	–
Barrington	11	1	39	0	21	13	17	0	3rd	283	358	137	–
Barber	11	8	12	0					4th	344	373	158	–
Parfitt					8	3	14	0	5th	361	386	158	–
Richardson					12	5	28	1	6th	365	414	159	–
Pullar					9	3	30	0	7th	393	418	184	–
									8th	–	422	191	–
PAKISTAN									9th	–	432	201	–
Munaf	30	5	55	1					10th	–	439	216	–
D'Souza	46	13	94	4									
Shujauddin	34	10	73	3									
Nasim	50	19	119	2	3	3	0	0					
Intikhab	9	0	43	0	5	0	16	0					
Saeed	12	3	18	0	4	2	2	0					
Burki					2	1	3	0					
Hanif					2	0	8	0					

Umpires: Daud Khan (7) and Shujauddin (6).

Close: 1st day – P(1) 175-2 (Hanif 64, Burki 30); 2nd – E(1) 57-0 (Pullar 31, Barber 23); 3rd – E(1) 333-1 (Pullar 160, Barrington 69); 4th – P(2) 28-0 (Hanif 18, Alimuddin 8).

PAKISTAN v ENGLAND 1961–62 (3rd Test)

Played at National Stadium, Karachi, on 2, 3, 4, 6, 7 February.
Toss: Pakistan.   Result: MATCH DRAWN.
Debuts: Nil.

White, who pulled a muscle and was unable to complete his third over, took the wicket of Imtiaz with his first ball. Dexter batted for 495 minutes for England's only double century in Pakistan and the highest innings of his first-class career. His partnership of 188 with Parfitt remains England's highest for the fourth wicket in this series. England's total was their highest in Pakistan until 1983-84 (*Test No. 979*). Hanif's aggregate of 407 runs remains the Pakistan record for any rubber against England.

PAKISTAN

Hanif Mohammad	c Dexter b Lock	67		c Dexter b Knight	89
Imtiaz Ahmed*†	b White	0	(5)	c Smith b Dexter	86
Saeed Ahmed	c Millman b Knight	16		c and b Barber	19
Javed Burki	c Millman b Dexter	3		c Millman b Dexter	44
Mushtaq Mohammad	lbw b Knight	14	(6)	b Lock	41
Alimuddin	c Lock b Knight	109	(2)	c Parfitt b Barber	53
Shujauddin	c Parfitt b Allen	15		c Lock b Barber	5
Nasim-ul-Ghani	b Barber	3		not out	41
Fazal Mahmood	b Knight	12		b Dexter	0
A. D'Souza	b Dexter	3		not out	10
Haseeb Ahsan	not out	4			
Extras	(B 2, LB 1, NB 4)	7		(B 8, LB 2, NB 6)	16
Total		**253**		(8 wickets)	**404**

ENGLAND

P.E. Richardson	c Alimuddin b Nasim	26
G. Pullar	c Alimuddin b Nasim	60
E.R. Dexter*	c Saeed b D'Souza	205
M.J.K. Smith	c Imtiaz b Nasim	56
P.H. Parfitt	c Saeed b D'Souza	111
R.W. Barber	st Imtiaz b Haseeb	23
B.R. Knight	c Imtiaz b D'Souza	6
D.A. Allen	c Imtiaz b D'Souza	1
G. Millman†	c Nasim b Haseeb	0
G.A.R. Lock	not out	0
D.W. White	b D'Souza	0
Extras	(B 7, LB 11, NB 1)	19
Total		**507**

ENGLAND	O	M	R	W	O	M	R	W	FALL OF WICKETS			
Knight	19	4	66	4	17	3	43	1		P	E	P
White	2·4	0	12	1					*Wkt*	*1st*	*1st*	*2nd*
Dexter	18·2	4	48	2	32	9	86	3	1st	2	77	91
Allen	27	14	51	1	35	19	42	0	2nd	25	107	129
Barber	14	1	44	1	41	7	117	3	3rd	36	250	211
Lock	14	8	25	1	37	16	86	1	4th	56	438	227
Parfitt					3	2	4	0	5th	148	493	256
Richardson					2	1	10	0	6th	183	497	337
									7th	196	502	373
PAKISTAN									8th	245	503	383
Fazal	63	23	98	0					9th	248	507	–
D'Souza	57·5	16	112	5					10th	253	507	–
Nasim	45	10	125	3								
Haseeb	36	7	68	2								
Shujauddin	27	5	63	0								
Saeed	3	0	12	0								
Mushtaq	2	0	10	0								

Umpires: Daud Khan (8) and Shujauddin (7).

Close: 1st day – P(1) 253 all out; 2nd – E(1) 219-2 (Dexter 87, Smith 42); 3rd – E(1) 453-4 (Parfitt 88, Barber 4); 4th – P(2) 147-2 (Hanif 58, Burki 10).

Test No. 520/10

SOUTH AFRICA v NEW ZEALAND 1961–62 (1st Test)

Played at Kingsmead, Durban, on 8, 9, 11, 12 December.
Toss: South Africa.   Result: SOUTH AFRICA won by 30 runs.
Debuts: South Africa – E.J. Barlow, K.C. Bland, H.D. Bromfield, M.K. Elgie, G.B. Lawrence,
P.M. Pollock, K.A. Walter; New Zealand – G.A. Bartlett, P.T. Barton, F.J. Cameron, A.E. Dick,
R.C. Motz.

Elgie represented Scotland at Rugby Union football. McGlew became the fourth South African after A.B.
Tancred, J.W. Zulch and T.L. Goddard to carry his bat through a completed Test innings. He remains the only
South African to score a century while doing so and 292 is the highest of the four innings totals involved; he
batted for 312 minutes and hit ten fours in registering South Africa's highest score in a home Test against New
Zealand. Needing 197 runs for their first Test victory overseas, New Zealand collapsed against the bowling of
Pollock, one of seven new Springbok caps. His analysis (6 for 38) remained the best of his 28-match Test career,
while his match figures of 9 for 99 were then the best by a genuinely fast bowler in any Test for South Africa.
Although this was the last Test match scheduled for Kingsmead, happily the venue of the longest cricket match
(*Test No. 271*) was reprieved.

SOUTH AFRICA

D.J. McGlew*	not out	127	b Motz	5
E.J. Barlow	b Motz	15	c Dick b Motz	10
J.H.B. Waite†	c Dick b Bartlett	25	c sub (G.T. Dowling) b Cameron	63
R.A. McLean	b Alabaster	63	c Bartlett b Motz	0
K.C. Bland	c Reid b Cameron	5	run out	30
M.K. Elgie	b Motz	1	st Dick b Alabaster	0
S. O'Linn	lbw b Cameron	8	c Cameron b Alabaster	6
P.M. Pollock	c Dick b Cameron	0	c Dick b Cameron	15
G.B. Lawrence	c Sparling b Alabaster	16	lbw b Alabaster	0
K.A. Walter	c Dick b Alabaster	0	c Dick b Cameron	1
H.D. Bromfield	lbw b Alabaster	0	not out	0
Extras	(B 11, LB 6, W 1, NB 14)	32	(B 2, LB 4, W 5, NB 8)	19
Total		**292**		**149**

NEW ZEALAND

J.W. Guy	c Walter b Pollock	8	c Bromfield b Pollock	1
J.T. Sparling	c Waite b Pollock	13	c Waite b Walter	10
P.T. Barton	c Elgie b Lawrence	54	c Waite b Pollock	23
S.N. McGregor	c Barlow b Walter	20	c Walter b Bromfield	55
J.R. Reid*	c Pollock b Lawrence	13	(6) c Waite b Pollock	16
P.G.Z. Harris	c Elgie b Walter	74	(5) lbw b Pollock	0
A.E. Dick†	c Waite b Pollock	3	c Waite b Pollock	2
R.C. Motz	c McGlew b Walter	0	(9) b Bromfield	10
G.A Bartlett	c Pollock b Walter	40	(8) c O'Linn b Bromfield	23
J.C. Alabaster	lbw b Lawrence	2	c Bromfield b Pollock	8
F.J. Cameron	not out	0	not out	1
Extras	(B 1, LB 1, NB 16)	18	(B 1, LB 1, NB 15)	17
Total		**245**		**166**

NEW ZEALAND	O	M	R	W	O	M	R	W					
Motz	23	3	64	2	20	1	51	3					
Bartlett	9	3	39	1	9	3	11	0					
Cameron	27	5	60	3	15·2	1	32	3					
Reid	11	1	38	0									
Alabaster	17·5	2	59	4	17	6	36	3					
Sparling	1	1	0	0									

FALL OF WICKETS

	SA	NZ	SA	NZ
Wkt	1st	1st	2nd	2nd
1st	20	20	17	7
2nd	82	33	38	23
3rd	185	63	38	53
4th	216	89	110	53
5th	233	150	113	100
6th	253	153	129	102
7th	263	162	137	137
8th	286	235	137	150
9th	292	245	144	162
10th	292	245	149	166

SOUTH AFRICA	O	M	R	W	O	M	R	W
Pollock	22	3	61	3	20·3	8	38	6
Walter	25·3	6	63	4	16	5	34	1
Lawrence	29	6	63	3	25	8	40	0
Barlow	8	3	17	0				
Bromfield	15	5	23	0	18	4	37	3

Umpires: W.P. Anderson (1) and D.R. Fell (1).

Close: 1st day – NZ(1) 31-1 (Guy 8, Barton 8); 2nd – SA(2) 13-0 (McGlew 5, Barlow 4); 3rd – NZ(2) 83-4
(McGregor 29, Reid 10).

SOUTH AFRICA v NEW ZEALAND 1961–62 (2nd Test)

Played at New Wanderers, Johannesburg, on 26, 27, 28, 29 December.
Toss: South Africa.   Result: MATCH DRAWN.
Debuts: New Zealand – G.T. Dowling.

Rain allowed only 79 minutes of play on the first day. Lawrence, a 6ft 5in Rhodesian, returned the best analysis by a fast bowler in Tests for South Africa and by any bowler for either side in this series. The last of Waite's four Test hundreds took 206 minutes. New Zealand were left four hours to score 278 runs.

SOUTH AFRICA

D.J. McGlew*	lbw b Motz	5		run out	38
E.J. Barlow	c Reid b Motz	47		c Dick b Motz	45
J.H.B. Waite†	c Dick b Cameron	101	(6)	c Dick b Bartlett	4
R.A. McLean	c Bartlett b Cameron	2		c and b Motz	45
K.C. Bland	c Barton b Cameron	0		c McGregor b Motz	24
S. O'Linn	b Cameron	17	(7)	not out	5
M.K. Elgie	b Bartlett	56	(3)	b Motz	0
P.M. Pollock	run out	37		not out	1
G.B. Lawrence	c Guy b Bartlett	22			
K.A. Walter	c Barton b Cameron	10			
H.D. Bromfield	not out	11			
Extras	(B 3, LB 9, NB 1, W 1)	14		(B 8, LB 4, NB 4)	16
Total		**322**		(6 wickets declared)	**178**

NEW ZEALAND

S.N. McGregor	c Walter b Lawrence	13		c Bromfield b Walter	11
G.T. Dowling	run out	74		c Waite b Pollock	58
P.T. Barton	c Waite b Lawrence	10		c Waite b Lawrence	11
J.R. Reid*	lbw b Lawrence	39		not out	75
J.W. Guy	c Waite b Lawrence	9		b Pollock	0
P.G.Z. Harris	c Elgie b Lawrence	0		not out	9
A.E. Dick†	b Bromfield	16			
G.A. Bartlett	c Waite b Lawrence	31			
R.C. Motz	c Waite b Lawrence	3			
J.C. Alabaster	c Barlow b Lawrence	17			
F.J. Cameron	not out	1			
Extras	(B 1, LB 6, NB 3)	10		(LB 1)	1
Total		**223**		(4 wickets)	**165**

NEW ZEALAND	O	M	R	W	O	M	R	W
Motz	27	4	70	2	17	2	68	4
Bartlett	21	2	82	2	13	1	44	1
Cameron	36·2	9	83	5	13	1	50	0
Reid	9	2	33	0				
Alabaster	10	2	40	0				
SOUTH AFRICA								
Pollock	20	4	49	0	14	6	18	2
Walter	23	4	62	0	18	5	38	1
Lawrence	30·3	12	53	8	22	4	45	1
Barlow	3	0	15	0	3	2	5	0
Bromfield	16	6	34	1	7	0	30	0
Elgie					4	0	28	0

FALL OF WICKETS				
	SA	NZ	SA	NZ
Wkt	1st	1st	2nd	2nd
1st	25	18	85	22
2nd	99	41	85	49
3rd	102	107	92	120
4th	102	132	168	124
5th	159	132	169	–
6th	188	163	177	–
7th	259	167	–	–
8th	287	187	–	–
9th	296	216	–	–
10th	322	223	–	–

Umpires: W.P. Anderson (2) and H.C. Kidson (1).

Close: 1st day – SA(1) 80-1 (Barlow 40, Waite 32); 2nd – NZ(1) 27-1 (Dowling 10, Barton 4); 3rd – SA(2) 59-0 (McGlew 25, Barlow 30).

SOUTH AFRICA v NEW ZEALAND 1961–62 (3rd Test)

Played at Newlands, Cape Town, on 1, 2, 3, 4 January.
Toss: New Zealand.   Result: NEW ZEALAND won by 72 runs.
Debuts: South Africa – S.F. Burke, W.S. Farrer.

New Zealand, who did not enforce the follow-on, gained their first Test victory against South Africa and only their second in all Test matches. Playing in his first Test, Burke (fast-medium) took 11 for 196 and remains the only bowler from either country to take ten wickets in a Test in this series. McGlew retired because of a finger injury when 11 and resumed at 100 for 3 in the second innings. Dick, who made his only half-century in Tests, and Cameron put on 49 in 42 minutes for the highest tenth-wicket partnership of this series. Harris compiled his only hundred for New Zealand and McLean made the last of his five for South Africa.

NEW ZEALAND

S.N. McGregor	b Burke	68	run out		20
G.T. Dowling	lbw b Lawrence	0	c Barlow b Burke		12
J.T. Sparling	c Elgie b Burke	19	c Waite b Burke		9
J.R. Reid*	c Bromfield b McKinnon	92	c Bromfield b Burke		14
P.G.Z. Harris	st Waite b Bromfield	101	c Bland b Burke		30
M.E. Chapple	c Waite b Burke	69	b Burke		33
A.E. Dick†	c Waite b Burke	4	(8) not out		50
G.A. Bartlett	c Waite b Burke	12	(7) st Waite b McKinnon		29
R.C. Motz	b Burke	0	c Barlow b Bromfield		0
J.C. Alabaster	c Farrer b Bromfield	1	st Waite b McKinnon		4
F.J. Cameron	not out	2	not out		10
Extras	(LB 8, NB 9)	17	(B 1)		1
Total		**385**	(9 wickets declared)		**212**

SOUTH AFRICA

D.J. McGlew*	c Bartlett b Motz	14	c Dick b Bartlett		63
E.J. Barlow	c Harris b Alabaster	51	c Reid b Alabaster		16
W.S. Farrer	c Dick b Alabaster	11	c Dowling b Alabaster		20
J.H.B. Waite†	c Chapple b Cameron	33	lbw b Alabaster		21
R.A. McLean	c Dick b Cameron	20	c Harris b Bartlett		113
K.C. Bland	b Alabaster	32	lbw b Reid		42
M.K. Elgie	c Chapple b Alabaster	6	c Harris b Cameron		12
S.F. Burke	c Dick b Cameron	0	c Motz b Sparling		12
G.B. Lawrence	c Reid b Cameron	4	c Harris b Reid		0
A.H. McKinnon	not out	9	b Alabaster		4
H.D. Bromfield	lbw b Cameron	1	not out		0
Extras	(B 6, LB 2, NB 1)	9	(B 14, LB 13, W 4, NB 1)		32
Total		**190**			**335**

SOUTH AFRICA	O	M	R	W	O	M	R	W		FALL OF WICKETS			
Burke	53·5	19	128	6	27·1	10	68	5		NZ	SA	NZ	SA
Lawrence	23	7	46	1					*Wkt*	*1st*	*1st*	*2nd*	*2nd*
McKinnon	19	6	42	1	17	7	32	2	1st	15	36	28	27
Barlow	9	0	40	0	20	2	53	0	2nd	59	67	40	54
Bromfield	46	11	94	2	24	3	58	1	3rd	116	85	44	100
Elgie	7	2	18	0					4th	209	124	61	201
									5th	357	157	106	273
NEW ZEALAND									6th	367	164	127	315
Motz	11	2	30	1	24	9	69	0	7th	369	165	158	317
Cameron	24·4	10	48	5	26	14	42	1	8th	369	173	159	331
Alabaster	21	4	61	4	50	12	119	4	9th	370	185	163	335
Bartlett	5	1	17	0	22	8	40	2	10th	385	190	–	335
Sparling	6	1	22	0	6	3	12	1					
Chapple	1	0	3	0									
Reid					14·2	8	21	2					

Umpires: D. Collins (10) and J.E. Warner (1).

Close: 1st day – NZ(1) 337-4 (Harris 91, Chapple 58); 2nd – NZ(2) 8-0 (McGregor 1, Dowling 7); 3rd – SA(2) 54-2 (Waite 5).

SOUTH AFRICA v NEW ZEALAND 1961–62 (4th Test)

Played at New Wanderers, Johannesburg, on 2, 3, 5 February.
Toss: New Zealand.   Result: SOUTH AFRICA won by an innings and 51 runs.
Debuts: South Africa – H.R. Lance.

Burke's reward for bowling 81 overs and taking eleven wickets in the previous Test was to be dropped from South Africa's team for three years. For the only time in 17 matches in this series both captains made hundreds, McGlew's being the last of his seven and in his penultimate Test. Reid, the victim of a sensational two-handed diving catch in the first innings, scored 142 out of 184 in 259 minutes with two sixes and 21 fours; he contributed half New Zealand's runs from the bat in this match. Adcock became the second South African to take 100 Test wickets when he dismissed Motz. Waite recaptured his world wicket-keeping record when he claimed his 24th dismissal of the rubber.

NEW ZEALAND

S.N. McGregor	c Waite b Lance	21		c McLean b Heine	0
G.T. Dowling	lbw b Lawrence	14		b Adcock	0
P.T. Barton	b Adcock	22	(7)	c Waite b Lance	9
J.R. Reid*	c Bland b Lawrence	60	(5)	c McGlew b Heine	142
P.G.Z. Harris	c Lawrence b Adcock	4	(3)	b Adcock	46
M.E. Chapple	c Lawrence b Lance	11	(4)	lbw b Lawrence	9
A.E. Dick†	b Lawrence	16	(6)	c McLean b Lawrence	1
G.A. Bartlett	c Waite b Lawrence	0		c Waite b Lawrence	33
J.C. Alabaster	c Bromfield b Lance	2		c Waite b Lawrence	3
R.C. Motz	not out	10		lbw b Adcock	0
F.J. Cameron	lbw b Lawrence	2		not out	0
Extras	(LB 1, NB 1)	2		(LB 2, NB 4)	6
Total		**164**			**249**

SOUTH AFRICA

D.J. McGlew*	run out	120
E.J. Barlow	c Dick b Reid	67
J.H.B. Waite†	c Dick b Alabaster	9
R.A. McLean	lbw b Motz	78
W.S. Farrer	c Bartlett b Alabaster	40
K.C. Bland	lbw b Reid	28
H.R. Lance	c Dick b Reid	7
G.B. Lawrence	c Harris b Motz	39
P.S. Heine	c Dick b Alabaster	31
N.A.T. Adcock	b Motz	17
H.D. Bromfield	not out	4
Extras	(B 1, LB 11, NB 7 W 5)	24
Total		**464**

SOUTH AFRICA	O	M	R	W	O	M	R	W	FALL OF WICKETS			
										NZ	SA	NZ
Heine	12	2	45	0	24	5	78	2	*Wkt*	*1st*	*1st*	*2nd*
Adcock	10	4	23	2	24	12	40	3	1st	36	134	0
Lawrence	16·1	3	52	5	22·2	10	57	4	2nd	40	170	23
Lance	13	6	30	3	13	0	50	1	3rd	76	282	38
Bromfield	2	0	12	0	5	2	18	0	4th	94	282	70
									5th	130	351	84
NEW ZEALAND									6th	150	363	138
Motz	26·2	2	86	3					7th	150	367	222
Cameron	30	6	84	0					8th	150	422	244
Bartlett	18	1	57	0					9th	157	445	245
Alabaster	31	4	143	3					10th	164	464	249
Reid	16	3	55	3								
Chapple	3	0	15	0								

Umpires: H.C. Kidson (2) and G. Parry (1).

Close: 1st day – SA(1) 134-1 (McGlew 62); 2nd – NZ(2) 51-3 (Harris 33, Reid 6).

SOUTH AFRICA v NEW ZEALAND 1961–62 (5th Test)

Played at St George's Park, Port Elizabeth, on 16, 17, 19, 20 February.
Toss· New Zealand.   Result: NEW ZEALAND won by 40 runs.
Debuts: Nil.

Victory with just 21 minutes to spare gave New Zealand an unprecedented second win and a share of the rubber. Barton batted 276 minutes and hit 20 fours in scoring a stylish and lone Test hundred. Waite extended his world record to 26 dismissals during the rubber; it remained intact, although equalled, until 1982-83. McGlew ended his 34-match international career with 2,440 runs, seven centuries – including the then national record score of 255 not out, a splinted thumb and a plaster-encased shoulder.

NEW ZEALAND

G.T. Dowling	lbw b Adcock	2	lbw b Lawrence	78
J.T. Sparling	c Lance b Pollock	3	c Bromfield b Pollock	4
P.T. Barton	c Bromfield b Lance	109	(4) lbw b Pollock	2
J.R. Reid*	b Adcock	26	(5) c Bromfield b Lance	69
S.N. McGregor	b Pollock	10	(6) b Lawrence	24
P.G.Z. Harris	c McGlew b Bromfield	7	(3) c Bland b Adcock	13
A.E. Dick†	c Waite b Pollock	46	lbw b Lance	1
G.A. Bartlett	hit wkt b Adcock	29	c Barlow b Lawrence	18
J.C. Alabaster	lbw b Lawrence	24	c Adcock b Lawrence	7
R.C. Motz	c McLean b Lawrence	2	c Waite b Pollock	0
F.J. Cameron	not out	1	not out	0
Extras	(B 1, LB 7, NB 8)	16	(B 4, LB 6, NB 2)	12
Total		**275**		**228**

SOUTH AFRICA

E.J. Barlow	c Dowling b Motz	20	b Reid	59
G.B. Lawrence	c Dick b Alabaster	43	(8) b Alabaster	17
J.H.B. Waite†	c Dowling b Cameron	0	(4) c Dowling b Reid	7
W.S. Farrer	c Dick b Motz	7	(2) lbw b Cameron	10
R.A. McLean	c McGregor b Bartlett	25	b Alabaster	10
K.C. Bland	lbw b Bartlett	12	lbw b Reid	32
H.R. Lance	st Dick b Reid	9	c Dick b Reid	9
D.J. McGlew*	not out	28	(3) run out	26
P.M. Pollock	lbw b Motz	8	not out	54
N.A.T. Adcock	c Dowling b Reid	5	b Motz	24
H.D. Bromfield	c Dick b Alabaster	21	c McGregor b Cameron	0
Extras	(LB 6, NB 6)	12	(B 6, LB 3, NB 14, W 2)	25
Total		**190**		**273**

SOUTH AFRICA	O	M	R	W	O	M	R	W
Adcock	27	11	60	3	21	11	25	1
Pollock	28	9	63	3	24·1	5	70	3
Lawrence	26·2	7	71	2	28	5	85	4
Lance	14	4	50	1	8	0	36	2
Bromfield	16	7	15	1	2	2	0	0
NEW ZEALAND								
Cameron	11	2	46	1	18	6	48	2
Bartlett	8	4	10	2	9	3	26	0
Motz	14	7	33	3	20	11	34	1
Alabaster	25·4	7	63	2	52	23	96	2
Reid	14	6	26	2	45	27	44	4

FALL OF WICKETS

Wkt	NZ 1st	SA 1st	NZ 2nd	SA 2nd
1st	4	34	4	57
2nd	20	39	37	101
3rd	82	65	50	117
4th	108	92	175	125
5th	115	112	185	133
6th	180	115	192	142
7th	225	125	216	193
8th	269	137	228	199
9th	272	143	228	259
10th	275	190	228	273

Umpires: G.D. Gibbon (1) and G. Parry (2).

Close: 1st day – NZ(1) 242-7 (Bartlett 19, Alabaster 8); 2nd – NZ(2) 36-1 (Dowling 19, Harris 12); 3rd – SA(2) 38-0 (Barlow 25, Farrer 8).

WEST INDIES v INDIA 1961–62 (1st Test)

Played at Queen's Park Oval, Port-of-Spain, Trinidad, on 16, 17, 19, 20 February.
Toss: India.   Result: WEST INDIES won by ten wickets.
Debuts: West Indies – J.L. Hendriks, S.C. Stayers.

Although unable to keep wicket after fracturing a finger on the first day (Smith deputised), Hendriks contributed his highest Test score and added 70 for the ninth wicket with Hall. India were dismissed for their lowest total (so far) after Hall had taken the wickets of Contractor, Manjrekar and Sardesai in four balls.

INDIA

N.J. Contractor*	c Sobers b Hall	10	b Hall	6
V.L. Mehra	c Hendriks b Hall	0	b Stayers	8
V.L. Manjrekar	b Stayers	19	hit wkt b Hall	0
D.N. Sardesai	c Solomon b Stayers	16	c Smith b Hall	2
P.R. Umrigar	c Sobers b Watson	2	c sub (W.V. Rodriguez) b Sobers	23
C.G. Borde	c Gibbs b Stayers	16	b Sobers	27
S.A. Durani	c and b Sobers	56	c Worrell b Sobers	7
R.F. Surti	st Smith b Sobers	57	c sub (W.V. Rodriguez) b Sobers	0
R.G. Nadkarni	run out	2	not out	12
F. M. Engineer†	c sub (W.V. Rodriguez) b Gibbs	3	c and b Gibbs	2
R.B. Desai	not out	4	c Kanhai b Gibbs	2
Extras	(B 11, LB 5, NB 2)	18	(LB 4, W 1, NB 4)	9
Total		**203**		**98**

WEST INDIES

C.C. Hunte	c and b Durani	58	not out	10
C.W. Smith	c Umrigar b Desai	12	not out	4
R.B. Kanhai	c and b Borde	24		
G. St A. Sobers	b Umrigar	40		
F.M.M. Worrell*	c Surti b Durani	0		
J.S. Solomon	c Engineer b Desai	43		
S.C. Stayers	c Borde b Durani	4		
J.L. Hendriks†	c Durani b Borde	64		
L.R. Gibbs	c Durani b Umrigar	0		
W.W. Hall	not out	37		
C.D. Watson	c Contractor b Durani	0		
Extras	(B 4, LB 3)	7	(NB 1)	1
Total		**289**	(0 wickets)	**15**

WEST INDIES	O	M	R	W	O	M	R	W	FALL OF WICKETS				
Hall	20	6	38	2	8	3	11	3		I	WI	I	WI
Watson	12	4	20	1	4	2	6	0	*Wkt*	*1st*	*1st*	*2nd*	*2nd*
Stayers	18	1	65	3	8	4	20	1	1st	7	13	6	–
Gibbs	14	4	34	1	7·5	1	16	2	2nd	32	67	6	–
Sobers	9·3	1	28	2	15	7	22	4	3rd	38	136	8	–
Worrell					8	2	14	0	4th	45	139	35	–
									5th	76	140	56	–
INDIA									6th	89	148	70	–
Desai	13	3	46	2	1	0	5	0	7th	170	212	70	–
Umrigar	35	8	77	2					8th	186	217	91	–
Durani	35·2	9	82	4					9th	194	287	96	–
Borde	25	4	65	2					10th	203	289	98	–
Nadkarni	3	2	1	0									
Surti	2	0	11	0	0·4	0	9	0					

Umpires: B. Jacelon (1) and H.B. de C. Jordan (8).

Close: 1st day – I(1) 114-6 (Durani 22, Surti 10); 2nd – WI(1) 148-6 (Solomon 4); 3rd – I(2) 49-4 (Umrigar 21, Borde 3).

WEST INDIES v INDIA 1961–62 (2nd Test)

Played at Sabina Park, Kingston, Jamaica, on 7, 8, 9, 10, 12 March.
Toss: India.   Result: WEST INDIES won by an innings and 18 runs.
Debuts: West Indies – I.L. Mendonça, W.V. Rodriguez.

Contractor celebrated his 28th birthday by winning his sixth consecutive toss for India. The partnership of 255 between McMorris and Kanhai remains a West Indies record for the second wicket against India. Sobers, who hit four sixes, used a runner on the third evening because of cramp in his thigh. When Solomon became the victim of the worst of many dubious decisions in the match on the third afternoon, there was a five-minute interruption due to a mild display of bottle-throwing. Hall's nine wickets took him past the 100-mark in his 20th Test. The West Indies total is their highest in a home Test against India.

INDIA

M.L. Jaisimha	c Gibbs b Stayers	28		b Hall	11
N.J. Contractor*	c Mendonça b Hall	1		b Hall	9
R.F. Surti	lbw b Sobers	35		lbw b Hall	26
V.L. Manjrekar	c Sobers b Gibbs	13	(6)	lbw b Sobers	19
P.R. Umrigar	lbw b Sobers	50		c Sobers b Gibbs	32
C.G. Borde	b Hall	93	(7)	c McMorris b Hall	0
S.A. Durani	lbw b Hall	17	(8)	b Gibbs	0
R.G. Nadkarni	not out	78	(4)	c Mendonça b Gibbs	35
F.M. Engineer†	st Mendonça b Gibbs	53		c Hunte b Hall	40
R.B. Desai	c Gibbs b Sobers	0		c Mendonça b Hall	20
E.A.S. Prasanna	c Mendonça b Sobers	6		not out	1
Extras	(B 14, LB 5, NB 2)	21		(B 18, LB 4, NB 2, W 1)	25
Total		**395**			**218**

WEST INDIES

C.C. Hunte	c Contractor b Desai	9
E.D.A. St J. McMorris	b Prasanna	125
R.B. Kanhai	c Umrigar b Prasanna	138
W.V. Rodriguez	c Umrigar b Prasanna	3
G. St A. Sobers	c Desai b Durani	153
J.S. Solomon	run out	9
F.M.M. Worrell*	b Durani	58
I.L. Mendonça†	b Nadkarni	78
S.C. Stayers	not out	35
L.R. Gibbs	) did not bat	
W.W. Hall	)	
Extras	(B 7, LB 15, W 1)	23
Total	(8 wickets declared)	**631**

WEST INDIES	O	M	R	W	O	M	R	W		FALL OF WICKETS		
Hall	28	4	79	3	20·5	5	49	6		I	WI	I
Stayers	23	4	76	1	10	0	25	0	*Wkt*	*1st*	*1st*	*2nd*
Worrell	9	1	35	0	10	1	26	0	1st	14	16	16
Gibbs	33	9	69	2	26	8	44	3	2nd	44	271	46
Sobers	39	8	75	4	17	3	41	1	3rd	79	282	50
Rodriguez	7	0	37	0	1	0	8	0	4th	89	293	116
Solomon	2	0	3	0					5th	183	320	137
									6th	234	430	138
INDIA									7th	263	557	141
Desai	20	6	84	1					8th	357	631	157
Surti	19	2	73	0					9th	358	–	205
Borde	31	6	93	0					10th	395	–	218
Durani	70	14	173	2								
Nadkarni	25·4	9	57	1								
Prasanna	50	14	122	3								
Contractor	2	0	6	0								

Umpires: R. Cole (1) and O. Davies (1).

Close: 1st day – I(1) 280-7 (Nadkarni 22, Engineer 6); 2nd – WI(1) 157-1 (McMorris 66, Kanhai 75); 3rd – WI(1) 398-5 (Sobers 63, Worrell 43); 4th – I(2) 83-3 (Nadkarni 9, Umrigar 12).

WEST INDIES v INDIA 1961–62 (3rd Test)

Played at Kensington Oval, Bridgetown, Barbados, on 23, 24, 26, 27, 28 March.
Toss: West Indies.   Result: WEST INDIES won by an innings and 30 runs.
Debuts: West Indies – D.W. Allan.

The Nawab of Pataudi led India in place of the injured N.J. Contractor and, at 21 years 77 days, became the youngest Test captain. Contractor, whose skull had been fractured by a ball from C.C. Griffith in the tourists' previous match against Barbados, underwent an emergency brain operation and played no further Test cricket. In the final session of this match, Gibbs achieved the outstanding analysis of 15·3–14–6–8. He was the first West Indies bowler to take eight wickets in a home Test.

INDIA

M.L. Jaisimha	c Allan b Hall	41	lbw b Stayers		0
D.N. Sardesai	c McMorris b Gibbs	31	c Sobers b Gibbs		60
R.F. Surti	lbw b Worrell	7	lbw b Stayers		36
V.L. Manjrekar	c Worrell b Hall	8	c Worrell b Gibbs		51
P.R. Umrigar	c Allan b Hall	8	c Allan b Gibbs		10
Nawab of Pataudi, jr*	c and b Valentine	48	c Sobers b Gibbs		0
C.G. Borde	c Allan b Sobers	19	c Worrell b Gibbs		8
R.G. Nadkarni	b Stayers	22	not out		2
F.M. Engineer†	c Worrell b Sobers	12	st Allan b Gibbs		0
S.A. Durani	not out	48	c Hunte b Gibbs		5
R.B. Desai	b Worrell	12	c Sobers b Gibbs		1
Extras	(NB 2)	2	(B 8, LB 3, W 2, NB 1)		14
Total		**258**			**187**

WEST INDIES

C.C. Hunte	c Engineer b Surti	59
E. D.A. St J. McMorris	c Engineer b Durani	39
R.B. Kanhai	run out	89
G. St A. Sobers	c Engineer b Nadkarni	42
J.S. Solomon	c Desai b Durani	96
L.R. Gibbs	b Borde	7
F.M.M. Worrell*	b Umrigar	77
S.C. Stayers	c Umrigar b Nadkarni	7
W.W. Hall	lbw b Umrigar	3
D.W. Allan†	not out	40
A.L. Valentine	b Borde	4
Extras	(LB 5, NB 7)	12
Total		**475**

WEST INDIES	O	M	R	W	O	M	R	W	FALL OF WICKETS			
										I	WI	I
Hall	22	4	64	3	10	3	17	0	*Wkt*	*1st*	*1st*	*2nd*
Stayers	11	0	81	1	18	8	24	2	1st	56	67	0
Worrell	7·1	3	12	2	27	18	16	0	2nd	76	152	60
Gibbs	16	7	25	1	53·3	37	38	8	3rd	82	226	158
Valentine	17	7	28	1	29	19	26	0	4th	89	255	159
Sobers	16	2	46	2	17	10	14	0	5th	112	282	159
Solomon					29	17	33	0	6th	153	378	174
Kanhai					2	1	5	0	7th	171	394	177
									8th	188	399	177
INDIA									9th	229	454	183
Desai	19	7	25	0					10th	258	475	187
Surti	29	6	80	1								
Durani	45	13	123	2								
Nadkarni	67	28	92	2								
Borde	31·3	4	89	2								
Jaisimha	1	0	6	0								
Umrigar	49	27	48	2								

Umpires: H.B. de C. Jordan (9) and J. Roberts (2).

Close: 1st day – WI(1) 5-0 (Hunte 4, McMorris 1); 2nd – WI(1) 263-4 (Solomon 23, Gibbs 1); 3rd – WI(1) 427-8 (Worrell 64, Allan 9); 4th – I(2) 104-2 (Sardesai 41, Manjrekar 14).

WEST INDIES v INDIA 1961–62 (4th Test)

Played at Queen's Park Oval, Port-of-Spain, Trinidad, on 4, 5, 6, 7, 9 April.
Toss: West Indies.   Result: WEST INDIES won by seven wickets.
Debuts: Nil.

Kanhai reached his first fifty in 67 minutes. Hall recorded his highest Test score, shared in what remains the highest West Indies partnership for the tenth wicket against all countries, and removed half the Indian batting order in a nine-over opening burst. Umrigar's twelfth and final three-figure innings for India was their highest in this series until 1970–71. He scored his runs out of 230 in 248 minutes.

WEST INDIES

C.C. Hunte	b Umrigar	28	c Kunderan b Durani	30
E.D.A. St J. McMorris	c Sardesai b Nadkarni	50	b Durani	56
R.B. Kanhai	lbw b Umrigar	139	c Nadkarni b Durani	20
S.M. Nurse	c and b Durani	1	not out	46
G. St A. Sobers	lbw b Jaisimha	19	not out	16
W.V. Rodriguez	b Umrigar	50		
I.L. Mendonça†	b Umrigar	3		
L.R. Gibbs	lbw b Nadkarni	15		
F.M.M. Worrell*	not out	73		
S.C. Stayers	c Surti b Umrigar	12		
W.W. Hall	not out	50		
Extras	(LB 4)	4	(B 3, LB 1, NB 4)	8
Total	(9 wickets declared)	**444**	(3 wickets)	**176**

INDIA

D.N. Sardesai	b Hall	0	(9)	c Worrell b Gibbs	0
V.L. Mehra	b Hall	14		b Hall	62
R.F. Surti	c Nurse b Hall	0	(7)	c Mendonça b Gibbs	2
V.L. Manjrekar	c Mendonça b Hall	4		c Nurse b Sobers	13
M.L. Jaisimha	c Mendonça b Hall	10	(1)	c Mendonça b Stayers	15
P.R. Umrigar	st Mendonça b Sobers	56		not out	172
Nawab of Pataudi, jr*	c Sobers b Rodriguez	47	(5)	c Kanhai b Sobers	1
C.G. Borde	c Nurse b Rodriguez	42		c Sobers b Gibbs	13
S.A. Durani	c Worrell b Rodriguez	12	(3)	c Rodriguez b Sobers	104
R.G. Nadkarni	c Rodriguez b Sobers	1		run out	23
B.K. Kunderan†	not out	4		c Rodriguez b Gibbs	4
Extras	(B 1, LB 4, NB 2)	7		(B 9, LB 3, NB 1)	13
Total		**197**			**422**

INDIA	O	M	R	W	O	M	R	W		FALL	OF	WICKETS	
Surti	26	4	81	0	21	7	48	0		WI	I	I	WI
Jaisimha	18	4	61	1	4	1	5	0	*Wkt*	*1st*	*1st*	*2nd*	*2nd*
Umrigar	56	24	107	5	16	8	17	0	1st	50	0	19	93
Durani	18	4	54	1	31	13	64	3	2nd	169	0	163	100
Borde	23	4	68	0	1	1	0	0	3rd	174	9	190	132
Nadkarni	35	14	69	2	28	13	34	0	4th	212	25	192	–
									5th	258	30	221	–
WEST INDIES									6th	265	124	236	–
Hall	9	3	20	5	18	3	74	1	7th	292	144	278	–
Stayers	8	1	23	0	10	2	50	1	8th	316	169	278	–
Gibbs	19	5	48	0	56·1	18	112	4	9th	346	175	371	–
Sobers	25	6	48	2	47	14	116	3	10th	–	197	422	–
Rodriguez	19·3	2	51	3	9	1	47	0					
Worrell					3	0	10	0					

Umpires: B. Jacelon (2) and H.B. de C. Jordan (10).

Close: 1st day – WI(1) 268-6 (Rodriguez 25, Gibbs 0); 2nd – I(1) 61-5 (Umrigar 9, Pataudi 19); 3rd – I(2) 186-2 (Durani 91, Manjrekar 9); 4th – WI(2) 23-0 (Hunte 11, McMorris 10).

WEST INDIES v INDIA 1961–62 (5th Test)

Played at Sabina Park, Kingston, Jamaica, on 13, 14, 16, 17, 18 April.
Toss: West Indies.   Result: WEST INDIES won by 123 runs.
Debuts: West Indies – L.A. King.

West Indies won the rubber by five victories to none and so emulated Australia (v England in 1920-21 and v South Africa in 1931-32) and England (v India in 1959). Sobers completed a fifth of his 13th Test century partnered by Valentine, the last man. King captured India's first five wickets during his first four overs as a Test bowler. Kanhai dropped down the order in the second innings because of a pulled thigh muscle.

WEST INDIES

C.C. Hunte	c Kunderan b Ranjane	1	c Kunderan b Surti	0
E.D.A. St J. McMorris	lbw b Durani	37	hit wkt b Borde	42
R.B. Kanhai	c and b Ranjane	44	(9) b Ranjane	41
J.S. Solomon	b Durani	0	(3) b Surti	0
G. St A. Sobers	c Manjrekar b Ranjane	104	(4) c Kunderan b Surti	50
F.M.M. Worrell*	lbw b Ranjane	26	(5) not out	98
W.W. Hall	c Kunderan b Nadkarni	20	(10) lbw b Ranjane	10
D.W. Allan†	c sub (E.A.S. Prasanna) b Borde	1	(6) lbw b Durani	2
L.R. Gibbs	lbw b Nadkarni	3	(7) lbw b Durani	0
L.A. King	b Nadkarni	0	(8) c Nadkarni b Durani	13
A.L. Valentine	not out	7	lbw b Nadkarni	7
Extras	(B 4, LB 2, NB 4)	10	(B 4, LB 5, NB 11)	20
Total		**253**		**283**

INDIA

M.L. Jaisimha	c Sobers b King	6	lbw b King	6
V.L. Mehra	c Allan b King	8	c Allan b Sobers	39
S.A. Durani	c Allan b King	6	lbw b King	4
V.L. Manjrekar	c Solomon b King	0	(5) lbw b Sobers	40
Nawab of Pataudi, jr*	c Kanhai b Hall	14	(6) b Sobers	4
C.G. Borde	c Hall b King	0	(4) b Sobers	26
R.G. Nadkarni	b Gibbs	61	(9) c Allan b Hall	0
R.F. Surti	b Gibbs	41	st Allan b Sobers	42
P.R. Umrigar	lbw b Gibbs	32	(7) b Hall	60
B.K. Kunderan†	c McMorris b Valentine	2	b Hall	1
V.B. Ranjane	not out	0	not out	0
Extras	(LB 6, NB 2)	8	(B 11, LB 1, NB 1)	13
Total		**178**		**235**

INDIA	O	M	R	W	O	M	R	W
Ranjane	19·2	2	72	4	28	3	81	2
Surti	6	0	25	0	18	3	56	3
Nadkarni	17	3	50	3	9	3	13	1
Durani	18	6	56	2	12	3	48	3
Borde	12	2	33	1	21	5	65	1
Jaisimha	4	0	7	0				
WEST INDIES								
Hall	11	3	26	1	20·5	3	47	3
King	19	3	46	5	13	3	18	2
Worrell	5	0	8	0				
Gibbs	14·2	2	38	3	25	2	66	0
Valentine	12	4	32	1	14	9	28	0
Sobers	6	1	20	0	32	9	63	5

FALL OF WICKETS

Wkt	WI 1st	I 1st	WI 2nd	I 2nd
1st	2	11	1	15
2nd	64	22	1	21
3rd	64	22	75	77
4th	93	26	118	80
5th	140	26	138	86
6th	174	40	138	135
7th	201	112	154	218
8th	218	171	234	219
9th	218	178	248	230
10th	253	178	283	235

Umpires: O. Davies (2) and D. Sang Hue (1).

Close: 1st day – I(1) 33-5 (Pataudi 8, Nadkarni 0); 2nd – WI(2) 138-6 (Worrell 32, King 0); 3rd – I(2) 37-2 (Mehra 15, Borde 8); 4th – I(2) 131-5 (Manjrekar 36, Umrigar 11).

ENGLAND v PAKISTAN 1962 (1st Test)

Played at Edgbaston, Birmingham, on 31 May, 1, 2, 4 June.
Toss: England.   Result: ENGLAND won by an innings and 24 runs.
Debuts: Nil.

England won with over a day and a half to spare after scoring their highest total for five years. Imtiaz conceded no byes during that mammoth innings; it is still the highest total without byes against Pakistan. The unbroken partnership of 153 between Parfitt, who scored his second successive hundred, and Allen remains England's highest for the sixth wicket against Pakistan.

ENGLAND

G. Pullar	b D'Souza	22
M.C. Cowdrey	c Imtiaz b Intikhab	159
E.R. Dexter*	c Burki b Intikhab	72
T.W. Graveney	c Ijaz Butt b Mahmood	97
K.F. Barrington	lbw b Mahmood	9
P.H. Parfitt	not out	101
D.A. Allen	not out	79
G. Millman†	)	
G.A.R. Lock	) did not bat	
F.S. Trueman	)	
J.B. Statham	)	
Extras	(LB 5)	5
Total	(5 wickets declared)	**544**

PAKISTAN

Hanif Mohammad	c Millman b Allen	47	c Cowdrey b Allen		31
Ijaz Butt	c Lock b Statham	10	c Trueman b Allen		33
Saeed Ahmed	c Graveney b Trueman	5	(5) c Parfitt b Lock		65
Mushtaq Mohammad	c Cowdrey b Lock	63	c Millman b Allen		8
Javed Burki*	c Barrington b Allen	13	(6) b Statham		19
Imtiaz Ahmed†	b Trueman	39	(3) c Graveney b Lock		46
W. Mathias	b Statham	21	b Statham		4
Nasim-ul-Ghani	b Statham	0	c Parfitt b Trueman		35
Intikhab Alam	b Lock	16	c Cowdrey b Lock		0
Mahmood Hussain	b Statham	0	c Graveney b Trueman		22
A. D'Souza	not out	23	not out		9
Extras	(B 8, LB 1)	9	(B 1, LB 1)		2
Total		**246**			**274**

PAKISTAN	O	M	R	W	O	M	R	W		FALL OF WICKETS		
Mahmood Hussain	43	14	130	2						E	P	P
D'Souza	46	9	161	1					*Wkt*	*1st*	*1st*	*2nd*
Intikhab	25	2	117	2					1st	31	11	60
Nasim	30	7	109	0					2nd	197	30	77
Saeed	2	0	22	0					3rd	304	108	119
ENGLAND									4th	330	144	127
Statham	21	9	54	4	19	6	32	2	5th	391	146	187
Trueman	13	3	59	2	24	5	70	2	6th	–	202	199
Dexter	12	6	23	0	7	2	16	0	7th	–	206	207
Allen	32	16	62	2	36	16	73	3	8th	–	206	207
Lock	19	8	37	2	36	14	80	3	9th	–	206	257
Parfitt	2	1	2	0					10th	–	246	274
Barrington	2	2	0	0								
Cowdrey					1	0	1	0				

Umpires: J.S. Buller (12) and C.S. Elliott (11).

Close: 1st day – E(1) 386-4 (Graveney 96, Parfitt 23); 2nd – P(1) 149-5 (Imtiaz 1, Mathias 2); 3rd – P(2) 158-4 (Saeed 30, Burki 9).

ENGLAND v PAKISTAN 1962 (2nd Test)

Played at Lord's, London, on 21, 22, 23 June.
Toss: Pakistan.   Result: ENGLAND won by nine wickets.
Debuts: England – L.J. Coldwell, M.J. Stewart.

Trueman took his 200th wicket in 47 Test matches when he dismissed Javed Burki and later shared with Graveney in a record ninth-wicket partnership against Pakistan which added 76 runs. Nasim became the first Pakistan batsman to score a Test hundred in England. His fifth-wicket partnership of 197 with Javed Burki was then Pakistan's record for that wicket in all Tests and remains so against England. Nasim was promoted two places as 'night-watchman' and scored his maiden hundred in first-class cricket. Coldwell bowled Imtiaz with his fifth ball in Test cricket.

PAKISTAN

Hanif Mohammad	c Cowdrey b Trueman	13	lbw b Coldwell		24
Imtiaz Ahmed†	b Coldwell	1	(7) c Trueman b Coldwell		33
Saeed Ahmed	b Dexter	10	b Coldwell		20
Javed Burki*	c Dexter b Trueman	5	(5) lbw b Coldwell		101
Mushtaq Mohammad	c Cowdrey b Trueman	7	(4) c Millman b Trueman		18
Alimuddin	b Coldwell	9	(2) c Graveney b Allen		10
W. Mathias	b Trueman	15	(8) c Graveney b Trueman		1
Nasim-ul-Ghani	c Millman b Trueman	17	(6) c Graveney b Coldwell		101
Mahmood Hussain	c Cowdrey b Coldwell	1	b Coldwell		20
A. D'Souza	not out	6	not out		12
Mohammad Farooq	c Stewart b Trueman	13	b Trueman		1
Extras	(B 1, LB 2)	3	(B 6, LB 4, W 4)		14
Total		**100**			**355**

ENGLAND

M.J. Stewart	c Imtiaz b D'Souza	39	not out		34
M.C. Cowdrey	c D'Souza b Farooq	41	c Imtiaz b D'Souza		20
E.R. Dexter*	c Imtiaz b Farooq	65	not out		32
T.W. Graveney	b D'Souza	153			
K.F. Barrington	c Imtiaz b Farooq	0			
D.A. Allen	lbw b Farooq	2			
P.H. Parfitt	b Mahmood	16			
G. Millman†	c Hanif b Mahmood	7			
G.A.R. Lock	c Mathias b Saeed	7			
F.S. Trueman	lbw b Saeed	29			
L.J. Coldwell	not out	0			
Extras	(B 1, LB 5, NB 5)	11			
Total		**370**	(1 wicket)		**86**

ENGLAND	O	M	R	W	O	M	R	W		FALL OF WICKETS			
Trueman	17·4	6	31	6	33·3	6	85	3		P	E	P	E
Coldwell	14	2	25	3	41	13	85	6	*Wkt*	*1st*	*1st*	*2nd*	*2nd*
Dexter	12	3	41	1	15	4	44	0	1st	2	59	36	36
Allen					15	6	41	1	2nd	23	137	36	–
Lock					14	1	78	0	3rd	25	168	57	–
Barrington					1	0	8	0	4th	31	168	77	–
									5th	36	184	274	–
PAKISTAN									6th	51	221	299	–
Mahmood Hussain	40	9	106	2					7th	77	247	300	–
Farooq	19	4	70	4	7	1	37	0	8th	78	290	333	–
D'Souza	35·4	3	147	2	7	0	29	1	9th	78	366	354	–
Nasim	2	0	15	0					10th	100	370	355	–
Saeed	5	1	21	2	2	0	12	0					
Mushtaq					1	0	8	0					

Umpires: J.S. Buller (13) and N. Oldfield (2).

Close: 1st day – E(1) 174-4 (Graveney 23, Allen 0); 2nd – P(2) 103-4 (Burki 15, Nasim 23).

ENGLAND v PAKISTAN 1962 (3rd Test)

Played at Headingley, Leeds, on 5, 6, 7 July.
Toss: Pakistan.   Result: ENGLAND won by an innings and 117 runs.
Debuts: Pakistan – Javed Akhtar (*his first match in England*).

Cowdrey ended his run of nine consecutive successes with the toss in Test matches. Parfitt and Allen shared what is still England's highest eighth-wicket partnership against Pakistan (99). For the fifth successive Test at Leeds, the match ended within three days' actual play. Pakistan were without Imtiaz Ahmed for the first time in 40 matches since their elevation to full Test status in 1952.

ENGLAND

M.J. Stewart	lbw b Munir	86
M.C. Cowdrey*	c Saeed b Mahmood	7
E.R. Dexter	b Mahmood	20
T.W. Graveney	c Ijaz Butt b Munir	37
K.F. Barrington	c Mushtaq b Farooq	1
P.H. Parfitt	c and b Nasim	119
F.J. Titmus	c and b Munir	2
J.T. Murray†	c and b Nasim	29
D.A. Allen	c Ijaz Butt b Munir	62
F.S. Trueman	lbw b Munir	20
J.B. Statham	not out	26
Extras	(B 6, LB 9, W 1, NB 3)	19
Total		**428**

PAKISTAN

Alimuddin	c Barrington b Titmus	50	c Titmus b Allen	60
Ijaz Butt†	b Trueman	1	b Trueman	6
Saeed Ahmed	c Trueman b Statham	16	(5) c Cowdrey b Statham	54
Mushtaq Mohammad	c Murray b Dexter	27	c Trueman b Allen	8
Hanif Mohammad	b Statham	9	(6) c Barrington b Allen	4
Javed Burki*	b Trueman	1	(7) c Murray b Statham	21
Nasim-ul-Ghani	c Graveney b Titmus	5	(3) lbw b Statham	19
Mahmood Hussain	not out	0	c and b Dexter	0
Munir Malik	b Dexter	3	b Statham	4
Javed Akhtar	b Dexter	2	not out	2
Mohammad Farooq	c Statham b Dexter	8	c Statham b Trueman	0
Extras	(B 8, NB 1)	9	(LB 2)	2
Total		**131**		**180**

PAKISTAN	O	M	R	W	O	M	R	W
Farooq	28	8	74	1				
Mahmood Hussain	25	5	87	2				
Munir	49	11	128	5				
Akhtar	16	5	52	0				
Nasim	14	2	68	2				
ENGLAND								
Trueman	23	6	55	2	10·4	3	33	2
Statham	20	9	40	2	20	3	50	4
Dexter	9·1	3	10	4	8	1	24	1
Allen	9	6	14	0	24	11	47	3
Titmus	4	1	3	2	11	2	20	0
Barrington					1	0	4	0

FALL OF WICKETS			
	E	P	P
Wkt	1st	1st	2nd
1st	7	13	10
2nd	43	51	40
3rd	108	72	57
4th	117	88	130
5th	177	118	136
6th	180	118	163
7th	247	118	178
8th	346	121	179
9th	377	123	179
10th	428	131	180

Umpires: J.G. Langridge (5) and W.E. Phillipson (8).

Close: 1st day – E(1) 194-6 (Parfitt 31, Murray 3); 2nd – P(1) 73-3 (Mushtaq 2, Hanif 0).

ENGLAND v PAKISTAN 1962 (4th Test)

Played at Trent Bridge. Nottingham, on 26 (*no play*), 27, 28, 30, 31 July.
Toss: Pakistan.   Result: MATCH DRAWN.
Debuts: Pakistan – Shahid Mahmood.

After a blank first day, rain reduced play to 195 minutes on the fourth day. Parfitt's hundred was his sixth in seven successive first-class innings against Pakistani bowling and his third in three innings against the tourists within a week. Statham exceeded R.R. Lindwall's record aggregate of Test wickets by a fast bowler (228) when he dismissed Imtiaz. Mushtaq, Test cricket's youngest century-maker (*Test No. 501*), scored his second hundred for Pakistan at the age of 18 years 251 days. No other batsman has scored a Test hundred before his 19th birthday.

ENGLAND

G. Pullar	lbw b Munir	5
Rev. D.S. Sheppard	c Imtiaz b Intikhab	83
E.R. Dexter*	c Burki b Fazal	85
T.W. Graveney	c Intikhab b Fazal	114
P.H. Parfitt	not out	101
B.R. Knight	c Saeed b Fazal	14
F.J. Titmus	not out	11
J.T. Murray†	)	
F.S. Trueman	) did not bat	
G.A.R. Lock	)	
J.B. Statham	)	
Extras	(LB 13, NB 2)	15
Total	**(5 wickets declared)**	**428**

PAKISTAN

Hanif Mohammad	c Titmus b Trueman	0		c and b Trueman	3
Shahid Mahmood	c Graveney b Trueman	16	(7)	c Statham b Dexter	9
Mushtaq Mohammad	c Lock b Knight	55		not out	100
Javed Burki*	c Murray b Knight	19		c sub (C.J. Poole) b Titmus	28
Saeed Ahmed	c Murray b Statham	43		c Trueman b Lock	64
Imtiaz Ahmed†	lbw b Trueman	15		lbw b Statham	1
Alimuddin	b Trueman	0	(2)	c Murray b Statham	11
Nasim-ul-Ghani	c Murray b Knight	41		not out	0
Intikhab Alam	c Murray b Statham	14			
Fazal Mahmood	lbw b Knight	2			
Munir Malik	not out	0			
Extras	(B 2, LB 10, NB 2)	14			14
Total		**219**		**(6 wickets)**	**216**

PAKISTAN	O	M	R	W	O	M	R	W		FALL OF WICKETS		
Fazal	60	15	130	3						E	P	P
Munir	34	4	130	1					*Wkt*	*1st*	*1st*	*2nd*
Nasim	20·2	1	76	0					1st	11	0	4
Intikhab	14	3	49	1					2nd	172	39	22
Shahid	6	1	23	0					3rd	185	95	78
Saeed	2	0	5	0					4th	369	98	185
									5th	388	120	187
ENGLAND									6th	–	120	216
Trueman	24	3	71	4	19	5	35	1	7th	–	171	–
Statham	18·1	5	55	2	22	8	47	2	8th	–	213	–
Knight	17	1	38	4	21	6	48	0	9th	–	217	–
Lock	14	5	19	0	15	4	27	1	10th	–	219	–
Titmus	13	2	22	0	16	7	29	1				
Dexter					7	0	25	1				
Parfitt					1	0	5	0				

Umpires: F.S. Lee (28) and W.E. Phillipson (9).

Close: 1st day – no play; 2nd – E(1) 310-3 (Graveney 89, Parfitt 38); 3rd – P(1) 127-6 (Saeed 13, Nasim 2); 4th – P(2) 11-1 (Alimuddin 3, Mushtaq 5).

ENGLAND v PAKISTAN 1962 (5th Test)

Played at Kennington Oval, London, on 16, 17, 18, 20 August.
Toss: England.   Result: ENGLAND won by ten wickets.
Debuts: England – J.D.F. Larter.

Cowdrey, who scored the highest of his 22 Test hundreds, and Dexter shared what is still England's highest second-wicket partnership against Pakistan (248). Imtiaz became the second batsman after Hanif Mohammad to score 2,000 runs for Pakistan. Larter (6ft 7½in tall) took nine wickets in his first Test match. Fazal Mahmood ended the last of his 34 Tests with the then record aggregate for Pakistan of 139 wickets. Mushtaq (401 runs) and Trueman (22 wickets) set the present record aggregates for their respective countries in a rubber between them in England.

ENGLAND

Batsman	Dismissal	Score	2nd innings	Score
Rev. D.S. Sheppard	c Fazal b Nasim	57	not out	9
M.C. Cowdrey	c Hanif b Fazal	182		
E.R. Dexter*	b Fazal	172		
K.F. Barrington	not out	50		
P.H. Parfitt	c Imtiaz b D'Souza	3		
B.R. Knight	b D'Souza	3		
R. Illingworth	not out	2		
J.T. Murray†	)		(2) not out	14
D.A. Allen	) did not bat			
L.J. Coldwell	)			
J.D.F. Larter	)			
Extras	(B 4, LB 5, NB 2)	11	(B 4)	4
Total	(5 wickets declared)	**480**	(0 wickets)	**27**

PAKISTAN

Batsman	Dismissal	Score	2nd innings	Score
Ijaz Butt	c Cowdrey b Larter	10	run out	6
Imtiaz Ahmed†	c Murray b Knight	49	c Cowdrey b Larter	98
Mushtaq Mohammad	lbw b Larter	43	b Illingworth	72
Javed Burki*	b Larter	3	(6) c Parfitt b Knight	42
Saeed Ahmed	c Parfitt b Allen	21	c Knight b Allen	4
Hanif Mohammad	b Larter	46	(4) c Dexter b Larter	0
W. Mathias	c Murray b Larter	0	run out	48
A. D'Souza	c Parfitt b Coldwell	1	(10) not out	2
Nasim-ul-Ghani	c Murray b Coldwell	5	(8) b Coldwell	24
Intikhab Alam	not out	3	(9) b Larter	12
Fazal Mahmood	b Coldwell	0	b Larter	5
Extras	(NB 2)	2	(B 4, LB 5, NB 1)	10
Total		**183**		**323**

PAKISTAN	O	M	R	W	O	M	R	W
Fazal	49	9	192	2	4	1	10	0
D'Souza	42	9	116	2	3	1	8	0
Intikhab	38	5	109	0				
Burki	1	0	12	0	1	0	2	0
Nasim	9	1	39	1				
Saeed	1	0	1	0				
Mushtaq					0·3	0	3	0
ENGLAND								
Coldwell	28	11	53	3	23	4	60	1
Larter	25	4	57	5	21·1	0	88	4
Allen	22	9	33	1	27	14	52	1
Knight	9	5	11	1	11	3	33	1
Illingworth	13	5	27	0	21	9	54	1
Dexter					6	1	16	0
Barrington					2	0	10	0

FALL OF WICKETS

Wkt	E 1st	P 1st	P 2nd	E 2nd
1st	117	11	34	–
2nd	365	93	171	–
3rd	441	102	171	–
4th	444	115	180	–
5th	452	165	186	–
6th	–	168	250	–
7th	–	175	294	–
8th	–	179	316	–
9th	–	183	316	–
10th	–	183	323	–

Umpires: C.S. Elliott (12) and F.S. Lee (29).

Close: 1st day – E(1) 406-2 (Dexter 144, Barrington 13); 2nd – P(1) 178-6 (Hanif 46, D'Souza 1); 3rd – P(2) 289-6 (Mathias 43, Nasim 17).

AUSTRALIA v ENGLAND 1962–63 (1st Test)

Played at Woolloongabba, Brisbane, on 30 November, 1, 3, 4, 5 December.
Toss: Australia.   Result: MATCH DRAWN.
Debuts: England – A.C. Smith.

Six playing hours per day were scheduled for the first time in Test matches in Australia. England were set 378 runs to win at 63 per hour. Fourteen fifties were scored in the match, equalling the record for this series set at Leeds in 1948 (*Test No. 302*).

AUSTRALIA

W.M. Lawry	c Smith b Trueman	5	c Sheppard b Titmus		98
R.B. Simpson	c Trueman b Dexter	50	c Smith b Dexter		71
N.C. O'Neill	c Statham b Trueman	19	lbw b Statham		56
R.N. Harvey	b Statham	39	c Statham b Dexter		57
P.J.P. Burge	c Dexter b Trueman	6	not out		47
B.C. Booth	c Dexter b Titmus	112	not out		19
A.K. Davidson	c Trueman b Barrington	23			
K.D. Mackay	not out	86			
R. Benaud*	c Smith b Knight	51			
G.D. McKenzie	c and b Knight	4			
B.N. Jarman†	c Barrington b Knight	2			
Extras	(B 5, LB 1, NB 1)	7	(B 4, LB 10)		14
Total		**404**	(4 wickets declared)		**362**

ENGLAND

G. Pullar	c and b Benaud	33	c and b Davidson		56
Rev. D.S. Sheppard	c McKenzie b Benaud	31	c Benaud b Davidson		53
E.R. Dexter*	b Benaud	70	b McKenzie		99
M.C. Cowdrey	c Lawry b Simpson	21	c and b Benaud		9
K.F. Barrington	c Burge b Benaud	78	c McKenzie b Davidson		23
A.C. Smith†	c Jarman b McKenzie	21			
P.H. Parfitt	c Davidson b Benaud	80	(6) c Jarman b McKenzie		4
F.J. Titmus	c Simpson b Benaud	21	(7) not out		3
B.R. Knight	c Davidson b McKenzie	0	(8) not out		4
F.S. Trueman	c Jarman b McKenzie	19			
J.B. Statham	not out	8			
Extras	(B 4, LB 2, W 1)	7	(B 15, LB 10, NB 2)		27
Total		**389**	(6 wickets)		**278**

ENGLAND	O	M	R	W	O	M	R	W		FALL OF WICKETS			
Statham	16	1	75	1	16	1	67	1		A	E	A	E
Trueman	18	0	76	3	15	0	59	0	Wkt	1st	1st	2nd	2nd
Knight	17.5	2	65	3	14	1	63	0	1st	5	62	136	114
Titmus	33	8	91	1	26	3	81	1	2nd	46	65	216	135
Dexter	10	0	46	1	16	0	78	2	3rd	92	145	241	191
Barrington	12	3	44	1					4th	101	169	325	257
									5th	140	220	–	257
AUSTRALIA									6th	194	297	–	261
Davidson	21	4	77	0	20	6	43	3	7th	297	361	–	–
McKenzie	25.3	2	78	3	20	4	61	2	8th	388	362	–	–
Mackay	28	7	55	0	7	0	28	0	9th	392	362	–	–
Benaud	42	12	115	6	27	7	71	1	10th	404	389	–	–
Simpson	18	6	52	1	7	0	48	0					
O'Neill	1	0	5	0	2	2	0	0					

Umpires: C.J. Egar (6) and E.F. Wykes (1).

Close: 1st day – A(1) 321-7 (Mackay 51, Benaud 13); 2nd – E(1) 169-4 (Barrington 13, Smith 0); 3rd – A(2) 16-0 (Lawry 7, Simpson 7); 4th – A(2) 362-4 (Burge 47, Booth 19).

AUSTRALIA v ENGLAND 1962–63 (2nd Test)

Played at Melbourne Cricket Ground on 29, 31 December, 1, 2, 3 January.
Toss: Australia.   Result: ENGLAND won by seven wickets.
Debuts: Nil.

England won their first Test in Australia since 1954-55 and with 75 minutes to spare. On the last day they scored 226 runs for the loss of only two wickets – both being run out. Cowdrey compiled the highest of his five hundreds against Australia and added 175 in 198 minutes with Dexter. Lawry's second fifty of the match took 275 minutes and remains the slowest on record for Australia. After scoring nought in the first innings and dropping two catches, Sheppard made amends with the last of his three Test hundreds. After 301 minutes at the crease, he was run out going for the winning single.

AUSTRALIA

W.M. Lawry	b Trueman	52	b Dexter		57
R.B. Simpson	c Smith b Coldwell	38	b Trueman		14
N.C. O'Neill	c Graveney b Statham	19	c Cowdrey b Trueman		0
R.N. Harvey	b Coldwell	0	run out		10
P.J.P. Burge	lbw b Titmus	23	b Statham		14
B.C. Booth	c Barrington b Titmus	27	c Trueman b Statham		103
A.K. Davidson	c Smith b Trueman	40	c Smith b Titmus		17
K.D. Mackay	lbw b Titmus	49	lbw b Trueman		9
R. Benaud*	c Barrington b Titmus	36	c Cowdrey b Trueman		4
G.D. McKenzie	b Trueman	16	b Trueman		0
B.N. Jarman†	not out	10	not out		11
Extras	(B 2, LB 4)	6	(B 4, LB 5)		9
Total		**316**			**248**

ENGLAND

Rev. D.S. Sheppard	lbw b Davidson	0	run out		113
G. Pullar	b Davidson	11	c Jarman b McKenzie		5
E.R. Dexter*	c Simpson b Benaud	93	run out		52
M.C. Cowdrey	c Burge b McKenzie	113	not out		58
K.F. Barrington	lbw b McKenzie	35	not out		0
T.W. Graveney	run out	41			
F.J. Titmus	c Jarman b Davidson	15			
A.C. Smith†	not out	6			
F.S. Trueman	c O'Neill b Davidson	6			
J.B. Statham	b Davidson	1			
L.J. Coldwell	c Benaud b Davidson	1			
Extras	(B 4, LB 4, NB 1)	9	(B 5, LB 3, NB 1)		9
Total		**331**	(3 wickets)		**237**

ENGLAND	O	M	R	W	O	M	R	W
Trueman	23	1	83	3	20	1	62	5
Statham	22	2	83	1	23	1	52	2
Coldwell	17	2	58	2	25	2	60	0
Barrington	6	0	23	0	5	0	22	0
Dexter	6	1	10	0	9	2	18	1
Titmus	15	2	43	4	14	4	25	1
Graveney	3	1	10	0				
AUSTRALIA								
Davidson	23·1	4	75	6	19	2	53	0
McKenzie	29	3	95	2	20	3	58	1
Mackay	6	2	17	0	9	0	34	0
Benaud	18	3	82	1	14	1	69	0
Simpson	7	1	34	0	2	0	10	0
O'Neill	5	1	19	0				
Booth					0·2	0	4	0

FALL OF WICKETS

	A	E	A	E
Wkt	1st	1st	2nd	2nd
1st	62	0	30	5
2nd	111	19	30	129
3rd	112	194	46	233
4th	112	254	69	–
5th	155	255	161	–
6th	164	292	193	–
7th	237	315	212	–
8th	289	324	228	–
9th	294	327	228	–
10th	316	331	248	–

Umpires: C.J. Egar (7) and W. Smyth (1).

Close: 1st day – A(1) 243-7 (Mackay 37, Benaud 21); 2nd – E(1) 210-3 (Cowdrey 94, Barrington 11); 3rd – A(2) 105-4 (Lawry 41, Booth 19); 4th – E(2) 9-1 (Sheppard 1, Dexter 3).

AUSTRALIA v ENGLAND 1962–63 (3rd Test)

Played at Sydney Cricket Ground on 11, 12, 14, 15 January.
Toss: England.   Result: AUSTRALIA won by eight wickets.
Debuts: Australia – C.E.J. Guest, B.K. Shepherd.

Australia squared the rubber at 2.15 pm on the fourth day. Parfitt kept wicket after Murray injured his shoulder when he caught Lawry. On the second day Titmus took four wickets for five runs in 58 balls; both he and Simpson recorded their best innings analyses in Test cricket. Murray, defending one-handed, spent 74 minutes before scoring and survived 100 minutes for his three runs.

ENGLAND

G. Pullar	c Benaud b Simpson	53	b Davidson	0
Rev. D.S. Sheppard	c McKenzie b Davidson	3	c Simpson b Davidson	12
E.R. Dexter*	c Lawry b Benaud	32	c Simpson b Davidson	11
M.C. Cowdrey	c Jarman b Simpson	85	c Simpson b Benaud	8
K.F. Barrington	lbw b Davidson	35	b McKenzie	21
P.H. Parfitt	c Lawry b Simpson	0	c O'Neill b McKenzie	28
F.J. Titmus	b Davidson	32	c Booth b O'Neill	6
J.T. Murray†	lbw b Davidson	0	not out	3
F.S. Trueman	b Simpson	32	c Jarman b McKenzie	9
J.B. Statham	c Benaud b Simpson	0	b Davidson	2
L.J. Coldwell	not out	2	c Shepherd b Davidson	0
Extras	(LB 3, W 2)	5	(B 2, LB 2)	4
Total		**279**		**104**

AUSTRALIA

W.M. Lawry	c Murray b Coldwell	8	b Trueman	8
R.B. Simpson	b Titmus	91	not out	34
R.N. Harvey	c Barrington b Titmus	64	lbw b Trueman	15
B.C. Booth	c Trueman b Titmus	16	not out	5
N.C. O'Neill	b Titmus	3		
B.K. Shepherd	not out	71		
B.N. Jarman†	run out	0		
A.K. Davidson	c Trueman b Titmus	15		
R. Benaud*	c and b Titmus	15		
G.D. McKenzie	lbw b Titmus	4		
C.E.J. Guest	b Statham	11		
Extras	(B 10, LB 11)	21	(B 5)	5
Total		**319**	(2 wickets)	**67**

AUSTRALIA	O	M	R	W	O	M	R	W
Davidson	24·5	7	54	4	10·6	2	25	5
McKenzie	15	3	52	0	14	3	26	3
Guest	16	0	51	0	2	0	8	0
Benaud	16	2	60	1	19	10	29	1
Simpson	15	3	57	5	4	2	5	0
O'Neill					7	5	7	1
ENGLAND								
Trueman	20	2	68	0	6	1	20	2
Statham	21·2	2	67	1	3	0	15	0
Coldwell	15	1	41	1				
Titmus	37	14	79	7				
Barrington	8	0	43	0				
Dexter					3·2	0	27	0

FALL OF WICKETS

	E	A	E	A
Wkt	1st	1st	2nd	2nd
1st	4	14	0	28
2nd	65	174	20	54
3rd	132	177	25	–
4th	201	187	37	–
5th	203	212	53	–
6th	221	216	71	–
7th	221	242	90	–
8th	272	274	100	–
9th	272	280	104	–
10th	279	319	104	–

Umpires: L.P. Rowan (1) and W. Smyth (2).

Close: 1st day – E(1) 256-7 (Titmus 28, Trueman 16); 2nd – A(1) 212-5 (Shepherd 18, Jarman 0); 3rd – E(2) 86-6 (Parfitt 26, Murray 0).

Test No. 538/187

AUSTRALIA v ENGLAND 1962–63 (4th Test)

Played at Adelaide Oval on 25, 26, 28, 29, 30 January.
Toss: Australia.   Result: MATCH DRAWN.
Debuts: Nil.

Rain reduced play by three hours on the third day. Barrington became the second batsman after J. Darling in 1897-98 (*Test No. 55*) to reach a hundred in this series of Tests with a six. Statham overtook A.V. Bedser's world record of 236 Test wickets when he dismissed Shepherd. Davidson pulled a hamstring and was unable to complete his fourth over. Harvey's century was the last of his 21 for Australia and his sixth against England.

AUSTRALIA

W.M. Lawry	b Illingworth	10	c Graveney b Trueman		16
R.B. Simpson	c Smith b Statham	0	c Smith b Dexter		71
R.N. Harvey	c Statham b Dexter	154	c Barrington b Statham		6
B.C. Booth	c Cowdrey b Titmus	34	c Smith b Dexter		77
N.C. O'Neill	c Cowdrey b Dexter	100	c Cowdrey b Trueman		23
A.K. Davidson	b Statham	46	(10) b Statham		2
B.K. Shepherd	c Trueman b Statham	10	(6) c Titmus b Dexter		13
K.D. Mackay	c Smith b Trueman	1	(7) c Graveney b Trueman		3
R. Benaud*	b Dexter	16	(8) c Barrington b Trueman		48
G.D. McKenzie	c Sheppard b Titmus	15	(9) c Smith b Statham		13
A.T.W. Grout†	not out	1	not out		16
Extras	(LB 5, W 1)	6	(B 1, LB 4)		5
Total		**393**			**293**

ENGLAND

G. Pullar	b McKenzie	9	c Simpson b McKenzie		3
Rev. D.S. Sheppard	st Grout b Benaud	30	c Grout b Mackay		1
K.F. Barrington	b Simpson	63	not out		132
M.C. Cowdrey	c Grout b McKenzie	13	run out		32
E.R. Dexter*	c Grout b McKenzie	61	c Simpson b Benaud		10
T.W. Graveney	c Booth b McKenzie	22	not out		36
F.J. Titmus	not out	59			
R. Illingworth	c Grout b McKenzie	12			
A.C. Smith†	c Lawry b Mackay	13			
F.S. Trueman	c Benaud b Mackay	38			
J.B. Statham	b Mackay	1			
Extras	(B 5, LB 5)	10	(B 4, W 5)		9
Total		**331**	(4 wickets)		**223**

ENGLAND	O	M	R	W	O	M	R	W
Trueman	19	1	54	1	23·3	3	60	4
Statham	21	5	66	3	21	2	71	3
Illingworth	20	3	85	1	5	1	23	0
Dexter	23	1	94	3	17	0	65	3
Titmus	20·1	2	88	2	24	5	69	0
AUSTRALIA								
Davidson	3·4	0	30	0				
McKenzie	33	3	89	5	14	0	64	1
Mackay	27·6	8	80	3	8	2	13	1
Benaud	18	3	82	1	15	3	38	1
Simpson	8	1	40	1	10	1	50	0
O'Neill					8	0	49	0
Lawry					1	1	0	0
Harvey					1	1	0	0

FALL OF WICKETS

	A	E	A	E
Wkt	1st	1st	2nd	2nd
1st	2	17	27	2
2nd	16	84	37	4
3rd	101	117	170	98
4th	295	119	175	122
5th	302	165	199	–
6th	331	226	205	–
7th	336	246	228	–
8th	366	275	254	–
9th	383	327	258	–
10th	393	331	293	–

Umpires: C.J. Egar (8) and A. Mackley (1).

Close: 1st day – A(1) 322-5 (Davidson 16, Shepherd 4); 2nd – E(1) 192-5 (Dexter 50, Titmus 2); 3rd – E(1) 328-9 (Titmus 57, Statham 0); 4th – A(2) 225-6 (O'Neill 22, Benaud 13).

AUSTRALIA v ENGLAND 1962–63 (5th Test)

Played at Sydney Cricket Ground on 15, 16, 18, 19, 20 February.
Toss: England.   Result: MATCH DRAWN.
Debuts: Australia – N.J.N. Hawke.

For the first time a five-match series in Australia ended with the sides level. Dexter's aggregate of 481 remains the record by an England captain in a rubber in Australia. O'Neill registered the 1,000th score of 50 or more in this series. Harvey and Davidson ended distinguished careers for Australia. Harvey, whose 79 appearances then constituted the national record, scored 6,149 runs (average 48·41), with 21 hundreds, and held 64 catches – six of them in this match. In 44 Tests, Davidson scored 1,328 runs and took 186 wickets, the last of them with his final ball.

ENGLAND

Rev. D.S. Sheppard	c and b Hawke	19	c Harvey b Benaud	68
M.C. Cowdrey	c Harvey b Davidson	2	(5) c Benaud b Davidson	53
K.F. Barrington	c Harvey b Benaud	101	c Grout b McKenzie	94
E.R. Dexter*	c Simpson b O'Neill	47	st Grout b Benaud	6
T.W. Graveney	c Harvey b McKenzie	14	(6) c and b Davidson	3
R. Illingworth	c Grout b Davidson	27	(2) c Hawke b Benaud	18
F.J. Titmus	c Grout b Hawke	34	not out	12
F.S. Trueman	c Harvey b Benaud	30	c Harvey b McKenzie	8
A.C. Smith†	b Simpson	6	c Simpson b Davidson	1
D.A. Allen	c Benaud b Davidson	14		
J.B. Statham	not out	17		
Extras	(B 4, LB 6)	10	(B 1, LB 4)	5
Total		**321**	(8 wickets declared)	**268**

AUSTRALIA

W.M. Lawry	c Smith b Trueman	11	not out	45
R.B. Simpson	c Trueman b Titmus	32	b Trueman	0
B.C. Booth	b Titmus	11	(5) b Allen	0
N.C. O'Neill	c Graveney b Allen	73	c Smith b Allen	17
P.J.P. Burge	lbw b Titmus	103	(6) not out	52
R.N. Harvey	c sub (P.H. Parfitt) b Statham	22	(3) b Allen	28
A.K. Davidson	c Allen b Dexter	15		
R. Benaud*	c Graveney b Allen	57		
G.D. McKenzie	c and b Titmus	0		
N.J.N. Hawke	c Graveney b Titmus	14		
A.T.W. Grout†	not out	0		
Extras	(B 6, LB 5)	11	(B 4, LB 6)	10
Total		**349**	(4 wickets)	**152**

AUSTRALIA	O	M	R	W	O	M	R	W
Davidson	25·6	4	43	3	28	1	80	3
McKenzie	27	4	57	1	8	0	39	2
Hawke	20	1	51	2	9	0	38	0
Benaud	34	9	71	2	30	8	71	3
Simpson	18	4	51	1	4	0	22	0
O'Neill	10	0	38	1				
Harvey					3	0	13	0
ENGLAND								
Trueman	11	0	33	1	3	0	6	1
Statham	18	1	76	1	4	1	8	0
Dexter	7	1	24	1	4	1	11	0
Titmus	47·2	9	103	5	20	7	37	0
Allen	43	15	87	2	19	11	26	3
Illingworth	5	1	15	0	10	5	8	0
Barrington					8	3	22	0
Graveney					4	0	24	0

FALL OF WICKETS

	E	A	E	A
Wkt	1st	1st	2nd	2nd
1st	5	28	40	0
2nd	39	50	137	39
3rd	129	71	145	70
4th	177	180	239	70
5th	189	231	247	–
6th	224	271	249	–
7th	276	299	257	–
8th	286	303	268	–
9th	293	347	–	–
10th	321	349	–	–

Umpires: C.J. Egar (9) and L.P. Rowan (2).

Close: 1st day – E(1) 195-5 (Illingworth 10, Titmus 0); 2nd – A(1) 74-3 (O'Neill 18, Burge 0); 3rd – A(1) 285-6 (Burge 98, Benaud 13); 4th – E(2) 165-3 (Barrington 87, Cowdrey 12).

NEW ZEALAND v ENGLAND 1962–63 (1st Test)

Played at Eden Park, Auckland, on 23, 25, 26, 27 February.
Toss: England.   Result: ENGLAND won by an innings and 215 runs.
Debuts: New Zealand – B.W. Sinclair, B.W. Yuile.

England's total was then their highest against New Zealand, 240 of the runs coming in a partnership between Parfitt and Knight which is still England's highest for the sixth wicket against all countries. An intriguing umpiring error by Shortt allowed Sparling to bowl eleven balls (excluding no-balls and wides) in his sixth over. The match ended after 66 minutes of play on the last day.

ENGLAND

Rev. D.S. Sheppard	c Dick b Cameron	12
R. Illingworth	c Reid b Cameron	20
K.F. Barrington	c Playle b Cameron	126
E.R. Dexter*	c Barton b Yuile	7
M.C. Cowdrey	c Barton b Cameron	86
P.H. Parfitt	not out	131
B.R. Knight	b Alabaster	125
F.J. Titmus	st Dick b Sparling	26
J.T. Murray†	not out	9
J.D.F. Larter	) did not bat	
L.J. Coldwell	)	
Extras	(B 18, LB 1, NB 1)	20
Total	(7 wickets declared)	**562**

NEW ZEALAND

G.T. Dowling	b Coldwell	3		b Illingworth	14
W.R. Playle	c Dexter b Larter	0		c Dexter b Coldwell	4
P.T. Barton	c Sheppard b Larter	3		lbw b Titmus	16
J.R. Reid*	b Titmus	59	(6)	not out	21
B.W. Sinclair	c Coldwell b Titmus	24		b Larter	2
J.T. Sparling	c Murray b Larter	3	(4)	c Barrington b Illingworth	0
A.E. Dick†	run out	29		c Illingworth b Larter	0
B.W. Yuile	run out	64		lbw b Larter	1
R.C. Motz	c Murray b Knight	60		c and b Illingworth	20
J.C. Alabaster	b Knight	2		c Titmus b Illingworth	0
F.J. Cameron	not out	0		b Larter	1
Extras	(B 5, LB 3, W 1, NB 2)	11		(B 2, LB 8)	10
Total		**258**			**89**

NEW ZEALAND	O	M	R	W	O	M	R	W
Motz	42	12	98	0				
Cameron	43	7	118	4				
Alabaster	40	6	130	1				
Yuile	21	4	77	1				
Reid	28	8	67	0				
Sparling	12	2	52	1				
ENGLAND								
Coldwell	27	9	66	1	5	2	4	1
Larter	26	12	51	3	14·1	3	26	4
Knight	10·4	2	23	2	10	2	13	0
Titmus	25	9	44	2	6	5	2	1
Barrington	12	4	38	0				
Dexter	9	4	20	0				
Illingworth	1	0	5	0	18	7	34	4

FALL OF WICKETS

Wkt	E 1st	NZ 1st	NZ 2nd
1st	24	0	15
2nd	45	7	42
3rd	63	7	42
4th	229	62	42
5th	258	71	46
6th	498	109	46
7th	535	161	56
8th	–	256	83
9th	–	258	83
10th	–	258	89

Umpires: J.M.A. Brown (1) and R.W.R. Shortt (2).

Close: 1st day – E(1) 328-5 (Parfitt 33, Knight 39); 2nd – NZ(1) 66-4 (Reid 34, Sparling 0); 3rd – NZ(2) 42-4 (Sinclair 0).

NEW ZEALAND v ENGLAND 1962–63 (2nd Test)

Played at Basin Reserve, Wellington, on 1, 2, 4 March.
Toss: England.   Result: ENGLAND won by an innings and 47 runs.
Debuts: New Zealand – B.D. Morrison, M.J.F. Shrimpton.

Cowdrey and Smith shared an unbroken partnership of 163 in 161 minutes to set a world Test record for the ninth wicket. It remains the England record for that wicket and has been bettered only by the partnership of 190 between Asif Iqbal and Intikhab Alam for Pakistan v England at The Oval in 1967 (*Test No. 623*).

NEW ZEALAND

G.T. Dowling	c Smith b Trueman	12	c Knight b Trueman	2
W.R. Playle	c Smith b Knight	23	c and b Illingworth	65
P.T. Barton	c Cowdrey b Trueman	0	c Barrington b Knight	3
J.R. Reid*	c Smith b Knight	0	c Barrington b Titmus	9
B.W. Sinclair	b Trueman	4	c and b Barrington	36
M.J.F. Shrimpton	lbw b Knight	28	c Parfitt b Barrington	10
A.E. Dick†	c Sheppard b Trueman	7	not out	38
B.W. Yuile	c Illingworth b Titmus	13	b Titmus	0
R.W. Blair	not out	64	c Larter b Titmus	5
B.D. Morrison	run out	10	c Larter b Titmus	0
F.J. Cameron	lbw b Barrington	12	lbw b Barrington	0
Extras	(B 13, LB 5, NB 3)	21	(B 13, LB 4, NB 2)	19
Total		**194**		**187**

ENGLAND

Rev. D.S. Sheppard	b Blair	0
R. Illingworth	c Morrison b Blair	46
K.F. Barrington	c Dick b Reid	76
E.R. Dexter*	b Morrison	31
P.H. Parfitt	c Dick b Morrison	0
B.R. Knight	c Dick b Cameron	31
F.J. Titmus	run out	33
M.C. Cowdrey	not out	128
F.S. Trueman	b Cameron	3
A.C. Smith†	not out	69
J.D.F. Larter	did not bat	
Extras	(B 3, LB 6, NB 2)	11
Total	(8 wickets declared)	**428**

ENGLAND	O	M	R	W	O	M	R	W	FALL OF WICKETS			
										NZ	E	NZ
Trueman	20	5	46	4	18	7	27	1				
Larter	14	2	52	0	7	1	18	0	*Wkt*	*1st*	*1st*	*2nd*
Knight	21	8	32	3	4	1	7	1	1st	32	0	15
Titmus	18	3	40	1	31	15	50	4	2nd	32	77	18
Barrington	2·3	1	1	1	11	3	32	3	3rd	35	125	41
Dexter	1	0	2	0					4th	40	125	122
Illingworth					27	14	34	1	5th	61	173	126
									6th	74	197	158
NEW ZEALAND									7th	96	258	159
Blair	33	11	81	2					8th	129	265	171
Morrison	31	5	129	2					9th	150	–	179
Cameron	43	16	98	2					10th	194	–	187
Reid	32	8	73	1								
Yuile	10	1	36	0								

Umpires: D.P. Dumbleton (1) and W.T. Martin (1).

Close: 1st day – E(1) 74-1 (Illingworth 43, Barrington 29); 2nd – E(1) 410-8 (Cowdrey 114, Smith 61).

NEW ZEALAND v ENGLAND 1962–63 (3rd Test)

Played at Lancaster Park, Christchurch, on 15, 16, 18, 19 March.
Toss: New Zealand.   Result: ENGLAND won by seven wickets.
Debuts: Nil.

Knight completed England's 3-0 victory in this rubber by hitting 14 runs (6, 4, 4) off successive balls from Alabaster. Trueman overtook J.B. Statham's world record of 242 Test wickets and ended his 56th Test with an aggregate of 250. His analysis of 7 for 75 is the best by an England bowler in a Test in New Zealand.

NEW ZEALAND

G.T. Dowling	c Dexter b Titmus	40	c Smith b Larter		22
W.R. Playle	c Barrington b Trueman	0	c Smith b Trueman		3
B.W. Sinclair	hit wkt b Trueman	44	lbw b Larter		0
J.R. Reid*	c Parfitt b Knight	74	b Titmus		100
P.T. Barton	c Smith b Knight	11	lbw b Knight		12
M.J.F. Shrimpton	c Knight b Trueman	31	b Titmus		8
A.E. Dick†	b Trueman	16	c Parfitt b Titmus		1
R.C. Motz	c Parfitt b Trueman	7	b Larter		3
R.W. Blair	c Parfitt b Trueman	0	b Titmus		0
J.C. Alabaster	not out	20	c Parfitt b Trueman		1
F.J. Cameron	c Smith b Trueman	1	not out		0
Extras	(B 1, LB 9, W 3, NB 9)	22	(LB 7, NB 2)		9
Total		**266**			**159**

ENGLAND

Rev. D.S. Sheppard	b Cameron	42	(2) b Alabaster		31
R. Illingworth	c Dick b Cameron	2			
K.F. Barrington	lbw b Motz	47	(1) c Reid b Blair		45
E.R. Dexter*	b Alabaster	46			
M.C. Cowdrey	c Motz b Blair	43	(4) not out		35
P.H. Parfitt	lbw b Reid	4	(3) c Shrimpton b Alabaster		31
B.R. Knight	b Blair	32	(5) not out		20
F.J. Titmus	c Dick b Motz	4			
F.S. Trueman	c Reid b Alabaster	11			
A.C. Smith†	not out	2			
J.D.F. Larter	b Motz	2			
Extras	(B 4, LB 6, W 5, NB 3)	18	(B 9, NB 2)		11
Total		**253**	(3 wickets)		**173**

ENGLAND	O	M	R	W	O	M	R	W
Trueman	30·2	9	75	7	19·4	8	16	2
Larter	21	5	59	0	23	8	32	3
Knight	23	5	39	2	10	3	38	1
Titmus	30	13	45	1	21	8	46	4
Dexter	9	3	8	0	10	2	18	0
Barrington	5	0	18	0				
NEW ZEALAND								
Motz	19·5	3	68	3	20	6	33	0
Cameron	24	6	47	2	12	3	38	0
Blair	24	12	42	2	12	3	34	1
Alabaster	20	6	47	2	15·3	5	57	2
Reid	8	1	31	1				

FALL OF WICKETS

Wkt	NZ 1st	E 1st	NZ 2nd	E 2nd
1st	3	11	16	70
2nd	83	87	17	96
3rd	98	103	66	149
4th	128	186	91	–
5th	195	188	129	–
6th	234	210	133	–
7th	235	225	151	–
8th	235	244	154	–
9th	251	250	159	–
10th	266	253	159	–

Umpires: L.C. Johnston (1) and W.T. Martin (2).

Close: 1st day – NZ(1) 238-8 (Motz 1, Alabaster 2); 2nd – E(1) 244-8 (Knight 31, Smith 0); 3rd – E(2) 41-0 (Barrington 30, Sheppard 8).

ENGLAND v WEST INDIES 1963 (1st Test)

Played at Old Trafford, Manchester, on 6, 7, 8, 10 June.
Toss: West Indies.   Result: WEST INDIES won by ten wickets.
Debuts: England – J.H. Edrich; West Indies – M.C. Carew, D.L. Murray.

West Indies gained their first victory in a Test at Old Trafford. Following their 5-0 defeat of India in 1961-62, this win gave West Indies six consecutive Test victories for the first time. Hunte's 182 was then the highest score against England at Manchester. For the first time in England three players from the same county, Stewart, Edrich and Barrington of Surrey, occupied the first three places in England's batting order. Gibbs, 11 for 157, returned the best match analysis of a career involving 79 Test matches.

WEST INDIES

C.C. Hunte	c Titmus b Allen	182	not out		1
M.C. Carew	c Andrew b Trueman	16	not out		0
R.B. Kanhai	run out	90			
B.F. Butcher	lbw b Trueman	22			
G. St A. Sobers	c Edrich b Allen	64			
J.S. Solomon	lbw b Titmus	35			
F.M.M. Worrell*	not out	74			
D.L. Murray†	not out	7			
W.W. Hall	)				
C.C. Griffith	) did not bat				
L.R. Gibbs	)				
Extras	(B 3, LB 7, NB 1)	11			
Total	(6 wickets declared)	**501**	(0 wickets)		**1**

ENGLAND

M.J. Stewart	c Murray b Gibbs	37	c Murray b Gibbs		87
J.H. Edrich	c Murray b Hall	20	c Hunte b Worrell		38
K.F. Barrington	c Murray b Hall	16	(4) b Gibbs		8
M.C. Cowdrey	b Hall	4	(5) c Hunte b Gibbs		12
E.R. Dexter*	c Worrell b Sobers	73	(6) c Murray b Gibbs		35
D.B. Close	c Hunte b Gibbs	30	(7) c Sobers b Gibbs		32
F.J. Titmus	c Sobers b Gibbs	0	(8) b Sobers		17
D.A. Allen	c Sobers b Gibbs	5	(9) b Gibbs		1
F.S. Trueman	c Worrell b Sobers	5	(10) not out		29
K.V. Andrew†	not out	3	(3) c Murray b Sobers		15
J.B. Statham	b Gibbs	0	b Griffith		7
Extras	(B 2, LB 7, NB 3)	12	(B 10, LB 4, NB 1)		15
Total		**205**			**296**

ENGLAND	O	M	R	W	O	M	R	W	FALL OF WICKETS				
										WI	E	E	WI
Trueman	40	7	95	2					Wkt	1st	1st	2nd	2nd
Statham	37	6	121	0					1st	37	34	93	–
Titmus	40	13	105	1					2nd	188	61	131	–
Close	10	2	31	0					3rd	239	67	160	–
Allen	57	22	122	2	0·1	0	1	0	4th	359	108	165	–
Dexter	12	4	16	0					5th	398	181	186	–
WEST INDIES									6th	479	190	231	–
Hall	17	4	51	3	14	0	39	0	7th	–	192	254	–
Griffith	21	4	37	0	8·5	4	11	1	8th	–	202	256	–
Gibbs	29·3	9	59	5	46	16	98	6	9th	–	202	268	–
Sobers	22	11	34	2	37	4	122	2	10th	–	205	296	–
Worrell	1	0	12	0	4	2	11	1					

Umpires: C.S. Elliott (13) and J.G. Langridge (6).

Close: 1st day – WI(1) 244-3 (Hunte 104, Sobers 3); 2nd – E(1) 31-0 (Stewart 7, Edrich 20); 3rd – E(2) 97-1 (Stewart 44, Andrew 4).

ENGLAND v WEST INDIES 1963 (2nd Test)

Played at Lord's, London, on 20, 21, 22, 24, 25 June.
Toss: West Indies.   Result: MATCH DRAWN.
Debuts: Nil.

This was one of the most dramatic of cricket matches with any of the four results possible as the last ball was being bowled. England needed six runs to win with their last pair together as Allen played Hall's final ball defensively to draw the match. His partner, Cowdrey, had his fractured left arm in plaster and intended to bat left-handed, but using only his right arm, had he been called upon to face the bowling. Hall bowled throughout the 200 minutes of play possible after rain had delayed the start of the last day. Shackleton ended West Indies' first innings by taking three wickets in four balls.

WEST INDIES

C.C. Hunte	c Close b Trueman	44		c Cowdrey b Shackleton	7
E.D.A. St J. McMorris	lbw b Trueman	16		c Cowdrey b Trueman	8
G. St A. Sobers	c Cowdrey b Allen	42	(5)	c Parks b Trueman	8
R.B. Kanhai	c Edrich b Trueman	73	(3)	c Cowdrey b Shackleton	21
B.F. Butcher	c Barrington b Trueman	14	(4)	lbw b Shackleton	133
J.S. Solomon	lbw b Shackleton	56		c Stewart b Allen	5
F.M.M. Worrell*	b Trueman	0		c Stewart b Trueman	33
D.L. Murray†	c Cowdrey b Trueman	20		c Parks b Trueman	2
W.W. Hall	not out	25		c Parks b Trueman	2
C.C. Griffith	c Cowdrey b Shackleton	0		b Shackleton	1
L.R. Gibbs	c Stewart b Shackleton	0		not out	1
Extras	(B 10, LB 1)	11		(B 5, LB 2, NB 1)	8
Total		**301**			**229**

ENGLAND

M.J. Stewart	c Kanhai b Griffith	2		c Solomon b Hall	17
J.H. Edrich	c Murray b Griffith	0		c Murray b Hall	8
E.R. Dexter*	lbw b Sobers	70		b Gibbs	2
K.F. Barrington	c Sobers b Worrell	80		c Murray b Griffith	60
M.C. Cowdrey	b Gibbs	4		not out	19
D.B. Close	c Murray b Griffith	9		c Murray b Griffith	70
J.M. Parks†	b Worrell	35		lbw b Griffith	17
F.J. Titmus	not out	52		c McMorris b Hall	11
F.S. Trueman	b Hall	10		c Murray b Hall	0
D.A. Allen	lbw b Griffith	2		not out	4
D. Shackleton	b Griffith	8		run out	4
Extras	(B 8, LB 8, NB 9)	25		(B 5, LB 8, NB 3)	16
Total		**297**		(9 wickets)	**228**

ENGLAND	O	M	R	W	O	M	R	W		FALL OF WICKETS			
										WI	E	WI	E
Trueman	44	16	100	6	26	9	52	5	*Wkt*	*1st*	*1st*	*2nd*	*2nd*
Shackleton	50·2	22	93	3	34	14	72	4	1st	51	2	15	15
Dexter	20	6	41	0					2nd	64	20	15	27
Close	9	3	21	0					3rd	127	102	64	31
Allen	10	3	35	1	21	7	50	1	4th	145	115	84	130
Titmus					17	3	47	0	5th	219	151	104	158
WEST INDIES									6th	219	206	214	203
Hall	18	2	65	1	40	9	93	4	7th	263	235	224	203
Griffith	26	6	91	5	30	7	59	3	8th	297	271	226	219
Sobers	18	4	45	1	4	1	4	0	9th	297	274	228	228
Gibbs	27	9	59	1	17	7	56	1	10th	301	297	229	–
Worrell	13	6	12	2									

Umpires: J.S. Buller (14) and W.E. Phillipson (10).

Close: 1st day – WI(1) 245-6 (Solomon 34, Murray 12); 2nd – E(1) 244-7 (Titmus 23, Trueman 5); 3rd – WI(2) 214-5 (Butcher 129, Worrell 33); 4th – E(2) 116-3 (Barrington 55, Close 7).

ENGLAND v WEST INDIES 1963 (3rd Test)

Played at Edgbaston, Birmingham, on 4, 5, 6, 8, 9 July.
Toss: England.   Result: ENGLAND won by 217 runs.
Debuts: England – P.J. Sharpe.

Rain curtailed play on each of the first three days. England's victory maintained their unbeaten run at Edgbaston. Trueman is the only bowler to take 12 wickets in any Birmingham Test or against West Indies in England. His match analysis remained the best of his career and brought his tally of wickets in two successive Tests to 23. His last six wickets were taken in a 24-ball spell which cost him just one scoring stroke for four runs by Gibbs. Lock scored his first fifty in Test cricket.

ENGLAND

P.E. Richardson	b Hall	2	c Murray b Griffith	14
M.J. Stewart	lbw b Sobers	39	c Murray b Griffith	27
E.R. Dexter*	b Sobers	29	(5) st Murray b Gibbs	57
K.F. Barrington	b Sobers	9	(3) b Sobers	1
D.B. Close	lbw b Sobers	55	(4) c Sobers b Griffith	13
P.J. Sharpe	c Kanhai b Gibbs	23	not out	85
J.M. Parks†	c Murray b Sobers	12	c Sobers b Gibbs	5
F.J. Titmus	c Griffith b Hall	27	b Gibbs	0
F.S. Trueman	b Griffith	4	c Gibbs b Sobers	1
G.A.R. Lock	b Griffith	1	b Gibbs	56
D. Shackleton	not out	6		
Extras	(LB 6, NB 3)	9	(B 9, LB 9, NB 1)	19
Total		**216**	(9 wickets declared)	**278**

WEST INDIES

C.C. Hunte	b Trueman	18	c Barrington b Trueman	5
M.C. Carew	c and b Trueman	40	lbw b Shackleton	1
R.B. Kanhai	c Lock b Shackleton	32	c Lock b Trueman	38
B.F. Butcher	lbw b Dexter	15	b Dexter	14
J.S. Solomon	lbw b Dexter	0	(6) c Parks b Trueman	14
G. St A. Sobers	b Trueman	19	(5) c Sharpe b Shackleton	9
F.M.M. Worrell*	b Dexter	1	c Parks b Trueman	0
D.L. Murray†	not out	20	c Parks b Trueman	3
W.W. Hall	c Sharpe b Dexter	28	b Trueman	0
C.C. Griffith	lbw b Trueman	5	lbw b Trueman	0
L.R. Gibbs	b Trueman	0	not out	4
Extras	(LB 7, W 1)	8	(LB 2, W 1)	3
Total		**186**		**91**

WEST INDIES	O	M	R	W	O	M	R	W	FALL OF WICKETS				
Hall	16·4	2	56	2	16	1	47	0		E	WI	E	WI
Griffith	21	5	48	2	28	7	55	3	*Wkt*	*1st*	*1st*	*2nd*	*2nd*
Sobers	31	10	60	5	27	4	80	2	1st	2	42	30	2
Worrell	14	5	15	0	8	3	28	0	2nd	50	79	31	10
Gibbs	16	7	28	1	26·2	4	49	4	3rd	72	108	60	38
									4th	89	109	69	64
ENGLAND									5th	129	128	170	78
Trueman	26	5	75	5	14·3	2	44	7	6th	172	130	184	80
Shackleton	21	9	60	1	17	4	37	2	7th	187	130	184	86
Lock	2	1	5	0					8th	194	178	189	86
Dexter	20	5	38	4	3	1	7	1	9th	200	186	278	86
									10th	216	186	–	91

Umpires: C.S. Elliott (14) and L.H. Gray (2).

Close: 1st day – E(1) 157-5 (Close 41, Parks 7); 2nd – E(1) 216 all out; 3rd – WI(1) 110-4 (Butcher 14, Sobers 1); 4th – E(2) 226-8 (Sharpe 69, Lock 23).

ENGLAND v WEST INDIES 1963 (4th Test)

Played at Headingley, Leeds, on 25, 26, 27, 29 July.
Toss: West Indies.   Result: WEST INDIES won by 221 runs.
Debuts: England – J.B. Bolus.

In his fiftieth Test, Worrell won first use of a pitch expected to assist spin eventually. Sobers completed 4,000 runs in Tests when he had made 82. Bolus on-drove his first ball in Test cricket to the boundary off Hall. Lock produced his second half-century in successive innings for England before becoming the final victim in a career-best analysis for Griffith.

WEST INDIES

C.C. Hunte	c Parks b Trueman	22	b Trueman	4
E.D.A. St J. McMorris	c Barrington b Shackleton	11	lbw b Trueman	1
R.B. Kanhai	b Lock	92	lbw b Shackleton	44
B.F. Butcher	c Parks b Dexter	23	c Dexter b Shackleton	78
G. St A. Sobers	c and b Lock	102	c Sharpe b Titmus	52
J.S. Solomon	c Stewart b Trueman	62	c Titmus b Shackleton	16
D.L. Murray†	lbw b Titmus	34	(8) c Lock b Titmus	2
F.M.M. Worrell*	c Close b Lock	25	(7) c Parks b Titmus	0
W.W. Hall	c Shackleton b Trueman	15	c Trueman b Titmus	7
C.C. Griffith	c Stewart b Trueman	1	not out	12
L.R. Gibbs	not out	0	c Sharpe b Lock	6
Extras	(B 4, LB 5, W 1)	10	(LB 7)	7
Total		**397**		**229**

ENGLAND

M.J. Stewart	c Gibbs b Griffith	2	b Sobers	0
J.B. Bolus	c Hunte b Hall	14	c Gibbs b Sobers	43
E.R. Dexter*	b Griffith	8	lbw b Griffith	10
K.F. Barrington	c Worrell b Gibbs	25	lbw b Sobers	32
D.B. Close	b Griffith	0	c Solomon b Griffith	56
P.J. Sharpe	c Kanhai b Griffith	0	c Kanhai b Gibbs	13
J.M. Parks†	c Gibbs b Griffith	22	lbw b Gibbs	57
F.J. Titmus	lbw b Gibbs	33	st Murray b Gibbs	5
F.S. Trueman	c Hall b Gibbs	4	c Griffith b Gibbs	5
G.A.R. Lock	b Griffith	53	c Murray b Griffith	1
D. Shackleton	not out	1	not out	1
Extras	(B 4, LB 6, NB 2)	12	(B 3, LB 5)	8
Total		**174**		**231**

ENGLAND	O	M	R	W	O	M	R	W
Trueman	46	10	117	4	13	1	46	2
Shackleton	42	10	88	1	26	2	63	3
Dexter	23	4	68	1	2	0	15	0
Titmus	25	5	60	1	19	2	44	4
Lock	28·4	9	54	3	7·1	0	54	1
WEST INDIES								
Hall	13	2	61	1	5	1	12	0
Griffith	21	5	36	6	18	5	45	3
Gibbs	14	2	50	3	37·4	12	76	4
Sobers	6	1	15	0	32	5	90	3

FALL OF WICKETS

Wkt	WI 1st	E 1st	WI 2nd	E 2nd
1st	28	13	1	0
2nd	42	19	20	23
3rd	71	32	85	82
4th	214	32	181	95
5th	287	34	186	130
6th	348	69	188	199
7th	355	87	196	221
8th	379	93	206	224
9th	389	172	212	225
10th	397	174	229	231

Umpires: J.G. Langridge (7) and W.E. Phillipson (11).

Close: 1st day – WI(1) 294-5 (Solomon 39, Murray 0); 2nd – E(1) 169-8 (Titmus 31, Lock 51); 3rd – E(2) 113-4 (Close 14, Sharpe 9).

ENGLAND v WEST INDIES 1963 (5th Test)

Played at Kennington Oval, London, 22, 23, 24, 26 August.
Toss: England.   Result: WEST INDIES won by eight wickets.
Debuts: Nil.

West Indies became the first holders of the Wisden Trophy by three Tests to one. Although a bruised ankle bone limited his second-innings spell to one over, Trueman set a new record for this series by taking 34 wickets. Murray made 24 dismissals in his first Test rubber. Close kept wicket on the second morning after Parks had been struck on the left foot by a yorker from Hall.

ENGLAND

J.B. Bolus	c Murray b Sobers	33	c Gibbs b Sobers	15
J.H. Edrich	c Murray b Sobers	25	c Murray b Griffith	12
E.R. Dexter*	c and b Griffith	29	c Murray b Sobers	27
K.F. Barrington	c Sobers b Gibbs	16	b Griffith	28
D.B. Close	b Griffith	46	lbw b Sobers	4
P.J. Sharpe	c Murray b Griffith	63	c Murray b Hall	83
J.M. Parks†	c Kanhai b Griffith	19	lbw b Griffith	23
F.S. Trueman	b Griffith	19	c Sobers b Hall	5
G.A.R. Lock	hit wkt b Griffith	4	b Hall	0
J.B. Statham	b Hall	8	b Hall	14
D. Shackleton	not out	0	not out	0
Extras	(B 4, LB 2, NB 7)	13	(B 5, LB 3, NB 4)	12
Total		**275**		**223**

WEST INDIES

C.C. Hunte	c Parks b Shackleton	80	not out	108
W.V. Rodriguez	c Lock b Statham	5	c Lock b Dexter	28
R.B. Kanhai	b Lock	30	c Bolus b Lock	77
B.F. Butcher	run out	53	not out	31
G. St A. Sobers	run out	26		
J.S. Solomon	c Trueman b Statham	16		
F.M.M. Worrell*	b Statham	9		
D.L. Murray†	c Lock b Trueman	5		
W.W. Hall	b Trueman	2		
C.C. Griffith	not out	13		
L.R. Gibbs	b Trueman	4		
Extras	(LB 3)	3	(B 4, LB 7)	11
Total		**246**	(2 wickets)	**255**

WEST INDIES	O	M	R	W	O	M	R	W		FALL OF WICKETS			
Hall	22·2	2	71	1	16	3	39	4		E	WI	E	WI
Griffith	27	4	71	6	23	7	66	3	*Wkt*	*1st*	*1st*	*2nd*	*2nd*
Sobers	21	4	44	2	33	6	77	3	1st	59	10	29	78
Gibbs	27	7	50	1	9	1	29	0	2nd	64	72	31	191
Worrell	5	0	26	0					3rd	103	152	64	–
									4th	115	185	69	–
ENGLAND									5th	216	198	121	–
Trueman	26·1	2	65	3	1	1	0	0	6th	224	214	173	–
Statham	22	3	68	3	22	2	54	0	7th	254	221	196	–
Shackleton	21	5	37	1	32	7	68	0	8th	258	225	196	–
Lock	29	6	65	1	25	8	52	1	9th	275	233	218	–
Dexter	6	1	8	0	9	1	34	1	10th	275	246	223	–
Close					6	0	36	0					

Umpires: J.S. Buller (15) and A.E.G. Rhodes (1).

Close: 1st day – E(1) 275 all out; 2nd – WI(1) 231-8 (Solomon 15, Griffith 3); 3rd – WI(2) 5-0 (Hunte 5, Rodriguez 0).

AUSTRALIA v SOUTH AFRICA 1963–64 (1st Test)

Played at Woolloongabba, Brisbane, on 6, 7, 9 (*no play*), 10, 11 December.
Toss: Australia.   Result: MATCH DRAWN.
Debuts: Australia – A.N. Connolly. T.R. Veivers; South Africa – D.T. Lindsay, J.T. Partridge,
D.B. Pithey, R.G. Pollock, M.A. Seymour, P.L. van der Merwe.

Torrential rain ended play soon after lunch on the last day. Meckiff (left-arm fast) announced his retirement from all classes of cricket after being no-balled for throwing four times in his only over by umpire Egar. Barlow remains the only South African to score a hundred in his first Test against Australia. Benaud, captaining Australia for the last time, scored his 2000th run and became the only Australian to achieve the double double of 2,000 runs and 200 wickets.

AUSTRALIA

W.M. Lawry	c R.G. Pollock b Barlow	43	not out	87
R.B. Simpson	c Waite b P.M. Pollock	12	c sub (K.C. Bland) b Partridge	34
N.C. O'Neill	c Barlow b P.M. Pollock	82	not out	19
P.J.P. Burge	run out	13		
B.C. Booth	c Barlow b P.M. Pollock	169		
R. Benaud*	lbw b Goddard	43		
G.D. McKenzie	c P.M. Pollock b Goddard	39		
T.R. Veivers	c Goddard b P.M. Pollock	14		
A.T.W. Grout†	c Seymour b P.M. Pollock	6		
I. Meckiff	b P.M. Pollock	7		
A.N. Connolly	not out	1		
Extras	(B 1, LB 5)	6	(LB 4)	4
Total		**435**	(1 wicket declared)	**144**

SOUTH AFRICA

T.L.Goddard*	c Meckiff b Benaud	52	not out	8
E.J. Barlow	b Benaud	114	c Simpson b McKenzie	0
P.R. Carlstein	c and b Benaud	0	not out	1
R.G. Pollock	b McKenzie	25		
D.T. Lindsay	lbw b Benaud	17		
J.H.B. Waite†	lbw b Connolly	66		
P.L. van der Merwe	b O'Neill	17		
D.B. Pithey	c Meckiff b Veivers	18		
P.M. Pollock	lbw b Benaud	8		
M.A. Seymour	b Simpson	10		
J.T. Partridge	not out	3		
Extras	(B 3, LB 5, NB 8)	16	(B 4)	4
Total		**346**	(1 wicket)	**13**

SOUTH AFRICA	O	M	R	W	O	M	R	W					
P.M. Pollock	22·6	0	95	6	6	0	26	0					
Partridge	25	3	87	0	17	1	50	1					
Goddard	24	6	52	2	7	0	34	0					
Barlow	9	0	71	1									
Seymour	11	0	39	0									
Pithey	23	6	85	0	5	0	30	0					
AUSTRALIA													
McKenzie	23	1	88	1	3·3	1	3	1					
Meckiff	1	0	8	0									
Connolly	19	4	46	1	1	0	2	0					
Veivers	34	15	48	1									
Benaud	33	10	68	5	2	1	4	0					
Simpson	18·5	5	52	1									
O'Neill	7	0	20	1									

FALL OF WICKETS

Wkt	A 1st	SA 1st	A 2nd	SA 2nd
1st	39	74	83	1
2nd	73	78	–	–
3rd	88	120	–	–
4th	208	157	–	–
5th	310	239	–	–
6th	394	272	–	–
7th	415	321	–·	–
8th	427	325	–	–
9th	434	335	–	–
10th	435	346	–	–

Umpires: C.J. Egar (10) and L.P. Rowan (3).

Close: 1st day – A(1) 337-5 (Booth 128, McKenzie 14); 2nd – SA(1) 157-4 (Barlow 56); 3rd – no play; 4th – A(2) 25-0 (Lawry 12, Simpson 12).

AUSTRALIA v SOUTH AFRICA 1963–64 (2nd Test)

Played at Melbourne Cricket Ground on 1, 2, 3, 4, 6 January.
Toss: Australia.   Result: AUSTRALIA won by eight wickets.
Debuts: Australia – I.R. Redpath.

Simpson, in his first Test as captain, put South Africa in to bat and made the winning hit on the morning of the fifth day. Barlow became the only South African to score hundreds in his first two Tests against Australia. Lawry and Redpath recorded Australia's highest opening partnership (219) in any home Test. It was beaten by Lawry and Simpson when they scored 244 against England in 1965-66 (*Test No. 600*). South Africa provided the third instance of a side playing two pairs of brothers in the same Test (also *Tests No. 134 and 232*). Injuries prevented Peter Pollock and Seymour from bowling in the second innings.

SOUTH AFRICA

T.L. Goddard*	c Grout b McKenzie	17	lbw b Hawke		8
E.J. Barlow	c Connolly b McKenzie	109	run out		54
A.J. Pithey	lbw b Connolly	21	c Grout b Connolly		76
R.G. Pollock	c Simpson b McKenzie	16	c Martin b Connolly		2
J.H.B. Waite†	c Grout b Hawke	14	b McKenzie		77
P.L. van der Merwe	st Grout b Martin	14	c Grout b Martin		31
K.C. Bland	run out	50	c and b Martin		22
D.B. Pithey	c Grout b McKenzie	0	c Martin b Hawke		4
P.M. Pollock	c Simpson b Martin	14	(10) b Hawke		0
M.A. Seymour	not out	7	(11) not out		11
J.T. Partridge	run out	9	(9) b McKenzie		12
Extras	(LB 3)	3	(B 2, LB 3, W 2, NB 2)		9
Total		**274**			**306**

AUSTRALIA

W.M. Lawry	c sub (P.R. Carlstein) b Partridge	157	b Partridge		20
I.R. Redpath	b Partridge	97	c Van der Merwe b Barlow		25
R.B. Simpson*	b P.M. Pollock	0	not out		55
P.J.P. Burge	c Bland b P.M. Pollock	23	not out		26
B.K. Shepherd	c D.B. Pithey b Barlow	96			
A.T.W. Grout†	c Waite b P.M. Pollock	3			
T.R. Veivers	c Waite b Partridge	19			
G.D. McKenzie	c Partridge b Seymour	2			
N.J.N. Hawke	b Barlow	24			
J.W. Martin	c D.B. Pithey b Partridge	17			
A.N. Connolly	not out	0			
Extras	(B 1, LB 2, NB 6)	9	(B 5, LB 2, W 1, NB 2)		10
Total		**447**	(2 wickets)		**136**

AUSTRALIA	O	M	R	W	O	M	R	W		FALL OF WICKETS			
McKenzie	19	1	82	4	25	1	81	2		SA	A	SA	A
Hawke	20	2	77	1	19	1	53	3	*Wkt*	*1st*	*1st*	*2nd*	*2nd*
Connolly	18	2	62	1	18	2	49	2	1st	26	219	35	33
Martin	16	3	44	2	27	4	83	2	2nd	74	222	83	75
Veivers	5	1	6	0					3rd	100	270	85	–
Simpson					12	2	31	0	4th	129	291	213	–
									5th	179	301	233	–
SOUTH AFRICA									6th	201	340	273	–
P.M. Pollock	20·5	1	98	3					7th	201	357	282	–
Partridge	34	4	108	4	17	1	49	1	8th	256	413	282	–
Bland	11	2	35	0	2	0	6	0	9th	256	439	282	–
Goddard	21	2	70	0	1	1	0	0	10th	274	447	306	–
D.B. Pithey	5	1	20	0	6	0	18	0					
Seymour	19	2	56	1									
Barlow	7·6	0	51	2	11	0	49	1					
Van der Merwe					0·1	0	4	0					

Umpires: C.J. Egar (11) and L.P. Rowan (4).

Close: 1st day – A(1) 4-0 (Lawry 4, Redpath 0); 2nd – A(1) 308-5 (Shepherd 19, Veivers 3); 3rd – SA(2) 127-3 (A.J. Pithey 42, Waite 19); 4th – A(2) 92-2 (Simpson 32, Burge 7).

AUSTRALIA v SOUTH AFRICA 1963–64 (3rd Test)

Played at Sydney Cricket Ground on 10, 11, 13, 14, 15 January.
Toss: Australia.   Result: MATCH DRAWN.
Debuts: South Africa – C.G. Halse.

Australia set South Africa to score 409 runs in 430 minutes. Australia's partnership of 160 between Benaud and McKenzie remains their highest for the seventh wicket against South Africa. Graeme Pollock, aged 19 years 318 days, became the youngest South African to score a hundred in Test cricket – a record he still holds. He batted for 221 minutes and scored his 122 runs out of 186 made while he was at the wicket. Simpson retained the Australian captaincy as Benaud, although recovered from injury, had announced his intention to retire after this rubber.

AUSTRALIA

R.B. Simpson*	c Goddard b P.M. Pollock	58	lbw b Halse	31
W.M. Lawry	b Partridge	23	c R.G. Pollock b Goddard	89
N.C. O'Neill	c Goddard b Halse	3	c Barlow b Partridge	88
P.J.P. Burge	b Partridge	36	c Waite b P.M. Pollock	13
B.C. Booth	b Partridge	75	b Partridge	16
B.K. Shepherd	c Waite b P.M. Pollock	0	c Waite b Partridge	11
R. Benaud	c Bland b P.M. Pollock	43	c D.B. Pithey b P.M. Pollock	90
G.D. McKenzie	c Goddard b Partridge	3	c Van der Merwe b Partridge	76
N.J.N. Hawke	c Goddard b P.M. Pollock	2	not out	6
A.T.W. Grout†	c Partridge b P.M. Pollock	1	c Bland b Partridge	8
A.N. Connolly	not out	3		
Extras	(B 5, LB 6, W 1, NB 1)	13	(B 8, LB 8, W 1, NB 5)	22
Total		**260**	(9 wickets declared)	**450**

SOUTH AFRICA

T.L. Goddard*	c Connolly b Benaud	80	lbw b Simpson	84
E.J. Barlow	c Grout b Connolly	6	c Simpson b Hawke	35
A.J. Pithey	c Grout b Hawke	9	(6) not out	53
R.G. Pollock	c McKenzie b Connolly	122	c Grout b Hawke	42
J.H.B. Waite†	b McKenzie	8		
P.L. van der Merwe	b McKenzie	0	(7) not out	13
K.C. Bland	c McKenzie b Benaud	51	(5) c Benaud b O'Neill	85
D.B. Pithey	c Lawry b Benaud	10	(3) b McKenzie	7
P.M. Pollock	c Grout b Hawke	1		
J.T. Partridge	b McKenzie	7		
C.G. Halse	not out	1		
Extras	(B 3, LB 4)	7	(B 2, LB 5)	7
Total		**302**	(5 wickets)	**326**

SOUTH AFRICA	O	M	R	W	O	M	R	W
P.M. Pollock	18	2	83	5	24	0	129	2
Partridge	19·6	2	88	4	32·5	4	123	5
Goddard	10	1	24	0	11	3	20	1
Halse	11	1	36	1	15	2	58	1
Bland	2	0	7	0	1	0	7	0
Barlow	2	0	9	0	1	0	5	0
D.B. Pithey					16	1	86	0

AUSTRALIA	O	M	R	W	O	M	R	W
McKenzie	19	2	70	3	14	2	61	1
Connolly	19	2	66	2	13	0	41	0
Hawke	18	1	56	2	19	5	43	2
Simpson	9	2	32	0	23	8	48	1
Benaud	24·1	4	55	3	30	8	61	0
O'Neill	3	0	16	0	16	1	59	1
Booth					1	0	3	0
Shepherd					1	0	3	0

FALL OF WICKETS

	A	SA	A	SA
Wkt	1st	1st	2nd	2nd
1st	59	10	58	57
2nd	66	58	198	67
3rd	108	137	235	141
4th	128	162	235	201
5th	129	162	259	291
6th	229	244	264	–
7th	238	277	424	–
8th	248	278	436	–
9th	256	300	450	–
10th	260	302	–	–

Umpires: C.J. Egar (12) and L.P. Rowan (5).

Close: 1st day – SA(1) 11-1 (Goddard 5, A.J. Pithey 0); 2nd – SA(1) 294-8 (Bland 49, Partridge 5); 3rd – A(2) 243-4 (Booth 4, Shepherd 4); 4th – SA(2) 61-1 (Goddard 24, D.B. Pithey 2).

AUSTRALIA v SOUTH AFRICA 1963–64 (4th Test)

Played at Adelaide Oval on 24, 25, 27, 28, 29 January.
Toss: Australia.   Result: SOUTH AFRICA won by ten wickets.
Debuts: Nil.

South Africa levelled the rubber with an emphatic pre-lunch victory on the fifth day after recording their highest total in Test cricket to date; it is still their highest in Australia. Barlow, who batted for 392 minutes and hit 27 fours, was the third South African after G.A. Faulkner and A.D. Nourse to score a double-century against Australia. His partnership of 341 in 283 minutes with Graeme Pollock remains South Africa's highest for any wicket in all Tests. At 19 years 333 days, Pollock became the third player after R.N. Harvey and Mushtaq Mohammad to score two Test hundreds before his 20th birthday. His century came in 126 minutes and he batted in all for 283 minutes, hitting three sixes and 18 fours. Grout beat W.A.S. Oldfield's Australian Test record of 130 dismissals when he caught Pithey.

AUSTRALIA

R.B. Simpson*	b Goddard	78	c Lindsay b Halse		34
W.M. Lawry	c Partridge b P.M. Pollock	14	c Goddard b P.M. Pollock		38
N.C. O'Neill	c Goddard b P.M. Pollock	0	c Partridge b Halse		66
P.J.P. Burge	c Halse b P.M. Pollock	91	run out		20
B.C. Booth	c Lindsay b Goddard	58	lbw b P.M. Pollock		24
B.K. Shepherd	lbw b Goddard	70	c Lindsay b Barlow		78
R. Benaud	b Partridge	7	b Barlow		34
G.D. McKenzie	c Lindsay b Goddard	12	c and b Barlow		4
A.T.W. Grout†	c P.M. Pollock b Goddard	0	(10) c Pithey b Halse		23
N.J.N. Hawke	not out	0	(9) c Carlstein b Seymour		0
R.A. Gaunt	run out	1	not out		2
Extras	(B 1, LB 8, NB 5)	14	(LB 4, W 1, NB 3)		8
Total		**345**			**331**

SOUTH AFRICA

T.L. Goddard*	b Hawke	34	not out	34
E.J. Barlow	lbw b Hawke	201	not out	47
A.J. Pithey	c Grout b Hawke	0		
R.G. Pollock	b Hawke	175		
K.C. Bland	c Grout b Gaunt	33		
P.R. Carlstein	c Benaud b Gaunt	37		
D.T. Lindsay†	b Simpson	41		
P.M. Pollock	c Benaud b Hawke	21		
M.A. Seymour	c Simpson b Hawke	3		
J.T. Partridge	b McKenzie	6		
C.G. Halse	not out	19		
Extras	(B 7, LB 8, W 3, NB 7)	25	(W 1)	1
Total		**595**	(0 wickets)	**82**

SOUTH AFRICA	O	M	R	W	O	M	R	W		FALL OF WICKETS				
P.M. Pollock	21	1	96	3	14	1	73	2			A	SA	A	SA
Partridge	22	4	76	1	17	3	76	0	*Wkt*	*1st*	*1st*	*2nd*	*2nd*
Halse	13	1	54	0	13·3	0	50	3	1st	35	70	72	–
Goddard	24·6	4	60	5	21	3	64	0	2nd	37	70	81	–
Seymour	12	2	38	0	19	1	54	1	3rd	141	411	125	–
Bland	1	0	7	0					4th	225	437	178	–
Barlow					5	2	6	3	5th	279	500	210	–
									6th	290	501	301	–
AUSTRALIA									7th	333	559	301	–
Gaunt	24	2	115	2	4	0	22	0	8th	333	568	302	–
McKenzie	30·1	2	156	1	4	0	22	0	9th	344	575	310	–
Hawke	39	5	139	6	6	0	20	0	10th	345	595	331	–
Benaud	20	1	101	0	3	1	17	0					
Simpson	10	1	59	1									

Umpires: C.J. Egar (13) and L.P. Rowan (6).

Close: 1st day – A(1) 281-5 (Shepherd 25, Benaud 2); 2nd – SA(1) 295-2 (Barlow 125, R.G. Pollock 120); 3rd – A(2) 48-0 (Simpson 19, Lawry 28); 4th – A(2) 317-9 (Grout 11, Gaunt 0).

AUSTRALIA v SOUTH AFRICA 1963–64 (5th Test)

Played at Sydney Cricket Ground on 7, 8, 10, 11, 12 February.
Toss: South Africa.   Result: MATCH DRAWN.
Debuts: Nil.

South Africa were left to score 171 runs in 85 minutes to win the rubber after Veivers and Hawke had frustrated them with a last-wicket partnership of 45 in 75 minutes. Unfortunately, Graeme Pollock had fractured a finger when dropping Grout, thus removing their main attacking batsman. In producing his best performance in Tests, Partridge enjoyed a spell of 3 for 0 in nine balls. Benaud ended his distinguished 63-match Test career (28 of them as captain), with 2,201 runs and 248 wickets.

AUSTRALIA

W.M. Lawry*	b Halse	13	c Waite b P.M. Pollock	12
R.B. Simpson*	c Lindsay b Partridge	28	lbw b Partridge	31
N.C. O'Neill	b P.M. Pollock	21	(7) b P.M. Pollock	6
P.J.P. Burge	b Partridge	56	c Partridge b Seymour	39
B.C. Booth	not out	102	(3) c sub (P.R. Carlstein) b Seymour	87
B.K. Shepherd	lbw b Partridge	1	c Bland b Goddard	12
R. Benaud	b Goddard	11	(5) c sub (P.R. Carlstein) b Seymour	3
T.R. Veivers	b Partridge	43	c Barlow b Goddard	39
G.D. McKenzie	b Partridge	0	c Bland b P.M. Pollock	0
N.J.N. Hawke	c Lindsay b Partridge	0	(11) not out	16
A.T.W. Grout†	c Waite b Partridge	29	(10) c Barlow b Partridge	14
Extras	(LB 2, NB 5)	7	(B 5, LB 4, NB 2)	11
Total		**311**		**270**

SOUTH AFRICA

T.L. Goddard*	c Grout b Veivers	93	not out	44
E.J. Barlow	c Benaud b O'Neill	5	not out	32
A.J. Pithey	c Grout b McKenzie	49		
R.G. Pollock	c and b Veivers	17		
K.C. Bland	c Booth b Benaud	126		
J.H.B. Waite†	c Simpson b McKenzie	19		
D.T. Lindsay	c sub (A.N. Connolly) b Benaud	65		
P.M. Pollock	c Lawry b Benaud	6		
M.A. Seymour	c Benaud b McKenzie	0		
J.T. Partridge	lbw b Benaud	6		
C.G. Halse	not out	10		
Extras	(B 4, LB 4, W 1, NB 6)	15		
Total		**411**	(0 wickets)	**76**

SOUTH AFRICA	O	M	R	W	O	M	R	W
P.M. Pollock	22	5	75	1	11	1	35	3
Partridge	31·1	6	91	7	32	5	85	2
Halse	14	3	40	1	7	0	22	0
Goddard	16	1	67	1	24·7	10	29	2
Barlow	9	1	31	0	1	0	8	0
Seymour					38	9	80	3
AUSTRALIA								
McKenzie	37	4	110	3	4	0	16	0
Hawke	22	4	69	0	4	0	16	0
O'Neill	2	0	2	1				
Benaud	49	10	118	4	8	2	25	0
Veivers	35	5	97	2	8	0	19	0

FALL OF WICKETS

Wkt	A 1st	SA 1st	A 2nd	SA 2nd
1st	42	18	29	–
2nd	44	142	49	–
3rd	103	157	132	–
4th	142	182	152	–
5th	144	223	181	–
6th	179	341	189	–
7th	263	365	207	–
8th	263	368	209	–
9th	265	389	225	–
10th	311	411	270	–

Umpires: C.J. Egar (14) and L.P. Rowan (7).

Close: 1st day – A(1) 223-6 (Booth 60, Veivers 27); 2nd – SA(1) 40-1 (Goddard 23, Pithey 8); 3rd – SA(1) 297-5 (Bland 68, Lindsay 34); 4th – A(2) 141-3 (Booth 57, Benaud 0).

INDIA v ENGLAND 1963–64 (1st Test)

Played at Corporation Stadium, Madras, on 10, 11, 12, 14, 15 January.
Toss: India.   Result: MATCH DRAWN.
Debuts: England – D. Wilson.

England, set to score 293 runs in 265 minutes on a dusting pitch and with several players suffering from stomach indispositions, did well to finish 52 runs short of victory and with five wickets intact. Kunderan scored 170 not out off 91 overs in 330 minutes on the first day and went on to record India's highest score against England (subsequently beaten in this rubber). Nadkarni bowled 21 consecutive maiden overs to establish the record for six-ball overs in all first-class cricket. His spell of 131 balls without conceding a run has been beaten only by H.J. Tayfield (137 balls, 16 eight-ball maidens) in *Test No. 436.*

INDIA

V.L. Mehra	c Parks b Titmus	17	run out		26
B.K. Kunderan†	b Titmus	192	lbw b Titmus		38
D.N. Sardesai	b Titmus	65	(4) st Parks b Mortimore		2
V.L. Manjrekar	c Smith b Knight	108	(7) run out		0
Nawab of Pataudi, jr*	lbw b Titmus	0	(6) c Bolus b Titmus		18
S.A. Durani	lbw b Smith	8	(5) c Parks b Mortimore		3
M.L. Jaisimha	lbw b Wilson	51	(3) b Titmus		35
A.G. Kripal Singh	not out	2	b Wilson		10
C.G. Borde	not out	8	not out		11
R.G. Nadkarni	) did not bat		c Parks b Titmus		7
V.B. Ranjane	)				
Extras	(B 1, LB 5)	6	(LB 2)		2
Total	(7 wickets declared)	**457**	(9 wickets declared)		**152**

ENGLAND

J.B. Bolus	lbw b Durani	88	st Kunderan b Borde		22
M.J.K. Smith*	c Kunderan b Ranjane	3	c Kunderan b Nadkarni		57
P.J. Sharpe	lbw b Borde	27	(7) not out		31
D. Wilson	c Manjrekar b Durani	42			
K.F. Barrington	c and b Borde	80			
B.R. Knight	b Durani	6	(4) c Kunderan b Kripal Singh		7
J.M. Parks†	b Borde	27	(3) c Kunderan b Nadkarni		30
F.J. Titmus	c Pataudi b Kripal Singh	14	(6) b Kripal Singh		10
J.B. Mortimore	c and b Borde	0	(5) not out		73
M.J. Stewart	st Kunderan b Borde	15			
J.D.F. Larter	not out	2			
Extras	(B 6, LB 5, NB 2)	13	(B 6, LB 2, NB 3)		11
Total		**317**	(5 wickets)		**241**

ENGLAND	O	M	R	W	O	M	R	W
Larter	19	2	62	0	11	3	33	0
Knight	27	7	73	1	7	1	22	0
Wilson	24	6	67	1	4	2	2	1
Titmus	50	14	116	5	19·5	4	46	4
Mortimore	38	7	110	0	15	3	41	2
Barrington	4	0	23	0	2	0	6	0
INDIA								
Ranjane	16	2	46	1	2	0	14	0
Jaisimha	7	3	16	0	4	2	8	0
Borde	67·4	30	88	5	22	7	44	1
Durani	43	13	97	3	21	8	64	0
Nadkarni	32	27	5	0	6	4	6	2
Kripal Singh	25	10	52	1	26	7	66	2
Manjrekar					3	0	3	0
Mehra					1	0	2	0
Sardesai					1	0	14	0
Pataudi					1	0	9	0

FALL OF WICKETS

	I	E	I	E
Wkt	1st	1st	2nd	2nd
1st	85	12	59	67
2nd	228	49	77	105
3rd	323	116	82	120
4th	323	235	100	123
5th	343	251	104	155
6th	431	263	106	–
7th	447	287	125	–
8th	–	287	135	–
9th	–	314	152	–
10th	–	317	–	–

Umpires: S.K. Banerjee (1) and I. Gopalakrishnan (3).

Close: 1st day – I(1) 277-2 (Kunderan 170, Manjrekar 20); 2nd – E(1) 63-2 (Bolus 25, Wilson 2); 3rd – E(1) 235-4 (Barrington 64, Knight 0); 4th – I(2) 116-6 (Pataudi 7, Kripal Singh 5).

INDIA v ENGLAND 1963–64 (2nd Test)

Played at Brabourne Stadium, Bombay, on 21, 22, 23, 25, 26 January.
Toss: India.   Result: MATCH DRAWN.
Debuts: India – B.S. Chandrasekhar, Rajinder Pal; England – J.G. Binks, I.J. Jones, J.S.E. Price.

A superb performance by England earned the touring team a draw after they had been deprived of the services of Barrington (fractured finger), Edrich, Sharpe and Mortimore (stomach disorders). Barrington and Stewart (who retired from the match with dysentery at tea on the first day) took no further part in the tour. England's ten-man team comprised two specialist batsmen, two wicket-keepers, four fast-medium bowlers and two spinners. The partnership of 153 by Borde and Durani was the highest for the seventh wicket by either side in this series until 1981-82 (*Test No. 917*).

INDIA

V.L. Mehra	lbw b Knight	9	lbw b Titmus	35
B.K. Kunderan†	c Wilson b Price	29	c Titmus b Price	16
D.N. Sardesai	b Price	12	run out	66
V.L. Manjrekar	c Binks b Titmus	0	(8) not out	43
Nawab of Pataudi, jr*	c Titmus b Knight	10	(4) b Price	. 0
M.L. Jaisimha	c Price b Titmus	23	(5) c Larter b Knight	66
C.G. Borde	c Binks b Wilson	84	c Smith b Titmus	7
S.A. Durani	c Binks b Price	90	(6) c Knight b Titmus	3
R.G. Nadkarni	not out	26	lbw b Knight	0
Rajinder Pal	lbw b Larter	3	not out	3
B.S. Chandrasekhar	b Larter	0		
Extras	(B 2, LB 9, NB 3)	14	(LB 4, W 1, NB 5)	10
Total		**300**	(8 wickets declared)	**249**

ENGLAND

J.B. Bolus	c Chandrasekhar b Durani	25	c Pataudi b Durani	57
M.J.K. Smith*	c Borde b Chandrasekhar	46	(4) not out	31
J.M. Parks	run out	1	(5) not out	40
B.R. Knight	b Chandrasekhar	12		
F.J. Titmus	not out	84		
D. Wilson	c and b Durani	1	(3) c Pataudi b Chandrasekhar	2
J.G. Binks†	b Chandrasekhar	10	(2) c Borde b Jaisimha	55
J.S.E. Price	b Chandrasekhar	32		
J.D.F. Larter	c Borde b Durani	0		
I.J. Jones	run out	5		
M.J. Stewart	absent ill	–		
Extras	(B 4, LB 7, NB 6)	17	(B 12, LB 7, W 1, NB 1)	21
Total		**233**	(3 wickets)	**206**

ENGLAND	O	M	R	W	O	M	R	W		FALL OF WICKETS			
Knight	20	3	53	2	13	2	28	2		I	E	I	E
Larter	10·3	2	35	2	5	0	13	0	*Wkt*	*1st*	*1st*	*2nd*	*2nd*
Jones	13	0	48	0	11	1	31	0	1st	20	42	23	125
Price	19	2	66	3	17	1	47	2	2nd	55	48	104	127
Titmus	36	17	56	2	46	18	79	3	3rd	56	82	107	134
Wilson	15	5	28	1	23	10	41	0	4th	58	91	140	–
									5th	75	98	152	–
INDIA									6th	99	116	180	–
Rajinder Pal	11	4	19	0	2	0	3	0	7th	252	184	231	–
Jaisimha	3	1	9	0	22	9	36	1	8th	284	185	231	–
Durani	38	15	59	3	29	12	35	1	9th	300	233	–	–
Borde	34	12	54	0	37	12	38	0	10th	300	–	–	–
Chandrasekhar	40	16	67	4	22	5	40	1					
Nadkarni	4	2	8	0	14	11	3	0					
Sardesai					3	2	6	0					
Mehra					2	1	1	0					
Pataudi					3	0	23	0					

Umpires: H.E. Choudhury (3) and A.M. Mamsa (1).

Close: 1st day – I(1) 225-6 (Borde 58, Durani 73); 2nd – E(1) 144-6 (Titmus 19, Price 21); 3rd – I(2) 91-1 (Mehra 31, Sardesai 42); 4th – E(2) 17-0 (Bolus 7, Binks 5).

INDIA v ENGLAND 1963–64 (3rd Test)

Played at Eden Gardens, Calcutta, on 29, 30 January, 1, 2, 3 February.
Toss: India.   Result: MATCH DRAWN.
Debuts: Nil.

Reinforced by the arrival of Cowdrey and Parfitt, England achieved a first-innings lead of 26. India did not begin their second innings until the fourth day and the match never promised a definite result. 150 minutes of play were lost on the third day when the umpires decided that a shower of rain had rendered the ground unfit. The partnership of 51 between Nadkarni and Chandrasekhar is India's highest for the tenth wicket against England (since equalled).

INDIA

M.L. Jaisimha	c Binks b Price	33	c Larter b Titmus		129
B.K. Kunderan†	c Binks b Price	23	lbw b Wilson		27
D.N. Sardesai	c Binks b Larter	54	c and b Parfitt		36
V.L. Manjrekar	c and b Price	25	b Parfitt		16
R.F. Surti	b Price	0			
C.G. Borde	c Cowdrey b Wilson	21	c Parks b Titmus		8
Nawab of Pataudi, jr*	c Binks b Wilson	2	(5) c Smith b Larter		31
S.A. Durani	c Binks b Price	8	(7) c Cowdrey b Larter		25
R.G. Nadkarni	not out	43	(8) not out		10
R.B. Desai	lbw b Titmus	11	(9) not out		2
B.S. Chandrasekhar	c Cowdrey b Knight	16			
Extras	(LB 1, NB 4)	5	(B 7, LB 5, NB 4)		16
Total		**241**	(7 wickets declared)		**300**

ENGLAND

J.B. Bolus	c and b Durani	39	c Jaisimha b Borde		35
J.G. Binks†	c Desai b Durani	13	b Durani		13
M.J.K. Smith*	c Jaisimha b Borde	19	not out		75
M.C. Cowdrey	c Pataudi b Desai	107	not out		13
J.M. Parks	lbw b Nadkarni	30			
P.H. Parfitt	c and b Desai	4			
D. Wilson	st Kunderan b Chandrasekhar	1			
B.R. Knight	c Manjrekar b Nadkarni	13			
F.J. Titmus	b Desai	26			
J.S.E. Price	not out	1			
J.D.F. Larter	c Manjrekar b Desai	0			
Extras	(B 6, LB 5, NB 3)	14	(B 9)		9
Total		**267**	(2 wickets)		**145**

ENGLAND	O	M	R	W	O	M	R	W	FALL OF WICKETS				
										I	E	I	E
Knight	13·2	5	39	1	4	0	33	0	Wkt	1st	1st	2nd	2nd
Price	23	4	73	5	7	0	31	0	1st	47	40	80	30
Larter	18	4	61	1	8	0	27	2	2nd	61	74	161	87
Titmus	15	4	46	1	46	23	67	2	3rd	103	77	217	–
Wilson	16	10	17	2	21	7	55	1	4th	103	158	218	–
Parfitt					34	16	71	2	5th	150	175	237	–
									6th	158	193	272	–
INDIA									7th	169	214	289	–
Desai	22·5	3	62	4	5	0	12	0	8th	169	258	–	–
Surti	6	2	8	0					9th	190	267	–	–
Jaisimha	4	1	10	0	13	5	32	0	10th	241	267	–	–
Durani	22	7	59	2	8	3	15	1					
Borde	31	14	40	1	15	5	39	1					
Chandrasekhar	21	5	36	1	8	2	20	0					
Nadkarni	42	24	38	2									
Pataudi					3	1	8	0					
Sardesai					3	0	10	0					

Umpires: M.V. Nagendra (1) and S. Roy (2).

Close: 1st day – I(1) 230-9 (Nadkarni 33, Chandrasekhar 15); 2nd – E(1) 149-3 (Cowdrey 41, Parks 29); 3rd – E(1) 235-7 (Cowdrey 90, Titmus 12); 4th – I(2) 180-2 (Jaisimha 103, Manjrekar 4).

INDIA v ENGLAND 1963–64 (4th Test)

Played at Feroz Shah Kotla, Delhi, on 8, 9, 11, 12, 13 February.
Toss: India.   Result: MATCH DRAWN.
Debuts: India – Hanumant Singh.

Hanumant Singh became the third Indian after L. Amarnath and A.A. Baig to score a hundred against England in his first Test match. Pataudi scored India's first double-century against England; his unbroken partnership of 190 with Borde was then India's highest for the fifth wicket against England. Cowdrey scored hundreds in his first two Test innings in India.

INDIA

M.L. Jaisimha	b Titmus	47	st Parks b Parfitt	50
B.K. Kunderan†	b Titmus	40	lbw b Price	100
D.N. Sardesai	c Parks b Mortimore	44	b Wilson	4
Nawab of Pataudi, jr*	b Titmus	13	not out	203
Hanumant Singh	c and b Mortimore	105	c Mortimore b Wilson	23
C.G. Borde	b Price	26	not out	67
S.A. Durani	c Smith b Wilson	16		
A.G. Kripal Singh	b Mortimore	0		
R.G. Nadkarni	run out	34		
R.B. Desai	not out	14		
B.S. Chandrasekhar	run out	0		
Extras	(LB 3, NB 2)	5	(B 5, LB 9, NB 2)	16
Total		**344**	(4 wickets)	**463**

ENGLAND

J.B. Bolus	lbw b Kripal Singh	58
J.H. Edrich	c and b Kripal Singh	41
M.J.K. Smith*	c Pataudi b Kripal Singh	37
D. Wilson	c Pataudi b Chandrasekhar	6
P.H. Parfitt	c Kunderan b Durani	67
M.C. Cowdrey	lbw b Nadkarni	151
J.M. Parks†	c sub (P.C. Poddar) b Chandrasekhar	32
B.R. Knight	c Desai b Nadkarni	21
J.B. Mortimore	c Hanumant b Nadkarni	21
F.J. Titmus	not out	4
J.S.E. Price	b Chandrasekhar	0
Extras	(B 8, LB 3, NB 2)	13
Total		**451**

ENGLAND	O	M	R	W	O	M	R	W
Price	23	3	71	1	9	1	36	1
Knight	11	0	46	0	8	1	47	0
Wilson	22	9	41	1	41	17	74	2
Titmus	49	15	100	3	43	12	105	0
Mortimore	38	13	74	3	32	11	52	0
Parfitt	5	2	7	0	19	3	81	1
Smith					13	0	52	0
INDIA								
Desai	9	2	23	0				
Jaisimha	4	0	14	0				
Kripal Singh	36	13	90	3				
Chandrasekhar	34·3	11	79	3				
Borde	12	2	42	0				
Durani	33	5	93	1				
Nadkarni	57	30	97	3				

FALL OF WICKETS

	I	E	I
Wkt	1st	1st	2nd
1st	81	101	74
2nd	90	114	101
3rd	116	134	226
4th	201	153	273
5th	267	268	–
6th	283	354	–
7th	283	397	–
8th	307	438	–
9th	344	451	–
10th	344	451	–

Umpires: S.P. Pan (3) and B. Satyaji Rao (3).

Close: 1st day – I(1) 247-4 (Hanumant 79, Borde 22); 2nd – E(1) 124-2 (Smith 16, Wilson 2); 3rd – E(1) 254-5 (Cowdrey 102, Parks 32); 4th – I(2) 166-2 (Kunderan 73, Pataudi 31).

INDIA v ENGLAND 1963–64 (5th Test)

Played at Green Park, Kanpur, on 15, 16, 18, 19, 20 February.
Toss: India.   Result: MATCH DRAWN.
Debuts: Nil.

Pataudi won the toss for the fifth time in the rubber. England's total was their highest in India until 1984-85. With the match devoid of interest, Durani reached his fifty in 29 minutes against the bowling of Cowdrey and Parks. It was one minute slower than the fastest Test fifty which J.T. Brown scored for England against Australia in 1894-95 (*Test No. 46*). The third day produced only 136 Indian runs in $5\frac{1}{2}$ hours. Kunderan (525) became the first wicket-keeper to score 500 runs in a Test rubber.

ENGLAND

J.B. Bolus	c Hanumant b Nadkarni	67
J.H. Edrich	c Pataudi b Borde	35
M.J.K. Smith*	c Borde b Gupte	38
B.R. Knight	c Manjrekar b Jaisimha	127
P.H. Parfitt	lbw b Jaisimha	121
M.C. Cowdrey	lbw b Pataudi	38
J.M. Parks†	not out	51
J.B. Mortimore	b Chandrasekhar	19
F.J. Titmus	c and b Nadkarni	5
D. Wilson	not out	18
J.S.E. Price	did not bat	
Extras	(B 29, LB 9, NB 2)	40
Total	(8 wickets declared)	**559**

INDIA

M.L. Jaisimha	c Parks b Titmus	5	c Cowdrey b Titmus	5
B.K. Kunderan†	b Price	5	lbw b Parfitt	55
V.L. Manjrekar	c and b Titmus	33		
D.N. Sardesai	c Mortimore b Parfitt	79	c Edrich b Parks	87
Hanumant Singh	c Parks b Titmus	24		
Nawab of Pataudi, jr*	b Titmus	31		
C.G. Borde	b Titmus	0		
S.A. Durani	b Mortimore	16	(5) not out	61
R.G. Nadkarni	not out	52	(3) not out	122
B.P. Gupte	c and b Titmus	8		
B.S. Chandrasekhar	b Price	3		
Extras	(B 5, LB 1, NB 4)	10	(B 5, LB 11, NB 1)	17
Total		**266**	(3 wickets)	**347**

INDIA	O	M	R	W	O	M	R	W
Jaisimha	19	4	54	2				
Durani	25	8	49	0				
Chandrasekhar	36	7	97	1				
Gupte	40	9	115	1				
Borde	23	4	73	1				
Nadkarni	57	22	121	2				
Pataudi	3	1	10	1				
ENGLAND								
Price	16·1	5	32	2	10	2	27	0
Knight	1	0	4	0	2	0	12	0
Titmus	60	37	73	6	34	12	59	1
Mortimore	48	31	39	1	23	14	28	0
Wilson	27	9	47	0	19	10	26	0
Parfitt	30	12	61	1	27	7	68	1
Edrich					4	1	17	0
Bolus					3	0	16	0
Parks					6	0	43	1
Cowdrey					5	0	34	0

FALL OF WICKETS

Wkt	E 1st	I 1st	I 2nd
1st	63	9	17
2nd	134	17	126
3rd	174	96	270
4th	365	135	–
5th	458	182	–
6th	474	182	–
7th	520	188	–
8th	531	229	–
9th	–	245	–
10th	–	266	–

Umpires: S. Bhattacharya (1) and S.K. Raghunatha Rao (4).

Close: 1st day – E(1) 252-3 (Knight 65, Parfitt 20); 2nd – I(1) 9-1 (Kunderan 4); 3rd – I(1) 145-4 (Sardesai 66, Pataudi 6); 4th – I(2) 86-1 (Kunderan 30, Nadkarni 39).

NEW ZEALAND v SOUTH AFRICA 1963–64 (1st Test)

Played at Basin Reserve, Wellington, on 21, 22, 24, 25 February.
Toss: South Africa.   Result: MATCH DRAWN.
Debuts: New Zealand – S.G. Gedye, J.T. Ward.

Anti-apartheid demonstrators damaged the pitch but failed to prevent the match from starting on time in cold weather and on a very slow surface. Pollock took the last four wickets for 10 runs in 18 balls to produce South Africa's best analysis in a Test in New Zealand. The batting highlight of this dour contest occurred on the last morning when Farrer and Bland added 75 runs in 45 minutes. Against accurate bowling, New Zealand were never on terms with the task of scoring 268 runs in four hours.

SOUTH AFRICA

T.L. Goddard*	b Cameron	24	b Reid	40
E.J. Barlow	b Cameron	22	c Ward b Cameron	92
A.J. Pithey	c Chapple b Motz	31		
W.S. Farrer	b Reid	30	(3) not out	38
K.C. Bland	c Ward b Blair	40	(4) not out	46
J.H.B. Waite†	b Blair	30		
D.T. Lindsay	b Cameron	27		
P.L. van der Merwe	b Motz	44		
D.B. Pithey	b Blair	7		
P.M. Pollock	c Dowling b Reid	24		
J.T. Partridge	not out	2		
Extras	(B 9, LB 3, NB 9)	21	(B 2)	2
Total		**302**	(2 wickets declared)	**218**

NEW ZEALAND

G.T. Dowling	b Pollock	1	lbw b Bland	32
S.G. Gedye	lbw b Pollock	10	c Van der Merwe b Pollock	52
B.W. Sinclair	lbw b D.B. Pithey	44	b Bland	0
J.R. Reid*	c Barlow b Partridge	16	b Goddard	12
S.N. McGregor	b D.B. Pithey	39	lbw b Van der Merwe	24
J.T. Sparling	lbw b Pollock	49	c Van der Merwe b Pollock	1
M.E. Chapple	c Goddard b Partridge	59	not out	0
R.C. Motz	c D.B. Pithey b Pollock	2	not out	0
J.T. Ward†	b Pollock	5		
R.W. Blair	b Pollock	5		
F.J. Cameron	not out	1		
Extras	(B 10, LB 5, NB 7)	22	(B 6, LB 7, W 1, NB 3)	17
Total		**253**	(6 wickets)	**138**

NEW ZEALAND	O	M	R	W	O	M	R	W		FALL OF WICKETS			
Motz	25	3	68	2	15	2	53	0		SA	NZ	SA	NZ
Cameron	30	13	58	3	19	6	60	1	*Wkt*	*1st*	*1st*	*2nd*	*2nd*
Blair	41	10	86	3	11	0	48	0	1st	41	14	117	64
Reid	29·5	12	47	2	21	8	55	1	2nd	56	17	143	64
Sparling	6	1	22	0					3rd	97	49	–	79
									4th	121	112	–	134
SOUTH AFRICA									5th	189	148	–	136
Pollock	31·5	9	47	6	16	4	31	2	6th	198	234	–	138
Partridge	45	24	50	2	14	8	10	0	7th	233	242	–	–
Goddard	38	21	42	0	16	10	11	1	8th	257	243	–	–
Barlow	11	0	38	0	2	1	13	0	9th	292	252	–	–
D.B. Pithey	24	11	53	2	14	3	34	0	10th	302	253	–	–
Bland	3	2	1	0	9	3	16	2					
Van der Merwe					5	4	6	1					

Umpires: D.P. Dumbleton (2) and W.T. Martin (3).

Close: 1st day – SA(1) 233-7 (Van der Merwe 11, D.B. Pithey 0); 2nd – NZ(1) 117-4 (McGregor 27, Sparling 4); 3rd – SA(2) 79-0 (Goddard 30, Barlow 47).

NEW ZEALAND v SOUTH AFRICA 1963–64 (2nd Test)

Played at Carisbrook, Dunedin, on 28 (*no play*), 29 February, 2, 3 March.
Toss: New Zealand.   Result: MATCH DRAWN.
Debuts: New Zealand – W.P. Bradburn.

This match, played in cold and grizzly weather, was overshadowed by the tragic death of P.R. Carlstein's wife and three of his four children in a South African motor accident. Only four hours of play was possible on the first two days. Both sides registered their lowest totals for this series in New Zealand. Remarkably, the second wicket mini-partnership of 51 between Bradburn and Sinclair was a record against South Africa. Reid and Pithey produced the best analyses of their Test careers, Reid's being New Zealand's best effort in all Tests against South Africa. After a spirited attempt, South Africa failed to score 65 runs in the last 27 minutes.

NEW ZEALAND

S.G. Gedye	c Waite b Partridge	6		b D.B. Pithey	25
W.P. Bradburn	b Pollock	32		lbw b D.B. Pithey	14
B.W. Sinclair	c Lindsay b Goddard	52		lbw b Goddard	11
J.R. Reid*	b Pollock	2	(7)	c Bland b D.B. Pithey	2
S.N. McGregor	run out	3	(4)	run out	11
J.T. Sparling	b Pollock	1	(5)	b D.B. Pithey	1
M.E. Chapple	c Farrer b D.B. Pithey	37	(6)	b D.B. Pithey	7
A.E. Dick†	c D.B. Pithey b Partridge	3		lbw b D.B. Pithey	22
R.C. Motz	c D.B. Pithey b Partridge	3		lbw b Pollock	0
R.W. Blair	b Partridge	0		not out	26
F.J. Cameron	not out	1		b Pollock	8
Extras	(B 3, LB 3, NB 3)	9		(LB 7, NB 4)	11
Total		**149**			**138**

SOUTH AFRICA

T.L. Goddard*	c Dick b Reid	63			
E.J. Barlow	b Reid	49		hit wkt b Cameron	13
A.J. Pithey	run out	1			
W.S. Farrer	run out	39			
K.C. Bland	lbw b Reid	1	(1)	not out	16
J.H.B. Waite†	c Sparling b Reid	4			
D.T. Lindsay	c Motz b Reid	20	(3)	b Blair	1
P.L. van der Merwe	c Sinclair b Reid	8	(4)	b Blair	0
D.B. Pithey	c Bradburn b Sparling	9	(5)	not out	8
P.M. Pollock	b Cameron	6			
J.T. Partridge	not out	8			
Extras	(B 6, LB 4, NB 5)	15		(LB 4)	4
Total		**223**		(3 wickets)	**42**

SOUTH AFRICA	O	M	R	W	O	M	R	W	FALL OF WICKETS				
										NZ	SA	NZ	SA
Pollock	27	13	53	3	10·5	2	25	2	*Wkt*	*1st*	*1st*	*2nd*	*2nd*
Partridge	34	15	51	4	5	4	3	0	1st	11	117	38	18
Bland	9	4	9	0					2nd	62	124	42	23
Goddard	17	14	10	1	26	10	29	1	3rd	64	124	63	25
Barlow	3	0	11	0					4th	98	130	64	–
D.B. Pithey	4	1	6	1	35	11	58	6	5th	100	134	67	–
Van der Merwe					8	3	12	0	6th	100	158	72	–
									7th	132	168	73	–
NEW ZEALAND									8th	142	185	79	–
Motz	6	1	23	0					9th	148	209	111	–
Cameron	17·2	3	40	1	4	0	22	1	10th	149	223	138	–
Blair	13	3	35	0	3	0	16	2					
Reid	35	15	60	6									
Chapple	27	14	41	0									
Sparling	7	2	9	1									

Umpires: D.C. Burns (1) and H.B. Cassie (1).

Close: 1st day – no play; 2nd – NZ(1) 114-6 (Chapple 11, Dick 3); 3rd – SA(1) 209-9 (Farrer 33, Partridge 0).

Test No. 560/17

NEW ZEALAND v SOUTH AFRICA 1963–64 (3rd Test)

Played at Eden Park, Auckland, on 13, 14, 16, 17 March.
Toss: New Zealand.   Result: MATCH DRAWN.
Debuts: New Zealand – R.S. Cunis.

New Zealand, set to score 309 runs in 313 minutes, managed to avoid defeat when the last 13 minutes of play were lost to rain. The Pollock and Pithey brothers provided the last instance of two pairs of brothers in one team in a Test. Sinclair batted for 345 minutes and hit 22 fours in compiling New Zealand's highest score in a home Test until 1967-68 (*Test No. 633*). His partnership of 171 with McGregor is the fourth-wicket record for this series. In the same innings, Bland and Lindsay added a record sixth-wicket stand of 83. Blair's analysis of 7 for 142 is New Zealand's best in a home Test in this series, this being the final encounter before South Africa were banished from official Test cricket.

SOUTH AFRICA

T.L. Goddard*	c Sinclair b Cameron	73		c McGregor b Blair	33
E.J. Barlow	c Shrimpton b Blair	61		b Blair	58
A.J. Pithey	c Bradburn b Blair	13			
R.G. Pollock	b Reid	30		c Sinclair b Cunis	23
K.C. Bland	lbw b Cameron	83		not out	21
J.H.B. Waite	c Dick b Cameron	28	(3)	c Sinclair b Blair	41
D.T. Lindsay†	b Blair	37	(6)	b Cunis	1
W.S. Farrer	lbw b Reid	21	(7)	not out	5
D.B. Pithey	c Dick b Blair	1			
P.M. Pollock	c and b Reid	2			
J.T. Partridge	not out	0			
Extras	(B 2, LB 16, NB 4)	22		(LB 17, NB 1)	18
Total		**371**		(5 wickets declared)	**200**

NEW ZEALAND

S.G. Gedye	c Lindsay b Partridge	18	b Partridge	55
W.P. Bradburn	b Partridge	2	c Lindsay b D.B. Pithey	14
B.W. Sinclair	c A.J. Pithey b Barlow	138	c Partridge b D.B. Pithey	19
J.R. Reid*	c Lindsay b Partridge	19	b Goddard	37
S.N. McGregor	hit wkt b P.M. Pollock	62	c Barlow b D.B. Pithey	29
M.J.F. Shrimpton	lbw b Barlow	0	b Goddard	0
M.E. Chapple	b Partridge	4	lbw b Goddard	20
A.E. Dick†	b P.M. Pollock	1	not out	4
R.W. Blair	b Partridge	0	b Goddard	0
R.S. Cunis	lbw b Partridge	0	not out	4
F.J. Cameron	not out	0		
Extras	(B 4, LB 7, NB 8)	19	(B 3, LB 2, NB 4)	9
Total		**263**	(8 wickets)	**191**

NEW ZEALAND	O	M	R	W	O	M	R	W
Cunis	21	2	80	0	17·4	0	47	2
Cameron	39	8	107	3	13	1	39	0
Reid	29·5	12	77	3	13	2	39	0
Blair	36	8	85	4	21	2	57	3
SOUTH AFRICA								
P.M. Pollock	28·3	13	60	2	16	3	42	0
Partridge	40	10	86	6	24	8	47	1
Goddard	26	17	32	0	17	9	18	4
D.B. Pithey	12	3	33	0	25	13	40	3
Barlow	12	5	20	2	16	8	19	0
Bland	13	6	13	0				
R.G. Pollock					3	0	16	0

FALL OF WICKETS

Wkt	SA 1st	NZ 1st	SA 2nd	NZ 2nd
1st	115	7	92	49
2nd	149	34	105	89
3rd	158	76	165	95
4th	202	247	187	145
5th	256	247	190	145
6th	339	260	–	180
7th	357	262	–	182
8th	362	263	–	185
9th	371	263	–	–
10th	371	263	–	–

Umpires: J.M.A. Brown (2) and E.C.A. MacKintosh (1).

Close: 1st day – SA(1) 327-5 (Bland 73, Lindsay 29); 2nd – NZ(1) 185-3 (Sinclair 104, McGregor 34); 3rd – SA(2) 163-2 (Waite 37, R.G. Pollock 23).

ENGLAND v AUSTRALIA 1964 (1st Test)

Played at Trent Bridge, Nottingham, on 4, 5, 6 *(no play)*, 8, 9 June.
Toss: England.   Result: MATCH DRAWN.
Debuts: England – G. Boycott; Australia – G.E. Corling.

Rain interrupted every day except the fourth, a total of $14\frac{3}{4}$ hours being lost. Titmus, who improvised as an opening batsman after Edrich had reported unfit shortly before the start, escaped being run out when Grout declined to break the wicket after the batsman had collided with the bowler in responding to a call for a quick single. Boycott began his crusade in search of the record Test match batting aggregate by steering a boundary off the 16th ball he faced. He was deprived of his second innings by a fielding accident which fractured a finger. When Australia attempted to score 242 runs in 195 minutes, the ever-threatening rain aborted their efforts after 45 minutes. In that period O'Neill hooked the first four balls of Trueman's second over to the boundary before a ball from Flavell damaged his hand and caused his retirement.

ENGLAND

G. Boycott	c Simpson b Corling	48			
F.J. Titmus	c Redpath b Hawke	16		lbw b McKenzie	17
E.R. Dexter*	c Grout b Hawke	9	(1)	c O'Neill b McKenzie	68
M.C. Cowdrey	b Hawke	32	(3)	b McKenzie	33
K.F. Barrington	c Lawry b Veivers	22	(4)	lbw b Corling	33
P.J. Sharpe	not out	35		c and b Veivers	1
J.M. Parks†	c Booth b Veivers	15	(5)	c Hawke b Veivers	19
F.S. Trueman	c Simpson b Veivers	0	(7)	c Grout b McKenzie	4
D.A. Allen	c Grout b McKenzie	21	(8)	lbw b McKenzie	3
L.J. Coldwell	not out	0		not out	0
J.A. Flavell	did not bat		(9)	c Booth b Corling	7
Extras	(B 5, LB 11, NB 2)	18		(B 2, LB 2, W 1, NB 3)	8
Total	(8 wickets declared)	**216**		(9 wickets declared)	**193**

AUSTRALIA

W.M. Lawry	c Barrington b Coldwell	11	run out	3
I.R. Redpath	b Trueman	6	c Parks b Flavell	2
N.C. O'Neill	b Allen	26	retired hurt	24
P.J.P. Burge	lbw b Trueman	31	not out	4
B.C. Booth	run out	0	not out	6
R.B. Simpson*	c Barrington b Titmus	50		
T.R. Veivers	c Trueman b Flavell	8		
G.D. McKenzie	c Parks b Coldwell	4		
N.J.N. Hawke	not out	10		
A.T.W. Grout†	c Parks b Coldwell	13		
G.E. Corling	b Trueman	3		
Extras	(LB 1, NB 5)	6	(NB 1)	1
Total		**168**	(2 wickets)	**40**

AUSTRALIA	O	M	R	W	O	M	R	W
McKenzie	28	7	53	1	24	5	53	5
Corling	23	7	38	1	15·5	4	54	2
Hawke	35	15	68	3	19	5	53	0
Veivers	16	2	39	3	8	0	25	2
ENGLAND								
Trueman	20·3	3	58	3	5	0	28	0
Coldwell	22	3	48	3				
Allen	16	8	22	1				
Flavell	16	3	28	1	4·2	0	11	1
Titmus	4	1	6	1				

FALL OF WICKETS

Wkt	E 1st	A 1st	E 2nd	A 2nd
1st	38	8	90	3
2nd	70	37	95	25
3rd	90	57	147	–
4th	135	61	174	–
5th	141	91	179	–
6th	164	118	180	–
7th	165	137	186	–
8th	212	141	187	–
9th	–	165	193	–
10th	–	168	–	–

Umpires: J.S. Buller (16) and C.S. Elliott (15).

Close: 1st day – E(1) 52-1 (Boycott 23, Dexter 6); 2nd – E(1) 216-8 (Sharpe 35, Coldwell 0); 3rd – no play; 4th – E(2) 71-0 (Dexter 56, Titmus 13).

ENGLAND v AUSTRALIA 1964 (2nd Test)

Played at Lord's, London, on 18 *(no play)*, 19 *(no play)*, 20, 22, 23 June.
Toss: England.   Result: MATCH DRAWN.
Debuts: England – N. Gifford.

Over half the possible playing time was lost to rain which prevented a start until the third day and ended the match just before 2.30 on the fifth afternoon. John Edrich, a cousin of W.J., completed a century in his first Test against Australia shortly after The Queen arrived. He batted for 379 minutes and hit two sixes and nine fours. Redpath was becalmed on 36 for the last 53 minutes of his 3¾-hour innings.

AUSTRALIA

W.M. Lawry	b Trueman	4	c Dexter b Gifford		20
I.R. Redpath	c Parfitt b Coldwell	30	lbw b Titmus		36
N.C. O'Neill	c Titmus b Dexter	26	c Parfitt b Trueman		22
P.J.P. Burge	lbw b Dexter	1	c Parfitt b Titmus		59
B.C. Booth	lbw b Trueman	14	not out		2
R.B. Simpson*	c Parfitt b Trueman	0	not out		15
T.R. Veivers	b Gifford	54			
G.D. McKenzie	b Trueman	10			
A.T.W. Grout†	c Dexter b Gifford	14			
N.J.N. Hawke	not out	5			
G.E. Corling	b Trueman	0			
Extras	(B 8, LB 5, NB 5)	18	(B 8, LB 4, NB 2)		14
Total		**176**	(4 wickets)		**168**

ENGLAND

E.R. Dexter*	b McKenzie	2
J.H. Edrich	c Redpath b McKenzie	120
M.C. Cowdrey	c Burge b Hawke	10
K.F. Barrington	lbw b McKenzie	5
P.H. Parfitt	lbw b Corling	20
P.J. Sharpe	lbw b Hawke	35
J.M. Parks†	c Simpson b Hawke	12
F.J. Titmus	b Corling	15
F.S. Trueman	b Corling	8
N. Gifford	c Hawke b Corling	5
L.J. Coldwell	not out	6
Extras	(LB 7, NB 1)	8
Total		**246**

ENGLAND	O	M	R	W	O	M	R	W
Trueman	25	8	48	5	18	6	52	1
Coldwell	23	7	51	1	19	4	59	0
Gifford	12	6	14	2	17	9	17	1
Dexter	7	1	16	2	3	0	5	0
Titmus	17	6	29	0	17	7	21	2
AUSTRALIA								
McKenzie	26	8	69	3				
Corling	27·3	9	60	4				
Hawke	16	4	41	3				
Veivers	9	4	17	0				
Simpson	21	8	51	0				

FALL OF WICKETS

	A	E	A
Wkt	1st	1st	2nd
1st	8	2	35
2nd	46	33	76
3rd	58	42	143
4th	84	83	148
5th	84	138	–
6th	88	170	–
7th	132	227	–
8th	163	229	–
9th	167	235	–
10th	176	246	–

Umpires: J.S. Buller (17) and J.F. Crapp (1).

Close: 1st day – no play; 2nd – no play; 3rd – E(1) 26-1 (Edrich 15, Cowdrey 9); 4th – A(2) 49-1 (Redpath 15, O'Neill 9).

ENGLAND v AUSTRALIA 1964 (3rd Test)

Played at Headingley, Leeds, on 2, 3, 4, 6 July.
Toss: England.   Result: AUSTRALIA won by seven wickets.
Debuts: Australia – R.M. Cowper.

Australia achieved the only victory of the rubber and so retained the Ashes. Dexter took the second new ball when Australia's first innings total was 187 for 7, and, after struggling against the off-spin of Titmus, Burge (then 38 not out) took his score to 160 ($5\frac{1}{4}$ hours, 24 fours) and added a further 202 runs. The first seven overs of the new ball conceded 42 runs. In the second innings Titmus, who took the new ball in the absence of Flavell (strained Achilles tendon), conceded only 12 runs in his first 24 overs. Parfitt had his knuckle broken by the first ball he received in the second innings, retired at 13 and returned at the fall of the seventh wicket.

ENGLAND

G. Boycott	c Simpson b Corling	38	c Simpson b Corling	4
J.H. Edrich	c Veivers b McKenzie	3	c Grout b McKenzie	32
E.R. Dexter*	c Grout b McKenzie	66	(5) c Redpath b Veivers	17
K.F. Barrington	b McKenzie	29	lbw b Veivers	85
P.H. Parfitt	b Hawke	32	(3) c Redpath b Hawke	6
K. Taylor	c Grout b Hawke	9	(8) b Veivers	15
J.M. Parks†	c Redpath b Hawke	68	(6) c Booth b McKenzie	23
F.J. Titmus	c Burge b McKenzie	3	(9) c Cowper b Corling	14
F.S. Trueman	c Cowper b Hawke	4	(10) not out	12
N. Gifford	not out	1	(7) b McKenzie	1
J.A. Flavell	c Redpath b Hawke	5	c Simpson b Corling	5
Extras	(LB 9, NB 1)	10	(B 6, LB 6, W 1, NB 2)	15
Total		**268**		**229**

AUSTRALIA

W.M. Lawry	run out	78	c Gifford b Trueman	1
R.B. Simpson*	b Gifford	24	c Barrington b Titmus	30
I.R. Redpath	b Gifford	20	not out	58
P.J.P. Burge	c sub (A. Rees) b Trueman	160	b Titmus	8
B.C. Booth	st Parks b Titmus	4	not out	12
R.M. Cowper	b Trueman	2		
T.R. Veivers	c Parks b Titmus	8		
G.D. McKenzie	b Titmus	0		
N.J.N. Hawke	c Parfitt b Trueman	37		
A.T.W. Grout†	lbw b Titmus	37		
G.E. Corling	not out	2		
Extras	(B 1, LB 8, W 2, NB 6)	17	(B 1, LB 1)	2
Total		**389**	(3 wickets)	**111**

AUSTRALIA	O	M	R	W	O	M	R	W	FALL OF WICKETS				
McKenzie	26	7	74	4	28	8	53	3		E	A	E	A
Hawke	31·3	11	75	5	13	1	28	1	*Wkt*	*1st*	*1st*	*2nd*	*2nd*
Corling	24	7	50	1	17·5	6	52	3	1st	17	50	13	3
Veivers	17	3	35	0	30	12	70	3	2nd	74	124	88	45
Simpson	5	0	24	0	1	0	11	0	3rd	129	129	145	64
									4th	138	154	156	–
ENGLAND									5th	163	157	169	–
Trueman	24·3	2	98	3	7	0	28	1	6th	215	178	184	–
Flavell	29	5	97	0					7th	232	178	192	–
Gifford	34	15	62	2	20	5	47	0	8th	260	283	199	–
Dexter	19	5	40	0	3	0	9	0	9th	263	372	212	–
Titmus	50	24	69	4	27	19	25	2	10th	268	389	229	–
Taylor	2	0	6	0									

Umpires: C.S. Elliott (16) and W.F.F. Price (1).

Close: 1st day – E(1) 268 all out; 2nd – A(1) 283-8 (Burge 100); 3rd – E(2) 157-4 (Parks 8, Gifford 0).

ENGLAND v AUSTRALIA 1964 (4th Test)

Played at Old Trafford, Manchester, on 23, 24, 25, 27, 28 July.
Toss: Australia.   Result: MATCH DRAWN.
Debuts: England -- T.W. Cartwright, F.E. Rumsey.

Australia's total of 656 for 8 declared remains the highest in any Manchester Test. Simpson scored his maiden Test hundred in his 52nd innings; his 311 is still the highest score in an Old Trafford Test and the highest by a Test captain. Only Bradman (334 in *Test No. 196*) has made a higher score for Australia. His innings lasted 762 minutes, remains the longest against England and was then the third-longest in all first-class cricket. His partnership of 201 with Lawry was then an Australian first-wicket record against England. Barrington's tenth Test hundred was his first in England and his score of 256 remains England's highest at Manchester. Veivers, brought on for just one over, established a record for this series by bowling 571 balls in an innings, including a spell of 51 overs unchanged. Only S. Ramadhin (588 balls in *Test No. 439*) has bowled more overs in a first-class innings. This is the only instance in Test cricket of both sides scoring over 600 runs in one innings.

AUSTRALIA

W.M. Lawry	run out	106	not out	0
R.B. Simpson*	c Parks b Price	311	not out	4
I.R. Redpath	lbw b Cartwright	19		
N.C. O'Neill	b Price	47		
P.J.P. Burge	c Price b Cartwright	34		
B.C. Booth	c and b Price	98		
T.R. Veivers	c Edrich b Rumsey	22		
A.T.W. Grout†	c Dexter b Rumsey	0		
G.D. McKenzie	not out	0		
N.J.N. Hawke	} did not bat			
G.E. Corling	}			
Extras	(B 1, LB 9, NB 9)	19		
Total	(8 wickets declared)	**656**	(0 wickets)	**4**

ENGLAND

G. Boycott	b McKenzie	58
J.H. Edrich	c Redpath b McKenzie	.6
E.R. Dexter*	b Veivers	174
K.F. Barrington	lbw b McKenzie	256
P.H. Parfitt	c Grout b McKenzie	12
J.M. Parks†	c Hawke b Veivers	60
F.J. Titmus	c Simpson b McKenzie	9
J.B. Mortimore	c Burge b McKenzie	12
T.W. Cartwright	b McKenzie	4
J.S.E. Price	b Veivers	1
F.E. Rumsey	not out	3
Extras	(B 5, LB 11)	16
Total		**611**

ENGLAND	O	M	R	W	O	M	R	W
Rumsey	35·5	4	99	2				
Price	45	4	183	3				
Cartwright	77	32	118	2				
Titmus	44	14	100	0	1	1	0	0
Dexter	4	0	12	0				
Mortimore	49	13	122	0				
Boycott	1	0	3	0				
Barrington					1	0	4	0
AUSTRALIA								
McKenzie	60	15	153	7				
Corling	46	11	96	0				
Hawke	63	28	95	0				
Simpson	19	4	59	0				
Veivers	95·1	36	155	3				
O'Neill	10	0	37	0				

FALL OF WICKETS

	A	E	A
Wkt	1st	1st	2nd
1st	201	15	–
2nd	233	126	–
3rd	318	372	–
4th	382	417	–
5th	601	560	–
6th	646	589	–
7th	652	594	–
8th	656	602	–
9th	–	607	–
10th	–	611	–

Umpires: J.S. Buller (18) and W.F.F. Price (2).

Close: 1st day – A(1) 253-2 (Simpson 109, O'Neill 10); 2nd – A(1) 570-4 (Simpson 265, Booth 82); 3rd – E(1) 162-2 (Dexter 71, Barrington 20); 4th – E(1) 411-3 (Barrington 153, Parfitt 12).

ENGLAND v AUSTRALIA 1964 (5th Test)

Played at Kennington Oval, London, on 13, 14, 15, 17, 18 (*no play*) August.
Toss: England.   Result: MATCH DRAWN.
Debuts: Nil.

Trueman became the first bowler to take 300 wickets in Test matches when he had Hawke caught by Cowdrey at first slip on the third afternoon. Barrington scored his 4,000th run in Test cricket during the first innings and Cowdrey his 5,000th during the second. Boycott produced the first of his 22 hundreds for England before rain washed out the final day with England 184 runs in front. McKenzie's 29 wickets equalled the current record set by C.V. Grimmett in 1930 as the most by an Australian in a rubber in England.

ENGLAND

G. Boycott	b Hawke	30	c Redpath b Simpson	113
R.W. Barber	b Hawke	24	lbw b McKenzie	29
E.R. Dexter*	c Booth b Hawke	23	c Simpson b McKenzie	25
M.C. Cowdrey	c Grout b McKenzie	20	(5) not out	93
K.F. Barrington	c Simpson b Hawke	47	(6) not out	54
P.H. Parfitt	b McKenzie	3		
J.M. Parks†	c Simpson b Corling	10		
F.J. Titmus	c Grout b Hawke	8	(4) b McKenzie	56
F.S. Trueman	c Redpath b Hawke	14		
T.W. Cartwright	c Grout b McKenzie	0		
J.S.E. Price	not out	0		
Extras	(LB 3)	3	(B 6, LB 4, NB 1)	11
Total		**182**	(4 wickets)	**381**

AUSTRALIA

R.B. Simpson*	c Dexter b Cartwright	24
W.M. Lawry	c Trueman b Dexter	94
N.C. O'Neill	c Parfitt b Cartwright	11
P.J.P. Burge	lbw b Titmus	25
B.C. Booth	c Trueman b Price	74
I.R. Redpath	b Trueman	45
A.T.W. Grout†	b Cartwright	20
T.R. Veivers	not out	67
G.D. McKenzie	c Cowdrey b Trueman	0
N.J.N. Hawke	c Cowdrey b Trueman	14
G.E. Corling	c Parfitt b Trueman	0
Extras	(B 4, LB 1)	5
Total		**379**

AUSTRALIA	O	M	R	W	O	M	R	W
McKenzie	26	6	87	3	38	5	112	3
Corling	14	2	32	1	25	4	65	0
Hawke	25·4	8	47	6	39	8	89	0
Veivers	6	1	13	0	47	15	90	0
Simpson					14	7	14	1
ENGLAND								
Trueman	33·3	6	87	4				
Price	21	2	67	1				
Cartwright	62	23	110	3				
Titmus	42	20	51	1				
Barber	6	1	23	0				
Dexter	13	1	36	1				

FALL OF WICKETS

	E	A	E
Wkt	1st	1st	2nd
1st	44	45	80
2nd	61	57	120
3rd	82	96	200
4th	111	202	255
5th	117	245	–
6th	141	279	–
7th	160	343	–
8th	173	343	–
9th	174	367	–
10th	182	379	–

Umpires: J.F. Crapp (2) and C.S. Elliott (17).

Close: 1st day – A(1) 3-0 (Simpson 0, Lawry 3); 2nd – A(1) 245-5 (Redpath 13, Grout 0); 3rd – E(2) 132-2 (Boycott 74, Titmus 0); 4th – E(2) 381-4 (Cowdrey 93, Barrington 54).

INDIA v AUSTRALIA 1964–65 (1st Test)

Played at Corporation Stadium, Madras, on 2, 3, 4, 6, 7 October.
Toss: Australia.   Result: AUSTRALIA won by 139 runs.
Debuts: India – K.S. Indrajitsinhji.

Australia won their third consecutive Test at Madras. They completed their victory with 109 minutes to spare after India had been left to score 333 runs in 390 minutes. Pataudi's 128 not out remains the highest score by an Indian captain against Australia. He emulated his father by scoring a hundred in his first innings against Australia (*see Test No. 220*). In the second innings, Veivers shared in two record Australian partnerships against India: 64 with Martin for the seventh wicket, and 73 for the eighth with McKenzie.

AUSTRALIA

W.M. Lawry	b Nadkarni	62	c sub (R.F. Surti) b Nadkarni		41
R.B. Simpson*	st Indrajitsinhji b Durani	30	run out		77
N.C. O'Neill	b Durani	40	b Nadkarni		0
P.J.P. Burge	b Nadkarni	20	lbw b Nadkarni		60
B.C. Booth	lbw b Nadkarni	8	c Indrajitsinhji b Durani		29
J.W. Martin	c Indrajitsinhji b Kripal Singh	20	(8) c Nadkarni b Ranjane		39
I.R. Redpath	c Hanumant b Nadkarni	10	(6) c Indrajitsinhji b Nadkarni		0
T.R. Veivers	b Kripal Singh	0	(7) c Pataudi b Nadkarni		74
G.D. McKenzie	not out	8	c Sardesai b Ranjane		27
A.T.W. Grout†	c Jaisimha b Nadkarni	0	c Hanumant b Nadkarni		12
N.J.N. Hawke	b Kripal Singh	0	not out		1
Extras	(LB 6, NB 7)	13	(B 15, LB 11, NB 11)		37
Total		**211**			**397**

INDIA

M.L. Jaisimha	lbw b McKenzie	29	b McKenzie		0
K.S. Indrajitsinhji†	c Grout b Hawke	4	b Hawke		0
D.N. Sardesai	b McKenzie	0	c Redpath b Martin		14
V.L. Manjrekar	c Grout b Martin	33	c Simpson b O'Neill		40
Hanumant Singh	c Grout b Martin	0	(6) c O'Neill b Veivers		94
Nawab of Pataudi, jr*	not out	128	(7) b McKenzie		1
C.G. Borde	c Simpson b McKenzie	49	(8) b McKenzie		0
S.A. Durani	c Grout b McKenzie	5	(10) c O'Neill b Veivers		10
R.G. Nadkarni	lbw b Hawke	3	c Simpson b Hawke		20
A.G. Kripal Singh	b McKenzie	0	(5) b McKenzie		1
V.B. Ranjane	c Redpath b McKenzie	2	not out		0
Extras	(B 13, LB 9, NB 1)	23	(B 11, LB 2)		13
Total		**276**			**193**

INDIA	O	M	R	W	O	M	R	W		FALL OF WICKETS			
Ranjane	7	0	30	0	12	1	53	2		A	I	A	I
Jaisimha	4	1	13	0	9	2	13	0	*Wkt*	*1st*	*1st*	*2nd*	*2nd*
Durani	21	5	68	2	40	9	102	1	1st	66	12	91	0
Kripal Singh	18	5	43	3	38	13	91	0	2nd	127	13	91	0
Borde	4	2	13	0	5	2	10	0	3rd	139	55	175	23
Nadkarni	18	6	31	5	54·4	21	91	6	4th	161	56	228	24
									5th	174	76	232	117
AUSTRALIA									6th	203	218	237	130
McKenzie	32·3	8	58	6	20	9	33	4	7th	203	232	301	130
Hawke	33	13	55	2	17	7	26	2	8th	203	249	374	168
Redpath	2	1	1	0					9th	209	256	392	191
Simpson	12	3	23	0	5	3	9	0	10th	211	276	397	193
Martin	26	11	63	2	16	4	43	1					
Booth	10	4	14	0	3	0	10	0					
Veivers	10	2	20	0	10	4	18	2					
O'Neill	7	3	19	0	9	3	41	1					

Umpires: M.V. Nagendra (2) and S. Roy (3).

Close: 1st day – I(1) 34-2 (Jaisimha 13, Manjrekar 12); 2nd – I(1) 241-7 (Pataudi 98, Nadkarni 1); 3rd – A(2) 154-2 (Simpson 67, Burge 33); 4th – I(2) 24-4 (Manjrekar 8, Hanumant 0).

INDIA v AUSTRALIA 1964–65 (2nd Test)

Played at Brabourne Stadium, Bombay, on 10, 11, 12, 14, 15 October.
Toss: Australia.   Result: INDIA won by two wickets.
Debuts: Nil.

A last-day crowd of 42,000 saw India gain only their second victory in 15 Tests against Australia. They accomplished this with just two wickets and half an hour to spare. The result might well have been reversed if O'Neill had not succumbed to an indigenous internal malady on the first morning. Curiously, none of the 11 fifties made in this match was converted into a hundred.

AUSTRALIA

W.M. Lawry	c Indrajitsinhji b Durani	16	lbw b Chandrasekhar	68
R.B. Simpson*	b Chandrasekhar	27	c Hanumant b Surti	20
B.C. Booth	b Chandrasekhar	1	(5) st Indrajitsinhji b Nadkarni	74
P.J.P. Burge	c Chandrasekhar b Borde	80	b Chandrasekhar	0
R.M. Cowper	lbw b Nadkarni	20	(3) c Indrajitsinhji b Nadkarni	81
T.R. Veivers	c Borde b Chandrasekhar	67	lbw b Chandrasekhar	0
B.N. Jarman†	c Durani b Surti	78	b Chandrasekhar	0
J.W. Martin	c Nadkarni b Chandrasekhar	0	c Surti b Nadkarni	16
G.D. McKenzie	b Nadkarni	17	c Surti b Nadkarni	4
A.N. Connolly	not out	0	not out	0
N.C. O'Neill	absent ill	–	absent ill	–
Extras	(B 7, LB 4, NB 3)	14	(B 4, NB 7)	11
Total		**320**		**274**

INDIA

D.N. Sardesai	c Simpson b Connolly	3	lbw b McKenzie	56
M.L. Jaisimha	b Veivers	66	c Jarman b Connolly	0
S.A. Durani	c Jarman b Simpson	12	c Cowper b Simpson	31
V.L. Manjrekar	c Cowper b Veivers	59	(8) c Simpson b Connolly	39
Hanumant Singh	b Veivers	14	(6) b McKenzie	11
Nawab of Pataudi, jr*	c McKenzie b Veivers	86	(7) c Burge b Connolly	53
C.G. Borde	c Simpson b Martin	4	(9) not out	30
R.F. Surti	c Jarman b Connolly	21	(5) c Booth b Veivers	10
R.G. Nadkarni	c Jarman b Martin	34	(4) c Simpson b Veivers	0
K.S. Indrajitsinhji†	c sub (I.R. Redpath) b Connolly	23	not out	3
B.S. Chandrasekhar	not out	1		
Extras	(B 4, LB 8, NB 6)	18	(B 15, LB 8)	23
Total		**341**	(8 wickets)	**256**

INDIA	O	M	R	W	O	M	R	W		FALL OF WICKETS			
Surti	18	1	70	1	21	5	77	1		A	I	A	I
Jaisimha	8	1	20	0	11	4	18	0	Wkt	1st	1st	2nd	2nd
Durani	20	5	78	1	15	3	48	0	1st	35	7	59	4
Chandrasekhar	26	10	50	4	30	11	73	4	2nd	36	30	121	70
Nadkarni	24·5	6	65	2	20·4	10	33	4	3rd	53	142	121	71
Borde	7	0	23	1	2	0	14	0	4th	142	149	246	99
									5th	146	181	247	113
AUSTRALIA									6th	297	188	247	122
McKenzie	22	2	49	0	21	6	43	2	7th	303	255	257	215
Connolly	22·3	5	66	3	18	8	24	3	8th	304	293	265	224
Martin	34	11	72	2	14	2	35	0	9th	320	331	274	–
Simpson	13	1	40	1	24	12	34	1	10th	–	341	–	–
Veivers	48	20	68	4	43·4	12	82	2					
Cowper	13	3	28	0	4	0	14	0					
Booth					4	3	1	0					

Umpires: H.E. Choudhury (4) and S.K. Raghunatha Rao (5).

Close: 1st day – A(1) 301-6 (Veivers 65, Martin 0); 2nd – I(1) 178-4 (Hanumant 11, Pataudi 17); 3rd – A(2) 112-1 (Lawry 63, Cowper 22); 4th – I(2) 74-3 (Sardesai 36, Surti 1).

INDIA v AUSTRALIA 1964–65 (3rd Test)

Played at Eden Gardens, Calcutta, on 17, 18, 20, 21 (*no play*), 22 (*no play*) October.
Toss: India.   Result: MATCH DRAWN.
Debuts: Australia – R.H.D. Sellers.

For only the third time in 54 Tests staged in India, rain seriously interrupted play. As on both previous occasions, in *Tests No. 358* and *515*, two days were completely lost. Durani, slow left-arm, returned a career-best analysis to bring about Australia's dramatic first innings collapse which saw all ten wickets fall for 77 – some 20 runs fewer than the opening partnership.

AUSTRALIA

W.M. Lawry	b Durani	50	not out	47
R.B. Simpson*	lbw b Surti	67	c Hanumant b Surti	71
R.M. Cowper	c Nadkarni b Durani	4	not out	14
P.J.P. Burge	c Hanumant b Durani	4		
B.C. Booth	b Durani	0		
I.R. Redpath	not out	32		
T.R. Veivers	c Pataudi b Durani	2		
B.N. Jarman†	b Durani	1		
G.D. McKenzie	st Indrajitsinhji b Surti	0		
R.H.D. Sellers	b Surti	0		
A.N. Connolly	c Hanumant b Chandrasekhar	0		
Extras	(B 1, LB 8, NB 5)	14	(B 6, NB 5)	11
Total		**174**	(1 wicket)	**143**

INDIA

D.N. Sardesai	c Veivers b Booth	42
M.L. Jaisimha	c Booth b Simpson	57
S.A. Durani	c Simpson b Veivers	12
V.L. Manjrekar	lbw b Veivers	9
Hanumant Singh	c Burge b Veivers	5
Nawab of Pataudi, jr*	b Simpson	2
R.G. Nadkarni	b McKenzie	24
C.G. Borde	not out	68
R.F. Surti	c Sellers b Simpson	9
K.S. Indrajitsinhji†	st Jarman b Booth	2
B.S. Chandrasekhar	b Simpson	1
Extras	(B 4)	4
Total		**235**

INDIA	O	M	R	W	O	M	R	W		FALL OF WICKETS		
										A	I	A
Surti	21	7	38	3	10	2	37	1	*Wkt*	*1st*	*1st*	*2nd*
Jaisimha	5	3	2	0	2	1	4	0	1st	97	60	115
Durani	28	11	73	6	18	3	59	0	2nd	104	97	–
Chandrasekhar	28·5	15	39	1	8	3	27	0	3rd	109	119	–
Nadkarni	2	0	8	0	8	6	5	0	4th	109	127	–
									5th	145	129	–
AUSTRALIA									6th	165	133	–
McKenzie	13	1	31	1					7th	167	166	–
Connolly	8	4	10	0					8th	167	187	–
Veivers	52	18	81	3					9th	169	196	–
Sellers	5	1	17	0					10th	174	235	–
Booth	18	10	33	2								
Cowper	6	0	14	0								
Simpson	28	12	45	4								

Umpires: S.P. Pan (4) and B. Satyaji Rao (4).

Close: 1st day – A(1) 167-6 (Redpath 25, Jarman 1); 2nd – I(1) 130-5 (Pataudi 1, Nadkarni 0); 3rd – A(2) 143-1 (Lawry 47, Cowper 14); 4th – no play.

PAKISTAN v AUSTRALIA 1964–65 (Only Test)

Played at National Stadium, Karachi, on 24, 25, 27, 28, 29 October.
Toss: Pakistan.   Results: MATCH DRAWN.
Debuts: Pakistan – Abdul Kadir, Asif Iqbal (*who played Ranji Trophy cricket for Hyderabad as 'A.I. Razvi'*), Khalid Ibadulla (*who played for Warwickshire, Tasmania and Otago as 'K. Ibadulla'*), Majid Jahangir Khan (*who has appeared as 'Majid Jahangir' and as 'M.J. Khan' for Cambridge University and Glamorgan; he is shown throughout this book as 'Majid Khan'*), Pervez Sajjad, Shafqat Rana.

Khalid Ibadulla became the first Pakistan batsman to score a hundred in his first Test match and he equalled Saeed Ahmed's current record score of 166 (*Test No. 480*) for Pakistan against Australia. His partnership of 249 with Abdul Kadir set a new Pakistan record for any wicket and remains their first-wicket record in all Tests. Simpson was the first visiting batsman to score a hundred in each innings of a Test in Pakistan. Australia were set to score 342 runs in 290 minutes.

PAKISTAN

Khalid Ibadulla	c Grout b McKenzie	166	c Redpath b McKenzie		3
Abdul Kadir†	run out	95	hit wkt b Veivers		26
Saeed Ahmed	c Redpath b Martin	7	(4) c sub (R.H.D. Sellers) b Martin		35
Javed Burki	hit wkt b McKenzie	8	(5) c Grout b Cowper		62
Hanif Mohammad*	c and b McKenzie	2	(6) c McKenzie b Booth		40
Shafqat Rana	c Grout b McKenzie	0	(7) lbw b McKenzie		24
Nasim-ul-Ghani	c Redpath b Hawke	15	(8) c Grout b Veivers		22
Majid Khan	lbw b Martin	0			
Intikhab Alam	c Grout b McKenzie	53	not out		21
Asif Iqbal	c Booth b McKenzie	41	(3) c and b Simpson		36
Pervez Sajjad	not out	3			
Extras	(B 9, LB 12, NB 3)	24	(B 1, LB 6, NB 3)		10
Total		**414**	(8 wickets declared)		**279**

AUSTRALIA

W.M. Lawry	hit wkt b Majid	7	c Ibadulla b Majid		22
R.B. Simpson*	c Pervez b Saeed	153	c Ibadulla b Nasim		115
I.R. Redpath	lbw b Intikhab	19	not out		40
P.J.P. Burge	c Majid b Pervez	54	not out		28
B.C. Booth	c Asif b Majid	15			
R.M. Cowper	b Asif	16			
T.R. Veivers	st Kadir b Saeed	25			
J.W. Martin	b Asif	26			
A.T.W. Grout†	c Asif b Saeed	0			
G.D. McKenzie	lbw b Intikhab	2			
N.J.N. Hawke	not out	8			
Extras	(B 12, LB 8, NB 7)	27	(LB 14, NB 8)		22
Total		**352**	(2 wickets)		**227**

AUSTRALIA	O	M	R	W	O	M	R	W		FALL OF WICKETS			
McKenzie	30	9	69	6	25	5	62	2		P	A	P	A
Hawke	20	2	84	1	6	2	20	0	*Wkt*	*1st*	*1st*	*2nd*	*2nd*
Martin	36	11	106	2	17	4	42	1	1st	249	10	13	54
Veivers	16	5	33	0	30	16	44	2	2nd	266	78	65	173
Simpson	30	8	69	0	20	5	47	1	3rd	284	194	81	–
Booth	5	2	15	0	13	4	18	1	4th	296	228	118	–
Redpath	1	0	14	0					5th	296	257	202	–
Cowper					11	3	36	1	6th	301	315	224	–
PAKISTAN									7th	302	315	236	–
Majid	30	9	55	2	16	3	42	1	8th	334	315	279	–
Asif	23·5	5	68	2	12	4	28	0	9th	383	320	–	–
Pervez	22	5	52	1	8	2	17	0	10th	414	352	–	–
Intikhab	28	5	83	2	16	3	48	0					
Nasim	4	0	17	0	12	3	24	1					
Saeed	19	5	41	3	13	6	28	0					
Ibadulla	7	3	9	0	2	0	14	0					
Burki					2	1	3	0					
Shafqat					1	0	1	0					

Umpires: Daud Khan (9) and Shujauddin (8).

Close: 1st day – P(1) 284-3 (Burki 2); 2nd – A(1) 151-2 (Simpson 72, Burge 34); 3rd – P(2) 28-1 (Kadir 9, Asif 15); 4th – P(2) 248-7 (Nasim 10, Intikhab 3).

AUSTRALIA v PAKISTAN 1964–65 (Only Test)

Played at Melbourne Cricket Ground on 4, 5, 7, 8 December.
Toss: Australia.   Result: MATCH DRAWN.
Debuts: Australia – I.M. Chappell, D.J. Sincock; Pakistan – Arif Butt, Farooq Hamid, Mohammad Ilyas.

Hanif, captaining Pakistan in their first Test in Australia, made top score in both innings, became the first Pakistan batsman to score 3,000 runs in Tests, and kept wicket throughout in place of Abdul Kadir, who was injured while batting. Two series partnership records were set which still survive; Cowper and Veivers added 139 for Australia's sixth wicket, before Intikhab and Afaq put on 56 for the ninth in Pakistan's second innings. Arif Butt's analysis of 6 for 89 was the best by a Pakistan bowler on debut until 1969-70 (*Test No. 662*).

PAKISTAN

Abdul Kadir†	c Chappell b McKenzie	0	(7) c Jarman b Hawke	35
Mohammad Ilyas	run out	6	lbw b McKenzie	3
Saeed Ahmed	c Chappell b Hawke	80	c Chappell b McKenzie	24
Javed Burki	c Simpson b McKenzie	29	b Hawke	47
Hanif Mohammad*	c McKenzie b Sincock	104	st Jarman b Veivers	93
Nasim-ul-Ghani	b McKenzie	27	b Sincock	10
Asif Iqbal	c McKenzie b Hawke	1	(8) c Jarman b Hawke	15
Intikhab Alam	c Shepherd b Hawke	13	(9) c Simpson b Hawke	61
Afaq Hussain	not out	8	(10) not out	13
Arif Butt	c Chappell b Sincock	7	(1) c Jarman b McKenzie	12
Farooq Hamid	b Sincock	0	b McKenzie	3
Extras	(B 4, LB 4, W 3, NB 1)	12	(B 5, LB 2, W 2, NB 1)	10
Total		**287**		**326**

AUSTRALIA

R.B. Simpson*	b Arif	47	c Hanif b Arif	1
W.M. Lawry	c Hanif b Arif	41	run out	19
I.M. Chappell	c Hanif b Farooq	11		
B.K. Shepherd	c sub (Ghulam Abbas) b Asif	55	(3) not out	43
B.C. Booth	c Hanif b Arif	57		
R.M. Cowper	c Intikhab b Saeed	83		
T.R. Veivers	c Hanif b Arif	88	(4) not out	16
B.N. Jarman†	b Asif	33		
D.J. Sincock	b Arif	7		
G.D. McKenzie	b Arif	1		
N.J.N. Hawke	not out	1		
Extras	(B 6, LB 3, W 1, NB 14)	24	(B 2, LB 4, W 2, NB 1)	9
Total		**448**	(2 wickets)	**88**

AUSTRALIA	O	M	R	W	O	M	R	W					
McKenzie	22	5	66	3	24·4	1	74	4					
Hawke	21	1	69	3	21	2	72	4					
Sincock	17·6	0	67	3	28	5	102	1					
Simpson	9	1	21	0									
Chappell	15	2	49	0	11	2	31	0					
Veivers	3	2	3	0	12	4	37	1					
PAKISTAN													
Farooq	19	1	82	1	4	0	25	0					
Asif	19	1	90	2	2	0	25	0					
Arif	21·3	1	89	6	5·5	0	29	1					
Afaq	9	1	45	0									
Intikhab	10	0	51	0									
Saeed	10	0	31	1									
Nasim	4	0	36	0									

FALL OF WICKETS

Wkt	P 1st	A 1st	P 2nd	A 2nd
1st	0	81	6	12
2nd	18	105	37	55
3rd	112	105	46	–
4th	127	200	130	–
5th	225	233	152	–
6th	226	372	198	–
7th	255	418	229	–
8th	275	434	267	–
9th	287	446	323	–
10th	287	448	326	–

Umpires: C.J. Egar (15) and W. Smyth (3).

Close: 1st day – P(1) 287-9 (Afaq 8); 2nd – A(1) 255-5 (Cowper 24, Veivers 5); 3rd – P(2) 130-3 (Burki 47, Hanif 41).

SOUTH AFRICA v ENGLAND 1964–65 (1st Test)

Played at Kingsmead, Durban, on 4, 5, 7, 8 December.
Toss: England.   Result: ENGLAND won by an innings and 104 runs.
Debuts: South Africa – G.D. Varnals; England – N.I. Thomson.

England's victory, gained shortly after lunch on the penultimate day, ended a run of 12 consecutive matches without a win – at that time their longest sequence without a success. The unbroken partnership of 206 between Barrington and Parks remains the sixth-wicket record for this series. Barrington's hundred was his eleventh for England and his tenth overseas. He became the first to score a Test hundred in all seven Test-playing countries.

ENGLAND

G. Boycott	lbw b Partridge	73
R.W. Barber	b Goddard	74
E.R. Dexter	c and b Seymour	28
K.F. Barrington	not out	148
P.H. Parfitt	c Goddard b Partridge	0
M.J.K. Smith*	c Lindsay b Partridge	35
J.M. Parks†	not out	108
F.J. Titmus	)	
D.A. Allen	) did not bat	
N.I. Thomson	)	
J.S.E. Price	)	
Extras	(B 2, LB 1, NB 16)	19
Total	(5 wickets declared)	**485**

SOUTH AFRICA

T.L. Goddard*	c Smith b Price	8	c Thomson b Titmus	15
E.J. Barlow	b Thomson	2	c Barrington b Price	0
A.J. Pithey	b Allen	15	c Dexter b Allen	43
R.G. Pollock	b Titmus	5	c Smith b Titmus	0
K.C. Bland	c Barber b Allen	26	c Barber b Titmus	68
D.T. Lindsay†	c Price b Barber	38	c Dexter b Titmus	10
R.A. McLean	c Smith b Allen	30	c Smith b Allen	9
G.D. Varnals	b Allen	3	c Parks b Thomson	11
M.A. Seymour	not out	15	b Titmus	36
P.M. Pollock	c Dexter b Barber	3	not out	18
J.T. Partridge	b Allen	6	run out	1
Extras	(B 4)	4	(B 9, LB 6)	15
Total		**155**		**226**

SOUTH AFRICA	O	M	R	W	O	M	R	W		FALL OF WICKETS		
P.M. Pollock	33	11	80	0						E	SA	SA
Partridge	45	14	85	3					*Wkt*	*1st*	*1st*	*2nd*
Barlow	20	5	36	0					1st	120	10	4
Seymour	46	4	144	1					2nd	169	10	28
Goddard	32	8	79	1					3rd	205	19	28
R.G. Pollock	10	1	32	0					4th	206	54	123
Bland	4	1	10	0					5th	279	67	142
									6th	–	120	145
ENGLAND									7th	–	130	157
Price	6	2	19	1	9	7	7	1	8th	–	131	178
Thomson	15	5	23	1	13	6	25	1	9th	–	142	225
Titmus	20	9	20	1	45·5	19	66	5	10th	–	155	226
Allen	19·5	5	41	5	47	15	99	2				
Barber	14	1	48	2	6	2	8	0				
Parfitt					2	0	6	0				

Umpires: J.G. Draper (1) and H.C. Kidson (3).

Close: 1st day – E(1) 260-4 (Barrington 48, Smith 27); 2nd – SA(1) 20-3 (Pithey 5, Bland 0); 3rd – SA(2) 122-3 (Pithey 42, Bland 58).

SOUTH AFRICA v ENGLAND 1964–65 (2nd Test)

Played at New Wanderers, Johannesburg, on 23, 24, 26, 28, 29 December.
Toss: England.   Result: MATCH DRAWN.
Debuts: Nil.

England again enforced the follow-on and Barrington scored his second hundred in consecutive innings. Rain and bad light prevented play after tea on the fifth day. The last of Dexter's nine Test hundreds completed his set of centuries against the other six current Test-playing nations. Bland ensured a draw for South Africa by batting for 248 minutes (two sixes and 17 fours) and producing the highest of his three Test hundreds.

ENGLAND

G. Boycott	c Lindsay b P.M. Pollock	4
R.W. Barber	b Seymour	97
E.R. Dexter	c Lindsay b R.G. Pollock	172
K.F. Barrington	c R.G. Pollock b P.M. Pollock	121
P.H. Parfitt	c Goddard b Partridge	52
M.J.K. Smith*	c McLean b Goodard	25
J.M. Parks†	lbw b R.G. Pollock	26
F.J. Titmus	b P.M. Pollock	2
D.A. Allen	lbw b P.M. Pollock	2
N.I. Thomson	not out	27
J.S.E. Price	b P.M. Pollock	0
Extras	(LB 3)	3
Total		**531**

SOUTH AFRICA

T.L. Goddard*	b Titmus	40	c Smith b Allen		50
E.J. Barlow	c Price b Titmus	71	c Smith b Allen		15
A.J. Pithey	b Allen	85	c Dexter b Allen		6
R.G. Pollock	c Smith b Titmus	12	(5) b Allen		55
K.C. Bland	c Thomson b Price	29	(6) not out		144
R.A. McLean	lbw b Barber	12	(4) b Titmus		24
G.D. Varnals	b Price	21	c Parks b Dexter		23
D.T. Lindsay†	b Thomson	10	not out		4
M.A. Seymour	run out	2			
P.M. Pollock	c Smith b Titmus	20			
J.T. Partridge	not out	13			
Extras	(LB 2)	2	(B 4, LB 8, NB 3)		15
Total		**317**	(6 wickets)		**336**

SOUTH AFRICA	O	M	R	W	O	M	R	W
P.M. Pollock	38·3	10	129	5				
Partridge	40	10	106	1				
Goddard	31	8	90	1				
Seymour	35	10	109	1				
Barlow	8	2	33	0				
R.G. Pollock	11	1	50	2				
Bland	3	0	11	0				
ENGLAND								
Price	32	11	66	2	15	3	49	0
Thomson	23	8	47	1	16	5	36	0
Titmus	39·5	15	73	4	45	18	101	1
Dexter	4	0	16	0	8	0	33	1
Allen	39	19	45	1	49	17	87	4
Barrington	4	0	29	0				
Barber	14	1	33	1	2	0	12	0
Parfitt	4	2	6	0				
Boycott					5	3	3	0

FALL OF WICKETS

	E	SA	SA
Wkt	1st	1st	2nd
1st	10	78	50
2nd	146	139	74
3rd	337	153	75
4th	419	211	109
5th	467	231	196
6th	477	271	320
7th	484	271	–
8th	490	282	–
9th	526	285	–
10th	531	317	–

Umpires: L.M. Baxter (1) and H.C. Kidson (4).

Close: 1st day – E(1) 329-2 (Dexter 147, Barrington 59); 2nd – SA(1) 9-0 (Goddard 0, Barlow 9); 3rd – SA(1) 261-5 (Pithey 80, Varnals 16); 4th – SA(2) 146-4 (R.G. Pollock 37, Bland 10).

SOUTH AFRICA v ENGLAND 1964–65 (3rd Test)

Played at Newlands, Cape Town, on 1, 2, 4, 5, 6 January.
Toss: South Africa.   Result: MATCH DRAWN.
Debuts: South Africa – G.G. Hall.

South Africa won their first toss in eight Tests against England. Barrington 'walked' after being given not out. For the first time in Test cricket, 20 players bowled in the match, the two excluded being the wicket-keepers, Parks and Lindsay. In a stalemate on the final day, eight occasional bowlers were called upon; Barrington and Boycott seized this opportunity to record their best analyses for England.

SOUTH AFRICA

T.L. Goddard*	b Titmus	40	c Parfitt b Price	6
E.J. Barlow	c Parks b Thomson	138	c Parks b Dexter	78
A.J. Pithey	c Barber b Allen	154	c Parks b Thomson	2
R.G. Pollock	c Parks b Allen	31	(5) b Boycott	73
K.C. Bland	run out	78	(6) b Boycott	64
D.T. Lindsay†	lbw b Thomson	2	(7) b Barrington	50
G.D. Varnals	c Smith b Titmus	19	(4) c Smith b Parfitt	20
S.F. Burke	not out	10	c Barber b Boycott	20
P.M. Pollock	)		lbw b Barrington	7
H.D. Bromfield	) did not bat		not out	12
G.G. Hall	)		b Barrington	0
Extras	(B 5, LB 11, W 1, NB 12)	29	(B 1, LB 9, W 1, NB 3)	14
Total	(7 wickets declared)	**501**		**346**

ENGLAND

G. Boycott	c Barlow b Bromfield	15	not out	1
R.W. Barber	lbw b Goddard	58		
E.R. Dexter	c and b Bromfield	61		
K.F. Barrington	c Lindsay b P.M. Pollock	49	(2) not out	14
P.H. Parfitt	b Hall	44		
M.J.K. Smith*	c Goddard b Bromfield	121		
J.M. Parks†	c Lindsay b Barlow	59		
F.J. Titmus	c Lindsay b P.M. Pollock	4		
D.A. Allen	c Barlow b Bromfield	22		
N.I. Thomson	c R.G. Pollock b Bromfield	0		
J.S.E. Price	not out	0		
Extras	(B 2, LB 5, NB 2)	9		
Total		**442**	(0 wickets)	**15**

ENGLAND	O	M	R	W	O	M	R	W		FALL OF WICKETS			
										SA	E	SA	E
Price	34	6	133	0	11	4	19	1	Wkt	1st	1st	2nd	2nd
Thomson	45	19	89	2	14	4	31	1	1st	80	72	10	–
Titmus	50·2	11	133	2	6	2	21	0	2nd	252	80	13	–
Dexter	2	0	10	0	17	3	64	1	3rd	313	170	86	–
Allen	40	14	79	2	17	6	27	0	4th	430	206	144	–
Parfitt	8	0	28	0	19	4	74	1	5th	439	243	231	–
Barber					1	0	2	0	6th	470	360	256	–
Boycott					20	5	47	3	7th	501	368	310	–
Smith					11	1	43	0	8th	–	438	331	–
Barrington					3·1	1	4	3	9th	–	440	334	–
SOUTH AFRICA									10th	–	442	346	–
P.M. Pollock	39	14	89	2									
Burke	29	8	61	0									
Bromfield	57·2	26	88	5									
Hall	31	7	94	1									
Goddard	37	13	64	1									
Barlow	12	3	37	1									
Bland					2	0	3	0					
R.G. Pollock					2	1	5	0					
Pithey					2	0	5	0					
Varnals					2	1	2	0					

Umpires: V. Costello (6) and J.E. Warner (2).

Close: 1st day – SA(1) 252-1 (Barlow 138, Pithey 59); 2nd – E(1) 24-0 (Boycott 11, Barber 11); 3rd – E(1) 240-4 (Parfitt 43, Smith 13); 4th – SA(2) 39-2 (Barlow 22, Varnals 4).

SOUTH AFRICA v ENGLAND 1964–65 (4th Test)

Played at New Wanderers, Johannesburg, on 22, 23, 25, 26, 27 January.
Toss: England.   Result: MATCH DRAWN.
Debuts: Nil.

England elected to field in South Africa for the first time since 1930-31 (*Test No. 208*). Rain caused the loss of 195 minutes of play during the first two days. The partnership of 157 between Pithey and Waite remains South Africa's highest for the fifth wicket against England. Goddard scored his first Test hundred in his 62nd innings. In the first innings, Van der Merwe (leg slip) threw down the wicket after the ball had been tossed to him by the wicket-keeper. The batsman, Smith, who had gone down the pitch 'gardening', was given out by umpire Kidson but was recalled after Goddard had asked for the appeal to be revoked. Barber fractured a finger when fielding and was unable to bat in the second innings.

SOUTH AFRICA

T.L. Goddard*	run out	60	c Barber b Price		112
E.J. Barlow	c and b Cartwright	96	c Barber b Titmus		42
K.C. Bland	c Parks b Price	55	(5) not out		38
A.J. Pithey	c Cartwright b Titmus	95	(3) b Cartwright		39
R.G. Pollock	c Parks b Price	4	(4) not out		65
J.H.B. Waite†	run out	64			
P.L. van der Merwe	not out	5			
P.M. Pollock	not out	0			
H.D. Bromfield	)				
A.K. McKinnon	) did not bat				
J.T. Partridge	)				
Extras	(LB 7, NB 4)	11	(LB 7, NB 4)		11
Total	(6 wickets declared)	**390**	(3 wickets declared)		**307**

ENGLAND

G. Boycott	c Barlow b Partridge	5	not out		76
R.W. Barber	lbw b McKinnon	61			
E.R. Dexter	c Waite b Goddard	38	c R.G. Pollock b P.M. Pollock		0
K.F. Barrington	c Waite b Barlow	93	c Bromfield b McKinnon		11
P.H. Parfitt	not out	122	c Barlow b McKinnon		22
M.J.K. Smith*	c R.G. Pollock b McKinnon	42	b Bromfield		8
J.M. Parks†	c Barlow b Partridge	0	c R.G. Pollock b McKinnon		10
F.J. Titmus	lbw b McKinnon	1	(2) c Van der Merwe b P.M. Pollock	13
T.W. Cartwright	b McKinnon	9	(8) not out		8
N.I. Thomson	c Barlow b P.M. Pollock	3			
J.S.E. Price	c Bromfield b P.M. Pollock	0			
Extras	(B 1, LB 5, W 1, NB 3)	10	(LB 5)		5
Total		**384**	(6 wickets)		**153**

ENGLAND	O	M	R	W	O	M	R	W
Price	17	1	68	2	14	1	56	1
Thomson	31	3	91	0	19	4	43	0
Cartwright	55	18	97	1	24	6	99	1
Dexter	6	0	30	0				
Titmus	29	2	68	1	31	4	98	1
Boycott	8	1	25	0				
SOUTH AFRICA								
P.M. Pollock	15·2	4	42	2	11	3	27	2
Partridge	30	6	92	2	7	4	10	0
Barlow	18	5	34	1				
Goddard	16	4	35	1	6	4	5	0
McKinnon	51	13	128	4	35	17	44	3
R.G. Pollock	4	0	12	0	11	2	35	0
Bromfield	13	4	31	0	17	8	27	1

FALL OF WICKETS

Wkt	SA 1st	E 1st	SA 2nd	E 2nd
1st	134	7	65	21
2nd	189	78	180	21
3rd	222	144	211	33
4th	226	244	–	80
5th	383	333	–	107
6th	389	333	–	124
7th	–	338	–	–
8th	–	350	–	–
9th	–	374	–	–
10th	–	384	–	–

Umpires: L.M. Baxter (2) and H.C. Kidson (5).

Close: 1st day – SA(1) 192-2 (Bland 32, Pithey 0); 2nd – SA(1) 390-6 (Van der Merwe 5, P.M. Pollock 0); 3rd – E(1) 297-4 (Parfitt 67, Smith 24); 4th – SA(2) 171-1 (Goddard 89, Pithey 35).

SOUTH AFRICA v ENGLAND 1964–65 (5th Test)

Played at St. George's Park, Port Elizabeth, on 12, 13, 15, 16, 17 February.
Toss: South Africa.   Result: MATCH DRAWN.
Debuts: South Africa – M.J. Macaulay; England – K.E. Palmer.

England's thirteenth draw in fifteen matches secured a 1-0 victory in the rubber. With Price, Brown and Cartwright injured, England called upon Palmer who had been coaching in Johannesburg. Graeme Pollock became the second player after G.A. Headley to score three hundreds before attaining the age of 21. Rain restricted play to 19·2 overs after lunch on the fifth day, England having been set to score 246 runs in 233 minutes. This match marked the retirement of South Africa's most experienced wicket-keeper batsman, John Waite. In 50 Tests he scored 2,405 runs and four centuries, and made 141 dismissals.

SOUTH AFRICA

T.L. Goddard*	c Boycott b Allen	61	c Boycott b Thomson		13
E.J. Barlow	c Parfitt b Boycott	69	b Titmus		47
K.C. Bland	c Parfitt b Titmus	48	c and b Thomson		22
R.G. Pollock	c and b Allen	137	not out		77
A.J. Pithey	c Barrington b Allen	23			
J.H.B. Waite†	run out	6			
P.L. van der Merwe	c Barrington b Palmer	66			
P.M. Pollock	c Titmus b Thomson	18			
M.J. Macaulay	b Titmus	21	(5) c Titmus b Boycott		12
A.H. McKinnon	run out	27	(6) not out		0
H.D. Bromfield	not out	1			
Extras	(B 10, LB 11, NB 4)	25	(B 1, LB 4, NB 2)		7
Total		**502**	(4 wickets declared)		**178**

ENGLAND

G. Boycott	c Van der Merwe b Bromfield	117	c Waite b Macaulay		7
J.T. Murray	lbw b Macaulay	4	not out		8
F.J. Titmus	b P.M. Pollock	12			
E.R. Dexter	run out	40	(3) not out		5
K.F. Barrington	c Van der Merwe b Goddard	72			
N.I. Thomson	c Barlow b McKinnon	39			
M.J.K. Smith*	c Waite b Barlow	26			
P.H. Parfitt	lbw b Barlow	0			
J.M. Parks†	c Waite b Barlow	35			
D.A. Allen	not out	38·			
K.E. Palmer	lbw b Goddard	10			
Extras	(B 7, LB 14, W 2, NB 19)	42	(B 7, LB 2)		9
Total		**435**	(1 wicket)		**29**

ENGLAND	O	M	R	W	O	M	R	W		FALL OF WICKETS			
Thomson	47	7	128	1	25	7	55	2			SA	E	SA	E
Palmer	35	6	113	1	28	1	76	0	*Wkt*	*1st*	*1st*	*2nd*	*2nd*
Boycott	26	7	69	1	2	0	13	1	1st	114	28	30	17
Titmus	37·1	7	87	2	5	0	27	1	2nd	171	52	69	–
Allen	44	13	80	3					3rd	185	115	124	–
SOUTH AFRICA									4th	268	272	171	–
P.M. Pollock	27	8	71	1	5·2	1	7	0	5th	276	277	–	–
Macaulay	37	13	63	1	9	4	10	1	6th	389	346	–	–
Goddard	35·5	18	34	2	5	3	3	0	7th	447	346	–	–
McKinnon	46	17	99	1					8th	455	346	–	–
Barlow	22	2	55	3					9th	498	410	–	–
Bromfield	33	14	57	1					10th	502	435	–	–
R.G. Pollock	7	3	14	0									

Umpires: L.M. Baxter (3) and H.C. Kidson (6).

Close: 1st day – SA(1) 261-3 (R.G. Pollock 56, Pithey 22); 2nd – E(1) 29-1 (Boycott 23, Titmus 0); 3rd – E(1) 278-5 (Thomson 1, Smith 0); 4th – SA(2) 62-1 (Barlow 28, Bland 19).

NEW ZEALAND v PAKISTAN 1964–65 (1st Test)

Played at Basin Reserve, Wellington, on 22, 23, 25, 26 January.
Toss: Pakistan.   Result: MATCH DRAWN.
Debuts: New Zealand – R.O. Collinge, B.E. Congdon; Pakistan – Naushad Ali.

Only two hours of play were possible on the first day. New Zealand's last six wickets fell for the addition of just five runs, the last four falling in five balls. Pakistan, set to score 259 runs in 188 minutes, lost seven wickets for 104 before their eighth-wicket pair played out the last 34 minutes. Asif Iqbal achieved his best bowling analysis in 45 Tests.

NEW ZEALAND

S.G. Gedye	b Asif	1	b Arif		26
G.T. Dowling	c Burki b Pervez	29	b Arif		19
B.W. Sinclair	c Nasim b Saeed	65	c Saeed b Pervez		17
B.E. Congdon	c Naushad b Asif	42	b Asif		30
J.R. Reid*	b Arif	97	c Saeed b Pervez		14
S.N. McGregor	lbw b Asif	11	not out		37
B.W. Yuile	b Asif	4	(8) run out		7
A.E. Dick†	b Arif	1			
R.C. Motz	b Asif	0	(7) b Arif		13
R.O. Collinge	not out	0			
F.J. Cameron	lbw b Arif	0			
Extras	(B 2, LB 14)	16	(B 12, LB 3, NB 1)		16
Total		**266**	(7 wickets declared)		**179**

PAKISTAN

Naushad Ali†	run out	11	c and b Motz		3
Mohammad Ilyas	b Collinge	13	c Reid b Motz		4
Saeed Ahmed	c Congdon b Motz	11	c Yuile b Collinge		4
Javed Burki	b Motz	0	c Dick b Collinge		0
Hanif Mohammad*	b Collinge	5	b Collinge		25
Abdul Kadir	c and b Motz	46	b Motz		0
Nasim-ul-Ghani	b Cameron	16	c Dowling b Reid		23
Asif Iqbal	c Sinclair b Yuile	30	not out		52
Intikhab Alam	b Motz	28	not out		13
Arif Butt	b Yuile	20			
Pervez Sajjad	not out	1			
Extras	(B 2, LB 4)	6	(B 8, LB 6, W 1, NB 1)		16
Total		**187**	(7 wickets)		**140**

PAKISTAN	O	M	R	W	O	M	R	W
Arif	22·2	10	46	3	29	10	62	3
Asif	25	11	48	5	20·4	6	33	1
Pervez	24	7	48	1	25	5	61	2
Intikhab	17	6	35	0	5	1	7	0
Saeed	16	7	40	1	1	1	0	0
Nasim	3	1	5	0				
Ilyas	7	1	28	0				
NEW ZEALAND								
Collinge	17	6	51	2	13	3	43	3
Cameron	19	11	33	1	8	5	10	0
Motz	20	9	45	4	15	6	34	3
Yuile	26	16	28	2	8	2	21	0
Reid	13	6	24	0	8	3	16	1

FALL OF WICKETS

	NZ	P	NZ	P
Wkt	1st	1st	2nd	2nd
1st	1	26	35	3
2nd	82	26	62	8
3rd	114	26	83	10
4th	223	41	102	17
5th	261	47	140	19
6th	261	64	156	64
7th	266	114	179	104
8th	266	144	–	–
9th	266	179	–	–
10th	266	187	–	–

Umpires: D.E.A. Copps (1) and W.T. Martin (4).

Close: 1st day – NZ(1) 54-1 (Dowling 19, Sinclair 31); 2nd – P(1) 26-0 (Naushad 11, Ilyas 13); 3rd – NZ(2) 64-2 (Gedye 17, Congdon 2).

NEW ZEALAND v PAKISTAN 1964–65 (2nd Test)

Played at Eden Park, Auckland, on 29, 30 January, 1, 2 February.
Toss: Pakistan.   Result: MATCH DRAWN.
Debuts: New Zealand – R.W. Morgan.

Pakistan scored only 161 for 8 off 131 overs, including 71 maidens, on the first day. Intikhab and Arif Butt set the present ninth-wicket record for Pakistan in this series by adding 52 together. Cameron's innings analysis (5 for 34) is the best against Pakistan in New Zealand, while his match figures (9 for 70) are New Zealand's best in this series in either country. New Zealand needed 220 runs to win in four hours. Pervez took four wickets for no runs in ten balls.

PAKISTAN

Naushad Ali†	b Yuile	14	c Yuile b Reid	8
Abdul Kadir	c and b Yuile	12	b Collinge	58
Saeed Ahmed	c Dick b Yuile	17	c Dick b Cameron	16
Javed Burki	c sub (S.G. Gedye) b Cameron	63	c Congdon b Collinge	15
Nasim-ul-Ghani	c Dowling b Yuile	2	lbw b Cameron	14
Hanif Mohammad*	b Collinge	27	c Congdon b Collinge	27
Mohammad Ilyas	lbw b Cameron	10	lbw b Reid	36
Asif Iqbal	c Morgan b Collinge	3	b Cameron	0
Intikhab Alam	lbw b Cameron	45	c Morgan b Cameron	7
Arif Butt	b Cameron	20	c Dick b Cameron	0
Pervez Sajjad	not out	2	not out	0
Extras	(B 5, LB 4, NB 2)	11	(B 9, LB 8, NB 9)	26
Total		**226**		**207**

NEW ZEALAND

G.T. Dowling	lbw b Asif	0	c Asif b Nasim	62
B.E. Congdon	b Asif	9	c Intikhab b Pervez	42
R.W. Morgan	b Pervez	66	b Asif	5
J.R. Reid*	run out	52	b Pervez	11
S.N. McGregor	c Hanif b Saeed	1	c Saeed b Pervez	0
P.G.Z. Harris	c Hanif b Asif	1	b Pervez	0
B.W. Yuile	b Asif	0	(8) not out	30
A.E. Dick†	b Saeed	19	(9) not out	3
R.C. Motz	c Naushad b Asif	31	(7) c Intikhab b Pervez	0
R.O. Collinge	b Arif	13		
F.J. Cameron	not out	5		
Extras	(B 7, LB 8, NB 2)	17	(B 6, LB 2, NB 5)	13
Total		**214**	(7 wickets)	**166**

NEW ZEALAND	O	M	R	W	O	M	R	W
Collinge	28	8	57	2	22·1	9	41	3
Motz	12	4	15	0	6	1	15	0
Cameron	26	11	36	4	23	11	34	5
Yuile	54	38	43	4	30	15	39	0
Reid	20	14	26	0	19	7	52	2
Harris	7	2	14	0				
Morgan	7	3	24	0				
PAKISTAN								
Arif	17·4	4	43	1	6	1	19	0
Asif	27	6	52	5	18	4	40	1
Intikhab	29	10	52	0	15	7	17	0
Pervez	15	4	35	1	25	7	42	5
Saeed	10	4	15	2	9	3	14	0
Ilyas					2	0	12	0
Nasim					5	2	9	1

FALL OF WICKETS

	P	NZ	P	NZ
Wkt	*1st*	*1st*	*2nd*	*2nd*
1st	19	9	25	68
2nd	44	25	51	82
3rd	70	101	75	102
4th	99	113	95	102
5th	129	125	139	102
6th	151	127	197	102
7th	156	148	200	150
8th	159	195	207	–
9th	211	195	207	–
10th	226	214	207	–

Umpires: E.C.A. MacKintosh (2) and R.W.R. Shortt (3).

Close: 1st day – P(1) 161-8 (Intikhab 4, Arif 0); 2nd – NZ(1) 122-4 (Morgan 5, Harris 1); 3rd – P(2) 129-4 (Kadir 43, Hanif 19).

NEW ZEALAND v PAKISTAN 1964–65 (3rd Test)

Played at Lancaster Park, Christchurch, on 12, 13, 15, 16 February.
Toss: Pakistan.   Result: MATCH DRAWN.
Debuts: New Zealand – P.B. Truscott; Pakistan – Mufasir-ul-Haq.

Rain ended the first day's play at 3.21 pm. Sinclair, who was struck in the face by a ball from Mufasir in the first innings, retired hurt and resumed his innings at the fall of the sixth wicket. New Zealand were set to score 314 runs in 243 minutes.

PAKISTAN

Khalid Ibadulla	c Ward b Cameron	28	b Collinge	9
Naushad Ali†	c Truscott b Motz	12	c Collinge b Yuile	20
Javed Burki	b Collinge	4	(4) b Collinge	12
Saeed Ahmed	c Ward b Cameron	1	(3) lbw b Reid	87
Hanif Mohammad*	c and b Collinge	10	not out	100
Mohammad Ilyas	st Ward b Yuile	88	b Yuile	13
Nasim-ul-Ghani	b Motz	5	b Collinge	12
Asif Iqbal	c Motz b Yuile	3	c Bartlett b Cameron	20
Intikhab Alam	c Sinclair b Yuile	27	c Reid b Yuile	15
Pervez Sajjad	b Motz	9	not out	0
Mufasir-ul-Haq	not out	8		
Extras	(LB 4, NB 7)	11	(B 9, LB 6, W 1, NB 5)	21
Total		**206**	(8 wickets declared)	**309**

NEW ZEALAND

B.E. Congdon	b Mufasir	21	c Hanif b Asif	8
P.B. Truscott	lbw b Asif	3	c and b Asif	26
B.W. Sinclair	c Naushad b Intikhab	46	(6) not out	7
R.W. Morgan	c Nasim b Mufasir	19	(3) c and b Mufasir	97
J.R. Reid*	b Asif	27	(4) c Ilyas b Intikhab	28
B.W. Yuile	c Hanif b Nasim	7	(5) c Ilyas b Pervez	42
G.A. Bartlett	b Pervez	1	not out	4
R.C. Motz	c Naushad b Pervez	21		
J.T. Ward†	c Naushad b Asif	2		
R.O. Collinge	c Hanif b Asif	32		
F.J. Cameron	not out	8		
Extras	(B 3, LB 3, W 1, NB 8)	15	(B 7, NB 4)	11
Total		**202**	(5 wickets)	**223**

NEW ZEALAND	O	M	R	W	O	M	R	W
Bartlett	18	6	47	0	14·3	2	46	0
Collinge	12	3	23	2	17	3	50	3
Cameron	24	15	29	2	14	2	61	1
Motz	18	4	48	3	17	7	43	0
Yuile	11	3	48	3	20	9	64	3
Reid					11	5	24	1
PAKISTAN								
Asif	25·5	9	46	4	16	6	29	2
Mufasir	29	11	50	2	8	1	34	1
Ibadulla	9	5	17	0	3	0	12	0
Pervez	21	6	53	2	21	8	33	1
Intikhab	7	1	17	1	21	6	60	1
Nasim	4	3	3	1	3	1	5	0
Saeed	3	2	1	0	8	1	25	0
Ilyas					3	0	14	0

FALL OF WICKETS

	P	NZ	P	NZ
Wkt	1st	1st	2nd	2nd
1st	36	7	27	18
2nd	41	34	58	41
3rd	42	76	97	98
4th	62	81	159	179
5th	66	83	199	219
6th	78	112	222	–
7th	81	129	254	–
8th	132	137	300	–
9th	160	178	–	–
10th	206	202	–	–

Umpires: F.R. Goodall (1) and W.T. Martin (5).

Close: 1st day – P(1) 109-7 (Ilyas 16, Intikhab 22); 2nd – NZ(1) 130-7 (Sinclair 21, Ward 0); 3rd – P(2) 181-4 (Hanif 27, Ilyas 13).

INDIA v NEW ZEALAND 1964–65 (1st Test)

Played at Corporation Stadium, Madras, on 27, 28 February, 1, 2 March.
Toss: India.   Result: MATCH DRAWN.
Debuts: India – S. Venkataraghavan; New Zealand – T.W. Jarvis, V. Pollard.

The partnership of 143 between Nadkarni and Engineer (whose 90 was scored in 115 minutes) remains India's highest eighth-wicket stand against all countries. Jarvis batted for 125 minutes for nine runs in the first innings. Sardesai retired hurt after being struck on the knee in Motz's opening over with one run scored. Manjrekar scored his seventh Test hundred in his final Test innings. Ward and Collinge added 61 in 72 minutes for the record last-wicket partnership in this series. Pataudi left New Zealand an hour in which to score 282 runs.

INDIA

D.N. Sardesai	b Pollard	22	retired hurt	0
M.L. Jaisimha	c Morgan b Motz	51	c Collinge b Yuile	49
V.L. Manjrekar	c Dowling b Pollard	19	not out	102
C.G. Borde	c Reid b Motz	68	b Pollard	20
Nawab of Pataudi, jr*	b Motz	9		
Hanumant Singh	c Ward b Pollard	0		
S.A. Durani	b Reid	34		
R.G. Nadkarni	c Collinge b Yuile	75		
F.M. Engineer†	c Pollard b Yuile	90		
R.F. Surti	not out	9	(5) not out	17
S. Venkataraghavan	b Collinge	4		
Extras	(B 10, LB 1, NB 5)	16	(B 3, LB 1, NB 7)	11
Total		**397**	(2 wickets declared)	**199**

NEW ZEALAND

T.W. Jarvis	b Durani	9	not out	40
G.T. Dowling	b Venkataraghavan	29	not out	21
B.W. Sinclair	b Venkataraghavan	30		
J.R. Reid*	lbw b Nadkarni	42		
R.W. Morgan	lbw b Durani	39		
B. Sutcliffe	b Surti	56		
B.W. Yuile	c Nadkarni b Durani	0		
V. Pollard	c Venkataraghavan b Jaisimha	3		
R.C. Motz	b Nadkarni	11		
J.T. Ward†	not out	35		
R.O. Collinge	lbw b Borde	34		
Extras	(B 8, LB 10, W 3, NB 6)	27	(NB 1)	1
Total		**315**	(0 wickets)	**62**

NEW ZEALAND	O	M	R	W	O	M	R	W	FALL OF WICKETS				
Collinge	22·5	5	55	1	9	2	29	0		I	NZ	I	NZ
Motz	30	6	87	3	19	1	57	0	*Wkt*	*1st*	*1st*	*2nd*	*2nd*
Reid	30	11	70	1					1st	51	38	88	–
Yuile	20	7	62	2	11·1	0	53	1	2nd	94	58	130	–
Pollard	34	16	90	3	14	4	32	1	3rd	94	119	–	–
Morgan	7	2	17	0	5	2	17	0	4th	107	139	–	–
									5th	114	200	–	–
INDIA									6th	202	200	–	–
Jaisimha	12	4	30	1	4	2	8	0	7th	232	227	–	–
Surti	33	12	55	1	1	0	10	0	8th	375	227	–	–
Durani	45	23	53	3	1	0	4	0	9th	378	254	–	–
Venkataraghavan	48	23	90	2					10th	397	315	–	–
Nadkarni	36	21	42	2									
Borde	5	2	18	1									
Pataudi					3	2	9	0					
Hanumant Singh					6	0	19	0					
Manjrekar					6	4	11	0					

Umpires: Mahomed Yunus (5) and S.K. Raghunatha Rao (6).

Close: 1st day – I(1) 225-6 (Borde 68, Nadkarni 14); 2nd – NZ(1) 93-2 (Sinclair 25, Reid 16); 3rd – NZ(1) 283-9 (Ward 20, Collinge 20).

INDIA v NEW ZEALAND 1964–65 (2nd Test)

Played at Eden Gardens, Calcutta, on 5, 6, 7, 8 March.
Toss: New Zealand.   Result: MATCH DRAWN.
Debuts: New Zealand – B.R. Taylor, G.E. Vivian.

Vivian, aged 19 years 5 days, made his first-class debut in this match. Taylor, a last-minute replacement for Sinclair (ill), became the second New Zealander after J.E. Mills to score a hundred on his first appearance in Test cricket. He batted for 158 minutes, hit three sixes and 14 fours, and added 163 runs with Sutcliffe in New Zealand's (then) highest seventh-wicket partnership in all Tests. It was Taylor's first hundred in first-class cricket. He remains the only player to score a century and take five wickets in an innings in his first Test. Pollard and Vivian contributed a record eighth-wicket stand for this series, 81 in 83 minutes. New Zealand's first innings total remains their highest in Tests in India. Morgan kept wicket in the second innings.

NEW ZEALAND

G.T. Dowling	lbw b Venkataraghavan	27	c Engineer b Gupte	23
B.E. Congdon	b Desai	9	c Borde b Desai	0
R.W. Morgan	c Engineer b Desai	20	(4) b Durani	33
J.R. Reid*	c Borde b Venkataraghavan	82	(5) lbw b Venkataraghavan	11
B. Sutcliffe	not out	151	(6) c Hanumant b Venkataraghavan	6
B.W. Yuile	b Gupte	1	(3) lbw b Venkataraghavan	21
V. Pollard	c Jaisimha b Desai	31	b Jaisimha	43
B.R. Taylor	c Kunderan b Nadkarni	105	(10) not out	0
G.E. Vivian	b Desai	1	c Jaisimha b Nadkarni	43
R.C. Motz	lbw b Venkataraghavan	21	(8) c Nadkarni b Durani	0
J.T. Ward†	not out	1		
Extras	(B 10, LB 3)	13	(B 10, NB 1)	11
Total	(9 wickets declared)	**462**	(9 wickets declared)	**191**

INDIA

M.L. Jaisimha	b Motz	22	c Morgan b Congdon	0
B.K. Kunderan	b Congdon	36	not out	12
F.M. Engineer†	c Pollard b Taylor	10	c Pollard b Dowling	45
C.G. Borde	c Pollard b Taylor	62		
R.G. Nadkarni	b Taylor	0		
Nawab of Pataudi, jr*	c Ward b Taylor	153		
Hanumant Singh	c sub (T.W. Jarvis) b Yuile	31		
S.A. Durani	c sub (T.W. Jarvis) b Yuile	20	(4) b Vivian	23
R.B. Desai	c Ward b Yuile	0		
S. Venkataraghavan	b Taylor	7	(5) not out	0
B.P. Gupte	not out	3		
Extras	(B 23, LB 2, NB 11)	36	(B 11, LB 1)	12
Total		**380**	(3 wickets)	**92**

INDIA	O	M	R	W	O	M	R	W
Desai	33	6	128	4	12	6	32	1
Jaisimha	20	6	73	0	15·1	12	21	1
Durani	15	3	49	0	18	10	34	2
Nadkarni	35	12	59	1	7	4	14	1
Gupte	16	3	54	1	22	7	64	1
Venkataraghavan	41	18	86	3	17	11	15	3
NEW ZEALAND								
Motz	21	3	74	1				
Taylor	23·5	2	86	5				
Congdon	18	5	49	1	5	0	33	1
Pollard	15	1	50	0				
Vivian	12	3	37	0	3	0	14	1
Reid	2	1	5	0				
Yuile	14	3	43	3				
Dowling					6	2	19	1
Sutcliffe					3	2	14	0

FALL OF WICKETS

Wkt	NZ 1st	I 1st	NZ 2nd	I 2nd
1st	13	45	4	3
2nd	37	61	37	52
3rd	138	100	61	92
4th	139	101	83	–
5th	152	211	97	–
6th	233	301	103	–
7th	396	357	103	–
8th	407	357	184	–
9th	450	371	191	–
10th	–	380	–	–

Umpires: S.K. Ganguli (10) and A.R. Joshi (12).

Close: 1st day – NZ(1) 259-6 (Sutcliffe 74, Taylor 13); 2nd – I(1) 101-4 (Borde 21); 3rd – NZ(2) 4-1 (Dowling 4, Yuile 0).

INDIA v NEW ZEALAND 1964–65 (3rd Test)

Played at Brabourne Stadium, Bombay, on 12, 13, 14, 15 March.
Toss: New Zealand.　Result: MATCH DRAWN.
Debuts: Nil.

India were dismissed for their lowest total in any home Test until 1976-77, when England bowled them out for 83 (*Test No. 790*), and the lowest by any side in a Test in Bombay. Sardesai and Hanumant Singh added 193 in 181 minutes in an unbroken partnership which was then India's record for the sixth wicket against all countries. Taylor's analysis of 5 for 26 was the best by a New Zealand bowler in a Test in India until 1988-89. Sardesai batted for 550 minutes and hit 25 fours for his first three-figure innings in Tests; his last 50 took 42 minutes. New Zealand were left $2\frac{1}{2}$ hours to score 255.

NEW ZEALAND

G.T. Dowling	b Desai	129	c Engineer b Jaisimha		0
B.E. Congdon	c Engineer b Desai	3	c Hanumant b Durani		14
B.W. Sinclair	b Desai	9	c Venkataraghavan b Desai		0
R.W. Morgan	b Chandrasekhar	71	b Chandrasekhar		11
B. Sutcliffe	run out	4	(6) c Durani b Chandrasekhar		1
V. Pollard	c Jaisimha b Desai	26	(7) c Borde b Durani		4
J.R. Reid*	lbw b Desai	22	(5) c Borde b Chandrasekhar		10
B.R. Taylor	c Hanumant b Desai	8	b Venkataraghavan		21
B.W. Yuile	lbw b Durani	2	not out		8
R.C. Motz	not out	5			
J.T. Ward†	b Durani	0	(10) not out		4
Extras	(B 4, LB 13, NB 1)	18	(B 5, NB 2)		7
Total		**297**	(8 wickets)		**80**

INDIA

D.N. Sardesai	c Ward b Motz	4	not out		200
M.L. Jaisimha	c Ward b Taylor	4	(4) c Ward b Pollard		47
S.A. Durani	c Morgan b Taylor	4	c Ward b Taylor		6
C.G. Borde	c Ward b Taylor	25	(5) c Yuile b Taylor		109
Hanumant Singh	hit wkt b Taylor	0	(7) not out		75
Nawab of Pataudi, jr*	c Ward b Congdon	9	b Motz		3
R.G. Nadkarni	lbw b Congdon	7			
F.M. Engineer†	run out	17	(2) c Reid b Taylor		6
R.B. Desai	c Reid b Motz	0			
S. Venkataraghavan	c Congdon b Taylor	7			
B.S. Chandrasekhar	not out	4			
Extras	(LB 4, NB 3)	7	(B 4, LB 5, W 1, NB 7)		17
Total		**88**	(5 wickets declared)		**463**

INDIA	O	M	R	W	O	M	R	W	FALL OF WICKETS				
Desai	25	9	56	6	9	5	18	1		NZ	I	I	NZ
Jaisimha	17	6	53	0	6	5	4	1	*Wkt*	*1st*	*1st*	*2nd*	*2nd*
Chandrasekhar	23	6	76	1	14	7	25	3	1st	13	4	8	0
Durani	20·2	10	26	2	7	2	16	2	2nd	31	8	18	0
Venkataraghavan	32	13	46	0	7	3	10	1	3rd	165	13	107	18
Nadkarni	12	7	22	0					4th	170	23	261	34
									5th	227	38	270	37
NEW ZEALAND									6th	256	48	–	45
Motz	15	4	30	2	29·4	11	63	1	7th	276	71	–	46
Taylor	7·3	2	26	5	29	5	76	3	8th	281	76	–	76
Congdon	9	5	21	2	17	6	44	0	9th	297	77	–	–
Pollard	2	1	4	0	29	6	95	1	10th	297	88	–	–
Yuile					25	8	76	0					
Morgan					18	3	54	0					
Reid					3	1	8	0					
Sutcliffe					4	0	30	0					

Umpires: M.V. Nagendra (3) and S. Roy (4).

Close: 1st day – NZ(1) 227-5 (Dowling 109); 2nd – I(2) 18-1 (Sardesai 6, Durani 6); 3rd – I(2) 281-5 (Sardesai 97, Hanumant 3).

INDIA v NEW ZEALAND 1964–65 (4th Test)

Played at Feroz Shah Kotla, Delhi, on 19, 20, 21, 22 March.
Toss: New Zealand.   Result: INDIA won by seven wickets.
Debuts: India – V. Subramanya.

Needing to score 70 runs in an hour, India won with 13 minutes to spare and so gained a 1–0 victory in the rubber. Venkataraghavan's innings analysis of 8 for 72 and match figures of 12 for 152 remain the best performances by a bowler from either country in this series. Congdon caught Hanumant Singh while keeping wicket after Ward had been injured.

NEW ZEALAND

Batsman	Dismissal 1	R	Dismissal 2	R
G.T Dowling	lbw b Venkataraghavan	7	lbw b Subramanya	0
T.W. Jarvis	b Venkataraghavan	34	b Venkataraghavan	77
R.W. Morgan	lbw b Venkataraghavan	82	c Venkataraghavan b Desai	4
B.E. Congdon	c Chandrasekhar b Venkataraghavan	48	b Chandrasekhar	7
J.R. Reid*	b Chandrasekhar	9	b Venkataraghavan	22
B. Sutcliffe	b Venkataraghavan	2	c Engineer b Chandrasekhar	54
B.R. Taylor	c Borde b Chandrasekhar	21	c Sardesai b Venkataraghavan	3
V. Pollard	b Venkataraghavan	27	c Engineer b Subramanya	6
J.T. Ward†	lbw b Venkataraghavan	11	(11) run out	0
R.O. Collinge	not out	4	(9) c Engineer b Venkataraghavan	54
F.J. Cameron	b Venkataraghavan	0	(10) not out	27
Extras	(B 8, LB 6, NB 3)	17	(B 15, LB 1, NB 2)	18
Total		262		272

INDIA

Batsman	Dismissal 1	R	Dismissal 2	R
D.N. Sardesai	c Jarvis b Morgan	106	not out	28
M.L. Jaisimha	c Dowling b Reid	10	(3) hit wkt b Cameron	1
Hanumant Singh	c Congdon b Collinge	82	(5) not out	7
C.G. Borde	c Jarvis b Cameron	87		
Nawab of Pataudi, jr*	b Collinge	113	(4) b Reid	29
V. Subramanya	b Taylor	9		
F.M. Engineer†	b Collinge	5	(2) b Taylor	2
R.G. Nadkarni	not out	14		
R.B. Desai	b Collinge	7		
S. Venkataraghavan	) did not bat			
B.S. Chandrasekhar	)			
Extras	(B 23, LB 4, W 1, NB 4)	32	(LB 4, NB 2)	6
Total	(8 wickets declared)	465	(3 wickets)	73

INDIA	O	M	R	W	O	M	R	W
Desai	9	2	36	0	18	3	35	1
Jaisimha	5	2	12	0	1	0	2	0
Subramanya	5	2	3	0	16	5	32	2
Venkataraghavan	51·1	26	72	8	61·2	30	80	4
Chandrasekhar	37	14	96	2	34	14	95	2
Nadkarni	16	8	21	0	19	13	10	0
Hanumant Singh	2	0	5	0				

NEW ZEALAND	O	M	R	W	O	M	R	W
Taylor	18	4	57	1	4	0	31	1
Collinge	20·4	4	89	4				
Reid	24	4	89	1	1	0	3	1
Cameron	26	5	86	1	4	0	29	1
Morgan	15	1	68	1				
Pollard	10	1	44	0				
Sutcliffe					0·1	0	4	0

FALL OF WICKETS

Wkt	NZ 1st	I 1st	NZ 2nd	I 2nd
1st	27	56	1	9
2nd	54	179	10	13
3rd	108	240	22	66
4th	117	378	68	–
5th	130	414	172	–
6th	157	421	178	–
7th	194	457	179	–
8th	256	465	213	–
9th	260	–	264	–
10th	262	–	272	–

Umpires: S.P. Pan (5) and B. Satyaji Rao (5).

Close: 1st day – NZ(1) 235-7 (Morgan 68, Ward 7); 2nd – I(1) 340-3 (Borde 73, Pataudi 49); 3rd – NZ(2) 95-4 (Jarvis 40, Sutcliffe 15).

WEST INDIES v AUSTRALIA 1964–65 (1st Test)

Played at Sabina Park, Kingston, Jamaica, on 3, 4, 5, 6, 8 March.
Toss: West Indies.   Result: WEST INDIES won by 179 runs.
Debuts: West Indies – A.W. White; Australia – L.C. Mayne, P.I. Philpott, G. Thomas.

West Indies gained their first home win against Australia and led them in a rubber for the first time. Captaining West Indies for the first time, Sobers took his 100th Test wicket when he dismissed Philpott and became the first player to complete a double of 4,000 runs and 100 wickets in Tests.

WEST INDIES

C.C. Hunte	c Grout b Philpott	41	c Simpson b Mayne	81
S.M. Nurse	c Grout b Hawke	15	run out	17
R.B. Kanhai	c Philpott b McKenzie	17	c and b Philpott	16
B.F. Butcher	b Mayne	39	c Booth b Philpott	71
G. St A. Sobers*	lbw b Simpson	30	(6) c Simpson b Philpott	27
J.S. Solomon	c Grout b Mayne	0	(7) c Grout b Mayne	76
J.L. Hendriks†	b Philpott	11	(8) b O'Neill	30
A.W. White	not out	57	(9) st Grout b Philpott	3
W.W. Hall	b Hawke	9	(10) b Mayne	16
C.C. Griffith	b Mayne	6	(11) not out	1
L.R. Gibbs	b Mayne	6	(5) b Mayne	5
Extras	(B 4, LB 3, W 1)	8	(B 20, LB 7, W 1, NB 2)	30
Total		**239**		**373**

AUSTRALIA

W.M. Lawry	lbw b Hall	19	b Griffith	17
R.B. Simpson*	c Kanhai b Hall	11	c Hendriks b Hall	16
R.M. Cowper	c Nurse b Hall	26	(4) lbw b Hall	2
N.C. O'Neill	c Butcher b White	40	(5) c Nurse b Gibbs	22
B.C. Booth	b Griffith	2	(6) b Griffith	56
G. Thomas	b Griffith	23	(7) b Hall	15
P.I. Philpott	c White b Hall	22	(8) c Kanhai b Sobers	9
N.J.N. Hawke	not out	45	(3) b Solomon	33
A.T.W. Grout†	c Nurse b Hall	5	lbw b Hall	2
G.D. McKenzie	b White	0	c Hall b White	20
L.C. Mayne	b Sobers	9	not out	11
Extras	(B 2, LB 8, NB 5)	15	(NB 13)	13
Total		**217**		**216**

AUSTRALIA	O	M	R	W	O	M	R	W		FALL OF WICKETS			
McKenzie	20	2	70	1	33	7	56	0		WI	A	WI	A
Hawke	14	4	47	2	18	5	25	0	*Wkt*	*1st*	*1st*	*2nd*	*2nd*
Mayne	17·2	2	43	4	23·4	5	56	4	1st	48	32	50	39
Philpott	14	2	56	2	47	10	109	4	2nd	70	39	78	40
Simpson	4	2	15	1	15	2	36	0	3rd	82	42	194	43
Cowper					9	1	27	0	4th	149	80	211	75
O'Neill					7	0	34	1	5th	149	96	226	144
									6th	149	136	247	167
WEST INDIES									7th	181	176	311	180
Hall	24	0	60	5	19	5	45	4	8th	211	192	314	184
Griffith	20	2	59	2	14	3	36	2	9th	229	193	372	192
Sobers	20·4	7	30	1	17	2	64	1	10th	239	217	373	216
Gibbs	16	8	19	0	9	1	21	1					
White	15	4	34	2	14·5	8	14	1					
Solomon					5	0	23	1					

Umpires: O. Davies (3) and D. Sang Hue (2).

Close: 1st day – A(1) 32-0 (Lawry 18, Simpson 11); 2nd – A(1) 211-9 (Hawke 44, Mayne 4); 3rd – WI(2) 199-3 (Hunte 74, Gibbs 0); 4th – A(2) 42-2 (Hawke 0, Cowper 2).

WEST INDIES v AUSTRALIA 1964-65 (2nd Test)

Played at Queen's Park Oval, Port-of-Spain, Trinidad, on 26, 27, 29, 30, 31 March, 1 April.
Toss: Australia.   Result: MATCH DRAWN.
Debuts: West Indies – B.A. Davis.

Simpson was only the second captain to invite the West Indies to bat in a Test in the Caribbean; R.E.S. Wyatt having done so twice in 1934-35. Cowper and Booth added 225 runs for the third wicket after O'Neill had retired hurt at 63 (struck on the left arm while protecting his head from a Griffith bouncer). Cowper batted for 343 minutes and hit 18 fours in his first three-figure score in Tests. On the last day he dislocated his left shoulder diving for a catch. With Philpott and Booth also unwell, Australia fielded three substitutes.

WEST INDIES

C.C. Hunte	c Simpson b McKenzie	89	b Philpott	53
B.A. Davis	c Simpson b McKenzie	54	c Simpson b O'Neill	58
R.B. Kanhai	c Grout b Cowper	27	c McKenzie b Philpott	53
B.F. Butcher	run out	117	c Thomas b Mayne	47
G. St A. Sobers*	run out	69	lbw b Simpson	24
J.S. Solomon	not out	31	c Booth b Simpson	48
J.L. Hendriks†	c Philpott b O'Neill	2	c Grout b Hawke	22
A.W. White	c Grout b Philpott	7	lbw b Hawke	4
W.W. Hall	c Booth b O'Neill	4	c Mayne b Simpson	37
C.C. Griffith	b O'Neill	12	not out	18
L.R. Gibbs	st Grout b O'Neill	1	c Booth b Simpson	1
Extras	(B 4, LB 9, W 2, NB 1)	16	(B 11, LB 8, NB 2)	21
Total		**429**		**386**

AUSTRALIA

W.M. Lawry	c Davis b Griffith	1
R.B. Simpson*	b Griffith	30
R.M. Cowper	run out	143
N.C. O'Neill	c Sobers b Hall	36
B.C. Booth	c Hendriks b Griffith	117
G. Thomas	c Hendriks b Hall	61
P.I. Philpott	c Sobers b Gibbs	19
N.J.N. Hawke	c Hall b Sobers	39
A.T.W. Grout†	c Hendriks b Sobers	35
G.D. McKenzie	c Butcher b Sobers	13
L.C. Mayne	not out	1
Extras	(B 8, LB 3, NB 10)	21
Total		**516**

AUSTRALIA	O	M	R	W	O	M	R	W		FALL OF WICKETS		
										WI	A	WI
McKenzie	36	9	94	2	21	5	62	0	*Wkt*	*1st*	*1st*	*2nd*
Hawke	23	4	50	0	21	4	42	2	1st	116	15	91
Mayne	17	0	65	0	11	2	37	1	2nd	164	60	166
Philpott	36	10	82	1	28	4	57	2	3rd	205	288	166
Booth	2	0	5	0	5	1	14	0	4th	365	306	236
Simpson	8	1	28	0	36·5	5	83	4	5th	372	372	266
Cowper	12	1	48	1	1	0	5	0	6th	380	415	323
O'Neill	17·4	3	41	4	24	6	65	1	7th	393	431	327
									8th	404	489	328
WEST INDIES									9th	425	511	382
Hall	35	6	104	2					10th	429	516	386
Griffith	33	5	81	3								
Sobers	27·5	5	75	3								
Gibbs	66	22	129	1								
White	52	15	104	0								
Hunte	2	1	2	0								

Umpires: C.Z. Bain (1) and R. Gosein (1).

Close: 1st day – WI(1) 141-1 (Hunte 67, Kanhai 15); 2nd – WI(1) 400-7 (Solomon 17, Hall 4): 3rd – A(1) 212-2 (Cowper 106, Booth 67); 4th – A(1) 404-5 (Thomas 54, Philpott 8); 5th – WI(2) 125-1 (Hunte 38, Kanhai 27).

WEST INDIES v AUSTRALIA 1964–65 (3rd Test)

Played at Bourda, Georgetown, British Guiana, on 14, 15, 17, 19, 20 April.
Toss: West Indies.   Result: WEST INDIES won by 212 runs.
Debuts: Nil.

G.E. Gomez, the former West Indies all rounder who was currently a Test selector, was appointed as umpire after C.P. Kippins had withdrawn on the eve of the match. Kippins had done so only at the insistence of the British Guiana Umpires' Association who objected to the appointment of Jordan of Barbados. Gomez held an umpiring certificate although he had not previously officiated in a first-class match. Gibbs, who took his 100th Test wicket during the match, completed West Indies' second victory of the rubber with the second ball bowled on the fifth day; his innings and match analyses remain the best by a West Indies bowler in a home Test against Australia. Hawke's match figures of 10 for 115 are the best in Tests between these sides in the Caribbean and were the record for any Test at Georgetown until 1987-88.

WEST INDIES

C.C. Hunte	c McKenzie b Philpott	31	c Grout b Hawke	38
B.A. Davis	b Hawke	28	b McKenzie	17
R.B. Kanhai	b Hawke	89	b McKenzie	0
B.F. Butcher	run out	49	b Hawke	18
S.M. Nurse	c and b Hawke	42	st Grout b Philpott	6
G. St A. Sobers*	c Grout b Hawke	45	c Simpson b Philpott	42
J.S. Solomon	c Grout b Hawke	0	c Simpson b Philpott	17
J.L. Hendriks†	not out	31	c Grout b Hawke	2
W.W. Hall	c Mayne b Hawke	7	not out	20
C.C. Griffith	lbw b O'Neill	19	c Thomas b Philpott	13
L.R. Gibbs	b O'Neill	2	b Hawke	1
Extras	(B 7, LB 1, W 1, NB 3)	12	(LB 3, W 1, NB 2)	6
Totals		**355**		**180**

AUSTRALIA

R.B. Simpson*	b Sobers	7	b Griffith	23
W.M. Lawry	run out	20	b Gibbs	22
R.M. Cowper	c Hendriks b Gibbs	41	st Hendriks b Gibbs	30
N.C. O'Neill	b Griffith	27	c Sobers b Gibbs	16
P.I. Philpott	c Butcher b Sobers	5	(8) c Sobers b Gibbs	6
B.C. Booth	c Sobers b Gibbs	37	(5) c Hendriks b Gibbs	0
G. Thomas	b Hall	8	(6) st Hendriks b Solomon	5
N.J.N. Hawke	c Sobers b Hall	0	(7) c Hendriks b Sobers	14
A.T.W. Grout†	run out	19	b Sobers	8
G.D. McKenzie	not out	3	b Gibbs	6
L.C. Mayne	b Gibbs	5	not out	0
Extras	(LB 1, NB 6)	7	(B 4, LB 4, NB 6)	14
Total		**179**		**144**

AUSTRALIA	O	M	R	W	O	M	R	W		FALL OF WICKETS			
McKenzie	23	2	92	0	21	7	53	2		WI	A	WI	A
Hawke	32	8	72	6	20·4	7	43	4	*Wkt*	*1st*	*1st*	*2nd*	*2nd*
Mayne	12	1	54	0	2	1	6	0	1st	56	11	31	31
Philpott	26	5	75	1	16	3	49	4	2nd	68	68	31	88
O'Neill	6·2	1	26	2	1	0	4	0	3rd	203	71	62	91
Simpson	7	1	23	0	17	9	19	0	4th	210	85	69	104
Cowper	1	0	1	0					5th	290	116	125	109
									6th	290	127	129	115
WEST INDIES									7th	297	130	146	130
Hall	13	2	43	2	2	1	1	0	8th	309	170	146	130
Sobers	12	2	38	2	19	7	39	2	9th	353	171	176	144
Griffith	14	2	40	1	6	1	30	1	10th	355	179	180	144
Gibbs	25·5	9	51	3	22·2	9	29	6					
Solomon					9	2	31	1					

Umpires: G.E. Gomez (1) and H.B. de C. Jordan (11).

Close: 1st day – WI(1) 201-2 (Kanhai 88, Butcher 47); 2nd – A(1) 92-4 (O'Neill 10, Booth 7); 3rd – WI(2) 69-3 (Hunte 23, Nurse 6); 4th – A(2) 144-9 (McKenzie 6, Mayne 0).

WEST INDIES v AUSTRALIA 1964–65 (4th Test)

Played at Kensington Oval, Bridgetown, Barbados, on 5, 6, 7, 8, 10, 11 May.
Toss: Australia.   Result: MATCH DRAWN.
Debuts: Nil.

Lawry and Simpson, who batted throughout the first day to score 263, became the first opening pair to score double centuries in the same Test innings. Their stand of 382 remains Australia's highest first-wicket partnership and was only 31 runs short of the world Test record set by M.H. Mankad and Pankaj Roy in 1955-56 (*Test No. 420*). Lawry's score of 210 is the highest for Australia in a Test in the West Indies. Hunte (29) retired hurt in the first innings when he was hit in the face attempting to hook Hawke and resumed at 299. Lawry retired hurt at 139 in the second innings. Set to score 253 runs in 270 minutes, West Indies finished 11 runs short with five wickets in hand but, with a 2-0 lead in the rubber, became the first holders of the Frank Worrell Trophy. Hendriks retired after being struck on the head by a steeply lifting ball from McKenzie and Nurse kept wicket in the second innings.

AUSTRALIA

Batsman	Dismissal 1st	Score	Dismissal 2nd	Score
W.M. Lawry	c Sobers b Solomon	210	retired hurt	58
R.B. Simpson*	b Hall	201	c Nurse b Sobers	5
R.M. Cowper	b Sobers	102	c and b Hall	4
N.C. O'Neill	c Kanhai b Gibbs	51	not out	74
B.C. Booth	b Gibbs	5	c Sobers b Gibbs	17
G. Thomas	not out	27	b Gibbs	1
B.K. Shepherd	lbw b Hall	4		
N.J.N. Hawke	not out	8		
P.I. Philpott	)			
A.T.W. Grout†	) did not bat			
G.D. McKenzie	)			
Extras	(B 10, LB 12, W 2, NB 18)	42	(B 11, LB 3, W 1, NB 1)	16
Totals	(6 wickets declared)	**650**	(4 wickets declared)	**175**

WEST INDIES

Batsman	Dismissal 1st	Score	Dismissal 2nd	Score
C.C. Hunte	c Simpson b McKenzie	75	c Grout b McKenzie	81
B.A. Davis	b McKenzie	8	c sub (D.J. Sincock) b Philpott	68
R.B. Kanhai	c Hawke b McKenzie	129	lbw b McKenzie	1
B.F. Butcher	c Simpson b O'Neill	9	c Booth b Philpott	27
S.M. Nurse	c Simpson b Hawke	201	(6) lbw b Hawke	0
G. St A. Sobers*	c Grout b McKenzie	55	(5) not out	34
J.S. Solomon	c McKenzie b Hawke	1	not out	6
J.L. Hendriks†	retired hurt	4		
W.W. Hall	c Simpson b Hawke	3		
C.C. Griffith	run out	54		
L.R. Gibbs	not out	3		
Extras	(B 13, LB 12, W 1, NB 5)	31	(B 19, LB 3, W 2, NB 1)	25
Total		**573**	(5 wickets)	**242**

WEST INDIES	O	M	R	W	O	M	R	W
Hall	27	3	117	2	8	0	31	1
Griffith	35	3	131	0	7	0	38	0
Sobers	37	7	143	1	20	11	29	1
Gibbs	73	17	168	2	18·2	3	61	2
Solomon	14	1	42	1				
Hunte	3	1	7	0				
AUSTRALIA								
McKenzie	47	11	114	4	24	6	60	2
Hawke	49	11	135	3	15	4	37	1
Philpott	45	17	102	0	24	7	74	2
O'Neill	26	13	60	1				
Simpson	15	3	44	0	9	4	15	0
Cowper	21	6	64	0	8	4	19	0
Booth	6	2	17	0	5	1	12	0
Shepherd	3	1	6	0				

FALL OF WICKETS

Wkt	A 1st	WI 1st	A 2nd	WI 2nd
1st	382	13	7	145
2nd	522	99	13	146
3rd	583	299	160	183
4th	604	445	175	216
5th	615	448	–	217
6th	631	453	–	–
7th	–	474	–	–
8th	–	539	–	–
9th	–	573	–	–
10th	–	–	–	–

Umpires: H.B. de C. Jordan (12) and C.P. Kippins (4).

Close: 1st day – A(1) 263-0 (Lawry 102, Simpson 137); 2nd – A(1) 583-2 (Cowper 102, O'Neill 29); 3rd – WI(1) 165-2 (Kanhai 80, Nurse 31); 4th – WI(1) 424-3 (Nurse 183, Hunte 71); 5th – A(2) 139-2 (Lawry 58, O'Neill 56).

WEST INDIES v AUSTRALIA 1964–65 (5th Test)

Played at Queen's Park Oval, Port-of-Spain, Trinidad, on 14, 15, 17 May.
Toss: West Indies.   Result: AUSTRALIA won by ten wickets.
Debuts: Nil.

Although defeated by ten wickets and with three days to spare in this match, West Indies gained their first victory in a rubber against Australia. Hunte was the second batsman after F.M.M. Worrell (*Test No. 441*) to carry his bat through a completed West Indies innings. McKenzie ended the second innings by bowling Hall, Griffith and Gibbs with four consecutive balls.

WEST INDIES

C.C. Hunte	c Grout b Hawke	1	not out	60
B.A. Davis	c McKenzie b Hawke	4	lbw b Hawke	8
R.B. Kanhai	c Hawke b Cowper	121	b Hawke	9
B.F. Butcher	lbw b Hawke	2	c Cowper b Sincock	26
S.M. Nurse	b McKenzie	9	lbw b Hawke	1
G. St A. Sobers*	b Sincock	18	b McKenzie	8
W.V. Rodriguez	c and b Sincock	9	st Grout b Sincock	1
D.W. Allan†	run out	11	c Cowper b McKenzie	7
W.W. Hall	b Philpott	29	b McKenzie	8
C.C. Griffith	c Sincock b Philpott	11	b McKenzie	0
L.R. Gibbs	not out	0	b McKenzie	0
Extras	(B 4, LB 2, W 2, NB 1)	9	(B 2, W 1)	3
Total		**224**		**131**

AUSTRALIA

W.M. Lawry	c Allan b Griffith	3	not out	18
R.B. Simpson*	b Griffith	72	not out	34
R.M. Cowper	lbw b Sobers	69		
B.C. Booth	lbw b Griffith	0		
G. Thomas	c Allan b Griffith	38		
B.K. Shepherd	c sub (C.A. Davis) b Gibbs	38		
N.J.N. Hawke	b Griffith	3		
P.I. Philpott	b Gibbs	10		
A.T.W. Grout†	c Griffith b Gibbs	14		
D.J. Sincock	not out	17		
G.D. McKenzie	b Griffith	8		
Extras	(B 12, LB 3, W 1, NB 6)	22	(B 4, W 1, NB 6)	11
Total		**294**	(0 wickets)	**63**

AUSTRALIA	O	M	R	W	O	M	R	W
McKenzie	14	0	43	1	17	7	33	5
Hawke	13	3	42	3	13	2	31	3
Sincock	15	1	79	2	18	0	64	2
Philpott	7·3	0	25	2				
Cowper	6	0	26	1				
WEST INDIES								
Hall	14	2	46	0	4	0	7	0
Griffith	20	6	46	6	6	0	19	0
Gibbs	44	17	71	3	4	2	7	0
Rodriguez	13	2	44	0	1	0	8	0
Sobers	37	13	65	1	2	0	7	0
Kanhai					1	0	4	0

FALL OF WICKETS

	WI	A	WI	A
Wkt	*1st*	*1st*	*2nd*	*2nd*
1st	2	5	12	–
2nd	18	143	22	–
3rd	26	143	63	–
4th	64	167	66	–
5th	100	222	87	–
6th	114	230	92	–
7th	162	248	103	–
8th	202	261	131	–
9th	217	270	131	–
10th	224	294	131	–

Umpires: H.B. de C. Jordan (13) and C.P. Kippins (5).

Close: 1st day – A(1) 68-1 (Simpson 36, Cowper 22); 2nd – A(1) 294-9 (Sincock 17, McKenzie 8).

PAKISTAN v NEW ZEALAND 1964–65 (1st Test)

Played at Rawalpindi Club Ground, on 27, 28, 30 March.
Toss: Pakistan.   Result: PAKISTAN won by an innings and 64 runs.
Debuts: Pakistan – Salahuddin.

The only Test to be played at Rawalpindi brought Pakistan their first home win for six years and with over a day to spare. Reid made his 53rd consecutive appearance beating the Test record held jointly by F.E. Woolley and P.B.H. May. Salahuddin made his debut at the age of 18 years 41 days and shared in Pakistan's highest tenth-wicket stand against New Zealand – 65 with Mohammad Farooq. The partnership of 114 between Ilyas and Saeed is Pakistan's best for the second wicket in this series. New Zealand were dismissed in 173 minutes, their last seven wickets falling for just two runs. Pervez registered the cheapest four-wicket analysis in Tests.

NEW ZEALAND

G.T. Dowling	b Farooq	5	b Majid		0
T.W. Jarvis	c Naushad b Asif	4	c Majid b Salahuddin		17
B.W. Sinclair	b Farooq	22	c Salahuddin b Pervez		21
J.R. Reid*	b Salahuddin	4	(6) c Asif b Farooq		0
R.W. Morgan	c Farooq b Salahuddin	0	(4) b Pervez		6
B. Sutcliffe	b Pervez	7	(8) b Pervez		0
B.R. Taylor	b Pervez	76	(9) not out		7
A.E. Dick†	b Pervez	0	(7) b Farooq		0
V. Pollard	lbw b Pervez	15	(10) c Hanif b Pervez		0
B.W. Yuile	not out	11	(5) run out		1
R.O. Collinge	c Ilyas b Intikhab	15	c Asif b Farooq		8
Extras	(B 1, LB 7, NB 8)	16	(B 6, LB 10, NB 3)		19
Total		**175**			**79**

PAKISTAN

Mohammad Ilyas	c Pollard b Reid	56
Naushad Ali†	b Reid	2
Saeed Ahmed	b Taylor	68
Javed Burki	b Collinge	6
Asif Iqbal	b Taylor	51
Hanif Mohammad*	b Pollard	16
Majid Khan	b Collinge	11
Salahuddin	not out	34
Intikhab Alam	c Yuile b Reid	1
Pervez Sajjad	c Dick b Taylor	18
Mohammad Farooq	c Dowling b Morgan	47
Extras	(B 5, LB 3)	8
Total		**318**

PAKISTAN	O	M	R	W	O	M	R	W		FALL OF WICKETS		
Asif	4	1	7	1	4	3	4	0		NZ	P	NZ
Majid	4	2	11	0	5	2	9	1	Wkt	1st	1st	2nd
Farooq	16	3	57	2	12	3	25	3	1st	5	13	3
Salahuddin	15	5	36	2	11	5	16	1	2nd	24	127	42
Pervez	16	5	42	4	12	8	5	4	3rd	34	135	57
Intikhab	1·5	0	6	1	3	2	1	0	4th	39	145	58
									5th	39	177	59
NEW ZEALAND									6th	91	215	59
Collinge	21	9	36	2					7th	91	217	59
Taylor	15	3	38	3					8th	143	220	59
Pollard	22	6	80	1					9th	148	253	59
Reid	34	18	80	3					10th	175	318	79
Yuile	16	5	42	0								
Morgan	8·3	1	34	1								

Umpires: Qamaruddin Butt (1) and Shujauddin (9).

Close: 1st day – P(1) 135-3 (Burki 6, Asif 1); 2nd – NZ(2) 59-6 (Dick 0).

PAKISTAN v NEW ZEALAND 1964–65 (2nd Test)

Played at Lahore Stadium on 2, 3, 4, 6, 7 April.
Toss: New Zealand.   Result: MATCH DRAWN.
Debuts: Nil.

Hanif and Majid added 217 – still Pakistan's highest sixth-wicket partnership in all Tests – after New Zealand had elected to bowl on a rain-affected pitch. Hanif's highest score in a home Test took 445 minutes and included 33 fours. New Zealand's total is still their highest in Pakistan and the partnership of 178 between Sinclair and Reid is their best for the third wicket in this series. New Zealand fielded three substitutes on the final day, Jarvis, Dowling and Dick being unfit. Reid kept wicket until tea when Congdon took over. In stumping Pervez Sajjad, he became the second substitute fielder to make a stumping in a Test match – the first being N.C. Tufnell for England in South Africa in 1909-10 (*Test No. 107*).

PAKISTAN

Mohammad Ilyas	c Dick b Cameron	17	c sub (R.C. Motz) b Taylor	4
Naushad Ali†	c Collinge b Cameron	9	b Cameron	29
Saeed Ahmed	b Pollard	23	(8) c and b Sutcliffe	4
Salahuddin	c Dick b Taylor	23	(3) b Cameron	25
Javed Burki	c Dick b Cameron	10	(4) c Reid b Sinclair	14
Hanif Mohammad*	not out	203		
Majid Khan	c Reid b Taylor	80	(5) c Reid b Sutcliffe	44
Asif Iqbal	lbw b Cameron	4	(6) c Sutcliffe b Pollard	43
Intikhab Alam	not out	10	(7) not out	5
Pervez Sajjad	) did not bat		(9) st sub (B.E. Congdon) b Sinclair	16
Mohammad Farooq	)		(10) not out	0
Extras	(B 2, LB 3, NB 1)	6	(B 6, LB 3, NB 1)	10
Total	**(7 wickets declared)**	**385**	**(8 wickets declared)**	**194**

NEW ZEALAND

G.T. Dowling	c Naushad b Farooq	83
T.W. Jarvis	b Salahuddin	55
B.W. Sinclair	c Hanif b Intikhab	130
J.R. Reid*	lbw b Majid	88
R.W. Morgan	c Majid b Farooq	50
B. Sutcliffe	b Asif	23
B.R. Taylor	not out	25
V. Pollard	not out	8
A.E. Dick†	) did not bat	
F.J. Cameron	)	
R.O. Collinge	)	
Extras	(B 5, LB 8, NB 7)	20
Total	**(6 wickets declared)**	**482**

NEW ZEALAND	O	M	R	W	O	M	R	W
Collinge	27	6	85	0	11	4	11	0
Cameron	44	12	90	4	11	5	15	2
Reid	9	3	21	0				
Pollard	42	20	76	1	19	6	41	1
Morgan	17	8	46	0	8	1	32	0
Taylor	28	9	61	2	7	3	15	1
Sinclair					10	3	32	2
Sutcliffe					11	4	38	2

PAKISTAN	O	M	R	W
Asif	33	12	85	1
Majid	24	3	57	1
Farooq	41	12	71	2
Pervez	43	18	72	0
Salahuddin	33	8	76	1
Intikhab	33	5	92	1
Saeed	1	0	1	0
Ilyas	1	0	8	0

FALL OF WICKETS

	P	NZ	P
Wkt	1st	1st	2nd
1st	14	136	5
2nd	45	164	61
3rd	49	342	74
4th	62	391	99
5th	121	439	169
6th	338	469	169
7th	362	–	173
8th	–	–	194
9th	–	–	–
10th	–	–	–

Umpires: Akhtar Hussain (2) and Shujauddin (10).

Close: 1st day – P(1) 176-5 (Hanif 62, Majid 30); 2nd – NZ(1) 13-0 (Dowling 6, Jarvis 5); 3rd – NZ(1) 200-2 (Sinclair 28, Reid 21); 4th – NZ(1) 444-5 (Morgan 41, Taylor 4).

PAKISTAN v NEW ZEALAND 1964–65 (3rd Test)

Played at National Stadium, Karachi, on 9, 10, 11, 13, 14 April.
Toss: New Zealand.   Result: PAKISTAN won by eight wickets.
Debuts: Nil.

Pakistan, needing 202 runs in 330 minutes to win the rubber 2-0, reached their objective in only 205 minutes. Saeed batted for 350 minutes, hitting a six and 18 fours in the highest and last of his five centuries in Tests. Reid (296 runs) set a New Zealand record for any rubber against Pakistan.

NEW ZEALAND

T.W. Jarvis	lbw b Salahuddin	27	b Asif	0
A.E. Dick†	c Naushad b Asif	33	b Majid	2
B.W. Sinclair	c Majid b Farooq	24	lbw b Farooq	14
J.R. Reid*	b Asif	128	c Majid b Salahuddin	76
R.W. Morgan	lbw b Saeed	13	c Salahuddin b Pervez	25
B.E. Congdon	c sub (Masood-ul-Hasan) b Intikhab	17	(8) b Intikhab	57
B.R. Taylor	c Pervez b Intikhab	6	c Hanif b Intikhab	3
V. Pollard	b Farooq	1	(9) b Salahuddin	4
R.C. Motz	b Intikhab	0	(10) lbw b Intikhab	2
B. Sutcliffe	not out	13	(6) c Majid b Intikhab	18
F.J. Cameron	c Naushad b Asif	9	not out	10
Extras	(LB 2, NB 12)	14	(B 1, LB 3, NB 8)	12
Total		**285**		**223**

PAKISTAN

Mohammad Ilyas	lbw b Motz	20	st Dick b Reid	126
Naushad Ali†	c Taylor b Motz	9	c sub (G.E. Vivian) b Pollard	39
Saeed Ahmed	b Cameron	172	not out	19
Javed Burki	c Morgan b Pollard	29	not out	4
Hanif Mohammad*	b Reid	1		
Majid Khan	run out	12		
Salahuddin	not out	11		
Asif Iqbal	lbw b Cameron	4		
Intikhab Alam	c Dick b Congdon	3		
Pervez Sajjad	not out	8		
Mohammad Farooq	did not bat			
Extras	(B 17, LB 12, NB 9)	38	(B 8, LB 2, W 1, NB 3)	14
Total	(8 wickets declared)	**307**	(2 wickets)	**202**

PAKISTAN	O	M	R	W	O	M	R	W		FALL OF WICKETS			
Asif	11	3	35	3	14	7	29	1		NZ	P	NZ	P
Majid	20	1	63	0	8	0	30	1	*Wkt*	*1st*	*1st*	*2nd*	*2nd*
Farooq	21	5	59	2	17	5	41	1	1st	50	21	0	121
Salahuddin	6	4	3	1	26	5	56	2	2nd	76	84	10	198
Pervez	11	4	29	0	8	3	16	1	3rd	123	198	45	–
Intikhab	24	6	53	3	26·4	10	39	4	4th	167	201	93	–
Saeed	10	3	29	1					5th	206	248	129	–
									6th	220	286	133	–
NEW ZEALAND									7th	226	290	151	–
Motz	22	11	35	2					8th	233	297	157	–
Cameron	28	7	70	2	11	3	29	0	9th	268	–	160	–
Pollard	27	13	41	1	18	3	52	1	10th	285	–	223	–
Taylor	15	2	54	0	14	3	43	0					
Morgan	13	2	31	0	7	2	31	0					
Reid	10	5	28	1	1	0	6	1					
Congdon	6	3	10	1	9	2	27	0					

Umpires: Daud Khan (10) and Shujauddin (11).

Close: 1st day – NZ(1) 233-7 (Reid 101, Motz 0); 2nd – P(1) 140-2 (Saeed 75, Burki 16); 3rd – NZ(2) 5-1 (Dick 1, Sinclair 2); 4th – NZ(2) 223 all out.

ENGLAND v NEW ZEALAND 1965 (1st Test)

Played at Edgbaston, Birmingham, on 27, 28, 29, 31 May, 1 June.
Toss: England.   Result: ENGLAND won by nine wickets.
Debuts: Nil.

England maintained their unbeaten record at Birmingham, this being their seventh win in 11 Tests. Barrington's innings occupied 437 minutes and resulted in his omission from the next Test; his score remained at 85 for 62 minutes while 20 overs were bowled. Sutcliffe retired hurt after being hit on the right ear by a Trueman bouncer, came back at 115 for the last two minutes before lunch but was unfit to continue afterwards. Congdon retired at 63 in the second innings after edging a sweep against Barber into his face but he resumed at 105. The partnership of 104 between Sutcliffe and Pollard remains New Zealand's highest for the seventh wicket against England. This match was played in miserably cold weather; twice on the second day hot drinks were brought on to the field.

ENGLAND

G. Boycott	c Dick b Motz	23	not out		44
R.W. Barber	b Motz	31	c sub (G.E. Vivian) b Morgan		51
E.R. Dexter	c Dick b Motz	57	not out		0
K.F. Barrington	c Dick b Collinge	137			
M.C. Cowdrey	b Collinge	85			
M.J.K. Smith*	lbw b Collinge	0			
J.M. Parks†	c Cameron b Reid	34			
F.J. Titmus	c Congdon b Motz	13			
T.W. Cartwright	b Motz	4			
F.S. Trueman	c Pollard b Cameron	3			
F.E. Rumsey	not out	21			
Extras	(B 10, LB 6, NB 11)	27	(NB 1)		1
Total		**435**	(1 wicket)		**96**

NEW ZEALAND

G.T. Dowling	b Titmus	32	b Barber		41
B.E. Congdon	c Smith b Titmus	24	b Titmus		47
B.W. Sinclair	b Titmus	14	st Parks b Barber		2
J.R. Reid*	b Trueman	2	c Barrington b Titmus		44
B.Sutcliffe	retired hurt	4	(7) c Titmus b Dexter		53
R.W. Morgan	c Parks b Barber	22	(5) lbw b Trueman		43
A.E. Dick†	c Titmus b Cartwright	0	(6) b Barber		42
V. Pollard	lbw b Titmus	4	not out		81
R.C. Motz	c Trueman b Cartwright	0	c and b Barber		21
R.O. Collinge	c Dexter b Barber	4	c Parks b Trueman		9
F.J. Cameron	not out	4	b Trueman		0
Extras	(B 1, LB 1, NB 4)	6	(B 17, LB 11, NB 2)		30
Total		**116**			**413**

NEW ZEALAND	O	M	R	W	O	M	R	W
Collinge	29·4	8	63	3	5	1	14	0
Cameron	43	10	117	1	3	0	11	0
Motz	43	14	108	5	13	3	34	0
Pollard	18	4	60	0	1	0	5	0
Congdon	7	2	17	0	2	1	6	0
Reid	16	5	43	1	5	2	7	0
Morgan					1·5	0	18	1
ENGLAND								
Rumsey	9	2	22	0	17	5	32	0
Trueman	18	3	49	1	32·4	8	79	3
Titmus	26	17	18	4	59	30	85	2
Cartwright	7	3	14	2	12	6	12	0
Barber	3	2	7	2	45	15	132	4
Barrington					5	0	25	0
Dexter					5	1	18	1

FALL OF WICKETS

	E	NZ	NZ	E
Wkt	1st	1st	2nd	2nd
1st	54	54	72	92
2nd	76	63	105	–
3rd	164	67	131	–
4th	300	86	145	–
5th	300	97	220	–
6th	335	104	249	–
7th	368	105	353	–
8th	391	108	386	–
9th	394	115	413	–
10th	435	–	413	–

Umpires: C.S. Elliott (18) and W.F.F. Price (3).

Close: 1st day – E(1) 232-3 (Barrington 61, Cowdrey 44); 2nd – NZ(1) 59-1 (Dowling 30, Sinclair 4); 3rd – NZ(2) 215-4 (Morgan 33, Dick 41); 4th – E(2) 8-0 (Boycott 5, Barber 3).

ENGLAND v NEW ZEALAND 1965 (2nd Test)

Played at Lord's, London, on 17, 18, 19, 21, 22 June.
Toss: New Zealand.   Result: ENGLAND won by seven wickets.
Debuts: England – J.A. Snow.

England won with just 15 minutes to spare after rain had claimed over five hours of play during the last two days. In his 67th and final Test match Frederick Sewards Trueman took his total of Test wickets to 307 – an aggregate which remained unbeaten until 31st January, 1976, when L.R. Gibbs overtook it in his 79th match (*Test No. 769*).

NEW ZEALAND

B.E. Congdon	lbw b Rumsey	0	lbw b Titmus	26
G.T. Dowling	lbw b Rumsey	12	b Parfitt	66
B.W. Sinclair	b Rumsey	1	c Parks b Barber	72
J.R. Reid*	c Parks b Snow	21	b Titmus	22
R.W. Morgan	c Parfitt b Rumsey	0	lbw b Rumsey	35
V. Pollard	c and b Titmus	55	run out	55
A.E. Dick†	b Snow	7	c Parks b Snow	3
B.R. Taylor	b Trueman	51	c Smith b Snow	0
R.C. Motz	c Parks b Titmus	11	(10) c Snow b Barber	8
R.O. Collinge	b Trueman	7	(9) c Parks b Barber	21
F.J. Cameron	not out	3	not out	9
Extras	(B 3, LB 2, NB 2)	7	(B 8, LB 12, NB 10)	30
Total		**175**		**347**

ENGLAND

G. Boycott	c Dick b Motz	14	lbw b Motz	76
R.W. Barber	c Dick b Motz	13	b Motz	34
E.R. Dexter	c Dick b Taylor	62	(4) not out	80
M.C. Cowdrey	c sub (T.W. Jarvis) b Collinge	119	(5) not out	4
P.H. Parfitt	c Dick b Cameron	11		
M.J.K. Smith*	c sub (T.W. Jarvis) b Taylor	44		
J.M. Parks†	b Collinge	2		
F.J. Titmus	run out	13	(3) c Dick b Motz	1
F.S. Trueman	b Collinge	3		
F.E. Rumsey	b Collinge	3		
J.A. Snow	not out	2		
Extras	(B 1, LB 7, W 1, NB 12)	21	(B 9, LB 5, NB 9)	23
Total		**307**	(3 wickets)	**218**

ENGLAND	O	M	R	W	O	M	R	W		FALL OF WICKETS			
										NZ	E	NZ	E
Rumsey	13	4	25	4	26	10	42	1	*Wkt*	*1st*	*1st*	*2nd*	*2nd*
Trueman	19·5	8	40	2	26	4	69	0	1st	0	18	59	64
Dexter	8	2	27	0					2nd	4	38	149	70
Snow	11	2	27	2	24	4	53	2	3rd	24	131	196	196
Titmus	15	7	25	2	39	12	71	2	4th	28	166	206	–
Barber	8	2	24	0	28	10	57	3	5th	49	271	253	–
Parfitt					6	2	25	1	6th	62	285	258	–
									7th	154	292	259	–
NEW ZEALAND									8th	160	300	293	–
Collinge	28·2	4	85	4	15	1	43	0	9th	171	302	303	–
Motz	20	1	62	2	19	5	45	3	10th	175	307	347	–
Taylor	25	4	66	2	10	0	53	0					
Cameron	19	6	40	1	13	0	39	0					
Morgan	8	1	33	0	3	0	11	0					
Reid					0.5	0	4	0					

Umpires: J.S. Buller (19) and W.E. Phillipson (12).

Close: 1st day – E(1) 72-2 (Dexter 30, Cowdrey 10); 2nd – E(1) 307 all out; 3rd – NZ(2) 261-7 (Pollard 14, Collinge 0); 4th – E(2) 64-1 (Boycott 28, Titmus 0).

ENGLAND v NEW ZEALAND 1965 (3rd Test)

Played at Headingley, Leeds, on 8, 9, 10, 12, 13 July.
Toss: England.   Result: ENGLAND won by an innings and 187 runs.
Debuts: Nil.

Edrich scored England's only triple century since 1938, his 310 not out being the highest score by an Englishman in first-class cricket at Leeds. He batted for 532 minutes and hit five sixes and 52 fours – the highest number of boundaries in any Test innings. He was on the field throughout the match. His partnership of 369 in 339 minutes with Barrington remains the highest for any wicket by either country in this series. His score and England's total are the highest in a home Test against New Zealand. Titmus took the wickets of Yuile, Taylor, Motz and Collinge for no runs in his 21st over (WOWWOW). England completed their third victory of the rubber after 16 minutes on the fifth morning – just before rain waterlogged the ground.

ENGLAND

R.W. Barber	c Ward b Taylor	13
J.H. Edrich	not out	310
K.F. Barrington	c Ward b Motz	163
M.C. Cowdrey	b Taylor	13
P.H. Parfitt	b Collinge	32
M.J.K. Smith*	not out	2
J.M. Parks†	)	
R. Illingworth	)	
F.J. Titmus	) did not bat	
F.E. Rumsey	)	
J.D.F. Larter	)	
Extras	(B 4, LB 8, NB 1)	13
Total	(4 wickets declared)	**546**

NEW ZEALAND

G.T. Dowling	c Parks b Larter	5	b Rumsey		41
B.E. Congdon	c Parks b Rumsey	13	b Rumsey		1
B.W. Sinclair	c Smith b Larter	13	lbw b Larter		29
J.R. Reid*	lbw b Illingworth	54	c Barrington b Rumsey		5
R.W. Morgan	b Illingworth	1	(6) b Titmus		21
V. Pollard	run out	33	(5) c Cowdrey b Larter		53
B.W. Yuile	b Larter	46	c Cowdrey b Titmus		12
B.R. Taylor	c Parks b Illingworth	9	c and b Titmus		0
R.C. Motz	c Barber b Illingworth	3	c Barrington b Titmus		0
J.T. Ward†	not out	0	(11) not out		2
R.O. Collinge	b Larter	8	(10) b Titmus		0
Extras	(B 5, LB 1, W 2)	8	(NB 2)		2
Total		**193**			**166**

NEW ZEALAND	O	M	R	W	O	M	R	W
Motz	41	8	140	1				
Taylor	40	8	140	2				
Collinge	32	7	87	1				
Yuile	17	5	80	0				
Morgan	6	0	28	0				
Pollard	11	2	46	0				
Congdon	4	0	12	0				
ENGLAND								
Rumsey	24	6	59	1	15	5	49	3
Larter	28·1	6	66	4	22	10	54	2
Illingworth	28	14	42	4	7	0	28	0
Titmus	6	2	16	0	26	17	19	5
Barber	2	0	2	0	14	7	14	0

FALL OF WICKETS

Wkt	E 1st	NZ 1st	NZ 2nd
1st	13	15	4
2nd	382	19	67
3rd	407	53	75
4th	516	61	86
5th	–	100	111
6th	–	153	158
7th	–	165	158
8th	–	173	158
9th	–	181	158
10th	–	193	166

Umpires: J.F. Crapp (3) and C.S. Elliott (19).

Close: 1st day – E(1) 366-1 (Edrich 194, Barrington 152); 2nd – NZ(1) 100-5 (Pollard 12, Yuile 0); 3rd – NZ(2) 0-0 (Dowling 0, Congdon 0); 4th – NZ(2) 161-9 (Pollard 50, Ward 0).

Test No. 594/100

ENGLAND v SOUTH AFRICA 1965 (1st Test)

Played at Lord's, London on 22, 23, 24, 26, 27 July.
Toss: South Africa.   Result: MATCH DRAWN.
Debuts: England – D.J. Brown; South Africa – A. Bacher, J.T. Botten, R. Dumbrill.

Needing 191 runs to win in 235 minutes, England were never on terms with the required scoring rate. With seven
wickets down and Edrich unable to resume his innings after being hit on the side of the head by a ball from
Peter Pollock at 37, England did well to draw this 100th match between the two countries. Bland ran out
Barrington and Parks with two outstanding pieces of fielding which culminated in direct hits on the stumps.

SOUTH AFRICA

E.J. Barlow	c Barber b Rumsey	1	c Parks b Brown	52
H.R. Lance	c and b Brown	28	c Titmus b Brown	9
D.T. Lindsay†	c Titmus b Rumsey	40	c Parks b Larter	22
R.G. Pollock	c Barrington b Titmus	56	b Brown	5
K.C. Bland	b Brown	39	c Edrich b Barber	70
A. Bacher	lbw b Titmus	4	b Titmus	37
P.L. van der Merwe*	c Barrington b Rumsey	17	c Barrington b Rumsey	31
R. Dumbrill	b Barber	3	c Cowdrey b Rumsey	2
J.T. Botten	b Brown	33	b Rumsey	0
P.M. Pollock	st Parks b Barber	34	not out	14
H.D. Bromfield	not out	9	run out	0
Extras	(LB 14, NB 2)	16	(B 4, LB 2)	6
Total		**280**		**248**

ENGLAND

G. Boycott	c Barlow b Botten	31	c and b Dumbrill	28
R.W. Barber	b Bromfield	56	c Lindsay b P.M. Pollock	12
J.H. Edrich	lbw b P.M. Pollock	0	retired hurt	7
K.F. Barrington	run out	91	lbw b Dumbrill	18
M.C. Cowdrey	b Dumbrill	29	lbw b P.M. Pollock	37
M.J.K. Smith*	c Lindsay b Botten	26	c Lindsay b Dumbrill	13
J.M. Parks†	run out	32	c Van der Merwe b Dumbrill	7
F.J. Titmus	c P.M. Pollock b Bromfield	59	not out	9
D.J. Brown	c Bromfield b Dumbrill	1	c Barlow b R.G. Pollock	5
F.E. Rumsey	b Dumbrill	3	not out	0
J.D.F. Larter	not out	0		
Extras	(B 1, LB 4, W 1, NB 4)	10	(LB 7, W 1, NB 1)	9
Total		**338**	(7 wickets)	**145**

ENGLAND	O	M	R	W	O	M	R	W		FALL OF WICKETS			
Larter	26	10	47	0	17	2	67	1		SA	E	SA	E
Rumsey	30	9	84	3	21	8	49	3	Wkt	1st	1st	2nd	2nd
Brown	24	9	44	3	21	11	30	3	1st	1	82	55	23
Titmus	29	10	59	2	26	13	36	1	2nd	60	88	62	70
Barber	10·3	3	30	2	25	5	60	1	3rd	75	88	68	79
									4th	155	144	120	113
SOUTH AFRICA									5th	170	240	170	121
P.M. Pollock	39	12	91	1	20	6	52	2	6th	170	240	216	135
Botten	33	11	65	2	12	6	25	0	7th	178	294	230	140
Barlow	19	6	31	0	9	1	25	0	8th	212	314	230	–
Bromfield	25·2	5	71	2	5	4	4	0	9th	241	338	247	–
Dumbrill	24	11	31	3	18	8	30	4	10th	280	338	248	–
Lance	5	0	18	0									
R.G. Pollock	5	1	21	0	4	4	0	1					

Umpires: J.S. Buller (20) and A.E.G. Rhodes (2).

Close: 1st day – SA(1) 227-8 (Botten 27, P.M. Pollock 2); 2nd – E(1) 26-0 (Boycott 11, Barber 15); 3rd – E(1)
287-6 (Parks 25, Titmus 22); 4th – SA(2) 186-5 (Bacher 27, Van der Merwe 1).

ENGLAND v SOUTH AFRICA 1965 (2nd Test)

Played at Trent Bridge, Nottingham, on 5, 6, 7, 9 August.
Toss: South Africa.   Result: SOUTH AFRICA won by 94 runs.
Debuts: Nil.

This was England's first defeat in 15 matches under Smith's captaincy. It was brought about mainly by the performances of the Pollock brothers, Graeme scoring 184 runs and Peter taking 10 for 87 in 48 overs – South Africa's best Test match analysis in England. The former received 145 balls in the first innings, scoring 125 out of 160 with 21 boundaries; the last 91 of his runs were made off 90 balls in 70 minutes while his partner, Van der Merwe, scored 10. Cartwright (fractured thumb) was unable to bowl again after achieving his only five-wicket analysis in Tests.

SOUTH AFRICA

E.J. Barlow	c Cowdrey b Cartwright	19	(4) b Titmus		76
H.R. Lance	lbw b Cartwright	7	c Barber b Snow		0
D.T. Lindsay†	c Parks b Cartwright	0	(1) c Cowdrey b Larter		9
R.G. Pollock	c Cowdrey b Cartwright	125	(5) c Titmus b Larter		59
K.C. Bland	st Parks b Titmus	1	(6) b Snow		10
A. Bacher	b Snow	12	(3) lbw b Larter		67
P.L. van der Merwe*	run out	38	c Parfitt b Larter		4
R. Dumbrill	c Parfitt b Cartwright	30	b Snow		13
J.T. Botten	c Parks b Larter	10	b Larter		18
P.M. Pollock	c Larter b Cartweight	15	not out		12
A.H. McKinnon	not out	8	b Titmus		9
Extras	(LB 4)	4	(B 4, LB 5, NB 3)		12
Total		**269**			**289**

ENGLAND

G. Boycott	c Lance b P.M. Pollock	0	b McKinnon		16
R.W. Barber	c Bacher b Dumbrill	41	c Lindsay b P.M. Pollock		1
K.F. Barrington	b P.M. Pollock	1	(5) c Lindsay b P.M. Pollock		1
F.J. Titmus	c R.G. Pollock b McKinnon	20	(3) c Lindsay b McKinnon		4
M.C. Cowdrey	c Lindsay b Botten	105	(6) st Lindsay b McKinnon		20
P.H. Parfitt	c Dumbrill b P.M. Pollock	18	(7) b P.M. Pollock		86
M.J.K. Smith*	b P.M. Pollock	32	(8) lbw b R.G. Pollock		24
J.M. Parks†	c and b Botten	6	(9) not out		44
J.A. Snow	run out	3	(4) b Botten		0
J.D.F. Larter	b P.M. Pollock	2	(11) c Van der Merwe b P.M. Pollock	10
T.W. Cartwright	not out	1	(10) lbw b P.M. Pollock		0
Extras	(B 1, LB 3. W 1, NB 6)	11	(LB 5, W 2, NB 11)		18
Total		**240**			**224**

ENGLAND	O	M	R	W	O	M	R	W	FALL OF WICKETS				
Larter	17	6	25	1	29	7	68	5		SA	E	SA	E
Snow	22	6	63	1	33	6	83	3	*Wkt*	*1st*	*1st*	*2nd*	*2nd*
Cartwright	31·3	9	94	6					1st	16	0	2	1
Titmus	22	8	44	1	19·4	5	46	2	2nd	16	8	35	10
Barber	9	3	39	0	3	0	20	0	3rd	42	63	134	10
Boycott					26	10	60	0	4th	43	67	193	13
									5th	80	133	228	41
SOUTH AFRICA									6th	178	225	232	59
P.M. Pollock	23·5	8	53	5	24	15	34	5	7th	221	229	243	114
Botten	23	5	60	2	19	5	58	1	8th	242	236	265	207
McKinnon	28	11	54	1	27	12	50	3	9th	252	238	269	207
Dumbrill	18	3	60	1	16	4	40	0	10th	269	240	289	224
R.G. Pollock	1	0	2	0	5	2	4	1					
Barlow					7	1	20	0					

Umpires: J.F. Crapp (4) and C.S. Elliott (20).

Close: 1st day – E(1) 16-2 (Barber 8, Titmus 4); 2nd – SA(2) 27-1 (Lindsay 6, Bacher 18); 3rd – E(2) 10-2 (Boycott 3, Snow 0).

Test No. 596/102

ENGLAND v SOUTH AFRICA 1965 (3rd Test)

Played at Kennington Oval, London, on 26, 27, 28, 30, 31 August.
Toss: England.   Result: MATCH DRAWN.
Debuts: England – K. Higgs.

England needed 91 runs to win with 70 minutes left when heavy rain ensured that South Africa won their second rubber in England, the first being in 1935. Higgs took the wicket of Lindsay with his 16th ball in Test cricket. Recalled after an interval of two years and 20 Tests, Statham took seven wickets in his final match to bring his tally to 252 wickets in 70 Tests – an aggregate at the time exceeded only by F.S. Trueman (307). At the end of this final match between these two countries, England had gained 46 wins to South Africa's 18, with 38 games drawn. Because of political pressures tours scheduled for 1968-69 and 1970 were cancelled.

SOUTH AFRICA

E.J. Barlow	lbw b Statham	18	b Statham	18
D.T. Lindsay†	lbw b Higgs	4	b Brown	17
A. Bacher	lbw b Higgs	28	c Smith b Statham	70
R.G. Pollock	b Titmus	12	run out	34
K.C. Bland	lbw b Statham	39	c Titmus b Higgs	127
H.R. Lance	lbw b Statham	69	b Higgs	53
P.L. van der Merwe*	c Barrington b Higgs	20	b Higgs	0
R. Dumbrill	c Smith b Higgs	14	c Barrington b Brown	36
J.T. Botten	c Cowdrey b Statham	0	b Titmus	4
P.M. Pollock	b Statham	3	not out	9
A.H. McKinnon	not out	0	b Higgs	14
Extras	(NB 1)	1	(B 1, LB 7, NB 2)	10
Total		**208**		**392**

ENGLAND

R.W. Barber	st Lindsay b McKinnon	40	c and b P.M. Pollock	22
W.E. Russell	lbw b P.M. Pollock	0	c Bacher b McKinnon	70
K.F. Barrington	b Botten	18	(4) lbw b P.M. Pollock	73
M.C. Cowdrey	c Barlow b P.M. Pollock	58	(5) not out	78
P.H. Parfitt	c and b McKinnon	24	(3) lbw b Botten	46
M.J.K. Smith*	lbw b P.M. Pollock	7	not out	10
D.J. Brown	c Dumbrill b McKinnon	0		
J.M. Parks†	c Bland b Botten	42		
F.J. Titmus	not out	2		
K. Higgs	b P.M. Pollock	2		
J.B. Statham	b P.M. Pollock	0		
Extras	(LB 6, W 3)	9	(LB 6, NB 3)	9
Total		**202**	(4 wickets)	**308**

ENGLAND	O	M	R	W	O	M	R	W		FALL OF WICKETS			
Statham	24·2	11	40	5	29	1	105	2		SA	E	SA	E
Brown	22	4	63	0	23	3	63	2	Wkt	1st	1st	2nd	2nd
Higgs	24	4	47	4	41·1	10	96	4	1st	21	1	28	39
Titmus	26	12	57	1	27	3	74	1	2nd	23	42	61	138
Barber					13	1	44	0	3rd	60	76	123	144
									4th	86	125	164	279
SOUTH AFRICA									5th	109	141	260	–
P.M. Pollock	25·1	7	43	5	32·2	7	93	2	6th	156	142	260	–
Botten	27	6	56	2	24	4	73	1	7th	196	198	343	–
Barlow	11	1	27	0	6	1	22	0	8th	197	198	367	–
Dumbrill	6	2	11	0	9	1	30	0	9th	207	200	371	–
McKinnon	27	11	50	3	31	7	70	1	10th	208	202	392	–
Lance	2	0	6	0	2	0	11	0					

Umpires: J.S. Buller (21) and W.F.F. Price (4).

Close: 1st day – SA(1) 152-5 (Lance 30, Van der Merwe 20); 2nd – E(1) 142-6 (Cowdrey 45); 3rd – SA(2) 163-3 (Bacher 70, Bland 18); 4th – E(2) 64-1 (Russell 32, Parfitt 7).

AUSTRALIA v ENGLAND 1965–66 (1st Test)

Played at Woolloongabba, Brisbane, on 10, 11 (*no play*), 13, 14, 15 December.
Toss: Australia.   Result: MATCH DRAWN.
Debuts: Australia – P.J. Allan, K.D. Walters.

Rain restricted play on the first day to 111 minutes and washed out the second completely. Lawry, having survived a confident appeal for a catch at the wicket off Brown's seventh ball of the innings, batted 419 minutes and hit 23 fours. Walters was the fifth Australian to score a hundred in the first innings of his first Test; all five instances have been against England. At 19 years 357 days, Walters was the third-youngest Australian after R.N. Harvey and A. A. Jackson to score a Test hundred. Russell, who began the match with a fractured thumb, split the webbing of his right hand when fielding.

AUSTRALIA

W.M. Lawry	c Parks b Higgs	166		
I.R. Redpath	b Brown	17		
R.M. Cowper	c Barrington b Brown	22		
P.J.P. Burge	b Brown	0		
B.C. Booth*	c and b Titmus	16		
K.D. Walters	c Parks b Higgs	155		
T.R. Veivers	not out	56		
N.J.N. Hawke	not out	6		
P.I. Philpott	)			
A.T.W. Grout†	) did not bat			
P.J. Allan	)			
Extras	(LB 2, NB 3)	5		
Total	(6 wickets declared)	**443**		

ENGLAND

R.W. Barber	c Walters b Hawke	5	c Veivers b Walters	34
G. Boycott	b Philpott	45	not out	63
J.H. Edrich	c Lawry b Philpott	32	c Veivers b Philpott	37
K.F. Barrington	b Hawke	53	c Booth b Cowper	38
M.J.K. Smith*	b Allan	16	not out	10
J.M. Parks†	c Redpath b Philpott	52		
F.J. Titmus	st Grout b Philpott	60		
D.A. Allen	c Cowper b Walters	3		
D.J. Brown	b Philpott	3		
K. Higgs	lbw b Allan	4		
W.E. Russell	not out	0		
Extras	(B 4, NB 3)	7	(B 2, LB 2)	4
Total		**280**	(3 wickets)	**186**

ENGLAND	O	M	R	W	O	M	R	W
Brown	21	4	71	3				
Higgs	30	6	102	2				
Titmus	38	9	99	1				
Allen	39	12	108	0				
Barber	5	0	42	0				
Boycott	4	0	16	0				
AUSTRALIA								
Allan	21	6	58	2	3	0	25	0
Hawke	16	7	44	2	10	2	16	0
Walters	10	1	25	1	5	1	22	1
Philpott	28·1	3	90	5	14	1	62	1
Cowper	7	4	7	0	6	0	20	1
Veivers	11	1	49	0	12	0	37	0

FALL OF WICKETS

	A	E	E
Wkt	1st	1st	2nd
1st	51	5	46
2nd	90	75	114
3rd	90	86	168
4th	125	115	–
5th	312	191	–
6th	431	221	–
7th	–	232	–
8th	–	253	–
9th	–	272	–
10th	–	280	–

Umpires: C.J. Egar (16) and L.P. Rowan (8).

Close: 1st day – A(1) 79-1 (Lawry 40, Cowper 20); 2nd – no play; 3rd – A(1) 384-5 (Walters 119, Veivers 39); 4th – E(1) 197-5 (Barrington 44, Titmus 0).

AUSTRALIA v ENGLAND 1965–66 (2nd Test)

Played at Melbourne Cricket Ground on 30, 31 December, 1, 3, 4 January.
Toss: Australia.   Result: MATCH DRAWN.
Debuts: Nil.

Simpson, Australia's appointed captain, had recovered from the fractured wrist which prevented him from playing in the 1st Test. For a variety of reasons both sides had a complete change of opening bowlers for this match. Boycott and Barber scored 98 in 77 minutes for England's first wicket. Cowdrey's hundred was his fourth against Australia and his third at Melbourne. McKenzie bowled 35·5 overs but earlier in the innings retired after bowling five balls of an over. On the fourth day Barrington deputised for Parks (stomach upset) from the start of the innings until tea and caught Simpson. Parks returned after the interval but rain ended play after nine minutes. Parks missed a vital stumping chance off Barber when Burge was 34 and Australia 204 for 4 in the second innings. Walters was the second batsman after W.H. Ponsford to score hundreds in each of his first two Tests.

AUSTRALIA

R.B. Simpson*	c Edrich b Allen	59		c Barrington b Knight	67
W.M. Lawry	c Cowdrey b Allen	88		c Smith b Barber	78
P.J.P. Burge	b Jones	5	(4)	c Edrich b Boycott	120
R.M. Cowper	c Titmus b Jones	99	(3)	lbw b Jones	5
B.C. Booth	lbw b Jones	23		b Allen	10
K.D. Walters	c Parks b Knight	22		c and b Barrington	115
T.R. Veivers	run out	19		st Parks b Boycott	3
P.I. Philpott	b Knight	10		b Knight	2
A.T.W. Grout†	c Barber b Knight	11		c Allen b Barrington	16
G.D. McKenzie	not out	12		run out	2
A.N. Connolly	c Parks b Knight	0		not out	0
Extras	(B 2, LB 7, NB 1)	10		(B 1, LB 3, W 1 NB 3)	8
Total		**358**			**426**

ENGLAND

G. Boycott	c McKenzie b Walters	51		not out	5
R.W. Barber	c Grout b McKenzie	48		not out	0
J.H. Edrich	c and b Veivers	109			
K.F. Barrington	c Burge b Veivers	63			
M.C. Cowdrey	c Connolly b Cowper	104			
M.J.K. Smith*	c Grout b McKenzie	41			
J.M. Parks†	c Cowper b McKenzie	71			
B.R. Knight	c Simpson b McKenzie	1			
F.J. Titmus	not out	56			
D.A. Allen	c Grout b Connolly	2			
I.J. Jones	b McKenzie	1			
Extras	(B 4, LB 5, W 2)	11			
Total		**558**		(0 wickets)	**5**

ENGLAND	O	M	R	W	O	M	R	W		FALL OF WICKETS			
Jones	24	4	92	3	20	1	92	1		A	E	A	E
Knight	26·5	2	84	4	21	4	61	2	*Wkt*	*1st*	*1st*	*2nd*	*2nd*
Titmus	31	7	93	0	22	6	43	0	1st	93	98	120	–
Allen	20	4	55	2	18	3	48	1	2nd	109	110	141	–
Barber	6	1	24	0	17	0	87	1	3rd	203	228	163	–
Barrington					7·4	0	47	2	4th	262	333	176	–
Boycott					9	0	32	2	5th	297	409	374	–
Smith					2	0	8	0	6th	318	443	382	–
AUSTRALIA									7th	330	447	385	–
McKenzie	35·2	3	134	5	1	0	2	0	8th	342	540	417	–
Connolly	37	5	125	1	1	0	3	0	9th	352	551	426	–
Philpott	30	2	133	0					10th	358	558	426	–
Walters	10	2	32	1									
Simpson	16	4	61	0									
Veivers	12	3	46	2									
Cowper	3	0	16	1									

Umpires: C.J. Egar (17) and W. Smyth (4).

Close: 1st day – A(1) 278-4 (Cowper 90, Walters 7); 2nd – E(1) 208-2 (Edrich 48, Barrington 54); 3rd – E(1) 516-7 (Parks 66, Titmus 23); 4th – A(2) 131-1 (Lawry 61, Cowper 1).

AUSTRALIA v ENGLAND 1965–66 (3rd Test)

Played at Sydney Cricket Ground on 7, 8, 10, 11 January.
Toss: England.   Result: ENGLAND won by an innings and 93 runs.
Debuts: Nil.

England beat Australia for the first time in eleven matches since 1962-63 (*Test No. 536*); it was their first victory in Australia by an innings since 1936-37 (*Test No. 256*). Simpson was again an unfortunate and notable absentee, this time because of chickenpox. The opening partnership of 234 in 242 minutes between Boycott and Barber is England's third-highest against Australia. Barber reached his only Test hundred in 198 minutes. He batted 296 minutes, faced 255 balls and hit 19 fours in making his highest score in first-class cricket; it remains the highest score by an England batsman on the first day of a Test against Australia. Edrich scored his second Test hundred in successive innings. Titmus scored his 1,000th run and completed the 'double' in his 40th Test. Brown took the wickets of Sincock, Hawke and Grout with the second, seventh, and eighth balls of his first over with the second new ball.

ENGLAND

G. Boycott	c and b Philpott	84
R.W. Barber	b Hawke	185
J.H. Edrich	c and b Philpott	103
K.F. Barrington	c McKenzie b Hawke	1
M.C. Cowdrey	c Grout b Hawke	0
M.J.K. Smith*	c Grout b Hawke	6
D.J. Brown	c Grout b Hawke	1
J.M. Parks†	c Grout b Hawke	13
F.J. Titmus	c Grout b Walters	14
D.A. Allen	not out	50
I.J. Jones	b Hawke	16
Extras	(B 3, LB 8, W 2, NB 2)	15
Total		**488**

AUSTRALIA

W.M. Lawry	c Parks b Jones	0	c Cowdrey b Brown	33
G. Thomas	c Titmus b Brown	51	c Cowdrey b Titmus	25
R.M. Cowper	st Parks b Allen	60	c Boycott b Titmus	0
P.J.P. Burge	c Parks b Brown	6	run out	1
B.C. Booth*	c Cowdrey b Jones	8	b Allen	27
D.J. Sincock	c Parks b Brown	29	(7) c Smith b Allen	27
K.D. Walters	st Parks b Allen	23	(6) not out	35
N.J.N. Hawke	c Barber b Brown	0	(9) c Smith b Titmus	2
A.T.W. Grout†	b Brown	0	(10) c Smith b Allen	3
G.D. McKenzie	c Cowdrey b Barber	24	(11) c Barber b Titmus	12
P.I. Philpott	not out	5	(8) lbw b Allen	5
Extras	(B 7, LB 8)	15	(B 3, LB 1)	4
Total		**221**		**174**

AUSTRALIA	O	M	R	W	O	M	R	W
McKenzie	25	2	113	0				
Hawke	33·7	6	105	7				
Walters	10	1	38	1				
Philpott	28	3	86	2				
Sincock	20	1	98	0				
Cowper	6	1	33	0				
ENGLAND								
Jones	20	6	51	2	7	0	35	0
Brown	17	1	63	5	11	2	32	1
Boycott	3	1	8	0				
Titmus	23	8	40	0	17·3	4	40	4
Barber	2·1	1	2	1	5	0	16	0
Allen	19	5	42	2	20	8	47	4

FALL OF WICKETS

	E	A	A
Wkt	1st	1st	2nd
1st	234	0	46
2nd	303	81	50
3rd	309	91	51
4th	309	105	86
5th	317	155	86
6th	328	174	119
7th	358	174	131
8th	395	174	135
9th	433	203	140
10th	488	221	174

Umpires: C.J. Egar (18) and L.P. Rowan (9).

Close: 1st day – E(1) 328-5 (Edrich 40, Brown 1); 2nd – A(1) 113-4 (Cowper 46, Sincock 0); 3rd – A(2) 85-3 (Lawry 33, Booth 26).

AUSTRALIA v ENGLAND 1965–66 (4th Test)

Played at Adelaide Oval on 28, 29, 31 January, 1 February.
Toss: England.   Result: AUSTRALIA won by an innings and 9 runs.
Debuts: Australia – K.R. Stackpole.

Australia's opening partnership of 244 in 255 minutes between Simpson and Lawry was their highest for the first wicket against England until 1989 and remains their highest against all opponents in Australia. Simpson batted for 545 minutes and hit a six and 18 fours. Barrington, in his final Test appearance at Adelaide, extended his unique run of success by scoring his tenth consecutive fifty in first-class matches on that ground: 104, 52, 52 not out, 63, 132 not out (in 1962-63); 69, 51, 63, 60, 102 (in 1965-66). Jones became the only Glamorgan player to take five or more wickets in a Test innings for England.

ENGLAND

G. Boycott	c Chappell b Hawke	22	lbw b McKenzie		12
R.W. Barber	b McKenzie	0	c Grout b Hawke		19
J.H. Edrich	c Simpson b McKenzie	5	c Simpson b Hawke		1
K.F. Barrington	lbw b Walters	60	c Chappell b Hawke		102
M.C. Cowdrey	run out	38	c Grout b Stackpole		35
M.J.K. Smith*	b Veivers	29	c McKenzie b Stackpole		5
J.M. Parks†	c Stackpole b McKenzie	49	run out		16
F.J. Titmus	lbw b McKenzie	33	c Grout b Hawke		53
D.A. Allen	c Simpson b McKenzie	2	not out		5
D.J. Brown	c Thomas b McKenzie	1	c and b Hawke		0
I.J. Jones	not out	0	c Lawry b Veivers		8
Extras	(LB 2)	2	(LB 2, NB 8)		10
Total		**241**			**266**

AUSTRALIA

R.B. Simpson*	c Titmus b Jones	225
W.M. Lawry	b Titmus	119
G. Thomas	b Jones	52
T.R. Veivers	c Parks b Jones	1
P.J.P. Burge	c Parks b Jones	27
K.D. Walters	c Parks b Brown	0
I.M. Chappell	c Edrich b Jones	17
K.R. Stackpole	c Parks b Jones	43
N.J.N. Hawke	not out	20
A.T.W. Grout†	b Titmus	4
G.D. McKenzie	lbw b Titmus	1
Extras	(B 4, LB 3)	7
Total		**516**

AUSTRALIA	O	M	R	W	O	M	R	W		FALL OF WICKETS		
McKenzie	21·7	4	48	6	18	4	53	1		E	A	E
Hawke	23	2	69	1	21	6	54	5	*Wkt*	*1st*	*1st*	*2nd*
Walters	14	0	50	1	9	0	47	0	1st	7	244	23
Stackpole	5	0	30	0	14	3	33	2	2nd	25	331	31
Chappell	4	1	18	0	22	4	53	0	3rd	33	333	32
Veivers	13	3	24	1	3·7	0	16	1	4th	105	379	114
									5th	150	383	123
ENGLAND									6th	178	415	163
Jones	29	3	118	6					7th	210	480	244
Brown	28	4	109	1					8th	212	501	253
Boycott	7	3	33	0					9th	222	506	257
Titmus	37	6	116	3					10th	241	516	266
Allen	21	1	103	0								
Barber	4	0	30	0								

Umpires: C.J. Egar (19) and L.P. Rowan (10).

Close: 1st day – E(1) 240-9 (Titmus 32, Jones 0); 2nd – A(1) 333-3 (Simpson 159); 3rd - E(2) 64-3 (Barrington 14, Cowdrey 13).

AUSTRALIA v ENGLAND 1965–66 (5th Test)

Played at Melbourne Cricket Ground on 11, 12, 14, 15 (*no play*), 16 February.
Toss: England.   Result: MATCH DRAWN.
Debuts: Nil.

Cowper scored Australia's only triple hundred in a home Test. He hit 20 fours and batted for 727 minutes to record the longest first-class innings in Australia, the longest innings against England overseas, and the then fourth-longest innings in all first-class cricket. Barrington hit his 122nd ball for six to complete his second consecutive Test hundred in 149 minutes. He was the first to reach a hundred with a six twice in Tests between England and Australia (also *Test No. 538*). It was the last of his five hundreds against Australia. Lawry scored 979 runs (average 97.90) in first-class matches against this touring team and batted for a total of $41\frac{1}{2}$ hours at a rate of 23 runs per hour. Wally Grout made the last of his 51 appearances for Australia, finishing with 187 dismissals – the record for his country at that time. Less than three years later, this great wicket-keeper died after a heart attack at the age of 41.

ENGLAND

G. Boycott	c Stackpole b McKenzie	17	lbw b McKenzie	1
R.W. Barber	run out	17	b McKenzie	20
J.H. Edrich	c McKenzie b Walters	85	b McKenzie	3
K.F. Barrington	c Grout b Walters	115	not out	32
M.C. Cowdrey	c Grout b Walters	79	not out	11
M.J.K. Smith*	c Grout b Walters	0		
J.M. Parks†	run out	89		
F.J. Titmus	not out	42		
B.R. Knight	c Grout b Hawke	13		
D.J. Brown	c and b Chappell	12		
I.J. Jones	not out	4		
Extras	(B 9, LB 2, NB 1)	12	(LB 2)	2
Total	(9 wickets declared)	**485**	(3 wickets)	**69**

AUSTRALIA

W.M. Lawry	c Edrich b Jones	108
R.B. Simpson*	b Brown	4
G. Thomas	c Titmus b Jones	19
R.M. Cowper	b Knight	307
K.D. Walters	c and b Barber	60
I.M. Chappell	c Parks b Jones	19
K.R. Stackpole	b Knight	9
T.R. Veivers	b Titmus	4
N.J.N. Hawke	not out	0
A.T.W. Grout†	) did not bat	
G.D. McKenzie	)	
Extras	(B 6, LB 5, NB 2)	13
Total	(8 wickets declared)	**543**

AUSTRALIA	O	M	R	W	O	M	R	W
McKenzie	26	5	100	1	6	2	17	3
Hawke	35	5	109	1	4	1	22	0
Walters	19	3	53	4	2	0	16	0
Simpson	5	1	20	0				
Stackpole	10	2	43	0	3	0	10	0
Veivers	15	3	78	0				
Chappell	17	4	70	1	2	0	2	0
ENGLAND								
Brown	31	3	134	1				
Jones	29	1	145	3				
Knight	36·2	4	105	2				
Titmus	42	12	86	1				
Barber	16	0	60	1				

FALL OF WICKETS

	E	A	E
Wkt	1st	1st	2nd
1st	36	15	6
2nd	41	36	21
3rd	219	248	34
4th	254	420	–
5th	254	481	–
6th	392	532	–
7th	419	543	–
8th	449	543	–
9th	474	–	–
10th	–	–	–

Umpires: C.J. Egar (20) and L.P. Rowan (11).

Close: 1st day – E(1) 312-5 (Cowdrey 43, Parks 29); 2nd – A(1) 101-2 (Lawry 43, Cowper 32); 3rd – A(1) 333-3 (Cowper 159, Walters 35); 4th – no play.

NEW ZEALAND v ENGLAND 1965–66 (1st Test)

Played at Lancaster Park, Christchurch on 25, 26, 28 February, 1 March.
Toss: England.   Result: MATCH DRAWN.
Debuts: New Zealand – G.P. Bilby, N. Puna.

Cowdrey became the second non-wicket-keeper after W.R. Hammond to hold 100 catches in Test cricket when he caught Chapple at second slip. Nineteen years earlier, Hammond had held the last of his 110 catches for England in the slips on the same ground (*Test No. 284*). Allen, destined to be the last Gloucestershire player to appear for England until 1986, recorded his highest score in Tests. New Zealand needed 196 runs in 139 minutes.

ENGLAND

G. Boycott	c Petrie b Motz	4	run out	4
W.E. Russell	b Motz	30	b Bartlett	25
J.H. Edrich	c Bartlett b Motz	2	lbw b Cunis	2
M.C. Cowdrey	c Bilby b Cunis	0	c Pollard b Motz	21
M.J.K. Smith*	c Puna b Pollard	54	c Bilby b Puna	87
P.H. Parfitt	c Congdon b Bartlett	54	not out	46
J.M. Parks†	c Petrie b Chapple	30	not out	4
D.A. Allen	c Chapple b Bartlett	88		
D.J. Brown	b Cunis	44		
K. Higgs	not out	8		
I.J. Jones	b Bartlett	0		
Extras	(B 6, LB 6, NB 16)	28	(B 4, LB 1, NB 7)	12
Total		**342**	(5 wickets declared)	**201**

NEW ZEALAND

G.P. Bilby	c Parks b Higgs	28	c Parks b Brown	3
M.J.F. Shrimpton	c Parks b Brown	11	c Smith b Allen	13
B.E. Congdon	c Smith b Jones	104	c Cowdrey b Higgs	4
B.W. Sinclair	c and b Higgs	23	c Parks b Higgs	0
V. Pollard	lbw b Higgs	23	not out	6
M.E. Chapple*	c Cowdrey b Jones	15	(7) c Parks b Higgs	0
G.A. Bartlett	c Parks b Brown	0	(8) c Brown b Parfitt	0
E.C. Petrie†	c Parks b Brown	55	(6) lbw b Higgs	1
R.C. Motz	c Parks b Jones	58	c Russell b Parfitt	2
R.S. Cunis	not out	8	not out	16
N. Puna	c Smith b Jones	1		
Extras	(B 7, LB 13, NB 1)	21	(B 2, LB 1)	3
Total		**347**	(8 wickets)	**48**

NEW ZEALAND	O	M	R	W	O	M	R	W
Motz	31	9	83	3	20	6	38	1
Bartlett	33·2	6	63	3	14	2	44	1
Cunis	31	9	63	2	19	3	58	1
Puna	18	6	54	0	14	6	49	1
Chapple	9	3	24	1				
Pollard	5	1	27	1				
ENGLAND								
Brown	30	3	80	3	4	2	6	1
Jones	28·4	9	71	4	7	3	13	0
Higgs	30	6	51	3	9	7	5	4
Allen	40	14	80	0	19	15	8	1
Boycott	12	6	30	0				
Parfitt	3	0	14	0	6	3	5	2
Parks					3	1	8	0

FALL OF WICKETS

	E	NZ	E	NZ
Wkt	1st	1st	2nd	2nd
1st	19	39	18	5
2nd	28	41	32	19
3rd	47	112	48	21
4th	47	181	68	21
5th	160	202	193	22
6th	160	203	–	22
7th	209	237	–	22
8th	316	326	–	32
9th	342	344	–	–
10th	342	347	–	–

Umpires: F.R. Goodall (2) and W.T. Martin (6).

Close: 1st day – E(1) 242-7 (Allen 32, Brown 14); 2nd – NZ(1) 174-3 (Congdon 78, Pollard 21); 3rd – E(2) 32-2 (Russell 20, Cowdrey 0).

NEW ZEALAND v ENGLAND 1965–66 (2nd Test)

Played at Carisbrook, Dunedin, on 4, 5, 7, 8 March.
Toss: New Zealand.   Result: MATCH DRAWN.
Debuts: Nil.

Motz hit 22 runs (064066) off Allen's 26th over to establish the record for the most runs by one batsman off a six-ball over in Test matches until 1980–81 (*Test No. 896*). Rain restricted play to $3\frac{1}{4}$ hours on the first day and to just over two hours on the third. Allen's off-spin claimed three wickets during his first eight balls after tea on the last day. By this time Russell was keeping wicket in place of Murray, who had an infected finger. If England had managed to take New Zealand's last wicket at the first attempt, they would have needed 51 runs in the final 24 minutes. Chapple, the appointed captain, was unable to play because of injury.

NEW ZEALAND

G.P. Bilby	c Murray b Jones	3	c Parfitt b Higgs	21	
M.J.F. Shrimpton	c Boycott b Higgs	38	(6) b Allen	0	
B.E. Congdon	c Murray b Jones	0	b Parfitt	19	
B.W. Sinclair*	b Knight	33	c Knight b Jones	39	
V. Pollard	c Murray b Higgs	8	(2) b Higgs	2	
R.W. Morgan	c Murray b Higgs	0	(5) c Smith b Allen	3	
G.A. Bartlett	c Parfitt b Allen	6	c Knight b Allen	4	
E.C. Petrie†	c Smith b Jones	28	not out	13	
R.C. Motz	c Higgs b Knight	57	b Jones	1	
R.S. Cunis	c Boycott b Allen	8	lbw b Allen	9	
N. Puna	not out	3	not out	18	
Extras	(B 4, LB 4)	8	(B 10, LB 6, NB 2)	18	
Total		**192**	(9 wickets)	**147**	

ENGLAND

G. Boycott	b Bartlett	5
W.E. Russell	b Motz	11
J.H. Edrich	c Bilby b Cunis	36
M.C. Cowdrey	not out	89
M.J.K. Smith*	c Pollard b Bartlett	20
P.H. Parfitt	c Pollard b Puna	4
J.T. Murray†	c Sinclair b Puna	50
B.R. Knight	c Bartlett b Motz	12
D.A. Allen	b Cunis	9
K. Higgs	not out	0
I.J. Jones	did not bat	
Extras	(B 4, LB 6, NB 8)	18
Total	(8 wickets declared)	**254**

ENGLAND	O	M	R	W	O	M	R	W
Jones	26	11	46	3	15	4	32	2
Higgs	20	6	29	3	13	7	12	2
Knight	32	14	41	2	3	1	3	0
Allen	27·4	9	68	2	33	17	46	4
Parfitt					17	6	30	1
Edrich					1	0	6	0
NEW ZEALAND								
Motz	32	7	76	2				
Bartlett	29	4	70	2				
Cunis	28	7	49	2				
Puna	14	2	40	2				
Pollard	1	0	1	0				

FALL OF WICKETS

	NZ	E	NZ
Wkt	1st	1st	2nd
1st	4	9	8
2nd	6	32	27
3rd	66	72	66
4th	83	103	75
5th	83	119	75
6th	92	200	79
7th	100	213	100
8th	179	241	102
9th	181	–	112
10th	192	–	–

Umpires: W.J.C. Gwynne (3) and W.T. Martin (7).

Close: 1st day – NZ(1) 83-5 (Pollard 5, Bartlett 0); 2nd – E(1) 103-3 (Cowdrey 23, Smith 20); 3rd – E(1) 181-5 (Cowdrey 57, Murray 38).

NEW ZEALAND v ENGLAND 1965–66 (3rd Test)

Played at Eden Park, Auckland, on 11, 12, 14, 15 March.
Toss: New Zealand.   Result: MATCH DRAWN.
Debuts: Nil.

England needed 204 runs to win in $4\frac{1}{2}$ hours. Edrich was taken ill with appendicitis after the first day and operated upon before the start of the second. Brown severely strained his back and was unable to complete his ninth over. Sinclair retained the captaincy, even though Chapple was fit to play, and scored 114 out of 163. Cowdrey became the fifth batsman to score 6,000 runs in Tests when his score reached 34 in the first innings. His second innings was his 141st for England – one more than any other batsman had played in Test cricket.

NEW ZEALAND

T.W. Jarvis	c Parks b Jones	39	c Parks b Jones		0
M.J.F. Shrimpton	b Brown	6	lbw b Brown		0
B.E. Congdon	lbw b Higgs	64	run out		23
B.W. Sinclair*	c Russell b Jones	114	b Higgs		9
R.W. Morgan	c Smith b Allen	5	lbw b Knight		25
V. Pollard	c Knight b Allen	2	c Parks b Jones		25
E.C. Petrie†	c Smith b Higgs	12	(8) b Higgs		6
R.C. Motz	c Jones b Allen	16	(7) c Smith b Jones		14
B.R. Taylor	b Allen	18	b Higgs		6
R.S. Cunis	not out	6	c sub (J.T. Murray) b Allen		8
N. Puna	c Russell b Allen	7	not out		2
Extras	(B 1, LB 4, NB 2)	7	(B 2, LB 7, NB 2)		11
Total		**296**			**129**

ENGLAND

P.H. Parfitt	b Taylor	3	b Taylor		30
W.E. Russell	lbw b Motz	56	c Petrie b Taylor		1
M.C. Cowdrey	run out	59	lbw b Puna		27
M.J.K. Smith*	b Taylor	18	lbw b Cunis		30
J.M. Parks†	lbw b Taylor	38	not out		45
B.R. Knight	c Taylor b Pollard	25	not out		13
D.A. Allen	not out	7			
D.J. Brown	b Pollard	0			
K. Higgs	c Petrie b Pollard	0			
I.J. Jones	b Cunis	0			
J.H. Edrich	absent ill	–			
Extras	(B 11, LB 3, NB 2)	16	(B 4, LB 4, NB 5)		13
Total		**222**	(4 wickets)		**159**

ENGLAND	O	M	R	W	O	M	R	W					
Brown	18	6	32	1	8·1	3	8	1					
Jones	21	4	52	2	25	9	28	3					
Higgs	28	13	33	2	28	11	27	3					
Allen	47·5	12	123	5	23·3	7	34	1					
Knight	16	7	40	0	18	9	21	1					
Parfitt	2	0	9	0									

FALL OF WICKETS

Wkt	NZ 1st	E 1st	NZ 2nd	E 2nd
1st	22	3	0	2
2nd	99	121	0	50
3rd	142	128	20	79
4th	153	175	48	112
5th	189	195	68	–
6th	237	215	88	–
7th	262	215	109	–
8th	264	219	118	–
9th	288	222	121	–
10th	296	–	129	–

NEW ZEALAND	O	M	R	W	O	M	R	W
Motz	15	4	42	1	16	1	32	0
Taylor	21	6	46	3	12	4	20	2
Cunis	25·5	8	45	1	18	5	33	1
Puna	22	2	70	0	12	4	27	1
Pollard	5	2	3	3	14	3	30	0
Shrimpton					2	1	1	0
Jarvis					1	0	3	0

Umpires: W.T. Martin (8) and R.W.R. Shortt (4).

Close: 1st day – NZ(1) 237-6 (Sinclair 103, Motz 0); 2nd – E(1) 181-4 (Smith 10, Knight 3); 3rd – NZ(2) 105-6 (Pollard 22, Petrie 3).

ENGLAND v WEST INDIES 1966 (1st Test)

Played at Old Trafford, Manchester, on 2, 3, 4 June.
Toss: West Indies.   Result: WEST INDIES won by an innings and 40 runs.
Debuts: England – C. Milburn; West Indies – D.A.J. Holford.

Hunte square cut the first ball of the rubber for four runs. England were beaten in three days for the first time since 1938 (*Test No. 265*) and it was their first such defeat in a five-day Test. The weather was hot throughout. Gibbs took his tally of wickets in two Test appearances at Old Trafford to 21 (also *Test No. 543*). This match marked the end of Mike Smith's 25-match reign as England's captain, the last appearance of David Allen and the Editor's debut in the BBC commentary box. Holford bowled Titmus with his fourth ball in Test cricket.

WEST INDIES

C.C. Hunte	c Smith b Higgs	135
E.D.A. St J. McMorris	c Russell b Higgs	11
R.B. Kanhai	b Higgs	0
B.F. Butcher	c Parks b Titmus	44
S.M. Nurse	b Titmus	49
G. St A. Sobers*	c Cowdrey b Titmus	161
D.A.J. Holford	c Smith b Allen	32
D.W. Allan†	lbw b Titmus	1
C.C. Griffith	lbw b Titmus	30
W.W. Hall	b Allen	1
L.R. Gibbs	not out	1
Extras	(B 8, LB 10, NB 1)	19
Total		**484**

ENGLAND

C. Milburn	run out	0	b Gibbs	94
W.E. Russell	c Sobers b Gibbs	26	b Griffith	20
K.F. Barrington	c and b Griffith	5	c Nurse b Holford	30
M.C. Cowdrey	c and b Gibbs	12	c Butcher b Sobers	69
M.J.K. Smith*	c Butcher b Gibbs	5	b Gibbs	6
J.M. Parks†	c Nurse b Holford	43	c and b Sobers	11
F.J. Titmus	b Holford	15	c Butcher b Sobers	12
D.A. Allen	c Sobers b Gibbs	37	c Allan b Gibbs	1
D.J. Brown	b Gibbs	14	c Sobers b Gibbs	10
K. Higgs	c Sobers b Holford	1	st Allan b Gibbs	5
I.J. Jones	not out	0	not out	0
Extras	(B 1, LB 4, NB 4)	9	(B 11, LB 1, NB 7)	19
Total		**167**		**277**

ENGLAND	O	M	R	W	O	M	R	W
Jones	28	6	100	0				
Brown	28	4	84	0				
Higgs	31	5	94	3				
Allen	31·1	8	104	2				
Titmus	35	10	83	5				
WEST INDIES								
Hall	14	6	43	0	5	0	28	0
Griffith	10	3	28	1	6	1	25	1
Sobers	7	1	16	0	42	11	87	3
Gibbs	28·1	13	37	5	41	16	69	5
Holford	15	4	34	3	14	2	49	1

FALL OF WICKETS

Wkt	WI 1st	E 1st	E 2nd
1st	38	11	53
2nd	42	24	142
3rd	116	42	166
4th	215	48	184
5th	283	65	203
6th	410	85	217
7th	411	143	218
8th	471	153	268
9th	482	163	276
10th	484	167	277

Umpires: J.S. Buller (22) and C.S. Elliott (21).

Close: 1st day – WI(1) 343-5 (Sobers 83, Holford 6); 2nd – E(1) 163-8 (Brown 10, Higgs 1).

ENGLAND v WEST INDIES 1966 (2nd Test)

Played at Lord's, London, on 16, 17, 18, 20, 21 June.
Toss: West Indies.   Result: MATCH DRAWN.
Debuts: England – B.L. D'Oliveira.

England needed to score 284 runs in 240 minutes. The unbroken partnership of 274 between Sobers and his cousin, Holford, remains the highest for West Indies' sixth wicket in all Tests. Milburn and Graveney recorded England's highest fifth-wicket partnership against West Indies (130 unbroken). Both Holford and Milburn scored hundreds in their second Test match. Parks made his 100th dismissal as a wicket-keeper, and completed the double of 1,000 runs and 100 dismissals, when he caught Kanhai.

WEST INDIES

C.C. Hunte	c Parks b Higgs	18	c Milburn b Knight	13
M.C. Carew	c Parks b Higgs	2	c Knight b Higgs	0
R.B. Kanhai	c Titmus b Higgs	25	c Parks b Knight	40
B.F. Butcher	c Milburn b Knight	49	lbw b Higgs	3
S.M. Nurse	b D'Oliveira	64	c Parks b D'Oliveira	35
G. St A. Sobers*	lbw b Knight	46	not out	163
D.A.J. Holford	b Jones	26	not out	105
D.W. Allan†	c Titmus b Higgs	13		
C.C. Griffith	lbw b Higgs	5		
W.W. Hall	not out	8		
L.R. Gibbs	c Parks b Higgs	4		
Extras	(B 2, LB 7)	9	(LB 8, NB 2)	10
Total		**269**	(5 wickets declared)	**369**

ENGLAND

G. Boycott	c Griffith b Gibbs	60	c Allan b Griffith	25
C. Milburn	lbw b Hall	6	not out	126
T.W. Graveney	c Allan b Hall	96	(6) not out	30
K.F. Barrington	b Sobers	19	(3) b Griffith	5
M.C. Cowdrey*	c Gibbs b Hall	9	(4) c Allan b Hall	5
J.M. Parks†	lbw b Carew	91	(5) b Hall	0
B.L. D'Oliveira	run out	27		
B.R. Knight	b Griffith	6		
F.J. Titmus	c Allan b Hall	6		
K. Higgs	c Holford b Gibbs	13		
I.J. Jones	not out	0		
Extras	(B 7, LB 10, NB 5)	22	(B 4, LB 2)	6
Totals		**355**	(4 wickets)	**197**

ENGLAND	O	M	R	W	O	M	R	W
Jones	21	3	64	1	25	2	95	0
Higgs	33	9	91	6	34	5	82	2
Knight	21	0	63	2	30	3	106	2
Titmus	5	0	18	0	19	3	30	0
D'Oliveira	14	5	24	1	25	7	46	1

WEST INDIES	O	M	R	W	O	M	R	W
Sobers	39	12	89	1	8	4	8	0
Hall	36	2	106	4	14	1	65	2
Griffith	28	4	79	1	11	2	43	2
Gibbs	37·3	18	48	2	13	4	40	0
Carew	3	0	11	1				
Holford					9	1	35	0

FALL OF WICKETS

	WI	E	WI	E
Wkt	1st	1st	2nd	2nd
1st	8	8	2	37
2nd	42	123	22	43
3rd	53	164	25	67
4th	119	198	91	67
5th	205	203	95	–
6th	213	251	–	–
7th	252	266	–	–
8th	252	296	–	–
9th	261	355	–	–
10th	269	355	–	–

Umpires: J.S. Buller (23) and W.F.F. Price (5).

Close: 1st day – WI(1) 155-4 (Nurse 40, Sobers 16); 2nd – E(1) 145-2 (Graveney 65, Barrington 8); 3rd – WI(2) 18-1 (Hunte 11, Kanhai 7); 4th – WI(2) 288-5 (Sobers 121, Holford 71).

ENGLAND v WEST INDIES 1966 (3rd Test)

Played at Trent Bridge, Nottingham, on 30 June, 1, 2, 4, 5 July.
Toss: West Indies.   Result: WEST INDIES won by 139 runs.
Debuts: England – D.L. Underwood.

England, needing to score 393 runs in 389 minutes, were all out at 4.14 pm. Graveney scored his third hundred in consecutive Test appearances at Nottingham. Butcher, who batted for 461 minutes and hit 22 fours, shared in century partnerships for three successive wickets. Underwood, who, in the second innings, was struck in the face by a bouncer from Griffith, added 65 for the tenth wicket with D'Oliveira. It remained England's highest last-wicket stand against West Indies until the 5th Test. When he dismissed Milburn the second time, Hall became the leading West Indies wicket-taker; he overtook the 158 wickets in 43 Tests by S. Ramadhin in his 36th match.

WEST INDIES

C.C. Hunte	lbw b Higgs	9	c Graveney b D'Oliveira	12
P.D. Lashley	c Parks b Snow	49	lbw b D'Oliveira	23
R.B. Kanhai	c Underwood b Higgs	32	c Cowdrey b Higgs	63
B.F. Butcher	b Snow	5	not out	209
S.M. Nurse	c Illingworth b Snow	93	lbw b Higgs	53
G. St A. Sobers*	c Parks b Snow	3	c Underwood b Higgs	94
D.A.J. Holford	lbw b D'Oliveira	11	not out	17
J.L. Hendriks†	b D'Oliveira	2		
C.C. Griffith	c Cowdrey b Higgs	14		
W.W. Hall	b Higgs	12		
L.R. Gibbs	not out	0		
Extras	(B 3, LB 2)	5	(LB 6, W 5)	11
Total		**235**	(5 wickets declared)	**482**

ENGLAND

G. Boycott	lbw b Sobers	0	c Sobers b Griffith	71
C. Milburn	c Sobers b Hall	7	c Griffith b Hall	12
W.E. Russell	b Hall	4	c Sobers b Gibbs	11
T.W. Graveney	c Holford b Sobers	109	c Hendriks b Griffith	32
M.C. Cowdrey*	c Hendriks b Griffith	96	c Sobers b Gibbs	32
J.M. Parks†	c Butcher b Sobers	11	c Lashley b Hall	7
B.L. D'Oliveira	b Hall	76	lbw b Griffith	54
R. Illingworth	c Lashley b Griffith	0	c Lashley b Sobers	4
K. Higgs	c Lashley b Sobers	5	c Sobers b Gibbs	4
J.A. Snow	b Hall	0	b Griffith	3
D.L. Underwood	not out	12	not out	10
Extras	(LB 2, NB 3)	5	(B 8, LB 2, NB 3)	13
Total		**325**		**253**

ENGLAND	O	M	R	W	O	M	R	W		FALL OF WICKETS			
Snow	25	7	82	4	38	10	117	0		WI	E	WI	E
Higgs	25·4	3	71	4	38	6	109	3	*Wkt*	*1st*	*1st*	*2nd*	*2nd*
D'Oliveira	30	14	51	2	34	8	77	2	1st	19	0	29	32
Underwood	2	1	5	0	43	15	86	0	2nd	68	10	65	71
Illingworth	8	1	21	0	25	7	82	0	3rd	80	13	175	125
									4th	140	182	282	132
WEST INDIES									5th	144	221	455	142
Sobers	49	12	90	4	31	6	71	1	6th	180	238	–	176
Hall	34·3	8	105	4	16	3	52	2	7th	190	247	–	181
Griffith	20	5	62	2	13·3	3	34	4	8th	215	255	–	222
Gibbs	23	9	40	0	48	16	83	3	9th	228	260	–	240
Holford	8	2	23	0					10th	235	325	–	253

Umpires: C.S. Elliott (22) and A. Jepson (1).

Close: 1st day – E(1) 33-3 (Graveney 16, Cowdrey 6); 2nd – E(1) 254-7 (D'Oliveira 20, Higgs 4); 3rd – WI(2) 138-2 (Kanhai 50, Butcher 47); 4th – E(2) 30-0 (Boycott 19, Milburn 11).

ENGLAND v WEST INDIES 1966 (4th Test)

Played at Headingley, Leeds, on 4, 5, 6, 8 August.
Toss: West Indies.   Result: WEST INDIES won by an innings and 55 runs.
Debuts: Nil.

West Indies retained the Wisden Trophy, completing their third victory of the rubber at 3.07 pm on the fourth day. Sobers scored his third hundred of the rubber and hit 103 runs between lunch and tea on the second day. His highest Test innings in England took 240 minutes, included 24 fours and took him past 5,000 runs in Tests, 2,000 runs against England, 500 runs in the rubber and 1,000 runs for the tour. His partnership of 265 in 240 minutes with Nurse remains the West Indies fifth-wicket record in all Tests. He then produced his best bowling figures in Tests to date, took his 50th wicket against England, and tidied up their first innings with a spell of 3 for 0 in seven balls. Lashley dismissed Boycott with his third ball in Test cricket.

WEST INDIES

C.C. Hunte	lbw b Snow	48
P.D. Lashley	b Higgs	9
R.B. Kanhai	c Graveney b Underwood	45
B.F. Butcher	c Parks b Higgs	38
S.M. Nurse	c Titmus b Snow	137
G. St A. Sobers*	b Barber	174
D.A.J. Holford	b Higgs	24
C.C. Griffith	b Higgs	0
J.L. Hendriks†	not out	9
W.W. Hall	b Snow	1
L.R. Gibbs	not out	2
Extras	(B 1, LB 12)	13
Total	**(9 wickets declared)**	**500**

ENGLAND

G. Boycott	c Holford b Hall	12		c Hendriks b Lashley	14
R.W. Barber	c Hendriks b Griffith	6		b Sobers	55
C. Milburn	not out	29	(7)	b Gibbs	42
T.W. Graveney	b Hall	8		b Gibbs	19
M.C. Cowdrey*	b Hall	17		lbw b Gibbs	12
B.L. D'Oliveira	c Hall b Griffith	88	(3)	c Butcher b Sobers	7
J.M. Parks†	lbw b Sobers	2	(6)	c Nurse b Gibbs	16
F.J. Titmus	c Hendriks b Sobers	6		b Gibbs	22
K. Higgs	c Nurse b Sobers	49		c Hunte b Sobers	7
D.L. Underwood	c Gibbs b Sobers	0		c Kanhai b Gibbs	0
J.A. Snow	c Holford b Sobers	0		not out	0
Extras	(B 12, LB 11)	23		(B 8, LB 1, NB 2)	11
Total		**240**			**205**

ENGLAND	O	M	R	W	O	M	R	W
Snow	42	6	146	3				
Higgs	43	11	94	4				
D'Oliveira	19	3	52	0				
Titmus	22	7	59	0				
Underwood	24	9	81	1				
Barber	14	2	55	1				
WEST INDIES								
Hall	17	5	47	3	8	2	24	0
Griffith	12	2	37	2	12	0	52	0
Sobers	19·3	4	41	5	20·1	5	39	3
Gibbs	20	5	49	0	19	6	39	6
Holford	10	3	43	0	9	0	39	0
Lashley					3	2	1	1

FALL OF WICKETS

Wkt	WI 1st	E 1st	E 2nd
1st	37	10	28
2nd	102	18	70
3rd	122	42	84
4th	154	49	109
5th	419	63	128
6th	467	83	133
7th	467	179	184
8th	489	238	205
9th	491	240	205
10th	–	240	205

Umpires: J.S. Buller (24) and C.S. Elliott (23).

Close: 1st day – WI(1) 137-3 (Butcher 26, Nurse 8); 2nd – E(1) 4-0 (Boycott 4, Barber 0); 3rd – E(2) 40-1 (Barber 22, D'Oliveira 0).

ENGLAND v WEST INDIES 1966 (5th Test)

Played at Kennington Oval, London, on 18, 19, 20, 22 August.
Toss: West Indies.   Result: ENGLAND won by an innings and 34 runs.
Debuts: England – D.L. Amiss.

Sobers won the toss for the fifth time in the rubber. England's last three wickets added a record 361 runs and for the first time in Test cricket the last three batsmen scored one hundred and two fifties. The partnership of 217 in 235 minutes between Graveney and Murray remains England's highest for the eighth wicket against West Indies and second-highest in all Tests. Higgs and Snow each scored their maiden fifties in first-class cricket and their partnership of 128 in 140 minutes was only two runs short of the England tenth-wicket record by R.E. Foster and W. Rhodes against Australia in 1903-04 (*Test No. 78*). The contribution of Sobers to his team's success in this rubber was massive. In addition to his mastery of the toss, crucial at Manchester, he scored 722 runs (average 103·14), took 20 wickets, and held ten catches, several the product of brilliant anticipation or abnormal reflex action. His first-ball dismissal on the final day was untypically bizarre; he edged a hook at a short ball, which rebounded from his 'box' to short leg, and departed laughing.

WEST INDIES

C.C. Hunte	b Higgs	1	c Murray b Snow		7
E.D.A. St J. McMorris	b Snow	14	c Murray b Snow		1
R.B. Kanhai	c Graveney b Illingworth	104	b D'Oliveira		15
B.F. Butcher	c Illingworth b Close	12	c Barber b Illingworth		60
S.M. Nurse	c Graveney b D'Oliveira	0	c Edrich b Barber		70
G. St A. Sobers*	c Graveney b Barber	81	(7) c Close b Snow		0
D.A.J. Holford	c D'Oliveira b Illingworth	5	(6) run out		7
J.L. Hendriks†	b Barber	0	b Higgs		0
C.C. Griffith	c Higgs b Barber	4	not out		29
W.W. Hall	not out	30	c D'Oliveira b Illingworth		17
L.R. Gibbs	c Murray b Snow	12	c and b Barber		3
Extras	(B 1, LB 3, NB 1)	5	(B 1, LB 14, NB 1)		16
Total		**268**			**225**

ENGLAND

G. Boycott	b Hall	4
R.W. Barber	c Nurse b Sobers	36
J.H. Edrich	c Hendriks b Sobers	35
T.W. Graveney	run out	165
D.L. Amiss	lbw b Hall	17
B.L. D'Oliveira	b Hall	4
D.B. Close*	run out	4
R. Illingworth	c Hendriks b Griffith	3
J.T. Murray†	lbw b Sobers	112
K. Higgs	c and b Holford	63
J.A. Snow	not out	59
Extras	(B 8, LB 14, NB 3)	25
Total		**527**

ENGLAND	O	M	R	W	O	M	R	W
Snow	20·5	1	66	2	13	5	40	3
Higgs	17	4	52	1	15	6	18	1
D'Oliveira	21	7	35	1	17	4	44	1
Close	9	2	21	1	3	1	7	0
Barber	15	3	49	3	22·1	2	78	2
Illingworth	15	7	40	2	15	9	22	2
WEST INDIES								
Hall	31	8	85	3				
Griffith	32	7	78	1				
Sobers	54	23	104	3				
Holford	25·5	1	79	1				
Gibbs	44	16	115	0				
Hunte	13	2	41	0				

FALL OF WICKETS

	WI	E	WI
Wkt	*1st*	*1st*	*2nd*
1st	1	6	5
2nd	56	72	12
3rd	73	85	50
4th	74	126	107
5th	196	130	137
6th	218	150	137
7th	218	166	142
8th	223	383	168
9th	223	399	204
10th	268	527	225

Umpires: J.S. Buller (25) and C.S. Elliott (24).

Close: 1st day – E(1) 20-1 (Barber 11, Edrich 5); 2nd – E(1) 330-7 (Graveney 132, Murray 81); 3rd – WI(2) 135-4 (Nurse 41, Holford 5).

INDIA v WEST INDIES 1966–67 (1st Test)

Played at Brabourne Stadium, Bombay, on 13, 14, 16, 17, 18 December.
Toss: India.   Result: WEST INDIES won by six wickets.
Debuts: India – A.L. Wadekar; West Indies – C.H. Lloyd.

Hunte's century was his eighth and last in Tests. Clive Hubert Lloyd began his 110-match Test career by scoring 160 runs for once out and giving a brilliant display of fielding. Chandrasekhar (11 for 235) produced the best match analysis for India against West Indies and, until 1984-85, the best figures for India in any Test in Bombay.

INDIA

D.N. Sardesai	b Hall	6	b Sobers		26
M.L. Jaisimha	c Hendriks b Griffith	4	c Bynoe b Sobers		44
A.A. Baig	b Hall	0	c and b Holford		42
C.G. Borde	c Hendriks b Sobers	121	c Sobers b Gibbs		12
Nawab of Pataudi, jr*	b Holford	44	(6) b Gibbs		51
A.L. Wadekar	c Gibbs b Sobers	8	(5) c Sobers b Holford		4
S.A. Durani	b Sobers	55	c Hendriks b Gibbs		17
R.G. Nadkarni	c Sobers b Griffith	9	lbw b Holford		0
B.K. Kunderan†	lbw b Griffith	6	b Griffith		79
S. Venkataraghavan	not out	36	lbw b Gibbs		26
B.S. Chandrasekhar	c Gibbs b Holford	2	not out		2
Extras	(LB 3, NB 2)	5	(B 8, NB 5)		13
Total		**296**			**316**

WEST INDIES

C.C. Hunte	b Durani	101	c sub (R.F. Surti) b Chandrasekhar		40
M.R. Bynoe	c Venkataraghavan b Chandrasekhar	2	c Wadekar b Chandrasekhar		5
R.B. Kanhai	c Baig b Chandrasekhar	24			
B.F. Butcher	b Chandrasekhar	16	(3) lbw b Chandrasekhar		11
C.H. Lloyd	c Kunderan b Chandrasekhar	82	not out		78
G. St A. Sobers*	b Venkataraghavan	50	not out		53
D.A.J. Holford	b Chandrasekhar	80			
J.L. Hendriks†	b Chandrasekhar	48			
C.C. Griffith	b Chandrasekhar	12			
W.W. Hall	lbw b Venkataraghavan	1			
L.R. Gibbs	not out	1	(4) c Wadekar b Chandrasekhar		5
Extras	(LB 2, NB 2)	4			
Total		**421**	(4 wickets)		**192**

WEST INDIES	O	M	R	W	O	M	R	W
Hall	19	4	54	2	10	3	10	0
Griffith	21	6	63	3	11	4	53	1
Sobers	25	9	46	3	27	6	79	2
Gibbs	25	8	60	0	24·5	3	67	4
Holford	19·4	2	68	2	39	7	94	3
INDIA								
Jaisimha	2	0	5	0	1	0	3	0
Wadekar	1	0	5	0	0·1	0	4	0
Chandrasekhar	61·5	17	157	7	31	7	78	4
Venkataraghavan	52	17	120	2	19	2	65	0
Durani	30	6	83	1	13	4	42	0
Nadkarni	15	5	47	0				

FALL OF WICKETS

	I	WI	I	WI
Wkt	1st	1st	2nd	2nd
1st	10	12	74	11
2nd	10	52	92	25
3rd	14	82	119	51
4th	107	192	124	90
5th	138	242	141	–
6th	240	295	192	–
7th	242	378	193	–
8th	253	402	217	–
9th	260	409	312	–
10th	296	421	316	–

Umpires: A.M. Mamsa (2) and B. Satyaji Rao (6).

Close: 1st day – I(1) 241-6 (Borde 120, Nadkarni 0); 2nd – WI(1) 208-4 (Hunte 79, Sobers 2); 3rd – I(2) 44-0 (Sardesai 13, Jaisimha 26); 4th – WI(2) 25-2 (Hunte 9, Gibbs 0).

INDIA v WEST INDIES 1966–67 (2nd Test)

Played at Eden Gardens, Calcutta, on 31 December, 1 (*no play*), 3, 4, 5 January.
Toss: West Indies.   Result: WEST INDIES won by an innings and 45 runs.
Debuts: India – B.S. Bedi.

The second day's play was abandoned after a riot had prevented it from being started. The authorities had oversold the seating accommodation and disappointed spectators invaded the ground, clashed with police and set fire to several stands. West Indies gained their second victory at Calcutta after less than 18 hours of play. When his score reached 53, Kanhai became the third West Indian after E. de C. Weekes and Sobers to score 4,000 runs in Tests. Sobers won a vital toss which gave him maximum advantage on an underprepared pitch, scored 70 in 80 minutes, and, using both types of left-arm spin, shared 14 wickets with Gibbs, who turned the ball viciously.

WEST INDIES

C.C. Hunte	run out	43
M.R. Bynoe	run out	19
R.B. Kanhai	c Pataudi b Surti	90
B.F. Butcher	c Pataudi b Bedi	35
C.H. Lloyd	c Kunderan b Bedi	5
S.M. Nurse	c Surti b Jaisimha	56
G. St A. Sobers*	c Jaisimha b Chandrasekhar	70
J.L. Hendriks†	b Surti	5
W.W. Hall	c Subramanya b Chandrasekhar	35
L.R. Gibbs	lbw b Chandrasekhar	1
C.C. Griffith	not out	9
Extras	(B 7, LB 11, NB 4)	22
Total		**390**

INDIA

B.K. Kunderan†	b Hall	39	lbw b Hall	4
M.L. Jaisimha	b Gibbs	37	c and b Gibbs	31
R.F. Surti	lbw b Sobers	16	c Griffith b Sobers	31
C.G. Borde	run out	10	b Lloyd	28
Nawab of Pataudi, jr*	c Griffith b Gibbs	2	c Griffith b Lloyd	2
Hanumant Singh	c Bynoe b Gibbs	4	b Sobers	37
V. Subramanya	c Hendriks b Gibbs	12	run out	17
S. Venkataraghavan	b Sobers	18	(9) c Hendriks b Sobers	2
A.A. Baig	b Gibbs	4	(8) b Gibbs	6
B.S. Bedi	st Hendriks b Sobers	5	c Bynoe b Sobers	0
B.S. Chandrasekhar	not out	3	not out	1
Extras	(B 12, LB 1, NB 4)	17	(B 14, LB 2, NB 3)	19
Total		**167**		**178**

INDIA	O	M	R	W	O	M	R	W
Surti	30	3	106	2				
Subramanya	6	1	9	0				
Chandrasekhar	46	11	107	3				
Bedi	36	11	92	2				
Venkataraghavan	14	3	43	0				
Jaisimha	6	2	11	1				
WEST INDIES								
Sobers	28·5	16	42	3	20	2	56	4
Griffith	6	3	14	0	5	4	4	0
Gibbs	37	17	51	5	30·4	8	36	2
Hall	6	0	32	1	7	0	35	1
Lloyd	4	2	4	0	14	5	23	2
Nurse	4	1	7	0				
Hunte					1	0	5	0

FALL OF WICKETS

Wkt	WI 1st	I 1st	I 2nd
1st	43	60	4
2nd	76	98	62
3rd	133	100	89
4th	154	117	105
5th	259	119	108
6th	272	155	
7th	290	139	170
8th	362	157	176
9th	371	161	176
10th	390	167	178

Umpires: I. Gopalakrishnan (4) and S.P. Pan (6).

Close: 1st day – WI(1) 212-4 (Kanhai 78, Nurse 23); 2nd – no play; 3rd – I(1) 89-1 (Jaisimha 34, Surti 10); 4th – I(2) 133-5 (Hanumant 16, Subramanya 7).

INDIA v WEST INDIES 1966–67 (3rd Test)

Played at Chepauk, Madras, 13, 14, 15, 17, 18 January.
Toss: India.   Result: MATCH DRAWN.
Debuts: Nil.

Engineer was six runs short of becoming the first Indian batsman to score a Test match hundred before lunch. His partnership of 129 with Sardesai was a first-wicket record against West Indies until 1975-76 (*Test No. 776*). India came close to their first win in this series when West Indies, needing 322 for victory in $4\frac{1}{2}$ hours, lost their seventh wicket at 193. Griffith then partnered Sobers through the final 90 minutes, frustrating the Indian spinners by using his pads or, by kneeling or squatting, his body, to obstruct the ball. Earlier Borde had made the last of his five Test hundreds.

INDIA

D.N. Sardesai	c Hendriks b Gibbs	28	lbw b Hall	0
F.M. Engineer†	c Kanhai b Sobers	109	c Butcher b Hall	24
A.L. Wadekar	c Hendriks b Gibbs	0	c Sobers b Gibbs	67
C.G. Borde	c Kanhai b Hunte	125	c Lloyd b Gibbs	49
Nawab of Pataudi, jr*	b Hall	40	c Sobers b Gibbs	5
Hanumant Singh	c Kanhai b Griffith	7	b Griffith	50
V. Subramanya	c Sobers b Hall	17	c Lloyd b Griffith	61
R.F. Surti	not out	50	c Hendriks b Griffith	8
E.A.S. Prasanna	b Bynoe	1	c Sobers b Gibbs	24
B.S. Bedi	c Griffith b Gibbs	11	c Nurse b Griffith	8
B.S. Chandrasekhar	c Hendriks b Sobers	1	not out	10
Extras	(B 4, LB 2, NB 9)	15	(LB 13, W 1, NB 3)	17
Total		**404**		**323**

WEST INDIES

C.C. Hunte	c Subramanya b Chandrasekhar	49	c Surti b Prasanna	26
M.R. Bynoe	lbw b Chandrasekhar	48	c Surti b Bedi	36
R.B. Kanhai	c Borde b Surti	77	c Pataudi b Bedi	36
B.F. Butcher	b Prasanna	0	c Surti b Prasanna	24
C.H. Lloyd	b Surti	38	b Bedi	24
S.M. Nurse	b Chandrasekhar	26	lbw b Bedi	0
G. St A. Sobers*	c Engineer b Chandrasekhar	95	not out	74
J.L. Hendriks†	c Engineer b Surti	0	lbw b Prasanna	9
C.C. Griffith	c Surti b Bedi	27	not out	40
W.W. Hall	b Prasanna	31		
L.R. Gibbs	not out	1		
Extras	(B 5, LB 6, NB 3)	14	(NB 1)	1
Total		**406**	(7 wickets)	**270**

WEST INDIES	O	M	R	W	O	M	R	W		FALL OF WICKETS			
Hall	19	1	68	2	12	2	67	2		I	WI	I	WI
Griffith	23	4	96	1	14	2	61	4	*Wkt*	*1st*	*1st*	*2nd*	*2nd*
Sobers	27·2	7	69	2	27	11	58	0	1st	129	99	0	63
Gibbs	46	10	87	3	40·4	13	96	4	2nd	131	114	45	71
Lloyd	13	2	39	0	12	3	24	0	3rd	145	115	107	118
Hunte	10	2	25	1					4th	239	194	123	130
Bynoe	5	4	5	1					5th	257	246	192	131
INDIA									6th	292	246	245	166
Surti	19	2	68	3	9	1	27	0	7th	377	251	266	193
Subramanya	7	1	21	0	7	3	14	0	8th	382	324	281	–
Chandrasekhar	46	15	130	4	12	2	41	0	9th	403	404	297	–
Bedi	19	3	55	1	28	7	81	4	10th	404	406	323	–
Prasanna	41	11	118	2	37	9	106	3					

Umpires: S.K. Raghunatha Rao (7) and S. Roy (5).

Close: 1st day – I(1) 278-5 (Borde 72, Subramanya 11); 2nd – WI(1) 95-0 (Hunte 45, Bynoe 42); 3rd – WI(1) 406-9 (Sobers 95, Gibbs 1); 4th – I(2) 303-9 (Prasanna 14, Chandrasekhar 0).

SOUTH AFRICA v AUSTRALIA 1966–67 (1st Test)

Played at New Wanderers, Johannesburg, on 23, 24, 26, 27, 28 December.
Toss: South Africa.   Result: SOUTH AFRICA won by 233 runs.
Debuts: Australia – D.A. Renneberg, H.B. Taber.

South Africa gained their first home victory against Australia at the 22nd attempt and 64 years after this series began. South Africa's total of 620 was then their highest in Tests and it remains the third-highest second innings total in all Test matches. Lindsay's 182 was his first Test hundred; it took 274 minutes and included five sixes. He also equalled the (then) world Test wicket-keeping record of six dismissals in an innings. His partnership of 221 with Van der Merwe remains the highest for South Africa's seventh wicket against Australia. Taber made eight dismissals in the first Test match he had ever attended. Goddard, varying his pace and movement, returned his best analysis in 41 Tests.

SOUTH AFRICA

T.L. Goddard	c Taber b Hawke	5	c Simpson b Hawke	13
E.J. Barlow	c Taber b McKenzie	13	c Taber b Renneberg	50
A. Bacher	c Cowper b McKenzie	5	run out	63
R.G. Pollock	c McKenzie b Renneberg	5	b Cowper	90
K.C. Bland	lbw b McKenzie	0	c Simpson b Chappell	32
H.R. Lance	hit wkt b McKenzie	44	c Simpson b McKenzie	70
D.T. Lindsay†	c Taber b Renneberg	69	c Chappell b Stackpole	182
P.L. van der Merwe*	c Taber b Simpson	19	c Chappell b Simpson	76
R. Dumbrill	c Chappell b Simpson	19	c Taber b Chappell	29
P.M. Pollock	c Taber b McKenzie	6	st Taber b Simpson	2
A.H. McKinnon	not out	0	not out	0
Extras	(B 11, W 3)	14	(B 7, LB 5, W 1)	13
Total		**199**		**620**

AUSTRALIA

R.B. Simpson*	c Goddard b P.M. Pollock	65	run out	48
W.M. Lawry	c Lindsay b Goddard	98	b Mckinnon	27
I.R. Redpath	c Lindsay b Barlow	41	c Van der Merwe b Barlow	21
R.M. Cowper	c Lindsay b Barlow	0	c Lindsay b Goddard	1
K.R. Stackpole	c Lindsay b Barlow	0	b Goddard	9
I.M. Chappell	c Lindsay b Goddard	37	c Lindsay b Dumbrill	34
T.R. Veivers	b Lance	18	b Goddard	55
H.B. Taber†	c Lindsay b McKinnon	13	b Goddard	7
G.D. McKenzie	run out	16	c sub (M.J. Procter) b Goddard	34
N.J.N. Hawke	not out	18	c sub (M.J. Procter) b Goddard	13
D.A. Renneberg	c Goddard b McKinnon	9	not out	2
Extras	(LB 5, W 2, NB 3)	10	(LB 6, W 2, NB 2)	10
Total		**325**		**261**

AUSTRALIA	O	M	R	W	O	M	R	W
McKenzie	21·5	6	46	5	39	4	118	1
Hawke	8	1	25	1	14·2	1	46	1
Renneberg	16	3	54	2	32	8	96	1
Chappell	2	0	16	0	21	3	91	2
Veivers	9	1	13	0	18	3	59	0
Cowper	6	0	21	0	16	2	56	1
Simpson	4	1	10	2	16·1	3	66	2
Stackpole					21	6	75	1
SOUTH AFRICA								
P.M. Pollock	25	6	74	1	18	3	33	0
Dumbrill	18	3	55	0	16	6	43	1
Goddard	26	11	39	2	32·5	14	53	6
Lance	17	6	35	1	3	0	6	0
McKinnon	27·2	9	73	2	30	14	64	1
Barlow	17	3	39	3	15	1	47	1
R.G. Pollock					3	1	5	0

FALL OF WICKETS				
	SA	A	SA	A
Wkt	*1st*	*1st*	*2nd*	*2nd*
1st	14	118	29	62
2nd	31	204	87	97
3rd	31	207	178	98
4th	35	207	228	110
5th	41	218	268	112
6th	151	267	349	183
7th	156	267	570	210
8th	190	294	614	212
9th	199	299	620	248
10th	199	325	620	261

Umpires: L.M. Baxter (4) and H.C. Kidson (7).

Close: 1st day – A(1) 99-0 (Simpson 52, Lawry 41); 2nd – SA(2) 4-0 (Goddard 3, Barlow 1); 3rd – SA(2) 336-5 (Lance 66, Lindsay 20); 4th – A(2) 97-1 (Simpson 48, Redpath 17).

SOUTH AFRICA v AUSTRALIA 1966–67 (2nd Test)

Played at Newlands, Cape Town, on 31 December, 2, 3, 4, 5 January.
Toss: Australia.   Result: AUSTRALIA won by six wickets.
Debuts: Australia – G.D. Watson.

Australia completed their win with 24 minutes to spare. Simpson's sixth Test hundred was his first against South Africa and his 50th in first-class cricket. Graeme Pollock, handicapped by a thigh strain, scored his first hundred off 139 balls in 193 minutes; his innings of 209 (in 350 minutes with 30 fours), is the highest in any Test at Cape Town. The Pollocks' partnership of 85 remains the highest for the ninth wicket by either side in this series. Barlow produced his only five-wicket analysis in 30 Tests.

AUSTRALIA

R.B. Simpson*	c Lance b Barlow	153	c Goddard b P.M. Pollock	18
W.M. Lawry	lbw b P.M. Pollock	10	c P.M. Pollock b Goddard	39
I.R. Redpath	lbw b McKinnon	54	not out	69
R.M. Cowper	c Van der Merwe b Lance	36	c Lindsay b Goddard	4
I.M. Chappell	c Lindsay b Goddard	49	b McKinnon	7
T.R. Veivers	lbw b P.M. Pollock	30	not out	35
K.R. Stackpole	c Lindsay b Barlow	134		
G.D. Watson	c Lance b Barlow	50		
G.D. McKenzie	c and b Barlow	11		
H.B. Tabert	not out	2		
D.A. Renneberg	b Barlow	2		
Extras	(B 2, LB 7, W 2)	11	(LB 5, NB 3)	8
Total		**542**	(4 wickets)	**180**

SOUTH AFRICA

T.L. Goddard	c Stackpole b McKenzie	7	lbw b Simpson	37
E.J. Barlow	c Redpath b McKenzie	19	run out	17
A. Bacher	b McKenzie	0	c Simpson b McKenzie	4
R.G. Pollock	c Taber b Simpson	209	b Simpson	4
H.R. Lance	c Simpson b Chappell	2	run out	53
D.T. Lindsay†	c and b Renneberg	5	c Simpson b Cowper	81
P.L. van der Merwe*	c Cowper b Simpson	50	lbw b Chappell	18
D.B. Pithey	c Taber b McKenzie	4	c Redpath b Renneberg	55
R. Dumbrill	c Chappell b McKenzie	6	(10) b McKenzie	1
P.M. Pollock	c Stackpole b Veivers	41	(9) not out	75
A.H. McKinnon	not out	6	b McKenzie	8
Extras	(LB 4)	4	(B 5, LB 9)	14
Total		**353**		**367**

SOUTH AFRICA	O	M	R	W	O	M	R	W
P.M. Pollock	22	4	84	2	12	2	42	1
Dumbrill	11	2	36	0				
Goddard	42	15	79	1	29·1	10	67	2
Barlow	33·3	9	85	5	2	1	1	0
Pithey	22	5	59	0				
McKinnon	38	16	93	1	22	5	62	1
Lance	20	1	95	1				
AUSTRALIA								
McKenzie	33	10	65	5	39·3	11	67	3
Renneberg	18	6	51	1	24	2	63	1
Watson	11	2	27	0				
Chappell	13	4	51	1	39	17	71	1
Simpson	24	9	59	2	39	12	99	2
Veivers	8·1	2	32	1	7	2	21	0
Cowper	6	0	28	0	10	2	21	1
Stackpole	14	2	36	0	8	4	11	0

FALL OF WICKETS

	A	SA	SA	A
Wkt	1st	1st	2nd	2nd
1st	21	12	45	49
2nd	138	12	60	81
3rd	216	41	60	98
4th	310	66	64	119
5th	316	85	183	–
6th	368	197	211	–
7th	496	242	245	–
8th	537	258	331	–
9th	538	343	345	–
10th	542	353	367	–

Umpires: G. Goldman (1) and H.C. Kidson (8).

Close: 1st day – A(1) 292-3 (Simpson 139, Chappell 45); 2nd – SA(1) 56-3 (R.G. Pollock 28, Lance 2); 3rd – SA(2) 13-0 (Goddard 9, Barlow 4); 4th – SA(2) 288-7 (Pithey 38, P.M. Pollock 23).

SOUTH AFRICA v AUSTRALIA 1966–67 (3rd Test)

Played at Kingsmead, Durban, on 20, 21, 23, 24, 25 January.
Toss: Australia.   Result: SOUTH AFRICA won by eight wickets.
Debuts: South Africa – M.J. Procter, P.H.J. Trimborn.

South Africa completed their second home win against Australia soon after tea on the fifth day after Simpson had become the first captain since 1930-31 to elect to field in a Durban Test. Barlow was out to the first ball of the match. In the first innings, Lawry missed a hook at a lifting ball from Pollock in the seventh over and retired for ten stitches to be inserted in his head wound. By the time he returned, head swathed in bandages, to make top score, Goddard had dismissed Redpath and become the first South African to complete the Test double of 100 wickets and 1,000 runs.

SOUTH AFRICA

E.J. Barlow	c and b McKenzie	0	c Redpath b McKenzie		22
T.L. Goddard	b Cowper	19	c Taber b Cowper		33
A. Bacher	c Taber b McKenzie	47	not out		60
R.G. Pollock	c Redpath b Cowper	2	not out		67
H.R. Lance	c Taber b Cowper	13			
D.T. Lindsay†	c Chappell b Hawke	137			
M.J. Procter	b Renneberg	1			
P.L. van der Merwe*	run out	42			
D.B. Pithey	b Hawke	15			
P.M. Pollock	not out	12			
P.H.J. Trimborn	run out	2			
Extras	(B 3, LB 2, NB 5)	10	(LB 2, NB 1)		3
Total		**300**	(2 wickets)		**185**

AUSTRALIA

R.B. Simpson*	c Lindsay b Procter	6	lbw b Trimborn		94
W.M. Lawry	c Lindsay b Barlow	44	c Lindsay b Lance		34
I.R. Redpath	c Barlow b Goddard	7	c Barlow b P.M. Pollock		80
R.M. Cowper	c Goddard b Trimborn	19	c Lindsay b Lance		40
K.R. Stackpole	c Lindsay b Barlow	24	(7) c R.G. Pollock b P.M. Pollock		35
T.R. Veivers	b Goddard	6	c Lindsay b Procter		0
I.M. Chappell	run out	5	(5) c R.G. Pollock b Procter		25
G.D. McKenzie	lbw b Procter	17	b Procter		8
H.B. Taber†	c Bacher b Barlow	4	(10) c Trimborn b Procter		0
N.J.N. Hawke	not out	9	(9) b Goddard		5
D.A. Renneberg	b Procter	0	not out		0
Extras	(LB 1, NB 5)	6	(B 4, LB 4, NB 5)		13
Total		**147**			**334**

AUSTRALIA	O	M	R	W	O	M	R	W
McKenzie	31	7	93	2	20	7	36	1
Hawke	18	1	69	2	14	6	22	0
Renneberg	21	4	58	1	11	1	27	0
Cowper	37	14	57	3	17	9	29	1
Redpath	4	0	13	0				
Simpson					4	0	21	0
Chappell					7	0	39	0
Stackpole					2	0	8	0
SOUTH AFRICA								
P.M. Pollock	13	4	35	0	19	5	58	2
Procter	14	4	27	3	29·1	7	71	4
Trimborn	14	3	35	1	28	9	47	1
Goddard	17	6	26	2	27	15	23	1
Barlow	11	4	18	3	14	5	28	0
Pithey					28	12	55	0
Lance					15	4	39	2

FALL OF WICKETS

Wkt	SA 1st	A 1st	A 2nd	SA 2nd
1st	0	14	94	52
2nd	53	37	159	58
3rd	57	45	224	–
4th	83	74	266	–
5th	90	88	266	–
6th	94	96	317	–
7th	197	132	320	–
8th	286	137	334	–
9th	287	137	334	–
10th	300	147	334	–

Umpires: J.G. Draper (2) and H.C. Kidson (9).

Close: 1st day – SA(1) 268-7 (Lindsay 131, Pithey 5); 2nd – A(1) 147 all out; 3rd – A(2) 185-2 (Redpath 36, Cowper 14); 4th – SA(2) 42-0 (Barlow 18, Goddard 22).

SOUTH AFRICA v AUSTRALIA 1966–67 (4th Test)

Played at New Wanderers, Johannesburg, on 3, 4, 6, 7 (*no play*), 8 February.
Toss: Australia.   Result: MATCH DRAWN.
Debuts: South Africa – J.H. du Preez.

A rain storm allowed only three balls to be bowled after tea on the final day when two wickets separated Australia from an innings defeat. Lindsay took just 47 minutes to reach 50, went to his third hundred of the rubber with a six exactly an hour later, and scored 105 in a post-tea session shortened by eight minutes because of poor light. His remarkable innings included four sixes and broke the record for the most runs by a wicket-keeper in a Test rubber (525 by B.K. Kunderan for India against England in 1963–64).

AUSTRALIA

W.M. Lawry	c Bacher b Trimborn	17		b Procter	2
R.B. Simpson*	c Du Preez b Goddard	24		c Bacher b Procter	28
I.R. Redpath	c Lindsay b Barlow	14	(4)	c Trimborn b P.M. Pollock	46
R.M. Cowper	c Trimborn b Procter	25	(5)	b Du Preez	16
I.M. Chappell	lbw b Goddard	0	(6)	not out	13
K.R. Stackpole	b Goddard	4	(7)	c Goddard b Du Preez	5
T.R. Veivers	c Lindsay b Procter	19	(8)	c Lindsay b Goddard	21
G.D. Watson	c Lance b Procter	17	(9)	b Goddard	0
G.D. McKenzie	c R.G. Pollock b Procter	11	(10)	not out	0
H.B. Taber†	c Trimborn b P.M. Pollock	4	(3)	lbw b Goddard	14
D.A. Renneberg	not out	0			
Extras	(LB 6, W 1, NB 1)	8		(LB 2, NB 1)	3
Total		**143**		(8 wickets)	**148**

SOUTH AFRICA

T.L. Goddard	c Stackpole b Renneberg	47
E.J. Barlow	c Taber b Renneberg	4
A. Bacher	c Taber b Watson	22
R.G. Pollock	c Taber b Cowper	22
H.R. Lance	lbw b Watson	30
D.T. Lindsay†	c Simpson b Renneberg	131
M.J. Procter	lbw b Simpson	16
P.L. van der Merwe*	c Taber b Renneberg	12
J.H. du Preez	c Simpson b Renneberg	0
P.M. Pollock	not out	34
P.H.J. Trimborn	not out	11
Extras	(LB 3)	3
Total	(9 wickets declared)	**332**

SOUTH AFRICA	O	M	R	W	O	M	R	W	FALL OF WICKETS			
P.M. Pollock	12·1	3	21	1	14	6	24	1		A	SA	A
Procter	18	7	32	4	17	6	38	2	*Wkt*	*1st*	*1st*	*2nd*
Goddard	19	6	36	3	16·3	9	23	3	1st	33	8	11
Trimborn	10	3	21	1	7	3	14	0	2nd	59	39	41
Barlow	11	6	25	1	7	3	20	0	3rd	59	86	58
Du Preez					14	6	22	2	4th	59	120	94
Lance					3	1	4	0	5th	69	177	116
									6th	103	210	125
AUSTRALIA									7th	108	266	148
McKenzie	39	7	96	0					8th	139	272	148
Renneberg	25	3	97	5					9th	139	299	–
Watson	20	4	67	2					10th	143	–	–
Cowper	15	7	36	1								
Simpson	6	0	33	1								

Umpires: J.G. Draper (3) and H.C. Kidson (10).

Close: 1st day – A(1) 139-9 (Taber 0, Renneberg 0); 2nd – SA(1) 266-7 (Lindsay 111, Du Preez 0); 3rd – A(2) 13-1 (Simpson 9, Taber 2); 4th – no play.

SOUTH AFRICA v AUSTRALIA 1966–67 (5th Test)

Played at St George's Park, Port Elizabeth, on 24, 25, 27, 28 February.
Toss: South Africa.   Result: SOUTH AFRICA won by seven wickets.
Debuts: Nil.

South Africa won their first rubber against Australia when Lance completed this third victory with a six over mid-wicket on the fourth afternoon. Peter Pollock became the fourth (and youngest) South African to take a hundred Test wickets when he dismissed Redpath in the second innings. His brother celebrated his 23rd birthday by scoring his sixth Test century. Lindsay, applauded to the wicket, added only a single to his record aggregate for a wicket-keeper in any Test rubber. His 606 runs (average 86·57) is also the record for South Africa at home against Australia. He went on to set two more records when he took his tally of dismissals in the rubber to 24 – all caught: the most catches in any five-match rubber and the most dismissals for either country in this series.

AUSTRALIA

R.B. Simpson*	c Lindsay b P.M. Pollock	12	lbw b Goddard	35
W.M. Lawry	run out	0	c Bacher b Barlow	25
I.M. Chappell	c Bacher b Procter	11	lbw b Goddard	15
I.R. Redpath	c Du Preez b P.M. Pollock	26	lbw b P.M. Pollock	28
R.M. Cowper	c Lindsay b Trimborn	60	b Barlow	54
K.R. Stackpole	c R.G. Pollock b Goddard	24	c Lindsay b Trimborn	19
J.W. Martin	lbw b Goddard	0	c Lindsay b Goddard	20
G.D. Watson	c Barlow b Goddard	0	b P.M. Pollock	9
G.D. McKenzie	c Trimborn b Du Preez	14	c R.G. Pollock b Trimborn	29
H.B. Taber†	c Bacher b Procter	20	c Goddard b Trimborn	30
D.A. Renneberg	not out	0	not out	0
Extras	(W 1, NB 5)	6	(LB 2, W 1, NB 11)	14
Total		**173**		**278**

SOUTH AFRICA

T.L. Goddard	c Taber b McKenzie	74	c Taber b McKenzie	59
E.J. Barlow	lbw b McKenzie	46	c Chappell b McKenzie	15
A. Bacher	c Taber b McKenzie	3	c Martin b Chappell	40
R.G. Pollock	b Cowper	105	not out	33
H.R. Lance	c Renneberg b Simpson	21	not out	28
D.T. Lindsay†	c Redpath b McKenzie	1		
M.J. Procter	hit wkt b McKenzie	0		
P.L. van der Merwe*	lbw b Watson	8		
P.M. Pollock	c Lawry b Cowper	13		
J.H. du Preez	lbw b Cowper	0		
P.H.J. Trimborn	not out	0		
Extras	(B 1, LB 3, W 1)	5	(LB 1, W 2, NB 1)	4
Total		**276**	(3 wickets)	**179**

SOUTH AFRICA	O	M	R	W	O	M	R	W		FALL OF WICKETS			
P.M. Pollock	17	2	57	2	15	0	42	2		A	SA	A	SA
Procter	15·1	3	36	2	16	3	59	0	*Wkt*	*1st*	*1st*	*2nd*	*2nd*
Trimborn	18	4	37	1	10·1	4	12	3	1st	4	112	50	28
Goddard	10	3	13	3	36	12	63	3	2nd	17	124	74	109
Barlow	4	2	9	0	15	3	52	2	3rd	27	125	79	118
Lance	8	4	15	0	5	2	7	0	4th	89	175	144	–
Du Preez	2	2	0	1	8	4	29	0	5th	137	201	166	–
									6th	137	201	207	–
AUSTRALIA									7th	137	226	207	–
McKenzie	35	13	65	5	17	5	38	2	8th	137	271	229	–
Renneberg	19	6	44	0	12	1	38	0	9th	173	271	268	–
Watson	18	3	58	1	3	0	10	0	10th	173	276	278	–
Cowper	19·3	9	27	3	12	4	26	0					
Martin	17	1	64	0	5	0	25	0					
Simpson	8	2	13	1	5	0	10	0					
Chappell					7·1	2	28	1					

Umpires: J.G. Draper (4) and H.C. Kidson (11).

Close: 1st day – SA(1) 7-0 (Goddard 7, Barlow 0); 2nd – SA(1) 220-6 (R.G. Pollock 67, Van der Merwe 6); 3rd – A(2) 207-5 (Cowper 54, Martin 20).

ENGLAND v INDIA 1967 (1st Test)

Played at Headingley, Leeds, on 8, 9, 10, 12, 13 June.
Toss: England.   Result: ENGLAND won by six wickets.
Debuts: England – R.N.S. Hobbs; India – S. Guha, R.C. Saxena.

India, without a victory in any first-class match on the tour so far, lost the services of two key bowlers (Surti – bruised knee, Bedi – leg strain) from the first afternoon. Following on 386 in arrears, India retaliated with their highest total against England until 1984-85 and took the match to 2.59 on the fifth afternoon. Boycott's 246 not out was scored off 555 balls in 573 minutes and included a six and 29 fours; it remains the highest innings by either side in this series and he shared in hundred partnerships for three successive wickets. His first hundred occupied 341 minutes (316 balls) and he was excluded from the next Test as a disciplinary measure. England's total is their highest at Leeds. The stand of 168 between Engineer and Wadekar was the first hundred partnership of the tour and was then India's highest for the second wicket against England.

ENGLAND

J.H. Edrich	c Engineer b Surti	1	c Wadekar b Chandrasekhar	22
G. Boycott	not out	246		
K.F. Barrington	run out	93	(2) c Engineer b Chandrasekhar	46
T.W. Graveney	c sub (S. Venkataraghavan) b Chandrasekhar	59	(3) b Chandrasekhar	14
B.L. D'Oliveira	c sub(‡) b Chandrasekhar	109	(4) not out	24
D.B. Close*	not out	22		
J.T. Murray†	)		(5) c sub(‡) b Prasanna	4
R. Illingworth	)		(6) not out	12
K. Higgs	) did not bat			
J.A. Snow	)			
R.N.S. Hobbs	)			
Extras	(B 8, LB 12)	20	(B 3, LB 1)	4
Total	(4 wickets declared)	**550**	(4 wickets)	**126**

INDIA

F.M. Engineer†	c and b Illingworth	42	c and b Close	87
R.C. Saxena	b D'Oliveira	9	(7) b Snow	16
A.L. Wadekar	run out	0	c Close b Illingworth	91
C.G. Borde	b Snow	8	b Illingworth	33
Hanumant Singh	c D'Oliveira b Illingworth	9	c D'Oliveira b Illingworth	73
Nawab of Pataudi, jr*	c Barrington b Hobbs	64	b Illingworth	148
E.A.S. Prasanna	c Murray b Illingworth	0	(8) lbw b Close	19
S. Guha	b Snow	4	(9) b Higgs	1
R.F. Surti	c and b Hobbs	22	(2) c Murray b Snow	5
B.S. Bedi	lbw b Hobbs	0	c Snow b Hobbs	14
B.S. Chandrasekhar	not out	0	not out	0
Extras	(LB 6)	6	(B 10, LB 13)	23
Total		**164**		**510**

INDIA	O	M	R	W	O	M	R	W		FALL OF WICKETS			
Guha	43	10	105	0	5	0	10	0		E	I	I	E
Surti	11	2	25	1					*Wkt*	*1st*	*1st*	*2nd*	*2nd*
Chandrasekhar	45	9	121	2	19	8	50	3	1st	7	39	5	58
Bedi	15	8	32	0					2nd	146	40	173	78
Prasanna	59	8	187	0	21·3	5	54	1	3rd	253	59	217	87
Pataudi	4	1	13	0					4th	505	59	228	92
Wadekar	1	0	9	0	2	0	8	0	5th	–	81	362	–
Hanumant Singh	3	0	27	0					6th	–	81	388	–
Saxena	2	0	11	0					7th	–	92	448	–
ENGLAND									8th	–	151	469	–
Snow	17	7	34	2	41	11	108	2	9th	–	151	506	–
Higgs	14	8	19	0	24	3	71	1	10th	–	164	510	–
D'Oliveira	9	4	29	1	11	5	22	0					
Hobbs	22·2	9	45	3	45·2	13	100	1					
Illingworth	22	11	31	3	58	26	100	4					
Close	3	3	0	0	21	5	48	2					
Barrington					9	1	38	0					

Umpires: C.S. Elliott (25) and H. Yarnold (1).   ‡ V. Subramanya

Close: 1st day – E(1) 281-3 (Boycott 106, D'Oliveira 19); 2nd – I(1) 86-6 (Pataudi 14, Guha 4); 3rd – I(2) 198-2 (Wadekar 84, Borde 16); 4th – I(2) 475-8 (Pataudi 129, Bedi 0).

ENGLAND v INDIA 1967 (2nd Test)

Played at Lord's, London, on 22, 23, 24, 26 June.
Toss: India.   Result: ENGLAND won by an innings and 124 runs.
Debuts: Nil.

Although over six hours of play were lost to rain and bad light on the second and third days, England completed their innings victory at 3.08 on the fourth afternoon. Murray's six catches in the first innings equalled the (then) Test record held jointly by A.T.W. Grout and D.T. Lindsay. Sardesai retired hurt (when 9 and with India's total 22) after being struck on the right hand by a ball from Snow. He resumed at 102 but X-ray examinations subsequently revealed a fracture and he did not bat in the second innings.

INDIA

D.N. Sardesai	c Murray b Illingworth	28		absent hurt	–
F.M. Engineer†	c Murray b Brown	8	(1)	c Amiss b Snow	8
A.L. Wadekar	c Illingworth b D'Oliveira	57		b Illingworth	19
C.G. Borde	b Snow	0		c Snow b Close	1
Nawab of Pataudi, jr*	c Murray b Brown	5		c Graveney b Close	5
R.F. Surti	c Murray b D'Oliveira	6		c D'Oliveira b Illingworth	0
V. Subramanya	c Murray b Brown	0		c Edrich b Illingworth	1
B.K. Kunderan	c Murray b Snow	20	(2)	lbw b Illingworth	47
E.A.S. Prasanna	run out	17	(8)	c D'Oliveira b Illingworth	0
B.S. Bedi	c Amiss b Snow	5	(9)	b Illingworth	11
B.S. Chandrasekhar	not out	2	(10)	not out	3
Extras	(B 2, LB 2)	4		(B 11, LB 4)	15
Total		**152**			**110**

ENGLAND

J.H. Edrich	c and b Surti	12
K.F. Barrington	b Chandrasekhar	97
D.L. Amiss	b Chandrasekhar	29
T.W. Graveney	st Engineer b Bedi	151
B.L. D'Oliveira	c and b Chandrasekhar	33
D.B. Close*	c Borde b Prasanna	7
J.T. Murray†	b Chandrasekhar	7
R. Illingworth	lbw b Chandrasekhar	4
R.N.S. Hobbs	b Bedi	7
D.J. Brown	c Pataudi b Bedi	5
J.A. Snow	not out	8
Extras	(B 5, LB 18, W 1, NB 2)	26
Total		**386**

ENGLAND	O	M	R	W	O	M	R	W		FALL OF WICKETS		
Snow	20·4	5	49	3	8	4	12	1		I	E	I
Brown	18	3	61	3	5	2	10	0	*Wkt*	*1st*	*1st*	*2nd*
D'Oliveira	15	6	38	2					1st	12	46	8
Illingworth	2	2	0	1	22·3	12	29	6	2nd	24	107	60
Hobbs					6	1	16	0	3rd	29	185	67
Close					15	5	28	2	4th	45	307	79
									5th	58	334	80
INDIA									6th	102	359	86
Surti	31	10	67	1					7th	112	365	90
Subramanya	7	1	20	0					8th	144	372	101
Chandrasekhar	53	9	127	5					9th	145	372	110
Bedi	31·2	13	68	3					10th	152	386	–
Prasanna	32	5	78	1								

Umpires: J.S. Buller (26) and A. Jepson (2).

Close: 1st day – E(1) 107-2 (Barrington 54); 2nd – E(1) 252-3 (Graveney 74, D'Oliveira 27); 3rd – E(1) 386 all out.

ENGLAND v INDIA 1967 (3rd Test)

Played at Edgbaston, Birmingham, on 13, 14, 15 July.
Toss: England.   Result: ENGLAND won by 132 runs.
Debuts: Nil.

England achieved their third win in this three-match rubber at 6.18 on the third evening after 20 wickets had fallen on the second day. Murray and Hobbs shared a partnership of 57 which was England's highest for the tenth wicket against India until 1982 (*Test No. 928*). Boycott ended the match with a diving catch in front of the sightscreen.

ENGLAND

G. Boycott	st Engineer b Bedi	25	b Subramanya		6
C. Milburn	c Wadekar b Chandrasekhar	40	b Bedi		15
K.F. Barrington	c Wadekar b Prasanna	75	c Kunderan b Chandrasekhar		13
T.W. Graveney	c Venkataraghavan				
	b Chandrasekhar	10	c Subramanya b Prasanna		17
D.L. Amiss	c Wadekar b Venkataraghavan	5	c Wadekar b Prasanna		45
D.B. Close*	c Subramanya b Prasanna	26	c Chandrasekhar b Prasanna		47
J.T. Murray†	c Subramanya b Chandrasekhar	77	b Bedi		4
R. Illingworth	c Wadekar b Prasanna	2	c Pataudi b Prasanna		10
D.J. Brown	run out	3	not out		29
J.A. Snow	c Engineer b Bedi	10	c Borde b Chandrasekhar		9
R.N.S. Hobbs	not out	15	c Prasanna b Chandrasekhar		2
Extras	(B 5, LB 5)	10	(B 4, LB 2)		6
Total		**298**			**203**

INDIA

F.M. Engineer†	c Graveney b Brown	23	c Barrington b Hobbs		28
B.K. Kunderan	b Brown	2	c Murray b Close		33
A.L. Wadekar	c Amiss b Snow	5	c Boycott b Illingworth		70
C.G. Borde	b Snow	8	b Illingworth		10
Nawab of Pataudi, jr*	b Brown	0	c Hobbs b Close		47
Hanumant Singh	c Amiss b Illingworth	15	c Milburn b Illingworth		6
V. Subramanya	b Hobbs	10	c Milburn b Illingworth		4
S. Venkataraghavan	not out	19	c Hobbs b Close		17
E.A.S. Prasanna	b Illingworth	1	b Hobbs		15
B.S. Bedi	c and b Hobbs	1	not out		15
B.S. Chandrasekhar	st Murray b Hobbs	0	c Boycott b Close		22
Extras	(B 4, LB 2, NB 2)	8	(B 5, LB 5)		10
Total		**92**			**277**

INDIA	O	M	R	W	O	M	R	W		FALL OF WICKETS			
Subramanya	10	2	28	0	4	0	22	1		E	I	E	I
Kunderan	4	0	13	0					*Wkt*	*1st*	*1st*	*2nd*	*2nd*
Bedi	27	6	76	2	24	9	60	2	1st	63	9	6	48
Chandrasekhar	32	8	94	3	20·5	6	43	3	2nd	67	18	32	91
Venkataraghavan	13	3	26	1	2	1	4	0	3rd	89	35	34	102
Prasanna	20	5	51	3	24	9	60	4	4th	112	35	66	185
Pataudi					2	0	8	0	5th	182	41	144	201
									6th	183	66	149	203
ENGLAND									7th	186	72	149	207
Snow	12	3	28	2	14	0	33	0	8th	191	73	179	226
Brown	11	6	17	3	2	1	1	0	9th	241	82	193	240
Illingworth	7	4	14	2	43	13	92	4	10th	298	92	203	277
Hobbs	6·3	1	25	3	32	10	73	2					
Close					21·4	7	68	4					

Umpires: A.E. Fagg (1) and W.F.F. Price (6).

Close: 1st day – I(1) 9-0 (Engineer 6, Kunderan 2); 2nd – E(2) 203 all out.

ENGLAND v PAKISTAN 1967 (1st Test)

Played at Lord's, London, on 27, 28, 29, 31 July, 1 August.
Toss: England.　Result: MATCH DRAWN.
Debuts: Pakistan – Salim Altaf, Wasim Bari.

Five wickets fell for nine runs after Barrington and Graveney had established England's third-wicket record against Pakistan with a partnership of 201 in 223 minutes. Hanif's 187 not out, scored off 556 balls in 542 minutes, included 21 fours and was Pakistan's highest score against England until 1971 (*Test No. 687*). His partnership of 130 in 191 minutes with Asif is still Pakistan's record for the eighth wicket against all countries. Set 257 runs in 210 minutes, Pakistan scored only 88 in 165 minutes off 62 overs, 32 of which were maidens. Rain claimed 3 hours 37 minutes of the match.

ENGLAND

C. Milburn	c Wasim b Asif	3	c Asif b Majid	32
W.E. Russell	b Intikhab	43	b Majid	12
K.F. Barrington	c Wasim b Asif	148	b Intikhab	14
T.W. Graveney	b Salim	81	c Ibadulla b Asif	30
B.L. D'Oliveira	c Intikhab b Mushtaq	59	not out	81
D.B. Close*	c sub (Ghulam Abbas) b Salim	4	st Wasim b Nasim	36
J.T. Murray†	b Salim	0	c and b Nasim	0
R. Illingworth	b Asif	4	c and b Nasim	9
K. Higgs	lbw b Mushtaq	14	c Hanif b Intikhab	1
J.A. Snow	b Mushtaq	0	c Hanif b Mushtaq	7
R.N.S. Hobbs	not out	1	not out	1
Extras	(LB 5, NB 7)	12	(B 12, LB 5, NB 1)	18
Total		**369**	(9 wickets declared)	**241**

PAKISTAN

Khalid Ibadulla	b Higgs	8	c Close b Illingworth	32
Javed Burki	lbw b Higgs	31	c and b Barrington	13
Mushtaq Mohammad	c Murray b Higgs	4	(4) not out	30
Hanif Mohammad*	not out	187		
Majid Khan	c and b Hobbs	5	(3) c Close b Barrington	5
Nasim-ul-Ghani	c D'Oliveira b Snow	2		
Saeed Ahmed	c Graveney b Snow	6	(5) not out	6
Intikhab Alam	lbw b Illingworth	17		
Asif Iqbal	c Barrington b Illingworth	76		
Wasim Bari†	c Close b Barrington	13		
Salim Altaf	c Milburn b Snow	2		
Extras	(B 1, LB 2)	3	(B 1, LB 1)	2
Total		**354**	(3 wickets)	**88**

PAKISTAN	O	M	R	W	O	M	R	W		FALL OF WICKETS			
Salim	33	6	74	3	0·3	0	4	0		E	P	E	P
Asif	28	10	76	3	21	5	50	1	*Wkt*	*1st*	*1st*	*2nd*	*2nd*
Ibadulla	3	0	5	0					1st	5	19	33	27
Majid	11	2	28	0	10	1	32	2	2nd	82	25	48	39
Nasim	12	1	36	0	13	3	32	3	3rd	283	67	76	77
Intikhab	29	3	86	1	30	7	70	2	4th	283	76	95	–
Mushtaq	11·3	3	23	3	16	4	35	1	5th	287	91	199	–
Saeed	11	3	29	0					6th	287	99	201	–
									7th	292	139	215	–
ENGLAND									8th	352	269	220	–
Snow	45·1	11	120	3	4	2	6	0	9th	354	310	239	–
Higgs	39	12	81	3	6	3	6	0	10th	369	354	–	–
D'Oliveira	15	7	17	0									
Illingworth	31	14	48	2	15	11	10	1					
Hobbs	35	16	46	1	16	9	28	0					
Barrington	11	1	29	1	13	2	23	2					
Close	6	3	10	0	8	5	13	0					

Umpires: C.S. Elliott (26) and A. Jepson (3).

Close: 1st day – E(1) 282-2 (Barrington 147, Graveney 81); 2nd – P(1) 78-4 (Hanif 28, Nasim 2); 3rd – P(1) 233-7 (Hanif 102, Asif 56); 4th – E(2) 131-4 (D'Oliveira 21, Close 10).

ENGLAND v PAKISTAN 1967 (2nd Test)

Played at Trent Bridge, Nottingham, on 10, 11, 12, 14 (*no play*), 15 August.
Toss: Pakistan.   Result: ENGLAND won by ten wickets.
Debuts: England – G.G. Arnold, A.P.E. Knott; Pakistan – Niaz Ahmed.

Barrington reached his hundred off 344 balls and altogether batted for 409 minutes. The Nottingham Fire Brigade pumped 100,000 gallons of water off the ground after a violent thunderstorm soon after 5 pm on the first day had transformed the playing area into a lake. Play was able to restart at 12.45 pm on the second day. Alan Bull, a young recruit to the Nottinghamshire playing staff who was not destined to play in a first-class match, fielded substitute for D'Oliveira and caught Asif at long on. This was Hanif's first defeat in ten Tests as captain.

PAKISTAN

Khalid Ibadulla	c Knott b Higgs	2		c Knott b Close	5
Javed Burki	lbw b Arnold	1		c Knott b Higgs	3
Saeed Ahmed	c Knott b Arnold	44		c Arnold b Underwood	68
Mushtaq Mohammad	b Higgs	29	(6)	lbw b Underwood	0
Hanif Mohammad*	c Titmus b Underwood	16		c Knott b Higgs	4
Majid Khan	lbw b D'Oliveira	17	(7)	c Close b Underwood	5
Asif Iqbal	b Higgs	18	(8)	c sub (A. Bull) b Titmus	1
Nasim-ul-Ghani	run out	11	(4)	c Close b Titmus	6
Intikhab Alam	c Knott b Arnold	0		c Knott b Underwood	16
Wasim Bari†	b Higgs	0		c Barrington b Underwood	3
Niaz Ahmed	not out	0		not out	1
Extras	(LB 1, NB 1)	2		(LB 1, NB 1)	2
Total		**140**			**114**

ENGLAND

G. Boycott	b Asif	15	not out	1
M.C. Cowdrey	c Majid b Nasim	14	not out	2
K.F. Barrington	not out	109		
T.W. Graveney	c Niaz b Ibadulla	28		
B.L. D'Oliveira	run out	7		
D.B. Close*	c Wasim b Niaz	41		
F.J. Titmus	lbw b Asif	13		
A.P.E. Knott†	c Hanif b Mushtaq	0		
G.G. Arnold	lbw b Niaz	14		
K. Higgs	not out	0		
D.L. Underwood	did not bat			
Extras	(B 3, LB 3, W 1, NB 4)	11		
Total	(8 wickets declared)	**252**	(0 wickets)	**3**

ENGLAND	O	M	R	W	O	M	R	W		FALL OF WICKETS			
Arnold	17	5	35	3	5	3	5	0		P	E	P	E
Higgs	19	12	35	4	6	1	8	2	*Wkt*	*1st*	*1st*	*2nd*	*2nd*
D'Oliveira	18	9	27	1					1st	3	21	4	–
Close	3	0	12	0	4	1	11	1	2nd	21	31	35	–
Titmus	7	3	12	0	23	11	36	2	3rd	65	75	60	–
Underwood	5	2	17	1	26	8	52	5	4th	82	92	71	–
									5th	104	187	76	–
PAKISTAN									6th	116	213	89	–
Asif	39	10	72	2					7th	140	214	93	–
Niaz	37	10	72	2					8th	140	251	99	–
Nasim	8	2	20	1					9th	140	–	113	–
Saeed	2	2	0	0	1	1	0	0	10th	140	–	114	–
Intikhab	7	2	19	0									
Ibadulla	32	13	42	1									
Mushtaq	9·3	3	16	1	1·1	0	3	0					

Umpires: J.S. Buller (27) and W.F.F. Price (7).

Close: 1st day – E(1) 4-0 (Boycott 4, Cowdrey 0); 2nd – E(1) 119-4 (Barrington 34, Close 16); 3rd – E(1) 252-8 (Barrington 109, Higgs 0); 4th – no play.

ENGLAND v PAKISTAN 1967 (3rd Test)

Played at Kennington Oval, London, on 24, 25, 26, 28 August.
Toss: England.   Result: ENGLAND won by eight wickets.
Debuts: Pakistan – Ghulam Abbas.

Barrington's 19th Test hundred was his third in successive Tests and his first in a Test on his county ground. He thus became the first to score a Test hundred on each of England's six current Test grounds. It was his 52nd score of 50 or more and equalled L. Hutton's world Test record. Asif's 146 off 244 balls in 200 minutes included two sixes and 21 fours. His partnership of 190 in 170 minutes with Intikhab remains the highest for the ninth wicket in all Test cricket. England won at 5.11 on the fourth evening.

PAKISTAN

Hanif Mohammad*	b Higgs	3	(5) c Knott b Higgs	18
Mohammad Ilyas	b Arnold	2	c Cowdrey b Higgs	1
Saeed Ahmed	b Arnold	38	c Knott b Higgs	0
Majid Khan	c Knott b Arnold	6	b Higgs	0
Mushtaq Mohammad	lbw b Higgs	66	(7) c D'Oliveira b Underwood	17
Javed Burki	c D'Oliveira b Titmus	27	(8) b Underwood	7
Ghulam Abbas	c Underwood b Titmus	12	(6) c Knott b Higgs	0
Asif Iqbal	c Close b Arnold	26	(9) st Knott b Close	146
Intikhab Alam	b Higgs	20	(10) b Titmus	51
Wasim Bari†	c Knott b Arnold	1	(1) b Titmus	12
Salim Altaf	not out	7	not out	0
Extras	(B 5, LB 2, NB 1)	8	(B 1, LB 1, NB 1)	3
Total		**216**		**255**

ENGLAND

M.C. Cowdrey	c Mushtaq b Majid	16	c Intikhab b Asif	9
D.B. Close*	c Wasim b Asif	6	b Asif	8
K.F. Barrington	c Wasim b Salim	142	not out	13
T.W. Graveney	c Majid b Intikhab	77		
D.L. Amiss	c Saeed b Asif	26	(4) not out	3
B.L. D'Oliveira	c Mushtaq b Asif	3		
F.J. Titmus	c sub (Niaz Ahmed) b Mushtaq	65		
A.P.E. Knott†	c Ilyas b Mushtaq	28		
G.G. Arnold	c Majid b Mushtaq	59		
K. Higgs	b Mushtaq	7		
D.L. Underwood	not out	2		
Extras	(LB 4, NB 5)	9	(NB 1)	1
Total		**440**	(2 wickets)	**34**

ENGLAND	O	M	R	W	O	M	R	W		FALL OF WICKETS			
Arnold	29	9	58	5	17	5	49	0		P	E	P	E
Higgs	29	10	61	3	20	7	58	5	Wkt	1st	1st	2nd	2nd
D'Oliveira	17	6	41	0					1st	3	16	1	17
Close	5	1	15	0	1	0	4	1	2nd	5	35	5	20
Titmus	13	6	21	2	29·1	8	64	2	3rd	17	176	5	–
Underwood	9	5	12	0	26	12	48	2	4th	74	270	26	–
Barrington					8	2	29	0	5th	138	276	26	–
									6th	155	276	41	–
PAKISTAN									7th	182	323	53	–
Salim	40	14	94	1	2	1	8	0	8th	188	416	65	–
Asif	42	19	66	3	4	1	14	2	9th	194	437	255	–
Majid	10	0	29	1					10th	216	440	255	–
Mushtaq	26·4	7	80	4									
Saeed	21	5	69	0	2	0	7	0					
Intikhab	28	3	93	1									
Hanif					0·2	0	4	0					

Umpires: W.F.F. Price (8) and H. Yarnold (2).

Close: 1st day – P(1) 214-9 (Intikhab 19, Salim 6); 2nd – E(1) 257-3 (Barrington 129, Amiss 23); 3rd – P(2) 26-4 (Hanif 12, Ghulam 0).

AUSTRALIA v INDIA 1967–68 (1st Test)

Played at Adelaide Oval on 23, 25, 26, 27, 28 December.
Toss: Australia.   Result: AUSTRALIA won by 146 runs.
Debuts: Australia – J.W. Gleeson, A.P. Sheahan; India – S. Abid Ali, U.N. Kulkarni.

An injured left hamstring prevented Pataudi from playing and gave Borde his only experience of captaining India. Abid Ali's first bowl in Test cricket produced India's best analysis in Australia until 1977-78 (*Test No. 811*). Australia required 26 balls on the last day to remove India's last wicket, Renneberg returning his best analysis in Tests.

AUSTRALIA

R.B. Simpson*	c and b Abid Ali	55	b Surti	103
W.M. Lawry	c Engineer b Abid Ali	42	c Engineer b Kulkarni	0
A.P. Sheahan	lbw b Prasanna	81	lbw b Prasanna	35
R.M. Cowper	c Engineer b Abid Ali	92	b Abid Ali	108
I.R. Redpath	c Borde b Prasanna	0	(7) lbw b Surti	34
I.M. Chappell	c Borde b Prasanna	2	(5) b Surti	13
B.N. Jarman†	b Abid Ali	34	(6) c and b Surti	17
G.D. McKenzie	c Borde b Abid Ali	5	run out	28
J.W. Gleeson	lbw b Abid Ali	1	not out	18
A.N. Connolly	not out	7	c sub (R.B. Desai) b Surti	0
D.A. Renneberg	b Chandrasekhar	1	run out	0
Extras	(B 2, LB 10, NB 3)	15	(B 5, LB 6, NB 2)	13
Total		**335**		**369**

INDIA

F.M. Engineer†	c Jarman b McKenzie	89	run out	19
D.N. Sardesai	c Redpath b Renneberg	1	c Jarman b Renneberg	11
A.L. Wadekar	st Jarman b Connolly	28	c Jarman b Renneberg	0
C.G. Borde*	lbw b Gleeson	69	b Renneberg	12
R.F. Surti	b Simpson	70	c Redpath b Gleeson	53
R.G. Nadkarni	lbw b Gleeson	3	(8) b McKenzie	15
S. Abid Ali	c and b Connolly	33	(6) lbw b Renneberg	33
V. Subramanya	b Connolly	7	(7) run out	75
E.A.S. Prasanna	c Lawry b McKenzie	1	not out	18
U.N. Kulkarni	lbw b Connolly	0	(11) c Chappell b Renneberg	2
B.S. Chandrasekhar	not out	1	(10) c Simpson b Gleeson	0
Extras	(NB 5)	5	(B 3, LB 8, NB 2)	13
Total		**307**		**251**

INDIA	O	M	R	W	O	M	R	W		FALL OF WICKETS			
Kulkarni	5	0	25	0	4	1	12	1		A	I	A	I
Surti	7	0	30	0	20·1	6	74	5	*Wkt*	*1st*	*1st*	*2nd*	*2nd*
Abid Ali	17	2	55	6	16	2	61	1	1st	99	19	0	24
Nadkarni	17	2	68	0	9·4	3	24	0	2nd	109	80	61	24
Chandrasekhar	27·1	3	72	1	13	1	67	0	3rd	227	129	233	46
Prasanna	17	2	60	3	25	2	109	1	4th	227	250	263	49
Subramanya	2	0	10	0	1	0	9	0	5th	235	259	263	104
									6th	311	272	295	159
AUSTRALIA									7th	319	287	322	209
McKenzie	15	1	70	2	17	2	91	1	8th	324	288	364	232
Renneberg	6	0	45	1	14·2	2	39	5	9th	330	291	365	236
Connolly	12·4	1	54	4	3	0	21	0	10th	335	307	369	251
Gleeson	13	4	36	2	16	4	38	2					
Chappell	10	1	41	0	5	0	24	0					
Simpson	12	2	42	1	5	0	25	0					
Cowper	3	0	14	0									

Umpires: C.J. Egar (21) and L.P. Rowan (12).

Close: 1st day – A(1) 311-6 (Cowper 85); 2nd – I(1) 288-8 (Abid Ali 16); 3rd – A(2) 305-6 (Redpath 20, McKenzie 5); 4th – I(2) 236-9 (Prasanna 5, Kulkarni 0).

Test No. 625/18

AUSTRALIA v INDIA 1967–68 (2nd Test)

Played at Melbourne Cricket Ground on 30 December, 1, 2, 3 January.
Toss: India.   Result: AUSTRALIA won by an innings and 4 runs.
Debuts: Nil.

Batting for the first time in a first-class match in Australia, the Nawab of Pataudi achieved a match aggregate of 160 runs in spite of a damaged hamstring which reduced his running between the wickets to a gentle jog. Surti retired after being struck in the ribs and returned at 72. The partnership of 191 between Simpson and Lawry was then Australia's highest for the first wicket against India. Simpson, who was captaining Australia for a record 29th time, became the third Australian to score 4,000 runs in Tests.

INDIA

Batsman	Dismissal 1	Score	Dismissal 2	Score
D.N. Sardesai	b McKenzie	1	b McKenzie	5
F.M. Engineer†	c Connolly b McKenzie	9	c Chappell b Renneberg	42
S. Abid Ali	c Jarman b McKenzie	4	(8) lbw b Cowper	21
A.L. Wadekar	c Connolly b McKenzie	6	(3) c Sheahan b Simpson	99
R.F. Surti	lbw b Simpson	30	(4) c Jarman b McKenzie	43
C.G. Borde	c Redpath b McKenzie	0	c Redpath b Renneberg	6
Nawab of Pataudi, jr*	c Jarman b Renneberg	75	c Redpath b Simpson	85
V. Subramanya	b McKenzie	5	(9) lbw b McKenzie	10
E.A.S. Prasanna	c Chappell b Renneberg	14	(5) c Chappell b Simpson	21
R.B. Desai	not out	13	c Simpson b Connolly	14
B.S. Chandrasekhar	c Jarman b McKenzie	0	not out	0
Extras	(B 8, LB 2, NB 6)	16	(B 1, LB 4, NB 1)	6
Total		**173**		**352**

AUSTRALIA

R.B. Simpson*	b Surti	109
W.M. Lawry	st Engineer b Prasanna	100
A.P. Sheahan	c Engineer b Surti	24
R.M. Cowper	b Prasanna	12
I.M. Chappell	c Wadekar b Surti	151
I.R. Redpath	run out	26
B.N. Jarman†	b Prasanna	65
G.D. McKenzie	c sub (B.S. Bedi) b Prasanna	0
J.W. Gleeson	c Borde b Prasanna	13
A.N. Connolly	c sub (B.S. Bedi) b Prasanna	5
D.A. Renneberg	not out	8
Extras	(B 3, LB 10, NB 3)	16
Total		**529**

AUSTRALIA	O	M	R	W	O	M	R	W
McKenzie	21·4	2	66	7	19	2	85	3
Renneberg	15	4	37	2	14	1	98	2
Connolly	13	3	33	0	11·7	2	48	1
Gleeson	5	0	9	0	14	5	37	0
Chappell	1	0	7	0	4	0	14	0
Simpson	2	0	5	1	14	3	44	3
Cowper					8	2	20	1

INDIA	O	M	R	W
Desai	12	0	63	0
Surti	29·3	4	150	3
Abid Ali	20	0	106	0
Chandrasekhar	7	0	35	0
Prasanna	34	6	141	6
Subramanya	3	0	18	0

FALL OF WICKETS

Wkt	I 1st	A 1st	I 2nd
1st	2	191	11
2nd	10	233	66
3rd	18	246	182
4th	25	274	194
5th	25	329	217
6th	47	463	227
7th	72	463	276
8th	146	500	292
9th	162	508	346
10th	173	529	352

Umpires: C.J. Egar (22) and L.P. Rowan (13).

Close: 1st day – I(1) 156-8 (Pataudi 70, Desai 3); 2nd – A(1) 329-5 (Chappell 45, Jarman 0); 3rd – I(2) 190-3 (Wadekar 97, Prasanna 0).

637

AUSTRALIA v INDIA 1967–68 (3rd Test)

Played at Woolloongabba, Brisbane, on 19, 20, 22, 23, 24 January.
Toss: India. Result: AUSTRALIA won by 39 runs.
Debuts: Australia – E.W. Freeman.

Jaisimha scored 74 and 101 on his first-class debut in Australia only a few days after arriving from India. Freeman's first scoring stroke in Test cricket was a six over mid-wicket off Prasanna. He then took the wickets of Abid Ali and Engineer with his third and tenth balls. Lawry began his 25-match reign as Australia's captain. Private Walters, on leave from national service, contributed 155 runs for once out, a replica of his debut performance (*Test No. 597*).

AUSTRALIA

W.M. Lawry*	c Bedi b Nadkarni	64	c Engineer b Surti	45
I.R. Redpath	c Wadekar b Prasanna	41	lbw b Prasanna	79
R.M. Cowper	b Nadkarni	51	b Surti	25
A.P. Sheahan	st Engineer b Surti	58	c Surti b Bedi	26
I.M. Chappell	b Surti	17	b Prasanna	27
K.D. Walters	c Wadekar b Kulkarni	93	not out	62
B.N. Jarman†	lbw b Prasanna	2	c and b Prasanna	9
E.W. Freeman	b Surti	18	c Surti b Prasanna	8
J.W. Gleeson	run out	15	c Abid Ali b Surti	1
A.N. Connolly	c Pataudi b Kulkarni	14	b Prasanna	0
D.A. Renneberg	not out	0	c Surti b Prasanna	0
Extras	(B 1, LB 1, NB 4)	6	(B 1, LB 10, NB 1)	12
Total		**379**		**294**

INDIA

F.M. Engineer†	c Gleeson b Freeman	2	c Jarman b Renneberg	0
S. Abid Ali	c Redpath b Freeman	2	c Jarman b Connolly	47
A.L. Wadekar	c Jarman b Renneberg	1	c Connolly b Cowper	11
R.F. Surti	c Cowper b Chappell	52	b Cowper	64
Nawab of Pataudi, jr*	lbw b Freeman	74	b Walters	48
M.L. Jaisimha	c Lawry b Cowper	74	c Gleeson b Cowper	101
C.G. Borde	c and b Connolly	12	c Redpath b Cowper	63
R.G. Nadkarni	b Cowper	17	lbw b Gleeson	2
E.A.S. Prasanna	c Walters b Cowper	24	b Gleeson	4
B.S. Bedi	not out	2	c Lawry b Gleeson	0
U.N. Kulkarni	c Cowper b Connolly	7	not out	1
Extras	(B 6, LB 4, NB 2)	12	(B 4, LB 6, NB 4)	14
Total		**279**		**355**

INDIA	O	M	R	W	O	M	R	W
Kulkarni	8·2	1	37	2	4	0	22	0
Surti	26	2	102	3	16	4	59	3
Prasanna	38	6	114	2	33·4	9	104	6
Bedi	23	4	71	0	14	4	44	1
Abid Ali	2	0	9	0	1	0	6	0
Nadkarni	14	5	34	2	15	5	47	0
Jaisimha	1	0	6	0				
AUSTRALIA								
Renneberg	10	1	40	1	7	0	43	1
Freeman	21	1	56	3	8	2	29	0
Walters	6	0	22	0	11	2	33	1
Connolly	15	4	43	2	18	6	51	1
Gleeson	15	7	20	0	21	6	50	3
Cowper	15	5	31	3	39·6	8	104	4
Chappell	18	4	55	1	5	1	31	0

FALL OF WICKETS

	A	I	A	I
Wkt	1st	1st	2nd	2nd
1st	76	2	116	17
2nd	148	5	136	48
3rd	160	9	162	61
4th	215	137	196	154
5th	239	139	240	191
6th	250	165	266	310
7th	277	209	284	313
8th	323	268	293	323
9th	378	270	294	333
10th	379	279	294	355

Umpires: C.J. Egar (23) and L.P. Rowan (14).

Close: 1st day – A(1) 312-7 (Walters 51, Gleeson 7); 2nd – I(1) 169-6 (Jaisimha 16, Nadkarni 3); 3rd – A(2) 162-3 (Sheahan 8, Chappell 0); 4th – I(2) 177-4 (Surti 55, Jaisimha 5).

AUSTRALIA v INDIA 1967–68 (4th Test)

Played at Sydney Cricket Ground on 26, 27, 29, 30, 31 January.
Toss: India.   Result: AUSTRALIA won by 144 runs.
Debuts: Australia – L.R. Joslin.

This was India's seventh consecutive defeat, Australia's four victories in this rubber following three by England in 1967. Pataudi decided to field first for the second Test in succession. Simpson, brought back for what was intended to be his final Test, achieved his best match bowling figures and held his 99th catch, (he was recalled to lead a replacement Australian team after the World Series revolution in 1977). This match began with two left-handed opening pairs confronting each other. Cowper reached the last of his five Test centuries off 209 balls and went on to compile the highest score of the rubber.

AUSTRALIA

W.M. Lawry*	c Engineer b Prasanna	66	c sub (V. Subramanya) b Nadkarni	52
R.M. Cowper	b Abid Ali	32	st Engineer b Prasanna	165
A.P. Sheahan	c and b Bedi	72	(4) c Wadekar b Jaisimha	22
K.D. Walters	not out	94	(5) run out	5
L.R. Joslin	c Wadekar b Prasanna	7	(6) c Abid Ali b Bedi	2
R.B. Simpson	b Bedi	7	(3) run out	20
I.M. Chappell	run out	0	lbw b Prasanna	2
B.N. Jarman†	c Engineer b Surti	4	run out	5
E.W. Freeman	lbw b Kulkarni	11	c sub (R.C. Saxena) b Prasanna	8
N.J.N. Hawke	c Engineer b Kulkarni	1	c Abid Ali b Prasanna	4
J.W. Gleeson	lbw b Prasanna	14	not out	4
Extras	(B 2, LB 4, NB 3)	9	(B 1, LB 1, NB 1)	3
Total		**317**		**292**

INDIA

F.M. Engineer†	c Chappell b Walters	17	c Simpson b Gleeson	37
S. Abid Ali	hit wkt b Gleeson	78	c Simpson b Cowper	81
A.L. Wadekar	c and b Cowper	49	lbw b Cowper	18
R.F. Surti	b Simpson	29	c Chappell b Simpson	26
Nawab of Pataudi, jr*	c Simpson b Freeman	51	c Chappell b Simpson	6
M.L. Jaisimha	c Jarman b Simpson	0	c Gleeson b Cowper	13
R.G. Nadkarni	c Sheahan b Simpson	0	(8) c Sheahan b Simpson	6
E.A.S. Prasanna	c Cowper b Freeman	26	(9) b Simpson	0
C.G. Borde	lbw b Freeman	0	(7) c Simpson b Cowper	4
B.S. Bedi	c Simpson b Freeman	8	b Simpson	2
U.N. Kulkarni	not out	1	not out	1
Extras	(B 4, LB 2, NB 3)	9	(LB 3)	3
Total		**268**		**197**

INDIA	O	M	R	W	O	M	R	W		FALL OF WICKETS			
Kulkarni	17	0	73	2	8	0	31	0		A	I	A	I
Surti	11	1	64	1	8	1	49	0	*Wkt*	*1st*	*1st*	*2nd*	*2nd*
Abid Ali	15	1	58	1	2	0	7	0	1st	61	56	111	83
Jaisimha	2	0	9	0	1	0	2	1	2nd	136	111	166	120
Bedi	21	4	42	2	21	5	66	1	3rd	219	178	222	145
Prasanna	20·6	5	62	3	29·3	4	96	4	4th	228	178	240	164
Nadkarni					16	3	38	1	5th	239	184	243	175
									6th	242	184	260	180
AUSTRALIA									7th	256	236	271	193
Hawke	18	2	51	0	6	2	22	0	8th	275	236	278	193
Freeman	18·1	2	86	4	4	0	26	0	9th	277	267	286	195
Walters	4	0	20	1	3	1	11	0	10th	317	268	292	197
Gleeson	12	3	40	1	12	4	27	1					
Cowper	12	5	21	1	25·6	12	49	4					
Simpson	20	10	38	3	23	5	59	5					
Chappell	1	0	3	0									

Umpires: C.J. Egar (24) and L.P. Rowan (15).

Close: 1st day – A(1) 245-6 (Walters 50, Jarman 2); 2nd – I(1) 196-6 (Pataudi 14, Prasanna 4); 3rd – A(2) 222-3 (Cowper 126); 4th – I(2) 193-6 (Jaisimha 12, Nadkarni 6).

WEST INDIES v ENGLAND 1967–68 (1st Test)

Played at Queen's Park Oval, Port-of-Spain, Trinidad, on 19, 20, 22, 23, 24 January.
Toss: England.   Result: MATCH DRAWN.
Debuts: West Indies – G.S. Camacho.

England's total was their second-highest in the West Indies. Barrington reached his 20th and last hundred for England with a six; it was his fourth century in consecutive Tests. Lloyd became the fourth West Indies batsman to score a hundred in his first match against England. West Indies followed on for the first time in their 14 matches under the captaincy of Sobers. Brown dismissed Butcher, Murray and Griffith in the last over before tea but Hall partnered Sobers throughout the final session and avoided the possibility of an innings defeat. Their unbroken partnership of 63 was the highest for the West Indies ninth wicket against England until 1984 (*Test No. 989*).

ENGLAND

G. Boycott	lbw b Holford	68
J.H. Edrich	c Murray b Gibbs	25
M.C. Cowdrey*	c Murray b Griffith	72
K.F. Barrington	c Griffith b Gibbs	143
T.W. Graveney	b Gibbs	118
J.M. Parks†	lbw b Sobers	42
B.L. D'Oliveira	b Griffith	32
F.J. Titmus	lbw b Griffith	15
D.J. Brown	not out	22
R.N.S. Hobbs	c Butcher b Griffith	2
I.J. Jones	c Murray b Griffith	2
Extras	(B 8, LB 11, W 1, NB 7)	27
Total		**568**

WEST INDIES

S.M. Nurse	c Graveney b Titmus	41		b Titmus	42
G.S. Camacho	c Graveney b Brown	22		c Graveney b Barrington	43
R.B. Kanhai	c Cowdrey b D'Oliveira	85	(4)	c and b Hobbs	37
B.F. Butcher	lbw b Brown	14	(3)	lbw b Brown	52
C.H. Lloyd	b Jones	118		c Titmus b Jones	2
G. St A. Sobers*	c Graveney b Barrington	17	(7)	not out	33
D.A.J. Holford	run out	4	(6)	b Titmus	1
D.L. Murray†	c D'Oliveira b Hobbs	16		lbw b Brown	0
C.C. Griffith	c Parks b Jones	18		b Brown	0
W.W. Hall	not out	10		not out	26
L.R. Gibbs	b Jones	1			
Extras	(B 4, LB 6, NB 7)	17		(LB 5, NB 2)	7
Total		**363**		**(8 wickets)**	**243**

WEST INDIES	O	M	R	W	O	M	R	W
Hall	28	5	92	0				
Sobers	26	5	83	1				
Griffith	29·5	13	69	5				
Gibbs	63	15	147	3				
Holford	43	1	121	1				
Lloyd	8	3	17	0				
Camacho	3	1	12	0				
ENGLAND								
Brown	22	3	65	2	14	4	27	3
Jones	19	5	63	3	15	3	32	1
D'Oliveira	27	13	49	1	5	2	21	0
Titmus	34	9	91	1	27	13	42	2
Hobbs	15	1	34	1	13	2	44	1
Barrington	18	6	44	1	15	0	69	1
Cowdrey					1	0	1	0

FALL OF WICKETS

Wkt	E 1st	WI 1st	WI 2nd
1st	80	50	70
2nd	110	102	100
3rd	244	124	164
4th	432	240	167
5th	471	290	178
6th	511	294	180
7th	527	329	180
8th	554	352	180
9th	566	357	–
10th	568	363	–

Umpires: R. Gosein (2) and H.B. de C. Jordan (14).

Close: 1st day – E(1) 244-2 (Cowdrey 72, Barrington 71); 2nd – E(1) 546-7 (Titmus 11, Brown 12); 3rd – WI(1) 195-3 (Kanhai 66, Lloyd 36); 4th – WI(1) 363 all out.

WEST INDIES v ENGLAND 1967–68 (2nd Test)

Played at Sabina Park, Kingston, Jamaica, on 8, 9, 10, 12, 13, 14 February.
Toss: England.   Result: MATCH DRAWN.
Debuts: Nil.

West Indies followed on for the second Test running after Snow dismissed Sobers first ball for the second time in successive innings in which he had bowled to him. Butcher's second innings dismissal in mid-afternoon on the fourth day sparked off a bottle-throwing riot, with West Indies 204 for 5 and needing 29 runs to avoid an innings defeat. Play resumed after tea and it was agreed that the 75 minutes lost would be played on an extra (sixth) day.

ENGLAND

G. Boycott	b Hall	17	b Sobers		0
J.H. Edrich	c Kanhai b Sobers	96	b Hall		6
M.C. Cowdrey*	c Murray b Gibbs	101	lbw b Sobers		0
K.F. Barrington	c and b Holford	63	lbw b Griffith		13
T.W. Graveney	b Hall	30	c Griffith b Gibbs		21
J.M. Parks†	c Sobers b Holford	3	lbw b Gibbs		3
B.L. D'Oliveira	st Murray b Holford	0	not out		13
F.J. Titmus	lbw b Hall	19	c Camacho b Gibbs		4
D.J. Brown	c Murray b Hall	14	b Sobers		0
J.A. Snow	b Griffith	10			
I.J. Jones	not out	0			
Extras	(B 12, LB 7, NB 4)	23	(B 8)		8
Total		**376**	(8 wickets)		**68**

WEST INDIES

G.S. Camacho	b Snow	5	b D'Oliveira		25
D.L. Murray†	c D'Oliveira b Brown	0	(8) lbw b Brown		14
R.B. Kanhai	c Graveney b Snow	26	c Edrich b Jones		36
S.M. Nurse	b Jones	22	(2) b Snow		73
C.H. Lloyd	not out	34	b Brown		7
G. St A. Sobers*	lbw b Snow	0	not out		113
B.F. Butcher	c Parks b Snow	21	(4) c Parks b D'Oliveira		25
D.A.J. Holford	c Parks b Snow	6	(7) lbw b Titmus		35
C.C. Griffith	c D'Oliveira b Snow	8	lbw b Jones		14
W.W. Hall	b Snow	0	c Parks b Jones		0
L.R. Gibbs	c Parks b Jones	0	not out		1
Extras	(B 12, LB 5, W 1, NB 3)	21	(B 33, LB 10, NB 5)		48
Total		**143**	(9 wickets declared)		**391**

WEST INDIES	O	M	R	W	O	M	R	W
Hall	27	5	63	4	3	2	3	1
Griffith	31·2	7	72	1	5	2	13	1
Sobers	31	11	56	1	16·5	7	33	3
Gibbs	47	18	91	1	14	11	11	3
Holford	33	10	71	3				
ENGLAND								
Brown	13	1	34	1	33	9	65	2
Snow	21	7	49	7	27	4	91	1
Jones	14·1	4	39	2	30	4	90	3
D'Oliveira					32	12	51	2
Titmus					7	2	32	1
Barrington					6	1	14	0

FALL OF WICKETS

Wkt	E 1st	WI 1st	WI 2nd	E 2nd
1st	49	5	102	0
2nd	178	5	122	0
3rd	279	51	164	19
4th	310	80	174	19
5th	318	80	204	38
6th	318	120	314	51
7th	351	126	351	61
8th	352	142	388	68
9th	376	142	388	–
10th	376	143	–	–

Umpires: H.B. de C. Jordan (15) and D. Sang Hue (3).

Close: 1st day – E(1) 222-2 (Cowdrey 69, Barrington 24); 2nd – WI(1) 27-2 (Kanhai 5, Nurse 11); 3rd – WI(2) 81-0 (Camacho 19, Nurse 56); 4th – WI(2) 258-5 (Sobers 48, Holford 14); 5th – E(2) 19-4 (Graveney 0, Parks 0).

WEST INDIES v ENGLAND 1967–68 (3rd Test)

Played at Kensington Oval, Bridgetown, Barbados, on 29 February, 1, 2, 4, 5 March.
Toss: West Indies.   Result: MATCH DRAWN.
Debuts: England – P.I. Pocock.

Pocock replaced fellow off-spin bowler, Titmus, after the Middlesex player had lost four toes in a boating accident. Parks, playing in his final Test, became the second England wicket-keeper after T.G. Evans to hold 100 catches (excluding two he took in the field). Edrich scored his only century against West Indies.

WEST INDIES

S.M. Nurse	c Cowdrey b Brown	26		c Parks b Snow	19
G.S. Camacho	c Graveney b Barrington	57		lbw b Snow	18
R.B. Kanhai	c Parks b Snow	12		lbw b Snow	12
B.F. Butcher	lbw b Snow	86		run out	60
C.H. Lloyd	c and b Pocock	20		not out	113
G. St A. Sobers*	c Jones b Snow	68		b Brown	19
D.A.J. Holford	c Graveney b Snow	0			
D.L. Murray†	c Parks b Brown	27	(7)	c Snow b Pocock	18
C.C. Griffith	not out	16	(8)	not out	8
W.W. Hall	c Barrington b Snow	2			
L.R. Gibbs	b Jones	14			
Extras	(B 1, LB 14, NB 6)	21		(B 8, LB 3, NB 6)	17
Total		**349**		(6 wickets)	**284**

ENGLAND

J.H. Edrich	c Murray b Griffith	146
G. Boycott	lbw b Sobers	90
M.C. Cowdrey*	c Sobers b Griffith	1
K.F. Barrington	c Butcher b Hall	17
T.W. Graveney	c Sobers b Gibbs	55
J.M. Parks†	lbw b Gibbs	0
B.L. D'Oliveira	b Hall	51
D.J. Brown	b Griffith	1
J.A. Snow	c Nurse b Gibbs	37
P.I. Pocock	b Sobers	6
I.J. Jones	not out	1
Extras	(B 16, LB 9, NB 19)	44
Total		**449**

ENGLAND	O	M	R	W	O	M	R	W
Brown	32	10	66	2	11	0	61	1
Snow	35	11	86	5	10	2	39	3
D'Oliveira	19	5	36	0	4	0	19	0
Pocock	28	11	55	1	13	0	78	1
Jones	21·1	3	56	1	11	3	53	0
Barrington	8	1	29	1	4	0	17	0
WEST INDIES								
Sobers	41	10	76	2				
Hall	32	8	98	2				
Griffith	24	6	71	3				
Gibbs	47·5	16	98	3				
Holford	32	9	52	0				
Lloyd	3	0	10	0				
Nurse	1	1	0	0				

FALL OF WICKETS

	WI	E	WI
Wkt	1st	1st	2nd
1st	54	172	38
2nd	67	174	49
3rd	163	210	79
4th	198	319	180
5th	252	319	217
6th	252	349	274
7th	315	354	–
8th	315	411	–
9th	319	439	–
10th	349	449	–

Umpires: H.B. de C. Jordan (16) and D. Sang Hue (4).

Close: 1st day – WI(1) 86-2 (Camacho 33, Butcher 9); 2nd – WI(1) 311-6 (Sobers 64, Murray 27); 3rd – E(1) 169-0 (Edrich 64, Boycott 90); 4th – E(1) 412-8 (Snow 14, Pocock 0).

WEST INDIES v ENGLAND 1967–68 (4th Test)

Played at Queen's Park Oval, Port-of-Spain, Trinidad, on 14, 15, 16, 18, 19 March.
Toss: West Indies.   Result: ENGLAND won by seven wickets.
Debuts: Nil.

Butcher, whose leg-breaks had been allowed only one spell of six overs in his previous 31 Test matches, took five wickets for 15 runs in a spell of 8·3 overs. Carew set a West Indies record by bowling 15 consecutive maidens. England, set to score 215 runs in 165 minutes, won with three minutes to spare. Lock, who had just led Western Australia to the Sheffield Shield title, played in his first Test for 4½ years. Sobers, with his attack weakened by a thigh muscle injury to Griffith, gambled on a slight chance of winning rather than let the match stagnate. It was only the fourth instance in all Tests of a side winning against a second innings declaration, the last being in 1948-49 (*Test No. 313*).

WEST INDIES

G.S. Camacho	c Knott b Brown	87	c Graveney b Snow	31
M.C. Carew	c Lock b Brown	36	not out	40
S.M. Nurse	c Edrich b Barrington	136	run out	9
R.B. Kanhai	c Barrington b Lock	153	not out	2
C.H. Lloyd	b Jones	43		
G. St A. Sobers*	c Jones b Brown	48		
B.F. Butcher	not out	7		
W.V. Rodriguez	b Jones	0		
D.L. Murray†	not out	5		
C.C. Griffith	) did not bat			
L.R. Gibbs	)			
Extras	(LB 6, NB 5)	11	(B 1, LB 7, NB 2)	10
Total	(7 wickets declared)	**526**	(2 wickets declared)	**92**

ENGLAND

J.H. Edrich	c Lloyd b Carew	32	b Rodriguez	29
G. Boycott	c Nurse b Rodriguez	62	not out	80
M.C. Cowdrey*	c Murray b Butcher	148	c Sobers b Gibbs	71
K.F. Barrington	lbw b Gibbs	48		
T.W. Graveney	c Murray b Rodriguez	8	(4) b Gibbs	2
B.L. D'Oliveira	b Rodriguez	0	(5) not out	12
A.P.E. Knott†	not out	69		
J.A. Snow	b Butcher	0		
D.J. Brown	c Murray b Butcher	0		
G.A.R. Lock	lbw b Butcher	3		
I.J. Jones	b Butcher	1		
Extras	(B 13, LB 11, W 2, NB 7)	33	(B 11, LB 6, NB 4)	21
Total		**404**	(3 wickets)	**215**

ENGLAND	O	M	R	W	O	M	R	W		FALL OF WICKETS			
Brown	27	2	107	3	10	2	33	0		WI	E	WI	E
Snow	20	3	68	0	9	0	29	1	*Wkt*	*1st*	*1st*	*2nd*	*2nd*
Jones	29	1	108	2	11	2	20	0	1st	119	86	66	55
D'Oliveira	15	2	62	0					2nd	142	112	88	173
Lock	32	3	129	1					3rd	415	245	–	182
Barrington	10	2	41	1					4th	421	260	–	–
									5th	506	260	–	–
WEST INDIES									6th	513	373	–	–
Sobers	36	8	87	0	14	0	48	0	7th	514	377	–	–
Griffith	3	1	7	0					8th	–	377	–	–
Gibbs	57	24	68	1	16·4	1	76	2	9th	–	381	–	–
Rodriguez	35	4	145	3	10	1	34	1	10th	–	404	–	–
Carew	25	18	23	1	7	2	19	0					
Butcher	13·4	2	34	5	5	1	17	0					
Lloyd	4	2	7	0									
Nurse	2	2	0	0									

Umpires: R. Gosein (3) and D. Sang Hue (5).

Close: 1st day – WI(1) 168-2 (Nurse 23, Kanhai 16); 2nd – WI(1) 479-4 (Lloyd 27, Sobers 29); 3rd – E(1) 204-2 (Cowdrey 61, Barrington 28); 4th – WI(2) 6-0 (Camacho 5, Carew 1).

WEST INDIES v ENGLAND 1967–68 (5th Test)

Played at Bourda, Georgetown, Guyana, on 28, 29, 30 March, 1, 2, 3 April.
Toss: West Indies.   Result: MATCH DRAWN.
Debuts: Nil.

Sobers became the first to score 6,000 runs in Tests for West Indies. Pocock batted for 82 minutes before scoring his first run – the second-longest instance in Test cricket. His partnership of 109 with Lock, who made his highest first-class score on his final appearance for England, remains the highest for the ninth wicket in this series. Snow took 27 wickets in the rubber (in only four Tests) to beat England's previous best in the West Indies – 21 by F.S. Trueman in 1959-60.

WEST INDIES

S.M. Nurse	c Knott b Snow	17		lbw b Snow	49
G.S. Camacho	c and b Jones	14		c Graveney b Snow	26
R.B. Kanhai	c Edrich b Pocock	150		c Edrich b Jones	22
B.F. Butcher	run out	18	(6)	c Lock b Pocock	18
G. St A. Sobers*	c Cowdrey b Barrington	152		not out	95
C.H. Lloyd	b Lock	31		c Knott b Snow	1
D.A.J. Holford	lbw b Snow	1	(8)	b Lock	3
D.L. Murray†	c Knott b Lock	8	(7)	c Boycott b Pocock	16
L.A. King	b Snow	8		b Snow	20
W.W. Hall	not out	5		b Snow	7
L.R. Gibbs	b Snow	1		b Snow	0
Extras	(LB 3, W 2, NB 4)	9		(B 1, LB 2, W 1, NB 3)	7
Total		**414**			**264**

ENGLAND

J.H. Edrich	c Murray b Sobers	0	c Gibbs b Sobers	6
G. Boycott	c Murray b Hall	116	b Gibbs	30
M.C. Cowdrey*	lbw b Sobers	59	lbw b Gibbs	82
T.W. Graveney	c Murray b Hall	27	c Murray b Gibbs	0
K.F. Barrington	c Kanhai b Sobber	4	c Lloyd b Gibbs	0
B.L. D'Oliveira	c Nurse b Holford	27	c and b Gibbs	2
A.P.E. Knott†	lbw b Holford	7	not out	73
J.A. Snow	b Gibbs	0	lbw b Sobers	1
G.A.R. Lock	b King	89	c King b Sobers	2
P.I. Pocock	c and b King	13	c Lloyd b Gibbs	0
I.J. Jones	not out	0	not out	0
Extras	(B 12, LB 14, NB 3)	29	(B 9, W 1)	10
Total		**371**	(9 wickets)	**206**

ENGLAND	O	M	R	W	O	M	R	W		FALL OF WICKETS			
Snow	27·4	2	82	4	15·2	0	60	6		WI	E	WI	E
Jones	31	5	114	1	17	1	81	1	*Wkt*	*1st*	*1st*	*2nd*	*2nd*
D'Oliveira	8	1	27	0	8	0	28	0	1st	29	13	78	33
Pocock	38	11	78	1	17	1	66	2	2nd	35	185	84	37
Lock	28	7	61	2	9	1	22	1	3rd	72	185	86	37
Barrington	18	4	43	1					4th	322	194	133	39
									5th	385	240	171	41
WEST INDIES									6th	387	252	201	168
Sobers	37	15	72	3	31	16	53	3	7th	399	257	216	198
Hall	19	3	71	2	13	6	26	0	8th	400	259	252	200
King	38·2	11	79	2	9	1	11	0	9th	412	368	264	206
Holford	31	10	54	2	17	9	37	0	10th	414	371	264	–
Gibbs	33	9	59	1	40	20	60	6					
Butcher	5	3	7	0	10	7	9	0					

Umpires: H.B. de C. Jordan (17) and C.P. Kippins (6).

Close: 1st day – WI(1) 243-3 (Kanhai 113, Sobers 75); 2nd – E(1) 40-1 (Boycott 21, Cowdrey 13); 3rd – E(1) 146-1 (Boycott 93, Cowdrey 43); 4th – E(1) 352-8 (Lock 76, Pocock 7); 5th – WI(2) 264 all out.

NEW ZEALAND v INDIA 1967–68 (1st Test)

Played at Carisbrook, Dunedin, on 15, 16, 17, 19, 20 February.
Toss: New Zealand.   Result: INDIA won by five wickets.
Debuts: New Zealand – M.G. Burgess, R.I. Harford, B.A.G. Murray.

India's first Test in New Zealand brought them their first victory outside the sub-continent. The partnership of 155 between Dowling and Congdon was New Zealand's highest for the second wicket against all countries until 1978-79 (*Test No. 847*), with Dowling registering New Zealand's highest score in a home Test until he himself eclipsed it in the next match. All India's batsmen reached double figures in the first innings – the seventh instance in Test matches and the second by India. Desai continued batting after his jaw had been fractured by a ball from Motz and his partnership of 57 with Bedi remains the highest for India's tenth wicket against New Zealand. In the second innings, Motz's 22 included two sixes and was scored off five balls from Prasanna.

NEW ZEALAND

B.A.G. Murray	lbw b Desai	17	b Prasanna		54
G.T. Dowling	lbw b Abid Ali	143	c Borde b Nadkarni		10
B.E. Congdon	b Nadkarni	58	c Engineer b Prasanna		8
B.W. Sinclair*	c Wadekar b Bedi	0	run out		8
V. Pollard	b Abid Ali	20	(7) c Abid Ali b Bedi		15
M.G. Burgess	b Nadkarni	50	run out		39
B.W. Yuile	run out	4	(5) b Prasanna		2
B.R. Taylor	c Engineer b Abid Ali	7	(9) c Engineer b Prasanna		14
R.C. Motz	c Surti b Desai	10	(8) c sub (R.C. Saxena) b Prasanna		22
J.C. Alabaster	c Prasanna b Abid Ali	34	not out		13
R.I. Harford†	not out	0	lbw b Prasanna		6
Extras	(LB 5, NB 2)	7	(B 6, LB 6, NB 5)		17
Total		**350**			**208**

INDIA

S. Abid Ali	c Sinclair b Taylor	21	run out		10
F.M. Engineer†	b Motz	63	c and b Alabaster		29
A.L. Wadekar	c Harford b Alabaster	80	c Murray b Alabaster		71
R.F. Surti	c Harford b Motz	28	b Alabaster		44
E.A.S. Prasanna	b Motz	23			
Nawab of Pataudi, jr*	b Alabaster	24	(5) c and b Taylor		11
M.L. Jaisimha	c Yuile b Alabaster	17	(6) not out		11
C.G. Borde	c Pollard b Motz	21	(7) not out		15
R.G. Nadkarni	lbw b Taylor	12			
R.B. Desai	not out	32			
B.S. Bedi	c Yuile b Motz	22			
Extras	(B 2, LB 6, NB 8)	16	(B 1, LB 8)		9
Total		**359**	(5 wickets)		**200**

INDIA	O	M	R	W	O	M	R	W	FALL OF WICKETS				
Desai	21	3	61	2	7	1	15	0		NZ	I	NZ	I
Surti	11	1	51	0	4	1	3	0	*Wkt*	*1st*	*1st*	*2nd*	*2nd*
Abid Ali	15	6	26	4	19	9	22	0	1st	45	39	33	30
Bedi	37	10	90	1	22	11	44	1	2nd	200	118	57	49
Nadkarni	36·3	19	31	2	12	7	13	1	3rd	201	192	83	152
Prasanna	37	14	84	0	40	11	94	6	4th	243	215	91	163
									5th	246	224	92	169
NEW ZEALAND									6th	252	258	120	–
Motz	34	7	86	5	11	2	39	0	7th	264	279	142	–
Taylor	19	1	66	2	24	5	51	1	8th	281	300	187	–
Alabaster	24	6	66	3	22	9	48	3	9th	350	302	191	–
Pollard	19	5	55	0	10	1	30	0	10th	350	359	208	–
Yuile	28	9	70	0	5	1	17	0					
Congdon					1·4	1	6	0					
Burgess					1	1	0	0					

Umpires: D.E.A. Copps (2) and W.T. Martin (9).

Close: 1st day – NZ(1) 248-5 (Burgess 2, Yuile 2); 2nd – I(1) 202-3 (Surti 26, Prasanna 4); 3rd – NZ(2) 84-3 (Murray 51, Yuile 0); 4th – I(2) 161-3 (Wadekar 71, Pataudi 3).

NEW ZEALAND v INDIA 1967–68 (2nd Test)

Played at Lancaster Park, Christchurch, on 22, 23, 24, 26, 27 February.
Toss: India.   Result: NEW ZEALAND won by six wickets.
Debuts: New Zealand – K. Thomson.

New Zealand gained their fourth victory in 81 official Test matches and their first against India. Their second total of over 500 (first in New Zealand), owed much to their captain, Dowling, who batted for 556 minutes, faced 519 balls, hit five sixes, a five, and 28 fours, and set a new record (beaten by G.M. Turner in *Test No. 696*) for the highest Test innings by a New Zealander. His partnerships of 126 with Murray, 103 with Burgess, and 119 with Thomson are still New Zealand's highest against India for the first, fourth and fifth wickets respectively.

NEW ZEALAND

B.A.G. Murray	b Abid Ali	74	b Abid Ali	0
G.T. Dowling*	st Engineer b Prasanna	239	lbw b Bedi	5
B.E. Congdon	c Wadekar b Bedi	28	not out	61
V. Pollard	c Jaisimha b Bedi	1	c Jaisimha b Prasanna	9
M.G. Burgess	c Pataudi b Nadkarni	26	lbw b Bedi	1
K. Thomson	c Wadekar b Bedi	69	not out	0
G.A. Bartlett	c Wadekar b Bedi	22		
R.C. Motz	c sub (R.C. Saxena) b Bedi	1		
R.O. Collinge	c Pataudi b Nadkarni	11		
J.C. Alabaster	c Wadekar b Bedi	1		
R.I. Harford†	not out	0		
Extras	(B 1, LB 13, W 1, NB 15)	30	(B 8, LB 1, NB 3)	12
Total		**502**	(4 wickets)	**88**

INDIA

S. Abid Ali	c and b Motz	7	c Harford b Alabaster	16
F.M. Engineer†	c Congdon b Motz	12	c Burgess b Bartlett	63
A.L. Wadekar	b Motz	15	c Murray b Alabaster	8
R.F. Surti	c Pollard b Motz	67	lbw b Pollard	45
Nawab of Pataudi, jr*	c Murray b Pollard	52	b Bartlett	47
M.L. Jaisimha	c Murray b Collinge	1	(7) run out	15
C.G. Borde	lbw b Motz	57	(6) b Bartlett	33
R.G. Nadkarni	c Harford b Collinge	32	b Bartlett	29
E.A.S. Prasanna	c Dowling b Motz	7	c Pollard b Bartlett	7
B.S. Bedi	c Congdon b Collinge	3	c Murray b Bartlett	5
U.N. Kulkarni	not out	0	not out	1
Extras	(B 5, LB 8, NB 22)	35	(B 2, LB 11, NB 19)	32
Total		**288**		**301**

INDIA	O	M	R	W	O	M	R	W		FALL OF WICKETS			
Kulkarni	13	3	38	0						NZ	I	I	NZ
Surti	20	3	65	0	2·4	1	3	0	*Wkt*	*1st*	*1st*	*2nd*	*2nd*
Abid Ali	18	4	40	1	3	0	13	1	1st	126	7	56	0
Nadkarni	66	34	114	2	8	3	11	0	2nd	208	30	82	30
Bedi	47·3	11	127	6	17	9	21	2	3rd	214	50	107	70
Prasanna	19	2	83	1	8	1	18	1	4th	317	153	186	79
Jaisimha	3	1	5	0	2	0	10	0	5th	436	154	230	–
									6th	471	179	231	–
NEW ZEALAND									7th	473	270	264	–
Collinge	18·2	6	43	3	22	4	79	0	8th	498	281	278	–
Motz	21	6	63	6	14	5	37	0	9th	502	287	300	–
Bartlett	14	1	52	0	16·5	5	38	6	10th	502	288	301	–
Alabaster	15	7	36	0	31	13	63	2					
Pollard	24	7	59	1	15	2	52	1					

Umpires: F.R. Goodall (3) and R.W.R. Shortt (5).

Close: 1st day – NZ(1) 273-3 (Dowling 135, Burgess 13); 2nd – I(1) 8-1 (Engineer 0, Wadekar 1); 3rd – I(1) 288 all out; 4th – I(2) 283-8 (Nadkarni 17, Bedi 4).

NEW ZEALAND v INDIA 1967–68 (3rd Test)

Played at Basin Reserve, Wellington, on 29 February, 1, 2, 4 March.
Toss: New Zealand.   Result: INDIA won by eight wickets.
Debuts: Nil.

Wadekar's only hundred in Test cricket remains India's highest innings in New Zealand. Harford's five catches in the first innings established a New Zealand record and his seven in the match equalled A.E. Dick's performance in *Test No. 520*. Thomson and Murray both captured their first wickets in their first over in Test cricket. India won with over a day and a half to spare.

NEW ZEALAND

G.T. Dowling*	c Wadekar b Surti	15	c Abid Ali b Nadkarni	14
B.A.G. Murray	run out	10	c Pataudi b Nadkarni	22
B.E. Congdon	c Wadekar b Surti	4	c Jaisimha b Bedi	51
M.G. Burgess	c Surti b Prasanna	66	(5) c Pataudi b Nadkarni	60
K. Thomson	b Surti	25	(6) c Wadekar b Nadkarni	0
V. Pollard	c Engineer b Nadkarni	24	(4) c Abid Ali b Nadkarni	1
B.R. Taylor	st Engineer b Prasanna	17	c Subramanya b Prasanna	28
R.C. Motz	c Surti b Prasanna	5	c Subramanya b Prasanna	9
R.O. Collinge	c Wadekar b Prasanna	5	c sub (R.C. Saxena) b Nadkarni	5
J.C. Alabaster	not out	3	not out	2
R.I. Harford†	c Engineer b Prasanna	1	c Subramanya b Prasanna	0
Extras	(B 2, NB 9)	11	(B 5, LB 2)	7
Total		**186**		**199**

INDIA

S. Abid Ali	c Harford b Collinge	11	c Harford b Murray	36
F.M. Engineer†	run out	44	c Harford b Thomson	18
A.L. Wadekar	c Harford b Collinge	143	not out	5
R.F. Surti	c Congdon b Taylor	10	not out	0
Nawab of Pataudi, jr*	c Harford b Taylor	30		
C.G. Borde	c Harford b Collinge	10		
M.L. Jaisimha	c Harford b Alabaster	20		
R.G. Nadkarni	c Murray b Alabaster	3		
V. Subramanya	not out	32		
E.A.S. Prasanna	b Taylor	1		
B.S. Bedi	run out	8		
Extras	(LB 8, NB 7)	15		
Total		**327**	(2 wickets)	**59**

INDIA	O	M	R	W	O	M	R	W
Surti	22	6	44	3	8	1	31	0
Abid Ali	8	0	31	0				
Jaisimha	22	11	34	0	5	1	10	0
Bedi	2	0	12	0	16	5	42	1
Nadkarni	17	8	22	1	30	12	43	6
Prasanna	18·2	6	32	5	20·2	3	56	3
Subramanya					2	1	10	0
NEW ZEALAND								
Collinge	18	3	65	3	2	0	7	0
Motz	20	5	62	0	3	0	21	0
Taylor	27·1	9	59	3				
Alabaster	18	2	64	2	1	0	8	0
Pollard	25	6	62	0	1	0	7	0
Thomson					3·3	1	9	1
Burgess					2	0	7	0
Murray					1	1	0	1

FALL OF WICKETS

	NZ	I	NZ	I
Wkt	1st	1st	2nd	2nd
1st	24	18	35	43
2nd	30	78	42	57
3rd	33	97	49	–
4th	88	163	135	–
5th	154	186	148	–
6th	155	256	179	–
7th	160	268	192	–
8th	169	295	193	–
9th	182	296	199	–
10th	186	327	199	–

Umpires: D.E.A. Copps (3) and W.T. Martin (10).

Close: 1st day – NZ(1) 147-4 (Burgess 63, Pollard 20); 2nd – I(1) 200-5 (Wadekar 78, Jaisimha 5); 3rd – NZ(2) 143-4 (Burgess 50, Thomson 0).

NEW ZEALAND v INDIA 1967–68 (4th Test)

Played at Eden Park, Auckland, on 7, 8, 9, 11, 12 March.
Toss: New Zealand. Result: INDIA won by 272 runs.
Debuts: Nil.

Eight hours and 20 minutes of playing time were lost on the first two days. New Zealand, set 374 runs in 290 minutes, were all out 15 minutes after tea. This is the only rubber in which India have won three matches. Surti was destined to emulate N.W.D. Yardley (*Test No. 285*), J.E.F. Beck (*379*) and Maqsood Ahmed (*398*) by ending his Test career with a highest score of 99. Pataudi retired when 37 after being struck in the mouth by a ball from Bartlett.

INDIA

F.M. Engineer†	c Bartlett b Motz	44	c and b Alabaster	48
S. Abid Ali	c Dowling b Motz	1	c Murray b Taylor	22
A.L. Wadekar	c Ward b Bartlett	5	b Taylor	1
R.F. Surti	c Pollard b Bartlett	28	c Burgess b Bartlett	99
Nawab of Pataudi, jr*	c Pollard b Motz	51	lbw b Pollard	6
C.G. Borde	c Alabaster b Pollard	41	not out	65
M.L. Jaisimha	c Pollard b Alabaster	19	not out	1
V. Subramanya	run out	3		
R.G. Nadkarni	c Burgess b Bartlett	21		
E.A.S. Prasanna	not out	3		
B.S. Bedi	c Murray b Motz	0		
Extras	(B 9, LB 3, W 2, NB 22)	36	(B 6, LB 4, NB 9)	19
Total		**252**	(5 wickets declared)	**261**

NEW ZEALAND

G.T. Dowling*	c Engineer b Surti	8	b Bedi	37
B.A.G. Murray	c Engineer b Surti	17	c Jaisimha b Surti	3
B.E. Congdon	c Abid Ali b Nadkarni	27	c Surti b Nadkarni	3
M.G. Burgess	c Subramanya b Prasanna	11	c Bedi b Surti	18
B.W. Sinclair	b Bedi	20	b Prasanna	12
V. Pollard	run out	3	b Bedi	0
G.A. Bartlett	c Wadekar b Prasanna	0	(8) b Prasanna	11
B.R. Taylor	c Abid Ali b Bedi	7	(9) b Prasanna	0
R.C. Motz	c and b Prasanna	18	(10) c Engineer b Bedi	6
J.T. Ward†	not out	10	(7) b Prasanna	5
J.C. Alabaster	c Bedi b Prasanna	6	not out	0
Extras	(B 4, NB 9)	13	(B 3, LB 2, NB 1)	6
Total		**140**		**101**

NEW ZEALAND	O	M	R	W	O	M	R	W	FALL OF WICKETS				
Motz	26·4	12	51	4	16	4	44	0		I	NZ	I	NZ
Bartlett	26	11	66	3	15	1	40	1	*Wkt*	*1st*	*1st*	*2nd*	*2nd*
Taylor	17	4	49	0	22	4	60	2	1st	6	30	43	10
Pollard	8	4	9	1	21	8	42	1	2nd	13	33	48	15
Alabaster	13	0	41	1	22	4	56	1	3rd	69	67	112	55
INDIA									4th	132	74	127	74
Surti	10	2	32	2	11	2	30	2	5th	175	77	253	78
Jaisimha	7	3	14	0	3	1	5	0	6th	215	88	–	78
Nadkarni	14	6	16	1	2	1	1	1	7th	226	103	–	94
Prasanna	28·1	11	44	4	27	15	40	4	8th	244	106	–	95
Bedi	17	8	21	2	17·4	11	14	3	9th	251	124	–	101
Subramanya	1	1	0	0	1	0	5	0	10th	252	140	–	101

Umpires: D.E.A. Copps (4) and W.T. Martin (11).

Close: 1st day – I(1) 61-2 (Engineer 38, Surti 3); 2nd – I(1) 150-4 (Pataudi 37, Borde 8); 3rd – NZ(1) 101-6 (Sinclair 17, Taylor 5); 4th – I(2) 216-4 (Surti 81, Borde 43).

ENGLAND v AUSTRALIA 1968 (1st Test)

Played at Old Trafford, Manchester, on 6, 7, 8, 10, 11 June.
Toss: Australia.   Result: AUSTRALIA won by 159 runs.
Debuts: Nil.

England, needing 413 to win in 552 minutes, were dismissed at 1.02 pm on the fifth day. Walters enjoyed his most prolific match in England where, in 30 Test innings, he was destined never to reach 90. Neither D'Oliveira nor Pocock, England's main contributors in terms of runs and wickets respectively in this match, were retained for the next Test.

AUSTRALIA

W.M. Lawry*	c Boycott b Barber	81	c Pocock b D'Oliveira	16
I.R. Redpath	lbw b Snow	8	lbw b Snow	8
R.M. Cowper	b Snow	0	c and b Pocock	37
K.D. Walters	lbw b Barber	81	lbw b Pocock	86
A.P. Sheahan	c D'Oliveira b Snow	88	c Graveney b Pocock	8
I.M. Chappell	run out	73	c Knott b Pocock	9
B.N. Jarman†	c and b Higgs	12	b Pocock	41
N.J.N. Hawke	c Knott b Snow	5	c Edrich b Pocock	0
G.D. McKenzie	c Cowdrey b D'Oliveira	0	c Snow b Barber	0
J.W. Gleeson	c Knott b Higgs	0	run out	2
A.N. Connolly	not out	0	not out	2
Extras	(LB 7, NB 2)	9	(B 2, LB 9)	11
Total		**357**		**220**

ENGLAND

J.H. Edrich	run out	49	c Jarman b Cowper	38
G. Boycott	c Jarman b Cowper	35	c Redpath b McKenzie	11
M.C. Cowdrey*	c Lawry b McKenzie	4	c Jarman b McKenzie	11
T.W. Graveney	c McKenzie b Cowper	2	c Jarman b Gleeson	33
D.L. Amiss	c Cowper b McKenzie	0	b Cowper	0
R.W. Barber	c Sheahan b McKenzie	20	c Cowper b Hawke	46
B.L. D'Oliveira	b Connolly	9	not out	87
A.P.E. Knott†	c McKenzie b Cowper	5	lbw b Connolly	4
J.A. Snow	not out	18	c Lawry b Connolly	2
K. Higgs	lbw b Cowper	2	c Jarman b Gleeson	0
P.I. Pocock	c Redpath b Gleeson	6	lbw b Gleeson	10
Extras	(B 9, LB 3, W 3)	15	(B 5, LB 6)	11
Total		**165**		**253**

ENGLAND	O	M	R	W	O	M	R	W		FALL OF WICKETS			
Snow	34	5	97	4	17	2	51	1		A	E	A	E
Higgs	35·3	11	80	2	23	8	41	0	Wkt	1st	1st	2nd	2nd
D'Oliveira	25	11	38	1	5	3	7	1	1st	29	86	24	13
Pocock	25	5	77	0	33	10	79	6	2nd	29	87	24	25
Barber	11	0	56	2	10	1	31	1	3rd	173	89	106	91
									4th	174	90	122	91
AUSTRALIA									5th	326	97	140	105
McKenzie	28	11	33	3	18	3	52	2	6th	341	120	211	185
Hawke	15	7	18	0	8	4	15	1	7th	351	137	211	214
Connolly	28	15	26	1	13	4	35	2	8th	353	137	214	218
Gleeson	6·3	2	21	1	30	14	44	3	9th	357	144	214	219
Cowper	26	11	48	4	39	12	82	2	10th	357	165	220	253
Chappell	1	0	4	0	2	0	14	0					

Umpires: J.S. Buller (28) and C.S. Elliott (27).

Close: 1st day – A(1) 319-4 (Sheahan 74, Chappell 68); 2nd – E(1) 60-0 (Edrich 32, Boycott 26); 3rd – A(2) 60-2 (Cowper 14, Walters 19); 4th – E(2) 152-5 (Barber 29, D'Oliveira 21).

ENGLAND v AUSTRALIA 1968 (2nd Test)

Played at Lord's, London, on 20, 21, 22, 24, 25 June.
Toss: England.   Result: MATCH DRAWN.
Debuts: Nil.

After England had won their 103rd toss against Australia (with a gold sovereign presented by Sir Robert Menzies), rain reduced the playing time in this 200th match of the original series of Tests by over half, a total of 15 hours 3 minutes being lost, although some play was possible on each of the five days. Barrington (damaged finger) retired hurt at 271 when 61 and resumed at 330. Australia's total of 78 was their lowest since South Africa dismissed them for 75 in 1949-50 (*Test No. 320*), and their lowest in England since 1912 (*Test No. 129*). Cowdrey overtook W.R. Hammond's world Test record of 110 catches when he caught Gleeson at 1st slip. Knight took his 1,000th first-class wicket when he dismissed Sheahan. Jarman, who had fractured his right index finger when keeping wicket, retired at 78 after being hit on the same finger by the first ball he received. Brown's analysis remained his best in Tests. Sheahan batted 52 minutes and faced 44 balls without scoring on the final afternoon.

ENGLAND

J.H. Edrich	c Cowper b McKenzie	7
G. Boycott	c Sheahan b McKenzie	49
C. Milburn	c Walters b Gleeson	83
M.C. Cowdrey*	c Cowper b McKenzie	45
K.F. Barrington	c Jarman b Connolly	75
T.W. Graveney	c Jarman b Connolly	14
B.R. Knight	not out	27
A.P.E. Knott†	run out	33
J.A. Snow	not out	0
D.J. Brown	} did not bat	
D.L. Underwood		
Extras	(B 7, LB 5, W 1, NB 5)	18
Total	(7 wickets declared)	**351**

AUSTRALIA

W.M. Lawry*	c Knott b Brown	0	c Brown b Snow	28
I.R. Redpath	c Cowdrey b Brown	4	b Underwood	53
R.M. Cowper	c Graveney b Snow	8	c Underwood b Barrington	32
K.D. Walters	c Knight b Brown	26	b Underwood	0
A.P. Sheahan	c Knott b Knight	6	not out	0
I.M. Chappell	lbw b Knight	7	not out	12
N.J.N. Hawke	c Cowdrey b Knight	2		
G.D. McKenzie	b Brown	5		
J.W. Gleeson	c Cowdrey b Brown	14		
B.N. Jarman†	retired hurt	0		
A.N. Connolly	not out	0		
Extras	(LB 2, NB 4)	6	(NB 2)	2
Total		**78**	(4 wickets)	**127**

AUSTRALIA	O	M	R	W	O	M	R	W		FALL OF WICKETS			
McKenzie	45	18	111	3							E	A	A
Hawke	35	7	82	0						Wkt	1st	1st	2nd
Connolly	26·3	8	55	2						1st	10	1	66
Walters	3	2	2	0						2nd	142	12	93
Cowper	8	2	40	0						3rd	147	23	97
Gleeson	27	11	43	1						4th	244	46	115
										5th	271	52	–
ENGLAND										6th	330	58	–
Snow	9	5	14	1	12	5	30	1		7th	351	63	–
Brown	14	5	42	5	19	9	40	0		8th	–	78	–
Knight	10·4	5	16	3	16	9	35	0		9th	–	78	–
Underwood					18	15	8	2		10th	–	–	–
Barrington					2	0	12	1					

Umpires: J.S. Buller (29) and A.E. Fagg (2).

Close: 1st day – E(1) 53-1 (Boycott 27, Milburn 16); 2nd – E(1) 314-5 (Knight 8, Knott 30); 3rd – E(1) 351-7 (Knight 27, Snow 0); 4th – A(2) 50-0 (Lawry 25, Redpath 24).

ENGLAND v AUSTRALIA 1968 (3rd Test)

Played at Edgbaston, Birmingham, on 11 (*no play*), 12, 13, 15, 16 July.
Toss: England.   Result: MATCH DRAWN.
Debuts: Nil.

Cowdrey celebrated his becoming the first to appear in 100 Test matches by scoring his 21st hundred for England. He pulled a muscle in his left leg and used Boycott as his runner when he had scored 58. Two runs later he became the second batsman after W.R. Hammond to score 7,000 runs in Test cricket. Graveney assumed the captaincy when Cowdrey was unable to field. After scoring Australia's first six runs, Lawry retired when his right-hand little finger was fractured by a ball in Snow's opening over. McKenzie deputised as captain when Australia fielded again. Rain ended the match at 12.30 pm when Australia needed 262 runs to win in 270 minutes. For the first time in 13 Tests, Edgbaston lost a day's play.

ENGLAND

J.H. Edrich	c Taber b Freeman	88	c Cowper b Freeman		64
G. Boycott	lbw b Gleeson	36	c Taber b Connolly		31
M.C. Cowdrey*	b Freeman	104			
K.F. Barrington	lbw b Freeman	0			
T.W. Graveney	b Connolly	96	(3) not out		39
B.R. Knight	c Chappell b Connolly	6	(4) b Connolly		1
A.P.E. Knott†	b McKenzie	4	(5) not out		4
R. Illingworth	lbw b Gleeson	27			
D.J. Brown	b Connolly	0			
J.A. Snow	c Connolly b Freeman	19			
D.L. Underwood	not out	14			
Extras	(B 4, LB 6, W 1, NB 4)	15	(LB 2, NB 1)		3
Total		**409**	(3 wickets declared)		**142**

AUSTRALIA

W.M. Lawry*	retired hurt	6			
I.R. Redpath	b Brown	0	lbw b Snow		22
R.M. Cowper	b Snow	57	(1) not out		25
I.M. Chappell	b Knight	71	(3) not out		18
K.D. Walters	c and b Underwood	46			
A.P. Sheahan	b Underwood	4			
H.B. Taber†	c Barrington b Illingworth	16			
E.W. Freeman	b Illingworth	6			
G.D. McKenzie	not out	0			
J.W. Gleeson	c Illingworth b Underwood	3			
A.N. Connolly	b Illingworth	0			
Extras	(B 1, LB 10, NB 2)	13	(LB 1, NB 2)		3
Total		**222**	(1 wicket)		**68**

AUSTRALIA	O	M	R	W	O	M	R	W
McKenzie	47	14	115	1	18	1	57	0
Freeman	30·5	8	78	4	9	2	23	1
Connolly	35	8	84	3	15	3	59	2
Gleeson	46	19	84	2				
Cowper	7	1	25	0				
Walters	7	3	8	0				
ENGLAND								
Snow	17	3	46	1	9	1	32	1
Brown	13	2	44	1	6	1	15	0
Knight	14	2	34	1				
Underwood	25	9	48	3	8	4	14	0
Illingworth	22	10	37	3	5·2	2	4	0

FALL OF WICKETS

Wkt	E 1st	A 1st	E 2nd	A 2nd
1st	80	10	57	44
2nd	188	121	131	–
3rd	189	165	134	–
4th	282	176	–	–
5th	293	213	–	–
6th	323	213	–	–
7th	374	219	–	–
8th	374	222	–	–
9th	376	222	–	–
10th	409	–	–	–

Umpires: C.S. Elliott (28) and H. Yarnold (3).

Close: 1st day – no play; 2nd – E(1) 258-3 (Cowdrey 95, Graveney 32); 3rd – A(1) 109-1 (Cowper 54, Chappell 40); 4th – A(2) 9-0 (Redpath 6, Cowper 3).

ENGLAND v AUSTRALIA 1968 (4th Test)

Played at Headingley, Leeds, on 25, 26, 27, 29, 30 July.
Toss: Australia.   Result: MATCH DRAWN.
Debuts: England – K.W.R. Fletcher, R.M. Prideaux; Australia – R.J. Inverarity.

With Cowdrey and Lawry both injured, Graveney and Jarman were called upon to make their only appearances as Test captains. Australia retained the Ashes when England failed to score 326 runs in 295 minutes. Underwood's score of 45 not out is the highest by an England No. 11 against Australia.

AUSTRALIA

R.J. Inverarity	b Snow	8	lbw b Illingworth		34
R.M. Cowper	b Snow	27	st Knott b Illingworth		5
I.R. Redpath	b Illingworth	92	c Edrich b Snow		48
K.D. Walters	c Barrington b Underwood	42	c Graveney b Snow		56
I.M. Chappell	b Brown	65	c Barrington b Underwood		81
A.P. Sheahan	c Knott b Snow	38	st Knott b Illingworth		31
B.N. Jarman*†	c Dexter b Brown	10	st Knott b Illingworth		4
E.W. Freeman	b Underwood	21	b Illingworth		10
G.D. McKenzie	lbw b Underwood	5	c Snow b Illingworth		10
J.W. Gleeson	not out	2	c Knott b Underwood		7
A.N. Connolly	c Graveney b Underwood	0	not out		0
Extras	(LB 4, NB 1)	5	(B 13, LB 8, NB 5)		26
Total		**315**			**312**

ENGLAND

J.H. Edrich	c Jarman b McKenzie	62	c Jarman b Connolly		65
R.M. Prideaux	c Freeman b Gleeson	64	b McKenzie		2
E.R. Dexter	b McKenzie	10	b Connolly		38
T.W. Graveney*	c Cowper b Connolly	37	c and b Cowper		41
K.F. Barrington	b Connolly	49	not out		46
K.W.R. Fletcher	c Jarman b Connolly	0	not out		23
A.P.E. Knott†	lbw b Freeman	4			
R. Illingworth	c Gleeson b Connolly	6			
J.A. Snow	b Connolly	0			
D.J. Brown	b Cowper	14			
D.L. Underwood	not out	45			
Extras	(B 1, LB 7, NB 3)	11	(LB 7, NB 8)		15
Total		**302**	(4 wickets)		**230**

ENGLAND	O	M	R	W	O	M	R	W
Snow	35	3	98	3	24	3	51	2
Brown	35	4	99	2	27	5	79	0
Illingworth	29	15	47	1	51	22	87	6
Underwood	27·4	13	41	4	45·1	22	52	2
Dexter	7	0	25	0	1	0	3	0
Barrington					6	1	14	0
AUSTRALIA								
McKenzie	39	20	61	2	25	2	65	1
Freeman	22	6	60	1	6	1	25	0
Gleeson	25	5	68	1	11	4	26	0
Connolly	39	13	72	5	31	10	68	2
Cowper	18	10	24	1	5	0	22	1
Chappell	4	1	6	0	5	3	6	0
Inverarity					1	0	3	0

FALL OF WICKETS

	A	E	A	E
Wkt	1st	1st	2nd	2nd
1st	10	123	28	4
2nd	104	136	81	81
3rd	152	141	119	134
4th	188	209	198	168
5th	248	215	273	–
6th	267	235	281	–
7th	307	237	283	–
8th	309	241	296	–
9th	315	241	311	–
10th	315	302	312	–

Umpires: J.S. Buller (30) and A.E. Fagg (3).

Close: 1st day – A(1) 258-5 (Chappell 38, Jarman 8); 2nd – E(1) 163-3 (Graveney 10, Barrington 12); 3rd – A(2) 92-2 (Redpath 35, Walters 1); 4th – A(2) 283-6 (Jarman 4, Freeman 1).

ENGLAND v AUSTRALIA 1968 (5th Test)

Played at Kennington Oval, London, on 22, 23, 24, 26, 27 August.
Toss: England.   Result: ENGLAND won by 226 runs.
Debuts: Australia – A.A. Mallett.

England won with just five minutes to spare when Inverarity padded up to an 'arm' ball from Underwood after batting throughout Australia's 250-minute innings. Rain brought the players in to lunch a minute early on the final day. During the interval a freak storm completely flooded the playing area but the sun's reappearance, combined with heroic efforts by a groundstaff reinforced by volunteers from the crowd, enabled play to resume at 4.45 pm with Australia's score 86 for 5. Until D'Oliveira bowled Jarman at 5.24 pm they seemed to have saved the match. Cowdrey brought Underwood back to bowl the next over from the pavilion end and Mallett and McKenzie fell to the first and sixth balls. Gleeson survived until 5.48 pm. Seven minutes later Inverarity made his fatal lapse and England had taken five wickets and bowled 20·3 overs in the last hour of play. Earlier Mallett had dismissed Cowdrey with his fifth ball in Test cricket.

ENGLAND

J.H. Edrich	b Chappell	164	c Lawry b Mallett	17
C. Milburn	b Connolly	8	c Lawry b Connolly	18
E.R. Dexter	b Gleeson	21	b Connolly	28
M.C. Cowdrey*	lbw b Mallett	16	b Mallett	35
T.W. Graveney	c Redpath b McKenzie	63	run out	12
B.L. D'Oliveira	c Inverarity b Mallett	158	c Gleeson b Connolly	9
A.P.E. Knott†	c Jarman b Mallett	28	run out	34
R. Illingworth	lbw b Connolly	8	b Gleeson	10
J.A. Snow	run out	4	c Sheahan b Gleeson	13
D.L. Underwood	not out	9	not out	1
D.J. Brown	c Sheahan b Gleeson	2	b Connolly	1
Extras	(B 1, LB 11, W 1)	13	(LB 3)	3
Total		**494**		**181**

AUSTRALIA

W.M. Lawry*	c Knott b Snow	135	c Milburn b Brown	4
R.J. Inverarity	c Milburn b Snow	1	lbw b Underwood	56
I.R. Redpath	c Cowdrey b Snow	67	lbw b Underwood	8
I.M. Chappell	c Knott b Brown	10	lbw b Underwood	2
K.D. Walters	c Knott b Brown	5	c Knott b Underwood	1
A.P. Sheahan	b Illingworth	14	c Snow b Illingworth	24
B.N. Jarman†	st Knott b Illingworth	0	b D'Oliveira	21
G.D. McKenzie	b Brown	12	(9) c Brown b Underwood	0
A.A. Mallett	not out	43	(8) c Brown b Underwood	0
J.W. Gleeson	c Dexter b Underwood	19	b Underwood	5
A.N. Connolly	b Underwood	3	not out	0
Extras	(B 4, LB 7, NB 4)	15	(LB 4)	4
Total		**324**		**125**

AUSTRALIA	O	M	R	W	O	M	R	W
McKenzie	40	8	87	1	4	0	14	0
Connolly	57	12	127	2	22·4	2	65	4
Walters	6	2	17	0				
Gleeson	41·2	8	109	2	7	2	22	2
Mallett	36	11	87	3	25	4	77	2
Chappell	21	5	54	1				
ENGLAND								
Snow	35	12	67	3	11	5	22	0
Brown	22	5	63	3	8	3	19	1
Illingworth	48	15	87	2	28	18	29	1
Underwood	54·3	21	89	2	31·3	19	50	7
D'Oliveira	4	2	3	0	5	4	1	1

FALL OF WICKETS

	E	A	E	A
Wkt	1st	1st	2nd	2nd
1st	28	7	23	4
2nd	84	136	53	13
3rd	113	151	67	19
4th	238	161	90	29
5th	359	185	114	65
6th	421	188	126	110
7th	458	237	149	110
8th	468	269	179	110
9th	489	302	179	120
10th	494	324	181	125

Umpires: C.S. Elliott (29) and A.E. Fagg (4).

Close: 1st day – E(1) 272-4 (Edrich 130, D'Oliveira 24); 2nd – A(1) 43-1 (Lawry 19, Redpath 21); 3rd – A(1) 264-7 (Lawry 135, Mallett 7); 4th – A(2) 13-2 (Inverarity 1).

AUSTRALIA v WEST INDIES 1968–69 (1st Test)

Played at Woolloongabba, Brisbane, on 6, 7, 8, 10 December.
Toss: West Indies.   Result: WEST INDIES won by 125 runs.
Debuts: Nil.

West Indies gained their first victory in a Brisbane Test with a day and five minutes to spare. Chappell and Lloyd scored hundreds on their first appearances in this series. The partnership of 165 between Carew, subsequently demoted in the order because of an injured hand, and Kanhai was the highest for West Indies' second wicket against Australia until 1988-89. Sobers, mainly in his orthodox slower style, returned the best analysis of his 93-Test career. It included the freak dismissal of Chappell, caught via slip's right knee by a diving-on-the-run short third-man 20 yards away.

WEST INDIES

G.S. Camacho	b Gleeson	6	c Redpath b Connolly		40
M.C. Carew	run out	83	(8) not out		71
R.B. Kanhai	c Gleeson b Mallett	94	c Inverarity b Gleeson		29
S.M. Nurse	c Jarman b McKenzie	25	(2) c Mallett b Gleeson		16
B.F. Butcher	c Chappell b Connolly	22	(4) b Gleeson		1
G. St A. Sobers*	c Jarman b Connolly	2	c Jarman b Gleeson		36
C.H. Lloyd	c Jarman b Connolly	7	(5) lbw b McKenzie		129
D.A.J. Holford	c Jarman b Gleeson	6	(7) c Jarman b McKenzie		4
J.L. Hendriks†	not out	15	c Jarman b Chappell		10
C.C. Griffith	c Sheahan b Connolly	8	b Gleeson		1
L.R. Gibbs	b McKenzie	17	c Inverarity b Chappell		0
Extras	(B 1, LB 6, NB 4)	11	(B 4, LB 10, NB 2)		16
Total		**296**			**353**

AUSTRALIA

I.R. Redpath	c Hendriks b Sobers	0	c Lloyd b Sobers		18
W.M. Lawry*	c Sobers b Lloyd	105	b Gibbs		9
I.M. Chappell	c Sobers b Lloyd	117	c sub (C.A. Davis) b Sobers		50
K.R. Stackpole	c Holford b Gibbs	1	b Sobers		32
A.P. Sheahan	c Nurse b Holford	14	b Gibbs		34
R.J. Inverarity	c Holford b Gibbs	5	c Kanhai b Gibbs		9
B.N. Jarman†	c Sobers b Gibbs	17	st Hendriks b Sobers		4
G.D. McKenzie	c Gibbs b Holford	4	not out		38
A.A. Mallett	b Gibbs	6	lbw b Carew		19
J.W. Gleeson	not out	1	c sub (C.A. Davis) b Sobers		10
A.N. Connolly	lbw b Gibbs	0	c Holford b Sobers		0
Extras	(B 7, LB 1, NB 6)	14	(B 9, LB 7, NB 1)		17
Total		**284**			**240**

AUSTRALIA	O	M	R	W	O	M	R	W		FALL OF WICKETS			
McKenzie	21	5	55	2	16	2	55	2		WI	A	WI	A
Connolly	19	5	60	4	21	1	75	1	*Wkt*	*1st*	*1st*	*2nd*	*2nd*
Gleeson	28	7	72	2	33	5	122	5	1st	23	0	48	27
Mallett	14	2	54	1	4	0	32	0	2nd	188	217	92	29
Chappell	4	0	10	0	6	0	21	2	3rd	192	220	92	66
Stackpole	9	3	34	0	7	1	32	0	4th	241	246	93	137
									5th	243	255	165	161
WEST INDIES									6th	247	257	178	165
Sobers	14	5	30	1	33·6	12	73	6	7th	250	263	298	165
Griffith	12	1	47	0					8th	258	283	331	220
Gibbs	39·4	7	88	5	30	6	82	3	9th	267	284	350	238
Holford	25	6	88	2	14	1	31	0	10th	296	284	353	240
Lloyd	8	1	17	2	2	0	7	0					
Carew					9	1	30	1					

Umpires: C.J. Egar (25) and L.P. Rowan (16).

Close: 1st day – WI(1) 267-9 (Hendriks 3, Gibbs 0); 2nd – A(1) 255-5 (Sheahan 14, Jarman 0); 3rd – WI(2) 298-7 (Carew 29).

AUSTRALIA v WEST INDIES 1968–69 (2nd Test)

Played at Melbourne Cricket Ground on 26, 27, 28, 30 December.
Toss: Australia.   Result: AUSTRALIA won by an innings and 30 runs.
Debuts: West Indies – C.A. Davis, R.M. Edwards, R.C. Fredericks.

Australia won in the last over of the fourth (penultimate) day. McKenzie's analysis of 8 for 71 remains the best for either side in this series. Chappell scored the 1,000th hundred in Test cricket and made the same score as C. Bannerman achieved in the first Test match of all. His partnership of 298 in 310 minutes with Lawry is still the highest for the second wicket in this series. Lawry's 205 took 440 minutes and included a six and 12 fours. In the second innings, Nurse was caught at deep fine-leg after the ball had rebounded off the head of short fine-leg (Freeman).

WEST INDIES

G.S. Camacho	c Chappell b McKenzie	0		lbw b Gleeson	11
R.C. Fredericks	c Redpath b McKenzie	76		c Freeman b Gleeson	47
M.C. Carew	c Gleeson b McKenzie	7	(8)	b Stackpole	33
S.M. Nurse	c Jarman b Freeman	22	(5)	c Stackpole b Gleeson	74
B.F. Butcher	lbw b Gleeson	42	(7)	c Jarman b McKenzie	0
G. St A. Sobers*	b McKenzie	19		lbw b McKenzie	67
R.B. Kanhai	c Sheahan b McKenzie	5	(4)	c Redpath b Freeman	4
C.A. Davis	b McKenzie	18	(9)	c Redpath b Gleeson	10
J.L. Hendriks†	c Chappell b McKenzie	0	(10)	c Redpath b Gleeson	3
R.M. Edwards	not out	9	(3)	run out	21
L.R. Gibbs	b McKenzie	0		not out	0
Extras	(B 1, LB 1)	2		(B 7, LB 3)	10
Total		**200**			**280**

AUSTRALIA

I.R. Redpath	c Hendriks b Edwards	7
W.M. Lawry*	c Carew b Davis	205
I.M. Chappell	b Sobers	165
K.D. Walters	c Camacho b Sobers	76
K.R. Stackpole	b Gibbs	15
A.P. Sheahan	c and b Sobers	18
B.N. Jarman†	c Butcher b Gibbs	12
E.W. Freeman	c Carew b Gibbs	2
G.D. McKenzie	b Sobers	1
J.W. Gleeson	b Gibbs	0
A.N. Connolly	not out	3
Extras	(LB 4, NB 2)	6
Total		**510**

AUSTRALIA	O	M	R	W	O	M	R	W		FALL OF WICKETS		
McKenzie	28	5	71	8	20	2	88	2		WI	A	WI
Connolly	12	2	34	0	19	7	35	0	*Wkt*	*1st*	*1st*	*2nd*
Freeman	7	0	32	1	11	1	31	1	1st	0	14	23
Gleeson	25	8	49	1	26·4	9	61	5	2nd	14	312	76
Stackpole	1	0	12	0	13	9	19	1	3rd	42	435	85
Chappell					9	1	36	0	4th	135	453	85
									5th	158	488	219
WEST INDIES									6th	170	501	219
Sobers	33·3	4	97	4					7th	177	505	243
Edwards	26	1	128	1					8th	177	506	264
Davis	24	0	94	1					9th	200	506	278
Gibbs	43	8	139	4					10th	200	510	280
Carew	10	2	46	0								

Umpires: C.J. Egar (26) and L.P. Rowan (17).

Close: 1st day – WI(1) 176-6 (Fredericks 76, Davis 3); 2nd – A(1) 263-1 (Lawry 117, Chappell 133); 3rd – WI(2) 25-1 (Fredericks 13, Edwards 1).

AUSTRALIA v WEST INDIES 1968–69 (3rd Test)

Played at Sydney Cricket Ground on 3, 4, 5, 7, 8 January.
Toss: West Indies.   Result: AUSTRALIA won by ten wickets.
Debuts: Nil.

Australia completed their second comprehensive victory within ten days after 20 minutes on the final morning. The partnership of 73 between Gleeson and Connolly was a record for the tenth wicket by either side in this series until 1983-84 (*Test No. 981*).

WEST INDIES

R.C. Fredericks	c Chappell b McKenzie	26	c Redpath b Connolly		43
M.C. Carew	c Jarman b McKenzie	30	c Jarman b Freeman		10
R.B. Kanhai	b McKenzie	17	c Chappell b McKenzie		69
B.F. Butcher	b Stackpole	28	c and b Gleeson		101
S.M. Nurse	c Redpath b Connolly	3	c Stackpole b McKenzie		17
G. St A. Sobers*	b Freeman	49	c Chappell b Gleeson		36
C.H. Lloyd	c Jarman b Freeman	50	c Stackpole b Freeman		13
J.L. Hendriks†	c Stackpole b Freeman	4	c Connolly b Gleeson	(9)	22
R.M. Edwards	b Connolly	10	b Freeman	(8)	0
W.W. Hall	c Gleeson b McKenzie	33	st Jarman b Gleeson		5
L.R. Gibbs	not out	1	not out		1
Extras	(B 2, LB 10, NB 1)	13	(LB 3, NB 4)		7
Total		**264**			**324**

AUSTRALIA

W.M. Lawry*	c Carew b Edwards	29			
K.R. Stackpole	c Gibbs b Hall	58	not out		21
I.M. Chappell	c Kanhai b Gibbs	33			
I.R. Redpath	st Hendriks b Carew	80			
K.D. Walters	b Gibbs	118			
A.P. Sheahan	c Lloyd b Hall	47	not out	(1)	21
B.N. Jarman†	c Fredericks b Hall	0			
E.W. Freeman	b Edwards	76			
G.D. McKenzie	run out	10			
J.W. Gleeson	not out	42			
A.N. Connolly	run out	37			
Extras	(B 5, LB 11, W 1)	17			
Total		**547**	(0 wickets)		**42**

AUSTRALIA	O	M	R	W	O	M	R	W
McKenzie	22·1	3	85	4	24	2	80	2
Connolly	16	1	54	2	23	7	54	1
Freeman	13	2	57	3	15	3	59	3
Walters	2	1	3	0				
Gleeson	18	7	45	0	26	5	91	4
Stackpole	4	2	7	1	5	0	33	0
WEST INDIES								
Hall	26	2	113	3	2	0	8	0
Edwards	25	1	139	2	1	0	7	0
Sobers	21	4	109	0				
Gibbs	37·6	6	124	2				
Carew	12	1	45	1	2	0	9	0
Lloyd					2	0	8	0
Kanhai					1	0	10	0

FALL OF WICKETS

Wkt	WI 1st	A 1st	WI 2nd	A 2nd
1st	49	68	20	–
2nd	72	95	123	–
3rd	79	153	127	–
4th	85	235	168	–
5th	143	345	243	–
6th	181	349	263	–
7th	216	387	264	–
8th	217	418	318	–
9th	236	474	323	–
10th	264	547	324	–

Umpires: C.J. Egar (27) and L.P. Rowan (18).

Close: 1st day – WI(1) 218-8 (Edwards 0, Hall 1); 2nd – A(1) 280-4 (Walters 67, Sheahan 12); 3rd – WI(2) 65-1 (Fredericks 27, Kanhai 27); 4th – A(2) 15-0 (Sheahan 9, Stackpole 6).

AUSTRALIA v WEST INDIES 1968–69 (4th Test)

Played at Adelaide Oval on 24, 25, 27, 28, 29 January.
Toss: West Indies.   Result: MATCH DRAWN.
Debuts: Nil.

Although drawn, this match produced the most exciting finish of the rubber. Australia's tenth-wicket pair, Sheahan and Connolly, survived the last 26 balls – 16 of them bowled with a new ball by Sobers and Griffith. At the end of the highest scoring Test match in Australia only 20 runs and one wicket separated the two sides. West Indies' 616 remains their highest score against Australia and the highest second-innings total in any Test in that country. The partnership of 122 between Holford and Hendriks was then the highest for the West Indies' ninth wicket against any country and remains the record by either side in this series. Redpath, the non-striker, was run out by the bowler, Griffith, without a warning for backing-up before the ball had been bowled. W.A. Brown fell victim to a similar action by M.H. Mankad in *Test No. 291*. Nurse kept wicket after lunch in the second innings instead of Hendriks who had a sore foot.

WEST INDIES

R.C. Fredericks	lbw b Connolly	17	c Chappell b Connolly		23
M.C. Carew	c Chappell b Gleeson	36	c Chappell b Connolly		90
R.B. Kanhai	lbw b Connolly	11	b Connolly		80
B.F. Butcher	c Chappell b Gleeson	52	c Sheahan b McKenzie		118
S.M. Nurse	c and b McKenzie	5	(6) lbw b Gleeson		40
G. St A. Sobers*	b Freeman	110	(7) c Walters b Connolly		52
C.H. Lloyd	c Lawry b Gleeson	10	(8) c Redpath b Connolly		42
D.A.J. Holford	c McKenzie b Freeman	6	(9) c Stackpole b McKenzie		80
C.C. Griffith	b Freeman	7	(5) run out		24
J.L. Hendriks†	not out	10	not out		37
L.R. Gibbs	c Connolly b Freeman	4	b McKenzie		1
Extras	(B 5, LB 2, NB 1)	8	(B 5, LB 12, NB 12)		29
Total		**276**			**616**

AUSTRALIA

W.M. Lawry*	c Butcher b Sobers	62	c sub (C.A. Davis) b Sobers		89
K.R. Stackpole	c Hendriks b Holford	62	c Hendriks b Gibbs		50
I.M. Chappell	c Sobers b Gibbs	76	lbw b Griffith		96
I.R. Redpath	lbw b Carew	45	run out		9
K.D. Walters	c and b Griffith	110	run out		50
A.P. Sheahan	b Gibbs	51	not out		11
E.W. Freeman	lbw b Griffith	33	run out		1
B.N. Jarman†	c Hendriks b Gibbs	3	run out		4
G.D. McKenzie	c Nurse b Holford	59	c sub (G.S. Camacho) b Gibbs		4
J.W. Gleeson	b Gibbs	17	lbw b Griffith		0
A.N. Connolly	not out	1	not out		6
Extras	(B 3, LB 6, NB 5)	14	(B 8, LB 10, NB 1)		19
Total		**533**	(9 wickets)		**339**

AUSTRALIA	O	M	R	W	O	M	R	W		FALL OF WICKETS			
McKenzie	14	1	51	1	22·2	4	90	3		WI	A	WI	A
Connolly	13	3	61	2	34	7	122	5	*Wkt*	*1st*	*1st*	*2nd*	*2nd*
Freeman	10·3	0	52	4	18	3	96	0	1st	21	89	35	86
Gleeson	25	5	91	3	35	2	176	1	2nd	39	170	167	185
Stackpole	3	1	13	0	12	3	44	0	3rd	89	248	240	215
Chappell					14	0	50	0	4th	107	254	304	304
Walters					1	0	6	0	5th	199	347	376	315
Redpath					1	0	3	0	6th	215	424	404	318
WEST INDIES									7th	228	429	476	322
Sobers	28	4	106	1	22	1	107	1	8th	261	465	492	333
Griffith	22	4	94	2	19	2	73	2	9th	264	529	614	333
Holford	18·5	0	118	2	15	1	53	0	10th	276	533	616	–
Gibbs	43	8	145	4	26	7	79	2					
Carew	9	3	30	1	2	0	8	0					
Lloyd	6	0	26	0									

Umpires: C.J. Egar (28) and L.P. Rowan (19).

Close: 1st day – A(1) 37-0 (Lawry 4, Stackpole 30); 2nd – A(1) 424-6 (Walters 85, Jarman 0); 3rd – WI(2) 261-3 (Butcher 44, Griffith 10); 4th – WI(2) 614-9 (Hendriks 36).

AUSTRALIA v WEST INDIES 1968–69 (5th Test)

Played at Sydney Cricket Ground on 14, 15, 16, 18, 19, 20 February.
Toss: West Indies.   Result: AUSTRALIA won by 382 runs.
Debuts: Nil.

Australia gained the (then) biggest victory by a runs margin in this series in a match played over six days because the rubber had not been decided. Australia's total of 619 remains the highest by any side being put in to bat in a Test match and is also Australia's highest in a home Test against West Indies. Walters became the first to score a double-century and a century in the same Test; his score of 242 is the highest for either side in this series and the highest for Australia at Sydney. He was the second Australian after J. Ryder to score six fifties in consecutive innings and the first to score four hundreds in a rubber against West Indies. His partnership of 336 with Lawry, who batted for 487 minutes, remains the highest for the fourth wicket in this series. Hendriks conceded no byes in the first innings – only T.G. Evans had prevented any byes in a larger Test innings (*Test No. 280*).

AUSTRALIA

W.M. Lawry*	b Griffith	151	c Fredericks b Griffith		17
K.R. Stackpole	b Hall	20	c Carew b Hall		6
I.M. Chappell	lbw b Sobers	1	c Hendriks b Hall		10
I.R. Redpath	c Nurse b Sobers	0	c Sobers b Gibbs		132
K.D. Walters	b Gibbs	242	c Fredericks b Gibbs		103
A.P. Sheahan	c Fredericks b Griffith	27	c Hendriks b Sobers		34
E.W. Freeman	c Hendriks b Griffith	56	c Carew b Sobers		15
G.D. McKenzie	b Gibbs	19	c Carew b Sobers		40
H.B. Taber†	lbw b Hall	48	not out		15
J.W. Gleeson	c Hendriks b Hall	45	not out		5
A.N. Connolly	not out	1			
Extras	(LB 2, W 1, NB 6)	9	(B 4, LB 6, W 1, NB 6)		17
Total		**619**	(8 wickets declared)		**394**

WEST INDIES

R.C. Fredericks	c Taber b Connolly	39	c Taber b McKenzie		0
M.C. Carew	c Taber b Freeman	64	b Connolly		3
R.B. Kanhai	c Taber b Connolly	44	c Connolly b McKenzie		18
G. St A. Sobers*	c Taber b Connolly	13	(5) c Redpath b Gleeson		113
B.F. Butcher	c Sheahan b McKenzie	10	(4) c Gleeson b Stackpole		31
C.H. Lloyd	b McKenzie	53	c Freeman b Stackpole		11
S.M. Nurse	c Stackpole b Connolly	9	b Gleeson		137
J.L. Hendriks†	c Taber b McKenzie	1	c Stackpole b McKenzie		16
C.C. Griffith	c Freeman b Gleeson	27	b Gleeson		15
W.W. Hall	b Gleeson	1	c Sheahan b Chappell		0
L.R. Gibbs	not out	4	not out		0
Extras	(B 2, LB 4, NB 8)	14	(B 1, LB 5, NB 2)		8
Total		**279**			**352**

WEST INDIES	O	M	R	W	O	M	R	W
Hall	35·7	3	157	3	12	0	47	2
Griffith	37	1	175	3	14	0	41	1
Sobers	28	4	94	2	26	3	117	3
Gibbs	40	8	133	2	33	2	133	2
Carew	10	2	44	0	5	0	26	0
Lloyd	2	1	7	0	2	0	13	0
AUSTRALIA								
McKenzie	22·6	2	90	3	16	1	93	3
Connolly	17	2	61	4	18	4	72	1
Freeman	12	2	48	1	2	0	16	0
Gleeson	19	8	53	2	15·2	1	84	3
Chappell	6	1	13	0	6	0	22	1
Stackpole					7	0	57	2

FALL OF WICKETS

Wkt	A 1st	WI 1st	A 2nd	WI 2nd
1st	43	100	21	0
2nd	51	154	36	10
3rd	51	159	40	30
4th	387	179	250	76
5th	435	179	301	102
6th	453	190	329	220
7th	483	193	329	284
8th	543	257	388	351
9th	614	259	–	352
10th	619	279	–	352

Umpires: C.J. Egar (29) and L.P. Rowan (20).

Close: 1st day – A(1) 268-3 (Lawry 117, Walters 122); 2nd – A(1) 583-8 (Taber 34, Gleeson 24); 3rd – WI(1) 233-7 (Lloyd 27, Griffith 16); 4th – A(2) 239-3 (Redpath 96, Walters 100).

PAKISTAN v ENGLAND 1968–69 (1st Test)

Played at Lahore Stadium on 21, 22, 23, 24 February.
Toss: England.   Result: MATCH DRAWN.
Debuts: Pakistan – Aftab Gul, Asif Masood; England – R.M.H. Cottam.

Cowdrey's 22nd and last Test hundred equalled the England record held by W.R. Hammond. It was made in a match frequently interrupted by crowd invasions of the playing area and by minor riots and skirmishes. Pakistan were set to score 323 runs in 295 minutes. Graveney captained England throughout the final innings when Cowdrey went to hospital for treatment to a jarred nerve in the right forearm.

ENGLAND

J.H. Edrich	c Asif Masood b Intikhab	54	c Majid b Asif Masood		8
R.M. Prideaux	c Shafqat b Asif Masood	9	b Majid		5
M.C. Cowdrey*	c Wasim b Majid	100	c Wasim b Asif Masood		12
T.W. Graveney	c Asif Iqbal b Intikhab	13	run out		12
K.W.R. Fletcher	c Intikhab b Saeed	20	b Majid		83
B.L. D'Oliveira	c Ilyas b Intikhab	26	c Mushtaq b Saeed		5
A.P.E. Knott†	lbw b Saeed	52	b Asif Masood		30
D.L. Underwood	c Intikhab b Saeed	0	c Aftab b Mushtaq		6
D.J. Brown	b Saeed	7	not out		44
P.I. Pocock	b Intikhab	12	b Saeed		1
R.M.H. Cottam	not out	4			
Extras	(B 4, LB 2, NB 3)	9	(B 6, LB 9, NB 4)		19
Total		**306**	(9 wickets declared)		**225**

PAKISTAN

Mohammad Ilyas	lbw b Brown	0	c Fletcher b Brown		1
Aftab Gul	c D'Oliveira b Brown	12	c Pocock b Underwood		29
Saeed Ahmed*	c Knott b D'Oliveira	18	b Cottam		39
Asif Iqbal	c D'Oliveira b Cottam	70	c and b Cottam		0
Mushtaq Mohammad	c Fletcher b Cottam	4	not out		34
Hanif Mohammad	b Brown	7	(7) not out		23
Majid Khan	c Pocock b Underwood	18	(6) c Pocock b Brown		68
Shafqat Rana	c Knott b Cottam	30			
Intikhab Alam	c D'Oliveira b Pocock	12			
Wasim Bari†	not out	14			
Asif Masood	b Cottam	11			
Extras	(B 8, LB 4, NB 1)	13	(B 3, LB 5, NB 1)		9
Total		**209**	(5 wickets)		**203**

PAKISTAN	O	M	R	W	O	M	R	W		FALL OF WICKETS			
Asif Masood	21	5	59	1	25	4	68	3		E	P	E	P
Asif Iqbal	4	2	11	0					Wkt	1st	1st	2nd	2nd
Majid	18	8	25	1	20	5	41	2	1st	41	0	8	6
Intikhab	40·1	8	117	4	15	5	29	0	2nd	92	32	25	71
Saeed	20	5	64	4	15·5	3	44	2	3rd	113	32	41	71
Mushtaq	14	6	15	0	9	1	24	1	4th	182	52	46	71
Shafqat	2	0	6	0					5th	219	72	68	156
									6th	246	119	136	–
ENGLAND									7th	257	145	151	–
Brown	14	0	43	3	15	4	47	2	8th	287	176	201	–
Cottam	22·2	5	50	4	13	1	35	2	9th	294	187	225	–
D'Oliveira	8	2	28	1					10th	306	209	–	–
Underwood	16	4	36	1	19	8	29	1					
Pocock	10	3	39	1	16	4	41	0					
Fletcher					8	2	31	0					
Graveney					6	0	11	0					
Prideaux					2	2	0	0					

Umpires: Munawar Hussain (4) and Shujauddin (12).

Close: 1st day – E(1) 226-5 (D'Oliveira 16, Knott 5); 2nd – P(1) 71-4 (Asif 28, Hanif 7); 3rd – E(2) 174-7 (Fletcher 69, Brown 12).

PAKISTAN v ENGLAND 1968–69 (2nd Test)

Played at Dacca Stadium on 28 February, 1, 2, 3, March.
Toss: Pakistan.   Result: MATCH DRAWN.
Debuts: Nil.

The only riot-free match of this rubber was played in front of crowds controlled by the student leaders of East Pakistan and without either police or army presence. Partnered by Cottam for the last 34 runs of his innings, D'Oliveira scored 114 out of 174 on a pitch reminiscent of those on which he learnt his cricket in South Africa – pitted with holes all over.

PAKISTAN

Mohammad Ilyas	c Knott b Snow	20		c Snow b Cottam	21
Salahuddin	c Brown b Snow	6		lbw b Underwood	5
Saeed Ahmed*	b Brown	19	(5)	c Knott b Underwood	33
Asif Iqbal	b Brown	44	(3)	b Underwood	16
Mushtaq Mohammad	c Cottam b Snow	52	(4)	c D'Oliveira b Underwood	31
Majid Khan	c Knott b Brown	27		not out	49
Hanif Mohammad	lbw b Snow	8		lbw b Underwood	8
Intikhab Alam	lbw b Underwood	25		not out	19
Wasim Bari†	c Knott b Cottam	14			
Niaz Ahmed	not out	16			
Pervez Sajjad	b Cottam	2			
Extras	(B 4, LB 4, NB 5)	13		(LB 5, NB 8)	13
Total		**246**		(6 wickets declared)	**195**

ENGLAND

J.H. Edrich	c Mushtaq b Intikhab	24		not out	12
R.M. Prideaux	c Hanif b Pervez	4		not out	18
T.W. Graveney	b Pervez	46			
K.W.R. Fletcher	c Hanif b Saeed	16			
M.C. Cowdrey*	lbw b Pervez	7			
B.L. D'Oliveira	not out	114			
A.P.E. Knott†	c and b Pervez	2			
D.J. Brown	c Hanif b Saeed	4			
J.A. Snow	c Majid b Niaz	9			
D.L. Underwood	c Ilyas b Mushtaq	22			
R.M.H. Cottam	c Hanif b Saeed	4			
Extras	(B 14, LB 8)	22		(B 2, NB 1)	3
Total		**274**		(0 wickets)	**33**

ENGLAND	O	M	R	W	O	M	R	W
Snow	25	5	70	4	12	7	15	0
Brown	23	8	51	3	6	1	18	0
Underwood	27	13	45	1	44	15	94	5
Cottam	27·1	6	52	2	30	17	43	1
D'Oliveira	8	1	15	0	9	2	12	0

PAKISTAN	O	M	R	W	O	M	R	W
Niaz	10	4	20	1	2	0	2	0
Majid	11	4	15	0				
Pervez	37	8	75	4	3	2	1	0
Saeed	37·4	15	59	3	3	2	4	0
Intikhab	26	7	65	1	4	0	19	0
Mushtaq	11	3	18	1				
Asif					4	2	2	0
Hanif					3	2	1	0
Ilyas					1	0	1	0

FALL OF WICKETS

Wkt	P 1st	E 1st	P 2nd	E 2nd
1st	16	17	8	–
2nd	39	61	48	–
3rd	55	96	50	–
4th	123	100	97	–
5th	168	113	129	–
6th	184	117	147	–
7th	186	130	–	–
8th	211	170	–	–
9th	237	236	–	–
10th	246	274	–	–

Umpires: Gulzar (1) and Shujauddin (13).

Close: 1st day – P(1) 176-5 (Majid 24, Hanif 1); 2nd – E(1) 139-7 (D'Oliveira 16, Snow 7); 3rd – P(2) 77-3 (Mushtaq 18, Saeed 10).

PAKISTAN v ENGLAND 1968–69 (3rd Test)

Played at National Stadium, Karachi, on 6, 7, 8 March.
Toss: England.   Result: MATCH DRAWN – abandoned because of rioting.
Debuts: Pakistan – Sarfraz Nawaz.

The first five-day Test match to be scheduled without a rest day was abandoned shortly before lunch on the third day. A mob several hundred strong and bearing banners broke down the gates and stormed across the outfield when Knott needed four runs for his first hundred in Test cricket. Earlier Milburn, who had joined the MCC team from Western Australia where he had been playing in the Sheffield Shield, reached his hundred off 163 balls. It was his first innings in Pakistan and his last in Test cricket. Within a few weeks he had lost his left eye as a result of a car accident near Northampton. Graveney's sole hundred in Pakistan was the last of his 11 for England.

ENGLAND

C. Milburn	c Wasim b Asif Masood	139
J.H. Edrich	c Saeed b Intikhab	32
T.W. Graveney	c Asif Iqbal b Intikhab	105
M.C. Cowdrey*	c Hanif b Intikhab	14
K.W.R. Fletcher	b Mushtaq	38
B.L. D'Oliveira	c Aftab b Mushtaq	16
A.P.E. Knott†	not out	96
J.A. Snow	b Asif Masood	9
D.J. Brown	not out	25
D.L. Underwood	) did not bat	
R.N.S. Hobbs	)	
Extras	(B 5, LB 12, NB 11)	28
Total	(7 wickets)	**502**

PAKISTAN

Aftab Gul
Hanif Mohamad
Mushtaq Mohammad
Asif Iqbal
Saeed Ahmed*
Majid Khan
Shafqat Rana
Intikhab Alam
Wasim Bari†
Asif Masood
Sarfraz Nawaz

PAKISTAN	O	M	R	W
Asif Masood	28	2	94	2
Majid	20	5	51	0
Sarfraz	34	6	78	0
Intikhab	48	4	129	3
Saeed	22	5	53	0
Mushtaq	23·1	5	69	2

FALL OF WICKETS

	E
Wkt	1st
1st	78
2nd	234
3rd	286
4th	309
5th	360
6th	374
7th	427
8th	–
9th	–
10th	–

Umpires: Daud Khan (11) and Shujauddin (14).

Close: 1st day – E(1) 226-1 (Milburn 137, Graveney 51); 2nd – E(1) 412-6 (Knott 38, Snow 6).

NEW ZEALAND v WEST INDIES 1968–69 (1st Test)

Played at Eden Park, Auckland, on 27, 28, February, 1, 3 March.
Toss: West Indies.   Result: WEST INDIES won by five wickets.
Debuts: New Zealand – B.F. Hastings, B.D. Milburn, G.M. Turner.

West Indies won with three of the 15 mandatory last-hour overs to spare. Taylor batted only 86 minutes for New Zealand's first hundred against West Indies which he reached with a six; it remains the fifth-fastest century in Test cricket. His 124 took only 110 minutes and included five sixes and 14 fours. It was his second hundred in both first-class and Test cricket. His fifty took 30 minutes and remains the third-fastest in a Test match. The partnership of 174 between Nurse and Butcher took only 142 minutes and was then the highest for the third wicket by either side in this series.

NEW ZEALAND

G.T. Dowling*	c Hendriks b Edwards	18		b Edwards	71
G.M. Turner	c Sobers b Hall	0		b Edwards	40
B.E. Congdon	c Sobers b Gibbs	85		lbw b Edwards	7
B.F. Hastings	c Hendriks b Sobers	21		c Gibbs b Holford	31
M.G. Burgess	c Hendriks b Sobers	11		c Fredericks b Holford	30
V. Pollard	c and b Gibbs	4	(7)	not out	51
B.W. Yuile	c Lloyd b Holford	20	(8)	c Hendriks b Gibbs	1
B.R. Taylor	c Fredericks b Edwards	124	(6)	c Gibbs b Holford	9
R.C. Motz	c Hall b Edwards	13		lbw b Sobers	23
R.S. Cunis	c Fredericks b Gibbs	13		not out	20
B.D. Milburn†	not out	4			
Extras	(B 5, LB 2, NB 3)	10		(B 3, LB 2, NB 9)	14
Total		**323**		(8 wickets declared)	**297**

WEST INDIES

R.C. Fredericks	b Motz	6		c Turner b Pollard	23
M.C. Carew	c Burgess b Yuile	109		c Hastings b Cunis	38
S.M. Nurse	c Turner b Pollard	95		c Yuile b Motz	168
C.H. Lloyd	lbw b Yuile	3	(5)	run out	14
B.F. Butcher	c Hastings b Yuile	0	(4)	not out	78
G. St A. Sobers*	c Milburn b Pollard	11		lbw b Taylor	0
D.A.J. Holford	c Burgess b Taylor	18		not out	4
J.L. Hendriks†	c Dowling b Taylor	15			
R.M. Edwards	c Milburn b Motz	2			
W.W. Hall	b Motz	1			
L.R. Gibbs	not out	0			
Extras	(B 2, LB 9, NB 5)	16		(B 12, LB 10, NB 1)	23
Total		**276**		(5 wickets)	**348**

WEST INDIES	O	M	R	W	O	M	R	W	FALL OF WICKETS				
Hall	8	1	34	1	8·2	4	8	0		NZ	WI	NZ	WI
Edwards	16	2	58	3	24	4	71	3	*Wkt*	*1st*	*1st*	*2nd*	*2nd*
Gibbs	25·4	3	96	3	35	9	69	1	1st	8	25	112	50
Sobers	19	1	87	2	30	7	79	1	2nd	28	197	122	122
Holford	5	1	38	1	15	1	56	3	3rd	92	212	131	296
									4th	122	212	185	320
NEW ZEALAND									5th	135	225	200	320
Motz	19	3	70	3	12	0	85	1	6th	152	249	200	–
Taylor	16·7	2	48	2	11	1	54	1	7th	232	269	201	–
Cunis	9	2	36	0	20	1	80	1	8th	275	272	235	–
Yuile	15	2	64	3	14	2	58	0	9th	315	274	–	–
Pollard	20	5	42	2	12	1	48	1	10th	323	276	–	–

Umpires: E.C.A. MacKintosh (3) and R.W.R. Shortt (6).

Close: 1st day – WI(1) 53-1 (Carew 33, Nurse 11); 2nd – NZ(2) 12-0 (Dowling 6, Turner 5); 3rd – NZ(2) 259-8 (Pollard 25, Cunis 8).

NEW ZEALAND v WEST INDIES 1968–69 (2nd Test)

Played at Basin Reserve, Wellington, on 7, 8, 10, 11 March.
Toss: New Zealand.   Result: NEW ZEALAND won by six wickets.
Debuts: Nil.

New Zealand gained their fifth Test victory and their first at Wellington at 2.26 on the last afternoon. Motz passed J.R. Reid's New Zealand record of 85 wickets when he dismissed Griffith. Gibbs, in his 46th match, became the first West Indies bowler to take 200 Test wickets.

WEST INDIES

R.C. Fredericks	c Milburn b Motz	15	c Hastings b Motz	2
M.C. Carew	c Taylor b Motz	17	run out	1
S.M. Nurse	b Motz	21	c Congdon b Cunis	16
B.F. Butcher	lbw b Motz	50	lbw b Yuile	59
C.H. Lloyd	c Milburn b Cunis	44	b Cunis	1
G. St A. Sobers*	c Morgan b Motz	20	c Pollard b Cunis	39
D.A.J. Holford	lbw b Cunis	1	b Yuile	12
J.L. Hendriks†	not out	54	b Motz	5
C.C. Griffith	c Congdon b Motz	31	b Yuile	4
R.M. Edwards	run out	22	run out	1
L.R. Gibbs	c Milburn b Yuile	2	not out	1
Extras	(B 3, LB 6, W 1, NB 10)	20	(NB 7)	7
Total		**297**		**148**

NEW ZEALAND

G.T. Dowling*	c Gibbs b Griffith	21	c Hendriks b Griffith	23
G.M. Turner	c Sobers b Edwards	74	c Griffith b Edwards	1
B.E. Congdon	c Sobers b Carew	52	c Griffith b Edwards	4
B.F. Hastings	c Hendriks b Edwards	8	not out	62
V. Pollard	c Hendriks b Griffith	9		
R.W. Morgan	c Gibbs b Edwards	0	not out	16
B.W. Yuile	c Hendriks b Sobers	33	(5) lbw b Gibbs	37
B.R. Taylor	c Holford b Griffith	33		
R.G. Motz	c Gibbs b Edwards	18		
R.S. Cunis	lbw b Edwards	5		
B.D. Milburn†	not out	4		
Extras	(LB 7, NB 18)	25	(B 13, LB 4, W 1, NB 5)	23
Total		**282**	(4 wickets)	**166**

NEW ZEALAND	O	M	R	W	O	M	R	W
Motz	18	2	69	6	13	3	44	2
Taylor	14	1	67	0	6	0	36	0
Cunis	18	4	76	2	12	2	36	3
Yuile	9·4	4	27	1	6·4	0	25	3
Pollard	2	0	19	0				
Morgan	4	0	19	0				
WEST INDIES								
Griffith	26	2	92	3	15	6	29	1
Edwards	24·7	5	84	5	11	2	42	2
Sobers	9	2	22	1	8	2	22	0
Gibbs	14	3	41	0	14·5	3	50	1
Carew	10	3	18	1				

FALL OF WICKETS

	WI	NZ	WI	NZ
Wkt	*1st*	*1st*	*2nd*	*2nd*
1st	27	41	2	20
2nd	58	137	17	32
3rd	67	152	36	39
4th	130	169	38	113
5th	174	169	92	–
6th	177	194	116	–
7th	181	224	140	–
8th	241	262	140	–
9th	287	270	144	–
10th	297	282	148	–

Umpires: E.C.A. MacKintosh (4) and R.W.R. Shortt (7).

Close: 1st day – NZ(1) 2-0 (Dowling 1, Turner 0); 2nd – NZ(1) 257-7 (Taylor 22, Motz 16); 3rd – NZ(2) 40-3 (Hastings 0, Yuile 1).

NEW ZEALAND v WEST INDIES 1968–69 (3rd Test)

Played at Lancaster Park, Christchurch, on 13, 14, 15, 17 March.
Toss: West Indies.   Result: MATCH DRAWN.
Debuts: Nil.

Making his final appearance in Test cricket, Nurse batted for 476 minutes and hit a six and 34 fours in the highest innings in any Test at Christchurch. It also remains the highest score for West Indies against New Zealand. His partnership of 231 with Carew was the record for the second wicket in this series until 1971-72 (*Test No. 693*). Motz took the wickets of Lloyd, Sobers and Holford in six balls. In the course of his first Test hundred, Hastings shared in (then) record partnerships within this series of 75 for the third wicket with Congdon and 110 for the fifth with Pollard.

WEST INDIES

R.C. Fredericks	c Turner b Motz	4
M.C. Carew	c Turner b Pollard	91
S.M. Nurse	st Milburn b Yuile	258
B.F. Butcher	lbw b Motz	29
C.H. Lloyd	c Yuile b Motz	3
G. St A. Sobers*	b Motz	0
D.A.J. Holford	b Motz	0
J.L. Hendriks†	c Milburn b Taylor	10
C.C. Griffith	c Pollard b Taylor	8
R.M. Edwards	st Milburn b Yuile	0
L.R. Gibbs	not out	0
Extras	(B 4, LB 9, NB 1)	14
Total		**417**

NEW ZEALAND

G.T. Dowling*	lbw b Edwards	23		lbw b Sobers	76
G.M. Turner	b Gibbs	30		c Holford b Sobers	38
B.W. Yuile	lbw b Carew	17	(7)	b Griffith	20
B.E. Congdon	b Gibbs	42	(3)	b Sobers	43
B.F. Hastings	b Holford	0	(4)	not out	117
M.G. Burgess	b Edwards	26	(5)	c Sobers b Holford	2
V. Pollard	b Holford	21	(6)	b Carew	44
B.R. Taylor	not out	43		not out	0
R.C. Motz	c Fredericks b Holford	6			
R.S. Cunis	c Carew b Holford	0			
B.D. Milburn†	c Holford b Gibbs	0			
Extras	(B 5, LB 3, W 1)	9		(B 10, LB 14, NB 3)	27
Total		**217**		**(6 wickets)**	**367**

NEW ZEALAND	O	M	R	W	O	M	R	W
Motz	27	3	113	5				
Cunis	22	2	93	0				
Taylor	14·4	0	63	2				
Pollard	18	6	64	1				
Yuile	20	5	70	2				
WEST INDIES								
Sobers	8	3	21	0	31	8	70	3
Griffith	5	2	15	0	13·4	1	55	1
Edwards	15	4	30	2	21	6	67	0
Gibbs	24·3	6	64	3	19	4	42	0
Holford	20	5	66	4	25	5	82	1
Carew	8	2	12	1	9	4	24	1

FALL OF WICKETS

Wkt	WI 1st	NZ 1st	NZ 2nd
1st	16	55	115
2nd	247	63	128
3rd	326	95	203
4th	340	117	210
5th	350	119	320
6th	350	160	363
7th	382	182	–
8th	413	200	–
9th	417	216	–
10th	417	217	–

Umpires: E.C.A. MacKintosh (5) and W.T. Martin (12).

Close: 1st day – WI(1) 212-1 (Carew 81, Nurse 122); 2nd – NZ(1) 63-2 (Yuile 5); 3rd – NZ(2) 115-0 (Dowling 73, Turner 38).

ENGLAND v WEST INDIES 1969 (1st Test)

Played at Old Trafford, Manchester, on 12, 13, 14, 16, 17 June.
Toss: England.   Result: ENGLAND won by ten wickets.
Debuts: West Indies – M.L.C. Foster, V.A. Holder, J.N. Shepherd.

England's win, completed at 12.02 pm on the fifth day, was their first at Old Trafford since they beat India there in 1959. Cowdrey having torn his left Achilles tendon while batting in a Sunday League game on 25 May, Illingworth began his 31-match tenure of the England captaincy by winning England's first toss in Manchester since 1960.

ENGLAND

G. Boycott	lbw b Shepherd	128	not out		1
J.H. Edrich	run out	58	not out		9
P.J. Sharpe	b Gibbs	2			
T.W. Graveney	b Holder	75			
B.L. D'Oliveira	c Hendriks b Shepherd	57			
A.P.E. Knott†	c Gibbs b Shepherd	0			
R. Illingworth*	c and b Gibbs	21			
B.R. Knight	lbw b Shepherd	31			
D.J. Brown	b Sobers	15			
D.L. Underwood	not out	11			
J.A. Snow	b Shepherd	0			
Extras	(B 5, LB 9, W 1)	15	(LB 1, NB 1)		2
Total		**413**	(0 wickets)		**12**

WEST INDIES

R.C. Fredericks	c Graveney b Snow	0	c Illingworth b Underwood		64
M.C. Carew	b Brown	1	c Sharpe b D'Oliveira		44
B.F. Butcher	lbw b Snow	31	lbw b Knight		48
C.A. Davis	c D'Oliveira b Brown	34	c Underwood b Illingworth		24
G. St A. Sobers*	c Edrich b Brown	10	c Sharpe b Knight		48
C.H. Lloyd	b Snow	32	c Knott b Brown		13
M.L.C. Foster	st Knott b Underwood	4	lbw b Brown		3
J.N. Shepherd	c Illingworth b Snow	9	lbw b Snow		13
J.L. Hendriks†	c Edrich b Brown	1	not out		5
V.A. Holder	run out	19	lbw b Brown		0
L.R. Gibbs	not out	1	b Snow		0
Extras	(LB 3, NB 2)	5	(B 4, LB 8, NB 1)		13
Total		**147**			**275**

WEST INDIES	O	M	R	W	O	M	R	W		FALL OF WICKETS			
Sobers	27	7	78	1	2	1	1	0		E	WI	WI	E
Holder	38	11	93	1	2·5	1	9	0	*Wkt*	*1st*	*1st*	*2nd*	*2nd*
Shepherd	58·5	19	104	5					1st	112	0	92	–
Gibbs	60	22	96	2					2nd	121	5	138	–
Davis	1	0	1	0					3rd	249	58	180	–
Carew	11	3	19	0					4th	307	72	202	–
Foster	2	0	7	0					5th	314	83	234	–
									6th	343	92	256	–
ENGLAND									7th	365	119	258	–
Snow	15	2	54	4	22·3	4	76	2	8th	390	126	273	–
Brown	13	1	39	4	22	3	59	3	9th	411	139	274	–
Knight	2	0	11	0	12	3	15	2	10th	413	147	275	–
Illingworth	6	2	23	0	30	12	52	1					
Underwood	12	6	15	1	19	11	31	1					
D'Oliveira					9	2	29	1					

Umpires: J.S. Buller (31) and C.S. Elliott (30).

Close: 1st day – E(1) 261-3 (Graveney 56, D'Oliveira 6); 2nd – WI(1) 104-6 (Lloyd 17, Shepherd 5); 3rd – WI(2) 215-4 (Sobers 14, Lloyd 9); 4th – WI(2) 258-7 (Shepherd 1, Hendriks 0).

ENGLAND v WEST INDIES 1969 (2nd Test)

Played at Lord's, London, on 26, 27, 28, 30 June, 1 July.
Toss: West Indies.   Result: MATCH DRAWN.
Debuts: England – J.H. Hampshire; West Indies – T.M. Findlay, G.C. Shillingford.

England required 332 runs in 240 minutes plus 20 overs. Hampshire became the first England batsman to score a hundred in his first Test, that match being at Lord's. His 107 took 288 minutes, came off 258 balls and included 15 fours. In England's first innings, Gibbs assumed the captaincy when Sobers left the field at 241 for 6 because of a strained thigh. It was only the second time in 75 Tests that the latter had required a substitute. In the second innings Sobers batted with Camacho as his runner throughout but later on the same day bowled 29 overs when England batted again.

WEST INDIES

R.C. Fredericks	c Hampshire b Knight	63	c Hampshire b Illingworth		60
G.S. Camacho	c Sharpe b Snow	67	b D'Oliveira		45
C.A. Davis	c Knott b Brown	103	c Illingworth b D'Oliveira		0
B.F. Butcher	c Hampshire b Brown	9	b Illingworth		24
G. St A. Sobers*	run out	29	(7) not out		50
C.H. Lloyd	c Illingworth b Brown	18	(5) c Knott b Snow		70
J.N. Shepherd	c Edrich b Snow	32	(6) c Sharpe b Illingworth		11
T.M. Findlay†	b Snow	23	c Sharpe b Knight		11
V.A. Holder	lbw b Snow	6	run out		7
L.R. Gibbs	not out	18	b Knight		5
G.C. Shillingford	c Knott b Snow	3			
Extras	(B 5, LB 4)	9	(B 4, LB 7, NB 1)		12
Total		**380**	(9 wickets declared)		**295**

ENGLAND

G. Boycott	c Findlay b Shepherd	23	c Butcher b Shillingford		106
J.H. Edrich	c Fredericks b Holder	7	c Camacho b Holder		1
P.H. Parfitt	c Davis b Sobers	4	c Findlay b Shepherd		39
B.L. D'Oliveira	c Shepherd b Sobers	0	c Fredericks b Gibbs		18
P.J. Sharpe	b Holder	11	c Davis b Sobers		86
J.H. Hampshire	lbw b Shepherd	107	run out		5
A.P.E. Knott†	b Shillingford	53	(8) b Shillingford		11
R. Illingworth*	c and b Gibbs	113	(7) not out		9
B.R. Knight	lbw b Shillingford	0	not out		1
D.J. Brown	c Findlay b Shepherd	1			
J.A. Snow	not out	9			
Extras	(B 1, LB 5, NB 10)	16	(B 9, LB 5, NB 5)		19
Total		**344**	(7 wickets)		**295**

ENGLAND	O	M	R	W	O	M	R	W	FALL OF WICKETS				
Snow	39	5	114	5	22	4	69	1		WI	E	WI	E
Brown	38	8	99	3	9	3	25	0	*Wkt*	*1st*	*1st*	*2nd*	*2nd*
Knight	38	11	65	1	27·5	6	78	2	1st	106	19	73	1
D'Oliveira	26	10	46	0	15	2	45	2	2nd	151	37	73	94
Illingworth	16	4	39	0	27	9	66	3	3rd	167	37	128	137
Parfitt	1	0	8	0					4th	217	37	135	263
									5th	247	61	191	271
WEST INDIES									6th	324	189	232	272
Sobers	26	12	57	2	29	8	72	1	7th	336	249	263	292
Holder	38	16	83	2	11	4	36	1	8th	343	250	280	–
Shillingford	19	4	53	2	13	4	30	2	9th	376	261	295	–
Shepherd	43	14	74	3	12	3	45	1	10th	380	344	–	–
Gibbs	27·4	9	53	1	41	14	93	1					
Davis	1	0	2	0									
Butcher	3	1	6	0									

Umpires: J.S. Buller (32) and A.E. Fagg (5).

Close: 1st day – WI(1) 246-4 (Davis 57, Lloyd 17); 2nd – E(1) 46-4 (Sharpe 6, Hampshire 3); 3rd – E(1) 321-9 (Illingworth 97, Snow 2); 4th – WI(2) 247-6 (Sobers 26, Findlay 1).

ENGLAND v WEST INDIES 1969 (3rd Test)

Played at Headingley, Leeds, on 10, 11, 12, 14, 15 July.
Toss: England.   Result: ENGLAND won by 30 runs.
Debuts: Nil.

England completed their second win in the three-match rubber at 12.16 pm on the fifth day and so retained the Wisden Trophy convincingly. For the first time since 1957 they won two matches in a rubber against West Indies. Butcher's Test career ended with a disputed catch after a brilliant innings lasting 154 minutes and containing 16 fours.

ENGLAND

G. Boycott	lbw b Sobers	12	c Findlay b Sobers	0
J.H. Edrich	lbw b Shepherd	79	lbw b Sobers	15
P.J. Sharpe	c Findlay b Holder	6	lbw b Sobers	15
J.H. Hampshire	c Findlay b Holder	1	lbw b Shillingford	22
B.L. D'Oliveira	c Sobers b Shepherd	48	c Sobers b Davis	39
A.P.E. Knott†	c Findlay b Sobers	44	c Findlay b Sobers	31
R. Illingworth*	b Shepherd	1	c Lloyd b Holder	19
B.R. Knight	c Fredericks b Gibbs	7	c Holder b Gibbs	27
D.L. Underwood	c Findlay b Holder	4	b Sobers	16
D.J. Brown	b Holder	12	b Shillingford	34
J.A. Snow	not out	1	not out	15
Extras	(B 4, LB 3, NB 1)	8	(LB 5, W 1, NB 1)	7
Total		**223**		**240**

WEST INDIES

R.C. Fredericks	lbw b Knight	11	c Sharpe b Snow	6
G.S. Camacho	c Knott b Knight	4	c Hampshire b Underwood	71
C.A. Davis	c Underwood b Knight	18	c and b Underwood	29
B.F. Butcher	b Snow	35	c Knott b Underwood	91
G. St A. Sobers*	c Sharpe b Knight	13	(6) b Knight	0
C.H. Lloyd	c Snow b Brown	27	(5) c Knott b Illingworth	23
T.M. Findlay†	lbw b D'Oliveira	1	lbw b Knight	16
V.A. Holder	b Snow	35	(9) c Sharpe b Brown	13
L.R. Gibbs	not out	6	(10) c Knott b Brown	4
G.C. Shillingford	c Knott b Brown	3	(11) not out	5
J.N. Shepherd	absent hurt	–	(8) c Knott b Underwood	0
Extras	(LB 7, NB 1)	8	(LB 11, NB 3)	14
Total		**161**		**272**

WEST INDIES	O	M	R	W	O	M	R	W	FALL OF WICKETS				
Sobers	21	1	68	2	40	18	42	5		E	WI	E	WI
Holder	26	7	48	4	33	13	66	1	*Wkt*	*1st*	*1st*	*2nd*	*2nd*
Shillingford	7	0	21	0	20·4	4	56	2	1st	30	17	0	8
Gibbs	19	6	33	1	21	6	42	1	2nd	52	37	23	69
Shepherd	24	8	43	3					3rd	64	46	42	177
Davis	1	0	2	0	17	8	27	1	4th	140	80	58	219
									5th	165	88	102	224
ENGLAND									6th	167	91	147	228
Snow	20	4	50	2	21	7	43	1	7th	182	151	147	228
Brown	7·3	2	13	2	21	8	53	2	8th	199	153	171	251
Knight	22	5	63	4	18·2	4	47	2	9th	217	161	203	255
D'Oliveira	15	8	27	1	10	3	22	0	10th	223	–	240	272
Illingworth					14	5	38	1					
Underwood					22	12	55	4					

Umpires: C.S. Elliott (31) and A.E. Fagg (6).

Close: 1st day – E(1) 194-7 (Knott 29, Underwood 3); 2nd – E(2) 13-1 (Edrich 6, Sharpe 7); 3rd – E(2) 214-9 (Brown 24, Snow 0); 4th – WI(2) 240-7 (Findlay 1, Holder 7).

ENGLAND v NEW ZEALAND 1969 (1st Test)

Played at Lord's, London, on 24, 25, 26, 28 July.
Toss: England.   Result: ENGLAND won by 230 runs.
Debuts: England – Alan Ward (*England's first 'A. Ward', Albert, appeared in Tests 40-46 inclusive*);
New Zealand – D.R. Hadlee, H.J. Howarth, K.J. Wadsworth.

England won at 6.00 on the fourth evening. Effectively they won with 30 minutes to spare as rain would have prevented any play on the fifth day. Turner was the first to carry his bat throughout a completed innings for New Zealand. At 22 years 63 days he remains the youngest player to achieve this feat in a Test. He batted for 253 minutes, faced 226 balls and hit five fours. Underwood's analysis of 7 for 32 is still the best for either country in this series.

ENGLAND

G. Boycott	c Congdon b Motz	0	c Turner b Pollard		47
J.H. Edrich	c Motz b Taylor	16	c Wadsworth b Hadlee		115
P.J. Sharpe	c Turner b Taylor	20	c Congdon b Howarth		46
K.W.R. Fletcher	b Motz	9	b Howarth		7
B.L. D'Oliveira	run out	37	c Wadsworth b Taylor		12
A.P.E. Knott†	c and b Hadlee	8	lbw b Howarth		10
R. Illingworth*	c Wadsworth b Howarth	53	c Wadsworth b Taylor		0
B.R. Knight	c Hadlee b Pollard	29	b Motz		49
D.J. Brown	not out	11	c Wadsworth b Taylor		7
D.L. Underwood	c Pollard b Howarth	1	b Motz		4
A. Ward	b Taylor	0	not out		19
Extras	(B 1, LB 3, W 1, NB 1)	6	(B 4, LB 15, NB 5)		24
Total		**190**			**340**

NEW ZEALAND

G.T. Dowling*	c Illingworth b Underwood	41	c Knott b Ward		4
G.M. Turner	c Knott b Ward	5	not out		43
B.E. Congdon	c Sharpe b Ward	41	c Fletcher b Underwood		17
B.F. Hastings	c Ward b Illingworth	23	c Knott b Underwood		0
V. Pollard	c Ward b Underwood	8	lbw b Underwood		0
M.G. Burgess	lbw b Illingworth	10	lbw b Underwood		6
K.J. Wadsworth†	lbw b Illingworth	14	(8) b Underwood		5
B.R. Taylor	c Brown b Illingworth	3	(7) b Underwood		0
R.C. Motz	b Underwood	15	c Knott b Underwood		23
D.R. Hadlee	c Illingworth b Underwood	1	c Sharpe b D'Oliveira		19
H.J. Howarth	not out	0	b Ward		4
Extras	(B 4, LB 4)	8	(B 5, LB 4, NB 1)		10
Total		**169**			**131**

NEW ZEALAND	O	M	R	W	O	M	R	W
Motz	19	5	46	2	39·4	17	78	2
Hadlee	14	2	48	1	16	5	43	1
Taylor	13·5	4	35	3	25	4	62	3
Howarth	19	9	24	2	49	20	102	3
Pollard	9	1	31	1	8	2	20	1
Burgess					3	0	11	0
ENGLAND								
Brown	12	5	17	0	5	3	6	0
Ward	14	2	49	2	10·5	0	48	2
Underwood	29·3	16	38	4	31	18	32	7
Knight	10	3	20	0	3	1	5	0
Illingworth	22	8	37	4	18	9	24	0
D'Oliveira					8	3	6	1

FALL OF WICKETS

Wkt	E 1st	NZ 1st	E 2nd	NZ 2nd
1st	0	14	125	5
2nd	27	76	199	27
3rd	47	92	234	45
4th	47	101	243	45
5th	63	126	259	67
6th	113	137	259	67
7th	158	146	259	73
8th	186	150	284	101
9th	188	168	300	126
10th	190	169	340	131

Umpires: J.S. Buller (33) and A. Jepson (4).

Close: 1st day – NZ(1) 5-0 (Dowling, 4, Turner 1); 2nd – E(2) 21-0 (Boycott 12, Edrich 8); 3rd – E(2) 301-9 (Knight 31, Ward 0).

ENGLAND v NEW ZEALAND 1969 (2nd Test)

Played at Trent Bridge, Nottingham, on 7, 8, 9, 11, 12 August.
Toss: New Zealand.   Result: MATCH DRAWN.
Debuts: Nil.

Eleven hours 48 minutes of playing time were lost in this match which was abandoned at 4.35 on the final afternoon. The third-wicket partnership of 150 between Congdon and Hastings was then the highest for any New Zealand wicket in a Test in England. Edrich scored his second hundred in successive Test innings on his first appearance for England at Trent Bridge, and reached 25,000 runs in first-class cricket. His partnership of 249 with Sharpe, who made his only Test century, lasted 267 minutes.

NEW ZEALAND

G.T. Dowling*	b Ward	18	b Illingworth		22
B.A.G. Murray	c Knight b D'Oliveira	23	not out		40
B.E. Congdon	c Knott b Illingworth	66	not out		1
B.F. Hastings	c Sharpe b Illingworth	83			
V. Pollard	c Fletcher b Underwood	8			
M.G. Burgess	c Knight b Ward	2			
K.J. Wadsworth†	c D'Oliveira b Ward	21			
D.R. Hadlee	not out	35			
R.O. Collinge	c Knott b Knight	19			
R.C. Motz	b Ward	1			
H.J. Howarth	b Knight	3			
Extras	(B 1, LB 12, NB 2)	15	(LB 1, NB 2)		3
Total		**294**	(1 wicket)		**66**

ENGLAND

G. Boycott	b Motz	0
J.H. Edrich	b Hadlee	155
P.J. Sharpe	c and b Howarth	111
K.W.R. Fletcher	b Hadlee	31
B.L. D'Oliveira	c and b Hadlee	45
A.P.E. Knott†	c Burgess b Motz	15
R. Illingworth*	lbw b Collinge	33
B.R. Knight	not out	18
D.L. Underwood	c Collinge b Hadlee	16
J.A. Snow	not out	4
A. Ward	did not bat	
Extras	(B 6, LB 12, W 1, NB 4)	23
Total	(8 wicket declared)	**451**

ENGLAND	O	M	R	W	O	M	R	W	FALL OF WICKETS			
Snow	24	4	61	0	6	2	19	0		NZ	E	NZ
Ward	23	3	61	4	3	0	14	0	*Wkt*	*1st*	*1st*	*2nd*
Knight	18·5	4	44	2	4	0	14	0	1st	47	2	61
D'Oliveira	25	9	40	1	5	0	8	0	2nd	53	251	–
Underwood	22	8	44	1	3	1	5	0	3rd	203	301	–
Illingworth	12	4	15	2	2	0	3	1	4th	206	314	–
Fletcher	3	1	14	0					5th	212	344	–
									6th	229	408	–
NEW ZEALAND									7th	244	408	–
Motz	36	5	97	2					8th	280	441	–
Collinge	29	6	88	1					9th	285	–	–
Hadlee	25	3	88	4					10th	294	–	–
Howarth	41	14	89	1								
Pollard	10	2	26	1								
Burgess	14	4	40	0								

Umpires: C.S. Elliott (32) and A.E.G. Rhodes (3).

Close: 1st day – NZ(1) 231-6 (Wadsworth 16, Hadlee 0); 2nd – E(1) 227-1 (Edrich 117, Sharpe 103); 3rd – E(1) 241-1 (Edrich 128, Sharpe 106); 4th – NZ(2) 37-0 (Murray 24, Dowling 10).

ENGLAND v NEW ZEALAND 1969 (3rd Test)

Played at Kennington Oval, London, on 21, 22, 23, 25, 26 August.
Toss: New Zealand.   Result: ENGLAND won by eight wickets.
Debuts: England – M.H. Denness.

England completed their second win in this rubber at 2.30 on the fifth afternoon. When he dismissed Sharpe, Motz became the first bowler to take 100 wickets in Test matches for New Zealand. Underwood's match analysis of 12 for 101 remains the best against New Zealand in England and was the series record until 1970–71 when he took 12 for 97 at Christchurch (*Test No. 685*).

NEW ZEALAND

B.A.G. Murray	b Snow	2	c and b Underwood		5
G.M. Turner	c Sharpe b Underwood	53	b Underwood		25
B.E. Congdon	c Sharpe b Underwood	24	c Knott b Ward		30
G.T. Dowling*	c Edrich b Illingworth	14	lbw b Snow		30
B.F. Hastings	b Illingworth	21	c Knott b Ward		61
V. Pollard	st Knott b Illingworth	13	c Denness b Underwood		9
B.R. Taylor	c Denness b Underwood	0	st Knott b Underwood		4
K.J. Wadsworth†	c Arnold b Underwood	2	c Knott b Snow		10
R.C. Motz	c Arnold b Underwood	16	c Denness b Underwood		11
R.S. Cunis	c Illingworth b Underwood	0	lbw b Underwood		7
H.J. Howarth	not out	0	not out		4
Extras	(NB 5)	5	(B 3, LB 11, NB 19)		33
Total		**150**			**229**

ENGLAND

J.H. Edrich	b Howarth	68	c Wadsworth b Cunis		22
G. Boycott	b Cunis	46	b Cunis		8
M.H. Denness	c Wadsworth b Cunis	2	not out		55
P.J. Sharpe	lbw b Motz	48	not out		45
B.L. D'Oliveira	c Cunis b Howarth	1			
A.P.E. Knott†	c Murray b Taylor	21			
R. Illingworth*	c Wadsworth b Taylor	4			
G.G. Arnold	b Taylor	1			
D.L. Underwood	lbw b Taylor	3			
J.A. Snow	not out	21			
A. Ward	c Turner b Cunis	21			
Extras	(LB 5, NB 1)	6	(B 2, LB 4, NB 2)		8
Total		**242**	(2 wickets)		**138**

ENGLAND	O	M	R	W	O	M	R	W		FALL OF WICKETS			
Arnold	8	2	13	0	10	3	17	0		NZ	E	NZ	E
Snow	10	4	22	1	21	4	52	2	*Wkt*	*1st*	*1st*	*2nd*	*2nd*
Ward	5	0	10	0	18	10	28	2	1st	3	88	22	19
Illingworth	32·3	13	55	3	15	9	20	0	2nd	77	118	39	56
Underwood	26	12	41	6	38·3	15	60	6	3rd	90	118	88	–
D'Oliveira	1	0	4	0	14	9	19	0	4th	96	131	124	–
									5th	118	174	153	–
NEW ZEALAND									6th	119	180	159	–
Motz	19	6	54	1	9·3	1	35	0	7th	123	188	200	–
Taylor	21	9	47	4	4	0	11	0	8th	150	192	206	–
Cunis	19	3	49	3	11	3	36	2	9th	150	202	224	–
Howarth	34	14	66	2	23	10	32	0	10th	150	242	229	–
Pollard	5	1	20	0	5	1	16	0					

Umpires: A.E. Fagg (7) and T.W. Spencer (2).

Close: 1st day – NZ(1) 123-7 (Hastings 11); 2nd – E(1) 174-5 (Sharpe 34, Illingworth 0); 3rd – NZ(2) 71-2 (Congdon 18, Dowling 13); 4th – E(2) 32-1 (Edrich 18, Denness 4).

INDIA v NEW ZEALAND 1969–70 (1st Test)

Played at Brabourne Stadium, Bombay, on 25, 26, 27, 28, 30 September.
Toss: India.   Result: INDIA won by 60 runs.
Debuts: India – C.P.S. Chauhan, A.V. Mankad, A.M. Pai.

Serious rioting in Ahmedabad prevented that city from staging its first Test match. Transferred to Bombay at short notice, it was played on an under-prepared pitch. New Zealand's total of 127 was their lowest in India until 1988-89. The largest crowd ever to watch New Zealand, 47,000, attended the fourth day.

INDIA

S. Abid Ali	c Congdon b Hadlee	3	run out		27
C.P.S. Chauhan	c Murray b Cunis	18	c Wadsworth b Burgess		34
A.L. Wadekar	c Congdon b Cunis	49	c Wadsworth b Taylor		40
R.F. Surti	c Hastings b Congdon	6	b Hadlee		1
Nawab of Pataudi, jr*	c Congdon b Hadlee	18	c Howarth b Taylor		67
Hanumant Singh	c Wadsworth b Hadlee	1	c Wadsworth b Hadlee		13
A.V. Mankad	not out	19	(8) c and b Howarth		29
F.M. Engineer†	run out	20	(7) b Taylor		9
A.M. Pai	b Congdon	1	b Howarth		9
E.A.S. Prasanna	c Turner b Congdon	12	not out		17
B.S. Bedi	lbw b Taylor	4	c Wadsworth b Hadlee		4
Extras	(NB 5)	5	(LB 4, NB 6)		10
Total		**156**			**260**

NEW ZEALAND

G.M. Turner	c Surti b Prasanna	24	c Surti b Prasanna		5
B.A.G. Murray	c Chauhan b Pai	17	c Surti b Prasanna		11
G.T. Dowling*	c Surti b Prasanna	32	(4) not out		36
B.E. Congdon	c Wadekar b Bedi	78	(5) c Surti b Bedi		4
B.F. Hastings	b Abid Ali	11	(6) c Wadekar b Bedi		7
M.G. Burgess	c Abid Ali b Pai	10	(7) c and b Bedi		0
K.J. Wadsworth†	c Wadekar b Bedi	14	(8) c Pataudi b Prasanna		13
H.J. Howarth	c Bedi b Prasanna	1	(11) c Engineer b Bedi		3
B.R. Taylor	c Mankad b Prasanna	21	c Abid Ali b Bedi		9
D.R. Hadlee	not out	0	c Pataudi b Prasanna		21
R.S. Cunis	run out	2	(3) c Wadekar b Bedi		12
Extras	(B 8, LB 5, NB 6)	19	(LB 1, NB 5)		6
Total		**229**			**127**

NEW ZEALAND	O	M	R	W	O	M	R	W	FALL OF WICKETS				
										I	NZ	I	NZ
Taylor	12·2	2	37	1	18	8	30	3	*Wkt*	*1st*	*1st*	*2nd*	*2nd*
Hadlee	11	7	17	3	25·2	7	57	3	1st	4	27	44	10
Cunis	14	5	31	2	22	6	50	0	2nd	34	78	105	31
Congdon	15	3	33	3	6	1	14	0	3rd	45	97	105	31
Howarth	14	5	33	0	45	21	69	2	4th	99	125	111	35
Burgess					20	9	30	1	5th	99	165	151	49
INDIA									6th	102	203	165	49
Pai	17	4	29	2	2	1	2	0	7th	131	204	229	76
Abid Ali	11	1	23	1	2	1	1	0	8th	132	227	233	88
Surti	6	2	10	0	2	1	2	0	9th	151	227	243	115
Bedi	37	19	51	2	30·5	16	42	6	10th	156	229	260	127
Prasanna	46·3	16	97	4	33	13	74	4					

Umpires: A.M. Mamsa (3) and B. Satyaji Rao (7).

Close: 1st day –NZ(1) 21-0 (Turner 4, Murray 12); 2nd – NZ(1) 204-6 (Wadsworth 14, Howarth 0); 3rd – I(2) 127-4 (Pataudi 12, Hanumant 6); 4th – NZ(2) 12-1 (Murray 4, Cunis 0).

INDIA v NEW ZEALAND 1969–70 (2nd Test)

Played at Vidarbha C.A. Ground, Nagpur, on 3, 4, 5, 7, 8 October.
Toss: New Zealand.   Result: NEW ZEALAND won by 167 runs.
Debuts: India – A. Roy.

New Zealand gained their first success in India, in the only Test match to be played at Nagpur until 1983-84, after just 40 minutes' play on the fifth morning. Howarth's match analysis of 9 for 100 was New Zealand's best in India until 1988-89. Engineer batted with a runner in the second innings because of an injured ankle.

NEW ZEALAND

G.T. Dowling*	lbw b Venkataraghavan	69	c Engineer b Venkataraghavan	18
B.A.G. Murray	c Abid Ali b Prasanna	30	lbw b Abid Ali	2
B.E. Congdon	c Engineer b Bedi	64	(4) c Abid Ali b Bedi	7
M.G. Burgess	lbw b Prasanna	89	(5) c Chauhan b Venkataraghavan	12
G.M. Turner	c Surti b Bedi	2	(3) c Chauhan b Venkataraghavan	57
V. Pollard	c Wadekar b Abid Ali	10	c Wadekar b Prasanna	29
B.W. Yuile	b Bedi	9	b Prasanna	10
K.J. Wadsworth†	c and b Bedi	1	lbw b Venkataraghavan	5
D.R. Hadlee	c Chauhan b Venkataraghavan	26	c and b Venkataraghavan	32
R.S. Cunis	lbw b Venkataraghavan	7	c Chauhan b Venkataraghavan	2
H.J. Howarth	not out	0	not out	17
Extras	(B 4, LB 6, NB 2)	12	(B 12, LB 8, NB 3)	23
Total		**319**		**214**

INDIA

S. Abid Ali	c Dowling b Pollard	63	c Congdon b Cunis	0
C.P.S. Chauhan	c Turner b Yuile	14	c Congdon b Howarth	19
A.L. Wadekar	b Burgess	32	c and b Howarth	23
R.F. Surti	b Howarth	26	c Murray b Howarth	0
S. Venkataraghavan	c Turner b Burgess	0	(8) lbw b Burgess	4
Nawab of Pataudi, jr*	c Wadsworth b Burgess	7	(5) lbw b Howarth	28
A.V. Mankad	c and b Howarth	10	(6) c Congdon b Pollard	7
A. Roy	b Pollard	48	(7) c and b Howarth	2
F.M. Engineer†	b Howarth	40	st Wadsworth b Pollard	19
E.A.S. Prasanna	lbw b Howarth	3	b Pollard	0
B.S. Bedi	not out	0	not out	5
Extras	(B 4, LB 7, NB 3)	14	(B 2)	2
Total		**257**		**109**

INDIA	O	M	R	W	O	M	R	W	FALL OF WICKETS				
										NZ	I	NZ	I
Surti	9	3	27	0	3	0	3	0					
Abid Ali	12	2	31	1	9	4	7	1	*Wkt*	*1st*	*1st*	*2nd*	*2nd*
Venkataraghavan	31	9	59	3	30·1	8	74	6	1st	74	55	5	1
Bedi	45	18	98	4	32	13	46	1	2nd	123	95	41	44
Prasanna	33	10	92	2	31	10	61	2	3rd	206	139	59	44
									4th	208	143	79	49
NEW ZEALAND									5th	244	145	144	60
Hadlee	12	2	32	0	5	2	14	0	6th	284	150	146	79
Cunis	15	6	45	0	4	2	8	1	7th	286	161	152	84
Pollard	19·2	6	36	2	11·5	4	21	3	8th	288	234	168	102
Howarth	30	5	66	4	23	11	34	5	9th	316	243	171	104
Yuile	15	6	41	1	3	1	8	0	10th	319	257	214	109
Burgess	8	4	23	3	6	0	18	1					
Congdon					3	1	4	0					

Umpires: S.P. Pan (7) and V. Rajagopal (1).

Close: 1st day – NZ(1) 252-5 (Burgess 66, Yuile 0); 2nd – I(1) 143-4 (Surti 25); 3rd – NZ(2) 81-4 (Turner 30, Pollard 0); 4th – I(2) 86-7 (Pataudi 27, Engineer 2).

INDIA v NEW ZEALAND 1969–70 (3rd Test)

Played at Lal Bahadur Stadium, Hyderabad, on 15, 16 (*no play*), 18, 19, 20 October.
Toss: New Zealand. Result: MATCH DRAWN.
Debuts: India – A. Gandotra, E.D. Solkar.

New Zealand's attempt to win their first Test rubber was frustrated by the weather, the crowd and by the umpires, who forgot to arrange for the pitch to be cut on the rest day. Dowling, quite correctly, refused to allow the error to be compounded when the umpires wanted it cut on the third morning. Batting on a pitch unmown for three days, India were dismissed for the lowest total in a Test at Hyderabad. Rioting prevented New Zealand from starting their innings on the third evening. Their declaration set India 268 to win on the final day (5½ hours). At 2.26 pm, after 190 minutes of play, heavy rain brought the teams off with New Zealand just three wickets short of an historic victory. Little effort was made to restart play, even though sun baked the ground from 3.00 pm. This ground, redeveloped since the only previous Test (*No. 416*) was played on it in November 1955, was formerly known as Fateh Maidan.

NEW ZEALAND

G.T. Dowling*	run out	42		lbw b Abid Ali	60
B.A.G. Murray	c Jaisimha b Prasanna	80		lbw b Prasanna	26
G.M. Turner	c Indrajitsinhji b Bedi	2	(9)	not out	15
B.E. Congdon	c Pataudi b Prasanna	3	(3)	c Prasanna b Venkataraghavan	18
B.F. Hastings	c Venkataraghavan b Prasanna	2	(4)	c Venkataraghavan b Prasanna	21
M.G. Burgess	lbw b Bedi	2	(5)	b Abid Ali	3
B.R. Taylor	c Gandotra b Prasanna	16		b Venkataraghavan	18
D.R. Hadlee	c Pataudi b Prasanna	1		b Abid Ali	0
K.J. Wadsworth†	run out	14	(6)	lbw b Prasanna	5
R.S. Cunis	c Solkar b Abid Ali	7		not out	0
H.J. Howarth	not out	5			
Extras	(LB 7)	7		(B 6, LB 3)	9
Total		**181**		(8 wickets declared)	**175**

INDIA

S. Abid Ali	b Taylor	4		c Howarth b Taylor	5
K.S. Indrajitsinhji†	lbw b Cunis	7		c Dowling b Cunis	12
A.L. Wadekar	c Congdon b Hadlee	9		c Wadsworth b Hadlee	14
M.L. Jaisimha	c Hastings b Cunis	0		c Taylor b Hadlee	0
Nawab of Pataudi, jr*	c Murray b Hadlee	0		lbw b Cunis	9
A. Roy	c Wadsworth b Hadlee	0		c Wadsworth b Hadlee	4
A. Gandotra	c Wadsworth b Howarth	18		b Cunis	15
E.D. Solkar	c Murray b Cunis	0		not out	13
S. Venkataraghavan	not out	25		not out	2
E.A.S. Prasanna	b Hadlee	2			
B.S. Bedi	c Dowling b Congdon	20			
Extras	(B 1, LB 3)	4		(LB 2)	2
Total		**89**		(7 wickets)	**76**

INDIA	O	M	R	W	O	M	R	W	FALL OF WICKETS				
Jaisimha	4	0	13	0	4	2	2	0		NZ	I	NZ	I
Abid Ali	12·1	5	17	1	27	7	47	3	*Wkt*	*1st*	*1st*	*2nd*	*2nd*
Venkataraghavan	17	5	33	0	16	3	40	2	1st	106	5	45	10
Bedi	34	14	52	2	9	2	19	0	2nd	122	21	86	20
Solkar	3	1	8	0					3rd	128	21	127	21
Prasanna	29	13	51	5	26	7	58	3	4th	132	21	133	34
									5th	133	21	141	44
NEW ZEALAND									6th	135	27	141	50
Hadlee	17	5	30	4	10·4	2	31	3	7th	136	28	144	66
Taylor	10	2	20	1	8	2	18	1	8th	158	46	175	–
Cunis	14	7	12	3	12	5	12	3	9th	166	49	–	–
Congdon	3·2	1	7	1	5	3	4	0	10th	181	89	–	–
Howarth	9	2	12	1	5	2	4	0					
Burgess	1	0	4	0	6	3	5	0					

Umpires: S. Bhattacharya (2) and M.V. Nagendra (4).

Close: 1st day – NZ(1) 181-9 (Cunis 7, Howarth 5); 2nd – no play; 3rd – I(1) 89 all out; 4th – NZ(2) 175-8 (Turner 15, Cunis 0).

PAKISTAN v NEW ZEALAND 1969–70 (1st Test)

Played at National Stadium, Karachi, on 24, 25, 26, 27 October.
Toss: Pakistan.   Result: MATCH DRAWN.
Debuts: Pakistan – Mohammad Nazir, Sadiq Mohammad, Younis Ahmed, Zaheer Abbas.

New Zealand needed to score 230 runs in 195 minutes. This match provided the third instance of three brothers playing in the same Test, with the Mohammads emulating the Graces (*Test No. 4*) and the Hearnes (*No. 38*). The Pakistan family is alone in providing Test cricket with four brothers (Wazir, Hanif, Mushtaq and Sadiq) and a fifth, Raees, was 12th man in an official Test. This was Hanif's last appearance in Test cricket; he played in all but two of Pakistan's first 57 official matches. The partnership of 100 between Yuile and Hadlee remains the highest for the eighth wicket in this series. Mohammad Nazir's analysis of 7 for 99 in his first Test was the record for this series in Pakistan until Pervez improved upon it in the next match; it remains the best return by any Pakistan bowler in his first Test.

PAKISTAN

Hanif Mohammad	c Yuile b Howarth	22		lbw b Yuile	35
Sadiq Mohammad	b Howarth	69		run out	37
Younis Ahmed	c Dowling b Howarth	8	(5)	c Dowling b Cunis	62
Mushtaq Mohammad	b Yuile	14		c Murray b Howarth	19
Zaheer Abbas	c Murray b Yuile	12	(6)	c Burgess b Hadlee	27
Asif Iqbal	st Wadsworth b Howarth	22	(3)	c Hastings b Yuile	0
Intikhab Alam*	c Congdon b Howarth	0	(8)	c Yuile b Cunis	47
Wasim Barit†	c Murray b Hadlee	15	(7)	c Congdon b Howarth	19
Mohammad Nazir	not out	29		not out	17
Pervez Sajjad	b Hadlee	0			
Asif Masood	c Howarth b Hadlee	17			
Extras	(B 2, LB 10)	12		(B 13, LB 7)	20
Total		**220**		(8 wickets declared)	**283**

NEW ZEALAND

G.T. Dowling*	b Nazir	40		lbw b Pervez	3
B.A.G. Murray	c Hanif b Nazir	50		c Asif Iqbal b Pervez	6
B.E. Congdon	c Sadiq b Pervez	20		c Sadiq b Pervez	2
B.F. Hastings	b Nazir	22		b Pervez	9
M.G. Burgess	b Nazir	21		c Asif Iqbal b Pervez	45
V. Pollard	b Nazir	2		not out	28
B.W. Yuile	not out	47		not out	5
K.J. Wadsworth†	st Wasim b Pervez	0			
D.R. Hadlee	lbw b Mushtaq	56			
R.S. Cunis	b Nazir	5			
H.J. Howarth	b Nazir	0			
Extras	(B 6, LB 3, NB 2)	11		(B 12, LB 2)	14
Total		**274**		(5 wickets)	**112**

NEW ZEALAND	O	M	R	W	O	M	R	W			FALL OF WICKETS		
Hadlee	17·2	5	27	3	16	5	31	1			P	NZ	P	NZ
Cunis	11	5	18	0	15·4	4	38	2	*Wkt*	*1st*	*1st*	*2nd*	*2nd*
Congdon	8	5	14	0					1st	55	92	75	9
Howarth	33	10	80	5	31	13	60	2	2nd	78	99	75	10
Pollard	15	5	34	0	31	11	50	0	3rd	111	125	83	11
Yuile	13	3	35	2	35	13	70	2	4th	121	139	133	44
Burgess					6	1	14	0	5th	135	144	183	92
									6th	142	163	195	–
PAKISTAN									7th	153	164	244	–
Asif Masood	3	0	18	0	2	1	7	0	8th	191	264	283	–
Asif Iqbal	3	0	12	0	2	0	2	0	9th	191	273	–	–
Intikhab	13	3	51	0	5	1	18	0	10th	220	274	–	–
Nazir	30·1	3	99	7	14	5	15	0					
Pervez	31	7	71	2	24	12	33	5					
Mushtaq	5	0	12	1	12	5	20	0					
Sadiq					2	0	2	0					
Hanif					2	1	1	0					

Umpires: Idris Beg (9) and Munawar Hussain (5).

Close: 1st day – P(1) 199-9 (Nazir 22, Asif Masood 5); 2nd – P(2) 0-0 (Hanif 0, Sadiq 0); 3rd – P(2) 186-5 (Zaheer 19, Wasim 2).

PAKISTAN v NEW ZEALAND 1969–70 (2nd Test)

Played at Lahore Stadium on 30, 31 October, 1, 2 November.
Toss: Pakistan.   Result: NEW ZEALAND won by five wickets.
Debuts: Nil.

New Zealand's first win against Pakistan came after they had dismissed the home side for what is still their lowest total in this series. Pervez Sajjad's innings analysis of 7 for 74 and match analysis of 9 for 112 were the records for any Test at Lahore until 1981-82 (*Test No. 927*).

PAKISTAN

Sadiq Mohammad	b Congdon	16		c and b Howarth	17
Salahuddin	c Wadsworth b Taylor	2		b Taylor	11
Younis Ahmed	b Hadlee	0	(5)	c Murray b Pollard	19
Mushtaq Mohammad	c Wadsworth b Pollard	25		c Yuile b Howarth	1
Shafqat Rana	c Murray b Congdon	4	(6)	c Hastings b Hadlee	95
Asif Iqbal	c Murray b Pollard	20	(3)	c Congdon b Yuile	22
Intikhab Alam*	c Dowling b Howarth	6		b Pollard	11
Wasim Bari†	c Burgess b Pollard	7		c Murray b Hadlee	11
Salim Altaf	c Hastings b Howarth	1		lbw b Hadlee	0
Mohammad Nazir	c Wadsworth b Howarth	12		not out	4
Pervez Sajjad	not out	6		lbw b Taylor	2
Extras	(B 9, LB 6)	15		(B 4, LB 9, NB 2)	15
Total		**114**			**208**

NEW ZEALAND

G.T. Dowling*	b Salim	10		c Salahuddin b Pervez	9
B.A.G. Murray	c Shafqat b Pervez	90		c Asif b Pervez	8
B.E. Congdon	lbw b Pervez	22		c Shafqat b Nazir	5
B.F. Hastings	not out	80		c Mushtaq b Nazir	16
M.G. Burgess	c Mushtaq b Pervez	0		not out	29
V. Pollard	c Wasim b Pervez	11		st Wasim b Nazir	0
B.W. Yuile	c Asif b Pervez	2		not out	4
D.R. Hadlee	c and b Pervez	0			
B.R. Taylor	b Pervez	0			
K.J. Wadsworth†	b Salim	13			
H.J. Howarth	b Salim	4			
Extras	(B 1, LB 6, NB 2)	9		(B 4, LB 5, NB 2)	11
Total		**241**		(5 wickets)	**82**

NEW ZEALAND	O	M	R	W	O	M	R	W
Hadlee	7	3	10	1	17	4	27	3
Taylor	9	3	12	1	19·5	7	27	2
Congdon	10	4	15	2	8	4	17	0
Howarth	21·4	13	35	3	26	7	63	2
Pollard	20	7	27	3	20	7	32	2
Yuile					14	6	16	1
Burgess					1	0	11	0
PAKISTAN								
Salim	17	3	33	3	4	0	12	0
Asif	4	0	6	0	2	1	2	0
Pervez	40	15	74	7	14	6	38	2
Nazir	36	15	54	0	12·3	4	19	3
Mushtaq	8	1	34	0				
Intikhab	10	2	31	0				

FALL OF WICKETS

Wkt	P 1st	NZ 1st	P 2nd	NZ 2nd
1st	8	20	30	19
2nd	13	61	48	28
3rd	33	162	56	29
4th	39	162	66	66
5th	70	184	85	78
6th	83	186	117	–
7th	87	188	194	–
8th	90	188	194	–
9th	100	230	205	–
10th	114	241	208	–

Umpires: Akhtar Hussain (3) and Omar Khan (1).

Close: 1st day – NZ(1) 52-1 (Murray 23, Congdon 19); 2nd – P(2) 17-0 (Sadiq 9, Salahuddin 4); 3rd – P(2) 202-8 (Shafqat 91, Nazir 4).

PAKISTAN v NEW ZEALAND 1969–70 (3rd Test)

Played at Dacca Stadium on 8, 9, 10, 11 November.
Toss: New Zealand.   Result: MATCH DRAWN.
Debuts: Pakistan – Aftab Baloch.

This result gave New Zealand their first victory in a Test rubber; they had waited for 40 years. New Zealand's then record ninth-wicket partnership against all countries of 96 between Burgess and Cunis left the home side to score 184 runs in 2½ hours. Bad light stopped play with 90 minutes left but minor rioting and an invasion of the playing area caused the match to be abandoned 65 minutes before the scheduled close. Turner was the first New Zealander to score a century in his first match against Pakistan. This was the last Test match to be played at Dacca; since 16 December 1971 it has been within the People's Republic of Bangladesh.

NEW ZEALAND

B.A.G. Murray	b Asif	7	c Asif b Intikhab	2
G.M. Turner	c Shafqat b Pervez	110	c Intikhab b Pervez	26
G.T. Dowling*	c Asif b Intikhab	15	c Wasim b Intikhab	2
B.E. Congdon	c Pervez b Intikhab	6	b Pervez	0
B.F. Hastings	b Intikhab	22	b Pervez	3
M.G. Burgess	c Wasim b Pervez	59	not out	119
V. Pollard	c Shafqat b Intikhab	2	b Intikhab	11
D.R. Hadlee	c Burki b Intikhab	16	lbw b Intikhab	0
K.J. Wadsworth†	c Wasim b Salim	7	c Aftab Gul b Pervez	0
R.S. Cunis	lbw b Salim	0	b Shafqat	23
H.J. Howarth	not out	0	c Wasim b Intikhab	2
Extras	(B 14, LB 11, NB 4)	29	(B 2, LB 8, NB 2)	12
Total		**273**		**200**

PAKISTAN

Aftab Gul	c and b Howarth	30	b Cunis	5
Sadiq Mohammad	c Turner b Pollard	21	b Cunis	3
Javed Burki	c Turner b Howarth	22	not out	17
Shafqat Rana	run out	65	(5) c Dowling b Cunis	3
Aftab Baloch	lbw b Pollard	25		
Asif Iqbal	c Wadsworth b Howarth	92	(4) b Cunis	16
Intikhab Alam*	b Howarth	20	(6) not out	3
Wasim Bari†	not out	6		
Salim Altaf	)			
Mohammad Nazir	) did not bat			
Pervez Sajjad	)			
Extras	(B 6, LB 3)	9	(B 1, LB 3)	4
Total	(7 wickets declared)	**290**	(4 wickets)	**51**

PAKISTAN	O	M	R	W	O	M	R	W		FALL OF WICKETS			
Salim	19·3	6	27	2	11	4	18	0		NZ	P	NZ	P
Asif	13	4	22	1	7	2	8	0	*Wkt*	*1st*	*1st*	*2nd*	*2nd*
Pervez	48	20	66	2	34	11	60	4	1st	13	53	12	7
Intikhab	56	26	91	5	39·4	13	91	5	2nd	67	55	14	12
Nazir	30	15	38	0	3	1	3	0	3rd	99	81	17	40
Sadiq					2	1	4	0	4th	147	150	25	46
Aftab Baloch					2	0	2	0	5th	226	201	70	–
Shafqat					3	1	2	1	6th	241	277	92	–
NEW ZEALAND									7th	251	290	92	–
Hadlee	17	2	41	0	7	0	17	0	8th	271	–	101	–
Cunis	23	5	65	0	7	0	21	4	9th	272	–	197	–
Congdon	14	2	41	0					10th	273	–	200	–
Howarth	33·1	8	85	4									
Pollard	14	2	49	2	1	0	9	0					

Umpires: Daud Khan (12) and Shujauddin (15).

Close: 1st day – NZ(1) 172-4 (Turner 99, Burgess 5); 2nd – P(1) 92-3 (Shafqat 11, Aftab Baloch 6); 3rd – NZ(2) 55-4 (Turner 22, Burgess 22).

INDIA v AUSTRALIA 1969–70 (1st Test)

Played at Brabourne Stadium, Bombay, on 4, 5, 7, 8, 9 November.
Toss: India.   Result: AUSTRALIA won by eight wickets.
Debuts: Nil.

Australia gained their first Test victory at Bombay soon after lunch on the fifth day. The omission of S. Venkataraghavan from India's side caused such a public outcry that S. Guha agreed to stand down from the selected team. The partnership of 146 between Mankad and Pataudi was India's highest for the fourth wicket against Australia until 1979-80 (*Test No. 856*). Stackpole became the second Australian after D.G. Bradman to score a hundred in his first Test against India. On the fourth day, the last hour of play endured through a riot resulting from Venkataraghavan's second innings dismissal.

INDIA

D.N. Sardesai	b McKenzie	20	c Taber b Gleeson	3
F.M. Engineer†	c Redpath b McKenzie	19	c McKenzie b Mallett	28
A.V. Mankad	b McKenzie	74	b Gleeson	8
C.G. Borde	c Chappell b McKenzie	2	c Redpath b Gleeson	18
Nawab of Pataudi, jr*	c Lawry b Gleeson	95	c Stackpole b Gleeson	0
A.L. Wadekar	lbw b Connolly	9	c McKenzie b Stackpole	46
R.F. Surti	st Taber b Gleeson	4	lbw b Connolly	13
S. Abid Ali	c Stackpole b McKenzie	3	lbw b Connolly	2
S. Venkataraghavan	c Taber b Connolly	2	c Taber b Connolly	9
E.A.S. Prasanna	not out	12	b Mallett	3
B.S. Bedi	c McKenzie b Gleeson	7	not out	1
Extras	(B 15, LB 4, NB 5)	24	(B 4, NB 2)	6
Total		**271**		**137**

AUSTRALIA

W.M. Lawry*	b Prasanna	25	b Surti	2
K.R. Stackpole	c Surti b Prasanna	103	lbw b Surti	11
I.M. Chappell	b Prasanna	31	not out	31
K.D. Walters	c Venkataraghavan b Bedi	48	not out	22
I.R. Redpath	c Wadekar b Venkataraghavan	77		
A.P. Sheahan	lbw b Venkataraghavan	14		
G.D. McKenzie	c Borde b Prasanna	16		
H.B. Taber†	c Surti b Bedi	5		
A.A. Mallett	not out	10		
J.W. Gleeson	c Borde b Prasanna	0		
A.N. Connolly	c sub (E.D. Solkar) b Bedi	8	(B 1)	1
Extras	(B 4, NB 4)	8		
Total		**345**	(2 wickets)	**67**

AUSTRALIA	O	M	R	W	O	M	R	W	FALL OF WICKETS				
										I	A	I	A
McKenzie	29	7	69	5	16	4	33	0	*Wkt*	*1st*	*1st*	*2nd*	*2nd*
Connolly	31	11	55	2	20	10	20	3	1st	39	81	19	8
Gleeson	35·4	18	52	3	32	17	56	4	2nd	40	164	37	13
Walters	6	0	13	0					3rd	42	167	55	–
Mallett	30	19	43	0	21	9	22	2	4th	188	285	56	–
Stackpole	3	1	8	0	1·2	1	0	1	5th	239	297	59	–
Chappell	1	0	7	0					6th	245	322	87	–
INDIA									7th	246	322	89	–
Abid Ali	18	3	52	0	3	0	14	0	8th	249	337	114	–
Surti	9	2	23	0	4	1	9	2	9th	252	337	125	–
Venkataraghavan	31	11	67	2	1	0	2	0	10th	271	345	137	–
Bedi	62·4	33	74	3	9	5	11	0					
Prasanna	49	19	121	5	9	3	20	0					
Mankad					0·5	0	10	0					

Umpires: I. Gopalakrishnan (5) and S.P. Pan (8).

Close: 1st day – I(1) 202-4 (Pataudi 73, Wadekar 1); 2nd – A(1) 93-1 (Stackpole 57, Chappell 4); 3rd – A(1) 322-7 (Taber 0, Mallett 0); 4th – I(2) 125-9 (Wadekar 37).

INDIA v AUSTRALIA 1969–70 (2nd Test)

Played at Green Park, Kanpur, on 15, 16, 18, 19, 20 November.
Toss: India.   Result: MATCH DRAWN.
Debuts: India – G.R. Viswanath.

Viswanath became the sixth batsman to score a hundred on his Test debut for India and the first to do so against Australia. His innings of 137, scored in 354 minutes and including 25 fours, was India's highest against Australia in a home Test until he scored 161 not out in 1979-80 (*Test No. 856*). Sheahan delighted with a chanceless 226-minute innings; his first Test hundred, it contained 20 boundaries.

INDIA

F.M. Engineer†	c and b Stackpole	77	c Gleeson b Connolly	21
A.V. Mankad	c and b Mallett	64	b McKenzie	68
A.L. Wadekar	c Mallett b Connolly	27	c Chappell b Connolly	12
G.R. Viswanath	c Redpath b Connolly	0	lbw b Mallett	137
Nawab of Pataudi, jr*	c Redpath b McKenzie	38	lbw b McKenzie	0
A. Gandotra	c Taber b Connolly	13	c Chappell b Gleeson	8
E.D. Solkar	b Connolly	44	c Taber b McKenzie	35
S. Venkataraghavan	run out	17	not out	20
S. Guha	lbw b Mallett	6	not out	1
E.A.S. Prasanna	c McKenzie b Mallett	22		
B.S. Bedi	not out	1		
Extras	(LB 5, NB 6)	11	(LB 1, NB 9)	10
Total		**320**	(7 wickets declared)	**312**

AUSTRALIA

K.R. Stackpole	run out	40	not out	37
W.M. Lawry*	c Solkar b Venkataraghavan	14	not out	56
I.M. Chappell	lbw b Prasanna	16		
K.D. Walters	b Bedi	53		
I.R. Redpath	c Guha b Solkar	70		
A.P. Sheahan	c Engineer b Guha	114		
A.A. Mallett	b Venkataraghavan	4		
G.D. McKenzie	lbw b Prasanna	0		
H.B. Taber†	c Viswanath b Venkataraghavan	1		
J.W. Gleeson	b Guha	13		
A.N. Connolly	not out	7		
Extras	(B 4, LB 7, NB 5)	16	(NB 2)	2
Total		**348**	(0 wickets)	**95**

AUSTRALIA	O	M	R	W	O	M	R	W		FALL OF WICKETS			
McKenzie	25	7	70	1	34	13	63	3			I	A	I	A
Connolly	36	13	91	4	36	7	69	2	*Wkt*	*1st*	*1st*	*2nd*	*2nd*
Gleeson	29	5	79	0	35	11	74	1	1st	111	48	43	–
Mallett	51·5	30	58	3	36	18	62	1	2nd	167	56	94	–
Stackpole	2	1	4	1	7	1	21	0	3rd	171	93	125	–
Walters	2	1	7	0	3	1	7	0	4th	171	140	125	–
Lawry					1	0	6	0	5th	197	271	147	–
									6th	239	287	257	–
INDIA									7th	285	290	306	–
Guha	21·2	6	55	2	5	1	7	0	8th	287	297	–	–
Solkar	19	7	44	1	12	3	37	0	9th	315	331	–	–
Bedi	49	21	82	1	3	1	8	0	10th	320	348	–	–
Prasanna	39	18	71	2	15	6	17	0					
Venkataraghavan	37	16	76	3	4	1	11	0					
Viswanath	1	0	4	0	1	0	4	0					
Pataudi					1	0	4	0					
Mankad					1	1	0	0					
Gandotra					1	0	5	0					
Wadekar					1	1	0	0					

Umpires: A.M. Mamsa (4) and B. Satyaji Rao (8).

Close: 1st day – I(1) 237-5 (Pataudi 36, Solkar 15); 2nd – A(1) 105-3 (Walters 29, Redpath 4); 3rd – A(1) 348 all out; 4th – I(2) 204-5 (Viswanath 69, Solkar 20).

INDIA v AUSTRALIA 1969–70 (3rd Test)

Played at Feroz Shah Kotla, Delhi, on 28, 29, 30 November, 2 December.
Toss: Australia.   Result: INDIA won by seven wickets.
Debuts: Nil.

India gained their third victory against Australia and with more than a day to spare. Australia's total of 107 was the lowest in any Test at Delhi until 1987-88. Lawry, who batted for 195 minutes, became the sixth Australian to carry his bat through a complete innings and the second batsman after Nazar Mohammad of Pakistan (*Test No. 356*) to do so against India. Prasanna took his 100th Test wicket when he dismissed Sheahan.

AUSTRALIA

K.R. Stackpole	st Engineer b Bedi	61		b Prasanna	9
W.M. Lawry*	b Guha	6		not out	49
I.M. Chappell	b Bedi	138		c Solkar b Bedi	0
K.D. Walters	c Solkar b Prasanna	4		b Bedi	0
I.R. Redpath	c Bedi b Prasanna	6		b Bedi	4
A.P. Sheahan	b Bedi	4		c Venkataraghavan b Prasanna	15
H.B. Taber†	st Engineer b Bedi	46		c and b Prasanna	7
A.A. Mallett	b Venkataraghavan	2	(9)	c Venkataraghavan b Prasanna	0
G.D. McKenzie	lbw b Prasanna	20	(8)	lbw b Bedi	7
J.W. Gleeson	c Solkar b Prasanna	1		c Viswanath b Bedi	1
A.N. Connolly	not out	4		c and b Prasanna	11
Extras	(B 2, LB 1, NB 1)	4		(B 4)	4
Total		**296**			**107**

INDIA

F.M. Engineer†	b Connolly	38		c McKenzie b Mallett	6
A.V. Mankad	c Walters b Mallett	97		b Mallett	7
A.L. Wadekar	c and b Stackpole	22	(4)	not out	91
G.R. Viswanath	b Gleeson	29	(5)	not out	44
S. Venkataraghavan	c Walters b Mallett	0			
Nawab of Pataudi, jr*	c Chappell b Mallett	8			
A. Roy	c Taber b Mallett	0			
E.D. Solkar	not out	13			
S. Guha	b Mallett	0			
E.A.S. Prasanna	lbw b Gleeson	1			
B.S. Bedi	b Mallett	6	(3)	b Connolly	20
Extras	(B 3, LB 1, NB 5)	9		(B 9, LB 2, NB 2)	13
Total		**223**		(3 wickets)	**181**

INDIA	O	M	R	W	O	M	R	W	FALL OF WICKETS				
Guha	14	0	47	1	2	0	7	0		A	I	A	I
Solkar	11	1	43	0	1	1	0	0	*Wkt*	*1st*	*1st*	*2nd*	*2nd*
Bedi	42	15	71	4	23	11	37	5	1st	33	85	15	13
Prasanna	38·4	9	111	4	24·2	10	42	5	2nd	100	124	16	18
Venkataraghavan	14	4	20	1	8	2	17	0	3rd	105	176	16	61
									4th	117	177	24	–
AUSTRALIA									5th	133	197	61	–
McKenzie	12	4	22	0	13·4	5	19	0	6th	251	202	81	–
Connolly	20	4	43	1	16	5	35	1	7th	260	207	88	–
Gleeson	34	14	62	2	12	5	24	0	8th	283	207	89	–
Mallett	32·3	10	64	6	29	10	60	2	9th	291	208	92	–
Stackpole	10	4	23	1	8	4	13	0	10th	296	223	107	–
Chappell					2	0	17	0					

Umpires: I. Gopalakrishnan (6) and S. Roy (6).

Close: 1st day – A(1) 261-7 (Taber 36, McKenzie 0); 2nd – I(1) 183-4 (Mankad 89, Pataudi 0); 3rd – I(2) 13-1 (Mankad 2, Bedi 0).

INDIA v AUSTRALIA 1969–70 (4th Test)

Played at Eden Gardens, Calcutta, on 12, 13, 14, 16 December.
Toss: Australia.   Result: AUSTRALIA won by ten wickets.
Debuts: Nil.

Australia completed this convincing victory with more than a day to spare. Bad light claimed $2\frac{1}{2}$ hours of playing time on the first three days and a minor riot caused a 15-minute interruption on the fourth. Connolly struck three sixes off Prasanna and a fourth off Bedi, whose analysis was the best of his 67-match Test career. Lawry was the first visiting captain to elect to field first in a Test in India.

INDIA

F.M. Engineer†	c Stackpole b McKenzie	0	c Redpath b Freeman	10
A.V. Mankad	c Stackpole b McKenzie	9	c Taber b McKenzie	20
A.L. Wadekar	c Freeman b McKenzie	0	lbw b Freeman	62
G.R. Viswanath	c Taber b Mallett	54	b Freeman	5
Nawab of Pataudi, jr*	c Chappell b Mallett	15	(6) c Connolly b Mallett	1
A. Roy	c Taber b McKenzie	18	(7) c Sheahan b Connolly	19
E.D. Solkar	c Taber b McKenzie	42	(5) lbw b Connolly	21
S. Venkataraghavan	c Stackpole b Mallett	24	b Connolly	0
E.A.S. Prasanna	run out	26	c Stackpole b Freeman	0
S. Guha	b McKenzie	4	(11) not out	1
B.S. Bedi	not out	9	(10) c Chappell b Connolly	7
Extras	(B 5, LB 1, W 1, NB 4)	11	(B 6, LB 4, NB 5)	15
Total		**212**		**161**

AUSTRALIA

W.M. Lawry*	c Solkar b Bedi	35	not out	17
K.R. Stackpole	run out	41	not out	25
I.M. Chappell	c Wadekar b Bedi	99		
K.D. Walters	st Engineer b Bedi	56		
I.R. Redpath	c Wadekar b Bedi	0		
A.P. Sheahan	run out	32		
E.W. Freeman	c Prasanna b Bedi	29		
H.B. Taber†	b Bedi	2		
G.D. McKenzie	c Pataudi b Bedi	0		
A.A. Mallett	not out	2		
A.N. Connolly	c Guha b Solkar	31		
Extras	(B 4, LB 2, NB 2)	8		
Total		**335**	(0 wickets)	**42**

AUSTRALIA	O	M	R	W	O	M	R	W					
McKenzie	33·4	12	67	6	18	4	34	1					
Freeman	17	6	43	0	26	7	54	4					
Connolly	17	5	27	0	16·1	3	31	4					
Mallett	27	9	55	3	17	5	27	1					
Stackpole	2	0	9	0									

FALL OF WICKETS

Wkt	I 1st	A 1st	I 2nd	A 2nd
1st	0	65	29	–
2nd	0	84	31	–
3rd	22	185	40	–
4th	64	185	90	–
5th	103	257	93	–
6th	103	279	141	–
7th	154	302	141	–
8th	178	302	142	–
9th	184	302	159	–
10th	212	335	161	–

INDIA	O	M	R	W	O	M	R	W
Guha	19	5	55	0	3	1	25	0
Solkar	9·1	1	28	1				
Prasanna	49	15	116	0				
Venkataraghavan	16	6	30	0				
Bedi	50	19	98	7				
Wadekar					2	0	17	0

Umpires: S.P. Pan (9) and J. Reuben (1).

Close: 1st day – I(1) 176-7 (Solkar 41, Prasanna 5); 2nd – A(1) 95-2 (Chappell 10, Walters 5); 3rd – I(2) 12-0 (Engineer 5, Mankad 7).

INDIA v AUSTRALIA 1969–70 (5th Test)

Played at Chepauk, Madras, on 24, 25, 27, 28 December.
Toss: Australia.   Result: AUSTRALIA won by 77 runs.
Debuts: India – M. Amarnath.

Australia won this six-day match an hour after lunch on the fourth afternoon and so gained a 3-1 victory in the rubber and their fourth successive victory at Madras. Walters survived a stumping chance when he had scored four; his century was his only one in ten Tests against India.

AUSTRALIA

K.R. Stackpole	c Solkar b Venkataraghavan	37	b Amarnath	4
W.M. Lawry*	c Bedi b Prasanna	33	b Prasanna	2
I.M. Chappell	b Prasanna	4	b Amarnath	5
K.D. Walters	c Venkataraghavan b Bedi	102	c Solkar b Prasanna	1
A.P. Sheahan	c Solkar b Prasanna	1	(6) st Engineer b Prasanna	8
I.R. Redpath	c Engineer b Prasanna	33	(5) lbw b Prasanna	63
H.B. Tabert	lbw b Venkataraghavan	10	c Solkar b Prasanna	0
G.D. McKenzie	lbw b Venkataraghavan	2	lbw b Venkataraghavan	24
L.C. Mayne	c Chauhan b Venkataraghavan	10	c Viswanath b Prasanna	13
A.A. Mallett	not out	2	not out	11
A.N. Connolly	c and b Solkar	11	c Engineer b Venkataraghavan	8
Extras	(B 11, LB 2)	13	(B 8, LB 5, NB 1)	14
Total		**258**		**153**

INDIA

C.P.S. Chauhan	c Chappell b Mallett	19	c Redpath b McKenzie	1
A.V. Mankad	c Taber b Mayne	0	c Redpath b McKenzie	10
A.L. Wadekar	c Chappell b Mallett	12	c Stackpole b Mayne	55
G.R. Viswanath	b Mallett	6	c Redpath b Mallett	59
F.M. Engineert	c Connolly b Mallett	32	c and b McKenzie	3
Nawab of Pataudi, jr*	c Sheahan b McKenzie	59	c Chappell b Mallett	4
E.D. Solkar	c Taber b Mallett	11	c and b Mallett	12
M. Amarnath	not out	16	c Taber b Mayne	0
S. Venkataraghavan	run out	2	b Mallett	13
E.A.S. Prasanna	c Chappell b McKenzie	0	c McKenzie b Mallett	5
B.S. Bedi	absent ill	–	not out	0
Extras	(LB 5, NB 1)	6	(LB 4, NB 5)	9
Total		**163**		**171**

INDIA	O	M	R	W	O	M	R	W
Amarnath	7	0	21	0	24	11	31	2
Solkar	8·2	5	8	1	4	2	2	0
Bedi	26	10	45	1	9	5	6	0
Prasanna	40	13	100	4	31	14	74	6
Venkataraghavan	34	13	71	4	12·5	2	26	2
AUSTRALIA								
McKenzie	16·4	8	19	2	24	9	45	3
Mayne	7	2	21	1	18	8	32	2
Connolly	14	5	26	0	9	4	18	0
Mallett	25	7	91	5	29·2	12	53	5
Stackpole					5	2	14	0

FALL OF WICKETS

Wkt	A 1st	I 1st	A 2nd	I 2nd
1st	60	0	4	3
2nd	69	30	12	12
3rd	78	33	15	114
4th	82	40	16	119
5th	184	96	24	135
6th	219	128	24	142
7th	225	158	57	144
8th	243	163	107	159
9th	245	163	140	169
10th	258	–	153	171

Umpires: I. Gopalakrishnan (7) and B. Satyaji Rao (9).

Close: 1st day – A(1) 243-8 (Mayne 8, Mallett 0); 2nd – A(2) 14-2 (Lawry 1, Walters 0); 3rd – I(2) 82-2 (Wadekar 36, Viswanath 31).

SOUTH AFRICA v AUSTRALIA 1969–70 (1st Test)

Played at Newlands, Cape Town, on 22, 23, 24, 26, 27 January.
Toss: South Africa.   Result: SOUTH AFRICA won by 170 runs.
Debuts: South Africa – G.A. Chevalier, D. Gamsy, B.L. Irvine, B.A. Richards.

South Africa beat Australia at Newlands for the first time, having lost all six previous encounters dating back to 1902-03. Barlow's fifth Test hundred was his fourth against Australia and South Africa's 100th in 169 Tests. Chevalier took the wicket of Sheahan with his fifth ball in Test cricket.

SOUTH AFRICA

Batsman	Dismissal 1	R	Dismissal 2	R
B.A Richards	b Connolly	29	c Taber b Connolly	32
T.L. Goddard	c Taber b Walters	16	c Lawry b Mallett	17
A. Bacher*	lbw b Connolly	57	lbw b Gleeson	16
R.G. Pollock	c Chappell b Walters	49	c Walters b Connolly	50
E.J. Barlow	c Chappell b Gleeson	127	c Taber b Gleeson	16
B.L. Irvine	c Gleeson b Mallett	42	c Walters b Connolly	19
M.J. Procter	b Mallett	22	c Taber b Connolly	48
D. Gamsy†	not out	30	c Taber b Gleeson	2
P.M. Pollock	lbw b Mallett	1	b Gleeson	25
M.A. Seymour	c Lawry b Mallett	0	c Lawry b Connolly	0
G.A. Chevalier	c Chappell b Mallett	0	not out	0
Extras	(B 2, LB 5, NB 2)	9	(B 1, LB 4, NB 2)	7
Total		**382**		**232**

AUSTRALIA

Batsman	Dismissal 1	R	Dismissal 2	R
K.R. Stackpole	c Barlow b Procter	19	c Barlow b Goddard	29
W.M. Lawry*	b P.M. Pollock	2	lbw b Procter	83
I.M. Chappell	c Chevalier b P.M. Pollock	0	b Chevalier	13
K.D. Walters	c Irvine b P.M. Pollock	73	c Irvine b Procter	4
I.R. Redpath	c Barlow b Procter	0	not out	47
A.P. Sheahan	c Barlow b Chevalier	8	b Seymour	16
H.B. Taber†	lbw b Seymour	11	lbw b Procter	15
G.D. McKenzie	c R.G. Pollock b P.M. Pollock	5	(9) c R.G. Pollock b Chevalier	19
A.A. Mallett	c Goddard b Chevalier	19	(8) c P.M. Pollock b Procter	5
J.W. Gleeson	b Goddard	17	b Richards	10
A.N. Connolly	not out	0	b Chevalier	25
Extras	(B 1, NB 9)	10	(B 7, LB 2, NB 5)	14
Total		**164**		**280**

AUSTRALIA	O	M	R	W	O	M	R	W
McKenzie	30	8	74	0	8	0	29	0
Connolly	29	12	62	2	26	10	47	5
Walters	8	1	19	2				
Gleeson	45	17	92	1	30	11	70	4
Mallett	55·1	16	126	5	32	10	79	1
SOUTH AFRICA								
Procter	12	4	30	2	17	4	47	4
P.M. Pollock	12	4	20	4	18	12	19	0
Goddard	19·4	9	29	1	32	12	66	1
Chevalier	11	2	32	2	31·1	9	68	3
Seymour	11	2	28	1	19	6	40	1
Barlow	1	0	15	0	6	2	14	0
Richards					6	1	12	1

FALL OF WICKETS

	SA	A	SA	A
Wkt	1st	1st	2nd	2nd
1st	21	5	52	75
2nd	96	5	91	131
3rd	111	38	91	131
4th	187	39	121	136
5th	281	58	147	161
6th	323	92	171	188
7th	363	123	187	198
8th	364	134	222	228
9th	374	164	226	239
10th	382	164	232	280

Umpires: G. Goldman (2) and W.W. Wade (1).

Close: 1st day – SA(1) 254-4 (Barlow 66, Irvine 31); 2nd – A(1) 108-6 (Walters 58, McKenzie 0); 3rd – SA(2) 179-6 (Procter 23, Gamsy 0); 4th – A(2) 181-5 (Redpath 19, Taber 9).

SOUTH AFRICA v AUSTRALIA 1969–70 (2nd Test)

Played at Kingsmead, Durban, on 5, 6, 7, 9 February.
Toss: South Africa.   Result: SOUTH AFRICA won by an innings and 129 runs.
Debuts: South Africa – A.J. Traicos.

South Africa's first victory by an innings margin against Australia was achieved with over a day to spare. It remains their largest margin of victory in a home Test. South Africa's total is their highest in all Test cricket. Graeme Pollock batted for 417 minutes; his innings of 274 included a five and 43 fours and is the highest score for South Africa in Test matches (beating D.J. McGlew's 255 not out in *Test No. 370*). It is also the record score by any batsman in a Test in South Africa. He completed 2,000 runs in Tests and took 307 minutes to record his second double century for South Africa. His partnership of 200 with Lance is South Africa's highest for the sixth wicket in any Test. Richards reached his first Test hundred off 116 balls. The highest innings of his tragically brief Test career involved only 164 deliveries and produced a six and 20 fours.

SOUTH AFRICA

B.A. Richards	b Freeman	140
T.L. Goddard	c Lawry b Gleeson	17
A. Bacher*	b Connolly	9
R.G. Pollock	c and b Stackpole	274
E.J. Barlow	lbw b Freeman	1
B.L. Irvine	b Gleeson	13
H.R. Lance	st Taber b Gleeson	61
M.J. Procter	c Connolly b Stackpole	32
D. Gamsy†	lbw b Connolly	7
P.M. Pollock	not out	36
A.J. Traicos	not out	5
Extras	(B 1, LB 3, NB 23)	27
Total	(9 wickets declared)	**622**

AUSTRALIA

K.R. Stackpole	c Gamsy b Goddard	27	lbw b Traicos		71
W.M. Lawry*	lbw b Barlow	15	c Gamsy b Goddard		14
I.M. Chappell	c Gamsy b Barlow	0	c Gamsy b P.M. Pollock		14
K.D. Walters	c Traicos b Barlow	4	c R.G. Pollock b Traicos		74
I.R. Redpath	c Richards b Procter	4	not out		74
A.P. Sheahan	c Traicos b Goddard	62	c Barlow b Procter		4
E.W. Freeman	c Traicos b P.M. Pollock	5	b Barlow		18
H.B. Taber†	c and b P.M. Pollock	6	c Lance b Barlow		0
G.D. McKenzie	c Traicos b Procter	1	lbw b Barlow		4
J.W. Gleeson	not out	4	c Gamsy b Procter		24
A.N. Connolly	c Bacher b Traicos	14	lbw b Procter		0
Extras	(LB 5, NB 10)	15	(B 9, LB 8, NB 22)		39
Total		**157**			**336**

AUSTRALIA	O	M	R	W	O	M	R	W
McKenzie	25·5	3	92	0				
Connolly	33	7	104	2				
Freeman	28	4	120	2				
Gleeson	51	9	160	3				
Walters	9	0	44	0				
Stackpole	21	2	75	2				
SOUTH AFRICA								
Procter	11	2	39	2	18·5	5	62	3
P.M. Pollock	10	3	31	2	21·3	4	45	1
Goddard	7	4	10	2	17	7	30	1
Barlow	10	3	24	3	31	10	63	3
Traicos	8·2	3	27	1	30	8	70	2
Lance	2	0	11	0	7	4	11	0
Richards					3	1	8	0
R.G. Pollock					3	1	8	0

FALL OF WICKETS			
	SA	A	A
Wkt	1st	1st	2nd
1st	88	44	65
2nd	126	44	83
3rd	229	44	151
4th	231	48	208
5th	281	56	222
6th	481	79	264
7th	558	100	264
8th	575	114	268
9th	580	139	336
10th	–	157	336

Umpires: C.M.P. Coetzee (1) and J.G. Draper (5).

Close: 1st day – SA(1) 386-5 (R.G. Pollock 160, Lance 14); 2nd – A(1) 48-4 (Redpath 0, Sheahan 0); 3rd – A(2) 100-2 (Stackpole 55, Walters 8).

Test No. 672/52

SOUTH AFRICA v AUSTRALIA 1969–70 (3rd Test)

Played at New Wanderers, Johannesburg, on 19, 20, 21, 23, 24 February.
Toss: South Africa.   Result: SOUTH AFRICA won by 307 runs.
Debuts: Nil.

South Africa's victory remained their record by a runs margin in all Tests for just one match. Freeman was run out when his runner, Sheahan, attempted an impossible second run. Goddard took his 123rd wicket with his final ball in Test cricket; because he had announced that he would not be available for the scheduled tour of England, he was dropped for the final Test.

SOUTH AFRICA

B.A. Richards	c Taber b Connolly	65		c Taber b Mayne	35
T.L. Goddard	c Walters b Connolly	6	(9)	c Taber b Connolly	2
A. Bacher*	lbw b Mayne	30		b Connolly	15
R.G. Pollock	c Taber b Freeman	52		b Freeman	87
E.J. Barlow	st Taber b Gleeson	6	(2)	c Lawry b Gleeson	110
B.L. Irvine	c Stackpole b Gleeson	79	(5)	c Lawry b Gleeson	73
H.R. Lance	run out	8		lbw b Gleeson	30
D.T. Lindsay†	c Stackpole b Gleeson	0	(6)	b Gleeson	6
M.J. Procter	c Chappell b Walters	22	(8)	not out	36
P.M. Pollock	c Taber b Walters	0		c Taber b Gleeson	1
A.J. Traicos	not out	1		lbw b Mayne	0
Extras	(LB 7, W 1, NB 2)	10		(LB 8, NB 5)	13
Total		**279**			**408**

AUSTRALIA

K.R. Stackpole	c Lindsay b Procter	5	c Lindsay b Procter	1
W.M. Lawry*	c Lindsay b P.M. Pollock	1	c R.G. Pollock b Barlow	17
I.R. Redpath	lbw b Procter	0	b Goddard	66
I.M. Chappell	c Lance b Goddard	34	b Barlow	0
K.D. Walters	c Procter b P.M. Pollock	64	b Procter	15
A.P. Sheahan	b P.M. Pollock	44	b Procter	0
E.W. Freeman	c Goddard b P.M. Pollock	10	run out	18
L.C. Mayne	run out	0	c Procter b Traicos	2
H.B. Taber†	not out	26	not out	18
J.W. Gleeson	b Procter	0	b Goddard	0
A.N. Connolly	c Richards b P.M. Pollock	3	c Richards b Goddard	36
Extras	(LB 4, W 1, NB 10)	15	(W 2, NB 3)	5
Total		**202**		**178**

AUSTRALIA	O	M	R	W	O	M	R	W		FALL OF WICKETS			
Mayne	26	5	83	1	18·3	1	77	2		SA	A	SA	A
Connolly	30	10	49	2	32	6	83	2	Wkt	1st	1st	2nd	2nd
Freeman	20	4	60	1	19	4	77	1	1st	56	7	76	11
Gleeson	21·4	2	61	3	45	15	125	5	2nd	85	7	102	43
Walters	5	1	16	2	7	1	33	0	3rd	141	12	241	43
SOUTH AFRICA									4th	162	109	269	73
									5th	170	112	275	73
Procter	21	5	48	3	14	8	24	3	6th	194	139	349	122
P.M. Pollock	23·2	10	39	5	15	4	56	0	7th	194	140	372	124
Barlow	12	5	31	0	7	3	17	2	8th	238	194	375	126
Goddard	26	10	41	1	24·5	16	27	3	9th	246	195	380	126
Lance	3	1	5	0					10th	279	202	408	178
Traicos	6	3	23	0	17	4	49	1					

Umpires: C.M.P. Coetzee (2) and A.J. Warner (1).

Close: 1st day – SA(1) 191-5 (Irvine 17, Lance 8); 2nd – A(1) 122-5 (Sheahan 3, Freeman 2); 3rd – SA(2) 162-2 (Barlow 64, R.G. Pollock 46); 4th – A(2) 88-5 (Redpath 50, Freeman 0).

SOUTH AFRICA v AUSTRALIA 1969–70 (4th Test)

Played at St George's Park, Port Elizabeth, on 5, 6, 7, 9, 10 March.
Toss: South Africa.   Result: SOUTH AFRICA won by 323 runs.
Debuts: Nil.

South Africa won the last of their 172 Test matches prior to excommunication by their record margin of runs. It was the first time that they had won every match in a rubber of more than two matches and the first time they had won four matches in a rubber against Australia. Connolly took his 100th Test wicket when he dismissed Traicos. Richards (508 runs, average 72·57) is the only batsman to score 500 runs in his first rubber for South Africa. Peter Pollock pulled a hamstring muscle and was unable to complete his last over in Test cricket. Bacher's highest Test innings ended when his foot slipped and removed a bail as he played forward; his dismissal gave McKenzie his only wicket of the rubber at a cost of 333 runs. Lindsay conceded no byes in the last four Tests of his career. South Africa's Test cricket ended on the ground where it began, with the Union's initial first-class match, almost exactly 81 years earlier.

SOUTH AFRICA

B.A. Richards	c Taber b Connolly	81	c Chappell b Mayne		126
E.J. Barlow	c McKenzie b Connolly	73	c Stackpole b Walters		27
A. Bacher*	run out	17	hit wkt b McKenzie		73
R.G. Pollock	c Taber b Gleeson	1	b Mayne		4
B.L. Irvine	c Redpath b Gleeson	25	c Gleeson b Mayne		102
D.T. Lindsay†	c Taber b Connolly	43	b Connolly		60
H.R. Lance	b Mayne	21	run out		19
M.J. Procter	c Taber b Connolly	26	c Mayne b Gleeson		23
P.M. Pollock	not out	4	not out		7
P.H.J. Trimborn	b Connolly	0			
A.J. Traicos	c Taber b Connolly	2			
Extras	(B 4, LB 3, NB 11)	18	(LB 9, NB 20)		29
Total		**311**	(8 wickets declared)		**470**

AUSTRALIA

K.R. Stackpole	c Barlow b Procter	15	b Procter		20
W.M. Lawry*	c Lindsay b Lance	18	c Lindsay b Barlow		43
I.R. Redpath	c Trimborn b Procter	55	c Barlow b Procter		37
I.M. Chappell	c Procter b Trimborn	17	c Trimborn b Barlow		14
K.D. Walters	c Lindsay b Trimborn	1	b Procter		23
A.P. Sheahan	c Procter b P.M. Pollock	67	c Lindsay b Trimborn		46
H.B. Taber†	lbw b Barlow	3	not out		30
L.C. Mayne	b Procter	13	c Lindsay b Procter		12
G.D. McKenzie	c Barlow b P.M. Pollock	0	c Lindsay b Procter		2
J.W. Gleeson	c Lindsay b P.M. Pollock	8	b Procter		0
A.N. Connolly	not out	2	c Bacher b Trimborn		3
Extras	(LB 3, W 1, NB 9)	13	(LB 2, NB 14)		16
Total		**212**			**246**

AUSTRALIA	O	M	R	W	O	M	R	W		FALL OF WICKETS			
McKenzie	27	7	66	0	20	3	72	1			SA	A	SA	A
Mayne	27	4	71	1	29	6	83	3	Wkt	1st	1st	2nd	2nd
Connolly	28·2	9	47	6	36	3	130	1	1st	157	27	73	22
Walters	9	1	19	0	5	2	14	1	2nd	158	46	199	98
Gleeson	32	9	90	2	30·2	5	142	1	3rd	159	80	213	116
Redpath					1	1	0	0	4th	183	82	279	130
									5th	208	152	367	189
SOUTH AFRICA									6th	259	177	440	207
P.M. Pollock	14	2	46	3	1·1	0	2	0	7th	294	191	440	234
Procter	25·1	11	30	3	24	11	73	6	8th	305	195	470	243
Barlow	9	1	27	1	18	3	66	2	9th	305	208	–	243
Lance	8	1	32	1	10	4	18	0	10th	311	212	–	246
Trimborn	17	1	47	2	20·2	4	44	2					
Traicos	3	1	17	0	14	5	21	0					
Richards					3	1	6	0					

Umpires: C.M.P. Coetzee (3) and A.J. Warner (2).

Close: 1st day – SA(1) 249-5 (Lindsay 23, Lance 17); 2nd – A(1) 189-6 (Sheahan 66, Mayne 2); 3rd – SA(2) 235-3 (Bacher 52, Irvine 9); 4th – A(2) 134-4 (Walters 7, Sheahan 4).

AUSTRALIA v ENGLAND 1970–71 (1st Test)

Played at Woolloongabba, Brisbane, on 27, 28, 29 November, 1, 2 December.
Toss: Australia.   Result: MATCH DRAWN.
Debuts: Australia – T.J. Jenner, R.W. Marsh, A.L. Thomson; England – B.W. Luckhurst,
K. Shuttleworth.

Stackpole, favoured by a run out decision when he had scored 18, became the first to score a double century in an Australia v England Test at Brisbane; only Bradman (twice) has played a higher innings there. Stackpole batted for 440 minutes and hit a six and 25 fours. Australia's last seven first innings wickets fell for 15 runs in 47 minutes – Underwood claiming those of Redpath, Sheahan and Walters in seven balls without conceding a run. On the third day, Cowdrey passed W.R. Hammond's world Test record aggregate of 7,249 runs when he had scored 22.

AUSTRALIA

W.M. Lawry*	c Knott b Snow	4	c Snow b Fletcher		84
K.R. Stackpole	c Knott b Snow	207	c Knott b Shuttleworth		8
I.M. Chappell	run out	59	st Knott b Illingworth		10
K.D. Walters	b Underwood	112	c Luckhurst b Snow		7
I.R. Redpath	c Illingworth b Underwood	22	c and b Underwood		28
A.P. Sheahan	c Knott b Underwood	0	c Shuttleworth b Snow		36
R.W. Marsh†	b Snow	9	b Shuttleworth		14
T.J. Jenner	c Cowdrey b Snow	0	c Boycott b Shuttleworth		2
G.D. McKenzie	not out	3	b Shuttleworth		1
J.W. Gleeson	c Cowdrey b Snow	0	b Shuttleworth		6
A.L. Thomson	b Snow	0	not out		4
Extras	(B 7, LB 4, NB 6)	17	(B 4, LB 3, NB 7)		14
Total		**433**			**214**

ENGLAND

G. Boycott	c Marsh b Gleeson	37	c and b Jenner		16
B.W. Luckhurst	run out	74	not out		20
A.P.E. Knott†	c Lawry b Walters	73			
J.H. Edrich	c Chappell b Jenner	79			
M.C. Cowdrey	c Chappell b Gleeson	28			
K.W.R. Fletcher	c Marsh b McKenzie	34			
B.L. D'Oliveira	c Sheahan b McKenzie	57			
R. Illingworth*	c Marsh b Thomson	8			
J.A. Snow	c Marsh b Walters	34			
D.L. Underwood	not out	2			
K. Shuttleworth	c Lawry b Walters	7			
Extras	(B 2, LB 7, NB 22)	31	(LB 3)		3
Total		**464**	(1 wicket)		**39**

ENGLAND	O	M	R	W	O	M	R	W
Snow	32·3	6	114	6	20	3	48	2
Shuttleworth	27	6	81	0	17·5	2	47	5
D'Oliveira	16	2	63	0	7	5	7	0
Illingworth	11	1	47	0	18	11	19	1
Underwood	28	6	101	3	20	10	23	1
Cowdrey	1	0	10	0	2	0	8	0
Fletcher					9	1	48	1
AUSTRALIA								
McKenzie	28	5	90	2	3	0	6	0
Thomson	43	8	136	1	4	0	20	0
Gleeson	42	15	97	2				
Jenner	24	5	86	1	4·6	2	9	1
Stackpole	4	0	12	0	4	3	1	0
Walters	5·5	0	12	3				

FALL OF WICKETS

	A	E	A	E
Wkt	1st	1st	2nd	2nd
1st	12	92	30	39
2nd	163	136	47	–
3rd	372	245	64	–
4th	418	284	137	–
5th	418	336	152	–
6th	421	346	193	–
7th	422	371	199	–
8th	433	449	201	–
9th	433	456	208	–
10th	433	464	214	–

Umpires: T.F. Brooks (1) and L.P. Rowan (21).

Close: 1st day – A(1) 308-2 (Stackpole 175, Walters 55); 2nd – E(1) 99-1 (Luckhurst 52, Knott 6); 3rd – E(1) 365-6 (D'Oliveira 11, Illingworth 7); 4th – A(2) 56-2 (Lawry 29, Walters 3).

AUSTRALIA v ENGLAND 1970–71 (2nd Test)

Played at W.A.C.A. Ground, Perth, on 11, 12, 13, 15, 16 December.
Toss: Australia.   Result: MATCH DRAWN.
Debuts: Australia – G.S. Chappell; England – P. Lever.

Perth's first Test match attracted nearly 85,000 spectators and produced receipts approaching £50,000. Luckhurst, his thumb damaged early in his innings, scored a hundred in his second Test. Greg Chappell became the sixth Australian to score a hundred in his first Test innings. When Australia were asked to score 245 runs in 145 minutes, Lawry managed only six runs in the first 68 minutes; the second of them was his 5,000th in Test cricket and the third was his 2,000th against England.

ENGLAND

G. Boycott	c McKenzie b Gleeson	70	st Marsh b Gleeson		50
B.W. Luckhurst	b McKenzie	131	c Stackpole b Walters		19
J.H. Edrich	run out	47	not out		115
A.P.E. Knott†	c Stackpole b Thomson	24	(8) not out		30
K.W.R. Fletcher	b Walters	22	(4) lbw b Gleeson		0
M.C. Cowdrey	c and b G.S. Chappell	40	(5) c Marsh b Thomson		1
B.L. D'Oliveira	c Stackpole b Thomson	8	(6) b Gleeson		31
R. Illingworth*	b McKenzie	34	(7) c Marsh b Stackpole		29
J.A. Snow	not out	4			
K. Shuttleworth	b McKenzie	2			
P. Lever	b McKenzie	2			
Extras	(LB 8, W 1, NB 4)	13	(B 2, LB 3, NB 7)		12
Total		**397**	(6 wickets declared)		**287**

AUSTRALIA

W.M. Lawry*	c Illingworth b Snow	0	not out		38
K.R. Stackpole	c Lever b Snow	5	c sub (J.H. Hampshire) b Snow		0
I.M. Chappell	c Knott b Snow	50	c sub (J.H. Hampshire) b Snow		17
K.D. Walters	c Knott b Lever	7	b Lever		8
I.R. Redpath	c and b Illingworth	171	not out		26
A.P. Sheahan	run out	2			
G.S. Chappell	c Luckhurst b Shuttleworth	108			
R.W. Marsh†	c D'Oliveira b Shuttleworth	44			
G.D. McKenzie	c Lever b D'Oliveira	7			
J.W. Gleeson	c Knott b Snow	15			
A.L. Thomson	not out	12			
Extras	(B 5, LB 4, NB 10)	19	(B 4, LB 4, NB 3)		11
Total		**440**	(3 wickets)		**100**

AUSTRALIA	O	M	R	W	O	M	R	W
McKenzie	31·4	4	66	4	18	2	50	0
Thomson	24	4	118	2	25	3	71	1
G.S. Chappell	24	4	54	1	4	1	17	0
Gleeson	32	10	78	1	32	11	68	3
Walters	11	1	35	1	7	1	26	1
Stackpole	11	2	33	0	15	3	43	1
ENGLAND								
Snow	33·5	3	143	4	9	4	17	2
Shuttleworth	28	4	105	2	3	1	9	0
Lever	21	3	78	1	5	2	10	1
D'Oliveira	17	1	41	1	4	2	5	0
Illingworth	13	2	43	1	4	2	12	0
Boycott	1	0	7	0				
Fletcher	1	0	4	0	4	0	18	0
Cowdrey					3	0	18	0

FALL OF WICKETS

	E	A	E	A
Wkt	1st	1st	2nd	2nd
1st	171	5	60	0
2nd	243	8	98	20
3rd	281	17	98	40
4th	291	105	101	–
5th	310	107	152	–
6th	327	326	209	–
7th	389	393	–	–
8th	389	408	–	–
9th	393	426	–	–
10th	397	440	–	–

Umpires: T.F. Brooks (2) and L.P. Rowan (22).

Close: 1st day – E(1) 257-2 (Edrich 39, Knott 6); 2nd – A(1) 84-3 (I.M. Chappell 43, Redpath 24); 3rd – A(1) 355-6 (Redpath 159, Marsh 6); 4th – E(2) 137-4 (Edrich 38, D'Oliveira 22).

The 3rd Test at Melbourne Cricket Ground, scheduled for 31 December, 1, 2, 4, 5 January was abandoned on the third day without a ball being bowled (see page 816).

AUSTRALIA v ENGLAND 1970–71 (4th Test)

Played at Sydney Cricket Ground on 9, 10, 11, 13, 14 January.
Toss: England.   Result: ENGLAND won by 299 runs.
Debuts: England – R.G.D. Willis.

England achieved their largest victory against Australia by a runs margin since 1936-37 (*Test No. 255*). Lawry carried his bat through a completed Test innings – the first Australian to do so at Sydney and the second after W.M. Woodfull to achieve this feat twice. McKenzie, playing in the last of his 60 Tests, took his 246th wicket before being hit in the face by a short ball from Snow and retiring at 107. Willis, a replacement for the injured Alan Ward, took the first of his 325 Test wickets after beginning his quest for the world record of 'not out' innings.

ENGLAND

G. Boycott	c Gleeson b Connolly	77	not out		142
B.W. Luckhurst	lbw b Gleeson	38	c I.M. Chappell b McKenzie		5
J.H. Edrich	c Gleeson b G.S. Chappell	55	run out		12
K.W.R. Fletcher	c Walters b Mallett	23	c Stackpole b Mallett		8
B.L. D'Oliveira	c Connolly b Mallett	0	c I.M. Chappell b G.S. Chappell		56
R. Illingworth*	b Gleeson	25	st Marsh b Mallett		53
A.P.E. Knott†	st Marsh b Mallett	6	not out		21
J.A. Snow	c Lawry b Gleeson	37			
P. Lever	c Connolly b Mallett	36			
D.L. Underwood	c G.S. Chappell b Gleeson	0			
R.G.D. Willis	not out	15			
Extras	(B 5, LB 2, W 1, NB 12)	20	(B 9, LB 4, NB 9)		22
Total		**332**	(5 wickets declared)		**319**

AUSTRALIA

W.M. Lawry*	c Edrich b Lever	9	not out		60
I.M. Chappell	c Underwood b Snow	12	c D'Oliveira b Snow		0
I.R. Redpath	c Fletcher b D'Oliveira	64	c Edrich b Snow		6
K.D. Walters	c Luckhurst b Illingworth	55	c Knott b Lever		3
G.S. Chappell	c and b Underwood	15	b Snow		2
K.R. Stackpole	c Boycott b Underwood	33	c Lever b Snow		30
R.W. Marsh†	c D'Oliveira b Underwood	8	c Willis b Snow		0
A.A. Mallett	b Underwood	4	c Knott b Willis		6
G.D. McKenzie	not out	11	retired hurt		6
J.W. Gleeson	c Fletcher b D'Oliveira	0	b Snow		0
A.N. Connolly	b Lever	14	c Knott b Snow		0
Extras	(NB 11)	11	(B 2, NB 1)		3
Total		**236**			**116**

AUSTRALIA	O	M	R	W	O	M	R	W		FALL OF WICKETS			
McKenzie	15	3	74	0	15	0	65	1		E	A	E	A
Connolly	13	2	43	1	14	1	38	0	*Wkt*	*1st*	*1st*	*2nd*	*2nd*
Gleeson	29	7	83	4	23	4	54	0	1st	116	14	7	1
G.S. Chappell	11	4	30	1	15	5	24	1	2nd	130	38	35	11
Mallett	16·7	5	40	4	19	1	85	2	3rd	201	137	48	14
Walters	3	1	11	0	2	0	14	0	4th	205	160	181	21
Stackpole	7	2	31	0	6	1	17	0	5th	208	189	276	66
									6th	219	199	–	66
ENGLAND									7th	262	208	–	86
Snow	14	6	23	1	17·5	5	40	7	8th	291	208	–	116
Willis	9	2	26	0	3	2	1	1	9th	291	219	–	116
Lever	8·6	1	31	2	11	1	24	1	10th	332	236	–	–
Underwood	22	7	66	4	8	2	17	0					
Illingworth	14	3	59	1	9	5	9	0					
D'Oliveira	9	2	20	2	7	3	16	0					
Fletcher					1	0	6	0					

Umpires: T.F. Brooks (3) and L.P. Rowan (23).

Close: 1st day – E(1) 267-7 (Snow 25, Lever 1); 2nd – A(1) 189-4 (Redpath 64, Stackpole 26); 3rd – E(2) 178-3 (Boycott 84, D'Oliveira 56); 4th – A(2) 64-4 (Lawry 24, Stackpole 28).

AUSTRALIA v ENGLAND 1970–71 (5th Test)

Played at Melbourne Cricket Ground on 21, 22, 23, 25, 26 January.
Toss: Australia.   Result: MATCH DRAWN.
Debuts: Australia – J.R.F. Duncan, K.J. O'Keeffe.

This additional Test match was arranged after the 3rd Test had been abandoned without a ball being bowled; it replaced the touring team's four-day return match with Victoria and a one-day game at Euroa. On the first day, when England missed six catches, Lawry retired at 86 when 38, to have a finger X-rayed; he returned when the second wicket fell. Ian Chappell's second hundred took 57 minutes and was greeted by an invasion of many hundreds, whose bounty included the caps of Chappell and Cowdrey plus one stump. Lawry's declaration temporarily deprived Marsh of the opportunity of becoming the first Australian wicket-keeper to score a Test hundred. Luckhurst scored his second hundred of the rubber despite fracturing his left little finger early in his innings. The third day produced receipts of £25,070 – then a world record. With Luckhurst and D'Oliveira injured, England ignored the possibility of scoring 271 runs in four hours.

AUSTRALIA

K.R. Stackpole	c Lever b D'Oliveira	30	c Knott b Willis		18
W.M. Lawry*	c Snow b Willis	56	c sub (K. Shuttleworth) b Snow		42
I.M. Chappell	c Luckhurst b Snow	111	b Underwood		30
I.R. Redpath	b Snow	72	c Knott b Snow		5
K.D. Walters	b Underwood	55	not out		39
G.S. Chappell	c Edrich b Willis	3	not out		20
R.W. Marsh†	not out	92			
K.J. O'Keeffe	c Luckhurst b Illingworth	27			
J.W. Gleeson	c Cowdrey b Willis	5			
J.R.F. Duncan	c Edrich b Illingworth	3			
A.L. Thomson	not out	0			
Extras	(B 10, LB 17, NB 12)	39	(B 8, LB 3, NB 4)		15
Total	(9 wickets declared)	**493**	(4 wickets declared)		**169**

ENGLAND

G. Boycott	c Redpath b Thomson	12	not out		76
B.W. Luckhurst	b Walters	109			
J.H. Edrich	c Marsh b Thomson	9	(2) not out		74
M.C. Cowdrey	c and b Gleeson	13			
B.L. D'Oliveira	c Marsh b Thomson	117			
R. Illingworth*	c Redpath b Gleeson	41			
A.P.E. Knott†	lbw b Stackpole	19			
J.A. Snow	b I.M. Chappell	1			
P. Lever	run out	19			
D.L. Underwood	c and b Gleeson	5			
R.G.D. Willis	not out	5			
Extras	(B 17, LB 14, NB 11)	42	(B 1, LB 8, NB 2)		11
Total		**392**	(0 wickets)		**161**

ENGLAND	O	M	R	W	O	M	R	W
Snow	29	6	94	2	12	4	21	2
Lever	25	6	79	0	12	1	53	0
D'Oliveira	22	6	71	1				
Willis	20	5	73	3	10	1	42	1
Underwood	19	4	78	1	12	0	38	1
Illingworth	13	0	59	2				
AUSTRALIA								
Thomson	34	5	110	3	11	5	26	0
Duncan	14	4	30	0				
G.S. Chappell	8	0	21	0	5	0	19	0
O'Keeffe	31	11	71	0	19	3	45	0
Gleeson	25	7	60	3	3	1	18	0
Stackpole	17·5	4	41	1	13	2	28	0
Walters	5	2	7	1	7	1	14	0
I.M. Chappell	3	0	10	1				

FALL OF WICKETS

Wkt	A 1st	E 1st	A 2nd	E 2nd
1st	64	40	51	–
2nd	266	64	84	–
3rd	269	88	91	–
4th	310	228	132	–
5th	314	306	–	–
6th	374	340	–	–
7th	471	354	–	–
8th	477	362	–	–
9th	480	379	–	–
10th	–	392	–	–

Umpires: M.G. O'Connell (1) and L.P. Rowan (24).

Close: 1st day – A(1) 260-1 (I.M. Chappell 105, Redpath 70); 2nd – E(1) 28-0 (Boycott 10, Luckhurst 17); 3rd – E(1) 258-4 (D'Oliveira 72, Illingworth 16); 4th – A(2) 70-1 (Lawry 39, I.M. Chappell 4).

AUSTRALIA v ENGLAND 1970–71 (6th Test)

Played at Adelaide Oval on 29, 30 January, 1, 2, 3 February.
Toss: England.   Result: MATCH DRAWN.
Debuts: Australia – D.K. Lillee.

After deciding not to enforce the follow-on, England set Australia to score 469 runs in 500 minutes. Boycott and Edrich became the third opening pair to share century partnerships in both innings of a Test against Australia; the others were J.B. Hobbs and H. Sutcliffe, and L. Hutton and C. Washbrook (twice). Lillee took five wickets in his first Test innings.

ENGLAND

G. Boycott	run out	58	not out	119
J.H. Edrich	c Stackpole b Lillee	130	b Thomson	40
K.W.R. Fletcher	b Thomson	80	b Gleeson	5
A.P.E. Knott†	c Redpath b Lillee	7		
B.L. D'Oliveira	c Marsh b G.S. Chappell	47	(4) c Walters b Thomson	5
J.H. Hampshire	c Lillee b G.S. Chappell	55	(5) lbw b Thomson	3
R. Illingworth*	b Lillee	24	(6) not out	48
J.A. Snow	b Lillee	38		
P. Lever	b Thomson	5		
D.L. Underwood	not out	1		
R.G.D. Willis	c Walters b Lillee	4		
Extras	(B 1, LB 5, W 4, NB 11)	21	(LB 4, W 1, NB 8)	13
Total		**470**	(4 wickets declared)	**233**

AUSTRALIA

K.R. Stackpole	b Underwood	87	b Snow	136
W.M. Lawry*	c Knott b Snow	10	c Knott b Willis	21
I.M. Chappell	c Knott b Lever	28	c Willis b Underwood	104
I.R. Redpath	c Lever b Illingworth	9	not out	21
K.D. Walters	c Knott b Lever	8	not out	36
G.S. Chappell	c Edrich b Lever	0		
R.W. Marsh†	c Knott b Willis	28		
A.A. Mallett	c Illingworth b Snow	28		
J.W. Gleeson	c Boycott b Willis	16		
D.K. Lillee	c Boycott b Lever	10		
A.L. Thomson	not out	6		
Extras	(LB 2, NB 3)	5	(B 2, LB 3, NB 5)	10
Total		**235**	(3 wickets)	**328**

AUSTRALIA	O	M	R	W	O	M	R	W
Thomson	29·7	6	94	2	19	2	79	3
Lillee	28·3	0	84	5	7	0	40	0
Walters	9	2	29	0	3	0	5	0
G.S. Chappell	18	1	54	2	5	0	27	0
Gleeson	19	1	78	0	16	1	69	1
Mallett	20	1	63	0	1	1	0	0
Stackpole	12	2	47	0				
ENGLAND								
Snow	21	4	73	2	17	3	60	1
Lever	17·1	2	49	4	17	4	49	0
Underwood	21	6	45	1	35	7	85	1
Willis	12	3	49	2	13	1	48	1
Illingworth	5	2	14	1	14	7	32	0
D'Oliveira					15	4	28	0
Fletcher					4	0	16	0

FALL OF WICKETS

	E	A	E	A
Wkt	1st	1st	2nd	2nd
1st	107	61	103	65
2nd	276	117	128	267
3rd	289	131	143	271
4th	289	141	151	–
5th	385	145	–	–
6th	402	163	–	–
7th	458	180	–	–
8th	465	219	–	–
9th	465	221	–	–
10th	470	235	–	–

Umpires: T.F. Brooks (4) and M.G. O'Connell (2).

Close: 1st day – E(1) 276-2 (Fletcher 75, Knott 0); 2nd – A(1) 50-0 (Stackpole 41, Lawry 8); 3rd – E(2) 47-0 (Boycott 27, Edrich 18); 4th – A (2) 104-1 (Stackpole 65, I.M. Chappell 16).

AUSTRALIA v ENGLAND 1970–71 (7th Test)

Played at Sydney Cricket Ground on 12, 13, 14, 16, 17 February.
Toss: Australia.   Result: ENGLAND won by 62 runs.
Debuts: Australia – A.R. Dell, K.H. Eastwood.

England regained the Ashes at 12.36 pm on the fifth day of this six-day Test after the longest rubber in Test history. Chappell emulated P.S. McDonnell, G. Giffen and R.B. Simpson when he invited the opposition to bat in his first Test as Australia's captain. Crowd disturbances around 5.00 pm on the second day, after Snow had hit Jenner on the head with a short-pitched ball, led to Illingworth leading the England team off the field. They returned when the playing area had been cleared of missiles. Jenner retired when 8, at 195, and resumed at 235. In the second innings Snow fractured and dislocated his right little finger when he collided with the fencing in trying to catch Stackpole. Knott's total of 24 dismissals remains the England record for any rubber. No 'lbw' appeal was upheld against an Australian batsman in the entire rubber.

ENGLAND

J.H. Edrich	c G.S. Chappell b Dell	30	c I.M. Chappell b O'Keeffe	57
B.W. Luckhurst	c Redpath b Walters	0	c Lillee b O'Keeffe	59
K.W.R. Fletcher	c Stackpole b O'Keeffe	33	c Stackpole b Eastwood	20
J.H. Hampshire	c Marsh b Lillee	10	c I.M. Chappell b O'Keeffe	24
B.L. D'Oliveira	b Dell	1	c I.M. Chappell b Lillee	47
R. Illingworth*	b Jenner	42	lbw b Lillee	29
A.P.E. Knott†	c Stackpole b O'Keeffe	27	b Dell	15
J.A. Snow	b Jenner	7	c Stackpole b Dell	20
P. Lever	c Jenner b O'Keeffe	4	c Redpath b Jenner	17
D.L. Underwood	not out	8	c Marsh b Dell	0
R.G.D. Willis	b Jenner	11	not out	2
Extras	(B 4, LB 4, W 1, NB 2)	11	(B 3, LB 3, NB 6)	12
Total		**184**		**302**

AUSTRALIA

K.H. Eastwood	c Knott b Lever	5	b Snow	0
K.R. Stackpole	b Snow	6	b Illingworth	67
R.W. Marsh†	c Willis b Lever	4	(7) b Underwood	16
I.M. Chappell*	b Willis	25	(3) c Knott b Lever	6
I.R. Redpath	c and b Underwood	59	(4) c Hampshire b Illingworth	14
K.D. Walters	st Knott b Underwood	42	(5) c D'Oliveira b Willis	1
G.S. Chappell	b Willis	65	(6) st Knott b Illingworth	30
K.J. O'Keeffe	c Knott b Illingworth	3	c sub(‡) b D'Oliveira	12
T.J. Jenner	b Lever	30	c Fletcher b Underwood	4
D.K. Lillee	c Knott b Willis	6	c Hampshire b D'Oliveira	0
A.R. Dell	not out	3	not out	3
Extras	(LB 5, W 1, NB 10)	16	(B 2, NB 5)	7
Total		**264**		**160**

AUSTRALIA	O	M	R	W	O	M	R	W	FALL OF WICKETS				
Lillee	13	5	32	1	14	0	43	2		E	A	E	A
Dell	16	8	32	2	26·7	3	65	3	*Wkt*	*1st*	*1st*	*2nd*	*2nd*
Walters	4	0	10	1	5	0	18	0	1st	5	11	94	0
G.S. Chappell	3	0	9	0					2nd	60	13	130	22
Jenner	16	3	42	3	21	5	39	1	3rd	68	32	158	71
O'Keeffe	24	8	48	3	26	8	96	3	4th	69	66	165	82
Eastwood					5	0	21	1	5th	98	147	234	96
Stackpole					3	1	8	0	6th	145	162	251	131
ENGLAND									7th	156	178	276	142
Snow	18	2	68	1	2	1	7	1	8th	165	235	298	154
Lever	14·6	3	43	3	12	2	23	1	9th	165	239	299	154
D'Oliveira	12	2	24	0	5	1	15	2	10th	184	264	302	160
Willis	12	1	58	3	9	1	32	1					
Underwood	16	3	39	2	13·6	5	28	2					
Illingworth	11	3	16	1	20	7	39	3					
Fletcher					1	0	9	0					

Umpires: T.F. Brooks (5) and L.P. Rowan (25).   ‡ K. Shuttleworth

Close: 1st day – A(1) 13-2 (Marsh 2, I.M. Chappell 0); 2nd – A(1) 235-7 (G.S. Chappell 62, Lillee 6); 3rd – E(2) 229-4 (D'Oliveira 37, Illingworth 25); 4th – A(2) 123-5 (G.S. Chappell 19, Marsh 12).

WEST INDIES v INDIA 1970–71 (1st Test)

Played at Sabina Park, Kingston, Jamaica, on 18 (*no play*), 19, 20, 22, 23 February.
Toss: West Indies.   Result: MATCH DRAWN.
Debuts: West Indies – A.G. Barrett, J.M. Noreiga; India – K. Jayantilal, P. Krishnamurthy.

Because of rain this match began 35 minutes after the scheduled start on the second day. Sardesai batted for just over eight hours and hit a six and 17 fours in scoring India's first double century against West Indies. His partnerships of 137 with Solkar and 122 with Prasanna were India's best against West Indies for the sixth and ninth wickets respectively until 1983-84 (*Test No. 969*). India enforced the follow-on after gaining a first innings lead against West Indies for the first time in 24 Tests dating back to 1948-49.

INDIA

S. Abid Ali	c Camacho b Shillingford	6
K. Jayantilal	c Sobers b Shillingford	5
A.L. Wadekar*	c Fredericks b Holder	8
D.N. Sardesai	c Findlay b Holder	212
S.A. Durani	b Barrett	13
M.L. Jaisimha	b Holder	3
E.D. Solkar	b Sobers	61
S. Venkataraghavan	c Findlay b Sobers	4
P. Krishnamurthy†	b Noreiga	10
E.A.S. Prasanna	b Holder	25
B.S. Bedi	not out	5
Extras	(B 9, LB 6, NB 20)	35
Total		**387**

WEST INDIES

R.C. Fredericks	c Abid Ali b Prasanna	45	c Krishnamurthy b Bedi	16
G.S. Camacho	c Wadekar b Prasanna	35	c Abid Ali b Venkataraghavan	12
R.B. Kanhai	c sub (D. Govindraj) b Venkataraghavan	56	not out	158
C.H. Lloyd	run out	15	run out	57
G. St A. Sobers*	c Abid Ali b Prasanna	44	c Krishnamurthy b Solkar	93
M.C. Carew	c Wadekar b Prasanna	3		
A.G. Barrett	c Solkar b Venkataraghavan	2	(6) c Abid Ali b Solkar	4
T.M. Findlay†	b Bedi	6	(7) not out	30
V.A. Holder	b Venkataraghavan	7		
G.C. Shillingford	b Bedi	0		
J.M. Noreiga	not out	0		
Extras	(B 4)	4	(B 9, LB 5, NB 1)	15
Total		**217**	(5 wickets)	**385**

WEST INDIES	O	M	R	W	O	M	R	W
Holder	27·4	9	60	4				
Shillingford	26	2	70	2				
Sobers	30	8	57	2				
Noreiga	31	7	69	1				
Barrett	35	6	86	1				
Lloyd	4	1	7	0				
Carew	5	2	3	0				
INDIA								
Abid Ali	9	2	30	0	5	2	11	0
Solkar	2	0	9	0	22	4	56	2
Bedi	31·5	12	63	2	24	5	63	1
Prasanna	33	12	65	4	21	5	72	0
Venkataraghavan	18	5	46	3	37	8	94	1
Durani					14	0	42	0
Jaisimha					13	1	32	0

FALL OF WICKETS

	I	WI	WI
Wkt	1st	1st	2nd
1st	10	73	18
2nd	13	90	32
3rd	36	119	147
4th	66	183	320
5th	75	202	326
6th	212	203	–
7th	222	205	–
8th	260	217	–
9th	382	217	–
10th	387	217	–

Umpires: R. Gosein (4) and D. Sang Hue (6).

Close: 1st day – no play; 2nd – I(1) 183-5 (Sardesai 81, Solkar 50); 3rd – WI(1) 36-0 (Fredericks 19, Camacho 17); 4th – WI(2) 72-2 (Kanhai 31, Lloyd 9).

WEST INDIES v INDIA 1970–71 (2nd Test)

Played at Queen's Park Oval, Port-of-Spain, Trinidad, on 6, 7, 9, 10 March.
Toss: West Indies.   Result: INDIA won by seven wickets.
Debuts: India – S.M. Gavaskar.

India gained their first victory against West Indies at their 25th attempt and with over a day to spare. Gavaskar completed a memorable debut by hitting the winning boundary. West Indies were dismissed for their lowest total against India until 1987-88 and it is still their lowest for this series in a home Test. Fredericks was bowled by the first ball of the match. Noreiga, a 34-year-old off-spinner playing in his second Test match, became the first bowler to take nine wickets in an innings for West Indies. His analysis is the record for a Test in Trinidad. Davis, 33 overnight, was struck over his right eye while batting in the nets before the start of the fourth day's play when West Indies were 150 for 1, and was taken to hospital to have the wound stitched. He resumed at the fall of the fifth wicket.

WEST INDIES

R.C. Fredericks	b Abid Ali	0		run out	80
G.S. Camacho	c Solkar b Bedi	18	(6)	b Venkataraghavan	3
R.B. Kanhai	c Solkar b Prasanna	37	(2)	c Venkataraghavan b Bedi	27
C.H. Lloyd	b Abid Ali	7		c Wadekar b Durani	15
C.A. Davis	not out	71	(3)	not out	74
G. St A. Sobers*	b Venkataraghavan	29	(5)	b Durani	0
A.G. Barrett	c Solkar b Prasanna	8		b Venkataraghavan	19
T.M. Findlay†	b Bedi	1		c Solkar b Venkataraghavan	0
V.A. Holder	c Krishnamurthy b Bedi	14		b Venkataraghavan	14
G.C. Shillingford	c Solkar b Prasanna	25		c Durani b Venkataraghavan	1
J.M. Noreiga	b Prasanna	0		c Solkar b Bedi	2
Extras	(B 2, LB 2)	4		(B 18, LB 7, NB 1)	26
Total		**214**			**261**

INDIA

A.V. Mankad	b Shillingford	44	c sub (S.A. Gomes) b Barrett	29
S.M. Gavaskar	c Lloyd b Noreiga	65	not out	67
S.A. Durani	c and b Noreiga	9	b Barrett	0
D.N. Sardesai	c Shillingford b Noreiga	112	c Findlay b Barrett	3
A.L. Wadekar*	c Kanhai b Noreiga	0		
E.D. Solkar	c and b Noreiga	55		
S. Abid Ali	c Shillingford b Noreiga	20	(5) not out	21
S. Venkataraghavan	st Findlay b Noreiga	5		
P. Krishnamurthy†	c sub (S.A. Gomes) b Noreiga	0		
E.A.S. Prasanna	not out	10		
B.S. Bedi	c Holder b Noreiga	4		
Extras	(B 18, LB 2, NB 8)	28	(B 2, LB 2, NB 1)	5
Total		**352**	(3 wickets)	**125**

INDIA	O	M	R	W	O	M	R	W	FALL OF WICKETS				
										WI	I	WI	I
Abid Ali	20	4	54	2	5	2	3	0	*Wkt*	*1st*	*1st*	*2nd*	*2nd*
Solkar	3	0	12	0	7	2	19	0	1st	0	68	73	74
Gavaskar	1	0	9	0					2nd	42	90	150	74
Bedi	16	5	46	3	29·5	11	50	2	3rd	62	186	152	84
Prasanna	19·5	3	54	4	16	5	47	0	4th	62	186	169	–
Venkataraghavan	13	0	35	1	36	11	95	5	5th	108	300	169	–
Durani					17	8	21	2	6th	132	330	218	–
WEST INDIES									7th	133	337	222	–
Holder	19	8	37	0	2	0	12	0	8th	161	337	254	–
Shillingford	20	3	45	1	6	2	13	0	9th	214	342	256	–
Sobers	28	7	65	0	15	5	16	0	10th	214	352	261	–
Noreiga	49·4	16	95	9	18	4	36	0					
Barrett	37	13	65	0	8·4	0	43	3					
Davis	3	1	11	0									
Lloyd	1	0	6	0									

Umpires: R. Gosein (5) and S. Ishmael (1).

Close: 1st day – WI(1) 214 all out; 2nd – I(1) 247-4 (Sardesai 83, Solkar 24); 3rd – WI(2) 150-1 (Fredericks 80, Davis 33).

WEST INDIES v INDIA 1970–71 (3rd Test)

Played at Bourda, Georgetown, Guyana, on 19, 20, 21, 23, 24 March.
Toss: West Indies.   Result: MATCH DRAWN.
Debuts: West Indies – K.D. Boyce, D.M. Lewis.

India were left 90 minutes in which to score 295 runs to win. Gavaskar scored his first Test hundred in his second match. Sobers scored 99 runs between lunch and tea on the fifth day, taking his score from 9 to 108. When he had scored 54 in that innings he became the third player after W.R. Hammond and M.C. Cowdrey to score 7,000 runs in official Tests.

WEST INDIES

R.C. Fredericks	c Abid Ali b Venkataraghavan	47	lbw b Solkar	5
M.C. Carew	c Mankad b Durani	41	c Durani b Bedi	45
R.B. Kanhai	c Krishnamurthy b Bedi	25		
C.H. Lloyd	run out	60	c Krishnamurthy b Bedi	9
C.A. Davis	lbw b Solkar	34	(3) not out	125
G. St A. Sobers*	c Venkataraghavan b Bedi	4	(5) not out	108
D.M. Lewis†	not out	81		
K.D. Boyce	c Gavaskar b Venkataraghavan	9		
G.C. Shillingford	c Bedi b Venkataraghavan	5		
L.R. Gibbs	run out	25		
J.M. Noreiga	run out	9		
Extras	(B 11, LB 9, NB 3)	23	(B 5, LB 6, NB 4)	15
Total		**363**	(3 wickets declared)	**307**

INDIA

A.V. Mankad	b Noreiga	40	not out	53
S.M. Gavaskar	c Carew b Sobers	116	not out	64
A.L. Wadekar*	b Sobers	16		
G.R. Viswanath	b Boyce	50		
S.A. Durani	lbw b Sobers	2		
D.N. Sardesai	run out	45		
E.D. Solkar	run out	16		
S. Abid Ali	not out	50		
S. Venkataraghavan	lbw b Shillingford	12		
P. Krishnamurthy†	run out	0		
B.S. Bedi	lbw b Boyce	2		
Extras	(B 5, LB 6, W 1, NB 15)	27	(B 4, W 1, NB 1)	6
Total		**376**	(0 wickets)	**123**

INDIA	O	M	R	W	O	M	R	W	FALL OF WICKETS				
										WI	I	WI	I
Abid Ali	13·2	5	42	0	14	2	55	0	*Wkt*	*1st*	*1st*	*2nd*	*2nd*
Solkar	17	3	34	1	16	4	43	1	1st	78	72	11	–
Venkataraghavan	59	14	128	3	20	10	47	0	2nd	119	116	114	–
Bedi	55	18	85	2	26	9	55	2	3rd	135	228	137	–
Durani	14	3	51	1	16	2	47	0	4th	213	244	–	–
Mankad					5	0	33	0	5th	226	246	–	–
Wadekar					3	0	12	0	6th	231	278	–	–
									7th	246	339	–	–
WEST INDIES									8th	256	370	–	–
Boyce	20·4	5	47	2	2	0	12	0	9th	340	374	–	–
Shillingford	21	2	76	1	2	0	13	0	10th	363	376	–	–
Sobers	43	15	72	3	5	1	14	0					
Gibbs	39	17	61	0	1	0	4	0					
Noreiga	42	9	91	1	10	0	30	0					
Carew	2	0	2	0									
Lloyd					3	0	20	0					
Fredericks					4	0	9	0					
Davis					3	0	15	0					

Umpires: R. Gosein (6) and C.P. Kippins (7).

Close: 1st day – WI(1) 231-6 (Lewis 1); 2nd – I(1) 114-1 (Gavaskar 48, Wadekar 16); 3rd – I(1) 256-5 (Sardesai 5, Solkar 6); 4th – WI(2) 63-1 (Carew 21, Davis 34).

WEST INDIES v INDIA 1970–71 (4th Test)

Played at Kensington Oval, Bridgetown, Barbados, on 1, 2, 3, 4, 6 April.
Toss: India.   Result: MATCH DRAWN.
Debuts: West Indies – Inshan Ali, U.G. Dowe.

Sobers scored his third hundred in successive first-class innings against India, having made 135 for Barbados in the intervening match. He took his 200th wicket in 80 matches when he dismissed Viswanath in the first innings and became the second player after R. Benaud to score 2,000 runs and take 200 wickets in Test cricket. Sardesai shared record India partnerships for this series of 186 with Solkar and 62 with Bedi for the seventh and tenth wickets respectively. His stand with Solkar was India's highest for the seventh wicket against all countries until 1984-85.

WEST INDIES

R.C. Fredericks	b Abid Ali	1	b Venkataraghavan	48
D.M. Lewis†	b Bedi	88	b Abid Ali	14
R.B. Kanhai	c Mankad b Venkataraghavan	85	c Krishnamurthy b Solkar	11
C.A. Davis	c Venkataraghavan b Abid Ali	79	(8) not out	22
G. St A. Sobers*	not out	178	c Bedi b Abid Ali	9
C.H. Lloyd	c Mankad b Bedi	19	(4) c Venkataraghavan b Abid Ali	43
M.L.C. Foster	not out	36	not out	24
J.N. Shepherd	)		(6) c Solkar b Venkataraghavan	3
Inshan Ali	) did not bat			
V.A. Holder	)			
U.G. Dowe	)			
Extras	(B 10, LB 4, NB 1)	15	(B 2, LB 3, NB 1)	6
Total	(5 wickets declared)	**501**	(6 wickets declared)	**180**

INDIA

A.V. Mankad	c Lewis b Holder	6	c Shepherd b Ali	8
S.M. Gavaskar	c Holder b Dowe	1	not out	117
P. Krishnamurthy†	c Ali b Dowe	1		
A.L. Wadekar*	c Lewis b Sobers	28	(3) c Lloyd b Sobers	17
G.R. Viswanath	c Lewis b Sobers	25	(4) c Shepherd b Sobers	0
D.N. Sardesai	lbw b Holder	150	c Fredericks b Shepherd	24
M.L. Jaisimha	b Dowe	0	(5) lbw b Dowe	17
E.D. Solkar	c Lewis b Dowe	65	(7) not out	10
S. Abid Ali	run out	9		
S. Venkataraghavan	b Shepherd	12		
B.S. Bedi	not out	20		
Extras	(B 6, LB 6, NB 18)	30	(B 2, LB 8, W 1, NB 17)	28
Total		**347**	(5 wickets)	**221**

INDIA	O	M	R	W	O	M	R	W
Abid Ali	31	1	127	2	21	3	70	3
Solkar	19	4	40	0	14	0	73	1
Jaisimha	10	2	32	0				
Bedi	54	15	124	2	1	0	6	0
Venkataraghavan	57	12	163	1	7	0	25	2
WEST INDIES								
Holder	25·4	7	70	2	8	4	13	0
Dowe	23	7	69	4	11	5	22	1
Shepherd	24	4	54	1	20	7	36	1
Sobers	20	9	34	2	23	8	31	2
Ali	20	4	60	0	18	1	65	1
Foster	11	3	28	0	14	7	10	0
Davis	2	0	2	0	3	2	1	0
Lloyd					4	0	13	0
Fredericks					1	0	1	0
Kanhai					1	0	1	0

FALL OF WICKETS				
	WI	I	WI	I
Wkt	1st	1st	2nd	2nd
1st	4	2	17	35
2nd	170	5	36	71
3rd	179	20	112	79
4th	346	64	126	132
5th	394	69	132	192
6th	–	70	133	–
7th	–	256	–	–
8th	–	269	–	–
9th	–	285	–	–
10th	–	347	–	–

Umpires: H.B. de C. Jordan (18) and D. Sang Hue (7).

Close: 1st day – WI(1) 224-3 (Davis 25, Sobers 21); 2nd – I(1) 2-1 (Mankad 1); 3rd – I(1) 157-6 (Sardesai 58, Solkar 29); 4th – WI(2) 175-6 (Foster 22, Davis 19).

WEST INDIES v INDIA 1970–71 (5th Test)

Played at Queen's Park Oval, Port-of-Spain, Trinidad, on 13, 14, 15, 17, 18, 19 April.
Toss: India.   Result: MATCH DRAWN.
Debuts: Nil.

After rain had extended the lunch interval by 20 minutes, West Indies needed to score 262 runs in 155 minutes. This draw gave India their first victory in a rubber against West Indies. Gavaskar became the second batsman after K.D. Walters to score a century and a double century in the same Test, the second Indian after V.S. Hazare to score hundreds in both innings of a Test, and the third Indian after Hazare and P.R. Umrigar to score three hundreds in successive Test innings. His aggregate of 774 (average 154·80) remains India's record for a rubber against West Indies and the world record for any batsman playing in his first rubber. His innings of 220 made in 505 minutes with 22 fours, was India's highest in any first class-match in the Caribbean until 1988-89, the highest in any Test in Trinidad, and was their highest against West Indies until he scored 236 not out in 1983-84 (*Test No. 969*); he was suffering from severe toothache throughout it. He is the only Indian to score four hundreds in a rubber.

INDIA

S. Abid Ali	c Davis b Sobers	10	lbw b Sobers	3
S.M. Gavaskar	c Lewis b Holford	124	b Shepherd	220
A.L. Wadekar*	c Sobers b Shepherd	28	c Shepherd b Noreiga	54
D.N. Sardesai	c Lewis b Holford	75	c and b Foster	21
G.R. Viswanath	c Lewis b Shepherd	22	b Sobers	38
M.L. Jaisimha	c Carew b Dowe	0	lbw b Shepherd	23
E.D. Solkar	c sub (R.C. Fredericks) b Dowe	3	c Sobers b Noreiga	14
S. Venkataraghavan	c Carew b Shepherd	51	b Noreiga	21
P. Krishnamurthy†	c Lewis b Noreiga	20	c sub (S.A. Gomes) b Noreiga	2
E.A.S. Prasanna	c Lloyd b Holford	16	not out	10
B.S. Bedi	not out	1	c Sobers b Noreiga	5
Extras	(LB 1, NB 9)	10	(B 6, LB 8, NB 2)	16
Total		**360**		**427**

WEST INDIES

M.C. Carew	c Wadekar b Prasanna	28	run out	4
D.M. Lewis†	c Krishnamurthy b Bedi	72	(9) not out	4
R.B. Kanhai	run out	13	(4) b Abid Ali	21
C.A. Davis	c Solkar b Venkataraghavan	105	(8) c Viswanath b Venkataraghavan	19
C.H. Lloyd	c Venkataraghavan b Prasanna	6	(3) c Wadekar b Venkataraghavan	64
G. St A. Sobers*	b Prasanna	132	(5) b Abid Ali	0
M.L.C. Foster	b Abid Ali	99	(6) run out	18
D.A.J. Holford	st Krishnamurthy b Venkataraghavan	44	(7) c Bedi b Solkar	9
J.N. Shepherd	c Abid Ali b Venkataraghavan	0	(2) c and b Abid Ali	9
U.G. Dowe	lbw b Venkataraghavan	3	not out	0
J.M. Noreiga	not out	0		
Extras	(B 14, LB 8, NB 2)	24	(B 9, LB 8)	17
Total		**526**	**(8 wickets)**	**165**

WEST INDIES	O	M	R	W	O	M	R	W	FALL OF WICKETS			
Sobers	13	3	30	1	42	14	82	2		I	WI	I	WI
Dowe	29	1	99	2	22	2	55	0	*Wkt*	*1st*	*1st*	*2nd*	*2nd*
Shepherd	35	7	78	3	24	8	45	2	1st	26	52	11	10
Davis	10	0	28	0	10	2	12	0	2nd	68	94	159	16
Noreiga	16	3	43	1	53·4	8	129	5	3rd	190	142	194	50
Holford	28·3	5	68	3	27	3	63	0	4th	238	153	293	50
Foster	2	0	4	0	12	4	10	1	5th	239	330	374	101
Carew					7	2	15	0	6th	247	424	377	114
INDIA									7th	296	517	409	152
Abid Ali	31	7	58	1	15	1	73	3	8th	335	522	412	161
Solkar	11	1	35	0	13	1	40	1	9th	354	523	413	–
Bedi	71	19	163	1	2	1	1	0	10th	360	526	427	–
Prasanna	65	15	146	3	5	0	23	0					
Venkataraghavan	37·3	6	100	4	5	1	11	2					
Jaisimha	1	1	0	0									

Umpires: R. Gosein (7) and D. Sang Hue (8).

Close: 1st day – I(1) 247-5 (Gavaskar 102, Solkar 3); 2nd – WI(1) 117-2 (Lewis 59, Davis 16); 3rd – WI(1) 377-5 (Sobers 114, Foster 26); 4th – I(2) 324-4 (Gavaskar 180, Jaisimha 12).

NEW ZEALAND v ENGLAND 1970–71 (1st Test)

Played at Lancaster Park, Christchurch, on 25, 26, 27 February, 1 March.
Toss: New Zealand.   Result: ENGLAND won by eight wickets.
Debuts: England – R.W. Taylor.

New Zealand were dismissed for the lowest total in any Test at Christchurch and their third-lowest against England. Underwood took his 1,000th first-class wicket when he dismissed Shrimpton in the second innings. His match analysis of 12 for 97 is the record for any Test at Christchurch. The last of D'Oliveira's five Test hundreds was his first against New Zealand; a masterly 211-minute innings on a sub-standard pitch, it included two sixes and 13 fours. C.S. Elliott, in New Zealand on a Churchill Fellowship, was invited to umpire by the New Zealand Cricket Council.

NEW ZEALAND

G.T. Dowling*	c Edrich b Underwood	13	c Luckhurst b Lever	1
B.A.G. Murray	c Taylor b Shuttleworth	1	b Shuttleworth	1
B.E. Congdon	c Taylor b Shuttleworth	1	b Underwood	55
R.W. Morgan	c Luckhurst b Shuttleworth	6	(5) b Underwood	0
M.J.F. Shrimpton	c Fletcher b Underwood	0	(6) c Illingworth b Underwood	8
G.M. Turner	b Underwood	11	(4) b Underwood	76
V. Pollard	b Wilson	18	lbw b Underwood	34
K.J. Wadsworth†	c Fletcher b Underwood	0	c Fletcher b Wilson	1
R.S. Cunis	b Underwood	0	b Shuttleworth	35
H.J. Howarth	st Taylor b Underwood	0	c Illingworth b Underwood	25
R.O. Collinge	not out	3	not out	7
Extras	(B 9, LB 1, W 1, NB 1)	12	(B 6, LB 3, W 1, NB 1)	11
Total		**65**		**254**

ENGLAND

B.W. Luckhurst	c Wadsworth b Collinge	10	not out	29
J.H. Edrich	lbw b Cunis	12	c Wadsworth b Collinge	2
K.W.R. Fletcher	b Collinge	4	c Howarth b Collinge	2
J.H. Hampshire	c Turner b Howarth	40	not out	51
B.L. D'Oliveira	b Shrimpton	100		
R. Illingworth*	b Shrimpton	36		
R.W. Taylor†	st Wadsworth b Howarth	4		
D. Wilson	c Murray b Howarth	5		
P. Lever	b Howarth	4		
K. Shuttleworth	b Shrimpton	5		
D.L. Underwood	not out	0		
Extras	(B 1, LB 9, NB 1)	11	(B 1, LB 4)	5
Total		**231**	(2 wickets)	**89**

ENGLAND	O	M	R	W	O	M	R	W			FALL OF WICKETS		
Lever	5	4	1	0	15	3	30	1		NZ	E	NZ	E
Shuttleworth	8	1	14	3	12	1	27	2	*Wkt*	*1st*	*1st*	*2nd*	*2nd*
D'Oliveira	3	1	2	0					1st	4	20	1	3
Underwood	11·6	7	12	6	32·3	7	85	6	2nd	7	26	6	11
Illingworth	6	3	12	0	17	5	45	0	3rd	19	31	83	–
Wilson	4	2	12	1	21	6	56	1	4th	28	95	83	–
NEW ZEALAND									5th	33	188	99	–
Collinge	12	2	39	2	7	2	20	2	6th	54	213	151	–
Cunis	13	2	44	1	8	0	17	0	7th	54	220	152	–
Howarth	19	7	46	4	4	0	17	0	8th	62	224	209	–
Pollard	9	3	45	0	3	1	9	0	9th	62	231	231	–
Shrimpton	11·5	0	35	3	3	0	21	0	10th	65	231	254	–
Congdon	3	0	11	0									

Umpires: C.S. Elliott (33) and W.T. Martin (13).

Close: 1st day – E(1) 56-3 (Hampshire 19, D'Oliveira 9); 2nd – NZ(2) 54-2 (Congdon 34, Turner 15); 3rd – NZ(2) 212-8 (Cunis 27, Howarth 0).

NEW ZEALAND v ENGLAND 1970–71 (2nd Test)

Played at Eden Park, Auckland, on 5, 6, 7, 8 March.
Toss: New Zealand.   Result: MATCH DRAWN.
Debuts: New Zealand – M.G. Webb.

New Zealand were unable to include either B.A.G. Murray or V. Pollard in their team as neither would play on a Sunday. Burgess scored his second hundred in successive Test innings, following his 119 not out in *Test No. 664*. His stand of 141 with Shrimpton was New Zealand's highest for the fifth wicket against England until 1973 (*Test No. 722*). Cunis achieved his only innings analysis of five or more wickets in 20 appearances. Knott narrowly missed becoming the first wicket-keeper to score a hundred in each innings of a Test. His partnership of 149 with Lever remains the highest for the seventh wicket in this series.

ENGLAND

J.H. Edrich	c Morgan b Webb	1	c Burgess b Collinge	24
B.W. Luckhurst	c Dowling b Cunis	14	c Wadsworth b Webb	15
M.C. Cowdrey	c Congdon b Cunis	54	(6) b Collinge	45
J.H. Hampshire	c Turner b Cunis	9	(3) c Wadsworth b Cunis	0
B.L. D'Oliveira	c Morgan b Congdon	58	(9) b Collinge	5
R. Illingworth*	c Wadsworth b Cunis	0	(4) c Turner b Collinge	22
A.P.E. Knott†	b Collinge	101	(5) b Cunis	96
P. Lever	c Wadsworth b Cunis	64	(7) lbw b Howarth	0
K. Shuttleworth	c Wadsworth b Cunis	0	(8) c Wadsworth b Morgan	11
R.G.D. Willis	c Burgess b Collinge	7	lbw b Cunis	3
D.L. Underwood	not out	1	not out	8
Extras	(B 1, LB 4, NB 7)	12	(B 5, LB 3)	8
Total		**321**		**237**

NEW ZEALAND

G.M. Turner	c and b Underwood	65	not out	8
G.T. Dowling*	c and b Underwood	53	not out	31
B.E. Congdon	b Underwood	0		
R.W. Morgan	c and b Underwood	8		
M.G. Burgess	c Edrich b Willis	104		
M.J.F. Shrimpton	lbw b Underwood	46		
K.J. Wadsworth†	c Hampshire b Willis	16		
R.S. Cunis	not out	5		
H.J. Howarth	not out	2		
R.O. Collinge	} did not bat			
M.G. Webb	}			
Extras	(B 7, LB 4, NB 3)	14	(LB 1)	1
Total	(7 wickets declared)	**313**	(0 wickets)	**40**

NEW ZEALAND	O	M	R	W	O	M	R	W
Webb	18	0	94	1	11	0	50	1
Collinge	18·6	5	51	2	19	6	41	4
Cunis	24	4	76	6	21·7	5	52	3
Howarth	7	0	41	0	21	8	37	1
Congdon	2	0	18	1				
Shrimpton	3	0	29	0	6	0	33	0
Morgan					6	0	16	1
ENGLAND								
Lever	19	3	43	0	2	0	6	0
Shuttleworth	17	3	49	0	4	0	12	0
Willis	14	2	54	2	6	1	15	0
Underwood	38	12	108	5	2	2	0	0
Illingworth	18	4	45	0				
Luckhurst					2	0	6	0

FALL OF WICKETS

	E	NZ	E	NZ
Wkt	1st	1st	2nd	2nd
1st	8	91	26	–
2nd	38	91	27	–
3rd	59	121	62	–
4th	111	142	67	–
5th	111	283	143	–
6th	145	302	152	–
7th	294	307	177	–
8th	297	–	199	–
9th	317	–	218	–
10th	321	–	237	–

Umpires: E.C.A. MacKintosh (6) and R.W.R. Shortt (8).

Close: 1st day – E(1) 317-9 (Willis 4, Underwood 0); 2nd – NZ(1) 208-4 (Burgess 50, Shrimpton 20); 3rd – E(2) 78-4 (Knott 12, Cowdrey 2).

ENGLAND v PAKISTAN 1971 (1st Test)

Played at Edgbaston, Birmingham on 3, 4, 5, 7, 8 June.
Toss: Pakistan.   Result: MATCH DRAWN.
Debuts: Pakistan – Imran Khan.

Following on for the first time against Pakistan, England, 184 for 3, were still 71 runs behind the (then) highest total in an Edgbaston Test at the end of the fourth day. Rain prevented a second Pakistan victory in this series by allowing only a further 14·5 overs of play. Zaheer scored Pakistan's first double century against England and his partnership of 291 with Mushtaq remains his country's record for the second wicket in all Tests. His innings (544 minutes, 467 balls, 38 fours) remains the highest for Pakistan against England and the record for any batsman in his first innings against England. Pakistan's total is the highest of this series. The partnership of 159 between Knott and Lever was the seventh-wicket record for this series until 1983-84 (*Test No. 979*). Aftab (0) retired when one run had been scored after being struck on the head by Ward's third ball of the innings. He resumed at 469. Cowdrey made his last appearance in a Test in England.

PAKISTAN

Aftab Gul	b D'Oliveira	28
Sadiq Mohammad	c and b Lever	17
Zaheer Abbas	c Luckhurst b Illingworth	274
Mushtaq Mohammad	c Cowdrey b Illingworth	100
Majid Khan	c Lever b Illingworth	35
Asif Iqbal	not out	104
Intikhab Alam*	c Underwood b D'Oliveira	9
Imran Khan	run out	5
Wasim Bari†	not out	4
Asif Masood	} did not bat	
Pervez Sajjad	}	
Extras	(B 6, LB 14, NB 12)	32
Total	(7 wickets declared)	**608**

ENGLAND

J.H. Edrich	c Zaheer b Asif Masood	0	c Wasim b Asif Masood	15
B.W. Luckhurst	c Sadiq b Pervez	35	not out	108
M.C. Cowdrey	b Asif Masood	16	b Asif Masood	34
D.L. Amiss	b Asif Masood	4	c Pervez b Asif Masood	22
B.L. D'Oliveira	c Mushtaq b Intikhab	73	c Mushtaq b Asif Iqbal	22
R. Illingworth*	b Intikhab	1	c Wasim b Asif Masood	1
A.P.E. Knott†	b Asif Masood	116	not out	4
P. Lever	c Pervez b Asif Masood	47		
K. Shuttleworth	c Imran b Pervez	21		
D.L. Underwood	not out	9		
A. Ward	c Mushtaq b Pervez	0		
Extras	(B 16, LB 6, W 3, NB 6)	31	(B 4, LB 5, W 6, NB 8)	23
Total		**353**	(5 wickets)	**229**

ENGLAND	O	M	R	W	O	M	R	W
Ward	29	3	115	0				
Lever	38	7	126	1				
Shuttleworth	23	2	83	0				
D'Oliveira	38	17	78	2				
Underwood	41	13	102	0				
Illingworth	26	5	72	3				
PAKISTAN								
Asif Masood	34	6	111	5	23·5	7	49	4
Imran	23	9	36	0	5	0	19	0
Majid	4	1	8	0				
Intikhab	31	13	82	2	20	8	52	0
Pervez	15·5	6	46	3	14	4	27	0
Mushtaq	13	3	39	0	8	2	23	0
Asif Iqbal					20	6	36	1

FALL OF WICKETS

	P	E	E
Wkt	1st	1st	2nd
1st	68	0	34
2nd	359	29	114
3rd	441	46	169
4th	456	112	218
5th	469	127	221
6th	567	148	–
7th	581	307	–
8th	–	324	–
9th	–	351	–
10th	–	353	–

Umpires: C.S. Elliott (34) and T.W. Spencer (3).

Close: 1st day – P(1) 270-1 (Zaheer 159, Mushtaq 72); 2nd – P(1) 602-7 (Asif Iqbal 98, Wasim 4); 3rd – E(1) 320-7 (Knott 114, Shuttleworth 7); 4th – E(2) 184-3 (Luckhurst 87, D'Oliveira 6).

ENGLAND v PAKISTAN 1971 (2nd Test)

Played at Lord's, London, on 17, 18, 19 *(no play)*, 21, 22 June.
Toss: England.   Result: MATCH DRAWN.
Debuts: England – R.A. Hutton.

Rain claimed 17 hours 17 minutes of playing time during the match; play started at 3.30 on the first afternoon, at 2.30 on the fourth, not at all on the third, and there was only 23 minutes of cricket on the second. Price dismissed Wasim Bari and Asif Masood with successive balls but was denied the chance of a hat-trick by Pervez's illness (swollen feet and ankles). Luckhurst shared in century opening partnerships in both innings, his second partner being the elder son of Sir Leonard Hutton.

ENGLAND

G. Boycott	not out	121		
B.W. Luckhurst	c Wasim b Salim	46	(1) not out	53
J.H. Edrich	c Asif Masood b Pervez	37		
D.L. Amiss	not out	19		
R.A. Hutton	)		(2) not out	58
B.L. D'Oliveira	)			
R. Illingworth*	)			
A.P.E. Knott†	) did not bat			
P. Lever	)			
N. Gifford	)			
J.S.E. Price	)			
Extras	(B 6, LB 2, W 5, NB 5)	18	(B 1, LB 1, NB 4)	6
Total	(2 wickets declared)	**241**	(0 wickets)	**117**

PAKISTAN

Aftab Gul	c Knott b Hutton	33
Sadiq Mohammad	c Knott b D'Oliveira	28
Zaheer Abbas	c Hutton b Lever	40
Mushtaq Mohammad	c Amiss b Hutton	2
Asif Iqbal	c Knott b Gifford	9
Majid Khan	c Edrich b Price	9
Intikhab Alam*	c Gifford b Lever	18
Wasim Bari†	c Knott b Price	0
Salim Altaf	not out	0
Asif Masood	b Price	0
Pervez Sajjad	absent ill	–
Extras	(LB 5, W 1, NB 3)	9
Total		**148**

PAKISTAN	O	M	R	W	O	M	R	W
Asif Masood	21	3	60	0	3	1	3	0
Salim	19	5	42	1	5	2	11	0
Asif Iqbal	13	2	24	0	4	1	11	0
Majid	4	0	16	0	6	2	7	0
Intikhab	20	2	64	0	9	1	26	0
Pervez	6	2	17	1				
Mushtaq					11	3	31	0
Sadiq					5	1	17	0
Aftab					1	0	4	0
Zaheer					1	0	1	0
ENGLAND								
Price	11·4	5	29	3				
Lever	16	3	38	2				
Gifford	12	6	13	1				
Illingworth	7	6	1	0				
Hutton	16	5	36	2				
D'Oliveira	10	5	22	1				

FALL OF WICKETS

	E	P	E
Wkt	1st	1st	2nd
1st	124	57	–
2nd	205	66	–
3rd	–	97	–
4th	–	117	–
5th	–	119	–
6th	–	146	–
7th	–	148	–
8th	–	148	–
9th	–	148	–
10th	–	–	–

Umpires: A.E. Fagg (8) and A.E.G. Rhodes (4).

Close: 1st day – E(1) 118-0 (Boycott 61, Luckhurst 46); 2nd – E(1) 133-1 (Boycott 72, Edrich 0); 3rd – no play; 4th – P(1) 49-0 (Aftab 20, Sadiq 28).

ENGLAND v PAKISTAN 1971 (3rd Test)

Played at Headingley, Leeds, on 8, 9, 10, 12, 13 July.
Toss: England.   Result: ENGLAND won by 25 runs.
Debuts: Nil.

England won the rubber at 3.49 on the fifth afternoon when Pakistan narrowly failed to score 231 runs in 385 minutes. Boycott's tenth Test hundred was his third in successive innings. Only 159 runs were scored off 107·4 overs on the third day (Pakistan 142 for 6, England 17 for 1) – the slowest full day of Test cricket in England until 1978 (*Test No. 830*). Wasim Bari equalled the (then) Test record by holding eight catches in the match, which ended when Lever took three wickets in four balls. Illingworth completed the double in his 47th Test when he dismissed Aftab. Salim split his trousers and left the field after the first ball of his sixth over in the first innings.

ENGLAND

G. Boycott	c Wasim b Intikhab	112	c Mushtaq b Asif Masood	13
B.W. Luckhurst	c Wasim b Salim	0	c Wasim b Asif Masood	0
J.H. Edrich	c Wasim b Asif Masood	2	c Mushtaq b Intikhab	33
D.L. Amiss	c Wasim b Pervez	23	c and b Saeed	56
B.L. D'Oliveira	b Intikhab	74	c Wasim b Salim	72
A.P.E. Knott†	b Asif Masood	10	c Zaheer b Intikhab	7
R. Illingworth*	b Asif Iqbal	20	c Wasim b Salim	45
R.A. Hutton	c Sadiq b Asif Iqbal	28	c Zaheer b Intikhab	4
R.N.S. Hobbs	c Wasim b Asif Iqbal	6	b Salim	0
P. Lever	c Salim b Intikhab	19	b Salim	8
N. Gifford	not out	3	not out	2
Extras	(B 5, LB 5, NB 9)	19	(B 6, LB 11, W 2, NB 5)	24
Total		**316**		**264**

PAKISTAN

Aftab Gul	b Gifford	27	c Hobbs b Illingworth	18
Sadiq Mohammad	c Knott b Gifford	28	c and b D'Oliveira	91
Zaheer Abbas	c Edrich b Lever	72	c Luckhurst b Illingworth	0
Mushtaq Mohammad	c Knott b Hutton	57	c Edrich b Illingworth	5
Saeed Ahmed	c Knott b D'Oliveira	22	c D'Oliveira b Gifford	5
Asif Iqbal	c Hutton b D'Oliveira	14	st Knott b Gifford	33
Intikhab Alam*	c Hobbs b D'Oliveira	17	c Hutton b D'Oliveira	4
Wasim Bari†	c Edrich b Gifford	63	c Knott b Lever	10
Salim Altaf	c Knott b Hutton	22	not out	8
Asif Masood	c and b Hutton	0	c Knott b Lever	1
Pervez Sajjad	not out	9	lbw b Lever	0
Extras	(B 6, LB 11, W 1, NB 1)	19	(B 17, LB 9, W 1, NB 3)	30
Total		**350**		**205**

PAKISTAN	O	M	R	W	O	M	R	W		FALL OF WICKETS			
Asif Masood	18	2	75	2	20	7	46	2		E	P	E	P
Salim	20·1	4	46	1	14·3	9	11	4	*Wkt*	*1st*	*1st*	*2nd*	*2nd*
Asif Iqbal	13	2	37	3					1st	4	54	0	25
Pervez	20	2	65	1	16	3	46	0	2nd	10	69	21	25
Intikhab	27·1	12	51	3	36	10	91	3	3rd	74	198	112	54
Saeed	4	0	13	0	15	4	30	1	4th	209	198	120	65
Mushtaq	3	1	10	0	6	1	16	0	5th	234	223	142	160
									6th	234	249	248	184
ENGLAND									7th	283	256	252	187
Lever	31	9	65	1	3·3	1	10	3	8th	286	313	252	203
Hutton	41	8	72	3	6	0	18	0	9th	294	313	262	205
Gifford	53·4	26	69	3	34	14	51	2	10th	316	350	264	205
Illingworth	28	14	31	0	26	11	58	3					
Hobbs	20	5	48	0	4	0	22	0					
D'Oliveira	36	18	46	3	15	7	16	2					

Umpires: D.J. Constant (1) and A.E. Fagg (9).

Close: 1st day – E(1) 309-9 (Lever 16, Gifford 1); 2nd – P(1) 208-4 (Saeed 1, Asif Iqbal 9); 3rd – E(2) 17-1 (Boycott 10, Edrich 5); 4th – P(2) 25-0 (Aftab 18, Sadiq 2).

ENGLAND v INDIA 1971 (1st Test)

Played at Lord's, London, on 22, 23, 24, 26, 27 July.
Toss: England.   Result: MATCH DRAWN.
Debuts: Nil.

Rain prevented play after tea on the fifth day when India wanted 38 runs with two wickets left to win their first Test in England. 304 minutes were lost during the match. Snow made his highest score in first-class cricket but was excluded from the next Test as a disciplinary measure for colliding with Gavaskar as the latter was completing a fast single in the second innings. Six years later he scored 73 not out, statistically a higher score, for Sussex against Worcestershire.

ENGLAND

G. Boycott	c Engineer b Abid Ali	3	c Wadekar b Venkataraghavan		33
B.W. Luckhurst	c Solkar b Chandrasekhar	30	b Solkar		1
J.H. Edrich	c Venkataraghavan b Bedi	18	c Engineer b Bedi		62
D.L. Amiss	c Engineer b Bedi	9	run out		0
B.L. D'Oliveira	c Solkar b Chandrasekhar	4	b Bedi		30
A.P.E. Knott†	c Wadekar b Venkataraghavan	67	c Wadekar b Chandrasekhar		24
R. Illingworth*	c Engineer b Bedi	33	c Wadekar b Venkataraghavan		20
R.A. Hutton	b Venkataraghavan	20	b Chandrasekhar		0
J.A. Snow	c Abid Ali b Chandrasekhar	73	c Chandrasekhar b Venkataraghavan		9
N. Gifford	b Bedi	17	not out		7
J.S.E. Price	not out	5	c Abid Ali b Venkataraghavan		0
Extras	(B 8, LB 12, NB 5)	25	(LB 5)		5
Total		**304**			**191**

INDIA

A.V. Mankad	c Gifford b Snow	1	c Knott b Snow		5
S.M. Gavaskar	c Amiss b Price	4	c Edrich b Gifford		53
A.L. Wadekar*	c Illingworth b Gifford	85	c Boycott b Price		5
D.N. Sardesai	c Illingworth b Gifford	25	(6) b Illingworth		1
G.R. Viswanath	c Knott b Hutton	68	c Amiss b Gifford		9
F.M. Engineer†	c Illingworth b Hutton	28	(4) st Knott b Gifford		35
E.D. Solkar	c Knott b Gifford	67	not out		6
S. Abid Ali	c Luckhurst b Snow	6	c Snow b Illingworth		14
S. Venkataraghavan	c Hutton b Price	11	c Hutton b Gifford		7
B.S. Bedi	c Price b Gifford	0	not out		2
B.S. Chandrasekhar	not out	0			
Extras	(B 7, LB 9, NB 2)	18	(LB 7, NB 1)		8
Total		**313**	(8 wickets)		**145**

INDIA	O	M	R	W	O	M	R	W		FALL OF WICKETS			
Abid Ali	15	3	38	1	9	1	20	0		E	I	E	I
Solkar	8	3	17	0	6	3	13	1	Wkt	1st	1st	2nd	2nd
Venkataraghavan	28	8	44	2	30·5	11	52	4	1st	18	1	4	8
Chandrasekhar	49	10	110	3	23	7	60	2	2nd	46	29	65	21
Bedi	39·3	18	70	4	30	13	41	2	3rd	56	108	70	87
									4th	61	125	117	101
ENGLAND									5th	71	175	145	108
Price	25	9	46	2	4	0	26	1	6th	161	267	153	114
Snow	31	9	64	2	8	0	23	1	7th	183	279	153	135
Hutton	24	8	38	2	3	0	12	0	8th	223	302	174	142
Gifford	45·3	14	84	4	19	4	43	4	9th	294	311	189	–
D'Oliveira	15	7	20	0					10th	304	313	191	–
Illingworth	25	12	43	0	16	2	33	2					

Umpires: D.J. Constant (2) and C.S. Elliott (35).

Close: 1st day – E(1) 252-8 (Snow 51, Gifford 4); 2nd – I(1) 179-5 (Viswanath 24, Solkar 0); 3rd – I(1) 313 all out; 4th – E(2) 145-5 (Knott 17).

ENGLAND v INDIA 1971 (2nd Test)

Played at Old Trafford, Manchester, on 5, 6, 7, 9, 10 *(no play)* August.
Toss: England.   Result: MATCH DRAWN.
Debuts: England – J.A. Jameson.

Rain, which began at 10.30 the previous night, caused the fifth day's play to be abandoned and rescued India from probable defeat after they had been left to score 420 runs in 475 minutes. Lever batted 227 minutes for his highest score in first-class cricket and shared with Illingworth in the highest eighth-wicket partnership by either country in this series (168). Gifford fractured his thumb while fielding and was unable to bowl in the match. This result extended to 26 England's unbroken run of official Tests without defeat since the Manchester Test against Australia in 1968. Until 1984-85, when the West Indies increased it to 27, this constituted the record, beating Australia's run of 25 matches from Wellington 1945-46 to Adelaide 1950-51.

ENGLAND

B.W. Luckhurst	c Viswanath b Bedi	78	st Engineer b Solkar	101
J.A. Jameson	c Gavaskar b Abid Ali	15	run out	28
J.H. Edrich	c Engineer b Abid Ali	0	b Bedi	59
K.W.R. Fletcher	lbw b Abid Ali	1	not out	28
B.L. D'Oliveira	c Gavaskar b Abid Ali	12	not out	23
A.P.E. Knott†	b Venkataraghavan	41		
R. Illingworth*	c Gavaskar b Venkataraghavan	107		
R.A. Hutton	c and b Venkataraghavan	15		
P. Lever	not out	88		
N. Gifford	c Engineer b Solkar	8		
J.S.E. Price	run out	0		
Extras	(B 6, LB 12, W 1, NB 2)	21	(LB 5, NB 1)	6
Total		**386**	(3 wickets declared)	**245**

INDIA

A.V. Mankad	c Knott b Lever	8	b Price	7
S.M. Gavaskar	c Knott b Price	57	c Knott b Hutton	24
A.L. Wadekar*	c Knott b Hutton	12	b Price	9
D.N. Sardesai	b Lever	14	not out	13
G.R. Viswanath	b Lever	10	not out	8
F.M. Engineer†	c Edrich b Lever	22		
E.D. Solkar	c Hutton b D'Oliveira	50		
S. Abid Ali	b D'Oliveira	0		
S. Venkataraghavan	c Knott b Lever	20		
B.S. Bedi	b Price	8		
B.S. Chandrasekhar	not out	4		
Extras	(B 1, LB 4, NB 2)	7	(LB 2, NB 2)	4
Total		**212**	(3 wickets)	**65**

INDIA	O	M	R	W	O	M	R	W
Abid Ali	32·4	5	64	4	26	2	95	0
Solkar	21	5	46	1	5	0	23	1
Chandrasekhar	30	6	90	0	2	0	5	0
Bedi	40	10	72	1	5	0	21	1
Venkataraghavan	35	9	89	3	16	3	58	0
Gavaskar	2	0	4	0	12	3	37	0
ENGLAND								
Price	22	7	44	2	10	3	30	2
Lever	26	4	70	5	7	3	14	0
D'Oliveira	24	11	40	2	3	2	1	0
Hutton	14	3	35	1	7	1	16	1
Illingworth	7	2	16	0				

FALL OF WICKETS

Wkt	E 1st	I 1st	E 2nd	I 2nd
1st	21	19	44	9
2nd	21	52	167	22
3rd	25	90	212	50
4th	41	103	–	–
5th	116	104	–	–
6th	168	163	–	–
7th	187	164	–	–
8th	355	194	–	–
9th	384	200	–	–
10th	386	212	–	–

Umpires: A.E. Fagg (10) and T.W. Spencer (4).

Close: 1st day – E(1) 219-7 (Illingworth 27, Lever 16); 2nd – I(1) 8-0 (Mankad 4, Gavaskar 4); 3rd – I(1) 212 all out; 4th – I(2) 65-3 (Sardesai 13, Viswanath 8).

ENGLAND v INDIA 1971 (3rd Test)

Played at Kennington Oval, London, on 19, 20 *(no play)*, 21, 23, 24 August.
Toss: England.   Result: INDIA won by four wickets.
Debuts: Nil.

Abid Ali cut Luckhurst to the boundary at 2.42 on the fifth afternoon to give India her first victory in 22 Tests in England dating back to 1932. It ended England's record run by any country of 26 official matches without defeat and was their first reversal in 20 Tests under Illingworth's captaincy. The partnership of 103 in 66 minutes between Knott and Hutton was England's highest for the seventh wicket against India until 1982 *(Test No. 928)*. England's total of 101 is still their lowest against India. Chandrasekhar's match analysis of 8 for 114 remains India's best in England.

ENGLAND

B.W. Luckhurst	c Gavaskar b Solkar	1	c Venkataraghavan b Chandrasekhar	33
J.A. Jameson	run out	82	run out	16
J.H. Edrich	c Engineer b Bedi	41	b Chandrasekhar	0
K.W.R. Fletcher	c Gavaskar b Bedi	1	c Solkar b Chandrasekhar	0
B.L. D'Oliveira	c Mankad b Chandrasekhar	2	c sub (K. Jayantilal) b Venkataraghavan	17
A.P.E. Knott†	c and b Solkar	90	c Solkar b Venkataraghavan	1
R. Illingworth*	b Chandrasekhar	11	c and b Chandrasekhar	4
R.A. Hutton	b Venkataraghavan	81	not out	13
J.A. Snow	c Engineer b Solkar	3	c and b Chandrasekhar	0
D.L. Underwood	c Wadekar b Venkataraghavan	22	c Mankad b Bedi	11
J.S.E. Price	not out	1	lbw b Chandrasekhar	3
Extras	(B 4, LB 15, W 1)	20	(LB 3)	3
Total		**355**		**101**

INDIA

S.M. Gavaskar	b Snow	6	lbw b Snow	0
A.V. Mankad	b Price	10	c Hutton b Underwood	11
A.L. Wadekar*	c Hutton b Illingworth	48	run out	45
D.N. Sardesai	b Illingworth	54	c Knott b Underwood	40
G.R. Viswanath	b Illingworth	0	c Knott b Luckhurst	33
E.D. Solkar	c Fletcher b D'Oliveira	44	c and b Underwood	1
F.M. Engineer†	c Illingworth b Snow	59	not out	28
S. Abid Ali	b Illingworth	26	not out	4
S. Venkataraghavan	lbw b Underwood	24		
B.S. Bedi	c D'Oliveira b Illingworth	2		
B.S. Chandrasekhar	not out	0		
Extras	(B 6, LB 4, NB 1)	11	(B 6, LB 5, NB 1)	12
Total		**284**	(6 wickets)	**174**

INDIA	O	M	R	W	O	M	R	W
Abid Ali	12	2	47	0	3	1	5	0
Solkar	15	4	28	3	3	1	10	0
Gavaskar	1	0	1	0				
Bedi	36	5	120	2	1	0	1	1
Chandrasekhar	24	6	76	2	18·1	3	38	6
Venkataraghavan	20·4	3	63	2	20	4	44	2
ENGLAND								
Snow	24	5	68	2	11	7	14	1
Price	15	2	51	1	5	0	10	0
Hutton	12	2	30	0				
D'Oliveira	7	5	5	1	9	3	17	0
Illingworth	34·3	12	70	5	36	15	40	0
Underwood	25	6	49	1	38	14	72	3
Luckhurst					2	0	9	1

FALL OF WICKETS

Wkt	E 1st	I 1st	E 2nd	I 2nd
1st	5	17	23	2
2nd	111	21	24	37
3rd	135	114	24	76
4th	139	118	49	124
5th	143	125	54	134
6th	175	222	65	170
7th	278	230	72	–
8th	284	278	72	–
9th	352	284	96	–
10th	355	284	101	–

Umpires: C.S. Elliott (36) and A.E.G. Rhodes (5).

Close: 1st day – E(1) 355 all out; 2nd – no play; 3rd – I(1) 234-7 (Abid Ali 2, Venkataraghavan 3); 4th – I(2) 76-2 (Wadekar 45, Sardesai 13).

WEST INDIES v NEW ZEALAND 1971–72 (1st Test)

Played at Sabina Park, Kingston, Jamaica, on 16, 17, 18, 19, 21 February.
Toss: West Indies.   Result: MATCH DRAWN.
Debuts: West Indies – L.G. Rowe.

Lawrence George Rowe, a 23-year-old right-handed batsman playing in the town of his birth, became the first player to score hundreds in both innings of his first Test match. He was the third after K.D. Walters and S.M. Gavaskar to score a century and a double century in the same Test and his match aggregate of 314 is the record for any debutant. Rowe's 214 was scored in 427 minutes and included a six and 19 fours. His partnership of 269 with Fredericks remains the highest for any West Indies wicket against New Zealand. Turner carried his bat throughout New Zealand's innings for the highest score by any batsman achieving this feat in a Test. It was the second time he had carried his bat for New Zealand (also *Test No. 656*). He batted for 572 minutes and hit a five and 26 fours. His partnership of 220 with Wadsworth was a new record for New Zealand overseas and was then New Zealand's highest for the sixth wicket in all Tests. Rowe and Turner had both scored double centuries in their last first-class innings before this match. New Zealand were asked to score 341 runs in 310 minutes.

WEST INDIES

R.C. Fredericks	c and b Howarth	163	b Congdon	33
M.C. Carew	lbw b Congdon	43	b Congdon	22
L.G. Rowe	c Dowling b Howarth	214	not out	100
C.A. Davis	c Turner b Cunis	31	b Howarth	41
M.L.C. Foster	not out	28	not out	13
G. St A. Sobers*	not out	13		
D.A.J. Holford	)			
T.M. Findlay†	)			
L.R. Gibbs	) did not bat			
G.C. Shillingford	)			
U.G. Dowe	)			
Extras	(B 1, LB 11, NB 4)	16	(B 9)	9
Total	(4 wickets declared)	**508**	(3 wickets declared)	**218**

NEW ZEALAND

G.T. Dowling*	lbw b Dowe	4	b Holford	23
G.M. Turner	not out	223	b Holford	21
T.W. Jarvis	b Shillingford	7	(6) lbw b Holford	0
M.G. Burgess	b Dowe	15	c and b Dowe	101
B.E. Congdon	c and b Holford	11	(3) run out	16
B.F. Hastings	c Sobers b Gibbs	16	(5) b Holford	13
K.J. Wadsworth†	c Fredericks b Dowe	78	not out	36
R.S. Cunis	c Findlay b Shillingford	0	not out	13
H.J. Howarth	lbw b Holford	16		
J.C. Alabaster	c Dowe b Gibbs	2		
M.G. Webb	lbw b Shillingford	0		
Extras	(B 9, LB 1, NB 4)	14	(B 5, LB 6, NB 2)	13
Total		**386**	(6 wickets)	**236**

NEW ZEALAND	O	M	R	W	O	M	R	W
Webb	25	4	86	0	5	1	34	0
Cunis	34	3	118	1	20·4	2	87	0
Congdon	23	2	55	1	11	2	45	2
Alabaster	25	4	110	0				
Howarth	44	6	108	2	17	6	43	1
Burgess	2	0	15	0				

WEST INDIES	O	M	R	W	O	M	R	W
Dowe	29	5	75	3	13	3	46	1
Shillingford	26·5	8	63	3	11	2	32	0
Sobers	11	3	20	0	13	5	16	0
Holford	44	18	64	2	33	12	55	4
Gibbs	45	9	94	2	21	8	42	0
Foster	14	8	20	0	9	5	12	0
Fredericks	4	1	5	0	4	0	14	0
Carew	9	0	29	0	4	1	6	0
Davis	5	3	2	0				

FALL OF WICKETS

	WI	NZ	WI	NZ
Wkt	1st	1st	2nd	2nd
1st	78	4	44	50
2nd	347	25	57	51
3rd	428	48	155	96
4th	488	75	–	131
5th	–	108	–	135
6th	–	328	–	214
7th	–	329	–	–
8th	–	361	–	–
9th	–	364	–	–
10th	–	386	–	–

Umpires: J.R. Gayle (1) and D. Sang Hue (9).

Close: 1st day – WI(1) 274-1 (Fredericks 126, Rowe 94); 2nd – NZ(1) 49-3 (Turner 20, Congdon 1); 3rd – NZ(1) 280-5 (Turner 164, Wadsworth 50); 4th – WI(2) 168-3 (Rowe 67, Foster 1).

WEST INDIES v NEW ZEALAND 1971–72 (2nd Test)

Played at Queen's Park Oval, Port-of-Spain, Trinidad, on 9, 10, 11, 12, 14 March.
Toss: West Indies.   Result: MATCH DRAWN.
Debuts: Nil.

Dowling's declaration left West Indies 170 minutes in which to score 296, with a minimum of 20 overs to be bowled in the last hour. Congdon's partnership of 136 with Cunis remains New Zealand's highest for the eighth wicket in all Tests, and his stand of 139 with Turner in the second innings was then their highest for the second wicket in this series.

NEW ZEALAND

G.T. Dowling*	c Carew b Sobers	8	c Holder b Gibbs	10
G.M. Turner	c Carew b Sobers	2	b Sobers	95
B.E. Congdon	not out	166	c Holford b Ali	82
M.G. Burgess	c Findlay b Holder	32	not out	62
B.F. Hastings	c Rowe b Ali	3	not out	29
G.E. Vivian	lbw b Holder	0		
K.J. Wadsworth†	c and b Holford	7		
B.R. Taylor	b Foster	46		
R.S. Cunis	c and b Holder	51		
H.J. Howarth	lbw b Holder	0		
J.C. Alabaster	c Carew b Ali	18		
Extras	(B 6, NB 9)	15	(B 3, NB 7)	10
Total		**348**	(3 wickets declared)	**288**

WEST INDIES

R.C. Fredericks	c Wadsworth b Howarth	69	c Hastings b Taylor	31
M.C. Carew	lbw b Taylor	4	c Vivian b Taylor	28
L.G. Rowe	b Congdon	22	c and b Howarth	1
C.A. Davis	c Turner b Howarth	90	not out	29
M.L.C. Foster	b Howarth	23	c Burgess b Taylor	3
G. St A. Sobers*	c Wadsworth b Congdon	19	b Alabaster	9
D.A.J. Holford	lbw b Congdon	14	not out	9
T.M. Findlay†	b Taylor	16		
Inshan Ali	c Burgess b Taylor	25		
V.A. Holder	b Taylor	30		
L.R. Gibbs	not out	3		
Extras	(B 12, LB 9, W 1, NB 4)	26	(B 8, W 1, NB 2)	11
Total		**341**	(5 wickets)	**121**

WEST INDIES	O	M	R	W	O	M	R	W		FALL OF WICKETS			
Holder	32	13	60	4	15	5	17	0		NZ	WI	NZ	WI
Sobers	26	7	40	2	20	3	54	1	*Wkt*	*1st*	*1st*	*2nd*	*2nd*
Gibbs	29	6	64	0	35	14	67	1	1st	5	18	35	59
Ali	46·5	10	92	2	33	8	60	1	2nd	16	65	174	66
Holford	22	6	45	1	17	2	50	0	3rd	66	143	218	68
Davis	3	1	9	0	4	2	5	0	4th	77	200	–	73
Foster	9	5	12	1	7	2	9	0	5th	78	239	–	95
Carew	3	0	8	0	5	0	10	0	6th	99	245	–	–
Fredericks	5	3	3	0	4	2	6	0	7th	168	270	–	–
									8th	304	281	–	–
NEW ZEALAND									9th	307	327	–	–
Cunis	22	5	67	0	5	0	33	0	10th	348	341	–	–
Taylor	20·1	9	41	4	12	2	26	3					
Howarth	53	17	102	3	20	8	36	1					
Congdon	39	19	56	3	1	1	0	0					
Alabaster	21	7	49	0	4	2	5	1					
Vivian					4	2	10	0					

Umpires: R. Gosein (8) and D. Sang Hue (10).

Close: 1st day – NZ(1) 211-7 (Congdon 85, Cunis 20); 2nd – WI(1) 68-2 (Fredericks 35, Davis 0); 3rd – WI(1) 245-6 (Holford 1); 4th – NZ(2) 112-1 (Turner 65, Congdon 30).

WEST INDIES v NEW ZEALAND 1971–72 (3rd Test)

Played at Kensington Oval, Bridgetown, Barbados, on 23, 24, 25, 26, 28 March.
Toss: West Indies.   Result: MATCH DRAWN.
Debuts: Nil.

Taylor's innings analysis of 7 for 74 remains the best for New Zealand in this series. West Indies recorded their lowest total in a home Test against New Zealand. The partnership of 175 between Congdon and Hastings was New Zealand's highest for the fourth wicket in all Tests and remains the record by either side in this series – as does the sixth-wicket stand of 254 which Davis and Sobers shared in 363 minutes. West Indies scored their highest second innings total in any home Test. Sobers passed M.C. Cowdrey's world record aggregate of 7,459 when he had scored 11 in the second innings. Cowdrey subsequently scored a further 165 runs against Australia in 1974-75, but the record remained with Sobers until G. Boycott overtook his final aggregate of 8,032 in 1981-82 (*Test No. 914*).

WEST INDIES

R.C. Fredericks	c Hastings b Cunis	5	lbw b Cunis		28
M.C. Carew	c Morgan b Taylor	1	c Turner b Howarth		45
L.G. Rowe	c Wadsworth bTaylor	0	lbw b Congdon		51
C.A. Davis	c Jarvis b Taylor	1	(5) run out		183
G. St A. Sobers*	c Wadsworth b Congdon	35	(7) c Vivian b Taylor		142
M.L.C. Foster	c Wadsworth b Taylor	22	lbw b Taylor		4
D.A.J. Holford	c Wadsworth b Taylor	3	(8) c Wadsworth b Congdon		50
T.M. Findlay†	not out	44	(4) c Morgan b Howarth		9
Inshan Ali	b Taylor	3	not out		12
V.A. Holder	b Congdon	3	not out		16
G.C. Shillingford	c Morgan b Taylor	15			
Extras	(NB 1)	1	(B 6, LB 9, W 1, NB 8)		24
Total		**133**	(8 wickets)		**564**

NEW ZEALAND

G.M. Turner	c Holford b Holder	21
T.W. Jarvis	lbw b Shillingford	26
B.E. Congdon*	lbw b Holder	126
M.G. Burgess	c Fredericks b Sobers	19
B.F. Hastings	lbw b Sobers	105
R.W. Morgan	c Fredericks b Ali	2
G.E. Vivian	b Sobers	38
K.J. Wadsworth†	not out	15
B.R. Taylor	lbw b Sobers	0
R.S. Cunis	c Findlay b Holder	27
H.J. Howarth	b Shillingford	8
Extras	(LB 13, NB 22)	35
Total		**422**

NEW ZEALAND	O	M	R	W	O	M	R	W
Cunis	10	3	26	1	38	8	130	1
Taylor	20·3	6	74	7	33	3	108	2
Congdon	16	3	26	2	31	7	66	2
Howarth	3	1	6	0	74	24	138	2
Morgan					30	8	78	0
Vivian					8	2	20	0

WEST INDIES	O	M	R	W
Holder	40	13	91	3
Sobers	29	6	64	4
Shillingford	24·2	7	65	2
Davis	10	3	19	0
Ali	35	11	81	1
Holford	9	0	20	0
Foster	14	2	40	0
Fredericks	2	0	7	0

FALL OF WICKETS

	WI	NZ	WI
Wkt	*1st*	*1st*	*2nd*
1st	6	54	48
2nd	6	68	91
3rd	6	112	105
4th	12	287	163
5th	44	293	171
6th	52	356	425
7th	83	369	518
8th	99	369	544
9th	102	412	–
10th	.133	422	–

Umpires: H.B. de C. Jordan (19) and C.P. Kippins (8).

Close: 1st day – NZ(1) 31-0 (Turner 4, Jarvis 20); 2nd – NZ(1) 297-5 (Hastings 81, Vivian 1); 3rd – WI(2) 98-2 (Rowe 15, Findlay 3); 4th – WI(2) 297-5 (Davis 72, Sobers 74).

Test No. 696/13

WEST INDIES v NEW ZEALAND 1971–72 (4th Test)

Played at Bourda, Georgetown, Guyana, on 6, 7, 8, 9, 11 April.
Toss: West Indies.   Result: MATCH DRAWN.
Debuts: West Indies – G.A. Greenidge, A.B. Howard, A.I. Kallicharran.
West Indies declared on the third day after Kallicharran had completed a hundred in his first Test. The innings, which lasted 522 minutes, had been suspended for 16 minutes when bottles had been thrown on to the playing area after Lloyd's dismissal. New Zealand declared after batting for 780 minutes and reaching what was then their highest total in any Test; it remains the highest total in a Test at Georgetown. Turner's score of 259 is the highest for New Zealand in all Tests (beating G.T. Dowling's 239 in *Test No. 634*), the highest in any Test in Guyana and the record for either side in this series. He batted for 704 minutes and hit 22 fours. In his previous innings he had compiled the identical score against Guyana on the same ground. His partnership of 387 in 540 minutes with Jarvis remains the highest first-wicket partnership by New Zealand batsmen in all first-class cricket and the record for any wicket by either side in this series.

WEST INDIES

R.C. Fredericks	c Turner b Cunis	41	not out	42
G.A. Greenidge	c Wadsworth b Taylor	50	not out	35
L.G. Rowe	b Congdon	31		
C.H. Lloyd	run out	43		
C.A. Davis	c Wadsworth b Taylor	28		
A.I. Kallicharran	not out	100		
G. St A. Sobers*	c Burgess b Taylor	5		
D.A.J. Holford	lbw b Congdon	28		
T.M. Findlay†	not out	15		
V.A. Holder	) did not bat			
A.B. Howard	)			
Extras	(B 10, LB 5, W 1, NB 8)	24	(B 4, LB 2, W 1, NB 2)	9
Total	(7 wickets declared)	**365**	(0 wickets)	**86**

NEW ZEALAND

G.M. Turner	lbw b Howard	259
T.W. Jarvis	c Greenidge b Holford	182
B.E. Congdon*	not out	61
M.G. Burgess	b Howard	8
B.F. Hastings	not out	18
R.W. Morgan	)	
G.E. Vivian	)	
K.J. Wadsworth†	) did not bat	
B.R. Taylor	)	
R.S. Cunis	)	
H.J. Howarth	)	
Extras	(LB 11, NB 4)	15
Total	(3 wickets declared)	**543**

NEW ZEALAND	O	M	R	W	O	M	R	W		FALL OF WICKETS		
										WI	NZ	WI
Cunis	24	5	61	1	5	2	13	0	*Wkt*	*1st*	*1st*	*2nd*
Taylor	37	7	105	3	6	3	9	0	1st	79	387	–
Congdon	33	7	86	2					2nd	103	482	–
Howarth	38	10	79	0	9	3	12	0	3rd	160	496	–
Vivian	3	0	10	0	3	0	16	0	4th	178	–	–
Morgan					9	3	10	0	5th	237	–	–
Burgess					5	3	12	0	6th	244	–	–
Turner					2	1	5	0	7th	305	–	–
Jarvis					1	1	0	0	8th	–	–	–
WEST INDIES									9th	–	–	–
Holder	24	8	39	0					10th	–	–	–
Sobers	42	15	76	0								
Lloyd	36	11	74	0								
Howard	62	16	140	2								
Holford	54	24	78	1								
Greenidge	14	4	34	0								
Davis	25	8	42	0								
Kallicharran	6	1	17	0								
Rowe	5	0	28	0								

Umpires: H.B. de C. Jordan (20) and C.P. Kippins (9).

Close: 1st day – WI(1) 201-4 (Davis 14, Kallicharran 14); 2nd – WI(1) 310-7 (Kallicharran 59, Findlay 5): 3rd – NZ(1) 163-0 (Turner 87, Jarvis 71); 4th – NZ(1) 410-1 (Turner 210, Congdon 4).

WEST INDIES v NEW ZEALAND 1971–72 (5th Test)

Played at Queen's Park Oval, Port-of-Spain, Trinidad, on 20, 21, 22, 23, 25, 26 April.
Toss: West Indies.   Result: MATCH DRAWN.
Debuts: West Indies – R.R. Jumadeen.

Sobers became the first captain to win all five tosses in a rubber twice; he had been equally successful in England in 1966. Kallicharran was the second batsman after Rowe to score hundreds in his first two innings in Test cricket: Rowe had done so in his first match (*Test No. 693*). West Indies did not enforce the follow on and New Zealand were eventually left 605 minutes in which to score 401 to win the rubber. Wadsworth and Taylor batted out the last 106 minutes to earn a draw. Sobers made his 85th consecutive appearance for West Indies in this match – the world Test record until G.R. Viswanath improved upon it in 1982-83 (*Test No. 947*). His 39 successive Tests as captain remained the world record until 1989. Knee surgery caused him to miss the 1972-73 home rubber against Australia.

WEST INDIES

R.C. Fredericks	run out	60		c Turner b Taylor	15
G.A. Greenidge	c Hastings b Howarth	38		c Wadsworth b Taylor	21
A.I. Kallicharran	c Wadsworth b Cunis	101		c Vivian b Taylor	18
C.A. Davis	c Hastings b Morgan	40		c Taylor b Howarth	23
C.H. Lloyd	c Howarth b Taylor	18		c Congdon b Howarth	5
T.M. Findlay†	b Congdon	9	(7)	lbw b Howarth	6
D.A.J. Holford	retired hurt	46	(9)	run out	25
G. St A. Sobers*	c Hastings b Howarth	28	(6)	b Taylor	2
Inshan Ali	c Wadsworth b Taylor	0	(8)	lbw b Taylor	16
V.A. Holder	c and b Taylor	12		b Cunis	42
R.R. Jumadeen	not out	3		not out	2
Extras	(B 2, LB 6, NB 5)	13		(B 5, LB 12, NB 2)	19
Total		**368**			**194**

NEW ZEALAND

G.M. Turner	b Holder	1		c Findlay b Holder	50
T.W. Jarvis	c Sobers b Ali	40		lbw b Ali	22
B.E. Congdon*	c Findlay b Lloyd	11		b Sobers	58
M.G. Burgess	b Ali	5		c Greenidge b Ali	6
R.S. Cunis	c Findlay b Ali	2			
B.F. Hastings	c Findlay b Jumadeen	27	(5)	c Lloyd b Holder	11
G.E. Vivian	b Sobers	24	(6)	lbw b Holder	4
B.R. Taylor	b Sobers	26	(9)	not out	42
R.W. Morgan	c Holder b Ali	4	(8)	b Holder	2
K.J. Wadsworth†	st Findlay b Ali	1	(7)	not out	40
H.J. Howarth	not out	0			
Extras	(B 3, LB 6, NB 12)	21		(B 2, LB 1, W 1, NB 14)	18
Total		**162**		(7 wickets)	**253**

NEW ZEALAND	O	M	R	W	O	M	R	W		FALL OF WICKETS			
Cunis	20	5	61	1	4·2	0	21	1		WI	NZ	WI	NZ
Taylor	19·4	1	74	3	24	8	41	5	*Wkt*	*1st*	*1st*	*2nd*	*2nd*
Congdon	31	6	73	1	15	2	39	0	1st	92	18	35	62
Howarth	51	17	109	2	29	8	70	3	2nd	107	39	48	105
Morgan	7	0	38	1	2	1	4	0	3rd	208	51	66	122
									4th	265	53	73	157
WEST INDIES									5th	265	86	90	157
Holder	16	1	37	1	26	12	41	4	6th	312	106	90	181
Sobers	11	5	17	2	29	12	45	1	7th	348	142	97	188
Lloyd	3	0	10	1					8th	360	150	123	–
Ali	26·4	8	59	5	51	16	99	2	9th	368	162	179	–
Jumadeen	19	9	18	1	45	22	46	0	10th	–	162	194	–
Greenidge					1	0	2	0					
Fredericks					2	1	2	0					
Kallicharran					1	1	0	0					

Umpires: R. Gosein (9) and D. Sang Hue (11).

Close: 1st day – WI(1) 278-5 (Findlay 2, Holford 10); 2nd – NZ(1) 53-4 (Jarvis 26, Hastings 0); 3rd – NZ(1) 162 all out; 4th – WI(2) 192-9 (Holder 41, Jumadeen 2); 5th – NZ(2) 51-0 (Turner 31, Jarvis 17).

ENGLAND v AUSTRALIA 1972 (1st Test)

Played at Old Trafford, Manchester, on 8, 9, 10, 12, 13 June.
Toss: England.   Result: ENGLAND won by 89 runs.
Debuts: England – A.W. Greig; Australia – D.J. Colley, B.C. Francis.

At 3.12 on the fifth afternoon England gained their first victory in the first Test of a home series against Australia since 1930. Illingworth won the toss on his 40th birthday. Soon after the start, which had been delayed 90 minutes because of a wet outfield, Boycott was struck above the left elbow by a ball from Lillee. He retired (3) at lunch, when England had scored 13, and resumed at 118. Greig was top scorer in both innings of his first official Test. England lost their last four second innings wickets to the first six deliveries with the second new ball, including those of Illingworth, Snow and Gifford to four balls from Lillee. Marsh, who equalled the series record with five catches in the second innings, scored 91 off 111 balls in 123 minutes and hit four sixes and nine fours. His partnership of 104 in 82 minutes with Gleeson was Australia's highest for the ninth wicket in all Tests outside Australia.

ENGLAND

G. Boycott	c Stackpole b Gleeson	8	lbw b Gleeson		47
J.H. Edrich	run out	49	c Marsh b Watson		26
B.W. Luckhurst	b Colley	14	c Marsh b Colley		0
M.J.K. Smith	lbw b Lillee	10	c Marsh b Lillee		34
B.L. D'Oliveira	b G.S. Chappell	23	c Watson b Lillee		37
A.W. Greig	lbw b Colley	57	b G.S. Chappell		62
A.P.E. Knott†	c Marsh b Lillee	18	c Marsh b Lillee		1
R. Illingworth*	not out	26	c I.M. Chappell b Lillee		14
J.A. Snow	b Colley	3	lbw b Lillee		0
N. Gifford	run out	15	c Marsh b Lillee		0
G.G. Arnold	c Francis b Gleeson	1	not out		0
Extras	(B 10, LB 9, W 2, NB 4)	25	(B 4, LB 8, NB 1)		13
Total		**249**			**234**

AUSTRALIA

K.R. Stackpole	lbw b Arnold	53	b Greig		67
B.C. Francis	lbw b D'Oliveira	27	lbw b Snow		6
I.M. Chappell*	c Smith b Greig	0	c Knott b Snow		7
G.S. Chappell	c Greig b Snow	24	c D'Oliveira b Arnold		23
G.D. Watson	c Knott b Arnold	2	c and b Snow		0
K.D. Walters	c Illingworth b Snow	17	b Greig		20
R.J. Inverarity	c Knott b Arnold	4	c Luckhurst b D'Oliveira		3
R.W. Marsh†	c Edrich b Arnold	8	c Knott b Greig		91
D.J. Colley	b Snow	1	c Greig b Snow		4
J.W. Gleeson	b Snow	0	b Greig		30
D.K. Lillee	not out	1	not out		0
Extras	(B 1, LB 4)	5	(W 1)		1
Total		**142**			**252**

AUSTRALIA	O	M	R	W	O	M	R	W
Lillee	29	14	40	2	30	8	66	6
Colley	33	3	83	3	23	3	68	1
G.S. Chappell	16	6	28	1	21·2	6	42	1
Walters	5	1	7	0				
Watson	4	2	8	0	5	0	29	1
Gleeson	24·4	10	45	2	7	3	16	1
Inverarity	9	3	13	0				
ENGLAND								
Snow	20	7	41	4	27	2	87	4
Arnold	25	4	62	4	20	2	59	1
Greig	7	1	21	1	19·2	7	53	4
D'Oliveira	6	1	13	1	16	4	23	1
Gifford					3	0	29	0

FALL OF WICKETS

	E	A	E	A
Wkt	1st	1st	2nd	2nd
1st	50	68	60	9
2nd	86	69	65	31
3rd	99	91	81	77
4th	118	99	140	78
5th	127	119	182	115
6th	190	124	192	120
7th	200	134	234	136
8th	209	137	234	147
9th	243	137	234	251
10th	249	142	234	252

Umpires: C.S. Elliott (37) and T.W. Spencer (5).

Close: 1st day – E(1) 147-5 (Greig 26, Knott 3); 2nd – A(1) 103-4 (G.S. Chappell 15, Walters 1); 3rd – E(2) 136-3 (Smith 18, D'Oliveira 35); 4th – A(2) 57-2 (Stackpole 28, G.S. Chappell 16).

ENGLAND v AUSTRALIA 1972 (2nd Test)

Played at Lord's, London, on 22, 23, 24, 26 June.
Toss: England.   Result: AUSTRALIA won by eight wickets.
Debuts: Australia – R. Edwards, R.A.L. Massie.

Australia won what has become known as 'Massie's Match' at 2.34 on the fourth afternoon. Robert Arnold Lockyer Massie, a 25-year-old Western Australian from Perth, returned match figures of 16 for 137 on his first appearance in Test cricket. His analysis remains the record for any bowler in his first Test and for any Test at Lord's; only J.C. Laker and S.F. Barnes have taken more wickets in a Test. Only three other bowlers A.E. Trott, A.L. Valentine and N.D. Hirwani, have taken eight wickets in an innings in their first Test. In 1970 the right-arm fast-medium swing bowling of Massie produced figures of 3 for 166 in two matches for Northamptonshire Second Eleven and he was not offered a contract by the county. This result ended Australia's longest run without a victory against England – 11 matches since Manchester 1968 (*Test No. 637*) had produced four defeats and seven draws.

ENGLAND

G. Boycott	b Massie	11	b Lillee		6
J.H. Edrich	lbw b Lillee	10	c Marsh b Massie		6
B.W. Luckhurst	b Lillee	1	c Marsh b Lillee		4
M.J.K. Smith	b Massie	34	c Edwards b Massie		30
B.L. D'Oliveira	lbw b Massie	32	c G.S. Chappell b Massie		3
A.W. Greig	c Marsh b Massie	54	c I.M. Chappell b Massie		3
A.P.E. Knott†	c Colley b Massie	43	c G.S. Chappell b Massie		12
R. Illingworth*	lbw b Massie	30	c Stackpole b Massie		12
J.A. Snow	b Massie	37	c Marsh b Massie		0
N. Gifford	c Marsh b Massie	3	not out		16
J.S.E. Price	not out	4	c G.S. Chappell b Massie		19
Extras	(LB 6, W 1, NB 6)	13	(W 1, NB 4)		5
Total		**272**			**116**

AUSTRALIA

K.R. Stackpole	c Gifford b Price	5	not out		57
B.C. Francis	b Snow	0	c Knott b Price		9
I.M. Chappell*	c Smith b Snow	56	c Luckhurst b D'Oliveira		6
G.S. Chappell	b D'Oliveira	131	not out		7
K.D. Walters	c Illingworth b Snow	1			
R. Edwards	c Smith b Illingworth	28			
J.W. Gleeson	c Knott b Greig	1			
R.W. Marsh†	c Greig b Snow	50			
D.J. Colley	c Greig b Price	25			
R.A.L. Massie	c Knott b Snow	0			
D.K. Lillee	not out	2			
Extras	(LB 7, NB 2)	9	(LB 2)		2
Total		**308**	(2 wickets)		**81**

AUSTRALIA	O	M	R	W	O	M	R	W
Lillee	28	3	90	2	21	6	50	2
Massie	32·5	7	84	8	27·2	9	53	8
Colley	16	2	42	0	7	1	8	0
G.S. Chappell	6	1	18	0				
Gleeson	9	1	25	0				
ENGLAND								
Snow	32	13	57	5	8	2	15	0
Price	26·1	5	87	2	7	0	28	1
Greig	29	6	74	1	3	0	17	0
D'Oliveira	17	5	48	1	8	3	14	1
Gifford	11	4	20	0				
Illingworth	7	2	13	1				
Luckhurst					0·5	0	5	0

FALL OF WICKETS

	E	A	E	A
Wkt	1st	1st	2nd	2nd
1st	22	1	12	20
2nd	23	7	16	51
3rd	28	82	18	–
4th	84	84	25	–
5th	97	190	31	–
6th	193	212	52	–
7th	200	250	74	–
8th	260	290	74	–
9th	265	290	81	–
10th	272	308	116	–

Umpires: D.J. Constant (3) and A.E. Fagg (11).

Close: 1st day – E(1) 249-7 (Illingworth 23, Snow 28); 2nd – A(1) 201-5 (G.S. Chappell 105, Gleeson 0); 3rd – E(2) 86-9 (Gifford 3, Price 2).

Test No. 700/212

ENGLAND v AUSTRALIA 1972 (3rd Test)

Played at Trent Bridge, Nottingham, on 13, 14, 15, 17, 18 July.
Toss: England.   Result: MATCH DRAWN.
Debuts: Nil.

England were set 451 runs in 569 minutes after Illingworth had become the first England captain to invite the opposition to bat in a Test at Trent Bridge. For the second time in the rubber Marsh equalled the series record by holding five catches in an innings. England were set 451 runs in a minimum of 569 minutes. Luckhurst's defiant 325-minute vigil produced England's highest individual score of the summer. Massie's tally of 21 wickets so far in the rubber is the most taken by any bowler in his first two Tests against England.

AUSTRALIA

K.R. Stackpole	c Parfitt b Greig	114	c Luckhurst b Snow		12
B.C. Francis	c Smith b Lever	10			
I.M. Chappell*	c Knott b Snow	34	lbw b Illingworth		50
G.S. Chappell	c Parfitt b Snow	26	b Snow		72
K.D. Walters	c Parfitt b Snow	2	c Gifford b Snow		7
R. Edwards	c Knott b Snow	13	(2) not out		170
R.W. Marsh†	c D'Oliveira b Gifford	41	(6) not out		7
D.J. Colley	c Greig b D'Oliveira	54			
R.A.L. Massie	c Parfitt b Snow	0			
J.W. Gleeson	not out	6			
D.K. Lillee	c Knott b Greig	0			
Extras	(B 4, LB 6, NB 5)	15	(LB 4, W 1, NB 1)		6
Total		**315**	(4 wickets declared)		**324**

ENGLAND

B.W. Luckhurst	lbw b Lillee	23	c G.S. Chappell b I.M. Chappell		96
J.H. Edrich	c Marsh b Colley	37	b Massie		15
P.H. Parfitt	b Massie	0	b Lillee		46
M.J.K. Smith	b Lillee	17	lbw b Lillee		15
B.L. D'Oliveira	lbw b Lillee	29	not out		50
N. Gifford	c Marsh b Massie	16			
A.W. Greig	c Marsh b Massie	7	(6) not out		36
A.P.E. Knott†	c Marsh b Massie	0			
R. Illingworth*	not out	24			
J.A. Snow	c Marsh b Lillee	6			
P. Lever	c Walters b Colley	9			
Extras	(B 5, LB 2, W 1, NB 13)	21	(B 17, LB 9, W 4, NB 2)		32
Total		**189**	(4 wickets)		**290**

ENGLAND	O	M	R	W	O	M	R	W		FALL OF WICKETS			
Snow	31	8	92	5	24	1	94	3		A	E	A	E
Lever	26	8	61	1	19	3	76	0	Wkt	1st	1st	2nd	2nd
Greig	38·4	9	88	2	12	1	46	0	1st	16	55	15	50
D'Oliveira	18	5	41	1	7	0	12	0	2nd	98	60	139	167
Gifford	5	1	18	1	15	1	49	0	3rd	157	74	285	200
Illingworth					15	4	41	1	4th	165	111	295	201
									5th	189	133	–	–
AUSTRALIA									6th	227	145	–	–
Lillee	29	15	35	4	25	10	40	2	7th	289	145	–	–
Massie	30	10	43	4	36	13	49	1	8th	298	155	–	–
Colley	23·3	5	68	2	19	6	43	0	9th	315	166	–	–
Gleeson	6	1	22	0	30	13	49	0	10th	315	189	–	–
I.M.Chappell					12	5	26	1					
G.S.Chappell					9	4	16	0					
Stackpole					17	7	35	0					

Umpires: A.E.G. Rhodes (6) and T.W. Spencer (6).

Close: 1st day – A(1) 249-6 (Marsh 17, Colley 18); 2nd – E(1) 117-4 (D'Oliveira 25, Gifford 0); 3rd – A(2) 157-2 (Edwards 90, G.S. Chappell 0); 4th – E(2) 111-1 (Luckhurst 60, Parfitt 14).

ENGLAND v AUSTRALIA 1972 (4th Test)

Played at Headingley, Leeds, on 27, 28, 29 July.
Toss: Australia.   Result: ENGLAND won by nine wickets.
Debuts: Nil.

England retained the Ashes at 5.04 on the third evening. The pitch took spin from the first morning and was the subject of much criticism. It had been flooded by a freak storm the previous weekend and the weather had prevented the use of a heavy roller; it was also grassless – the result, apparently, of an attack of *Fusarium Oxysporum*, a fungus that thrives on soil temperatures of above 75°F – not the most likely denizen to be found in Leeds. Underwood was the third bowler after J.C. Laker (1956) and F.S. Trueman (1961) to take ten or more wickets against Australia at Headingley.

AUSTRALIA

K.R. Stackpole	c Knott b Underwood	52	lbw b Underwood	28
R. Edwards	c Knott b Snow	0	c Knott b Arnold	0
I.M. Chappell*	c and b Illingworth	26	c Knott b Arnold	0
G.S. Chappell	lbw b Underwood	12	c D'Oliveira b Underwood	13
A.P. Sheahan	c Illingworth b Underwood	0	not out	41
K.D. Walters	b Illingworth	4	c Parfitt b Underwood	3
R.W. Marsh†	c Illingworth b Underwood	1	c Knott b Underwood	1
R.J. Inverarity	not out	26	c Illingworth b Underwood	0
A.A. Mallett	lbw b Snow	20	b Illingworth	9
R.A.L. Massie	b Arnold	0	(11) b Illingworth	18
D.K. Lillee	c Greig b Arnold	0	(10) b Underwood	7
Extras	(LB 2, NB 3)	5	(LB 12, NB 4)	16
Total		**146**		**136**

ENGLAND

B.W. Luckhurst	c G.S. Chappell b Mallett	18	not out	12
J.H. Edrich	c I.M. Chappell b Mallett	45	lbw b Lillee	4
P.H. Parfitt	c Marsh b Lillee	2	not out	0
K.W.R. Fletcher	lbw b Mallett	5		
B.L. D'Oliveira	b Mallett	12		
A.W. Greig	c G.S. Chappell b Inverarity	24		
A.P.E. Knott†	st Marsh b Mallett	0		
R. Illingworth*	lbw b Lillee	57		
J.A. Snow	st Marsh b Inverarity	48		
D.L. Underwood	c I.M. Chappell b Inverarity	5		
G.G. Arnold	not out	1		
Extras	(B 19, LB 15, W 4, NB 8)	46	(LB 3, NB 2)	5
Total		**263**	(1 wicket)	**21**

ENGLAND	O	M	R	W	O	M	R	W		FALL OF WICKETS			
Arnold	9·5	2	28	2	6	1	17	2		A	E	A	E
Snow	13	5	11	2	10	2	26	0	*Wkt*	*1st*	*1st*	*2nd*	*2nd*
Greig	10	1	25	0					1st	10	43	5	7
Illingworth	21	11	32	2	19·1	5	32	2	2nd	79	52	7	–
Underwood	31	16	37	4	21	6	45	6	3rd	93	66	31	–
D'Oliveira	2	1	8	0					4th	93	76	51	–
									5th	97	108	63	–
AUSTRALIA									6th	98	108	69	–
Lillee	26·1	10	39	2	5	2	7	1	7th	98	128	69	–
Massie	14	4	34	0					8th	145	232	93	–
Mallett	52	20	114	5	5	1	9	0	9th	146	246	111	–
Inverarity	33	19	26	3					10th	146	263	136	–
I.M. Chappell	3	2	1	0									
G.S. Chappell	2	0	3	0									

Umpires: D.J. Constant (4) and C.S. Elliott (38).

Close: 1st day – E(1) 43-0 (Luckhurst 18, Edrich 21); 2nd – E(1) 252-9 (Illingworth 54, Arnold 0).

ENGLAND v AUSTRALIA 1972 (5th Test)

Played at Kennington Oval, London, on 10, 11, 12, 14, 15, 16 August.
Toss: England.   Result: AUSTRALIA won by five wickets.
Debuts: England – B. Wood.

Australia won at 2.49 on the sixth afternoon and so squared the rubber. Lillee dismissed Parfitt, Illingworth and Snow to take three wickets in four balls for the second time in the rubber. His 31 wickets in this rubber was the record for Australia in England until 1981. The Chappells provided the first instance in Test cricket of brothers each scoring hundreds in the same innings. Marsh's 23 dismissals established the record for Australia in a rubber in England. Illingworth caught his foot in the bowlers' rough, strained a tendon in his right ankle and was unable to complete his ninth over. From 5.30 on the fourth evening, Edrich led an England team bereft of three bowlers: Illingworth, Snow (bruised arm), and D'Oliveira (strained back muscle). The second six-day Test in England (also *Test No. 198*) was the first to feature an Australian team without a New South Wales representative. More than 15 million calls were made to the Post Office scores service during the rubber.

ENGLAND

B. Wood	c Marsh b Watson	26	lbw b Massie		90
J.H. Edrich	lbw b Lillee	8	b Lillee		18
P.H. Parfitt	b Lillee	51	b Lillee		18
J.H. Hampshire	c Inverarity b Mallett	42	c I.M. Chappell b Watson		20
B.L. D'Oliveira	c G.S. Chappell b Mallett	4	c I.M. Chappell b Massie		43
A.W. Greig	c Stackpole b Mallett	16	c Marsh b Lillee		29
R. Illingworth*	c G.S. Chappell b Lillee	0	lbw b Lillee		31
A.P.E. Knott†	c Marsh b Lillee	92	b Lillee		63
J.A. Snow	c Marsh b Lillee	3	c Stackpole b Mallett		14
G.G. Arnold	b Inverarity	22	lbw b Mallett		4
D.L. Underwood	not out	3	not out		0
Extras	(LB 8, W 1, NB 8)	17	(B 11, LB 8, NB 7)		26
Total		**284**			**356**

AUSTRALIA

G.D. Watson	c Knott b Arnold	13	lbw b Arnold		6
K.R. Stackpole	b Snow	18	c Knott b Greig		79
I.M. Chappell*	c Snow b Arnold	118	c sub (R.G.D. Willis) b Underwood		37
G.S. Chappell	c Greig b Illingworth	113	lbw b Underwood		16
R. Edwards	b Underwood	79	lbw b Greig		1
A.P. Sheahan	c Hampshire b Underwood	5	not out		44
R.W. Marsh†	b Underwood	0	not out		43
R.J. Inverarity	c Greig b Underwood	28			
A.A. Mallett	run out	5			
R.A.L. Massie	b Arnold	4			
D.K. Lillee	not out	0			
Extras	(LB 8, W 1, NB 7)	16	(LB 6, NB 10)		16
Total		**399**	(5 wickets)		**242**

AUSTRALIA	O	M	R	W	O	M	R	W		FALL OF WICKETS			
Lillee	24·2	7	58	5	32·2	8	123	5		E	A	E	A
Massie	27	5	69	0	32	10	77	2	Wkt	1st	1st	2nd	2nd
Watson	12	4	23	1	19	8	32	1	1st	25	24	56	16
Mallett	23	4	80	3	23	7	66	2	2nd	50	34	81	132
G.S. Chappell	2	0	18	0					3rd	133	235	114	136
Inverarity	4	0	19	1	15	4	32	0	4th	142	296	194	137
									5th	145	310	205	171
ENGLAND									6th	145	310	270	–
Arnold	35	11	87	3	15	5	26	1	7th	159	383	271	–
Snow	34·5	5	111	1	6	1	21	0	8th	181	387	333	–
Greig	18	9	25	0	25·3	10	49	2	9th	262	399	356	–
D'Oliveira	9	4	17	0					10th	284	399	356	–
Underwood	38	16	90	4	35	11	94	2					
Illingworth	17	4	53	1	8·5	2	26	0					
Parfitt					2	0	10	0					

Umpires: A.E. Fagg (12) and A.E.G. Rhodes (7).

Close: 1st day – E(1) 267-9 (Knott 78, Underwood 3); 2nd – A(1) 274-3 (I.M. Chappell 107, Edwards 16); 3rd – A(1) 394-8 (Mallett 3, Massie 2); 4th – E(2) 227-5 (Greig 13, Illingworth 10); 5th – A(2) 116-1 (Stackpole 70, I.M. Chappell 29).

INDIA v ENGLAND 1972–73 (1st Test)

Played at Feroz Shah Kotla, Delhi, on 20, 21, 23, 24, 25 December.
Toss: India.   Result: ENGLAND won by six wickets.
Debuts: India – R.D. Parkar; England – A.R. Lewis.

Lewis captained England in his first Test and shared with Greig an unbroken fifth-wicket partnership of 101 which, shortly after lunch on Christmas Day, took England to their first victory in Delhi and their first in India since 1951–52 (*Test No. 342*). Chandrasekhar achieved his best innings analysis in Test matches. Bedi took his 100th Test wicket when he dismissed Fletcher.

INDIA

S.M. Gavaskar	c Greig b Arnold	12	c Greig b Underwood		8
R.D. Parkar	c Pocock b Arnold	4	lbw b Arnold		35
A.L. Wadekar*	b Arnold	3	st Knott b Pocock		24
D.N. Sardesai	b Arnold	12	c Greig b Underwood		10
G.R. Viswanath	c Knott b Greig	27	b Underwood		3
E.D. Solkar	c Knott b Greig	20	c sub (G.R.J. Roope) b Arnold		75
F.M. Engineer†	b Cottam	15	c Knott b Underwood		63
S. Abid Ali	c Greig b Cottam	58	c Fletcher b Pocock		0
S. Venkataraghavan	c Greig b Arnold	17	b Pocock		0
B.S. Bedi	not out	4	b Arnold		2
B.S. Chandrasekhar	b Arnold	0	not out		1
Extras	(LB 1)	1	(B 8, LB 2, NB 2)		12
Total		**173**			**233**

ENGLAND

B. Wood	c Venkataraghavan b Chandrasekhar	19	c Solkar b Bedi		45
D.L. Amiss	st Engineer b Bedi	46	c Chandrasekhar b Bedi		9
K.W.R. Fletcher	b Chandrasekhar	2	c Wadekar b Bedi		0
M.H. Denness	c Engineer b Bedi	16	c Viswanath b Chandrasekhar		35
A.R. Lewis*	lbw b Chandrasekhar	0	not out		70
A.W. Greig	not out	68	not out		40
A.P.E. Knott†	c Solkar b Chandrasekhar	4			
G.G. Arnold	c Abid Ali b Chandrasekhar	12			
P.I. Pocock	lbw b Chandrasekhar	0			
D.L. Underwood	c Solkar b Chandrasekhar	6			
R.M.H. Cottam	c Abid Ali b Chandrasekhar	3			
Extras	(B 4, LB 17, NB 3)	24	(LB 9)		9
Total		**200**	(4 wickets)		**208**

ENGLAND	O	M	R	W	O	M	R	W
Arnold	23·4	7	45	6	20·4	6	46	3
Cottam	23	5	66	2	7	1	18	0
Greig	23	8	32	2	6	1	16	0
Pocock	6	1	13	0	33	7	72	3
Underwood	9	1	16	0	30	13	56	4
Wood					2	0	13	0
INDIA								
Abid Ali	9	5	13	0	4	2	6	0
Solkar	3	0	8	0	3	0	13	0
Bedi	47	23	59	2	39	20	50	3
Chandrasekhar	41·5	18	79	8	24	7	70	1
Venkataraghavan	8	2	17	0	16	0	47	0
Sardesai					1·5	0	12	0
Gavaskar					1	0	1	0

FALL OF WICKETS

	I	E	I	E
Wkt	1st	1st	2nd	2nd
1st	7	61	26	18
2nd	15	69	59	20
3rd	20	71	82	76
4th	43	71	86	107
5th	59	119	103	–
6th	80	123	206	–
7th	123	152	207	–
8th	169	160	211	–
9th	169	180	215	–
10th	173	200	233	–

Umpires: M.V. Nagendra (5) and B. Satyaji Rao (10).

Close: 1st day – I(1) 156-7 (Abid Ali 47, Venkataraghavan 15); 2nd – E(1) 151-6 (Greig 43, Arnold 12); 3rd – I(2) 123-5 (Solkar 30, Engineer 3); 4th – E(2) 106-3 (Wood 45, Lewis 17).

INDIA v ENGLAND 1972–73 (2nd Test)

Played at Eden Gardens, Calcutta, on 30, 31 December, 1, 3, 4 January.
Toss: India.   Result: INDIA won by 28 runs.
Debuts: England – C.M. Old.

India won in the first over after lunch on the fifth day. Durani (strained thigh) batted with Gavaskar as his runner in the second innings. Engineer captained India on the field for most of the match after Wadekar had been taken ill with influenza.

INDIA

S.M. Gavaskar	c Old b Underwood	18	lbw b Old	2
R.D. Parkar	c Knott b Old	26	c Fletcher b Old	15
A.L. Wadekar*	run out	44	(7) lbw b Greig	0
G.R. Viswanath	c Wood b Cottam	3	c Fletcher b Old	34
S.A. Durani	b Greig	4	(3) c Fletcher b Greig	53
E.D. Solkar	b Old	19	c Knott b Greig	6
F.M. Engineer†	b Underwood	75	(5) c Knott b Underwood	17
S. Abid Ali	b Cottam	3	c Amiss b Old	3
E.A.S. Prasanna	lbw b Cottam	6	b Greig	0
B.S. Bedi	run out	0	not out	9
B.S. Chandrasekhar	not out	1	b Greig	1
Extras	(LB 3, NB 8)	11	(B 8, LB 2, NB 5)	15
Total		**210**		**155**

ENGLAND

B. Wood	b Bedi	11	b Abid Ali	1
D.L. Amiss	c Solkar b Chandrasekhar	11	c Engineer b Bedi	1
K.W.R. Fletcher	c Gavaskar b Prasanna	16	lbw b Bedi	5
M.H. Denness	c Solkar b Chandrasekhar	21	lbw b Chandrasekhar	32
A.R. Lewis*	lbw b Bedi	4	c Solkar b Bedi	3
A.W. Greig	c sub (S. Venkataraghavan) b Prasanna	29	lbw b Chandrasekhar	67
A.P.E. Knott†	st Engineer b Chandrasekhar	35	c Durani b Chandrasekhar	2
C.M. Old	not out	33	not out	17
P.I. Pocock	b Prasanna	3	c and b Bedi	5
D.L. Underwood	c Solkar b Chandrasekhar	0	c Wadekar b Bedi	4
R.M.H. Cottam	lbw b Chandrasekhar	3	lbw b Chandrasekhar	13
Extras	(LB 4, NB 4)	8	(B 6, LB 5, NB 2)	13
Total		**174**		**163**

ENGLAND	O	M	R	W	O	M	R	W
Old	26	7	72	2	21	6	43	4
Cottam	23	6	45	3	5	0	18	0
Underwood	20·4	11	43	2	14	4	36	1
Pocock	19	10	26	0	8	1	19	0
Greig	9	1	13	1	19·5	9	24	5
INDIA								
Abid Ali	4	1	4	0	8	2	12	1
Solkar	3	1	5	0	1	1	0	0
Bedi	26	7	59	2	40	12	63	5
Chandrasekhar	26·2	5	65	5	29	14	42	4
Prasanna	16	4	33	3	9	0	19	0
Durani					4	1	14	0

FALL OF WICKETS

Wkt	I 1st	E 1st	I 2nd	E 2nd
1st	29	18	2	3
2nd	68	37	33	8
3rd	78	47	104	11
4th	99	56	112	17
5th	100	84	133	114
6th	163	117	133	119
7th	176	144	135	123
8th	192	153	135	130
9th	192	154	147	138
10th	210	174	155	163

Umpires: A.M. Mamsa (5) and J. Reuben (2).

Close: 1st day – I(1) 148-5 (Solkar 19, Engineer 26); 2nd – E(1) 126-6 (Knott 23, Old 4); 3rd – I(2) 121-4 (Engineer 10, Solkar 2); 4th – E(2) 105-4 (Denness 28, Greig 60).

INDIA v ENGLAND 1972–73 (3rd Test)

Played at Chepauk, Madras, on 12, 13, 14, 16, 17 January.
Toss: England.   Result: INDIA won by four wickets.
Debuts: Nil.

India won shortly before lunch on the fifth day. Chandrasekhar took his 100th wicket in Test matches when he dismissed Amiss in the second innings. The Nawab of Pataudi had been stripped of his royal title by the Indian government since making his last appearance in Test cricket in 1969. Although he played in this and the 1974-75 rubber against West Indies as 'Mansur Ali Khan', he is given his original title throughout to avoid confusion. The partnership of 83 between Fletcher and Gifford is England's highest against India for the ninth wicket.

ENGLAND

B. Wood	c Engineer b Bedi	20	c sub (R.D. Parkar) b Bedi	5
D.L. Amiss	c Solkar b Chandrasekhar	15	c Engineer b Chandrasekhar	8
A.P.E. Knott†	c Pataudi b Bedi	10	c Chandrasekhar b Bedi	13
M.H. Denness	b Prasanna	17	c Solkar b Prasanna	76
K.W.R. Fletcher	not out	97	c Chauhan b Bedi	21
A.W. Greig	lbw b Chandrasekhar	17	c Solkar b Durani	5
A.R. Lewis*	c Solkar b Chandrasekhar	4	c Chauhan b Bedi	11
C.M. Old	c Durani b Chandrasekhar	4	c Bedi b Prasanna	9
G.G. Arnold	c Solkar b Prasanna	17	c Wadekar b Prasanna	0
N. Gifford	lbw b Chandrasekhar	19	not out	3
P.I. Pocock	lbw b Chandrasekhar	2	c Wadekar b Prasanna	0
Extras	(B 8, LB 11, NB 1)	20	(B 2, LB 3, NB 3)	8
Total		**242**		**159**

INDIA

C.P.S. Chauhan	c Knott b Arnold	0	c Knott b Pocock	11
S.M. Gavaskar	c Greig b Gifford	20	(8) not out	0
A.L. Wadekar*	c Wood b Pocock	44	c Greig b Old	0
S.A. Durani	c and b Gifford	38	lbw b Pocock	38
Nawab of Pataudi, jr	c sub (R.W. Tolchard) b Pocock	73	(6) not out	14
G.R. Viswanath	c Old b Pocock	37	(5) b Pocock	0
F.M. Engineer†	c Wood b Gifford	31	(2) lbw b Old	10
E.D. Solkar	b Pocock	10	(7) c Denness b Pocock	7
E.A.S. Prasanna	lbw b Arnold	37		
B.S. Bedi	b Arnold	5		
B.S. Chandrasekhar	not out	3		
Extras	(B 6, LB 3, NB 9)	18	(LB 1, NB 5)	6
Total		**316**	(6 wickets)	**86**

INDIA	O	M	R	W	O	M	R	W		FALL OF WICKETS			
Solkar	2	0	13	0	2	2	0	0		E	I	E	I
Gavaskar	1	0	6	0					Wkt	1st	1st	2nd	2nd
Bedi	30	9	66	2	43	24	38	4	1st	33	4	14	11
Chandrasekhar	38·5	9	90	6	35	9	69	1	2nd	47	28	14	11
Prasanna	15	3	47	2	10	5	16	4	3rd	52	89	30	44
Pataudi					1	0	4	0	4th	69	155	77	51
Durani					15	5	24	1	5th	98	220	97	67
									6th	106	224	126	78
ENGLAND									7th	110	247	152	–
Arnold	23·1	12	34	3	4	1	11	0	8th	151	288	152	–
Old	20	4	51	0	9	3	19	2	9th	234	303	159	–
Gifford	34	15	64	3	7·5	2	22	0	10th	242	316	159	–
Greig	12	1	35	0									
Pocock	46	15	114	4	13	3	28	4					

Umpires: A.M. Mamsa (6) and M.V. Nagendra (6).

Close: 1st day – I(1) 4-0 (Chauhan 0, Gavaskar 4); 2nd – I(1) 175-4 (Pataudi 53, Viswanath 9); 3rd – E(2) 52-3 (Denness 10, Fletcher 15); 4th – I(2) 32-2 (Chauhan 7, Durani 13).

INDIA v ENGLAND 1972–73 (4th Test)

Played at Green Park, Kanpur, on 25, 27, 28, 29, 30 January.
Toss: India.   Result: MATCH DRAWN.
Debuts: England – J. Birkenshaw, G.R.J. Roope.

Lewis batted for 267 minutes and hit a six and 16 fours in his innings of 125. It was the first hundred by an England batsman for ten Test matches. Gifford fractured his left-hand little finger when fielding before lunch on the first day and took no further part in the match.

INDIA

C.P.S. Chauhan	c Old b Underwood	22	c Roope b Arnold	1
S.M. Gavaskar	c Greig b Birkenshaw	69	c sub (B. Wood) b Underwood	24
A.L. Wadekar*	c Fletcher b Greig	90	c and b Underwood	9
G.R. Viswanath	c Denness b Old	25	not out	75
Nawab of Pataudi, jr	lbw b Arnold	54		
E.D. Solkar	b Underwood	10	c Greig b Birkenshaw	26
F.M. Engineer†	b Underwood	15	(5) c Old b Birkenshaw	2
S. Abid Ali	b Old	41	(7) b Greig	36
E.A.S. Prasanna	c Knott b Old	0	(8) not out	2
B.S. Bedi	not out	4		
B.S. Chandrasekhar	b Old	0		
Extras	(B 1, LB 9, NB 17)	27	(B 5, LB 4, NB 2)	11
Total		**357**	(6 wickets)	**186**

ENGLAND

M.H. Denness	c Abid Ali b Chandrasekhar	31
G.R.J. Roope†	c Abid Ali b Chandrasekhar	11
A.P.E. Knott†	c Gavaskar b Prasanna	40
A.R. Lewis*	b Abid Ali	125
K.W.R. Fletcher	c Chandrasekhar b Bedi	58
A.W. Greig	c Chauhan b Bedi	8
J. Birkenshaw	c Abid Ali b Chandrasekhar	64
C.M. Old	lbw b Chandrasekhar	4
G.G. Arnold	b Bedi	45
D.L. Underwood	not out	0
N. Gifford	absent hurt	–
Extras	(B 1, LB 8, W 1, NB 1)	11
Total		**397**

ENGLAND	O	M	R	W	O	M	R	W
Arnold	35	10	72	1	7	3	15	1
Old	24	5	69	4	11	3	28	0
Underwood	51	20	90	3	26	11	46	2
Greig	29	11	40	1	10	7	6	1
Gifford	8	2	17	0				
Birkenshaw	20	6	42	1	25	5	66	2
Roope					5	1	14	0
INDIA								
Abid Ali	22	3	55	1				
Solkar	5	0	14	0				
Bedi	68·5	15	134	3				
Chandrasekhar	41	12	86	4				
Prasanna	34	4	87	1				
Viswanath	2	0	10	0				

FALL OF WICKETS

	I	E	I
Wkt	1st	1st	2nd
1st	85	37	8
2nd	109	48	33
3rd	179	118	36
4th	265	262	39
5th	292	274	103
6th	296	288	181
7th	326	301	–
8th	345	397	–
9th	357	397	–
10th	357	–	–

Umpires: M.V. Gothoskar (1) and J. Reuben (3).

Close: 1st day – I(1) 168-2 (Wadekar 41, Viswanath 24); 2nd – I(1) 332-7 (Abid Ali 20, Prasanna 0); 3rd – E(1) 198-3 (Lewis 86, Fletcher 28); 4th – E(1) 390-7 (Birkenshaw 59, Arnold 45).

INDIA v ENGLAND 1972–73 (5th Test)

Played at Brabourne Stadium, Bombay, on 6, 7, 8, 10, 11 February.
Toss: India.   Result: MATCH DRAWN.
Debuts: Nil.

India won the rubber 2-1 when England were unable to score 213 runs in 90 minutes. Viswanath became the first of six Indian batsmen who scored a hundred on Test debut to reach a second century for their country. The partnership of 192 between Engineer and Wadekar is still India's highest for the second wicket against England. Fletcher, who scored his first century in his 20th Test, and Greig shared a partnership of 254 which remains England's highest for the fifth wicket in all Test matches. In the second innings Pataudi batted 95 minutes for five runs and did not score for the last 65 minutes of his innings. Chandrasekhar took 35 wickets in this rubber to set a new record for India against all countries. Knott led England when Lewis and Denness were off the field on the fourth evening. Abid Ali kept wicket in the second innings when Engineer was injured.

INDIA

F.M. Engineer†	c Roope b Birkenshaw	121	b Underwood	66
S.M. Gavaskar	b Old	4	c and b Underwood	67
A.L. Wadekar*	c Old b Birkenshaw	87	(6) not out	11
S.A. Durani	c Underwood b Pocock	73	(3) c Knott b Pocock	37
Nawab of Pataudi, jr	b Underwood	1	b Pocock	5
G.R. Viswanath	b Arnold	113	(4) c Knott b Greig	48
E.D. Solkar	c Denness b Old	6	not out	6
S. Abid Ali	c Roope b Arnold	15		
S. Venkataraghavan	not out	11		
B.S. Bedi	b Arnold	0		
B.S. Chandrasekhar	c Fletcher b Old	3		
Extras	(B 4, LB 4, NB 6)	14	(LB 4)	4
Total		**448**	(5 wickets declared)	**244**

ENGLAND

A.R. Lewis*	b Abid Ali	0	(4) not out	17
G.R.J. Roope	c Abid Ali b Chandrasekhar	10	not out	26
A.P.E. Knott†	lbw b Chandrasekhar	56	b Chandrasekhar	8
D.L. Underwood	c Abid Ali b Bedi	9		
K.W.R. Fletcher	lbw b Bedi	113		
A.W. Greig	lbw b Chandrasekhar	148		
M.H. Denness	c Venkataraghavan b Bedi	29		
J. Birkenshaw	b Chandrasekhar	36	(1) b Bedi	12
C.M. Old	c and b Venkataraghavan	28		
G.G. Arnold	lbw b Chandrasekhar	27		
P.I. Pocock	not out	0		
Extras	(B 13, LB 5, NB 6)	24	(B 3, LB 1)	4
Total		**480**	(2 wickets)	**67**

ENGLAND	O	M	R	W	O	M	R	W		FALL OF WICKETS			
Arnold	21	3	64	3	3	0	13	0		I	E	I	E
Old	21·2	2	78	3	3	1	11	0	*Wkt*	*1st*	*1st*	*2nd*	*2nd*
Underwood	26	6	100	1	38	16	70	2	1st	25	0	135	23
Greig	22	7	62	0	13	7	19	1	2nd	217	38	136	37
Pocock	25	7	63	1	27	5	75	2	3rd	220	67	198	–
Birkenshaw	23	2	67	2	12	1	52	0	4th	221	79	227	–
									5th	371	333	233	–
INDIA									6th	395	381	–	–
Abid Ali	15	2	60	1					7th	427	397	–	–
Solkar	4	0	16	0	2	0	4	0	8th	435	442	–	–
Bedi	69	20	138	3	10	4	25	1	9th	439	479	–	–
Chandrasekhar	46·1	8	135	5	9	1	26	1	10th	448	480	–	–
Durani	4	0	21	0									
Venkataraghavan	25	1	86	1	5	1	8	0					
Gavaskar					2	2	0	0					
Pataudi					1	1	0	0					

Umpires: M.V. Gothoskar (2) and J. Reuben (4).

Close: 1st day – I(1) 250-4 (Durani 20, Viswanath 10); 2nd – E (1) 41-2 (Knott 29, Underwood 1); 3rd – E(1) 333-5 (Greig 126); 4th – I(2) 102-0 (Engineer 47, Gavaskar 53).

AUSTRALIA v PAKISTAN 1972–73 (1st Test)

Played at Adelaide Oval on 22, 23, 24, 26, 27 December.
Toss: Pakistan.   Result: AUSTRALIA won by an innings and 114 runs.
Debuts: Australia – J. Benaud; Pakistan – Talat Ali.

Australia's first win against Pakistan in a home Test was gained off the 14th ball of the fifth morning. Ian Chappell's highest Test innings was then the record for this series, as was Australia's total of 585 which is still their highest against Pakistan in Australia and included three hundred partnerships. The partnership of 104 between Intikhab and Wasim Bari remains Pakistan's highest for the seventh wicket against Australia. Marsh, playing in his first Test against Pakistan, became the first Australian wicket-keeper to score a Test hundred. Mallett's analysis of 8 for 59 remained his best in Test matches and is still Australia's record for this series. Talat Ali, his right thumb fractured by a ball from Lillee, batted one-handed in the second innings to take the match into the last day.

PAKISTAN

Sadiq Mohammad	c G.S. Chappell b Massie	11		c and b Mallett	81
Talat Ali	retired hurt	7	(11)	c Edwards b Mallett	0
Zaheer Abbas	c Marsh b Lillee	7		c Marsh b O'Keeffe	0
Majid Khan	c Sheahan b Massie	11		c I.M. Chappell b Mallett	11
Mushtaq Mohammad	c G.S. Chappell b Lillee	3		lbw b Mallett	32
Saeed Ahmed	c Marsh b Massie	36	(2)	lbw b Mallett	39
Asif Iqbal	c Marsh b Massie	16	(6)	c G.S. Chappell b Mallett	0
Intikhab Alam*	c Edwards b Lillee	64	(7)	c G.S. Chappell b Lillee	30
Wasim Bari†	c Redpath b Mallett	72	(8)	c O'Keeffe b Mallett	0
Salim Altaf	not out	17	(9)	not out	9
Asif Masood	c Marsh b Lillee	0	(10)	c Marsh b Mallett	1
Extras	(B 4, LB 3, W 4, NB 2)	13		(B 3, LB 4, W 1, NB 3)	11
Total		**257**			**214**

AUSTRALIA

A.P. Sheahan	b Asif Masood	44
I.R. Redpath	c Wasim b Asif Masood	2
I.M. Chappell*	c Asif Iqbal b Majid	196
G.S. Chappell	lbw b Salim	28
R. Edwards	lbw b Asif Masood	89
J. Benaud	lbw b Salim	24
R.W. Marsh†	b Mushtaq	118
K.J. O'Keeffe	b Mushtaq	40
A.A. Mallett	c sub (Sarfraz Nawaz) b Majid	0
D.K. Lillee	c Saeed b Mushtaq	14
R.A.L. Massie	not out	12
Extras	(B 2, LB 12, NB 4)	18
Total		**585**

AUSTRALIA	O	M	R	W	O	M	R	W
Lillee	20·3	7	49	4	15	3	53	1
Massie	24	3	70	4	9	3	26	0
G.S. Chappell	11	2	29	0	4	0	21	0
Mallett	12	3	52	1	23·6	6	59	8
O'Keeffe	8	1	44	0	14	1	44	1
PAKISTAN								
Asif Masood	19	1	110	3				
Salim	25	1	83	2				
Asif Iqbal	14	0	76	0				
Intikhab	18	2	115	0				
Saeed	3	0	28	0				
Majid	20	1	88	2				
Mushtaq	11·2	0	67	3				

FALL OF WICKETS			
	P	A	P
Wkt	1st	1st	2nd
1st	30	3	88
2nd	30	103	89
3rd	33	158	111
4th	74	330	162
5th	95	390	162
6th	104	413	182
7th	208	533	182
8th	255	534	211
9th	257	566	214
10th	–	585	214

Umpires: M.G. O'Connell (3) and N. Townsend (1).

Close: 1st day – P(1) 255-7 (Intikhab 64, Salim 15); 2nd – A(1) 363-4 (Edwards 78, Benaud 7); 3rd – P(2) 111-3 (Sadiq 59); 4th – P(2) 214-9 (Salim 9, Talat 0).

AUSTRALIA v PAKISTAN 1972–73 (2nd Test)

Played at Melbourne Cricket Ground on 29, 30 December, 1, 2, 3 January.
Toss: Australia.   Result: AUSTRALIA won by 92 runs.
Debuts: Australia – J.R. Thomson, M.H.N. Walker.

Pakistan's total remained their highest in Australia until 1983-84 (*Test No. 972*), in which match the partnership of 195 between Sadiq and Majid, until then Pakistan's best for the second wicket in this series, was also beaten. Saeed (18) retired at 31 after being hit on the right hand, hooking Lillee. Majid's first Test hundred, scored in his 20th innings and eight years after his debut, remains Pakistan's highest score in a Test in Australia. Benaud's hundred in his second Test included 93 before lunch on the fourth day after being told that he had not been selected for the next Test. His second-wicket partnership of 233 with Sheahan was Australia's highest for any wicket in this series until 1983-84 (*Test No. 970*).

AUSTRALIA

I.R. Redpath	c Saeed b Intikhab	135	c Wasim b Salim		6
A.P. Sheahan	run out	23	c Sarfraz b Asif Masood		127
I.M. Chappell*	c Wasim b Sarfraz	66	(4) st Wasim b Majid		9
G.S. Chappell	not out	116	(5) run out		62
J. Benaud	c Sarfraz b Intikhab	13	(3) c Wasim b Salim		142
R.W. Marsh†	c Wasim b Sarfraz	74	c Asif Iqbal b Asif Masood		3
K.J. O'Keeffe	)		b Sarfraz		24
A.A. Mallett	)		c Wasim b Sarfraz		8
M.H.N. Walker	) did not bat		run out		11
J.R. Thomson	)		not out		19
D.K. Lillee	)		c Mushtaq b Intikhab		2
Extras	(B 1, LB 6, NB 7)	14	(LB 3, NB 9)		12
Total	(5 wickets declared)	**441**			**425**

PAKISTAN

Sadiq Mohammad	lbw b Lillee	137	c Marsh b Walker	5
Saeed Ahmed	c G.S. Chappell b Walker	50	c Mallett b Lillee	6
Zaheer Abbas	run out	51	run out	25
Majid Khan	c Marsh b Walker	158	c Marsh b Lillee	47
Mushtaq Mohammad	c Marsh b O'Keeffe	60	run out	13
Asif Iqbal	c Lillee b Mallett	7	c Redpath b Walker	37
Intikhab Alam*	c Sheahan b Mallett	68	c I.M. Chappell b Mallett	48
Wasim Bari†	b Mallett	7	b Walker	0
Salim Altaf	not out	13	b O'Keeffe	10
Sarfraz Nawaz	not out	0	run out	8
Asif Masood	did not bat		not out	1
Extras	(B 12, LB 7, W 1, NB 3)	23		–
Total	(8 wickets declared)	**574**		**200**

PAKISTAN	O	M	R	W	O	M	R	W		FALL OF WICKETS			
Asif Masood	17	0	97	0	12	0	100	2		A	P	A	P
Salim	9	0	49	0	14	0	50	2	*Wkt*	*1st*	*1st*	*2nd*	*2nd*
Sarfraz	22·5	4	100	2	22	2	99	2	1st	60	128	18	11
Intikhab	16	0	101	2	15·6	3	70	1	2nd	183	323	251	15
Majid	21	2	80	0	17	1	61	1	3rd	273	395	288	80
Mushtaq					7	0	33	0	4th	295	416	298	83
									5th	441	429	305	128
AUSTRALIA									6th	–	519	375	138
Lillee	16·6	1	90	1	11	1	59	2	7th	–	541	391	138
Thomson	17	1	100	0	2	0	10	0	8th	–	572	392	161
Walker	24	1	112	2	14	0	39	3	9th	–	–	418	181
Mallett	38	4	124	3	17·5	3	56	1	10th	–	–	425	200
O'Keeffe	23	1	94	1	9	4	10	1					
I.M. Chappell	5	0	21	0	3	0	16	0					
Redpath	1	0	10	0									
G.S. Chappell					1	0	10	0					

Umpires: J.R. Collins (1) and P.R. Enright (1).

Close: 1st day – A(1) 349-4 (G.S. Chappell 71, Marsh 27); 2nd – P(1) 292-1 (Sadiq 125, Majid 92); 3rd – A(2) 47-1 (Sheahan 27, Benaud 11); 4th – A(2) 416-8 (Walker 10, Thomson 15).

AUSTRALIA v PAKISTAN 1972–73 (3rd Test)

Played at Sydney Cricket Ground on 6, 7, 8, 10, 11 January.
Toss: Pakistan.   Result: AUSTRALIA won by 52 runs.
Debuts: Australia – J.R. Watkins.

Australia gained a remarkable victory to win the rubber 3-0. Pakistan needed to score only 159 runs in their second innings, despite a record ninth-wicket partnership of 83 in 150 minutes between Watkins and Massie. Walker, who took five wickets for three runs with his last 30 balls, and Lillee, restricted by a vertebral injury, bowled unchanged throughout the 138 minutes of play on the final day to dismiss Pakistan for their lowest score in this series until 1981-82 (*Test No. 909*). The partnership of 139 between Mushtaq and Asif was Pakistan's highest for the fifth wicket against Australia until 1983-84 (*Test No. 972*).

AUSTRALIA

K.R. Stackpole	c Wasim b Sarfraz	28	c Intikhab b Salim	9
I.R. Redpath	run out	79	c Nasim b Sarfraz	18
I.M. Chappell*	lbw b Sarfraz	43	c Wasim b Sarfraz	27
G.S. Chappell	b Majid	30	(6) lbw b Sarfraz	6
R. Edwards	c Wasim b Salim	69	(4) lbw b Salim	3
K.D. Walters	b Asif Iqbal	19	(5) lbw b Salim	6
R.W. Marsh†	c Wasim b Salim	15	c Zaheer b Salim	0
M.H.N. Walker	c Majid b Sarfraz	5	c Mushtaq b Sarfraz	16
J.R. Watkins	not out	3	c Zaheer b Intikhab	36
D.K. Lillee	b Sarfraz	2	(11) not out	0
R.A.L. Massie	b Salim	2	(10) c Sadiq b Mushtaq	42
Extras	(B 18, LB 8, W 4, NB 9)	39	(B 10, LB 3, NB 8)	21
Total		**334**		**184**

PAKISTAN

Sadiq Mohammad	c G.S. Chappell b Lillee	30	c Edwards b Massie	6
Nasim-ul-Ghani	c Redpath c G.S. Chappell	64	b Lillee	5
Zaheer Abbas	c Marsh b Massie	14	c Redpath b Lillee	47
Majid Khan	b Massie	0	lbw b Walker	12
Mushtaq Mohammad	c Walker b G.S. Chappell	121	c Marsh b Lillee	15
Asif Iqbal	c Marsh b G.S. Chappell	65	c Marsh b Walker	5
Intikhab Alam*	c Marsh b Massie	9	c Watkins b Walker	8
Wasim Bari†	b G.S. Chappell	1	c Edwards b Walker	0
Salim Altaf	c Marsh b Walker	12	c Massie b Walker	0
Sarfraz Nawaz	b G.S. Chappell	12	c Redpath b Walker	1
Asif Masood	not out	1	not out	3
Extras	(B 12, LB 10, W 6, NB 3)	31	(LB 2, W 1, NB 1)	4
Total		**360**		**106**

PAKISTAN	O	M	R	W	O	M	R	W	FALL OF WICKETS				
Asif Masood	18	1	81	0	3	0	15	0		A	P	A	P
Salim	21·5	3	71	3	20	5	60	4	*Wkt*	*1st*	*1st*	*2nd*	*2nd*
Sarfraz	19	3	53	4	21	7	56	4	1st	56	56	29	7
Majid	18	1	66	1					2nd	138	79	31	11
Intikhab	2	0	13	0	4	2	9	1	3rd	196	83	34	52
Asif Iqbal	2	0	11	1	2	0	10	0	4th	220	131	44	83
Mushtaq					3·1	0	13	1	5th	271	270	70	88
									6th	315	279	73	93
AUSTRALIA									7th	324	280	94	95
Lillee	10	2	34	1	23	5	68	3	8th	327	336	101	95
Massie	28	6	123	3	7	4	19	1	9th	329	349	184	103
Walker	16	2	65	1	16	8	15	6	10th	334	360	184	106
G.S. Chappell	18·6	5	61	5									
Walters	9	3	25	0									
Watkins	6	1	21	0									
I.M. Chappell	1	1	0	0									

Umpires: T.F. Brooks (6) and J.R. Collins (2).

Close: 1st day – A(1) 306-5 (Edwards 69, Marsh 7); 2nd – P(1) 250-4 (Mushtaq 69, Asif Iqbal 47); 3rd – A(2) 94-7 (Walker 15); 4th – P(2) 48-2 (Zaheer 26, Majid 11).

NEW ZEALAND v PAKISTAN 1972–73 (1st Test)

Played at Basin Reserve, Wellington, on 2, 3, 4, 5 February.
Toss: Pakistan.   Result: MATCH DRAWN.
Debuts: New Zealand – R.J. Hadlee, J.M. Parker; Pakistan – Wasim Raja.

New Zealand were asked to score 323 runs to win in 121 minutes. Wasim Bari was taken to hospital after being hit in the face by a bouncer from Collinge. Majid kept wicket at the start of the first innings and caught Jarvis. Parker fractured a bone in his hand while fielding and was unable to bat in his first Test. Sadiq compiled the highest of his five Test hundreds. His partnership of 171 with Majid was Pakistan's record for the third wicket against New Zealand until 1984-85. Hastings and Burgess shared the best fourth-wicket New Zealand stand (128) for this series.

PAKISTAN

Sadiq Mohammad	c sub (D.R. O'Sullivan) b Hadlee	166	c Congdon b Howarth	68
Talat Ali	c Turner b Collinge	6	lbw b Taylor	2
Zaheer Abbas	c Hadlee b Taylor	2	c Wadsworth b Collinge	8
Majid Khan	c Congdon b Taylor	79	c Burgess b Howarth	79
Asif Iqbal	c and b Hadlee	39	c Hastings b Howarth	23
Wasim Raja	c Congdon b Taylor	10	c sub (D.R. O'Sullivan) b Howarth	41
Intikhab Alam*	run out	16	not out	53
Wasim Bari†	retired hurt	13		
Salim Altaf	c Howarth b Taylor	14	(8) not out	6
Sarfraz Nawaz	c Wadsworth b Collinge	0		
Pervez Sajjad	not out	1		
Extras	(B 1, LB 5, NB 5)	11	(B 4, LB 2, NB 4)	10
Total		**357**	(6 wickets declared)	**290**

NEW ZEALAND

G.M. Turner	c Intikhab b Sarfraz	43	not out	49
T.W. Jarvis	c Majid b Sarfraz	0	c Majid b Salim	0
B.E. Congdon*	run out	19	c and b Salim	0
B.F. Hastings	c Majid b Sarfraz	72	c Wasim Bari b Salim	0
M.G. Burgess	c and b Intikhab	79	not out	21
B.R. Taylor	c Zaheer b Majid	5		
K.J. Wadsworth†	c Asif b Sarfraz	28		
R.J. Hadlee	c Asif b Salim	46		
H.J. Howarth	not out	3		
R.O. Collinge	b Salim	0		
J.M. Parker	absent hurt	–		
Extras	(B 9, LB 9, NB 12)	30	(LB 1, W 1, NB 6)	8
Total		**325**	(3 wickets)	**78**

NEW ZEALAND	O	M	R	W	O	M	R	W	FALL OF WICKETS				
Hadlee	18	0	84	2	7	0	28	0		P	NZ	P	NZ
Collinge	20	1	63	2	13	1	50	1	*Wkt*	*1st*	*1st*	*2nd*	*2nd*
Taylor	24·4	1	110	4	11	2	63	1	1st	20	4	20	1
Howarth	25	6	73	0	31	7	99	4	2nd	26	55	35	1
Congdon	3	0	16	0	9	0	40	0	3rd	197	88	129	11
									4th	271	216	177	–
PAKISTAN									5th	308	221	202	–
Salim	16·4	3	70	2	6	1	15	3	6th	308	261	255	–
Sarfraz	29	5	126	4	5	1	15	0	7th	334	302	–	–
Asif	2	1	6	0					8th	342	325	–	–
Intikhab	13	1	55	1	3	0	11	0	9th	357	325	–	–
Pervez	5	0	19	0	4	1	5	0	10th	–	–	–	–
Majid	9	2	19	1									
Wasim Raja					4	0	10	0					
Sadiq					3	0	13	0					
Talat					1	0	1	0					

Umpires: E.C.A. MacKintosh (7) and W.T. Martin (14).

Close: 1st day – P(1) 196-2 (Sadiq 107, Majid 78); 2nd – NZ(1) 77-2 (Turner 41, Hastings 7); 3rd – P(2) 64-2 (Sadiq 42, Majid 9).

NEW ZEALAND v PAKISTAN 1972–73 (2nd Test)

Played at Carisbrook, Dunedin, on 7, 8, 9, 10 February.
Toss: Pakistan.   Result: PAKISTAN won by an innings and 166 runs.
Debuts: New Zealand – D.R. O'Sullivan.

Pakistan gained their first victory in New Zealand after 55 minutes of play on the fourth morning and by their biggest margin in all Tests. Their total of 507 was the highest by either country in this series in New Zealand until 1988-89. Mushtaq batted 383 minutes and hit 20 fours in scoring Pakistan's first double century in New Zealand and his highest score in Test cricket. His partnership of 350 in 275 minutes with Asif Iqbal was Pakistan's highest for any wicket in all Test matches until 1982-83 (*Test No. 946*) and remains their highest for the fourth wicket in all first-class cricket. Mushtaq was the second player after D. St E. Atkinson (*Test No. 406*) to score a double century and take five wickets in an innings in the same Test. Intikhab (11 for 130) returned the best match analysis for any Test in Dunedin until 1979-80 (*Test No. 873*).

PAKISTAN

Sadiq Mohammad	b Hadlee	61
Zaheer Abbas	c Wadsworth b Hadlee	15
Majid Khan	c and b Taylor	26
Mushtaq Mohammad	c Wadsworth b Congdon	201
Asif Iqbal	c Hastings b Taylor	175
Wasim Raja	not out	8
Intikhab Alam*	c Pollard b Howarth	3
Wasim Bari†	not out	2
Salim Altaf	)	
Sarfraz Nawaz	) did not bat	
Pervez Sajjad	)	
Extras	(LB 13, NB 3)	16
Total	(6 wickets declared)	**507**

NEW ZEALAND

G.M. Turner	c Mushtaq b Intikhab	37	c Mushtaq b Intikhab		24
T.W. Jarvis	c Mushtaq b Sarfraz	7	c Wasim Bari b Mushtaq		39
B.E. Congdon*	c Wasim Bari b Intikhab	35	c Majid b Mushtaq		7
B.F. Hastings	c Sarfraz b Intikhab	4	b Mushtaq		9
M.G. Burgess	b Intikhab	10	c Pervez b Intikhab		4
V. Pollard	c Sarfraz b Intikhab	3	b Intikhab		61
B.R. Taylor	c Sarfraz b Intikhab	0	(8) run out		3
K.J. Wadsworth†	b Mushtaq	45	(7) c Majid b Intikhab		17
D.R. Hadlee	st Wasim Bari b Intikhab	1	c Majid b Mushtaq		0
D.R. O'Sullivan	c Wasim Raja b Mushtaq	4	b Mushtaq		1
H.J. Howarth	not out	4	not out		7
Extras	(B 1, LB 2, NB 3)	6	(B 5, LB 7, NB 1)		13
Total		**156**			**185**

NEW ZEALAND	O	M	R	W	O	M	R	W
Hadlee	24	3	100	2				
Taylor	22	3	91	2				
Congdon	17	1	72	1				
Howarth	29	6	83	1				
Pollard	13	2	64	0				
O'Sullivan	18	2	81	0				
PAKISTAN								
Salim	5	0	23	0	4	2	11	0
Sarfraz	5	0	20	1	4	0	16	0
Intikhab	21	3	52	7	18·4	2	78	4
Pervez	17	5	40	0	3	0	10	0
Mushtaq	3·5	1	15	2	18	2	49	5
Wasim Raja					2	0	8	0

FALL OF WICKETS

Wkt	P 1st	NZ 1st	NZ 2nd
1st	23	15	48
2nd	81	73	57
3rd	126	84	78
4th	476	87	87
5th	500	99	91
6th	504	99	127
7th	–	104	150
8th	–	116	159
9th	–	139	169
10th	–	156	185

Umpires: D.E.A. Copps (5) and R.W.R. Shortt (9).

Close: 1st day – P(1) 107-2 (Sadiq 52, Mushtaq 6); 2nd – P(1) 507-6 dec; 3rd – NZ(2) 123-5 (Pollard 23, Wadsworth 13).

NEW ZEALAND v PAKISTAN 1972–73 (3rd Test)

Played at Eden Park, Auckland, on 16, 17, 18, 19 February.
Toss: Pakistan.   Result MATCH DRAWN.
Debuts: New Zealand – R.E. Redmond.

Pakistan won their first Test rubber outside their own country. Redmond, in his only Test, became the third New Zealander after J.E. Mills and B.R. Taylor to score a hundred (in 136 minutes) in his first Test; all three were left-handed. His innings of 107, New Zealand's first hundred in a home Test against Pakistan, took 145 minutes and included a five and 20 fours. His partnership of 159 with Turner is the highest for the first wicket in this series. Hastings and Collinge set the present world Test record for the tenth wicket with their partnership of 151 runs in 155 minutes; it beat the 130 added by R.E. Foster and W. Rhodes against Australia in 1903-04 (*Test No. 78*). Collinge registered the highest score by a number eleven batsman in Test cricket. Taylor became the second bowler after R.C. Motz to take 100 Test wickets for New Zealand. His next wicket gave him the New Zealand record. Wadsworth became New Zealand's most successful wicket-keeper when he passed A.E. Dick's record of 51 Test match dismissals. For only the third time a Test match first innings was tied.

PAKISTAN

Sadiq Mohammad	c Wadsworth b Collinge	33	c Hadlee b Taylor		38
Zaheer Abbas	c Turner b Taylor	10	c Turner b Taylor		0
Majid Khan	c Wadsworth b Taylor	110	c Wadsworth b Howarth		33
Mushtaq Mohammad	c Hastings b Congdon	61	b Howarth		52
Asif Iqbal	b Taylor	34	(6) lbw b Congdon		39
Wasim Raja	c Wadsworth b Collinge	1	(7) b Collinge		49
Intikhab Alam*	c Wadsworth b Taylor	34	(8) b Howarth		2
Wasim Bari†	c and b Howarth	30	(9) lbw b Hadlee		27
Salim Altaf	not out	53	(5) lbw b Congdon		11
Sarfraz Nawaz	c Wadsworth b Howarth	2	c Taylor b Collinge		4
Pervez Sajjad	lbw b Congdon	24	not out		8
Extras	(B 1, LB 3, NB 6)	10	(B 3, LB 3, NB 2)		8
Total		**402**			**271**

NEW ZEALAND

R.E. Redmond	c Mushtaq b Pervez	107	c Intikhab b Wasim Raja		56
G.M. Turner	c Sarfraz b Intikhab	58	b Wasim Raja		24
B.E. Congdon*	b Intikhab	24	not out		6
B.F. Hastings	b Wasim Raja	110	(5) not out		4
M.G. Burgess	b Intikhab	2	(4) c Mushtaq b Wasim Raja		1
T.W. Jarvis	lbw b Intikhab	0			
K.J. Wadsworth†	c Sadiq b Intikhab	6			
B.R. Taylor	c Majid b Pervez	2			
D.R. Hadlee	b Intikhab	0			
H.J. Howarth	c Majid b Mushtaq	8			
R.O. Collinge	not out	68			
Extras	(B 8, LB 6, NB 3)	17	(B 1)		1
Total		**402**	(3 wickets)		**92**

NEW ZEALAND	O	M	R	W	O	M	R	W		FALL OF WICKETS			
Collinge	24	2	72	2	7	2	19	2		P	NZ	P	NZ
Hadlee	18	3	100	0	5·7	0	35	1	*Wkt*	*1st*	*1st*	*2nd*	*2nd*
Taylor	32	9	86	4	19	5	66	2	1st	43	159	4	80
Howarth	32	5	86	2	31	11	99	3	2nd	43	180	61	81
Congdon	11·5	0	48	2	16	3	44	2	3rd	147	203	71	87
									4th	233	205	116	–
PAKISTAN									5th	238	205	159	–
Salim	20	1	58	0	4	0	17	0	6th	267	225	203	–
Sarfraz	16	1	85	0	4	0	13	0	7th	295	235	206	–
Intikhab	30	4	127	6					8th	342	236	238	–
Majid	3	0	30	0	3	0	11	0	9th	354	251	242	–
Pervez	15	3	50	2					10th	402	402	271	–
Mushtaq	5	0	26	1									
Wasim Raja	1·6	0	9	1	8	2	32	3					
Sadiq					5	1	18	0					

Umpires: E.C.A. MacKintosh (8) and W.T. Martin (15).

Close: 1st day – P(1) 300-7 (Wasim Bari 6, Salim 5); 2nd – NZ(1) 180-2 (Congdon 6); 3rd – P(2) 73-3 (Mushtaq 0, Salim 2).

WEST INDIES v AUSTRALIA 1972–73 (1st Test)

Played at Sabina Park, Kingston, Jamaica, on 16, 17, 18, 20, 21 February.
Toss: Australia.   Result: MATCH DRAWN.
Debuts: Australia – J.R. Hammond.

Foster scored a hundred in his first Test against Australia and with Kanhai shared a partnership of 210 which remains the West Indies fifth-wicket record for this series. For the first time since 1954-55, West Indies were without G. St A. Sobers. Stackpole savaged Dowe's bowling to such an extent that a section of the crowd arrived the following day with banners proclaiming an eleventh Commandment: 'Dowe Shall Not Bowl'.

AUSTRALIA

K.R. Stackpole	b Foster	44	c Rowe b Holder		142
I.R. Redpath	b Gibbs	46	c Kanhai b Gibbs		60
I.M. Chappell*	c Dowe b Ali	19	not out		38
G.S. Chappell	c Kallicharran b Gibbs	42	not out		14
R. Edwards	c and b Gibbs	63			
K.D. Walters	c Kanhai b Gibbs	72			
R.W. Marsh†	hit wkt b Dowe	97			
K.J. O'Keeffe	not out	19			
M.H.N. Walker	)				
J.R. Hammond	) did not bat				
D.K. Lillee	)				
Extras	(B 6, LB 12, W 1, NB 7)	26	(LB 2, NB 4)		6
Total	(7 wickets declared)	**428**	(2 wickets declared)		**260**

WEST INDIES

R.C. Fredericks	c O'Keeffe b Walker	31	c Marsh b G.S. Chappell		21
G.A. Greenidge	b Walker	0			
L.G. Rowe	c Stackpole b Walker	76	c G.S. Chappell b Hammond		4
A.I. Kallicharran	c Marsh b Hammond	50	not out		7
R.B. Kanhai*	c Marsh b Hammond	84			
M.L.C. Foster	b Walker	125	(5) not out		18
T.M. Findlay†	c Marsh b Walker	12	(2) c Marsh b G.S. Chappell		13
Inshan Ali	c Marsh b Walker	10			
V.A. Holder	lbw b Hammond	12			
L.R. Gibbs	c O'Keeffe b Hammond	5			
U.G. Dowe	not out	5			
Extras	(LB 9, NB 9)	18	(B 1, W 1, NB 2)		4
Total		**428**	(3 wickets)		**67**

WEST INDIES	O	M	R	W	O	M	R	W		FALL OF WICKETS			
Holder	26	5	55	0	19	5	34	1		A	WI	A	WI
Dowe	21	3	96	1	21	4	72	0	*Wkt*	*1st*	*1st*	*2nd*	*2nd*
Foster	44	18	84	1	22	7	71	0	1st	66	6	161	35
Gibbs	41	14	85	4	15	4	40	1	2nd	106	49	230	36
Ali	25	5	82	1	4	0	28	0	3rd	128	165	–	42
Fredericks					1	0	9	0	4th	179	165	–	–
									5th	271	375	–	–
AUSTRALIA									6th	365	385	–	–
Lillee	26	4	112	0	6	1	20	0	7th	428	400	–	–
Walker	39	10	114	6	6	3	8	0	8th	–	417	–	–
Hammond	28·5	5	79	4	10	4	17	1	9th	–	423	–	–
O'Keeffe	18	1	71	0					10th	–	428	–	–
I.M. Chappell	11	3	30	0									
G.S. Chappell	2	0	4	0	10	4	18	2					
Walters					1	1	0	0					

Umpires: R. Gosein (10) and D. Sang Hue (12).

Close: 1st day – A(1) 190-4 (Edwards 20, Walters 9); 2nd – WI(1) 39-1 (Fredericks 22, Rowe 15); 3rd – WI(1) 300-4 (Kanhai 60, Foster 69); 4th – A(2) 96-0 (Stackpole 58, Redpath 33).

WEST INDIES v AUSTRALIA 1972–73 (2nd Test)

Played at Kensington Oval, Bridgetown, Barbados, on 9, 10, 11, 13, 14 March.
Toss: Australia.   Result: MATCH DRAWN.
Debuts: West Indies – E.T. Willett.

This was the 15th drawn match out of the last 17 Tests played in the West Indies. Australia did not begin their second innings until the last session of the fourth day. The partnership of 165 between Kanhai and Murray is the West Indies sixth-wicket record for this series.

AUSTRALIA

K.R. Stackpole	c Kanhai b Holder	1	b Foster		53
I.R. Redpath	c Kanhai b Boyce	6	c Greenidge b Gibbs		20
I.M. Chappell*	run out	72	not out		106
G.S. Chappell	c Murray b Holder	106			
R. Edwards	c Murray b Boyce	15			
K.D. Walters	c Kanhai b Gibbs	1	(4) not out		102
R.W. Marsh†	c Rowe b Willett	78			
K.J. O'Keeffe	b Willett	21			
J.R. Hammond	lbw b Boyce	0			
T.J. Jenner	not out	10			
M.H.N. Walker	b Gibbs	0			
Extras	(NB 14)	14	(B 1, LB 6, NB 12)		19
Total		**324**	(2 wickets declared)		**300**

WEST INDIES

R.C. Fredericks	lbw b Hammond	98	not out		22
G.A. Greenidge	lbw b Walker	9	not out		10
L.G. Rowe	c Stackpole b Walker	16			
A.I. Kallicharran	b Walker	14			
R.B. Kanhai*	lbw b I.M. Chappell	105			
M.L.C. Foster	b Jenner	12			
D.L. Murray†	c Redpath b Jenner	90			
K.D. Boyce	lbw b Walker	10			
E.T. Willett	c Stackpole b Jenner	0			
V.A. Holder	b Walker	1			
L.R. Gibbs	not out	0			
Extras	(B 13, LB 5, W 4, NB 14)	36	(LB 2, W 1, NB 1)		4
Total		**391**	(0 wickets)		**36**

WEST INDIES	O	M	R	W	O	M	R	W	FALL OF WICKETS				
										A	WI	A	WI
Holder	21	5	49	2	21	5	52	0	*Wkt*	*1st*	*1st*	*2nd*	*2nd*
Boyce	22	5	68	3	18	4	54	0	1st	2	19	79	–
Foster	15	4	35	0	13	4	29	1	2nd	19	77	108	–
Willett	37	11	79	2	28	15	45	0	3rd	148	118	–	–
Gibbs	36	9	79	2	25	10	55	1	4th	189	162	–	–
Fredericks					1	0	3	0	5th	194	179	–	–
Greenidge					7	0	24	0	6th	218	344	–	–
Kanhai					6·1	1	19	0	7th	264	385	–	–
									8th	283	386	–	–
AUSTRALIA									9th	320	391	–	–
Hammond	31	9	114	1	4	1	10	0	10th	324	391	–	–
Walker	51·4	20	97	5	4	3	1	0					
G.S. Chappell	22	11	37	0									
Jenner	28	9	65	3									
O'Keeffe	10	3	18	0	6	2	15	0					
Walters	2	0	7	0									
I.M. Chappell	8	3	17	1									
Stackpole					5	3	6	0					

Umpires: H.B. de C. Jordan (21) and D. Sang Hue (13).

Close: 1st day – A(1) 243-6 (Marsh 19, O'Keeffe 11); 2nd – WI(1) 52-1 (Fredericks 32, Rowe 8); 3rd – WI(1) 241-5 (Kanhai 60, Murray 15); 4th – A(2) 84-1 (Redpath 18, I.M. Chappell 3).

WEST INDIES v AUSTRALIA 1972–73 (3rd Test)

Played at Queen's Park Oval, Port-of-Spain, Trinidad, on 23, 24, 25, 27, 28 March.
Toss: Australia.   Result: AUSTRALIA won by 44 runs.
Debuts: Nil.

This defeat ended a record sequence of ten successive drawn matches by West Indies. Walters scored 100 runs (out of 130) between lunch and tea on the first day. Rowe fell while fielding on the first evening, damaged ligaments in his right ankle, and took no further part in the rubber.

AUSTRALIA

K.R. Stackpole	c Foster b Boyce	0		c Fredericks b Boyce	18
I.R. Redpath	run out	66		c Kanhai b Willett	44
G.S. Chappell	c Kallicharran b Gibbs	56	(4)	c and b Gibbs	1
K.D. Walters	c Fredericks b Ali	112	(5)	c Gibbs b Willett	32
R. Edwards	lbw b Boyce	12	(6)	b Gibbs	14
I.M. Chappell*	c and b Ali	8	(3)	c Fredericks b Willett	97
R.W. Marsh†	b Ali	14		b Ali	8
K.J. O'Keeffe	run out	37		c Kallicharran b Gibbs	7
T.J. Jenner	lbw b Gibbs	2		b Gibbs	6
M.H.N. Walker	b Gibbs	0	(11)	not out	23
J.R. Hammond	not out	2	(10)	c Kanhai b Gibbs	19
Extras	(B 10, LB 7, NB 6)	23		(B 5, LB 7)	12
Total		**332**			**281**

WEST INDIES

R.C. Fredericks	c I.M. Chappell b Jenner	16		c Redpath b Stackpole	76
M.L.C. Foster	lbw b Jenner	25	(6)	c G.S. Chappell b O'Keeffe	34
A.I. Kallicharran	c G.S. Chappell b Jenner	53		c Marsh b Walker	91
C.H. Lloyd	c and b G.S. Chappell	20	(5)	c Stackpole b O'Keeffe	15
R.B. Kanhai*	c Redpath b O'Keeffe	56	(4)	b G.S. Chappell	14
D.L. Murray†	lbw b Hammond	40	(2)	c Redpath b Walker	7
K.D. Boyce	c Marsh b O'Keeffe	12		c I.M. Chappell b O'Keeffe	11
Inshan Ali	c Marsh b Walker	15		b Walker	2
E.T. Willett	not out	4		b O'Keeffe	0
L.R. Gibbs	c O'Keeffe b Jenner	6		not out	0
L.G. Rowe	absent hurt	–		absent hurt	–
Extras	(B 17, LB 11, W 1, NB 4)	33		(B 19, LB 13, NB 7)	39
Total		**280**			**289**

WEST INDIES	O	M	R	W	O	M	R	W		FALL OF WICKETS			
Boyce	18	4	54	2	10	1	41	1		A	WI	A	WI
Lloyd	7	3	13	0	3	1	11	0	*Wkt*	*1st*	*1st*	*2nd*	*2nd*
Gibbs	38	11	79	3	45	14	102	5	1st	1	33	31	39
Willett	19	3	62	0	28	15	33	3	2nd	108	44	96	141
Ali	41·1	11	89	3	21	2	82	1	3rd	181	100	99	177
Foster	6	2	12	0					4th	240	149	156	219
									5th	257	206	185	268
AUSTRALIA									6th	262	230	208	274
Walker	30	8	55	1	25	6	43	3	7th	312	265	231	281
Hammond	7	3	7	1	6	3	12	0	8th	321	267	231	288
Jenner	38·3	7	98	4	15	2	46	0	9th	321	280	248	289
O'Keeffe	28	10	62	2	24·1	5	57	4	10th	332	–	281	–
G.S. Chappell	14	8	16	1	32	10	65	1					
Stackpole	2	0	8	0	11	4	27	1					
I.M. Chappell	2	1	1	0									

Umpires: R. Gosein (11) and D. Sang Hue (14).

Close: 1st day – A(1) 308-6 (Marsh 12, O'Keeffe 27); 2nd – WI(1) 210-5 (Murray 16, Boyce 2); 3rd – A(2) 174-4 (I.M. Chappell 67, Edwards 5); 4th – WI(2) 188-3 (Kallicharran 61, Lloyd 1).

WEST INDIES v AUSTRALIA 1972–73 (4th Test)

Played at Bourda, Georgetown, Guyana, on 6, 7, 8, 10, 11 April.
Toss: West Indies.   Result: AUSTRALIA won by ten wickets.
Debuts: Nil.

Australia won their second rubber in the West Indies after 20 minutes of play on the fifth morning. West Indies were dismissed for their second-lowest total in a home Test – they scored only 102 against England at Bridgetown in 1934-35 (*Test No. 238*). Lloyd batted $5\frac{3}{4}$ hours and included a six and 24 fours in his highest innings in a Test in the Caribbean.

WEST INDIES

R.C. Fredericks	c I.M. Chappell b Walters	30	c Marsh b Hammond		6
G.A. Greenidge	b Walters	22	b Hammond		24
A.I. Kallicharran	run out	13	c Walker b Hammond		8
C.H. Lloyd	b Hammond	178	c Marsh b Hammond		3
R.B. Kanhai*	c O'Keeffe b Hammond	57	lbw b Walker		23
C.A. Davis	lbw b Walker	5	c Marsh b Walker		16
D.L. Murray†	c I.M. Chappell b Hammond	1	c Marsh b Walker		3
K.D. Boyce	c Edwards b Walters	23	c G.S. Chappell b Walters		10
E.T. Willett	lbw b Walters	12	not out		3
V.A. Holder	not out	9	b Walters		3
L.R. Gibbs	b Walters	1	b Walker		7
Extras	(B 5, LB 6, W 2, NB 2)	15	(LB 3)		3
Total		**366**			**109**

AUSTRALIA

K.R. Stackpole	lbw b Boyce	1	not out		76
I.R. Redpath	c Fredericks b Holder	22	not out		57
I.M. Chappell*	b Gibbs	109			
G.S. Chappell	b Willett	51			
K.D. Walters	c Murray b Gibbs	81			
R. Edwards	c Murray b Boyce	13			
R.W. Marsh†	lbw b Willett	23			
K.J. O'Keeffe	b Gibbs	5			
T.J. Jenner	c Kallicharran b Boyce	10			
J.R. Hammond	run out	1			
M.H.N. Walker	not out	2			
Extras	(B 9, LB 7, W 4, NB 3)	23	(LB 2)		2
Total		**341**	(0 wickets)		**135**

AUSTRALIA	O	M	R	W	O	M	R	W
Hammond	33	6	110	3	16	4	38	4
Walker	38	11	77	1	23·3	4	45	4
G.S. Chappell	16	4	56	0				
Walters	18·2	1	66	5	13	3	23	2
O'Keeffe	8	1	27	0				
Jenner	7	0	15	0				
I.M. Chappell	1	1	0	0				
WEST INDIES								
Holder	35	6	64	1	7	2	21	0
Boyce	24·4	6	69	3	8	1	33	0
Davis	6	0	15	0	3	2	5	0
Willett	27	3	88	2	6	2	20	0
Gibbs	36	15	67	3	5	4	9	0
Lloyd	7	1	15	0	5	1	15	0
Kanhai					5	1	15	0
Greenidge					4	0	15	0

FALL OF WICKETS

	WI	A	WI	A
Wkt	*1st*	*1st*	*2nd*	*2nd*
1st	55	5	12	–
2nd	56	36	30	–
3rd	90	157	39	–
4th	277	229	42	–
5th	307	262	77	–
6th	310	306	82	–
7th	337	316	91	–
8th	347	334	95	–
9th	356	336	100	–
10th	366	341	109	–

Umpires: C.P. Kippins (10) and D. Sang Hue (15).

Close: 1st day – WI(1) 269-3 (Lloyd 139, Kanhai 53); 2nd – A(1) 99-2 (I.M. Chappell 40, G.S. Chappell 21); 3rd – WI(2) 3-0 (Fredericks 3, Greenidge 0); 4th – A(2) 105-0 (Stackpole 66, Redpath 37).

WEST INDIES v AUSTRALIA 1972–73 (5th Test)

Played at Queen's Park Oval, Port-of-Spain, Trinidad, on 21, 22, 23, 25, 26 April.
Toss: Australia.   Result: MATCH DRAWN.
Debuts: Nil.

West Indies were asked to score 319 runs in 270 minutes. Rain curtailed the second day by 175 minutes and ended play on the third day 25 minutes before tea. In this match, Gibbs became the first bowler to bowl 20,000 balls in Test cricket. He and Walker each took 26 wickets in the rubber to share the record for this series in the West Indies until 1983-84 when J. Garner took 31. During the rubber, the Post Office scores service received 15,500,500 calls.

AUSTRALIA

I.R. Redpath	c Fredericks b Gibbs	36	c Boyce b Foster		24
R. Edwards	c Fredericks b Jumadeen	74	c Kallicharran b Ali		14
I.M. Chappell*	c Kallicharran b Ali	56	c Kallicharran b Gibbs		37
G.S. Chappell	c Fredericks b Gibbs	41	c Fredericks b Gibbs		31
K.D. Walters	c Fredericks b Gibbs	70	c Murray b Gibbs		27
J. Benaud	c and b Ali	8	c Davis b Ali		36
R.W. Marsh†	c Ali b Jumadeen	56	not out		21
K.J. O'Keeffe	b Ali	37	c Lloyd b Gibbs		0
T.J. Jenner	not out	27	not out		11
J.R. Hammond	not out	6			
M.H.N. Walker	did not bat				
Extras	(B 5, LB 1, NB 2)	8	(B 13, LB 2, W 1, NB 1)		17
Total	(8 wickets declared)	**419**	(7 wickets declared)		**218**

WEST INDIES

R.C. Fredericks	c Edwards b Jenner	73	c Marsh b Hammond		8
M.L.C. Foster	c Marsh b Walker	29	c I.M. Chappell b Walker		19
C.A. Davis	c Marsh b Walker	25	b Benaud		24
A.I. Kallicharran	c Hammond b Jenner	32	c O'Keeffe b Benaud		26
R.B. Kanhai*	b Jenner	3	(6) not out		16
C.H. Lloyd	c Redpath b Walker	59	(7) not out		22
D.L. Murray†	c Marsh b Walker	34	(5) c I.M. Chappell b Jenner		7
K.D. Boyce	b Jenner	31			
Inshan Ali	c G.S. Chappell b Walker	0			
R.R. Jumadeen	not out	11			
L.R. Gibbs	c Hammond b Jenner	6			
Extras	(B 6, LB 4, W 1, NB 5)	16	(B 10, NB 3)		13
Total		**319**	(5 wickets)		**135**

WEST INDIES	O	M	R	W	O	M	R	W		FALL OF WICKETS			
Boyce	10	3	21	0						A	WI	A	WI
Lloyd	12	6	19	0	3	0	16	0	*Wkt*	*1st*	*1st*	*2nd*	*2nd*
Davis	5	0	22	0	5	0	16	0	1st	50	48	37	25
Gibbs	52	15	114	3	32	12	66	4	2nd	159	88	49	30
Jumadeen	40	8	89	2	18	5	32	0	3rd	169	151	101	81
Ali	44	4	124	3	19	2	68	2	4th	280	171	114	86
Foster	8	3	15	0	3	1	3	1	5th	281	180	157	96
Fredericks	2	0	7	0					6th	293	270	195	–
									7th	379	271	197	–
AUSTRALIA									8th	395	271	–	–
Hammond	21	4	76	0	15	8	25	1	9th	–	303	–	–
Walker	37	10	75	5	17	8	24	1	10th	–	319	–	–
G.S. Chappell	7	2	21	0	6	2	11	0					
Walters	3	2	5	0									
Jenner	32·2	9	90	5	17	7	33	1					
O'Keeffe	11	1	36	0	10	5	17	0					
Benaud					4	1	12	2					

Umpires: R. Gosein (12) and D. Sang Hue (16).

Close: 1st day – A(1) 300-6 (Marsh 4, O'Keeffe 3); 2nd – WI(1) 15-0 (Fredericks 11, Foster 3); 3rd – WI(1) 193-5 (Lloyd 13, Murray 8); 4th – A(2) 145-4 (Walters 21, Benaud 14).

PAKISTAN v ENGLAND 1972–73 (1st Test)

Played at Gaddafi Stadium, Lahore, on 2, 3, 4, 6, 7 March.
Toss: England.   Result: MATCH DRAWN.
Debuts: Nil.

Pakistan were left 145 minutes in which to score 240 runs. Amiss scored the first of his 11 Test hundreds in his 22nd innings. Sadiq and Majid both scored their 1,000th run in Test cricket during the first innings. When 22, Mushtaq scored his 1,040th run against England and overtook the record held by his elder brother, Hanif. Lahore Stadium had been renamed since it staged its last Test in November 1969 (*Test No. 663*).

ENGLAND

M.H. Denness	lbw b Salim	50	c Wasim Bari b Intikhab	68
D.L. Amiss	b Salim	112	c Mushtaq b Intikhab	16
G.R.J. Roope	c Wasim Bari b Pervez	15	st Wasim Bari b Intikhab	0
A.R. Lewis*	b Wasim Raja	29	b Salim	74
K.W.R. Fletcher	c Wasim Bari b Pervez	55	c Majid b Intikhab	12
A.W. Greig	c Majid b Sarfraz	41	c Talat b Mushtaq	72
A.P.E. Knott†	c Wasim Bari b Mushtaq	29	c Majid b Mushtaq	34
C.M. Old	b Pervez	0	not out	17
G.G. Arnold	c Sarfraz b Mushtaq	0	not out	3
D.L. Underwood	not out	5		
P.I. Pocock	c Talat b Mushtaq	5		
Extras	(LB 11, NB 3)	14	(B 6, LB 3, NB 1)	10
Total		**355**	(7 wickets declared)	**306**

PAKISTAN

Sadiq Mohammad	c Roope b Greig	119	c Roope b Greig	9
Talat Ali	c Greig b Arnold	35	c and b Pocock	57
Majid Khan*	run out	32	c and b Greig	43
Mushtaq Mohammad	b Underwood	66	not out	5
Asif Iqbal	c Denness b Arnold	102		
Intikhab Alam	b Underwood	3		
Wasim Raja	c Roope b Greig	23	(5) not out	6
Salim Altaf	not out	11		
Wasim Bari†	b Underwood	7		
Sarfraz Nawaz	b Greig	8		
Pervez Sajjad	lbw b Greig	4		
Extras	(B 1, LB 6, NB 5)	12	(LB 4)	4
Total		**422**	(3 wickets)	**124**

PAKISTAN	O	M	R	W	O	M	R	W	FALL OF WICKETS				
Salim	28	3	80	2	11	2	24	1		E	P	E	P
Sarfraz	31	14	51	1	17	7	41	0	*Wkt*	*1st*	*1st*	*2nd*	*2nd*
Wasim Raja	21	0	69	1	14	7	36	0	1st	105	99	63	9
Pervez	23	9	58	3	23	9	37	0	2nd	147	155	102	102
Intikhab	32	14	62	0	35	10	80	4	3rd	201	222	108	114
Mushtaq	8·3	1	21	3	16	2	66	2	4th	219	294	154	–
Majid					3	1	12	0	5th	286	310	203	–
									6th	333	383	282	–
ENGLAND									7th	333	391	287	–
Arnold	43	10	95	2	4	1	12	0	8th	334	404	–	–
Old	27	2	98	0					9th	345	413	–	–
Underwood	35	15	58	3	13	5	38	0	10th	355	422	–	–
Pocock	24	6	73	0	15	3	42	1					
Greig	29·2	5	86	4	6	0	28	2					

Umpires: Daud Khan (13) and Shujauddin (16).

Close: 1st day – E(1) 272-4 (Fletcher 24, Greig 30; 2nd – P(1) 96-0 (Sadiq 63, Talat 32); 3rd – P(1) 347-5 (Asif 77, Wasim Raja 6); 4th – E(2) 134-3 (Lewis 34, Fletcher 6).

PAKISTAN v ENGLAND 1972–73 (2nd Test)

Played at Niaz Stadium, Hyderabad, on 16, 17, 18, 20, 21 March.
Toss: England.   Result: MATCH DRAWN.
Debuts: Nil.

Hyderabad's first Test match provided Pakistan with their highest total in a home Test against England. Mushtaq and Intikhab shared a partnership of 145 which remains the highest for Pakistan's sixth wicket against England. Mushtaq's 157 is the highest score against England in Pakistan. Intikhab's only Test hundred included four sixes and 15 fours. Mohammad Aslam Khokhar, who made his debut as a Test umpire in this match, played in one Test (*Test No. 388*) as 'Mohammad Aslam'.

ENGLAND

M.H. Denness	b Salim	8	c Mushtaq b Salim		0
D.L. Amiss	st Wasim b Mushtaq	158	c Sadiq b Intikhab		0
K.W.R. Fletcher	c Zaheer b Intikhab	78	c Asif b Intikhab		21
A.R. Lewis*	c Wasim b Mushtaq	7	c Pervez b Intikhab		21
G.R.J. Roope	st Wasim b Intikhab	27	b Mushtaq		18
A.W. Greig	b Mushtaq	36	c Wasim b Asif		64
A.P.E. Knott†	c Nazir b Mushtaq	71	not out		63
G.G. Arnold	c Wasim b Intikhab	8	not out		19
N. Gifford	b Intikhab	24			
D.L. Underwood	not out	20			
P.I. Pocock	b Pervez	33			
Extras	(B 2, LB 11, NB 4)	17	(B 1, LB 5, NB 6)		12
Total		**487**	(6 wickets)		**218**

PAKISTAN

Sadiq Mohammad	c Knott b Pocock	30
Talat Ali	c Fletcher b Gifford	22
Majid Khan*	c Knott b Pocock	17
Mushtaq Mohammad	lbw b Gifford	157
Zaheer Abbas	c Roope b Pocock	24
Asif Iqbal	c Roope b Pocock	68
Intikhab Alam	b Arnold	138
Salim Altaf	c Gifford b Pocock	2
Wasim Bari†	c Pocock b Gifford	48
Mohammad Nazir	not out	22
Pervez Sajjad	not out	10
Extras	(B 14, LB 10, NB 7)	31
Total	(9 wickets declared)	**569**

PAKISTAN	O	M	R	W	O	M	R	W
Salim	29	10	63	1	10	1	40	1
Asif	11	5	31	0	1	0	3	1
Intikhab	65	17	137	4	19	5	44	3
Nazir	36	9	84	0	16	3	41	0
Pervez	21·2	5	56	1	11	5	11	0
Mushtaq	35	10	93	4	20	5	42	1
Sadiq	3	1	6	0	3	0	14	0
Majid					2	0	4	0
Talat					2	1	6	0
Zaheer					1	0	1	0

ENGLAND	O	M	R	W
Arnold	24	2	78	1
Greig	13	2	39	0
Pocock	52	9	169	5
Gifford	52	16	111	3
Underwood	48	15	119	0
Fletcher	3	0	22	0

FALL OF WICKETS

Wkt	E 1st	P 1st	E 2nd
1st	22	53	0
2nd	190	66	0
3rd	250	77	34
4th	259	139	52
5th	319	292	77
6th	343	437	189
7th	364	449	–
8th	428	514	–
9th	432	553	–
10th	487	–	–

Umpires: Mohammad Aslam Khokhar (1) and Shujauddin (17).

Close: 1st day – E(1) 288-4 (Roope 21, Greig 10); 2nd – P(1) 16-0 (Sadiq 9, Talat 6); 3rd – P(1) 266-4 (Mushtaq 93, Asif 61); 4th – P(1) 561-9 (Nazir 20, Pervez 4).

PAKISTAN v ENGLAND 1972–73 (3rd Test)

Played at National Stadium, Karachi, on 24, 25, 27, 28, 29 March.
Toss: Pakistan.   Result: MATCH DRAWN.
Debuts: Nil.

This match and the rubber were left drawn when play was abandoned 45 minutes early because of a dust storm. Sundry riots and crowd incursions lost nearly two hours of playing time earlier in the match. Amiss failed by one run to score his third hundred in successive Tests. His aggregate of 406 (average 81·20) was England's highest in a rubber in Pakistan until D.I. Gower scored 449 in 1983-84; his previous 12 Test matches produced only 348 runs (average 18·31). Amiss was one of three batsmen to be out for 99 in the match – a unique record in Test cricket. Pakistan's total of 199 is their lowest in a home Test against England. This was the eighth successive drawn Test involving these countries in Pakistan.

PAKISTAN

Sadiq Mohammad	c Denness b Gifford	89	(6) b Gifford	1
Talat Ali	c Amiss b Gifford	33	b Gifford	39
Majid Khan*	c Amiss b Pocock	99	(1) b Gifford	23
Mushtaq Mohammad	run out	99	(5) c Denness b Birkenshaw	0
Asif Iqbal	c and b Pocock	6	(4) c Fletcher b Gifford	36
Intikhab Alam	c and b Birkenshaw	61	(7) c Greig b Birkenshaw	0
Zaheer Abbas	not out	22	(3) c Knott b Gifford	4
Wasim Bari†	not out	17	c Denness b Birkenshaw	41
Salim Altaf	)		c Knott b Birkenshaw	13
Sarfraz Nawaz	) did not bat		not out	33
Asif Masood	)		c Gifford b Birkenshaw	0
Extras	(B 4, LB 9, NB 6)	19	(LB 4, NB 5)	9
Total	(6 wickets declared)	**445**		**199**

ENGLAND

B. Wood	c Sarfraz b Asif Masood	3	c Asif Masood b Salim	5
D.L. Amiss	c Sarfraz b Intikhab	99	not out	21
K.W.R. Fletcher	c Talat b Intikhab	54	not out	1
M.H. Denness	lbw b Asif Masood	47		
A.R. Lewis*	c Asif Iqbal b Intikhab	88		
P.I. Pocock	c Sarfraz b Mushtaq	4		
A.W. Greig	b Majid	48		
A.P.E. Knott†	b Majid	2		
J. Birkenshaw	c Majid b Mushtaq	21		
G.G. Arnold	c Mushtaq b Intikhab	2		
N. Gifford	not out	4		
Extras	(B 3, LB 3, NB 8)	14	(NB 3)	3
Total		**386**	(1 wicket)	**30**

ENGLAND	O	M	R	W	O	M	R	W
Arnold	19	2	69	0	15	2	52	0
Greig	20	1	76	0	10	2	26	0
Pocock	38	7	93	2				
Gifford	46	12	99	2	29	9	55	5
Birkenshaw	31	5	89	1	18·3	5	57	5
PAKISTAN								
Salim	15	3	38	0	5	1	16	1
Asif Masood	21	4	41	2	4	1	11	0
Intikhab	39	8	105	4				
Sarfraz	25	3	64	0	1	1	0	0
Mushtaq	34·3	9	73	2				
Majid	22	5	51	2				

FALL OF WICKETS

	P	E	P	E
Wkt	1st	1st	2nd	2nd
1st	79	13	39	27
2nd	176	143	51	–
3rd	297	182	105	–
4th	307	220	106	–
5th	389	323	106	–
6th	413	331	106	–
7th	–	370	108	–
8th	–	373	129	–
9th	–	381	198	–
10th	–	386	199	–

Umpires: Daud Khan (14) and Mohammad Aslam Khokhar (2).

Close: 1st day – P(1) 201-2 (Majid 50, Mushtaq 12); 2nd – E(1) 10-0 (Wood 2, Amiss 8); 3rd – E(1) 223-4 (Lewis 10, Pocock 3); 4th – P(2) 55-2 (Talat 23, Asif Iqbal 1).

ENGLAND v NEW ZEALAND 1973 (1st Test)

Played at Trent Bridge, Nottingham, on 7, 8, 9, 11, 12 June.
Toss: England.   Result: ENGLAND won by 38 runs.
Debuts: Nil.

England won at 3.33 on the fifth afternoon after New Zealand had scored the then second-highest total in the fourth innings of any Test match; it was then the highest fourth innings total by a losing team in Test cricket. Congdon, who scored New Zealand's first century in England since 1949, and Pollard, whose hundred was his first in 56 innings in 30 Tests, shared a partnership of 177 which was then New Zealand's highest for the fifth wicket in all Tests and which remains their record for that wicket against England. New Zealand's first innings was then the highest in all Test matches in which extras have made the largest contribution. The partnership of 59 by Knott and Gifford remains the record for the tenth wicket by either side in this series.

ENGLAND

G. Boycott	lbw b Taylor	51	run out	1
D.L. Amiss	c Wadsworth b Taylor	42	not out	138
G.R.J. Roope	lbw b D.R. Hadlee	28	c Wadsworth b Collinge	2
A.R. Lewis	c Wadsworth b Taylor	2	c Wadsworth b Taylor	2
K.W.R. Fletcher	lbw b D.R. Hadlee	17	b D.R. Hadlee	8
A.W. Greig	c Parker b Collinge	2	lbw b Collinge	139
R. Illingworth*	b D.R. Hadlee	8	c Parker b Pollard	3
A.P.E. Knott†	b Congdon	49	c Hastings b Pollard	2
J.A. Snow	b D.R. Hadlee	8	b R.J. Hadlee	7
G.G. Arnold	c Wadsworth b Taylor	1	not out	10
N. Gifford	not out	25		
Extras	(LB 10, NB 7)	17	(B 4, LB 6, NB 3)	13
Total		**250**	(8 wickets declared)	**325**

NEW ZEALAND

G.M. Turner	c Roope b Greig	11	c Roope b Arnold	9
J.M. Parker	c Knott b Greig	2	c Illingworth b Snow	6
B.E. Congdon*	run out	9	b Arnold	176
B.F. Hastings	c Roope b Arnold	3	lbw b Arnold	11
M.G. Burgess	c Knott b Arnold	0	c Knott b Arnold	26
V. Pollard	not out	16	lbw b Greig	116
K.J. Wadsworth†	c Knott b Greig	0	c Roope b Arnold	46
B.R. Taylor	c Knott b Snow	19	lbw b Snow	11
D.R. Hadlee	b Snow	0	hit wkt b Greig	14
R.J. Hadlee	b Snow	0	not out	4
R.O. Collinge	b Greig	17	b Greig	0
Extras	(B 8, LB 6, NB 6)	20	(LB 13, W 1, NB 7)	21
Total		**97**		**440**

NEW ZEALAND	O	M	R	W	O	M	R	W
Collinge	27	6	62	1	24	7	43	2
R.J. Hadlee	26	5	64	0	19	3	79	1
Taylor	29	7	53	4	23	3	87	1
D.R. Hadlee	19	6	42	4	13	2	51	1
Congdon	6·4	1	12	1	9	1	28	0
Pollard					9	3	24	2
ENGLAND								
Snow	13	5	21	3	43	10	104	2
Arnold	18	8	23	2	53	15	131	5
Greig	10·4	0	33	4	45·1	10	101	3
Roope					9	2	17	0
Gifford					17	7	35	0
Illingworth					21	7	31	0

FALL OF WICKETS

Wkt	E 1st	NZ 1st	E 2nd	NZ 2nd
1st	92	24	2	16
2nd	106	31	8	16
3rd	108	34	11	68
4th	140	34	24	130
5th	147	45	234	307
6th	161	45	241	402
7th	162	71	263	414
8th	184	72	311	431
9th	191	72	–	440
10th	250	97	–	440

Umpires: D.J. Constant (5) and A.E.G. Rhodes (8).

Close: 1st day – E(1) 216-9 (Knott 32, Gifford 10); 2nd – E(2) 72-4 (Amiss 22, Greig 33); 3rd – NZ(2) 56-2 (Congdon 29, Hastings 9); 4th – NZ(2) 317-5 (Pollard 74, Wadsworth 3).

ENGLAND v NEW ZEALAND 1973 (2nd Test)

Played at Lord's, London, on 21, 22, 23, 25, 26 June.
Toss: New Zealand.   Result: MATCH DRAWN.
Debuts: Nil.

New Zealand scored their highest total in all Tests until 1985-86 after winning the toss for the first time in ten matches. This was the first instance of three batsmen scoring hundreds in the same innings for New Zealand. The partnerships of 190 between Congdon and Hastings and 117 between Burgess and Pollard were then New Zealand's highest against England for the third and sixth wickets respectively. A stand of 92 in 87 minutes between Fletcher, who batted 379 minutes and hit two sixes and 21 fours, and Arnold saved England from their first defeat in this series.

ENGLAND

G. Boycott	c Parker b Collinge	61	c and b Howarth		92
D.L. Amiss	c Howarth b Hadlee	9	c and b Howarth		53
G.R.J. Roope	lbw b Howarth	56	c Parker b Taylor		51
K.W.R. Fletcher	c Hastings b Howarth	25	c Taylor b Collinge		178
A.W. Greig	c Howarth b Collinge	63	c Wadsworth b Hadlee		12
R. Illingworth*	c Collinge b Hadlee	3	c Turner b Howarth		22
A.P.E. Knott†	b Hadlee	0	c Congdon b Howarth		0
C.M. Old	b Howarth	7	c Congdon b Pollard		7
J.A. Snow	b Taylor	2	c Hastings b Pollard		0
G.G. Arnold	not out	8	not out		23
N. Gifford	c Wadsworth b Collinge	8	not out		2
Extras	(LB 1, W 1, NB 9)	11	(B 8, LB 3, NB 12)		23
Total		**253**	(9 wickets)		**463**

NEW ZEALAND

G.M. Turner	c Greig b Arnold	4
J.M. Parker	c Knott b Snow	3
B.E. Congdon*	c Knott b Old	175
B.F. Hastings	lbw b Snow	86
H.J. Howarth	hit wkt b Old	17
M.G. Burgess	b Snow	105
V.Pollard	not out	105
K.J. Wadsworth†	c Knott b Old	27
B.R. Taylor	b Old	11
D.R. Hadlee	c Fletcher b Old	6
R.O. Collinge	did not bat	
Extras	(LB 5, NB 7)	12
Total	(9 wickets declared)	**551**

NEW ZEALAND	O	M	R	W	O	M	R	W	FALL OF WICKETS			
										E	NZ	E
Collinge	31	8	69	3	19	4	41	1	*Wkt*	*1st*	*1st*	*2nd*
Taylor	19	1	54	1	34	10	90	1	1st	24	5	112
Hadlee	26	4	70	3	25	2	79	1	2nd	116	10	185
Congdon	5	2	7	0	8	3	22	0	3rd	148	200	250
Howarth	25	6	42	3	70	24	144	4	4th	165	249	274
Pollard					39	11	61	2	5th	171	330	335
Hastings					1	0	3	0	6th	175	447	339
ENGLAND									7th	195	523	352
Snow	38	4	109	3					8th	217	535	368
Arnold	41	6	108	1					9th	237	551	460
Old	41·5	7	113	5					10th	253	–	–
Roope	6	1	15	0								
Gifford	39	6	107	0								
Illingworth	39	12	87	0								

Umpires: A.E. Fagg (13) and T.W. Spencer (7).

Close: 1st day – E(1) 240-9 (Arnold 2, Gifford 2); 2nd – NZ(1) 200-3 (Congdon 100, Howarth 0); 3rd – NZ(1) 492-6 (Pollard 77, Wadsworth 14); 4th – E(2) 224-2 (Roope 41, Fletcher 28).

ENGLAND v NEW ZEALAND 1973 (3rd Test)

Played at Headingley, Leeds, on 5, 6, 7, 9, 10 July.
Toss: New Zealand.   Result: ENGLAND won by an innings and one run.
Debuts: Nil.

England won after 13 minutes (21 balls) of play on the fifth morning. Turner narrowly missed becoming the first batsman to carry his bat through a completed Test innings on three occasions; he was last out after batting for 274 minutes in the second innings. Rain prevented any play after lunch on the second day.

NEW ZEALAND

G.M. Turner	lbw b Old	11	lbw b Snow	81
J.M. Parker	c Knott b Arnold	8	c Knott b Arnold	4
B.E. Congdon*	c Knott b Arnold	0	c Knott b Arnold	2
B.F. Hastings	lbw b Arnold	18	b Old	10
M.G. Burgess	c Roope b Old	87	lbw b Old	18
V. Pollard	c Boycott b Old	62	c Roope b Arnold	3
K.J. Wadsworth†	b Old	8	b Arnold	5
B.R. Taylor	c Fletcher b Greig	20	c Roope b Snow	1
D.R. Hadlee	b Snow	34	lbw b Snow	0
R.O. Collinge	b Snow	5	b Arnold	0
H.J. Howarth	not out	8	not out	15
Extras	(B 5, LB 7, W 1, NB 2)	15	(B 1, LB 2)	3
Total		**276**		**142**

ENGLAND

G. Boycott	c Parker b Congdon	115
D.L. Amiss	lbw b Collinge	8
G.R.J. Roope	c Turner b Collinge	18
K.W.R. Fletcher	c Howarth b Collinge	81
A.W. Greig	c Howarth b Congdon	0
R. Illingworth*	lbw b Taylor	65
A.P.E. Knott†	c Wadsworth b Taylor	21
C.M. Old	lbw b Collinge	34
J.A. Snow	c Howarth b Collinge	6
G.G. Arnold	c Wadsworth b Hadlee	26
D.L. Underwood	not out	20
Extras	(B 5, LB 16, W 1, NB 3)	25
Total		**419**

ENGLAND	O	M	R	W	O	M	R	W		FALL OF WICKETS		
										NZ	E	NZ
Snow	21·4	4	52	2	19·3	4	34	3	*Wkt*	*1st*	*1st*	*2nd*
Arnold	27	8	62	3	22	11	27	5	1st	24	23	16
Old	20	4	71	4	14	1	41	2	2nd	24	71	20
Underwood	11	4	27	0	7	2	14	0	3rd	24	190	39
Greig	13	4	29	1	6	1	22	0	4th	78	190	85
Illingworth	6	0	20	0	2	1	1	0	5th	184	280	88
									6th	202	300	94
NEW ZEALAND									7th	215	339	95
Collinge	34	7	74	5					8th	227	346	97
Taylor	31	3	111	2					9th	233	365	106
Hadlee	23·1	2	98	1					10th	276	419	142
Congdon	32	10	54	2								
Howarth	18	6	44	0								
Pollard	7	4	13	0								

Umpires: H.D. Bird (1) and C.S. Elliott (39).

Close: 1st day – NZ(1) 262-9 (Hadlee 25, Howarth 8); 2nd – E(1) 70-1 (Boycott 45, Roope 17); 3rd – E(1) 337-6 (Knott 20, Old 16); 4th – NZ(2) 138-9 (Turner 80, Howarth 13).

ENGLAND v WEST INDIES 1973 (1st Test)

Played at Kennington Oval, London, on 26, 27, 28, 30, 31 July.
Toss: West Indies.   Result: WEST INDIES won by 158 runs.
Debuts: England – F.C. Hayes; West Indies – R.G.A. Headley, B.D. Julien.

West Indies won at 2.26 on the fifth afternoon to end a run of 20 Test matches without a victory. Hayes scored a hundred in his first Test after batting for exactly four hours and hitting 12 fours. Boyce's match analysis of 11 for 147 was then the best for West Indies in this series. Greig dislocated a finger and left the field after bowling three balls of his 16th over on the first afternoon.

WEST INDIES

R.C. Fredericks	lbw b Arnold	35	c Hayes b Arnold	3
R.G.A. Headley	lbw b Greig	8	b Arnold	42
R.B. Kanhai*	b Greig	10	c Knott b Snow	0
C.H. Lloyd	lbw b Arnold	132	c Greig b Snow	14
A.I. Kallicharran	c Knott b Arnold	80	b Illingworth	80
D.L. Murray†	c Roope b Arnold	28	(7) c Roope b Underwood	4
G. St A. Sobers	run out	10	(6) c Underwood b Snow	51
B.D. Julien	lbw b Arnold	11	b Illingworth	23
K.D. Boyce	b Underwood	72	b Illingworth	9
Inshan Ali	c Boycott b Underwood	15	not out	5
L.R. Gibbs	not out	1	c Knott b Arnold	3
Extras	(B 1, LB 2, NB 10)	13	(B 2, LB 13, NB 6)	21
Total		**415**		**255**

ENGLAND

G. Boycott	c Murray b Julien	97	c and b Gibbs	30
D.L. Amiss	b Boyce	29	c Kanhai b Boyce	15
G.R.J. Roope	b Boyce	9	c and b Gibbs	31
F.C. Hayes	c Lloyd b Sobers	16	not out	106
K.W.R. Fletcher	c Lloyd b Julien	11	c Kallicharran b Gibbs	5
A.W. Greig	c Sobers b Boyce	38	c Gibbs b Ali	0
R. Illingworth*	lbw b Sobers	27	(8) b Boyce	40
A.P.E. Knott†	not out	4	(9) lbw b Boyce	5
J.A. Snow	b Boyce	0	(11) b Boyce	1
G.G. Arnold	c Kallicharran b Boyce	4	c Headley b Boyce	4
D.L. Underwood	c Headley b Sobers	0	(7) lbw b Boyce	7
Extras	(B 2, LB 7, W 2, NB 11)	22	(LB 5, W 1, NB 5)	11
Total		**257**		**255**

ENGLAND	O	M	R	W	O	M	R	W	FALL OF WICKETS				
Snow	31	8	71	0	18	4	62	3		WI	E	WI	E
Arnold	39	10	113	5	18·1	7	49	3	*Wkt*	*1st*	*1st*	*2nd*	*2nd*
Greig	30·3	6	81	2	8	1	22	0	1st	33	50	9	36
Roope	6	1	26	0					2nd	47	95	31	66
Underwood	23·3	8	68	2	19	5	51	1	3rd	64	134	52	91
Illingworth	15	3	43	0	24	8	50	3	4th	272	163	117	97
									5th	275	185	177	107
WEST INDIES									6th	297	247	184	136
Sobers	22·1	13	27	3	11	3	22	0	7th	309	247	215	229
Boyce	22	4	70	5	21·1	4	77	6	8th	346	247	232	239
Julien	20	6	49	2	17	4	35	0	9th	405	257	252	253
Gibbs	23	8	37	0	33	9	61	3	10th	415	257	255	255
Ali	11	3	52	0	23	6	49	1					

Umpires: D.J. Constant (6) and T.W. Spencer (8).

Close: 1st day – WI(1) 275-4 (Lloyd 132, Murray 1); 2nd – E(1) 117-2 (Boycott 55, Hayes 14); 3rd – WI(2) 95-3 (Headley 40, Kallicharran 23); 4th – E(2) 126-5 (Hayes 37, Underwood 3).

ENGLAND v WEST INDIES 1973 (2nd Test)

Played at Edgbaston, Birmingham, on 9, 10, 11, 13, 14 August.
Toss: West Indies.   Result: MATCH DRAWN.
Debuts: Nil.

England needed to score 325 runs to win in 227 minutes. Boycott (54) retired at 105 because of bruised ribs, resumed at 249, but retired at the same total when he was hit on the arm first ball by Holder. He returned again at 299. A.S.M. Oakman, a former first-class umpire, deputised for the first over of the third day, when A.E. Fagg refused to umpire because of dissent shown by Kanhai when he did not uphold an appeal against Boycott for a catch by Murray on the second afternoon.

WEST INDIES

Batsman	Dismissal	Score	Dismissal (2nd)	Score
R.C. Fredericks	c Amiss b Underwood	150	c Knott b Arnold	12
R.G.A. Headley	b Old	1	c Knott b Old	11
R.B. Kanhai*	c Greig b Arnold	2	c Arnold b Illingworth	54
C.H. Lloyd	lbw b Old	15	c Knott b Underwood	94
A.I. Kallicharran	c Hayes b Arnold	34	b Underwood	4
G. St A. Sobers	b Old	21	b Arnold	74
D.L. Murray†	b Underwood	25	hit wkt b Arnold	15
B.D. Julien	c Greig b Arnold	54	b Greig	11
K.D. Boyce	lbw b Illingworth	12	c Knott b Arnold	0
V.A. Holder	c Boycott b Underwood	6	c Luckhurst b Greig	10
L.R. Gibbs	not out	1	not out	3
Extras	(LB 2, W 1, NB 3)	6	(LB 10, NB 4)	14
Total		**327**		**302**

ENGLAND

Batsman	Dismissal	Score	Dismissal (2nd)	Score
G. Boycott	not out	56		
D.L. Amiss	c Murray b Julien	56	not out	86
B.W. Luckhurst	lbw b Sobers	12	(1) c Murray b Lloyd	42
F.C. Hayes	c Kallicharran b Holder	29	(3) lbw b Lloyd	0
A.W. Greig	c Fredericks b Julien	27		
A.P.E. Knott†	b Holder	0		
K.W.R. Fletcher	c Holder b Sobers	52	(4) not out	44
R. Illingworth*	lbw b Holder	27		
C.M. Old	run out	0		
G.G. Arnold	c Kallicharran b Sobers	24		
D.L. Underwood	c Murray b Gibbs	2		
Extras	(B 4, LB 1, NB 15)	20	(B 8, NB 2)	10
Total		**305**	(2 wickets)	**182**

ENGLAND	O	M	R	W	O	M	R	W
Arnold	37	13	74	3	20	1	43	4
Old	30	3	86	3	14	0	65	1
Greig	26	3	84	0	7·4	0	35	2
Illingworth	32	19	37	1	26	6	67	1
Underwood	24·3	10	40	3	32	9	66	2
Luckhurst					4	2	12	0
WEST INDIES								
Holder	44	16	83	3	7	1	17	0
Sobers	30	6	62	3	7	1	21	0
Boyce	19	2	48	0				
Julien	26	8	55	2	18	3	32	0
Gibbs	35·4	21	32	1	12	2	32	0
Lloyd	2	0	5	0	12	3	26	2
Fredericks					4	0	23	0
Kanhai					7	1	21	0

FALL OF WICKETS

	WI	E	WI	E
Wkt	1st	1st	2nd	2nd
1st	14	119	24	96
2nd	17	139	42	100
3rd	39	191	136	–
4th	93	191	152	–
5th	128	197	197	–
6th	242	249	247	–
7th	280	249	283	–
8th	302	299	283	–
9th	325	302	293	–
10th	327	305	302	–

Umpires: H.D. Bird (2) and A.E. Fagg (14).

Close: 1st day – WI(1) 190-5 (Fredericks 98, Murray 15); 2nd – E(1) 96-0 (Boycott 52, Amiss 42); 3rd – E(1) 265-7 (Fletcher 37, Arnold 3); 4th – WI(2) 205-5 (Sobers 21, Murray 0).

ENGLAND v WEST INDIES 1973 (3rd Test)

Played at Lord's, London, on 23, 24, 25, 27 August.
Toss: West Indies.   Result: WEST INDIES won by an innings and 226 runs.
Debuts: Nil.

West Indies gained their largest margin of victory over England after scoring what was then their highest total in England. The match ended at 2.56 on the fourth afternoon. Sobers (132) retired at 528 because of a stomach disorder after sharing an unbroken partnership of 155 in 113 minutes with Julien; it remains the West Indies record for the seventh wicket against England. He resumed at 604 and altogether batted for 288 minutes (227 balls) and hit 19 fours; it was his 26th and last hundred in official Tests – only S.M. Gavaskar (30 before the 1984-85 season) and Sir Donald Bradman (29) have scored more. Earlier Kanhai, during the last of his 15 centuries, had become the second batsman after Sobers to score 6,000 runs for West Indies. Julien reached his first hundred in first-class cricket off 127 balls. For the second time (also *Test No. 407*), five bowlers conceded a hundred runs in the same Test innings. A bomb alert at 2.42 on the third afternoon resulted in 89 minutes being lost but an hour of this time was subsequently made up. The six Tests of the 1973 season attracted 19,935,000 calls to the Post Office scores service.

WEST INDIES

R.C. Fredericks	c Underwood b Willis	51
D.L. Murray†	b Willis	4
R.B. Kanhai*	c Greig b Willis	157
C.H. Lloyd	c and b Willis	63
A.I. Kallicharran	c Arnold b Illingworth	14
G. St A. Sobers	not out	150
M.L.C. Foster	c Willis b Greig	9
B.D. Julien	c and b Greig	121
K.D. Boyce	c Amiss b Greig	36
V.A. Holder	not out	23
L.R. Gibbs	did not bat	
Extras	(B 1, LB 14, W 1, NB 8)	24
Total	(8 wickets declared)	**652**

ENGLAND

G. Boycott	c Kanhai b Holder	4	c Kallicharran b Boyce		15
D.L. Amiss	c Sobers b Holder	35	c Sobers b Boyce		10
B.W. Luckhurst	c Murray b Boyce	1	(4) c Sobers b Julien		12
F.C. Hayes	c Fredericks b Holder	8	(5) c Holder b Boyce		0
K.W.R. Fletcher	c Sobers b Gibbs	68	(6) not out		86
A.W. Greig	c Sobers b Boyce	44	(7) lbw b Julien		13
R. Illingworth*	c Sobers b Gibbs	0	(8) c Kanhai b Gibbs		13
A.P.E. Knott†	c Murray b Boyce	21	(3) c Murray b Boyce		5
G.G. Arnold	c Murray b Boyce	5	c Fredericks b Gibbs		1
R.G.D. Willis	not out	5	c Fredericks b Julien		0
D.L. Underwood	c Gibbs b Holder	12	b Gibbs		14
Extras	(B 6, LB 4, W 3, NB 17)	30	(B 9, W 1, NB 14)		24
Total		**233**			**193**

ENGLAND	O	M	R	W	O	M	R	W
Arnold	35	6	111	0				
Willis	35	3	118	4				
Greig	33	2	180	3				
Underwood	34	6	105	0				
Illingworth	31·4	3	114	1				
WEST INDIES								
Holder	15	3	56	4	14	4	18	0
Boyce	20	7	50	4	16	5	49	4
Julien	11	4	26	0	18	2	69	3
Gibbs	18	3	39	2	13·3	3	26	3
Sobers	8	0	30	0	4	1	7	0
Foster	1	0	2	0				

FALL OF WICKETS	WI	E	E
Wkt	*1st*	*1st*	*2nd*
1st	8	5	32
2nd	87	7	38
3rd	225	29	42
4th	256	97	49
5th	339	176	63
6th	373	176	87
7th	604	187	132
8th	610	205	143
9th	–	213	146
10th	–	233	193

Umpires: H.D. Bird (3) and C.S. Elliott (40).

Close: 1st day – WI(1) 335-4 (Kanhai 156, Sobers 31); 2nd – E(1) 88-3 (Amiss 32, Fletcher 30); 3rd – E(2) 42-3 (Luckhurst 2).

AUSTRALIA v NEW ZEALAND 1973–74 (1st Test)

Played at Melbourne Cricket Ground on 29, 30 December, 1, 2 January.
Toss: Australia.   Result: AUSTRALIA won by an innings and 25 runs.
Debuts: Australia – I.C. Davis, G.J. Gilmour; New Zealand – B. Andrews, J.F.M. Morrison.

Remarkably this was New Zealand's first official Test in Australia, the only previous match in this series being played at Wellington in 1945–46 when Australia won in two days. Stackpole scored the first hundred of the series and Wadsworth became the first New Zealander to score a fifty against Australia. Turner fractured a finger on his right-hand for the second time on the tour when he was hit by a ball from Dell.

AUSTRALIA

K.R. Stackpole	c Parker b Shrimpton	122
A.P. Sheahan	c Wadsworth b D.R. Hadlee	28
I.M. Chappell*	c R.J. Hadlee b Shrimpton	54
G.S. Chappell	c Wadsworth b Congdon	60
K.D. Walters	c Wadsworth b D.R. Hadlee	79
I.C. Davis	c Wadsworth b D.R. Hadlee	15
R.W. Marsh†	c Parker b D.R. Hadlee	6
K.J. O'Keeffe	not out	40
G.J. Gilmour	b Congdon	52
A.A. Mallett	) did not bat	
A.R. Dell	) did not bat	
Extras	(LB 4, W 1, NB 1)	6
Total	(8 wickets declared)	**462**

NEW ZEALAND

G.M. Turner	c Gilmour b Dell	6		absent hurt	–
J.M. Parker	c I.M. Chappell b O'Keeffe	27	(1)	c I.M. Chappell b Walters	23
M.J.F. Shrimpton	c Marsh b Gilmour	16		b Walters	22
B.F. Hastings	b O'Keeffe	1		c Marsh b Mallett	22
B.E. Congdon*	st Marsh b Mallett	31		c Marsh b Mallett	14
J.F.M. Morrison	c Marsh b Gilmour	44	(2)	c Marsh b Walters	16
K.J. Wadsworth†	c G.S. Chappell b Gilmour	80	(6)	c Stackpole b Mallett	30
R.J. Hadlee	c Marsh b Gilmour	9	(7)	c I.M. Chappell b O'Keeffe	6
D.R. Hadlee	run out	2	(8)	c and b O'Keeffe	37
D.R. O'Sullivan	c Davis b Mallett	6	(9)	c and b Mallett	8
B. Andrews	not out	0	(10)	not out	5
Extras	(B 8, LB 5, NB 2)	15		(B 8, LB 9)	17
Total		**237**			**200**

NEW ZEALAND	O	M	R	W	O	M	R	W
R.J. Hadlee	25	4	104	0				
Andrews	19	2	100	0				
D.R. Hadlee	20	2	102	4				
O'Sullivan	22	3	80	0				
Shrimpton	7	0	39	2				
Congdon	8·5	1	31	2				
AUSTRALIA								
Dell	22	7	54	1	5	0	9	0
Gilmour	22	4	75	4	3	0	16	0
G.S. Chappell	4	2	4	0	7	3	18	0
Mallett	16·7	2	46	2	24	4	63	4
O'Keeffe	14	4	40	2	29·6	12	51	2
I.M. Chappell	1	0	3	0				
Walters					13	4	26	3

FALL OF WICKETS

Wkt	A 1st	NZ 1st	NZ 2nd
1st	75	19	37
2nd	203	47	54
3rd	212	51	83
4th	304	56	109
5th	345	100	113
6th	363	189	134
7th	381	215	150
8th	462	230	188
9th	–	237	200
10th	–	237	–

Umpires: T.F. Brooks (7) and J.R. Collins (3).

Close: 1st day – A(1) 335-4 (Walters 52, Davis 15); 2nd – NZ(1) 51-3 (Parker 26); 3rd – NZ(2) 85-3 (Hastings 12, Congdon 1).

AUSTRALIA v NEW ZEALAND 1973–74 (2nd Test)

Played at Sydney Cricket Ground on 5, 6, 7 (*no play*), 9, 10 (*no play*) January.
Toss: Australia.   Result: MATCH DRAWN.
Debuts: New Zealand – J.V. Coney.

Australia were 425 runs behind with eight second innings wickets left when rain prevented any play on the fifth day. Parker scored New Zealand's first hundred of the series. A groin injury prevented Walker from bowling in the second innings when Morrison scored a hundred in his second Test match.

NEW ZEALAND

J.M. Parker	c Marsh b Walker	108	c Marsh b G.S. Chappell		11
J.F.M. Morrison	c G.S. Chappell b Walters	28	c Davis b I.M. Chappell		117
M.J.F. Shrimpton	b Walters	0	c and b Walters		28
B.E. Congdon*	c Marsh b Walters	4	b Gilmour		17
B.F. Hastings	c Marsh b Walker	16	b G.S. Chappell		83
J.V. Coney	c Stackpole b O'Keeffe	45	(7) c Davis b G.S. Chappell		11
K.J. Wadsworth†	c Marsh b Walters	54	(6) c G.S. Chappell b Gilmour		2
D.R. Hadlee	c and b G.S. Chappell	14	(9) not out		18
R.J. Hadlee	c I.M. Chappell b G.S. Chappell	17	(8) run out		1
D.R. O'Sullivan	not out	3	lbw b Gilmour		1
B. Andrews	c Marsh b Gilmour	17			
Extras	(LB 2, NB 4)	6	(B 4, LB 11, W 1)		16
Total		**312**	(9 wickets declared)		**305**

AUSTRALIA

A.P. Sheahan	c Coney b Andrews	7	not out	14
K.R. Stackpole	c Morrison b R.J. Hadlee	8	lbw b R.J. Hadlee	2
I.M. Chappell*	c Hastings b D.R. Hadlee	45	lbw b R.J. Hadlee	6
G.S. Chappell	c Coney b Andrews	0	not out	8
K.D. Walters	c Coney b D.R. Hadlee	41		
I.C. Davis	c Andrews b R.J. Hadlee	29		
R.W. Marsh†	c Wadsworth b D.R. Hadlee	10		
K.J. O'Keeffe	c Wadsworth b R.J. Hadlee	9		
G.J. Gilmour	c Wadsworth b Congdon	3		
A.A. Mallett	lbw b R.J. Hadlee	0		
M.H.N. Walker	not out	2		
Extras	(LB 5, NB 3)	8		
Total		**162**	(2 wickets)	**30**

AUSTRALIA	O	M	R	W	O	M	R	W		FALL OF WICKETS			
Gilmour	18·6	3	70	1	21·2	1	70	3		NZ	A	NZ	A
Walker	22	2	71	2					*Wkt*	*1st*	*1st*	*2nd*	*2nd*
G.S. Chappell	19	2	76	2	16	3	54	3	1st	78	20	23	10
Walters	11	0	39	4	11	0	54	1	2nd	78	20	94	22
Mallett	8	0	30	0	14	1	65	0	3rd	90	21	120	–
O'Keeffe	8	2	20	1	10	0	40	0	4th	113	98	244	–
I.M. Chappell					3	0	6	1	5th	193	115	255	–
									6th	221	133	276	–
NEW ZEALAND									7th	268	150	282	–
R.J. Hadlee	9·4	2	33	4	4·3	0	16	2	8th	292	157	292	–
Andrews	9	1	40	2	4	0	14	0	9th	293	160	305	–
D.R. Hadlee	13	3	52	3					10th	312	162	–	–
Congdon	13	2	29	1									

Umpires: P.R. Enright (2) and M.G. O'Connell (4).

Close: 1st day – NZ(1) 273-7 (D.R. Hadlee 7, R.J.Hadlee 5); 2nd – NZ(2) 10-0 (Parker 2, Morrison 7); 3rd – no play; 4th – A(2) 30-2 (Sheahan 14, G.S. Chappell 8).

AUSTRALIA v NEW ZEALAND 1973–74 (3rd Test)

Played at Adelaide Oval on 26, 27, 28, 30 (*no play*), 31 January.
Toss: Australia.   Result: AUSTRALIA won by an innings and 57 runs.
Debuts: Australia – G. Dymock, A.G. Hurst, A.J. Woodcock; New Zealand – B.L. Cairns.

Australia gained their third victory by an innings margin in four matches against New Zealand. A blank fourth day and stoppages amounting to 95 minutes on the fifth extended the match until 5.02 on the final evening. The seventh-wicket partnership of 168 between Marsh and O'Keeffe was an Australian record, subsequently beaten, in all Tests, improving on the one of 165 between C. Hill and H. Trumble against England in 1897-98 (*Test No. 56*). Dymock took the wicket of Parker with his second ball in Test cricket.

AUSTRALIA

K.R. Stackpole	c Parker b D.R. Hadlee	15
A.J. Woodcock	c Coney b Cairns	27
I.M. Chappell*	c R.J. Hadlee b Cairns	22
G.S. Chappell	b Congdon	42
K.D. Walters	b O'Sullivan	94
I.C. Davis	c Congdon b O'Sullivan	15
R.W. Marsh†	st Wadsworth b O'Sullivan	132
K.J. O'Keeffe	lbw b R.J.Hadlee	85
A.A. Mallett	c Wadsworth b O'Sullivan	11
A.G. Hurst	c Hastings b O'Sullivan	16
G. Dymock	not out	0
Extras	(B 3, LB 6, NB 9)	18
Total		**477**

NEW ZEALAND

J.M. Parker	c Marsh b Dymock	0	c I.M. Chappell b Dymock	22
G.M. Turner	lbw b Hurst	20	c O'Keeffe b Dymock	34
J.F.M. Morrison	c I.M. Chappell b O'Keeffe	40	c I.M. Chappell b O'Keeffe	4
B.F. Hastings	c Woodcock b O'Keeffe	23	c Stackpole b Dymock	7
B.E. Congdon*	run out	13	not out	71
J.V. Coney	c Marsh b Dymock	8	b Dymock	17
K.J. Wadsworth†	lbw b I.M. Chappell	48	c Marsh b O'Keeffe	16
D.R. Hadlee	c G.S. Chappell b Mallett	29	c G.S. Chappell b Mallett	0
R.J. Hadlee	c I.M. Chappell b Mallett	20	c Marsh b O'Keeffe	15
D.R. O'Sullivan	b O'Keeffe	2	c I.M. Chappell b Dymock	4
B.L.Cairns	not out	4	c I.M. Chappell b Mallett	0
Extras	(B 4, LB 4, NB 3)	11	(B 2, LB 8, NB 2)	12
Total		**218**		**202**

NEW ZEALAND	O	M	R	W	O	M	R	W
R.J. Hadlee	28	3	102	1				
D.R. Hadlee	21	2	76	1				
Cairns	21	4	73	2				
O'Sullivan	35·5	4	148	5				
Congdon	15	1	60	1				
AUSTRALIA								
Hurst	19	3	56	1	10	2	17	0
Dymock	19	5	44	2	27	7	58	5
Walters	1	0	2	0	3	0	17	0
Mallett	23	6	46	2	21·5	9	47	2
O'Keeffe	24·3	9	55	3	28	12	51	3
I.M. Chappell	1	0	4	1				

FALL OF WICKETS

Wkt	A 1st	NZ 1st	NZ 2nd
1st	21	1	56
2nd	67	35	65
3rd	73	84	65
4th	173	89	73
5th	221	107	105
6th	232	110	130
7th	400	176	143
8th	452	209	170
9th	472	214	197
10th	477	218	202

Umpires: J.R. Collins (4) and P.R. Enright (3).

Close: 1st day – A(1) 332-6 (Marsh 44, O'Keeffe 58); 2nd – NZ(1) 104-4 (Congdon 13, Coney 5); 3rd – NZ (2) 98-4 (Congdon 9, Coney 17); 4th – no play.

WEST INDIES v ENGLAND 1973–74 (1st Test)

Played at Queen's Park Oval, Port-of-Spain, Trinidad, on 2, 3, 5, 6, 7 February.
Toss: West Indies.   Result: WEST INDIES won by seven wickets.
Debuts: Nil.

This result ended a run of 22 home Tests without victory for West Indies and an unbeaten run of 13 Tests in the West Indies for England. When Julien played the last ball of the second day down the pitch, Greig picked it up and, seeing Kallicharran (142) out of his ground, threw down the bowler's stumps and appealed. Kallicharran was given 'run out' by umpire Sang Hue. After a lengthy off-the-field conference between the captains, administrators, and umpires, the appeal was withdrawn in the interests of the rubber. When he bowled Greig, Gibbs became the first bowler to take 250 Test wickets for West Indies.

ENGLAND

G. Boycott	c Julien b Boyce	6	c Fredericks b Gibbs	93
D.L. Amiss	c Murray b Sobers	6	lbw b Sobers	174
M.H. Denness*	b Julien	9	run out	44
F.C. Hayes	c Fredericks b Sobers	12	b Sobers	8
K.W.R. Fletcher	b Julien	4	c Rowe b Sobers	0
A.W. Greig	c Murray b Boyce	37	b Gibbs	20
A.P.E. Knott†	b Boyce	7	c Rowe b Gibbs	21
C.M. Old	c Fredericks b Ali	11	c and b Gibbs	3
P.I. Pocock	b Boyce	2	c Fredericks b Gibbs	0
D.L. Underwood	not out	10	c Kanhai b Gibbs	9
R.G.D. Willis	b Gibbs	6	not out	0
Extras	(B 1, LB 8, NB 12)	21	(B 5, LB 5, NB 10)	20
Total		**131**		**392**

WEST INDIES

R.C. Fredericks	c Knott b Old	5	not out	65
L.G. Rowe	c Knott b Willis	13	c Hayes b Pocock	5
A.I. Kallicharran	c Underwood b Pocock	158	c Greig b Underwood	21
C.H. Lloyd	c Denness b Old	18	c Hayes b Underwood	0
R.B. Kanhai*	b Pocock	8	not out	39
G. St A. Sobers	c Denness b Underwood	23		
D.L. Murray†	c Fletcher b Pocock	19		
B.D. Julien	not out	86		
K.D. Boyce	c Boycott b Pocock	26		
Inshan Ali	c Knott b Pocock	9		
L.R. Gibbs	b Old	2		
Extras	(B 3, LB 6, NB 16)	25	(LB 1, NB 1)	2
Total		**392**	(3 wickets)	**132**

WEST INDIES	O	M	R	W	O	M	R	W		FALL OF WICKETS			
										E	WI	E	WI
Boyce	19	4	42	4	10	1	36	0	*Wkt*	*1st*	*1st*	*2nd*	*2nd*
Julien	12	5	14	2	15	2	48	0	1st	6	14	209	15
Sobers	14	3	37	2	34	15	54	3	2nd	22	27	328	77
Gibbs	3	1	5	1	57·2	15	108	6	3rd	23	63	338	77
Ali	7	5	12	1	37	5	99	0	4th	30	106	338	–
Fredericks					10	2	24	0	5th	71	147	349	–
Lloyd					3	1	3	0	6th	90	196	366	–
									7th	100	296	378	–
ENGLAND									8th	108	324	378	–
Willis	19	5	52	1	4	1	6	0	9th	116	373	391	–
Old	20·4	2	89	3	3	0	18	0	10th	131	392	392	–
Greig	17	3	60	0	2	1	4	0					
Pocock	43	12	110	5	16	6	49	1					
Underwood	23	8	56	1	12	2	48	2					
Fletcher					0·5	0	5	0					

Umpires: R. Gosein (13) and D. Sang Hue (17).

Close: 1st day – WI(1) 14-0 (Fredericks 5, Rowe 8); 2nd – WI(1) 274-6 (Kallicharran 142, Julien 22); 3rd – E(2) 201-0 (Boycott 91, Amiss 92); 4th – WI(2) 77-1 (Fredericks 49, Kallicharran 21).

WEST INDIES v ENGLAND 1973–74 (2nd Test)

Played at Sabina Park, Kingston, Jamaica, on 16, 17, 19, 20, 21 February.
Toss: England.   Result: MATCH DRAWN.
Debuts: Nil.

The partnership of 206 between Fredericks and Rowe remains the first-wicket record for West Indies against England. On the fourth day Sobers became the first batsman to score 8,000 runs in Tests. Amiss batted 570 minutes, received 563 balls and hit a six and 40 fours in the highest innings of his first-class career. Only an unbeaten innings lasting 53 minutes by Willis prevented his becoming the fourth batsman to carry his bat through a completed innings for England; it would have been the highest score by anyone achieving this feat in Test cricket. This innings gave Amiss a Test aggregate of 1,356 within a period of twelve months. Pocock scored four singles off 88 balls in 83 minutes in the second innings.

ENGLAND

G. Boycott	c Kanhai b Sobers	68		c Murray b Boyce	5
D.L. Amiss	c Kanhai b Barrett	27		not out	262
J.A. Jameson	st Murray b Gibbs	23		c Rowe b Barrett	38
F.C. Hayes	c Boyce b Sobers	10		run out	0
M.H. Denness*	c Fredericks b Boyce	67		c Rowe b Barrett	28
A.W. Greig	c Fredericks b Barrett	45		b Gibbs	14
A.P.E. Knott†	c Murray b Barrett	39	(8)	run out	6
C.M. Old	c Murray b Julien	2	(9)	b Barrett	19
D.L. Underwood	c Fredericks b Sobers	24	(7)	c Murray b Sobers	12
P.I. Pocock	c Gibbs b Julien	23		c sub (V.A. Holder) b Boyce	4
R.G.D. Willis	not out	6		not out	3
Extras	(LB 7, NB 12)	19		(B 10, LB 11, W 1, NB 19)	41
Total		**353**		**(9 wickets)**	**432**

WEST INDIES

R.C. Fredericks	b Old	94
L.G. Rowe	lbw b Willis	120
A.I. Kallicharran	c Denness b Old	93
C.H. Lloyd	b Jameson	49
R.B. Kanhai*	c Willis b Greig	39
G. St A. Sobers	c Willis b Greig	57
B.D. Julien	c Denness b Greig	66
K.D. Boyce	c Greig b Willis	8
D.L. Murray†	not out	6
A.G. Barrett	lbw b Willis	0
L.R. Gibbs	not out	6
Extras	(B 16, LB 18, NB 11)	45
Total	**(9 wickets declared)**	**583**

WEST INDIES	O	M	R	W	O	M	R	W
Boyce	19	2	52	1	21	4	70	2
Julien	18	3	40	2	13	3	36	0
Sobers	33	11	65	3	34	13	73	1
Barrett	39	16	86	3	54	24	87	3
Gibbs	40	16	78	1	44	15	82	1
Fredericks	4	0	11	0	6	1	17	0
Lloyd	4	2	2	0	3	1	5	0
Kanhai					3	1	8	0
Rowe					2	1	1	0
Kallicharran					3	0	12	0

ENGLAND	O	M	R	W
Willis	24	5	97	3
Old	23	6	72	2
Pocock	57	14	152	0
Underwood	36	12	98	0
Greig	49	14	102	3
Jameson	7	2	17	1

FALL OF WICKETS

Wkt	E 1st	WI 1st	E 2nd
1st	68	206	32
2nd	104	226	102
3rd	133	338	107
4th	134	401	176
5th	224	439	217
6th	278	551	258
7th	286	563	271
8th	322	567	343
9th	333	574	392
10th	353	–	–

Umpires: H.B. de C. Jordan (22) and D. Sang Hue (18).

Close: 1st day – E(1) 251-5 (Denness 51, Knott 13); 2nd – WI(1) 159-0 (Fredericks 72, Rowe 80); 3rd – WI(1) 434-4 (Kallicharran 89, Sobers 8); 4th – E(2) 218-5 (Amiss 123, Underwood 1).

WEST INDIES v ENGLAND 1973–74 (3rd Test)

Played at Kensington Oval, Bridgetown, Barbados, on 6, 7, 9, 10, 11 March.
Toss: West Indies.   Result: MATCH DRAWN.
Debuts: West Indies – A.M.E. Roberts.

Roberts was the first Antiguan to play Test cricket. Greig and Knott shared an England sixth-wicket record partnership for this series of 163. Rowe batted for 612 minutes, received 430 balls, and hit a six and 36 fours in scoring the first triple century for West Indies against England. His previous ten first-class hundreds had all been scored at Sabina Park. His partnership of 249 with Kallicharran was the highest for the second wicket by West Indies in this series until 1984 (*Test No. 990*). Greig became the first to score a century and take five wickets in an innings of the same Test for England. The match produced 99 calls of 'no ball' (runs being scored off 20 of them) – a record for Test cricket until 1976-77 (*Test No. 798*). West Indies bowlers were responsible for 47 such infringements.

ENGLAND

M.H. Denness*	c Murray b Sobers	24	lbw b Holder		0
D.L. Amiss	b Julien	12	c Julien b Roberts		4
J.A. Jameson	c Fredericks b Julien	3	lbw b Roberts		9
G. Boycott	c Murray b Julien	10	c Kanhai b Sobers		13
K.W.R. Fletcher	c Murray b Julien	37	not out		129
A.W. Greig	c Sobers b Julien	148	c Roberts b Gibbs		25
A.P.E. Knott†	b Gibbs	87	lbw b Lloyd		67
C.M. Old	c Murray b Roberts	1	b Lloyd		0
G.G. Arnold	b Holder	12	not out		2
P.I. Pocock	c Lloyd b Gibbs	18			
R.G.D. Willis	not out	10			
Extras	(LB 5, NB 28)	33	(B 7, LB 5, NB 16)		28
Total		**395**	(7 wickets)		**277**

WEST INDIES

R.C. Fredericks	b Greig	32
L.G. Rowe	c Arnold b Greig	302
A.I. Kallicharran	b Greig	119
C.H. Lloyd	c Fletcher b Greig	8
V.A. Holder	c and b Greig	8
R.B. Kanhai*	b Arnold	18
G. St A. Sobers	c Greig b Willis	0
D.L. Murray†	not out	53
B.D. Julien	c Willis b Greig	1
A.M.E. Roberts	not out	9
L.R. Gibbs	did not bat	
Extras	(B 3, LB 8, NB 35)	46
Total	(8 wickets declared)	**596**

WEST INDIES	O	M	R	W	O	M	R	W		FALL OF WICKETS		
Holder	27	6	68	1	15	6	37	1		E	WI	E
Roberts	33	8	75	1	17	4	49	2	*Wkt*	*1st*	*1st*	*2nd*
Julien	26	9	57	5	11	4	21	0	1st	28	126	4
Sobers	18	4	57	1	35	21	55	1	2nd	34	375	8
Gibbs	33·4	10	91	2	28·3	15	40	1	3rd	53	390	29
Lloyd	4	2	9	0	12	4	13	2	4th	68	420	40
Fredericks	3	0	5	0	6	2	24	0	5th	130	465	106
Rowe					1	0	5	0	6th	293	466	248
Kallicharran					1	0	5	0	7th	306	551	248
									8th	344	556	–
ENGLAND									9th	371	–	–
Arnold	26	5	91	1					10th	395	–	–
Willis	26	4	100	1								
Greig	46	2	164	6								
Old	28	4	102	0								
Pocock	28	4	93	0								

Umpires: S.E. Parris (1) and D. Sang Hue (19).

Close: 1st day – E(1) 219-5 (Greig 65, Knott 47); 2nd – WI(1) 83-0 (Fredericks 24, Rowe 48); 3rd – WI(1) 394-3 (Rowe 202, Holder 4); 4th – E(2) 72-4 (Fletcher 23, Greig 13).

WEST INDIES v ENGLAND 1973–74 (4th Test)

Played at Bourda, Georgetown, Guyana, on 22, 23, 24, 26 *(no play)*, 27 March.
Toss: England.   Result: MATCH DRAWN.
Debuts: Nil.

Rain and poor drainage accounted for 13 hours and 26 minutes of playing time being lost. Amiss was the first England batsman to score three hundreds in a rubber against West Indies.

ENGLAND

G. Boycott	b Julien	15
D.L. Amiss	c Murray b Boyce	118
M.H. Denness*	b Barrett	42
K.W.R. Fletcher	c Murray b Julien	41
A.W. Greig	b Boyce	121
F.C. Hayes	c and b Gibbs	6
A.P.E. Knott†	c Julien b Gibbs	61
J. Birkenshaw	c Murray b Fredericks	0
C.M. Old	c Kanhai b Boyce	14
G.G. Arnold	run out	1
D.L. Underwood	not out	7
Extras	(B 1, LB 13, NB 8)	22
Total		**448**

WEST INDIES

R.C. Fredericks	c and b Greig	98
L.G. Rowe	b Greig	28
A.I. Kallicharran	b Birkenshaw	6
R.B. Kanhai*	b Underwood	44
C.H. Lloyd	not out	7
M.L.C. Foster	)	
D.L. Murray†	)	
B.D. Julien	)	
K.D. Boyce	) did not bat	
A.G. Barrett	)	
L.R. Gibbs	)	
Extras	(B 6, LB 4, NB 5)	15
Total	(4 wickets)	**198**

WEST INDIES	O	M	R	W
Boyce	27·4	6	70	3
Julien	36	10	96	2
Lloyd	19	5	27	0
Foster	16	5	32	0
Gibbs	37	5	102	2
Barrett	31	6	87	1
Fredericks	5	2	12	1
ENGLAND				
Arnold	10	5	17	0
Old	13	3	32	0
Underwood	17·5	4	36	1
Greig	24	8	57	2
Birkenshaw	22	7	41	1

FALL OF WICKETS

	E	WI
Wkt	1st	1st
1st	41	73
2nd	128	90
3rd	228	179
4th	244	198
5th	257	–
6th	376	–
7th	377	–
8th	410	–
9th	428	–
10th	448	–

Umpires: D. Sang Hue (20) and C. F. Vyfhuis (1).

Close: 1st day – E(1) 218-2 (Amiss 106, Fletcher 39); 2nd – E(1) 448 all out; 3rd – WI(1) 110-2 (Fredericks 58, Kanhai 11); 4th – no play.

WEST INDIES v ENGLAND 1973–74 (5th Test)

Played at Queen's Park Oval, Port-of-Spain, Trinidad, on 30, 31 March, 2, 3, 4, 5 April.
Toss: England.   Result: ENGLAND won by 26 runs.
Debuts: Nil.

England won this six-day Test with an hour to spare and so squared the rubber. Sobers, playing in the last of his 93 Test matches, became the first bowler to take 100 wickets for West Indies against England when he dismissed Amiss. Gibbs became the second to do so when he bowled Boycott, who failed by just one run to be the first to score a hundred in both innings for England in this series. Greig's innings analysis of 8 for 86 and match analysis of 13 for 156 are the best by an England bowler against West Indies. His match figures are also a record for any Test in Trinidad. Kanhai, also making his last Test appearance, caught Amiss when he kept wicket for part of the first day after Murray had sustained a cut head.

ENGLAND

G. Boycott	c Murray b Julien	99	b Gibbs	112
D.L. Amiss	c Kanhai b Sobers	44	b Lloyd	16
M.H. Denness*	c Fredericks b Ali	13	run out	4
K.W.R. Fletcher	c Kanhai b Gibbs	6	b Julien	45
A.W. Greig	lbw b Gibbs	19	(6) c Fredericks b Julien	1
F.C. Hayes	c Rowe b Ali	24	(7) lbw b Julien	0
A.P.E. Knott†	not out	33	(8) lbw b Sobers	44
J. Birkenshaw	c Lloyd b Julien	8	(9) c Gibbs b Ali	7
G.G. Arnold	run out	6	(10) b Sobers	13
P.I. Pocock	c Lloyd b Ali	0	(5) c Kallicharran b Boyce	5
D.L. Underwood	b Gibbs	4	not out	1
Extras	(B 2, LB 3, NB 6)	11	(LB 4, NB 11)	15
Total		**267**		**263**

WEST INDIES

R.C. Fredericks	c Fletcher b Pocock	67	run out	36
L.G. Rowe	c Boycott b Greig	123	lbw b Birkenshaw	25
A.I. Kallicharran	c and b Pocock	0	c Fletcher b Greig	0
C.H. Lloyd	c Knott b Greig	52	c and b Greig	13
G. St A. Sobers	c Birkenshaw b Greig	0	(6) b Underwood	20
R.B. Kanhai*	c and b Greig	2	(5) c Fletcher b Greig	7
D.L. Murray†	c Pocock b Greig	2	c Fletcher b Greig	33
B.D. Julien	c Birkenshaw b Greig	17	c Denness b Pocock	2
K.D. Boyce	c Pocock b Greig	19	not out	34
Inshan Ali	lbw b Greig	5	c Underwood b Greig	15
L.R. Gibbs	not out	0	b Arnold	1
Extras	(B 11, LB 4, NB 3)	18	(B 9, LB 2, NB 2)	13
Total		**305**		**199**

WEST INDIES	O	M	R	W	O	M	R	W		FALL OF WICKETS			
Boyce	10	3	14	0	12	3	40	1		E	WI	E	WI
Julien	21	8	35	2	22	7	31	3	Wkt	1st	1st	2nd	2nd
Sobers	31	16	44	1	24·2	9	36	2	1st	83	110	39	63
Ali	35	12	86	3	34	12	51	1	2nd	114	122	44	64
Gibbs	34·3	10	70	3	50	15	85	1	3rd	133	224	145	65
Lloyd	4	2	7	0	7	4	5	1	4th	165	224	169	84
									5th	204	226	174	85
ENGLAND									6th	212	232	176	135
Arnold	8	0	27	0	5·3	1	13	1	7th	244	270	213	138
Greig	36·1	10	86	8	33	7	70	5	8th	257	300	226	166
Pocock	31	7	86	2	25	7	60	1	9th	260	300	258	197
Underwood	34	12	57	0	15	7	19	1	10th	267	305	263	199
Birkenshaw	8	1	31	0	10	1	24	1					

Umpires: S. Ishmael (2) and D. Sang Hue (21).

Close: 1st day – E(1) 198-4 (Boycott 97, Hayes 12); 2nd – WI(1) 174-2 (Rowe 75, Lloyd 21); 3rd – E(2) 23-0 (Boycott 11, Amiss 10); 4th – E(2) 158-3 (Boycott 81, Pocock 3); 5th – WI(2) 30-0 (Fredericks 13, Rowe 13).

NEW ZEALAND v AUSTRALIA 1973–74 (1st Test)

Played at Basin Reserve, Wellington, on 1, 2, 3, 5, 6 March.
Toss: Australia.   Result: MATCH DRAWN.
Debuts: Nil.

Gregory Stephen Chappell set the present record for the most runs in a Test match by scoring 380 to beat the 375 (325 and 50) by A. Sandham at Kingston in 1929-30 (*Test No. 193*). He was the fourth batsman after K.D. Walters, S.M. Gavaskar and L.G. Rowe to score a double century and a century in the same Test match. He batted for 410 minutes for his highest innings in first-class cricket which included a six and 29 fours. With Ian Michael Chappell he provided only the second instance in all first-class cricket of brothers each scoring a hundred in both innings of a match; R.E. and W.L. Foster were the first to achieve this feat, for Worcestershire against Hampshire at Worcester in 1899. The Chappells' partnership of 264 remains the highest for any wicket by either country in this series. New Zealand's record fourth-wicket partnership of 229 between Congdon and Hastings is their highest for any wicket against Australia. The match aggregate of 1,455 is the highest for any Test in New Zealand and includes that country's highest total against Australia at home. Hastings was dismissed by the ninth ball of Dymock's over.

AUSTRALIA

K.R. Stackpole	b Webb	10	b Collinge		27
I.R. Redpath	c Coney b Hadlee	19	c Howarth b Congdon		93
I.M. Chappell*	c Wadsworth b Webb	145	c Hadlee b Howarth		121
G.S. Chappell	not out	247	c Wadsworth b Collinge		133
I.C. Davis	c Wadsworth b Hadlee	16	c Wadsworth b Howarth		8
K.D. Walters	c Howarth b Collinge	32	c Morrison b Hadlee		8
R.W. Marsh†	lbw b Congdon	22	c Collinge b Congdon		17
K.J. O'Keeffe			c Howarth b Congdon		2
M.H.N. Walker	did not bat		not out		22
A.A. Mallett			not out		4
G. Dymock					
Extras	(B 1, LB 4, NB 15)	20	(B 4, LB 4, W 1, NB 16)		25
Total	(6 wickets declared)	**511**	(8 wickets)		**460**

NEW ZEALAND

G.M. Turner	c Redpath b O'Keeffe	79
J.M. Parker	lbw b Walker	10
J.F.M. Morrison	b Walker	66
B.E. Congdon*	c Davis b Mallett	132
B.F. Hastings	c I.M. Chappell b Dymock	101
J.V. Coney	c G.S. Chappell b Walker	13
K.J. Wadsworth†	b Dymock	5
D.R. Hadlee	c Davis b O'Keeffe	9
R.O. Collinge	run out	2
H.J. Howarth	not out	29
M.G. Webb	c O'Keeffe b Dymock	12
Extras	(B 10, LB 5, NB 11)	26
Total		**484**

NEW ZEALAND	O	M	R	W	O	M	R	W
Webb	21	1	114	2	19	0	93	0
Collinge	24	3	103	1	19	3	60	2
Hadlee	27	7	107	2	21	2	106	1
Howarth	21	0	113	0	25	3	97	2
Congdon	12·5	0	54	1	13	1	60	3
Coney					2	0	13	0
Hastings					2	0	6	0

AUSTRALIA	O	M	R	W
Walker	41	11	107	3
Dymock	35	7	77	3
Walters	8	1	39	0
Mallett	41	8	117	1
O'Keeffe	33	9	83	2
G.S. Chappell	7	0	27	0
I.M. Chappell	4	0	8	0

FALL OF WICKETS

	A	NZ	A
Wkt	1st	1st	2nd
1st	13	28	67
2nd	55	136	208
3rd	319	169	294
4th	359	398	318
5th	431	409	359
6th	511	423	414
7th	–	423	433
8th	–	430	433
9th	–	437	–
10th	–	484	–

Umpires: D.E.A. Copps (6) and F.R. Goodall (4).

Close: 1st day – A(1) 372-4 (G.S. Chappell 162, Walters 6); 2nd – NZ(1) 161-2 (Morrison 62, Congdon 7); 3rd – NZ(1) 364-3 (Congdon 108, Hastings 86); 4th – A(2) 86-1 (Redpath 35, I.M. Chappell 12).

NEW ZEALAND v AUSTRALIA 1973–74 (2nd Test)

Played at Lancaster Park, Christchurch, on 8, 9, 10, 12, 13 March.
Toss: New Zealand.   Result: NEW ZEALAND won by five wickets.
Debuts: Nil.

When Wadsworth hit the winning boundary after 92 minutes of play on the fifth morning, New Zealand gained their first success in this series and their eighth in 113 official Tests. They had beaten every country except England. Turner became the first to score a hundred in each innings of a Test for New Zealand.

AUSTRALIA

K.R. Stackpole	b Collinge	4	c Wadsworth b Collinge		9
I.R. Redpath	c and b Collinge	71	c Howarth b R.J. Hadlee		58
I.M. Chappell*	b R.J. Hadlee	20	b Collinge		1
G.S. Chappell	c Howarth b Congdon	25	c Coney b R.J. Hadlee		6
I.C. Davis	lbw b R.J. Hadlee	5	c Congdon b R.J. Hadlee		50
K.D. Walters	b R.J. Hadlee	6	lbw b D.R. Hadlee		65
R.W. Marsh†	b Congdon	38	c and b D.R. Hadlee		4
K.J. O'Keeffe	c Wadsworth b Congdon	3	not out		23
M.H.N. Walker	not out	18	c Howarth b D.R. Hadlee		4
A.A. Mallett	b Collinge	1	(11) c Wadsworth b R.J. Hadlee		11
G. Dymock	c Congdon b D.R. Hadlee	13	(10) c Wadsworth b D.R. Hadlee		0
Extras	(B 1, LB 6, NB 12)	19	(B 16, LB 4, NB 8)		28
Total		**223**			**259**

NEW ZEALAND

G.M. Turner	c Stackpole b G.S. Chappell	101	not out	110
J.M. Parker	lbw b Dymock	18	c Marsh b Walker	26
J.F.M. Morrison	c Marsh b G.S. Chappell	12	lbw b Walker	0
B.E. Congdon*	c I.M. Chappell b Walker	8	run out	2
B.F. Hastings	c Marsh b Walker	19	b Mallett	46
J.V. Coney	c Marsh b Dymock	15	c Marsh b G.S. Chappell	14
K.J. Wadsworth†	c Marsh b Mallett	24	not out	9
D.R. Hadlee	c Marsh b Dymock	11		
R.J. Hadlee	lbw b Walker	23		
H.J. Howarth	c I.M. Chappell b Walker	0		
R.O. Collinge	not out	1		
Extras	(B 4, LB 8, NB 11)	23	(B 4, LB 14, NB 5)	23
Total		**255**	(5 wickets)	**230**

NEW ZEALAND	O	M	R	W	O	M	R	W	FALL OF WICKETS				
R.J. Hadlee	14	2	59	3	18·4	3	71	4		A	NZ	A	NZ
Collinge	21	4	70	3	9	0	37	2	*Wkt*	*1st*	*1st*	*2nd*	*2nd*
D.R. Hadlee	12·2	2	42	1	20	2	75	4	1st	8	59	12	51
Congdon	11	2	33	3	9	3	26	0	2nd	45	90	26	55
Howarth					11	2	22	0	3rd	101	104	33	62
									4th	120	136	139	177
AUSTRALIA									5th	128	171	142	206
Walker	19·6	5	60	4	28	10	50	2	6th	181	213	160	–
Dymock	24	6	59	3	25	5	84	0	7th	190	220	232	–
Walters	7	1	34	0					8th	194	241	238	–
G.S. Chappell	20	2	76	2	17·6	5	38	1	9th	196	242	239	–
Mallett	3	1	3	1	13	4	35	1	10th	223	255	259	–

Umpires: J.B.R. Hastie (1) and R.L. Monteith (1).

Close: 1st day – A(1) 128-5 (Redpath 55); 2nd – NZ(1) 194-5 (Turner 99, Wadsworth 9); 3rd – A(2) 211-6 (Walters 52, O'Keeffe 6); 4th – NZ(2) 177-4 (Turner 85).

NEW ZEALAND v AUSTRALIA 1973–74 (3rd Test)

Played at Eden Park, Auckland, on 22, 23, 24 March.
Toss: New Zealand.　　Result: AUSTRALIA won by 297 runs.
Debuts: Nil.

Australia's victory on the third evening squared the rubber with two days to spare. Stackpole was out to the first ball of the match. A record Auckland crowd of 35,000 saw Redpath become the first player to carry his bat through a completed innings of a Test in New Zealand. He batted for 348 minutes and hit 20 fours. Marsh made his 100th dismissal in Test matches when he caught Congdon.

AUSTRALIA

K.R. Stackpole	c Parker b R.J. Hadlee	0	c Congdon b Collinge		0
I.R. Redpath	c Wadsworth b Collinge	13	not out		159
I.M. Chappell*	c Turner b Collinge	37	lbw b Collinge		35
G.S. Chappell	c Howarth b Collinge	0	c Wadsworth b Howarth		38
I.C. Davis	c Hastings b Collinge	0	c Parker b Howarth		5
K.D. Walters	not out	104	c Parker b Congdon		5
R.W. Marsh†	c Hastings b Collinge	45	c R.J. Hadlee b Howarth		47
K.J. O'Keeffe	c Morrison b Congdon	0	c Burgess b Collinge		32
G.J. Gilmour	c Morrison b Congdon	1	b R.J. Hadlee		4
M.H.N. Walker	c Burgess b Congdon	7	b R.J. Hadlee		0
A.A. Mallett	c Turner b Congdon	7	c Parker b Collinge		6
Extras	(B 4, LB 1, NB 2)	7	(B 4, LB 4, W 1, NB 6)		15
Total		**221**			**346**

NEW ZEALAND

G.M. Turner	c G.S. Chappell b Mallett	41	c I.M. Chappell b Walker		72
J.M. Parker	lbw b Gilmour	11	c Marsh b Gilmour		34
J.F.M. Morrison	c Marsh b Walker	9	c Marsh b Gilmour		0
B.E. Congdon*	lbw b Gilmour	4	c Marsh b Walker		4
B.F. Hastings	b Gilmour	0	lbw b Walker		1
M.G. Burgess	c Marsh b Gilmour	7	c Stackpole b Walker		6
K.J. Wadsworth†	c Marsh b Gilmour	0	c G.S. Chappell b Mallett		21
H.J. Howarth	c Gilmour b Mallett	0	(10) not out		3
D.R. Hadlee	b Mallett	4	(8) c Walters b Mallett		4
R.J. Hadlee	c I.M. Chappell b Mallett	13	(9) b O'Keeffe		1
R.O. Collinge	not out	8	c I.M. Chappell b O'Keeffe		4
Extras	(B 4, LB 1, NB 10)	15	(B 3, LB 2, NB 3)		8
Total		**112**			**158**

NEW ZEALAND	O	M	R	W	O	M	R	W
R.J. Hadlee	9	1	45	1	9	1	50	2
Collinge	18	4	82	5	16·4	0	84	4
D.R. Hadlee	9	0	41	0	7	0	48	0
Congdon	10·2	0	46	4	19	1	66	1
Howarth					28	5	83	3
AUSTRALIA								
Walker	10	4	11	1	19	8	39	4
Gilmour	15	3	64	5	16	0	52	2
Mallett	5·2	0	22	4	13	6	51	2
O'Keeffe					5	1	8	2

FALL OF WICKETS

Wkt	A 1st	NZ 1st	A 2nd	NZ 2nd
1st	0	16	2	107
2nd	32	28	69	107
3rd	37	34	118	112
4th	37	40	132	115
5th	64	62	143	116
6th	150	62	230	127
7th	154	63	315	145
8th	162	72	330	147
9th	191	102	330	147
10th	221	112	346	158

Umpires: D.E.A. Copps (7) and W.R.C. Gardiner (1).

Close: 1st day – NZ(1) 85-8 (Turner 34, R.J. Hadlee 4); 2nd – A(2) 330-9 (Redpath 150, Mallett 0).

ENGLAND v INDIA 1974 (1st Test)

Played at Old Trafford, Manchester, on 6, 7, 8, 10, 11 June.
Toss: England.   Result: ENGLAND won by 113 runs.
Debuts: England – M. Hendrick; India – Madan Lal, B.P. Patel.

England won at 5.19 on the fifth evening with 15·5 of the mandatory last 20 overs in hand. Rain claimed five hours 38 minutes of playing time. This was the first match to be played under regulations providing for an hour's extension of play on any of the first four days of a Test in England when more than one hour of that day's playing time had been lost for any reason other than the normal intervals. This regulation was invoked on the first and third days, play continuing until 7.30 pm. Edrich's 11th Test hundred was his first in eight matches against India and in seven Tests at Old Trafford. Knott, who holds the England record for most wicket-keeping dismissals (269), made five in an innings for the only time in 95 Tests. Earlier Hendrick had dismissed Solkar with his third ball in Test cricket.

ENGLAND

G. Boycott	lbw b Abid Ali	10	c Engineer b Solkar	6
D.L. Amiss	c Madan Lal b Chandrasekhar	56	c Gavaskar b Bedi	47
J.H. Edrich	b Abid Ali	7	(4) not out	100
M.H. Denness*	b Bedi	26	(5) not out	45
K.W.R. Fletcher	not out	123		
D.L. Underwood	c Solkar b Bedi	7	(3) c Engineer b Abid Ali	9
A.W. Greig	c Engineer b Madan Lal	53		
A.P.E. Knott†	lbw b Madan Lal	0		
C.M. Old	c Engineer b Chandrasekhar	12		
R.G.D. Willis	lbw b Abid Ali	24		
M. Hendrick	did not bat			
Extras	(B 1, LB 7, W 1, NB 1)	10	(B 4, LB 2)	6
Total	(9 wickets declared)	**328**	(3 wickets declared)	**213**

INDIA

S.M. Gavaskar	run out	101	c Hendrick b Old	58
E.D. Solkar	c Willis b Hendrick	7	c Hendrick b Underwood	19
S. Venkataraghavan	b Willis	3	(9) not out	5
A.L. Wadekar*	c Hendrick b Old	6	(3) c Knott b Greig	14
G.R. Viswanath	b Underwood	40	(4) c Knott b Old	50
B.P. Patel	c Knott b Willis	5	(5) c Knott b Old	3
F.M. Engineer†	b Willis	0	(6) c Knott b Hendrick	12
Madan Lal	b Hendrick	2	(7) hit wkt b Willis	7
S. Abid Ali	c Knott b Hendrick	71	(8) c Boycott b Greig	4
B. S. Bedi	b Willis	0	b Old	0
B.S. Chandrasekhar	not out	0	st Knott b Greig	0
Extras	(B 3, LB 3, NB 5)	11	(B 1, LB 2, NB 7)	10
Total		**246**		**182**

INDIA	O	M	R	W	O	M	R	W		FALL OF WICKETS			
Abid Ali	30·3	6	79	3	11	2	31	1		E	I	E	I
Solkar	13	4	33	0	7	0	24	1	*Wkt*	*1st*	*1st*	*2nd*	*2nd*
Madan Lal	31	11	56	2	12	2	39	0	1st	18	22	13	32
Venkataraghavan	5	1	8	0	9	1	17	0	2nd	28	25	30	68
Bedi	43	14	87	2	20	2	58	1	3rd	90	32	104	103
Chandrasekhar	21	4	55	2	11	2	38	0	4th	104	105	–	111
									5th	127	129	–	139
ENGLAND									6th	231	135	–	157
Willis	24	3	64	4	12	5	33	1	7th	231	143	–	165
Old	16	0	46	1	16	7	20	4	8th	265	228	–	180
Hendrick	20	4	57	3	17	1	39	1	9th	328	228	–	180
Underwood	19	7	50	1	15	4	45	1	10th	–	246	–	182
Greig	5	1	18	0	25·1	8	35	3					

Umpires: H.D. Bird (4) and D.J. Constant (7).

Close: 1st day – E(1) 116-4 (Fletcher 11, Underwood 4); 2nd – I(1) 25-2 (Gavaskar 13); 3rd – E(2) 18-1 (Amiss 7, Underwood 5); 4th – E(2) 213-3 (Edrich 100, Denness 45).

ENGLAND v INDIA 1974 (2nd Test)

Played at Lord's, London, on 20, 21, 22, 24 June.
Toss: England.   Result: ENGLAND won by an innings and 285 runs.
Debuts: England – D. Lloyd.

England gained their second-largest margin of victory in all Tests at 12·39 p.m. on the fourth day. England's total of 629, scored in 650 minutes, remains their highest at Lord's, and was their highest in all post-war Tests and their highest against India until 1979 (*Test No. 851*). The partnership of 221 in 226 minutes between Amiss and Edrich was then England's highest for the second wicket in this series and remains their highest in all Tests at Lord's. Bedi became the first bowler to concede 200 runs in a Test at Lord's. India were dismissed in 77 minutes in their second innings for their lowest total in Test cricket and the lowest total in all Test matches at Lord's. Chandrasekhar retired in the middle of his tenth over after injuring his right hand.

ENGLAND

D.L. Amiss	lbw b Prasanna	188
D.Lloyd	c Solkar b Prasanna	46
J.H. Edrich	lbw b Bedi	96
M.H. Denness*	c sub (S. Venkataraghavan) b Bedi	118
K.W.R. Fletcher	c Solkar b Bedi	15
A.W. Greig	c and b Abid Ali	106
A.P.E. Knott†	c and b Bedi	26
C.M. Old	b Abid Ali	3
G.G. Arnold	b Bedi	5
D.L. Underwood	c Solkar b Bedi	9
M. Hendrick	not out	1
Extras	(B 8, LB 4, W 2, NB 2)	16
Total		**629**

INDIA

S.M. Gavaskar	c Knott b Old	49	lbw b Arnold	5
F.M. Engineer†	c Denness b Old	86	lbw b Arnold	0
A.L. Wadekar*	c Underwood b Hendrick	18	b Old	3
G.R. Viswanath	b Underwood	52	c Knott b Arnold	5
B.P. Patel	c Fletcher b Greig	1	c Knott b Arnold	1
E.D. Solkar	c Underwood b Hendrick	43	not out	18
S. Abid Ali	c Arnold b Old	14	c Knott b Old	3
Madan Lal	c Knott b Old	0	c Hendrick b Old	2
E.A.S. Prasanna	c Denness b Hendrick	0	b Old	5
B.S. Bedi	b Arnold	14	b Old	0
B.S. Chandrasekhar	not out	2	absent hurt	–
Extras	(B 4, LB 7, NB 12)	23		–
Total		**302**		**42**

INDIA	O	M	R	W	O	M	R	W		FALL OF WICKETS		
Abid Ali	22	2	79	2						E	I	I
Solkar	6	2	16	0					*Wkt*	*1st*	*1st*	*2nd*
Madan Lal	30	6	93	0					1st	116	131	2
Bedi	64·2	8	226	6					2nd	337	149	5
Chandrasekhar	9·3	1	33	0					3rd	339	183	12
Prasanna	51	6	166	2					4th	369	188	14
									5th	571	250	25
ENGLAND									6th	591	280	28
Arnold	24·5	6	81	1	8	1	19	4	7th	604	281	30
Old	21	6	67	4	8	3	21	5	8th	611	286	42
Hendrick	18	4	46	3	1	0	2	0	9th	624	286	42
Greig	21	4	63	1					10th	629	302	–
Underwood	15	10	18	1								
Lloyd	2	0	4	0								

Umpires: A.E. Fagg (15) and T.W. Spencer (9).

Close: 1st day – E(1) 334-1 (Amiss 187, Edrich 93); 2nd – I(1) 51-0 (Gavaskar 17, Engineer 33); 3rd – I(2) 2-0 (Gavaskar 2, Engineer 0).

ENGLAND v INDIA 1974 (3rd Test)

Played at Edgbaston, Birmingham, on 4 (*no play*), 5, 6, 8 July.
Toss: India.   Result: ENGLAND won by an innings and 78 runs.
Debuts: India – S.S. Naik.

England won at 4.10 on the fourth afternoon in spite of a blank first day. It was the third time that a side had won a Test after losing only two wickets in the match; the other instances were both by England, against South Africa at Lord's in 1924 and against New Zealand at Leeds in 1958. Gavaskar was out to the first ball of the match, umpire Alley being called upon to make a decision about his first ball in Test cricket. Lloyd batted for 448 minutes, received 396 balls and hit 17 fours in making the highest score of his first-class career. He was on the field throughout his second Test match. Edrich, who took his Test aggregate past 4,000 runs in the previous match, was not called upon to bat.

INDIA

S.M. Gavaskar	c Knott b Arnold	0	c Knott b Old	4
S.S. Naik	b Arnold	4	lbw b Greig	77
A.L. Wadekar*	c Knott b Hendrick	36	(4) lbw b Old	5
G.R. Viswanath	b Hendrick	28	(5) c Greig b Hendrick	25
A.V. Mankad	c Knott b Arnold	14	(6) hit wkt b Old	43
F.M. Engineer†	not out	64	(7) lbw b Hendrick	33
E.D. Solkar	lbw b Old	3	(8) c Edrich b Arnold	8
S. Abid Ali	run out	6	(3) b Arnold	3
S. Venkataraghavan	b Underwood	0	c Lloyd b Greig	5
E.A.S. Prasanna	c Greig b Hendrick	0	b Hendrick	4
B.S. Bedi	c Old b Hendrick	0	not out	1
Extras	(B 1, LB 1, NB 8)	10	(LB 3, NB 5)	8
Total		**165**		**216**

ENGLAND

D.L. Amiss	c Mankad b Prasanna	79
D. Lloyd	not out	214
M.H. Denness*	c and b Bedi	100
K.W.R. Fletcher	not out	51
J.H. Edrich	)	
A.W. Greig	)	
A.P.E. Knott†	)	
C.M. Old	) did not bat	
G.G. Arnold	)	
D.L. Underwood	)	
M. Hendrick	)	
Extras	(B 4, LB 5, W 1, NB 5)	15
Total	(2 wickets declared)	**459**

ENGLAND	O	M	R	W	O	M	R	W	FALL OF WICKETS			
Arnold	14	3	43	3	19	3	61	2		I	E	I
Old	13	0	43	1	15	3	52	3	*Wkt*	*1st*	*1st*	*2nd*
Hendrick	14·2	1	28	4	14·4	4	43	3	1st	0	157	6
Greig	3	0	11	0	16	3	49	2	2nd	17	368	12
Underwood	15	3	30	1	3	1	3	0	3rd	62	–	21
									4th	81	–	59
INDIA									5th	115	–	146
Abid Ali	18	2	63	0					6th	129	–	172
Solkar	18	5	52	0					7th	153	–	183
Bedi	45	4	152	1					8th	156	–	196
Venkataraghavan	23	1	71	0					9th	165	–	211
Prasanna	35	4	101	1					10th	165	–	216
Gavaskar	1	0	5	0								

Umpires: W.E. Alley (1) and C.S. Elliott (41).

Close: 1st day – no play; 2nd – E(1) 117-0 (Amiss 57, Lloyd 53); 3rd – I(2) 12-2 (Naik 3).

ENGLAND v PAKISTAN 1974 (1st Test)

Played at Headingley, Leeds, on 25, 26, 27, 29, 30 (*no play*) July.
Toss: Pakistan.   Result: MATCH DRAWN.
Debuts: Pakistan – Shafiq Ahmed.

This was England's 500th official Test, excluding the three abandoned without a ball being bowled. England needed to score 44 runs with four wickets in hand when rain ended the match prematurely. If England had reached their target of 282 runs, they would have scored their highest fourth innings total to win a Test at home. The partnership of 62 between Sarfraz and Asif Masood was the highest for the tenth wicket by either side in this series until 1982 (*Test No. 931*). A bomb alert at 11.50 on the first morning caused play to be suspended for 14 minutes.

PAKISTAN

Sadiq Mohammad	c Lloyd b Hendrick	28	c Greig b Old		12
Shafiq Ahmed	b Old	7	c Greig b Arnold		18
Majid Khan	c and b Greig	75	c Knott b Arnold		4
Mushtaq Mohammad	c Fletcher b Underwood	6	c Greig b Hendrick		43
Zaheer Abbas	c Knott b Hendrick	48	c Knott b Greig		19
Asif Iqbal	c Knott b Arnold	14	b Old		8
Intikhab Alam*	c Knott b Arnold	3	lbw b Old		10
Imran Khan	c Greig b Old	23	c Greig b Hendrick		31
Wasim Bari†	c Denness b Old	2	b Hendrick		3
Sarfraz Nawaz	b Arnold	53	c Fletcher b Arnold		2
Asif Masood	not out	4	not out		2
Extras	(LB 5, W 2, NB 15)	22	(LB 14, W 1, NB 12)		27
Total		**285**			**179**

ENGLAND

D.L. Amiss	c Sadiq b Sarfraz	13	lbw b Sarfraz		8
D. Lloyd	c Sadiq b Asif Masood	48	c Wasim b Sarfraz		9
J.H. Edrich	c Asif Iqbal b Asif Masood	9	c Sadiq b Imran		70
M.H. Denness*	b Asif Masood	9	c Sarfraz b Intikhab		44
K.W.R. Fletcher	lbw b Sarfraz	11	not out		67
A.W. Greig	c Wasim b Imran	37	c Majid b Sarfraz		12
A.P.E. Knott†	c Wasim b Asif Iqbal	35	c Majid b Sarfraz		5
C.M. Old	c Asif Masood b Imran	0	not out		10
G.G. Arnold	c Intikhab b Sarfraz	1			
D.L. Underwood	run out	9			
M. Hendrick	not out	1			
Extras	(B 1, LB 3, W 4, NB 2)	10	(B 4, LB 3, W 1, NB 5)		13
Total		**183**	(6 wickets)		**238**

ENGLAND	O	M	R	W	O	M	R	W	FALL OF WICKETS				
Arnold	31·5	8	67	3	23·1	11	36	3		P	E	P	E
Old	21	4	65	3	17	0	54	3	*Wkt*	*1st*	*1st*	*2nd*	*2nd*
Hendrick	26	4	91	2	18	6	39	3	1st	12	25	24	17
Underwood	12	6	26	1	1	1	0	0	2nd	60	69	35	22
Greig	11	4	14	1	9	3	23	1	3rd	70	79	38	94
									4th	170	84	83	174
PAKISTAN									5th	182	100	97	198
Asif Masood	16	3	50	3	19	2	63	0	6th	189	172	115	213
Sarfraz	22	4	51	3	36	14	56	4	7th	198	172	154	–
Imran	21	1	55	2	29	7	55	1	8th	209	172	168	–
Mushtaq	1	1	0	0	4	1	8	0	9th	223	182	177	–
Intikhab	6	2	14	0	14	4	25	1	10th	285	183	179	–
Asif Iqbal	6	3	3	1	5	1	18	0					

Umpires: A.E. Fagg (16) and T.W. Spencer (10).

Close: 1st day – P(1) 227-9 (Sarfraz 5, Asif Masood 1); 2nd – P(2) 20-0 (Sadiq 8, Shafiq 10); 3rd – E(2) 38-2 (Edrich 8, Denness 6); 4th – E(2) 238-6 (Fletcher 67, Old 10).

ENGLAND v PAKISTAN 1974 (2nd Test)

Played at Lord's, London, on 8, 9, 10, 12, 13 (*no play*) August.
Toss: Pakistan.   Result: MATCH DRAWN.
Debuts: Nil.

England needed 60 runs to win when rain caused the final day to be abandoned for the second Test in succession, bringing the total time lost in the match to 13 hours 11 minutes. Underwood, presented with a drying wicket after rain had seeped under the covers during an overnight storm, returned the best innings and match analyses of his career. The first bowler to take eight wickets in an innings in this series, that analysis included a spell of 6 for 2 in 51 balls. He is the only England bowler to take 13 wickets in a match against Pakistan.

PAKISTAN

Sadiq Mohammad	lbw b Hendrick	40		lbw b Arnold	43
Majid Khan	c Old b Greig	48		lbw b Underwood	19
Zaheer Abbas	c Hendrick b Underwood	1		c Greig b Underwood	1
Mushtaq Mohammad	c Greig b Underwood	0		c Denness b Greig	76
Wasim Raja	c Greig b Underwood	24		c Lloyd b Underwood	53
Asif Iqbal	c Amiss b Underwood	2		c Greig b Underwood	0
Intikhab Alam*	b Underwood	5	(8)	b Underwood	0
Imran Khan	c Hendrick b Greig	4	(7)	c Lloyd b Underwood	0
Wasim Bari†	lbw b Greig	4	(10)	lbw b Underwood	1
Sarfraz Nawaz	not out	0	(9)	c Lloyd b Underwood	1
Asif Masood	did not bat			not out	17
Extras	(NB 2)	2		(LB 8, NB 7)	15
Total	(9 wickets declared)	**130**			**226**

ENGLAND

D.L. Amiss	c Sadiq b Asif Masood	2		not out	14
D. Lloyd	c Zaheer b Sarfraz	23		not out	12
J.H. Edrich	c Sadiq b Intikhab	40			
M.H. Denness*	b Imran	20			
K.W.R. Fletcher	lbw b Imran	8			
A.W. Greig	run out	9			
A.P.E. Knott†	c Wasim Bari b Asif Masood	83			
C.M. Old	c Wasim Bari b Mushtaq	41			
G.G. Arnold	c Wasim Bari b Asif Masood	10			
D.L. Underwood	not out	12			
M. Hendrick	c Imran b Intikhab	6			
Extras	(LB 14, W 1, NB 1)	16		(NB 1)	1
Total		**270**		(0 wickets)	**27**

ENGLAND	O	M	R	W	O	M	R	W	FALL OF WICKETS				
Arnold	8	1	32	0	15	3	37	1		P	E	P	E
Old	5	0	17	0	14	1	39	0	*Wkt*	*1st*	*1st*	*2nd*	*2nd*
Hendrick	9	2	36	1	15	4	29	0	1st	71	2	55	–
Underwood	14	8	20	5	34·5	17	51	8	2nd	91	52	61	–
Greig	8·5	4	23	3	19	6	55	1	3rd	91	90	77	–
									4th	91	94	192	–
PAKISTAN									5th	103	100	192	–
Asif Masood	25	10	47	3	4	0	9	0	6th	111	118	200	–
Sarfraz	22	8	42	1	3	0	7	0	7th	116	187	200	–
Intikhab	26	4	80	2	1	1	0	0	8th	130	231	206	–
Wasim Raja	2	0	8	0					9th	130	254	208	–
Mushtaq	7	3	16	1					10th	–	270	226	–
Imran	18	2	48	2									
Asif Iqbal	5	0	13	0									
Majid					2	0	10	0					

Umpires: D.J. Constant (8) and C.S. Elliott (42).

Close: 1st day – E(1) 42-1 (Lloyd 18, Edrich 22); 2nd – E(1) 270 all out; 3rd – P(2) 173-3 (Mushtaq 55, Wasim Raja 44); 4th – E(2) 27-0 (Amiss 14, Lloyd 12).

ENGLAND v PAKISTAN 1974 (3rd Test)

Played at Kennington Oval, London, on 22, 23, 24, 26, 27 August.
Toss: Pakistan.   Result: MATCH DRAWN.
Debuts: Nil.

The first four days of play, during which only 74 minutes were lost to rain, produced 1,038 runs and only 13 wickets. Pakistan batted for 670 minutes, Zaheer's second double-century innings taking 545 minutes (410 balls) and including 22 fours. His partnership of 172 in 202 minutes with Mushtaq was then Pakistan's highest for the third wicket in all Tests. England saved the follow-on at 6.19 on the fourth evening. Fletcher took 458 minutes to reach his hundred and set a new record for the slowest first-class century in England. His innings lasted 513 minutes, he faced 377 balls and hit ten fours. Intikhab took his 100th Test wicket and became the first to complete the Test 'double' of 100 wickets and 1,000 runs for Pakistan, when he bowled Knott. Amiss (178) retired at 305 after being hit in the face by a bouncer from Sarfraz and returned at 539. Intikhab won his seventh successive toss for Pakistan. His team emulated the 1948 Australians by completing their first-class tour without a defeat.

PAKISTAN

Sadiq Mohammad	c Old b Willis	21	c and b Arnold	4
Majid Khan	b Underwood	98	c Denness b Old	18
Zaheer Abbas	b Underwood	240	c Knott b Arnold	15
Mushtaq Mohammad	b Arnold	76	b Underwood	8
Asif Iqbal	c and b Greig	29		
Wasim Raja	c Denness b Greig	28	(5) not out	30
Imran Khan	c Knott b Willis	24	(6) not out	10
Intikhab Alam*	not out	32		
Sarfraz Nawaz	not out	14		
Wasim Bari†	) did not bat			
Asif Masood	)			
Extras	(B 6, LB 18, NB 14)	38	(B 5, NB 4)	9
Total	(7 wickets declared)	**600**	(4 wickets)	**94**

ENGLAND

D.L. Amiss	c Majid b Intikhab	183
D. Lloyd	c Sadiq b Sarfraz	4
D.L. Underwood	lbw b Wasim Raja	43
J.H. Edrich	c Wasim Bari b Intikhab	25
M.H. Denness*	c Imran b Asif Masood	18
K.W.R. Fletcher	run out	122
A.W. Greig	b Intikhab	32
A.P.E. Knott†	b Intikhab	9
C.M. Old	lbw b Intikhab	65
G.G. Arnold	c Wasim Bari b Mushtaq	2
R.G.D. Willis	not out	1
Extras	(B 8, LB 13, NB 20)	41
Total		**545**

ENGLAND	O	M	R	W	O	M	R	W
Arnold	37	5	106	1	6	0	22	2
Willis	28	3	102	2	7	1	27	0
Old	29·3	3	143	0	2	0	6	1
Underwood	44	14	106	2	8	2	15	1
Greig	25	5	92	2	7	1	15	0
Lloyd	2	0	13	0				

PAKISTAN	O	M	R	W
Asif Masood	40	13	66	1
Sarfraz	38	8	103	1
Intikhab	51·4	14	116	5
Imran	44	16	100	0
Mushtaq	29	12	51	1
Wasim Raja	23	6	68	1

FALL OF WICKETS

	P	E	P
Wkt	1st	1st	2nd
1st	66	14	8
2nd	166	143	33
3rd	338	209	41
4th	431	244	68
5th	503	383	–
6th	550	401	–
7th	550	531	–
8th	–	539	–
9th	–	539	–
10th	–	545	–

Umpires: W.E. Alley (2) and H.D. Bird (5).

Close: 1st day – P(1) 317-2 (Zaheer 118, Mushtaq 67); 2nd – E(1) 15-1 (Amiss 8, Underwood 1); 3rd – E(1) 293-4 (Amiss 168, Fletcher 12); 4th – E(1) 438-6 (Fletcher 76, Old 18).

INDIA v WEST INDIES 1974–75 (1st Test)

Played at Karnataka State C.A. Stadium, Bangalore, on 22, 23, 24, 26, 27 November.
Toss: India.   Result: WEST INDIES won by 267 runs.
Debuts: India – H.S. Kanitkar; West Indies – C.G. Greenidge, I.V.A. Richards.

West Indies won the first Test to be played at Bangalore, completing their victory before lunch on the fifth day. Pataudi (dislocated finger) and Engineer (hit over the eye) had suffered their injuries while fielding, Kanitkar deputised as wicket-keeper during the second innings. Unseasonal rain delayed the start on the first day until 20 minutes before lunch and no play was possible on the second until after the interval. Fredericks (23) tore ligaments in his ankle, retired at 38 and returned at 264. Greenidge became the first West Indies player to score a hundred on his Test debut, that match being overseas. Lloyd reached his hundred off 85 balls with a six and 18 fours. India's total of 118 was their lowest against West Indies in a home Test until 1983-84 (*Test No. 966*). Bedi's run of 30 consecutive Test appearances for India was ended when he was banned from selection for this match by the President of the Indian Board of Control as a disciplinary measure for giving a live television interview during India's tour of England earlier in the year.

WEST INDIES

R.C. Fredericks	c Patel b Venkataraghavan	23		
C.G. Greenidge	run out	93	(1) c Gavaskar b Venkataraghavan	107
A.I. Kallicharran	c Engineer b Prasanna	124	lbw b Prasanna	29
I.V.A. Richards	c Prasanna b Chandrasekhar	4	c Abid Ali b Chandrasekhar	3
C.H. Lloyd*	c Abid Ali b Venkataraghavan	30	c Solkar b Chandrasekhar	163
D.L. Murray†	c Solkar b Venkataraghavan	0	(2) lbw b Abid Ali	0
K.D. Boyce	b Chandrasekhar	4	(6) c Pataudi b Venkataraghavan	4
A.G. Barrett	c Patel b Chandrasekhar	2	not out	5
V.A. Holder	b Chandrasekhar	0	(7) not out	26
L.R. Gibbs	c Solkar b Venkataraghavan	2		
A.M.E. Roberts	not out	0		
Extras	(B 5, LB 1, NB 1)	7	(LB 15, NB 4)	19
Total		**289**	(6 wickets declared)	**356**

INDIA

S.M. Gavaskar	c Richards b Holder	14	c Murray b Boyce	0
F.M. Engineer†	c Richards b Roberts	3	absent hurt	–
H.S. Kanitkar	st Murray b Barrett	65	(2) c Kallicharran b Holder	18
G.R. Viswanath	lbw b Gibbs	29	b Holder	22
Nawab of Pataudi, jr*	c Lloyd b Holder	22	absent hurt	–
B.P. Patel	c Murray b Holder	2	(5) lbw b Roberts	22
E.D. Solkar	run out	14	(3) c Murray b Boyce	15
S. Abid Ali	run out	49	(6) c sub (D. A. Murray) b Boyce	1
S. Venkataraghavan	b Roberts	1	(7) lbw b Roberts	7
E.A.S. Prasanna	c Kallicharran b Roberts	23	(8) not out	12
B.S. Chandrasekhar	not out	5	(9) b Roberts	0
Extras	(B 4, LB 8, W 4, NB 17)	33	(B 1, LB 5, NB 15)	21
Total		**260**		**118**

INDIA	O	M	R	W	O	M	R	W
Abid Ali	8	1	21	0	19	1	92	1
Solkar	7	1	28	0	2	0	7	0
Chandrasekhar	28	5	112	4	23	3	102	2
Prasanna	22·2	4	46	1	18	3	57	1
Venkataraghavan	30	8	75	4	21	4	79	2
WEST INDIES								
Roberts	22	5	65	3	10·5	4	24	3
Holder	20·5	7	37	3	10	3	18	2
Gibbs	15	4	39	1	1	0	1	0
Boyce	12	1	51	0	13	3	43	3
Barrett	14	3	35	1	8	3	11	0

FALL OF WICKETS

Wkt	WI 1st	I 1st	WI 2nd	I 2nd
1st	177	23	5	5
2nd	181	23	71	25
3rd	230	112	75	54
4th	236	154	282	69
5th	245	157	301	71
6th	255	163	340	96
7th	255	197	–	118
8th	264	199	–	118
9th	289	241	–	–
10th	289	260	–	–

Umpires: M.V. Nagendra (7) and J. Reuben (5).

Close: 1st day – WI(1) 212-2 (Kallicharran 64, Lloyd 21); 2nd – I(1) 43-2 (Kanitkar 6, Viswanath 4); 3rd – WI(2) 40-1 (Greenidge 29, Kallicharran 10); 4th – I(2) 36-2 (Kanitkar 9, Viswanath 5).

INDIA v WEST INDIES 1974–75 (2nd Test)

Played at Feroz Shah Kotla, Delhi, on 11, 12, 14, 15 December.
Toss: India.   Result: WEST INDIES won by an innings and 17 runs.
Debuts: India – P. Sharma.

West Indies won after an hour's play on the fourth day. Richards batted for five hours and hit six sixes and 20 fours in his second Test match. His partnership of 124 with Boyce is the highest for the eighth wicket by either side in this series.

INDIA

S.S. Naik	lbw b Boyce	48	b Julien		6
F.M. Engineer†	b Julien	17	b Gibbs		75
H.S. Kanitkar	lbw b Roberts	8	b Gibbs		20
G.R. Viswanath	c Murray b Julien	32	c Lloyd b Gibbs		39
P. Sharma	c Julien b Willett	54	run out		49
B.P. Patel	c Kallicharran b Willett	11	c and b Roberts		29
E.D. Solkar	c Lloyd b Gibbs	1	c Kallicharran b Gibbs		8
S. Abid Ali	c Boyce b Gibbs	8	run out		4
S. Venkataraghavan*	c Greenidge b Roberts	13	c Richards b Gibbs		5
E.A.S. Prasanna	not out	8	not out		0
B.S. Bedi	b Roberts	0	c Greenidge b Gibbs		0
Extras	(B 1, LB 3, NB 16)	20	(B 5, LB 8, W 1, NB 7)		21
Total		**220**			**256**

WEST INDIES

C.G. Greenidge	c Engineer b Prasanna	31
D.L. Murray†	c Patel b Solkar	0
E.T. Willett	b Prasanna	26
A.I. Kallicharran	c Patel b Bedi	44
I.V.A. Richards	not out	192
C.H. Lloyd*	lbw b Solkar	71
R.C. Fredericks	c Engineer b Venkataraghavan	5
B.D. Julien	c Bedi b Prasanna	45
K.D. Boyce	c Patel b Prasanna	68
L.R. Gibbs	run out	6
A.M.E. Roberts	run out	2
Extras	(B 2, LB 1)	3
Total		**493**

WEST INDIES	O	M	R	W	O	M	R	W		FALL OF WICKETS		
Roberts	17·3	3	51	3	16	6	43	1		I	WI	I
Boyce	11	2	41	1	3	0	10	0	*Wkt*	*1st*	*1st*	*2nd*
Julien	16	3	38	2	9	2	33	1	1st	36	2	9
Gibbs	29	17	40	2	40·5	17	76	6	2nd	51	50	81
Willett	13	3	30	2	26	9	61	0	3rd	104	73	103
Fredericks					2	0	12	0	4th	132	123	204
									5th	164	243	214
INDIA									6th	173	248	246
Abid Ali	7	0	47	0					7th	189	320	249
Solkar	13	3	43	2					8th	196	444	252
Bedi	53	13	146	1					9th	220	467	256
Prasanna	34	7	147	4					10th	220	493	256
Venkataraghavan	34	6	107	1								

Umpires: M.V. Gothoskar (3) and B. Satyaji Rao (11).

Close: 1st day – WI(1) 4-1 (Greenidge 4, Willett 0); 2nd – WI(1) 378-7 (Richards 118, Boyce 36); 3rd – I(2) 239-5 (Patel 25, Solkar 5).

INDIA v WEST INDIES 1974–75 (3rd Test)

Played at Eden Gardens, Calcutta, on 27, 28, 29, 31 December, 1 January.
Toss: India.   Result: INDIA won by 85 runs.
Debuts: India – A.D. Gaekwad, K.D. Ghavri.

At five minutes before lunch on the fifth day India beat West Indies in a home Test for the first time in 16 attempts. This success ended a run of five successive Test defeats. Naik was out to the first ball of the match. Viswanath's innings of 139, scored in $6\frac{1}{4}$ hours and including 22 fours, was India's highest score against West Indies in a home Test until 1978-79 (*Test No. 840*).

INDIA

S.S. Naik	c Murray b Roberts	0	c Fredericks b Roberts	6
F.M. Engineer†	c Lloyd b Roberts	24	c Lloyd b Willett	61
P. Sharma	b Julien	6	run out	9
G.R. Viswanath	lbw b Gibbs	52	b Holder	139
Nawab of Pataudi, jr*	b Roberts	36	c Holder b Willett	8
A.D. Gaekwad	c Murray b Fredericks	36	c Greenidge b Gibbs	4
Madan Lal	c Murray b Holder	48	b Roberts	15
K.D. Ghavri	b Holder	3	b Roberts	27
E.A.S. Prasanna	c Greenidge b Roberts	17	lbw b Holder	2
B.S. Bedi	b Roberts	0	c Julien b Holder	5
B.S. Chandrasekhar	not out	4	not out	7
Extras	(LB 1, NB 6)	7	(B 3, LB 13, NB 17)	33
Total		**233**		**316**

WEST INDIES

R.C. Fredericks	c Viswanath b Madan Lal	100	b Bedi	21
C.G. Greenidge	c Bedi b Madan Lal	20	lbw b Ghavri	3
A.I. Kallicharran	c Pataudi b Madan Lal	0	c Viswanath b Chandrasekhar	57
I.V.A. Richards	run out	15	b Madan Lal	47
C.H. Lloyd*	c Engineer b Bedi	19	b Chandrasekhar	28
D.L. Murray†	run out	24	lbw b Bedi	13
B.D. Julien	c Viswanath b Bedi	19	lbw b Chandrasekhar	7
E.T. Willett	b Ghavri	13	not out	16
V.A. Holder	b Chandrasekhar	2	run out	0
L.R. Gibbs	not out	6	c Prasanna b Bedi	3
A.M.E. Roberts	lbw b Madan Lal	1	b Bedi	6
Extras	(B 6, LB 11, NB 4)	21	(B 8, LB 10, NB 5)	23
Total		**240**		**224**

WEST INDIES	O	M	R	W	O	M	R	W		FALL OF WICKETS			
Roberts	19·3	6	50	5	31	6	88	3		I	WI	I	WI
Julien	12	1	57	1	17	8	29	0	*Wkt*	*1st*	*1st*	*2nd*	*2nd*
Holder	16	3	48	2	27·2	5	61	3	1st	0	42	19	5
Fredericks	9	4	24	1	1	0	1	0	2nd	23	42	46	41
Gibbs	17	6	34	1	37	17	53	1	3rd	32	66	120	125
Willett	7	3	13	0	30	14	51	2	4th	94	115	138	163
									5th	169	189	152	178
INDIA									6th	169	212	192	186
Ghavri	7	1	28	1	7	0	18	1	7th	180	219	283	198
Madal Lal	16·1	5	22	4	6	1	23	1	8th	224	221	301	203
Bedi	25	8	68	2	26·2	13	52	4	9th	224	235	303	213
Chandrasekhar	22	6	80	1	20	3	66	3	10th	233	240	316	224
Prasanna	11	4	21	0	25	12	42	0					

Umpires: J. Reuben (6) and H.P. Sharma (1).

Close: 1st day – WI(1) 14-0 (Fredericks 11, Greenidge 2); 2nd – I(2) 8-0 (Naik 2, Engineer 6); 3rd – I(2) 206-6 (Viswanath 75, Ghavri 5); 4th – WI(2) 146-3 (Kallicharran 48, Lloyd 13).

INDIA v WEST INDIES 1974–75 (4th Test)

Played at Chepauk, Madras, on 11, 12, 14, 15 January.
Toss: India.   Result: INDIA won by 100 runs.
Debuts: Nil.

India drew level in the rubber 45 minutes after lunch on the fourth day after dismissing West Indies for their two lowest totals of this series until 1978-79 (*Test No. 843*). Roberts was the first bowler to take 12 wickets in a Test for West Indies and his analysis of 12 for 121 in this match was the record for this series until 1987-88. His first innings analysis of 7 for 64 is the best for West Indies in India.

INDIA

F.M. Engineer†	c Greenidge b Julien	14		b Holder	28
E.D. Solkar	c Kallicharran b Julien	4		c Kallicharran b Julien	15
A.D. Gaekwad	lbw b Roberts	7	(7)	run out	80
G.R. Viswanath	not out	97		c Murray b Roberts	46
Nawab of Pataudi, jr*	lbw b Roberts	6		lbw b Roberts	4
A.V. Mankad	c Fredericks b Roberts	19	(3)	b Boyce	20
Madan Lal	b Roberts	0	(8)	c Murray b Roberts	5
K.D. Ghavri	b Roberts	12	(9)	not out	35
E.A.S. Prasanna	c Murray b Roberts	0	(6)	lbw b Boyce	0
B.S. Bedi	b Gibbs	14		c Murray b Roberts	0
B.S. Chandrasekhar	c Lloyd b Roberts	1		b Roberts	0
Extras	(B 1, LB 6, NB 9)	16		(B 12, LB 3, NB 8)	23
Total		**190**			**256**

WEST INDIES

R.C. Fredericks	c Solkar b Ghavri	14		c Solkar b Prasanna	19
C.G. Greenidge	c Prasanna b Bedi	14		b Chandrasekhar	17
A.I. Kallicharran	c Viswanath b Bedi	17	(4)	run out	51
V.A. Holder	hit wkt b Bedi	0	(10)	c Viswanath b Bedi	4
I.V.A. Richards	c Chandrasekhar b Prasanna	50		c Engineer b Prasanna	2
C.H. Lloyd*	c Viswanath b Prasanna	39		st Engineer b Prasanna	7
D.L. Murray†	c Engineer b Prasanna	8		c Solkar b Bedi	18
B.D. Julien	c and b Prasanna	2		not out	14
K.D. Boyce	c Bedi b Prasanna	0		lbw b Prasanna	4
L.R. Gibbs	not out	14	(3)	c Solkar b Chandrasekhar	3
A.M.E. Roberts	lbw b Chandrasekhar	17		lbw b Bedi	0
Extras	(B 7, LB 10)	17		(B 14, LB 1)	15
Total		**192**			**154**

WEST INDIES	O	M	R	W	O	M	R	W		FALL OF WICKETS			
Roberts	20·5	5	64	7	21·4	6	57	5		I	WI	I	WI
Julien	6	2	12	2	13	4	31	1	*Wkt*	*1st*	*1st*	*2nd*	*2nd*
Boyce	11	3	40	0	15	4	61	2	1st	21	20	40	32
Holder	9	1	26	0	24	8	40	1	2nd	24	35	65	45
Gibbs	12	1	32	1	26	11	36	0	3rd	30	35	73	62
Fredericks					5	2	8	0	4th	41	70	85	65
									5th	74	138	85	85
INDIA									6th	76	155	178	125
Ghavri	6	0	25	1	2	0	13	0	7th	117	160	188	133
Madan Lal	2	0	7	0	2	0	5	0	8th	117	160	256	138
Prasanna	23	6	70	5	24	8	41	4	9th	169	165	256	152
Bedi	19	7	40	3	19	8	29	3	10th	190	192	256	154
Chandrasekhar	9·2	1	33	1	20	6	51	2					

Umpires: B. Satyaji Rao (12) and M.S. Sivasankariah (1).

Close: 1st day – WI(1) 36-3 (Kallicharran 6, Richards 1); 2nd – I(2) 85-4 (Viswanath 10, Prasanna 0); 3rd – WI(2) 38-1 (Greenidge 15, Gibbs 0).

INDIA v WEST INDIES 1974–75 (5th Test)

Played at Wankhede Stadium, Bombay, on 23, 24, 25, 27, 28, 29 January.
Toss: West Indies.   Result: WEST INDIES won by 201 runs.
Debuts: Nil.

West Indies gained their victory 72 minutes after lunch on the final afternoon of this six-day Test to win their fourth rubber in four visits to India. This was the first Test match to be played at the new stadium named after the president of the Bombay Cricket Association. Bombay thus equalled Johannesburg in playing Test cricket on three different grounds. Lloyd's innings of 242 not out is the highest on any of them; he batted for 429 minutes and hit four sixes and 19 fours. His partnership of 250 with Murray is the record for the sixth wicket in this series. Police brutality involving a young spectator, when Lloyd reached his double century, resulted in rioting and the loss of 90 minutes of play after tea on the second day. Roberts, with 32 wickets in the rubber, set a record for this series which stood until M.D. Marshall took 33 in 1983-84.

WEST INDIES

R.C. Fredericks	c Solkar b Bedi	104	b Ghavri	37
C.G. Greenidge	c Engineer b Ghavri	32	c Patel b Bedi	54
A.I. Kallicharran	c Viswanath b Ghavri	98	not out	34
C.H. Lloyd*	not out	242	c Patel b Ghavri	37
V.A. Holder	c Chandrasekhar b Ghavri	5		
I.V.A. Richards	c Engineer b Chandrasekhar	1	(5) not out	39
D.L. Murray†	c Patel b Ghavri	91		
B.D. Julien	not out	6		
A.G. Barrett	)			
L.R. Gibbs	) did not bat			
A.M.E. Roberts	)			
Extras	(B 12, LB 10, NB 3)	25	(LB 4)	4
Total	(6 wickets declared)	**604**	(3 wickets declared)	**205**

INDIA

S.M. Gavaskar	b Gibbs	86	c Fredericks b Roberts	8
F.M. Engineer†	c Richards b Julien	0	b Julien	0
E.D. Solkar	b Barrett	102	lbw b Holder	25
E.A.S. Prasanna	c Murray b Gibbs	4	(5) b Holder	1
G.R. Viswanath	c Fredericks b Gibbs	95	(4) b Holder	17
A.D. Gaekwad	c Richards b Gibbs	51	b Gibbs	42
B.P. Patel	b Gibbs	5	(8) not out	73
B.S. Bedi	lbw b Roberts	13	(10) c Julien b Holder	13
Nawab of Pataudi, jr*	b Gibbs	9	(7) lbw b Gibbs	9
K.D. Ghavri	c Kallicharran b Gibbs	9	(9) c Murray b Holder	1
B.S. Chandrasekhar	not out	0	c Murray b Holder	0
Extras	(B 16, LB 9, W 1, NB 6)	32	(LB 3, NB 10)	13
Total		**406**		**202**

INDIA	O	M	R	W	O	M	R	W
Ghavri	35	8	140	4	17	1	92	2
Solkar	16	2	57	0	6	2	14	0
Prasanna	45	5	149	0	5	0	28	0
Chandrasekhar	35	3	135	1				
Bedi	30	4	98	1	11	2	66	1
Gaekwad					1	0	1	0
WEST INDIES								
Roberts	31·1	6	79	1	18	4	64	1
Julien	19	8	34	1	7	2	16	1
Holder	23	8	46	0	20·1	6	39	6
Gibbs	59	20	98	7	23	10	45	2
Barrett	35	10	85	1	7	2	18	0
Fredericks	7	0	22	0	2	0	7	0
Richards	7	2	10	0				

FALL OF WICKETS				
	WI	I	WI	I
Wkt	1st	1st	2nd	2nd
1st	81	0	75	2
2nd	194	168	105	17
3rd	298	180	149	46
4th	323	238	–	56
5th	341	359	–	59
6th	591	373	–	89
7th	–	374	–	161
8th	–	392	–	167
9th	–	406	–	188
10th	–	406	–	202

Umpires: M.V. Nagendra (8) and J. Reuben (7).

Close: 1st day – WI(1) 309-3 (Lloyd 64, Holder 3); 2nd – WI(1) 528-5 (Lloyd 201, Murray 67); 3rd – I(1) 171-2 (Solkar 76, Prasanna 0); 4th – I(1) 373-6 (Gaekwad 51, Bedi 0); 5th – I(2) 53-3 (Solkar 22, Prasanna 1).

AUSTRALIA v ENGLAND 1974–75 (1st Test)

Played at Woolloongabba, Brisbane, on 29, 30 November, 1, 3, 4 December.
Toss: Australia.   Result: AUSTRALIA won by 166 runs.
Debuts: Australia – W.J. Edwards.

With 80 minutes of the last day to spare, Australia completed their fifth victory in eight post-war Tests against England at Brisbane. Knott overtook the world Test record of 173 catches by T.G. Evans when he caught Ross Edwards in the second innings. Greig's hundred was the first for England at Brisbane since 1936-37. Alderman Clem Jones, Lord Mayor of Brisbane and future rebuilder of a demolished Darwin, acting in his capacity as a member of the cricket ground trust, dismissed the curator eight days before this Test (because he rolled the pitch sideways), and prepared the surface himself. It provided a perfect launching pad for the most lethal post-war fast bowling partnership: 'Ashes to Ashes. Dust to Dust. If Thommo don't get you, then Lillee must'. Amiss (thumb) and Edrich (hand) sustained fractures in the first innings.

AUSTRALIA

I.R. Redpath	b Willis	5	b Willis		25
W.J. Edwards	c Amiss b Hendrick	4	c Knott b Willis		5
I.M. Chappell*	c Greig b Willis	90	c Fletcher b Underwood		11
G.S. Chappell	c Fletcher b Underwood	58	b Underwood		71
R. Edwards	c Knott b Underwood	32	c Knott b Willis		53
K.D. Walters	c Lever b Willis	3	not out		62
R.W. Marsh†	c Denness b Hendrick	14	not out		46
T.J. Jenner	c Lever b Willis	12			
D.K. Lillee	c Knott b Greig	15			
M.H.N. Walker	not out	41			
J.R. Thomson	run out	23			
Extras	(LB 4, NB 8)	12	(B 1, LB 7, W 1, NB 6)		15
Total		**309**	(5 wickets declared)		**288**

ENGLAND

D.L. Amiss	c Jenner b Thomson	7	c Walters b Thomson	25
B.W. Luckhurst	c Marsh b Thomson	1	c I.M. Chappell b Lillee	3
J.H. Edrich	c I.M. Chappell b Thomson	48	b Thomson	6
M.H. Denness*	lbw b Walker	6	c Walters b Thomson	27
K.W.R. Fletcher	b Lillee	17	c G.S. Chappell b Jenner	19
A.W. Greig	c Marsh b Lillee	110	b Thomson	2
A.P.E. Knott†	c Jenner b Walker	12	b Thomson	19
P. Lever	c I.M. Chappell b Walker	4	c Redpath b Lillee	14
D.L. Underwood	c Redpath b Walters	25	c Walker b Jenner	30
R.G.D. Willis	not out	13	not out	3
M. Hendrick	c Redpath b Walker	4	b Thomson	0
Extras	(B 5, LB 2, W 3, NB 8)	18	(B 8, LB 3, W 2, NB 5)	18
Total		**265**		**166**

ENGLAND	O	M	R	W	O	M	R	W
Willis	21·5	3	56	4	15	3	45	3
Lever	16	1	53	0	18	4	58	0
Hendrick	19	3	64	2	13	2	47	0
Greig	16	2	70	1	13	2	60	0
Underwood	20	6	54	2	26	6	63	2
AUSTRALIA								
Lillee	23	6	73	2	12	2	25	2
Thomson	21	5	59	3	17·5	3	46	6
Walker	24·5	2	73	4	9	4	32	0
Walters	6	1	18	1	2	2	0	0
Jenner	6	1	24	0	16	5	45	2

FALL OF WICKETS

	A	E	A	E
Wkt	1st	1st	2nd	2nd
1st	7	9	15	18
2nd	10	10	39	40
3rd	110	33	59	44
4th	197	57	173	92
5th	202	130	190	94
6th	205	162	–	94
7th	228	168	–	115
8th	229	226	–	162
9th	257	248	–	163
10th	309	265	–	166

Umpires: R.C. Bailhache (1) and T.F. Brooks (8).

Close: 1st day – A(1) 219-6 (Marsh 8, Jenner 8); 2nd – E(1) 114-4 (Edrich 40, Greig 34); 3rd – A(2) 51-2 (Redpath 24, G.S. Chappell 7); 4th – E(2) 10-0 (Amiss 9, Luckhurst 0).

AUSTRALIA v ENGLAND 1974–75 (2nd Test)

Played at W.A.C.A. Ground, Perth, on 13, 14, 15, 17 December.
Toss: Australia.   Result: AUSTRALIA won by nine wickets.
Debuts: Nil.

Australia's first win against England in Perth was gained with a day and 50 minutes to spare. Hand fractures sustained by Amiss and Edrich in the first Test resulted in Cowdrey making his first Test appearance since June 1971 just four days after arriving in Australia. This was his sixth tour of that continent, equalling the record of J. Briggs. Walters scored 100 runs between tea and the close of play on the second day; he took his score to 103 with a six off the last ball of the session. Greg Chappell set the present record (seven) for the most catches by a non-wicket-keeper in a Test match. He was the third after S.J.E. Loxton and R.N. Harvey to hold four in an England innings in this series. Lloyd (17) retired at 52 in the second innings, after being hit in the groin by a ball from Thomson, and resumed at 106. Titmus made his first appearance since losing four toes in a boating accident off Barbados in February 1968.

ENGLAND

D. Lloyd	c G.S. Chappell b Thomson	49		c G.S. Chappell b Walker	35
B.W. Luckhurst	c Mallett b Walker	27	(7)	c Mallett b Lillee	23
M.C. Cowdrey	b Thomson	22	(2)	lbw b Thomson	41
A.W. Greig	c Mallett b Walker	23		c G.S. Chappell b Thomson	32
K.W.R. Fletcher	c Redpath b Lillee	4		c Marsh b Thomson	0
M.H. Denness*	c G.S. Chappell b Lillee	2	(3)	c Redpath b Thomson	20
A.P.E. Knott†	c Redpath b Walters	51	(6)	c G.S. Chappell b Lillee	18
F.J. Titmus	c Redpath b Walters	10		c G.S. Chappell b Mallett	61
C.M. Old	c G.S. Chappell b I.M. Chappell	7		c Thomson b Mallett	43
G.G. Arnold	run out	1		c Mallett b Thomson	4
R.G.D. Willis	not out	4		not out	0
Extras	(W 3, NB 5)	8		(LB 4, W 1, NB 11)	16
Total		**208**			**293**

AUSTRALIA

I.R. Redpath	st Knott b Titmus	41	not out	12
W.J. Edwards	c Lloyd b Greig	30	lbw b Arnold	0
I.M. Chappell*	c Knott b Arnold	25	not out	11
G.S. Chappell	c Greig b Willis	62		
R. Edwards	b Arnold	115		
K.D. Walters	c Fletcher b Willis	103		
R.W. Marsh†	c Lloyd b Titmus	41		
M.H.N. Walker	c Knott b Old	19		
D.K. Lillee	b Old	11		
A.A. Mallett	c Knott b Old	0		
J.R. Thomson	not out	11		
Extras	(B 7, LB 14, NB 2)	23		
Total		**481**	(1 wicket)	**23**

AUSTRALIA	O	M	R	W	O	M	R	W		FALL OF WICKETS			
Lillee	16	4	48	2	22	5	59	2		E	A	E	A
Thomson	15	6	45	2	25	4	93	5	Wkt	1st	1st	2nd	2nd
Walker	20	5	49	2	24	7	76	1	1st	44	64	62	4
Mallett	10	3	35	0	11·1	4	32	2	2nd	99	101	106	–
Walters	2·3	0	13	2	9	4	17	0	3rd	119	113	124	–
I.M. Chappell	2	0	10	1					4th	128	192	124	–
									5th	132	362	154	–
ENGLAND									6th	132	416	156	–
Willis	22	0	91	2	2	0	8	0	7th	194	449	219	–
Arnold	27	1	129	2	1·7	0	15	1	8th	201	462	285	–
Old	22·6	3	85	3					9th	202	462	293	–
Greig	9	0	69	1					10th	208	481	293	–
Titmus	28	3	84	2									

Umpires: R.C. Bailhache (2) and T.F. Brooks (9).

Close: 1st day – A(1) 1-0 (Redpath 1, W.J. Edwards 0); 2nd – A(1) 352-4 (R. Edwards 79, Walters 103); 3rd – E(2) 102-1 (Denness 13, Greig 28).

AUSTRALIA v ENGLAND 1974–75 (3rd Test)

Played at Melbourne Cricket Ground on 26, 27, 28, 30, 31 December.
Toss: Australia.   Result: MATCH DRAWN.
Debuts: Nil.

Australia, needing to score 246 runs to win, were 4 for no wicket when the last day began and needed 55 in the last hour with four wickets left. Amiss took his aggregate of runs in Test cricket in 1974 to 1,379 – just two runs short of the record for a calendar year which R.B. Simpson had set in 1964. Hendrick damaged a hamstring muscle and was unable to complete his third over. Ian Chappell became the first captain to put the opposition in to bat in successive Ashes Tests.

ENGLAND

D.L. Amiss	c Walters b Lillee	4	c I.M. Chappell b Mallett		90
D. Lloyd	c Mallett b Thomson	14	c and b Mallett		44
M.C. Cowdrey	lbw b Thomson	35	c G.S. Chappell b Lillee		8
J.H. Edrich	c Marsh b Mallett	49	c Marsh b Thomson		4
M.H. Denness*	c Marsh b Mallett	8	c I.M. Chappell b Thomson		2
A.W. Greig	run out	28	c G.S. Chappell b Lillee		60
A.P.E. Knott†	b Thomson	52	c Marsh b Thomson		4
F.J. Titmus	c Mallett b Lillee	10	b Mallett		0
D.L. Underwood	c Marsh b Walker	9	c I.M. Chappell b Mallett		4
R.G.D. Willis	c Walters b Thomson	13	b Thomson		15
M. Hendrick	not out	8	not out		0
Extras	(LB 2, W 1, NB 9)	12	(B 2, LB 9, W 2)		13
Total		**242**			**244**

AUSTRALIA

I.R. Redpath	c Knott b Greig	55	run out		39
W.J. Edwards	c Denness b Willis	29	lbw b Greig		0
G.S. Chappell	c Greig b Willis	2	(4) lbw b Titmus		61
R. Edwards	c Cowdrey b Titmus	1	(5) c Lloyd b Titmus		10
K.D. Walters	c Lloyd b Greig	36	(6) c Denness b Greig		32
I.M. Chappell*	lbw b Willis	36	(3) lbw b Willis		0
R.W. Marsh†	c Knott b Titmus	44	c Knott b Greig		40
M.H.N. Walker	c Knott b Willis	30	not out		23
D.K. Lillee	not out	2	c Denness b Greig		14
A.A. Mallett	run out	0	not out		0
J.R. Thomson	b Willis	2			
Extras	(B 2, LB 2)	4	(B 6, LB 9, NB 4)		19
Total		**241**	(8 wickets)		**238**

AUSTRALIA	O	M	R	W	O	M	R	W
Lillee	20	2	70	2	17	3	55	2
Thomson	22·4	4	72	4	17	1	71	4
Walker	24	10	36	1	11	0	45	0
Walters	7	2	15	0				
Mallett	15	3	37	2	24	6	60	4
ENGLAND								
Willis	21·7	4	61	5	14	2	56	1
Hendrick	2·6	1	8	0				
Underwood	22	6	62	0	19	7	43	0
Greig	24	2	63	2	18	2	56	4
Titmus	22	11	43	2	29	10	64	2

FALL OF WICKETS

	E	A	E	A
Wkt	1st	1st	2nd	2nd
1st	4	65	115	4
2nd	34	67	134	5
3rd	110	68	152	106
4th	110	156	120	
5th	141	126	158	121
6th	157	173	165	171
7th	176	237	178	208
8th	213	237	182	235
9th	232	238	238	–
10th	242	241	244	–

Umpires: R.C. Bailhache (3) and T.F. Brooks (10).

Close: 1st day – E(1) 176-7 (Knott 18); 2nd – A(1) 63-0 (Redpath 34, W.J. Edwards 28); 3rd – E(2) 1-0 (Amiss 1, Lloyd 0); 4th – A(2) 4-0 (Redpath 0, W. J. Edwards 0).

AUSTRALIA v ENGLAND 1974–75 (4th Test)

Played at Sydney Cricket Ground on 4, 5, 6, 8, 9 January.
Toss: Australia.   Result: AUSTRALIA won by 171 runs.
Debuts: Australia – R.B. McCosker.

With 4·3 of the mandatory last 15 overs to spare, Mallett had Arnold caught at short-leg to regain the Ashes which had been lost three years and 326 days previously. It was Mallett's 100th wicket in 23 Tests. Arnold took his 100th wicket in 29 Tests when he dismissed Greg Chappell in the first innings. The partnership of 220 between Redpath and Greg Chappell is a record for the second wicket against England in Australia. Edrich, who captained England in this match when Denness decided to drop himself after scoring only 65 runs in six innings, was hit in the ribs by the first ball he received (from Lillee) in the second innings, and retired to hospital at 70. He resumed at 156 with two fractures.

AUSTRALIA

I.R. Redpath	hit wkt b Titmus	33	c sub (C.M. Old) b Underwood	105
R.B. McCosker	c Knott b Greig	80		
I.M. Chappell*	c Knott b Arnold	53	(2) c Lloyd b Willis	5
G.S. Chappell	c Greig b Arnold	84	(3) c Lloyd b Arnold	144
R. Edwards	b Greig	15	not out	17
K.D. Walters	lbw b Arnold	1	(4) b Underwood	5
R.W. Marsh†	b Greig	30	(6) not out	7
M.H.N. Walker	c Greig b Arnold	30		
D.K. Lillee	b Arnold	8		
A.A. Mallett	lbw b Greig	31		
J.R. Thomson	not out	24		
Extras	(LB 4, W 1, NB 11)	16	(LB 2, W 1, NB 3)	6
Total		**405**	(4 wickets declared)	**289**

ENGLAND

D.L. Amiss	c Mallett b Walker	12	c Marsh b Lillee	37
D. Lloyd	c Thomson b Lillee	19	c G.S. Chappell b Thomson	26
M.C. Cowdrey	c McCosker b Thomson	22	c I.M. Chappell b Walker	1
J.H. Edrich*	c Marsh b Walters	50	not out	33
K.W.R. Fletcher	c Redpath b Walker	24	c Redpath b Thomson	11
A.W. Greig	c G.S. Chappell b Thomson	9	st Marsh b Mallett	54
A.P.E. Knott†	b Thomson	82	c Redpath b Mallett	10
F.J. Titmus	c Marsh b Walters	22	c Thomson b Mallett	4
D.L. Underwood	c Walker b Lillee	27	c and b Walker	5
R.G.D. Willis	b Thomson	2	b Lillee	12
G.G. Arnold	not out	3	c G.S. Chappell b Mallett	14
Extras	(B 15, LB 7, W 1)	23	(B 13, LB 3, NB 5)	21
Total		**295**		**228**

ENGLAND	O	M	R	W	O	M	R	W		FALL OF WICKETS			
Willis	18	2	80	0	11	1	52	1		A	E	A	E
Arnold	29	7	86	5	22	3	78	1	*Wkt*	*1st*	*1st*	*2nd*	*2nd*
Greig	22·7	2	104	4	12	1	64	0	1st	96	36	15	68
Underwood	13	3	54	0	12	1	65	2	2nd	142	46	235	70
Titmus	16	2	65	1	7·3	2	24	0	3rd	199	69	242	74
									4th	251	108	280	103
AUSTRALIA									5th	255	123	–	136
Lillee	19·1	2	66	2	21	5	65	2	6th	305	180	–	156
Thomson	19	3	74	4	23	7	74	2	7th	310	240	–	158
Walker	23	2	77	2	16	5	46	2	8th	332	273	–	175
Mallett	1	0	8	0	16·5	9	21	4	9th	368	285	–	201
Walters	7	2	26	2					10th	405	295	–	228
I.M. Chappell	4	0	21	0	3	2	1	0					

Umpires: R.C. Bailhache (4) and T.F. Brooks (11).

Close: 1st day – A(1) 251-4 (G.S. Chappell 59, Walters 0); 2nd – E(1) 106-3 (Edrich 13, Fletcher 23); 3rd – A(2) 123-1 (Redpath 47, G.S. Chappell 69); 4th – E(2) 33-0 (Amiss 14, Lloyd 15).

AUSTRALIA v ENGLAND 1974–75 (5th Test)

Played at Adelaide Oval on 25 (*no play*), 26, 27, 29, 30 January.
Toss: England.   Result: AUSTRALIA won by 163 runs.
Debuts: Nil.

Australia's fourth victory in the rubber was gained with two hours and 40 minutes to spare, despite the loss of the first day after overnight rain had seeped under the covers. Knott became the second wicket-keeper after T.G. Evans to make 200 dismissals in Test cricket, when he caught Ian Chappell in the first innings. Later Knott scored the second hundred by a wicket-keeper in this series, L.E.G. Ames having scored the first in 1934 (*Test No. 234*). Underwood's match analysis of 11 for 215 was England's best in Australia since 1928-29. Thomson tore fibres in his right shoulder when playing tennis on the rest day and was unable to bowl in the second innings. His total of 33 wickets in the rubber was Australia's third-highest in this series (A.A. Mailey 36 in 1920-21, G. Giffen 34 in 1894-95). Cowdrey's 42nd appearance against Australia beat the record previously held jointly by W. Rhodes and J.B. Hobbs. Willis damaged his knee in Australia's second innings.

AUSTRALIA

I.R. Redpath	c Greig b Underwood	21		b Underwood	52
R.B. McCosker	c Cowdrey b Underwood	35		c Knott b Arnold	11
I.M. Chappell*	c Knott b Underwood	0		c Knott b Underwood	41
G.S. Chappell	lbw b Underwood	5		c Greig b Underwood	18
K.D. Walters	c Willis b Underwood	55		not out	71
R.W. Marsh†	c Greig b Underwood	6		c Greig b Underwood	55
T.J. Jenner	b Underwood	74		not out	14
M.H.N. Walker	run out	41			
D.K. Lillee	b Willis	26			
A.A. Mallett	not out	23			
J.R. Thomson	b Arnold	5			
Extras	(B 4, LB 4, NB 5)	13		(LB 4, NB 6)	10
Total		**304**		(5 wickets declared)	**272**

ENGLAND

D.L. Amiss	c I.M. Chappell b Lillee	0		c Marsh b Lillee	0
D. Lloyd	c Marsh b Lillee	4		c Walters b Walker	5
M.C. Cowdrey	c Walker b Thomson	26		c Mallett b Lillee	3
M.H. Denness*	c Marsh b Thomson	51		c Jenner b Lillee	14
K.W.R. Fletcher	c I.M. Chappell b Thomson	40		lbw b Lillee	63
A.W. Greig	c Marsh b Lillee	19		lbw b Walker	20
A.P.E. Knott†	c Lillee b Mallett	5		not out	106
F.J. Titmus	c G.S. Chappell b Mallett	11		lbw b Jenner	20
D.L. Underwood	c Lillee b Mallett	0		c I.M. Chappell b Mallett	0
G.G. Arnold	b Lillee	0		b Mallett	0
R.G.D. Willis	not out	11		b Walker	3
Extras	(LB 2, NB 3)	5		(B 3, LB 3, NB 1)	7
Total		**172**			**241**

ENGLAND	O	M	R	W	O	M	R	W
Willis	10	0	46	1	5	0	27	0
Arnold	12·2	3	42	1	20	1	71	1
Underwood	29	3	113	7	26	5	102	4
Greig	10	0	63	0	2	0	9	0
Titmus	7	1	27	0	13	1	53	0
AUSTRALIA								
Lillee	12·5	2	49	4	14	3	69	4
Thomson	15	1	58	3				
Walker	5	1	18	0	20	3	89	3
Jenner	5	0	28	0	15	4	39	1
Mallett	9	4	14	3	25	10	36	2
I.M. Chappell					1	0	1	0

FALL OF WICKETS

Wkt	A 1st	E 1st	A 2nd	E 2nd
1st	52	2	16	0
2nd	52	19	92	8
3rd	58	66	128	10
4th	77	90	133	33
5th	84	130	245	76
6th	164	147	–	144
7th	241	155	–	212
8th	259	156	–	213
9th	295	161	–	217
10th	304	172	–	241

Umpires: R.C. Bailhache (5) and T.F. Brooks (12).

Close: 1st day – no play; 2nd – E(1) 2-0 (Amiss 0, Lloyd 0); 3rd – A(2) 111-2 (Redpath 47, G.S. Chappell 6); 4th – E(2) 94-5 (Fletcher 39, Knott 9).

AUSTRALIA v ENGLAND 1974–75 (6th Test)

Played at Melbourne Cricket Ground on 8, 9, 10, 12, 13 February.
Toss: Australia.   Result: ENGLAND won by an innings and 4 runs.
Debuts: Nil.

England gained their solitary success in this rubber 35 minutes after lunch on the fifth day. Denness made the highest score by an England captain in Australia, his 188 improving upon A.E. Stoddart's 173 in 1894-95 (*Test No. 43*). Lillee bruised his right foot and left the field after bowling six overs. Cowdrey ended his Test career after a record 114 matches with 7,624 runs (the England record until G. Boycott passed it in 1981 – *Test No. 907*), 22 hundreds (the England record shared with W.R. Hammond and, eventually, Boycott), and 120 catches (the world record until G.S. Chappell overtook it in his final Test in 1983-84 – *Test No. 974*). Lever's 4 for 5 spell led to his best figures in Tests. Walker was the third Australian to take eight England wickets in an innings at home, and the first since A.A. Mailey in 1920-21 (*Test No. 138*).

AUSTRALIA

I.R. Redpath	c Greig b Lever	1	c Amiss b Greig		83
R.B. McCosker	c Greig b Lever	0	c Cowdrey b Arnold		76
I.M. Chappell*	c Knott b Old	65	c Knott b Greig		50
G.S. Chappell	c Denness b Lever	1	b Lever		102
R. Edwards	c Amiss b Lever	0	c Knott b Arnold		18
K.D. Walters	c Edrich b Old	12	b Arnold		3
R.W. Marsh†	b Old	29	c Denness b Lever		1
M.H.N. Walker	not out	20	c and b Greig		17
D.K. Lillee	c Knott b Lever	12	(11) not out		0
A.A. Mallett	b Lever	7	(9) c Edrich b Greig		0
G. Dymock	c Knott b Greig	0	(10) c Knott b Lever		0
Extras	(B 2, LB 1, NB 2)	5	(B 9, LB 5, W 4, NB 5)		23
Total		**152**			**373**

ENGLAND

D.L. Amiss	lbw b Lillee	0
M.C. Cowdrey	c Marsh b Walker	7
J.H. Edrich	c I.M. Chappell b Walker	70
M.H. Denness*	c and b Walker	188
K.W.R. Fletcher	c Redpath b Walker	146
A.W. Greig	c sub (T.J. Jenner) b Walker	89
A.P.E. Knott†	c Marsh b Walker	5
C.M. Old	b Dymock	0
D.L. Underwood	b Walker	11
G.G. Arnold	c Marsh b Walker	0
P. Lever	not out	6
Extras	(B 4, LB 2, NB 1)	7
Total		**529**

ENGLAND	O	M	R	W	O	M	R	W
Arnold	6	2	24	0	23	6	83	3
Lever	11	2	38	6	16	1	65	3
Old	11	0	50	3	18	1	75	0
Greig	8·7	1	35	1	31·7	7	88	4
Underwood					18	5	39	0
AUSTRALIA								
Lillee	6	2	17	1				
Walker	42·2	7	143	8				
Dymock	39	6	130	1				
Walters	23	3	86	0				
Mallett	29	8	96	0				
I.M. Chappell	12	1	50	0				

FALL OF WICKETS

	A	E	A
Wkt	1st	1st	2nd
1st	0	4	111
2nd	5	18	215
3rd	19	167	248
4th	23	359	289
5th	50	507	297
6th	104	507	306
7th	115	508	367
8th	141	514	373
9th	149	514	373
10th	152	529	373

Umpires: R.C. Bailhache (6) and T.F. Brooks (13).

Close: 1st day – E(1) 15-1 (Cowdrey 5, Edrich 6); 2nd – E(1) 273-3 (Denness 133, Fletcher 56); 3rd – A(2) 32-0 (Redpath 10, McCosker 22); 4th – A(2) 274-3 (G.S. Chappell 39, Edwards 9).

PAKISTAN v WEST INDIES 1974–75 (1st Test)

Played at Gaddafi Stadium, Lahore, on 15, 16, 17, 19, 20 February.
Toss: West Indies.   Result: MATCH DRAWN.
Debuts: Pakistan – Agha Zahid; West Indies – L. Baichan.

This first meeting between these countries since March 1959 was left drawn when Baichan batted throughout the fifth day and shared a match-saving partnership with his captain. He was the ninth West Indies player to score a hundred in his first Test match and the first overseas batsman to do so in Pakistan. The innings and match analyses by Roberts are the best for West Indies in Pakistan. Mushtaq played the highest Test innings against West Indies in Pakistan (equalled by Imran Khan in 1980-81 – *Test No. 886*).

PAKISTAN

Majid Khan	c Murray b Roberts	2	b Roberts	17
Agha Zahid	c Gibbs b Roberts	14	lbw b Roberts	1
Zaheer Abbas	c Murray b Roberts	18	lbw b Holder	33
Mushtaq Mohammad	c Murray b Gibbs	27	b Holder	123
Asif Iqbal	c Lloyd b Roberts	25	b Roberts	52
Wasim Raja	c Fredericks b Boyce	13	b Holder	35
Aftab Baloch	c Holder b Boyce	12	not out	60
Intikhab Alam*	b Gibbs	29	c Gibbs b Roberts	19
Wasim Bari†	lbw b Boyce	8	not out	1
Sarfraz Nawaz	c Richards b Roberts	1		
Asif Masood	not out	30		
Extras	(B 1, LB 3, NB 16)	20	(B 4, LB 5, NB 23)	32
Total		**199**	(7 wickets declared)	**373**

WEST INDIES

R.C. Fredericks	lbw b Sarfraz	44	lbw b Sarfraz	14
L. Baichan	c Majid b Sarfraz	20	not out	105
A.I. Kallicharran	not out	92	c Wasim Bari b Intikhab	44
I.V.A. Richards	b Asif Masood	7	lbw b Intikhab	0
C.H. Lloyd*	b Sarfraz	8	c Wasim Bari b Asif Masood	83
D.L. Murray†	run out	10	not out	1
B.D. Julien	b Sarfraz	2		
K.D. Boyce	lbw b Sarfraz	13		
V.A. Holder	lbw b Intikhab	4		
A.M.E. Roberts	lbw b Sarfraz	0		
L.R. Gibbs	lbw b Asif Masood	0		
Extras	(B 6, LB 5, NB 3)	14	(B 1, LB 4, NB 6)	11
Total		**214**	(4 wickets)	**258**

WEST INDIES	O	M	R	W	O	M	R	W
Roberts	23	5	66	5	26	4	121	4
Julien	2	1	4	0	15	4	53	0
Holder	13	4	33	0	19·6	5	69	3
Boyce	15	1	55	3	14	4	47	0
Gibbs	6·4	0	21	2	20	4	51	0
PAKISTAN								
Asif Masood	19·5	0	63	2	17	2	70	1
Sarfraz	27	1	89	6	20	3	71	1
Asif Iqbal	2	0	16	0				
Wasim Raja	4	1	15	0	4	0	10	0
Intikhab	9	2	17	1	18	3	61	2
Mushtaq					6	0	20	0
Aftab Baloch					4	0	15	0

FALL OF WICKETS

Wkt	P 1st	WI 1st	P 2nd	WI 2nd
1st	2	66	8	30
2nd	35	83	53	89
3rd	40	92	58	89
4th	92	105	137	253
5th	98	141	214	–
6th	117	156	330	–
7th	130	199	370	–
8th	140	212	–	–
9th	142	213	–	–
10th	199	214	–	–

Umpires: Amanullah Khan (1) and Shakoor Rana (1).

Close: 1st day – P(1) 111-5 (Wasim Raja 6, Aftab 8); 2nd – WI(1) 139-4 (Kallicharran 40, Murray 8); 3rd – P(2) 153-4 (Mushtaq 35, Wasim Raja 5); 4th – WI(2) 15-0 (Fredericks 10, Baichan 4).

PAKISTAN v WEST INDIES 1974–75 (2nd Test)

Played at National Stadium, Karachi, on 1, 2, 3, 5, 6 March.
Toss: Pakistan.   Result: MATCH DRAWN.
Debuts: Pakistan – Liaquat Ali (*not Liaqat*).

Rioting, which followed spectator intrusions when Wasim Raja completed his hundred, caused $2\frac{1}{2}$ hours to be lost on the second day. As West Indies eventually had only 25 minutes in which to score 170 for victory, this interruption greatly influenced the result of the match. The partnership of 128 between Wasim Raja and Wasim Bari is the highest by either side for the seventh wicket in this series. Both sides scored their highest totals of the series for matches played in Pakistan. Sadiq, unable to turn his head after being hit in the neck when fielding, batted in pain for 315 minutes. Wasim Raja, whose ankle was put in plaster after he had damaged ligaments when bowling his fifth over, was unable to survive sufficiently long to allow Sadiq to reach his hundred.

PAKISTAN

Majid Khan	c Baichan b Gibbs	100	(2) run out	18
Sadiq Mohammad	c Murray b Roberts	27	(7) not out	98
Zaheer Abbas	c Murray b Gibbs	18	(1) c Fredericks b Roberts	2
Mushtaq Mohammad	c Murray b Holder	5	(3) c Kallicharran b Boyce	1
Asif Iqbal	c Boyce b Holder	3	(4) c Holder b Julien	77
Wasim Raja	not out	107	(11) b Gibbs	1
Intikhab Alam*	c Fredericks b Julien	34	(5) c Richards b Fredericks	6
Wasim Bari†	c Baichan b Roberts	58	(6) run out	0
Sarfraz Nawaz	b Gibbs	0	(8) run out	15
Asif Masood	not out	5	(9) c Julien b Gibbs	0
Liaquat Ali	did not bat		(10) c and b Richards	12
Extras	(B 1, LB 16, NB 32)	49	(B 6, LB 6, NB 14)	26
Total	(8 wickets declared)	**406**		**256**

WEST INDIES

R.C. Fredericks	c Liaquat b Intikhab	77	not out	0
L. Baichan	c Wasim Bari b Intikhab	36	not out	0
A.I. Kallicharran	c Zaheer b Sarfraz	115		
I.V.A. Richards	lbw b Mushtaq	10		
C.H. Lloyd*	c Sadiq b Asif Masood	73		
D.L. Murray†	c Majid b Intikhab	19		
B.D. Julien	b Asif Masood	101		
K.D. Boyce	run out	2		
V.A. Holder	lbw b Liaquat	29		
A.M.E. Roberts	run out	6		
L.R. Gibbs	not out	4		
Extras	(B 1, LB 2, NB 18)	21	(NB 1)	1
Total		**493**	(0 wickets)	**1**

WEST INDIES	O	M	R	W	O	M	R	W		FALL OF WICKETS			
										P	WI	P	WI
Roberts	25	3	81	2	16	0	54	1		*1st*	*1st*	*2nd*	*2nd*
Julien	11	0	51	1	16	7	37	1	*Wkt*				
Holder	19	2	66	2	6	3	19	0	1st	94	95	2	–
Boyce	12	1	60	0	3	0	15	1	2nd	144	136	11	–
Fredericks	1	0	10	0	12	3	39	1	3rd	167	151	61	–
Gibbs	26	4	89	3	37·1	19	49	2	4th	170	290	88	–
Richards					9	2	17	1	5th	178	336	90	–
									6th	246	391	148	–
PAKISTAN									7th	374	399	212	–
Asif Masood	15·2	2	76	2					8th	393	449	213	–
Sarfraz	21	1	106	1					9th	–	474	253	–
Liaquat	19	1	90	1					10th	–	493	256	–
Intikhab	28	1	122	3									
Mushtaq	15	4	56	1									
Wasim Raja	4·7	0	22	0									
Zaheer					1	1	0	0					

Umpires: Amanullah Khan (2) and Mahboob Shah (1).

Close: 1st day – P(1) 271-6 (Wasim Raja 40, Wasim Bari 14); 2nd – P(1) 406-8 (Wasim Raja 107, Asif Masood 5); 3rd – WI(1) 319-4 (Kallicharran 103, Murray 7); 4th – P(2) 90-4 (Asif Iqbal 51, Wasim Bari 0).

Test No. 758/46

NEW ZEALAND v ENGLAND 1974–75 (1st Test)

Played at Eden Park, Auckland, on 20, 21, 22, 23, 25 February.
Toss: England.   Result: ENGLAND won by an innings and 83 runs.
Debuts: New Zealand – E.J. Chatfield, G.P. Howarth.

The match ended after 47 minutes of play on the fifth morning when Chatfield deflected a bouncer from Lever into his left temple and collapsed unconscious with a hairline fracture of the skull. Chatfield's heart stopped beating for several seconds and only heart massage and mouth-to-mouth resuscitation by Bernard Thomas, the MCC physiotherapist, saved his life. England's total is the highest by either country in this series. Wood, who arrived three days earlier after a 63-hour flight from the West Indies, was out first ball. Denness (414 minutes, 25 fours) and Fletcher (443 minutes, 30 fours) added 266 runs to set a new record for the fourth wicket in this series. Greig took his 100th wicket in 37 official Tests when he dismissed Howarth and became the third player after W. Rhodes and T.E. Bailey to score 2,000 runs and take 100 wickets for England.

ENGLAND

D.L. Amiss	c Wadsworth b Hadlee	19
B. Wood	c Parker b Hadlee	0
J.H. Edrich	c Congdon b H.J. Howarth	64
M.H. Denness*	c Parker b Congdon	181
K.W.R. Fletcher	c Hadlee b Congdon	216
A.W. Greig	b G.P. Howarth	51
A.P.E. Knott†	not out	29
C.M. Old	not out	9
D.L. Underwood	)	
G.G. Arnold	) did not bat	
P. Lever	)	
Extras	(B 2, LB 14, NB 8)	24
Total	(6 wickets declared)	**593**

NEW ZEALAND

J.F.M. Morrison	c Amiss b Greig	58		c Fletcher b Greig	58
G.M. Turner	c Amiss b Arnold	8		c Knott b Lever	2
J.M. Parker	c Knott b Underwood	121	(5)	c Edrich b Greig	13
B.E. Congdon*	c Old b Greig	2	(3)	b Underwood	18
B.F. Hastings	c Knott b Old	13	(4)	c Amiss b Lever	0
G.P. Howarth	c Wood b Greig	6		not out	51
K.J. Wadsworth†	lbw b Underwood	58		c Fletcher b Underwood	6
D.R. Hadlee	c sub (B.W. Luckhurst) b Underwood	22		c Edrich b Greig	1
H.J. Howarth	c Fletcher b Greig	9		b Greig	4
R.O. Collinge	not out	0		c Fletcher b Greig	0
E.J. Chatfield	c Fletcher b Greig	0		retired hurt	13
Extras	(B 5, LB 4, NB 20)	29		(LB 6, NB 12)	18
Total		**326**			**184**

NEW ZEALAND	O	M	R	W	O	M	R	W
Collinge	24	6	75	0				
Hadlee	20	2	102	2				
Chatfield	19	2	95	0				
Congdon	30	3	115	2				
H.J. Howarth	46	9	135	1				
G.P. Howarth	14	1	47	1				
ENGLAND								
Arnold	20	4	69	1	6	1	31	0
Lever	20	4	75	0	11·5	0	37	2
Greig	26	4	98	5	15	3	51	5
Underwood	16	6	38	3	25	9	47	2
Old	7	3	17	1				

FALL OF WICKETS

	E	NZ	NZ
Wkt	1st	1st	2nd
1st	4	9	3
2nd	36	125	42
3rd	153	131	46
4th	419	166	99
5th	497	173	102
6th	578	285	131
7th	–	315	134
8th	–	326	140
9th	–	326	140
10th	–	326	–

Umpires: D.E.A. Copps (8) and W.R.C. Gardiner (2).

Close: 1st day – E(1) 319-3 (Denness 149, Fletcher 76); 2nd – NZ(1) 31-1 (Morrison 7, Parker 9); 3rd – NZ(1) 285-5 (Parker 121, Wadsworth 49); 4th – NZ(2) 161-9 (G.P. Howarth 38, Chatfield 4).

NEW ZEALAND v ENGLAND 1974–75 (2nd Test)

Played at Lancaster Park, Christchurch, on 28 February *(no play)*, 1 *(no play)*, 2, 3, 4, 5 *(no play)*
  March.
Toss: England.   Result: MATCH DRAWN.
Debuts: Nil.

To compensate for the loss of the first two days to rain, play began, after an early lunch, on the scheduled rest
day. Morrison was out to the first ball of the match – the first New Zealand batsman to suffer this fate. Arnold,
who dismissed S.M. Gavaskar with the first ball of *Test No. 741*, is the only bowler to achieve this feat twice
in Tests.

NEW ZEALAND

J.F.M. Morrison	c Hendrick b Arnold	0
G.M. Turner	lbw b Arnold	98
B.E. Congdon*	c Wood b Hendrick	38
B.F. Hastings	c Wood b Lever	0
J.M. Parker	c Edrich b Greig	41
G.P. Howarth	b Underwood	11
K.J. Wadsworth†	c Lever b Greig	58
D.R. Hadlee	c Greig b Arnold	22
B.L. Cairns	c and b Hendrick	39
H.J. Howarth	lbw b Underwood	9
R.O. Collinge	not out	0
Extras	(B 3, LB 9, W 1, NB 13)	26
Total		**342**

ENGLAND

D.L. Amiss	not out	164
B. Wood	c Wadsworth b Hadlee	33
J.H. Edrich	c Hadlee b H.J. Howarth	11
M.H. Denness*	not out	59
K.W.R. Fletcher	)	
A.W. Greig	)	
A.P.E. Knott†	)	
D.L. Underwood	) did not bat	
G.G. Arnold	)	
P. Lever	)	
M. Hendrick	)	
Extras	(LB 3, NB 2)	5
Total	(2 wickets)	**272**

ENGLAND	O	M	R	W
Arnold	25	5	80	3
Lever	18	2	66	1
Hendrick	20	2	89	2
Underwood	13·5	3	·35	2
Greig	9	1	27	2
Wood	4	0	19	0
NEW ZEALAND				
Collinge	19	3	63	0
Hadlee	19	2	61	1
Cairns	13	5	44	0
Congdon	7	2	27	0
H.J. Howarth	18	5	53	1
G.P. Howarth	7	0	19	0

FALL OF WICKETS

Wkt	NZ 1st	E 1st
1st	0	80
2nd	64	121
3rd	66	–
4th	181	–
5th	208	–
6th	212	–
7th	267	–
8th	318	–
9th	338	–
10th	342	–

Umpires: D.E.A. Copps (9) and W.R.C. Gardiner (3).

Close: 1st day – no play; 2nd – no play; 3rd – NZ(1) 140-3 (Turner 62, Parker 21); 4th – E(1) 57-0 (Amiss 33,
Wood 24); 5th – E(1) 272-2 (Amiss 164, Denness 59).

ENGLAND v AUSTRALIA 1975 (1st Test)

Played at Edgbaston, Birmingham, on 10, 11, 12, 14 July.
Toss: England. Result: AUSTRALIA won by an innings and 85 runs.
Debuts: England – G.A. Gooch; Australia – A. Turner.

This four-match rubber was played after the first Prudential World Cup competition. Australia's victory, completed at 3.05 on the fourth afternoon, was the first by any visiting country in a Test at Edgbaston. Denness became the first England captain to elect to field in a Birmingham Test. A thunderstorm at 2.55 on the second afternoon, after England had batted for one over, provided the Australian bowlers with a rain-affected pitch. A.S.M. Oakman, formerly a first-class umpire, deputised for H.D. Bird (injured back) after tea on the third day. T.W. Spencer took his place on the fourth day. In the second innings, Amiss (2) ducked into a short ball from Lillee, retired at 7 with a bruised left elbow, and returned at 100. Gooch bagged a 'pair' in his first Test.

AUSTRALIA

R.B. McCosker	b Arnold	59
A. Turner	c Denness b Snow	37
I.M. Chappell*	c Fletcher b Snow	52
G.S. Chappell	lbw b Old	0
R. Edwards	c Gooch b Old	56
K.D. Walters	c Old b Greig	14
R.W. Marsh†	c Fletcher b Arnold	61
M.H.N. Walker	c Knott b Snow	7
J.R. Thomson	c Arnold b Underwood	49
D.K. Lillee	c Knott b Arnold	3
A.A. Mallett	not out	3
Extras	(B 1, LB 8, NB 9)	18
Total		**359**

ENGLAND

J.H. Edrich	lbw b Lillee	34	c Marsh b Walker		5
D.L. Amiss	c Thomson b Lillee	4	c sub (G.J. Gilmour) b Thomson		5
K.W.R. Fletcher	c Mallett b Walker	6	c Walters b Lillee		51
M.H. Denness*	c G.S. Chappell b Walker	3	b Thomson		8
G.A. Gooch	c Marsh b Walker	0	c Marsh b Thomson		0
A.W. Greig	c Marsh b Walker	8	c Marsh b Walker		7
A.P.E. Knott†	b Lillee	14	c McCosker b Thomson		38
D.L. Underwood	b Lillee	10	(10) b Mallett		3
C.M. Old	c G.S. Chappell b Walker	13	(8) c Walters b Lillee		7
J.A. Snow	lbw b Lillee	0	(9) c Marsh b Thomson		34
G.G. Arnold	not out	0	not out		6
Extras	(LB 3, W 5, NB 1)	9	(LB 5, W 2, NB 2)		9
Total		**101**			**173**

ENGLAND	O	M	R	W	O	M	R	W
Arnold	33	3	91	3				
Snow	33	6	86	3				
Old	33	7	111	2				
Greig	15	2	43	1				
Underwood	7	3	10	1				
AUSTRALIA								
Lillee	15	8	15	5	20	8	45	2
Thomson	10	3	21	0	18	8	38	5
Walker	17·3	5	48	5	24	9	47	2
Mallett	3	1	8	0	13·2	6	34	1

FALL OF WICKETS

Wkt	A 1st	E 1st	E 2nd
1st	80	9	7
2nd	126	24	18
3rd	135	46	20
4th	161	46	52
5th	186	54	90
6th	265	75	100
7th	286	78	122
8th	332	87	151
9th	343	97	167
10th	359	101	173

Umpires: H.D. Bird (6) and A.E. Fagg (17) (A.S.M. Oakman and T.W. Spencer deputised).

Close: 1st day – A(1) 243-5 (Edwards 22, Marsh 47); 2nd – E(1) 83-7 (Underwood 8, Old 0); 3rd – E(2) 93-5 (Knott 10, Old 2).

ENGLAND v AUSTRALIA 1975 (2nd Test)

Played at Lord's, London, on 31 July, 1, 2, 4, 5 August.
Toss: England.   Result: MATCH DRAWN.
Debuts: England – D.S. Steele, R.A. Woolmer.

Australia were set to score 484 runs in a minimum of 500 minutes. Lillee faced 103 balls and hit three sixes and eight fours in what remained the highest score of his first-class career. Edrich batted 538 minutes, faced 420 balls and hit 21 fours in compiling the highest of his seven hundreds against Australia; it was the last of his 12 Test centuries. Thomson was no-balled 22 times on the first day, and also conceded four wides. Michael Angelow, a cook in the Merchant Navy, became the first streaker to intrude upon the field of play during a Test in England. With perfect timing he hurdled over each set of stumps at 3.20 on the fourth afternoon while John Arlott was commentating for BBC Radio's 'Test Match Special'. Earlier, Steele (33) had followed up his 163-minute half-century by dismissing Mallett with his fourth ball in Test cricket.

ENGLAND

B. Wood	lbw b Lillee	6	c Marsh b Thomson	52
J.H. Edrich	lbw b Lillee	9	c Thomson b Mallett	175
D.S. Steele	b Thomson	50	c and b Walters	45
D.L. Amiss	lbw b Lillee	0	c G.S. Chappell b Lillee	10
G.A. Gooch	c Marsh b Lillee	6	b Mallett	31
A.W. Greig*	c I.M. Chappell b Walker	96	c Walters b I.M. Chappell	41
A.P.E. Knott†	lbw b Thomson	69	not out	22
R.A. Woolmer	c Turner b Mallett	33	b Mallett	31
J.A. Snow	c Walker b Mallett	11		
D.L. Underwood	not out	0		
P. Lever	lbw b Walker	4		
Extras	(B 3, LB 1, W 4, NB 23)	31	(LB 18, W 2, NB 9)	29
Total		**315**	(7 wickets declared)	**436**

AUSTRALIA

R.B. McCosker	c and b Lever	29	lbw b Steele	79
A. Turner	lbw b Snow	9	c Gooch b Greig	21
I.M. Chappell*	c Knott b Snow	2	lbw b Greig	86
G.S. Chappell	lbw b Snow	4	not out	73
R. Edwards	lbw b Woolmer	99	not out	52
K.D. Walters	c Greig b Lever	2		
R.W. Marsh†	c Amiss b Greig	3		
M.H.N. Walker	b Snow	5		
J.R. Thomson	b Underwood	17		
D.K. Lillee	not out	73		
A.A. Mallett	lbw b Steele	14		
Extras	(LB 5, NB 6)	11	(B 4, NB 14)	18
Total		**268**	(3 wickets)	**329**

AUSTRALIA	O	M	R	W	O	M	R	W		FALL OF WICKETS			
Lillee	20	4	84	4	33	10	80	1		E	A	E	A
Thomson	24	7	92	2	29	8	73	1	*Wkt*	*1st*	*1st*	*2nd*	*2nd*
Walker	21·4	7	52	2	37	8	95	0	1st	10	21	111	50
Mallett	22	4	56	2	36·4	10	127	3	2nd	29	29	215	169
I.M. Chappell					10	2	26	1	3rd	31	37	249	222
Walters					2	0	6	1	4th	49	54	315	–
									5th	145	56	380	–
ENGLAND									6th	222	64	387	–
Snow	21	4	66	4	19	3	82	0	7th	288	81	436	–
Lever	15	0	83	2	20	5	55	0	8th	309	133	–	–
Woolmer	13	5	31	1	3	1	3	0	9th	310	199	–	–
Greig	15	5	47	1	26	6	82	2	10th	315	268	–	–
Underwood	13	5	29	1	31	14	64	0					
Steele	0·4	0	1	1	9	4	19	1					
Wood					1	0	6	0					

Umpires: W.E. Alley (3) and T.W. Spencer (11).

Close: 1st day – E(1) 313-9 (Underwood 0, Lever 2); 2nd – E(2) 5-0 (Wood 5, Edrich 0); 3rd – E(2) 230-2 (Edrich 104, Amiss 6); 4th – A(2) 97-1 (McCosker 46, I.M. Chappell 25).

ENGLAND v AUSTRALIA 1975 (3rd Test)

Played at Headingley, Leeds, on 14, 15, 16, 18, 19 (*no play*) August.
Toss: England.   Result: MATCH DRAWN.
Debuts: England – P.H. Edmonds.

This match was abandoned as a draw after vandals, campaigning for the release from prison of a convicted criminal, sabotaged the rugby ground end of the pitch with knives and oil. Rain, which fell from noon until 4.00 pm, would probably have produced the same result. The day should have started with Australia needing 225 runs to win with seven wickets to fall, and with McCosker five runs short of his first Test hundred. Edmonds took five wickets, including those of Ian Chappell and Edwards with successive balls, in his first Test innings. In the second innings of his 57th match, Underwood became the fourth bowler after A.V. Bedser, F.S. Trueman, and J.B. Statham to take 200 wickets in official Tests for England.

ENGLAND

B. Wood	lbw b Gilmour	9		lbw b Walker	25
J.H. Edrich	c Mallett b Thomson	62		b Mallett	35
D.S. Steele	c Walters b Thomson	73		c G.S. Chappell b Gilmour	92
J.H. Hampshire	lbw b Gilmour	14	(7)	c G.S. Chappell b Thomson	0
K.W.R. Fletcher	c Mallett b Lillee	8	(4)	c G.S. Chappell b Lillee	14
A.W. Greig*	run out	51	(5)	c and b Mallett	49
A.P.E. Knott†	lbw b Gilmour	14	(8)	c Thomson b Lillee	31
P.H. Edmonds	not out	13	(9)	c sub (A. Turner) b Gilmour	8
C.M. Old	b Gilmour	5	(6)	st Marsh b Mallett	10
J.A. Snow	c Walters b Gilmour	0		c Marsh b Gilmour	9
D.L. Underwood	c G.S. Chappell b Gilmour	0		not out	0
Extras	(B 4, LB 15, W 11, NB 9)	39		(B 5, LB 2, W 2, NB 9)	18
Total		**288**			**291**

AUSTRALIA

R.B. McCosker	c Hampshire b Old	0		not out	95
R.W. Marsh†	b Snow	25		b Underwood	12
I.M. Chappell*	b Edmonds	35		lbw b Old	62
G.S. Chappell	c Underwood b Edmonds	13		c Steele b Edmonds	12
R. Edwards	lbw b Edmonds	0			
K.D. Walters	lbw b Edmonds	19	(5)	not out	25
G.J. Gilmour	c Greig b Underwood	6			
M.H.N. Walker	c Old b Edmonds	0			
J.R. Thomson	c Steele b Snow	16			
D.K. Lillee	b Snow	11			
A.A. Mallett	not out	1			
Extras	(LB 5, W 1, NB 3)	9		(B 4, LB 8, NB 2)	14
Total		**135**		(3 wickets)	**220**

AUSTRALIA	O	M	R	W	O	M	R	W		FALL OF WICKETS			
Lillee	28	12	53	1	20	5	48	2		E	A	E	A
Thomson	22	8	53	2	20	6	67	1	Wkt	1st	1st	2nd	2nd
Gilmour	31·2	10	85	6	20	5	72	3	1st	25	8	55	55
Walker	18	4	54	0	15	4	36	1	2nd	137	53	70	161
I.M. Chappell	2	0	4	0					3rd	159	78	103	174
Mallett					19	4	50	3	4th	189	78	197	–
									5th	213	81	209	–
ENGLAND									6th	268	96	210	–
Snow	18·5	7	22	3	15	6	21	0	7th	269	104	272	–
Old	11	3	30	1	17	5	61	1	8th	284	107	276	–
Greig	3	0	14	0	9	3	20	0	9th	284	128	285	–
Wood	5	2	10	0					10th	288	135	291	–
Underwood	19	12	22	1	15	4	40	1					
Edmonds	20	7	28	5	17	4	64	1					

Umpires: D.J. Constant (9) and A.E. Fagg (18).

Close: 1st day – E(1) 251-5 (Greig 46, Knott 7); 2nd – A(1) 107-8 (Thomson 3, Lillee 0); 3rd – E(2) 184-3 (Steele 59, Greig 38); 4th – A(2) 220-3 (McCosker 95, Walters 25).

ENGLAND v AUSTRALIA 1975 (4th Test)

Played at Kennington Oval, London, on 28, 29, 30 August, 1, 2, 3 September.
Toss: Australia.   Result: MATCH DRAWN.
Debuts: Nil.

Following on 341 runs behind on the first innings, England scored their highest second innings total against Australia. The innings lasted 886 minutes. Woolmer took 394 minutes to reach his hundred, the slowest century of the series (previously 362 minutes by M.C. Cowdrey in 1958-59 in *Test No. 466*) until 1978-79 (*Test No. 834*). McCosker scored a hundred to compensate for the one he had been deprived of at Leeds, and shared with Ian Chappell a second-wicket partnership of 277 in 343 minutes. England's massive recovery left Australia with a minimum of 85 minutes to score 198 runs. This third and last six-day Test in England produced that country's longest first-class match. Actual playing time, excluding 187 minutes lost and breaks between innings, amounted to 32 hours 17 minutes.

AUSTRALIA

R.B. McCosker	c Roope b Old	127	not out	25
A. Turner	c Steele b Old	2	c Woolmer b Greig	8
I.M. Chappell*	c Greig b Woolmer	192		
G.S. Chappell	c Knott b Old	0	not out	4
R. Edwards	c Edrich b Snow	44	(3) c Old b Underwood	2
K.D. Walters	b Underwood	65		
R.W. Marsh†	c and b Greig	32		
M.H.N. Walker	c Steele b Greig	13		
J.R. Thomson	c Old b Greig	0		
D.K. Lillee	not out	28		
A.A. Mallett	not out	5		
Extras	(LB 5, W 2, NB 17)	24	(LB 1)	1
Total	(9 wickets declared)	**532**	(2 wickets)	**40**

ENGLAND

B. Wood	b Walker	32	lbw b Thomson	22
J.H. Edrich	lbw b Walker	12	b Lillee	96
D.S. Steele	b Lillee	39	c Marsh b Lillee	66
G.R.J. Roope	c Turner b Walker	0	b Lillee	77
R.A. Woolmer	c Mallett b Thomson	5	lbw b Walters	149
A.W. Greig*	c Marsh b Lillee	17	c Marsh b Lillee	15
A.P.E. Knott†	lbw b Walker	9	c Marsh b Walters	64
P.H. Edmonds	c Marsh b Thomson	4	(9) run out	7
C.M. Old	not out	25	(8) c I.M. Chappell b Walters	0
J.A. Snow	c G.S. Chappell b Thomson	30	c and b Walters	0
D.L. Underwood	c G.S. Chappell b Thomson	0	not out	3
Extras	(LB 3, W 3, NB 12)	18	(B 2, LB 15, W 5, NB 17)	39
Total		**191**		**538**

ENGLAND	O	M	R	W	O	M	R	W
Old	28	7	74	3	2	0	7	0
Snow	27	4	74	1	2	1	4	0
Woolmer	18	3	38	1				
Edmonds	38	7	118	0	6·1	2	14	0
Underwood	44	13	96	1	2	0	5	1
Greig	24	5	107	3	5	2	9	1
Steele	2	1	1	0				
AUSTRALIA								
Lillee	19	7	44	2	52	18	91	4
Thomson	22·1	7	50	4	30	9	63	1
Walker	25	7	63	4	46	15	91	0
Mallett	3	1	16	0	64	31	95	0
I.M. Chappell					17	6	52	0
Walters					10·5	3	34	4
G.S. Chappell					12	2	53	0
Edwards					2	0	20	0

FALL OF WICKETS

	A	E	E	A
Wkt	1st	1st	2nd	2nd
1st	7	45	77	22
2nd	284	78	202	33
3rd	286	83	209	–
4th	356	96	331	–
5th	396	103	371	–
6th	441	125	522	–
7th	477	131	522	–
8th	477	147	533	–
9th	501	190	533	–
10th	–	191	538	–

Umpires: H.D. Bird (7) and T.W. Spencer (12).

Close: 1st day – A(1) 280-1 (McCosker 126, I.M. Chappell 142); 2nd – E(1) 19-1 (Wood 16, Edrich 0); 3rd – E(1) 169-8 (Old 21, Snow 13); 4th – E(2) 179-1 (Edrich 91, Steele 52); 5th – E(2) 333-4 (Woolmer 37, Greig 1).

AUSTRALIA v WEST INDIES 1975–76 (1st Test)

Played at Woolloongabba, Brisbane, on 28, 29, 30 November, 2 December.
Toss: West Indies.   Result: AUSTRALIA won by eight wickets.
Debuts: West Indies – M.A. Holding.

Greg Chappell became the first player to score hundreds in both innings of his first Test as captain. He was the first Australian to achieve this feat twice in Test cricket having done so against New Zealand in 1973–74 (*Test No. 736*). He also made the winning hit with a day and 38 minutes to spare. Lillee took his 100th wicket in his 22nd Test when he dismissed Richards. The partnership of 198 between Rowe and Kallicharran is the highest for the fourth wicket by West Indies in this series. Inshan Ali (24) retired at 308 after being struck on his injured hand by a Thomson bouncer; he survived only one ball after resuming at 346.

WEST INDIES

R.C. Fredericks	c Marsh b Gilmour	46	c Marsh b Gilmour		7
C.G. Greenidge	lbw b Lillee	0	c McCosker b Gilmour		0
L.G. Rowe	run out	28	(4) c I.M. Chappell b Jenner		107
A.I. Kallicharran	c Turner b Lillee	4	(5) b Mallett		101
I.V.A. Richards	c Gilmour b Lillee	0	(7) run out		12
C.H. Lloyd*	c Marsh b Gilmour	7	c Redpath b Jenner		0
D.L. Murray†	c Mallett b Gilmour	66	(8) c and b Mallett		55
M.A. Holding	c G.S. Chappell b Gilmour	34	(3) c Turner b Lillee		19
Inshan Ali	c Redpath b Thomson	12	b Lillee		24
A.M.E. Roberts	c I.M. Chappell b Mallett	3	lbw b Lillee		3
L.R. Gibbs	not out	11	not out		4
Extras	(LB 1, NB 2)	3	(B 4, LB 15, W 5, NB 14)		38
Total		**214**			**370**

AUSTRALIA

I.R. Redpath	run out	39			
A. Turner	b Roberts	81	b Gibbs		26
I.M. Chappell	lbw b Gibbs	41	not out		74
G.S. Chappell*	c Greenidge b Roberts	123	not out		109
R.B. McCosker	c Kallicharran b Ali	1	(1) c Murray b Roberts		2
R.W. Marsh†	c Murray b Gibbs	48			
G.J. Gilmour	c Lloyd b Gibbs	13			
T.J. Jenner	not out	6			
D.K. Lillee	b Roberts	1			
J.R. Thomson	lbw b Gibbs	4			
A.A. Mallett	c Fredericks b Gibbs	0			
Extras	(LB 5, NB 4)	9	(B 5, LB 2, NB 1)		8
Total		**366**	(2 wickets)		**219**

AUSTRALIA	O	M	R	W	O	M	R	W
Lillee	11	0	84	3	16	3	72	3
Thomson	10	0	69	1	18	3	89	0
Gilmour	12	1	42	4	11	4	26	2
Jenner	4	1	15	0	20	2	75	2
Mallett	0·5	0	1	1	21·4	6	70	2
WEST INDIES								
Roberts	25	2	85	3	14	2	47	1
Holding	20	4	81	0	10	0	46	0
Gibbs	38	7	102	5	20	8	48	1
Ali	17	1	67	1	10	0	57	0
Lloyd	6	1	22	0				
Fredericks					2	0	12	0
Kallicharran					0·2	0	1	0

FALL OF WICKETS

	WI	A	WI	A
Wkt	1st	1st	2nd	2nd
1st	3	99	6	7
2nd	63	142	12	60
3rd	70	178	50	–
4th	70	195	248	–
5th	81	317	248	–
6th	99	350	269	–
7th	171	354	275	–
8th	199	361	346	–
9th	199	366	348	–
10th	214	366	370	–

Umpires: R.C. Bailhache (7) and T.F. Brooks (14).

Close: 1st day – A(1) 94-0 (Redpath 38, Turner 55); 2nd – WI(2) 8-1 (Fredericks 4, Holding 0); 3rd – WI(2) 318-7 (Murray 17, Roberts 0).

AUSTRALIA v WEST INDIES 1975–76 (2nd Test)

Played at W.A.C.A. Ground, Perth, on 12, 13, 14, 16 December.
Toss: Australia.   Result: WEST INDIES won by an innings and 87 runs.
Debuts: Nil.

West Indies won their first Test match in Perth and, at 12.29 pm on the fourth day, gained their first victory by an innings in this series. Ian Chappell became the fourth Australian after D.G. Bradman, R.N. Harvey and W.M. Lawry to score 5,000 runs in Test cricket. Playing in his 75th Test, Gibbs became the second bowler after F.S. Trueman to take 300 wickets. West Indies scored the (then) highest total in a Perth Test and their second-highest in this series. Fredericks batted 212 minutes and scored 169 runs off 145 balls with a six and 27 fours. He reached 50 in 45 minutes off 33 balls and 100 in 116 minutes off 71 balls. Kallicharran retired when 46 (at 271) to spend a night in hospital after fracturing his nose attempting to hook a bouncer from Lillee. He resumed at 522. Lloyd took his score from 42 to 140 before lunch on the third day. Roberts achieved the best analysis for West Indies against Australia. Holding pulled a groin muscle and retired without completing his 11th over in the second innings.

AUSTRALIA

R.B. McCosker	lbw b Roberts	0	c Rowe b Roberts		13
A. Turner	c Gibbs b Roberts	23	c Murray b Roberts		0
I.M. Chappell	b Holding	156	c sub (C.G. Greenidge) b Roberts		20
G.S. Chappell*	c Murray b Julien	13	c Rowe b Roberts		43
I.R. Redpath	c Murray b Julien	33	lbw b Roberts		0
R.W. Marsh†	c Julien b Boyce	23	c Murray b Roberts		39
G.J. Gilmour	c Julien b Gibbs	45	c Fredericks b Roberts		3
M.H.N. Walker	c Richards b Holding	1	c sub (C.G. Greenidge) b Julien		3
D.K. Lillee	not out	12	c Lloyd b Julien		4
J.R. Thomson	b Holding	0	b Julien		9
A.A. Mallett	b Holding	0	not out		18
Extras	(B 12, LB 5, NB 6)	23	(B 13, LB 2, NB 2)		17
Total		**329**			**169**

WEST INDIES

R.C. Fredericks	c G.S. Chappell b Lillee	169
B.D. Julien	c Mallett b Gilmour	25
L.G. Rowe	c Marsh b Thomson	19
A.I. Kallicharran	c I.M. Chappell b Walker	57
I.V.A. Richards	c Gilmour b Thomson	12
C.H. Lloyd*	b Gilmour	149
D.L. Murray†	c Marsh b Lillee	63
M.A. Holding	c Marsh b Thomson	0
K.D. Boyce	not out	49
A.M.E. Roberts	b Walker	0
L.R. Gibbs	run out	13
Extras	(B 2, LB 16, NB 11)	29
Total		**585**

WEST INDIES	O	M	R	W	O	M	R	W
Roberts	13	1	65	2	14	3	54	7
Boyce	12	2	53	1	2	0	8	0
Holding	18·7	1	88	4	10·6	1	53	0
Julien	12	0	51	2	10·1	1	32	3
Gibbs	14	4	49	1	3	1	3	0
Fredericks					1	0	2	0

AUSTRALIA	O	M	R	W
Lillee	20	0	123	2
Thomson	17	0	128	3
Gilmour	14	0	103	2
Walker	17	1	99	2
Mallett	26	4	103	0
I.M. Chappell	1·4	1	0	0

FALL OF WICKETS

	A	WI	A
Wkt	1st	1st	2nd
1st	0	91	0
2nd	37	134	25
3rd	70	258	45
4th	149	297	45
5th	189	461	124
6th	277	461	128
7th	285	522	132
8th	329	548	142
9th	329	548	146
10th	329	585	169

Umpires: R.R. Ledwidge (1) and M.G. O'Connell (5).

Close: 1st day – A(1) 317-7 (I.M. Chappell 148, Lillee 9); 2nd – WI(1) 350-4 (Lloyd 42, Murray 21); 3rd – A(2) 104-4 (G.S. Chappell 32, Marsh 23).

AUSTRALIA v WEST INDIES 1975–76 (3rd Test)

Played at Melbourne Cricket Ground on 26, 27, 28, 30 December.
Toss: Australia.   Result: AUSTRALIA won by eight wickets.
Debuts: Australia – G.J. Cosier.

Australia won at 5.11 on the fourth evening. Ian Chappell became the first Australian to hold 100 catches in Test cricket when he caught Rowe at first slip. Cosier was the seventh batsman to score a hundred in his first Test innings for Australia and the first to achieve the feat in this series. Fredericks batted with a runner in the second innings.

WEST INDIES

Batsman	Dismissal	R	Dismissal (2nd)	R
R.C. Fredericks	c McCosker b Thomson	59	b G.S. Chappell	26
C.G. Greenidge	c Marsh b Thomson	3	c Marsh b Walker	8
L.G. Rowe	c I.M. Chappell b Thomson	0	c Marsh b Lillee	8
A.I. Kallicharran	c Marsh b Thomson	20	c Marsh b Lillee	32
I.V.A. Richards	b Lillee	41	c Marsh b Thomson	36
C.H. Lloyd*	c G.S. Chappell b Thomson	2	c Lillee b Mallett	102
D.L. Murray†	c Walker b Lillee	24	c Marsh b Lillee	22
B.D. Julien	c Mallett b Lillee	18	b Walker	27
V.A. Holder	b Walker	24	run out	15
A.M.E. Roberts	c Marsh b Lillee	6	c Mallett b I.M. Chappell	5
L.R. Gibbs	not out	0	not out	5
Extras	(LB 4, W 1, NB 22)	27	(B 8, LB 4, NB 14)	26
Total		**224**		**312**

AUSTRALIA

Batsman	Dismissal	R	Dismissal (2nd)	R
I.R. Redpath	b Roberts	102	(3) c sub (K.D. Boyce) b Julien	9
A. Turner	b Roberts	21	b Roberts	7
R.B. McCosker	c Murray b Julien	4	(1) not out	22
I.M. Chappell	c Kallicharran b Gibbs	35	not out	13
G.S. Chappell*	c Murray b Julien	52		
G.J. Cosier	c Kallicharran b Roberts	109		
R.W. Marsh†	c and b Gibbs	56		
M.H.N. Walker	c Murray b Roberts	1		
D.K. Lillee	c Richards b Holder	25		
J.R. Thomson	lbw b Julien	44		
A.A. Mallett	not out	3		
Extras	(B 5, LB 6, NB 22)	33	(LB 1, NB 3)	4
Total		**485**	(2 wickets)	**55**

AUSTRALIA	O	M	R	W	O	M	R	W
Lillee	14	2	56	4	15	1	70	3
Thomson	11	1	62	5	9	0	51	1
Walker	13	1	46	1	19	1	74	2
Cosier	4	0	15	0				
Mallett	5	1	18	0	14	0	61	1
G.S. Chappell					7	1	23	1
I.M. Chappell					5·2	3	7	1
WEST INDIES								
Roberts	32	2	126	4	3	0	19	1
Holder	27	2	123	1				
Julien	28·3	5	120	3	3	0	13	1
Gibbs	30	9	81	2				
Richards	1	0	2	0				
Greenidge					1	1	0	0
Rowe					1	0	6	0
Kallicharran					0·7	0	13	0

FALL OF WICKETS

Wkt	WI 1st	A 1st	WI 2nd	A 2nd
1st	22	49	14	23
2nd	22	61	48	36
3rd	91	151	48	–
4th	103	188	99	–
5th	108	302	151	–
6th	167	390	229	–
7th	172	392	278	–
8th	199	415	288	–
9th	218	471	297	–
10th	224	485	312	–

Umpires: R.C. Bailhache (8) and J.R. Collins (5).

Close: 1st day – A(1) 38-0 (Redpath 16, Turner 16); 2nd – A(1) 270-4 (G.S. Chappell 42, Cosier 44); 3rd – WI(2) 92-3 (Kallicharran 9, Richards 34).

AUSTRALIA v WEST INDIES 1975–76 (4th Test)

Played at Sydney Cricket Ground on 3, 4, 5, 7 January.
Toss: Australia.   Result: AUSTRALIA won by seven wickets.
Debuts: Australia – G.N. Yallop.

At 4.45 on the fourth afternoon Australia took a 3–1 lead in the six-match series and retained the Frank Worrell Trophy. Three West Indies players retired hurt during the first innings: Julien (7) fractured his right thumb at 15 and resumed batting one-handed at 286; Lloyd (0) was struck on the jaw at 166 and resumed at 233; and Holding (2) was hit in the face at 286 and resumed at 321. The umpires ruled that Holding, who had retired hurt off the last ball of the day, could not resume at the start of the next morning, but allowed Julien, who had also retired hurt, to return instead. The Law then allowed an injured player to resume his innings 'only on the fall of a wicket'. Walker, playing his 24th Test, took his 100th wicket when he dismissed Roberts in the first innings. Murray, who scored his 1,000th run in this Test, became the first West Indies player to make 100 dismissals and complete the wicket-keeper's 'double' when he caught Turner.

WEST INDIES

R.C. Fredericks	c I.M. Chappell b Thomson	48		c Turner b Gilmour	24
B.D. Julien	not out	46	(9)	lbw b Walker	8
A.I. Kallicharran	c Redpath b Thomson	9	(2)	c Walker b Thomson	7
L.G. Rowe	b Walker	67		c Marsh b Thomson	7
I.V.A. Richards	c I.M. Chappell b G.S. Chappell	44	(3)	c Thomson b Gilmour	2
C.H. Lloyd*	c Turner b Walker	51		c Marsh b Thomson	19
D.L. Murray†	c Thomson b Walker	32		b Thomson	50
K.D. Boyce	c and b Mallett	16		c Redpath b Thomson	0
M.A. Holding	hit wkt b Thomson	2	(5)	b Thomson	9
A.M.E. Roberts	c Marsh b Walker	4		b Walker	2
L.R. Gibbs	c Marsh b G.S. Chappell	5		not out	0
Extras	(B 5, LB 14, W 9, NB 3)	31			–
Total		**355**			**128**

AUSTRALIA

I.R. Redpath	c Murray b Holding	25		b Boyce	28
A. Turner	c Lloyd b Boyce	53		c Murray b Holding	15
G.N. Yallop	c Murray b Julien	16		not out	16
I.M. Chappell	c Murray b Holding	4		c sub (C.G. Greenidge) b Kallicharran	9
G.S. Chappell*	not out	182		not out	6
G.J. Cosier	b Holding	28			
R.W. Marsh†	c Gibbs b Julien	38			
G.J. Gilmour	run out	20			
M.H.N. Walker	c Lloyd b Roberts	8			
J.R. Thomson	c Richards b Roberts	0			
A.A. Mallett	lbw b Roberts	13			
Extras	(B 3, LB 8, W 2, NB 5)	18		(LB 4, W 4)	8
Total		**405**		(3 wickets)	**82**

AUSTRALIA	O	M	R	W	O	M	R	W		FALL OF WICKETS			
Thomson	25	5	117	3	15	4	50	6			WI	A	WI	A
Gilmour	13	2	54	0	12	4	40	2	*Wkt*	*1st*	*1st*	*2nd*	*2nd*
Walker	21	8	70	4	9·3	3	31	2	1st	44	70	23	45
Cosier	3	1	13	0					2nd	87	93	32	51
Mallett	13	4	50	1	1	0	2	0	3rd	160	103	33	67
G.S. Chappell	4·2	0	10	2	2	0	5	0	4th	213	103	47	–
I.M. Chappell	1	0	10	0					5th	233	202	52	–
									6th	259	319	95	–
WEST INDIES									7th	321	348	95	–
Roberts	20·6	3	94	3	4	1	12	0	8th	321	377	120	–
Holding	21	2	79	3	7	0	33	1	9th	346	377	126	–
Boyce	16	1	75	1	4	0	14	1	10th	355	405	128	–
Gibbs	18	3	52	0	1	0	4	0					
Julien	15	2	87	2									
Kallicharran					2	1	7	1					
Richards					0·1	0	4	0					

Umpires: T.F. Brooks (15) and R.R. Ledwidge (2).

Close: 1st day – WI(1) 286-6 (Lloyd 38, Holding 2); 2nd – A(1) 164-4 (G.S. Chappell 38, Cosier 19); 3rd – WI(2) 33-3 (Rowe 0, Holding 0).

AUSTRALIA v WEST INDIES 1975–76 (5th Test)

Played at Adelaide Oval on 23, 24, 26, 27, 28 January.
Toss: Australia.   Result: AUSTRALIA won by 190 runs.
Debuts: Nil.

Australia won the rubber at 11.43 on the fifth morning. Redpath, playing his 117th innings in 65 Tests, hit the only two sixes of his Test career. Gibbs (78 Tests) equalled the world record of F.S. Trueman (67 Tests) when he dismissed Mallett to take his 307th wicket. Boyce took his first innings score from 65 to 95 with last man Gibbs as his partner but was destined never to make a Test century.

AUSTRALIA

I.R. Redpath	b Gibbs	103	c Lloyd b Gibbs		65
A. Turner	b Boyce	26	c Richards b Gibbs		136
G.N. Yallop	c Richards b Holder	47	lbw b Holder		43
I.M. Chappell	lbw b Holder	42	run out		23
G.S. Chappell*	c Richards b Holder	4	not out		48
G.J. Cosier	c Murray b Holder	37			
R.W. Marsh†	b Roberts	24	(6) c Murray b Holder		1
G.J. Gilmour	c Holding b Gibbs	95	(7) c Fredericks b Holder		0
A.A. Mallett	c Fredericks b Holding	5	(8) c Murray b Gibbs		11
J.R. Thomson	c Murray b Holder	6			
D.K. Lillee	not out	16			
Extras	(B 1, LB 9, W 1, NB 2)	13	(LB 7, NB 11)		18
Total		**418**	(7 wickets declared)		**345**

WEST INDIES

R.C. Fredericks	lbw b Gilmour	0	lbw b Lillee		10
I.V.A. Richards	c Yallop b Thomson	30	b Lillee		101
L.G. Rowe	run out	7	c G.S. Chappell b Thomson		15
A.I. Kallicharran	lbw b Thomson	76	c Redpath b Mallett		67
C.H. Lloyd*	lbw b Lillee	6	b Mallett		5
D.L. Murray†	c Mallett b Lillee	18	c Marsh b Thomson		6
K.D. Boyce	not out	95	c sub (M.H.N. Walker) b Mallett	69
M.A. Holding	c Mallett b Thomson	8	c I.M. Chappell b Gilmour		10
V.A. Holder	lbw b Thomson	0	c Marsh b Gilmour		7
A.M.E. Roberts	c Redpath b I.M. Chappell	17	c and b Gilmour		0
L.R. Gibbs	b Gilmour	3	not out		0
Extras	(LB 1, NB 13)	14	(B 1, LB 2, W 1, NB 5)		9
Total		**274**			**299**

WEST INDIES	O	M	R	W	O	M	R	W
Roberts	12	1	54	1	4	0	24	0
Holding	22	3	126	1	14	0	55	0
Boyce	7	0	40	1	5	0	22	0
Holder	21	1	108	5	23	2	115	3
Gibbs	26	4	77	2	32·5	5	106	3
Fredericks					1	0	5	0
AUSTRALIA								
Gilmour	8·2	1	37	2	10·4	1	44	3
Thomson	11	0	68	4	13	2	66	2
Lillee	10	0	68	2	14	0	64	2
Cosier	5	0	23	0				
Mallett	5	0	37	0	20	3	91	3
I.M. Chappell	2	0	23	1	1	0	4	0
G.S. Chappell	1	0	4	0	5	0	21	0

FALL OF WICKETS

Wkt	A 1st	WI 1st	A 2nd	WI 2nd
1st	43	0	148	23
2nd	171	21	253	55
3rd	190	50	261	182
4th	199	78	302	189
5th	259	110	318	212
6th	272	149	318	216
7th	327	171	345	265
8th	355	171	–	285
9th	362	239	–	299
10th	418	274	–	299

Umpires: T.F. Brooks (16) and M.G. O'Connell (6).

Close: 1st day – A(1) 301-6 (Marsh 17, Gilmour 17); 2nd – WI(1) 274-9 (Boyce 95, Gibbs 3); 3rd – A(2) 302-4 (G.S. Chappell 19); 4th – WI(2) 257-6 (Boyce 36, Holding 9).

AUSTRALIA v WEST INDIES 1975–76 (6th Test)

Played at Melbourne Cricket Ground on 31 January, 1, 2, 4, 5 February.
Toss: Australia.   Result: AUSTRALIA won by 165 runs.
Debuts: Nil.

Australia won at 12.02 pm on the fifth day. West Indies lost five matches in a rubber for the first time. Gibbs became the leading wicket-taker in Test cricket when he had Redpath caught on the long-on boundary at 5.25 on the first evening and passed F.S. Trueman's record of 307 wickets. Gibbs ended his Test career with 309 wickets, average 29·09, in this his 79th match. Trueman bowled 15,178 balls; Gibbs took his 308th wicket with his 26,853rd ball, Marsh made 26 dismissals in the six-match rubber to equal the record set by J.H.B. Waite for South Africa in the five-match rubber against New Zealand in 1961-62.

AUSTRALIA

I.R. Redpath	c Holding b Gibbs	101	c sub (C.G. Greenidge) b Holder	70
A. Turner	c Gibbs b Holder	30	lbw b Boyce	21
R.B. McCosker	b Boyce	21	not out	109
I.M. Chappell	b Holder	1	c Holder b Boyce	31
G.S. Chappell*	c Boyce b Fredericks	68	not out	54
G.N. Yallop	c Holding b Boyce	57		
R.W. Marsh†	b Holding	7		
G.J. Gilmour	lbw b Gibbs	9		
A.A. Mallett	lbw b Boyce	16		
J.R. Thomson	lbw b Holder	0		
D.K. Lillee	not out	19		
Extras	(B 4, LB 11, NB 7)	22	(B 5, LB 9, NB 1)	15
Total		**351**	(3 wickets declared)	**300**

WEST INDIES

R.C. Fredericks	c Thomson b Gilmour	22	b Thomson	6
I.V.A. Richards	c Marsh b Lillee	50	c G.S. Chappell b Lillee	98
L. Baichan	c G.S. Chappell b Gilmour	3	b Thomson	20
A.I. Kallicharran	b Gilmour	4	c McCosker b Lillee	44
C.H. Lloyd*	c Redpath b Lillee	37	not out	91
L.G. Rowe	c Marsh b Gilmour	6	c Redpath b Mallett	6
D.L. Murray†	c Marsh b Lillee	1	c Marsh b Lillee	5
K.D. Boyce	lbw b Gilmour	0	c G.S. Chappell b Mallett	11
M.A. Holding	b Lillee	9	c Gilmour b Mallett	4
V.A. Holder	not out	14	b Thomson	22
L.R. Gibbs	c Marsh b Lillee	2	c Marsh b Thomson	0
Extras	(LB 5, W 1, NB 6)	12	(B 6, LB 10, NB 3)	19
Total		**160**		**326**

WEST INDIES	O	M	R	W	O	M	R	W
Boyce	17·2	1	75	3	19	2	74	2
Holding	16	4	51	1	1	0	2	0
Holder	20	2	86	3	18	0	81	1
Lloyd	7	2	20	0	4	1	14	0
Fredericks	6	0	29	1	3	1	14	0
Gibbs	24	4	68	2	26	3	62	0
Richards					7	0	38	0

AUSTRALIA	O	M	R	W	O	M	R	W
Thomson	9	0	51	0	12·5	0	80	4
Lillee	11·3	0	63	5	18	1	112	3
Gilmour	10	3	34	5	7	1	26	0
G.S. Chappell					2	0	6	0
I.M. Chappell					2	0	10	0
Mallett					13	1	73	3

FALL OF WICKETS

Wkt	A 1st	WI 1st	A 2nd	WI 2nd
1st	44	44	53	6
2nd	92	49	132	53
3rd	96	53	190	170
4th	220	99	–	175
5th	250	110	–	186
6th	261	113	–	199
7th	277	118	–	226
8th	317	140	–	238
9th	323	151	–	326
10th	351	160	–	326

Umpires: T.F. Brooks (17) and M.G. O'Connell (7).

Close: 1st day – A(1) 263-6 (Yallop 21, Gilmour 1); 2nd – WI(1) 32-0 (Fredericks 19, Richards 11); 3rd – A(2) 163-2 (McCosker 50, I.M. Chappell 11); 4th – WI(2) 248-8 (Lloyd 42, Holder 0).

NEW ZEALAND v INDIA 1975–76 (1st Test)

Played at Eden Park, Auckland, on 24, 25, 26, 28 January.
Toss: New Zealand.   Result: INDIA won by eight wickets.
Debuts: India – S. Amarnath, S.M.H. Kirmani, D.B. Vengsarkar.

India's second victory in successive Tests at Auckland was completed at 2.08 on the fourth afternoon, with more than a day and a half to spare. Surinder Amarnath became the fourth to score a hundred in his first Test innings for India and the first to achieve the feat in New Zealand. He was also the first to emulate his father by scoring a hundred in his first Test, Lala Amarnath having scored 118 in the second innings of India's first home Test in 1933-34 (*Test No. 230*). His partnership of 204 with Gavaskar is the highest for the second wicket by either side in this series. Prasanna's analysis of 8 for 76 is the best in any Auckland Test. His country's total of 414, his match figures of 11 for 140 and his second innings analysis are all Indian records for Tests in New Zealand. Gavaskar led India in B.S. Bedi's absence (leg injury).

NEW ZEALAND

J.F.M. Morrison	c and b Chandrasekhar	46	c Viswanath b Prasanna		23
G.M. Turner*	c Gavaskar b Chandrasekhar	23	c Madan Lal b Prasanna		13
B.E. Congdon	c Madan Lal b Prasanna	54	c Gavaskar b Prasanna		54
J.M. Parker	b Chandrasekhar	17	c Vengsarkar b Prasanna		70
B.F. Hastings	lbw b Prasanna	8	b Prasanna		1
M.G. Burgess	c Prasanna b Venkataraghavan	31	lbw b Chandrasekhar		6
K.J. Wadsworth†	c Gavaskar b Prasanna	41	b Chandrasekhar		19
D.R. Hadlee	b Chandrasekhar	24	c Vengsarkar b Prasanna		0
D.R. O'Sullivan	c S. Amarnath b Chandrasekhar	0	c S. Amarnath b Prasanna		1
H.J. Howarth	c and b Chandrasekhar	0	(11) not out		1
R.O. Collinge	not out	3	(10) c S. Amarnath b Prasanna		13
Extras	(B 5, LB 12, NB 2)	19	(B 4, LB 8, NB 2)		14
Total		**266**			**215**

INDIA

S.M. Gavaskar*	c Turner b Howarth	116	not out		35
D.B. Vengsarkar	lbw b Collinge	7	c Turner b Howarth		6
S. Amarnath	c sub (G.N. Edwards) b Hadlee	124	lbw b Howarth		9
G.R. Viswanath	c Wadsworth b Hadlee	0	not out		11
B.P. Patel	c Morrison b Congdon	10			
S. Venkataraghavan	c Congdon b Howarth	1			
M. Amarnath	b Congdon	64			
Madan Lal	c Turner b Congdon	27			
S.M.H. Kirmani†	b Congdon	14			
E.A.S. Prasanna	not out	25			
B.S. Chandrasekhar	b Congdon	0			
Extras	(B 13, LB 9, NB 4)	26	(B 7, NB 3)		10
Total		**414**	(2 wickets)		**71**

INDIA	O	M	R	W	O	M	R	W		FALL OF WICKETS			
Madan Lal	5	0	14	0	4	4	0	0		NZ	I	NZ	I
M. Amarnath	4	1	16	0	2	0	8	0	*Wkt*	*1st*	*1st*	*2nd*	*2nd*
Chandrasekhar	30	6	94	6	22·2	2	85	2	1st	38	16	32	38
Venkataraghavan	24	4	59	1	19	8	32	0	2nd	110	220	39	56
Prasanna	24	5	64	3	23	5	76	8	3rd	144	220	161	–
NEW ZEALAND									4th	145	270	169	–
Collinge	19	3	61	1	2	0	14	0	5th	155	270	180	–
Hadlee	18	3	71	2	3	0	15	0	6th	211	275	180	–
Congdon	26·7	3	65	5					7th	263	368	180	–
Howarth	29	6	97	2	5·2	3	15	2	8th	263	369	182	–
O'Sullivan	29	4	94	0	4	1	17	0	9th	263	414	214	–
									10th	266	414	215	–

Umpires: D.E.A. Copps (10) and R.L. Monteith (2).

Close: 1st day – I(1) 16-0 (Gavaskar 8, Vengsarkar 7); 2nd – I(1) 279-6 (M. Amarnath 8, Madan Lal 0); 3rd – NZ(2) 161-2 (Congdon 46, Parker 70).

NEW ZEALAND v INDIA 1975–76 (2nd Test)

Played at Lancaster Park, Christchurch, on 5, 6, 7 *(no play)*, 8, 9, 10 February.
Toss: India.   Result: MATCH DRAWN.
Debuts: New Zealand – A.D.G. Roberts.

When the third day (Saturday) was lost to rain, the scheduled rest day (Monday) became a playing day under the tour regulations. Kirmani equalled the Test match wicket-keeping record (then) of six dismissals in an innings, shared by A.T.W. Grout, D.T. Lindsay and J.T. Murray. During his third hundred in four Test innings at Christchurch (he scored 98 in the other one), Turner became the first to score 1,000 runs in a season of first-class cricket in New Zealand.

INDIA

S.M. Gavaskar	c Burgess b Collinge	22	c Howarth b D.R. Hadlee	71
D.B. Vengsarkar	c Wadsworth b Collinge	16	c Wadsworth b R.J. Hadlee	30
S. Amarnath	b Collinge	11	c Wadsworth b Collinge	21
G.R. Viswanath	c Turner b D.R. Hadlee	83	c Wadsworth b Roberts	79
B.P. Patel	c Burgess b Collinge	8	c Morrison b Parker	7
M. Amarnath	lbw b Congdon	45	c Wadsworth b Howarth	30
Madan Lal	c Wadsworth b D.R. Hadlee	5	not out	4
S.M.H. Kirmani†	lbw b Collinge	27	not out	1
E.A.S. Prasanna	c Roberts b D.R. Hadlee	1		
B.S. Bedi*	c Howarth b Collinge	30		
B.S. Chandrasekhar	not out	2		
Extras	(B 6, LB 4, NB 10)	20	(B 2, LB 3, W 1, NB 6)	12
Total		**270**	(6 wickets)	**255**

NEW ZEALAND

J.F.M. Morrison	lbw b Madan Lal	31
G.M. Turner*	c Kirmani b M. Amarnath	117
B.E. Congdon	st Kirmani b Bedi	58
J.M. Parker	c Bedi b M. Amarnath	44
M.G. Burgess	c and b Madan Lal	31
A.D.G. Roberts	lbw b Madan Lal	17
K.J. Wadsworth†	c Kirmani b Madan Lal	29
D.R. Hadlee	c Kirmani b Madan Lal	10
R.J. Hadlee	c Kirmani b M. Amarnath	33
R.O. Collinge	c Kirmani b M. Amarnath	0
H.J. Howarth	not out	8
Extras	(B 8, LB 14, LB 3)	25
Total		**403**

NEW ZEALAND	O	M	R	W	O	M	R	W		FALL OF WICKETS		
Collinge	16·6	0	63	6	14	1	36	1		I	NZ	I
R.J. Hadlee	12	1	75	0	14	2	64	1	*Wkt*	*1st*	*1st*	*2nd*
D.R. Hadlee	16	0	76	3	12	1	52	1	1st	32	56	60
Congdon	16	3	36	1	5	2	5	0	2nd	41	170	97
Howarth					22	7	48	1	3rd	52	254	138
Parker					5	2	24	1	4th	98	260	175
Roberts					5	1	12	1	5th	196	293	250
Burgess					2	1	2	0	6th	204	325	250
									7th	204	347	–
INDIA									8th	206	360	–
Madan Lal	43	9	134	5					9th	258	361	–
M. Amarnath	25·1	5	63	4					10th	270	403	–
Chandrasekhar	15	2	60	0								
Bedi	33	7	59	1								
Prasanna	16	1	62	0								

Umpires: D.E.A. Copps (11) and W.R.C. Gardiner (4).

Close: 1st day – NZ(1) 26-0 (Morrison 11, Turner 9); 2nd – NZ(1) 237-2 (Turner 101, Parker 39); 3rd – no play; 4th – NZ(1) 361-9 (R.J. Hadlee 5); 5th – I(2) 16-0 (Gavaskar 5, Vengsarkar 9).

NEW ZEALAND v INDIA 1975–76 (3rd Test)

Played at Basin Reserve, Wellington, on 13, 14, 15, 17 February.
Toss: India.   Result: NEW ZEALAND won by an innings and 33 runs.
Debuts: Nil.

New Zealand won this six-day match at 2.31 on the fourth afternoon to gain their ninth Test victory and their first by an innings. The partnership of 116 between Patel and Kirmani is India's highest for the seventh wicket in this series. On the third day, Bedi was confined to bed with a chill, Mohinder Amarnath (migraine) retired after starting his 19th over, and Gavaskar was taken to hospital for surgery after being hit on the right cheek-bone. In the second innings, India were dismissed for the lowest total by either country in this series. Richard John Hadlee returned the best innings (7 for 23) and match (11 for 58) analyses by a New Zealand bowler in Test cricket until 1985-86 when he surpassed them himself. They are also the records for any Test at Wellington. Wadsworth made the last of his 33 appearances for New Zealand, extending the national record for most wicket-keeping dismissals to 96. Six months later he died of cancer at the age of 29.

INDIA

S.M. Gavaskar	c Wadsworth b R.J. Hadlee	22		absent hurt	–
D.B. Vengsarkar	c Wadsworth b R.J. Hadlee	20	(1)	c Turnter b Collinge	4
S. Amarnath	c Roberts b R.J. Hadlee	2	(2)	c Burgess b R.J. Hadlee	27
G.R. Viswanath	c Turner b D.R. Hadlee	4	(3)	c Congdon b R.J. Hadlee	20
B.P. Patel	c Congdon b Cairns	81	(4)	c Wadsworth b R.J. Hadlee	3
M. Amarnath	lbw b Collinge	26	(5)	c Roberts b D.R. Hadlee	13
Madan Lal	b D.R. Hadlee	3		not out	2
S.M.H. Kirmani†	c Wadsworth b R.J. Hadlee	49	(6)	c Burgess b R.J. Hadlee	1
E.A.S. Prasanna	not out	0	(8)	b R.J. Hadlee	0
B.S. Bedi*	run out	2	(9)	b R.J. Hadlee	2
B.S. Chandrasekhar	b Cairns	0	(10)	b R.J. Hadlee	0
Extras	(LB 8, NB 3)	11		(B 5, LB 2, NB 2)	9
Total		**220**			**81**

NEW ZEALAND

G.M. Turner*	st Kirmani b Bedi	64
J.F.M. Morrison	c Kirmani b Madan Lal	12
B.E. Congdon	c Viswanath b Chandrasekhar	52
J.M. Parker	c Gavaskar b Bedi	5
M.G. Burgess	lbw b Madan Lal	95
A.D.G. Roberts	c Kirmani b Chandrasekhar	0
K.J. Wadsworth†	c Gavaskar b Bedi	10
B.L. Cairns	c sub(E.D. Solkar) b M. Amarnath	47
R.J. Hadlee	c Prasanna b Madan Lal	12
D.R. Hadlee	c Kirmani b Chandrasekhar	13
R.O. Collinge	not out	5
Extras	(LB 15, NB 4)	19
Total		**334**

NEW ZEALAND	O	M	R	W	O	M	R	W		FALL OF WICKETS		
Collinge	12	1	33	1	5	0	21	1		I	NZ	I
Cairns	20·7	2	57	2	4	1	9	0	*Wkt*	*1st*	*1st*	*2nd*
D.R. Hadlee	18	1	51	2	9	2	19	1	1st	40	55	10
R.J. Hadlee	14	1	35	4	8·3	0	23	7	2nd	46	103	46
Congdon	9	1	33	0					3rd	47	117	62
									4th	50	155	75
INDIA									5th	92	155	77
M. Amarnath	18·2	2	60	1					6th	101	180	77
Madan Lal	38	4	116	3					7th	217	270	77
Bedi	27	6	63	3					8th	218	301	79
Chandrasekhar	22·5	2	55	3					9th	220	324	81
Prasanna	8	2	21	0					10th	220	334	–

Umpires: W.R.C. Gardiner (5) and R.L. Monteith (3).

Close: 1st day – I(1) 220 all out; 2nd – NZ(1) 170-5 (Burgess 23, Wadsworth 4); 3rd – NZ(1) 333-9 (D.R. Hadlee 12, Collinge 5).

WEST INDIES v INDIA 1975–76 (1st Test)

Played at Kensington Oval, Bridgetown, Barbados, on 10, 11, 13 March.
Toss: India.   Result. WEST INDIES won by an innings and 97 runs.
Debuts: Nil.

West Indies won with two days and 12 minutes to spare to end a run of six drawn Tests at Bridgetown. They gained their largest margin of victory against India in a home Test. The partnership of 220 between Richards and Kallicharran is the highest for the third wicket by either side in this series. Lloyd, playing in his 50th Test match, scored his tenth hundred for West Indies.

INDIA

S.M. Gavaskar	lbw b Roberts	37	c Jumadeen b Roberts		1
P. Sharma	c Fredericks b Holding	6	c Murray b Holding		1
A.D. Gaekwad	c Murray b Julien	16	c Murray b Roberts		14
G.R. Viswanath	c Rowe b Holford	11	lbw b Roberts		62
S. Amarnath	c Richards b Holford	0	b Jumadeen		8
M. Amarnath	b Holding	26	c Rowe b Jumadeen		25
Madan Lal	b Holford	45	not out		55
S.M.H. Kirmani†	b Roberts	8	lbw b Holford		15
E.A.S. Prasanna	c Richards b Holford	3	absent hurt		–
B.S. Bedi*	c Julien b Holford	0	(9) c Murray b Jumadeen		10
B.S. Chandrasekhar	not out	1	(10) b Holding		0
Extras	(B 2, LB 7, NB 15)	24	(B 7, LB 3, NB 13)		23
Total		**177**			**214**

WEST INDIES

R.C. Fredericks	c M. Amarnath b Chandrasekhar	54
L.G. Rowe	lbw b Chandrasekhar	30
I.V.A. Richards	c Kirmani b M. Amarnath	142
A.I. Kallicharran	c Viswanath b M. Amarnath	93
C.H. Lloyd*	st Kirmani b Bedi	102
D.L. Murray†	b Bedi	27
D.A.J. Holford	c Kirmani b Chandrasekhar	9
B.D. Julien	not out	13
M.A. Holding	lbw b Chandrasekhar	0
A.M.E. Roberts	c S. Amarnath b Bedi	0
R.R. Jumadeen	did not bat	
Extras	(B 7, LB 7, NB 4)	18
Total	(9 wickets declared)	**488**

WEST INDIES	O	M	R	W	O	M	R	W
Roberts	11	2	48	2	14	4	51	3
Holding	15	10	24	2	13	6	22	2
Julien	15	5	46	1	4	2	8	0
Holford	8·1	1	23	5	17	1	52	1
Jumadeen	5	1	12	0	24	7	57	3
Fredericks					1	0	1	0
INDIA								
Madan Lal	16	1	61	0				
M. Amarnath	12	2	53	2				
Bedi	43·5	8	113	3				
Chandrasekhar	39	5	163	4				
Prasanna	24	2	66	0				
Gaekwad	4	0	14	0				

FALL OF WICKETS

	I	WI	I
Wkt	1st	1st	2nd
1st	51	58	4
2nd	57	108	9
3rd	74	328	40
4th	74	337	66
5th	103	417	117
6th	133	446	146
7th	162	482	184
8th	171	483	213
9th	176	488	214
10th	177	–	–

Umpires: S.E. Parris (2) and D. Sang Hue (22).

Close: 1st day – WI(1) 97-1 (Fredericks 45, Richards 14); 2nd – WI(1) 439-5 (Lloyd 73, Holford 5).

WEST INDIES v INDIA 1975–76 (2nd Test)

Played at Queen's Park Oval, Port-of-Spain, Trinidad, on 24 *(no play)*, 25, 27, 28, 29 March.
Toss: India. Result: MATCH DRAWN.
Debuts: Nil.

The partnership of 204 between Gavaskar and Patel was then India's highest for the fifth wicket against all countries. Gavaskar scored his third hundred in successive Test innings at Queen's Park Oval. Richards, who had strained a thigh muscle when fielding, retired hurt at 34 after facing five balls in the second innings, and resumed at 112. Fredericks was bowled by the second ball of the match.

WEST INDIES

R.C. Fredericks	b Madan Lal	0	lbw b Venkataraghavan		8
L.G. Rowe	b M. Amarnath	4	b Venkataraghavan		47
I.V.A. Richards	b Bedi	130	(4) run out		20
A.I. Kallicharran	c Madan Lal b Bedi	17	(5) c Venkataraghavan		
			b Chandrasekhar		12
C.H. Lloyd*	b Chandrasekhar	7	(6) c M. Amarnath b Bedi		70
D.L. Murray†	c Kirmani b Bedi	46	(7) c Vengsarkar b Bedi		9
B.D. Julien	run out	28	(8) not out		12
D.A.J. Holford	b Bedi	4	(9) b Bedi		0
M.A. Holding	c Viswanath b Bedi	1	(3) b Chandrasekhar		3
A.M.E. Roberts	c Vengsarkar b Chandrasekhar	1	not out		4
R.R. Jumadeen	not out	1			
Extras	(LB 1, NB 1)	2	(B 14, LB 15, NB 1)		30
Total		**241**	(8 wickets)		**215**

INDIA

S.M. Gavaskar	c Murray b Holding	156
D.B. Vengsarkar	c Murray b Roberts	0
M. Amarnath	c Murray b Jumadeen	19
G.R. Viswanath	c Murray b Holding	21
S. Amarnath	c Rowe b Jumadeen	21
B.P. Patel	not out	115
Madan Lal	not out	33
S. Venkataraghavan	)	
S.M.H. Kirmani†	) did not bat	
B.S. Bedi*	)	
B.S. Chandrasekhar	)	
Extras	(B 11, LB 10, NB 16)	37
Total	(5 wickets declared)	**402**

INDIA	O	M	R	W	O	M	R	W		FALL OF WICKETS		
										WI	I	WI
Madan Lal	9	3	16	1	4	2	2	0				
M. Amarnath	5	1	13	1	3	0	11	0	*Wkt*	*1st*	*1st*	*2nd*
Chandrasekhar	21	2	64	2	40	16	68	2	1st	0	1	23
Bedi	34	11	82	5	36	18	44	3	2nd	4	35	30
Venkataraghavan	28	5	64	0	41	19	60	2	3rd	39	77	52
									4th	52	126	112
WEST INDIES									5th	174	330	137
Roberts	28	6	77	1					6th	212	–	185
Holding	27	8	68	2					7th	236	–	188
Julien	30	7	63	0					8th	238	–	194
Jumadeen	42	12	79	2					9th	239	–	–
Richards	6	0	17	0					10th	241	–	–
Holford	20	5	51	0								
Lloyd	3	0	10	0								

Umpires: R. Gosein (14) and D. Sang Hue (23).

Close: 1st day – no play; 2nd – WI(1) 237-7 (Holford 3, Holding 1); 3rd – I(1) 217-4 (Gavaskar 90, Patel 42); 4th – WI(2) 29-1 (Rowe 16, Holding 2).

WEST INDIES v INDIA 1975–76 (3rd Test)

Played at Queen's Park Oval, Port-of-Spain, Trinidad, on 7, 8, 10, 11, 12 April.
Toss: West Indies.   Result: INDIA won by six wickets.
Debuts: West Indies – Imtiaz Ali, A.L. Padmore.

This match, scheduled for Georgetown, had to be moved to Trinidad because of incessant rain in Guyana. India achieved one of Test cricket's most remarkable victories; set to score 403 runs to win in a minimum of 595 minutes, India reached their target with seven of the mandatory last 20 overs to spare. Their total of 406 for 4 remains the highest in the fourth innings to win a Test match. There has been only one other instance of a side scoring over 400 in the fourth innings to win a Test: Australia scored 404 for 3 at Leeds in 1948 (*Test No. 302*). The partnership of 159 between Amarnath and Viswanath is India's highest for the third wicket against West Indies.

WEST INDIES

R.C. Fredericks	c Amarnath b Chandrasekhar	27	c Solkar b Chandrasekhar		25
L.G. Rowe	c Viswanath b Chandrasekhar	18	c Kirmani b Venkataraghavan		27
I.V.A. Richards	c Chandrasekhar b Bedi	177	c Solkar b Venkataraghavan		23
A.I. Kallicharran	b Chandrasekhar	0	not out		103
C.H. Lloyd*	c Gaekwad b Chandrasekhar	68	c Viswanath b Chandrasekhar		36
D.L. Murray†	b Chandrasekhar	11	c Solkar b Bedi		25
B.D. Julien	c Viswanath b Bedi	47	c Kirmani b Venkataraghavan		6
M.A. Holding	lbw b Bedi	1	not out		17
Imtiaz Ali	not out	1			
A.L. Padmore	c Gavaskar b Bedi	0			
R.R. Jumadeen	lbw b Chandrasekhar	0			
Extras	(LB 7, NB 2)	9	(B 1, LB 7, NB 1)		9
Total		**359**	(6 wickets declared)		**271**

INDIA

S.M. Gavaskar	lbw b Holding	26	c Murray b Jumadeen		102
A.D. Gaekwad	c Murray b Julien	6	c Kallicharran b Jumadeen		28
M. Amarnath	st Murray b Padmore	25	run out		85
G.R. Viswanath	b Ali	41	run out		112
E.D. Solkar	b Holding	13			
B.P. Patel	c Fredericks b Holding	29	(5) not out		49
Madan Lal	c Richards b Holding	42	(6) not out		1
S. Venkataraghavan	b Ali	13			
S.M.H. Kirmani†	lbw b Holding	12			
B.S. Bedi*	b Holding	0			
B.S. Chandrasekhar	not out	0			
Extras	(B 11, LB 6, W 4)	21	(B 8, LB 12, W 1, NB 8)		29
Total		**228**	(4 wickets)		**406**

INDIA	O	M	R	W	O	M	R	W
Madan Lal	6	1	22	0	11	2	14	0
Amarnath	5	0	26	0	11	3	19	0
Solkar	9	2	40	0				
Bedi	30	11	73	4	25	3	76	1
Chandrasekhar	32·2	8	120	6	27	5	88	2
Venkataraghavan	27	7	69	0	30·3	5	65	3
WEST INDIES								
Julien	13	4	35	1	13	3	52	0
Holding	26·4	3	65	6	21	1	82	0
Lloyd	1	0	1	0	6	1	22	0
Padmore	29	11	36	1	47	10	98	0
Ali	17	7	37	2	17	3	52	0
Jumadeen	16	7	33	0	41	13	70	2
Fredericks					2	1	1	0

FALL OF WICKETS

	WI	I	WI	I
Wkt	1st	1st	2nd	2nd
1st	45	22	41	69
2nd	50	50	78	177
3rd	52	52	86	336
4th	176	112	162	392
5th	227	147	214	–
6th	334	182	230	–
7th	357	203	–	–
8th	358	225	–	–
9th	358	227	–	–
10th	359	228	–	–

Umpires: R. Gosein (15) and C.F. Vyfhuis (2).

Close: 1st day – WI(1) 320-5 (Richards 151, Julien 37); 2nd – I(1) 169-5 (Patel 27, Madan Lal 13); 3rd – WI(2) 132-3 (Kallicharran 32, Lloyd 19); 4th – I(2) 134-1 (Gavaskar 86, Amarnath 14).

WEST INDIES v INDIA 1975–76 (4th Test)

Played at Sabina Park, Kingston, Jamaica, on 21, 22, 24, 25 April.
Toss: West Indies.   Result: WEST INDIES won by ten wickets.
Debuts: West Indies – W.W. Daniel.
West Indies won this six-day Test with over two days to spare and so gained a 2–1 victory in the rubber. The recently relaid pitch, with its unpredictable bounce which differed vastly at each end, encouraged a surfeit of short-pitched bowling, particularly from Holding. Three batsmen were injured in the first innings and took no further part in the match: Viswanath was dismissed by a ball that fractured and dislocated his right middle finger, Gaekwad was struck on the left ear and spent two days in hospital, and Patel had three stitches inserted in a cut in his mouth. Gaekwad retired at 237 and Patel at 273. Bedi declared his first innings closed as a protest against the intimidatory bowling. At the time it was thought that he also declared his second innings closed for the same reason. He later denied this, stating that neither he nor Chandrasekhar was fit to bat because of hand injuries sustained when fielding. India's second innings total, albeit with five men absent, is their lowest in the West Indies and the lowest in any Test at Kingston. All 17 members of the touring party fielded at some stage during the match; Surinder Amarnath, who fielded as substitute for much of the first innings, was operated on for appendicitis on the fourth day.

INDIA

S.M. Gavaskar	b Holding	66	c Julien b Holding	2
A.D. Gaekwad	retired hurt	81	absent hurt	–
M. Amarnath	c Julien b Holding	39	st Murray b Jumadeen	60
G.R. Viswanath	c Julien b Holding	8	absent hurt	–
D.B. Vengsarkar	b Holding	39	(2) lbw b Jumadeen	21
B.P. Patel	retired hurt	14	absent hurt	–
Madan Lal	lbw b Daniel	5	(4) b Holding	8
S. Venkataraghavan	lbw b Daniel	9	(5) b Holding	0
S.M.H. Kirmani†	not out	0	(6) not out	0
B.S. Bedi*	} did not bat		absent hurt	–
B.S. Chandrasekhar	}		absent hurt	–
Extras	(B 6, LB 6, W 12, NB 21)	45	(NB 6)	6
Total	(6 wickets declared)	**306**		**97**

WEST INDIES

R.C. Fredericks	run out	82	not out	6
L.G. Rowe	st Kirmani b Bedi	47	not out	6
I.V.A. Richards	b Chandrasekhar	64		
A.I. Kallicharran	b Chandrasekhar	12		
C.H. Lloyd*	c and b Chandrasekhar	0		
D.L. Murray†	c sub (E.D. Solkar) b Chandrasekhar	71		
B.D. Julien	b Chandrasekhar	5		
M.A. Holding	c sub (P. Sharma) b Bedi	55		
V.A. Holder	not out	36		
R.R. Jumadeen	c Gavaskar b Venkataraghavan	3		
W.W. Daniel	c Amarnath b Venkataraghavan	11		
Extras	(B 1, LB 2, NB 2)	5	(NB 1)	1
Total		**391**	(0 wickets)	**13**

WEST INDIES	O	M	R	W	O	M	R	W
Holding	28	7	82	4	7·2	0	35	3
Daniel	20·2	7	52	2	3	0	12	0
Julien	23	10	53	0	3	0	13	0
Holder	27	4	58	0	6	2	12	0
Jumadeen	3	1	8	0	7	3	19	2
Fredericks	3	1	8	0				
INDIA								
Madan Lal	7	1	25	0	1	0	5	0
Amarnath	8	1	28	0				
Chandrasekhar	42	7	153	5				
Bedi	32	10	68	2				
Venkataraghavan	51·3	12	112	2				
Vengsarkar					0·5	0	7	0

FALL OF WICKETS

Wkt	I 1st	WI 1st	I 2nd	WI 2nd
1st	136	105	5	–
2nd	205	186	68	–
3rd	216	197	97	–
4th	280	206	97	–
5th	306	209	97	–
6th	306	217	–	–
7th	–	324	–	–
8th	–	345	–	–
9th	–	352	–	–
10th	–	391	–	–

Umpires: R. Gosein (16) and D. Sang Hue (24).

Close: 1st day – I(1) 175-1 (Gaekwad 58, Amarnath 25); 2nd – WI(1) 82-0 (Fredericks 44, Rowe 37); 3rd – WI(1) 320-6 (Murray 54, Holding 53).

ENGLAND v WEST INDIES 1976 (1st Test)

Played at Trent Bridge, Nottingham, on 3, 4, 5, 7, 8 June.
Toss: West Indies.   Result: MATCH DRAWN.
Debuts: England – J.M. Brearley; West Indies – H.A. Gomes.

England needed to score 339 runs in 315 minutes to win. Richards scored his fifth Test hundred of 1976 and took his Test aggregate for the calendar year past 1,000 runs. He batted for 438 minutes, faced 313 balls, and hit four sixes and 31 fours. Both Richards and Steele scored hundreds in their first innings in this series. Knott, playing in his 74th Test, became the first to hold 200 catches when he dismissed Julien. Edrich scored his 5,000th run in 76 Tests. In the second innings, the umpires refused to allow the West Indies' twelfth man, C.L. King, to act as runner for Greenidge (injured leg). Gomes took his place for Greenidge's last ten runs. Old retired when 9, his left wrist bruised by a bouncer from Roberts, and returned at 279.

WEST INDIES

Batsman	Dismissal	R	Dismissal 2	R2
R.C. Fredericks	c Hendrick b Greig	42	b Snow	15
C.G. Greenidge	c Edrich b Hendrick	22	c and b Old	23
I.V.A. Richards	c Greig b Underwood	232	lbw b Snow	63
A.I. Kallicharran	c Steele b Underwood	97	(6) not out	29
C.H. Lloyd*	c Hendrick b Underwood	16	(4) c Brearley b Snow	21
B.D. Julien	c Knott b Old	21	(5) c Hendrick b Snow	13
H.A. Gomes	c Close b Underwood	0		
D.L. Murray†	c Close b Snow	19		
V.A. Holder	not out	19		
A.M.E. Roberts	b Old	1		
W.W. Daniel	c Knott b Old	4		
Extras	(LB 12, W 1, NB 8)	21	(LB 6, W 2, NB 4)	12
Total		**494**	(5 wickets declared)	**176**

ENGLAND

Batsman	Dismissal	R	Dismissal 2	R2
J.H. Edrich	c Murray b Daniel	37	not out	76
J.M. Brearley	c Richards b Julien	0	c Murray b Holder	17
D.S. Steele	c Roberts b Daniel	106	c Julien b Roberts	6
D.B. Close	c Murray b Daniel	2	not out	36
R.A. Woolmer	lbw b Julien	82		
A.W. Greig*	b Roberts	0		
A.P.E. Knott†	c sub (C.L. King) b Holder	9		
C.M. Old	b Daniel	33		
J.A. Snow	not out	20		
D.L. Underwood	c Murray b Holder	0		
M. Hendrick	c Daniel b Fredericks	5		
Extras	(B 5, LB 1, W 3, NB 29)	38	(B 9, W 2, NB 10)	21
Total		**332**	(2 wickets)	**156**

ENGLAND	O	M	R	W	O	M	R	W
Snow	31	5	123	1	11	2	53	4
Hendrick	24	7	59	1	7	2	22	0
Old	34·3	7	80	3	10	0	64	1
Greig	27	4	82	1	1	0	16	0
Woolmer	10	2	47	0				
Underwood	27	8	82	4	7	3	9	0
WEST INDIES								
Roberts	34	15	53	1	9	3	20	1
Julien	34	9	75	2	16	8	19	0
Holder	25	5	66	2	12	6	12	1
Daniel	23	8	53	4	10	2	20	0
Fredericks	8·4	2	24	1	9	1	21	0
Richards	3	1	8	0	3	1	7	0
Gomes	4	1	8	0	9	1	18	0
Lloyd	3	1	7	0				
Kallicharran					10	3	18	0

FALL OF WICKETS

Wkt	WI 1st	E 1st	WI 2nd	E 2nd
1st	36	0	33	38
2nd	105	98	77	55
3rd	408	105	109	–
4th	423	226	124	–
5th	432	229	176	–
6th	432	255	–	–
7th	458	278	–	–
8th	481	279	–	–
9th	488	318	–	--
10th	494	332	–	–

Umpires: H.D. Bird (8) and T.W. Spencer (13).

Close: 1st day – WI(1) 274-2 (Richards 143, Kallicharran 52); 2nd – E(1) 0-0 (Edrich 0, Brearley 0); 3rd – E(1) 221-3 (Steele 105, Woolmer 52); 4th – WI(2) 124-3 (Richards 42, Julien 13).

ENGLAND v WEST INDIES 1976 (2nd Test)

Played at Lord's, London, on 17, 18, 19 *(no play)*, 21, 22 June.
Toss: England.   Result: MATCH DRAWN.
Debuts: Nil.

West Indies needed 323 runs to win in a minimum of 294 minutes. Lloyd claimed the last half hour when West Indies were 210 for 2 with 11 overs left but wanted to end the match when he was out (233 for 4) with 6·5 overs left. Greig insisted on continuing into the last of the mandatory 20 overs of the final hour and captured two more wickets. Wood (10) retired at 19 after twice being struck on the right hand by balls from Roberts in the second innings, and resumed at 207.

ENGLAND

B. Wood	c Murray b Roberts	6	c Murray b Holding	30
J.M. Brearley	b Roberts	40	b Holding	13
D.S. Steele	lbw b Roberts	7	(4) c Jumadeen b Roberts	64
D.B. Close	c Holder b Jumadeen	60	(5) c and b Holder	46
R.A. Woolmer	c Murray b Holding	38	(6) c Murray b Roberts	29
A.W. Greig*	c Lloyd b Roberts	6	(7) c Gomes b Holder	20
A.P.E. Knott†	b Holder	17	(8) lbw b Roberts	4
C.M. Old	b Holder	19	(9) run out	13
J.A. Snow	b Roberts	0	(10) not out	6
D.L. Underwood	b Holder	31	(11) b Roberts	2
P.I. Pocock	not out	0	(3) c Jumadeen b Roberts	3
Extras	(B 7, LB 5, W 5, NB 9)	26	(B 7, LB 7, NB 10)	24
Total		**250**		**254**

WEST INDIES

R.C. Fredericks	c Snow b Old	0	c Greig b Old	138
C.G. Greenidge	c Snow b Underwood	84	c Close b Pocock	22
H.A. Gomes	c Woolmer b Snow	11	(7) b Underwood	0
A.I. Kallicharran	c Old b Snow	0	(3) b Greig	34
C.H. Lloyd*	c Knott b Underwood	50	(4) b Greig	33
D.L. Murray†	b Snow	2	not out	7
B.D. Julien	lbw b Snow	3	(5) b Underwood	1
M.A. Holding	b Underwood	0		
V.A. Holder	c Woolmer b Underwood	12	(8) not out	0
A.M.E. Roberts	b Underwood	16		
R.R. Jumadeen	not out	0		
Extras	(B 2, NB 2)	4	(B 3, LB 2, NB 1)	6
Total		**182**	(6 wickets)	**241**

WEST INDIES	O	M	R	W	O	M	R	W
Roberts	23	6	60	5	29·5	10	63	5
Holding	19	4	52	1	27	10	56	2
Julien	23	6	54	0	13	5	20	0
Holder	18·4	7	35	3	19	2	50	2
Jumadeen	12	4	23	1	16	4	41	0
ENGLAND								
Old	10	0	58	1	14	4	46	1
Snow	19	3	68	4	7	2	22	0
Underwood	18·4	7	39	5	24·3	8	73	2
Pocock	3	0	13	0	27	9	52	1
Greig					14	3	42	2

FALL OF WICKETS

	E	WI	E	WI
Wkt	1st	1st	2nd	2nd
1st	15	0	29	41
2nd	31	28	29	154
3rd	115	40	112	230
4th	153	139	169	233
5th	161	141	186	238
6th	188	145	207	238
7th	196	146	215	–
8th	197	153	245	–
9th	249	178	249	–
10th	250	182	254	–

Umpires: H.D. Bird (9) and D.J. Constant (10).

Close: 1st day – E(1) 197-8 (Old 0); 2nd – E(2) 27-0 (Brearley 12, Pocock 2); 3rd – no play; 4th – E(2) 223-7 (Wood 14, Old 7).

ENGLAND v WEST INDIES 1976 (3rd Test)

Played at Old Trafford, Manchester, on 8, 9, 10, 12, 13 July.
Toss: West Indies.   Result: WEST INDIES won by 425 runs.
Debuts: England – M.W.W. Selvey; West Indies – C.L. King.

West Indies won at 11.12 on the fifth morning; it was their largest victory by a runs margin in this series. Selvey took a wicket with his sixth ball in Test cricket and 3 for 6 in his first 20 balls. Greenidge scored 63.5% of his side's total in the first innings; only C. Bannerman, who scored 67.3% in *Test No. 1*, has exceeded this contribution in a Test match. Greenidge was the second West Indies batsman after G.A. Headley to score a hundred in each innings of a Test in this series. England's 71 is the lowest total by either side in this series; only Australia (seven occasions) had dismissed England for a lower total at that time. Underwood emulated R. Peel and R.W. Blair by being dismissed for a 'pair' three times in Test matches. Extras were the main contributor to England's second innings (fourth instance) and to their match aggregate (unique at Test level). West Indies' second innings included the Test record for leg byes in an innings.

WEST INDIES

R.C. Fredericks	c Underwood b Selvey	0	hit wkt b Hendrick		50
C.G. Greenidge	b Underwood	134	b Selvey		101
I.V.A. Richards	b Selvey	4	lbw b Pocock		135
A.I. Kallicharran	b Selvey	0	(5) c Close b Pocock		20
C.H. Lloyd*	c Hayes b Hendrick	2	(4) c Underwood b Selvey		43
C.L. King	c Greig b Underwood	32	not out		14
D.L. Murray†	c Greig b Hendrick	1	not out		7
M.A. Holding	b Selvey	3			
A.M.E. Roberts	c Steele b Pocock	6			
A.L. Padmore	not out	8			
W.W. Daniel	lbw b Underwood	10			
Extras	(LB 8, NB 3)	11	(B 5, LB 30, W 1, NB 5)		41
Total		**211**	(5 wickets declared)		**411**

ENGLAND

J.H. Edrich	c Murray b Roberts	8	b Daniel		24
D.B. Close	lbw b Daniel	2	b Roberts		20
D.S. Steele	lbw b Roberts	20	c Roberts b Holding		15
P.I. Pocock	c Kallicharran b Holding	7	(10) c King b Daniel		3
R.A. Woolmer	c Murray b Holding	3	(4) lbw b Roberts		0
F.C. Hayes	c Lloyd b Roberts	0	(5) c Greenidge b Roberts		18
A.W. Greig*	b Daniel	9	(6) b Holding		3
A.P.E. Knott†	c Greenidge b Holding	1	(7) c Fredericks b Roberts		14
D.L. Underwood	b Holding	0	(8) c King b Roberts		0
M.W.W. Selvey	not out	2	(9) c Greenidge b Roberts		4
M. Hendrick	b Holding	0	not out		0
Extras	(B 8, NB 11)	19	(B 4, LB 1, NB 20)		25
Total		**71**			**126**

ENGLAND	O	M	R	W	O	M	R	W			FALL OF WICKETS		
Hendrick	14	1	48	2	24	4	63	1			WI	E	WI	E
Selvey	17	4	41	4	26	3	111	2	*Wkt*	*1st*	*1st*	*2nd*	*2nd*
Greig	8	1	24	0	2	0	8	0	1st	1	9	116	54
Woolmer	3	0	22	0					2nd	15	36	224	60
Underwood	24	5	55	3	35	9	90	0	3rd	19	46	356	60
Pocock	4	2	10	1	27	4	98	2	4th	26	48	385	80
									5th	137	48	388	94
WEST INDIES									6th	154	65	–	112
Roberts	12	4	22	3	20·5	8	37	6	7th	167	66	–	112
Holding	14·5	7	17	5	23	15	24	2	8th	193	67	–	118
Daniel	6	2	13	2	17	8	39	2	9th	193	71	–	124
Padmore					3	2	1	0	10th	211	71	–	126

Umpires: W.E. Alley (4) and W.L. Budd (1).

Close: 1st day – E(1) 37-2 (Edrich 6, Pocock 1); 2nd – WI(2) 163-1 (Greenidge 71, Richards 28); 3rd – E(2) 21-0 (Edrich 10, Close 1); 4th – E(2) 125-9 (Selvey 3, Hendrick 0).

ENGLAND v WEST INDIES 1976 (4th Test)

Played at Headingley, Leeds, on 22, 23, 24, 26, 27 July.
Toss: West Indies.   Result: WEST INDIES won by 55 runs.
Debuts: England – J.C. Balderstone, P. Willey.

West Indies retained the Wisden Trophy when they completed this victory at 12.22 pm on the fifth day. Knott equalled the Test wicket-keeping record held by T.G. Evans, his only dismissal bringing his aggregate to 219. Greenidge became the first to score three hundreds in successive innings against England since A. Melville in 1947. Richards took his aggregate from Tests during 1976 beyond R.B. Simpson's record (1,381 in 1964) with the first run of his second innings. West Indies scored 437 for 9 off 83 overs in 360 minutes on the first day. Snow took his 200th wicket in 49 Tests when he bowled Roberts; he was the fifth England bowler to achieve this feat. Knott's hundred included a seven (one, plus two overthrows, plus four boundary overthrows). Roberts took his 100th wicket in 19 Tests when he dismissed Steele. Murray's five catches in the second innings equalled the West Indies record set by F.C.M. Alexander in 1959-60 (*Test No. 487*). King's fifty came off only 39 balls in 59 minutes.

WEST INDIES

R.C. Fredericks	b Willis	109	b Snow	6
C.G. Greenidge	c Ward b Snow	115	lbw b Ward	6
I.V.A. Richards	c Knott b Willis	66	b Willis	38
L.G. Rowe	c Greig b Woolmer	50	run out	6
C.H. Lloyd*	c Steele b Ward	18	b Ward	29
C.L. King	c Hayes b Ward	0	c Greig b Snow	58
D.L. Murray†	c Willis b Snow	33	b Willis	18
M.A. Holding	b Snow	2	(9) lbw b Willis	4
V.A. Holder	c Hayes b Willis	1	(8) b Willis	5
A.M.E. Roberts	b Snow	19	b Willis	3
W.W. Daniel	not out	4	not out	0
Extras	(B 1, LB 15, W 2, NB 15)	33	(B 4, LB 6, W 1, NB 12)	23
Total		**450**		**196**

ENGLAND

R.A. Woolmer	c Greenidge b Holder	18	lbw b Holder	37
D.S. Steele	b Holding	4	c Murray b Roberts	0
F.C. Hayes	c Murray b Daniel	7	c Richards b Roberts	0
J.C. Balderstone	c Murray b Roberts	35	c Murray b Roberts	4
P. Willey	lbw b Roberts	36	c Roberts b Holding	45
A.W. Greig*	c Lloyd b Daniel	116	not out	76
A.P.E. Knott†	c Daniel b Holder	116	(8) c Murray b Daniel	2
J.A. Snow	c Fredericks b Holder	20	(9) c Greenidge b Daniel	8
D.L. Underwood	c Lloyd b King	1	(7) c Murray b Daniel	0
A. Ward	lbw b Roberts	0	c Murray b Holding	0
R.G.D. Willis	not out	0	lbw b Holding	0
Extras	(B 2, LB 7, W 2, NB 23)	34	(B 12, LB 5, W 7, NB 8)	32
Total		**387**		**204**

ENGLAND	O	M	R	W	O	M	R	W		FALL OF WICKETS			
Willis	20	2	71	3	15·3	6	42	5		WI	E	WI	E
Snow	18·4	3	77	4	20	1	80	2	*Wkt*	*1st*	*1st*	*2nd*	*2nd*
Underwood	18	2	80	0					1st	192	4	13	5
Ward	15	0	103	2	9	2	25	2	2nd	287	24	23	12
Greig	10	2	57	0					3rd	330	32	60	23
Woolmer	6	0	25	1	7	0	26	0	4th	370	80	72	80
Willey	1	0	4	0					5th	370	169	121	140
									6th	413	321	178	148
WEST INDIES									7th	421	364	184	150
Roberts	35	7	102	3	18	8	41	3	8th	423	367	188	158
Holding	8	2	14	1	14	1	44	3	9th	433	379	193	204
Daniel	29	7	102	2	13	0	60	3	10th	450	387	196	204
Holder	30·3	13	73	3	11	3	27	1					
King	26	6	56	1									
Fredericks	3	1	5	0									
Lloyd	2	1	1	0									

Umpires: D.J. Constant (11) and T.W. Spencer (14).

Close: 1st day – WI(1) 437-9 (Roberts 9, Daniel 1); 2nd – E(1) 238-5 (Greig 89, Knott 30); 3rd – WI(2) 56-2 (Richards 32, Rowe 4); 4th – E(2) 146-5 (Greig 35, Underwood 0).

ENGLAND v WEST INDIES 1976 (5th Test)

Played at Kennington Oval, London, on 12, 13, 14, 16, 17 August.
Toss: West Indies.   Result: WEST INDIES won by 231 runs.
Debuts: England – G. Miller.

West Indies won the rubber 3–0 at 4.20 on the fifth afternoon after setting England to score 435 runs in a minimum of 380 minutes. Their highest total against England was scored in 650 minutes and included hundred partnerships for three successive wickets. Richards (472 minutes, 386 balls, 38 fours) made the highest score of the series in England to bring his record total of runs in a calendar year to 1,710. His aggregate of 829 runs is the fourth highest in any Test rubber and a record for the West Indies. Playing in his 78th match, Knott beat T.G. Evans' world Test record of 219 dismissals in 91 Tests when he stumped Rowe. Holding's analysis of 8 for 92 is the best by a West Indies bowler against England. He became the first West Indian to take more than 12 wickets in a Test against any country when he achieved match figures of 14 for 149. The umpires suspended play for nine minutes on the third evening when several dozen spectators invaded the field of play after Greig had been dismissed.

WEST INDIES

R.C. Fredericks	c Balderstone b Miller	71	not out	86
C.G. Greenidge	lbw b Willis	0	not out	85
I.V.A. Richards	b Greig	291		
L.G. Rowe	st Knott b Underwood	70		
C.H. Lloyd*	c Knott b Greig	84		
C.L. King	c Selvey b Balderstone	63		
D.L. Murray†	c and b Underwood	36		
V.A. Holder	not out	13		
M.A. Holding	b Underwood	32		
A.M.E. Roberts	} did not bat			
W.W. Daniel	}			
Extras	(B 1, LB 17, NB 9)	27	(B 4, LB 1, W 1, NB 5)	11
Total	(8 wickets declared)	**687**	(0 wickets declared)	**182**

ENGLAND

R.A. Woolmer	lbw b Holding	8	c Murray b Holding	30
D.L. Amiss	b Holding	203	c Greenidge b Holding	16
D.S. Steele	lbw b Holding	44	c Murray b Holder	42
J.C. Balderstone	b Holding	0	b Holding	0
P. Willey	c Fredericks b King	33	c Greenidge b Holder	1
A.W. Greig*	b Holding	12	b Holding	1
D.L. Underwood	b Holding	4	(9) c Lloyd b Roberts	2
A.P.E. Knott†	b Holding	50	(7) b Holding	57
G. Miller	c sub (B.D. Julien) b Holder	36	(8) b Richards	24
M.W.W. Selvey	b Holding	0	not out	4
R.G.D. Willis	not out	5	lbw b Holding	0
Extras	(B 8, LB 11, NB 21)	40	(B 15, LB 3, W 8)	26
Total		**435**		**203**

ENGLAND	O	M	R	W	O	M	R	W
Willis	15	3	73	1	7	0	48	0
Selvey	15	0	67	0	9	1	44	0
Underwood	60·5	15	165	3	9	2	38	0
Woolmer	9	0	44	0	5	0	30	0
Miller	27	4	106	1				
Balderstone	16	0	80	1				
Greig	34	5	96	2	2	0	11	0
Willey	3	0	11	0				
Steele	3	0	18	0				
WEST INDIES								
Roberts	27	4	102	0	13	4	37	1
Holding	33	9	92	8	20·4	6	57	6
Holder	27·5	7	75	1	14	5	29	2
Daniel	10	1	30	0				
Fredericks	11	2	36	0	12	5	33	0
Richards	14	4	30	0	11	6	11	1
King	7	3	30	1	6	2	9	0
Lloyd					2	1	1	0

FALL OF WICKETS

	WI	E	WI	E
Wkt	1st	1st	2nd	2nd
1st	5	47	–	49
2nd	159	147	–	54
3rd	350	151	–	64
4th	524	279	–	77
5th	547	303	–	78
6th	640	323	–	148
7th	642	342	–	196
8th	687	411	–	196
9th	–	411	–	202
10th	–	435	–	203

Umpires: W.E. Alley (5) and H.D. Bird (10).

Close: 1st day – WI(1) 373-3 (Richards 200, Lloyd 15); 2nd – E(1) 34-0 (Woolmer 6, Amiss 22); 3rd – E(1) 304-5 (Amiss 176, Underwood 1); 4th – E(2) 43-0 (Woolmer 21, Amiss 14).

PAKISTAN v NEW ZEALAND 1976–77 (1st Test)

Played at Gaddafi Stadium, Lahore, on 9, 10, 11, 13 October.
Toss: Pakistan.   Result: PAKISTAN won by six wickets.
Debuts: Pakistan – Javed Miandad; New Zealand – R.W. Anderson, W.K. Lees, P.J. Petherick.

Pakistan won with a day and three hours to spare. Javed Miandad became the second batsman after Khalid Ibadulla to score a hundred in his first innings for Pakistan. His partnership of 281 with Asif Iqbal is the highest for the fifth wicket by Pakistan in all Test matches. Petherick's offspin dismissed Miandad, Wasim Raja and Intikhab in successive balls on the first day. It was the second hat-trick by a bowler playing in his first Test: M.J.C. Allom also achieved the feat on his debut in 1929-30 (*Test No. 186*). The partnership of 183 between Burgess and Anderson, who scored 92 in his first Test, is New Zealand's highest for the fifth wicket against all countries.

PAKISTAN

Majid Khan	c Lees b Hadlee	23	c Turner b Collinge	21
Sadiq Mohammad	c Burgess b Hadlee	5	c Parker b Howarth	38
Zaheer Abbas	b Burgess	15	c Morrison b Petherick	15
Mushtaq Mohammad*	b Hadlee	4	(5) c Morrison b Petherick	5
Javed Miandad	c Hadlee b Petherick	163	(4) not out	25
Asif Iqbal	b Hadlee	166	not out	1
Wasim Raja	c and b Petherick	0		
Intikhab Alam	c Howarth b Petherick	0		
Imran Khan	c Burgess b Hadlee	29		
Sarfraz Nawaz	lbw b O'Sullivan	4		
Wasim Bari†	not out	2		
Extras	(B 1, LB 2, NB 3)	6		
Total		**417**	(4 wickets)	**105**

NEW ZEALAND

G.M. Turner*	c Wasim Raja b Sarfraz	8	b Imran	1
J.F.M. Morrison	c Wasim Bari b Sarfraz	3	c Zaheer b Sarfraz	0
G.P. Howarth	c and b Intikhab	38	c Sadiq b Sarfraz	0
J.M. Parker	c Wasim Bari b Imran	9	lbw b Imran	22
M.G. Burgess	b Imran	17	b Intikhab	111
R.W. Anderson	c Mushtaq b Intikhab	14	c Majid b Mushtaq	92
W.K. Lees†	st Wasim Bari b Intikhab	8	c Mushtaq b Imran	42
R.J. Hadlee	c Wasim Raja b Mushtaq	27	c Majid b Miandad	42
D.R. O'Sullivan	c Miandad b Mushtaq	8	(11) not out	23
R.O. Collinge	c Wasim Bari b Intikhab	8	(9) b Imran	0
P.J. Petherick	not out	1	(10) c Mushtaq b Sarfraz	1
Extras	(B 1, LB 4, NB 11)	16	(B 4, LB 11, NB 11)	26
Total		**157**		**360**

NEW ZEALAND	O	M	R	W	O	M	R	W
Collinge	14	0	81	0	6	0	30	1
Hadlee	19	0	121	5	5	0	36	0
Burgess	4	1	20	1				
O'Sullivan	25·5	3	86	1				
Petherick	18	1	103	3	4·7	2	26	2
Howarth					3	0	13	1
PAKISTAN								
Sarfraz	13	5	33	2	18	1	69	3
Imran	15	1	57	2	21	4	59	4
Asif	2	0	10	0				
Intikhab	16·4	6	35	4	26	4	85	1
Mushtaq	3	0	6	2	13	2	56	1
Wasim Raja					7	0	31	0
Miandad					7·4	1	34	1

FALL OF WICKETS

Wkt	P 1st	NZ 1st	NZ 2nd	P 2nd
1st	23	9	1	49
2nd	33	26	1	74
3rd	44	64	1	74
4th	55	72	62	96
5th	336	99	245	–
6th	336	105	245	–
7th	336	106	306	–
8th	408	146	306	–
9th	413	149	315	–
10th	417	157	360	–

Umpires: Amanullah Khan (3) and Shujauddin (18).

Close: 1st day – P(1) 349-7 (Asif 128, Imran 5); 2nd – NZ(2) 1-1 (Turner 1, Howarth 0); 3rd – NZ(2) 299-6 (Lees 38, Hadlee 12).

PAKISTAN v NEW ZEALAND 1976–77 (2nd Test)

Played at Niaz Stadium, Hyderabad, on 23, 24, 25, 27 October.
Toss: Pakistan.   Result: PAKISTAN won by ten wickets.
Debuts: Pakistan – Farrukh Zaman.

A boundary off the bowling of the wicket-keeper gave Pakistan victory in their first match against New Zealand at Hyderabad soon after tea on the penultimate day. This was their first successful home rubber since 1964-65. Sadiq (56) retired with cramp in his leg at 136 and resumed at 384. Sadiq and Mushtaq Mohammad became the second pair of brothers after G.S. and I.M. Chappell to score hundreds in the same Test match.

PAKISTAN

Sadiq Mohammad	not out	103		
Majid Khan	st Lees b O'Sullivan	98		
Zaheer Abbas	lbw b Roberts	11		
Javed Miandad	c sub (N.M. Parker) b Cairns	25		
Mushtaq Mohammad*	run out	101		
Asif Iqbal	st Lees b Petherick	73		
Imran Khan	c Turner b O'Sullivan	13		
Intikhab Alam	lbw b Hadlee	4		
Sarfraz Nawaz	c Turner b Petherick	10	(1) not out	4
Wasim Bari†	not out	13	(2) not out	0
Farrukh Zaman	did not bat			
Extras	(B 17, LB 3, NB 2)	22		
Total	(8 wickets declared)	**473**	(0 wickets)	**4**

NEW ZEALAND

G.M. Turner*	c Wasim b Imran	49	b Sarfraz	2
G.P. Howarth	b Sarfraz	0	c Miandad b Mushtaq	23
J.M. Parker	c Miandad b Imran	7	c Mushtaq b Miandad	82
A.D.G. Roberts	c Wasim b Sarfraz	8	b Miandad	33
M.G. Burgess	c Wasim b Imran	33	c sub (Wasim Raja) b Intikhab	21
R.W. Anderson	b Intikhab	30	c Zaheer b Intikhab	4
W.K. Lees†	lbw b Intikhab	15	c sub (Mohsin Khan) b Miandad	29
B.L. Cairns	c Majid b Miandad	18	lbw b Intikhab	3
R.J. Hadlee	not out	28	c Wasim b Intikhab	0
D.R. O'Sullivan	b Miandad	4	b Sarfraz	23
P.J. Petherick	b Sarfraz	0	not out	12
Extras	(B 13, LB 8, NB 6)	27	(B 15, LB 2, NB 5)	22
Total		**219**		**254**

NEW ZEALAND	O	M	R	W	O	M	R	W
Hadlee	19	1	77	1				
Cairns	26	7	101	1				
Roberts	8	1	23	1				
Petherick	36	5	158	2				
O'Sullivan	39	10	92	2				
Lees					0·5	0	4	0
PAKISTAN								
Sarfraz	17.7	5	53	3	10·4	1	45	2
Imran	15	4	41	3	16	1	53	0
Intikhab	20	7	51	2	20	7	44	4
Farrukh	6	1	8	0	4	1	7	0
Miandad	8	1	20	2	19	2	74	3
Mushtaq	7	2	19	0	9	4	9	1
Majid					2	2	0	0

FALL OF WICKETS

	P	NZ	NZ	P
Wkt	1st	1st	2nd	2nd
1st	164	5	5	–
2nd	176	27	70	–
3rd	220	38	147	–
4th	384	101	158	–
5th	387	111	172	–
6th	410	161	190	–
7th	415	178	193	–
8th	427	200	193	–
9th	–	208	226	–
10th	–	219	254	–

Umpires: Amanullah Khan (4) and Shakoor Rana (2).

Close: 1st day – P(1) 289-3 (Mushtaq 57, Asif 24); 2nd – NZ(1) 75-3 (Turner 32, Burgess 18); 3rd – NZ(2) 75-2 (Parker 40, Roberts 3).

PAKISTAN v NEW ZEALAND 1976–77 (3rd Test)

Played at National Stadium, Karachi, on 30, 31 October, 1, 3, 4 November.
Toss: Pakistan.   Result: MATCH DRAWN.
Debuts: Pakistan – Shahid Israr, Sikander Bakht; New Zealand – N.M. Parker.

This match produced the highest aggregate of runs for any Test on the Indian sub-continent: 1,585. Pakistan's total of 565 was then the highest by either country in this series and remains the record for any Test in Karachi. Majid reached his hundred in 112 minutes off 77 balls before lunch on the first day and was 108 at the interval. Only three others – V.T. Trumper, C.G. Macartney and D.G. Bradman, all Australians playing against England – have scored a hundred before lunch on the first day of a Test match. Javed Miandad, who batted for 410 minutes and hit two sixes and 29 fours, is the youngest to score a double century in Test cricket (19 years and 141 days). Lees completed his first hundred in first-class cricket, recorded New Zealand's highest score against Pakistan, and shared with Hadlee New Zealand's highest seventh-wicket partnership (186) in all Tests. In the first innings, Imran was banned from bowling after being warned by both umpires for bowling too many short-pitched balls.

PAKISTAN

Sadiq Mohammad	c Burgess b Hadlee	34	c Lees b Collinge	31
Majid Khan	c Burgess b Collinge	112	run out	50
Zaheer Abbas	b O'Sullivan	3	c Lees b O'Sullivan	16
Javed Miandad	c Hadlee b Collinge	206	(5) st Lees b O'Sullivan	85
Mushtaq Mohammad*	c Lees b Hadlee	107	(6) not out	67
Asif Iqbal	c Lees b Hadlee	12	(4) st Lees b Roberts	30
Imran Khan	c O'Sullivan b Hadlee	59	not out	4
Intikhab Alam	lbw b O'Sullivan	0		
Sarfraz Nawaz	lbw b Cairns	15		
Shahid Israr†	not out	7		
Sikander Bakht	did not bat			
Extras	(B 3, LB 5, NB 2)	10	(LB 4, NB 3)	7
Total	(9 wickets declared)	**565**	(5 wickets declared)	**290**

NEW ZEALAND

J.F.M. Morrison	b Sarfraz	4	c Mushtaq b Sikander	31
N.M. Parker	c Shahid b Sarfraz	2	c Imran b Intikhab	40
J.M. Parker*	c Majid b Imran	24	c Sadiq b Miandad	16
A.D.G. Roberts	b Imran	39	b Sikander	45
M.G. Burgess	c Miandad b Sarfraz	44	c Majid b Miandad	1
R.W. Anderson	lbw b Imran	8	lbw b Imran	30
W.K. Lees†	b Sikander	152	c Asif b Imran	46
R.J. Hadlee	c Shahid b Intikhab	87	not out	30
B.L. Cairns	not out	52	not out	9
D.R. O'Sullivan	c Mushtaq b Intikhab	1		
R.O. Collinge	b Intikhab	3		
Extras	(B 12, LB 7, NB 33)	52	(B 4, LB 5, NB 5)	14
Total		**468**	(7 wickets)	**262**

NEW ZEALAND	O	M	R	W	O	M	R	W
Collinge	21	1	141	2	12	0	88	1
Hadlee	20·2	1	138	4	12	0	75	0
Cairns	28	2	142	1				
O'Sullivan	35	6	131	2	17	0	96	2
Morrison	1	0	3	0	2	0	6	0
Roberts					4·4	2	18	1

PAKISTAN	O	M	R	W	O	M	R	W
Sarfraz	20	1	84	3				
Imran	24·6	4	107	3	21·6	1	104	2
Sikander	16	3	68	1	8	2	38	2
Intikhab	20·7	5	76	3	17	5	42	1
Mushtaq	6	2	30	0	6	2	9	0
Miandad	10	3	34	0	17	4	45	2
Majid	5	2	17	0	9	4	6	0
Sadiq	1	1	0	0	1	0	4	0

FALL OF WICKETS

Wkt	P 1st	NZ 1st	P 2nd	NZ 2nd
1st	147	5	76	43
2nd	151	10	88	90
3rd	161	78	117	91
4th	413	93	137	93
5th	427	104	275	140
6th	524	195	–	200
7th	525	381	–	241
8th	548	433	–	–
9th	565	434	–	–
10th	–	468	–	–

Umpires: Shakoor Rana (3) and Shujauddin (19).

Close: 1st day – P(1) 338-3 (Miandad 110, Mushtaq 73); 2nd – NZ(1) 67-2 (J.M. Parker 12, Roberts 35); 3rd – NZ(1) 398-7 (Lees 140, Cairns 3); 4th – P(2) 290-5 (Mushtaq 67, Imran 4).

INDIA v NEW ZEALAND 1976–77 (1st Test)

Played at Wankhede Stadium, Bombay, on 10, 11, 13, 14, 15 November.
Toss: India.   Result: INDIA won by 162 runs.
Debuts: Nil.

After setting New Zealand 304 to win in a minimum of 290 minutes, India won with 10.4 of the final hour's mandatory 20 overs to spare. Gavaskar's ninth Test hundred was his first in India. Kirmani and Bedi shared a record Indian ninth-wicket partnership of 105 against New Zealand (equalled in 1980-81 – *Test No. 902*). Venkataraghavan's dismissal of Hadlee brought him his 100th wicket in 33 Tests. Gaekwad was taken ill on the third day.

INDIA

S.M. Gavaskar	c Cairns b Petherick	119	c Burgess b Hadlee	14
A.D. Gaekwad	lbw b O'Sullivan	42		
M. Amarnath	c O'Sullivan b Hadlee	45	(2) c Roberts b Collinge	30
G.R. Viswanath	b Petherick	10	(3) st Lees b Petherick	39
B.P. Patel	b Cairns	4	(4) c sub (R.W. Anderson) b Collinge	82
A.V. Mankad	c and b Hadlee	16	(5) not out	27
Madan Lal	c N.M. Parker b Hadlee	8	(6) not out	8
S.M.H. Kirmani†	c J.M. Parker b Petherick	88		
S. Venkataraghavan	c Turner b Hadlee	3		
B.S. Bedi*	c J.M. Parker b Cairns	36		
B.S. Chandrasekhar	not out	20		
Extras	(B 2, LB 1, NB 5)	8	(LB 1, NB 1)	2
Total		**399**	(4 wickets declared)	**202**

NEW ZEALAND

G.M. Turner*	c Amarnath b Venkataraghavan	65	c Gavaskar b Madan Lal	6
N.M. Parker	c Kirmani b Chandrasekhar	9	c Amarnath b Chandrasekhar	14
J.M. Parker	run out	104	b Bedi	7
M.G. Burgess	c sub (K.D. Ghavri) b Bedi	42	c Gavaskar b Bedi	0
A.D.G. Roberts	lbw b Chandrasekhar	2	c Mankad b Bedi	16
W.K. Lees†	c Kirmani b Chandrasekhar	7	b Venkataraghavan	42
R.J. Hadlee	c Kirmani b Venkataraghavan	17	c Patel b Bedi	7
B.L. Cairns	b Chandrasekhar	12	st Kirmani b Venkataraghavan	1
D.R. O'Sullivan	c Venkataraghavan b Bedi	3	(10) not out	7
R.O. Collinge	c Kirmani b Venkataraghavan	26	(9) c Madan Lal b Bedi	36
P.J. Petherick	not out	0	c Amarnath b Chandrasekhar	1
Extras	(B 1, LB 6, NB 4)	11	(B 4)	4
Total		**298**		**141**

NEW ZEALAND	O	M	R	W	O	M	R	W
Collinge	15	5	41	0	12	2	45	2
Hadlee	29	5	95	4	16	0	76	1
Cairns	34	8	76	2				
Roberts	6	0	27	0	6	1	13	0
O'Sullivan	27	9	62	1	10	6	21	0
Petherick	31·5	6	90	3	14	4	45	1
INDIA								
Madan Lal	9	2	27	0	6	0	13	1
Amarnath	13	3	33	0	3	0	9	0
Bedi	50·3	22	71	2	33	18	27	5
Chandrasekhar	44	13	77	4	19·2	5	59	2
Venkataraghavan	37	11	79	3	19	9	29	2

FALL OF WICKETS

	I	NZ	I	NZ
Wkt	1st	1st	2nd	2nd
1st	120	37	24	6
2nd	188	143	63	25
3rd	218	220	118	27
4th	218	228	175	27
5th	239	238	–	50
6th	241	239	–	64
7th	247	267	–	67
8th	252	267	–	132
9th	357	298	–	136
10th	399	298	–	141

Umpires: J. Reuben (8) and B. Satyaji Rao (13).

Close: 1st day – I(1) 228-4 (Patel 4, Mankad 6); 2nd – NZ(1) 48-1 (Turner 29, J.M. Parker 6); 3rd – NZ(1) 234-4 (Roberts 2, Lees 3); 4th – I(2) 178-4 (Mankad 10, Madan Lal 1).

INDIA v NEW ZEALAND 1976–77 (2nd Test)

Played at Green Park, Kanpur, on 18, 19, 20, 21, 23 November.
Toss: India.   Result: MATCH DRAWN.
Debuts: New Zealand – G.B. Troup.

New Zealand's eighth-wicket pair survived for the final 118 minutes of the match to earn a draw. India's total of 524 is the highest in Test cricket in which no batsman has scored a century. It provided the eighth instance of all 11 batsmen reaching double figures in a Test innings.

INDIA

Batsman	Dismissal	Score	2nd Dismissal	2nd Score
S.M. Gavaskar	b O'Sullivan	66	b Hadlee	15
A.D. Gaekwad	c Lees b Hadlee	43	not out	77
M. Amarnath	b O'Sullivan	70	c N.M. Parker b Hadlee	8
G.R. Viswanath	lbw b Roberts	68	not out	103
B.P. Patel	b Petherick	13		
A.V. Mankad	lbw b Troup	50		
S.M.H. Kirmani†	c Turner b O'Sullivan	64		
K.D. Ghavri	c Troup b Petherick	37		
S. Venkataraghavan	c and b Petherick	27		
B.S. Bedi*	not out	50		
B.S. Chandrasekhar	not out	10		
Extras	(B 17, LB 4, W 1, NB 4)	26	(LB 4, NB 1)	5
Total	(9 wickets declared)	**524**	(2 wickets declared)	**208**

NEW ZEALAND

Batsman	Dismissal	Score	2nd Dismissal	2nd Score
G.M. Turner*	c Viswanath b Bedi	113	(2) c Venkataraghavan b Bedi	35
G.P. Howarth	c Kirmani b Ghavri	19	(6) c Mankad b Venkataraghavan	4
J.M. Parker	c Ghavri b Bedi	34	lbw b Bedi	17
M.G. Burgess	c Ghavri b Bedi	54	lbw b Venkataraghavan	24
A.D.G. Roberts	not out	84	c Mankad b Chandrasekhar	9
N.M. Parker	lbw b Venkataraghavan	6	(1) lbw b Chandrasekhar	18
W.K. Lees†	b Chandrasekhar	3	not out	49
R.J. Hadlee	b Chandrasekhar	0	c Venkataraghavan b Bedi	10
D.R. O'Sullivan	c Chandrasekhar b Venkataraghavan	15	not out	23
G.B. Troup	c Amarnath b Venkataraghavan	0		
P.J. Petherick	c Kirmani b Chandrasekhar	13		
Extras	(LB 9)	9	(LB 4)	4
Total		**350**	(7 wickets)	**193**

NEW ZEALAND	O	M	R	W	O	M	R	W
Hadlee	29	2	121	1	15	1	56	2
Troup	20	3	69	1	10	0	47	0
Roberts	19	5	53	1				
O'Sullivan	50	14	125	3	16	1	49	0
Petherick	45	12	109	3	11	0	51	0
Howarth	5	0	21	0				
INDIA								
Ghavri	12	3	16	1	6	2	35	0
Amarnath	5	0	23	0	4	2	5	0
Bedi	41	12	80	3	40	23	42	3
Chandrasekhar	36·5	6	102	3	33	15	61	2
Venkataraghavan	48	9	120	3	34	20	46	2

FALL OF WICKETS

Wkt	I 1st	NZ 1st	I 2nd	NZ 2nd
1st	79	54	23	43
2nd	193	118	45	59
3rd	196	224	–	86
4th	217	225	–	97
5th	312	241	–	110
6th	341	250	–	114
7th	413	250	–	134
8th	450	291	–	–
9th	493	298	–	–
10th	–	350	–	–

Umpires: M.V. Nagendra (9) and M.S. Sivasankariah (2).

Close: 1st day – I(1) 304-4 (Viswanath 50, Mankad 42); 2nd – NZ(1) 52-0 (Turner 31, Howarth 17); 3rd – NZ(1) 265-7 (Roberts 19, O'Sullivan 11); 4th – I(2) 208-2 (Gaekwad 77, Viswanath 103).

INDIA v NEW ZEALAND 1976–77 (3rd Test)

Played at Chepauk, Madras, on 26 (*no play*), 27, 28, 30 November, 1, 2 December.
Toss: India.   Result: INDIA won by 216 runs.
Debuts: Nil.

Heavy rain, which had flooded the ground, prevented a start until 11.15 on the second morning. Besides winning all three tosses, leading India to a 2–0 win in the rubber, and scoring his only fifty in Tests, Bedi took 22 wickets, average 13·18, in the three matches. M.V. Gothoskar (ill) and H.P. Sharma (stranded 100 miles away) were the originally appointed umpires.

INDIA

S.M. Gavaskar	b Cairns	2	st Lees b O'Sullivan	43
A.D. Gaekwad	c Parker b Cairns	0	b Hadlee	11
M. Amarnath	c Petherick b Cairns	21	c Morrison b Hadlee	55
G.R. Viswanath	c Lees b Hadlee	87	st Lees b O'Sullivan	17
B.P. Patel	run out	33	not out	40
A.V. Mankad	b Cairns	14	c Burgess b Petherick	21
S.M.H. Kirmani†	lbw b Petherick	44		
K.D. Ghavri	c Petherick b Hadlee	8		
S. Venkataraghavan	c sub (R.O. Collinge) b Cairns	64		
B.S. Bedi*	c Cairns b Hadlee	5		
B.S. Chandrasekhar	not out	1		
Extras	(B 7, LB 8, W 1, NB 3)	19	(B 11, LB 2, NB 1)	14
Total		**298**	(5 wickets declared)	**201**

NEW ZEALAND

G.M. Turner*	c Kirmani b Chandrasekhar	37	c Amarnath b Chandrasekhar	5
J.F.M. Morrison	c Kirmani b Ghavri	7	c Chandrasekhar b Ghavri	1
J.M. Parker	c Patel b Ghavri	9	c Kirmani b Chandrasekhar	38
M.G. Burgess	b Bedi	40	run out	15
A.D.G. Roberts	c Venkataraghavan b Chandrasekhar	1	c Gavaskar b Bedi	0
G.P. Howarth	c Venkataraghavan b Bedi	3	c Chandrasekhar b Bedi	18
W.K. Lees†	c Venkataraghavan b Bedi	9	c sub (Madan Lal) b Bedi	21
R.J. Hadlee	c Gaekwad b Bedi	21	c Amarnath b Bedi	5
B.L. Cairns	c Mankad b Bedi	5	not out	8
D.R. O'Sullivan	c Venkataraghavan b Chandrasekhar	0	c Patel b Chandrasekhar	21
P.J. Petherick	not out	0	lbw b Venkataraghavan	1
Extras	(B 1, LB 2, NB 5)	8	(B 7, LB 1, NB 2)	10
Total		**140**		**143**

NEW ZEALAND	O	M	R	W	O	M	R	W		FALL OF WICKETS			
										I	NZ	I	NZ
Hadlee	21	7	37	3	17	3	52	2	*Wkt*	*1st*	*1st*	*2nd*	*2nd*
Cairns	33·1	11	55	5	16	2	49	0	1st	0	17	33	2
Roberts	17	5	32	0	2	0	4	0	2nd	3	37	21	21
O'Sullivan	34	9	69	0	20	3	70	2	3rd	60	91	118	50
Petherick	25	5	77	1	6·5	0	12	1	4th	137	99	142	53
Howarth	3	1	9	0					5th	167	101	201	79
									6th	167	103	–	85
INDIA									7th	181	133	–	103
Ghavri	13	3	32	2	8	4	14	1	8th	255	133	–	114
Amarnath	8	3	17	0	3	1	6	0	9th	276	136	–	142
Bedi	16·4	4	48	5	22	12	22	4	10th	298	140	–	143
Chandrasekhar	16	5	28	3	20	3	64	3					
Venkataraghavan	2	0	7	0	14	8	27	1					

Umpires: Mohammad Ghouse (1) and K.B. Ramaswami (1).

Close: 1st day – no play; 2nd – I(1) 162-4 (Viswanath 82, Mankad 14); 3rd – NZ(1) 13-0 (Turner 6, Morrison 7); 4th – NZ(1) 84-2 (Turner 33, Burgess 30); 5th – I(2) 201-5 (Patel 40).

INDIA v ENGLAND 1976–77 (1st Test)

Played at Feroz Shah Kotla, Delhi, on 17, 18, 19, 21, 22 December.
Toss: England.   Result: ENGLAND won by an innings and 25 runs.
Debuts: England – G.D. Barlow, J.K. Lever.

This was England's first victory by an innings in India and only their fifth success in 24 Tests there. Amiss reached his hundred with a six and made England's highest score in a Test in India until 1984-85. Gavaskar became the first Indian to score 1,000 runs in a calendar year, taking his aggregate for 1976 to 1,024. Lever was the sixth Englishman to take ten wickets in his first Test; only A.L. Valentine and R.A.L. Massie had then achieved better figures than his 7 for 46 in their first Test innings. Bedi became the fourth player after R. Peel, R.W. Blair and D.L. Underwood to be dismissed for a 'pair' three times in Test matches.

ENGLAND

D.L. Amiss	c Sharma b Venkataraghavan	179
J.M. Brearley	run out	5
G.D. Barlow	c Amarnath b Bedi	0
R.A. Woolmer	lbw b Chandrasekhar	4
K.W.R. Fletcher	b Chandrasekhar	8
A.W. Greig*	lbw b Venkataraghavan	25
A.P.E. Knott†	st Kirmani b Bedi	75
C.M. Old	c Viswanath b Bedi	15
J.K. Lever	c Bedi b Chandrasekhar	53
R.G.D. Willis	c Venkataraghavan b Bedi	1
D.L. Underwood	not out	7
Extras	(B 1, LB 5, W 1, NB 2)	9
Total		**381**

INDIA

S.M. Gavaskar	c Willis b Lever	38	c Woolmer b Underwood		71
A.D. Gaekwad	lbw b Lever	20	b Willis		11
M. Amarnath	lbw b Lever	0	(6) c sub (D.W. Randall) b Underwood		24
G.R. Viswanath	lbw b Lever	3	c Knott b Greig		18
S. Venkataraghavan	b Lever	0	(9) c Knott b Lever		4
B.P. Patel	c Knott b Lever	33	(5) c and b Underwood		14
P. Sharma	c Willis b Underwood	4	(3) c Fletcher b Underwood		29
S.M.H. Kirmani†	b Lever	13	(7) c Lever b Greig		10
K.D. Ghavri	not out	3	(8) not out		35
B.S. Bedi*	c Greig b Old	0	b Lever		0
B.S. Chandrasekhar	b Old	0	b Lever		0
Extras	(LB 4, W 1, NB 3)	8	(B 3, LB 8, NB 7)		18
Total		**122**			**234**

INDIA	O	M	R	W	O	M	R	W
Ghavri	14	3	50	0				
Amarnath	8	2	12	0				
Bedi	59	22	92	4				
Chandrasekhar	32·5	6	117	3				
Venkataraghavan	34	6	94	2				
Gaekwad	1	0	1	0				
Sharma	3	0	6	0				
ENGLAND								
Old	12·5	0	28	2	4	2	6	0
Willis	7	3	21	0	9	3	24	1
Lever	23	6	46	7	13·4	6	24	3
Underwood	9	3	19	1	44	15	78	4
Greig					40	11	84	2

FALL OF WICKETS

Wkt	E 1st	I 1st	I 2nd
1st	34	43	20
2nd	34	43	110
3rd	51	49	133
4th	65	49	153
5th	125	96	163
6th	226	99	182
7th	263	103	190
8th	357	121	226
9th	363	122	226
10th	381	122	234

Umpires: M.V. Nagendra (10) and J. Reuben (9).

Close: 1st day – E(1) 239-6 (Amiss 109, Old 5); 2nd – I(1) 51-4 (Gavaskar 22, Patel 2); 3rd – I(2) 82-1 (Gavaskar 40, Sharma 24); 4th – I(2) 216-7 (Ghavri 23, Venkataraghavan 3).

INDIA v ENGLAND 1976–77 (2nd Test)

Played at Eden Gardens, Calcutta, on 1, 2, 3, 5, 6 January.
Toss: India.   Result: ENGLAND won by ten wickets.
Debuts: England – D.W. Randall, R.W. Tolchard.

England won successive Tests in India for the first time; it was also their first victory in six Tests in Calcutta. Greig reached his hundred in 413 minutes, then the fourth-slowest for England. When he had made 3, he scored his 3,000th run in 49 Tests and became the first to achieve a double of 3,000 runs and 100 wickets for England.

INDIA

S.M. Gavaskar	c Old b Willis	0	b Underwood	18
A.D. Gaekwad	b Lever	32	c Tolchard b Greig	8
P. Sharma	c Greig b Lever	9	c Knott b Willis	20
G.R. Viswanath	c Tolchard b Underwood	35	c Lever b Greig	3
B.P. Patel	hit wkt b Willis	21	lbw b Old	56
E.D. Solkar	c Greig b Willis	2	c Knott b Willis	3
Madan Lal	c Knott b Old	17	c Brearley b Old	16
S.M.H. Kirmani†	not out	25	b Old	0
E.A.S. Prasanna	b Willis	2	c Brearley b Underwood	13
B.S. Bedi*	c Lever b Old	1	b Underwood	18
B.S. Chandrasekhar	b Willis	1	not out	4
Extras	(LB 2, NB 8)	10	(B 2, LB 4, NB 16)	22
Total		**155**		**181**

ENGLAND

D.L. Amiss	c Kirmani b Prasanna	35	not out	7
G.D. Barlow	c Kirmani b Madan Lal	4	not out	7
J.M. Brearley	c Solkar b Bedi	5		
D.W. Randall	lbw b Prasanna	37		
R.W. Tolchard	b Bedi	67		
A.W. Greig*	lbw b Prasanna	103		
A.P.E. Knott†	c Gavaskar b Bedi	2		
C.M. Old	c Madan Lal b Prasanna	52		
J.K. Lever	c Gavaskar b Bedi	2		
D.L. Underwood	c Gavaskar b Bedi	4		
R.G.D. Willis	not out	0		
Extras	(B 5, LB 5)	10	(LB 1, NB 1)	2
Total		**321**	(0 wickets)	**16**

ENGLAND	O	M	R	W	O	M	R	W	FALL OF WICKETS				
Willis	20	3	27	5	13	1	32	2		I	E	I	E
Lever	22	2	57	2	3	0	12	0	*Wkt*	*1st*	*1st*	*2nd*	*2nd*
Underwood	13	5	24	1	32·5	18	50	3	1st	1	7	31	–
Old	20	5	37	2	12	4	38	3	2nd	23	14	33	–
Greig					10	0	27	2	3rd	65	81	36	–
									4th	92	90	60	–
INDIA									5th	99	232	70	–
Madan Lal	17	4	25	1	1	0	3	0	6th	106	234	97	–
Solkar	6	1	15	0					7th	136	298	97	–
Bedi	64	25	110	5	1·4	0	6	0	8th	147	307	146	–
Chandrasekhar	33	9	66	0					9th	149	321	171	–
Prasanna	57·4	16	93	4	1	0	5	0	10th	155	321	181	–
Sharma	1	0	2	0									

Umpires: B. Satyaji Rao (14) and H.P. Sharma (2).

Close: 1st day – I(1) 146-7 (Kirmani 20, Prasanna 1); 2nd – E(1) 136-4 (Tolchard 31, Greig 19); 3rd – E(1) 285-6 (Greig 94, Old 35); 4th – I(2) 145-7 (Patel 48, Prasanna 12).

INDIA v ENGLAND 1976–77 (3rd Test)

Played at Chepauk, Madras, on 14, 15, 16, 18, 19 January.
Toss: England.   Result: ENGLAND won by 200 runs.
Debuts: Nil.

England won their first rubber in India since 1933-34. It was the first time that India had lost the first three matches in any home rubber. Bedi, playing in his 51st match, became the first bowler to take 200 wickets in Tests for India when he dismissed Greig. In the first innings, Tolchard (1) retired at 33 after being hit on the back of his right hand by a ball from Amarnath, and resumed at 209. India's total of 83 was then the lowest by any side in a Test match in India. Vengsarkar, struck on the hand by his first ball from Willis, retired at the tea interval when India were 10 for 0.

ENGLAND

D.L. Amiss	lbw b Madan Lal	4		c Amarnath b Chandrasekhar	46
R.A. Woolmer	c Gavaskar b Madan Lal	22		lbw b Prasanna	16
J.M. Brearley	c and b Prasanna	59	(4)	b Chandrasekhar	29
D.W. Randall	run out	2	(5)	c Kirmani b Chandrasekhar	0
R.W. Tolchard	not out	8	(9)	not out	10
A.W. Greig*	c Viswanath b Bedi	54		lbw b Prasanna	41
A.P.E. Knott†	c Viswanath b Bedi	45		c Patel b Prasanna	11
J.K. Lever	c Kirmani b Bedi	23	(3)	c Amarnath b Chandrasekhar	2
C.M. Old	c Amarnath b Bedi	2	(8)	c Chandrasekhar b Prasanna	4
D.L. Underwood	b Prasanna	23		st Kirmani b Chandrasekhar	8
R.G.D. Willis	run out	7		not out	4
Extras	(B 5, LB 8)	13		(B 14)	14
Total		**262**		(9 wickets declared)	**185**

INDIA

S.M. Gavaskar	c Brearley b Old	39		c Woolmer b Underwood	24
M. Amarnath	b Old	0	(3)	c Woolmer b Underwood	12
G.R. Viswanath	c Knott b Lever	9	(4)	c Brearley b Underwood	6
A.V. Mankad	b Lever	0	(7)	c Old b Lever	4
B.P. Patel	b Underwood	32	(6)	c Old b Willis	4
D.B. Vengsarkar	c Randall b Lever	8	(2)	retired hurt	1
Madan Lal	c Underwood b Willis	12	(9)	c Knott b Willis	6
S.M.H. Kirmani†	c Brearley b Lever	27		c Brearley b Willis	1
E.A.S. Prasanna	c and b Underwood	13	(5)	c Brearley b Underwood	0
B.S. Bedi*	c sub (G.D. Barlow) b Lever	5		not out	11
B.S. Chandrasekhar	not out	1		b Lever	6
Extras	(LB 1, NB 17)	18		(B 5, LB 1, NB 2)	8
Total		**164**			**83**

INDIA	O	M	R	W	O	M	R	W
Madan Lal	21	5	43	2	9	2	15	0
Amarnath	14	3	26	0	7	2	18	0
Chandrasekhar	25	4	63	0	20·5	4	50	5
Bedi	38·5	16	72	4	13	3	33	0
Prasanna	27	11	45	2	22	5	55	4
ENGLAND								
Willis	19	5	46	1	13	4	18	3
Old	13	4	19	2	5	1	11	0
Lever	19·5	2	59	5	6·5	0	18	2
Woolmer	1	0	2	0				
Greig	4	1	4	0				
Underwood	17	9	16	2	14	7	28	4

FALL OF WICKETS

Wkt	E 1st	I 1st	E 2nd	I 2nd
1st	14	5	39	40
2nd	29	17	54	45
3rd	31	17	83	45
4th	142	69	83	54
5th	162	86	124	54
6th	201	114	135	57
7th	209	115	141	66
8th	228	151	169	71
9th	253	161	180	83
10th	262	164	–	–

Umpires: J. Reuben (10) and M.S. Sivasankariah (3).

Close: 1st day – E(1) 171-5 (Knott 21, Lever 0); 2nd – I(1) 58-3 (Gavaskar 13, Patel 27); 3rd – E(2) 44-1 (Amiss 24, Lever 0); 4th – I(2) 45-3 (Viswanath 2).

INDIA v ENGLAND 1976–77 (4th Test)

Played at Karnataka State C.A. Stadium, Bangalore, on 28, 29, 30 January, 1, 2 February.
Toss: India.   Result: INDIA won by 140 runs.
Debuts: India – Yajurvindra Singh.

This was England's first Test match in Bangalore. On only one previous occasion in all Test matches has England's fourth wicket fallen for eight runs or less; against Australia in 1903-04 (*Test No. 82*) their first four wickets fell for five runs. Playing in his first Test match, Yajurvindra Singh equalled the innings and match catching records for non-wicket-keepers; his five catches in the first innings equalled V.Y. Richardson's feat in 1935-36 (*Test No. 251*), and his seven in the match enabled him to share G.S. Chappell's record set in 1974–75 (*Test No. 751*).

INDIA

S.M. Gavaskar	c Underwood b Lever	4	c Brearley b Underwood	50
A.D. Gaekwad	c Tolchard b Greig	39	b Old	9
S. Amarnath	b Greig	63	c Tolchard b Willis	14
G.R. Viswanath	c Brearley b Underwood	13	(7) not out	79
B.P. Patel	c Randall b Willis	23	(4) c Knott b Underwood	17
Yajurvindra Singh	c Knott b Willis	8	(5) c Fletcher b Underwood	15
S.M.H. Kirmani†	b Willis	52	(8) c Randall b Underwood	21
K.D. Ghavri	c Knott b Willis	16	(9) c Amiss b Lever	12
E.A.S. Prasanna	c Greig b Willis	6	(6) c Old b Willis	12
B.S. Bedi*	not out	8	run out	15
B.S. Chandrasekhar	c Knott b Willis	1	not out	0
Extras	(B 8, LB 6, NB 6)	20	(B 1, LB 6, NB 8)	15
Total		**253**	(9 wickets declared)	**259**

ENGLAND

D.L. Amiss	c Yajurvindra b Chandrasekhar	82	c Yajurvindra b Ghavri	0
J.M. Brearley	c Viswanath b Chandrasekhar	4	c Gaekwad b Bedi	4
K.W.R. Fletcher	c Yajurvindra b Prasanna	10	c Yajurvindra b Chandrasekhar	1
D.W. Randall	c Yajurvindra b Prasanna	10	c Gaekwad b Bedi	0
R.W. Tolchard	b Chandrasekhar	0	lbw b Chandrasekhar	14
A.W. Greig*	c Yajurvindra b Chandrasekhar	2	st Kirmani b Bedi	31
A.P.E. Knott†	b Bedi	29	not out	81
C.M. Old	lbw b Prasanna	9	lbw b Chandrasekhar	13
J.K. Lever	not out	20	c Ghavri b Bedi	11
D.L. Underwood	c Yajurvindra b Chandrasekhar	12	c Patel b Bedi	10
R.G.D. Willis	lbw b Chandrasekhar	7	st Kirmani b Bedi	0
Extras	(B 3, LB 5, NB 2)	10	(B 5, LB 6, NB 1)	12
Total		**195**		**177**

ENGLAND	O	M	R	W	O	M	R	W
Willis	17	2	53	6	18	2	47	2
Lever	17	2	48	1	9	1	28	1
Old	12	0	43	0	10	4	19	1
Underwood	21	7	45	1	31	8	76	4
Greig	18	5	44	2	23	2	74	0
INDIA								
Ghavri	13	3	31	0	4	1	4	1
Yajurvindra Singh	1	0	2	0				
Bedi	23	11	29	1	21·3	4	71	6
Chandrasekhar	31·2	7	76	6	15	3	55	3
Prasanna	28	10	47	3	15	5	35	0
Gavaskar					2	2	0	0

FALL OF WICKETS				
	I	E	I	E
Wkt	1st	1st	2nd	2nd
1st	9	13	31	0
2nd	102	34	80	7
3rd	124	64	82	7
4th	134	65	104	8
5th	153	67	124	35
6th	170	137	154	61
7th	236	146	189	105
8th	240	154	223	148
9th	249	175	257	166
10th	253	195	–	177

Umpires: Mohammad Ghouse (2) and M.V. Nagendra (11).

Close: 1st day – I(1) 205-6 (Kirmani 31, Ghavri 9); 2nd – E(1) 138-6 (Amiss 76, Old 0); 3rd – I(2) 105-4 (Yajurvindra 7, Prasanna 1); 4th – E(2) 34-4 (Tolchard 14, Greig 12).

INDIA v ENGLAND 1976–77 (5th Test)

Played at Wankhede Stadium, Bombay, on 11, 12, 14, 15, 16 February.
Toss: India.   Result: MATCH DRAWN.
Debuts: Nil.

India used only one ball in England's first innings which lasted 154 overs. Underwood took 29 wickets in the rubber to equal F.S. Trueman's record for England against India set in 1952.

INDIA

S.M. Gavaskar	c and b Underwood	108	c Willis b Underwood		42
A.D. Gaekwad	c Tolchard b Lever	21	st Knott b Underwood		25
S. Amarnath	b Underwood	40	run out		63
G.R. Viswanath	c and b Lever	4	c Lever b Greig	(5)	5
B.P. Patel	st Knott b Greig	83	c Fletcher b Underwood	(4)	3
Yajurvindra Singh	b Greig	6	run out		21
S.M.H. Kirmani†	c Knott b Underwood	8	c Greig b Underwood		10
K.D. Ghavri	lbw b Greig	25	c Fletcher b Underwood		8
E.A.S. Prasanna	b Underwood	9	not out		0
B.S. Bedi*	not out	20	lbw b Lever		3
B.S. Chandrasekhar	b Lever	3	b Lever		4
Extras	(LB 9, NB 2)	11	(B 4, LB 1, NB 3)		8
Total		**338**			**192**

ENGLAND

D.L. Amiss	c Viswanath b Bedi	50	c Viswanath b Bedi	14
J.M. Brearley	st Kirmani b Prasanna	91	c Yajurvindra b Prasanna	18
D.W. Randall	c Gaekwad b Prasanna	22	c Kirmani b Ghavri	15
K.W.R. Fletcher	c Viswanath b Chandrasekhar	14	not out	58
A.W. Greig*	b Prasanna	76	c Bedi b Ghavri	10
A.P.E. Knott†	b Chandrasekhar	24	b Ghavri	1
R.W. Tolchard	st Kirmani b Prasanna	4	c Gavaskar b Ghavri	26
J.K. Lever	c Gavaskar b Bedi	7	c Patel b Ghavri	4
D.L. Underwood	b Bedi	7		
M.W.W. Selvey	not out	5		
R.G.D. Willis	c Gavaskar b Bedi	0		
Extras	(B 1, LB 13, NB 3)	17	(B 2, LB 3, NB 1)	6
Total		**317**	(7 wickets)	**152**

ENGLAND	O	M	R	W	O	M	R	W
Willis	13	1	52	0	6	1	15	0
Lever	17·4	4	42	3	17·4	6	46	2
Selvey	15	1	80	0				
Underwood	38	13	89	4	33	10	84	5
Greig	22	6	64	3	14	3	39	1
INDIA								
Ghavri	12	2	31	0	15	6	33	5
Gavaskar	2	0	2	0	1	1	0	0
Bedi	56	20	109	4	21	5	52	1
Chandrasekhar	32	7	85	2	4	0	25	0
Prasanna	52	20	73	4	30	12	36	1

FALL OF WICKETS

	I	E	I	E
Wkt	1st	1st	2nd	2nd
1st	52	146	68	34
2nd	115	175	72	38
3rd	122	180	80	86
4th	261	206	92	112
5th	267	247	136	113
6th	273	256	156	148
7th	289	290	182	152
8th	303	300	185	–
9th	321	312	188	–
10th	338	317	192	–

Umpires: B. Satyaji Rao (15) and H.P. Sharma (3).

Close: 1st day – I(1) 261-4 (Gavaskar 103); 2nd – E(1) 99-0 (Amiss 26, Brearley 68); 3rd – E(1) 285-6 (Greig 57, Lever 7); 4th – I(2) 140-5 (Amarnath 36, Kirmani 1).

AUSTRALIA v PAKISTAN 1976–77 (1st Test)

Played at Adelaide Oval on 24, 26, 27, 28, 29 December.
Toss: Pakistan.   Result: MATCH DRAWN.
Debuts: Pakistan – Iqbal Qasim, Mudassar Nazar.

Australia's seventh-wicket pair needed to score 56 runs to win the match when the first of the mandatory last 15 overs began. They were content with a draw and finished 24 runs short of their target. Thomson, attempting to catch Zaheer off his own bowling, collided with Turner (short leg) and dislocated his collar bone. He took no further part in the rubber. The partnership of 87 between Asif and Iqbal Qasim (whose contribution was 4), remains the highest for the tenth wicket in this series.

PAKISTAN

Majid Khan	c McCosker b Thomson	15	lbw b Lillee	47
Mudassar Nazar	c Marsh b Gilmour	13	c Marsh b O'Keeffe	22
Zaheer Abbas	c Walters b O'Keeffe	85	c Davis b Lillee	101
Mushtaq Mohammad*	c McCosker b Thomson	18	c Marsh b Lillee	37
Javed Miandad	b O'Keeffe	15	b Gilmour	54
Asif Iqbal	c Marsh b O'Keeffe	0	not out	152
Imran Khan	b Chappell	48	b O'Keeffe	5
Salim Altaf	c Davis b Chappell	16	c Turner b Lillee	21
Wasim Bari†	run out	21	lbw b Lillee	0
Sarfraz Nawaz	c Marsh b Lillee	29	c Lillee b O'Keeffe	0
Iqbal Qasim	not out	1	run out	4
Extras	(LB 6, NB 5)	11	(B 14, LB 1, NB 8)	23
Total		**272**		**466**

AUSTRALIA

I.C. Davis	c Mushtaq b Miandad	105	b Sarfraz	0
A. Turner	c Zaheer b Imran	33	c Sarfraz b Miandad	48
R.B. McCosker	b Mushtaq	65	c Wasim b Qasim	42
G.S. Chappell*	c Zaheer b Miandad	52	c Mushtaq b Qasim	70
K.D. Walters	c Miandad b Sarfraz	107	c Wasim b Qasim	51
G.J. Cosier	c Asif b Miandad	33	(7) not out	25
R.W. Marsh†	b Mushtaq	36	(8) not out	13
G.J. Gilmour	c Qasim b Mushtaq	3	(6) b Qasim	5
K.J. O'Keeffe	not out	3		
D.K. Lillee	c Majid b Mushtaq	0		
J.R. Thomson	absent hurt	–		
Extras	(LB 4, NB 13)	17	(B 1, LB 3, NB 3)	7
Total		**454**	(6 wickets)	**261**

AUSTRALIA	O	M	R	W	O	M	R	W		FALL OF WICKETS			
Lillee	19	1	104	1	47·7	10	163	5		P	A	P	A
Thomson	8·5	2	34	2					*Wkt*	*1st*	*1st*	*2nd*	*2nd*
Gilmour	14·2	1	55	1	14	1	67	1	1st	19	63	58	0
Walters	3	0	12	0	2	1	5	0	2nd	56	188	92	92
O'Keeffe	19	5	42	3	53	12	166	3	3rd	98	244	182	100
Chappell	7	2	14	2	11	3	31	0	4th	140	278	236	201
Cosier					5	1	11	0	5th	152	366	293	219
									6th	157	445	298	228
PAKISTAN									7th	220	451	368	–
Sarfraz	24	3	75	1	8	1	24	1	8th	221	451	378	–
Salim	15	0	71	0					9th	271	454	379	–
Imran	22	2	92	1	5	0	25	0	10th	272	–	466	–
Qasim	14	0	56	0	30	6	84	4					
Miandad	25	3	85	3	21	6	71	1					
Mushtaq	19·4	2	58	4	9	1	50	0					

Umpires: R.C. Bailhache (9) and M.G. O'Connell (8).

Close: 1st day – P(1) 272 all out; 2nd – A(1) 310-4 (Walters 35, Cosier 8); 3rd – P(2) 140-2 (Zaheer 36, Mushtaq 28): 4th – P(2) 437-9 (Asif 124, Qasim 4).

AUSTRALIA v PAKISTAN 1976–77 (2nd Test)

Played at Melbourne Cricket Ground on 1, 2, 3, 5, 6 January.
Toss: Australia.   Result: AUSTRALIA won by 348 runs.
Debuts: Nil.

In the first innings Australia achieved their highest partnerships against Pakistan for the first, fifth and eighth wickets: 134 by Davis and Turner; 171 by Chappell and Cosier; and 117 by Cosier and O'Keeffe. Lillee's match figures of 10 for 135 were the best for Australia in this series until 1979-80 (*Test No. 877*). This remains Pakistan's heaviest defeat by a runs margin.

AUSTRALIA

I.C. Davis	c Imran b Asif Iqbal	56	c Asif Iqbal b Qasim		88
A. Turner	b Asif Iqbal	82	lbw b Imran		5
R.B. McCosker	lbw b Asif Iqbal	0	st Wasim b Qasim		105
G.S. Chappell*	c Wasim b Qasim	121	c Majid b Imran		67
K.D. Walters	st Wasim b Qasim	42	b Imran		0
G.J. Cosier	c Asif Masood b Majid	168	b Imran		8
R.W. Marsh†	lbw b Qasim	2	st Wasim b Qasim		13
G.J. Gilmour	st Wasim b Qasim	0	not out		7
K.J. O'Keeffe	not out	28	(9) b Imran		6
D.K. Lillee	) did not bat				
M.H.N. Walker	)				
Extras	(B 3, LB 7, W 1, NB 7)	18	(B 2, LB 11, NB 3)		16
Total	(8 wickets declared)	**517**	(8 wickets declared)		**315**

PAKISTAN

Majid Khan	c Marsh b Lillee	76	b Lillee	35
Sadiq Mohammad	c McCosker b O'Keeffe	105	c Walters b Gilmour	0
Zaheer Abbas	b Gilmour	90	lbw b Walker	58
Mushtaq Mohammad*	lbw b Lillee	9	c Chappell b Lillee	4
Javed Miandad	lbw b Lillee	5	c Turner b O'Keeffe	10
Asif Iqbal	c sub (K.J. Hughes) b Gilmour	35	lbw b Lillee	6
Imran Khan	c Marsh b Lillee	5	c and b O'Keeffe	28
Salim Altaf	c Chappell b Lillee	0	b O'Keeffe	0
Wasim Bari†	lbw b Lillee	0	c Walker b O'Keeffe	2
Iqbal Qasim	run out	1	c Marsh b Lillee	1
Asif Masood	not out	0	not out	0
Extras	(LB 2, NB 5)	7	(B 1, LB 6)	7
Total		**333**		**151**

PAKISTAN	O	M	R	W	O	M	R	W
Imran	22	0	115	0	25·5	2	122	5
Salim	17	2	117	0	6	1	28	0
Asif Masood	13	1	79	0				
Asif Iqbal	16	3	52	3				
Miandad	2	0	15	0				
Qasim	21	5	111	4	25	2	119	3
Majid	1·6	0	10	1	2	0	12	0
Mushtaq					3	0	18	0
AUSTRALIA								
Lillee	23	4	82	6	14	1	53	4
Gilmour	16·1	2	78	2	3	0	19	1
Walker	22	1	93	0	9	2	34	1
O'Keeffe	21	4	63	1	18·1	5	38	4
Cosier	2	0	10	0				

FALL OF WICKETS

	A	P	A	P
Wkt	1st	1st	2nd	2nd
1st	134	113	6	4
2nd	134	241	182	86
3rd	151	270	223	99
4th	227	285	226	104
5th	398	292	244	120
6th	400	303	301	124
7th	400	303	301	128
8th	517	303	315	136
9th	–	332	–	145
10th	–	333	–	151

Umpires: T.F. Brooks (18) and M.G. O'Connell (9).

Close: 1st day – A(1) 322-4 (Chappell 80, Cosier 50); 2nd – P(1) 186-1 (Sadiq 78, Zaheer 30); 3rd – A(2) 122-1 (Davis 53, McCosker 56); 4th – P(2) 128-7 (Imran 8).

AUSTRALIA v PAKISTAN 1976–77 (3rd Test)

Played at Sydney Cricket Ground on 14, 15, 16, 18 January.
Toss: Australia.   Result: PAKISTAN won by eight wickets.
Debuts: Pakistan – Haroon Rashid.

Pakistan gained their first Test victory in Australia and only their second of this series. Imran's match analysis (12 for 165) remains Pakistan's best in Australia. The partnership of 115 by Asif Iqbal and Javed Miandad is Pakistan's highest for the sixth wicket against Australia.

AUSTRALIA

I.C. Davis	b Sarfraz	20	c Haroon b Imran	25
A. Turner	c Wasim b Sarfraz	0	c Majid b Sarfraz	11
R.B. McCosker	c Mushtaq b Imran	8	c Wasim b Imran	8
G.S. Chappell*	c Zaheer b Imran	28	c Wasim b Sarfraz	5
K.D. Walters	c Wasim b Imran	2	c Wasim b Imran	38
G.J. Cosier	c Wasim b Imran	50	c Wasim b Sarfraz	4
R.W. Marsh†	c and b Imran	14	run out	41
G.J. Gilmour	c Miandad b Sarfraz	32	c Zaheer b Imran	0
K.J. O'Keeffe	c Asif b Imran	1	c Haroon b Imran	7
D.K. Lillee	lbw b Miandad	14	c Zaheer b Imran	27
M.H.N. Walker	not out	34	not out	3
Extras	(B 5, NB 3)	8	(B 7, NB 4)	11
Total		**211**		**180**

PAKISTAN

Majid Khan	c Marsh b Walker	48	not out	26
Sadiq Mohammad	c Cosier b Walker	25	c Marsh b Lillee	0
Zaheer Abbas	c Turner b Lillee	5	c Walters b Lillee	4
Mushtaq Mohammad*	c Turner b Lillee	9	not out	0
Haroon Rashid	c Marsh b Gilmour	57		
Asif Iqbal	b Gilmour	120		
Javed Miandad	c Walters b Walker	64		
Imran Khan	c Turner b Gilmour	0		
Sarfraz Nawaz	c Turner b Walker	13		
Wasim Bari†	c Walters b Lillee	5		
Iqbal Qasim	not out	0		
Extras	(B 6, LB 6, NB 2)	14	(B 1, NB 1)	2
Total		**360**	(2 wickets)	**32**

PAKISTAN	O	M	R	W	O	M	R	W
Sarfraz	16	4	42	3	15	3	77	3
Imran	26	6	102	6	19·7	3	63	6
Asif	15	5	53	0				
Mushtaq	2	1	2	0				
Qasim	4	3	2	0	2	1	2	0
Miandad	1·2	0	2	1	5	0	27	0
AUSTRALIA								
Lillee	22·3	0	114	3	4	0	24	2
Gilmour	16	1	81	3				
Walker	29	4	112	4	3·2	1	6	0
Walters	4	1	7	0				
O'Keeffe	11	2	32	0				

FALL OF WICKETS

	A	P	A	P
Wkt	*1st*	*1st*	*2nd*	*2nd*
1st	3	42	32	1
2nd	26	51	41	22
3rd	28	77	51	–
4th	38	111	61	–
5th	100	205	75	–
6th	125	320	99	–
7th	138	322	99	–
8th	146	339	115	–
9th	159	360	177	–
10th	211	360	180	–

Umpires: T.F. Brooks (19) and R.R. Ledwidge (3).

Close: 1st day – A(1) 198-9 (Lillee 11, Walker 28): 2nd – P(1) 281-5 (Asif 93, Miandad 36); 3rd – A(2) 180-9 (Lillee 27, Walker 3).

NEW ZEALAND v AUSTRALIA 1976–77 (1st Test)

Played at Lancaster Park, Christchurch, on 18, 19, 20, 22, 23 February.
Toss: New Zealand.   Result: MATCH DRAWN.
Debuts: New Zealand – G.N. Edwards.

New Zealand were set to score 350 runs in 390 minutes. Congdon (297 minutes) and D.R. Hadlee (52 minutes) earned a draw after the final hour had begun with their total at 260 for 8. Australia's 552 and Walters' score of 250, the highest in Test cricket by a number six batsman, are records for this series. Walters batted for 394 minutes and hit two sixes and 30 fours in the highest of his 15 Test hundreds. His partnership of 217 in 187 minutes with Gilmour is Australia's highest for the seventh wicket against all countries.

AUSTRALIA

A. Turner	b Chatfield	3	lbw b D.R. Hadlee		20
I.C. Davis	c G.P. Howarth b R.J. Hadlee	34	c Lees b R.J. Hadlee		22
R.B. McCosker	c Parker b D.R. Hadlee	37	not out		77
G.S. Chappell*	c Turner b R.J. Hadlee	44	c Parker b H.J. Howarth		0
G.J. Cosier	b R.J. Hadlee	23	run out		2
K.D. Walters	c H.J. Howarth b D.R. Hadlee	250	not out		20
R.W. Marsh†	c Parker b H.J. Howarth	2			
G.J. Gilmour	b Chatfield	101			
K.J. O'Keeffe	run out	8			
D.K. Lillee	c R.J. Hadlee b Chatfield	19			
M.H.N. Walker	not out	10			
Extras	(B 7, LB 10, NB 4)	21	(LB 10, NB 3)		13
Total		**552**	(4 wickets declared)		**154**

NEW ZEALAND

G.M. Turner*	c Turner b O'Keeffe	15	c and b O'Keeffe		36
G.P. Howarth	c Marsh b O'Keeffe	42	c Marsh b Gilmour		28
B.E. Congdon	c Gilmour b Walker	23	not out		107
J.M. Parker	c Marsh b O'Keeffe	34	c McCosker b Walker		21
M.G. Burgess	c Marsh b Walker	66	c McCosker b Walker		39
G.N. Edwards	c Gilmour b O'Keeffe	34	c Marsh b Walker		15
W.K. Lees†	c Marsh b Lillee	14	c Marsh b Lillee		3
R.J. Hadlee	c Marsh b O'Keeffe	3	(9) c Cosier b Walker		15
H.J. Howarth	b Walker	61	(8) b Lillee		0
D.R. Hadlee	not out	37	not out		8
E.J. Chatfield	b Lillee	5			
Extras	(LB 9, W 2, NB 12)	23	(LB 12, W 1, NB 8)		21
Total		**357**	(8 wickets)		**293**

NEW ZEALAND	O	M	R	W	O	M	R	W
R.J. Hadlee	29	1	155	3	13	4	41	1
Chatfield	31	4	125	3	11	1	34	0
D.R. Hadlee	24·5	1	130	2	8	0	28	1
Congdon	7	0	27	0	1	0	1	0
H.J. Howarth	19	2	94	1	10	0	37	1
AUSTRALIA								
Lillee	31·2	6	119	2	18	1	70	2
Gilmour	10	0	48	0	10	0	48	1
Walker	26	7	66	3	25	4	65	4
O'Keeffe	28	5	101	5	20	4	56	1
Chappell					11	0	33	0

FALL OF WICKETS

Wkt	A 1st	NZ 1st	A 2nd	NZ 2nd
1st	9	60	37	70
2nd	76	65	67	70
3rd	78	91	68	128
4th	112	189	82	218
5th	205	193	–	238
6th	208	220	–	245
7th	425	223	–	245
8th	454	265	–	260
9th	504	338	–	–
10th	552	357	–	–

Umpires: D.E.A. Copps (12) and F.R. Goodall (5).

Close: 1st day – A(1) 345-6 (Walters 129, Gilmour 65); 2nd – NZ(1) 106-3 (Parker 6, Burgess 10); 3rd – NZ(1) 324-8 (H.J. Howarth 55, D.R. Hadlee 18); 4th – NZ(2) 12-0 (Turner 4, G.P. Howarth 5).

NEW ZEALAND v AUSTRALIA 1976–77 (2nd Test)

Played at Eden Park, Auckland, on 25, 26, 27 February, 1 March.
Toss: Australia.   Result: AUSTRALIA won by ten wickets.
Debuts: Nil.

Australia gained their fifth victory in nine Tests against New Zealand and with almost two days to spare. Lillee took his 150th wicket in 31 Tests. His match figures of 11 for 123 were then the record for this series and remain the best in Tests at Auckland.

NEW ZEALAND

G.M. Turner*	c Marsh b Walker	4	c Walters b Lillee		23
G.P. Howarth	c McCosker b Lillee	59	c Turner b Lillee		2
B.E. Congdon	c Marsh b Lillee	25	c McCosker b Lillee		1
J.M. Parker	c Cosier b Lillee	20	c Turner b Walker		5
M.G. Burgess	c Marsh b Walters	1	b Walker		38
G.N. Edwards†	c Lillee b Gilmour	51	c Marsh b Lillee		0
R.J. Hadlee	c McCosker b Lillee	44	b Chappell		81
B.L. Cairns	b Chappell	2	c Lillee b Walker		7
H.J. Howarth	b Walker	5	lbw b Lillee		6
P.J. Petherick	c Marsh b Lillee	4	b Lillee		1
E.J. Chatfield	not out	0	not out		4
Extras	(LB 7, NB 7)	14	(B 4, LB 2, NB 1)		7
Total		**229**			**175**

AUSTRALIA

I.C. Davis	b Chatfield	13	not out	6
A. Turner	c Edwards b Cairns	30	not out	20
R.B. McCosker	c Edwards b Cairns	84		
G.S. Chappell*	run out	58		
G.J. Cosier	c and b Cairns	21		
K.D. Walters	c Hadlee b Chatfield	16		
R.W. Marsh†	lbw b Hadlee	4		
G.J. Gilmour	b Chatfield	64		
K.J. O'Keeffe	c Congdon b Hadlee	32		
D.K. Lillee	not out	23		
M.H.N. Walker	c Turner b Chatfield	9		
Extras	(B 9, LB 9, NB 5)	23	(LB 1, NB 1)	2
Total		**377**	(0 wickets)	**28**

AUSTRALIA	O	M	R	W	O	M	R	W
Lillee	17·3	4	51	5	15·7	2	72	6
Walker	24	6	60	2	17	4	70	3
Gilmour	7	0	56	1	1	0	11	0
Chappell	13	4	28	1	9	4	15	1
Walters	4	1	20	1				
O'Keeffe	1	1	0	0				
NEW ZEALAND								
Hadlee	28	2	147	2	2	0	11	0
Chatfield	27·1	3	100	4	1·5	0	15	0
Cairns	28	9	69	3				
Congdon	5	1	8	0				
H.J. Howarth	5	1	16	0				
Petherick	4	2	14	0				

FALL OF WICKETS

Wkt	NZ 1st	A 1st	NZ 2nd	A 2nd
1st	6	31	10	–
2nd	63	56	12	–
3rd	112	171	23	–
4th	113	202	31	–
5th	121	217	31	–
6th	177	221	136	–
7th	202	245	162	–
8th	211	338	163	–
9th	228	364	169	–
10th	229	377	175	–

Umpires: D.E.A. Copps (13) and W.R.C. Gardiner (6).

Close: 1st day – NZ(1) 229 all out; 2nd – A(1) 281-7 (Gilmour 29, O'Keeffe 10); 3rd – NZ(2) 175 all out.

WEST INDIES v PAKISTAN 1976–77 (1st Test)

Played at Kensington Oval, Bridgetown, Barbados, on 18, 19, 20, 22, 23 February.
Toss: Pakistan.   Result: MATCH DRAWN.
Debuts: West Indies – C.E.H. Croft, J. Garner.

West Indies, needing 306 for victory, came close to losing their first Test at Bridgetown since 1934-35. Their last three batsmen survived the final 20 mandatory overs plus 15 minutes. The partnership of 133 in 110 minutes between Wasim Raja and Wasim Bari is Pakistan's highest for the tenth wicket in all Tests. Bari was batting last after a swimming incident the previous day when he had been rescued from the sea by a lifeguard. The match aggregate of extras (173) and no-balls (103) are records for all Test cricket, as was the total of 68 extras conceded by West Indies in the second innings. Partnership records for this series were set for West Indies by Lloyd with Murray (151 – sixth) and Garner (70 – seventh), and for Pakistan by Wasim Raja and Sarfraz (73 – ninth).

PAKISTAN

Batsman	Dismissal	Score	Dismissal 2	Score 2
Majid Khan	b Garner	88	c Garner b Croft	28
Sadiq Mohammad	c Croft b Garner	37	c Garner b Croft	9
Haroon Rashid	c Kallicharran b Foster	33	b Roberts	39
Mushtaq Mohammad*	c Murray b Croft	0	c Murray b Roberts	6
Asif Iqbal	c Murray b Croft	36	b Croft	0
Javed Miandad	lbw b Garner	2	c Greenidge b Croft	1
Wasim Raja	not out	117	c Garner b Foster	71
Imran Khan	c Garner b Roberts	20	c Fredericks b Garner	1
Salim Altaf	lbw b Garner	19	b Garner	2
Sarfraz Nawaz	c Kallicharran b Foster	38	c Murray b Roberts	6
Wasim Bari†	lbw b Croft	10	not out	60
Extras	(B 5, LB 6, W 1, NB 23)	35	(B 29, LB 11, NB 28)	68
Total		**435**		**291**

WEST INDIES

Batsman	Dismissal	Score	Dismissal 2	Score 2
R.C. Fredericks	c and b Sarfraz	24	b Sarfraz	52
C.G. Greenidge	c Majid b Imran	47	c Wasim Raja b Sarfraz	2
I.V.A. Richards	c Salim b Sarfraz	32	c Sadiq b Sarfraz	92
A.I. Kallicharran	c Sarfraz b Imran	17	c Wasim Bari b Salim	9
C.H. Lloyd*	c Sadiq b Salim	157	c Wasim Bari b Imran	11
M.L.C. Foster	b Sarfraz	15	b Sarfraz	4
D.L. Murray†	c Mushtaq b Imran	52	c Wasim Bari b Salim	20
J. Garner	b Miandad	43	b Salim	0
A.M.E. Roberts	c Wasim Bari b Salim	4	not out	9
C.E.H. Croft	not out	1	(11) not out	5
V.A. Holder	absent hurt	–	(10) b Imran	6
Extras	(B 2, LB 6, NB 21)	29	(B 1, LB 8, W 1, NB 31)	41
Total		**421**	(9 wickets)	**251**

WEST INDIES	O	M	R	W	O	M	R	W
Roberts	30	3	124	1	25	5	66	3
Croft	31·4	6	85	3	15	3	47	4
Holder	4	0	13	0				
Garner	37	7	130	4	17	4	60	2
Foster	27	13	41	2	8	2	34	1
Richards	3	1	3	0	2	0	16	0
Fredericks	1	0	4	0				
PAKISTAN								
Imran	28	3	147	3	32	16	58	2
Sarfraz	29	3	125	3	34	10	79	4
Salim	21	3	70	2	21	7	33	3
Miandad	10·4	3	22	1	11	4	31	0
Mushtaq	5	0	27	0				
Majid	1	0	1	0	1	0	1	0
Asif					1	0	8	0

FALL OF WICKETS

Wkt	P 1st	WI 1st	P 2nd	WI 2nd
1st	72	59	29	12
2nd	148	91	68	142
3rd	149	120	102	166
4th	186	134	103	179
5th	207	183	108	185
6th	233	334	113	206
7th	271	404	126	210
8th	335	418	146	217
9th	408	421	158	237
10th	435	–	291	–

Umpires: R. Gosein (17) and D. Sang Hue (25).

Close: 1st day – P(1) 269-6 (Wasim Raja 31, Imran 19); 2nd – WI(1) 109-2 (Richards 22, Kallicharran 6); 3rd – P(2) 18-0 (Majid 10, Sadiq 5); 4th – WI(2) 41-1 (Fredericks 21, Richards 14).

WEST INDIES v PAKISTAN 1976–77 (2nd Test)

Played at Queen's Park Oval, Port-of-Spain, Trinidad, on 4, 5, 6, 8, 9 March.
Toss: Pakistan.   Result: WEST INDIES won by six wickets.
Debuts: West Indies – I.T. Shillingford.

Croft, playing in his second match, achieved the best analysis by a West Indies fast bowler in Test cricket. In that innings, Sadiq (0) retired at 6 after being hit on the arm by a ball from Croft and resumed at 112. Wasim Raja was top scorer in both innings for the second Test in succession. Fredericks (4,000 runs) and Mushtaq (3,000 runs) achieved notable Test career landmarks. Intikhab, who scored 1,493 runs, took 125 wickets, and captained Pakistan 17 times, made the last of his 47 Test appearances.

PAKISTAN

Majid Khan	lbw b Garner	47		c Kallicharran b Jumadeen	54
Sadiq Mohammad	c and b Croft	17		c Kallicharran b Garner	81
Haroon Rashid	c Lloyd b Croft	4		lbw b Fredericks	7
Mushtaq Mohammad*	c Richards b Croft	9		c Greenidge b Roberts	21
Asif Iqbal	c Murray b Croft	0		b Garner	12
Wasim Raja	b Croft	65		c Garner b Croft	84
Imran Khan	c Fredericks b Jumadeen	1	(8)	c Murray b Roberts	35
Intikhab Alam	b Croft	0	(9)	b Garner	12
Wasim Bari†	c Murray b Croft	21	(10)	c Fredericks b Roberts	2
Salim Altaf	b Croft	1	(11)	not out	0
Iqbal Qasim	not out	0	(7)	b Roberts	4
Extras	(B 3, LB 3, NB 9)	15		(B 13, LB 4, NB 11)	28
Total		**180**			**340**

WEST INDIES

R.C. Fredericks	c Sadiq b Mushtaq	120		c Asif b Wasim Raja	57
C.G. Greenidge	b Salim	5		c Wasim Bari b Imran	70
I.V.A. Richards	b Salim	4		b Imran	30
A.I. Kallicharran	c Wasim Bari b Intikhab	37		not out	11
I.T. Shillingford	lbw b Mushtaq	39		c Wasim Bari b Imran	2
C.H. Lloyd*	c Haroon b Intikhab	22		not out	23
D.L. Murray†	b Mushtaq	10			
J. Garner	lbw b Imran	36			
A.M.E. Roberts	b Mushtaq	4			
C.E.H. Croft	not out	23			
R.R. Jumadeen	lbw b Imran	0			
Extras	(B 5, LB 11)	16		(B 1, LB 11, W 1)	13
Total		**316**		(4 wickets)	**206**

WEST INDIES	O	M	R	W	O	M	R	W	FALL OF WICKETS				
Roberts	17	2	34	0	26	4	85	4		P	WI	P	WI
Croft	18·5	7	29	8	25	3	66	1	*Wkt*	*1st*	*1st*	*2nd*	*2nd*
Garner	16	1	47	1	20·1	6	48	3	1st	10	18	123	97
Jumadeen	16	3	55	1	35	13	72	1	2nd	21	22	155	159
Fredericks					6	2	14	1	3rd	21	102	167	166
Richards					12	4	27	0	4th	103	183	181	170
									5th	112	216	223	–
PAKISTAN									6th	150	243	239	–
Imran	21	5	50	2	24	8	59	3	7th	154	258	315	–
Salim	18	3	44	2	21	3	58	0	8th	159	270	334	–
Intikhab	29	6	90	2	2	1	6	0	9th	161	316	340	–
Majid	8	3	9	0					10th	180	316	340	–
Qasim	10	2	26	0	13	6	30	0					
Mushtaq	20	7	50	4	9	1	27	0					
Wasim Raja	10	1	31	0	5	1	13	1					

Umpires: R. Gosein (18) and D. Sang Hue (26).

Close: 1st day – WI(1) 35-2 (Fredericks 19, Kallicharran 7); 2nd – WI(1) 301-8 (Garner 33, Croft 11); 3rd – P(2) 223-5 (Wasim Raja 24, Qasim 0); 4th – WI(2) 148-1 (Greenidge 65, Richards 18).

WEST INDIES v PAKISTAN 1976–77 (3rd Test)

Played at Bourda, Georgetown, Guyana, on 18, 19, 20, 22, 23 March.
Toss: West Indies.   Result: MATCH DRAWN.
Debuts: Nil.

Lloyd tore a hamstring muscle after only 20 minutes of play on the first day and Murray assumed the West Indies captaincy on the field. Sadiq (22) retired at 60 after being hit on the jaw when attempting a hook against Roberts, and returned at 311. Majid and Zaheer added a further 159 to set a new first wicket record for Pakistan in this series. A bottle-throwing incident caused play to be suspended for 20 minutes on the second day. Majid achieved Test career-best performances with both bat and ball in this match.

PAKISTAN

Majid Khan	c Murray b Roberts	23		c Greenidge b Roberts	167
Sadiq Mohammad	c Murray b Garner	12		lbw b Croft	48
Zaheer Abbas	b Garner	0		c Fredericks b Croft	80
Haroon Rashid	c Murray b Croft	32	(5)	c and b Garner	60
Mushtaq Mohammad*	c Murray b Julien	41	(4)	b Roberts	19
Asif Iqbal	c and b Croft	15	(7)	lbw b Garner	35
Wasim Raja	c and b Croft	5	(8)	b Garner	0
Imran Khan	c Shillingford b Roberts	47	(9)	lbw b Roberts	35
Sarfraz Nawaz	c Kallicharran b Garner	6	(10)	c Kallicharran b Fredericks	25
Wasim Bari†	c Murray b Garner	1	(11)	not out	25
Salim Altaf	not out	0	(6)	lbw b Garner	6
Extras	(LB 5, NB 7)	12		(B 13, LB 7, W 1, NB 19)	40
Total		**194**			**540**

WEST INDIES

R.C. Fredericks	c Majid b Sarfraz	5		not out	52
C.G. Greenidge	b Majid	91		c Haroon b Imran	96
I.V.A. Richards	lbw b Imran	50			
A.I. Kallicharran	lbw b Imran	72			
I.T. Shillingford	c Haroon b Sarfraz	120			
B.D. Julien	b Salim	5			
D.L. Murray†	c Zaheer b Majid	42			
J. Garner	b Majid	4			
C.H. Lloyd*	c Imran b Majid	14			
A.M.E. Roberts	not out	20			
C.E.H. Croft	b Mushtaq	6			
Extras	(B 1, LB 9, W 3, NB 6)	19		(LB 5, NB 1)	6
Total		**448**		(1 wicket)	**154**

WEST INDIES	O	M	R	W	O	M	R	W		FALL OF WICKETS			
Roberts	16·3	3	49	2	45	6	174	3		P	WI	P	WI
Croft	15	3	60	3	35	7	119	2	*Wkt*	*1st*	*1st*	*2nd*	*2nd*
Garner	16	4	48	4	39	8	100	4	1st	36	11	219	154
Julien	9	2	25	1	28	3	63	0	2nd	40	94	304	–
Richards					5	0	11	0	3rd	46	193	311	–
Fredericks					11·3	2	33	1	4th	96	244	381	–
									5th	125	255	404	–
PAKISTAN									6th	133	378	417	–
Imran	31	6	119	2	12·5	0	79	1	7th	143	390	417	–
Sarfraz	45	16	105	2	9	0	58	0	8th	174	422	471	–
Salim	29	6	71	1					9th	188	422	491	–
Asif	4	1	15	0					10th	194	448	540	–
Mushtaq	29·3	7	74	1									
Majid	24	9	45	4	3	0	11	0					

Umpires: C. Paynter (1) and C.F. Vyfhuis (3).

Close: 1st day – WI(1) 68-1 (Greenidge 30, Richards 31); 2nd – WI(1) 278-5 (Shillingford 31, Murray 9); 3rd – P(2) 113-0 (Majid 69, Zaheer 18); 4th – P(2) 398-4 (Haroon 55, Salim 2).

WEST INDIES v PAKISTAN 1976–77 (4th Test)

Played at Queen's Park Oval, Port-of-Spain, on 1, 2, 3, 5, 6 April.
Toss: West Indies.   Result: PAKISTAN won by 266 runs.
Debuts: Nil.

Pakistan drew level in the rubber with their second victory in the West Indies. Mushtaq became the second all-rounder after G.St A. Sobers to score a hundred and take five wickets in an innings of the same Test on two occasions. Imran and Sarfraz added 73 for the record Pakistan eighth-wicket partnership in this series until 1987-88.

PAKISTAN

Majid Khan	c Murray b Croft	92	c Murray b Croft	16
Sadiq Mohammad	c Lloyd b Roberts	0	b Ali	24
Zaheer Abbas	b Roberts	14	lbw b Garner	9
Haroon Rashid	c Kallicharran b Ali	11	lbw b Garner	11
Mushtaq Mohammad*	c Greenidge b Richards	121	c Fredericks b Roberts	56
Asif Iqbal	c Ali b Roberts	11	c and b Ali	10
Wasim Raja	c and b Ali	28	b Garner	70
Imran Khan	c Greenidge b Ali	1	c and b Croft	30
Sarfraz Nawaz	c Richards b Croft	29	c Lloyd b Croft	51
Wasim Bari†	not out	5	not out	2
Iqbal Qasim	b Richards	2		
Extras	(B 4, LB 8, NB 15)	27	(B 8, LB 11, NB 3)	22
Total		**341**	(9 wickets declared)	**301**

WEST INDIES

R.C. Fredericks	b Imran	41	c Majid b Qasim	17
C.G. Greenidge	b Qasim	32	c Majid b Sarfraz	11
I.V.A. Richards	b Imran	4	st Wasim Bari b Mushtaq	33
A.I. Kallicharran	c Sarfraz b Mushtaq	11	c Asif b Mushtaq	45
I.T. Shillingford	st Wasim Bari b Mushtaq	15	c Qasim b Mushtaq	23
J. Garner	c Qasim b Mushtaq	0	(8) b Sarfraz	0
C.H. Lloyd*	lbw b Imran	22	(6) b Sarfraz	17
D.L. Murray†	lbw b Imran	0	(7) c Sadiq b Wasim Raja	30
A.M.E. Roberts	c Qasim b Mushtaq	6	c Majid b Wasim Raja	35
Inshan Ali	c Qasim b Mushtaq	4	c Sadiq b Wasim Raja	0
C.E.H. Croft	not out	0	not out	0
Extras	(B 11, LB 2, NB 6)	19	(B 7, LB 1, NB 3)	11
Total		**154**		**222**

WEST INDIES	O	M	R	W	O	M	R	W
Roberts	25	2	82	3	20	2	56	1
Croft	21	4	56	2	22·5	6	79	3
Garner	24	6	55	0	23	4	71	3
Ali	32	9	86	3	20	2	73	2
Richards	18·3	6	34	2				
Fredericks	1	0	1	0				
PAKISTAN								
Imran	21	6	64	4	21	5	46	0
Sarfraz	10	4	17	0	19	10	21	3
Qasim	13	6	26	1	20	6	50	1
Mushtaq	10·5	3	28	5	31	9	69	3
Wasim Raja	1	1	0	0	3·5	1	22	3
Majid					10	8	3	0

FALL OF WICKETS

Wkt	P 1st	WI 1st	P 2nd	WI 2nd
1st	1	73	25	24
2nd	19	77	46	42
3rd	51	82	58	82
4th	159	106	74	126
5th	191	106	95	148
6th	246	122	211	154
7th	252	125	213	154
8th	320	144	286	196
9th	331	154	301	196
10th	341	154	–	222

Umpires: R. Gosein (19) and C.F. Vyfhuis (4).

Close: 1st day – P(1) 225-5 (Mushtaq 80, Wasim Raja 10); 2nd – WI(1) 107-5 (Shillingford 10, Lloyd 0); 3rd – P(2) 152-5 (Mushtaq 44, Wasim Raja 29); 4th – WI(2) 146-4 (Kallicharran 45, Lloyd 12).

WEST INDIES v PAKISTAN 1976–77 (5th Test)

Played at Sabina Park, Kingston, Jamaica, on 15, 16, 17, 19, 20 April.
Toss: West Indies.   Result: WEST INDIES won by 140 runs.
Debuts: Nil.

Soon after the start of the fifth day's play West Indies won their second rubber against Pakistan. Wasim Bari, who became the first wicket-keeper to make 100 dismissals for Pakistan, retired at 197 after being hit in the face attempting a hook against Croft. Majid kept wicket for part of the second innings and held four catches. Croft emulated A.L. Valentine by taking 33 wickets in his first rubber. Pakistan scored 300 runs in the fourth innings of a Test for the first time. Asif Iqbal ended an unbroken run of 45 matches which was then the Pakistan record for most consecutive Test appearances.

WEST INDIES

Batsman	1st innings		2nd innings	
R.C. Fredericks	c and b Imran	6	c Majid b Wasim Raja	83
C.G. Greenidge	c Wasim Bari b Sikander	100	c Majid b Sikander	82
I.V.A. Richards	c Wasim Bari b Imran	5	b Wasim Raja	7
C.H. Lloyd*	c Zaheer b Imran	22	c Asif b Wasim Raja	48
A.I. Kallicharran	c Wasim Bari b Imran	34	c Majid b Sikander	22
C.L. King	c Wasim Bari b Sikander	41	c Majid b Sikander	3
D.L. Murray†	c Sikander b Imran	31	c Wasim Bari b Imran	33
D.A.J. Holford	c Majid b Imran	2	c Wasim Bari b Sarfraz	37
J. Garner	c Mushtaq b Sarfraz	9	c Sadiq b Imran	0
A.M.E. Roberts	b Sarfraz	7	c Wasim Bari b Sarfraz	2
C.E.H. Croft	not out	6	not out	12
Extras	(LB 9, NB 8)	17	(B 13, LB 7, NB 10)	30
Total		**280**		**359**

PAKISTAN

Batsman	1st innings		2nd innings	
Majid Khan	c Richards b Croft	11	c Fredericks b Croft	4
Sadiq Mohammad	b Roberts	3	c Greenidge b Croft	14
Zaheer Abbas	lbw b Roberts	28	c Richards b Croft	0
Haroon Rashid	c Greenidge b Croft	72	c Greenidge b Garner	31
Mushtaq Mohammad*	c Lloyd b Garner	24	hit wkt b Garner	17
Asif Iqbal	c Kallicharran b Holford	5	st Murray b Holford	135
Wasim Raja	c King b Holford	13	c Fredericks b Holford	64
Imran Khan	c and b Croft	23	c Lloyd b Holford	22
Sarfraz Nawaz	c Holford b Croft	8	b Garner	9
Wasim Bari†	retired hurt	0	run out	0
Sikander Bakht	not out	1	not out	0
Extras	(LB 1, NB 9)	10	(B 3, NB 2)	5
Total		**198**		**301**

PAKISTAN	O	M	R	W	O	M	R	W
Imran	18	2	90	6	27·2	3	78	2
Sarfraz	24·3	5	81	2	27	6	93	2
Sikander	12	0	71	2	16	3	55	3
Asif	4	1	6	0				
Mushtaq	7	2	15	0	11	3	38	0
Wasim Raja					21	5	65	3
WEST INDIES								
Roberts	14	4	36	2	18	6	57	0
Croft	13·3	1	49	4	20	5	86	3
Garner	9	1	57	1	18·2	0	72	3
Holford	16	3	40	2	18	3	69	3
King	4	2	6	0	3	0	12	0

FALL OF WICKETS

	WI	P	WI	P
Wkt	1st	1st	2nd	2nd
1st	6	11	182	5
2nd	22	26	182	9
3rd	56	47	193	32
4th	146	106	252	51
5th	200	122	260	138
6th	229	140	269	253
7th	252	174	335	289
8th	254	190	343	296
9th	268	198	345	301
10th	280	–	359	301

Umpires: R. Gosein (20) and D. Sang Hue (27).

Close: 1st day – P(1) 25-1 (Majid 10, Zaheer 10); 2nd – WI(2) 118-0 (Fredericks 54, Greenidge 51); 3rd – WI(2) 324-6 (Murray 32, Holford 23): 4th – P(2) 289-7 (Asif 132).